The History of German Literature on Film

HISTORY OF WORLD LITERATURES ON FILM

Series Editors:
Greg M. Colón Semenza
Bob Hasenfratz

Also Published in the Series

The History of British Literature on Film, 1895–2015
Greg M. Colón Semenza and Bob Hasenfratz
The History of American Literature on Film
Thomas Leitch
The History of French Literature on Film
Kate Griffiths and Andrew Watts

Forthcoming Volumes in the Series

The History of Russian Literature on Film
David Gillespie and Marina Korneeva
The History of Sub-Saharan African Literatures on Film
Sara Hanaburgh

The History of German Literature on Film

Christiane Schönfeld

BLOOMSBURY ACADEMIC
NEW YORK • LONDON • OXFORD • NEW DELHI • SYDNEY

BLOOMSBURY ACADEMIC
Bloomsbury Publishing Inc
1385 Broadway, New York, NY 10018, USA
50 Bedford Square, London, WC1B 3DP, UK
29 Earlsfort Terrace, Dublin 2, Ireland

BLOOMSBURY, BLOOMSBURY ACADEMIC and the Diana logo are
trademarks of Bloomsbury Publishing Plc

First published in the United States of America 2023
Paperback edition published in 2025

Copyright © Christiane Schönfeld, 2023

For legal purposes the Acknowledgments on pp. xi–xiii constitute
an extension of this copyright page.

Cover images (clockwise from top left): Angela Winkler in *The Lost Honour of Katharina Blum*, 1975, dir. Volker Schlöndorff and Margarethe von Trotta © Bioskop Film / Paramount Orion / Collection Christophel / ArenaPAL / www.arenapal.com; Henny Porten and Alexander Wirth in *Rose Bernd*, 1919, dir. Alfred Halm; Mads Mikkelsen in *Age of Uprising: The Legend of Michael Kohlhaas*, 2013, dir. Arnaud des Pallières © Looks Film produktionen/ Les Films d ici /Collection Christophel / ArenaPAL / www.arenapal.com; Gösta Ekman as old Faust in *Faust*, 1926, dir. F.W. Murnau.

All rights reserved. No part of this publication may be reproduced or
transmitted in any form or by any means, electronic or mechanical, including
photocopying, recording, or any information storage or retrieval system,
without prior permission in writing from the publishers.

Bloomsbury Publishing Inc does not have any control over, or responsibility for,
any third-party websites referred to or in this book. All internet addresses given
in this book were correct at the time of going to press. The author and publisher
regret any inconvenience caused if addresses have changed or sites have ceased
to exist, but can accept no responsibility for any such changes.

Library of Congress Cataloging-in-Publication Data
Names: Schönfeld, Christiane, author.
Title: The history of German literature on film / Christiane Schönfeld.
Description: New York : Bloomsbury Academic, 2023. |
Series: The history of world literatures on film | Includes bibliographical references and index.
Identifiers: LCCN 2022044831 (print) | LCCN 2022044832 (ebook) |
ISBN 9781628923766 (hardback) | ISBN 9781501399572 (paperback) |
ISBN 9781628923759 (ebook) | ISBN 9781628923742 (pdf) | ISBN 9781501396564 (ebook other)
Subjects: LCSH: German literature—Film adaptations. | Motion pictures and literature. |
Film adaptations. | Motion pictures—adaptatHistory.
Classification: LCC PN1995.3 .S32 2023 (print) | LCC PN1995.3 (ebook) |
DDC 791.430943–dc23/eng/20221121
LC record available at https://lccn.loc.gov/2022044831
LC ebook record available at https://lccn.loc.gov/2022044832

ISBN:	HB:	978-1-6289-2376-6
	PB:	978-1-5013-9957-2
	ePDF:	978-1-6289-2374-2
	eBook:	978-1-6289-2375-9

Typeset by Integra Software Services Pvt. Ltd.

To find out more about our authors and books visit www.bloomsbury.com
and sign up for our newsletters.

In memory of
Eoin Bourke (1939–2017)
Martin Schönfeld (1963–2020)
Ernst Schürer (1933–2021)
Wolfram Renger (1965–2022)

CONTENTS

List of Figures viii
Acknowledgments xi
List of Abbreviations xiv

Introduction 1

1   The Beginnings of German-language Literature on Film (1897–1906) 11

2   Early Transnational Narrative Cinema and the Impact of the First World War (1907–18) 33

3   The 'Golden Age' of Silent Cinema: Literary Adaptation, Radicalism, and Censorship (1919–29) 89

4   Literary Talkies: Sound and Internationalization (1922–32) 171

5   The Other German Cinema: Exile and the Second World War (1933–45) 243

6   A History of Abuse: German-language Literature in Nazi Cinema (1933–45) 275

7   The Postwar Period: Reconstructions and Deconstructions (1946–61) 333

8   Split Screens: Continuities and a New German Cinema (1962–89) 429

9   The Walls Come Down: Entrepreneurs, Auteurs, and Art-house Cinema (1990–2021) 499

Bibliography 583
Index 600

FIGURES

1.1 Méliès as Mephistopheles in *Faust aux enfers* (FR, Georges Méliès, 1903) 19

1.2 *Faust et Méphistophélès* (FR, Alice Guy, 1903) 23

2.1 *Atlantis* (DK, August Blom, 1913) 48

2.2 *Der Student von Prag* (DE, Stellan Rye, 1913) 53

2.3 *Dida Ibsens Geschichte* (DE, Richard Oswald, 1918) 70

3.1 *Rose Bernd* (DE, Alfred Halm, 1919) 99

3.2 *Von morgens bis mitternachts* (DE, Karlheinz Martin, 1920) 104

3.3 *Der böse Geist Lumpaci Vagabundus* (DE, Carl Wilhelm, 1922) 107

3.4 *Buddenbrooks* (DE, Gerhard Lamprecht, 1923) 110

3.5 *Die Nibelungen* (DE, Fritz Lang, 1924) 116

3.6 *Varieté* (DE, Ewald André Dupont, 1925) 123

3.7 *Die Weber* (DE, Friedrich Zelnik, 1927) 127

3.8 *Faust* (DE, F. W. Murnau, 1926) 132

4.1 *Alraune* (DE, Richard Oswald, 1930) 179

4.2 *Cyankali* (DE, Hans Tintner, 1931) 185

4.3 *Der blaue Engel* (DE, Josef von Sternberg, 1930) 188

4.4 *All Quiet on the Western Front* (US, Lewis Milestone, 1930) 201

4.5 *Grand Hotel* (US, Edmund Goulding, 1932) 208

5.1 *Pastor Hall* (GB, Roy Boulting, 1940) 255

5.2 *Восстание рыбаков* (USSR, Erwin Piscator, 1934) 257

5.3 *The Seventh Cross* (US, Fred Zinnemann, 1944) 263

6.1 *Der Schimmelreiter* (DE, Hans Deppe/Curt Oertel, 1934) 286

6.2 *Wilhelm Tell* (DE/CH, Heinz Paul, 1934) 294

6.3 *Rotkäppchen* (DE, Fritz Genschow, 1937) 299

6.4 *Der Fuchs von Glenarvon* (DE, Max W. Kimmich, 1940) 302

6.5 *Jud Süß* (DE, Veit Harlan, 1940) 316

7.1 *Und über uns der Himmel* (DE, Josef von Baky, 1947) 341

7.2 *Liebe 47* (DE, Wolfgang Liebeneiner, 1949) 345

7.3 *The Tales of Hoffmann* (GB, Michael Powell/Emeric Pressburger, 1951) 350

7.4 *Arch of Triumph* (US, Lewis Milestone, 1948) 358

7.5 *Der Untertan* (GDR, Wolfgang Staudte, 1951) 372

7.6 *08/15* (FRG, Paul May, 1954) 390

7.7 *Die Brücke* (FRG, Bernhard Wicki, 1959) 392

8.1 *Professor Mamlock* (GDR, Konrad Wolf, 1961) 430

8.2 *The Trial* (US/FR/FRG/IT, Orson Welles, 1962) 435

8.3 *Ragtime* (US, Miloš Forman, 1981) 437

8.4 *Winnetou* (FRG, Harald Reinl, 1962) 448

8.5 *Der junge Törless* (FRG, Volker Schlöndorff, 1966) 453

8.6 *Falsche Bewegung* (FRG, Wim Wenders, 1975) 457

8.7 *Gruppenbild mit Dame* (FRG/FR, Aleksandar Petrović, 1977) 461

8.8 *Die Blechtrommel* (FRG, Volker Schlöndorff, 1979) 470

8.9 *Fontane Effi Briest* (FRG, Rainer Werner Fassbinder, 1974) 474

9.1 *Timm Thaler oder Das verkaufte Lachen* (DE, Andreas Dresen, 2017) 504

9.2 *Berlin Alexanderplatz* (DE, Burhan Qurbani, 2020) 511

9.3 *Transit* (DE, Christian Petzold, 2018) 523

9.4 *Undine* (DE, Christian Petzold, 2020) 525

9.5 *The Reader* (US/DE, Stephen Daldry, 2008) 530

9.6 *Hyènes* (SN, Djibril Diop Mambéty, 1992) 532

9.7 *Die Wand* (AT/DE, Roman Pölsler, 2012) 544

9.8 *Fabian oder Der Gang vor die Hunde* (DE, Dominik Graf, 2021) 555

NB: Illustrations in this book are either screen grabs, photographs provided by the Deutsche Kinemathek, or scans of photographs from my grandfather and early film buff Willi Schönfeld's movie stills collection. I tried to identify the rights holders of all archival photographs kindly provided by the Deutsche Kinemathek. Their support of this project is gratefully acknowledged.

ACKNOWLEDGMENTS

Many people contributed to this book in a myriad of ways and helped bring it to fruition.

My thanks are due to Craig Semenza and Bob Hasenfratz for inviting me to take on this project, and for their meticulous editing work and helpful advice; and to Katie Gallof and her team at Bloomsbury for backing this series and for all the assistance along the way. I gratefully acknowledge a Senior Research Fellowship award by the DAAD, and the support provided by MIC (Mary Immaculate College, University of Limerick) in the form of several seed funding awards for archival visits as well as a research sabbatical, without which this major research undertaking would not have been possible.

I am grateful to my students—from undergraduate students to postgraduate assistants for their questions and many productive conversations—and to the many colleagues and associations that invited me to present research and enabled me to profit from ensuing debates, among them especially the Association for German Studies in Britain and Ireland (AGS), Women in German Studies (WiGS), the German Studies Association of Ireland (GSAI), Gesellschaft für interkulturelle Germanistik (GiG), IMLR School of Advanced Study (University of London), and the Konrad Adenauer Stiftung (KAS).

I would also like to acknowledge the Deutsche Kinemathek in Berlin as an invaluable resource for research and the preservation of film heritage. Many thanks to all the staff in the Kinemathek's film archive, document archive, photo archive, and library. Other archives that also provided support and resources include the BFI (London), dff Deutsches Filminstitut, Danske Film Institut, La Cinémathèque française, Filminstitut Hannover, The Internet Archive, Filmarchiv Austria, and the US National Archive & Records Administration (NARA, Maryland). Many individuals generously shared their knowledge and suggested adaptations or texts to look at, especially, in alphabetical order, Gerald Bär (Lisbon), Eoin and Eva Bourke (Galway/Berlin), Michael Braun (Cologne), Elisabeth Bronfen (Zurich), Erica Carter (London), Sarah Colvin (Cambridge), Steffan Davies (Bristol), Sabine Egger (Limerick), Anne Fuchs (Dublin), François Genton (Grenoble), Helmut Grugger (Limerick), Ernest Hess-Lüttich (Berlin/GiG), Gisela Holfter (Limerick), Klaus Kiefer (Munich), Henrike Lähnemann (Oxford), Karina von Lindeiner-Stráský (Milton

Keynes), Robert G. Moeller (Irvine), Stephan Mühr (Pretoria), Maria Müller-Sommer (Kiepenheuer Berlin), Stefan Neuhaus (Koblenz), Bill Niven (Nottingham), Sonja Novak (Osijek), Pól Ó Dochartaigh (Galway), Ernst Offermanns (Berlin), Gillian Pye (Dublin), Wolfram Renger (Halle/Tirol), Volker Schlöndorff (Potsdam), Paulo Soethe (Curitiba), Tony Tracy (Galway), Ian Wallace (Bath), and Godela Weiss-Sussex (London/Cambridge).

For their enlightening publications that helped me better understand and contextualize the role of literature in over 120 years of cinema history, I am indebted particularly to Hester Baer, Tim Bergfelder, Hans-Michael Bock, Stephen Brockmann, Erica Carter, Paul Cooke, Timothy Corrigan, Thomas Elsaesser, Jaimey Fisher, Norbert Grob, Sabine Hake, Wolfgang Jakobsen, Anton Kaes, Jennifer Kapczynski, Hans Helmut Prinzler, Eric Rentschler, Michael Töteberg, and Michael Wedel. Greg Semenza, Bob Hasenfratz, Thomas Leitch, Kate Griffiths, and Andrew Watts, the other authors in this series, also provided inspiration and furthered my understanding of this field. Some of my own published research has provided the foundation for a few of the sections in this volume and I gratefully acknowledge the relevant journals, edited books, and publishers in endnotes as appropriate.

I am very grateful to the Irish-German poet and translator Eva Bourke for her invaluable help with some of the translations. For their assistance with Excel templates and for entering substantial chunks of the 2,000+ adaptations into the spreadsheet, my sincere thanks to Magdalena Glaab and Susanne Mödl.

As I might not get another opportunity to do so, I would also like to thank my inspiring teachers, who pushed me to read and look closely while not losing sight of the bigger picture; among them Norbert Cabla, Hanno König and Stefan Kummer, Hiltrud Gnüg and Tilmann Buddensieg, Jacques Derrida, Tom Beebee, Peter Gould, Tony Cutler, Joseph Kockelmans, and, especially, Ernst Schürer.

To my family and friends, thank you for your encouragement, generosity, and love!

Whether it was an inspiring email from a colleague somewhere on the globe telling me about a new adaptation they had just seen, a letter from my dear father with carefully collected newspaper clippings about the premiere of yet another German-language novel on screen, my wonderful sons saying they are proud of their Mom when she felt guilty about working too much, a new article by one of the great scholars in this exciting interdisciplinary field of inquiry, or all the support I received from my friends and family during good times and bad—this book could not have been completed without it and I am so grateful for it all.

Last but certainly not least, I would like to thank Ulf Strohmayer (Galway), who has supported me—and this book project—with patience, passion, and great intelligence, with countless helpful conversations, ideas, questions and by simply being there with so much love and good humor, sharing the everyday. I dedicate this book to him—and to the memory of dear friends and inspiring colleagues Eoin Bourke (NUIG) and Ernst Schürer (PSU), and of my dear brother Martin (USF) and my friend since childhood, the artist and writer Wolfram Renger.

ABBREVIATIONS

The countries of a film's production are given in round brackets and are normally abbreviated according to the ISO codes below (ISO 3166 international standard), unless divisions necessitate differentiation:

Argentina – AR

Austria – AT

Australia – AU

Bangladesh – BD

Belgium – BE

Brazil – BR

Bulgaria – BG

Canada – CA

Chile – CL

China – CN

Croatia – HR

Czechoslovakia (Československá socialistická republika, 1918–93) – ČSSR

Czech Republic (from 1993) – CZ

Denmark – DK

Egypt – EG

Finland – FI

ABBREVIATIONS

France – FR

Germany (until the country's division in 1949; and again from 1990) – DE

Germany East (1949–89) – GDR

Germany West (1949–89) – FRG

Greece – GR

Hungary – HU

India – IN

Iran – IR

Ireland – IE

Italy – IT

Japan – JP

Liechtenstein – LI

Luxembourg – LU

Mexico – MX

Netherlands (the) – NL

New Zealand – NZ

Norway – NO

Poland – PO

Portugal – PT

Russia – RU

Soviet Union (1922–91) – USSR

Senegal – SN

Spain – ES

Sweden – SE

Switzerland – CH

Turkey – TR

United Kingdom of Great Britain and Northern Ireland – GB

United States of America – US

Further Abbreviations

ARD	Broadcaster and first television channel (also called Das Erste, FRG/DE; ARD stands for Arbeitsgemeinschaft der öffentlich-rechtlichen Rundfunkanstalten der Bundesrepublik Deutschland/ German Association of Public Broadcasters)
BPB	Bundeszentrale für politische Bildung/Federal Agency for Civic Education (FRG/DE)
DEFA	Deutsche Film Anstalt (GDR)
DFF	Deutscher Fernsehfunk (GDR)
DK	Deutsche Kinemathek, Schriftgut Archiv/document archive
FFA	Filmförderungsanstalt, Germany's federal film subsidy board (FRG/DE)
IMDb	Internet Movie Database
MLV	Multiple-language versions
NARA	The U.S. National Archives and Records Administration
NDR	Norddeutscher Rundfunk/public Northern Germany's Broadcasting Company (FRG/DE)
OMGUS	Office of Military Government for Germany (US)

PAGU	Projektions-AG Union (1911–24)
RAF	Rote Armee Fraktion/Red Army Faction
SDR	Süddeutscher Rundfunk (SDR)/public broadcasting company of northern Baden-Württembergs (1949–98)
SMAD	Soviet Military Administration in Germany (1945–9)
SWR	Südwest Rundfunk/public South-western Broadcasting Company (FRG/DE)
Ufa	Universum Film AG (1917–91);
UFA	UFA Film & TV Produktion GmbH (1991–4); UFA GmbH (1994–present)
Ufi	Ufa-Film GmbH (1942–5)
WDR	Westdeutscher Rundfunk/public Western German Broadcasting Company (FRG/DE)
ZDF	Zweites Deutsches Fernsehen/German public-service television broadcaster and second public television channel (FRG/DE)

NB:

Original quotes are in double quotation marks.

Single quotation marks identify quotes translated into English by the author of this book.

Translations of literary texts and date (year) of first publication or performance are given in parentheses.

Translations of film titles are given in [brackets] followed by (country, director, year of premiere).

Introduction

This book is a first attempt to present the overall development of German-language literature on film and to shed light not only on its role within cinema history, but also on the different factors that shaped relevant adaptations from those first *Faust* films in the late nineteenth century to remakes and movies for cinema as well as television series based on both canonical and contemporary literatures in the twenty-first century. When we speak of German literature, we usually refer to the language in which the text was written, not to a flawed definition of a national canon. Goethe, Schiller, Storm, Nestroy, Anzengruber, Schnitzler, Spyri, and Kästner are among the most frequently adapted German-language authors, but Germany as a nation did not exist prior to 1871 and only materialized in its current form in 1990. The borders of the Empire of Austria changed significantly during the eighteenth and nineteenth centuries due to wars and subsequent treaties. The First World War left the Habsburg Empire a rump state of German-speaking Austria, which emerged into the First Austrian Republic in 1919 until it became part of the German Reich in 1938. Following the Second World War and occupation, Austria became a neutral, democratic state in 1955. Only Switzerland and Liechtenstein, the other two German-speaking countries in Europe, did not undergo major changes regarding their borders. In 1815, the Congress of Vienna re-established Swiss autonomy. By then, Liechtenstein had been a principality for nearly a century and became sovereign in the early nineteenth century.

"When a German meets a real-life Siegfried, it's kind of a big deal," Dr. King Schultz (Christoph Waltz) says to Django (Jamie Foxx) in Quentin Tarantino's *Django Unchained* (US, 2012). The revisionist Western pays homage to Italy's famous Spaghetti Westerns and refers to the medieval hero of the *Nibelungenlied*. An epic poem written in Middle High German over 800 years ago, the *Song of the Nibelungs* inspired not only Richard Wagner's *Ring* operas and Fritz Lang's *Nibelungen* film but continues to echo through visual and literary culture to this day.[1] German-language culture is inherently transnational, but so is 'German' culture. Countless motifs and themes in German literature originated in earlier texts, as long ago as the *Gilgamesh* epic (of around 3000 BC), the Bible (especially the Old Testament), Homer's *Iliad* and *Odyssey* (eighth century BC) to Egyptian, Arabian, and Indian tales, or Roman and Greek myths. Stories survived due to a dynamic transcultural oral tradition that fed into an emerging market for written texts. For centuries, literature reinvented stories to entertain, criticize, and educate—adapting and shaping pre-existing narratives in order to communicate their essence or speak to them anew. During the past 125 years, the baton was passed on to visual culture and it was film, adaptations of literary texts, folk and fairy tales for the cinema and, increasingly, television that kept these stories alive. The art of storytelling became the essence of cinema. Catering to the different needs and interests of children and adults, the flexibility of transposition processes that brought literature to film and its enormous popularity now ensures the continued narration of those themes and motifs that, in their essence, are today as relevant as they were thousands of years ago. This is not to say that all written texts can be traced to myths and fairy tales—but there is a significant proportion of films based on literary texts that draw upon and reinvent these narratives.

The great mobility among German-speaking creatives has added transnational and intercultural contexts and aspects to their works, even prior to 1933, when Hitler and his willing henchmen turned many of the most talented writers and filmmakers into stateless refugees. As a result, German culture advanced outside the expanding borders of the German Reich—in Paris, London, New York, Los Angeles, and other places of exile. Unsurprisingly, the role of literature originally written in the German language in cinema is deeply connected to key foundational events and historical moments. Processes of adaptation, however, are as much shaped by global catastrophes and the emergence of nations, as they are by materialist conditions and economic goals, political agendas, the mobility of individuals, and the desire to create reflective surfaces and, sometimes, art.[2]

Both the number of films based on German-language literature and the impact of adaptations on film history have long been underestimated.[3] German-language literature was for decades core to the visual culture of, especially, German-speaking countries, and adaptations still amount to a significant percentage of film productions today. German cinematic narratives depended heavily on literature from film's inception, and for more than a century at this stage, literary texts originally written in German were adapted by some of the most respected filmmakers—from Georges Méliès, Fritz Lang, Max Ophüls, and Rainer Werner Fassbinder to Lewis Milestone, Orson Welles, Stanley Kubrick, and Tom Tykwer—to great national and international acclaim. In several cases, an outstanding literary work is remembered mostly due to its adaptation, for example Heinrich Mann's novel *Professor Unrat* (*Small Town Tyrant*, 1905), which was a success in

German-speaking countries prior to the First World War but became an international sensation when Sternberg's *Der blaue Engel/The Blue Angel* (1930), starring Marlene Dietrich and Emil Jannings, hit the cinema screens.

During the twentieth century, cinema developed from a technical novelty to mass entertainment and frequently served as a projection screen for the public sphere. While contributing to memory culture and the maintenance of literary heritage, the film industry time and again made use of familiar narratives to communicate both content and opinions. Jürgen Habermas famously differentiated between the public sphere in pubs, coffeehouses, and on the street, and the 'organized presence of the public in theater and film performances'.[4] The latter is an 'abstract public' produced via mass media and, as German filmmaker Alexander Kluge notes, it is a public sphere that can be purchased.[5] For over a century, filmmakers utilized this function and several examples in this book highlight their thematical range. Source texts are normally either contemporary literature or masterpieces of the literary canon, but children's and youth literature and popular literature have been considered in this volume when their adaptations made a significant contribution to film history or were otherwise relevant in this context. The frequent labeling of women writers' works as 'trivial' and, especially by the far-right in the 1920s and 1930s, as 'asphalt literature' excluded authors like Vicki Baum, Gina Kaus, or Gabriele Tergit from the canon of German-language literature for many decades, even though this categorization has been called into question by scholars since the 1990s. Apart from a few notable exceptions such as Johanna Spyri's *Heidi*, adaptations of German-language literature in international cinema demonstrate a literary canon that is almost exclusively male.

Since the beginning of film, cinema has been a contested space. At the same time, transnational literature and adaptations helped to bridge the gap between high culture and mass entertainment, feeding the medium's hunger for narratives to this day. This book generally follows a simple chronology of German-language literature on cinema screens, while foregrounding the range of adaptations and investigating the films' complex functions within specific cultural, political, economic, and even personal contexts. It begins with a focus on the rise of narrative integration in early film and traces the transnational and intercultural trajectory of adaptations of German-language literature (Chapter 1), before examining early twentieth-century adaptations and adaptation criticism in Germany and outlining both cultural contexts and legal frameworks that shaped early film adaptations of German literary texts (Chapter 2). After the First World War, cinema became the most popular mass entertainment medium in Europe and the United States. Film functioned as productive commodity and provider of escapist leisure, and literary texts were adapted to all genres. In German-language countries, filmmakers frequently turned to literature when seeking to mediate values, shape public discourses via cinema screens, and thus contribute to civil society. But film also became art and cinema began to affect the literature of the avant-garde. German-language literature was integral to productions of the so-called 'Golden Age' of silent cinema (Chapter 3) and served as inspiration for hugely successful early talkies within the German film industry and abroad (Chapter 4). The lure of Hollywood and the mobility of directors such as Ernst Lubitsch, or actors such as Marlene Dietrich and screenwriters such as Vicki Baum contributed to the internationalization of German film. Hitler's rise to power in 1933 accelerated this move of talent across the Atlantic, with nearly all outstanding German filmmakers and writers being forced into exile, many of whom gratefully accepting a temporary home and workplace in the film industry in Paris and Hollywood, but also in Shanghai or Bollywood (Chapter 5).

In the German Reich, adaptations were to help make Nazi propaganda palpable. Nazi cinema's (ab)use of German literature included classical playwrights such as Schiller and canonical authors Storm and Fontane, but also a novel by world-renowned writer and Jewish exile Lion Feuchtwanger. Chapter 6 examines the mechanisms by which cultural products of the time were ruthlessly shaped by ideological convictions and political opportunism. The following chapters repeatedly reflect on the role of literary heritage and contemporary literature on film as cultural intervention. After 1945 the manifold consequences of the Second World War and the Holocaust, the physical and material as well as the psychological and moral devastation experienced by millions led to a new engagement with literary texts by producers and makers of German film. National Socialism and Hitler's reign had caused the most significant ruptures in cultural production processes, which directly affected German culture for decades to come. It required not only trials that shed light on the crimes committed and passed judgment on some of the perpetrators, but decades of relentless information campaigns, supported by political leaders as well as educators.

'Schuld' in German means both guilt and debt, and German culture has been haunted by its own history. The second half of this book examines adaptations in the context of their narrative potential within varying degrees of willingness to work through a horrifying past. Understandably, the international community had only little patience for adaptations of German-language literature after 1945. In Germany and Austria, the trauma of war and Holocaust impacted film production, and the literary texts chosen for adaptation reveal much about the nations' anxiety regarding their shameful history (Chapter 7). At the same time, German literature once again became a vehicle for the communication of certain values that were now for the most part intended to stabilize, distract, and comfort. Tracing adaptations produced in East and West Germany allows for fascinating insights into the role of literature in the contexts of Holocaust memory, antiwar activism, cultural heritage, and nation building in a divided country with differing ideological outlooks.

In the 1960s German literature became core to New German Cinema, as Chapter 8 outlines.

Questions regarding the time and place of adaptations of particular literary texts have been central to my inquiry. Socio-political conditions, the market, but also the availability of public funding influenced both choices regarding source texts and cinema history. Subsidies from federal and local governments are vital for filmmakers and have enabled some of the most creative engagements with the medium—films of New German Cinema in the 1960s and 1970s being a case in point. Literature played a central role in this revival of art cinema in Germany. Changes in national funding policies and subvention schemes in 1984 saw a profit-driven film industry looking to maximize returns by tapping into markets beyond the German-language area, while auteur filmmakers like Werner Herzog and Volker Schlöndorff left for the United States. The ways in which literature contributed to Germany's neoliberal cinema from the 1990s is the focus of the final chapter, while a list of 'solitaires'—adaptations that in my view stand out and deserve further attention—concludes my inquiry.

Some of the literary texts mentioned in this book appear repeatedly during the twentieth and twenty-first centuries. Why certain novels or plays have had this multiplicatory effect that repeatedly prompted filmmakers to adapt the text for cinema and later television screens is a recurring query in this volume. Georg Büchner's story of insanity and artistic genius *Lenz* (1835/39), which was turned into film at least ten times, or the numerous adaptations based on Heinrich von Kleist's novella *Michael Kohlhaas* (1808/1810)—the tale of a man's resolute if hopeless fight for justice[6]—indicates the role of adaptation in the context of our need (and the creative industries' awareness thereof) to reflect on human nature and on the essence of relationships, our desire to continuously re-imagine ourselves and the communities we live in. Not being considered producers of a lesser art, German filmmakers have often displayed an uncommon confidence regarding the use of literature for film, and their adaptation projects have had a significant impact on the history of German film from its inception in the late nineteenth century to the present day. Filmmakers have been turning to literature not only for inspiration or economic success, but because certain stories not only are great entertainment, but deserve or even need to be re-seen and, as Walter Benjamin had hoped, re-read.

The editors of this series, Greg Semenza and Bob Hasenfratz, convincingly argued for the need of adaptation studies to look beyond the source text or "cinematic adaptations of a particular canonical literary author" and account for the role of literary films "within movie history itself."[7] As I embarked on this project, I soon realized I could not tell the story of adaptation in this context without exploring, for example, the interplay between literary and film texts, commercial interests, or how the literary text itself inspired a film's aesthetic and new forms. Throughout this book, literary sources shine through, while the focus remains on processes of adaptation, trends within the industry, and reception histories. German-language literature was adapted for many reasons, from commercial to political, pragmatic, and aesthetic ones. This book hopes to shed some light on the role of both literary heritage and contemporary literature from the first pioneering adaptations of the late nineteenth century to its place in both twenty-first-century neoliberal film industries and art cinema.

When Sergei Eisenstein quoted Goethe in the preface to his "A Dialectic Approach to Film Form" (1949)—"In nature we never see anything isolated, but everything in connection with something else which is before it, beside it, under it, and over it."—the German writer's understanding of the creative process matched Eisenstein's own take on filmmaking as a palimpsest of narrative substance that could be communicated via montage. Adaptations are multi-layered narratives that intersect the past with the present while providing creative and reflective spaces for the future.[8] The contemporaneity of many of the adaptations discussed in this volume that reflect this 'passion for the present' with a view toward the past that 'crosses' or 'thwarts one's horizon'[9] should not divert from relevant "materialist conditions,"[10] but it is much more than commercial interests that shaped film history.

As this book will highlight in some detail, the history of German-language literature on film was dramatically influenced by twelve long years under Hitler's reign and far-right politics which led to another even more horrific war and genocide. Even more so than its military defeat, Germany's moral downfall is the undercurrent to many of the creative engagements with literature for film during the second half of the twentieth century. After having destabilized the world so dramatically with its expansionist war of aggression, mass murder, and the Holocaust, adaptations contributed to processes that helped Germany emerge from isolation and work through cultural anxiety and its bloody past, while communicating a critical awareness of the constructedness of their historical depictions. From the 1960s, a new generation of young German and Austrian filmmakers turned to literature, producing reflections and cinematic analysis of the horror emanating from Germany during the twentieth century, its willing collaborators, and misguided ideologies. Films like Volker Schlöndorff's *Der junge Törless* [Young Törless] (FRG/FR, 1966) based on Robert Musil's 1906 novel, or his adaptation of Günter Grass' bestselling *Die Blechtrommel* [The Tin Drum] (FRG/FR/YU, 1979) won globally recognized awards in Cannes and, in 1980, even an Academy Award for Best Foreign Film. The success of his adaptations helped to further re-integration and to restore to some degree the international community's view of German culture.

In his play *Das Leben des Galilei* (The Life of Galilei, 1938), Brecht has the seventeenth-century philosopher Galileo Galilei say: "Unhappy the land that needs heroes." This rings true when considering the many literary narratives adapted to film screens since 1945. Even in run-of-the mill postwar *Heimat*-films both national heritage and gender identities are often negotiated before a backdrop of heroic masculinities turned into cannon fodder. The history of German literature on film is shaped by its continuities, but even more so by its ruptures. Many of the adaptations mentioned in this book allow their viewers to see the literary text in an entirely new light, unveiling its obscured wisdom and profound complexities. More often than not, however, the laws of the medium and its industry make an adaptation seem naïve, unsophisticated, and even strained. This book focuses not only on those outstanding adaptations that brought literature to life on screen, that progressed the medium and the genre, and reshaped viewers' experience of the literary text.[11] Many films today forgotten or overlooked will be remembered on the pages to come, for it is their creators' multifaceted achievements that contributed to aesthetic shifts and made the history of German literature on film. Some adaptations and their remakes time and again remind us of the lessons of history and the gifts of democracy and peace within specific cultural and sociopolitical contexts.

Despite my best efforts to not only illuminate general trends but also put a spotlight on the many and often forgotten adaptations of German-language literature, this book cannot be exhaustive. But I hope that this volume will contribute to a better understanding of the history of German-language literature on film, and of the complexities and nature of specific adaptive relationships. My research is embedded in cultural and historical contexts as they shaped and are reflected in relevant adaptations and their reception.[12] Numerous writers and scholars—among them Ernst Toller in 1924 and Arjun Appandurai in 2017—highlighted the significance of mass culture and the diegetic function of even spectacular film narratives as the communication of values, truth, realities, and justice.[13] This is conveyed in many adaptations discussed in this volume, and their fidelity to the literary text is of little relevance in this context. Some adaptations remain so close to their source that they appear like a calque translation. Others are perhaps reminiscent of surrealist painter Max Ernst's *graffage* process by which the surface pattern of an underlying fabric, leaf, or wood is incorporated into the work of art like a story that is told in two different media at the same time, one shining or chiming through the other. And while conventional filmmaking, franchise productions, and brand building dominate much of the bestseller adaptation landscape of popular crime novels and children's and youth literatures today, some films inspired by German-language literature are works of art and evidence to the possibility of creative freedom and playful experimentation in adaptative practices.

Notes

1. See, for example, Felicitas Hoppe's new novel *Die Nibelungen. Ein deutscher Stummfilm* [The Nibelungs. A German Silent Movie] (Frankfurt/M.: Fischer, 2021).
2. See for example Michael Wedel, *Filmgeschichte als Krisengeschichte* (Bielefeld: transcript, 2011); Thomas Elsaesser, *European Cinema: Face to Face with Hollywood* (Amsterdam: Amsterdam University Press, 2005); Jennifer Kapczynski and Michael D. Richardson, eds., *A New History of German Cinema* (Rochester: Camden House, 2012); Michael Braun, *Prometheus unchained: Beiträge zum Film* (Würzburg: Königshausen & Neumann, 2016); Stefan Neuhaus, ed., *Literatur im Film. Beispiele einer Medienbeziehung* (Würzburg: Königshausen & Neumann, 2000); etc.
3. Hester Baer points to the "substantial number of films produced across national borders since the beginning of cinema that have been adaptations" and quotes Carolyn Anderson ["Film and Literature," in *Film and the Arts in Symbiosis*, ed. Gary R. Edgerton (New York: Greenwood, 1988), 97–132; quoted in Kyle Edwards, "Brand-Name Literature: Film Adaptation and Selznick International Pictures' *Rebecca* (1940)," *Cinema Journal* 45.3 (2006): 32], who estimates that "more than a third of classical Hollywood films were adapted from novels." She also refers to Eric Rentschler's estimation in 1985 of around 800 adaptations of German-language literature, and rightly notes that "[e]ven the number 800 is low, since Rentschler did not conduct an entirely systematic or exhaustive count." Eric Rentschler, ed., *German Film & Literature: Adaptations and Transformations* (London: Routledge, 1986); Hester Baer, "Producing Adaptations: Bernd Eichinger, *Christiane F.*, and German Film History," in *Generic Histories of German Cinema: Genre and Its Deviations*, ed. Jaimey Fisher (Rochester: Camden House, 2013), 173–96, here 181–2.
4. Jürgen Habermas, *Strukturwandel der Öffentlichkeit* [1962]; trans. Thomas Burger and Frederick Lawrence as *The Structural Transformation of the Public Sphere* (Cambridge: Polity, 1989); Alexander Kluge, *Geschichten vom Kino* (Frankfurt/M.: Suhrkamp, 2007), 33.
5. Kluge, *Geschichten vom Kino*, 33.
6. Georg Büchner's *Lenz* was adapted by G. Moorse, 1971; A. Rockwell, 1981; O. Hockenhull, 1985; A. Szirtes, 1987; J. Lodemann, 1988; E. Günther, 1992; D. Marchais, 2003; M. Franchini, 2004; T. Imbach, 2006; and A. Morell, 2009, and by Isabelle Krötsch in her experimental documentary *Büchner.Lenz. Leben*, 2013. Kleist's *Michael Kohlhaas* was adapted by W. Vollmar, 1967; V. Schlöndorff, 1969; J. Badham, 1999; A. Lehmann, 2013; A. des Pallières, 2013.
7. Greg Semenza and Bob Hasenfratz, *The History of British Literature on Film (1895–2015)* (New York: Bloomsbury, 2015), 5.
8. See especially Sandro Zanetti, "Poetische Zeitgenossenschaft," *Variations* 19 (2011): 39–53; Giorgio Agamben, "Was ist Zeitgenossenschaft?," in *Nacktheiten*, trans. Andreas Hiepko (Frankfurt/M.: Fischer, 2010), 21–36.
9. Zanetti, "Poetische Zeitgenossenschaft," 53. As noted above, single quotation marks refer to my own translations from the German original.

10 Thomas Elsaesser, *Weimar Cinema and After: Germany's Historical Imaginary* (New York: Routledge, 2000), 438.
11 Jed Pearl, *Authority and Freedom* (New York: Knopf, 2021).
12 While this book is focused on adaptations in their historical contexts rather than on theories on adaptation, the latter published by especially Dudley Andrew, Deborah Cartmell and Imelda Whelahan, Kamilla Elliott, Linda Hutcheon, Thomas Leitch, Laurence Raw, Julie Sanders, and Robert Stam have been very useful and shaped my understanding.
13 Ernst Toller outlined his view of cinema's potential in an article on "Film und Staat" in 1924. See my article on "Ernst Toller und das Kino," *text+kritik* 223 (2019): 47–57. Arjun Appandurai defined the significance of film as such in his lecture at Humboldt University in Berlin on July 14, 2017.

1

The Beginnings of German-language Literature on Film (1897–1906)

> *I address you all tonight as you truly are:*
> *wizards, mermaids, travelers, adventurers and magicians.*
> GEORGES MÉLIÈS IN BRIAN SELZNICK'S *THE INVENTION OF HUGO CABRET*[1]

In 1903, one of the most creative pioneers of early silent cinema Georges Méliès presented a short film entitled *La laterne magique*.[2] It opens with a clown and a *pierrot* who are busy assembling a large magic lantern. Once put together, the device magically projects images of the past and subsequently the present until, surprisingly, the two characters themselves appear as projections. Clearly unsettled by this sudden doubling, the two frantically set out to dismantle this indeed magic device. But instead of a flame, its center miraculously reveals another narrative and layer of early cinema history in the form of an enthusiastic group of six beautiful chorus girls and one soloist. The story of projection is here equipped with additional attractions and light-hearted entertainment as the soloist performs cartwheels and somersaults while the six women do the cancan. Their performance reenacts what cinema's pioneers would often have captured on film and later screened as a spectacular conclusion to a variety show, hereby doubling both the performance of cinematic action and the pleasure of entertainment.

In German-language literature light-projected entertainment technology, such as the *laterna magica* or magic lantern, played a role long before the birth of cinema or, to be more precise, before the first public screening of a series of short celluloid film strips by Max Skladanowsky on the Skladanowsky brothers' Bioskop projector for a variety show in Berlin's

Wintergarten theater on November 1, 1895. Johann Wolfgang von Goethe and E.T.A. Hoffmann, for example, describe the effect of seemingly magical projections on individuals in their texts when cinema as a mass entertainment medium could hardly have been imagined.[3] From the first moments moving images flickered across a makeshift screen in Berlin and Paris, London and New York, cinema amused, surprised, and enchanted audiences. But some considered film screenings light entertainment at best and any encroachment of the medium into the realm of high culture a provocation, while the conditions of film screenings—men and women sitting in dark spaces and in close proximity—seemed incompatible with bourgeois morality and filled many in the middle and upper classes with anxiety. In addition, the blaze at the 1897 Bazar de la Charité in Paris caused by a Cinematographe installation catching fire and resulting in more than 120 deaths among (mainly aristocratic) women while hundreds more suffered burns and smoke inhalation heightened the fears associated with the new medium. Nonetheless, moving pictures were sensational and the first narratives on film proved most attractive commodities. Soon film began to offer reflections on the human condition and reimagined culture in a myriad of ways. Literature and the practice of adaptation are at the core of early narrative cinema, but so is the enchantment deriving from film's endless possibilities, as Méliès suggests in his short film about the magic lantern. Just like a good novel or play, the brand-new medium had the potential to create spaces of illusion that have since continuously sparked our imagination and brightened our world.

As other volumes in this series indicate, the practice and process of adaptation have been an integral part of filmmaking nearly from its very beginning, shaping the history of cinema in various ways. The reasons for early silent cinema's turn toward literary narratives—or, rather, toward popular protagonists and key moments based on well-known source texts—with a focus on the most prominent examples of German-language literature on film will be the preoccupation of this first chapter. Looking at cinema's infancy and literature as complex cultural palimpsests in general and at adaptations of Goethe's *Faust* in particular, the following pages query the function of German literature in those early narrative films.

Within little over a year following the first public film screenings in Berlin and Paris, adaptations of *Faust* and other classics negotiated the tension arising from traditional high culture and cinema as *vaudeville*. Following their first experiments with documentary film, pioneers of cinema soon used canonical narratives to entertain and, by linking their short films to popular plays and operas, to tempt the educated middle and upper classes to take a closer look at the new medium. Their short films communicated elements of the literary canon to the masses—and, ideally, across the social spectrum.[4] Even during this first decade, adaptations served to address bourgeois audiences' apprehensions regarding this new technology. By then countries such as France and Germany were significantly shaped by industrialization and urbanization, but also by an ever so swiftly progressing secularization. The ensuing destabilization of traditions, political and economic systems, as well as changes to work practices, social structures, and individual interpretations of the everyday led to an amplified sense of insecurity and uncertainty. Both swiftly growing cities and modern entertainment industries provided especially the bourgeoisie with anxiety.

The consumption of high culture had been the privilege of the educated classes. As Jörg Schweinitz[5] points out in his collection of essays on early film, the purpose of this consumption was primarily an intellectual engagement of the upper classes. The awakening of the imagination and the practice of contemplation were considered important constituents of an educated mind. Around 1900 cinema transgressed into the cultural realm with irritating speed and surprising efficacy. The popularity of the new medium quickly became the cultural icon of the modern, industrialized, and highly capitalized society. Film was synonymous with both entertainment/culture and capitalism, i.e., the commodification of culture. Considered a *parvenu*[6] or illegitimate upstart, early twentieth-century films provided plenty of cause for angry articles condemning the new mass medium that offered such fascinating entertainment for millions every day. In early narrative cinema, texts like *Faust*—a folk tale that inspired the most widely known play in the German language as well as art songs, symphonies, and operas across Europe—clearly profited from their inherent spatial and national hybridity or transcultural rootedness.

The creativity with which literary narratives were transposed onto cinema screens is stunning, fascinating, and often hilarious. Choosing novels and plays, lengthy and wordy genres of literature, for a minute-long, silent medium is bound to challenge the viewers. Hence a critical debate emerged that became particularly heated in the early twentieth century and today provides valuable insights into the struggle to make film mainstream. German authors like Goethe, Schiller, or Hoffmann[7] used the *laterna magica* as both metaphor and narrative device in their literary texts; soon pioneers of filmmaking and entrepreneurs such as Louis Lumière, Alice Guy, and Georges Méliès in France turned to these authors in particular not least because "the German Reich was undoubtedly a most attractive market."[8] But also George Albert Smith and Robert W. Paul in Britain or Thomas Edison and Edwin S. Porter in the United States used German literature to communicate the magic of cinema via narratives that would have been known to the majority of respective audiences.

These very early shorts could only offer a moment's glimpse of a literary text, of course, but a viewer's ability to place a short film narrative into an imaginary and yet familiar, i.e. much more elaborate plot, equipped the early and so-called "cinema of attraction"[9] with narrative complexity that was as yet impossible to produce on (one-shot) film. For that first generation of filmmakers, literary texts offered inspiration and a good yarn at once. Of course, there was no need in fact for the audience to be familiar with the adapted text, as one could be quite sure that cinema at that time would have been extraordinary and spectacular no matter what. But the film pioneers' choice of only the best-known literary texts indicates both their rootedness in literary culture and their expectation that even a title reference to a well-known text would benefit the commercial viability of their new product. In addition, these very first adaptations for variety or sideshow presentations reflect a desire to integrate film into the other forms of cultural expression. Film was indeed a sensation and attraction as film scholars such as Tom Gunning and André Gaudreault have pointed out. But, as Thomas Elsaesser[10] and others have emphasized, at the same time the ambition to be producers of art is apparent in many of the films and adaptations from the beginning.

Pioneers of Filmmaking

My story starts in France, not in Germany, as it is in the country of some of those most gifted and innovative pioneers that German-language literature appeared on film for the first time. In the beginning, films were shot with a stationary camera and usually presented as unedited, continuous footage lasting often only a few seconds or, if projected at a slower speed, provided fascinating entertainment for up to a minute.[11] How quickly cinema technology advanced during this early period becomes evident when looking at 1897 adaptations of German literature that already last up to a couple of minutes. Even then, the use of literature on film indicates the filmmakers' desire to develop cinema into an art form. Documentary footage or short narratives of amusing mishaps entertained, but the most outstanding pioneers of early silent film envisaged a cinema of spectacle and wonder that could be rooted in literary and high culture. By attempting to bridge the gap between spectacular entertainment and literature, they doubled the imaginary and, sometimes, economic impulse that was to shape adaptations during the years to come.

The pace and range of the development of moving images to film narrative during those first few years of filmmaking are staggering and reflect the enthusiasm, creativity, and inventiveness of cinema's pioneers. Photographer and inventor Eadweard Muybridge, to name just one of the medium's creating forerunners, had already presented sensational chronophotographic pictures in motion from the beginning of the 1880s. His Zoopraxiscope was a device for the display of moving images that had taken inspiration from the *laterna magica*. Muybridge traveled back and forth between the United States and Europe to advertise his work (much of it during the 1880s, partly enabled due to sponsorship by the University of Pennsylvania). He met and worked with, for example, the French photographer Étienne-Jules Marey and inspired the German film pioneer Oskar Messter,[12] who "perfected" Muybridge's Zoopraxiscope system.[13] Much of the work of pioneers such as Wordsworth Donisthorpe in England, Louis Le Prince in France, or Scotsman William Kennedy Dickson in the United States impacted on the history of cinema as it changed once and for all the imaginary possibility and promise of visual representation. Inventors like Dickson, an employee of Thomas Edison, or Charles Moisson, who worked in Lyon for the brothers Lumière, were eager to explore further technological possibilities to record and project a mobile world. Edison's and Dickson's Kinetoscope or kinematographic camera or the Lumière brothers' Cinématographe was among the first motion picture cameras ever built.

It was the Cinématographe of the Lumière brothers—camera, projector, and film printer in one—that proved the most practical and popular of all projection devices developed at the time. Soon the most widely used projector in Europe, it made the production and projection of film a highly profitable business. After first shorts in 1895 such as *La Sortie des ouvriers de l'usine Lumière* [Workers Leaving the Lumière Factory]—the first 'film' (and the first remake) as we understand it—and *L'Arrivé d'un train en gare* [Arrival of a Train in the Station] that famously sent spectators in the first rows ducking, it was the introduction of narrative that impacted even more greatly on the popularity of these early films. Louis Lumière's *L'Arroseur arrosé* [The Sprinkler Sprinkled] (1895) that saw a gardener inspect the water-less garden hose—only to get splashed in the face every time his apprentice lifts his foot off the hose—was copied many times and proved an enormous success. The ensuing growth of the profitable industry encouraged others to take the leap into this novel enterprise that continued to gain in popularity across the social spectrum, especially among working and lower middle classes.[14]

Probably the most outstanding narrative artist of early cinema was Georges Méliès (1861–1938), a professional magician, actor, illustrator, and owner/operator of the Théâtre Robert-Houdin in Paris, who encountered film for the first time at a Lumière side-show presentation in 1895. Immediately realizing the great "illusionist potential"[15] of this invention, Méliès' sought to acquire a Cinématographe projector for his and his wife Eugénie Génin's theater. He spoke to the Lumière brothers but was refused as the entrepreneurs were probably trying to minimize their competition. But Méliès was hooked, sourced an Animatograph projector from the British inventor Robert Paul and used it to build his own movie camera.[16] And, as David Cook emphasizes, "by April 1896 Méliès was showing his own productions in his own theater. In time, he would become the cinema's first important narrative artist as well, but not before he had done some apprentice work in the manner of the Lumières and Edison by filming a series of *actualités,* comic episodes, and stage conjurer's tricks for projection in his theater."[17] Both Louis Lumière and Georges Méliès, however, turned to literature almost as soon as they began experimenting with film.[18]

Early films by Lumière in France, Edison in the United States, or Max and Emil Skladanowsky in Germany were not only very short, but the camera was static and unwieldy. The camera distance was always the same unless the camera was physically moved, which meant that little alteration of camera distances, i.e. reframing of action, was done in films prior to the turn of the century. Providing audiences with references to a current opera production or a well-known play on film was a logical step that would at once allow for additional complexity of a simple, continuous narrative, while curbing the effects of the static camera's limitations and ensuring early cinema's continued popularity and economic success. It is perhaps a reflection of the seductiveness of the new medium also for its creators that the most internationally popular of the literary narratives adapted to early cinema was *Faust*.

Faust on Film

It was J.W. v. Goethe who turned the story of Johann Georg Faust—the topic of many representations in popular culture since the sixteenth century—into a literary sensation. Johann Spies had published his *Historia von d. Johann Fausten* (the 'Volksbuch') in 1587, warning the reader of the dire, hellish consequences of a lack of virtue and humility. Johann Fausten's insatiable desire for knowledge, power, and pleasure makes him enter into a pact with the devil. His hubris becomes the downfall of this respected and valuable member of society. Inspired either by a German version of the Faust legend or by *The English Faust Book* (1592), the story was dramatized for the Elizabethan stage by the playwright Christopher Marlowe shortly before his death in 1593 as the *Tragical History of the Life and Death of Doctor Faustus*. Marlowe's adaptation remained popular for centuries, until Goethe's tragedy (first published in 1808 with a second part to follow shortly after the author's death in 1832, i.e., *Faust I* and *Faust II*) turned the text into one of the most influential pieces of German-language literature to date. Goethe (1749–1832) was a celebrity and the most distinguished German writer of his time, which surely helped in the international distribution of his tragic play about an individual's descent—"Vom Himmel durch die Welt zur Hölle"[19] as Goethe put it—'from heaven though the world to hell'. The story of human weakness, the bet between Mephistopheles and God in Heaven, and the toxic pact between Faust and the devil on Earth has inspired adaptations from the very beginning of cinema history to this very day. Perhaps it was not only the awareness of the universal and timeless relevance of this tale, but also the deep fascination with cinema technology and the seductive force of moving pictures that suggested the Faust narrative to early film pioneers like Lumière and Méliès. They would likely have been familiar with the tale from Gerard de Nerval's work—a surrealist *avant la lettre* and famous for taking his pet lobster for walks in the Palais Royal—who had translated Goethe's *Faust I* into French, despite claiming that his German was only rudimentary. Goethe, however, who had good French, attested to Nerval that he had perfectly captured the spirit of his play.[20]

Nerval's translation of Goethe's text into French in 1828 (and the revised version published in 1840) became bestsellers. Further translations into English and other European languages and, in addition, adaptations in music continuously lifted and enriched the aura of Goethe's masterpiece. Whether it was songs based on *Faust* by Franz Schubert, an oratorio by Robert Schumann, or a *Faust Symphony* (1857) by Franz Liszt, *La damnation de Faust* (1846) by Hector Berlioz, Charles Gounod's *Faust* (1859), or Arrigo Boito's *Mefistofele* opera (1868; 1875), performances of these various pieces and operas in cities like Paris, Berlin, New York, Vienna, and London as well as countless popular representations and re-narrations ensured the public's familiarity with the *Faust* narrative and, at least implicitly, Goethe's tragic play.

It was especially the popularity and continuing success of Gounod's *Faust* opera that prepared the ground for adaptation. Early filmmakers were entrepreneurs who sought to minimize the economic risk of costly narrative films by referring to already successful and widely known cultural products in their adaptations. Hence—and within little over twelve months after the so-called 'birth of cinema'—Goethe's *Faust* was adapted to film by both the Societé Lumière and Georges Méliès. Their short *Faust* films, which succinctly staged key moments of the narrative, were swiftly followed by additional adaptations of Goethe's play.

Georges Hatot worked for Louis Lumière's production company in Lyon and, in 1897, filmed the seduction of the extremely learned but increasingly frustrated Faust in *Apparition de Méphistophélès* [Appartition of Mephisto], followed by Faust's transformation and first encounter with Gretchen in *Métamorphose de Faust et apparition de Marguerite* [Transformation of Faust and appearance of Gretchen]. The magical appearance of Mephistopheles and the depiction of Faust's honest efforts to resist the devil's draw in this short film would have been astounding visualizations of a narrative familiar to many at the time.

Méliès and *Faust*

Whether or not Georges Méliès saw the Lumière production before starting his own adaptation of the text cannot be said for certain. But his *Faust*-films are truly spectacular. By turning to literature, the fabulously creative entertainer Méliès doubled the magic. He shaped new and exciting illusory worlds on film while cinema was still in its infancy, and seemed to tap into those imaginary worlds within his viewers. At a time of growing awareness regarding the human psyche, due to the lectures and publications by Sigmund Freud especially, Méliès referred to German literature repeatedly. His appreciation of both story-telling and literary traditions, his passion for film, and his utilization of a range of source materials beyond literature are all apparent already in his early *Faust* adaptations.[21] But it is also his innovative creativity that enabled representations of human torment and the frailty of man's soul even with the most rudimentary cinema technology.

The magic of Mephistopheles' sudden appearance or disappearance and his mystical powers must have appealed to Méliès the magician, but a coincidence enabled him to equip film with equally 'supernatural' powers. As Méliès explained in his memoirs[22] the camera, placed by the side of the road, jammed one day while he was shooting traffic. He continued shooting from the same spot shortly after and realized upon inspecting the footage that the recorded material suggested an omnibus had miraculously disappeared or had suddenly turned into a hearse, creating the first and entirely accidental jump cut. Absolutely delighted in his discovery, Méliès made the most of this new possibility of optical illusion and *Faust* provided just the yarn. Unfortunately, his *Le Cabinet de Méphistophélès* [Mephisto's Laboratory], *Faust et Marguerite* (both 1897), and his Berlioz and Goethe inspired *La Damnation de Faust* (1898) appear to be lost, but according to archival records, Méliès developed the storyline, starred as Mephistopheles, arranged and edited the footage. He used disappearing and reappearing effects, often by way of small explosions, puffs of smoke, and stop motion photography.

With his technologically innovative takes on Goethe's tragedy, Méliès produced a visual sensation, which at the same time highlighted cinema's narrative potential years before narrative film became the norm. Five years later, he presented Faust's damnation as a multi-shot narrative with fantastic backgrounds and plenty of drama in over six minutes. In *Faust aux enfers* [Faust in Hell; released in the United States as *The Damnation of Faust*] (FR, 1903), Méliès and his crew show off an array of tricks, especially during the cinematographically spectacular descent into the depths of hell that features violent waterfalls, sudden bursts of white smoke, scarring and abruptly changing scenery. Phantasmagoric backgrounds of infernal landscapes dominated by harsh contrasts and razor-sharp angles overwhelm the small figure of Faust as he is being dragged along by Mephistopheles.

FIGURE 1.1 *Méliès as Mephistopheles in* Faust aux enfers *(FR, Georges Méliès, 1903).*

In the depths of this unstable netherworld, fire and endless caves with stalactites sharp as knives give way to beautifully dancing women, perhaps meant to distract or calm the clearly distressed Faust. But this sequence evoking entertainment is hardly what it suggests. This is not a cabaret like the Moulin Rouge but a place of damnation. Here an attractive female dancer suddenly turns into a frowning octopus or volatile spider-like monster before transforming once again—this time into a male human form. There is no humor, but only Faustus' highly entertaining horror as the shocking instability of gender in this scene takes root. Finally, Mephistopheles grabs his victim and disappears into a hole in the ground while flames and smoke emanate from those frightening imaginary depths of hell. Upward moving panes to both sides of the two seemingly floating figures emphasize both their long descent and Faust's catastrophic fall. Having arrived in the core of Mephistopheles' infernal home, dancing women swarm around the devil as he spreads his threateningly large, black wings that will, eventually, drown out all light and thereby conclude the narrative.

In 1904, surely due to the popularity of his *Faust* films, Méliès reshot the sequence in hell for his *Damnation du docteur Faust*. The film now told the Faust narrative in nearly fifteen minutes and was promoted in France as fantastic play in twenty scenes—"a pièce fantastique à grand spectacle en 20 tableaux (d'après le roman de Goethe)"—clearly linking the film to both theater and Goethe's text. In contrast, advertisements in the United States foregrounded Gounod's opera rather than Goethe's *Faust* as source text.[23]

Méliès' *Faust* films are performative spectacles and, in this sense, belong to the aforementioned "cinema of attractions." But even his earlier *Faust*-adaptations as 'moving tableaux' convey narrative elements of *Faust* and together present a sequence of dramatic scenes. From 1902/3, the multi-shot format allowed Méliès to convey a sense of narrative continuity, as well as an illusion of visual and narrative mobility, despite the fact that each individual shot was taken from a fixed point of view. The camera is still 'chained', motionless, but the sequence of shots and the 'magic' of special effects such as stop-action or substitution splices, multiple exposures, dissolves, and fades create the illusion of visual mobility and ensure the continued fascination of audiences at the time. Méliès' eye-level shots and the viewers' familiarity with a literary figure or text allowed for an affective communication of much more than a 'sensation' or 'attraction' but, rather, for a multi-layered narrative on screen. As argued by Andrew Watts in *The History of French Literature on Film*, adapting well-respected literary texts became a profitable endeavor for early filmmakers, not only in financial terms, but by associating film with traditional culture and thus legitimizing the new medium within modern society.[24]

Faust on International Screens

The first *Faust* film by British magic lantern lecturer and film pioneer George Albert Smith was an 1898 copy of the French adaptation, which highlights the success of both the Lumière and Méliès' productions abroad. By 1902 Méliès' Star Film had become one of the major players in international motion picture distribution with offices in Berlin, London, Barcelona, and New York.[25] His films were so popular that he reshot some of them, such as his *Faust* adaptations, partly in order to update them as the art of editing advanced rapidly. But he also wished to remind international audiences of his original work, as other international *Faust* adaptations were being presented to audiences and sold abroad. G. A. Smith had produced not only his 'own' *Faust*-film, but also an American adaptation of Goethe's play or, rather, of Méliès' film, copyrighted by Thomas Edison and, possibly, produced and/or directed by Edwin S. Porter premiered on February 28, 1900, in the United States.

While it is unclear if it was indeed Porter[26] who directed the film, we know that he worked as a projectionist and in 1901 became head of production for Edison's Skylight Studio, but also continued to work as cameraman and director in the company. He often copied commercially successful European films—especially by pioneer Méliès, whom he particularly admired—a common practice prior to the establishment of internationally binding copyright laws.[27] This first American *Faust and Marguerite* adaptation recounts the tale of Gretchen and Faust, however, with a twist. Here, Faust resists Mephistopheles' seduction. When he is handed a sword and enticed by the devil to kill Gretchen by beheading her, Faust remains steadfast and refuses. Mephistopheles then miraculously turns into Faust and a skeleton appears in his stead. In the end, after further tricks and jump-cut transformations, Mephistopheles seems abandoned, and Faust and Marguerite are wed by a priest.[28] But having witnessed the role reversals only seconds before, who can be sure that poor Gretchen indeed married Faust and not the devil?

While implicitly a tribute to Méliès and, more than likely, also an effort to replicate his financial success, the narrative in this film is almost secondary as it shows off the technical possibilities of the new medium at the time. These quick-fire transformations created by splicing together shots and therefore manipulating and compressing time itself could not be performed in theater, the filmmaker seems to tell us, and it is therefore cinema, and not the theater, that will be the art form of the new century. This level of mobility and flexibility of identity, time and space due to tricks and editing, i.e. the arrangements of shots in a particular sequence, was indeed not available to traditional stage productions, and this magic drew ever-growing numbers to screenings of these early films.

During this first decade, Faustus appeared on short silent films in Europe and the United States at least a dozen times.[29] Méliès' updated and extended remakes of his own *Faust* films from 1903 onward are full of enchanted transpositions from one sphere or body to another. In his *Faust aux enfers* (1903; released in the United States as *The Damnation of Faust* and in the UK as *The Condemnation of Faust*—also inspired by Hector Berlioz's operatic 'dramatic legend' *La damnation de Faust*, 1846, inspired by Goethe) and *Damnation du docteur Faust* (1904; released in the United States as *Faust and Marguerite* and in the UK simply as *Faust*), for instance, Méliès displays the full range of his editing skills, from substitution splices to superimpositions and dissolves and, of course, his much-loved pyrotechnical repertoire of tricks. In Méliès' new version of *Faust and Marguerite*, Faust is visibly burdened by age and longs for youth. The devil provides him with the latter in exchange for his soul. As part of the seduction of Faust, an image of Gretchen at the spinning wheel appears—as in Goethe's *Faust*, in the scene in 'Gretchen's Room', when the girl laments that her 'peace is gone' and her 'heart is sore'. The image in the background not only doubles Faust's imaginary longing, but—for those familiar with Goethe's play—the illusionary superimposition could be read as a forewarning as it predicts the loss of peace and the heartache, if not the damnation, to come.

But Faust is desperate and one look at Gretchen suffices to make him kneel before Mephistopheles kissing his hand. Gretchen, in contrast, is much more steadfast (as long as there is no magic involved) and refuses the now young and beautiful Faust when he first approaches her outside the church with the crowds looking on.

Alice Guy's *Faust and Mephisto* (1903)

The same year Méliès' *Faust aux enfers* premiered, Alice Guy[30]—the first female film director among the pioneers of cinema, who had displayed narratives on screen as early as 1896[31]—presented her first *Faust* adaptation. Having to earn her keep by working as a stenographer from age seventeen after the deaths of her father and brother, she began her career at a photography equipment company (Comptoir general de Photographie) as a secretary to Léon Gaumont. Gaumont not only offered her a job when he set up his own company but supported her wish to become a filmmaker. She had been fascinated by moving pictures from her first encounter when the Lumière brothers presented their Cinématographe at an internal presentation months prior to the first public screening in December 1895. Two years later, Guy was appointed head of production at Gaumont. Unlike the Skladanowsky brothers, whose short films at the time provided audiences with fascinating documentaries like busy traffic on Berlin's streets and amusing scenes with a boxing kangaroo or a couple performing tricks on a high bar, Guy[32] wanted her moving pictures to tell stories. Like Méliès, she wrote her own scripts, experimented with variations in camera distance, hand-tinted color, and utilized editing to structure her short narratives.[33]

Her 1903 *Faust et Méphistophélès* relies heavily on stop-motion 'magic' and presents Mephistopheles as the necromancer who overwhelms poor old Faust with an array of different characters and life options. Faust is bored, depressed, and ready to give up on his failing scholarly endeavors, he longs for change and distraction. Mephistopheles' cunning presentation leaves its mark and Faust, like a first-time moviegoer, is initially terrified, then pleasantly surprised, only to become increasingly fascinated by those constantly changing identities and scenarios unfolding in front of him. But it is only when the devil offers a superimposed glimpse of Gretchen that Faust's resistance falters. Guy, however, offers a happy end, when evil seems to be defeated by the cross and Faust emerges with Gretchen by his side.

Like cinema itself, her *Faust et Méphistophélès* is such a wonder of changing scenarios and magical entertainment that one forgets the immobile camera and the stage-like space. By 1903, the first female film director uses a bestselling literary text derived from a popular tale and adapted to great acclaim for the opera, and not only replaces traditional

FIGURE 1.2 Faust et Méphistophélès *(FR, Alice Guy, 1903)*.

forms of entertainment with film, but reflects on Faust's escapist desire in a highly industrialized society well aware of the seductive challenges facing humankind.

Cinema versus High Culture

As cinema became increasingly popular in the public sphere, film and industrial mass entertainment turned into a highly contested space. And it was especially the transfer of literary texts to cinema screens that prompted outcries by critics about those 'modern' cultural products' reductive expediency. Turning a bestselling play into a popular opera was one thing, but reducing *Faust* to a few minutes of 'silent' moving pictures quite another. The mass appeal of cinema only strengthened, however, due to filmmakers like Guy or Méliès turning to literature for narrative inspiration. And slowly, as the first decade of cinema came to a close, at least for some of the educated middle and upper classes, the literary source began to function as a bridge to the new medium. Soon advocates of the new medium argued that the less educated thereby gained access to the cultural canon, as the following chapter will highlight in more detail.[34] Adaptations therefore, at least potentially, had a leveling effect, which did not translate into economic or social power of course, but just as the cinema space was possibly shared across social divides, representations of 'high culture' could now be accessed by a mass audience.

Strongly believing in their own intellectual superiority, the bourgeois "Bildungsphilister" or educated philistines (as Nietzsche had called them a generation earlier) harshly criticized the commodity aspect of cinema. Films based on *Faust* or other transpositions of the canon of (trans)national literatures pushed the uncomfortable realization that productions of plays by stars like Goethe or operas like those by Gounod were commodities intended to provide public entertainment in modern societies. In this respect, they did not differ from a film shown in one of the growing numbers of new and purpose-built cinemas in all major cities, from Paris to London, New York to Berlin. Goethe's tragedy *Faust I* in fact opens with a poem highlighting the creative process as reflective practice (as we would call it today), and the "Vorspiel" features a theater director, a poet, and a comedian who discuss the intention of their creative product. Soon they decide that their interests are all valid. Whatever they produce should be art, but also entertainment, and needs to be economically sound. But this only applies to theatrical spaces or Goethe's "Bretter," i.e., the boards that mean to be the world. Goethe continues his *Faust* tale in heaven, where further complexities are highlighted, and representation as such is questioned by Mephistopheles. It comes as no surprise that these questions appealed to the pioneers of filmmaking. The literary texts chosen for early film plots reveal much about their desire to produce art, entertainment, and an attractive commodity at the same time.

Thus, the Lumières', Méliès', and Guy's short *Faust* movies were not the only adaptations of Goethe's play, Berlioz's musical *légende dramatique*, or Gounod's opera. In 1906 Léon Gaumont presented *Faust* and *Mignon*, both based on Goethe, followed by another *Faust*-adaption by the Pathé brothers a year later. Méliès again retaliated with another *Faust* film in 1909, but an ever-increasing number of competitors both in France and abroad had discovered Goethe and produced films in quick succession.[35] All those moving pictures taking inspiration from Goethe's *Faust* were, however, only a few among hundreds of wonderful short narrative films at the time. As Cook rightly emphasized, it was, of course, theater that had provided the inspiration for early cinema's narrative mode. Wholly familiar with the narrative structure and theatrical performance of plays, Méliès, for example, "conceived all of his films in terms of dramatic scenes played out from beginning to end, rather than in terms of shots, or individual perspectives on a scene."[36] The practice of adapting the literary canon, however, was not only considered cultural trespassing by a growing number of critics of the new medium. It also indicates the experience of cinema as a cultural rupture that accompanied the beginning of the new century and beyond.[37] Early adaptations of literary texts especially were criticized as 'hailstorms of stimuli'[38] that provided short summaries of the literary canon to the modern city-dwellers in this accelerated century of extracts and disconnect. Guy's *Faust*, who recounted the entire tale in barely two minutes, could be considered the perfect example of the speed challenging modern city-dwellers in their everyday and around the clock, leading to the love-hate relationship with the city by its inhabitants so innovatively portrayed by German Expressionists from 1907. The success of these early films fueled the rage of many conservative critics.

Turning to literature for narrative substance did little to ease the resistance toward this new medium and novel form of entertainment. But at the same time, adaptations not only aided in the communication of a complex tale during this era of relatively limited means of film production, but as early cinema supporters argued, the translation of literary texts into moving pictures also improved the literacy of audiences regarding the new medium of cinema and could be viewed as thoroughly educational. The apprehension regarding cinema's corrupting influence, based on questionable storylines and on the proximity of human bodies in dark spaces, could be relieved to some degree by transposing highly respected literary texts and projecting them onto cinema screens. The moral and educational value of classics like *Faust* would have been undisputed and the use of characters such as Faust, Gretchen, and Mephistopheles during the infancy of cinema illustrates not only the talent of film pioneers such as Méliès and Eugénie Genin, the brothers Lumière, Léon Gaumont, and Alice Guy as entrepreneurs, but also as communicators of a new form of cultural representation.

Schiller on Film

Early adaptations of Goethe's *Faust* highlight both the opportunity and calamity inherent in using the literary canon for film. It was not only Goethe, of course, who inspired early filmmakers but also, unsurprisingly, his contemporary Friedrich Schiller (1759–1805), the other celebrity playwright of nineteenth-century German-language culture. Already in 1898, Méliès took the mickey out of the Swiss national hero Wilhelm Tell—and, by implication, Friedrich Schiller's famous 1804 play—illustrating not only his well-known talent for comedy but socio-political criticism. In his gloriously bonkers *Guillaume Tell et le clown* (1898), Tell is a puppet that comes to life after having been put together by an industrious clown. Whenever the fool turns his back on the 'legend', however, he gets smacked. Méliès once again uses stop motion jump cuts or substitution splices to create his own satirical and delightfully disrespectful magic of the Tell legend. The film not only uses slapstick to entertain—men hitting one another over the head with whatever tool they can find has been a popular instrument for entertainment almost from the inception of moving pictures and seems to continue as a source of amusement in both television and cinema to this day. But Méliès' film also deconstructs a national icon in the context of the *über*-masculine Swiss hero and his revered, nation-building Rütli-oath. Here, the legendary fourteenth-century freedom fighter and symbol of Swiss patriotism is involved in a ridiculous struggle with an annoyingly patronizing clown. One could interpret Méliès' depiction as critique of the many and often quite hagiographic cultural Tell representations, from monuments to operas and plays, that were created throughout the nineteenth century in order to strengthen national identity in Switzerland and beyond. Méliès' criticism might also have been directed at nationalism as such or at the 'clowns' that do not tire of fanning its dangerous flame. In the end, it is the clown, having put together the legend or hero's statue in the first place, who gets a proper thrashing by no one lesser than Tell himself. But, perhaps, it was all just a bit of fun, like Faust and Mephistopheles had been throughout the late Middle Ages, when the legend or its first printed versions such as the *Historia von D. Johann Fausten* (The Story of D. Johann Fausten, 1587), *Das Widmann'sche Faustbuch* (Widmann's Faustbook, 1599) or, to name but one more, *Dr. Fausts großer und gewaltiger Höllenzwang* (Dr. Faust's great and enormous coercion of hell, 1609) were adapted for puppet theater. Faust, who according to the legend arrogantly chose limitless human over divine knowledge, earthly pleasures over moral integrity, gets his comeuppance in the end, and his punishment was surely greeted with enthusiasm by audiences of the puppet plays, especially if Faust's final downward spiral into hell included a good hiding or other bits of vulgar fun just like in Méliès' *Guillaume Tell et le clown*.

Méliès and the Magic of E.T.A. Hoffmann

In 1900 Méliès had turned his attention also to E.T.A. Hoffmann and produced *Coppélia ou la Poupée animée* based on motifs taken from Hoffmann's "Der Sandmann" (The Sandman, 1816) and most likely inspired by the revered ballet *Coppélia ou La Fille aux yeux d'émail* that had premiered in Paris in 1870 and became part of the standard repertoire of the Opera. Soon after, Jacques Offenbach's *Les contes d'Hoffmann*—an opéra fantastique based on three of Hoffmann's stories, which premiered in Paris in February 1881—included the dance of Olimpia, a moving puppet. The attraction to the automaton, the will to control the machine, the difference between illusion and reality are all motifs in Hoffmann's "Sandmann"-tale. Here, when Nathanael sees Olimpia for the first time, he notices that her eyes seem dead, as if asleep. Only when he looks at Olimpia through a telescope bought from Coppelius—a mysterious salesman who offers 'pretty eyes, pretty eyes!'—the object of his desire seems to come to life. The harder he looks, the more it seems as if the power of her gaze is ignited, 'more and more alive burned her looks'.[39] The deep attraction to the automaton, like the movie camera, is its ability to bring imagination to life, to make a vision reality, like a dark power reminiscent of the visions offered to Faust by Mephistopheles.

Méliès' famous 1902 film *A Trip to the Moon* (Star Film 399–411), inspired by Jules Verne and others, could also be considered a response to

Hoffmann's "Sandmann." In Hoffmann's story, the protagonist and student Nathanael recounts his fear of the "Sandman" who, according to his parents, came to children who insisted on staying awake at night and refused to go to bed. The Sandman would steal their eyes and use them to feed his own kids who lived on the moon. Perhaps Méliès' answer to this tale of terror and horrifying threat of blindness was to send a space capsule shaped like a bullet filled with astronomers to the moon and land it smack in one of the moon's blinking eyes as retaliation. As mentioned above, Hoffmann's tale focuses on the fantastical versus reality, the automaton versus the human being, enlightenment, and the dark power of the look. For the filmmaker unfolding stories through the lens of the camera is at the center of the process of storytelling on film. The fascination and dependency on the machine, the increasing blurriness of distinction between the real and the imagined could drive one to *luna*cy—as poor young Nathanael, who loses his mind when the eyes of his beloved (automaton) roll on the floor before him. He recovers only to be driven to madness once again when looking at his soon-to-be betrothed Clara through the looking glass (which he had used before to longingly gaze at the automaton Olimpia). In Méliès' films, the impossibility to distinguish between reality and illusion should not be cause for alarm, their creator seems to tell us. The rocket to the moon is the vehicle to a magical world just like the cinema is a place of dreams. Where is the fun in always knowing the subject of our gaze, Méliès the magician might ask. Cinema's magic lies in its light-hearted ability to have us pick up Olimpia's eyes and juggle.

Méliès' *Coppélia ou la Poupée animée* and *La laterne magique* might serve as examples of early silent cinema's power to confront viewers with their doubles or *Doppelgängers*. And already in 1906, Ernst Jentsch, the forgotten father of a psychology of the uncanny, published his "Zur Psychologie des Unheimlichen," which addresses the public's fear of automatons and doubles. He explains this fear as an inability to uphold their imaginary defenses that clearly distinguish between us and them, between real and imaginary, familiar and strange.[40]

Conclusion

The literary canon becomes early silent cinema's vital tool in addressing potential audiences' apprehensions regarding this new technology. At the same time, the aforementioned film pioneers' capacity to turn literary imagination into visual power could be considered a critique of the arrogance of those guardians and executors of the 'arts', i.e. traditional forms of 'high' culture such as literature, and the bourgeoisie's disdain for street entertainment such as cinema. Those early filmmakers were manifestly ready for that fight. Looking at Goethe and Schiller adaptations alone, it is clear directors were not shying away from the literary canon, but rather using it to make their point, highlighting film's potential to bring it once again to life for a modern mass consumer. Alice Guy, for example, followed Méliès with her own adaptation of Schiller's *Guillaume Tell* (1900), the same year as the London-based film pioneer Robert W. Paul brought his own version of the Swiss hero's tale to British audiences. Lucien Nonguet released his *Tell* version in 1903.

Looking at early silent cinema through the lens of adaptation unveils much about the cultural currency of both literature and film, and the motivations of those pioneers of filmmaking such as Lumière, Méliès, Guy, and others during this initial period. When pioneering filmmakers established their first production companies, presenting profitable commodities was fundamental to their economic survival. As other books in this series highlight, at first the most widely known literary texts were brought to film. Not surprisingly, it was Goethe—a literary genius comparable to Shakespeare and, like him, a most prominent part of cultural history—who dominates the beginning of the history of German-language literature on film. His *Faust* plays and adaptations like Gounod's opera inspired some of the earliest examples of narrative cinema from 1897 onwards.

Tapping into already popular sources could maximize potential audiences and secure financial profits. But the literary canon also served as a useful vehicle in other ways. Adaptations in music (especially opera) and popular (folk) culture had increased the currency of particular narratives while early silent films were struggling to tell complex tales. Even before the turn of the century—when filmmakers began more actively to associate cinema with literary classics and thus 'high' culture by way of adaption as the second chapter will argue—the storytelling impulse of early silent cinema is as apparent as the desire to present the new medium in an implicit dialogue with some of the masterpieces of literature. In the context of German-language literature, Goethe and Schiller offered significant cultural capital even to filmmakers abroad, especially in France, Britain, and the United States.[41] One of the strongest motifs for bringing literary masterpieces such as *Faust* to film was their international popularity, which served to widen the appeal of cinema while potentially lending cultural credibility to the new medium.[42]

But it was not only cultural prestige filmmakers like Méliès were after. His *Faust* films imply an interest in communicating the potentially complex narrative capacities of the new medium even in those first one-shot films (by way of sequels) and, from 1902, in multi-shot narrative films.[43] There was little concern with fidelity, of course, as the short format of these early film necessarily confined the sources text to its key moments. Nonetheless, as adaptations in other genres, they could serve as a playground for film's potential and attesting to early filmmakers' creativity.[44] Adapting a flagship of literary culture, such as *Faust* within little over a year of the first public screening and so-called birth of cinema, also indicates a critical engagement with the separation of culture into high art and lowbrow, unsophisticated forms of entertainment, which reflects a class-based categorization of its consumers along social hierarchies. Already during the first decade literature on early cinema screens helped to bridge the divide between traditional culture and modern entertainment, and challenged class-based divisions in modern society by offering moments of interaction across both cultural and social boundaries.

Notes

1   Georges Méliès in Brian Selznick, *The Invention of Hugo Cabret* (New York: Scholastic Press, 2007), 506.
2   Jacques Malthête and Laurent Mannoni, *L'oeuvre de Georges Méliès* (Paris: Éditions de la Martinière, 2008).
3   See, for example, Goethe's *Die Leiden des jungen Werthers* (1774) in *Sämtliche Werke*, ed. Eduard von der Hellen, Stuttgart-Berlin 1904–1905, Bd. XVI, S. 42: "Wilhelm, was ist unserm Herzen die Welt ohne Liebe! Was eine Zauberlaterne ist ohne Licht!" and E.T.A. Hoffmann's early nineteenth-century *Fantasie- und Nachtstücke* (1815–17). Cf. Friedrich A. Kittler on Hoffmann's *Fantasie- und Nachtstücke* in "'Das Phantom unseres Ichs' und die Literaturpsychologie," in *Urszenen*, ed. F. Kittler and Horst Turk (Frankfurt/M.: Suhrkamp, 1977), 162–4.
4   The concept of adaptation as a rarity in silent film has been proven wrong. See Timothy Corrigan, "Literature on Screen, a History: In the Gap," in *The Cambridge Companion to Literature on Screen*, ed. Deborah Cartmell and Imelda Whelehan (Cambridge University Press, 2007), 29–43.
5   Schweinitz, "Vorwort," in *Prolog vor dem Film* (Leipzig: Reclam, 1992), 5–14, here p. 6.
6   Ibid., 7.
7   See, for example, Friedrich Kittler's article "Die Laterna magica der Literatur: Schillers und Hoffmanns Medienstrategien," http://edoc.hu-berlin.de/hostings/athenaeum/documents/athenaeum/1994-4/kittler-friedrich-219/PDF/kittler.pdf.
8   Frank Kessler and Sabine Lenk, "The French Connection: Franco-German Film Relations before World War I," in *A Second Life: German Cinema's First Decades*, ed. Thomas Elsaesser (Amsterdam: Amsterdam University Press, 1996), 62–71, here p. 64.
9   This term was first coined by film scholars Tom Gunning and André Gaudreault in Gunning's 1986 essays on "The Cinema of Attraction: Early Film, Its Spectator and the Avant-Garde" and in the co-authored (with A. Gaudreault) "Le cinema des premiers temps: un défi à l'histoire du cinema?" of the same year.

10   Elsaesser, *A Second Life: German Cinema's First Decades*; for further reading see relevant publications by Heide Schlüpmann, Thomas Koebner, Sabine Hake, Rainer Rother, Deniz Göktürk, Anton Kaes, Wolfgang Jacobsen, Harro Segeberg, and Karsten Witte in the bibliography.
11   David A. Cook, *A History of Narrative Film* (New York and London: Norton, ³1996), 8; Douglas Gomery and Clara Pafort-Overduin, *Movie History: A Survey* (New York: Routledge, ²2011), 7–28. For more information regarding early film in Germany, see also Wolfgang Jacobsen, "Frühgeschichte des deutschen Films," in *Geschichte des deutschen Films*, ed. Wolfgang Jacobsen, Anton Kaes, Hans Helmut Prinzler (Stuttgart: Metzler, 1993), 13–38; Sabine Hake, *German National Cinema* (London: Routledge, 2008), 8–17.
12   The correct spelling is Meßter, but since Messter is more common in English-language publication, the adapted spelling is used here.
13   Cook, *A History of Narrative Film*, 9.
14   For further information regarding early silent film, see Lee Grieveston and Peter Krämer, eds., *The Silent Cinema Reader* (London: Routledge, 2004; especially Richard Abel's "The Cinema of Attractions in France, 1896–1904," 63–76; and Joseph Garncarz, "Art and Industry: German Cinema of the 1920s," 389–400); Simon Popple and Joe Kember, eds., *Early Cinema: From Factory Gate to Dream Factory* (London: Wallflower, 2004); Elsaesser, *A Second Life: German Cinema's First Decades*.
15   Cook, *A History of Narrative Film*, 13. Cook recognizes the narrative potential of early silent film and includes pioneers such as Méliès in his study. He avoids the common designation of the early decade of filmmaking as a cinema of sensation (rather than narration). When focusing on literature on film, the problematic nature of this category becomes particularly apparent.
16   Méliès "simply reversed its mechanical principle to design his own camera, which was constructed for him by the instrument-maker Lucien Korsten." Cook, *A History of Narrative Film*, 14.
17   Cook, *A History of Narrative Film*, 14.
18   Méliès, cinema's great early pioneer, often based his short films on often extensive literary texts from Jonathan Swift's *Gullivers Travels* (1726, amended 1735) as *Le voyage de Gulliver à Lilliput et chez les géants* (1902); Daniel Defoe's *Robinson Crusoe* (1719) as *Les aventueres de Robinson Crusoé* (1903); Miguel de Cervantes's *El ingenioso hidalgo don Quijote de la Mancha* (1605/1615) as *Don Quichotte* (1908); *20000 lieues sous les mers* by Jules Verne and William Shakespeare's *Hamlet* and *The Death of Julius Cesar* (all 1907).
19   In a letter Goethe's to Eckermann, January 25, 1827.
20   Nerval's first translation of *Faust* was published in 1828, with a revised version available in 1840. Johann Wolfgang von Goethe, *Le "Faust" de Goethe*, trans. Gérard de Nerval, ed. Lieven d'Hulst (Paris: Fayard, 2002); cf. Léon Cellier, *Gérard de Nerval: L'homme et l'oeuvre* (Paris: Hatier-Boivin, 1956); Louis Betz, "Goethe und Gérard de Nerval," *Goethe Jahrbuch* 18 (1897): 197–217; Oskar Seidlin, "Goethe über Goethe auf Französisch," *The Germanic Review* 21 (1946): 241–6.

21   For more context and further useful information about Méliès, see Andrew Watts' first chapter of *The History of French Literature on Film* (New York: Bloomsbury, 2021); "The Currency of Adaptation: Art and Money in Silent Cinema (1899–1929)," 19–62.
22   Méliès, *Mes Memoires* (orig. publ. Rome 1938); see Cook, *A History of Narrative Film*, 14.
23   Malthête and Mannoni, *L'oeuvre de Georges Méliès*, 164.
24   Watts, "The Currency of Adaptation," 20f.
25   Cook, *A History of Narrative Film*, 15f.
26   According to the Library of Congress, the film was copyrighted to Thomas A. Edison on 28th February 1900 (D4734). "According to Musser's *Edison motion pictures 1890–1900*, although this film was copyrighted by Edison, it does not appear to have been made at the Edison studio, or by Edison producers or affiliated filmmakers. Maybe a foreign production. According to some sources, including early motion pictures, this film was produced by Edwin S. Porter. However, according to Musser's *Edison motion pictures 1890–1900*, p. 675, Porter was not hired by the Edison Manufacturing Company until November 29, 1900, nine months after this film was made and copyrighted." See (including the film itself) https://www.loc.gov/item/00694201.
27   For further information about the lack of copyright legislation and Méliès' efforts to distribute his own films internationally, see Matthew Solomon, "Negotiating the Bounds of Transnational Cinema with Georges Méliès, 1986–1908," *Early Popular Visual Culture* 14.2 (2016): 155–67.
28   See https://de.wikipedia.org/wiki/Faust_and_Marguerite.
29   This assessment is based on films that either survived in archives or are listed in filmographies. The actual number, however, was most likely higher.
30   Alice Guy married in 1907 and was then known as Alice Guy-Blaché. For further information about her life as she saw it, see Alice Guy, *Autobiographie einer Filmpionierin. 1873–1968* (Münster: Tende, 1981).
31   See a.o. Victor Bachy, *Alice Guy-Blaché (1873–1968): la première femme cinéaste du monde* (Perpignan: Institut Jean Vigo, 1993); Alison McMahan, "Alice Guy Blaché," in *Women Film Pioneers Project*, ed. Jane Gaines, Radha Vatsal and Monica Dall'Asta (New York: Center for Digital Research and Scholarship, Columbia University Libraries, 2013); https://wfpp.cdrs.columbia.edu/pioneer/ccp-alice-guy-blache/.
32   Following her marriage to Herbert Blaché, Guy had to give up her position at Gaumont. In subsequent films she is named Mme Blaché or Alice Guy-Blaché.
33   See Alison McMahan, *Alice Guy-Blaché: Lost Visionary of the Cinema* (New York: Bloomsbury, 2002); Marquise Lepage's 1995 documentary *The Lost Garden: The Life and Cinema of Alice Guy-Blaché* (the film is available on DVD and via nfb.ca: https://www.nfb.ca/film/lost_garden_life_cinema_alice_guy_blache/).
34   Cf. for example, Franz Pfemfert, "Kino als Erzieher" [Cinema as Educator], *Die Aktion* 18 (June 19, 1911), 560–3.
35   See Ernest Prodolliet, *Faust im Kino* (Freiburg/CH: Universitätsverlag, 1978); Hauke Lange-Fuchs, *Ja wäre nur ein Zaubermantel mein! Faust im Film* (Bonn: InterNationes, 1985).

36 Cook, *A History of Narrative Film*, 14.
37 As Chapter 2 outlines, by 1910 cinemas had become 'sworn enemies of the theater,' because they offered much better entertainment for a lot less money as the critic, writer and film author Hans Land declared. Cf. Hans Land, "Lichtspiele," *Die Schaubühne* 6 (1910): 963–4. Also quoted in Schweinitz, *Prolog vor dem* Film, 18–20.
38 Quoted in Schweinitz, *Prolog vor dem* Film, 8.
39 E.T.A. Hoffmann, *Der Sandmann* (Stuttgart: Reclam, 2017), 17–28.
40 Ernst Jentsch, "Zur Psychologie des Unheimlichen," *Psychiatrisch-neurologische Wochenschrift* 22 (1906): 195. Quoted and discussed in Kittler, *Die Wahrheit der technischen Welt* (Frankfurt/M.: Suhrkamp, 2013), 93–103.
41 Semenza/Hasenfratz discuss literature as cultural capital in *The History of British Literature on Film* repeatedly; Watts engages with Pierre Bourdieu's theories more explicitly in the first chapter of *The History of French Literature on Film*.
42 Regarding the cultural privilege of source texts, see Corrigan, "Literature on Screen," 33; quoted by Semenza/Hasenfratz, *The History of British Literature on Film*, 13.
43 Semenza/Hasenfratz, *The History of British Literature on Film*, 30.
44 Cf. Semenza/Hasenfratz, *The History of British Literature on Film*, 28. *Faust* adaptations functioned less as advertisements, as Semenza and Hasenfratz imply in the context of first adaptations of British literature, than as a transmedial dialogue with cultural representations. The idea of cultural capital is also central to Watts' argument in "The Currency of Adaptation," 20–62. Watts builds his chapter around Pierre Bourdieu's theory of cultural, social, and economic capital and beautifully teases out the relationship between them in the context of the 'currency' derived from early cinema. Having looked at adaptations of German literature in early French cinema, I can only agree with his assessment.

2

Early Transnational Narrative Cinema and the Impact of the First World War (1907–18)

> *Cinema is the people's most treacherous educator.*
> FRANZ PFEMFERT, 1909[1]

> *There are people who never go to the movies. There are also people who never take a bath. I find both types rather disagreeable.*
> HANNS HEINZ EWERS, 1910[2]

This chapter looks in detail at the most important examples of early narrative cinema based on German-language literature. Some of these films are lost, others long forgotten, but they deserve to be rediscovered, not least because they shed light on both the critical and the affirmative function of adaptation in this early period.[3] Increasing numbers of adaptations based on the literary canon reflect filmmakers' creative engagement not only with the Empire's imagined literary heritage, but with the objections to the new mass medium by critics and reformers. The Wilhelmine era's cinema reform movement gained momentum in 1907 following the patronage of German teachers' associations. Supporting the medium in view of its educational potential, cinema reformers at the time nonetheless warned of the moral dangers inherent in the consumption of light entertainment—such as, especially, titillating melodramas and vulgar comedies—in crowded nickelodeons or *Kintopps*.[4]

Foregrounding examples of bourgeois culture on film and marketing strategies that implied cinema as high art served to legitimize the new medium during this era, even though its opponents were not easily swayed.⁵ The following pages are preoccupied with filmmakers' creative use of film as high culture within German-speaking countries and abroad, which—as Joachim Paech and others have argued—led to a literarization of film, and thus potentially altered not only the conditions for "Zerstreuung"⁶ or distraction, but also both the range of potential audiences and the public function of cinema at the time.⁷ The transnational significance of German-language literature and the impact of the First World War are further prominent themes of this chapter.

The desire to tell stories that would capture the viewers' imagination is reflected in the work of film pioneers on both sides of the Atlantic. In Europe, France and soon Denmark emerged as dominant players in the cinema landscape during the early years of the twentieth century. But not surprisingly, it was particularly in Germany, as Anton Kaes points out, that "filmmakers were eager to explore the artistic potential of the new medium in order to prove to a skeptical *Bildungsbürgertum* [i.e., the educated middle-class] that film could be more than just a technological fairground amusement for the masses."⁸ Reflecting a sense of competition with the theater and even the opera,⁹ adaptations produced during this second decade of filmmaking thus celebrated their solid footing in one of the other arts, namely literature. Gradually, moving pictures based on German-language texts began confidently to unfold into works of art in their own right, while indicating cross-fertilization, transnational influences, and, further, national or even local intertexts. In addition, the German-language plays or prose texts chosen were often cultural palimpsests layered with further literary narratives or previous adaptations and variations in other arts, thereby gently guiding more discerning audiences already familiar with adaptations of German literature in other cultural realms such as the opera, toward an appreciation of film.

Considering key moments that impacted the cultural currency of adaptation, Timothy Corrigan mentions the "emergence of the scriptwriter, and the necessity of scripts and screenplays as key components in the production of films" after the premiere of *Ben Hur* (US, Sidney Olcott, 1907) and its subsequent copyright lawsuit.¹⁰ Corrigan is right to point to the 'scriptwriter' when highlighting a professionalization of the transposition process that affected the position of literature within the motion picture industry, and to the early twentieth century as an "especially active period in the cultural disciplining of film through the adaptation of material and practices from older literary or artistic heritages."¹¹ The year 1907 might seem of little significance at first glance, but with regard to cultural representation, it marks a most radical and cathartic re-imagination of everyday life. Key moments range from Pablo Picasso's first cubist painting *Les Demoiselles d'Avignon* to Oskar Kokoschka's first expressionist play *Mörder, Hoffnung der Frauen* (Murderers, Women's Hope). At the time, increasing numbers of visual artists and writers produced provocative and outrageous works that reflected the tensions and challenges of modern society and culture in novel and audacious ways.[12]

Marginalized figures of society had been moving into the center of canvases already during the nineteenth century, from Jean-François Millet's *Les Glaneuses* (The Gleaners, 1857) and, especially, since the exhibition of Édouard Manet's scandalizing *Olympia* in 1863. In German literature Gerhart Hauptmann's naturalistic play *Die Weber* (The Weavers, 1892) put disadvantaged workers and exploitative practices center-stage in Germany and Silesia, giving dignity and attention to the invisible members of industrialized, capitalized society since its premiere in 1894. By 1907, the plight of women and the systemic corruption of the modern subject were becoming the most dominant themes in avant-garde German-language literature. Contemporary author Margarete Böhme published *Dida Ibsens Geschichte* (Dida Ibsen's Story, 1907), a novel that confronted sexual and physical abuse in marriage head-on while highlighting bourgeois society's double moral standards that contributed to women's exploitation and ill-treatment. The same year, Hugo von Hofmannsthal wrote *Furcht. Das Gespräch der Tänzerinnen* (Fear. A Dancers' Dialogue) inspired predominantly by the Syrian satirist Lucian of Samosata's Ἑταιρικοὶ Διάλογοι (Dialogues of the Courtesans, around 160 AD) and Heinrich von Kleist's *Über das Marionettentheater* (On the Marionette Theater, 1810). Here a conversation between two prostitutes about their hopes and fears and the significance of dance in society and for themselves reflects the experience of modernity and the value of myths, the power dynamics of social order, body and mind, and dance as a 'vision of pure presence'.[13]

From 1907 onwards, an increasingly confident and highly critical engagement with modern society by a new generation of young artists, writers, and filmmakers depicted 'fallen women' and prostitutes,[14] but also criminals and mental patients, in order to question the sanity of a society that not only tolerates, but administers marginalization, discrimination, and injustice. Other members of the avant-garde questioned representation as such and pushed the boundaries of film's mimetic potential. An early Vitagraph-film featuring stop-motion animation, James Stuart Blackton's *The Haunted Hotel*, premiered in Paris in April 1907, inspiring the young cartoon artist Émile Cohl to create *Fantasmagorie*, the first entirely animated film lasting nearly two minutes and consisting of approximately 700 drawings, designating Cohl the "father of animation."[15] While cubism and expressionism challenged visual and literary representation from 1907 in theater performances, art exhibitions, and publications, new levels of abstraction in narrative cinema only captured the imagination of moviegoers from 1920 onwards, beginning with *Das Cabinet des Dr. Caligari* (DE, Robert Wiene, 1920) and in *Von morgens bis mitternachts* [From Morning to Midnight] (DE, Karlheinz Martin, 1920).[16] Meanwhile narrative cinema was becoming the most popular mode of entertainment of the working and lower middle classes, especially in Europe's and the United States' urban centers.

The number of cinemas in Germany, Italy, France, Denmark, and other European countries, but also in the United States and Russia had been growing at a remarkable speed. And after a decade of mobile film screenings as part of variety shows, the popular medium began to settle down. By the end of 1907 proper cinemas had opened in all major cities in Germany, and they multiplied 'like rabbits' as one critic put it.[17] There were nickelodeons or *Kintöppe*, as the cheaper, unventilated cinemas for the lower classes were called, and *Lichtspiele* for the more discerning and higher earners. Soon imposing *Filmpaläste* [film palaces] marked the gradual leveling of film and other arts performed in theaters or opera houses.[18] As Emilie Altenloh argued in her 1914 PhD thesis on the *Soziologie des Kinos*, these luxurious *Filmpaläste* imitated "respectable theaters (displaying cloakrooms, bars, program notes, ushers and orchestras) making the cinema a fad among the urban upper and upper middle classes, bringing them up to date on fashions and sentiments and linking them to the international world of cultural consumption."[19]

The Canon of German-language Theater and Popular Literature on Film

Cinema had developed from an act in a variety show to an indispensable contributor to a mass entertainment industry. Offering recreation inspired by its nearest competitor, the theater, the new art form now produced moving pictures that were often structured like plays, dividing its narrative into a number of acts—such as the five "Bilder" [pictures/images/acts] in Schiller's *Die Räuber* of 1907—and intertitles. The latter created an unambiguous link to the literary text, frequently offering direct quotes from the play in question, but also allowing for further narrative complexity. The year Rudyard Kipling was awarded the Nobel prize for literature for his "power of observation, originality of imagination, virility of ideas and remarkable talent for narration,"[20] adaptations of German literature focused predominantly on theater classics. Another *Faust* by the Pathé brothers in France and Schiller adaptations by motion picture production companies in Germany and other European countries reflect a continuing appetite for the literary canon, but also an appreciation of narrative entertainment.[21] Schiller's *Wilhelm Tell*, for example, previously adapted by pioneers such as Georges Méliès, Alice Guy, Robert W. Paul, and Lucien Nonguet, was filmed once again in 1908 by French screenwriter, actor, director, and producer Albert Capellani. Viggo Larsen followed with another *Wilhelm Tell* film in Denmark the same year. In Italy, Mario Caserini adapted *Don*

Carlos[22] in 1909 and, again in France, André Calmettes filmed *Don Carlos* in 1910, swiftly followed by a first *Cabale et Amour* in 1911. The same year, *Guglielmo Tell* was adapted in Italy, and *Wallenstein* in Germany.

The first German adaptation of Schiller's highly emotional and melodramatic 'Sturm und Drang' play *Die Räuber* (*The Robbers*, 1781) was filmed in the young German Empire by the Internationale Cinematographen- und Licht-Effect-Gesellschaft in 1907. While the adaptation cannot compare to Méliès' or Guy's technological and creative genius, this rather theatrical Schiller film is equipped with a sort of happy ending catering to the *Kintopp* audience's desire for retribution.[23] But it was particularly the creative freedom of those early filmmakers that exasperated bourgeois and upper-class guardians of 'high culture', who regarded the new medium as utterly suspect and considered canonical texts on cinema screens not only reductive, but reprehensible.[24] Around 1912/13, as Miriam Hansen notes, the cinema reform movement's second wave "crystallized around issues of artistic quality and cultural value."[25] Early reformers had called for cinema to serve popular education, especially of the working class. With adaptations infringing on depictions of cultural heritage, the debate shifted to "a more abstract ethics of culture. The cinema's poaching on the domain of high art was considered reprehensible only insofar as it violated the authority and integrity of the literary classics."[26]

Nonetheless, several famous stage actors and well-known authors—such as Gerhart Hauptmann or Hugo von Hofmannsthal—were drawn to film productions. And while Goethe[27] still topped the list of internationally adapted German-language writers at the time, with Schiller[28] and Lessing[29] following suit, an increasing number of contemporary novels by popular authors such as Hermann Sudermann[30] or Margarete Böhme were being adapted to film. In Germany and Austria, however, many journalists, novelists, and playwrights voiced concerns regarding this rapidly expanding entertainment industry, outlining the dire consequences for the education and literacy of especially the lower classes, i.e., the main consumers of the medium. Other writers—like Robert Walser[31]—despaired in light of all those unlikely narrative turns and implausible plots in most of the quickly produced moving pictures being screened for a mass audience, i.e., the cinematic equivalent of a *Groschenroman* or dime novel. And while some demonized film as the brutal butcher of culture and respectable entertainment, others such as journalist and publicist Hugo Landsberger celebrated film's ability for lifelike representation and recognized the medium's narrative possibilities. He adapted his own novel *Stürme* [Storms] in 1913 (as Hans Land), praised the 'immediacy' and the 'splendid realism' of moving pictures, and acknowledged cinema's power and theater's most noteworthy competitor. For film, in his opinion, provided 'better entertainment for far less money'.[32]

The *Faust* narrative continued to be a source of inspiration for filmmakers—especially in France from Henri Andréani (*Faust*, 1910) to Jean Durand (*Faust et Marguerite*, 1911). The aforementioned pioneer of animation Émile Cohl even produced a puppet film on the topic (*Le tout petit Faust*, 1910).[33] Stories of seduction and dark powers appear like red threads throughout German literary and adaptation history. Johann Nepomuk Nestroy's magical farce *Der böse Geist Lumpazivagabundus* (The evil spirit Lumpazivagabundus, 1833/5) was adapted for the first time in Denmark in 1911/12 as *Lumpazivagabundus* or *Haandvaerkersvendens Eventyr* [The Journeymen's Adventure], starring Oscar Stribolt under the direction of Sören Nielsen.[34] Many adaptations of Nestroy's *Lumpazivagabundus*-play would follow. Is it simply a morbid fascination with the weakness of human spirit or perhaps a reflection of the seductive experience of urban, 'modern' life?

Cinema, Modern Life, and Censorship

German philosopher and sociologist Georg Simmel reiterated the modern experience of destabilization and fragmentation, and suggested the proximity between urban living and the new medium of film in his famous essay "Die Großstädte und das Geistesleben" (The Metropolis and Mental Life, 1903).[35] Ludwig Rubiner and other critics at the time remarked on the contemporary demand for multifaceted, quick-fire entertainment, elucidating the popularity of variety performances and film screenings.[36] In 1910 an article in *Die Lichtbild-Bühne*[37] hinted at the experience of a new (film) aesthetic that matched the expectations and nature of the modern city-dweller: 'Cinema [...] responds to and is in line with our nervous impatience. We demand rapid developments: extracts, concentration, three-minute novels [...]',[38] and filmmakers at the time were clearly up for it. Soon Hermann Kienzl equated the fleeting, curious, and nervous 'soul' of the modern metropolis ("Großstadtseele") and its inhabitants with the soul of the cinematograph ("Kinematographenseele"),[39] while Egon Friedell celebrated the new medium, because 'it is short, rapid, almost in code, and it does not dwell. It is scarce, with military precision. It fits our time perfectly, as we live in a time of extracts.'[40]

The majority of critics in the German Empire, however, such as Walter von Molo, was appalled at the power of the film industry, which enthusiastically embraced German literary masterpieces such as *Faust* in order to turn them into silently moving pictures as fleeting entertainment. With 70,000 cinemas globally, as Molo[41] estimated in his article "Im Kino" [In the Cinema] in April 1912, film had undoubtedly become the 'theatre of the people'.[42] With dramatic hyperbole he declared the "Volksstück" [folk play] 'murdered' by the motion picture industry, as the public clearly preferred to be entertained in stuffy *Kintöppe* rather than in a theater.[43] At the same time, he had no doubt about the benefit and educational promise of motion pictures that could potentially provide realistic information about foreign cultures, industry, or the sciences. In Molo's opinion, this possibility was already lost due to the masses' desire for light entertainment and 'cheap' tricks. The kind of well-meaning educational intent by producers of literary adaptations, however, often caused even more uproar, especially when it came to favorite classics by Goethe or Schiller, or of the Middle High German heroic epic and foundational legend the *Nibelungenlied*. When Ulrich Rauscher saw the first adaptation of parts of the *Song of the Nibelungs* in Germany in 1913—*Sigfrido* (1912) by the Italian actor, screenwriter, and director Mario Caserini[44]—he balked at the 'culture-promoting mix of Kintopp and suburban carnival' and pronounced at length the utterly ruinous effect of cinema on this beloved medieval epic, which up to that point had been 'erroneously considered indestructible'.[45]

Calls for national censorship legislation were frequent. In Germany, as Wolfgang Mühl-Benninghaus put it, "film censorship is almost as old as the medium itself."[46] In the nationalist and militaristic German Empire, film came under scrutiny especially due to frequent protests voiced by representatives of the educated middle and upper classes, self-proclaimed guardians of written culture, and the pressure applied by the conservative press.[47] While film review offices were established in all German states—even in the "Grand Duchy Saxony-Weimar which only had four cinemas"[48] in total—film censorship varied significantly between the different regions of the German Empire. Filmmakers even "filed suit against Berlin's censorship order" in 1906 arguing that the laws were based on the censorship of the press, which "had been done away with in the wake of the Press Law of 1874."[49] But to no avail. The Prussian Higher Administrative Court declared the censorship ruling as legal "since they were based on the Theater Censorship of 1850" rather than on press laws. By 1910 all jurisdictions across Germany were ordered to introduce film censorship, which was usually based on the Berlin legislation. The enforcement of these laws, however, not only differed greatly across the German Empire, but all national efforts to "battle against dirt in word and image" and to establish "tougher and more stream-lined surveillance of cinematographic theatre"[50] were only selectively implemented.

Contemporary Plays and Prose on Film

The fastest-growing industry in European capitals had an insatiable appetite for narrative. Following bitter competition between the theater and cinema during the first decade of the twentieth century—and numerous campaigns against the new medium every time a controversial adaptation of a beloved classic premiered in movie theaters—PAGU's Paul Davidson initiated a "truce between stage authors and the industry"[51] in 1912. Rather than bringing the canon of German-language literature to cinemas, producers now increased their efforts to involve well-known writers in the making of films. This led to a number of *Autorenfilme* such as Hanns Heinz Ewers' *Der Student von Prag* [The Student of Prague] (DE, H.H. Ewers/Stellan Rye, 1913) and Lindau's *Der Andere*.[52]

In support of Paul Lindau's reworking of his popular play *Der Andere* (The Other, 1893) into a script, which was filmed under the direction of Max Mack and due to premiere in Berlin in late January 1913, Germany's leading film journal *Der Kinematograph*[53] announced that the future of cinema hinged on 'famous authors'. Founded in 1907 the most prominent cinema journal emphasized the need for "Autorenfilme" [author's films].[54] Not only was it considered essential for the future of this new industry that popular authors were invited to contribute to film by producing original scripts. Writers were also encouraged to adapt their own novels or plays in order to maximize their own audience and at the same time contribute to the continued development of both the industry and a modern film aesthetic.

In an article about 'Speaking Pictures', the Viennese writer and critic Felix Salten—who would create *Bambi* a decade later—delights in those moving images that were 'so fabulously alive' during a presentation of Edison's sound film invention, the Kinetophon. But after ten minutes, he writes, one has become used to seeing realistic representations of speaking and singing human beings on a screen. Therefore, he concludes, this invention calls for excellent actors and writers as the new medium will be evidence for future generations and will 'expose our cultural standing'.[55] While the above-mentioned Hans Land or Paul Lindau certainly profited from their willingness to imagine their literary text on screen, a relatively small number of well-known writers followed suit at the time. Harry Geduld rightly points out that the "involvement of Author and Film began virtually with the inception of cinema in the 1890s,"[56] but considering adaptations such as *Den okända* [The Unknown] (SE, Mauritz Stiller, 1913), based on Hugo von Hofmannsthal's story *Das fremde Mädchen* (The Strange Girl, 1911), or the spectacular 'Gerhart-Hauptmann-film' *Atlantis* (DK, August Blom, 1913), one detects a growing interest in adaptations of, especially, contemporary German-language literature and collaborations with living authors from 1913 onwards. While numerous writers such as Hauptmann or Hofmannsthal initially rejoiced "in [their new muse's] magic and her vigor," however, Geduld also recounts their disenchantment and "disillusion with the industry's pusillanimous standards, its internal decadence and external puritanism, its prostitution of talent, disillusion with public taste and ultimately, by implication, with the integrity and value of anything that smacks of mass culture."[57] But despite a decidedly critical stance by the majority of novelists and playwrights, authors like Hauptmann, Clara

Viebig and Max Halbe, Bertha von Suttner, or Arthur Schnitzler were drawn to the new industry.[58] Whether they were interested in pursuing film projects as an additional source of income and possibly fame, or simply shared a fascination with the medium, film companies like Nordisk in Denmark provided ample opportunity for transnational, creative collaborations.

Arthur Schnitzler's *Liebelei* on Film

Because of the runaway success of Schnitzler's play *Liebelei* (Flirtation or dalliance, 1895)[59] in theaters across Europe, the Viennese company Wiener Kunstfilm had sought to purchase the adaptation rights from the author.[60] But it was Nordisk that secured the contract with the Austrian playwright, whose drama had been performed in theaters in Copenhagen from 1897.[61] Not only did the Danish company's Karl Ludwig Schröder pursue the production of a film based on Schnitzler's controversial but highly popular play, the author himself was invited to write the script for the film. After some negotiation, Schnitzler began working on a first draft in September 1912, but did not sign the contract with Nordisk until January 1913 and still made changes to the ending of the film script in February after a conversation with Salten as he records in his diary, finally proposing three different options for the final scene, as Claudia Wolf notes.[62] A remaining bone of contention was the inclusion of intertitles. Schnitzler considered it vital that the (visual) experience of the (silent) film remained unimpaired, and was fervently opposed to plates of (literary) text interrupting or obscuring the narrative on screen. In his opinion only films that 'consist of logical and self-explanatory images' will survive and be recognized as art.[63] He felt so strongly about this that he threatened to pull out of the contract as late as March 1913.[64]

Elskovsleg (Dalliance) based on Schnitzler's script and directed by August Blom was first presented in a special screening in December 1913, after which Schnitzler, an enthusiastic moviegoer himself,[65] noted in his diary his mere 'moderate pleasure' at the final result.[66] The picture—featuring Nordisk's most prolific actor (until his suicide in 1917) Valdemar Psilander, as well as Holger Reenberg, Christel Holch, and Frederik Jacobsen in the lead roles—recounts Schnitzler's play about extramarital relationships and the tragic fate of the 'sweet girl' Christine, the "süßes Mädel" in Austrian society, who did not know how to separate between a dalliance and love. The film focuses on Christine, the shy and inexperienced girl meant to be a mere distraction for Fritz who has an affair with a married woman. But Christine falls deeply for Fritz and loses everything when her beloved is killed in a duel by the jealous husband of his previous mistress. The film concludes with Christine's melodramatic collapse next to Fritz's coffin.

Schnitzler was well aware of the technical and aesthetic possibilities of film and made use of cinematic narrative tools like crosscutting and mobility with regard to time and space in his script. His demand for a complete omission of intertitles was not entirely followed through, but as Schnitzler notes in a letter to Schröder, those 'few prose titleplates in the first part of the film do not really interfere, but I still think they are completely superfluous'.[67] Schnitzler believed in film's ability to communicate a literary narrative in all its emotional, sociopolitical, and psychological complexity by way of live action, camera technique, editing and, in particular, by the actors' gestures, expressions, looks, and glances. While the plot of the film follows the play's narrative overall, Christine's suicide, implied in the conclusion of Schnitzler's original text, was omitted in the interest of a more visually dramatic and affective if somewhat maudlin ending. The film finally premiered in Denmark on January 22, 1914, and hit the screens in Austria and Germany in March that year.[68] Despite its impressive selection of indoor as well as outdoor scenes, varying camera distances, and a recognition of the dramatic events that are reflected in a 'naked and factual' manner, critic Wolfgang Ritscher bemoans the 'unfortunate relocation' of this 'typically Viennese' story to the Danish capital.[69]

Gerhart Hauptmann's *Atlantis* and Other Catastrophes

In contrast to Schnitzler's *Liebelei* or *Elskovsleg*, another Nordisk production of 1913 would fare better with regard to geographical authenticity and audience appreciation. It would do so despite its reliance on intertitles—six alone in the first two minutes and 128 in total, including one stating "Ogsaa det!" [that, too]! Hauptmann's novel *Atlantis* was produced and marketed as a sensational disaster movie of a spectacular two hours in length[70] by the recent Nobel Prize-winning author and groundbreaking playwright of Naturalism. Despite the fact that Hauptmann did not write the script but was paid royally for the rights,[71] the film was advertised as a Gerhart-Hauptmann-film. Hauptmann's story of a hitherto successful academic takes place in rural Germany, Berlin, Paris, and both New York City and State. It is the journey of Dr. Friedrich von Kammacher who leaves his family for a vacation in the city, where he becomes infatuated with a young dancer. He follows her to New York and after a number of misfortunes and a final breakdown, is saved by an independent, down-to-earth artist who accompanies him back home. While the plot is not as mundane as this short summary might suggest, the transposition to film of different psychopathologies described in the literary text is particularly innovative, but as a high-culture, mass-produced commodity aware of its own ambiguity, this generally underappreciated adaptation is truly remarkable.

Published in 1912, the text opens with a description of the ship that was to take von Kammacher to New York City. The opening paragraph reads like a harbinger of "Neue Sachlichkeit" or New Objectivity—the avant-garde German literary movement that dominated the 1920s—whose factual style was often compared to the documentary drift or actuality element of cinema:

> The German steamer "Roland" left Bremen on 23rd January 1892. It was one of the older ships of the Norddeutsche Schiffahrtsgesellschaft among those that provided transportation between Europe and New York. The crew of the ship consisted of the captain, four officers, six machinists, one provision manager and one paymaster, one provision and one paymaster assistant, the chief steward, the second steward, the head chef and the second cook, and finally the doctor.—Besides those people, who were entrusted with the welfare of this enormous floating house, there were sailors, stewards, stewardesses, kitchen assistants [...] and other employees on board, including several cabin boys and a nurse. The ship did not carry more than a hundred cabin passengers from Bremen. About four hundred passengers occupied the lower deck.[72]

Initially, the prose is occupied with facts; the reasons for Friedrich's travels from his home to Berlin, Paris, and, via Le Havre, to Southampton, where he is to board the 'Roland', are subsequently explained in retrospect.

In contrast to the literary text, the adaptation's narrative chronology (based on a script by the aforementioned Karl Ludwig Schröder and Axel Garde) is linear and begins with an introduction to Friedrich (played by Olaf Fønss, who in 1921 appeared as Herbert Rowland in Joe May's von Harbou-adaptation[73] *Das indische Grabmal*), his wife Angèle (Lily Frederiksen), and his parents (Marie Dinesen and Cajus Zeuthen Bruun), while the children remain in the background initially. Under the direction of August Blom (with assistant directors Mihály Kertész—who would later, as Michael Curtiz, become one of Hollywood's most prolific directors—and Robert Dinesen), the focus of the opening sequence is on the Kammachers' difficult home life due to Angèle's mental illness. Rather than communicating the details of her obsessive compulsive disorder on title plates, the camera centers on Angèle, who cannot stop frantically cutting pieces of cloth with a pair of scissors, until her caring husband takes the fabric away and his wife gently into his arms. Soon after as she approaches her sleeping husband with her favorite tool, unsettling both of them profoundly when he wakes, the fragmenting and devastating impact of her state on her family and herself is well illustrated. Despite the short scene's dramatic focus on Friedrich's terror when he wakes to the sight of his wife holding her scissors like a knife above him, the audience's gaze under Blom's direction remains at a distancing medium two shot. Angèle is portrayed as a victim deserving of our sympathy in this Nordisk production, while the earnest depiction of her condition reflects the growing awareness of psychopathologies in this age of Sigmund Freud. Angèle is treated with much love and tenderness by Friedrich and his parents, but Bloch also highlights the toll her serious condition is taking on her husband especially. Friedrich is the main character of Hauptmann's tale and of this first adaptation—a well-respected bacteriologist who had studied under Max Joseph Pettenkofer and Robert Koch, but whose research is considered too revolutionary by his academic peers. Exhausted and forlorn after his wife had to be committed to a psychiatric institution (where she is looked after by Friedrich's close friend Rasmussen), he travels to Berlin at the advice of his parents (in the film: his mother). Freud's article "'Civilized' Sexual Morality and Modern Nervous Illness," written in 1907 and published in 1908, is another intertext that could well have provided inspiration to both author and filmmakers.

Following a title plate informing us of Friedrich's accommodation in a Berlin hotel, the audience is provided not only with actual footage of Berlin but gets to observe Friedrich leaving his hotel and hesitating before stepping out into the busy street—an action performed by the local porter without the slightest issue just seconds earlier. Hereby, the contrast between the scientist's former rural family home and life in the German capital, the 'moloch' Berlin, is subtly emphasized. At the invitation of an acquaintance Friedrich diffidently steps out into a life-changing adventure, which is beautifully introduced by traveling shots of Berlin landmarks such as the Siegessäule (Heinrich Strack's Victory Column, 1873), the Tiergarten-park, and busy street scenes, and tracking shots that capture Friedrich's taxi passing through the Brandenburg Gate. His car maneuvers the city's traffic along Berlin's famous Unter den Linden, where the imperial castle, museums, and the Humboldt university are located, but also theaters and the opera. This is where the taxi comes to a halt and the film cuts to the inside of a theater. An intertitle informs the audience that it is young Ingigerd Hahlström, who is making her debut at this matinee.

Ingigerd is a young expression dancer who performs "Edderkoppens Offer" (translated as "The spider's victim" in the title plate). She dances a butterfly that is drawn to a large rose and intoxicated by its scent. When a sizeable spider descends from above to relax in the rose's blossom, Ingigerd's dance communicates her love for, and the seductive draw of, the 'rose' with clear sexual overtones, and the fear of the 'spider' that will undoubtedly bring about her downfall. Exhausted from her indecisive whirl, a toing and froing between safe distance and the poisoning draw of desire, the butterfly finally collapses. Based on dancers Isadora Duncan's and Rudolf von Laban's concepts of an unregimented and yet unifying system of natural body movement, expression dance had been a recent phenomenon in Germany that gained further popularity due to Émile Jaques-Dalcroze's schools of rhythmic education in Hellerau/Dresden, Berlin, and Frankfurt in 1911/12. Soon young German dancers such as Mary Wigman or Anita Berber performed pieces not too dissimilar from Ingigerd's 'spider dance' in *Atlantis*, often mesmerizing their audiences—a fact that was memorialized by Fritz Lang in *Metropolis* (1927) more than a decade later. In Hauptmann's novel the young dancer is the daughter of a circus performer, but in the film, her background is of no consequence.

A key intertitle reads: "Like a meteor from an unknown world Ingigerd slips into the grey and melancholy life of von Kammacher."[74] This implies the powerful impact of unrestricted modern urban creativity, epitomized by the young woman's expression dance, would have on Friedrich, the bourgeois and family-bound scientist. Some viewers at the time criticized the casting of Ida Orloff, however, as the 24-year-old mother failed to convince as 'the girl' ("das Mädchen") or 'the little one' (die "Kleine"), as Hauptmann describes the character repeatedly in his novel. As a mere sixteen-year-old and at the beginning of her career as an actress, Orloff had appeared in Wedekind's controversial play *Die Büchse der Pandora* [Pandora's Box] in Vienna in 1905. According to Hauptmann, her performance left its mark on the author and, supposedly, had a similar effect on the married writer at the time as his character Ingigerd had on Friedrich in his literary text. Hauptmann called Orloff his 'muse'[75] and made her his under-aged lover the same year. It was at the author's request eight years later that Nordisk employed Orloff to play the capricious virgin-*femme fatale* Ingigerd Hahlström. The portrayal of Friedrich as victim, who is smitten and struggles to find release from his passion for the young performer in both novel and film, is of course, highly problematic in terms of Hauptmann's position of authority and the sexual exploitation of a minor. Nonetheless, the film deserves our attention as the most expensive and courageous adaptation of a German-language text of its time.

As Deniz Göktürk points out, "[r]umors of colossal expenses and ambitious technology had been circulating for months before the film was released."[76] Nordisk had forwarded information about the enormity of this adaptation project to the press that duly reported the "high gross production costs (ca. 500,000 marks), the army of actors (close to eighty starring actors, one hundred supporting actors, and as many as five hundred extras for the ship scenes), as well as the chartered flotilla (including an ocean liner, three trans-Atlantic steamships, two tugboats, an extravagantly constructed wreck, and many motorboats)."[77] The implication was, of course, that quality productions by a modern media industry for mass audiences required this kind of significant investment and international outlook. Literary adaptations of this caliber, however, also necessitated a tempering of any overt eroticism in order to clearly distinguish a classy 'Gerhart-Hauptmann-film' from, for example, the highly popular *Afgrunden* [The Abyss] (DK, Urban Gad, 1910) that had sparked Asta Nielsen's international career amidst controversy.[78]

The ensuing relationship between Ingigerd and Friedrich in *Atlantis* appears platonic in the film, therefore, even though her flirtations with other men drive the fragile and underappreciated soul to seek refuge in distant Paris to get rid of his 'passion'. But his love for the sixteen-year-old 'had become an illness' as Hauptmann puts it. Hence, absence of proximity to the object of his desire is not enough, and when Friedrich reads in a newspaper that the young celebrity will be traveling to New York on the steamer "Roland," he spontaneously books a passage for the same date. The impact of the past on our present is a topic in both the novel and its film, but this adaptation also uses advances in film technology and references to cinematic history in order to fold another, entirely film-specific layer into Hauptmann's narrative. Once on the boat to Southampton, for example, Friedrich sits next to a group of 'card players', as such introduced by an intertitle. However unnecessary this confirmation in writing may be, the card players are thereby highlighted, and their presence (about twenty-eight minutes into the film) on the left half of the frame could be considered a reference to the beginning of cinema or, rather, an homage to Lumière's *Partie d'ecarte* [Card Party] of 1895. A pillar divides the frame in half and on the right a solitary Friedrich is reading a paper. As the editing speed of the film increases, the card players remain on the lower deck as static as the figures in a nineteenth-century photograph, as Friedrich and the Nordisk team have long rushed onto the upper deck awaiting the ocean liner. Soon "Roland,"[79] the huge steamer as a symbol of innovation and a better future, fills the upper half of the screen as passengers wave to one another across the divide. Nonetheless, the past cannot be left behind. On board of the ocean liner, the everyday business of a professional crew taking care of every whim of their first class passengers is foregrounded. Those on the lower decks survive in cramped conditions, including a woman reminiscent of Nielsen in *Afgrunden*—perhaps once more hinting at the fact that this is a tale for the more discerning viewers, a work of art by a 'first-class', ultra-modern culture industry.

Our hero, a representative of that upper middle class, is lost nonetheless, still captivated by Ingigert, who is as capricious as ever and surrounded by Friedrich's competition on the promenade deck (or even in her cabin). The immature celebrity's superficiality is placed in stark contrast with scenes highlighting the realism of the workings in the underbelly of the ship— sweaty men laboring in the boiler room—and of Friedrich's subconscious. Rather than depicting Friedrich's premonitions as described in the novel, Friedrich's thoughts and emotions are communicated to the viewer by way of double exposure. When he receives a letter from his mother informing him of Rasmussen's death and his wife's worsening condition, Friedrich imagines Rasmussen and his family at home. The filmmakers' choice of cinematic realism rather than supernatural visions by a psychic again indicates their collective efforts to distinguish *Atlantis* from other films of the entertainment industry. While the film shows off the entire repertoire of Danish filmmaking expertise at the time from stage-like performances, traveling shots, double exposure enabling paranormal visions and psychological insights, it also references art and thereby places itself alongside representations of bourgeois culture. A medium shot of Friedrich watching a sunset over the Atlantic is reminiscent of a Caspar David Friedrich painting, particularly of his *Wanderer above a Sea of Fog* (Der Wanderer über dem Nebelmeer, 1818). In this masterpiece of Romanticism an individual is depicted with his back turned and yet, by imitating his gaze, the viewer understands that the landscape maps the wanderer's soul, and gains insight not only into his, but their own subconscious and humanity.

While the Romantic painting encapsulates calm contemplation, in 1913, by contrast, there is no time. After a few short seconds a fellow traveler interrupts Friedrich's reflective stasis and the plot is driven toward its action-packed climax. A few minutes later, another short contemplative scene in which Friedrich looks out onto the sea at a fully rigged sailing vessel like a memento from a distant past is swiftly followed by a precursor of Eisenstein's collision montage: as first-class passengers are happily enjoying their luxurious dinner, a worker in the boiler room collapses and dies. This prepares the ground for an even greater catastrophe. During a night of fog, the ocean liner strikes a wreck and in a sequence of astonishing editing speed, the film cuts from men falling off their chairs due to the impact, to water pouring into the hull, frantic efforts by the crew to telegraph S.O.S., wake up passengers, and hand out life-vests. This staccato of crisis management comes to a sudden halt when the film cuts to Friedrich's cabin where he is still asleep. The alarm sounds, but he dreams of walking through the legendary sunken city-state of Atlantis together with his friend, Dr. Schmidt. Again Danish cinematographer Johan Ankerstjerne's use of double exposure merges dream and reality, fact and fiction, with the camera imitating the doubling of outer and inner spaces.

Significantly more than the attractive location footage of Berlin or New York or the fascinating depiction of psychopathologies by way of the latest film technology, it was the recent Titanic disaster that impacted the film's reception. Cross-cutting between scenes of cramped corridors with passengers wrangling about life-vests, falling over one another trying to get up the stairs, women in nightgowns and half-dressed men running onto the top deck, cramping into lifeboats while passengers in the lower decks wake to flooded halls, the film's quick succession of shots with camera-distances changing from close-ups of panicking passengers running for their lives (and affectively toward the camera), or long shots of people jumping from the sinking ship, provided audiences at the time with a hitherto unseen spectacle of the fear and chaos that must have ensued on

FIGURE 2.1 *Danish film poster for* Atlantis *(DK, August Blom, 1913)*.
Source: Det Danske Filminstitut.

the Titanic before the vast majority of those on board were to lose their lives. Panorama shots of the proud ocean liner slowly being submerged while the sea is dotted with small lifeboats are reminiscent of Wilhelm II's favorite artist Willy Stöwer's drawings depicting the catastrophe for *Die Gartenlaube* (1912), the most widely read and first successful mass-circulation newspaper in Germany. With the sinking of the Titanic in April 1912—which traveled from Southampton to New York just like the "Roland" in Hauptmann's novel and Nordisk's film—still fresh in people's minds, this must have been a shocking visualization of a disaster that shook the world at the time, with over 1,500 victims from across the world, but predominantly from North America, English-speaking Europe, and Scandinavia (with many Irish, and—as in this adaptation—Russian Jews in third class). The film takes its viewers straight into a cramped lifeboat, the waves shaking the small vessel and the camera capturing a sickening sense of exposure and frailty of life. The Norwegian censorship board banned the film, judging it tasteless to depict a ship's sinking so blatantly reminiscent of the recent tragedy.

In his novel, which appeared as a series in the *Berliner Tageblatt* a few weeks before the sinking of the RMS *Titanic*, Hauptmann reflects on the lure of personal and natural disaster and spectacle. In Chapter 5 of his novel, shortly after the sinking steamer provides a tragic climax to the narrative, he writes:

> 'Steamship "Roland" went down, it's in the papers. Oh, says the philistine in Berlin, the philistine in Hamburg and Amsterdam, takes another sip of coffee and draws on his cigar, before savoring all the details of the catastrophe [...]. And the hooray of the newspaper publishers! A sensation! New subscribers! This is the Medusa, whom we look into the eye and who tells us the true value of a ship's cargo of human lives.'

The writer reflects on the pull of sensationalism in modern society and on the commodification of human tragedy, while producing a commodity himself, of course, soon selling rights to his novel the highest bidder in the film industry. The silent movie, however, will not as yet turn on itself and mentions nothing of the commodification of tragedy in twentieth-century mass society. Instead, the film focuses on the lives of the few survivors, among them Ingigerd and Friedrich, and provides its viewers with everything from spectacular scenes of New York City to traveling shots from a train through stunning wintery landscapes, from innovative depictions of mental disintegration to Friedrich's final release and happy ending. The latter are achieved with the help of Miss Eva Burns, a beautiful and yet entirely practical and reasonable young sculptor.

Hauptmann's text incorporates the author's knowledge about psychopathologies, and reflects his awareness of an increasing Americanization and commodification within a modern media society. The enthusiasm for America and the suggestion that, ideally, we would all be 'americanised and then become new Europeans' or "Neueuropäer"[80] is missing in this Danish adaptation but, at the same time, the product with its enticing street scenes of Berlin and New York and its remarkable visualizations of Friedrich's mental state could be viewed as the growing Danish movie industry's nod toward those innovators like Max Skladanowsky in Germany and Louis Lumière, Georges Méliès, and Alice Guy in France.

But while celebrating innovations in cinema technology and marketing their new product as a 120-minute sensation, this silent picture criticizes Ingigerd's superficial need for amusement (highlighted in Friedrich's hallucinations) and, just like the bourgeoisie and their educated philistines, supposedly distances itself from other forms of 'light entertainment'. Instead, the focus is on values such as home and family, but also on mental health and happiness, and concludes with hope for a new life—not in America, but in the traditional setting of the family home. The closing sequence of Nordisk's *Atlantis* depicts Friedrich's joyful return home to his delighted parents and his giddy children, with Eva Burns by his side, who is lovingly welcomed by Friedrich's mother. Hence, as Göktürk remarks, by returning to Europe the "cultivated hero was [...] saved." She poignantly summarizes the ambivalent (doubling) effect of Hauptmann's novel as "it was *Atlantis*—with its rejection of the city and metropolitan mass culture—that inaugurated [the author's] occasional enterprises in the realm of the entertainment industry."[81]

The film was marketed as a "Großereignis" or major event in bourgeois newspapers, was distributed internationally, and became one of Nordisk's most successful film productions to date. The movie's critics, of course, did not shy away from expressing their scorn and mockery. *Atlantis* indicated all too well the narrative cinema's power and capability as a cultural product. The reactions of some members of the avant-garde reflect their "anxiety over cultural values" as cinema encroached on the domain of high art.[82] Journalist and writer Kurt Tucholsky ridiculed Hauptmann's tête-à-tête with the film industry and disapproved particularly of filmmakers' financial considerations when undertaking a new project. In his mind, art and commercial interests were mutually exclusive. Referring to the massive investment made by Nordisk, he dismissed *Atlantis* entirely: 'they spend all this money and then nothing really comes of it'.[83] If cinema were indeed serious about becoming a new art form, it must experiment, Tucholsky emphasizes, and push the boundaries of representation and form.

Doppelgänger and H.H. Ewers' *The Student from Prague*

While the dream sequences and visions in *Atlantis* could be deemed remarkable in their use of double exposure and thought provoking with regard to their visualization of Friedrich's mental state, they were not particularly groundbreaking in technical terms. Moreover, the *Doppelgänger* and uncanny visions of oneself or others had been common motifs in the literature of Romanticism, especially in E.T.A. Hoffmann's collection *Serapionsbrüder* (1819–21), and texts by one of his Serapion's Brethren Adelbert von Chamisso, who also described a case of uncanny doubling in his poem "Die Erscheinung" (The Vision, 1828). As Friedrich Kittler emphasizes, the concept of the *Doppelgänger*, or the doubling of identities, fascinated modern city-dwellers, and left its mark on early fantasy films.[84] Even prior to the First World War, some filmmakers sought to reflect the unsettling experience of modernity and turned to literature for inspiration.

As Chapter 3 outlines in more detail, the motif of the *Doppelgänger* in film is motivated by German Romanticism's fascination with dualism and serves to highlight the fragmentation experienced by the modern human being. The motif of doubling is central to the early horror film *Der Student von Prag*—taking inspiration from Dark Romanticism and *Faust*—and even prompted Austrian psychoanalyst Otto Rank to publish on the *Doppelgänger*.[85] Doubling also features prominently in other silent films at the time, for example in *Der Andere* [The Other] (DE, Max Mack, 1913), *Der Golem* (DE, Paul Wegener/Henrik Galeen, 1915), and in the six-part science fiction serial *Homunculus* (DE, Otto Rippert, 1916–17).[86]

Often coined an early auteur film and even the first German art film *Der Student von Prag* (1913) is a literary film that innovated cinematic adaptation techniques and movie technology, but also impacted the reception of adaptations of literary texts for the cinema. Ewers, writer and film enthusiast, based his exposé on literary texts by Hoffmann and Chamisso, but was not only inspired by German Romanticism, but by Alfred de Musset's poem "La Nuit de Décembre" (Night in December, 1835), Edgar Allen Poe's short story "William Wilson" (1839), and Oscar Wilde's *Dorian Gray* (1890)—all stories of doubling and inner turmoil. Sometimes the film is even interpreted as "a version of the Faust legend"[87]; as Faust, too, is torn between two worlds and within his own humanity, and famously declared "zwei Seelen wohnen, ach, in meiner Brust" [Two souls alas! are dwelling in my breast].[88] As Lotte Eisner emphasizes in her seminal *The Haunted Screen* book about Expressionism in German cinema:

> Ewers was evidently inspired by Peter Schlemihl, a story by Chamisso in which a young man sells his shadow, and by *Das Abenteuer der*

Sylvester-Nacht in which E.T.A. Hoffmann sends Chamisso's hero on a journey with his own Erasmus Spikher, 'the man who lost his reflection'. (The name Scapinelli, which Ewers gives to the diabolical and mysterious character who buys the reflection, is surely a harking back to the bewitched world of Hoffmann.)[89]

Eisner underlines the significance of literature for innovative auteur film projects such as *Der Student von Prag* as "it was immediately realized that the cinema could become the perfect medium for Romantic anguish, dream-states, and those hazy imaginings which shade so easily into the indefinite depths of that fragment of space-outside-time, the screen."[90]

Ewers, together with his co-director Stellan Rye and cinematographer Guido Seeber, was aware of the potential of film and the need for visual innovation in order to signify film as unique and on equal footing with other arts. The silent movie was to be accompanied not by bits and pieces of classical and popular music, but by an original score[91] for the entire feature-length film composed by Josef Weiss. Ewers' literary concoction tells the horror story of Balduin (played by Paul Wegener), a poor student who sells his mirror image to Scapinelli, a satanical magician, for the stunning sum of 100,000 Gulden. It is a tragic tale of a naïve young man's desire for success and social standing. Balduin wants to be someone, party with the upper class, and lead the life of a gentleman. When a Countesse falls for him, Balduin's social rise seems within his grasp. But his mirror image haunts him, not only ruining his chances with his soon to be betrothed, but causing his own death when Balduin shoots at his *Doppelgänger* and dies.

The movie was filmed primarily in the Bioscop studios in Neubabelsberg near Berlin and in Prague and, when it premiered in the Mozartsaal at Nollendorfplatz in Berlin on August 22, 1913, audiences were stunned, especially at the seemingly perfect doubling of actor Paul Wegener, who could suddenly be seen twice as he stepped out of the mirror to confront his alter ego.[92] The screen had indeed become 'haunted' as a doubling of a human being that acted naturally and seemed as 'real' as the other had never like this been seen before. Up to that point, it was only the imagination of the reader, say the tales of the Romantic *Serapion's Brethren*, that could convincingly furnish our minds with versions of ourselves. Now a modern industry with its rapidly developing technology was able to produce all kinds of *Doppelgänger* for the price of a cinema ticket.

Wegener recounted his fascination with this "strange mixture of the natural and the artificial, in theme as in setting" of the film and emphasized the significance of the camera for twentieth-century cinema:

> The real creator of the film must be the camera. Getting the spectator to change his point of view, using special effects to double the actor on the divided screen, superimposing other images—all this, technique,

FIGURE 2.2 *Paul Wegener (doubled) and Grete Berger in* Der Student von Prag *(DE, H.H. Ewers/S. Rye, 1913).*
Source: Det Danske Filminstitut.

form, gives the content its real meaning. [...] I realized that photographic technique was going to determine the destiny of the cinema. Light and darkness in the cinema play the same role as rhythm and cadence in music.[93]

In a public lecture delivered in Berlin in 1916, Wegener outlined the poetic potential of the film camera, convinced that film would eventually have us gaze in awe at cinema screens, where the hitherto unseen, the magical and unreal would fold seamlessly into the familiar and everyday.[94]

Film as Art and Commodity: Kellermann's *Der Tunnel* and the Coming of War

Not all adaptations of the works of E.T.A. Hoffmann, Adelbert von Chamisso, Friedrich Hebbel, Franz Grillparzer, or Gottfried August Bürger strove with such confidence for cinematographic innovation, but they do reflect filmmakers' choices based on magical or uncanny aspects of popular literary texts, giving them a canvas to show off their craft. At the same time, adaptations increasingly drew attention to socio-political discourses while a growing sense of instability—due to the effects of modernity from rapidly changing urban environments to industrialized work practices, and soon war—raised questions of nation and national culture while highlighting the meaning of family and community. Considering, for instance, the numerous movies based on Hermann Sudermann's bestselling novels, economic concerns and a commitment to the entertainment value of the modern industry were clearly prioritized.

In an article in *Bild und Film* (1913/14) it was estimated that 1,392,000 Germans per day consumed film in the Empire's approximately 2,900 cinemas. Forty big international film companies produced 6,000 meters of footage per day or 150 new films per week. The censorship board in Berlin alone dealt with 40,000 meters of film every week. The most successful films in Germany were seen by up to 13 million viewers, which was an enormous section of the population (of 64 million in total), when we consider that it was still primarily the working and lower middle class that frequented cinemas. There is no doubt that by now film was not only a 'significant economic factor',[95] but also becoming an attractive commodity for more discerning audiences of the middle and upper classes. Apart from a broadening interest in film as an art form, advertising had also undergone reform and presented films in tastefully designed posters (often without images) rather than the hitherto common and often sensationalist or bloodthirsty illustrated broadsheets.[96]

As Sabine Becker writes in *Experiment Weimar*, it was film (and the press) that affected literature and narrative strategies most remarkably. While her assessment is surely true with regard to the Weimar Republic's literary culture, the impact of modern industries is also reflected in a number of prose texts published prior to the First World War. Noteworthy in this context is especially Bernhard Kellermann's *Der Tunnel* (The Tunnel, 1913), a Jules Verne and H.G. Wells inspired science fiction novel that focuses on a massive engineering project, namely a tunnel to be built underneath the Atlantic Ocean.[97]

The visionary engineer Allan's trust in himself and in modern technology seems shatterproof, but shifting financial interests and a number of setbacks delay and eventually stall the major international building project causing a massive recession. The workers revolt and turn to violence. By the time the committed engineer is able to bring his project to completion nearly three decades later, huge rigid airships are able to cross the ocean in thirty-six hours and the tunnel is already obsolete the moment it is finally ready for use.

Kellermann's novel was tremendously successful and his publisher Fischer reported sales of 100,000 after barely six months. *Der Tunnel* was to become one of the most widely read novels until the Second World War and was considered for adaptation to the screen within a year of its publication. The Vitascope production under the direction of Rudolf Meinert was to be grandiose—a prestige production that would not only impress with its cinematography, realism, and large-scale sets built in Berlin-Weißensee, but with a linear narrative structure inspired by the novel that was to demonstrate the cultural reality of a 'natural' alignment of cinema and literature once and for all.[98] Usually D.W. Griffith is credited with adapting the source text's narrative structure into his 1915 *Birth of a Nation*, but clearly, similar efforts were underway on the other side of the Atlantic, too.

But in June 1914 the assassination of Austro-Hungarian Archduke Franz Ferdinand and soon the outbreak of the First World War impacted significantly on a number of large-scale film productions planned at the time. For internationally operating film industries, war meant an array of challenges and additional financial constraints, new taxes, import and export restrictions, and of course more stringent but often haphazard censorship regulation. Once the German Empire was placed under martial law, censorship became as much part of the war effort as the use of film as propaganda. Film production now had to focus on national needs rather than operate within an international market.[99] Not surprisingly, adaptations of German-language literature outside Germany and Austria soon all but disappeared.

Der Tunnel premiered in Berlin in September 1915 in a slimmed down and much less extravagant version. This first German-language science-fiction adaptation was directed by William Wauer, who had also written the script based on Kellermann's prose. Hermann Warm, who famously turned to expressionism for the design of *The Cabinet of Dr Caligari* four years later, was in charge of the futuristic set. Friedrich Kayßler played the visionary engineer Max Allan, and Hermann Vallentin and the well-known singer Fritzi Massary[100] appear as billionare Lloyd and his daughter. Clearly an advocate of technical progress and industrialization, the reviewer in the *Lichtbild-Bühne* praised the film's depiction of 'work' as the 'Song of Songs' and 'alpha and omega of progress', as well as 'the poetry of mechanical engineering and the imposing magic of gigantic large-scale industry'.[101] It was not until economic crises, hyperinflation, and mass unemployment hit Germany in the aftermath of the war and then, again, in 1929 that readers and viewers realized how prophetic elements of the novel and the film had been.

Literature, Film, and the Impact of War

Bertha von Suttner—pacifist, writer, and the first woman to receive the Nobel Peace Prize in 1905—published her antiwar novel *Die Waffen nieder!* (Down with the Weapons!, 1889) to great acclaim. With nationalism and political tensions ominously on the rise, Carl Theodor Dreyer wrote a film script based on her novel and Holger-Madsen directed *Ned med våbnene* (DK, 1914) for Nordisk. But their intent to amplify Suttner's antiwar message by putting it on screen came too late. Ads for the adaptation can be found in July 1914 editions of *Lichtbild-Bühne*, but following the beginning of war between the Triple Alliance of Austria-Hungary, Germany, and Italy and the Triple Entente of Britain, France, and Russia on the 28th of that month, no further mention of the project is made in the Berlin film journal. The antiwar film premiered in New York in August 1914; the event that was to frame the adaptation's international premiere originally—the World Peace Conference in Vienna—had been cancelled.[102] In Germany and Austria, no distributor dared to take on the silent movie as enthusiasm for war engulfed the masses. When the adaptation was finally screened as the First World War ended, reality had caught up with Suttner's cautionary tale and hardly anyone was interested. The reality and consequence of war had become all too painfully apparent.

The First World War affected silent film production, distribution and reception, adaptations of German-language literature, as well as the German film industry as a whole. Before 1914, not even a quarter of films screened in German cinemas were German productions. The majority of motion pictures distributed were "supplied by France (30%), the United States (25%), Italy (20%), Denmark and England, mostly by way of imports but also through local subsidiaries (e.g., Pathé and Nordisk)."[103]

When the war broke out, 'enemy' productions were suddenly banned. Not surprisingly, the German film industry could not keep up with demand and soon more than 20 percent of films screened in the Empire were distributed via (the neutral) Nordisk Film, making the company a major player in the German market and adaptation business.[104] Considering much of the motion picture industry superficial rubbish unbecoming in serious times of war, the German government also banned 'shallow entertainment' in December 1914, despite protests by film pioneer and entrepreneur Oskar Messter, who argued that entertaining features financed newsreels and war films.[105]

In August 1916, Lt. Ludwig Brauner sent an article from the front on 'Cinema Business after the War' to *Der Kinematograph*. Here he informs its readers that regular film screenings at the front and cinemas at the military bases had provided the film industry with a significant rise in ardent supporters. 'Many of those, for whom a visit to a cinema would have been extraordinary before, are now completely used to the screenings [...]', and film clearly had a positive impact on both the soldiers and the communities in which they were stationed, Brauner claims.[106] Films indeed became an integral part of life during the war—a fact that playwright Ernst Toller included in his tragedy *Der deutsche Hinkemann* (known in English as *Bloody Laughter* or *The Red Laugh*), written in 1921/2 during the author's and political activist's imprisonment in Niederschönenfeld Prison.

But in contrast to Lt. Brauner's account, Toller's 'Hinkemann' tells us: 'We spent the week at the front. And on Sunday we would go to a stuffy cinema and watch deceitful movies. About the lord of the castle who raised a poor girl from the dirt of the streets to his position, and other similarly stupid nonsense.'[107] For the most part, not literary adaptations but trashy formula films were preferred vehicles for light entertainment by the varied audiences at military bases and makeshift screenings at the front. The implementation of the ban of superficial amusement in cinemas was clearly secondary to providing escapist entertainment to the troops.

The newsreels, however, were appallingly unrealistic in the soldiers' opinions, according to Lt. Brauner, because filming was normally not allowed near the German front.[108] In the meantime, 'enemy nations' had begun to produce their own frontline footage. The power of film as a propaganda tool is highlighted in another *Kinematograph* article: 'We failed to see [...] film as a weapon [...] and, thereby, made a devastating mistake. [...] Film today, as the Member of Parliament Dr. Naumann told me so poignantly, is the <u>international language</u>. With this language one gets through, only with this language one speaks to peoples' hearts.'[109]

On January 30, 1917, the German Empire's Bild- und Filmamt (BUFA) was created and equipped with a significant budget in order to coordinate film production and distribution (particularly of documentary footage and newsreels) as well as censorship. Gustav Stresemann, member of the Reichstag who was to become Chancellor and Foreign Minister during the Weimar Republic, considered film 'the most powerful advertising tool of our time'.[110] Also being aware of the power of the moving image, especially with regard to the productive use of documentary footage across enemy lines, the Imperial Army's First Quartermaster-general Erich Ludendorff wrote to the German War Ministry on July 4, 1917, to push for the creation of a national film industry and the use of film for propaganda. In his letter, Ludendorff lists companies that should be bought in a clandestine operation—Deutsche Bioskop, Messter-Film, Eiko-Film, Projektions A.G.-Union (PAGU), and others.[111] His initiative led to the transformation of BUFA into Ufa (Universum Film AG) and to the creation of Germany's largest film company. With a phenomenal start-up capital of 25 million Marks, Ufa was designed as major film production and distribution business that was to include the creation or acquisition of cinema chains, as well as the production and trade of film technology.[112] Consolidating Messter's film business with Nordisk, and buying the majority of shares in Paul Davidson's Projektions AG Union (PAGU) and others, led to outstanding and popular talent from Ernst Lubitsch to Ossi Oswalda now being 'owned' by Ufa.[113]

The war stymied film production in Germany on several levels as mentioned above, but also impacted positively on cinema culture. Already in August 1914, an editorial entitled "War and Cinema" published in *Der Kinematograph* outlines how the onset of war had significantly increased ticket sales in cinemas as people were impatiently hoping for 'definite information' regarding the events unfolding on the military and political stages via newsreels, but also taking advantage of the escapist opportunities provided by cinematic entertainment—'to calm their fears, unease and restlessness with the help of flicking images'.[114] Cinema owners were encouraged to provide documentaries about the combatant nations alongside news items while offering light entertainment with longer features, now often more than seventy minutes long.

As a number of industrialist and other interest groups invested in film in order to prepare their markets abroad for the period after the war, suddenly financial backing for more complex projects and longer feature films was available to filmmakers,[115] evidenced by, for example, a large-scale adaptation of Wilhelm Hauff's *Mitteilungen aus den Memoiren des Satans* (The Devil's Memoirs, 1825ff.) as a four-part series written and directed by Robert Heymann entitled *Die Memoiren des Satans I: Dr. Mors* (1917), *Die Memoiren des Satans II: Fanatiker des Lebens* [Fanatics of Life] (1917), *Die Memoiren des Satans III: Der Fluchbeladene* [The Cursed] (1917/18), and *Der Sturz der Menschheit. Die Memoiren des Satans. 4. Teil* [The Fall of Mankind] (1918), all produced by Luna-Film in Berlin. A critic in the *Neue Kino-Rundschau* praised the series in January 1918 as a 'powerful and effective dramatically enhanced' adaptation of Hauff's work, because it presented 'self-contained' films that at the same time mirrored 'an exposition of the whole'. Its basic idea and theme were the capacity of 'pure sacrificial love to overcome whatever Mephisto, the enemy of humankind, does in order to bring sorrow and misery upon his victims.'[116] Indeterminate representations of evil and stories celebrating sacrificial love became common during the final phase of the First World War, mostly in trashy melodramas, but also in literary adaptations.

During this final year of the First World War, Max Mack also adapted both Shakespeare's play and Hauff's eponymous novella in his *Othello*, Reinhard Bruck turned to Kleist's *Das Erdbeben in Chile*, and Hubert Moest brought Lessing's *Emilia Galotti* to cinema screens, all three among the most dramatic tales of the literary canon. But wartime escapism and the audience's penchant for the cultural mode of melodramatic narratives also gave rise to numerous 'fallen woman' or 'threatened virtue' films. They were either so-called "Schundfilme"—trivial to trashy titillating entertainment— or for the more discerning cinemagoer, adaptations of German-language literature. Sometimes, they were both, like *Lulu,* directed by Alexander von Antalffy (DE, 1918), an adaptation loosely based on Wedekind's plays *Erdgeist* (Earth Spirit, 1895), and *Die Büchse der Pandora* (Pandora's Box, 1902), which the author had revised and republished as *Lulu. Tragödie in 5 Aufzügen* (Lulu, a tragedy in five acts, 1913).

Erna Morena played the lead in Antalffy's *Lulu*, and Emil Jannings appeared as a young man smitten with the seductive *femme fatale*. This film was considered highly provocative when it premiered in October 1917, and despite the obvious talent of the two leading actors, the picture was categorized as "Schundfilm" by critics upon its release by the censorship board that had slapped a youth ban on the picture. It is a story of love and deceit that focuses on the destructive impact of another capricious and deceptive young woman. Lulu works as a circus dancer,[117] and although she seems to be in love with a clown, she enters into a relationship with a nobleman who swiftly falls into debt in order to satisfy her material desires. When he commits suicide, she wastes no time before she seduces her next victim. But finally, the clown returns and Lulu resumes her relationship with him. When her current lover, a baron, catches the two and is killed in a violent argument, his son takes over the inheritance and kicks Lulu out. In the end she marries the clown, but dies soon after, thereby performing an act of retribution to satisfy the censors and the public.[118]

Even before the devastating First World War[119] had ended, adaptations of the German-language literary canon, always already markers of the folklore and heritage they sustained, served as potential platforms for a critical engagement with the Empire's authoritarianism and militarism, while highlighting the frailty of human nature and the deficiencies of contemporary society. Controversial contemporary literature on film in contrast—especially if the source text was known to have caused scandals—would have been economically risky. During wartime, adaptations of the literary canon were becoming welcome contributions to educational and high culture, while being consumed *en masse* as at once refreshing celebrations of the nation's literary tradition and escapist entertainment.

War-time Adaptations: National Heritage and Film as Culture

In 1915, Wegener, Rye, and Galeen turned their attention to Hoffmann's close friend and co-conspirator Chamisso to transpose *Peter Schlemihls wundersame Geschichte* (Peter Schlemihl's Miraculous Story, 1813/14) to screen. Peter Schlemihl, as mentioned above, sells his shadow to the devil for power and financial gain and spends the rest of his short life trying to get his shadow—and his humanity—back. Foregrounding an individual's effort to regain his heart, and thus his compassion, was contrary to the heroic tales in popular culture now regularly produced in war-time Germany. By adapting a well-known children's story with a humanist message by a Frenchman residing in Prussia during the time of the Napoleonic wars, the collaborators could well have risked a ban. But the popularity of *Kunstmärchen* or literary fairy tales by the cherished authors of German Romanticism clearly worked in their favor.

Wegener also drew attention to Gustav Meyrink's novel *Der Golem* (The Golem, first published in Kurt Wolff's *Die weißen Blätter* in 1913 and 1914), when releasing his and Galeen's silent horror movie of 1915 based on the Talmudic legend.[120] During the same year, Stellan Rye used Goethe's famous ballad "Der Erlkönig" (The Erlking, 1782) for his film *Erlkönigs Töchter* [Daughters of the Erlking], a story of a father's underestimation of the lurking threat at his child's peril. Friedrich Hebbel's epic poem "Mutter und Kind" (Mother and Child, 1859) was adapted under the direction of Hans Oberländer based on a script by Heinrich Lautensack, and celebrated compassion and the unbreakable bond between mother and child. The film, produced by Lloyd-Film in Berlin, was released by censors in October 1916.[121]

Four years earlier Oberländer had directed the Messter production of Friedrich Spielhagen's *Problematische Naturen* (Problematic Natures, 1861) with Carl Froelich at the camera and Erich Kaiser-Titz in the lead. After a screening in Vienna in 1915, the Austrian *Kinematographische Rundschau* hailed this first Spielhagen adaptation as a 'masterpiece of film art' and considered it further evidence that not only had moving pictures come a long way but also their critics. The article outlines the prolonged and punitive condemnation of the new medium by, especially, the educated classes in France and Germany, all too often wheedled and encouraged by the press. But 'there has been a major turnaround', the *Kinematographische Rundschau* reports:

> A few years ago, film was tolerated, but only spitefully, today, however, it is a recognized form of art; great intellectuals hold moving pictures in high regard [...]. Philosophy and psychology, ethics and aesthetics have taken possession of film, and cinema has become an educational apparatus just like a school, churches or a theater. Film theaters now maintain our heritage. It is the most valuable treasure that cannot be protected enough.[122]

And this is the core of the reviewer's enthusiasm for this particular adaptation: 'This film is folklore, it is artistic and it is of interest for the literary world', cinema is the place where literary tradition is preserved and can, once again, come alive. Therefore, readers of this Austrian publication are told that adaptations of literary texts could not be praised enough or held in higher regard.

Transposing German-language literature to cinema screens during times of war was considered a contribution to national culture. For filmmakers, adaptations of German-language texts were suddenly relatively safe economical and political choices, provided the literary text was in line with dominant culture. Notions of home and national belonging but also images of familiar landscapes shape, for example, a number of Ludwig

Anzengruber adaptations, such as *Der Pfarrer vom Kirchfeld* [The Priest of Kirchfeld] and *Der Meineidbauer* [The Perjuring Farmer] in 1914 and 1915, respectively. Even German emperor Wilhelm II's favorite writer Ernst von Wildenbruch, or rather his novella *Das wandernde Licht* [The Wandering Light] (DE, Robert Wiene, 1916), found its way onto nationalized, wartime cinema screens in Germany and Austria. The rather trivial story of a couple in a castle, upheaval caused by a mad servant, and the final return of order and love was produced by Messter in Berlin.[123] The film stars Henny Porten and Bruno Decarli as noble newlyweds, and Theodor Becker as the cracked butler. Especially the latter must have provided plenty of comedy and thus welcome relief when the movie premiered on September 1, 1916, in the dignified Mozartsaal in Berlin as the battles of the Somme were continuing.

Wiene collaborated with Messter on a number of entertaining features on the light but also satirical side—such as *Der wandernde Blumentopf* [The Wandering Flower Pot] in 1916—until he made film history with *Das Cabinet des Dr. Caligari* in 1920. Messter, who had taken over his father's company of lighting and optical instruments in 1892, soon experimented with moving images and film projection, produced and distributed short films, and opened his own cinema in September 1896. By the time the war broke out, Messters Projektion GmbH had grown into one of the most successful film businesses in the German Empire[124]—mostly due to Messter's knack for employing young and innovative talent: directors such as Ernst Lubitsch, Konrad Wiene, Joe May; actors like Emil Jannings, Henny Porten, Reinhold Schünzel, Fritz Kortner; and probably the most daring and original cameraman of his time, Karl Freund. Messter's film company produced a few adaptations of popular literature[125]—but left films based on the canon of German literature to another entrepreneur and innovator, who had begun to make a name for himself as both a director and 'adaptor' in the field: Richard Oswald.

Richard Oswald and Literature on Film

One of the most productive and innovative filmmakers of his time, Oswald began his career as an actor in several German and Austrian theaters and appeared on screen for the first time in 1911 in Reinhard Bruck's silent film *Halbwelt* [demi-monde]. From 1914 he worked as a screenwriter and successfully adapted numerous literary texts for the cinema screen—from four adaptations of Sir Arthur Conan Doyle's *The Hound of the Baskervilles* (1914/15) to Oscar Wilde's *Picture of Dorian Gray* (1917). He also started directing in 1914, his screenwriting/directing debut being *Das eiserne Kreuz* [The Iron Cross], a story of two innkeepers and best friends on both sides of the German/Belgian border. The film highlights the war's effect on their relationship and indicated that Oswald intended to use cinema as a tool for political education and civil engagement. War breeds only hatred, the film was supposed to tell its audience, war destroys human relationships and, therefore, the communities we live in. The final title plate reads "Wohin soll das noch führen?"—'Where is this going to lead?'[126] Not surprisingly—at a time when the German Empire's hubris suggested that the Reich's military power would surely guarantee the prominent standing of the young nation—the film was confiscated by German authorities due to its pacifist tendencies, and the censorship board banned two-thirds of the film from public exhibition, which meant it could not be screened at all.[127] The war changed the German cinema landscape profoundly. The early surge of enthusiasm for the war soon gave way to the reality of military conflict and its grim consequences. The desire to be entertained in cinemas, however, was growing steadily, and so was the demand on film companies to ensure supply of local produce now that imports of French, British, or US American pictures were no longer possible.

E.T.A. Hoffmann, Richard Oswald, and Adaptation as High Culture

Germany and Austria were at war with Britain and Oswald's adaptations of works by Arthur Conan Doyle and Robert Louis Stevenson were no longer flavor of the month. Ever the pragmatist or, rather, economically savvy, Oswald turned to projects that were relatively safe bets in yielding a profit. What is more, he pushed the imaginary boundary of cinema at the time, and presented his 1916 adaptation of *Hoffmanns Erzählungen* [The Tales of Hoffmann] as high culture rather than mass entertainment. According to reviews in cinema journals *Der Kinematograph* and *Lichtbild-Bühne* on February 26, 1916, the premiere of this moving picture in Marmorhaus-Lichtspiele, one of the major Berlin cinemas, was a grand affair, and the excitement among the audience was palpable. The upper class attended in droves, well-known journalists such as *Berliner Tageblatt*'s Fritz Engel and Professor Klahr of the *Vossische Zeitung* were there to report on the event before the midnight deadline; all in all it was a premiere atmosphere finally equal to any other opening of a 'high culture' event.

The reviewer of the cinema journal *Lichtbild-Bühne* reporting on the opening night was convinced that this project would be a success.[128] He points out that the plot of the film does not coincide fully with that of the well-known and very popular *Tales of Hoffmann* opera. But he is also quick to emphasize that this is entirely in the interest of Oswald's adaptation project. 'The free adaptation of the material was correctly recognized and undoubtedly necessary.' He even adds, 'What is so difficult to understand in opera clearly comes to the fore in the film.' Therefore, the film complements the opera perfectly and is, in the reviewer's opinion, undoubtedly destined "diese noch mehr dem Volke zuzuwenden", i.e., 'to turn it even more towards the people'. Here, the bridging effect of adaptation and its educational potential is unambiguously emphasized.

Oswald's skillful blending of the plot of Hoffmann's stories with well-known melodies from Jacques Offenbach's *Tales of Hoffmann* opera, the clever use of cinema technology, and careful synchronization of the moving images with Offenbach's music played by an orchestra opened doors and muffled the voices of some of the most ardent critics of cinema. Siegbert Goldschmidt had arranged the music, 'as if Offenbach had written it especially for the film', the critic notes. The picturesque mise-en-scène is applauded with 'each scene offering beautiful motifs'—an effort by the filmmaker to differentiate the medium from the aesthetics of the theater and present its improved, modern, and spectacular version to audiences across the social spectrum. The actors are praised, especially young Hoffmann (played by Kurt Wolowski), but also the rest of the team of actors, including Werner Krauß, who appeared as Graf Dapertutto in his first screen role. Oswald was applauded, because he managed to 'breathe love, care and artistic feeling' into the moving pictures and 'created a work that not only does him every credit, not only strengthens his reputation as a director, but will most certainly impact in the interest of cinematography and contribute to raising its profile.' The 'enemies of the cinema' must agree, he continues, that after viewing Oswald's adaptation no one can maintain 'that there was no art to be found in film'. In *Der Kinematograph* the movie and the premiere were thoroughly praised and labeled an "Ereignis"—a real event.[129]

Oswald, as was common among those early filmmakers, not only directed but had written the script of *Hoffmanns Erzählungen* in collaboration with Fritz Friedmann-Frederich. He also appears on screen himself introducing the narrative while standing next to the grave of Friedrich Schiller.

Despite the fact that Schiller's grave is in Weimar and not in Jena, where Hoffmann lived with his aunt and uncle as a young man, as Oswald tells us, the reference to Schiller makes sense. In 1789, the year of the French Revolution, Schiller was appointed (unpaid) professor of history at the University of Jena. But the reference to Schiller also indicates that Oswald wanted the audience to recognize his moving picture as high culture and art, inspired by two of the greats of German-language literature Schiller and Hoffmann. Moreover, Schiller had published an intriguing story entitled "Der Geisterseher" (The Ghost-Seer, 1787–9) in serialized form his journal *Thalia*, which proved his most successful prose text and was to have a lasting influence on Romanticism's Gothic fiction. The story of conspiracy, necromancy, and spiritism is written like an eyewitness report, and includes a mysterious Armenian. According to Adalbert von Hanstein, the figure is based on an infamous Italian imposter who called himself Count of Cagliostro.[130] Schiller's fiction of a prince in Venice, who falls prey to this count and a beautiful woman, paradoxically claims authenticity, while at the same time inviting readers to lose themselves in imagination.

Oswald was likely aware of the fact that Hoffmann himself refers to Schiller in the prologue of his "Die Abenteuer der Sylvester-Nacht" (New Year's Eve Adventures, 1815). Part 4 of the narrative contains "Die Geschichte vom verlornen Spiegelbilde" (A Story of Lost Reflection), another romantic ghost story whose narrator alleges reality and fact while offering an imagined world of fiction. Hoffmann's tale of the mirror image—that inspired the Guilietta-act in Offenbach's opera and *The Student of Prague* (1913) film discussed above—tells the story of Erasmus Spikher, who leaves wife and child to travel to Florence, where he meets 'miracle doctor' Dapertutto and beautiful Guilietta. Overcome with blazing desire for this stunning young woman and following a number of strange incidents and a murder, he agrees to give up his mirror image to console 'the clever courtisane'. But as soon as his mirror image steps into Guilietta's open arms, the two disappear accompanied by sounds of fiendish mockery and an oddly lingering smell.

When Erasmus returns home, the absence of his reflection frightens his wife and son. Again, Dapertutto appears miraculously and offers a solution. Erasmus only needs to untie the bond to wife and child and he would be free to return to Guilietta and his reflection. He hands him a vial of poison, but when Erasmus fails to kill his family, both Guilietta and Dapertutto try to force him to sign them over to the devil with a steel pen and his own blood for ink. Suddenly a vision of his wife appears and pleads with him, in Jesus' name, to stop this gruesome deed. Inspired, Erasmus violently frees himself from Guiletta's embrace and tells the devilish fiends to leave him be. Like Mephistopheles in Méliès's films mentioned in Chapter 1, they disappear in thick, stinking smoke that drowns out all the light. Finally free, his wife tells him he looked ridiculous without a reflection and he really should go and travel the world and, perhaps, he will be able to claim back his reflection from the devil. Wishing him a safe trip, she adds that he should send trousers for his son occasionally and, perhaps, a toy and a sweet.

The story ends with Erasmus wandering the wide world, and meeting Peter Schlemihl who had in a thoughtless act of comparable stupidity sold his shadow. The two flawed men's idea of walking in company and replacing one another's missing reflections does not quite work out, however, Hoffmann tells us in conclusion.[131] Having begun the tale with an acknowledgment of Schiller's story, he leaves his readers with reference to Chamisso's literary fairy tale *Peter Schlemihls wundersame Geschichte* and homage to its French-German author. As mentioned above, Chamisso was part of Hoffmann's circle of friends in Berlin—*The Serapion Brethren*—which became the title of Hoffmann's famous collection of fairytales and novellas (1819–21). The originally four volumes contained "Die Automate" (The Automaton), 'New Year's Eve Adventures', and other ghost stories.

Magical Doublings and Hoffmann on Film

A treasure-trove of automatons, magically appearing and disappearing beings, doubling visions of self, independently acting mirror images, and apparati with which one would see the world through different eyes or perceive an imaginary world as everyday reality, Hoffmann's compilation provided filmmakers such as Oswald with an abundance of fantastic narratives that were deemed ideal for adaptation. On screen, these tales could provide food for thought, entertainment, shock, and surprise, while showing off the magic of cinema and, thereby, demonstrating this art form's superiority. In the prologue of his *Hoffmanns Erzählungen* film, we are introduced to young Hoffmann, who encounters several dubious characters in his aunt and uncle's house; there is Coppelius (Friedrich Kühne), who deals in glasses and optical devices, museum director Spalanzani (Lupu Pick), faith healer Dr. Mirakel (Andreas von Horn), and Count Dapertutto (Werner Krauß). The following three acts focus on Hoffmann and show the author's entanglement with his own stories. Here it is the poet himself, not Nathanael of the "Sandman"-tale, who buys magical glasses from creepy Coppelius. When he looks through them, he feels elated and the world seems brighter and better and somehow complete. He is over the moon, as Méliès might have put it, when he watches Spalanzani's 'ward' Olimpia/Olympia, without realizing that she is not, indeed, alive. Just as film suggests fiction as reality, Coppelius' optical device leads Hoffmann to recognize the puppet in its human form, even though the jerky staccato of her dance movements are anything but natural. Poor Hoffmann's blind love and romantic longing for the silly robot, and enraged Coppelius' thundering destruction of the puppet, made for great entertainment to be sure. But Oswald also created another layer of meaning to the tale entirely situated within the new medium. It was Coppelius, of course, who provided the vision in the first place, and just like a director or filmmaker, he is allowed to edit, cut, and obliterate the image as he pleases. The film was a family affair—not only did scriptwriter/producer/director Richard Oswald appear in the prologue of the adaptation, but his wife Käte took on the role of Stella, and their three-year-old daughter Ruth played young Antonia Crespel. But the star of the film was to be Werner Krauß.

Celebrities of the Theater on Film: Werner Krauss

Krauß had been one of the leading actors on Max Reinhardt's stage for the past three years, was celebrated in numerous plays at the Deutsches Theater in Berlin, and had earned an excellent reputation as an actor. According to Krauß, it was Richard Oswald who offered the actor his first opportunity to act in front of a movie camera. In his memoir *Das Schauspiel meines Lebens* (The Play of My Life, 1958), Krauß recounts his initial meeting with the director: 'I came in, was excited, film was something new then [...]—Say, Mr. Krauß, what can you do? [Oswald asks]—Everything, I reply. So the case was closed and I entered the film industry.'[132]

When an intertitle in *Tales of Hoffmann* announces the arrival of "Conte Dapertutto," Krauß enters the scene with confidence, but exaggerates every move, as Michael Hanisch points out, rushing forward to join the two waiting figures, raising his arms, dancing forward, bending down—there was a star clearly determined to draw the eyes of the audience onto himself.[133] The camera is static and, for the most part, remains at the same distance, giving the audience the impression of sitting in a theater performance. Highlighting the movie actors' engagements at Berlin's theaters in the opening credits—Werner Krauß (Deutsches Theater), Erich Kaiser-Titz (Lessingtheater), and Lupu Pick (Kleines Theater)[134]—also served to raise the status of film to that of the other dramatic arts. Remaining formally in close proximity to the theater, the film nonetheless illuminated the fact that only cinema technology can compete with literary imagination and recreate those perplexing dream worlds and doublings of Romanticism.[135]

Special effects and mirror technology[136] enabled Oswald to breathe life into a doll as Hanisch emphasizes, and to visualize horror elements, especially when Coppelius and Spalanzani, realizing they are in need of eyes for their puppet, reach out and grab young Hoffmann, who had been watching their work on the life-like automaton.[137] In Oswald's film the puppet comes to life, three years prior to Lubitsch's famous 1919 comedy fantasy film *Die Puppe* [The Doll]. Incidentally, Lubitsch's film is also implicitly based on Hoffmann's stories as they inspired Edmond Audran's operetta *La poupée* (The Doll) and the ballet *Coppélia* mentioned in the previous chapter, which Lubitsch acknowledged as his sources. How much the film industry owed to Oswald at the time is reflected in typical Lubitsch humor, when he called the doll Ossi Hilarius—played by actress Ossi Oswalda, whose birth name was Oswalda Stäglich. She first appeared as a nineteen-year-old in Lubitsch's 1916 classic *Schuhpalast Pinkus* [Shoepalace Pinkus]—which features the director in the lead role—and played under his direction or by his side in almost every film until *Mephistophela* in 1920.

Literature and Social Hygiene Films

Richard Oswald in the meantime had turned to social hygiene films, a genre meant to provide information and thus improve the medical and social health of all citizens. These *Aufklärungsfilme* [lit. enlightenment films] were supported financially by the State, which promised both a stable income and normally a large audience. Initially working with 'Spalanzani's' Lupu

Pick and with E.A. Dupont on the scripts, with Max Faßbender on the camera, Oswald looked in particular at marginalized members of society, and released four *Es werde Licht!* [There Will be Light!] films between 1916 and 1918.

Oswald wanted to provide 'sensible public education' (while, of course, producing films that could be successful at the box office) and, at the same time, he wished to support the social-hygiene movement that set out to deliver information rather than a morality lesson. Using a dramatic narrative ("Tendenzdrama") to communicate health facts, his films were huge box-office hits. In December 1917, an article in *Der Film* highlights Oswald's success and advises military propaganda efforts to follow his lead for a much more affective and hence valuable 'secondary propaganda'.[138]

While using cinema as a space of agitation ("Agitationsraum") or the screen as "Tribüne" or platform—terms coined a few years later by theater director and producer Erwin Piscator for the politically engaged theater stage—Oswald did not intend to use his craft for the war effort, and could afford a certain degree of independence due to running his own production company Richard Oswald-Film GmbH, Berlin. Often contrary to public opinion and even existing laws, Oswald's films indeed requested tolerance and inclusive behavior toward marginalized and criminalized groups such as homosexuals or prostitutes. As Klaus Kreimeier put it in his contribution to the CineGraph volume dedicated to Richard Oswald, he wished to have a 'genuine educational impact within the context of bourgeois emancipatory ideas' and produced films that 'could function as platforms [...] for an urban democratization of the topics of love and sexuality'. In this respect a number of adaptations by Oswald should be recognized, Kreimeier suggests, as an 'element within the structural transformation of the public sphere (Habermas)'.[139]

The effect of literature on Oswald's work as a filmmaker has, so far, been largely ignored in adaptation research. However, even his social-hygiene films were inspired by literary texts, especially by one of his favorite authors, Margarete Böhme. The title of his film about the detrimental and destabilizing effects of the law on already marginalized, clandestine homosexuals *§175: Anders als die Anderen* [Different from the Others] (DE, 1919), is a direct quote from Böhme's aforementioned *Dida Ibsen* novel, in which the young protagonist falls in love with a woman and, after their first sexual encounter, asks herself if she is, therefore, 'different from the others'.[140] The third part of Oswald's *There will be light!* (1918) series, developed in cooperation with the first German "sexologist" Iwan Bloch[141] and supported by the Medical Society for Sexual Research, deals with venereal diseases (and the possibility of curing them through scientific methods), and borrows the figure of the sadistic landowner Waldemar Gorsky from Böhme's *Dida Ibsen* novel.

The film is a biting critique of state-endorsed sexual ethics of slavery by way of marriage at the heart of the empire. The depiction of a distressingly abusive husband and father, as well as the consequences of Gorsky's syphilis-induced insanity for the entire family (where the mother heartbreakingly gives her child away for protection), is an adaptation of the narrative strand centered on Heribert Gallen in Böhme's *Dida Ibsens Geschichte*, her novel printed in 1907 by the Berlin publisher "Es werde Licht" [There Will be Light]. Star actor Werner Krauß plays the insanely abusive husband both in the third part of Oswald's *There will be light* series and in Oswald's adaptation of Böhme's *Dida Ibsen* novel.

Margarete Böhme on Film

Both films, as well as Oswald's *Das Tagebuch einer Verlorenen* [Diary of a Lost Girl], were completed in 1918. *Das Tagebuch einer Verlorenen* and *Dida Ibsens Geschichte* [The Story of Dida Ibsen] are adaptations of novels by the German writer. Born in the Northern German town Husum,[142] Margarete Böhme was one of the most successful and most widely read German authors of the early twentieth century. She authored forty novels, as well as short stories, articles, and autobiographical sketches. She is best known for *The Diary of a Lost Girl*, first published in 1905 as *Tagebuch einer Verlorenen. Von einer Toten*—the subtitle 'by a dead woman' indicating the death of the author, however, not in a Roland Barthes' sense. Katharina Gerstenberger called the novel "[p]erhaps the most notorious and certainly the most commercially successful autobiographical narrative of the early twentieth century."[143]

In *Tagebuch einer Verlorenen* Böhme identifies herself simply as the editor of a diary entrusted to her by a so-called 'fallen' or 'lost' girl, in order to lend authenticity to the painful and devastating experiences of a teenager, who is raped by her father's assistant on her confirmation day—an event that leads to her continuous and multifaceted sexual exploitation and social marginalization, prostitution, and eventually her early death. Because of the appearance of the texts as a 'diary', whose authenticity is confirmed by Böhme in her preface, experiences described and thoughts conveyed in the text are to be read as intimate, private truths. This particular narrative strategy, of course, significantly enhanced the affective impact of the text at the time, and pushed the 'unspeakable' (rape, teenage sex/pregnancy, prostitution) into the center of public awareness and discourse. In her text Böhme repeatedly emphasizes the destructiveness of Victorian society's exploitative practices and its hypocritical "principle of secrecy" (Michel Foucault)[144] with regard to matters physical or sexual, and simultaneously breaks the implicit silence by making the text available in print.

The book was a sensation and could not be reprinted fast enough. By 1907, *Tagebuch einer Verlorenen* was in its 100th edition. The same year Böhme published *Dida Ibsens Geschichte*, which was announced as the sequel to and conclusion of *The Diary of a Lost Girl*. Here, the young protagonist Dida befriends Thymian (the protagonist of the previous novel) and Thymian's letters are included in Dida's account lending both authenticity to the story and emphasizing the precariousness of the situation both women find themselves in. Dida's story is also one of suffering, even if she only prostitutes herself once in order to help her parents out of a financial crisis. She incurs the wrath of society primarily due to her relationship with a married man. He is separated from his wife, but cannot avail himself of divorce; Dida moves in with him, soon they have a child and are in all relevant aspects a happy and well-functioning family. After a number of deeply scarring experiences and in order to protect their child from society's scorn and herself from continuous humiliation, Dida finally leaves her beloved partner and enters a marriage of convenience with Philip Galen, who turns out to be a sadistic and abusive madman.

Oswald adapted both novels during the First World War, but censorship offices in Berlin and Munich prevented screenings of the films until late 1918. Originially entitled *Tagebuch einer Toten* [A Dead Woman's Diary], *Das Tagebuch einer Verlorenen* premiered shortly before the armistice on November 11, 1918.[145] When the prolific filmmaker turned his attention to Böhme's text in 1917, he was undoubtedly aware of the immense popularity of the book prior to the war and of the potential market value of an adaptation. However, the critical potential of both novels was paramount for the director from the very beginning. Unfortunately, Oswald's adaptation of Böhme's *Diary of a Lost Girl* seems to be lost; just like a previous German film based on Böhme's text directed by Fritz Bernhardt in 1912. Remaining film fragments, production documents, and stills, however, indicate that Oswald followed Böhme's narrative and critique quite closely while especially highlighting the sanctity of motherhood and society's failure in protecting Thymian (played by Erna Morena) as a vulnerable teen and her child.

The loss of a child—because of adoption and subsequent death (Thymian), or because her daughter needed to be protected from her violent stepfather and is therefore removed (Dida)—is the sad climax in both of Oswald's Böhme-adaptations, thereby emphasizing the traumatic effect of an event that should never have occurred. Oswald portrays Thymian and Dida, the 'fallen girls', as victims of a prudish and harshly condemning society, whose prescribed role models, moral codes, and hypocrisy not only destroy individuals, but also render the public incapable of perceiving these young women as human beings. In both films, Oswald juxtaposes opening sequences depicting teenage girls full of life shot in natural light with scenes that are void of movement and confine their protagonists to a lifeless and meaningless stage to suitably claustrophobic effect.

His *Dida Ibsen* film for instance opens with Dida (played by expression dancer/actress/model Anita Berber[146]) running toward the camera as if into the viewers' arms, and clearly communicates Dida as a girl filled with joy and love for life. Oswald's film, however, soon turns away from the outdoors, from natural light and energetic physical movement, and focuses on the topic of an arranged marriage for money—or "Geldheirat"—in the closed environment of her parents' sitting room. Dida is pressured into a marriage for money because her parents are under severe financial pressure. The filmmaker here only seemingly replaces the act of prostitution depicted in the literary text as a means to deal with the parents' dilemma, with a barter deal, i.e., financial security and good standing for permission to marry the struggling parents' virgin daughter. In his *Philosophy of Money* (1900) the sociologist Georg Simmel had famously identified as a form of prostitution the very common practice of marrying for money and status among bourgeois families.

Dida, however, defies her parents and elopes with Eric Norrensen (Conrad Veidt). In the scenes following Dida's escape from a potentially disastrous but commonly accepted "Geldheirat," Oswald carefully constructs scenes that aim at normalizing Eric and Dida's relationship as a couple living together and making a home. He repeatedly highlights the happiness of the couple and, soon, the young family. Again, by way of juxtaposition, her subsequent marriage of convenience and protection from public scorn, which follows her idyllic relationship with her lover, are identified as madness—frighteningly personified by Dida's abusive husband (Werner Krauß). By implication, society's belief in the institution of marriage is here declared equally delusional.

The focus of the main part of the film is on the abusive relationship Dida endures and the impact it has on Dida's daughter (played by three-year-old Loni Nest[147]). In order to communicate his provocative message as well as Dida's growing fear and despair most effectively, Oswald captures the mother's deep pain and the child's anguish in a rare series of medium close-up shots reflecting the moments when Dida gives up her child to protect it from the sadistic stepfather.

FIGURE 2.3 *Dida saying goodbye to her child in* Dida Ibsens Geschichte *(l. to r.: Maria Forescu, Loni Nest, and Anita Berber; DE, Richard Oswald, 1918).*

The director usually minimizes melodramatic gestures (remaining stylistically in line with his *There will be light!* films) and maintains the same camera distance. He utilizes this sequence of medium close-ups to remind the audience of the happy, carefree girl at the beginning of the film and to draw attention to this painful climax in Dida's life. Oswald captures the essence of Böhme's social critique here by visually pausing on mother and child, emphasizing their despair. At that moment, time is briefly suspended and an affective image, as Gilles Deleuze[148] called it, is formed; in this pause between action and reaction, the essence of this particular human experience is communicated affectively. Furthermore, these uncommon medium close-up shots could also be read as a form of fragmentation that at least potentially, and if only for a moment, removes the protagonist from the fabric of the narrative and leaves only the despair and pain of this mother and child. Oswald wanted to educate, and thus created strong affective images to enable the communication of a tragedy, devoid of moral judgment and demanding critical re-evaluation.

At several instances in both novel and film, Böhme and Oswald highlighted the similarities between their marginalized female protagonists and 'normal' bourgeois girls and women, thereby questioning the basis for their difference and social exclusion. Moreover, Oswald foregrounds the human consequences of hypocritical and cruel social morals, depicting in *Tagebuch einer Verlorenen* how Thymian is denied access to her family home (as a raped teenager, but nonetheless 'fallen woman') and is forced to give up her child for adoption. Surviving still photos of the film reflect Thymian's journey from a happy, lively girl, giddily dancing on the table surrounded by actresses invited by her father (corresponding with a scene in the novel) to becoming a broken individual, who, despite the loving care of Dr. Julius (Conrad Veidt), becomes seriously ill and dies. The prevalent attitudes to morality are identified as both inhuman and illogical with reference to Thymian's role as a mother. It is precisely by denying this so-called 'fallen girl' the right to motherhood that her demise and eventually death is precipitated.

Oswald cleverly deals with popular, conservative voices on the theme of prostitution and takes issue with 'scientists' such as Cesare Lombroso and Guglielmo Ferrero. Lombroso's and his son-in-law Ferrero's questionable 'criminal-anthropological' *La Donna delinquente, la prostituta e la donna normale* (1893) was published in German as *Das Weib als Verbrecherin und Prostituirte* [sic] (Woman as Criminal and Prostitute, 1894) to great acclaim. The text defined 'perpetrator-types' according to their physiological characteristics, and denied these 'born prostitutes' the ability to experience deep emotions as 'they are lacking in maternal feelings, have no love for their families and are intent on ruthlessly satisfying their passions [...].'[149] Margarete Böhme had written her two novels also to rebuff Lombroso and

Ferrero's pseudo-scientific publication, and therefore placed the focus of her literary texts resolutely on her characters' experiences of maternal love, the deep pain caused by the loss of their children, and on their distress when denied the love and support of their families. Oswald deals with the theme of motherhood in his adaptations of her novels accordingly by making it a central dimension of the two female characters. Motherhood here is not abstract or 'sacred', but concrete and an innately human impulse. Thus he simultaneously criticizes the moral laws and the criminal anthropological 'sentencing' of these two mothers as both incorrect and unjust. Furthermore, he celebrates motherhood as the core of an emotionally bonding and melodramatic gesture.

Wartime Adaptations and Definitions of Alterity

The foregrounding of motherhood and of the society's failure to support those in need infers the functionality of Oswald's wartime films. Marriage is the theme of Oswald's adaptation *Jettchen Geberts Geschichte* [Jettchen Gebert's Story] (1918), a two-part feature based on Georg Hermann's novel, first published in 1906. It is a story of young woman's compliance regarding prescribed role models and the tragic consequences of her quest for self-determination. An arranged marriage with a man she does not love only ends in divorce due to open-minded and caring relatives. But when she is finally free to marry the man she had loved, Jettchen Gebert realizes that her desire for happiness can no longer be satisfied and she takes her own life.[150] Interestingly, the censors allowed this adaptation to be released prior to the end of the war. *Dida Ibsens Geschichte* remained banned until it finally premiered in Berlin's Marmorhaus on December 12, 1918. Oswald's Böhme adaptations, which focus emphatically on his female protagonists' humanity and highlight their likeness with other 'normal' girls and women, should be considered challenges of traditional (bourgeois) society's definition of alterity and social practices of marginalization and exclusion. Especially in light of dramatic sociopolitical changes experienced by German audiences at the time, one should not dismiss the impact of sentimental or melodramatic forms of narrative, as Christof Decker reminds us, as this particular cultural mode can uncover and enable 'hidden moral qualities' and not only highlight conflicts of values but support processes of intellectual and emotional understanding.[151] This strategy of 'generating feelings in order to influence actions or ideas and make moral corrections' becomes a widely used model in early film[152] on both sides of the Atlantic Ocean.

Conclusion

As support for the still young medium grew, filmmakers used new technical opportunities to develop more intricate storylines on screen. From 1907/8 establishing shots, continuity editing, varying camera distances, inter- or cross-cutting became increasingly common on both sides of the Atlantic. These editing techniques allowed two (or sometimes even three) storylines to unfold at the same time, thereby not only increasing suspense, but also the tempo at which the culmination of events unfolded. While the history of narrative integration begins with Méliès' and Lumière/Hatot's short moving pictures inspired by Goethe and Gounod, the representation of literary texts on film rapidly gains in complexity (and popularity) from year to year.

As this chapter hoped to show, early twentieth-century filmmakers were well on their way to transforming "the new medium from a mechanical recording instrument to a modern electrical *Gesamtkunstwerk* that combined the crafts of photography and cinematography, theater staging and acting, storytelling and writing, painting and set design,"[153] as Kaes puts it. Moreover, by using well-known texts belonging to the canon of German-language literature, as well as notorious plays and bestselling novels for their adaptations, these filmmakers contributed significantly to breaking "the resistance that German intellectuals and the educated middle class instinctively felt against the originally plebeian and unrefined mass entertainment of film."[154] This systematic cultural appropriation of the literary canon began to bridge the perceived cultural gap between film and other arts. But perhaps even more importantly than providing the new medium with cultural respectability, by formulating what we might call a cinematographic 'ethics of similarity', filmmakers like Oswald created awareness and at least tried to contribute to a more just, equal, and tolerant society.[155] Between 1907 and 1918 silent film would become the most popular mass medium in countries such as Germany, Austria, Britain, Denmark, Italy, France, and the United States.

While this chapter highlighted adaptation projects—some of which were destroyed or seem to be lost and could only be reconstructed through censorship reports, promotional materials, and reviews in the press— the majority of films at the time were comedies such as greatly popular Lubitsch/Ossi Oswalda features, romantic melodramas, or crime films such as a Lothar Schmidt adaptation *Ringende Seelen* [Struggling Souls] (DE, Eugen Illés, 1918). The outbreak of the First World War affected not only the narrative content of silent cinema in Germany and Austria, but economic contexts, as well as production, distribution, and exhibition patterns, not least due to a ban on the importation of 'enemy culture'. Between 1914 and 1918 adaptations of German-language literature were increasingly considered welcome educational endeavors while providing escapist entertainment. Adaptations of the canon of German and Austrian literature marked the new medium's ability to celebrate literary traditions and national heritage. The need to display national culture during the war contributed to the promotion of cinema as a significant contributor and aided in the consideration of film as (at least potentially) high culture. In Germany the number of adaptations of the German-language literary canon by Ufa, but also smaller, independent motion picture production companies, increased significantly for several reasons. Films based on Goethe, Schiller, and other internationally famous German-language authors were seen to celebrate national culture, fan patriotism and contribute to a sense of identity—both modern and rooted in national heritage—while helping to meet the enormous demand for new narratives on screens both at home and at the front, while foreign imports were banned. During the First World War, adaptations of the canon German-language literature were a safe choice for filmmakers, both economically and politically.

Potentially more controversial were adaptations of contemporary literature, and censors regularly prevented films that addressed social ills or criticized bourgeois moral codes from being screened in cinemas until the devastating First World War was about to end.[156] Combatting nations were well aware of the power of film as a propaganda medium and the value of the 'international language' of silent cinema. Among the few adaptations of German-language literature during the First World War by filmmakers abroad, only Hermann Sudermann's work left an impact—in the United States.

In 1916 Edgar Lewis directed an adaptation of Sudermann's *Johannisfeuer* (Fires of St. John, 1900) produced by Siegmund Lubin and the Lubin Manufacturing Company in Philadelphia. *The Flames of Johannis* was based on a script by Alfred Hickman and starred his wife Nance O'Neil. The following year *Magda*, based on Sudermann's play *Heimat* (Home/Homeland, 1893) or, rather, on the 1896 translation of the perhaps most successful play of the late nineteenth century by C.E.A. Winslow, was produced by Lewis J. Selznick's Clara Kimball Young Film Corporation and starred Clara Kimball Young, one of the most renowned American actors of the early silent era. Magda, the leading lady of this heart-wrenching drama, could be considered an early representation of the 'New Woman', which is an aspect of Sudermann's narrative that might well have been emphasized in the adaptation by the open-minded and controversial celebrity who played her.[157] Finally, Sudermann's novel *Das hohe Lied* provided the plot for a play written by Edward Sheldon, which was so successful on Broadway in 1914/15 that Famous Players-Lasky produced an adaptation directed by Joseph Kaufman based on a scenario written by Charles Maigne. The film starred Elsie Ferguson, Frank Losee, and Crauford Kent. Unfortunately all three of these American adaptations of Sudermann's work seem to be lost.

Literary responses to the First World War by German writers—from August Stramm's Expressionist poetry, Ernst Jünger's prose, or Ernst Toller's plays—were not considered for adaptation to cinema screens. German and Austrian filmmakers[158] saw little point in confronting their potential audiences with the traumatic events of the recent past. The vast majority of moviegoers were all too aware of the devastating consequences of war and hoped for entertainment and escape from the everyday in the cinema. Nonetheless, adaptations produced during the war in Germany feature recurring motifs. The preponderance of Mephistopheles, devils, and other evildoers is blatant, and narratives of fragmented identities and the seduction of unsuspecting and utterly naïve victims indicate adaptations' critical subtexts. At the same time, however, national legends and tales of sacrificial love contributed to the war effort, while raising the status of motion pictures and integrating cinema into the cultural landscape of postwar Europe. After the First World War cinema was no longer considered the 'theater of the small people', as writer Alfred Döblin called it in 1909, but a medium that now provided entertainment across social classes in a variety of venues.[159] This development was to no small degree due to adaptations of literary works with high production values based on the involvement of well-known writers and theater actors as well as innovative directors and cinematographers, which productively linked this industrial form of popular culture with high art.

Notes

1. Franz Pfemfert, "Kino als Erzieher," originally published in *Das Blaubuch* 4 (1909): 548–50. Pfemfert's article was included in an exhibition at the Deutsches Literaturarchiv, Schiller-Nationalmuseum Marbach/N. entitled: *Hätte ich das Kino! Die Schriftsteller und der Stummfilm*, April 24 to October 31, 1976. The exhibition catalogue was edited by Ludwig Greve, Margot Pehle, and Heidi Westhoff (Munich: Kösel, 1976). Cf. *Hätte ich das Kino*, 68.
2. Hanns Heinz Ewers, "Vom Kinema," *Der Kinematograph* 159 (January 12, 1910): n.p.
3. Here, Sabine Hake's analysis of early German cinema's self-referentiality is particularly useful and illuminating. Sabine Hake, "Self-Referentiality in Early German Cinema," in *A Second Life: German Cinema's First Decades*, ed. Thomas Elsaesser and Michael Wedel (Amsterdam: Amsterdam University Press, 1996), 237–45.
4. For an excellent comparative analysis of early cinema in the United States and in Germany in this context, see Miriam Hansen, "Early Silent Cinema: Whose Public Sphere?," *New German Critique* 29 (1983): 147–84, here p. 168.
5. Hansen already mentions the marketing strategies in her essay on "Early Silent Cinema," 151.

6   On the topic of 'Zerstreuung,' see Siegfried Kracauer, "Kult der Zerstreuung: Über die Berliner Lichtspielhäuser," *Ornament der Masse*, 311–17; Walter Benjamin, "The Work of Art in the Age of Mechanical Reproduction," in *Illuminations* (New York: Schocken Books, 1969), 217–51; both are quoted and further discussed in Hansen, "Early Silent Cinema," 150–1.
7   Joachim Paech, *Literatur und Film* (Stuttgart: Metzler, 1988) and, more recently, Christian Kiening, "Blick und Schrift. Das Cabinet des Dr. Caligari und die Medialität des frühen Spielfilms," *Poetica* 37 (2005): 119–46.
8   Anton Kaes, "Silent Cinema," *Monatshefte* 82.3 (1990): 246–56, here p. 246.
9   Kaes, "Silent Cinema," 246.
10 Corrigan, "Literature on Screen," 35.
11 Ibid.
12 The year of the premiere of Kokoschka's play is disputed and took place in either 1907 or 1908. Georg Jäger is a proponent of the latter date in "Kokoschkas 'Mörder Hoffnung der Frauen'," *Germanisch-Romanische Monatsschrift* 63 (1982): 215–33.
13 Cf. Gabriele Brandstetter, "Der Traum vom anderen Tanz. Hofmannsthals Ästhetik des Schöpferischen im Dialog 'Furcht'," in *Hugo von Hofmannsthal, Neue Wege der Forschung*, ed. Elsbeth Dangel-Pelloquin (Darmstadt: Wissenschaftliche Buchgesellschaft, 2007), 41–61.
14 My publications on the topic might be of interest for further information: *Practicing Modernity: Female Creativity in the Weimar Republic*, ed. with Carmel Finnan (Würzburg: Königshausen & Neumann, 2006); *Commodities of Desire: The Prostitute in Modern German Literature* (Columbia, SC: Camden House, 2000); "Under Construction: Gender and the Representation of the Prostitute in German Expressionism," in *Expressionism and Gender*, ed. Frank Krause (Göttingen: Vandenhoek & Ruprecht, 2010), 117–32; "Prostitution im Kino der Weimarer Republik," in *Körper kaufen? Prostitution in Literatur und Medien*, ed. Simone Sauer-Kretschmer (Berlin: Bachmann, 2016), 68–87.
15 See Donald Crafton, *Emile Cohl, Caricature, and Film* (Princeton, NJ: Princeton University Press, 1990), 198.
16 In the 1920s abstract animation films by experimental filmmakers such as Walter Ruttmann and Viking Eggeling proved very popular, especially screenings of *Der absolute Film* (a feature-length compilation consisting of experimental shorts by Hans Richter, Viking Eggeling, Walter Ruttmann, Oskar Fischinger, etc.). Hans Helmut Prinzler mentions sold-out screenings in the Ufa Theater am Kurfürstendamm in Berlin in May 1925. Cf. Prinzler's "Chronik" on filmportal.de.
17 Cf. Jörg Schweinitz, "Vorwort," in *Prolog vor dem Film*, 5–14, here p. 9.
18 Hence remedy for the fact that before adaptations "represented one of the most visible markers of the film industry's desire to improve its cultural status, explicitly invoking 'high' culture referents but offering them in a 'low' culture venue, the moving picture shows." Cf. Pearson and Uricchio, *Reframing Culture: The Case of the Vitagraph Quality Films* (Princeton, NJ: Princeton University Press, 1993), 5. Quoted in Greg M. Colón Semenza and Bob Hasenfratz, *The History of British Literature on Film*, 7. Timothy Corrigan indicated that Griffith's *Birth of a Nation* (1915) "led the way to movie-palace exhibition"

(Corrigan, "Literature on Screen," 33). In Europe, both adaptations with a narrative structure typical of nineteenth-century novels and extravagant premieres of films/adaptations in movie palaces in Berlin, Rome, Paris, or Vienna precede 1915.

19 Emilie Altenloh, *Zur Soziologie des Kino: Die Kino-Unternehmung und die sozialen Schichten ihrer Besucher*, PhD thesis, Heidelberg University (Leipzig: Spamersche Buchdruckerei, 1914); translated/summarized by and quoted from Hansen, "Early Silent Cinema," 177.
20 See www.nobelprize.org: "Nobel Prize in Literature 1907."
21 Cf. 1907 Schiller adaptations include *Kabale und Liebe* [Intrigue and Love] and *Die Räuber* [The Robbers] as well as an adaptation of Schiller's famous poem *Das Lied von der Glocke* as *Die Glocke* [The Bell] by a young Karl Freund for the Berlin film company Internationale Cinematographen- und Licht-Effekt-Gesellschaft. *Kabale und Liebe* was again adapted in Germany six years later (DE, Friedrich Féher, 1913). The production of the Internationale Cinematographen- und Licht-Effekt-Gesellschaft should not be confused with *The Robbers* produced by the Societa Italiana Pineschi Roma, a six-minute film about a robbery and kidnapping that ends well for the female victim due to a young boy, who belongs to the robbers but has empathy and helps to save the young woman. The film ends with a medium close-up of the boy smiling into the camera. This is not, however, an adaptation of Schiller.
22 Schiller's poetry was also quite popular: Arturo Ambrosio-Torino filmed *L´andata alla fucina* and *Il guanto* (IT, 1910) based on Schiller's ballads "Der Gang nach dem Eisenhammer" and "Der Handschuh" (The Glove) respectively. A further adaptation of Schiller's "Die Bürgschaft" (The Pledge, 1799) by the same director is mentioned in Alfred Estermann, *Die Verfilmung literarischer Werke* (Bonn: Bouvier, 1965), 20.
23 Estermann, *Die Verfilmung literarischer Werke*, 18.
24 Particularly useful are the collections of film reviews edited by Anton Kaes and Jörg Schweinitz; Anton Kaes, ed., *Kino-Debatte: Texte zum Verhältnis von Literatur und Film 1909–1929* (Munich: dtv, 1978); Schweinitz, *Prolog vor dem Film*.
25 Hansen, "Early German Cinema," 169.
26 Ibid.; as Hansen also notes, reformers like Victor Noack condemned "poets'dance around the Golden Calf," i.e., cinema, and Karl Kraus, criticized H. v. Hofmannsthal, who "enlisted his art in the service of film." For Kraus, this was "proof, not of the cinema's literary ambitions, but of Herr von Hofmansthal's commercial ambitions." Hansen, "Early German Cinema," 166.
27 In 1910, Goethe's *Götz von Berlichingen* was adapted in Italy and both Goethe's *Die Leiden des jungen Werther* and *Torquato Tasso* were made into films in France, with another version of the original *Torquato Tasso* following in 1913.
28 For example, numerous films about Jeanne d'Arc appeared in France, Germany, and Italy before the First World War, based on both French history and Schiller's play (from Georges Méliès version in 1900 and the Pathé brothers in 1903, to Mario Caserini's Italian *Giovanna d´Arco* of 1909). Viggo Larsen adapted *Wilhelm Tell* in Denmark in 1908. The following year saw adaptations of Schiller's ballad *Die Bürgschaft* (The Pledge) in Britian

and Italy, etc. (cf. Estermann, *Die Verfilmung literarischer Werke*, 20–7). In Germany, 1913 proved extremely productive with regard to cinematic Schiller adaptations. Phil Jutzi directed *Fiesko*, starring Wilhelm Dieterle; and Friedrich Fehér (best known for playing Francis in Robert Wiene's *Das Cabinet des Dr. Caligari*) directed and played the lead in both *Kabale und Liebe* and *Die Räuber*. According to archival records the fourth German *Wilhelm Tell*-adaptation hit cinema screens in 1914: Fehér's adaptation of Schiller's *Tell* premiered as *Die Befreiung der Schweiz* und *Die Sage von Wilhelm Tell*, in which Fehér himself plays Gessler and Karl Kienlechner appears as Wilhelm Tell. In 1916, Cecil B. de Mille's *Joan of Arc* and, a year later, *Joan the Woman* premiere.

29   Consider, for example, *Emilia Galotti* (DE, Friedrich Fehér, 1913), an adaptation of Lessing's tragedy. Lessing, the most important representative of German-language literature of the enlightenment, tells the story of the careless egotism of the nobility (represented by the Prince of Guastalla) and its destructive effect on the young, pure, and beautiful Emilia Galotti, whose destruction implies at the same time that of society, community, and family. Driven by his lust for the gorgeous virgin, the Prince discards his mistress and has the Count Appiani killed in order to prevent his imminent marriage to Emilia. The girl is brought to his palace, where she is stabbed, i.e., sacrificed by her father Odoardo to save her from her now seemingly inevitable fate of becoming the Prince's next sex toy. This highly dramatic plot could not be more suitable for early cinema, as it conveniently addresses the hugely popular 'threat to beautiful girl's virginity'-trope and, at the same time, critically examines the nobility's abuse of power. Thereby, the play and the film implicitly address both the aspirations of a rising bourgeoisie with regard to freedom and self-determination and its limitations. While the bourgeois Emilia is morally superior, the power over happiness and autonomy, life and death clearly lies with the nobility. The film and the play end tragically; any hope for betterment is in the hands of the audience. While the use of one of the best-known German plays provides a convenient cover, the filmmaker's critical stance toward the power of the nobility becomes nonetheless manifest on the cinema screen.

30   Notable early adaptations in Germany include the Oskar Messter production *Heimat* (DE, Adolf Gärtner, 1912), *Der Katzensteg* (DE, Alfred Halm, 1913; and a remake of the popular novel in 1915; dir. Max Mack), and *Stein unter Steinen* [Stone among Stones] (DE, Felix Basch, 1916; starring Emil Jannings and Paul Bildt). In Denmark, Urban Gad directed *Vorderhaus und Hinterhaus*, starring Asta Nielsen; Karl Freund was at the camera; the script is based on Sudermann's *Die Ehre* (Honor) in 1914. In the United States, *Flames of Johannis* (1916; dir. Siegmund Lubin; based on *Johannisfeuer*) and *Magda* (1917; dir. Emile Chautard; based on *Heimat*). I have been unable to locate *Casa paterna* (1910), which according to Estermann was an Italian adaptation of Sudermann's novel *Heimat* (Home). Cf. Estermann, *Die Verfilmung literarischer Werke*, 28–39; www.filmportal.de, and http://www.sudermannstiftung.de/verfilmungen/.

31   Robert Walser, "Kino" (1912), in Schweinitz, ed., *Prolog vor dem Film*, 26f.
32   Land in Schweinitz, ed., *Prolog vor dem Film*, 19.

33 The fact that the *Faust* narrative had been turned into music and was even available as an opera score meant that early sound film pioneers experimenting with the synchronization of image and music also turned to *Faust* for narrative depth as they were working on "opera films" [US], "Tonbilder" [Germany], and "Singing Pictures" [GB]. For further info on these early sound experiments on film, see Michael Wedel's essay "Messter's Silent Heirs: Sync Systems of the German Music Film 1914–1929," *Film History* 11.4 (1999): 464–76. See also Alfred Estermann, *Die Verfilmung literarischer Werke*, 18–37.
34 According to Estermann, *Die Verfilmung literarischer Werke*, 24.
35 Cf. Georg Simmel, *Brücke und Tor. Essays des Philosophen zur Geschichte, Religion, Kunst und Gesellschaft* (Stuttgart: Koehler, 1957), 227–42. Cf. also Anton Kaes, "Einführung," in *Kino-Debatte*, 1–36, here p. 6f.
36 Cf. Kaes, *Kino-Debattte*, 5; also Schweinitz, *Prolog vor dem Film*.
37 "Die Karriere des Kinematographen," *Die Lichtbild-Bühne* 124 (December 10, 1910), quoted in Kaes, *Kino-Debattte*, 5.
38 Refers to Heinrich Mann's 'Drei-Minuten-Roman,' in Heinrich Mann, *Flöten und Dolche. Novellen* (Munich: Langen, 1905), as Anton Kaes rightly points out in *Kino-Debatte*, 7.
39 Quoted in Kaes, *Kino-Debattte*, 6.
40 Egon Friedell, "Prolog vor dem Film," *Blätter des deutschen Theaters* 2 (1912): 509f. Quoted in Kaes, *Kino-Debatte*, 7. For an in-depth exploration of German film criticism, see Sabine Hake, *The Cinema's Third Machine: German Writings on Film 1907–1933* (Lincoln: University of Nebraska Press, 1993).
41 Walter von Molo was a German writer who later spent the Hitler era in Germany in a kind of subservient inner emigration and only entered German literary history due to his invitation to Thomas Mann to return to Germany after the collapse of the murderous regime in 1945. Mann famously replied that in his view all German cultural productions 1933 to 1945 are worthless and German culture will forever be soiled due to the crimes committed under Hitler's reign.
42 Walter von Molo's essay "Im Kino" (April 1912) was reprinted in Schweinitz, *Prolog vor dem Film*, 28–39, here p. 29.
43 Ibid., in Schweinitz, 36.
44 Mario Caserini had adapted a number of Shakespeare plays, but also turned to German literature, notably E.T.A. Hoffmann's *Das Fräulein von Scuderi* in 1911 as *Mademoiselle de Scudery*. His highly dramatic *Last Days of Pompeii* (1913) based on Edward Bulwer-Lytton's 1834 novel was a spectacular success.
45 "Siegfrieds Traum: Ein kinematographischer Albdruck" (1913), in *Prolog vor dem Film*, ed. Schweinitz, 39–42, here p. 42. *Les Hallucinations du baron de Münchhausen* (1911; a 10.26 minutes long Star Film directed by Méliès) also features a dragon reflecting filmmakers' interest in experimentation with large, moving models. Méliès' take on Münchhausen's tall tales does not really make reference to Gottfried August Bürger's *Wunderbare Reisen zu Wasser und zu Lande—Feldzüge und lustige Abenteuer des Freiherrn von Münchhausen* (1786), as he depicts a dream or incoherent nightmare sequence following a heavy meal that sees Münchhausen descend to hell like Faust or seduced by a

woman with tentacles just like the one in his earlier adaptation. There is even an animated dragon in Münchhausen's nightmare, that seems at least as alive as the one being killed by Siegfried in Fritz Lang's *Nibelungen* (1924). Méliès' film is listed on Wikipedia and in Estermann (p. 23) as the earliest adaptation of Bürger's text, but should rather be considered an amusing counter-fiction that uses Münchhausen's name for marketing purposes.

46 Wolfgang Mühl-Benninghaus, "German Film Censorship during World War I," *Film History* 9.1 (1997): 71–94, here p. 71.
47 Mühl-Benninghaus, "German Film Censorship," 71, and Thomas Nipperdey, *Deutsche Geschichte 1916–18*, vol. 1 (Munich: Beck, 1991), 817 (quoted by Mühl-Benninghaus).
48 Mühl-Benninghaus, "German Film Censorship," 71.
49 Ibid.
50 Bundesarchiv documents quoted in Mühl-Benninghaus, "German Film Censorship," 72.
51 Hansen, "Early Silent Cinema," 165.
52 Reinhold Keiner, *Hanns Heinz Ewers und der phantastische Film* (Hildesheim: Olms, 1987); Wolfgang Mühl-Benninghaus, "*Don Juan heiratet* und *Der Andere*. Zwei frühe filmische Theateradaptionen," in *Kino der Kaiserzeit. Zwischen Tradition und Moderne*, ed. Thomas Elsaesser and Michael Wedel (Munich: text+kritik, 2002), 337–48; Wilfried Kugel, *Der Unverantwortliche. Das Leben des Hanns Heinz Ewers* (Düsseldorf: Grupello, 1992).
53 Eduard Lintz published *Der Kinematograph* from January 6, 1907, the first German-language journal for film and film technology. *Der Kinematograph* appeared once a week until 1928, then daily Mondays to Saturdays. After the sacking of all Jewish employees in 1933 and further political streamlining under the ownership of Alfred Hugenberg, the journal went downhill and was closed in 1935. Cf. "Pionier der Filmpublizistik: Der Kinematograph," *Programmheft Deutsches Filmmuseum* (January 2007): 7. Also see text archive at Deutsches Film Institut, Frankfurt/M. in particular.
54 Cf. *Der Kinematograph*, January 1, 1913, and March 26, 1913 ("Der Autorenfilm und seine Bewertung"); quoted in Heinz B. Heller, "Buch und Schrift im bewegten Bild," in *Grauzonen*, ed. Stefan Keppler-Tasaki and Fabienne Liptay (Munich: text+kritik, 2010), 102–20, here p. 103. For further context see Helmut Diederich, "The Origins of the Autorenfilm," in *Before Caligari. German Cinema 1895–1920*, ed. Paolo Cherchi Usai and Lorenzo Codelli (Pordenone: Edizioni Biblioteca dell'Immagine, 1990), 380–401.
55 Felix Salten, "Die sprechenden Bilder. Vorführung des neuerfundenen Kinetophon" (25 August 1913); in Schweinitz, ed., *Prolog vor dem Film*, 46–51. Here pp. 48 and 50 resp.
56 Harry M. Geduld, "Introduction," in *Authors on Film*, ed. H. Geduld (Bloomington: Indiana University Press, 1972), xi.
57 Geduld, "Introduction," xi.
58 See also Anton Kaes, "Literary Intellectuals and the Cinema. Charting a Controversy (1909–1929)," *New German Critique* 40 (1987): 7–33; Sigfrid Hoefert, *Gerhart Hauptmann und der Film* (Berlin: Erich Schmidt, 1996).
59 *Liebelei* was written in 1894 and the play premiered at the Vienna Burgtheater on October 9, 1895. Wiener Kunstfilm planned a silent film recording of

the play in the Burgtheater, but the project was deemed 'humiliating' for the established actors and was dropped. Cf. Claudia Wolf, *Arthur Schnitzler und der Film* (Karlsruhe: KTI Scientific Publishing, online version; OpenEdition Books: January 16, 2017), 40f. The title is usually translated as *Flirtation*, but also as *The Reckoning*; the play was adapted as *Dalliance* by Tom Stoppard in 1986. Max Ophül's adaptation of Schnitzler's play will be discussed in Chapter 4.

60 According to Claudia Wolf, this Schnitzler noted in his diary on November 23, 1911 (vol. 4, p. 284); see Wolf, *Arthur Schnitzler und der Film*, 40.
61 Schnitzler's play was well known in Scandinavia. It also premiered in Sweden (Stockholm) in 1896 and in Norway (Oslo) in 1898. Cf. Daniel Göske, "Rezeption und Wirkung: Skandinavien," in *Schnitzler Handbuch: Leben—Werk—Wirkung*, ed. Christoph Jürgensen, Wolfgang Lukas, and Michael Scheffel (Stuttgart: Metzler, 2014), 372.
62 I'm again referring to quotes from Schnitzler's diary and letters held at the German literary archive in Marbach discussed in Wolf, *Arthur Schnitzler und der Film*, 43.
63 Schnitzler in a letter to Schröder, February 5, 1913. See Schnitzler, *Briefe II*, 9f.; quoted in Wolf, *Arthur Schnitzler und der Film*, 44.
64 Cf. Wolf, *Arthur Schnitzler und der Film*, 45.
65 See Julia Ilgner's chapter on "Ein Wiener 'Kinoniter!' Arthur Schnitzlers Filmgeschmack," in *Arthur Schnitzler und der Film*, ed. Achim Aurnhammer, Barbara Beßlich, and Rudolf Denk (Würzburg: Ergon, 2010), 15–44.
66 Arthur Schnitzler, *Liebelei*, in Peter Michael Braunwarth, Gerhard Hubmann, and Isabella Schwentner's critical edition (Berlin: De Gruyter, 2014), 1117f.
67 Letter to Karl Ludwig Schröder, December 23, 1913, Deutsches Literaturarchiv Marbach (Mappe 549); quoted in Wolf, *Arthur Schnitzler und der Film*, 50.
68 Cf. https://www.dfi.dk/viden-om-film/filmdatabasen/film/elskovsleg-0. According to the Danish Film Institute, only a fifteen-minute fragment of the 42-minute film remains.
69 Wolfgang Ritscher, "Schnitzlers Dramatik und der Kino," in *Kino-Debatte*, 110. Also quoted in Wolf, *Arthur Schnitzler und der Film*, 51.
70 Films had been growing in length steadily, but most films would have lasted thirty to sixty minutes, with cinemas showing one short movie after another. By 1913 more high-profile productions, such as *The Student of Prague* (eighty-five minutes), were nearing feature-length.
71 Dierk Rodewald and Corinna Fiedler, eds., *Samuel Fischer, Hedwig Frischer: Briefwechsel mit Autoren* (Frankfurt/M.: Fischer, 1989), 303; quoted in Deniz Göktürk, "18 December 1913: *Atlantis* Triggers Controversy about Sinking in Culture," in *A New History of German Cinema*, ed. Jennifer M. Kapczynski and Michael D. Richardson (Rochester, NY: Camden House, 2012), 51–6, here pp. 52, 56. Other Gerhart Hauptmann adaptations or films using motifs based on Hauptmann's literary works during the First World War include: *Sturmflut, ihr Söhne* (DE, Willy Zeyn, 1917) and *Graf Michael* (DE, H. Fredall, 1918). Cf. Estermann, *Die Verfilmung literarischer Werke*, 35, 37.
72 Hauptmann's novel is in the public domain and available online via the Gutenberg project; due to the author's international fame, but also the fact that part of the text takes place in the United States (which the author had

visited in 1892), the novel was included in the Reader's Digest 30 volume *Library of the World's Best Literature* in 1917. The 1912 translation by Adele and Thomas Seltzer (New York: Huebsch, 1912) can be accessed here: https://archive.org/stream/atlantisanovel00haupgoog#page/n8/mode/2up; as this English version diverts from the original text quite significantly, I am referring to my own close translation based on Hauptmann's novel.

73   Actor/writer Thea von Harbou's novel *Das indische Grabmal* (Berlin: Ullstein, 1918) was adapted to film by Harbou and Fritz Lang. Directed by Joe May, the film was screened in two parts and was a hit with moviegoers. Further adaptations of the novel were brought to cinemas in 1938 (DE, Richard Eichberg) and 1959 (DE, Fritz Lang).

74   There are several uploads of the film on YouTube. For the translations of all *Atlantis* intertitles into English, see here: https://www.youtube.com/watch?v=kk14s7JuWBo.

75   Gerhart Hauptmann published parts of his diary and correspondence in his *Gerhard Hauptmann und Ida Orloff: Dokumentation einer dichterischen Leidenschaft* (Berlin: Propyläen, 1969), which serves to highlight this fact.

76   Göktürk, "18 December 1913," 52.

77   Göktürk, "18 December 1913," 52; summary/translation of article in *Erste Internationale Film-Zeitung* (September 20, 1913): 31; cf. Göktürk, "18 December 1913," 56.

78   Cf. Heide Schlüpmann, "Asta Nielsen and Female Narration: The Early Films," in *A Second Life: German Cinema's First Decades*, ed. Thomas Elsaesser and Michael Wedel, 118–22; and Peter Lähn, "Paul Davidson, the Frankfurt Film Scene and 'Afgrunden' in Germany," in *A Second Life: German Cinema's First Decades*, 79–85.

79   The steamer is named after the early medieval hero Roland or Hruotland remembered in the old French *La Chanson de Roland* (around 1100) but also in sculptures of knights typically put up in medieval German cities marking the protection of their independence and freedom.

80   Hauptmann, *Atlantis,* chapter 10.

81   Göktürk, "18 December 1913," 55.

82   Hansen, "Early Silent Cinema," 170.

83   Quoted in Töteberg, "Nachwort," 123. "Nun geben sie all das viele Geld aus, und es wird doch nichts." For more information on Stellan Rye, see Casper Tybjerg, "The Faces of Stellan Rye," in *A Second Life: German Cinema's First Decades*, 151–9.

84   Friedrich A. Kittler, "Romantik—Psychoanalyse—Film: Eine Doppelgängergeschichte," in *Die Wahrheit der technischen Welt* (Berlin: Suhrkamp, ²2014), 93–112.

85   Rank's essay is available in English as "The Double. A Psychoanalytic Study," trans./ed./intro. by Harry Tucker (Chapel Hill: The University of North Carolina Press, 1971).

86   For more detail, see Dietrich Scheunemann, ed., *Expressionist Film* (Rochester, NY: Camden House, 2003), 134–6. The *Doppelgänger* continues to haunt literature throughout the nineteenth century. The impact of Dostoevsky's Gogol-inspired novella Двойник (The Double, 1846) and many others on cinema is worth a closer look.

87 http://muse.jhu.edu/journals/gyr/summary/v017/17.richter.html; *Goethe Yearbook* 17 (2010): 374–5; Simon Richter, "Faust," *Classics in Miniature* (review).
88 Goethe, *Faust I*, verse 1112.
89 Lotte H. Eisner, *The Haunted Screen: Expressionism in the German Cinema and the Influence of Max Reinhardt*, trans. Roger Greaves (Berkeley: University of California Press, 1969), 39f.
90 Eisner, *The Haunted Screen*, 40.
91 This new practice had been successfully initiated by Camille Saint-Saëns, who composed a fifteen-minute original score for the French silent movie *L'assassinat du duc de Guise* [The Assassination of the Duke de Guise] (FR, Charles Le Bargy, André Calmettes, 1908).
92 See Peter Beicken, *Wie interpretiert man einen Film?* (Stuttgart: Reclam, 2004); Iona Craciun, *Die Dekonstruktion des Bürgerlichen im Stummfilm der Weimarer Republik* (Heidelberg: Winter, 2015), 272.
93 Quoted by Eisner, *The Haunted Screen*, 40.
94 Young Lotte Reiniger was present during the lecture and later credited Wegener for influencing her path as a pioneer in animation. Paul Wegener, "Die künstlerischen Möglichkeiten des Films (Vortrag 1916)"; the eleven-page typescript of Wegener's talk can be accessed via Deutsches Filminstitut (Nachlass Paul Wegener) at filmportal.de: https://www.filmportal.de/sites/default/files/p000329_slg_wegener_filmschriften_01.pdf. For further detail see Aneka Meier and Christiane Schönfeld, "Lotte Reiniger and Female Creativity in the Weimar Republic," in *Beyond Prince Achmed: New Perspectives on Animation Pioneer Lotte Reiniger*, ed. Rada Bieberstein (Marburg: Schüren, 2021), 31–69, 34–8.
95 Cf. *Bild und Film* III, 3/4 (1913/14): 70.
96 Cf. C. Z. K., "Das Kinoplakat," *Bild und Film* III, 3/4 (1913/14): 70.
97 Not much secondary literature is available on Kellermann's novel or the adaptation. Cf. Werner Fuld, "Bis an die Knöchel im Geld, über Bernhard Kellermanns *Der Tunnel*," in *Romane von gestern—heute gelesen*, vol. 1 (1900–18), ed. Marcel Reich-Ranicki (Frankfurt/M.: Fischer, 1989), 180–6.
98 Cf. for example the review in *Lichtbild-Bühne* 37 (September 11, 1915).
99 See "Filmbranche und Propaganda 1914–1918," in *Filmportal Themen*, Deutsches Filminstitut, Frankfurt/M.; https://www.filmportal.de/thema/filmbranche-und-propaganda-1914-1918.
100 Fritzi Massary's daughter Liesl later married the writer Bruno Franck, a novelist, who later in exile adapted Victor Hugo's *Hunchback of Notre Dame* for William Dieterle's 1939 film.
101 Cf. *Lichtbild-Bühne* 37 (September 11, 1915), n.p.
102 Nikola Knoth, "Antikriegsfilm *Die Waffen nieder!*", *Deutschlandfunk Kultur*, https://www.hoerspielundfeature.de/antikriegsfilm-die-waffen-nieder-100.html.
103 Hansen, "Early Silent Cinema," 159–60.
104 Manfred Behn, "Filmfreunde. Die Gründung der Ufa," in *Das Ufa-Buch*, ed. Hans-Michael Bock and Michael Töteberg (Frankfurt/M.: Zweitausendeins, 1992), 30–5, here p. 31.

105 Ibid.
106 Ludwig Brauner, "Das Kinogeschäft nach dem Kriege," *Der Kinematograph* 505 (1916): 1–2.
107 Cf. Toller's play in the new edition of his collected works; Ernst Toller, *Sämtliche Werke. Kritische Ausgabe*, vol. 1 (Göttingen: Wallstein, 2015), 212.
108 Austria-Hungary, in contrast, used film as propaganda from 1915. The "kaiserlich und königliche Kriegspressequartier" (KPQ), the imperial and royal war information bureau organized news and propaganda from the beginning of the First World War and employed numerous artists and writers to support the war effort. In 1915, the founder/director of Sascha-Film Sascha Kolowrat-Krakowsky began to oversee film production for KPQ. Cf. Österreichisches Staatsarchiv/ Kriegsarchiv, Vienna.
109 Jos. Max Jacobi, "Der Triumph des Films," *Der Kinematograph* 563 (October 10, 1917): 1. Source: Deutsches Filminstitut—DIF e.V., Frankfurt/M.; emphasis in the original.
110 Gustav Stresemann, "Die Filmpropaganda für die deutsche Sache im Ausland," *Der Film* (April 7, 1917), reprinted in Bock/Töteberg, *Das Ufa-Buch*, 29.
111 Ludendorff's letter can be accessed via filmportal.de at: https://www.filmportal.de/material/der-weg-zur-ufa-der-ludendorff-brief.
112 Official commercial register entry of the company, Berlin, February 14, 1918. Quoted in Bock/Töteberg, *Das Ufa-Buch*, 31.
113 For further information on Ludendorff's consolidation of the media during the First World War, see Hans-Michael Bock and Michael Töteberg, "A History of Ufa," in *The German Cinema Book*, ed. Tim Bergfelder, Erica Carter, and Deniz Göktürk (London: BFI, 2002), 285–95, here 286f.; for a more in-depth history of the company, cf. Bock/Töteberg, *Das Ufa-Buch*. Wegener's adaptation of *Der Rattenfänger von Hameln* [The Pied Piper of Hamelin] (1918), a PAGU production, indicates not only the potential for innovation, but the use of a genre like fairy tales to introduce a critical subtext during the final period of the First World War. Wegener's film followed a first adaptation by Percy Stow (GB, 1907).
114 Anon., "Krieg und Kino," *Der Kinematograph* (August 5, 1914): 1.
115 The German government and industrialist (AEG, Bosch, Hapag, etc.) funded Ufa at first; in 1921 the government passed its share on to the Deutsche Bank; see Bock/Töteberg, "A History of Ufa," 286. The Deutsche Lichtbild Gesellschaft (Deulig), financed by German industrialists, produced propaganda films from December 1916 onwards. For an excellent summary used for this paragraph and links to archive material, see "Filmbranche und Propaganda 1914–1918," Filmportal Themen, Deutsches Filminstitut, Frankfurt/M.; https://www.filmportal.de/thema/filmbranche-und-propaganda-1914-1918.
116 Cf. *Neue Kino-Rundschau* (January 19, 1918): 58. Quoted on Wikipedia.
117 Perhaps also a reference to Hauptmann's *Atlantis,* where the young dancer Ingigerd is described as the daughter of a circus performer, which is omitted in the adaptation.

118 Cf. Silvia Bovenschen, *Die imaginierte Weiblichkeit* (Franfurt/M.: Suhrkamp, 1979), 43–59; Elisabeth Bronfen, *Over Her Dead Body: Death, Feminity and the Aesthetic* (London: Routledge, 1992).
119 Critical reflections on the First World War on both sides of the Atlantic by way of adaptations of German-language literature include *Faust* (US, 1917) by the Expressionist artist and director William Wauer in a mini-series that foregrounds the ruinous, catastrophic effect of man's hubris and, generally, any kind of pact with the devil, or Robert Heymann's aforementioned three films based on Wilhelm Hauff's *Die Memoiren des Satans* (1917).
120 Most of the original *Der Golem* and probably all of its 1917 sequel *Der Golem und die Tänzerin* [The Golem and the Dancing Girl] (DE, P. Wegener/Rochus Gliese) appear to be lost and therefore links to Meyrinck's supposed source text cannot be examined. Only the last part of Wegener's *Golem* trilogy survives (*Der Golem, wie er in die Welt kam*, 1920); for further information, see chapter 3.
121 Two years into the war, books and films began to capture the woman's perspective. Thea von Harbou, for example, published *Die deutsche Frau im Weltkrieg. Einblicke und Ausblicke* (Leipzig: Hesse & Becker, 1916).
122 Anon. "Problematische Naturen," *Kinematographische Rundschau* 358 (1915): 54.
123 For further information on Oskar Messter, see Martin Koerber, "Oskar Messter, Film Pioneer," in *A Second Life: German Cinema's First Decades*, ed. Thomas Elsaesser and Michael Wedel, 51–61.
124 Comparable only to Deutsche Bioscop, Vitascope and Union.
125 Messter's wartime adaptations include *Die Kunst zu heiraten* [The Art of Marrying] based on Max Kretzer's comedy and *Der Mann mit den sieben Masken* [The Man with Seven Masks], based on Erich Wulffen's novel, both directed by Viggo Larsen; *Die Sieger* [The Victors], based on Felix Philippi's novel, who also wrote the screenplay; and *Der Rubin-Salamander* [The Red Salamander], based on Paul Lindau's novel *Die Brüder* [The Brothers], both directed by Rudolf Biebrach.
126 Hans-Michael Bock, "Biografie," in *Richard Oswald. Regisseur und Produzent*, ed. Helga Belach and Wolfgang Jacobsen (Munich: text+kritik, 1990), 119–35, here p. 122.
127 Hans-Michael Bock, "Filmografie," in *Richard Oswald. Regisseur und Produzent*, 137–80, here p. 138.
128 Anon., "Hoffmanns Erzählungen," *Lichtbild-Bühne* 8 (February 26, 1916); https://www.filmportal.de/node/33909/material/723651.
129 *Der Kinematograph* 479 (March 1, 1916); https://www.filmportal.de/node/33909/material/723653.
130 Cf. Matthias Luserke-Jaqui, ed., *Schiller-Handbuch* (Stuttgart: Metzler, 2001), 312. Peter-André Alt, "Der Geisterseher," in *Schiller. Leben—Werk—Zeit*, vol. 1 (Munich: Beck, 2009), 572f.
131 The full story can be accessed online via the project Gutenberg.de at https://gutenberg.spiegel.de/buch/die-geschichte-vom-verlornen-spiegelbilde-3086/1; currently over 8,000 works by more than 1,700 German-language authors can be accessed for free via this brilliant online resource.

132 Quoted in Michael Hanisch's essay. Translation and emphasis are mine.
133 In contrast to Krauß, the rest of the ensemble seems rather reserved. Cf. Michael Hanisch's essay on *Hoffmanns Erzählungen* in Oswald cinegraph book; cf. Michael Hanisch, "Hoffmanns Erzählungen," in *Richard Oswald. Regisseur und Produzent*, 83–6, here p. 83. Hanisch detects the same desire to shine center stage in the Nazi propaganda film *Jud Süß* (1940), in which Krauß plays five different characters reinforcing antisemitic stereotypes. For more information, cf. Chapter 6.
134 Mentioned by Hanisch, "Hoffmanns Erzählungen," 84.
135 Ibid., 85.
136 Preceeding Eugen Schüfftan's innovative use of mirrors in Lang's *Metropolis* now known as the "Schüfftan process."
137 Cf. Hanisch, "Hoffmanns Erzählungen," 85.
138 "Filmbranche und Propaganda 1914–1918," *Filmportal Themen*, Deutsches Filminstitut, Frankfurt/M.; https://www.filmportal.de/thema/filmbranche-und-propaganda-1914-1918.
139 Cf. Klaus Kreimeier, "Aufklärung, Kommerzialismus und Demokratie. Oder: Der Bankrott des deutschen Mannes," in *Richard Oswald. Regisseur und Produzent*, 9f.
140 Margarete Böhme, *Dida Ibsens Geschichte. Ein Finale zum Tagebuch einer Verlorenen* (Berlin: Verlag Es werde Licht, ^{6}1921), 71.
141 Iwan Bloch had earned a name for himself as a controversial educator through various essays, such as *Der Ursprung der Syphilis* (The Cause of Syphilis, 1901), *Das Sexualleben unserer Zeit* (Sexual Life in Our Time, 1907) as well as *Die Prostitution* (1912), and had planned to write *Handbuch der gesamten Sexualwissenschaft in Einzeldarstellungen*, a multi-volume handbook on the sexual sciences.
142 Theodor Storm lived in the northern German town of Husum. Böhme was eleven when the famous writer died.
143 Katharina Gerstenberger, *Truth to Tell: German Women's Autobiographies and Turn-of-the-Century Culture* (Ann Arbor: University of Michigan Press, 2000), quoted by Thomas Gladysz in his introduction to *The Diary of a Lost Girl* by Margarete Böhme, translated (anonymously) by Ethel Colburn Mayne (London: Sisley, 1907; Rainier, OR: Pandora's Box, 2010), ix.
144 Michel Foucault, *Histoire de la sexualité. La volonté de savoir* (Paris: Gallimard, 1976); *The History of Sexuality*, vol. 1 (New York: Vintage, 1990), 3f.
145 Oswald made reference to the subtitle of Böhme's novel: *Tagebuch einer Verlorenen. Von einer Toten* [Diary of a Lost Woman/Girl. By someone deceased]; Böhme claimed the novel was merely the edited version of a real diary by a prostitute, who left her account to Böhme when she died.
146 Anita Berber was raised by her grandmother in Dresden, at the time a hotbed of avant-garde art and social-reform movements. She attended Émile Jacques-Dalcroze's first school in Germany for Eurhythmics, a method of experiencing space, time, one's own body in movement and learning music through movement. Dalcroze's eurhythmics was intended to address the rupture of modern life and human nature, and repair the separation of emotion and intellect. Three of the most significant pioneers of modern dance, Grete

Wiesenthal and Marie Wiegmann (Mary Wigman) and Anita Berber, were among the first pupils in the school. Cf. Lothar Fischer, *Anita Berber: Ein getanztes Leben* (Berlin: Bäßler, 2014), 18f.

147 Loni Nest was the daughter of actress Anni Nest and is especially remembered for playing the little girl who stops Paul Wegener's *Golem* (1920). She is also in F. W. Murnau's *Nosferatu* (1921) and with Asta Nielsen and the young Greta Garbo in Pabst's *Die freudlose Gasse / Joyless Street* (1925).

148 Gilles Deleuze, *Cinema 1: L'Image-Mouvement* (Paris: Minuit, 1983). Cf. *Cinema 1. The Movement Image* (London: Routledge, 2005), 89ff.

149 Cf. Cesare Lombroso/Gugliemo Ferrero, "Die geborene Prostituirte," in *Gebuchte Lust. Texte zur Prostitution*, ed. Dietmar Schmidt (Leipzig: Reclam, 1996), 58.

150 According to *Der Kinematograph* (October 16, 1918), the film premiered in October 1918 in Düsseldorf. Cf. Bock, "Filmografie," in *Richard Oswald. Regisseur und Produzent*, 150.

151 Christof Decker, *Hollywoods kritischer Blick: Das soziale Melodrama in der amerikanischen Kultur 1840–1950* (Frankfurt: Campus, 2003), 11; see also: Peter Brooks, *The Melodramatic Imagination. Balzac, Henry James, Melodrama, and the Mode of Excess* (New Haven: Yale University Press, 1976).

152 Decker, *Hollywoods kritischer Blick*, 11.

153 Kaes, "Silent Film," 246.

154 Ibid.

155 The term 'ethics of similarity' is inspired by the work of our Indian colleague Anil Bhatti. Cf. Anil Bhatti, "Heterogeneities and Homogeneities. On Similarities and Diversities," in *Understanding Multiculturalism and the Habsburg Central European Experience*, ed. Cohen Gary and Johannes Feichtinger (New York: Berghahn, 2014), 17–46.

156 See, for example, in 1917: William Wauer's aforementioned mini-series based on Goethe's *Faust* and Robert Heymann's three films based on Wilhelm Hauff's *Die Memoiren des Satans*.

157 Margaret Turnbull's script was directed by French-American filmmaker Émile Chautard.

158 Switzerland, which had remained neutral during the First World War, had no film industry of its own until the 1930s, hence my focus on Germany and Austria.

159 Hansen refers to Döblin in "Early Silent Cinema," 173.

3

The 'Golden Age' of Silent Cinema: Literary Adaptation, Radicalism, and Censorship (1919–29)

The basis for all future art is the cinema.
YVAN GOLL (1920)[1]

No longer willing to obey orders to engage in further battles, members of the German navy triggered the so-called November revolution, which spread across the German Empire like wildfire as the First World War drew to its chaotic close. Mutinies in the armed forces, mass demonstrations by the civil population, and workers' extensive industrial actions led to the abdication of Emperor Wilhelm II and announcements of a democratic parliamentary republic in November 1918. As German society grappled with the trauma of defeat as well as the multifaceted and devastating consequences of the war affecting people's lives, political unrest on the streets, strikes, and protests dominated the following few months. The murder of inspiring leaders such as Rosa Luxemburg and Karl Liebknecht in January 1919, and the violent containment of the socialist revolution across the country by early May caused further chaos and alienation, while the signing of the Treaty of Versailles in June indicated the defeated country's grim economic future.[2]

The declaration of the republic's constitution in Weimar in August 1919 provided only little comfort in this context, despite granting universal suffrage from the age of twenty and, in article 118, 'free expression of opinion in word, writing, print, image, or other forms, within the confines of the general law'. In short, the article reads: 'There is no censorship.'

Despite writers and filmmakers being granted the freedom of speech, the cinema was not entirely liberated: 'for film screenings diverging regulations may be issued. Legal measures are also permissible to combat literary trash and smut literature ["Schund- und Schmutzliteratur"] and to protect young people at public shows and performances.'[3]

Nonetheless, the political turmoil reigning in the crumbling German Empire and subsequently in the young republic created a short period during which films could be produced and exhibited freely. This autonomy to develop film as an art form and the medium as a mirror and accelerator of modernity is reflected in numerous movies considered masterpieces of German cinema. Representations of women in urban society are particularly prevalent during this decade. The Constitution provided a legal foundation for increasing equality for and independence of women. In the 1919 election, women voted for the first time, and 37 of 423 seats went to female candidates. Now, representatives of the bourgeois women's rights movement, founders of the Worker's Welfare Association, and other activists who had been fighting for the rights of the marginal and underprivileged did so in an official capacity in parliament. Woman's place in society was changing rapidly and traditional definitions of gender roles were being challenged by politicians, artists, writers, and filmmakers.[4]

This chapter looks at films based on German-language literature in this context and examines the function of adaptation during this decade of innovations as well as continuations of narrative practices on screen. The literary canon, avant-garde theater, serialized novels, even illustrated stories in verse or early comic books—like a first adaptation of Wilhelm Busch's *Max und Moritz* (DE, Curt Wolfram Kießlich, 1923)—provided source texts for silent film projects during this chaotic and yet, culturally, extraordinarily productive era.

Much has been written about this so-called 'golden age' of German cinema and the innovations in cinematography in some of the outstanding films of this period. As the following pages will argue, literature contributed to these advances and inspired representations of and critical engagements with modern, urban life. The way in which censorship—or the lack thereof—shaped film productions of the time is one of the preoccupations of this chapter, as controversial literary texts were now considered for adaptation. The majority of films produced in Germany after the First World War were aimed at mass entertainment and profit maximization, genres like romance and melodrama flourished. In the context of adaptation, source texts were often carefully chosen as valuable contributions to the young nation's public sphere. Whether we consider social problem films or adaptations of Germanic legends, literature clearly became an agent on cinema screens during a complex and chaotic nation building process.

The pages to follow will review film productions by some remaining independent companies but, especially, by a powerful Ufa and its growing number of subsidiaries, which continued to be backed financially by German industrialists.[5] In its 1920/1 catalogue, Ufa announced serial blockbusters by internationally renowned directors such as Ernst Lubitsch starring celebrities like Henny Porten or Ossi Oswalda. At a time of 'massive foreign competition' and suffering the 'bitter conditions of the peace treaty', the film industry must serve as 'an energetic reminder of everyone's inner strength', Ufa proclaimed. With a 200 million Reichsmark capital base the strongest film company of the immediate postwar era in Europe, Ufa here declared its 'cultural mission' in 1920 as follows: producing quality films that may contribute to 'instilling, consolidating and maintaining respect for German work.'[6] This included a marketing strategy focused on literature. Particularly adaptations of novels that proved popular with a wide readership were now being put on film.[7]

Publishers and the German Film Industry

Following war and revolution, the public's desire for entertainment during the early period of the newly formed Weimar Republic was enormous. Germans craved novelties and publishers as well as the film industry at the time noted a significant acceleration of consumption of both books and films.[8] New stories were constantly required, and film companies sought contracts with publishers in order to guarantee access to novels and short stories as soon as they had been tested by a mass readership.[9]

Known for publishing a range of popular genres, Ullstein had been offering options (for a few weeks or months) to film companies since the end of the First World War. Once options for a particular text expired, the right to adapt could be sold once again, which proved an attractive additional income source for the publisher. In order to secure access to any of Ullstein's publications, Jasmin Lange conveys, Ufa subsidiary Maxim film bought exclusive rights to the publisher's output. Their initial agreement, which expired on January 31, 1920, stipulated that at least eight weeks had to pass between the publication of the book and the premiere of the film. This detail not only indicates the book market's substitution fear in view of adaptations, but the speed at which mass entertainment was produced by the film industry at the time. In addition, the contract states that the author and title of the source text as well as Ullstein publishers had to be mentioned prominently not only in the credits but on each adaptation's marketing materials.[10]

The film industry's appetite for new narrative material was seemingly limitless and the competition for attractive literary texts was fierce. To increase its supply of popular literature, Ufa contacted newspaper editors and, for example, acquired the rights to serialized novels that appeared in the daily *Berliner Tageblatt*.[11] The collaboration between Ufa and Ullstein resulted in Uco-Productions,[12] an adaptation company, which brought silent gems like *Schloss Vogelöd* [Vogelöd Castle] (F.W. Murnau, 1921; adapted by Carl Mayer) and Karl Freund's innovative camera work in *Varieté* (E.A. Dupont, 1925; based on Felix Hollaender's *Der Eid des Stephan Huller*) to cinema. Probably the most gifted and sought-after screenwriter of his generation in Germany, Mayer also adapted Ludwig Fulda's hit comedy *Der Dummkopf* [The Blockhead] (Lupu Pick, 1921) for Pick's Rex Film Company.[13] The same year, Mayer signed a four-movie-script deal with Ufa with a brief to adapt literature to film.[14] When three of the four planned projects failed to materialize, however, Ufa ended their collaboration and sued the brilliant perfectionist successfully.[15]

Canonical and, increasingly, contemporary prose and plays were integral components of cinema at the time. Filmographies indicate that in 1920, two-thirds[16] of German film production was based on literature, from contemporary novels like, for example, Ernst Friedrich's *Das Mädchen aus der Ackerstraße* (The Girl from Ackerstreet,1919; DE, Reinhold Schünzel, 1920) to controversial Expressionist plays such as Georg Kaiser's *Von morgens bis mitternachts* (From Morning to Midnight, 1917; DE, Karl Heinz Martin, 1920).

Freedom of Expression and Adaptations in German Cinema (1919–20)

Censorship had been more or less abandoned by November 1918 with the collapse of the German Empire. An article in the cinema journal *Lichtbild-Bühne* indicates the delight by filmmakers to be rid of those 'annoying shackles', but the piece also reflects an awareness of the responsibility that comes with freedom: 'The film industry must prove its maturity in regulating itself.'[17] There was clearly an awareness of practices elsewhere, like in Hollywood, where producers and directors self-censored in order to maintain autonomy and avoid intervention by the state. This was the case in Germany, too, but for a brief period during the chaotic aftermath of the First World War, the acceleration of production and the virtual absence of censorship shaped film and adaptation projects.

While censorship boards continued to be in operation in places like Berlin during this brief period of very little and only local oversight, it seems these boards were as unsettled and disorganized as society around them. The production of silent films, now regularly more than an hour long, continued unimpeded in an ever-increasing number of film companies. The public's escapist desire after the war was at an all-time high, despite economic privation and widespread poverty, especially among the working class. A total of 615 applications for new cinemas in Berlin alone were submitted in 1919 in the midst of a severe housing crisis in the city.[18]

As indicated above, the demand for new screenplays was significant. Numerous contemporary plays and even operettas, popular with theater audiences, quickly found their way onto cinema screens. Intertitles were commonly used in silent film to convey the gist of the literary text, but as the expertise in narrating with objects and gestures in German cinema grew, many within the film and publishing industry criticized this disruption of the "Stimmung" or 'mood'—often very successfully cultivated by the visual narrative on screen and aurally by its musical accompaniment—and considered them, ideally, superfluous. Acclaimed author Gerhart Hauptmann commented at the time: 'Like a lead sinker, they burden the fleeting sequence of images.'[19] Most filmmakers thus tried to keep intertitles to a minimum.

In 1919, a year after Frank Wedekind's death, the (in)famous playwright's *König Nicolo oder So ist das Leben* (King Nicolo or That's Life, 1912) premiered in cinemas. Directed by Paul Legband and starring Wedekind's widow Tilly, the adaptation is evidence to the freedom filmmakers enjoyed now that Wilhelm II had abdicated. Ernst Stahl-Nachbaur starred as King Nicolo, a failure of a monarch, who lost his kingdom and now fears the citizens he does not know. When he discovers his talent for storytelling and acting, however, his performances enable proximity and communication with his former subjects. He begins to appreciate renarration as a gift that enables him to understand others—and himself. Accentuating the creative arts as stimulus for transformation, *König Nicolo* is about identity and adaptation, social hierarchies, and the precariousness as well as the meaning and value of life. It was a timely tale that delighted audiences.

Another story about life and cinema's ability to reflect on existential questions is treated with the humor Lubitsch thought this topic deserved. His film *Die Puppe* [The Doll][20] is loosely based on Alfred Maria Willner's *Eine lustige Geschichte aus einer Spielzeugschachtel* (A Funny Story from a Toy Box, 1899). Willner's operetta is a German version of Edmond Audran's opéra-comique *La Poupée* (The Puppet, 1896), which in turn was based on motifs by E.T.A. Hoffmann. Lubitsch's film opens with the director himself, who is setting the scene for his famous film. He unpacks a house, trees, and figures, and carefully places them on a small cardboard stage, creating 'a funny story from a toy box' indeed, as film posters at the time promised. Once the camera cuts to a close-up of the scene, the gaze of the audience is absorbed by that artificial universe, perhaps no longer aware of its 'real' surroundings (or the larger set for that matter) and, therefore, the difference between the two. Two actors now exit the house and immediately the clumsy one loses his footing and rolls down the hill only to land in a pool of water. Lubitsch caters to his audience's desire to be enchanted and provides plenty of laughs in this amusing and light-hearted film. The young man ('Lancelot' as he is ironically named in the film, played by Hermann Thimig) is obligingly dried by the sun, while releasing copious amounts of steam. The artificiality of the sets is matched by the narrative strand that focuses on an imitation: a life-like doll, which due to an accidental turn of events ends up being impersonated by the doll-makers daughter (Ossi Oswalda).

She pretends to be an automaton but falls out of that role occasionally for the great amusement of the audience. In addition to this fairytale love story with a very happy end that leaves Hoffmann's uncanny tale *Der Sandmann* (The Sandman, 1816) far behind, the film reflects on the fictional (literary) narrative on the cinema screen. It does not hide the artificiality of the world recreated on screen, but at the same time invites viewers to come close and enter this imaginary world for their distraction and a laugh. In his review entitled 'The Evil Darkroom', Martin Proskauer recounts the great success of the film that seemed to please everyone, bar a Catholic critic in Aachen, who revealed his anger at the film's satirical display of monastic life and values, criticizing the abbey scenes as 'scandalous' and filled with 'monastic hatred'. Deeply offended, he called on other Catholics to put an end to this and other disgraceful examples of this 'lowest' form of cinematic entertainment.[21]

Until the end of the First World War, censorship regulations prohibited children's access to mainstream films. Despite scenes viewed as 'scandalous' by some, *Die Puppe* was open to all ages when it was released in 1919, which contributed to the continued success of the film.[22]

Adaptation for a Better Society: Women on Screen (1919–20)

The role of women in the young republic and in growing urban centers was a recurring theme in contemporary literature and film. Now, representations of the devastating effects of repressive bourgeois principles and conservative morals on young, single women could be amplified by adaptation. Film writer, director, actor, and entrepreneur Richard Oswald made excellent use of this short-lived liberation of film, especially with his adaptations of Margarete Böhme's novels and his 'enlightenment films' discussed in the previous chapter.

In 1919, Carl Theodor Dreyer's compassionate *Praesidenten* [The President]—an adaptation of popular Austrian writer Karl Emil Franzos's

Der Präsident (1884)—raised issues such as the sexual exploitation of lower-class women and social consequences of illegitimate births. In his stunning directorial debut at Nordisk, Dreyer not only communicates the violence these girls endure, but highlights society's inhumanity and injustice as a consequence of the middle and upper classes' strict moral code. The film premiered in Denmark and was subsequently screened in Germany and Austria.

The same year, Oswald extended his aforementioned educational *There will be light!*-series with a two-part film on prostitution.[23] In collaboration with physician and sexologist Magnus Hirschfeld, Oswald addressed this highly controversial topic in his first film by way of a framing narrative focusing on a court case, and a number of episodes that illuminate in flashback the fate of 'fallen women'. The two women at the center of this narrative are Lola (played by Anita Berber) and Hedwig (Gussy Holl), daughters of an alcoholic and abusive father (Fritz Beckmann), who sold his children for sex to cater for his addiction.

After a first press screening, a number of journalists expressed their concern that the title "Prostitution" alone could provide 'enemies of cinema' with the necessary ammunition to reinstate censorship.[24] When the film was released as *Das gelbe Haus* [The Yellow House] (DE, Richard Oswald, 1919) with written assurances by the distributor that this film is not 'a wild sensationalist racket-piece' but instead a 'serious and important work in the battle [...] against regulated and unregulated prostitution',[25] it was a runaway success at the box-office. Nonetheless, the film was harshly criticized by the writer Kurt Tucholsky, who considered Oswald's work as offensive as a trashy novel. 'Since film censorship has fallen by the wayside', he wrote in the *Berliner Volkszeitung* (May 7, 1919), 'large film companies [...] stir a particular seasoning into the usual "Kinokitsch" [...] and that seasoning is sexuality.'[26] Like the novels by Böhme or Jerusalem, Oswald's films were considered a provocation, as they violated bourgeois society's "principle of secrecy"[27] with regard to all things sexual. His aforementioned *Anders als die Anderen* (1919) had hoped to overturn the prohibition on homosexual practices and caused a political scandal. His work on prostitution and the sexual exploitation of women fostered Oswald's notoriety.

Oswald hoped, however, to create "a greater awareness of the world in which we live"[28] and to contribute to civil society of the new Weimar Republic. Consequently, he visualized unspoken social practices and placed them into the spotlight of postwar Germany's mass media republic. He would have agreed with Carlo Mierendorff who stated in his *Hätte ich das Kino!* (If [Only] I Had the Cinema, 1920) that modern twentieth-century culture, even '[t]he earth would stand still if you removed the cinema', emphasizing the power of the new medium: 'Whoever controls the cinema, will leverage the world.'[29]

Oswald knew that by constructing not only informative but affective narratives, he could expand the dimensions of moral judgment by providing knowledge, inducing empathy, and, ideally, encouraging the autonomy of the new state to make legal changes to the Victorian system of regulation that at once criminalized prostitutes and ensured their availability to potential consumers in convenient environments.[30] His deconstructions of stereotypical images of marginal or so-called 'fallen' women can be interpreted as acts of resistance aiming at sociopolitical impact, but are always already commodities produced for profit. This dichotomy alone would have ensured that cinema remained a contested space during this immediate postwar era but, especially, adaptations of German-language literature time and again poured fuel into those ongoing and decidedly heated debates between representatives of the film industry and the educated middle and upper classes. The latter had only begun to accept cinema due to 'high-culture' entertainment such as star-studded adaptations of the literary canon available in newly built film palaces. Films about sexual exploitation, however, were deemed morally and politically unacceptable by the conservative bourgeoisie.

Franz Schönhuber, for instance, a teacher and school principal in Munich, published an eight-page "Denkschrift" or 'reflective pamphlet' entitled "Keine Zensur?" (No Censorship?) in April 1919, arguing for the need for strict control in the interest of raising film quality and moral standards. This, in his mind, was a task of utmost importance at a time of low self-esteem and general depression in Germany following the country's military defeat and economic collapse. Growing numbers of prostitutes and increases in sexually transmitted infections, which Schönhuber considered indisputable evidence for the alarmingly loose morals of the young republic, were in fact to a significant degree consequences of the war.[31]

Meanwhile, director Friedrich (Frederic) Zelnik, at this stage in his life still in Germany, filmed *Margarete—die Geschichte einer Gefallenen* [Margarete: A Fallen Woman's Tale] (1919) based on Marie von Ebner-Eschenbach's *Margarete*.[32] Considering the current cultural climate, this particularly well-chosen story of a single mother who loses her son and eventually herself provided Zelnik and his frequent collaborator scriptwriter/director/actor Alfred Halm with the perfect plot for a mass audience. One of the most respected female writers of the late nineteenth century, the Austrian Marie von Ebner-Eschenbach (1830–1916) had always aimed at communicating a kind of ethical humanism in her work. Zelnik was convinced that cinema could pick up the baton and thus become an important cultural constituent in this volatile postwar society.

Ebner-Eschenbach's melodramatic narrative briefly recounts the fate of a young wife, who flees domestic abuse, is cheated out of her inheritance, and ends up as a seamstress and single mother. The center of her life is her young son, who tragically dies after an accident involving a horse-drawn carriage.

Robert, one of the passengers in the stage-coach, carries the injured child (Georg) to his distraught mother (Margarete) and arranges for a doctor to look after the boy. But the physician takes a much keener interest in Margarete than in his young patient, calling her 'most beautiful' and 'heavenly'.[33] Aware of his intentions, she is even willing to give herself to him if he saves her boy,[34] but the child passes away. Robert, a kind and well-meaning nobleman, tries to support Margarete in her grief. Together with his new wife, the 'enlightened' couple offer Margarete an education as a way toward freedom and happiness. But the trauma of losing her son and also Robert, whom she loves, instead paves the way for another libidinous suitor. Margarete becomes the lover of a wealthy, shallow macho (Steinau), and Ebner-Eschenbach carefully juxtaposes her fate as a marginalized and judged sexual woman ('witch'/'devil') with an education that could open eyes and provide a degree of independence.[35] In her despair, Margarete seeks the detachment of light entertainment and lavish consumption. Steinau offers both, and presents Margarete as his prize possession at upper-class parties. Ebner-Eschenbach describes the "Schaulust der Menge," the voyeuristic pleasure experienced by the crowd watching the spectacular beauty in her expensive gown. But Margarete soon tires of this numbing life of cursory pleasures, puts on her old dress, and commits suicide next to the grave of her child.[36] In 1919 Halm and Zelnik's adaptation of this bestselling narrative became a box-office hit. The film's subliminal dialectic, however, its critical reflection of celebrity culture and the superficiality of viewing a spectacle, be it Margarete or the motion picture itself, was probably lost on the majority of the spectators. At the same time, their aim of creating a desirable (i.e., profitable) commodity is already evident when looking at the alluring subtitle added by the filmmakers—"the story of a fallen woman"—a suggestive promise to unveil hidden facts of both a marginal and scandalous existence.

Henny Porten, Stardom and the Fight for Marginal Women (1919–20)

Henny Porten became an international star after playing the lead in *Das Liebesglück der Blinden* [Blind Lover's Happiness] (DE, Heinrich Bolten-Baeckers/Curt A. Stark, 1910) alongside Fred Zelnik. It is a love story, written by her sister Rosa Porten,[37] between a blind woman and her doctor. The Oskar Messter production turned Henny Porten not only into one of Germany's greatest stars of the early twentieth century, but also into the most reliable export commodity. An outspoken women's rights activist, Porten regularly used her popularity to highlight social exploitation and female oppression. Seemingly untouched by war and political conflict, 'Henny

Porten films' sold out before and after the war, in Germany, Sweden, and the Soviet Union alike.[38] Her popularity extended to all ages and social classes, which made her, in critic Kurt Pinthus' opinion, the ideal candidate for the Reich presidency of the young Weimar Republic.[39] Comparing her to Gerhart Hauptmann, the "sixty-year-old poet of humanity," Pinthus writes, his "fame is but a breeze in the storm of the popularity that whirls around this woman."[40] His perhaps ironic hyperbole notwithstanding, Pinthus wonders in 1921: "Is it not a woman's business to govern? [...] Have nations not always blossomed at precisely those times when a woman served as their leader?"[41]

As Corinna Müller outlines, Ufa needed a star and Porten was their prime target. But Porten was not interested and under contract with Oskar Messter since 1917. But one day, she recounts, Messter ruefully told her 'I sold myself, Hennychen. And I sold you, too. There's nothing anyone can do about it.'[42] For Ufa, Porten was worth every penny. She even managed to persuade celebrated Nobel Prize-winning author Hauptmann to release the rights to *Rose Bernd*. It was the adaptation of his tragic play which became her—and Ufa's—first great success. Moreover, it communicated film as art, functioned as political weapon, and still excited the masses.[43] An international celebrity following the triumph of *Anna Boleyn* (DE, Ernst Lubitsch, 1920), Porten used her fame to shed critical light on woman's role in society. She invested into her own film production company and pushed literary texts such as *Die Geier-Wally* (DE, E.A. Dupont, 1921) based on the novel by Wilhelmine von Hillern and 'a great plea for equality and the peaceful coexistence of man and woman', as Müller argues.[44]

Hauptmann's *Rose Bernd* had premiered in Berlin and Vienna in 1903 and 1904, and its naturalistic depiction of the destruction of a young, beautiful 22-year-old woman shook theater audiences.[45] Pregnant and unmarried, Rose suffers extortion, sexual abuse and rape, slander and public humiliation. The play highlights male power and different facets of the patriarchal system that pushes a vulnerable young woman to the margins and into despair. Her employer gets her pregnant, her father wants her to marry pious and pasty Keil, Streckmann blackmails and abuses her, publicly denouncing her a whore. Giving birth to her child all alone in the woods, she succumbs to madness. The play ends with her admitting to having killed her newborn child.

Like *Margarete* based on a screenplay by Alfred Halm, the transposition of the tragic tale to screen functioned both as a vehicle for social criticism and as a profitable commodity offering to satisfy its viewers' voyeuristic desire. However, as in Oswald's and Zelnik's adaptations of Böhme and Ebner-Eschenbach before, Rose (Henny Porten) is depicted as a victim. Rather than focusing only on her youth and beauty, or the fact that she is expecting a child out of wedlock, the film emphasizes her kindness and compassion. This is highlighted further by the juxtaposition of good Rose with evil Arthur Streckmann (Emil Jannings), a devious character, who is driven by selfish jealousy and violent lust, and who takes full advantage of society's failure to protect 'women like her'. In Weimar cinema, the abused woman repeatedly served as signifier of man's—and society's—inhumanity.[46]

Halm's project indicates a conscious construction of both a successful product that could also leave its mark on civil society and induce change for the better. Not surprisingly, marketing of the adaptation focused on literary celebrity Gerhart Hauptmann, but ads highlighted in even bigger letters the 'stars' to be seen in this "Monumentalfilm": Henny Porten, Werner Krauß, Paul Bildt, and Emil Jannings. During a time of crisis, a movie ticket now also provided access to dreamy actors and a revered celebrity culture. Advertising strategies indicate the industry's move toward a star system and reflect its confidence in the value of screen entertainment for viewers who were increasingly derived from across the social spectrum. The willingness of the growing movie industry to make significant investments into high-caliber film projects led to the employment of numerous composers and artists, such as Guiseppe Becce, who composed an original score for *Margarete,* and the artist and writer Hans Baluschek who designed the set.

All too often, however, critics' responses still remained particularly unforgiving when the cultural divide between cinema and the 'high arts' was challenged by adaptation projects. Theater and film critic Herbert Ihering, for example, slammed Hauptmann for collaborating with the silent movie

FIGURE 3.1 *Henny Porten and Emil Jannings in* Rose Bernd *(DE, Alfred Halm, 1919).*

industry in his *Rose Bernd* review published in *Berliner Börsen-Courier* (October 21, 1919), and mocked the filmmakers who feel 'idealistic and artistic' when they 'throw the playwright's text amongst their images'. His criticism of film as a playground for utopian ideals and escapist practices while modernity demanded rational thought and action was echoed by numerous writers and journalists at the time, but was never voiced more passionately than in the context of adaptations of the literary canon for cinema.

Kurt Tucholsky (writing as Ignaz Wrobel, one of his *noms de plume*) accused filmmakers of being utilitarian profiteers who turned literary texts into shallow trivia that contained not even the slightest trace of the 'soul of the novel'.[47] His bone of contention this time was, in particular, a 'magnificent film in six acts' entitled *Prinz Kuckuck!* [Prince Cuckoo] (DE, Paul Leni, 1919) based on a text by Otto Julius Bierbaum.[48]

Literary Scandals, Adaptation, and Postwar Society

Barely remembered today, Bierbaum left his mark on literary history mainly as a journalist and editor-in-chief of *Neue Deutsche Rundschau, Pan*, or *Die Insel*. His successful three-volume novel *Prinz Kuckuck. Leben, Taten, Meinungen und Höllenfahrt eines Wollüstlings* (Life, Deeds, Opinions, and Descent into Hell of a Voluptuary, 1906–8) caused significant uproar upon its publication.

Suspected to be a roman à clef about Alfred Walter Heymel, the 'scandalous' novel tells the story of Henry Felix, adopted son of eccentric millionaire Kraker, who happily indulges in an unconstrained life of luxury and entertainment. When he inherits his adoptive father's fortune, Kraker's niece Berta and nephew Carl feel cheated out of their inheritance and go to great lengths to get their money, and Henry—the 'cuckoo'—out of their nest.[49] The novel (or at least its first half) was turned into a screenplay by Georg Kaiser for Gloria Film in Berlin. Hanns Lippmann produced and Paul Leni directed the movie with Carl Hoffmann at the camera and Friedrich Hollaender providing the musical score. Conrad Veidt, elegant as ever, starred as the millionaire's nephew Carl, who offers himself as constant companion to Kraker's adopted son (Niels Prien), aiming, of course, only to lead him astray and, by seducing him into all sorts of debauchery, eventually to destroy this competitor. In the end, the greedy nephew gets his comeuppance as his murder ploy results in his own death and Henry Felix continues to enjoy his carefree existence, which must have been the stuff of dreams for audiences in a time of economic hardship.

Cinema was, indeed, a place of 'refuge' for the working class especially, in a 'dark attempt to survive', where moving images and distracting narratives provided an essential 'substitute for dreams' as Hugo von Hofmannsthal famously wrote in 1921.⁵⁰ A public notice by the Hamburg-based distributor Hammonia-Film-Verleih refuting the claim that the film's 'deeply erotic images' could cause offence celebrated the 'literary Prince Cuckoo' as 'the lifework by one of our most prominent authors' and the film *Prinz Kuckuck* as 'the artwork of one of our most celebrated directors'.⁵¹

The film journal *Lichtbild-Bühne* had reported early on about the 'Venice' set built in Babelsberg outside Berlin for the *Prinz Kuckuck*-adaptation as it was impossible to take all the actors and film crew down to Italy in this time of *Ersatz* [substitution] and economic restraint.⁵² In *Der Kinematograph* the film was hailed as 'the greatest accomplishment!' especially in the context of 'the literary film'. Under the direction of 'painter-director' Paul Leni, the "Nachdichter" or adapter, and the "Neuschöpfer" or creator join forces ('hands') and achieve entirely 'new perspectives!'—

> Now we have it: It is not the slavish rendering of the narrative content that can conjure up psychological subtleties of the literary work on the screen; rather film technology and the image, i.e. the purely pictorial, is the main thing and together they facilitate the enjoyment of the psychological in cinema. [...] For the German industry, this film is a golden page in the book of its history.⁵³

The reviewer expected that 'foreign countries' would long to receive copies of the film and learn from its innovation and success, and he concludes emphatically (if rather hyperbolically): 'It is a work that stands out and apart from everything that cinematography created so far. Not only German cinematography, but cinematography as a whole.'⁵⁴ As the film seems to be lost, it has been impossible to estimate its impact. However, at the time, the enthusiasm for this film production was palpable. A planned sequel, an adaptation of the second part of the novel, however, was never realized.⁵⁵

On an international sphere, adaptations of German or Austrian literature—or cultural products of the Central Powers—so soon after the end of the First World War were very rare. Dreyer's *Praesidenten* in Denmark and another adaptation of Sudermann's *Heimat* produced by Cines-Film in Italy, also in 1919,⁵⁶ were exceptions. Filmmakers in Germany and Austria also looked mainly at their national literatures for source texts that could provide both entertainment and financial stability during these precarious times. Inspired by previous box-office successes and the lull in censorship, filmmakers like Friedrich Zelnik, Alfred Halm, Richard Oswald, Paul Leni, or Leopold Jessner repeatedly focused on topics likely to generate interest across gender and class divides, such as marginal women, social hierarchies, and patterns of exclusion.⁵⁷

Previous literary scandals also provided additional publicity, and in several instances, the prominence of an author's name was exploited by film companies, such as Luna-Film, for marketing purposes. Promo-Film's *Frühlings Erwachen* (Spring Awakening, 1923), for example, prompted an angry exchange of open letters published in *Süddeutsche Zeitung* between the producers and Tilly Wedekind, who considered their adaptation 'disrespectful' to her late husband's work.[58] Tilly Wedekind's dissatisfaction with this first 'adaptation' of Wedekind's "Kindertragödie" or 'Children's Tragedy' (1891) by the Austrian couple Luise and Jakob Fleck, who co-produced and directed the film (the screenplay was written by Jakob Fleck and Adolf Lantz), was triggered by the use of her husband's name for a film that had nothing in common with his tragic story while still availing of the names of the main characters. Even the Viennese *Film-Rundschau* reviewer considered this practice 'not nice'.[59] But, as Tilly Wedekind was informed by the anonymous Promo-Film A.G. representatives in their reply, once the film rights are sold, the author has no more jurisdiction regarding the use of their work, and is neither invited to provide instructions to the filmmakers nor in a position to demand redress if the outcome fails to meet their expectations. The latter, as the producers did not refrain from emphasizing, could not be established anyhow due to the author's death.

German Literature on Film and the Impact of Censorship Legislation

As German silent cinema of the 1920s grew into one of the most productive industries, keen on rivaling Hollywood, period films, but also transpositions of literary texts were abundant. Numerous film projects aimed at contributing to this experiment in democracy and civil society by depicting social deprivation, sexual exploitation, and marginalization, others focused on high-culture on screen in an effort to reawaken the nation's sense of identity and to cater to middle-class audience's desire "to combine entertainment with education."[60] They filmed classical literature and literary themes on the one hand—from numerous Schiller, Goethe, Kleist, or Büchner-adaptations and, of course, the *Nibelungen*-saga, reviving and reflecting on core elements of an imagined German identity—to more popular works by von Hillern, Sudermann, Schnitzler, or Hauptmann to name but a few.[61] The aesthetic backdrops of those enormously popular films discussed above not only generated socio-political reflections and impassioned 'cinema' debates, however, but also triggered national censorship legislation which standardized film censorship rules on May 12, 1920, for the entire Weimar Republic. A film's potential to 'cause offence', 'jeopardize public order or safety', to have a 'demoralizing effect' or even 'over-stimulate' younger audiences now automatically led to a ban. Non-compliance carried severe penalties.[62] This German "Lichtspielgesetz" [cinema law] impacted significantly on the way literary texts were chosen and adapted by the motion picture industry and caused programmatic re-coding in numerous adaptation projects.

Following film censorship legislation in the United States and Britain—which directly affected the international marketability of German films—the Weimar Republic's new censorship laws put an end to adaptations of German literary texts and other film projects that could be viewed as radical interventions, such as Oswald's *Dida Ibsen* discussed in the previous chapter. No doubt, the national legislation was aimed at protecting younger and more vulnerable audiences and upholding morale, but implicitly shaped the public's perception of contentious social issues highlighted first in literature. Of course, this was nothing new. From its beginning, film production and consumption were affected to some degree by regional or national censorship laws. Films were edited to suit potential censors, fragmented or prohibited by ill-disposed boards, or screened only where existing laws provided loopholes or where censors allowed for a more liberal approach.

After 1920, however, films that made any reference to sexuality were automatically rated 21, and still underwent severe cuts before securing a permit, which is clearly documented in censorship reports on the hearings of the Film Review Office regarding, for example, G.W. Pabst's *Freudlose Gasse* [Joyless Street], a film adaptation of Hugo Bettauer's socio-critical and extremely successful, serialized novel published in 1924.[63] Depictions of prostitution—for money or, as in the 1925 adaptation of the novel, also for meat—and references to sexual passion or scenes depicting the daily routine of a brothel usually led to an immediate ban. This was normally followed by appeals, a lengthy lawsuit, and, eventually, a court order to radically edit and cut all potentially offending sequences.

Film projects that critically explored the existing philistine morality or highlighted sexual exploitation did so at significant financial risk, and during the precarious postwar years, this had far-reaching consequences for the film industry as a whole. Censorship boards of the Weimar Republic were primarily to blame for the fact that a prostitute or sexually active, independent woman could now only be portrayed on cinema screens under certain narrative conditions. Films that successfully circumvented an unfavorable bearing of the censors indicate the following prerequisites: the woman's dream of climbing the social ladder was clearly and unambiguously shattered; the woman was killed or committed suicide; and/or the film reinforced the cliché of the *femme fatale* and could, therefore, function as a warning to audiences with regard to the threatening power and destructive impact of female sexuality, which for example the German neurologist Paul Möbius had been promulgating with significant success since the turn of the century.[64]

Films or scenes that could potentially offend were eliminated from public discourse. An adaptation of Georg Kaiser's expressionist play *Von morgens bis mitternachts* (From Morning to Midnight, 1912) by Karlheinz Martin in 1920 was only cleared for 'private screenings' at first and then struggled to find a distributor. The film was deemed lost until a version produced for the international market was discovered at Japan's National Film Center in Tokyo, where the film had had quite a successful run in the early 1920s.[65] Martin, who had been instrumental in bringing Expressionist plays to the stage—such as *Bürger Schippel* (Citizen Schippel, 1913) by Carl Sternheim in Frankfurt in 1915 or the 'sensational premiere' (as Erwin Piscator[66] put it) of Ernst Toller's *Die Wandlung* (Transformation, 1917/18) at the newly established *Tribüne* in Berlin in 1919—directed Kaiser's "Stationendrama" first on stage and subsequently as an Expressionist *Gesamtkunstwerk* for the cinema screen.[67] The set is similarly Expressionist in style as *Das Cabinet des Dr. Caligari* (1920), but focused more directly on dehumanizing norms and practices and an annihilation of humanity in modern, capitalist society. Even more radical in form and content than *Caligari*, Martin's Kaiser-adaptation provokes with a hitherto unseen level of abstraction in narrative cinema.

FIGURE 3.2 *Ernst Deutsch as bank teller in* Von morgens bis mitternachts *(DE, Karlheinz Martin, 1920)*.

Designed by Robert Neppach, white lines are carved into stylized and distorted sets and costumes alike. Black walls rhythmically obstruct views, and actors' anti-naturalist performances emphasize the main character's description in the play as a 'miraculous human being' whose 'mechanism' is fashioned on silent hinges: the automated human of modern capitalism.[68] Kaiser's play focuses on twenty-four hours in the life of a bank clerk or cashier ("Kassierer") who—longing for release and fulfillment—steals a large sum of money, initially to help a stunning Italian lady that had come into the bank to withdraw cash. After realizing that his plan of eloping with the alluring hottie was just a crazy dream, and no longer able to 'balance [life's] value and countervalue', he becomes 'unhinged'. When he returns home to his family, he challenges their superficiality and the banality of everyday routines, shocking his wife and daughters and, due to his deplorable intent to leave without first eating his lunch, causing the death of his mother. He flees to the city, where he visits the sports palace and a cycling race, a dance hall (where even the masked dancer's leg proves a prosthetic illusion) and, finally, a salvation army café, where the seemingly sympathetic and caring salvation army girl selfishly rats him out to the police for financial reward. The place of the narrative is 'the big city B.'—most likely Berlin—and, as the bank clerk says dispassionately already during the cycling race: 'Victims are inevitable where others live feverishly.'[69]

It is a depiction of alienation due to modernity's rule over time and space, of human beings mechanized by their own obsession with traditional everyday practices, the superficiality of conforming, keeping face, façades (and up with the Joneses), but also, and perhaps even more importantly, the greed and duplicity of them all, including those supposedly working tirelessly and selflessly to help only others. Nietzsche's call for self-realization is crushed by the soulless confinements of capitalist, bourgeois society. The sharp contrasts of light and dark dominate the Expressionist mise-en-scène, a clock is ticking in every scene, and time is running out, the stunning film warns its viewers. As a work of art that attempts to fold the Expressionist aesthetic and ethics into the movement's socio-political critique, this film was ahead of its time and sadly disappeared from screens before it could even leave its mark.

Filmmakers in the 1920s had no choice but to abide by the new censorship regulations and, rather than highlighting the plight of prostitutes or the insanity of society's false morality, now adapted popular *Heimat-* and adventure novels—such as Gorch Fock's *Seefahrt ist not!* (Seafaring is a necessity, 1913) in 1921 under the direction of Rudolf Biebrach. Gloomy thrillers also gained in popularity, like F. W. Murnau's psychodrama *Schloß Vogelöd* (1921) based on Rudolf Stratz's recent text and, of course, there were countless films based on bestselling dime novels: one with impact was Ernst Friedrich a.k.a. Hermann Fleischack's *Das Mädchen aus der Ackerstraße* (The Girl from Acker Street), a Pigmaleon-type story ending badly, starring

Rosa Valetti, Otto Gebühr, and Lilly Flohr (DE, Reinhold Schünzel, 1920).[70] Producing 'high culture' for cinema remained one of the aims of the film industry, however, especially of massive production companies like Ufa.

'High Culture' Adaptations of German-language Literature

By the early 1920s cinema was well established and a favorite pastime especially in urban centers. But even though the stories being discussed in public spaces were all too often cinematic narratives, a substantial part of conservative bourgeois households still considered film a lesser art and an ever-growing danger to German culture. Film producers were looking to neutralize publications like Willy Finger's "Kampfschrift" or 'combative pamphlet' *Deutschkunde und Kinodrama* (German Studies and Drama at the Cinema, 1921) by promoting adaptations of highly respected literary achievements, such as Schiller's epic poem *Die Glocke* [The Bell] (DE, Franz Hofer, 1921) or his drama *Die Verschwörung des Fiesco zu Genua* filmed as *Die Verschwörung zu Genua* [The Conspiracy in Genoa] (Paul Leni, 1921), Kleist's ground-breaking novella *Die Marquise von O.* (Paul Legband, 1920), Büchner's *Dantons Tod* [Danton's Death] (Dimitri Buchowetzki, 1920), or canonical stories of seduction such as *Der verlorene Schatten* [The Lost Shadow] (DE, Rochus Gliese, 1921; with Paul Wegener based on Adelbert von Chamisso's *Peter Schlemihl*) and Nestroy's *Lumpaci Vagabundus* (Carl Wilhelm, 1922), starring a young and vivacious Hans Albers.[71]

Social critique was to be avoided due to the offense it could cause, but nonetheless appeared regularly, either obliquely or subtly woven into the fabric of the script, such as in Manfred Noa's adaptation of Lessing's play *Nathan der Weise* (Nathan the Wise, 1779). Hans Kyser wrote the screenplay for the historical film that emphasizes the need for religious tolerance and starred celebrity actor Werner Krauß as wise Nathan. The Bavaria production could be viewed as a genre film based on one of the most important and widely respected literary texts in the German language that communicated core values of humanism and enlightenment. But the project was also cinema's response to the murder of Minister of Foreign Affairs Walther Rathenau on June 24, 1922, who was killed by members of the antisemitic, nationalistic 'Organisation Consul', a terrorist network that was later integrated into Nazi Germany's infamous paramilitary organizations.[72] When the film finally premiered in Munich in December, it caused violent protests. It had been denied clearance for public screening in the first instance, as its 'philo-Semitic nature' was considered detrimental to keeping the peace. When the film was granted approval following an

FIGURE 3.3 *Hans Albers as the amusing 'evil spirit' in* Der böse Geist Lumpaci Vagabundus *(DE, Carl Wilhelm, 1922).*

appeal, far-right extremists unsuccessfully tried to destroy the negatives and continued their protests once the film was screened in cinemas.[73]

A first adaptation of Thomas Mann's novel *Buddenbrooks* (1901) is perhaps the most interesting example of this strategy of weaving social criticism into a film narrative based on a canonical literary work. One of the most widely read works in Germany at the time, *Buddenbrooks* chronicles the gradual decline of a prosperous Hanseatic family over four generations. The only adaptation of the novel during the silent film era, produced by Albert Pommer for Dea-Film, premiered on August 31, 1923, in Ufa's Tauentzienpalast in Berlin.[74] Based on 'motifs' of the novel, the film was 'transposed into modern form for the film' as the title plate reads, preparing the audience for more than just cuts to the literary narrative—spanning generations in over several hundred pages—in the barely ninety-minute silent picture to come. It also indicates the production team's intention to offer a 'quality film'[75] and an independent product that made innovative use of film technology and design in order to express Mann's story through visual means.

Luise Heilborn-Körbitz wrote the screenplay in collaboration with Alfred Fekete. Heilborn-Körbitz was an experienced scriptwriter and had worked with director Gerhard Lamprecht on a number of projects in the early 1920s, namely *Erfolg verblüffend* [Astonishing Success], *Der Friedhof der Lebenden* [Cemetery of the Living], and *Das Haus ohne Lachen* [The House without Laughter]. Making a number of cuts and changes[76] to the screenplay, Lamprecht focused the film on one of the family's most prominent members Thomas Buddenbrook as *homo oeconomicus*, who misguidedly tries to secure the future of the family business through financially lucrative weddings. Lamprecht also foregrounded Lübeck as a commercial city, and the industrialization of the shipping business dominates the opening sequence of the film accordingly. Rather than suggesting a dehumanizing integration of the workforce into production processes as depicted in Fritz Lang's *Metropolis* (1927), Lamprecht documented economic processes in an aesthetic that anticipates the cinematic avant-garde of Walter Ruttmann, Dziga Vertov, or Sergei Eisenstein.

Lamprecht aimed for authenticity, or "Natürlichkeit" ('naturalness') as he put it,[77] and at the same time for innovative cinematic form. Inspired especially by Swedish directors such as Mauritz Stiller or Victor Sjöström, he uses montage to reflect meaning; centering his critique on money, or capital, as power and all-determining factor. Mann, a highly cultured bourgeois, both despised and loved the new medium, as he explained on several occasions.[78] His attitude to the *Buddenbrooks* project was equally ambivalent. Nonetheless, Mann traveled to Berlin in January 1923 to meet with Lamprecht and Heilborn-Körbitz, to be read the screenplay. While he seemed to have enjoyed the presentation greatly, as Lamprecht and Heilborn-Körbitz both recount, he refused[79] to support the team's plan for a costume drama. As inflation was reaching its climax in this postwar era, social and economic difficulties were rife. A more elaborate budget might have reduced the chances of the film project coming to fruition or, perhaps, 'costume' just seemed unnecessary for the story the filmmakers intended to tell.

The movie is structured in six acts and was filmed in Lübeck and in Ufa's new Tempelhof studios in Berlin. The opening sequence introduces Lübeck as a picturesque place of commerce, with a merchant vessel being pulled into the port by a tugboat from the end point of the Elbe-Trave canal—moving images that corresponded to depictions of the Hanseatic city port in engravings and photographs from around 1900—that delighted critics at the time. At first static, the movie camera serves as a reminder of the past, at least for a moment, before the viewer's gaze is guided responsively to the activities in the port itself, reflecting both technological and aesthetic progress. Mobility, also of work processes, determines the initial sequences of this film, and refers to people, goods, and capital. Lamprecht's depiction of the mechanization and industrialization of everyday life, even in this small, picturesque town, had a visible impact on documentaries such as Ruttmann's *Berlin, Sinfonie der Großstadt* (1927).

A long shot of the huge granary in the process of being filled by invisible hands through four enormous pipes reflects the mechanization of labor, as well as the accumulated wealth and business as foundations of the city. But soon enough these abstract processes become personal: sellers offer potential buyers samples of the grain that they rub and sniff in their hands, accountants bend over their bills and papers in the office, and finally we see Thomas Buddenbrook (Peter Esser) absorbed in his work in his stately private office. His right-hand man Marcus (Karl Platen) informs him (and the audience by intertitle) that Lübeck's Senate should be deciding on the 'major grain deal for the city' about now. This contract, which promises great profit but also poses enormous economic risk for the Buddenbrook family, is the narrative core of the film's plot that motivates each of the six acts in different ways.

Tony Buddenbrook (Hildegard Imhoff) is not the eight-year-old girl of the beginning of the novel, but already a young though as yet unmarried woman. Her best friend Gerda Arnoldsen (Mady Christians) and her father (Franz Egénieff) live next to the Buddenbrook residence, not in Amsterdam. This geographical focus on Lübeck had practical and financial reasons; the modification of Gerda's rapt, exotic beauty to average German looks, the elimination of a kiss between Gerda and her musical partner Renée Throta (Kurt Vespermann) marked in the screenplay, or the cutback on Thomas' unruly brother Christian's (Alfred Abel) nightlife, were pragmatic decisions in view of censorship regulations, but also enabled Lamprecht to focus his narrative more clearly on business considerations and the cycle of economic exchange.

Despite the Buddenbrook company's standing and Thomas' delight in having been awarded the contract, he has to approach his grandparents for a loan to secure the deal. But Consul Kröger's (Rudolf del Zopp) advice is simple: marry! Thus it is not the Thomas of the novel, enthusiastically in love with Gerda, who vows 'This or none, now or never!'[80] but a pragmatic merchant, driven by personal ambition and business interest, who proposes to the daughter of the rich owner of a shipping business. When she politely asks Thomas for patience, but confesses to her father: 'I cannot!', she is told that 'daughters of business men cannot always vote with their heart' as the intertitle clarifies, thereby doubling Tony's reaction to Grünlich's request in the novel.[81] This first act of the film thus swiftly concludes with a 'wedding between the houses Buddenbrook and Arnoldsen', as the intertitle announces, but there is no ceremony. Instead, the audience witnesses a far more significant exchange that instantly unveils the symbolic core of the wedding taking place. According to the script we see '[scene 33] a large safe.—Arnoldsen (in tails) approaches. He takes a stately bundle of banknotes from it and leaves [...]. [scene 34] Another safe. Thomas Buddenbrook approaches, also in a tailcoat. He holds the same bundle of banknotes in his hands. He slowly puts it into the safe, closes the door, and locks it tightly.'[82]

Lamprecht highlights this exchange of cash instead of a marriage vow by doubling the action: both carefully enter the combination on their respective safes, open the door without haste, remove (Arnoldsen)/deposit (Thomas) a cash box, and close the safe upon completion. Lamprecht slowed down the action significantly at this point to emphasize the focus of his adaptation and to mark money as capitalist society's highest good. Young women or daughters, consequently, are depicted as mere commodities.

Accordingly, Tony is to marry seemingly well-heeled Grünlich and despite initial protests, she finally gives in after Gerda, in another doubling, reminds Tony that 'as daughters of merchants we cannot always choose with our hearts'. Just like an economic transaction that replaces a wedding celebration—which throughout film history would often represent the climax of a film narrative—the melodrama of this scene indicated in the

FIGURE 3.4 *The 'wedding scene' in* Buddenbrooks *(DE, Gerhart Lamprecht, 1923).*

screenplay is eliminated in the interest of establishing critical distance and a narrative that calls into question capitalism. Anticipating not only *Neue Sachlichkeit* or New Objectivity on screen, but a form of 'epic' cinema that Brecht was only beginning to develop for the theater in Munich and, from 1924, in Berlin, Lamprecht stages the scene in an emphatically factual manner and, instead of passionate resentment, foregrounds the resignation of these two young women as domesticated (and valuable) objects. His use of narrative and visual doubling (Tony is soon likened to a piece of jewelry by her new husband), a distinct reduction of melodrama, and, instead, a documentation of focused action creates critical distance and, thereby, emphasizes the inhumanity of these marriage practices aimed at increasing capital. Even the birth of Hanno, which is a deeply emotional event for his father Thomas and a delight for the entire family in the novel, is thus subordinated to the economic primacy of the company in the film.

The final act of Lamprecht's *Buddenbrooks* adaptation focuses on Thomas' recognition of guilt, atonement, and rescue. Instead of the family's ultimate deterioration after Hanno's death, the film concludes with a happy ending, but not until providing remarkable excitement in the movie's most dramatic scene: Thomas, driven by existential angst and jealousy, puts an end to his wife's musical evenings with Throta. In consequence, Gerda leaves and his father-in-law denies Thomas financial aid because he has 'not made Gerda happy'. When Thomas realizes Gerda's absence, he races to Throta's house. In an extremely dynamic film sequence that includes close-up shots of the galloping horse's legs—perhaps in homage to Edward Muybridge's innovative photographs (1872/81)—Lamprecht anticipated the turmoil of marching boots in Eisenstein's *Battleship Potemkin* (orig. Броненосец Потёмкин/*Bronenosets Potyomkin*), 1925, as Zander suggests.[83] By intercutting almost completely static shots that show Gerda and her father sitting at the table waiting for Thomas, Lamprecht greatly emphasized the dynamic of the scene above, as well as editing and montage as essential dramatic devices in filmmaking. As one of the critics notes, audiences in 1923 regularly applauded this stunning sequence with great enthusiasm.[84]

When he cannot find Gerda in Throta's house and bedroom, Thomas finally realizes his aberration and is deeply embarrassed. But the musician, who is the civilizing artist depicted as a positive and creative counter-image to Thomas' *homo oeconomicus*, cordially and forgivingly shakes his hand. When admitting his culpability to his wife later that evening—'I am guilty ... I married Tony to an imposter ... I kicked Christian out of house and company ... I didn't make you happy ... Now everything around me has collapsed'—Thomas' *contritio cordis* provides the desired release. Touched by his despair, Gerda reaches out and (tenderly, submissively, and to the relief of the censors with suitable restraint) kisses his hand. Gerda's father, who heard Thomas' confession, saves the Buddenbrook's company the following morning with an impressive infusion of capital. Completing the circle with another doubling, the film ends as it began, the economic cycle remains unbroken, and the rotation continues: the clerks work in the office, the buyers and sellers go about their business, workers carry heavy sacks, and in the end, seemingly limitless amounts of grain fall into an enormous storage facility. Seen in the context of the Weimar Republic's catastrophic economic decline from the war-years until 1924 (when the Dawes' plan provided life-saving stabilization), the film's hopeful conclusion turns Lamprecht's critical staging of this cycle of economic existence into an idealized fiction. After years of inflation, dramatic economic slumps in 1921 and 1922, and hyperinflation in 1923,[85] which saw many, especially medium-sized businesses go bankrupt and child mortality rise to a postwar high, the psychological state of the nation was indeed fragile. Zander sees Lamprecht's *Buddenbrooks* as a reflection of Germany's 'inflation neurosis', at a time when the German film industry actually benefited from the crisis in terms of its production volume.[86]

As economic hardship and political chaos collided with people's desire for peace, safety, and comfort, Lamprecht and Heiborn-Körbitz constructed a narrative montage of opposing desires and demands—in business, career, marriage, and family—in order to drive their adaptation to its climax while reflecting the tensions inherent in a class-based, capitalist, and patriarchal society. Lamprecht eschews the melodramatic or even Expressionist staging proposed in parts of the screenplay in favor of restrained mise-en-scène and sequences that foreground money as an 'expression and means of human relationship [and], their relativity' (Georg Simmel). Repetitions and juxtapositions problematize both the identity of the modern capitalist and the bourgeois practice of "Geldheirat" or 'marriage for money', which was formulated by Simmel[87] and had triggered significant public debate.

All references in the script to sexuality, however (Christian's cane topped with a carved nude, pictures of naked women in suggestive poses in his desk, the passionate kiss and implied affair between Gerda and Throta), were eliminated by the director and/or producer in order to release the film without censorship-related delays. Critics' responses after the premiere were largely positive, even predicting the film's 'international success'. The film was 'rich in nuances', wrote Puszel in the communist *Die rote Fahne*, Fechter and Grossmann praised the morality and absence of "Oswalderei" (Richard Oswald-like melodrama), and even Ihering judged the film to be 'successful with regard to direction and photography'.[88] An anonymous reviewer reflected on the public's sense of ownership when it came to literary works such as *Buddenbrooks*, and another called the film groundbreaking and a 'prime example' of how 'the filming of a literary work must be done'. Only the 'happy, reconciling ending' caused much frustration, as it seemed to deprive the novel of 'its actual meaning'.[89] Mann himself later criticized the film in a number of essays and letters[90] as 'silly' and 'sentimental', but also proudly referred to all the money he 'already made and will continue to make' from this adaptation.[91] While believing that film had "little to do with art," Mann described in a later essay his increasing enthusiasm for the new medium film:

> I go often to the cinema; for hours on end I do not tire of the joys of spectacle spiced with music; whether it be traced pictures, scenes from the wild, the weekly news of the world, a diverting piece of tomfoolery, a 'thriller' or a 'shocker', or a touching tale of love. The actors must be good to look at, with a gift of expression, vain if you like but never unnatural; the 'story' itself may be vastly silly—as is nearly always the case to-day. The silliness or sentimentality is set in a frame of scenic and mimic detail, which is true to life and to reality, so that the human triumphs persistently over the crude falsity of the performance as a whole. [...] It is not art, it is life, it is actuality.[92]

But when it came to adaptations of his own works, Mann lamented: "As an author I have not as yet had much luck with the films."[93] The large majority of critics approved of *Buddenbrooks* as a welcomed 'cultural and historical document of the highest appeal',[94] and were particularly enthusiastic about its documentation of capitalist economic order and the movie's original aesthetic.

Adaptation and National Identity

Restrictions on foreign film imports put pressure on Ufa due to the company's Dafco (Danish-American Films-Corporation) distribution agreement. Postwar import laws stated that no more than 15 percent of all films screened in Germany could be foreign, and many films bought were never shown in German cinemas. At the same time, Ufa made every effort to profit from its investment by creating a subsidiary (Damra), reediting old Hollywood films, and presenting them once more to the German public. Charlie Chaplin films in particular proved an enormous success.[95]

The German economy had been devastated by the First World War, suffering the consequences of the nation's prolonged engagement with a military endeavor it could simply not afford. The value of the German currency plummeted and especially Hollywood realized the advantages of inflation for film production. In 1919/20 numerous production companies—such as Famous Players—either looked for collaborations with German companies such as Ufa or set up independent collaborative ventures such as the European Film Alliance (EFA). Because of the low value of Reichsmark, German movies became attractive commodities for American film distributors, who were able to import German films at a bargain and increase their profit margin significantly in the United States.

German cinema in the 1920s is often associated with a 'golden age' of stunning creativity and innovative visual and narrative forms. And, indeed, spectacular and momentous silent movies arose from the chaos like dancing stars.[96] Years of hardship and turmoil, the unsettling effect of loss—from personal to systemic—in postwar Germany had provided the fertile ground for new thought and avant-garde art, literature, and film. But from the ashes of the war and all the dead also rose a cultural capital of imaginative visual narrative firmly in the service of the communication of traditional values and foundational nationalism.

From 1922 onwards, Thea von Harbou tried to convince producers and filmmakers to support an adaptation of the middle-high German 'Song of the Nibelungs' but, as she recounted in a briefing for cinema owners[97] in 1924, 98 percent of her contacts refused the project to adapt the heroic legend and two others were merely skeptical. It was not until her husband Fritz Lang was commissioned to film *Nibelungen* (1924) by Decla-Ufa that her project and a grand cinema spectacle finally took shape.[98]

Decla's founder Erich Pommer had joined Ufa's board in 1923 and was instrumental in helping the company reach its apogee of internationally successful films in the 1920s.[99]

As Bock and Töteberg emphasize, Ufa's studio system as well as "its marketing, sales, and distribution practices always remained innovative. Long before such terms had been coined, Ufa practiced modern marketing, cross-media promotion campaigns, and product placement; developed new ideas for merchandising and tie-ins; and consistently prioritized a corporate identity."[100] While independent entrepreneurs and filmmakers such as Oswald struggled due to unsuccessful adaptations of the German literary canon in 1923/4—his *Faust* failed half-finished and his *Carlos und Elisabeth* based on Schiller tanked at the box office—the talent working with Pommer under the powerful auspices of Ufa had the financial backing to develop their projects in terms of both aesthetic innovation and economic success.

When compiling research for the screenplay and realizing the existence of about twenty different versions of the 'Song of the Nibelungs' alone (not counting the many adaptations in Scandinavian and other literatures), von Harbou decided 'to take the most beautiful and strongest elements from all those sources and to shape them into something new'. In her mind, only experts would be interested in the details (and accuracy) of the Germanic legend on film, but not the general public. Her assessment was spot on. Cinema audiences in Germany and abroad were much more likely to opt for *Kitsch* and genre films than high culture on screen.[101]

Friedrich Hebbel's 1861 play *Die Nibelungen*—consisting of "Der gehörnte Siegfried" [Duped Siegfried], "Siegfrieds Tod" [Siegfried's Death], and "Kriemhild's Rache" [Kriemhild's Vengeance]—and Richard Wagner's opera cycle *Der Ring des Nibelungen* (The Ring of the Nibelung, 1848–74) left their mark on Harbou's version, but are not mentioned by her as a source. Convinced that the "legend of the Nibelungen had 'chosen' her (not the other way around)",[102] she states her somewhat puffed-up wish to reveal to the German people the 'unspeakable magnificence of Kriemhild and Siegfried's world', as it corresponds to their longing for a miracle, as much as it does to their 'weariness and exhaustion'. In her mind, this 'great, tired and worn-out people is [...] unable to pick up a book after a long day's [...] work' and only film, 'the rhapsodist of the twentieth century', would be able to successfully communicate and revive this heroic legend. In usually pompous language she conveys her idea of the *Nibelungs*-film that at its core was meant to replace 'the singer, the narrating poet' and to reconnect audiences in Germany with this foundational 'song of songs of unconditional loyalty'. Lang picked up his wife's hyperbolic baton and in the same briefing outlined his sense of accountability in this process of adapting what he called 'the spiritual sanctuary of a nation'.[103] He wanted to be sure not to trivialize the "Heilig-Geistige" (holy-spiritual) and, instead, to create a film that would be accessible to (or rather 'owned' by) the people ("Volk") rather than by a 'very small number of privileged and cultivated brains'. Harbou and Lang dedicated the movie to the 'German people'.[104] Well aware of the potential criticism by film reviewers and reformers alike, Lang refused the idea of a costume drama or a "Sensationsfilm" for his first major film project, but still wanted to ensure the 'splendor' of the first and the thrilling and 'ravishing breath' of the latter. His main goal was to visualize the myth for the twentieth century, bringing it to life in a 'believable manner' while making people embrace once again the 'magic' of the legendary tale.[105]

His film introduces and entangles four different worlds, each one unique and complete in itself: Worms and its tired but highly cultured society; young Siegfried in a natural but also subterranean world of dragons and dwarfs; Brunhild and volcanic Isenland featuring 'humans looking like glass' in the 'strange, pale, icy air' with northern lights flickering in the skies; and finally the world of King Etzel and the Huns, dominated by his wife's Kriemhild's love for a dead man and a desire for revenge. As these worlds collide on tinted film stock, Lang highlighted the mood[106] and inexorable logic of their tragic fates.[107]

Siegfried premiered at the largest and most glamorous of all cinemas in Berlin, the Ufa-Palast am Zoo, on February 14, with part two *Kriemhilds Rache* [Kriemhild's Revenge] following on April 26, 1924. The *Nibelungen*, Pommer's most expensive production thus far, became Lang's second great success.[108] His adaptation of Norbert Jacques' novels, the two-part film *Dr. Mabuse, der Spieler* [Dr. Mabuse, the Gambler[109]] (1922), had focused on the psychoanalyst and megalomaniac Dr. Mabuse (Rudolf Klein-Rogge) whose proficiency in hypnosis and a double life as a criminal enables him to establish a wide-reaching power base within the state in a staccato of

FIGURE 3.5 *Paul Richter as Siegfried in* Die Nibelungen *(part 1:* Siegfried; *DE, Fritz Lang, 1924).*

ferocious action unfolding within modern, urban spaces. The screenplay by Lang and Harbou for this first of several *Mabuse*-adaptations concludes with the manipulative doctor succumbing to madness. Mabuse, who wanted to be 'a giant [...], a titan, who blows laws and gods around like dry leaves!!',[110] is at end of the film haunted by the ghosts of his victims and sitting ragged in a pile of cash. The film's ending bluntly but effectively symbolizes the lunacy caused by his extravagant desire for riches and complete control, and made for a satisfying narrative at times of economic hardship. Considering the German leadership's megalomania during the Hitler era, the adaptation appears gloomily prophetic.

Lang's and Harbou's *Dr. Mabuse* was a box-office hit, and their *Nibelungen*—which could be read as both "a balm to a wounded nation" and "a subtle critique of the decadent and ultimately self-destructive pursuit of fatalist glory"[111]—was considered a "watershed"[112] and indicated a new chapter in German cinema history that impacted particularly on Goebbels' imagined aesthetic for Nazi film nearly a decade before his appointment as Hitler's Propaganda Minister.[113] Modern and yet embedded in tradition and Germanic myth, the monumental story of violence, existential struggle, and death perfectly complemented the Nazi's logic of an aesthetic that inspired 'greatness' while feeding off a toxic sense of rootedness and exceptionalism.[114] Ending in downfall for both the Nibelungs and the Nazis, the logic was successfully refracted nearly a century later in Tarantino's *Nibelungen*-inspired *Inglorious Basterds* (US, 2018), which eliminates Nazis alongside the fascist corruption of visual culture in 1940s France.[115]

Also a story of lust for power starring Rudolf Klein-Rogge (now as King Etzel) *Nibelungen* was produced[116] for both national and international markets. With Ufa's generous financial backing the project was meant again to establish the German film industry globally as a major player that could rival Hollywood at a time when German stars such as Pola Negri[117] and Ernst Lubitsch were leaving for California. According to Adeline Mueller, Pommer had "engineered"[118] a sumptuous banquet after the premiere for the stars and filmmakers to celebrate the adaptation together with 170 leading figures of politics, business, and society. Foreign Minister Gustav Stresemann gave a speech in which he called *Die Nibelungen* "a masterpiece of education and edification for the German people and for the world, a means of bringing all nations closer together in mutual sympathy and understanding."[119] While the film challenges the dichotomy and naïve bifurcation of good and evil, it also accommodates readings that celebrate heroism and Germanness. Lang himself, however, took issue with the film's appropriation by "Rightist imbeciles before and under Hitler" insisting that it is "not at all a heroic poem of the *German people*,"[120] but rather a "cautionary tale."[121]

An original score composed by Gottfried Huppertz accompanied Lang's visualization of types and basic emotions conveyed in the Germanic legend, but rather than providing melodramatic monosemy, the music subverts the film's narrative authority.[122] Stylized images juxtapose light and dark, love and hate, success and failure, civilization and savagery. The director's vision was supported by a strong team of collaborators that included Carl Hoffmann and Günther Rittau at the camera, Otto Hunte (with Erich Kettelhut) responsible for the set, and costumes by Paul Gerd Guderian and Änne Willkomm. Part one follows Siegfried (played by Paul Richter) and his valiant deeds—including the killing of a large animatronic dragon designed by Karl Vollbrecht and reminiscent of Méliès' smaller version in his *Münchhausen*-comedy of 1911—until the hero's demise at the hands of Hagen (Hans Adalbert Schlettow), with Brunhild (Hanna Ralph) and Gunther (Theodor Loos) having been complicit in his death. The first part of the film ends with penitent Brunhild's suicide in the cathedral, where Siegfried's body is laid out. The film's conclusion in part two focuses on revenge, especially Kriemhild's (Margarete Schön) who avenges her beloved Siegfried's murder until the devastation is complete.

Herbert Ihering in *Berliner Börsen-Courier* praised Lang's intention to create a 'binding style', i.e., an aesthetic that draws from literature, painting, architecture, and mythology.[123] In his mind, however, the director failed in his endeavor because he cared too much about appealing to the audience. What was to be a folk film ("Volksfilm"), Ihering writes, became an 'aesthete's eclectic' version of the Germanic legend. Critic Kracauer was even less enthused when watching Lang and Harbou's 'sacred gala, which drags itself endlessly across the screen like a lindworm', as he wrote in *Frankfurter Zeitung* in 1924.[124] A keen observer, Kracauer[125] paid attention to detail and knew that taking myths too seriously caused only unintentional comedy and even a travesty of meaning. In his mind, the length of the film alone was a sign of arrogance that pointed ominously to an underlying desire to amplify German mythology and, by implication, nationalism. At a time of extremism and growing support for nationalists, this was indeed a questionable undertaking.

Overall, however, the project was celebrated as a proud as well as technologically and stylistically innovative masterpiece that translated the legend's 'blazing love and flaming hatred, victorious masculinity and eternal loyalty' into a modern film language. 'Hail to the one who dared to grasp' this opportunity, 'hail to us, if he succeeds', wrote Heinz Udo Brachvogel in *Lichtbild-Bühne* (February 14, 1924)[126] in a language already evoking Hitler's and Goebbels' speeches. Perhaps Lang was interested neither in celebrating Siegfried as an immaculate hero nor in creating a nationalistic monument to some mythical Germanic past. But at the same time, together with Harbou, he revived Siegfried and Hagen, thereby providing stunning imagery to a legend that helped fertilize the growing movement based on nationalistic, militaristic, racist, and antisemitic ideology. Siegfried, who slays the dragon, was the name chosen for the most important line of defense during the First World War—the *Siegfriedlinie*. When the German hero was betrayed and defeated, Hagen became his replacement: a much more ferocious, enigmatic, and menacing leader, utterly determined no matter the catastrophic outcome of his obsessive will to battle.[127] It would be Hitler himself who proclaimed on several occasions his 'faithfulness' to the fight and based his illusion of power and respectable masculinity on the promise of resistance. His madness resulted in mass murder and the death of over 70 million. While Lang and von Harbou could not have known the devastating outcome of Hitler's rise to power, it is impossible to watch their *Nibelungen* and not be reminded of the Nazi's genocidal ideology. The film's depictions of Siegfried and Hagen were useful bricks for blinding the masses with mythical heroism as they built their concentration camps and declared another, even more devastating world war.

Social Problem Films

But it was not only right-wing sympathizers such as von Harbou, of course, who had discovered film as an ideological weapon. Filmmakers like Oswald or famous writers such as Toller proposed film as the most effective tool in their fight for social justice. On February 5, 1924, a letter by the famous

Expressionist playwright appeared in the *Berliner Volks-Zeitung* on the topic of 'Film and State'. Toller here, once again, castigates the 'sentimental antirevolutionary kitsch, and law-and-order films', which are being fabricated by the 'Messrs film producers' for the screen. Film is the expression of the 'cultural leveling of this mechanistic age', Toller writes, because the film industry only cares about profit maximization.[128] He believed in the medium's potential to be an 'instrument of inestimable value for the struggle' since, for example, film footage of devastated cities and mutilated bodies could counteract militarism. Toller also suggested very astutely that filmmakers should cut documentary sequences depicting 'life in the slums of the city' into feature films to contrast the 'greedy dance of black marketeers and war profiteers, the stock-exchange speculators and currency traders in bars, luxury hotels, splendid halls'[129] for anti-capitalist effect.

This proposal not only anticipated Eisenstein's collision- and attraction-montages, but was immediately followed up by G.W. Pabst, who filmed and edited this sequence almost exactly as Toller had suggested and incorporated it in his 1925 adaptation of Hugo Bettauer's *Freudlose Gasse* (Joyless Street, 1924). It is the 'sensual, ocular effect' of the medium which makes it so suitable 'for educational, informational, campaign and propaganda purposes' in Toller's eyes. The outspoken anti-fascist's idea of a central administration for propaganda film production was put into practice by the Nazis only a few years later—a bitterly ironic twist of fate.

Social problem films were becoming an established genre in the 1920s, when increasing numbers of politically minded filmmakers used the medium to amplify society's shortcomings. *Die Gezeichneten* [The Stigmatized] (DE, Carl Theodor Dreyer, 1922) based on the Danish novel *Elsker hverandre* (Love each other, 1913) by Aage Madelung, for example, highlighted racial prejudice, which in this adaptation culminates in brutal antisemitic violence in Tsarist Russia. In the Soviet Union a few years later, Третья Мещанская (Tretya meshchanskaya)—released in English-speaking countries as *Bed and Sofa* (USSR, Abram Room, 1927)—corroborated the harsh realities of life of the working poor living in Moscow's Third Meshchanskaia Street. In the United States, addiction, domestic violence, and racism were put on screen in films such as *Ten Nights in a Barroom* (Roy Calnek, 1926) and *The Scar of Shame* (Frank Peregini, 1929). In Germany, it was especially G. W. Pabst, Richard Oswald, and Fred Zelnik, who used well-known and popular literary texts to diversify the genre and maximize potential viewers.

Pabst repeatedly used cinema to highlight poverty and to criticize society's hypocritical morality, sexual exploitation, and the marginalization of 'fallen' women in adaptations of Bettauer's *Freudlose Gasse* and, in 1929, of Wedekind's 'Lulu'-plays *Erdgeist* (Earth Spirit, 1895) and *Die Büchse der Pandora* (Pandora's Box, 1904), and in another adaptation of Böhme's *Tagebuch einer Verlorenen* (Diary of a Lost Girl, 1905). Prostitution is also the topic of Oswald's adaptation of Else Jerusalem's bestselling novel

Der heilige Skarabäus (The Sacred Scarab, 1909) in *Die Rothausgasse* (1928) or, alternatively entitled *Das Haus zur roten Laterne* [Red Lantern House], and internationally distributed as *Red House Lane*. In 1929 Oswald filmed another adaptation of Wedekind's tragic *Frühlings Erwachen* (Spring Awakening, 1891) and highlighted the problem of authoritarian education and repressive morality as potentially life-threatening as they leave children vulnerable and unable to make informed decisions.

Adaptations to Fight Antisemitism and Marginalization

Many films after the end of the First World War depicted devastation—not only of the built environment and nature, but of individuals—and sought ways to address society, its value system (and, by implication, its democracy) as inherently unstable. Heinrich Mann, bestselling author of *Professor Unrat* (Small Town Tyrant, 1905) and *Der Untertan* (The Loyal Subject, 1918), considered the cinema as a place of inspiration and film as a medium that 'could promote reconstruction, democratization, and understanding between classes and nations'. But in order to successfully impact on public opinion, he believed, film must be 'naïve, able to throw punches, [and convey] simple ideological content'.[130]

Hugo Bettauer was extremely successful in doing just that. Working as a journalist and highly productive author in Germany and Austria, he published provocative articles addressing social ills but also highly controversial topics such as homosexuality and abortion. Considered a member of the so-called 'Red Vienna' the left-wing author published numerous crime novels that doubled as social criticism. His novel *Stadt ohne Juden* (City without Jews, 1922) responded to the palpable increase in openly displayed antisemitism in Austria at the time. Populism reigned and Jews were made the scapegoats by feckless politicians for everything from military defeat to economic crisis. In his satire, Bettauer imagines a Vienna which, after expelling all the Jews, comes to a grinding halt culturally and economically, and suffers in virtually all other practical aspects as well. A sobering experience for the remaining city-dwellers, who in the end decide they need to get their Jewish citizens back. Criticized as 'trashy' by nationalists, Bettauer's dystopian novel had great popular appeal and became the topic of heated public debate. His depiction of the impact of antisemitism on families and individuals, on lovers, parents, and children, provided those easy-to-read punches that Mann had recommended. *Stadt ohne Juden* was quickly adapted for the cinema by Ida Jenbach (who, as a Jew, was murdered in a German concentration camp in 1942).

Her screenplay was filmed in 1924 under the direction of Hans Karl Breslauer, who aimed at maximum popular appeal.[131] The film, starring Hans Moser, Anny Miletty, and Ferdinand Maierhofer, exchanged Vienna for "Utopia" and turned the satire into a comedy, in order to minimize the currency of the film in light of right-wing protests and conservative censorship boards. The movie was thought to be lost until it was discovered at a flea market in Paris in 2015.[132] Four years later, in an article published in newspaper *Süddeutsche Zeitung*, Karl-Markus Gauß examines the mechanisms of incitement and the demagoguery of power-hungry politicians so cynically depicted in Bettauer's novel and, to a lesser degree, in Breslauer's film, in light of their alarming topicality.[133] Gauß's thought experiment focuses on a 'city without migrants', without those who, for instance, settled in Vienna during and after the war in former Yugoslavia, or those who fled Syria more recently. Without their contribution to society in hotels, restaurants, shops, Gauß suggests, without their presence and willingness to work jobs others shy away from, today's infrastructure in Vienna would simply collapse.

Because of Bettauer's courageous and provocatively uncompromising journalism, especially after he started publishing his own journal *Er und Sie* [He and She], a 'weekly magazine for life culture and eroticism' in 1924, he received death threats and was sued. A media campaign persistently demonized the (formerly Jewish) writer as a menace who jeopardized public decency, and on March 10, 1925, a young Austrian Nazi took violent action.[134] Bettauer was shot several times and died two weeks later, nearly two months before Pabst's adaptation of his novel premiered in Berlin's Mozartsaal.[135] While Bettauer's critics had tried to discredit him as a writer by calling him "Asphaltliteraten," who needlessly and provocatively focuses on the city's seedy underbelly,[136] the urban fabric itself became the melodramatic foundation of Pabst's *Die freudlose Gasse*. The leveling effect of economic and social crises sees girls threatened with the prospect or reality of lost virtue. The street is the looming abyss, leading Lotte Eisner to lament the lack of "restraint and humanity"[137] in Pabst's silent movie. But the director, "film history's ultimate nowhere man"[138] as Eric Rentschler calls him, was committed to highlighting the question of morality in the context of the plight of the working and middle classes suffering the greed of unscrupulous individuals. He is particularly focused on the plight of women, as captured so well by his three main actors Asta Nielsen, Valeska Gert, and Greta Garbo in her first major international role. Especially Nielsen and Garbo reveal intense emotions in close-up shots and thus communicate their despair. Two separate if interlinked stories center on Maria Lechner (Nielsen) and Grete Rumfort (Garbo), and highlight the dramatic consequences of poverty and repressive moral structures for individual women and girls from the working and the middle classes. While Maria finally resorts to selling herself in order to survive and escape domestic punishment, Grete's family's precarious financial situation soon sees the young middle-class virgin implicated in prostitution. Pabst communicates his critique of exploitative practices and social order in melodramatic mode, resorting to "cliché, overstatement and overemphasis"[139] in order to make his (and Bettauer's) point. Patrice Petro examines in detail the "melodramatic refusal of censorship and repression" that the film illustrates.[140] Censors on both sides of the Atlantic prohibited several scenes, and Britain banned the film altogether, despite the significant narrative alteration of the film's conclusion into a happy ending with Grete's virtue finally being rewarded.[141] Cuts demanded by censors left the film fragmented, however, which impacted its reception. The restored version available today reflects Pabst's powerful depiction of poverty, despair, and prostitution juxtaposed with scenes of carefree entertainment and luxury enjoyed by the bankers and asset managers inspired by Toller's aforementioned article on 'Film and State'.

New Perspectives: Mass Entertainment and Voyeurism

Bettauer's compelling critical assessment of capitalist society is remembered due to its adaptation, which also holds true for Felix Hollaender's little known novel *Der Eid des Stephan Huller* (The Oath of Stephan Huller, 1912). The dramaturge and stage producer under Max Reinhardt in Berlin, and also his close friend, Hollaender was appointed director of the Deutsches Theater in 1920. When Ewald André Dupont's *Varieté*—already the third[142] adaptation of Hollaender's novel—hit the cinema screens, Emil Jannings' spectacular portrayal of a volatile acrobat and Karl Freund's dizzying 'unchained' camera work in the heights of the trapeze made film history.[143]

Using 'motifs' of the literary text as stated in the opening credits, the "Triebdrama,"[144] as Kracauer called it, foregrounds basic human instincts or drives such as curiosity, affection, sexual desire, jealousy, and rivalry. But it also celebrates cinema, particularly in a sequence set in and around the Wintergarten in Berlin, where the first public screening of moving pictures had taken place in 1895. The novel begins with a description of celebrity culture, the making of stars, and a variety show in Berlin's famous temple of spectacular entertainment in the late 1880s.[145] In their film, in the first of three Wintergarten-sequences, Dupont and Freund not only present a kaleidoscope of different performances—from unicyclists to clowns, dancing girls and animal acts—but transport their audience into Berlin's famous varieté culture of the 1920s by providing glimpses of an Anita Berber/Sebastian Droste-style act and, thereby, the couple's famous 'Dances of Vice, Horror and Ecstasy' which had caused such an uproar in 1922/3.

By 1925 Droste had died of tuberculosis and Berber, a 'legend'[146] already in her mid-twenties, had returned to Berlin to perform with Henri Chatin Hofmann. The famous actress[147] and dancer had provided Berlin's bourgeois and upper-class society with plenty of titillating scandal since her rise to stardom in Oswald's films, particularly due to her drug use, bisexuality, cross-dressing, and, of course, her Expressionist dances, often performed with little more than a veil.

In *Varieté* Dupont not only invites his audience to share in the joy of entertainment of a Wintergarten-show, but reminds viewers of their seldom openly acknowledged gratification. Freund's camera pans along a row of heartily laughing spectators in medium close-up, but also cuts to collated images of voyeuristic pleasure, i.e., several men with binoculars reflecting the scantily-clad dancers in their lenses.

Together Freund and Dupont thus memorialized the entertainers, from clowns and acrobats to Anita Berber and the Skladanowsky brothers. The sequence also pays homage to these pioneers of cinema with a sequence of shots of Berlin's busy streets, reminiscent of Max Skladanowsky's original documentary footage of the 1890s. But this time, three decades later, the traffic could be filmed at night. It was possible only now, due to film stock sensitive to the full chromatic spectrum from light to dark.[148] Once again, Weimar cinema is, as Elsaesser so convincingly argues, self-referential.[149]

In *Varieté*, the desire to be entertained, aroused, and excited is universal, no matter if it is in the fancy Wintergarten theater or in 'Boss' Huller's cheap Reeperbahn show. The audience's attire might differ, but their experience of

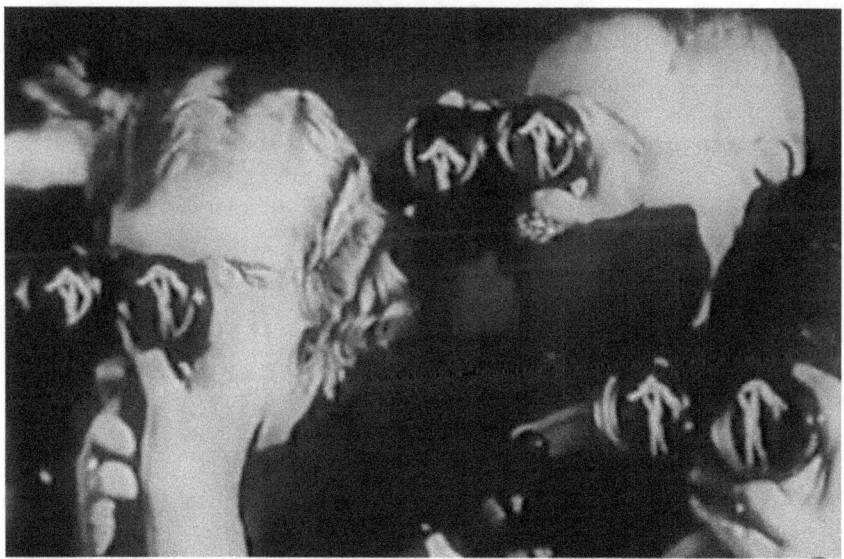

FIGURE 3.6 Varieté *(DE, Ewald André Dupont, 1925).*

entertainment does not. Dupont's film opens in a prison, where Jannings' former trapeze artist 'Boss' Huller is introduced as a number—"28"—in an Expressionist mise-en-scène evoking the dehumanizing control of punitive society and the loneliness of incarceration. A flashback reveals to the viewers the inmate's journey from being an honest, kind, life-loving entrepreneur, who ran a small dingy theatre in Hamburg's entertainment district that featured mostly half-naked female dancers. His wife (Maly Delschaft) and mother of their small child plays the piano in the establishment, until "das fremde Mädchen" (as Lya de Putti is called in the opening credits)—a 'strange girl'—is brought to him straight from the "Berta-Marie," a cargo ship. Soon Huller falls under the girl's spell or, as the intertitle reads, her "fremder Zauber" or 'strange magic'. Freund's camera highlights the inversion of the power relationship between the 'Boss' and the young castaway, as he becomes passionately and masochistically entangled with the exotic beauty. Their relationship is marked from the beginning as potentially hazardous as 'Boss' Huller leaves his wife and child and moves to Berlin with her, working once again as a fairground acrobat. The return of success, due to his stimulating and talented sidekick, peaks when they are invited to join famous Artinelli (Warwick Ward) in the trapeze at the Wintergarten in Berlin. Their highly publicized performance happens almost exactly at the film's half-way mark. While their trapeze act marks the turning point of the narrative, it is the unchained camera itself that is placed exactly at the film's climax if we accept Gustav Freytag's pyramid as blueprint for the film's dramatic structure. It is here that the audience share in the experience of a trapeze artist's perspective via breathtaking shots. This, *Varieté* emphasizes, is the spectacular and most modern form of entertainment that only cinema can provide. Point-of-view shots from a swing high above the audience, for instance, invite the spectator herself to embody the spectacle.

But public exhibition and intimate tragedy soon collide when 'Boss' assumes his adored partner is having an affair with their celebrity colleague. Love turns to overwhelming jealousy; Huller stabs and kills Artinelli, after first imagining his death during their final Wintergarten performance. Finally, he turns himself into the police, reconnecting the tragic tale with its framing narrative. Jannings' range of emotions from desperate humiliation to imploding, but also the dramatic function of objects signaled in close-up shots or implied in passing, particularly impressed critics at the time. The film transposes the novel's tragic conclusion into an aerial view revealing the oppressive power of prison—inspired by depictions of walls in Expressionist art and literature—in the opening shot, but also a painting by Van Gogh, as Lotte Eisner[150] notes, subtly implying 'Boss' Huller's mental breakdown.

The power of the camera not only communicates the suffering of the male lead but also reflects his—and the audience's—gaze. This gaze "fixes and isolates women,"[151] leading to their fragmentation in recurring close-up shots, especially of Lya de Putti's and other women's bare legs. G.W. Pabst would use Dupont's "leitmotif"[152] and Freund's camera technique in his adaptation of Frank Wedekind's *Pandora's Box* three years later, and its impact would still be visible in Sternberg's *The Blue Angel* (1930) and beyond. But it is also man's fragmentation that is captured in one of the most iconic images of this film, when Huller returns to the room he shares with his lover and places his hands in a washbasin. Close-ups of blood seeping into the water from his hands signal the final disintegration of relationships, individuals, and lives. Dupont and Freund are radically modern in their visualization of Hollaender's text, and their "courageous formal innovation"[153] on screen is reflective of ground-breaking developments in cinematic expression and visual culture.

Innovative narrative practices often increased the marketability of new films at the time, but already in 1922, Béla Balász had lamented in an article in the communist *Rote Fahne* the difficulty of breaking the spell of bourgeois showpieces that kept the 'weary proletariat'[154] pacified and politically unaware. He acknowledged their 'need of distraction' but suggested that entertainment, even representations of a glamorous upper-class lifestyle, could be used to raise 'class consciousness and combativeness'.[155] In 1927, an adaptation of Hauptmann's *Die Weber* (The Weavers) demonstrated the capacity of film to be (political) art that would still draw the masses into cinemas.

Ensemble Acting and Workers' Rights on Screen: Fred Zelnik's *The Weavers*

In 1893, Gerhart Hauptmann had brought *De Waber/Die Weber* (The Weavers) to the theater stage, a socio-political critique so true to life that it was soon considered the pinnacle of naturalism. His play depicts the increasingly inhumane working and living conditions of weavers in Silesia during the onset of industrialization and transposes their uprising in 1844. Together with Fanny Carlsen, Willy Haas wrote the script based on Hauptmann's play, which seemed a perfect fit. At the time Hauptmann's play had provided theater with new representational and political norms, just as Soviet films by Eisenstein and Pudovkin were proving in 1925/6 that films could be at once stunning political instruments and works of art.[156] In 1927, inspired by the Soviet filmmakers' innovative aesthetic and social awareness, Friedrich Zelnik directed *The Weavers* to great acclaim, with Paul Wegener and Valeska Stock playing industrialist Dreißiger and his wife, Wilhelm Dieterle and Theodor Loos playing the leaders of their opposition as Moritz Jäger and weaver Bäcker. The film opens with a stop-motion animated scene by Expressionist artist Georges Grosz, in which lines turn into forms and, finally, into a 'world'.[157] When the drawing of a group (standing in a room next to a table and scales) is complete, the film dissolves into live-action. The contrast between the art of drawing and the realism of those tired weavers' faces on film is striking. Zelnik and his cameramen Frederik Fuglsang and Friedrich Weinmann used editing, and particularly montage (Eisenstein) or linkage (Pudovkin), to critically highlight class difference, dependency, exploitative work practices, de-individualization, and dehumanization due to industrialization, capitalism, and social hierarchy.

As rolls of fabric are handed to the foreman in the live-action part of the opening sequence, the camera closes in on the weavers: individuals—from children to old men and women—carry the products of their labor; their work is individualized. When it is their turn at the counter the quality of the cloth and the price are decided, the weavers are entirely at the mercy of the well-dressed foreman. His harsh exactitude is judiciously juxtaposed by two panning shots along shelves filled with an abundance of rolls of new fabric and along the bare feet of the weavers. All their good work does not even provide for shoes and, as the following static shots of both old and young weavers reveal, this system of exploitation affects workers across generations. Only slightly elevated, the capitalist system's social hierarchy provides a boy at the scales with a sense of power, and he smiles self-importantly as he announces: 'Reimann is short in weight again!' The foreman thus reduces Reimann's pay, leaving the weaver perplexed. Indicating their dependence and vulnerability, the motionless group of weavers raise their heads, acknowledging this judgment before collapsing back into their bowed shapes. Having been denied payment altogether, a close-up of an old woman's tired face wet with tears affectively communicates the incalculable impact of this decision, further clarified by an intertitle that reads in dialect: 'My husband has been sick in bed for weeks .... I don't dare return home without money!'

Zelnik foregrounds the meaning of fair pay for the weavers' work—which is a question of life and death for those at the bottom of the social spectrum—and places it in critical contrast with industrialist Dreissiger's safe and abundant home. This technique is reminiscent of Thanhouser's *The Cry of the Children* (US, George O. Nichols, 1912), and the adaptation of Elizabeth Barrett Browning's reform poem might well have inspired Zelnik's Hauptmann film.[158] Cutting from a close-up shot of the two old weavers' faces (with the old woman still crying), we see a beautifully set table with white table cloth with a roast goose or large chicken, not a Sunday event, but everyday in this house. When tension between the weavers and their superiors rises, Zelnik uses simple but effective juxtapositions to emphasize class, injustice, and a crushing cycle of exploitation. As one of the weavers stands up to the foreman, a boy faints due to malnutrition. The emaciated little lad is carried into the apartment above and, once back on his feet with the help of a servant and some milk, marvels at the luxuriously decorated rooms. When spotting children's toys in the next room, he imagines himself sitting on the rocking horse, which caught his eye. The scene artfully communicates class difference by placing the thin boy in his tattered clothes and dirty feet on this beautifully decorated toy. But the scene is only an illusion—as is the implied access to a world of security and luxury for this child and those of his class—and thereby also conveys the lack of self-esteem of those caught in this cycle of exploitation. Inducing viewers' imagination of 'normal', child-like behavior that would see the boy trying to climb onto that rocking horse, this child's inaction and separation, i.e., class difference and exploitation, are implicitly marked as anomalous. Zelnik carefully avoids naïve political statements and instead creates visual and narrative complexity that reinvents Hauptmann's play and updates its socio-political critique.

At the same time and also in Berlin, Erwin Piscator and Ernst Toller were working toward a revolutionary, socialist theatre that made use of the central 'dramatic-functional significance' of film, aiming at an 'authentic' representation of contemporary socio-political problems and their historical significance by complementing acting with film screenings on stage. Zelnik, Piscator, and Toller agreed that film provided the perfect vehicle in the communication of socially relevant topics, as the new medium penetrated the intellectual and emotional reality of viewers, thereby not only providing information but also impacting on individuals' political understanding and decision-making processes, as Piscator emphasized.[159]

In *Die Weber*, Zelnik cuts from the boy's shattered dream to the harsh everyday reality of three women, who work in their small cottage, producing baskets in addition to spinning and weaving in order to make the rent, and still they are afraid to be short and without a home at the end of the month. When Moritz Jäger returns from service to his family, well-fed and in uniform, he barely recognizes their thin faces. His belief in the benevolence of the king is revealed as naïve in the montage to follow, as the film cuts from a newspaper article reporting on the king's "Schwanenorden" and its intent to 'rid the world of misery and poverty', to the members of the king's order, who sit around drinking champagne and discussing the need to send a mission to Africa to ensure a 'Christian, god-fearing education of negro-children'. The

FIGURE 3.7 Die Weber *(DE, Friedrich Zelnik, 1927); credits by George Grosz.*

order's luxuriously decked table blends into its utterly bare equivalent in the poor weavers' cottage just slowly enough for all to realize the inability of either class to imagine the vast difference between the reality of poverty and fear of one, and the comfort of luxury and security of the other.

Disgusted by the weavers' living and working conditions, Moritz encourages resistance, believing in their success if only they stick together. As his song about their right to judge those that consume the poor's "Hab und Gut" [Goods and Chattel] gains momentum, so does the film's editing speed, cutting from long shots of the group to extreme close-ups of their eyes and mouths. Live-action revolution is mirrored in animated title-plates communicating the text of the song with large letters and words coming together and becoming an abstract collection. Inspired by Soviet revolutionary films such as Eisenstein's *Potemkin* (1925) and Pudovkin's *Mother* (1926), both screened in Berlin, Zelnik composed mass scenes of weavers gathering and marching to face their suppressors—first Dreissiger and soon the factory and its machines, i.e., industrialization itself.

Despite the powerful triumvirate of industrialist/capital, police/state, and priest/church, the irresistible mass of workers manages to oust Dreissiger and push back armed troops with their commitment and their stones, at least for now. But when the weavers attack the machines calling them their 'worst enemies', a simple shot of a roll of fabric lying on the dirty ground reveals the incongruity of their action and incompatibility of their rage against the machine with their aim to improve working and living conditions for all. Industrialization is inevitable, Zelnik seems to say; not the machine is our enemy, but those that use them to exploit and suppress their workers refusing to pay a fair wage. After highlighting the tragic losses and suffering of innocents, Zelnik closes his film with the two leaders of the uprising Bäcker and Jäger, with Emma, Gottlieb, and his wife standing on the otherwise empty village square. Only rocks and few helmets are scattered around. In this final scene, the group is arranged like as a crucifixion ensemble; here, religious iconography not only foregrounds their sacrifice but also evokes Christian humanism as a value system.

In this reimagination of Hauptmann's play for the 1920s, Zelnik created for the cinema screen what Toller envisaged when he worked toward a collective drama for the young republic that would at once encompass the energy of large modern mass scenes while conveying the most intimate closeness, reflecting the psychology of its protagonists and thereby the consequences of their struggle.[160] As mentioned before, Soviet films such as *Potemkin* and *Mother* had a significant impact on filmmaking in Germany in particular. Hauptmann's play was an excellent thematic fit, but Zelnik's adaptation also reflects the impact of social problem films beginning with Thanhouser productions such as *The Actor's Children* (1910) and *The Cry of the Children* (1912) in the United States. In *Die Weber*, Soviet film style is prevalent, as Kracauer and others noted, especially with regard to varying camera distances, editing (montage), and the evocative representation of poverty and class difference. Content and composition reinforce one another and constitute a linear film narrative of great political significance. As Toller had hoped in 1924, the cinema screen here served as space of agitation and as a bridge between media and different audiences. Zelnik's film was a great success, not least because its political message resonated with both the masses and educated intellectuals, and was instrumentalized by both right- and left-wing activists. Particularly for an adaptation of a well-known play, the film's overall positive reception was nonetheless remarkable and reflected the aesthetic quality of the transposition.[161]

Overall, film production companies at the time fared better with adaptations of popular literature. This became particularly clear in 1926, when *Die Brüder Schellenberg* [The Brothers Schellenberg] and another *Faust* premiered the same year. A thrilling tale of adversity, violence, and madness *Die Brüder Schellenberg* (DE, Karl Grune, 1926), based on Bernhard Kellermann's new novel, was a box-office hit. It was in particular Conrad Veidt—playing two very different twin brothers and conflicting *Doppelgänger*—that delighted audiences and critics alike. As outlined in Chapter 2, the motif had been gaining popularity since Romanticism. Greater awareness of psychopathologies and publications in psychoanalysis inspired both literature and soon film. In 1912, for example, Gerhard Hauptmann described the main protagonist's disintegrating mental state in his novel *Atlantis*. Here, plagued by hallucinations, Friedrich's mirror image speaks to him: 'You have split into yourself and me before you could distinguish the individual qualities of your being, which only works as a whole, that is to say you could divide, that is to say you could split. Until you see yourself in the mirror, you see nothing of the world.'[162] As mentioned above, it was the Danish cinematographer Johan Ankerstjerne and his German colleague Guido Seeber, who produced *Doppelgänger* sequences for two of the most outstanding adaptations of 1913—*Atlantis* and *Der Student von Prag* respectively. Thirteen years later, cinematographer Karl Hasselmann also received much praise in reviews of *Die Brüder Schellenberg* for his use of double exposure. He also made use of some of Freund's creative use of a mobile camera, for example during a tracking shot as a plane departs.[163]

Goethe on Film: Murnau's 'Prestige Production' *Faust* (1926)

One of the most stunning scenes in Friedrich Wilhelm Murnau's last German film project—in *Faust*, one of the most canonical of literary texts—also involves a flight, but this time it is Mephisto who invites Faust to a new life as a confident, beautiful young man who can have what he desires. All they need to do is to step on and it will carry them through the air, he tells

Faust as he seductively lays out his coat.[164] Although the scene is Goethe, its power lies in remarkable aerial shots that imitate the odd couple's gaze as Mephisto and Faust fly over Europe. Yet critics and audiences now rarely responded to a film as film when the plot was derived from a cherished example of traditional high culture. Only belatedly did French *nouvelle vague* director Eric Rohmer call Murnau's *Faust* "the greatest film by the greatest film author," and yet more recently, Helmut Schanze labeled the film "one of the milestones in the history of cinema, one of the milestones in the history of adaptation of literature and theater to the new medium film, a milestone in the interplay of different media, and a milestone in Murnau's cinematographic work."[165]

Helped by Ufa's 2 million marks investment into the project (the most expensive Ufa project prior to *Metropolis*), *Faust* was to follow the *Nibelungs* as a major prestige production for the global market that coupled this revered representation of a national culture with an international cast and outlook. Subtitled 'A German Folk Tale' the screenplay by the German playwright and novelist Hans Kyser not only was based on Johann Wolfgang von Goethe's play, but also drew from Christopher Marlowe, as well as Ludwig Berger's manuscript for 'Das verlorene Paradies' (Paradise Lost).[166] Berger had worked with Erich Pommer for Decla-Bioscop as a screenwriter and director, but also published fairytales, plays, and poetry, and adapted *Cinderella* as a romantic silent movie entitled *Der verlorene Schuh* [The Lost Shoe] in 1923, which he also directed. Fairy tale motifs such as the flying item of clothing used by Goethe and Murnau were perfect for film as Berger notes: 'The fairy tale provides film with what film needs most: the simple theme with all the possibilities of colorful variations [...]. Film in turn gives the fairy tale what it needs: reality and credibility, tempo and buoyancy.'[167]

But Goethe's *Faust* was not a fairy tale but serious business for those cultured cinemagoers in 1926, even though the majority in the audience probably did not mind this 'simplification' of Goethe's play into a tragic but visually stunning and dramatically entertaining love story. Critics did, though, rejecting cinema's ability to bring a classical narrative belonging to the literary canon to life in those modern spaces of mass entertainment. Even internationally acclaimed author Thomas Mann elaborated on the difference between high-art/-culture and cinema:

> Say what you like, the atmosphere of art is cool; it is a sphere of spiritual valuations, of transmuted values; a world of style, a manuscript world, objectively, in the most personal sense, preoccupied with form; an intellectual sphere—'*denn sie kommt aus dem Verstande*' (deriving from the intellect) says Goethe. It is chaste and elegant, it is significant, it is serene; its agitations are kept sternly at bay; you are at court, you control

yourself. But take a pair of lovers on the cinema screen, two young folk as pretty as pictures, bidding each other an eternal farewell in a real garden, with the grass waving in the wind—to the accompaniment of the most agreeable music; who could resist them, who would not blissfully let flow the tear that wells to the eye? For it is all raw material, it has not been transmuted, it is life at first hand.[168]

While ignoring the careful and multi-facetted composition of most film narratives, Mann regards the creation of authenticity and immediacy of 'life at first hand' as cinema's greatest accomplishment that, at the same time, will always already manifest its separation from 'art'. Unlike Walter Benjamin, who suggested a "Fortleben"[169] or continuation of life in the context of a translation of a literary work and, therefore, recognized an opportunity in forms of adaptations, thinkers such as Mann (or Adorno, for that matter)[170] remained deeply skeptical of transpositions of literary works to silent film.

Making the most of recent developments in cinema technology and due to Murnau's keen sense for composition, this *Faust* film is visually powerful, evoking Expressionism[171] and avant-garde modernity, but also juxtaposing classicism[172] and romanticism in an array of references to literary and art history. When Mephistopheles (Emil Jannings) emerges from the shadows, he hovers over a small town tightly packed with houses (reminiscent of the opening scene in *The Cabinet of Dr. Caligari*) with a large church in its center. With his enormous black wings he covers almost two-thirds of the screen, and although the spire of the church tower points defiantly at him, his power is undeniable and unsettling. Having wagered with an archangel for the poor soul of Faust (played by the Swedish heartthrob Gösta Ekman), the film centers on Faust's pact with Mephisto, but develops two fairly separate narrative strands in order to highlight the impact of the old alchemist/scholar/doctor's choice.

The first part of the film carefully portrays old Faust, his gentle demeanor, his dedication to his work and desire to put his knowledge to good use, and his frustration when an epidemic breaks out. This feeling of utter helplessness at a time of increasing physical frailty provides the fertile ground for Faust's transgression. He is no easy catch for the devil, but eventually his fear of damnation is overcome by a desire for youth and prowess. The second part of the film is based primarily on Goethe's depiction of Gretchen's downfall and the tragic deaths of her mother, brother, child, and, finally, herself in *Faust I*. Influenced by Scandinavian filmmakers of the early twentieth century such as Mauritz Stiller, Victor Sjöström, Urban Gad, or Benjamin Christensen, as Lotte Eisner and, especially, Thomas Elsaesser[173] indicate, Murnau conveys emotional and psychological conflict in a relatively understated manner, thereby separating his adaptation from the melodramatic volume of 'fallen women' films.

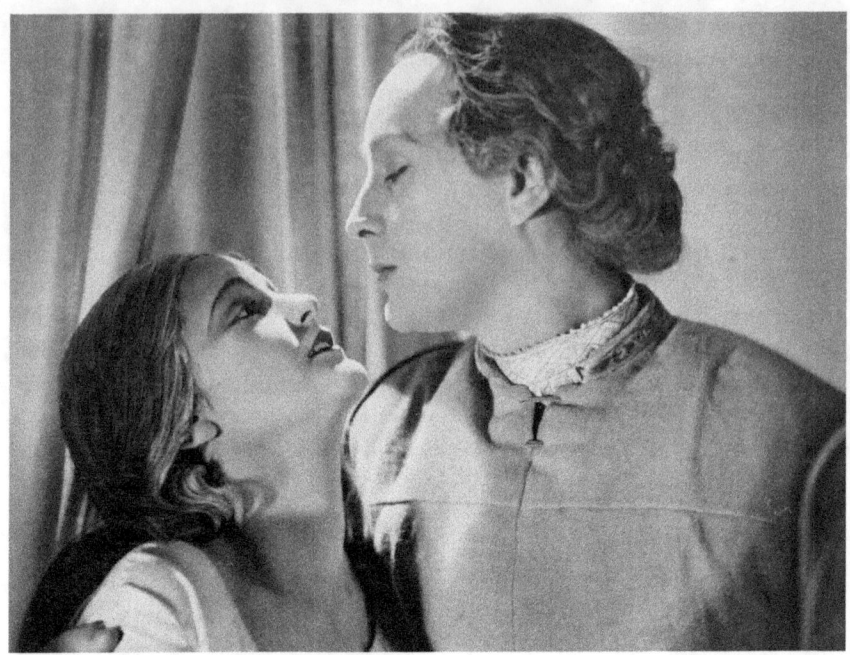

FIGURE 3.8 *Gösta Ekman and Camilla Horn as young Faust and Gretchen in* Faust *(DE, F. W. Murnau, 1926) [cf. Ekman as old Faust on the cover of this book].*

Gretchen (newcomer Camilla Horn, who replaced "First Lady of American Cinema"[174] Lillian Gish), however, is the real victim of this tale. Seduced by Faust and left pregnant and alone, Murnau takes his time when revealing the young mother's fate as the film draws to its tragic close. Clutching her newborn child and homeless in a winter's night, Gretchen knocks at many doors, but the 'fallen' woman is turned away by the town's cold-hearted, 'upright' citizens. Exhausted, her longing finally turns into a vision of a beautiful cradle, and she places her child tenderly into it before collapsing in the snow herself. The child dies of hypothermia and Gretchen is condemned to death for murder—to be burnt at the stake like a witch. Faust is filled with remorse and Emil Jannings' Mephisto (no longer his charismatic and seductive variation) angrily smashes the mirror holding Faust's youthful image, thus obliterating the enchantment. Once again a tired, old man, Faust hurries clumsily toward the pyre through the crowds who have amassed for the guilty pleasure of a heartrending spectacle. Gretchen, who had been violently dragged through the square by her chains to the place of execution, underscoring her vulnerability and critically, if indirectly, marking the horror of domestic and societal abuse, is already beginning to lose consciousness when Faust climbs onto the pyre toward her. For a brief moment she recognizes her love—highlighted in a double exposure unifying beautiful young Faust with the aged version at her feet—and they die in the flames together. As their spirits are welcomed in heaven, Mephisto is informed that 'Love has triumphed over all,' and his bet is lost. By merging the salvation of the two lovers Faust and Gretchen in the conclusion of his tragic magic tale, Kyser and Murnau blended the final proclamations of Goethe's *Faust I* [a cherubic voice informs the audience of Gretchen's safe arrival in heaven] and *Faust II* [angels carry Faust's soul to heaven]. As the face/body of old Faust fades, once again, into the attractive young lover in Gretchen's dying imagination, forgiveness and salvation here are based on both critical reflection and the possibility of love, but enabled or communicated by cinema technology, from double-exposures and fades to dissolves.

Intertitles for this film were composed by scriptwriter Kyser, but to Kyser's consternation Ufa decided that the Nobel Prize-winning author Gerhart Hauptmann would be better suited and should be commissioned with the task. Hauptmann obliged once Ufa doubled their offer to 40,000 marks, even though it seems he did not even believe in the benefit of titles for film narratives, as he wrote to his 'esteemed friend' Kyser: 'I have long been of the opinion that film titles were harming rather than aiding film. Their nature is de-illusionment ['Entillusionierung'] and disenchantment.'[175] Hauptmann finally submitted titles in doggerel verse so convoluted with cultural awareness and self-importance that Ufa's director Neumann finally wrote to Hauptmann's wife Margarete asking her to persuade her husband to 'popularize' his texts for the film. When Hauptmann refused, his verses were merely printed in a separate brochure for sale in cinemas screening *Faust*.[176] Because of a letter of protest written by Kyser and published in the *B.Z.* newspaper after Ufa's offer to Hauptmann, critics were well aware of the controversy relating to the *Faust*-titles. 'Step onto my coat and around you will circle the world,'[177] Mephisto says luringly on a title plate to Faust in Murnau's adaptation. Faust's journey and the audience's longing for entertainment and redemption were to be the focal points and center of this (cinematic) universe, but when it premiered, *Faust: A German Folk Tale* failed to convince.

Neither particularly popular with critics nor the wider public at the time, the most negative reviews focused on the film as adaptation: 'The programme made quite a few promises', Bernhard von Brentano wrote for instance in the *Frankfurter Zeitung* (October 18, 1926), while the film offered merely

> an illustration of Goethe's work with a number of changes made off the cuff by a carefree director. Did Mr. Murnau not know, that there is no word of Gretchen in the folk tale of Faust? That this is Goethe's original invention? He removed from Goethe what he did not understand, and added his own, which no one in the audience comprehended.

Clearly offended, Brentano snubs the film as 'falsification' and even 'blasphemy'. What angered him most was the fact that this Faust is a failure, who 'cannot do anything and therefore makes a pact with the devil. [...] What he does, defies all logic, because he [...] is not Goethe's grand, straying and searching man, but a weak scoundrel, who accepts the devil's advance so he can buy what he fancies.' And because the director and his screenwriters 'degraded Faust to a mere lecher, they raised Gretchen to be a heroine', he seethed. For Brentano, this film was 'an end. It cannot go any lower.' Likely the worst review the film received, one of Ufa's competitors sent copies of it to cinema owners with the most critical passages highlighted in red.[178]

Many others shared Brentano's outrage, and even Willy Haas criticized Murnau and Kyser for trying to adapt both the folk tale of Dr. Faustus and Goethe's narrative portraying Gretchen's tragic fate, doing justice to neither of the two texts.[179] In his seminal *From Caligari to Hitler* (1947) Kracauer slated not only the appropriation of this 'cultural monument' for profit, but in particular the trivialization of the eternal metaphysical conflict between good and evil in the interest of a tragic love story. After Germany's decent into Fascism, Faust's redemption (never mind his pact with the devil) and the heavenly union of the two lovers in death must have struck the exiled writer and critic as decidedly tasteless.[180] Murnau's *Faust* illustrates the domestic and international pressure that shaped much of Weimar cinema, with filmmakers facing a "twofold contest over cultural recognition at home and commercial success abroad," as Elsaesser outlines, while considering *Faust* "not only in subject matter a 'national' production, [but the] outstanding technical achievement[] of the Weimar cinema, with such dazzling display of special effects that it remained unsurpassed until Stanley Kubrick's *2001—A Space Odyssey,* almost fifty years later."[181]

After completing both *Tartüffe* (an adaptation of Molière's comedy) and *Faust*, Murnau left for Hollywood in 1926.

German Literature in Hollywood

William Fox of Fox Film had just purchased the US rights to the Tri-Ergon patent, and also bought sound-on-film patents from Case Research Lab, i.e., the Movietone sound film system in July 1926.[182] Fox's first original feature to use Movietone's synchronized soundtrack of sound effects and a musical score was Murnau's first Hollywood film: *Sunrise. A Song of Two Humans* (1927).[183] Fox, who admired Murnau's silent film work, calling the director the "German genius," offered him an exceptionally attractive contract and used the lure of brand-new technology to bring the German director to California. For his first film project in the United States, Murnau engaged a number of trusted former collaborators, such as Carl Mayer and Rochus Gliese. Mayer, with whom Murnau had worked on films such as *Der letzte Mann*—distributed internationally as *The Last Laugh* (1924)—and *Tartüffe* (1925), provided the script, but turned down the offer to join Murnau in Hollywood.[184] Gliese designed the impressive sets, as he had done before in *Das Cabinet des Dr. Caligari* (DE, Robert Wiene, 1920), *Der Golem* (DE, Paul Wegener, 1920), and in Murnau's 1922 film drama *Der brennende Acker* [The Burning Field].

The well-known German director "brought the studio great prestige" and was given "*carte blanche* by Fox" for *Sunrise* as Joel Finler confirms. The film was an expensive project, partly due to the "controlled world which he had created on some of the most elaborate exterior sets ever constructed for an American production. At Lake Arrowhead he and his German art director built a rural village, together with the downtown area of a city and Luna Park fairground; and he used many effects characteristic of the German Expressionist cinema."[185]

Based on Mayer's script, Murnau adapts *Reise nach Tilsit* (Journey to Tilsit, 1917), a short story by Hermann Sudermann about Ansas Balczus, a successful and confident fisherman in Wilwischken near the Curonian Lagoon, using its "original theme" for the film as the title plate informs the audience. Ansas is married to Indre Jaksztat, the beautiful daughter of a rich farmer from Minge, who contributes to their livelihood by selling her much sought-after produce such as butter and currant wine at the market. The third-person narrator describes her in the most complimentary tone and seems smitten with his fictional character. The couple have three gorgeous children and lead a happy marriage until—in a somewhat clichéd turn of events—another woman enters the scene. As soon as Busze is employed as a maid, Ansas begins to change and, after 'visiting her in her bedroom', completely falls under her spell. The devil brought Busze into this house, Sudermann writes, and she quickly corrupts their idyllic world. Ansas' marriage to Indre deteriorates dramatically and friends and neighbors, who side with silently suffering Indre, finally inform her powerful father of recent events. When Jaksztat arrives in a fine carriage, Busze approaches him and, without wasting any time, the old man lashes her across the face and arm with his whip. Furious, Busze drags him onto the ground and starts beating him with her fists until the coachman and Ansas put a stop to the spectacle. When confronted by his father-in-law, Ansas appears contrite and promises to mend his ways, but he is weak and once again fails to resist Busze's seductive power. She persuades Ansas to take his wife on a day-trip to Tilsit, capsize their sailing boat at a known danger-spot out at sea, and thereby make way for her as his new partner. He prepares everything as instructed, including two bunches of rushes, which he hides on the boat as an emergency floatation device for his own survival. The day in Tilsit, however, reminds him of his love for his wife and their joyous and blessed life together. Ansas finally sees clearly again and is utterly mortified at the realization of what he was about to do and what he had become. They buy cake and a bottle of sticky rose liqueur, and on the return journey, Ansas finally confesses his guilt and murderous intent. Indre, who never stopped loving him, forgives him. They pray together and talk, until beautiful song interrupts their conversation. They stop their sailboat to greet the group of *Dzimken* or raftsmen from Russia and offer them (including the Jew among them as Sudermann mentions) a glass of their liqueur and shake their hands when they leave. Indre and Ansas continue their journey home, but also their celebration of reconciliation. They finish the bottle, make love, and finally, despite their best intentions, fall soundly asleep. Indre's neighbor Ane Doczys wakes up in early hours worried about her friend and together with her husband she sails out to look for the couple. They find Indre drifting in the sea, having survived due to two bundles of rushes that Ansas had tied on to her after the boat had capsized. Ansas, however, is nowhere to be found, until two days later, when his body washes up near their home. His punishment is also his redemption. His widow gives birth to another child nine months later. She calls her son Galas, Lithuanian for 'end' or 'ending'. The story concludes with a brief description of Indre' children, who are now all grown up and lead fulfilled and honorable lives. Indre is now an old woman, living with her oldest son and respected by the entire community. She knows she will be reunited with Ansas soon, since God forgives all sinners. Sudermann closes with the hope that He will also forgive all our sins.

In his script for Murnau's *Sunrise* project, Mayer tells this dramatic story with a distinct twist that shines light on the tension between idyllic and peaceful country life and a woman from the 'city'. By using a popular symbolic figure—the *femme fatale*—Mayer foregrounds the destructive effect of urban, metropolitan influence on the traditional order still prevailing in Arcadian rural environments, and thus highlights the city's (and modernity's) destructive force.

The film opens with a title plate reading "This song of the 'Man and his Wife' is of no place and every place; you might hear it anywhere at any time," underscoring the universal nature of the narrative to follow. Despite the German/Austrian creative input and the omission of names in the interest of individuals' roles—popular among German Expressionist playwrights such as Kaiser or Toller—Mayer and Murnau here emphasize the relevance of their film for a first and foremost US American cinema audience, while identifying their tale as clearly transnational and not geographically bound: "For wherever the sun rises and sets ... in the city's turmoil or under the open sky on the farm, life is much the same; sometimes bitter, sometimes sweet." In its opening sequence, the film suggests mobility emphasized by an urban backdrop—a drawing of a big railway station and a "summer time ... vacation time" title, which then turns into life-action with a steaming locomotive leaving the large glass dome separating the station from modern apartment- and office-buildings, transporting tourists to the seaside. Double exposure emphasizes modes of travel and seaside destinations. Finally, tourists (with their delighted cinema audience in tow) arrive in a sleepy village now teeming with vacation activity. At the stern of the boat is a woman in a white dress and hat, waving enthusiastically at the people waiting at the small peer. Another title plate changes the lighthearted tone of this opening sequence: "Among the vacationists was a Woman of the City. Several weeks had passed since her coming and still she lingered." Like a bacterial infection that is nowhere near under control, this "Woman of the City" (played by Margaret Livingston) or "Großstadtgeschöpf" (lit. 'big city creature') as Carl Mayer called her in his screenplay is presented bouncing around her rented room, wearing only her undergarments and a dressing gown, lighting a cigarette at a candle sitting and brushing her short hair while glancing briefly at herself in the mirror. She appears in true metropolitan 'New Woman' attire downstairs while the elderly couple living in the cottage are just having their dinner. Her arrogant confidence and narcissistic tendency are emphasized when she complains about her dirty high-heeled shoe and the old woman swiftly rises to bow down and wipe away the dirt or sand inevitable in these parts—no 'asphalt' here.

In this adaptation, it is not the maid who plays the seductive mistress (Bodil Rosing) but, rather, "The Woman from the City." Like any wild beast, the urban predator goes straight for her prey. We see the husband, here called "the Man" (George O'Brien), sitting at his perfectly set table waiting for his angelic wife (Janet Gaynor) to serve dinner. When Woman from the City whistles outside, he briefly tries to resist. His wife lowers the bowl of soup in despair when she finds the room empty. Neighbors are talking already about the husband's failure, and in a brief flashback we are provided with a glimpse of the couple's past happiness and lightness of being. Now he "ruins himself for that woman from the city" and "money-lenders strip the farm." The man literally walks a dark path toward the other woman, while his wife cries next to their little child, who clumsily tries to comfort his mother. A close-up of the tears streaming down her beautiful face foregrounds the wife's suffering and the affective impact of this image communicates a tragedy in need of critical re-evaluation, while her husband enjoys the city-slicker's passionate embrace on the beach. She tempts him to sell his farm and come with her to the city in words that increase in size (and impact) on title plates. Murnau transposes her seductive kisses conveying a mood of urban excitement into a collage of cityscapes and nightly entertainment, a montage of images that overlap and merge into one another—humans, instruments, machines, all folded into the other visually and aurally. Here the accompanying score goes beyond extradiegetic classical orchestral music and merges with city sounds from cars to jazz music emanating from metropolitan nightclubs.

Man's rhetorical question "... and my wife?" is met with an immediate response—"Couldn't she be drowned?" in compellingly sinking letters. Man appears shocked and is raised, albeit briefly, from his passion-induced topor. He begins to strangle the 'Whore of Babylon', but she showers him with kisses and caresses and within seconds he is, once again, putty in her cunning hands. The triangular constellation is clearly constructed, but opposing moralities, geographies, as well as dynamics (from sexual passion to marital calm) are not as black and white as this brief summary might suggest. It is the wavering of Man between the two draws personified by the two women that provide the underlying tension in this film. The married couple's 'trip across the water' follows the structure of the literary narrative although this couple will be going not to Tilsit but to a geographically unspecific location. Allowing for visualizations of imaginary deeds the short story only insinuates, the adaptation presents a much more focused and tension-filled narrative. Juxtapositions particularly—of the two women, domesticity/marriage and savagery/affair, rural and urban space, etc.—construct a simple moral logic. Man's guilty conscience bends his spine as he rows bowed like Quasimodo. When Man gets up and moves toward his wife in seemingly monstrous intent, she pleads with her hands clasped in prayer, but he opens his hands until the sound [!] of church bells breaks his evil lover's spell. He covers his face in shame, moving back to his seat, rowing like a lunatic in order to get away from the sound of the bells still ringing loudly along with the musical score. His wife sits with her hands covering her face in desperate disappointment. Once the couple reach land, he reaches out to help her up, but she jumps off and runs away. When a tram appears and she gets on, he barely manages to catch the ride as it already begins to leave. A romantic score underlines the melodramatic narrative, indicating a turning point as the two villagers arrive in the city. A traveling shot—with the camera situated behind, i.e., replacing the conductor—takes the audience along on this journey, overcoming both the rural-urban-divide and the couple's struggle.

Diegetic sound marks the most important and emotionally charged scenes, and reminds Man of his humanity: to the sound of church bells he finally begins to take pity on his distraught wife, and a wedding and its accompanying tune draws the pair to a church reminding them of their love and vows. Once again reunited, symbolized by idyllic pastures that magically surround them, they move through the city traffic unharmed. When they stop to kiss in the middle of the street, they bring cars and trucks, a horse-drawn carriage, cyclists, and even a tram to a sudden halt. This depiction of urban traffic inspired Joe May's visually spectacular *Asphalt* (1929), but here the modern chaos is audible. Traffic approaches the reunited couple from all directions, loud sounds of horns honking, motorists screaming, but they do not hear a thing as the romantic score continues simultaneously. "Get out of here!," drivers shout, and finally the lovers hear the sounds around them—a new chapter in film history is sealed with a kiss.

Murnau's movie presents visual compositions as well as sound collages as high art. Musical scores harmonized with silent film were nothing new, but the combination of diegetic and non-diegetic sound with a range of aesthetic and affective images depicting different facets of the three individuals' lives, of emotions and environments, was groundbreaking. The married couple's happiness once they reconciled in the city is foregrounded by a harmonization of space and sound, especially during a rural folk dance in this utterly urban environment, or the dramatization of bad weather out at sea and in the city. On their way back, shortly before their boat capsizes, Man ties the bundles of rushes around his wife, as in the literary text. But here, he manages to swim to shore, raise the alarm, and villagers come running. The separation between Man and Woman from the City is indicated by Charles G. Rosher's and Karl Struss' cinematography long before the narrative concludes.

Woman from the City now remains a remote spectator, who watches from her window, offering a glimpse of her naked back and shortly after a naked limb as she is getting dressed, making the viewer complicit in Man's desire. Not to lend a helping hand but to share in another's voyeuristic gaze, she sneaks to the beach, and watches Man calling for his wife growing increasingly anxious as the camera moves closer to focus on the emotional veracity of Man's visible action. When loose rushes seem to indicate that his wife did not survive, Man returns home in utter desperation. When Woman from the City comes whistling, rage rises within him in true Expressionist style. She tries to flee, but he catches up and begins to strangle her. He would have murdered her had it not been for Mother's calls (a close-up of her smiling, her face wet with tears reveals the good news). He rushes back and indeed finds his wife alive. An old fisherman who 'know[s] the tides' did not give up hope, and fished her out of the sea still clutching a bundle of rushes. After a romantic reconciliation and a bit of comedic relief provided by the old fisherman, the film ends with the couple kissing once again in close-up as the sun rises. Despite the challenges of modernity—instability, chaos, swift changes, and new identities—their bond and family, and thus if implicitly, tradition prevail.

While Murnau used the new Movietone sound-on-film technology to incorporate the musical score, featuring Gounod and Chopin, as well as diegetic sound, he exploits silent film conventions in most other aspects of his film. The village church with its tower is included in numerous shots of the village, the sound of its bells providing warning or moral guidance as they had done in adaptations of Schiller's epic poem *Die Glocke* (The Bell) in 1917 and 1921 mentioned above, but this time they are heard, not read and imagined. The film premiered on November 29, 1927, in New York at a high-profile gala event. The innovative and high quality nature of both images and sound in *Sunset* ensured "a triumphant US debut."[186] Mordaunt Hall, the reviewer for *The New York Times* (October 3, 1927) attending the premiere, praised the "excellent Movietone features, in which the figurantes [such as Benito Mussolini, C.S.] were heard as well as seen," in a presentation of newsreel shorts that preceded the screening of *Sunrise*. But particularly Murnau's "masterpiece," "a mixture of Russian gloom and Berlin brightness," impressed the critic, who writes:

> Mr. Murnau shows himself to be an artist in camera studies, bringing forth marvelous results from lights, shadows and settings. He also proves himself to be a true story teller, and, incidentally, here is a narrative wherein the happy ending is welcome. [...] In a remarkable series of scenes one is taken through the city on a tram car, and then follow the adventures in an amusement park, in which a straying pig affords some of the comedy. Mr. Murnau does all his work quite differently from any other director and when he stoops to somewhat hilarious fun it does not matter, for it is filmed with astuteness and originality. [...] There is not a weak spot in any of the performances and the incidents are stamped with genuineness and simplicity. You find yourself thinking now and again that it is just the sort of thing farm people might do on going to Tilsit. Mr. Murnau proves by 'Sunrise' that he can do just as fine work in Hollywood as he ever did in Germany.[187]

Censors in Germany released the film in January 1928 but banned it for minors. Critics in Germany voiced their concern regarding the fidelity of the adaptation in view of the film's happy ending contrary to Sudermann's tragic story and narrative intent. But even the most disparaging of reviewers acknowledged the expressive aesthetic range and technological expertise of Murnau's movie and the stunning cinematography by Rosher and Struss. Heinrich Hauser, for example, wrote in *Frankfurter Zeitung* on January 11, 1928:

> Image after image is rich, possibly too rich in ideas. The abundance of aesthetic nuances, the care with which the essentials were teased out and the unimportant elements eliminated, it is so great that one can barely grasp it all as the plot moves on. We have never before seen such excellent cuts and overlaps or similarly animated landscapes. A tram going from the forest through suburbia and, after many bends, entering the center of a big city, is wonderful. Two human beings, who do nothing for a long time but breathe, breathing after a fast run, after a heavy blow, we have never seen anything like it.[188]

Eugen Gürster enthusiastically agreed with Hauser's review and wrote in the art journal *Kunstwart*: 'For the first time I experienced artistic processes only available to film—an indication of a purely cinematic psychology that virtually stands as a self-justified means of expression alongside the artistic elements such as the design of the epic narrative.'[189] Nonetheless, at a time of international successes of silent films produced in Germany, many in the industry were lulled into thinking that sound film would be a passing whim. Soon Ufa and other German film companies were seriously lagging behind in the race to bring talking pictures to national and international cinema screens, as the next chapter will outline in more detail.

Psychology, Doubles, and Adaptations

Writings and theories about the human mind have been prevalent since antiquity and the term 'psychology' as an academic inquiry into the workings of the soul was coined already in sixteenth-century humanism by Melanchthon. From around 1800, when the concept of a transcendental subject no longer provided comfort in a swiftly changing world, Dark Romanticism (L. Tieck, E.T.A. Hoffmann, M. Shelley, E.A. Poe, C. Baudelaire, etc.) explored subjectivity and human nature, often with a focus on an individual's torment and propensity for self-destruction. From the nineteenth century onwards the literary canon became increasingly populated with prose that offered stunning psychological penetration (Dostoevsky, Austen, Flaubert, L. Andreas-Salomé, etc.), while psychiatry impacted institutions and defined 'neuroses' and 'psychoses' as psychological ailments. By the time cinema came into being, psychology was still a young discipline that had already defined a number of different approaches and was being taught in a number of research institutes and universities on both sides of the Atlantic. In German-speaking countries, it was especially Sigmund Freud in Vienna, Wilhelm Wundt in Leipzig, Max Wertheimer in Berlin, and Oswald Külpe in Würzburg, who were instrumental not only in establishing psychology as an academic discipline but in communicating the relevance of their insights into a wider public.[190] The works of Musil, Schnitzler, Hesse, Thomas Mann, and many authors of literary modernity who addressed subjectivity in crisis were shaped significantly by the authors' interest in psychoanalysis.[191]

Not surprisingly, this interest in psychological processes is reflected on film, especially following the multi-facetted trauma of the First World War. Psychological dramas such as *Crainquebille* (FR, Jacques Feyder, 1922) or *L'Auberge rouge* (FR, Jean Epstein, 1923), *Greed* (US, Erich von Stroheim, 1924), and *Amok* (USSR, Kote Marjanishvili, 1927) may serve as evidence and highlight the impact of literature on early cinematic depictions of individuals in crisis, human ordeals, and the psychological effect of pain and trauma.[192] Like the other films mentioned, *Amok*—a silent Georgian psychological drama and adaptation—explores the topic of obsession. A first adaptation of Stefan Zweig's 1922 novella 'of passion', the film stars Nato Vachnadze as a woman seeking an abortion who becomes a doctor's (Aleksandre Imedashvili) object of sexual fixation. The novella subtly problematizes preoccupations with race and identity, while telling the story of a doctor from Leipzig who loses his footing after a number of lonely years working in Indonesia. Rather than exploring the protagonist's mental illness, however, the film focuses on the consequences of the drug-addicted doctor's indecent proposal made to the beautiful young woman seeking a termination of her pregnancy.

Obsession, sexual fixation, and the doubling of woman through this process of fetishization had already been explored in Hauptmann's novel *Phantom* (1915/23)[193] which was adapted for the cinema by Thea von Harbou and directed by F. W. Murnau in 1922. Screenwriter Willy Haas wrote at the time:

> Did Gerhart Hauptmann consider the film version when he wrote [his novel]? For it is an unparalleled 'film problem': this deepest emotional shock of a man whom the vision of a woman's body—unattainable, untouchable—hurls up into the heavens. And while he still exists in heaven, the physical phantom, the *Doppelgänger* offers herself to him, pushing him into the depths of hell. To possess the dream image; but only in the *Doppelgänger*; and thus not to possess it; and having to pay, having to steal, to become criminals for this tormenting body, through which one only gazes towards the other, the sacred one. This is one of the few, most complicated psychological conflicts attainable via film; a thousand times more attainable than via the theater stage. The *Doppelgänger* problem—we know it from Wegener's *Student of Prague*—is actually its own demonic, essentially spiritual film problem. The film problem of all film problems.'[194]

Haas not only highlights the cinematic practice of doubling and film as reality and fiction/fantasy at once, but also emphasizes cinema's role in representing both psychological disorders and the experience of modernity, even before the First World War.

The motif of the *Doppelgänger* was core to Wegener's and Ewers's early horror filmscript *Der Student von Prag* (DE, Stellan Rye, 1913)—inspired by *Faust* and the Dark Romanticism of Poe, Musset, and Hoffmann. The fantasy of doubling featured prominently in silent films such as *Der Andere* [The Other] (DE, Max Mack, 1913), *Der Golem* (DE, Paul Wegener/Henrik Galeen, 1915), *Homunculus* (6 parts, DE, Otto Rippert, 1916–17), *Lilith und Ly* (AT, Erich Kober, 1919; script by F. Lang), *Alraune und der Golem* (DE, Nils Chrisander, 1919), and *Das Cabinet des Dr. Caligari* to name some of the more prominent examples.[195] Whether it was the alienation of the worker from industrialized production processes, sweeping technological progress, mental illness as a result of (war) trauma, or the fragmentation experienced by city-dwellers due to the challenges of modern urban space, the motif captured the loss of a cohesive and balanced identity as a constituent of a peaceful and ordered society.

Romanticism is rife with examples of the "chronic dualism" (E.T.A. Hoffmann) of reality and fantasy that shapes, separates, and fragments the subject.[196] Austrian psychoanalysts and colleagues Otto Rank and Sigmund Freud both published on the *Doppelgänger*.[197] Rank's essay on the fantasy of the double (1914) was inspired by *Der Student von Prag* and influenced Sigmund Freund's article on "The Uncanny" (1919) that explores subjective identity, voyeurism, and repressed desire in the context of E.T.A. Hoffmann's *Der Sandmann* (1816). Cameraman Guido Seeber, who had filmed *Der Student von Prag* and the two *Golem* films, published an article in the journal *Die Kinotechnik* in 1919 on the technical intricacies of producing *Doppelgänger* images.[198] Throughout the 1920s, fragmented, uncertain, and dysfunctional identities and the motif of the *Doppelgänger* continue to haunt cinema.

Thea von Harbou's science fiction novel[199] and screenplay for Fritz Lang's *Metropolis* (1927) features a doubling of Maria (Brigitte Helm), the female protagonist, which leads to a dramatic confrontation between 'good' and 'evil' that nearly ends in catastrophe. Lang equips Maria's benevolent 'original' with plenty of religious iconography to communicate the ethics of her behavior. Soon, her spectacular, sexualized robot-double preaches hatred and incites violent action before performing as Anita Berber-look-alike in front of an all-male audience in the 'Casino'. Lang took inspiration from the famous dancer—who had appeared in all three of Lang's early *Mabuse*-films (1921–2)[200]—in terms of her art (choreography, style, costume) and sexual agency when creating this dance sequence of the monstrous-feminine.[201] Lang's formative science fiction dystopia not only includes a (more elaborate) enactment of a well-known Anita Berber performance, but also captures the male gaze and the audience's growing desire. Cameraman Gunther Rittau rewound the film several times for multiple exposures of close-ups of eyes and faces, thereby creating a collage that highlighted man's voyeuristic lust even more distinctly than in Dupont's aforementioned *Varieté*.

Moreover, the 'Casino' sequence could be read as a transposition of one of the poems in Berber's and Sebastian Droste's book of poetry and prose, photographs and drawings entitled *Die Tänze des Lasters, des Grauens und der Ekstase* (Dances of Vice, Horror, and Ecstasy, 1923).[202] Droste's choreography of Berber's 'Cocaine'-dance is included in their book as an Expressionist poem that features the lines: 'Many eyes/Millions of eyes/Woman/Nervously fluttering desire'.[203] Lang was not only entirely familiar with Berber's dance style and the couple's Expressionist choreographies, as Maria's dance reveals, but it seems also with this particular poem on the voyeuristic gaze struggling to dominate the female form in the spotlight. Taking cue from this poem, Maria's doubling into an evil performer and seductress thus not only differentiates between the pleasure principle (id) and moral authority (super-ego/"moralische Instanz") to use Sigmund Freud's psychic apparatus, but also places the audience as the 'I' (ego) in the midst of this entertaining spectacle. Thus any negotiation of the subject's desire according to the reality principle could intimate complex decision processes of modern individuals as well as the filmmaker's awareness of the workings of the human psyche, while consciously doubling the audience itself onto the multiply exposed cinema screen.[204] The ability of this highly accessible medium to survey and transmit the (mental) life of a human being and thus to confront viewers with their own fears and desires while reminding them of their (fragmented) humanity ensured film's impact on modern industrial society. As the decade drew to a close, representations of women as sexual beings and objects of voyeuristic lust became increasingly implicated in this debate.

Displaced Anxieties: Women and Sexuality at the End of the Decade

Richard Oswald, while sharing Toller's idea of a cinema that could provide both education and induce socio-political change, became increasingly pragmatic. Censors had begun to target particularly films about prostitutes and other 'fallen women', fearing their immoral effects on a rapidly changing society. Thus Oswald's aforementioned adaptation of Jerusalem's *Der heilige Skarabäus* (The Sacred Scarab, 1909) in *Die Rothausgasse* (1928) turned the story of Milada—the protagonist of Jerusalem's text who grew up in a brothel and worked as a prostitute from the age of sixteen—into a love story. While the novel sheds an unflinching light on prostitution as an everyday experience for the women and thereby normalizes their profession as work, Milada (Grete Mosheim) in Oswald's film enters (as a virgin) into a monogamous relationship with Gustel Brenner (Gustav Fröhlich), the son of the town's well-respected chief surgeon. Trying to leave the milieu she grew up in, the film foregrounds Milada's difficulties due to the prejudices of the town's upstanding citizens toward 'a girl from Red House Lane', but also highlights the conflict between Gustel and his highly educated bourgeois father, who initially opposed his son's relationship with Milada. Nonetheless, the film—after a number of melodramatic tribulations—ends happily and even includes the father's blessing of the happy couple.

Despite Oswald's efforts, however, the film was immediately banned by the Censorship Board in Berlin on March 2, 1928, on the grounds that the 'depiction of life in a brothel did not exert a sufficiently deterring effect'. Further criticism included the film's lack of 'will to purity' and the absence of a 'tragic moment'. Oswald's depictions of girls and young women—being assessed and priced 'as commodities' and pursuing their profession as a matter of course—were far too realistic and deemed unacceptable by the censors.[205] After its initial ban, *Die Rothausgasse* was only given a permit by the Supreme Board of Film Censors on September 12, 1928, after Richard Oswald Production LLC (G.m.b.H.) had lodged two further appeals. The permit was eventually granted on condition that all scenes were cut that highlighted the physicality of the prostitutes or suggested in any way sexual contact with clients, as scenes of this nature would—in the eyes of the censors—generate temptation. Knowing that brothels had been declared illegal in 1927, Oswald won his case against the censorship board based on the argument that 'there were no longer any brothels in Germany and therefore any temptation to go into one would surely have to remain unsatisfied!'

Nonetheless, the cuts made left the narrative fragmented and impinged significantly on both the affective communication of the novel's social criticism and the success of the adaptation in German cinemas. As Petro rightly points out, censorship of melodramatic films such as Karl Grune's *Die Strasse* [The Street] (DE, 1923), Bruno Rahn's *Dirnentragödie* [Tragedy of the Street/of the Prostitute] (DE, 1927)—or, indeed of adaptations such as Pabst's *Freudlose Gasse* or Oswald's *Die Rothausgasse*—indicates the displacement of anxieties about social justice, identity, or freedom onto "anxieties about women and sexual identity."[206]

Around the same time, G.W. Pabst turned again to literary texts that foreground the experience of 'fallen', marginalized women: Frank Wedekind's 'Lulu'-plays *Erdgeist* (Earth Spirit, 1895) and *Die Büchse der Pandora* (Pandora's Box, 1904) premiered as *Die Büchse der Pandora* on February 2, 1929, in Gloria-Palast in Berlin. At the time, he was already working on another adaptation of Margarete Böhme's *Tagebuch einer Verlorenen* [Diary of a Lost Girl], which was first brought to cinemas that autumn. In both films the American actor Louise Brooks plays the lead, a gorgeous visual symbol of the New Woman of the 1920s with her fashionably cropped hair and boyish figure—even though neither her Lulu nor her Thymian should be equated with simple indications of urban female emancipation or sexual liberation. Pabst's reimagination of Wedekind's 'Lulu'-plays on screen is visibly inspired by Leopold Jessner's 1923 film *Erdgeist* [Earth Spirit] starring Asta Nielsen. But Pabst's new adaptation unveils in stunning sophistication the making of a *femme fatale* on screen, whose death at the hands of Jack the Ripper in London is all but a logical consequence of her actions, yet with an undercurrent of ambiguity and deep "psychological penetration,"[207] as Eisner put it. Pabst foregrounded the destructive power of sexual desire rather than telling the ambivalent tale of dependency and passion inherent in Wedekind's plays. The narrative structure thus implies a logic of female (sexual) power being equated with and eradicated by death.[208]

While the film was criticized for its interpretation of Wedekind's plays that, according to one reviewer,[209] left all too little 'intact', it reflects the filmmakers' interest in testing "the limits of sexuality in relation to legal (or moral) jurisdiction."[210] Mary Ann Doane examines this "strategic immoralism" in the context of urban Weimar Germany's "pervasive sexual cynicism," which she reads as "a rejection of the romantic idealism and corresponding repression of an earlier era."[211] It is indeed Brooks' Lulu's ambivalence, her emotionally detached, manipulative "morbid sexuality,"[212] but also the "false dichotomy"[213] between good and evil that drives Pabst's *Pandora's Box*. While censors at the time had few objections relating to the overall femme fatale/delinquent woman[214] narrative due to her decisive elimination at the hands of Jack the Ripper as the film concludes, Lulu's sexual relationship with both Dr. Schön (Fritz Kortner) and his son Alwa (Franz/Francis Lederer) was judged offensive. Therefore, the son had to be reinvented as Dr. Schön's secretary on all title plates at the time, diminishing Wedekind's provocative intent and leaving Dr. Schön's paternal gestures toward his 'secretary' strangely ambiguous.[215]

Pabst's new *Tagebuch einer Verlorenen* takes leave from Oswald's predecessor film and adapts Böhme's literary text in a deeply personal and highly affective narrative on screen. In 1920s films such as *Freudlose Gasse* or *Abwege* [The Devious Path], the Austrian director had repeatedly dealt with the themes of 'fallen' girls or women to examine modern communities' (double) ethical standards and the social responsibility of an allegedly moral society. In his adaptation of Böhme's novel, Brooks plays Thymian as a serious, introverted girl who may seem curious, but does not at all appear hungry for life. The film begins with a close-up of a book being wrapped by an elderly lady (Aunt Frieda, played by Vera Pawlowa). It is the diary that will hold Thymian's secrets and record her (unspeakable) experiences. As Böhme had told her readers, she was only the editor of this authentic text; Pabst now foregrounds the journal—the written, supposedly 'genuine' text—as the basis of his film, thereby highlighting the link to both Böhme's work and, as the author had done, the authenticity of the narrative to follow.

The reference in the opening sequence to the material manifestation and record of society's failure of this young girl replaces Oswald's depiction of the lightness and exuberance of young Thymian prior to her rape a decade earlier. Pabst's Thymian does show feelings in the introductory sequence of the film, but they are restrained—polite gratitude on the day of her confirmation and obvious confusion when Elisabeth, the beloved housekeeper, is expelled from her home. Thymian cannot understand her departure and is visibly shaken by the news. A fade-in of a baby's jacket only visible to the viewer is an indication of her pregnancy (with her employer, Thymian's widowed father, the pharmacist Gotteball, played by Josef Rovenský, implicated as the father of the child). When the young woman's body is brought back to the house following her suicide, Thymian's deep shock upon recognizing Elisabeth prompts an immediate reaction: she runs from the scene. Later she faints at the sight of her father, who sits next to the new housekeeper Meta (Franziska Kinz) and, wasting no time in his pursuit of his sexual pleasure, has his arm around her. Meinert, her father's creepy assistant (Fritz Rasp), has his own intentions and leaves a note 'at half past seven in the pharmacy' in Thymian's diary. The girl is easy prey and obediently appears on time. Her self-pitying (intertitle) declaration 'I am all alone' is met with Meinert's assurance of care, and when she leans against the supposedly responsible and trustworthy adult, she faints once again. Meinert does not hesitate, carries her to his bed, and rapes her. A glass filled with red wine on the bedside table topples and falls as he pushes it away with Thymian's diary, causing dark stains on the white sheet.

How difficult it was in the late 1920s to depict sexual vulnerability and injury is reflected by the outcry of indignation that led to the shortening of this sequence on both sides of the Atlantic and the elimination of this 'staining' of the teenager by her rapist. With Sepp Allgeier[216] at the camera, Pabst directed our gaze to the blemish in a close-up, thus illustrating the forceful rupture of the unconscious girl's hymen causing her to bleed onto her rapist's sheets. The directness and clarity with which Pabst infuses this scene were too much for the censors, who also intervened elsewhere in the film and defused its critical intent.[217] In contrast to the novel, in which Thymian repeatedly states her (if ambivalent) yearning for alcohol and, especially, subsequent nocturnal meetings with Meinert, there is no expression of desire or lust in Pabst's film. Apart from a few short scenes that convey champagne-induced *joie de vivre* in a brothel, Thymian remains detached, almost like a bystander in a life she never got to choose.[218] Moments of pain, however, are clearly marked by an original pastiche of camera distances or mobile camera sequences—when having to leave her baby Erika at Widow Bolke's and, especially, after her escape from the reform school, when she is informed by her daughter's carer that the baby died and has just been taken away. Thymian subsequently ends up in a brothel, the only place where an unmarried 'fallen' woman and runaway from a reform school at the time would normally find shelter. Her first sexual encounter there is again marked by the young woman's powerlessness, followed by a close-up of Thymian's shocked expression in view of her symbolic objectification the next day, when the bawd joyfully presents her with an envelope containing banknotes.

Pabst not only points to the hopelessness of the situation of a 'fallen girl', but also criticizes society's double standards by contrasting the sexual behavior of men—like Thymian's father and his assistant Meinert, which is of no consequence for their social position—with the death of the pregnant housekeeper at the beginning and the plea for the raped and prostituted at the end of the film. In one of the most remarkable scenes in the movie, Thymian's well-meaning effort to help an overweight, middle-aged gentleman out of financial misery through a lottery with herself as the top prize in a nightclub leads to an encounter with the two men that had impacted most significantly on her life. For that evening, Thymian's father, his new wife Meta, and assistant Meinert had come into town for their annual visit and to this very establishment to marvel at 'the morass of the big city'. When the eyes of father and daughter meet, a sequence of shots communicates Thymian's longing, her suffering and isolation, ending with medium closeups of forlorn Thymian, but also of the rotund gentleman. There is sympathy for the latter in society despite its rigid morality, the film conveys, but not a tear is shed for the plight of someone like her. Subtly but unmistakably Pabst confronts viewers with affective economies in society's ambiguous system of determined and entirely gendered marginalization. At the beginning of the sequence Thymian tries to make her way through the dancing couples and even her father takes a step toward her. But all too quickly Gotteball is held back by his stern wife Meta, while Thymian stops in the middle of the dance floor. She is surrounded by life, laughter, and entertainment, but a close-up of her earnest face filled with sadness distances her from the hustle and bustle, and her gaze reveals only the child who wants to be with her father. But Meta and Meinert pull the pharmacist away, while their eye contact lingers for a moment longer. As he leaves with Meta and Meinert by his sides, Thymian's father turns around once more and looks at his daughter in a medium close-up shot. Their pain is visible, but bourgeois society upholds a moral system in which compassionate behavior seems impossible. Allgeier and Pabst record the cost of this hypocritical morality without melodramatic gestures, but in a no less affective manner. 'Yes, Thymian, <u>now</u> you are a lost girl', says the gentleman in tears, interpreting the concept of "being lost" not morally but as a tragic consequence of a family and a society that have turned their back on a vulnerable minor.

Brooks' mostly restrained depiction of Thymian is much more in line with Böhme's description of motherless Thymian who learnt to suppress her emotions already as a young child. Her rape by Meinert irretrievably changes her path. Only the generosity of an old count, willing to overlook the 'mistakes' of the young woman and who looks after her out of guilt, enables at least a partial reintegration into society. The film ends more positively than Böhme's text, but communicates a no less damning judgment on society's (bourgeois) institutions: the family, the reform school, the brothel.[219]

During Thymian's visit as a member of the 'Association for the Rescue of Endangered Girls' at the end of the film, the school presents a façade of loving care as an ironic duplication of a distorted reality that exposes 'the bacterial infection of treachery, hypocrisy, greed, cruelty and deceit'[220] at the heart of this institution and society as a whole, as Böhme put it. Böhme's

Thymian unveils this 'disease' as the actual social problem, responding to its lies with truth: Thymian exposes the performance of the school's management as a farce, revealing herself as a 'fallen one' and criticizes the 'foolishness' of those well-meaning women of the Rescue Association, whose moral upbringing will not help these girls in the slightest. In his film, Pabst foregrounds the young woman's pain. Apart from those few moments of lightheartedness that see Brooks' Thymian laughing straight into the camera, this adaptation emphasizes the young woman's deep sadness. Pabst thereby communicates Böhme's literary critique in no less affective if in more conciliatory terms. In his adaptation, the relationship between Thymian and the old count for example remains benevolent and asexual, in contrast to the novel, in which Thymian's sexual exploitation continues until her terminal illness finally changes the dynamics of her liaison with the old nobleman. Nonetheless Pabst's adaptation renewed Böhme's plea for a more humane and just society, and ensured the survival of the nearly forgotten literary text and former bestseller to this day.

When *Tagebuch einer Verlorenen* premiered first in Vienna (September 27, 1929) and in Berlin (October 14, 1929), the reception by both critics and audiences was lukewarm at best, even though the 'transposition of the diary' as a personal and intimate document and the degree of 'authenticity' that the moving pictures revealed were remarked upon.[221] Respective censorship boards had ordered massive cuts to remove 'offensive' passages and the film's critique of bourgeois society's ambiguous philistine morality, leaving the narrative truncated and in several instances difficult to follow. Rudolf Leonhardt reported to Lotte Eisner that when he saw the film in Paris, almost the entire second half had vanished. But even if the film had been spared such mutilations, it still lacked sound. And by 1929, sound film was becoming all the rage.

The final significant adaptation of German-language literature of this decade based on Arthur Schnitzler's 1924 novella *Fräulein Else* is still a silent movie, but not only displays the expertise and craft of its makers but also summarizes the decade's most captivating technological innovations and aesthetic imaginations. Thanks to a restored version[222] of the film, it is now easily available and will hopefully receive the attention it deserves.

Already in April 1927, Schnitzler had written to actor Elisabeth Bergner to inquire about the possibility of an adaptation for cinema with her in the lead role: 'You know, dear Fräulein, how much it would mean to me if you took on Else in a screen adaptation. I can hardly imagine her other than with you in the picture.'[223] Other letters in his estate indicate the author's interest and involvement in the process of bringing this project to fruition. Paul Czinner wrote the script and directed the film, and Elisabeth Bergner, who later married Czinner in London, played Else to the author's delight. On January 10, 1929, Schnitzler wrote to Bergner that Carl Mayer, probably the most prominent screenwriter of the Weimar Republic beginning with *The Cabinet of Dr. Caligari* (1920) and a fellow Austrian, had shared a "highly significant" idea for their *Fräulein Else*-adaptation, which indicates that the film could have served as a catalyst for a truly avant-garde sound film aesthetic.[224] Mayer had proposed creating an adaptation in which only Else is visible in a homogeneous space, surrounded by a soundscape of her thoughts, voices, and the noise of the everyday. His suggestion was both deeply literary and informed by the latest sound technology, taking its cue perhaps from James Joyce's *Ulysses* (which had been published in German in 1927)[225] and certainly from Schnitzler's own text. His novella *Fräulein Else* consists of mostly interior monologues—a new narrative mode, which Schnitzler had employed for the first time in his pioneering antihero tale *Lieutenant Gustl* in 1900.

His *Fräulein Else* is a young, bourgeois, well-educated Viennese, self-conscious but not naïve, who receives a letter from her mother while on holiday with relatives. In this letter, her mother informs her about her father's imminent financial (and social) ruin, and implores her to approach Mr. Dorsday, a rich art dealer also on vacation in the resort, to ask for a significant loan of 30,000 guilders. When Else finally approaches him to explain her family's crisis, Dorsday agrees to provide the loan—under one condition. He wants to see Else naked. After her initial indignation has passed, she begins to realize the dilemma she now faces. Will she reject Dorsday's offer and maintain her dignity and demonstrate her independence, thereby risking her father's future, or will she oblige and follow her sense of loyalty and commitment to her family? Torn between her longing for self-determination and her devotion to her parents, Else cannot decide. The thought of displaying her body for money deems her a deplorable form of prostitution, which is less a moral than an emancipatory issue for this young 1920s city-dweller. Most of the novella consists of Else's thoughts, emotions, her sense of self in a stream of consciousness that weighs all sides and reflects a range of psychological patterns of behavior[226] brought to the fore by this predicament.

Apart from a number of small adjustments with regard to the narrative, there are only two significant changes: in his script, Czinner established that the father's financial ruin was not caused by embezzlement but by an ill-advised stock market investment, which seemed fitting even though the film premiered on March 7, 1929, in Berlin, more than seven months prior to the devastating stock market crash and ensuing global economic crisis. In both novella and film Else resolves the quandary by displaying herself naked to Dorsday in public, thereby avoiding the potential intimacy of his room, and embodying his demand as she takes off her coat and stands naked for all to see. While both take Veronal, a strong soporific drug, Else in the literary text might only be slipping into a deep sleep. Else in Czinner's film dies from an overdose as the film concludes. In the end, she cannot sacrifice herself, so sacrifice remains the only option. The film explores this modern Möbius strip of Else's psyche, twisting itself around a kaleidoscope of contradictory emotions until its final disintegration provides the resolve it craves. Her unwillingness to become a rich man's possession and a lack of self-preservation drive her to suicide. Karl Freund peels away Else's outer layers until we begin to see who she is. His camera introduces Else as a carefree girl, full of the confidence of youth and life, and then follows Else along hotel corridors, capturing her hesitancy, revealing her shyness as she negotiates her own position between parental expectation and self-respecting independence.

Freund's position in modern celebrity culture is revealed in the opening credits, when his name as director of photography follows immediately after the three star actors: Elisabeth Bergner (Else), Albert Bassermann (her father, Dr. Alfred Thalhof), and Albert Steinrück (Herr von Dorsday, an art dealer). His innovative cinematography, beginning with his 'unchained' camera in *Der letzte Mann/The Last Laugh* and *Varieté*, continues here, but is elegant, subtle, impartial. This is the cinematography of New Objectivity, the dominant aesthetic of the late 1920s, that sought to reflect reality—not as a highly emotional outcry as in Expressionism, but in a detached, analytical manner.

Documentary footage of the 1928 Winter Olympics, which took place in St. Moritz in Switzerland, marks the place where Else, her aunt, and cousin spend their holiday. Their train journey, beautifully documented in traveling and tracking shots, the sports events, and the actors' enjoyment of their own spectatorship, is folded into the Else's very personal and lonely predicament. By intercutting documentary sequences of sports events, tourist attractions, or the everyday in their luxury accommodation, the film provides distance from Else's emotional conundrum, also thanks to Bergner, a "[v]ibrant, sensitive, [...] actress of great nervous intellectuality," as Eisner put it:

> Elisabeth Bergner had as it were taken up the mantle of Asta Nielsen in the second half of the twenties. Up to the advent of Hitler, she embodied the spirit of an age which was ardent, anguished, intensely spiritual and still very close to the expansive ecstasy of the immediate postwar years.[227]

But Else's anguish in Czinner's film remains internal and veiled, only revealed by a cinematography that avoids melodrama, but instead captures "latent mood with close-ups of faces in which the passage of an emotion was reflected like a cloud crossing a limpid sky,"[228] as Eisner expresses it so well. Together Czinner and Freund offered a level and depth of psychological realism in their cinematography, which was profoundly inspired by Else's internal monologues of Schnitzler's literary text: the timing of long sequences and varying camera distances; the camera's hesitant, careful approximation and then motionless gaze on increasingly desperate, young Else; its subtle trailing of the young woman for much of the film in a linear and yet discursive manner just like a train of thought; the symbolic engagement of landscape. Had their silent film not premiered at the onset of the era of sound cinema, the creativity of this adaptation could have provided visual stimuli for decades to come.

Conclusion

Economic and political chaos, social hardship, and a catastrophic sense of defeat were some of the dire realities for Germany after the First World War. But as this chapter hoped to highlight, the wide-ranging turmoil of this decade also prepared a most fertile ground for innovation and stunning developments in avant-garde culture. The immediate postwar period provided filmmakers with unknown liberties due to an absence of censorship until 1920, and controversial novels or plays could now be brought to cinemas. Several notable writers considered film the most effective medium for the communication of values required in a modern society, and some of the most prominent filmmakers adapted literature to highlight social problems and spark debates in Weimar Germany's public sphere. Literature and film became active agents in the construction of this young democracy. The years 1924 to 1929 offered a period of relative economic stability, which encouraged film companies to bring spectacular productions to a mass audience eager to partake in a growing celebrity culture and lavish 'prestige productions'. Numerous adaptations of this era—*Nibelungen, Varieté, Faust, Dr. Mabuse,* and the sci-fi masterpiece *Metropolis* to name but a few—have had a lasting impact on cinema and cultural history.

The crash at Wall Street in 1929 reignited not only economic anxieties, but a sense of unmerited, prolonged humiliation among increasing numbers of the young republic's citizens, many of whom would soon turn to Hitler's NSDAP for illusions of comfort and pride. During this period of instability of both the new democratic state and its modern subjects' sense of identity, the public's escapist desire was at an all-time high. Cinema provided mass entertainment from dazzling adventures to poignant melodramas but also continued its efforts to bridge the cultural divide in view of the 'high arts' with adaptations of the literary canon. For the most part, however, adaptations of works by Schiller, Goethe, Kleist, or Büchner reflect a lack of aesthetic and narrative autonomy as reviewers and educated bourgeois audiences—well familiar with these works—were generally quite obsessed with fidelity and more critical when the adaptation failed to be suitably faithful to the literary work. Others of course considered faithful adaptations completely tiresome and celebrated films like Lamprecht's *Buddenbrooks* precisely because it had no intention to abide by the fidelity camp's conservative demand of 'completeness' and instead presented a narrative with a clear focus and entirely suitable for cinema.[229]

Despite postwar volatility and hyperinflation in the early 1920s, the output of motion picture production companies and the number of cinemas grew steadily. The film industry's rapacious appetite for suitable narratives led to collaborations with writers, publishers, and newspaper editors and ensured a steady flow of adaptations of popular literature. Increasingly, contemporary German-language literature dominated cinema production in Germany and Austria. Serialized prose as well as well-known novels by bourgeois authors such as Thomas Mann and Stefan Zweig and controversial bestsellers by Else Jerusalem, Margarete Böhme, Hugo Bettauer, and others discussed above, were brought to cinema by some of the most outstanding and innovative screenwriters, directors, and cameramen of the time.[230]

The fabulous creativity and highly innovative performative practices of contemporary German theater—from Naturalist plays by Hauptmann to the works of avant-garde and Expressionist playwrights such as Wedekind, Sternheim, Kaiser, Toller, and Brecht—had a considerable impact on the rest of Europe.[231] The success of contemporary theater productions both within German-speaking countries and abroad explains the number of silent film adaptations of plays even prior to a more pronounced shift toward theater productions to be witnessed elsewhere following the introduction of sound. Filmmakers populated cinema screens with both conventional and marginal figures in socio-political tragedies, powerful thrillers, light-hearted comedies, entertaining or melodramatic love stories, but also subtle psychological dramas such as *Fräulein Else* based on Schnitzler. Ufa, Germany's largest and most powerful motion picture production company at the time, had a "penchant for monumentalism"[232] and supported grand cinema spectacles such as Lang's *Nibelungen* or Murnau's *Faust*. Literature served as inspiration, in terms of not only the narratives it offered, but aesthetically and politically. During this 'golden age' of silent cinema, more than a third of all films produced in Germany during the decade were based on literary texts. Overall, the majority of films produced in the 1920s still remembered today as innovative masterpieces are in fact adaptations. Many more are nearly forgotten, but perhaps this chapter will help to revive their memory.

Adaptations were shaped by postwar reality and often meant to serve as social commentary. Especially prior to the introduction of censorship legislation, adaptations of well-known, controversial literary texts could be interpreted as pragmatic and profit-driven. But filmmakers such as Oswald or producers like Porten clearly meant to intervene and their works made important contributions to debates on equality and justice. During a time of fundamental changes to woman's place in society and to definitions of traditional gender roles, for example, the fate of 'fallen girls' and the brutal marginalization of unconventional, sexually active women depicted in literature was brought to a mass audience and thus to the public sphere. The political spectrum of the Weimar Republic from left to extreme right was visible not only on the street, but on cinema screens, and is reflected in adaptations from social problem films and provocative displays of exploitation in, for example, Zelnik's *The Weavers*, to representations of mythical heroism in adaptations of national epics like Lang's *Nibelungen*.

Films of the decade offered an enormous range of plots and themes across all genres. The film industry's hunger for stories on the one hand and its interest in maximizing potential audiences across the social spectrum ensured the production of significant numbers of adaptations of both popular and classical literatures. The latter catered particularly to middle-class audiences' interest in high culture and educational, rather than frivolous, entertainment. Adaptations of the classics reinforced core elements of an imagined German identity during a time of dramatic uncertainty and transformation. The majority of notable adaptations produced during this decade, however, focus either on social problems to affect change or highlight the crisis of the modern subject. Authors like Toller or H. Mann considered film the medium that could help in the construction of a just, peaceful, and democratic society more than any other. Source texts chosen for adaptation reveal filmmakers' commitment to civil society and Germany's first experiment in democracy. Most prevalent among the recurring themes in films at the time are woman's place and role in society. Their experiences—sexual exploitation, repressive moral and patriarchal structures, the devastating marginalization of so-called 'fallen girls'—are depicted in a significant range of adaptations from Gretchen in *Faust* to Thymian in *Diary of a Lost Girl*. Their commodification and objectification highlighted by popular authors Bettauer or Böhme, artists like Berber, and implied even by T. Mann are foregrounded in adaptations of their works due to film technology and innovative camera perspectives.

Normative and repressive structures of society and the crisis of the modern individual are favorite themes of avant-garde filmmakers at the time and impact the choice of literary texts for adaptation. Depictions of automatons and *Doppelgänger*—reflecting the unstable modern self—were particularly popular, indicating cinemagoers' interest in the medium not merely as entertainment but as innovative visual and narrative practices. The study of adaptations and their source texts also clearly reveals the impact of censorship on potential depictions of sexually active women. Censors ensured 'moral decency' by eliminating indications of rape or survival sex but allowed film narratives that explored the destructive power of female sexuality and thus contributed to the prevalence of the *femme fatale* on cinema screens. Another adaptation of Ewers' *Alraune* (DE, Henrik Galeen, 1927) and other movies discussed in this chapter end in the death of the young vamp. She is the outsider, who represents instability, darkness, and chaos, and her suggested removal reinforces the repressive moralities avant-garde filmmakers sought to challenge. Often, it is only the camera of innovators like Karl Freund that contests perspectives and manifests the isolation and objectification of women at the time.

Finally, cinema's ability to entertain the masses secured its continued and profitable rise. Comedies that pushed the boundaries of censorship regulations while remaining just within their limits proved exceedingly popular. Especially humorous depictions of married life with just enough sexual connotations, and hilarious caricatures of the philistine spirit (bourgeois and yet subservient) were on the rise. When Sternheim's comedy *Die Hose* (The Pants) premiered in 1911 in theater, the play about a young but respectable woman losing her underpants in public caused considerable scandal and had to be shut down. In 1927/8, its transposition in a screenplay by Franz Schulz was filmed under the direction of Hans Behrendt.[233]

The silent movie featuring[234] Jenny Jugo as Luise Maske, Werner Krauß as her husband Theobald, and Christian Bummerstedt as the Prince became a box-office hit. The working- and lower-middle-class cinemagoers were delighted and grateful consumers of hilariously ironic portrayals of those guardians of culture that would have been instrumental in banning Sternberg's play from theaters in the first place. Having access to *Kintöppe* and other cheap cinemas, plays like *The Pants* could now be (re)integrated into a public sphere no longer dominated by conservative "Bildungsphilister" or educated philistines, as Nietzsche's Zarathustra called them. No other genre proved as perpetually valuable as comedy with its promise of laughter and light-hearted escapism.

Some of the most enduring highlights of German silent cinema were produced during this decade and brought international fame to numerous directors and actors—some of whom, like Murnau, continued their careers in Hollywood with adaptations of German-language literature. By the end of the decade in the United States, sound cinema was well established. In Europe, and especially in Germany, motion picture production companies scrambled to catch up, while even masterful silent films soon failed to secure sufficient interest among mass audiences.

Notes

1 "Basis für alle neue kommende Kunst ist das Kino." Yvan Goll, "Das Kinodram," *Die neue Schaubühne* 2.6 (June 1920): 142.
2 Demilitarization and the reduction of troops to 100,000 as well as the reduction of German landmass became major points of contestation and fuelled fascism and a growing Nazi movement in the 1920s.
3 The constitution of the Weimar republic can be accessed here: http://www.verfassungen.de/de19-33/verf19-i.htm. Universal suffrage is granted in article 22.

4   For further information, see for example my entry on "Women within the City (Berlin 1900–1933)," in *Encyclopedia of Urban Literary Studies*, ed. Jeremy Tambling (London: Palgrave, online 2021; print 2022); https://link.springer.com/referenceworkentry/10.1007/978-3-319-62592-8_197-1; and "Lotte Reiniger and Female Creativity in the Weimar Republic," co-author: Aneka Meier, in *Beyond Prince Achmed*, 31–69.
5   Bock/Töteberg, "A History of Ufa," 287.
6   Quoted by Michael Töteberg in "Ohne Rücksicht auf die Qualität," Bock/Töteberg, *Das Ufa-Buch*, 74.
7   Provider of popular literary escapism in over 200 novels, Hedwig Courths-Mahler was the most successful writer during this era in terms of book sales (approx. 80 million; cf. Andreas Graf, *Hedwig Courths-Mahler* (Munich: dtv, 2000), 8. The popularity of her rather formulaic romantic works led to numerous adaptations, among them: *Die Wilde Ursula* [Wild Ursula] (DE, Georg Victor Mendel, 1917), *Ich lasse dich nicht* [I Won't Let You Go] (DE, Franz Eckstein/Erik Eriksen, 1919), and *Die schöne Miss Lilian* [Beautiful Ms Lilian] (DE, Franz Eckstein, 1920). Franz Eckstein worked repeatedly with Henny Porten's sister and soon his wife Rosa Porten on Courths-Mahler adaptations: *Opfer der Liebe* [Victims of Love], *Durch Liebe erlöst* [Redeemed by Love], *Deines Bruders Weib* [Your Brother's Wife] (all 1921).
8   Jasmin Lange, *Der deutsche Buchhandel und der Siegeszug der Kinematographie 1895–1933: Reaktionen und strategische Konsequenzen* (Wiesbaden: Harrassowitz, 2010), 105–11, here 106. Lange quotes Ute Schneider, *Buchkäufer*, 154–6.
9   Cf. Lange, *Der deutsche Buchhandel und der Siegeszug der Kinematographie 1895–1933*, 105–11.
10 Ibid., 104 and 111.
11 Serialized novels published by historian George L. Mosse's grandfather Rudolf, for example, were bought by Ufa via its subsidiary Kronen-Filme. Cf. Töteberg, *Das Ufa-Buch*, 75.
12 For further information, see Klaus Kreimeier, *The Ufa Story: A History of Germany's Greatest Film Company, 1918–1945* (Berkeley: University of California Press, 1999), 74.
13 The adaptation was directed by Lupu Pick and starred Max Adalbert, Otto Treptow, and Eugen Rex for Pick's Rex-Film. Apart from being a bestselling prose author, Fulda was one of the most popular playwrights of his time. He failed to leave Nazi-Germany in time and took his own life in 1939, after being denied a visa to the United States.
14 Mayer successfully adapted Stendhal's novella *Vanina Vanini* for Ufa: *Vanina* (DE, Arthur von Gerlach, 1922).
15 Mayer suggested camera movements in his scripts, for example, to *Der letzte Mann* (1924) and *Tartüff* (1925, based on Molière). Töteberg, *Das Ufa-Buch*, 75.
16 See, for example, the filmography in Dietrich Scheunemann, ed., *Expressionist Film*.
17 *Lichtbild-Bühne* 11.46 (1918): 67. The article was included in an exhibition at the Deutsches Literaturarchiv, Schiller-Nationalmuseum Marbach/N. entitled: *Hätte ich das Kino! Die Schriftsteller und der Stummfilm*, April 24

to October 31, 1976. The exhibition catalogue was edited by Ludwig Greve, Margot Pehle, and Heidi Westhoff (Munich: Kösel, 1976). Cf. *Hätte ich das Kino*, p. 85f.

18 The political correspondent of the *Berliner Tageblatt*, Bruno Stümke, questioned the city's priorities in "Kino, Kabarett und Wohnungsnot" on October 11, 1919. The text is also included in Ludwig Greve, ed. et al., *Hätte ich das Kino*, 87.

19 Hauptmann in a letter to screenwriter Kyser; Greve, *Hätte ich das Kino!*, 264.

20 There are different versions of the film available in archives (DK, DFI, etc.) and on YouTube, which range from 63 to 107 minutes in length.

21 Martin Proskauer, "Eine bösartige Dunkelkammer," *Film-Kurier* 28 (February 3, 1920); https://www.filmportal.de/node/41585/material/613140.

22 In the early 1920s, the production of children's films in Germany was a marginal occupation at best. Lotte Reiniger's silhouette films *Aschenputtel* (Cinderella, 1922) and her ground-breaking animated feature *Die Abenteuer des Prinzen Achmed* (1926) are among the few exceptions. The success of Reiniger's *Prince Achmed* and a first adaptation of Waldemar Bonsels' bestselling children's book *Die Biene Maja und ihre Abenteuer* (Bee Maja and her adventures, 1912) the same year provided the necessary impetus for the industry to take note of a potential new market. Wolfram Junghans's film (1926) about the hardworking, cheeky, and adventurous bee established a new genre of educational children's films that wove plenty of information about nature, evolution, botany, and insects into the narrative fabric of Maja's adventurous journey. Cf. Karin Herbst-Messlinger, "Kindheit," in *Kino der Moderne. Film der Weimarer Republik* (exhibition catalogue; edited by Kunst- und Ausstellungshalle der Bundesrepublik Deutschland, Bonn, and Deutsche Kinemathek, Berlin; Dresden: Sandstein, 2018), 34–9, here p. 35.

23 The 'Berlin novel' *Das Mädchen mit dem Goldhelm* (The Girl with the Golden Helmet, 1918) by Hans Land (Hugo Landsberger) which was adapted by PAGU film in 1919 under the direction of Victor Janson was another adaptation to emerge during the immediate postwar period that portrayed the dire consequences of outmoded definitions of propriety for families.

24 *Der Kinematograph* 633 (February 19, 1919), cf. selection of reviews on filmportal.de.

25 Ibid., http://www.filmportal.de/node/26151/material/730289 (accessed January 5, 2015); see also Bock, "Filmographie," in Belach, ed. et al., *Richard Oswald*, 152.

26 Tucholsky's article can also be found in Greve, ed. et al., *Hätte ich das Kino*, 84.

27 Foucault, *History of Sexuality*, 3.

28 I'm borrowing the words of Bassnett and Lefevere here (foreword, p. ix) here, which is also quoted by Laurence Raw in his introduction to *Translation, Adaptation and Transformation* (New York: Bloomsbury, 2012), 1.

29 Carlo Mierendorff, *Hätte ich das Kino!* (Berlin: Erich Reiß, 1920), 10 and 44.

30 See for example Schönfeld, ed., *Commodities of Desire: The Prostitute in Modern German Literature*, 2000.

31 After the end of the war the German economy collapsed, inflation and unemployment soared, many families were left without a breadwinner, and the numbers of women that had to resort to occasional prostitution increased steadily. In addition, returning soldiers who had contracted STIs in brothels passed them on to their partners at home. See a.o. Michaela Freund-Widder, *Frauen unter Kontrolle: Prostitution und ihre staatliche Bekämpfung in Hamburg vom Ende des Kaiserreiches bis zu den Anfängen der Bundesrepublik* (Münster: Lit, 2003); Sabine Gleß, *Die Reglementierung von Prostitution in Deutschland* (Berlin: Duncker & Humblot, 1999); Victoria Harris, *Selling Sex in the Reich. Prostitutes in German Society, 1914–1945* (Oxford: Oxford University Press, 2010); Julia Roos, *Weimar through the Lens of Gender. Prostitution Reform, Woman's Emancipation, and German Democracy, 1919–33* (Ann Arbor: University of Michigan Press, 2010).
32 Marie von Ebner-Eschenbach, *Margarete* (Stuttgart: Cotta, 1897).
33 Ebner-Eschenbach, *Margarete*, 13 and 28.
34 Ibid., 31.
35 Ibid., 37 and 105.
36 Ibid., 144.
37 Rosa Porten was a pioneer of screenwriting in German from 1910, as Gabriele Hansch and Gerlinde Waz outline in their *Filmpionierinnen in Deutschland. Ein Beitrag zur Filmgeschichtsschreibung* (unpublished manuscript).
38 Corinna Müller, "Der verkaufte Star. Henny Porten—Schauspielerin und Kapitalanlage," in *Das Ufa-Buch*, 48–50, here p. 48.
39 Kurt Pinthus, "Henny Porten for President," first published in *Das Tage-Buch* 2.41 (October 15, 1921), 1243–7; an English translation is included in Anton Kaes, ed. et al., *The Promise of Cinema: German Film Theory, 1907–1933* (Berkeley: University of California Press, 2016), 319–23.
40 Pinthus, "Henny Porten for President," 320.
41 Ibid., 322.
42 This is Müller's account of the event in "Der verkaufte Star," 49.
43 Ibid.; as Müller rightly points out, Porten's international success in *Anna Boleyn* (DE, Ernst Lubitsch, 1920) consolidates her position as a "Künstlerin," i.e., film artist.
44 Müller, "Der verkaufte Star," 49. Müller emphasizes that it was her exceptional and very creative engagement with gender issues (cf. *Hintertreppe*, 1921), which leads to her company's bankruptcy.
45 Wolfgang Leppmann, *Gerhart Hauptmann* (Berlin: Ullstein, 2007), 235.
46 A recurring image in Weimar film, even in Schiller adaptations like *Wilhelm Tell* (1923).
47 Kurt Tucholsky, "Was fehlt dem Kino?" *Berliner Tageblatt* (November 2, 1919); excerpt included in Greve, ed. et al., *Hätte ich das Kino,* 163f.
48 Bierbaum wrote the first German travel 'by car' diary: *Eine empfindsame Reise im Automobil* (A Sentimental Journey in an Automobile, 1903).
49 Cf. Greve, ed. et al., *Hätte ich das Kino,* 163.
50 Marion Faber, "Hofmannsthal and the Film," *German Life and Letters* 32 (1979): 187–95.
51 This public notice was included in the aforementioned *Hätte ich das Kino* exhibition and catalogue. Cf. Greve, ed. et al., *Hätte ich das Kino,* 164.

52 *Lichtbild-Bühne* 26 (June 28, 1919); cf. materials available on filmportal.de.
53 https://www.filmportal.de/node/6393/material/682138: *Der Kinematograph* 656 (July 30, 1919).
54 Ibid.
55 According to filmportal.de; cf. https://www.filmportal.de/film/prinz-kuckuck_c92fbcf7a2324bd98a48944a8455d1c4.
56 According to Estermann, *Die Verfilmung literarischer Werke*, 42.
57 Cf. adaptations of works by, for example, Margarete Böhme, Frank Wedekind, or Arthur Schnitzler. While also fitting in this category, Oswald's *Reigen* (1920), however, is not an adaptation of Schnitzler's play, despite sometimes being listed as such.
58 Cf. *Süddeutsche Zeitung* 25 (1923): 3; Promo-Film's reply is included in Ludwig Greve, ed. et al., *Hätte ich das Kino*, 189.
59 See "Film-Rundschau," *Neue Freie Presse* 21317 (January 15, 1924): 16.
60 Sabine Hake, "Lubitsch's Period Films as Palimpsest: On Passion and Deception," in *Framing the Past: The Historiography of German Cinema and Television*, ed. Bruce A. Murray and Christopher J. Wickham (Carbondale: Southern Illinois University Press, 1992), 68–98, here p. 80. Hake recounts how the German press used Lubitsch's period films and their international success "to indulge a renewed sense of national pride". Ibid., 76f.
61 Cf. Estermann, *Die Verfilmung literarischer Werke*, 43–84.
62 Cf. §18 of the 1920 Cinema Act or "Lichtspielgesetz" and Ernst Seeger's legal elaborations in *Reichslichtspielgesetz vom 12. Mai 1920* (Berlin: Heymanns, 1923).
63 For further information see Sara Hall, "Inflation and Devaluation: Gender, Space and Economics in G.W. Pabst's *Joyless Street* (1925)," in *Weimar Cinema: An Essential Guide to Classic Films of the Era*, ed. Noah Isenberg (New York: Columbia University Press, 2008), 135–54.
64 Paul Möbius writes in his provocative essay, first published in 1900, *Über den physiologischen Schwachsinn des Weibes* (Halle: Marhold, ^{5}1903) about the 'unnatural aspirations' of feminists and 'modern women' that threaten the health of humanity. 'Nature [...] wanted women to be mothers. [...] If a woman denies this service to her species, if she wants to 'realize herself' as an individual, she will be overcome by illness.' Needless to say, Möbius also warned of the detrimental effects of 'abusing' women's brains (at a time when universities in Germany were beginning to allow women full access to third-level education, in some cases up to doctoral level). Cf. Möbius, as above, 28.
65 Cf. Review of "From Morning to Midnight" by Juliet Jacques in *Cineaste* 36.2 (Spring 2011), accessed online: https://www.cineaste.com/spring2011/from-morning-to-midnight-web-exclusive.
66 Piscator, "Mein Freund Toller," *Schriften*, 341–4, here p. 342.
67 Manfred Lichtenstein, "Von morgens bis mitternachts," in *Deutsche Spielfilme von den Anfängen bis 1933. Ein Filmführer*, ed. Günther Dahlke and Günter Karl (Berlin: Henschel, ^{2}1993), 44f.
68 Georg Kaiser, *Von morgens bis mitternachts*, part 1; see for example, the Reclam edition (Stuttgart: Reclam, 1987), 24.
69 Kaiser, *Von morgens bis mitternachts*, 42.

70 Werner Funck and Martin Harwig directed two sequels to the popular adaptation.
71 At the same time, Keller's *Kleider machen Leute* (DE, Hans Steinhoff, 1921) was produced in Vienna. Whether Richard Eichberg's 1921 film *Tod in Venedig* [Death in Venice] is in fact an adaptation of Thomas Mann's novella could not be verified. The film seems to be lost. See also *Die Entstehung der Eidgenossenschaft* (CH, Emil Harder, 1924) based on Schiller's *Wilhelm Tell*.
72 In 1927 Richard Oswald's silent film *Feme* premiered, based on Vicki Baum's 1922 novel that traces an assassination plot inspired by the murder of Walter Rathenau by right-wing extremists. Not only the film, but also the director and the author of the source text suffered severe criticism and numerous verbal attacks by the far-right and members of the NSDAP.
73 Stefan Drössler in the booklet accompanying the DVD, "Der Fall *Nathan der Weise*" (Munich: Filmmuseum München, 2006); for a summary, see https://www.edition-filmmuseum.com/product_info.php/info/p26_Nathan-der-Weise.html. For further context, see Siegbert S. Prawer, *Between Two Worlds: The Jewish Presence in German and Austrian Film, 1910–1933* (London: Berghahn Books, 2007), 20.
74 This section is based on my article "Buddenbrooks im Stummfilm," in *Metzler Handbuch: Thomas Manns Buddenbrooks*, ed. Stefan Neuhaus and Nicole Mattern (Stuttgart: Metzler, 2018), 58–63. Permission to reuse some of the content and Eva Bourke's translation of same is gratefully acknowledged.
75 Hake, *Film in Deutschland*, 67.
76 Lamprecht deleted, for example, the Travemünde storyline and the Schwarzkopf family in its entirety from the original script. Cf. Deutsche Kinemathek, Schriftgut Archiv/document archive (=DK).
77 Gerhard Lamprecht, "Letter to Carolyn Lamont," May 16, 1970, DK.
78 Thomas Mann, "Über den Film," *Internationale Filmschau* 11.12 (1929): 12–13, here p. 12.
79 Cf. transcript of interview, Gerhard Lamprecht and Luise Heilborn-Körbitz, September 4, 1957, DK.
80 Thomas Mann, *Buddenbrooks* (Frankfurt/M.: Fischer, ³1986), 289.
81 Mann, *Buddenbrooks*, 106f., 114f.
82 Luise Heilborn-Körbitz/Alfred Fekete, *Buddenbrooks* (screenplay), 1922/23, DK, 22–3.
83 Peter Zander notes this anticipation of Sergej Eisenstein's montage in Peter Zander, *Thomas Mann im Kino* (Berlin: Bertz+Fischer, 2005), 65.
84 Stefan Grossmann, "Buddenbrooks. Der verfilmte Thomas Mann," *Montag Morgen* (September 3, 1923), DK.
85 Also in 1923 E.A. Dupont directed *Die grüne Manuela—Ein Film aus dem Süden* [Green Manuela, a film from the South] based on Clara Ratzka's novel *Die grüne Manuela* (1919).
86 Anton Kaes, "Film in der Weimarer Republik," in *Geschichte des deutschen Films*, ed. Wolfgang Jacobsen, Anton Kaes, and Hans H. Prinzler (Stuttgart: Metzler, 1993), 39–100, here p. 71; See also Zander, *Thomas Mann im Kino*, 196.
87 Georg Simmel, *Philosophie des Geldes* (Frankfurt/M.: Suhrkamp, 1989), 179, 520; also 482–541.

88 Puszel, "Filmschau," *Die rote Fahne* (September 12, 1923); Herbert Ihering, "Die Buddenbrooks im Film," *Berliner Börsen-Courier* (September 1, 1923); M—s, H., "Buddenbrooks, Tauentzienpalast," *Film-Kurier* (September 1, 1923); Ng., "Der Film der Woche: Buddenbrooks," *Berliner Lokal-Anzeiger* (September 3, 1923); cf. document archive, DK.
89 A collection of reviews, including the Lübeck local press, can be found in the archives of the Deutsche Kinemathek in Berlin, which Gerhard Lamprecht served as its first director in the 1960s.
90 See, for example, the letter to Ernst Bertram (February 21, 1923) in Rudolf Hirsch and Hans Wysling, eds., *Dichter über ihre Dichtungen: Thomas Mann* (Frankfurt/M.: Fischer, 1975), 81.
91 Mann, "Über den Film," 13.
92 Harry Geduld, *Authors on Film* (Bloomington: Indiana University Press, 1972), 129–32, here p. 129f.
93 Ibid., 131; Thomas Mann, *Past Masters*, trans. H. T. Lowe-Porter (New York: Knopf, 1933).
94 Critic "–ng." in "Der Film der Woche: Buddenbrooks," *Berliner Lokal-Anzeiger* (September 3, 1923), DK; this material has been previously published in German in "Buddenbrooks im Stummfilm," 63.
95 Thomas P. Saudners, "Vom Dafco zu Damra," *Das Ufa-Buch*, 70–4, here p. 71; Sabine Hake, "Chaplin Reception in Weimar Germany," *New German Critique* 51 (1990): 87–111.
96 Cf. Nietzsche's *Also sprach Zarathustra*: "Ich sage euch: man muss noch Chaos in sich haben, um einen tanzenden Stern gebären zu können. Ich sage euch: ihr habt noch Chaos in euch." [I'm telling you: you must have chaos within to be able to give birth to a dancing star. I'm saying to you: you still have chaos within you.]
97 Thea von Harbou, "Thea von Harbou, die das Drehbuch schrieb," *Reklameratschläge für den Theaterbesitzer*; in *Die Nibelungen: Bilder von Liebe, Verrat und Untergang*, ed. Wolfgang Storch (Munich: Prestel, 1987), 96. The following quotes refer to this text.
98 Thea von Harbou was a writer who had published novels such as *Der belagerte Tempel* [The Besieged Temple] (Berlin: Ullstein, 1917) and novellas such as *Sonderbare Heilige* [Strange Saints] (Berlin: Scherl, 1919) prior to her relationship with Fritz Lang. Their subsequent collaboration led to the treatment for and a prose publication of *Metropolis* (Berlin: Scherl, 1926)—the work on the film lasted from 1924 to 1927—and an adaptation of her novel *Die Frau im Mond* [Woman in the Moon] (Berlin: Scherl, 1928) in 1929. She published her prose prior to but also in view of their film versions. Publications like *Das Nibelungenbuch* (Munich: Drei Masken, 1923) also served to manifest her standing as a writer and helped to market Lang's motion picture. Because of her enthusiastic support of Nazism following Hitler's rise to power, her literary work drifted into the shadows and remains underresearched.
99 Decla and the Deutsche Bioskop AG had joined forces in 1920, making it Germany's second largest film company after Ufa. While remaining a largely independent operation in the beginning, Decla-Bioskop—and implicitly the most promising talent of the day from directors Lang or Robert Wiene, scriptwriters Carl Mayer and Thea von Harbou, innovators at the camera Carl Hoffmann or Karl Freund—was bought by Ufa in November 1921; https://www.filmportal.de/person/erich-pommer_22ed13b8f7fa47fd85a52e8c98b64e77.

100 Bock/Töteberg, "A History of Ufa," 285.
101 In their inaugural book of this series, Semenza and Hasenfratz clearly show how in the 1910s the viewing public generally shunned literary films in favor of Westerns and other entertaining genre films. Semenza/Hasenfratz, *The History of British Literature on Film*, 80–1.
102 Adeline Mueller refers to Harbou's text for the program handed out at the premiere of *Nibelungen*. Cf. Adeline Mueller, "14 February 1924: *Die Nibelungen* Premieres, Foregrounds Germanness," in *A New History of German Cinema*, ed. Jennifer M. Kapczynski and Michael D. Richardson (Rochester, NY: Camden House, 2012), 136–41, here p. 137.
103 Fritz Lang: "Worauf es ankam," *Reklameratschläge für den Theaterbesitzer*; in *Die Nibelungen*, ed. W. Storch, 96–7. The following quotes refer to p. 96.
104 The first intertitle reads (in Gothic script): "Dem Deutschen Volke zu eigen."
105 Lang, "Worauf es ankam," 97.
106 Lotte Eisner examines Lang's and Kurtz's "Stimmungsbilder" or 'mood pictures' that were to help viewers understand "man's destiny." As she explains, "Stimmung" meaning "an atmosphere permeated in some sort by the emanations of the German *Gemüt*—a highly particular mixture of sensibility and sentimentality." Cf. Eisner, *The Haunted Screen*, 152.
107 Lang, "Worauf es ankam," 97.
108 For further discussion of the film, see Eisner, *The Haunted Screen*, 151–75.
109 "Spieler" in German means not only gambler, but actor, puppeteer, player, all fitting descriptions of Dr. Mabuse.
110 Title plate, part 2 [0:06:33]: "Jetzt soll die Welt erst erfahren, wer ich bin,—ich! Mabuse!—Ich will ein Gigant werden,—ein Titan, der Gesetze und Götter durcheinander wirbelt wie dürres Laub!!".
111 Mueller, "14 February 1924," 136f.
112 Ibid., 137.
113 On Goebbels' infatuation with *Nibelungen* and its aesthetic see Mueller, "14 February 1924," 138.
114 For more information, see Siegfried Kracauer, *From Caligari to Hitler: A Psychological History of the German Film* (Princeton: Princeton University Press, [1947] 2004); Eric Rentschler, *The Ministry of Illusion: Nazi Cinema and Its Afterlife* (Cambridge: Harvard University Press, 1996); Hinrich C. Seeba, "'Germany: A Literary Concept': The Myth of National Literature," *German Studies Review* 17.2 (1994): 353–69; Robert G. Lee and Sabine Wilke, "Forest as *Volk: Ewiger Wald* and the Religion of Nature in the Third Reich," *Journal of Social and Ecological Boundaries* 1.1 (2005): 21–46. Chapter 6 might also be useful in this context.
115 A. Dana Weber, "From Glorious Nibelungs to Inglorious Basterds: Quentin Tarantino's Refractive Retelling of Fritz Lang's Epic," *German Studies Review* 42.3 (2019): 537–60.
116 Pommer served as Ufa's head of production from 1923. An expansion of the studios in Berlin Neubabelsberg (the former Bioscop studios) in addition to their studios in Berlin's Tempelhof enabled Ufa to realize major productions (such as *Faust* or *Metropolis*).
117 The Polish stage actress Pola Negri, who had become a star in German silent films, signed with Paramount in 1922 and starred in *Lily of the Dust* (US,

Dimitri Buchowetzki, 1924) and many other Hollywood blockbusters. *Lily of the Dust* seems to be lost, but is an adaptation of Hermann Sudermann's *Das hohe Lied* (The Song of Songs) and the aforementioned Broadway play by E. Sheldon.

118 Mueller, "14 February 1924," 137.
119 Stresemann's speech as reported in "Der Wendepunkt," *Lichtbild-Bühne* 17 (February 16, 1924): 9, 12; quoted according to the English translation in Mueller, "14 February 1924," 137.
120 Fritz Lang in a letter to Lotte Eisner (October 3, 1968), included in *Fritz Lang: Leben und Werk*, ed. et al., Rolf Aurich, 97f.; quoted in Mueller, "14 February 1924," 138.
121 Mueller, "14 February 1924," 139. As Mueller notes, Tom Gunning supported this view of the film celebrating a mythical and heroic Germanness while at the same time turning against itself. Cf. Tom Gunning, *The Films of Fritz Lang* (London: BFI, 2000), 43f.
122 For further clarification, see Mueller, "14 February 1924," 139.
123 Iherings review appeared after the premiere of part 1 on February 15, 1924, DK. The review can also be accessed via filmportal.de: https://www.filmportal.de/node/26835/material/733050.
124 Siegfried Kracauer, "Der Mythos im Großfilm," Frankfurter Zeitung (May 7, 1924), in the appendix of reviews included in Kracauer, Von Caligari zu Hitler (Frankfurt: Suhrkamp, 1984), 397. Kracauer concludes his review by calling the adaptation of Nibelungen a 'violation' and 'kitsch.' Ibid., 398.
125 His friend Walter Benjamin called Kracauer a "Lumpensammler" or ragman of details of life in modern, urban environments. The best films of this era do just that and include those 'rags' or objects to provide another layer to the adapted narrative.
126 Cf. https://www.filmportal.de/node/26835/material/733052. The film journalist Heinz Udo Brachvogel (1889–1934) was the son of Jewish writer and activist Carry Brachvogel. After having banned her from publishing and removing her from public position in 1933, the Nazis deported the 78-year-old to Theresienstadt, the concentration camp where she died in 1942 shortly after. Her numerous literary works are only now being rediscovered.
127 Cf. Robert Minder, "Allemagnes et Allemands," Paris 1948; translated by Isabella v. Künsberg as "Hagen/Hitler," in Storch, ed., *Die Nibelungen*, 99.
128 Ernst Toller, "Film und Staat," *Berliner Volks-Zeitung* (February 5, 1924); see Ernst Toller, *Sämtliche Werke. Kritische Ausgabe*, vol. 4.1, ed. Martin Gerstenbräun, Michael Pilz, Gerhard Scholz, and Irene Zanol (Göttingen: Wallstein, 2015), 457–8. Cf. also Schönfeld, "Ernst Toller und das Kino," *text+kritik* 223 (2019): 47–57, here: p. 48f. I also published this section on Toller in "Ernst Toller's Film Projects," *German Life and Letters* 75.2 (2022): 250–65 (special volume on *Ernst Toller in Exile*, co-edited with Lisa Marie Anderson). Permission to reuse some of this material is gratefully acknowledged.
129 Toller, "Film und Staat," 458.
130 Heinrich Mann, "Film und Staat," *Berliner Volks-Zeitung* (February 5, 1924). Thanks to Michael Pilz for providing a copy of the article.

131 Breslauer remained in Austria and published mainly newspaper articles after Austria had become part of Hitler's Reich in 1938. Cf. Armin Loacker, "Johann Karl Breslauer," in *Die Stadt ohne Juden*, ed. Guntram Geser and Armin Loacker (Vienna: Verlag Filmarchiv Austria, 2000), 169–71.

132 Cf. Philip Oltermann, "Lost Austrian Film Predicting Rise of Nazism Restored and Relaunched," *The Guardian* (December 9, 2016), https://www.theguardian.com/world/2016/dec/09/lost-austrian-film-predicting-rise-of-nazism-restored-and-relaunched.

133 Karl-Markus Gauß, "Die unentbehrlichen Sündenböcke," *Süddeutsche Zeitung* (July 25, 2019), https://www.sueddeutsche.de/politik/karl-markus-gauss-antisemitismus-wien-juden-fluechtlinge-1.4539149.

134 Bettauer's murderer Otto Rothstock had left the NSDAP prior to the attack, but Nazi lawyers supported him during the trial. He only had to serve eighteen months in a psychiatric clinic before he was released and could rejoin the Nazi party and their malicious cause.

135 *Joyless Street* premiered on May 18, 1925. Further adaptations of Hugo Bettauer's works include: *Faustrecht* (DE/AT, Karl Ehmann, 1922), *Die schönste Frau der Welt* (DE, Richard Eichberg, 1924), *Die Stadt ohne Juden* (AT, Hans Karl Breslauer, 1924), *Das Abenteuer der Sybille Brant* (DE, Carl Froelich, 1925), *Der Bankkrach unter den Linden* (DE, Paul Merzbach, 1926), *Andere Frauen* (AT, Heinz Hanus, 1928). *La rue sans joie* (FR, André Hugon, 1938) is a French language version of *Joyless Street*.

136 Cf. Patrice Petro's Weimar street film book *Joyless Street*. Especially her examination of gender, spectatorship, and censorship in the context of this "highly melodramatic, cinematic genre" that draws attention to social conflict and "the drama of male symbolic defeat" is enlightening. Petro, *Joyless Street*, 163.

137 Eisner, *The Haunted Screen*, 256. Also quoted in Petro, "Film Censorship and the Female Spectator: *The Joyless Street* (1925)," in *The Films of G.W. Pabst*, ed. Eric Rentschler (New Brunswick: Rutgers University Press, 1990), 30–40, here p. 32.

138 Eric Rentschler, "The Problematic Pabst: An *Auteur* Directed by History," in *The Films of G.W. Pabst*, 1–23, here p. 1.

139 Petro, in reference to Peter Brooks, *The Melodramatic Imagination. Balzac, Henry James, Melodrama, and the Mode of Excess* (New Haven: Yale University Press, 1976); cf. Petro, "Film Censorship and the Female Spectator: *The Joyless Street* (1925)," 32.

140 Ibid., 38.

141 For further reading see especially Petro, *Joyless Street*, especially 204–19.

142 Viggo Larsen directed the first adaptation in 1912, the second adaptation followed under the direction of Reinhard Bruck in 1921.

143 Karl Freund had offered a first taste of his 'unchained camera' technique in *Der letzte Mann* (distributed as *The Last Laugh*; DE, F. W. Murnau, 1924). *Varieté* takes mobility in the context of his camera work and the notion of perspective even further; cf. Thomas Brandlmeier, "Fragmenting Space: On E.A. Dupont's *Varieté*," in *Expressionist Film: New Perspectives*, 213–21.

144 Trieb = instinct, drive; Kracauer, *From Caligari to Hitler*, 126.

145 Felix Hollaender, *Der Eid des Stephan Huller* (Berlin: Ullstein, 1912), 11f. The novel can be accessed via archive.org: https://archive.org/details/dereiddestepha00hollgoog/page/n14.
146 Leo Lania in his Anita Berber novel *Der Tanz ins Dunkel* (Dancing into Dark, 1929); quoted by Klaus Mann, "Erinnerung an Anita Berber," in *Heute und Morgen. Schriften zur Zeit* (Munich: Nymphenburger, 1969), 21–6.
147 Anita Berber was one of the best-known dancers in Europe at the time, and in Germany and Austria certainly the most controversial. By the time she was in her early twenties, Berber had already starred in twenty-four feature films, playing the lead roles in Richard Oswald's *Diary of a Lost Girl*, *The Yellow House*, etc.
148 Cf. Eastman's panchromatic stock.
149 Thomas Elsaesser, *Weimar Cinema and After. Germany's Historical Imaginary* (London: Routledge, 2000), here especially p. 5, but the entire book is relevant in this context.
150 Eisner, *The Haunted Screen*, 278.
151 Brandlmeier, "Fragmenting Space: On E. A. Dupont's *Varieté*," 215.
152 Ibid.
153 Ibid., 220, referring only to Dupont here, but in general giving Freund's camerawork ample credit.
154 Quoted in Peter Manz, "Soziales," in *Kino der Moderne. Film der Weimarer Republik*, 28–33, here p. 28.
155 Manz, "Soziales," 28.
156 The 1922 German-Soviet trade agreement had paved the way for new Soviet films to be screened in Germany and vice versa.
157 Animation in the opening sequence of a film is still used today. See for example *The Only Living Boy in New York* (US, Marc Webb, 2018).
158 Cf. Semenza/Hasenfratz, *The History of British Literature on Film*, 99–101, who provide a fascinating discussion of the 1912 adaptation of E. Barrett Browning's reform poem. Thanks to Greg Semenza for the suggestion.
159 Cf. Toller's aforementioned 'Film and State' article and Erwin Piscator, *Das politische Theater* (Berlin: Henschel, 1968; facsimile of the 1929 edition), 150f. Piscator and Toller were working on staging *Hoppla, wir leben!* in 1927.
160 See "Das neue Drama Tollers," in *Ernst Toller. Sämtliche Werke*, vol. 4.1, 464.
161 See, for example, the letter written to Heinrich Mann by the 'Filmmanuskript Vertriebsgesellschaft (Berlin)' on December 9, 1926, asking for an option on his novel *Professor Unrat*. Quoted in Michael Grisko, *Heinrich Mann und der Film* (Munich: Meidenbauer, 2008), 213.
162 Hauptmann, *Atlantis*, chapter 10.
163 Cf. Hans Wollenberg's review in *Lichtbild-Bühne 69* (March 23, 1926). Excerpts of reviews by Siegfried Kracauer, Oskar Kalbus, etc. are also available via https://de.wikipedia.org/wiki/Die_Brüder_Schellenberg.
164 Goethe, *Faust I*: "Wir breiten nur den Mantel aus, Der soll uns durch die Lüfte tragen." (Tübingen: Cotta. 1808), 126.
165 Rohmer is quoted by Helmut Schanze on the same page in "On Murnau's *Faust*: A Generic *Gesamtkunstwerk?*" in *Expressionist Film: New Perspectives*, ed. D. Scheunemann, 223–35.

166 https://www.filmportal.de/person/ludwig-berger_424168cbc5aa4ee5a8606a 9d1382df72. See also Eric C. Brown, *Milton on Film* (University Park: The Pennsylvania State University Press, 2015).

167 Berger introduces the film in the booklet provided by Decla-Bioscop upon the release of the film. Berger is quoted in Bernhard Zeller, ed., *Klassiker in finsteren Zeiten, 1933–1945. Eine Ausstellung des Deutschen Literaturarchivs im Schiller-Nationalmuseum, Marbach am Neckar* (Marbach: Deutsche Schillergesellschaft, 1983), 356; and by Horst Schäfer in: "Verkannt, vergessen, verschollen: Märchen-Stummfilme in Deutschland," in *Märchen im Medienwechsel: Zur Geschichte und Gegenwart des Märchenfilms*, ed. Ute Dettmar, Claudia Maria Pecher, and Ron Schlesinger (Stuttgart: Springer, 2018), 59–84, here p. 75f.

168 Mann, in Geduld, *Authors on Film*, 130.

169 Cf. Benjamin, *Illuminationen*, 53.

170 Cf. Max Horkheimer's and Theodor W. Adorno's *Dialektik der Aufklärung* (1947), but also Theodor W. Adorno, "Résumé über die Kulturindustrie," in *Gesammelte Schriften*, vol. 10 (Frankfurt: Suhrkamp, 1963), 337–45.

171 See Eisner's "The Climax of the Chiaroscuro" in her seminal *The Haunted Screen*, 285–94.

172 Helmut Schanze outlines "elements of classicist ordering of the moving camera" in his "On Murnau's *Faust*: A Generic *Gesamtkunstwerk?*," 223.

173 Elsaesser, *Weimar Cinema and After*, 228.

174 In a *Vanity Fair* article; cf. the tribute to Lillian Gish by the American Film Institution in 1984 on the occasion of her Life Achievement Award; https://www.afi.com/laa/laa84.aspx.

175 Hauptmann's draft letter to Kyser was included in the 1976 *Hätte ich das Kino!*-exhibition in Marbach/Neckar and can be found in the aforementioned catalogue, 264.

176 Ibid., 264f. The original letter can be found in Berlin (Staatsbibliothek Preußischer Kulturbesitz).

177 "Auf meinen Mantel tritt, und um dich kreist die Erde"; Goethe, *Faust II*, line 2065.

178 Brentano's review and this information are included in Greve, ed. et al., *Hätte ich das Kino*, 260f.

179 Willy Haas in his review of "Faust" published in *Die literarische Welt* 44 (1926): 7.

180 Kracauer, *Von Caligari zu Hitler*, 158f.

181 Elsaesser, *Weimar Cinema and After*, 5 and 242.

182 For ensuing legal battles over the use of sound film technology between Germany and the United States, see Brockmann, *A Critical History of German Film*, 54f. See also Donald Crafton, *The Talkies: American Cinema's Transition to Sound 1926–1931* (Berkeley: University of California Press, 1999).

183 Crafton, *The Talkies*, 94.

184 Cf. Carl Mayer's biography on filmportal: https://www.filmportal.de/person/carl-mayer_513179fd1e6d40c1b3d38b7bb7c310a9.

185 Joel Waldo Finler, *The Hollywood Story* (New York: Wallflower, 2003), 129.

186 Philip French in his *Sunset* review in *The Guardian* to be accessed at: https://www.theguardian.com/film/2014/aug/17/murnau-faust-dvd-classic-philip-french-symphony-light-darkness.
187 Mordaunt Hall, "The Screen," *The New York Times* (September 24, 1927): 38.
188 Included in Greve, *Hätte ich das Kino*, 373.
189 Eugen Gürster in *Kunstwart* 41.1 (1927/8): 404–6; excerpt available in *Hätte ich das Kino*, 373f.
190 Wolfgang Schönpflug provides a helpful overview in *Geschichte und Systematik der Psychologie* (Weinheim: Beltz, 2004).
191 See Thomas Anz's work in this area and his article "Psychoanalyse und literarische Moderne: Zu den Anfängen einer dramatischen Beziehung" published online at https://literaturkritik.de/id/5803; for the influence of Freud and psychoanalysis on Austrian literature, see Michael Worbs, *Nervenkunst. Literatur und Psychoanalyse im Wien der Jahrhundertwende* (Frankfurt/M.: Europäische Verlagsanstalt, 1983).
192 For further information on the French and American adaptations mentioned here, see Griffiths' and Watts' *The History of French Literature on Film* (2020) and Leitch's *The History of American Literature on Film* (2019).
193 Hauptmann had been working on his novel *Phantom. Aufzeichnungen eines ehemaligen Sträflings* (Phantom. Notes by a former prisoner) from 1915 to 1921. The novel was eventually published by S. Fischer Berlin in 1923. His previous *Dünnebeil* (1888) and *Karl Henning* (1912) are considered preliminary works. See Klaus Kanzog, "An der Literatur zeigen, was der Film kann: *Phantom* (1922)," in *Von den Anfängen bis zum etablierten Medium 1895–1924*, ed. Werner Faulstich and Helmut Korte (Frankfurt/ M.: Fischer, 1994), 377–93.
194 Willy Haas, "November-Filme," *Freie deutsche Bühne* 4 (1922/23): 129–34; in Greve, *Hätte ich das Kino!*, 172–3, here p. 172.
195 For more detail, see Scheunemann, *Expressionist Film*, 134–36.
196 Numerous scholars from Lotte Eisner to Jürgen Kasten (1990), Anton Kaes (1993), and Siegbert S. Prawer (1995) have published on the *Doppelgänger* as a signifier of modernity. Particularly useful in terms of literary contexts is Andrew J. Webber's chapter on "Gothic Revivals: The *Doppelgänger* in the Age of Modernism" in his book *The Doppelgänger: Double Visions in German Literature* (Oxford: Oxford University Press, 1996), 317–56, which offers the depth and much fascinating detail this short section unfortunately cannot provide.
197 Rank's essay is available in English as "The Double. A Psychoanalytic Study," trans./ed./intro. by Harry Tucker (Chapel Hill: The University of North Carolina Press, 1971); for Sigmund Freund's "The Uncanny," see *The Standard Edition of the Complete Psychological Works of Sigmund Freud*, trans. James Strachey, vol. XVII (London: Hogarth, 1953), 219–52. See also Webber, *The Doppelgänger*, 39–53.
198 Guido Seeber, "Doppelgängerbilder im Film," *Die Kinotechnik* 1 (1919): 12–17; also quoted in Scheunemann, *Expressionist Film*, 153.

199 Harbou repeatedly wrote a prose text on a film's proposed narrative prior to or while embarking on a new screenplay, which can be considered both part of the creative process and a marketing strategy. Her novel *Metropolis* was published by Scherl (Berlin) in 1926, prior to the release of the film in 1927.
200 Berber here appears in men's clothing (in 'tails'), long before Marlene Dietrich paid homage to her in *Morocco* (US, Josef von Sternberg, 1930) in similar attire.
201 See Barbara Creed, *The Monstrous-Feminine. Film, Feminism, Psychoanalysis* (London: Routledge, 1993).
202 Anita Berber and Sebastian Droste, *Die Tänze des Lasters, des Grauens und der Ekstase* (Vienna: Gloriette-Verlag, 1923). Droste was Berber's dance partner and (second) husband from 1922–3.
203 For an introduction see Mel Gordon, *The Seven Addictions and Five Professions of Anita Berber* (Port Townsend, WA: Feral House, 2006). Gordon's text includes a translation of Droste/Berber's book, "The Dances of Depravity, Horror and Exstasy," 173–95, for "Cocaine," cf. 177.
204 Partly due to massive overspending, especially on *Nibelungen* and *Metropolis*, Ufa faced bankruptcy. The film company was taken over by media mogul Alfred Hugenberg, owner of the Scherl-group and leader of the Deutschnationalen Volkspartei, who opened Ufa to his nationalistic agenda.
205 Cf. the reports by the censorship board, available via filmportal.de: http://www.filmportal.de/sites/default/files/Das%20Haus%20zur%20roten%20Laterne_O.00220_1928 and http://www.filmportal.de/sites/default/files/Die%20Rothausgasse_O.00775_1928.
206 Petro, *Joyless Streets*, xxi.
207 Eisner, *The Haunted Screen*, 172. Cf. her chapter on "Pabst and the Miracle of Louise Brooks," 295–307.
208 This was often the case at the time in films focusing on dominant women. Regarding the "suggestive equations between power, desire, and death," see Hake, "Lubitsch's Period Films," 84.
209 Review by "R-r" (February 12, 1929), included in Greve *Hätte ich das Kino!*, 172–3, here p. 172.
210 Mary Anne Doane, "The Erotic Barter: Pandora's Box (1929)," in *The Films of G.W. Pabst*, ed. Eric Rentschler, 62–79, here pp. 62 and 63.
211 Doane, "The Erotic Barter," 63.
212 Ibid., 71.
213 Thomas Elsaesser, "Lulu and the Meter Man," *Screen* 24.4–5 (1983): 4–36, here 15 and 25; quoted by Doane, "The Erotic Barter," 71f., who critically engages with Elsaesser's essay.
214 Cesare Lombroso and Gugliemo Ferrero had published their 'criminal-anthropological study' *La Donna delinquente, la prostituta e la donna normale* in 1893 that was translated into German the following year (*Das Weib als Verbrecherin und Prostituirte* [sic] [Woman as Criminal and Prostitute], 1894) to great acclaim. In this book, the authors identify 'types' of sexually independent, 'delinquent' women.
215 According to the author of the scenario Rudolf Leonhardt, as Lotte Eisner recounts in *The Haunted Screen*, 306.

216 Allgeier became a well-known director of photography while working with Arnold Fanck, especially due to stunning imagery of snow-covered mountain landscapes. He continued to work with Leni Riefenstahl and in Hitler's politically aligned film industry until 1945, failing to really find a footing again in the industry after the collapse of the Nazi regime.
217 The version available on DVD today contains a reconstruction probably quite close to the original version.
218 Brooks plays Thymian more than "enigmatically impassive." Cf. Eisner, *The Haunted Screen*, 296.
219 For a more detailed analysis of bourgeois institutions operating "as forms of sadism constituted by the cinematic apparatus," see Heide Schlüpmann, "The Brothel as an Arcadian Space? *Diary of a Lost Girl* (1929)," in *The Films of G. W. Pabst*, ed. E. Rentschler, 80–90, here p. 85.
220 Böhme, *Tagebuch einer Verlorenen*, 82.
221 For example, a critic in the *Hamburger Abendblatt* rejected the comparison with Böhme's novel but remarks, if somewhat sardonically: 'It would be wrong to compare the film with the novel. [...] The movie, written by Rudolf Leonhardt and directed by G. W. Pabst, has its own face. [...] The story told here, is the story that they all tell, and that nobody believes. But one also believes that the 'lost' themselves believe in their story. So the film transposes the diary [...] with complete authenticity [...]. Seen that way, the adaptation is a wonderful success.' *Hamburger Acht-Uhr-Abendblatt* (November 11, 1929), in Arno Bammé, ed., *Margarete Böhme. Die Erfolgsschriftstellerin aus Husum* (Munich: Profil, 1994), 48f.
222 A collaboration of the Italian Cineteca del Comune di Bologna, the German public television ZDF, and the German-French TV channel Arte, the film is based on a copy found at the Danish Film Institute and intertitles based on censorship documents held in the German national film archive Bundesarchiv/Filmarchiv Berlin.
223 Schnitzler's letter to Elisabeth Bergner on April 7, 1929, is included in Greve *Hätte ich das Kino!*, 202.
224 Schnitzler's letter to Elisabeth Bergner written on January 10, 1929, is included in Greve et al., *Hätte ich das Kino!,* 374. Schnitzler was fond of Mayer: 'But beyond all momentous encounters and even beyond art, I am delighted about the short meeting with him and the confirmation of warm friendship, which enriches my existence,' Schnitzler writes in the letter.
225 James Joyce, *Ulysses* (1918–20), trans. Georg Goyert (Basel: Rhein-Verlag, 1927).
226 Schnitzler and Freud both lived in Vienna and knew one another. Schnitzler was clearly aware of the psychologist's theories, who in a letter (May 14, 1922) called Schnitzler his literary double, his *Doppelgänger*. An English translation of the letter can be downloaded here: https://www.pep-web.org/document.php?id=zbk.051.0339a.
227 Eisner, *The Haunted Screen*, 197.
228 Ibid.
229 To widen the lens, see Semenza/Hasenfratz' discussion of 'the growing concern with fidelity' in *The History of British Literature on Film*, 94–103.

230 Corrigan argues that it is in the late 1920s and 1930s that "adaptations of contemporary literature become more popular than ever before, partly because the introduction of sound in 1927 allows movies to more fully recreate literary and theatrical dialogue, character psychology, and plot complexity found in novels." Corrigan, "Literature on Screen," 35.

231 See for example the reviewer of *Le Théâtre Allemand d'Aujourd'hui* René Lauret, "The German Theatre," *Irish Times* (April 14, 1934): 7.

232 Bock/Töteberg, "A History of Ufa," 285.

233 Behrendt's first adaptation (screenplay/dir.) brought Wilhelm Meyer-Förster's 1901 play *Alt-Heidelberg* to the screen (1923).

234 Rudolf Forster appears as the Bohémien Scarron and, also, Veit Harlan—who later became Hitler's most prolific Nazi director—in a minor role as the Jewish barber Mandelstam.

4

Literary Talkies: Sound and Internationalization (1922–32)

You ain't heard nothin' yet.
AL JOLSON IN *THE JAZZ SINGER* (1927)

The demand for amusement is universal.
ERICH POMMER (1932)[1]

The possibility of sound film changed both practices of and attitudes toward adaptation. Literary texts that would not have been considered for film before were suddenly attractive commodities. But it took nearly a decade and a dramatically changing landscape of film consumption for German cinema to abandon familiar practices for brand-new technologies. The year 1922 was the so-called 'miracle year of words'[2] that saw the publications of courageously innovative, modernist texts such as James Joyce's *Ulysses*, Virginia Woolf's *Jacob's Room*, and T.S. Elliot's *Wasteland*, but also of Hermann Hesse's *Siddharta* and Stefan Zweig's *Amok*. Cinema, too, was trying out new narrative formats, animation, abstraction, and fragmentation. As discussed in the previous chapter, the German film industry produced mass entertainment, but in 1922 also began to explore the possibility of talking pictures, while silent masterpieces like F.W. Murnau's *Der brennende Acker* [Burning Soil] and *Nosferatu*, Fritz Lang's *Dr. Mabuse*, Richard Oswald's *Lucrecia Borgia*, and Manfred Noa's *Nathan der Weise* premiered. The national and international success of German silent cinema was impressive and greatly influenced attitudes toward sound film and shaped investments into technology and expertise in the years to come.

In 1927, the *The Jazz Singer* (US, Alan Crosland) triumphed due to its spectacular use of sound, and by the end of the decade, the silent era had come to a grinding halt in the United States. But at that time, the majority of film industries around the globe were only beginning to come to grips with the new technology. While film screenings had never really been silent, with musicians providing accompanying soundscapes, early experiments with synchronized, pre-recorded sound by innovators such as William Kennedy Dickson, Eugène Lauste, or Josef Engl had failed to have any significant effect on adaptations of German-language literature. Spoiled by its own international silent movie successes throughout the 1920s due to high-budget, spectacular period films such as Lubitsch's *Madame Dubarry [Passion]* (DE, 1919), innovative Expressionist masterpieces such as *The Cabinet of Dr. Caligari* (DE, 1920), Wegener's fantastic horror feature *Der Golem* [The Golem] (DE, 1920; inspired by Gustav Meyrink's 1913/14 serialized novel),[3] or thrillers like Fritz Lang/Thea von Harbou's adaptation of Norbert Jacques' *Dr. Mabuse* narrative (1922), leading figures in the German film industry, including Ufa board members, simply underestimated the attraction of the new technology. When Warner Bros.' *The Jazz Singer* and *The Singing Fool* (US, Lloyd Bacon, 1928), using the company's patented Vitaphone sound-on-disk system, established the 'talking picture' as a marvelous mainstream attraction, the reality of their fundamental misjudgment began to sink in.

Once the phenomenal success of Al Jolson's lip-synched voice had heralded the beginning of a new age in cinemas in the United States and soon abroad, film companies in Germany were far behind in implementing the new technology in their productions, despite sufficient awareness and even some action by Ufa in the early to mid-1920s which will be discussed below. As adaptations of German literature had been rarely even considered by filmmakers outside Germany or Austria[4] since the First World War, the industry's lack of investment into the new technology impacted adaptation projects as much as film productions as a whole. The German film industry, which had grown into Hollywood's rival during the 'Golden Twenties', now paid dearly for its overconfidence.

It was remarkably innovative filmmakers such as Walter Ruttmann who had turned to sound film early on. Upon completion of his ground-breaking, feature-length documentary *Berlin. Sinfonie einer Großstadt* [Berlin. Symphony of a Metropolis] (1927), Ruttmann continued his experiments with animated film sequences[5] and explored in particular the application of montage to both image and sound. His documentary *Tönende Welle* [Sound Wave] premiered at the Berlin radio exhibition in 1928, and in October of the same year, Ruttmann presented a number of short sound films in Frankfurt/Main. Journalist and film critic Siegfried Kracauer,[6] who attended the screening in his hometown, compared the excitement at the event with the thrill of the first public screening of moving pictures at Berlin's Wintergarten in November 1895,[7] when those hitherto unimaginable future possibilities of film as art, entertainment, and cultural commodity had first been suggested. A year later, Ruttmann completed Germany's first feature length sound film *Melodie der Welt* [Melody of the World] (1929), which not only included an original score by Wolfgang Zeller, but invited its viewers on a journey to foreign lands, offering glimpses of far-away cultures in moving images and sound. Like fellow animator Lotte Reiniger a member of the Institut für Kulturforschung [institute for cultural research] in Berlin, Ruttmann was acutely aware of the intercultural dimension of film and sound technology. Values conveyed already in Reiniger's *Die Abenteuer des Prinzen Achmed* [The Adventures of Prince Ahmed] (1926) on which he collaborated, Ruttmann's *Melodie der Welt* invited interest in and tolerance toward the 'other'. But what was the impact of sound on adaptations of German literature, both within Germany and abroad?

Corrigan notes that, in "the late 1920s and 1930s, adaptations of contemporary literature become more popular than ever before, partly because the introduction of sound in 1927 allows movies to more fully recreate literary and theatrical dialogue, character psychology, and plot complexity found in novels."[8] As the following pages will illustrate, it was indeed popular, contemporary prose and plays rather than the canon of German-language literature that were brought to cinema screens especially from 1930, until the election of Adolf Hitler on January 30, 1933, fundamentally altered the conditions of life and work of so many creatives in Germany. By the early 1930s, a confident film industry made systematic use of literary production, primarily for commercial gain, which Bertolt Brecht would soon censure. But by turning to contemporary literature, Germany's and Austria's literary avant-garde and modern filmmakers intersected even more directly than before.

In contrast to those franchise adaptations of the classics of British and American literature common in 1930s Hollywood, discussed by Greg Semenza/Bob Hasenfratz and Tom Leitch in their respective volumes of this series, adaptations of German-language prose and plays in Germany were often shaped by their producers, and the political outlooks of members on film companies' boards. Film companies were constantly searching for "suitable screen stories"[9] and bestselling novels or hits on theater stages were of interest not only to local filmmakers in Germany and Austria, but to Hollywood studios—especially once a text had proven successful in English translation, and marketing of adaptations could be based on its reputation.[10]

This chapter opens with a flashback, tracing the gradual inclusion and impact of sound technology in productions based on German-language literary texts. The focus then shifts to avant-garde writers and filmmakers, whose work helped to establish a canon of German cinema. Soon, however, many of them would leave in ever greater numbers due to economic and political instability, increasing nationalism and antisemitism, and, from 1933 onwards, persecution in Hitler's swiftly expanding Reich. This migration of talent from Germany and soon Austria, which the following chapter will outline, affected not only other film industries, particularly in France and the United States, but brought German-language literature to the attention of powerful players in the movie business. Hollywood adaptations of novels such as Erich Maria Remarque's *Im Westen nichts Neues* (1929) into *All Quiet on the Western Front* (US, Lewis Milestone, 1930) in turn impacted an increasingly unstable Germany.

Sound Film Experiments in Germany in the 1920s

Sound was viewed as both a threat and opportunity to adaptations of German-language literature. Expectations relating to films based on literary texts that could now provide spoken dialogues were considerable, but in the beginning, the aesthetic and economic pitfalls of the new system seemed even greater. Using optical sound technology, the Tri-Ergon system—the work of three German inventors, namely Josef Engl, Joseph Massolle, and Hans Vogt—enabled the storage of photoelectric sound recordings on film and thus a synchronized presentation of moving image and sound.[11] Having been made aware of Tri-Ergon's technology as early as 1922, the board of Ufa, the largest and most financially stable German film company, put Guido Bagier in charge of assessing the economic prospects of the new system. But it took another three years for a contract between Ufa and Tri-Ergon to be drawn up. Talkies were clearly not high on the agenda of the swiftly growing film company. Once resources for this experiment were finally made available, a suitable studio space was found in Weißensee on the outskirts of Berlin, and a soundstage was constructed.[12] Finally, in July 1925, Ufa's brand-new Tri-Ergon department began producing a first short based on Hans Christian Andersen's fairy tale *The Little Match Girl* under the Bagier's direction.[13] Hans Kyser had supplied the script, and Joseph Engl was in charge of using Tri-Ergon's technology for synchronized sound. When the highly anticipated film premiered in Berlin's fashionable Mozartsaal on December 20, 1925, the visual projection worked flawlessly, but the sound suddenly began to dwindle and then failed entirely. This much anticipated presentation of the latest sound film technology ended in spectacular embarrassment for the entire team and its company. Despite claims of sabotage intended to cripple German sound film production, Ufa's executive took immediate and, in hindsight, misguided action by closing its Tri-Ergon department and terminating all contracts.[14] For Ufa, this calamity could not have happened at a worse time. As outlined in the previous chapter, due to overspending on impressive productions such as Murnau's *Faust* (1926) and, especially, on acquisitions of smaller competitors, Ufa was in a deep financial crisis, which led to a controversial partial buyout by Paramount and Metro-Goldwyn-Mayer or, rather, the joint distribution arrangement known as Parufamet.[15]

Beyond struggling Ufa, sound film experiments continued, driven by individuals and smaller, independent film companies. Carl Robert Blum, for example, patented his 'musical chronometer' in 1926 and developed processes designed to synchronize the rhythm of film images and musical scores.[16] As Wedel indicates, an updated version of Blum's invention[17] was tested by composer Edmund Meisel in preparation of the premiere of Ruttmann's *Berlin. Sinfonie einer Großstadt* in September 1927, but was then not utilized.[18] Perhaps, the *Little Match Girl* calamity was still too fresh in everyone's mind. Ufa owned the rights to the Tri-Ergon process in Germany until 1927, but as soon as its licensing entitlements expired, Tri-Ergon, produced and distributed by the inventors' company in Switzerland, was well on its way to becoming the most widely used sound process in German-language cinema among the well over a dozen other available systems at the time.[19] Soon, however, European patent holders became increasingly pragmatic in light of the pressure from across the Atlantic and decided to join forces.

Collaboration and Competition

The Ton-Bild-Syndikat AG [Sound Pictures Syndicate or Tobis] was created in 1928 in an effort to enable competition with Hollywood and end the film industries' process of 'continued self-destruction'.[20] In July 1928 representatives of Tri-Ergon, Lignose-Hörfilm, Deutsche Tonfilm A.G., Forest-Film, Terra, Küchenmeister, AEG, Siemens, Zeiß, and others met in order to enable the collaboration of patent holders. The development and promotion of sound film in Germany at Tobis under the leadership of Hans Henkel (formerly Ufa), Arthur Frischknecht, and Guido Bagier led to an agreement with the Dutch N.V. Küchenmeister's Internationale Maatschappij voor Sprekende Films Amsterdam, German Ultraphon-inventor Heinrich J. Küchenmeister's company. With it came further financial muscle to secure technology exchange and distribution agreements.[21]

By the end of the summer, the aforementioned Tri-Ergon-Musik-AG, the Küchenmeister-Tobis group, and other smaller firms holding sound recording and playback patents agreed to ensure standardization, and began producing a number of short sound films. Within a year, Ufa teamed up with Klangfilm GmbH [Sound Film Co.] in order to secure its rights to recording and projecting of talking pictures, and was in the process of building massive soundstages in Neubabelsberg outside Berlin.[22] Sound film was the future, even the most conservative members of the Ufa board agreed in light of films such as *Atlantik* (GB, E. A. Dupont, 1929), by far the most profitable talkie at the box office during the 1929/30 season in Germany. A British-German adaptation of Ernest Raymond's play *The Berg,* the German version of the disaster movie featured well-known theater and film personalities such as Elsa Wagner, Lucie Mannheim, Fritz Kortner, and Willi Forst. Hearing these silent film stars speak (German) on screen must have mesmerized audiences, since no one seemed to mind that all crowd scenes had only been recorded in English, a language only few Germans spoke at the time.

Because of the fact that not even Ufa had suitable purpose-built sound studios at the time, and compatibility issues often arose during screenings of these early talkies, the very first adaptations of German literature that made use of the new technology were rather flawed enterprises. *Land ohne Frauen* [Land without Women] (Carmine Gallone, 1929) was the first feature-length film in Germany that had been shot as a silent movie but was subsequently equipped with synchronized sound, both a pre-recorded musical score (composed by Wolfgang Zeller) and voice-overs by the film's actors Conradt Veidt, Elga Brink, Grete Berger, and others. Hungarian screenwriter Ladislaus Vajda, the prolific co-author of *Pandora's Box* (1929) and numerous other filmscripts, had written the script based on Peter Bolt's popular novel *Die Braut Nr. 68* (Bride No. 68; published in 1925 by Ullstein). He also wrote the script for Tobis' first major sound film *Der Günstling von Schönbrunn* [The Favorite of Schönbrunn] directed by Erich Waschneck with co-director Max Reichmann, who was responsible for the movie's sound sequences. While considering this project a step in the right direction, Siegfried Kracauer criticized the film upon its premiere in November 1929 in a review published in *Frankfurter Zeitung*. He highlighted in particular his difficulties in actually making out the human voice and complained about the artificiality of the soundscape due to muffled background noise. While drawing attention to the lack of expertise in this area in Germany at the time, Kracauer had little hope for the future, as in his opinion there would not be any sound film directors available in Germany for a while. At the moment, he concluded, the local film industry is seriously lacking both time and experience in this area.[23] Numbers clearly support Kracauer's estimation—in 1929 only eight of 183 films made in Germany were equipped with sound.[24] It was not until the following year that the first 'Tonfilmschule' or school for sound film opened in Berlin. Hugo Döblin[25] founded this technical college in an effort to provide the German film industry with a growing cohort of sound film experts.

In the meantime, competition with Hollywood was fierce as Europe was playing catch-up. Sound films from the United States were big hits and by the end of 1929, more than 220 cinemas in Germany had transferred to sound film projection. A year later, it was nearly 2,000.[26] When Tobis and Klangfilm agreed to join forces, their alliance enabled competition with Hollywood's Warner Bros., who used Western Electric's sound technology and were the dominant player in the industry at the time. Each companies' requirement to use the appropriate projection device when playing films recorded with their technology led to much discord on both sides of the Atlantic and to several lawsuits.[27] By July 1930 Western Electric and the Küchenmeister-Tobis-Klangfilm-group agreed in the so-called "Pariser Tonfilmfrieden" [lit. Paris Sound Film Peace] to share both sound technology patents and divide up the market between them. Other countries such as France or Italy had to pay hefty fees to be allowed to use the technology which impacted on soundfilm production elsewhere.[28] But the introduction of sound also affected the way films were to be distributed internationally, as borders now also meant language barriers that could not simply be overcome by translating a few title plates. Paris became the first hub of international sound film production, when both Tobis-Klangfilm and Paramount opened studios outside the French capital to shoot movies in different languages, using the same set and often crew, but mostly different actors, who would have been native speakers of the language in question and known to their respective audience.[29]

Remakes: Gendered Horror in Richard Oswald's *Alraune*

A number of successful silent films were remade as sound films, most notably in this early period *Alraune* [lit. Mandrake, English title *Unholy Love* or *The Daughter of Evil*] in 1930. Inspired by Mary Shelley's *Frankenstein*, Hanns Heinz Ewers's 1911 novel also tells the story of the creation of a 'hideous creature'—Alraune. She is the product of a genetic experiment, and Ewers foregrounds both the scientist and his creation. Professor ten Brinken uses the sperm of a condemned and hanged murderer to artificially inseminate a prostitute. He names the child after the magical root, thus linking science with witchcraft, and closely observes the creature's increasingly devastating effects on those around her as she grows into womanhood. In the end, Alraune's destructive urges and her insatiable sexual desire culminate in vampirism and, finally, death. The plot certainly lent itself to stimulating entertainment, but it was not until Richard Oswald took on the project that the novel was adapted into a psychologically motivated narrative and made use of sound to amplify its affective power.

As a critic noted in 1930, Ewers had created a 'vamp [...] before we even knew the term'.[30] His novel *Alraune* had been adapted first in 1918/19 in Germany (under the direction of Eugen Illiés[31]) and in Hungary (directed by Mihaly Kertész, i.e., Michael Curtiz). A third adaptation nearly a decade later—Henrik Galeen's two-hour *Alraune* (1927/28)—brought international acclaim to Ewers, and Galeen as both director and author of the screenplay. Brigitte Helm starred as Alraune, and Paul Wegener as the scientist Prof. Jakob ten Brinken. Despite numerous cuts required by censors nationally and internationally, particularly in Gt. Britain and the United

States, Galeen's audience-friendly variation of a *femme fatale* narrative included redemption and a happy ending, and did so well at the box office that filmmaker Oswald considered a remake with sound within a year of the earlier film's premiere. Oswald's adaptation was to precede Tod Browning's *Dracula* and James Whale's *Frankenstein* at Universal, and thus Carl Laemmle Jr.'s skillful reinvention of the horror-genre in 1931 as outlined by Semenza and Hasenfratz.[32]

Richard Oswald had realized numerous, successful adaptation projects in the past and clearly recognized the commercial potential of sound technology. He had already completed *Wien, du Stadt der Lieder* [Vienna, City of Songs] and *Dreyfus* (both in 1930) in rented Ufa studios equipped with Tobis-Klangfilm, i.e., European sound technology. Oswald directed his *Alraune* from late September to late October 1930, again in a rented studio in Neubabelsberg.[33] Brigitte Helm, who played the two Marias in Lang's *Metropolis* (1927), again starred as Alraune, and Albert Bassermann, one of the most prominent theater and film actors at the time, played the scientist and Privy Councillor ten Brinken. In typical early talkie fashion, Oswald's *Alraune* opens with music and song (the first work for German film by Polish composer Bronisław Kaper)—ten Brinken's nephew and his fraternity buddies are having themselves a good time in a pub, singing about women, who are the source of financial misery and all else: 'all because of a little girl, all because of a charming woman'. Soon we are informed of the geneticist's breakthrough development of 'artificial rats', followed by his nephew's suggestion or 'amusing idea' that one should produce human beings rather than rodents. He takes his uncle to a nightclub, where Alma (also played by Helm) works as a singer. Reminiscent of Marlene Dietrich's performance in the 'Blue Angel' nightclub but decidedly more provocative, Alma sings her song about infidelity and emphasizes in close-up her availability for the right price to all. With the help of Dr. Petersen, who gets Alma drunk and makes her sign a contract, the three men put her in the scientist's car. Shortly after, a hanged murderer is being donated to science. Alma's artificial insemination with the murderer's final ejaculate is only implied, but due to audiences' familiarity with the story, the framing narrative is kept suitably brief. 'Seventeen years later', Alraune is a moody, confident teenager. Privy Councillor ten Brinken raises the product of his experiment as his 'niece' in an educated, comfortable environment in order to investigate whether genes rather than upbringing mold an individual. Alraune provides ample evidence for a genetic predisposition, particularly as she reaches adolescence, remaining coldly puzzled by concepts of love or compassion while her sexual drive develops rapidly and excessively. Fearless and entirely void of empathy, the young woman is soon responsible for the deaths of several men, eventually including the Privy Councillor himself, who is as driven by cold professional ambition and sublimated sexual desire as he is helplessly dependent on his seductive creation. Only when

Alraune begins to trust, feel, and, perhaps, even love, the news of her origin as a 'scientific' experiment in genetic engineering deals her a devastating blow. Her suicide is implied in the final scene, which records her act of self-determination without melodrama as a rational, if tragic, conclusion to a failed experiment in line with Ewers' text.

Oswald once again recreates the myth of a sexual woman's dangerous and destructive nature. Together with his scriptwriters Robert Weisbach and Charlie K. Roellinghoff, however, he also reimagines Ewers' *Alraune* as a genetic as much as psychological experiment framed by a narrative that avoids superficial moralization.[34] The scene of her suicide in particular reveals the dangerous vamp not as a powerful harbinger of chaos, but as a lonely and devastated young woman. The mise-en-scène provides no support and the camera remains fashionably detached as Alraune, fatally undermined from the beginning, gives up. In an interview at the evening of the premiere, Oswald outlined the need to construct a narrative logic suitable for twentieth-century audiences—for people, that is, who do not believe in miracles anymore. After World War and economic disaster, these citizens of modern, urban spaces in his view were well capable of relating to the randomness of Alraune's fate.[35]

Film critics at the time praised particularly Helm as Alraune, whose depiction in Oswald's film differed significantly from Galeen's earlier adaptation as it reflected a range of psychological impediments that challenged

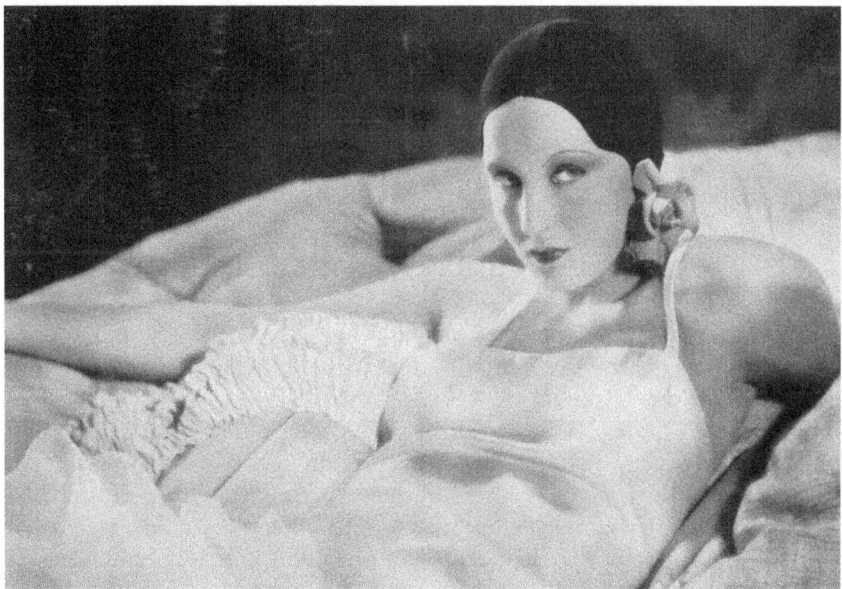

FIGURE 4.1 *Brigitte Helm as* Alraune *(DE, Richard Oswald, 1930)*.

the archetypal reading of Alraune. Rather than recreating a sexually driven vamp simply causing havoc, Helm's second interpretation focuses much more on the modern 'demonic' of ten Brinken's creation, which could be considered both a nod to the literary fashion of *Neue Sachlichkeit* [New Objectivity or New Sobriety] and an homage to expression dancer Anita Berber, whose performances put her own destructive demons center stage and often conveyed anxious self-examination in the modern city dwellers she entertained. Oswald foregrounds Alraune as an unstable self, an enticing, smug, ruthless, and entirely tentative product of ten Brinken's questionable 'science'. Helm examines Alraune's changeability from amiably innocent to deeply wicked. Her culpability, however, is only marginally lightened by her intentionally manufactured genetic make-up, so her evil seems as undeniable as it does inescapable and catastrophic. While the abuse of her mother is at least hinted at, Alraune is displayed as a victim only when her first awareness of love as a deeply human experience of vulnerability enables emotional growth almost at the same time as her existence is rendered unbearable due to male insensitivity and malice. Nonetheless, her death provides release and safety to those now no longer affected by her destructive power. Viewed in the context of growing antisemitism and racial ideologies spouted by Nazi demagogues at the time, both Ewers' novel and Oswald's adaptation are decidedly if, perhaps, inadvertently suspect. As a sound film, *Alraune* flopped. Too many words, too much dialogue, some songs for entertainment, in addition to visually overcharged mise-en-scènes and image composition—all in all a very imbalanced affair in the view of its critics. Only Helm's acting and, particularly, Bassermann's communication of despair by way of a single groan was celebrated; everyone in the audience understood the infinite possibility and thrilling promise of sound, which could shape palpable atmospheres and create a profound mood through only one audible whimper.[36]

Music(ians) and Operetta on Film

By 1930 increasing numbers of cinemas were equipped for sound and no longer needed live musical entertainment. For musicians employed full-time in film theaters, the introduction of sound was especially detrimental. In the United States alone, according to Richard Jewell, some 18,000 musicians lost their jobs, from those playing the piano or organ in smaller movie houses "to members of good-sized orchestras who performed in the urban film palaces."[37] Film studios alleviated this crisis somewhat by hiring musicians for the recording of soundtracks. In addition, an increasing number of films featured bands or orchestras on screen. There is no narrative requisite for an entire orchestra to play, for example, in the opening scene of the 1935 Gaumont-British remake[38] of Kellermann's famous science-fiction novel *Der Tunnel* as *Trans-Atlantic Tunnel* directed by Maurice Elvey; it even seems excessive considering the number of people to be entertained at the private party depicted. But this short sequence provided employment to musicians, who would here be paid for providing the musical score and for appearing as extras on screen. Like in many talkies of the time, the beauty of sound is foregrounded, and the audience's auditory sense emphasized as cinemagoers listened to the orchestra's music for the first ten seconds without any further sensory diversion as the screen remained black. The music continues during the opening credits until after well over a minute into the film when, finally, the orchestra can be seen. The conductor is placed in the center of the screen, with his back turned to the audience. But lest the harmonious ensemble of sound and image were to imply Romanticism's sublime in (human) nature, and hint at an individual's ability to draw inspiration from aural and visual stimulation, the camera draws back and then cuts to an elderly gentleman who leans over to the lady next to him, asking: "Does this tune ever end?" "It's Beethoven" she replies, adding, after a pause: "He is dead."—"Good!" he retorts. This short exchange reveals comedy as a necessary component of representations of high art in this modern mass medium, but at the same time points the finger at those that undercut individual creativity. In *Trans-Atlantic Tunnel* the creative spirit and innovation are celebrated while the spotlight is on the courage and sacrifice required by all to unite nations and safeguard peace, especially in light of the enormous economic pressures caused by ruthless financiers, who had recklessly undermined a momentary postwar stabilization.

Music was an integral part of early sound films and essential to maximizing profits. Orchestral music transcended language boundaries, but for songs to have the desired impact, multiple language versions had to be produced. Compared to Hollywood, potential German-language audiences in Germany, Austria, Switzerland, and Liechtenstein[39] were considered too small to generate sufficient income at the box office. Hence, larger companies such as Ufa deemed foreign distribution as essential, particularly for their costly 'prestige' productions. As Bock and Töteberg note, "Ufa's first all-talking feature, *Melodie des Herzens* (Melody of the Heart, Hanns Schwarz) starring Dita Parlo and Willy Fritsch, premiered on December 16, 1929. The film was produced—with foreign distribution in mind—in multiple language versions."[40]

Weimar cinema's most prominent producer Pommer oversaw *Melodie des Herzens*, and also produced *Liebeswalzer* [Waltz of Love] and *Die Drei von der Tankstelle* [The Three from the Filling Station] for Ufa in 1930. With the help of Austrian screenwriter and film director Wilhelm Thiele, who adapted the recipe of musical/part talkie blockbusters of US American productions—such as Warner Bros.' *The Singing Fool* (1928) or MGM's first "talking, singing, dancing" musical film *The Broadway Melody* (Harry Beaumont, 1929)—Pommer firmly established this new type of musical comedy in German-speaking countries. Thiele's films generated unforeseen profits for Ufa at the time, and the company soon launched a wave of entertaining operettas on cinema screens in Europe and the United States.

Both *Liebeswalzer* and *Die Drei von der Tankstelle* starred Lilian Harvey and Willy Fritsch, Ufa sound film's 'perfect couple.' Producer Pommer's dream team had appeared together already in three previous movies—including *Melodie des Herzens*, in which Fritsch had launched the German talkie with the unforgettable line: "Ich spare nämlich auf ein Pferd" ['I'm actually saving for a horse!']. In the English version of *Liebeswalzer*, released as *The Love Waltz* in London on July 24, 1930, Fritsch was replaced by John Batten, Anglo-German actress and singer Lilian Harvey starred in both versions. Fritsch and Harvey made nine more films together and were a hit with audiences even when there was no singing involved—such as in *Hokuspokus* (DE, Gustav Ucicky, 1930), a first adaptation of Swiss-German writer and actor Curt Goetz's 1926 lighthearted courtroom comedy, which was simultaneously produced for the English-language market as *The Temporary Widow*.

Die Drei von der Tankstelle also launched actor Heinz Rühmann's successful career, which was to last six decades across three political regimes. Because of the success of *Die Drei von der Tankstelle* and the subsequent *Die Privatsekretärin* [The Private Secretary] (DE, 1931), Thiele became known as "Ufa's most successful musical comedy specialist."[41] Bock and Töteberg underline the impact of Thiele's films, from *Liebeswalzer* onwards, as his "integration of musical numbers and narrative" not only became integral to, but "pre-empted an important element of subsequent Hollywood musicals."[42] According to Marian Winter,

> Wilhelm Thiele first achieved the successful film operetta using conventional music material, but so co-ordinated it with a plot adaptable to the camera, that a welcome effect of spontaneity and careless gaiety was attained. In *Drei von der Tankstelle* (1930), with pleasant music by Werner Heymann, the musical comedy *milieu* with its stage limitations was disregarded, and the camera endowed a stage form with new freedom.[43]

Incidentally, Winter notes, "Clair was in Berlin at the time Thiele was proving how deftly [sound] could be used, and to what degree spontaneity in film operetta could be achieved." René Clair's subsequent first sound film *Sous les Toits de Paris* [Under the Roofs of Paris] (FR, 1930), inspired by Thiele's work, almost instantly "became a classic."[44] Clair's *À nous la liberté* [Freedom for Us] (FR, 1931) was produced by Tobis-Tonbild Syndikat and filmed at

Tobis' Epinay Studios north of Paris. According to Winter, a decade into the establishment of the operetta film as a new genre, only three directors were considered successful in musical (operetta) films: Wilhelm Thiele, G.W. Pabst, and René Clair. The impact of their work on Hollywood was significant as "[i]t was the lessons learned from Thiele and Clair that freed American musical films of much that was cumbersome, and pointed the way for the spontaneity of Astaire-Rogers films."[45] Winter might also have mentioned Erik Charell's MLV-film *Der Kongreß tanzt* [Congress Dances] (1931/German and French versions, 1932/English), another international blockbuster success for Ufa and producer Pommer. The operetta film stars Harvey in all three versions as Christel/Chystel and, as Tzar Alexander and his double, Fritsch in the German, Henri Garat in the French and English versions.

During the 1920s, chorus lines of female dancers such as the Tiller Girls were labeled 'mass ornament' by critic Kracauer, who likened the rhythm of their movements to the actions performed in a factory by humans at conveyer belt or indeed by the machines themselves, thus providing "unmediated access to the fundamental substance of the state of things."[46] A decade later, the music of modern revue films and songs in musical comedies churned out by the entertainment industries both in the United States and in Europe gainfully addressed the modern, urban public's longing for order and stability particularly as their technological-functional societies[47] were becoming increasingly chaotic, ambivalent, and unstable. As for the aforementioned musicians, only a fraction of them were lucky enough to be hired for recordings of musical scores by film companies or as extras performing on film. The majority of "these talented individuals suddenly found themselves without employment just as the Depression was engulfing America."[48] This was just as true on the other side of the Atlantic Ocean as the major economic crisis following the Wall Street crash in October 1929 took hold of Europe. Especially larger cities like London, Berlin, or Paris were marked by mass unemployment and poverty. A severe housing crisis aggravated the crisis in Berlin and saw numbers of homeless families as well as infant mortality rising rapidly. Statistics also indicate an increase in fatalities among women due to illegally performed and botched abortions, which was an unmistakable indicator of growing despondency, especially among the lower classes.

Sound and Political Agency in German Literature/Film

In 1929, medical doctor, author, and political activist Friedrich Wolf wrote a so-called "Tendenzdrama" or tendencious play intended to provoke public debate around the §218 of the Weimar Republic's Criminal Code, which declared abortion illegal and punishable by imprisonment up to five years.[49] Wolf wanted to draw attention to the grim consequences of Germany's highly restrictive abortion legislation for women, who often found themselves in desperate circumstances and ended up availing of the services of untrained backstreet abortionists. Like Ernst Toller, Bertolt Brecht, Helene Weigel, Erwin Piscator, and others, Friedrich Wolf believed in the potential of all arts, but especially literature performed in theaters, to be a political weapon, as he had outlined in his *Kunst ist Waffe* in 1928.[50] Aware of the power of film, and in order to maximize the impact of the play, Hans Tintner adapted *Cyankali* originally written by Wolf for the cinema screen in collaboration with the author. When the film premiered in May 1930, it was advertised as a 'major sound and talking picture' ["Groß-Ton- und Sprechfilm"] based on the 'famous play by Dr. Friedrich Wolf'. Grete Mosheim was presented as the star of the picture, but a text on the poster announcing the film's premiere provided further information:

> German doctors anticipate about 1 million surreptitious abortions, of which 10 000 result in the death of the woman, and 50 000 of them end up seriously ill.—Would it not be better if the Government regulated and allowed birth control?

The text goes on to highlight the playwright's medical profession and emphasizes the fact that he was forced to witness those tragedies time and again. In its advertisement, the sound cinema 'Tonfilm-Bühne Babylon' at Bülowplatz in Berlin stated that this film *'speaks* [...] bitter earnestness and bitter truth'.

Cyankali had been filmed as a silent picture in Ufa's studios in Berlin Tempelhof and Neubabelsberg from January 1930. In April of the same year, sound elements were added to deepen the affective impact as the film draws to its tragic close. In agony after an illegal abortion and a poisonous dose of potassium cyanide dispensed by a backstreet abortionist, Hete (Grete Mosheim) now screams audibly for help as she is slowly dying with her powerless mother by her side. For the most part of the film, silent images and title plates reflect the story of Paul and Hete, a young couple still hopeful in the beginning that the ongoing factory workers' strike will result in better working conditions for all and enable them to afford the child Hete is expecting. But a lockout and subsequent loss of income quickly turn their everyday hardship into utter desperation in light of the young woman's pregnancy. Entirely in line with Wolf's play, Tintner's film is a deeply political, but also emotional plea for legal change. The addition of sound elements was geared toward attracting greater audiences but also aimed at maximizing the film's affective rhetoric as audiences watched Hete's excruciating end, with her inconsolable mother facing prison for having assisted Hete in taking the 'medicine'. Tintner's inclusion of new sound

FIGURE 4.2 *Grete Mosheim as Hete, crying for help in* Cyankali *(DE, Hans Tintner, 1931)*.

technology did amplify the movie's message and generated livid support for the modification of §218 wherever the film was screened. *Cyankali* had a very successful run in the German capital from May 23, 1930, despite a number of cuts required by Berlin's main censorship board. Locally, however, especially in Munich and other conservative towns in Bavaria and across Germany, the police frequently prohibited performances, and in 1933 the film was banned by the new Nazi-led government and disappeared from the public sphere.

The topic of unwanted pregnancy/illegal abortion was raised repeatedly in German-language literature at the time. Increasing numbers of female authors[51] contributed to the public sphere by publishing articles and literary texts, and women writers such as Vicki Baum and Irmgard Keun wove the abortion and single mother discourse into their literary narratives. The success of their literary publications brought them to the attention of the film industry, which was always interested in a good story, especially if it came with limited economic risk. As adaptations, these bestselling novels also lent legitimacy to the cinematic promotion of discourses on controversial issues such as unwanted pregnancy, abortion, and giving birth out of wedlock.

Baum, working for Ullstein in Berlin at the time, published her novel *Stud. chem. Helene Willfüer* first in serialized form in Ullstein's *Berliner Illustrierte Zeitung* in 1928/9, which was a breakthrough success for the working mother of two. In the novel, skilfully shaped and marketed by Ullstein[52] publishers, her protagonist Helene, a soon to be PhD in chemistry, struggles to succeed in a field dominated by men, and when she falls pregnant, she tries in vain to arrange for a termination. Baum draws attention to the desperation caused by pregnancy, the dangers of making illicit services available, and the serious hardship of single motherhood. However, misery rarely sells and, as the novel progresses, the author augments the narrative clarity of New Objectivity with fairy-tale or, perhaps, wishful thinking. Baum presents an unmarried Helene who prevails against all odds and finally achieves independence in a career of her choice. The novel does not end here, however, and makes a decidedly conventional turn when Helene eventually decides to leave her job and marry her old chemistry professor—a marketing decision that was to maximize Baum's readership. The adaptation, produced by Heinrich Nebenzahl and Gustav Schwab, premiered on March 3, 1930. The text was adapted by screenwriters Curt J. Braun and Herbert Rosenfeld and filmed under the direction of Fred Sauer, who had previously written and directed *Ledige Mütter* [Single Mothers] in 1928. *Stud. chem. Helene Willfüer* starred Olga Tschechowa (Chekhova) as the chemistry student Helene, who drops out when she falls pregnant and, again, cannot get an abortion. But on screen her redemption comes in the form of hardship as Helene works a variety of jobs to make ends meet, raising her child on her own. Finally, her old professor (Ernst Stahl-Nachbaur), no longer married, but now blind and in need of a career, marries her, providing a pragmatic end to this cautionary tale.

Irmgard Keun also raised the issue of unwanted pregnancy in her first novel *Gilgi. Eine von uns* (Gilgi, One of Us, 1931), while foregrounding a young woman's urban experience of modernity and reflecting on the social reality[53] of this type of 'New Woman'. Also written in the temperate and lucid style of New Objectivity, Gilgi is 'one of us' as the subtitle suggests, striving toward financial independence and sexual self-determination, a typical example of a working girl in a white-collar job enjoying a degree of independence and trying to succeed in the modern metropolis. Her dreams, however, are mass-produced by a star-studded entertainment industry and, hence, interchangeable, just like the 'tired, sullen faces' that surround her on the tram: 'always the same, always the same.'[54] As scholars such as Ritta Jo Horsley or Gerd-Peter Rutz point out, in modern Berlin, the younger generation, no matter whether working-class or white-collar employee, dreamt of breaking out of their routines and 'making it' in the big city.[55] For young women, dime novels, fashion magazines, and, especially, movies suggested that their bodies and outward appearance were their most important assets in this dream of social ascent, one fleeting relationship at a time. By tracing Gilgi's dreams, challenges, and failures, Keun reflects on the contradictions and instability of both the final years of the Weimar Republic and the sexually active New Woman, as Horsley[56] rightly emphasizes, but at this time of severe economic crisis the text also suggests a critical evaluation of the illusion of stardom and vast riches. The author thus recounts the aforementioned socio-political and cultural criticism of writers such as Ernst Toller, and takes the film industry to task when she indicates the paralyzing effect of escapist entertainment that feeds the masses with unrealistic stories and fairy-tale endings.[57] Undeterred, the sound film company T. K. Tonfilm under Felix Pfitzner secured the rights to the runaway bestseller *Gilgi*, and scriptwriters Irma von Cube and Emeric Pressburger adapted the popular novel for the cinema screen.

Eine von uns [One of Us] (DE, Johannes Meyer, 1932) is a conventional tale of a good girl from a stable middle-class home, who experiences some confusion and a bit of hardship, but when she gets pregnant, the travel writer and father of her unborn child (Gustav Diessl) does 'the right thing' and marries her. In the end, all is well and bourgeois order is restored. Following the successful recipe of Hollywood's early sound films, the film features an original score by Franz Grothe and songs written by Fritz Rotter. Brigitte Helm, who held a ten-year contract with Ufa since her portrayal of the two Marias in *Metropolis* (1927) and other successful leads in adaptations such as *Alraune* (1927 and 1930), plays Gilgi. T. K. Tonfilm, the company that emerged from the agreement between the aforementioned sound film patent holders Tobis, Klangfilm, General Electric, and Western Electric, produced the movie. The syndicate shared their patents and was now called Tobis-Klangfilm. The film was distributed internationally by Paramount.[58]

The success of *Eine von uns* was negligible, however, compared to another movie at the time that was to become one of the most widely known and discussed[59] adaptations of a German-language text following its premiere in 1930: *Der blaue Engel* [*The Blue Angel*] based on Heinrich Mann's *Professor Unrat oder das Ende eines Tyrannen* (*Small Town Tyrant*, lit. Professor Rubbish or the End of a Tyrant, 1905). The movie starred renowned theater and film actor Emil Jannings, and introduced Marlene Dietrich to an international audience.[60] Jannings had been eager to play the title role of the authoritarian Professor and encouraged Heinrich Mann as early as 1923/4 to pursue an adaptation of his novel.[61] The actor's great success in films such as *Der letzte Mann* [lit. The Last Man; *The Last Laugh*] (1924) and *Faust* (1926), however, prompted a contract offer by Paramount and Jannings decided to continue his career in Hollywood. Producer Pommer had already quit at Ufa after being blamed for the company's financial difficulties, especially in light of the costly production of *Metropolis*, and had joined former colleagues Lya de Putti, Lubitsch, and Murnau in California.[62]

Jannings starred across the Atlantic in films such as *The Way of All Flesh* (US, Victor Fleming, 1927), *The Patriot* (US, Ernst Lubitsch, 1928; Hanns

Kräly wrote the script largely based on Alfred Neumann's biographical narrative[63] about Paul I of Russia), and in John F. Goodrich/Herman J. Mankiewicz's Lajos Bíró adaptation *The Last Command* (US, Josef von Sternberg, 1928). His depiction of the Russian Emperor Czar Paul I in the latter film, the only silent film ever nominated for Best Picture,[64] won Jannings an Oscar for Best Actor in a Leading Role in 1929. Despite this phenomenal success, his career in Hollywood, however, was over. Silent films were no longer deemed worthy investments and, with Jannings' English-language skills being far too deficient for a sound film career in North America, a return to the country of his native tongue seemed the only sensible option. The introduction of sound, however, also impacted positively on Jannings' future. A *Professor Unrat*-adaptation, considered unworkable when Heinrich Mann and the actor discussed it in the mid-1920s, now became an attractive new project for veteran producer Pommer. Having worked for Paramount and MGM, Pommer returned to Germany with numerous Hollywood connections and plenty of knowledge regarding the latest innovations and advances in filmmaking.[65] It was the availability of sound film technology that finally brought *Professor Unrat* or, rather, *The Blue Angel* to the cinema screen.[66]

Back at Ufa in Berlin, Erich Pommer commissioned his former colleague, Austro-American Josef von Sternberg to direct the film on account of his Hollywood 'talkie' experience—a necessary measure in light of the existing gap in sound film expertise in Europe at the time as mentioned above. While there had been interest in experimenting with sound at Ufa from the mid-1920s onwards, the company was not only financially under enormous pressure[67] but also in terms of studio space. Existing studios had glass roofs to let in a maximum amount of light, but with the introduction of sound, every passing airplane and, especially, rainfall caused delays and necessitated retakes. In 1929 Ufa's board of directors cleared the way for four purpose-built sound film studios in Babelsberg outside Berlin. This "Tonkreuz" (referring to the shape of the four <u>sound</u> studios forming a <u>cross</u> around a courtyard) was around 38,000 square feet and provided a state-of-the-art soundproof environment.[68]

FIGURE 4.3 *Marlene Dietrich and the transformation of Emil Jannings in* Der blaue Engel *(DE, Josef von Sternberg, 1930)*.

Right-wing Leadership at Ufa: The Making and Impact of *The Blue Angel*

The industrialist, media mogul, and fervent nationalist Alfred Hugenberg had taken over Ufa in 1927, mainly in order to "save it from falling into American hands" as a British journalist noted at the time.[69] Hugenberg owned the Scherl-group—a newspaper empire that also published cinema journals such as *Filmwelt* and *Der Kinematograph*—and represented the DNVP [Deutschnationale Volkspartei or German National People's Party] in the Reichstag, i.e., German parliament. His right-wing outlook was in stark contrast to Heinrich Mann's leftist, anti-fascist leanings and literary works. In novels such as *Professor Unrat* and *Der Untertan* (*The Loyal Subject*, 1914–18) Mann had satirized Wilhelmine society and criticized the servility of the German bourgeoisie and its compliant philistines, all too easily manipulated by commanding suggestions of nationalism and social order. While the immense popularity of his novels recommended them for adaptation, even the support of big shots such as Pommer and Jannings seemed insufficient when the adaptation of *Professor Unrat* was first suggested to members of the Ufa-board under Hugenberg's right-wing leadership. Minutes of relevant board meetings reflect the amount of resistance the film project had to overcome, which was above all due to the literary source itself and, of course, its author. The novel was considered an 'evil attack of higher education' and the portrayal of grammar school teacher Professor "Unrat" or 'Rubbish' was deemed an 'exaggerated' and 'disagreeable' caricature by its left-wing, scandalizing author. Already in August 1929 Ufa's head of production Ernst Hugo Correll suggested that the plot of the novel would be 'completely reworked' and that the figure of the Professor would be portrayed in a 'humane and compassionate manner'.[70]

On September, 23, 1929, Ufa finally bought the rights to Heinrich Mann's novel for the stately sum of 25,000 Reichsmark. Another 10,000 Reichsmark were added in 1931 for the English-language version of the film, which was shot scene by scene in parallel.[71] At the same time, as Michael Grisko explains, Ufa's PR team was at pains to establish distance between the adaptation and the novel's author. Permission to publish a photograph showing Mann together with the two lead actors sought by *Frankfurter Illustrierte Zeitung*, for example, was refused, and not a single official photograph associating the film with Heinrich Mann seems to exist.[72] While it has been suggested that Mann produced a first screenplay for the film, which was subsequently mostly ignored by the three screenwriters Carl Zuckmayer, Robert Liebmann, and Karl Vollmöller, no material evidence for this claim still exists. However, the author did meet with the screenwriters on a number of occasions and was sometimes present during the filming of *Der blaue Engel/The Blue Angel*. The movie was to be available in both

German and English at first, with Jannings in particular speaking the foreign tongue with a heavy accent. His portrayal of Rath as an English (!) teacher in the German version of the movie provided welcome comic relief, while his authority was portrayed as somewhat hapless compared to the often rather malicious power he yields in the source text. In his autobiography *Fun in a Chinese Laundry* Sternberg[73] foregrounds his own vision for the film and indicates that the famous playwright Zuckmayer's mention as one of the scriptwriters was merely a strategy employed for marketing purposes.[74] This version of events is in stark contrast to Zuckmayer's own account, which might also be somewhat exaggerated. It is safe to assume, however, that the final screenplay was shaped by the input of all three screenwriters, Mann, and the director. Mann himself explained in a letter to Karl Lemke that the transposition from novel to film was accomplished "with the help of seven persons altogether. You must not think that the director himself made all the decisions. I had a voice, and so did, in addition, two other authors [Carl Zuckmayer and Karl Gustav Vollmöller], a script writer [Robert Liebmann], a representative of the UFA [Erich Pommer] and, finally, Jannings and Sternberg."[75]

In *Der blaue Engel/The Blue Angel*, however, Dietrich's Lola Lola has little in common with the single mother and occasional prostitute Rosa Fröhlich, the female protagonist in the novel. Mann's biting critique of a hypocritical bourgeoisie and its authoritarian, callous system of repression, as well as his at least partial cognizance of a marginal(ized) woman's precarious everyday is no longer represented in the film. Instead, the adaptation's 'Lola' evokes a history of scandalous and spectacular performers, such as Anita Berber, who appeared as 'Lola' in Richard Oswald's *The Yellow House* (aka *Prostitution*), a box office hit in 1919. It also makes reference to *Die tolle Lola* [Fabulous/Crazy[76] Lola] (DE, Richard Eichberg 1927), based on both the play *Der Weg zur Hölle* (The Road to Hell, 1906) by the Hungarian-German Jewish writer and actor Gustav Kadelburg, and on its even more successful adaptation as an operetta by Hugo Hirsch in 1919. Eichberg's *Die tolle Lola*-film starred the Anglo-German actor and singer Lilian Harvey as the entertainer and dancer Tilly Schneider who performs Spanish dances as 'Lola Cornero', inspired by another (in)famous Lola, i.e., Lola Montez and her gambits of the 1840s that included highly publicized affairs with well-known gentlemen such as the writers Dumas (both father and son) and king Ludwig I of Bavaria. Harvey, who had begun her career as a revue dancer, had starred in a number of silent films until her breakthrough in 1925 when she appeared as leading lady in two films directed by the aforementioned Eichberg—*Leidenschaft* [Passion] alongside with Otto Gebühr, and *Liebe und Trompetenblasen* [Love and Trumpets] together with Harry Liedtke and Harry Halm. By 1930, Harvey was an international celebrity.[77] The renaming of the female protagonist Rosa Fröhlich to Lola Lola though not only indicates the filmmakers' desire to maximize *The Blue Angel*'s potential profit by linking the commodity to other bestselling cultural products, but also signposts the most fundamental transformation of Mann's text into a new rendering of the age-old myth, with Lola Lola performing the new Pandora-type of the sound film era.

The Blue Angel tells the story of bourgeois schoolmaster Prof. Rath who becomes infatuated with the personification of his repressed desires embodied by the cabaret singer Lola Lola. Unable to think outside bourgeois norms and structures, Rath's attempt to legalize his relationship with a 'fallen' woman and, thereby, contain Lola's sexuality via the bourgeois institution of marriage proves to be fatal. Five years after his vitalistic liberation but incapable of growing into a self-determined individual, Rath is devoid of all dignity, a mere object, an attraction to be laughed at. In contrast, Lola Lola is loose woman, seductive performer, and (near-)average housewife in one. At the same time that Rath is publicly abused as the stage clown by the director of the troupe (Kurt Gerron), Lola is making out with another artist (Hans Albers), hence displaying her infidelity as inhumanity. After this final humiliation, Rath returns to his old school and dies at his desk, once more embraced by a beam of light, only this time it is the porter's flashlight that unambiguously links his death to the spotlight Lola shone on him during his first visit to the seedy 'Blue Angel' joint by the harbor.

Then, intrigued and concerned by photographs of Lola he had confiscated from his students, Professor Rath walked along a dark alley toward the bar, clearly out of his depth while a foghorn sounds warning. As Mann put it, he is about to enter an "abyss," an "alien milieu that is such a 'negation of his whole being' [...] that he is incapable of perceiving this vulgar, shrieking, voluptuous body, this 'something'," as Gilbert Carr writes in reference to both film and Mann's novel, comparing it to the seductive "false Maria's dance in Fritz Lang's *Metropolis*."[78] As soon as Rath enters this space, marked with symbolic images such as nets and cages in the film, his entanglement begins. This place of entertainment is a chaotic mess and further suggests that this might indeed be a dangerous trap leading to confusion, bondage, and disintegration. Match-cuts link the disoriented schoolmaster making his way through the chaos of the club and the performer on stage to whom he is inevitably drawn. For there, in the center of long shots to medium close-ups, scantily clad and singing in her huskily distinctive voice, visually and aurally erotic Marlene Dietrich is positioned for "the pleasure and reassurance of the male spectator."[79] A spectacle, further objectified by plenty of props surrounding her, she stands confidently in the middle of the stage with her hands on her hips and flaunting an outfit that reveals most of her attractive features. It is only during the initial moments of this first encounter with Lola Lola on stage that Rath communicates the dominating power of the male gaze. At this point, he still possesses economic and social superiority, but despite his repulsed confusion he adores Lola, who successfully functions as erotic object. But all too soon it is she who gazes and objectifies. While singing a song that establishes her as the dominant party—"Heute such' ich mir was aus! Einen Mann, einen richtigen Mann!" [Tonight I'll choose something! A man, a real man!]—she confines and objectifies the schoolmaster by way of a spotlight. What follows are dependency and increasing degradation after losing his job due to his marriage to Lola Lola, emphasizing a crisis of male identity so often depicted in films of the Weimar Republic.[80] When the troupe returns to his former hometown, his humiliation is highlighted again by way of juxtaposition. Similarly composed shots now confine him to a life on stage. Making use of the affective rhetoric of the melodrama, the former Professor now not only suffers the callousness of his unfaithful wife but is also at the mercy of the troupe's director and magician, who cracks eggs on the broken man's head and makes him croak like a rooster.

In the closing sequence of this film, it is the Professor's last journey back to his old school that is match-cut with Lola's wide-legged performance of her famous song known in the English version as "Falling in Love Again," emphasizing her interest in love making and nothing else. If men get burnt in the process, as she declares in the German version, that surely was not her problem—"Und wenn sie verbrennen, ja dafür kann ich nichts."

In this adaptation, the toppled authoritarian of the novel becomes the pitiable victim of a vamp who is the source of anarchy, chaos, and ultimately death. Lola Lola personifies the sexual/phallic woman that remains a deeply ambivalent figure: she gives liberation, life, and sensuality, but at the same time, she exudes danger and eventually brings ruin. The force and menace of female sexuality are once more emphasized by Lola Lola's final song. Clearly this woman is unwilling to preserve patriarchal law and sacrifice her desire to that of the male Other. Therefore, her actions must be labeled as negative which Sternberg achieves by constructing a vamp and confronting her sexual power with the heart-breaking destruction of a gentleman, educator, and upstanding member of bourgeois society.

Mann "felt sympathetic towards the film," as he said after the first screening, not least due to its "ingenious stage director," and remained publicly supportive of the adaptation after the movie's release in both Europe and the United States.[81] Mann stressed the proximity of the work of an author and a film director, but also his awareness for the need of a different perspective. In literature, "[w]e stage these events, although only verbally. Still, they are made visible to the imagination."[82] He accepted the changes to the narrative, as in his view

> this does not affect the characters, who remain basically the same. They now disport themselves in the film rather than in the novel, which changes their actions but not their nature. From another of his mental predispositions, Unrat [...] may well end as a clown (as he does in the movie) instead of as a croupier (as he does in the novel). The action unfolds along the same lines but is simplified in view of the fifty million viewers Sternberg envisages.[83]

In the same letter to Karl Lemke, he introduces a caveat as he proclaims not to know enough about the "transfer from the literary to the cinematographic medium." Nonetheless, the author seemed pleased that "the plot of the film differs only in the second half from that of my novel" and "even a few of my lines have been salvaged." Publicly, he remained convinced that the operation was successful in the case of *The Blue Angel*.

> Some sort of transition is imperative in every instance [...]. The adapters of the novel simply must build a bridge to the film, for a true novel cannot be filmed integrally [sic]. It has many sides, only one of which faces the film, which has to be shot in its own terms, as has here been the case in my opinion.[84]

Mann's enthusiasm for the adaptation was more than pragmatic, it seems. He was delighted with his characters' embodiment, particularly by Dietrich, "bursting forth with life."[85] Victor Mann confirmed his uncle's complete support of Marlene Dietrich's personification of his 'Artist Rosa Fröhlich' in his 1949 biography of the Mann family.[86]

Heinrich Mann was also delighted when seeing Jannings in the role of Professor Unrat: "A great actor, Emil Jannings, had borrowed his shape and was now displaying it to me. He had enlarged on the figure, following its innermost nature, for in the novel Unrat does not die; but Jannings knew and realized the manner of his death."[87] The way the nightclub's noises and jealousies, songs, and screams "had been revived in the studios of Neubabelsberg"[88] fascinated him, and the film undoubtedly profited from the author's full endorsement at the box office. The author's interest in adaptation is indicative of the changing role of cinema in the context of sound film. Writers like Heinrich Mann recognized and creatively embraced the opportunity to bring literature to another life on screen.

Today the film is sometimes described as "one of the great European films of the twentieth century."[89] At the time of its release, the movie was highly praised, not only by those writing for the more conservative papers. Kracauer, in contrast, called the film a 'prime example of insubstantiality' with its limpid aim not to criticize and reveal, but rather to veil and, of course, to entertain. Using the novel itself to inform and substantiate his criticism, he targets right-wing Hugenberg, the Ufa board, and their willing team of filmmakers. Together, Kracauer carped, they deliberately eliminated social critique and removed any insight into the Professor's 'dark psyche'[90] that in the 1905 novel captured the core of a system of repression, an ailing society, and a volatile bourgeoisie. This view was echoed abroad, especially when the English-language version was shown.

Despite impressive performances and a wide-ranging narrative integration of sound, the film was deemed too conventional by some critics abroad, and the actors' English for the most part unconvincing. A reviewer in *The Observer* wrote:

> This is not the film [...] that is likely to save Europe from American domination. It has plenty of effects, but no real spirit, [...] nothing [...] to muster followers, to stir up enthusiasms, as the Soviet directors know so well how to do. 'The Blue Angel' goes no further than its own little problems.[91]

But even this little enthused critic praised Dietrich as "a new and very exciting actress," who was able to convince even in the English version of the film.[92] Decades later, *The Blue Angel* is still being debated by scholars, yet not necessarily in the context of adaptation. And while Stephen Brockmann sees Lola Lola as the "quintessential 'New Woman' of the Weimar Republic," the conservative, patriarchal system still has the upper hand—for despite his torment and even in death "Rath continues to exercise supreme narrative authority," as Judith Mayne points out.[93] In 1931, Heinrich Mann reflected on the consequences of turning his satire into a melodrama and wrote to the writer Erich Ebermayer, who adapted *Professor Unrat* for the theater stage: 'as effective as Jannings played his death, letting Unrat die at his desk as a Clown was wrong'.[94]

Apart from bowing to Hugenberg's conservative agenda, the movie follows the basic principle of sound film as musical entertainment first established by *The Jazz Singer*. Sternberg himself used a method still common at the time "of building the main structure of his film on silence and introducing dialogue only at pivotal moments," as one of the film's London reviewers noted. Consequently, it is the absence of sound, which is, in the view of this critic, "for the first time [furnished] with a weighty meaning."[95] However, it was particularly sound as song that proved popular with cinemagoers from 1927 and well into the 1930s and 1940s.

In Germany, the box-office successes of the previous Dietrich film *Ich küsse Ihre Hand, Madame* [I Kiss Your Hand, Madame] (DE, Robert Land, 1929) and, especially, the operetta film *Die Drei von der Tankstelle*[96] indicated to media moguls and producers alike that the public wanted light, conventional entertainment that included songs. The latter would be played on the radio, and sung in cabarets and on the streets. The songs of *Ich küsse Ihre Hand, Madame* and *Die Drei von der Tankstelle* became bestsellers in music shops. As a film, *The Blue Angel/Der blaue Engel* exceeded commercial expectations on both sides of the Atlantic. But it was particularly the songs by Friedrich Hollaender that became global bestsellers on gramophone records, and turned Dietrich into an international celebrity. Following its premiere in London, *The Observer* noted that the film is "acknowledged by all the recognised critics to be the pick of existing German sound production."[97] As a sound film, it skillfully combined the latest technology with the aesthetic of 1920s German cinema: "The surface appearance of the old German cinema is there, the beautiful warm lighting, the romantic photography. There are camera angles and camera usages of the old school which the new cinema has forgotten and at the same time there is new and exciting use of incidental sound." After *The Blue Angel* there was no doubt in the minds of experienced producers such as Pommer that "the public prefers the entertaining story interwoven with music."[98]

But it was also Dietrich, who fascinated audiences as Lola Lola, depicting a familiar and yet novel female stereotype that, in this case, did not merely harken back to ancient myths but instead communicated the toughness of the working class, the fairytale of social mobility, and, most importantly, the ambivalence of Berlin's seedy and fabulous, creative and limitless nightlife. Balancing precariously on the edge of the volcano during this postwar era, Weimar society's dance was further intensified in its feverish desire for pleasure and entertainment after the Wall Street crash.[99] Dietrich was instrumental in the creation and establishment of this archetypal *femme fatale* in cinema. Dietrich's quintessential embodiment of the hauntingly alluring, but ultimately harmful and even lethal vamp impacted cinema to a significant degree, even more so than Louise Brooks' silent and eventually silenced *femme fatale* in Pabst's *Pandora's Box* (1929) based on Wedekind's plays.

After the German premiere of *Der blaue Engel*, Sternberg took Dietrich back with him to the United States and Hollywood's Paramount studios. In the following five years Sternberg directed *Morocco* (1930), *Dishonoured* (1931), *Shanghai Express* (1932), *Blonde Venus* (1932), *The Scarlet Empress* (1934), and *The Devil Is a Woman* (1935), all starring Dietrich and thus helping to firmly establish the image of the dangerous vamp and sexual predator in US American film production.[100] The *femme fatale* became the female archetype of *film noir*—*film noir*'s fantasy one might say—epitomized by Rita Hayworth, Barbara Stanwyck, and Joan Crawford. In the 1940s and 1950s, 'Black Widow' or 'Spider Woman' films were particularly popular, such as Roy William Neill's *Spider Woman* (1944), Arthur Lubin's sequel *The Spider Woman Strikes Back* (1946), or Nunnally Johnson's *Black Widow* (1954) with Ginger Rogers, based on the novel *Fatal Woman* by Patrick Quentin. *Femme fatale* films were produced regularly throughout the second half of the twentieth century and included box-office hits such as *Fatal Attraction* (US, Adrian Lyne, 1987). More recent but just as stereotypical reincarnations such as *Femme Fatale* (FR, Brian de Palma, 2002) or *Red Sparrow* (US, Francis Lawrence, 2018) have been less successful—perhaps indicating that particularly female audiences no longer appreciate this continuous cinematic feed of a threatening archetype in need of repression and control.

Adaptation Co-op: Christa Winsloe's and Leontine Sagan's *Girls in Uniform*

Heinrich Mann's criticism of the German Empire's school system, which produces bullies and future authoritarians, is included in Sternberg's adaptation *The Blue Angel* for mainly comedic effect. Filmmaker Leontine Sagan in contrast, who directed *Mädchen in Uniform* [Girls in Uniform] in 1931, puts the spotlight on a similarly repressive system of education that stifles emotion and physical contact with near-fatal consequence. Christa Winsloe wrote the script together with F.D. Andam (Friedrich Dammann), based on her own play *Children in Uniform* (the title of the London premiere in 1932), which was first performed in Leipzig as *Ritter Nérestan* (Knight Nérestan, 1930) and then in Berlin as *Gestern und heute* (Yesterday and Today, 1931).[101] Sagan's talkie is often discussed by film historians as the first representation of lesbian desire on film, for in this boarding school for girls structured by rigid discipline, demands of obedience, a vilification of the body, and double standards, there is one kind teacher who practices a more enlightened, compassionate education.

Using an all-female, largely unprofessional cast, Sagan's film uses sound to counter the stiff authoritarians' harsh bellowing with the voices of natural youth, lending it "a fresh and documentary-like tone," as Ruby Rich wrote in *Jump Cut* in 1981, hailing the film "key to establishing a history of lesbian cinema."[102] Sagan carefully frames the gentle, if intense attraction felt by fourteen-year-old pupil Manuela (Hertha Thiele) for her kindhearted teacher Fräulein von Bernburg (Dorothea Wieck), especially after being kissed goodnight by her—not on the forehead like the other girls, but on the lips—an act that, from a twenty-first-century perspective, considering the age of the pupil and the teacher's position of power is, of course, highly problematic. At the same time, the film is about empowerment, even at young age, and disobedience, which can be lifesaving.

Inspired by Soviet avant-garde filmmakers Pudovkin's and Eisenstein's work, Sagan's montage-inflected talkie places a thoughtful and open-minded child within an educational system that relies on rigidly authoritarian methods aimed at order, discipline, and complete submission. When Manuela publicly declares her love for her caring educator, the two systems and their representatives (Fräulein von Bernburg and the dictatorial head teacher, played by Emilie Unda) clash. In Winsloe's play, this conflict culminates in the suicide of the child due to the weakness of Bernburg, who fails to stand up for Manuela or herself. The adaptation strengthens Frl. von Bernburg's character's resolve to some degree, but especially that of

Manuela's classmates, who—in an act of resistance that defies one of the school's imperatives—take action to save their friend from jumping to her death from the top of a forbidden staircase.[103]

Also novel for a commercial feature in Germany, the picture was produced collectively by Winsloe, Sagan, actors, and crew, under the auspices of the small profit-sharing co-op Deutsche Film-Gemeinschaft GmbH (Berlin), i.e., Friedrich Pflughaupt, Walter Supper, and Frank Wysbar, with support and financial input provided by Carl Froelich. Sagan's Winsloe-adaptation premiered on November 27, 1931, in Berlin's Capitol cinema to great critical acclaim. A Tobis-Klangfilm talkie, sound is used pioneeringly and to great effect, "not only as a functional synchronous accompaniment, but also as a thematic element in its own right," as Rich emphasizes. Winter highlights the moment when a "*diminuendo* of voices calling 'Manuela!' as the child mounts the stairs to commit suicide gives a sense of height and severance from the earth" as the film approaches its climax.[104] In Eisner's estimation, with *Mädchen in Uniform*, the "pre-war German sound film reached its highest level."[105]

Sagan's *Girls in Uniform* does not follow Sternberg's desire for light entertainment in *The Blue Angel* or Pabst's 1929 silent parody of tyrannical authority culminating in the orgiastic drill of the 'fallen girls' during synchronized gymnastics in *Diary of a Lost Girl*. Instead, *Mädchen in Uniform* uses sound, but also light, to communicate affectively Manuela's fragile presence, her luminous face repeatedly recorded by Reimar Kuntze and Franz Weihmayr's camera in medium close-up in front of light backgrounds, as Kracauer commends. But in his important *From Caligari to Hitler* (1947), he also criticizes the film for not going far enough in its critical analysis of Prussian authoritarianism and, by implication, fascism, as it fails to outline more directly the horrific consequence of a people's timid conformity. He notes, however, that in Germany, *Mädchen in Uniform* was considered the best film of the year, with a similarly positive echo among critics and cinemagoers in the United States.

Together with Pabst's *Diary of a Lost Girl*, the film had a visible impact on Hollywood productions on the topic of single motherhood and reform schools.[106] From the 1970s, *Girls in Uniform* has been screened regularly at film festivals and discussed among scholars in journal articles and books, often highlighting the early talkie's remarkable cinematographic examination of patriarchy, same-sex love and its essential, if implicit, call for equality and democracy.[107] In 1933, Sagan turned to her story once again and reworked it into a novel entitled *Das Mädchen Manuela* [The Girl Manuela], "which returns to *Nérestan*'s tragic ending (Manuela's suicide) and to the choice of Voltaire's *Zaïre* (over Friedrich Schiller's *Don Carlos*) for the school play at the heart of the plot."[108]

Rising Fascism in Europe and German-language Literature in Hollywood

In Italy, Mussolini and his National Fascist Party had been in power since 1922. In Germany, Hitler's Nazi party (NSDAP/National Socialistist German Workers' Party) had been promoting a *völkisch* nationalism based on a claim of superiority of the Aryan master race since 1920. Inspired by their Italian friends, Hitler and his thugs attempted to launch a coup d'etat on November 8, 1923, but their so-called Beer Hall Putsch failed. Hitler and a number of his supporters were subsequently tried for treason but given lenient sentences by sympathetic judges. In prison, Hitler wrote his infamous semi-autobiographical *Mein Kampf* (*My Struggle*, 1925/6), which was handed out for free to anyone interested during the late 1920s, particularly to teenagers via Nazi youth groups. Hitler presented himself as anti-elite and anti-establishment, as a voice of the disenfranchised little people, who were left to suffer the consequences of the ruling classes' capitalist greed. Adding a potpourri of anti-communist, anti-bourgeois, and antisemitic rhetoric depending on his audience, Hitler and his Nazi movement began to gain significant popular support during the economic devastation that followed the Wall Street crash of 1929. Heinrich Brüning's weak minority government, mass unemployment, and growing numbers of bankruptcies among small business owners fed a growing desire for stability, particularly among the hardest hit economically, the working and lower middle classes.

In the United States, studios were under state and industrial pressures to avoid taking a stand on fascism. A number of talkies produced at the time, however, could be read as responses to the rise of fascism in Europe and efforts to communicate a more critical engagement with or even deliberate opposition to the hateful populist nationalism spouted by the far right. Two of the most successful of these films were adaptations of German literature, based on Erich Maria Remarque's *Im Westen nichts Neues* (lit. Nothing New in the West/*All Quiet on the Western Front*, 1929) and Vicki Baum's *Menschen im Hotel* (lit. Humans in a Hotel/*Grand Hotel*, 1929). The novels had been runaway bestsellers across Europe and the United States and certainly recommended themselves from a marketing perspective. But considering the fact that one was an antiwar novel and the other authored by a Jewish writer that included clear references to the utter devastation caused by war, both adaptations could be regarded as actions against the rise in nationalism, militarism, and antisemitism—in short, against fascism.

Throughout the 1920s, First World War films had done extremely well at the box office, with *The Big Parade* (US, King Vidor, 1925) becoming one of the most successful silent pictures of the era. *Seventh Heaven* (Frank Borzage), *Hotel Imperial* (Mauritz Stiller), and *Wings* (William Wellman) followed in 1927 with great acclaim. The latter in particular impressed due to the numerous Magnascope aerial shots and battle scenes involving up to 300 pilots. *Wings* won the first Academy Award for Best Picture in 1929 and launched Gary Cooper's career. When *Wings* was screened in Germany, however, the quality of the soundtrack was so deficient that cinema owners complained and Universal pulled the film. Michael Wedel points to the problems Universal was facing regarding its dubbed German-language versions:

> First, this practice conflicted with the international patent law situation in technical sound equipment and became entangled in the Tobis-Klangfilm group and the Western Electric/RCA Photophone group's fight over the European (and German) exhibition market. The second problem was German audience's low tolerance for foreign films dubbed into German.[109]

Wolfgang Mühl-Benninghaus and Wedel outline the "incompatibility of the American (Western Electric) sound recording system and the European (Tobis-Klangfilm) reproduction apparatus" and the consequences of the different sound technologies used in the United States and Europe, which led to "serious acoustic shortcomings."[110] Universal dealt with the problem by relocating its "production of dubbed language versions from Hollywood to Germany and, by doing so, moved from Western Electric to Tobis-Klangfilm recording technology" and subsequently "expanded its own distribution activities in the German market by affording Deutsche Universal a broader financial basis."[111] While other Hollywood studios focused on producing different language versions of their films, Universal decided to invest heavily into post-synchronized, dubbed versions recorded on systems "that were compatible with local sound reproduction technology and complied with German patent law."[112] But, as Wedel emphasizes, "multiple-language versions were the dominant solution for the German market. Only 10 percent of all foreign films entering the German market in German language versions in 1930–31 were dubbed."[113]

When Universal bought the rights to Remarque's First World War-bestseller, the decision to pursue an adaptation under the direction of Lewis Milestone was not just a clever investment, however, but aimed at creating "the most powerful antiwar film of the 1930s."[114] Remarque's *Im Westen nichts Neues* had been published in January 1929 and the first edition of 30,000 sold out within days. By May more than half a million books had been purchased and translations into twenty-six languages were underway[115] and, as *Film-Kurier* reported in July 1929, Universal considered an adaptation with German actors to be filmed in Germany.[116]

In the novel, first-person narrator Paul Bäumer describes the everyday of war, reflects on the past and the consequences of the present, and gives accounts of the deaths of his friends one by one until, finally, he himself is shot and dies. But in light of the millions devoured by war, the death of the individual is insignificant and hence, as the title indicates, 'nothing' was reported from the western front that day. Flashbacks inform the reader of the boys' naïve enthusiasm for male heroism and valiant war action instilled in Bäumer and his adolescent classmates, but the text also conveys the reality of military training, everyday hardship, and the horror of combat. It thereby exposes the mechanisms employed by those in authority: "the false promises of spiritual regeneration [that] are nothing more than a lure to coax innocent civilians into signing up for military service. Trying to salvage some kind of redemptive value from the ruins of military conflict is a doomed enterprise," Maria Tatar summarizes Remarque's message.[117] The first-person narrative further dismantles the classic 'us' and 'them' binary, which feeds the war machine, by realizing a shared understanding of this paradoxical and incongruous war experience by human beings. While the story is told from a German point of view, the experience and its likely consequences are the same, no matter which side you are on: 'Grenades, gas and tanks—crushing, corroding, death. Dysentery, influenza, typhoid—asphyxiation, burning, death. Trench, hospital, mass grave—there are no other options.'[118] The young narrator's account also illustrates how the soldiers' passion swiftly turns to pragmatism and soon blends into increasing callousness and general brutalization. Projected ideals of an 'iron youth' are dismantled, as their language, bodies, and humanity slowly but surely disintegrate. While a number of literary texts[119] had been published in the 1920s that presented the past war in a critical light, the First World War veteran Toller considered Remarque's novel the most convincing and authentic literary portrayal of war ever produced. This is fiction, Toller writes in his 1929 review, which reflects the truth of war and its effect on human nature. This book 'should be distributed in the millions, translated, read in schools, [...] bought and given away as gifts', and perhaps, Toller hoped, it may prevent our 'blindness' and save future generations from being butchered on the battlefield.[120] While the focus here is on a group of German schoolboys, like many others Toller considered their war experience as depicted by Remarque as universal—a monotonous and banal, frightening and horrific everyday of non-heroes that may not be forgotten.

As in the novel, Milestone's *All Quiet on the Western Front* presents the First World War through the eyes and experiences of young Bäumer and his friends as they "proceed from the safety of their schoolrooms to the slaughter of the killing fields."[121] The adaptation opens not at the front, but in a classroom, filled with boys not men, thus creating a chronologically more linear narrative. Sound is used for great effect not only during the battle scenes. Already in the opening sequence, as soldiers march past the school and the rhythmical tune of the military band seeps into the classroom, the music and the voice of their teacher further ignite the pupils' desire to join the fight. Having been fed a diet of nationalism and heroic sacrifice, five of the boys enthusiastically sign up to make good on the promise of their

FIGURE 4.4 Lew Ayres *in* All Quiet on the Western Front *(US, Lewis Milestone, 1930).*

'iron youth'. But soon the everyday of war, filmed with great attention to detail, the cries of the wounded and the stillness of death unveil to them the vanity and emptiness of those stories of adventure, valor, and epic triumph. As in Remarque's novel, none of the boys live to see the end of the war. As Richard Jewell points out, the "indictment of war in *All Quiet* was arguably the most forceful that had ever been seen on the screen, but its sentiments were neither fresh nor unusual. Rather, they were in keeping with the genre's dominant ideological position, a position that had been well established since the early 1920s."[122]

In the adaptation, however, Hollywood's pacifist message was even more pronounced as Milestone carefully safeguarded the author's compelling demolition of war as adventure, of heroism as masculine virtue, or death on the battlefield as a glorious finale of a true hero's life. Employing several former German officers as advisors, the director's emphasis on realism—particularly regarding the sets and military action—as well as the transnational perspective was groundbreaking. When the 140-minute movie was released in the United States (as a talkie, and as a silent film for those cinemas still lacking sound equipment), it surpassed all box-office expectations and recuperated its production costs of 1.25 million dollars within a few weeks. The talkie was nominated for six Academy Awards, taking home the Oscar for 'Best Film' and 'Best Director'.

In the United States, censors had insisted on ten minutes of the original film to be cut. For the version to be screened in Germany, further cuts were made, among them an instance of vehement insubordination, a conversation critical of the Emperor that deems Wilhelm II responsible for the war, as well as the repeated appearance of a pair of good boots that is passed on from one soldier to the next, serving every temporary owner well until he, too, is killed.[123] At a time of growing nationalist sentiments in Germany though, where right-wing politicians and the conservative public frequently called for remilitarization and an end to the 'humiliation' of defeat that had become manifest in the treaty of Versailles, *All Quiet on the Western Front* was considered an intervention sure to cause discord. But the backlash to the first screenings of the film was more forceful and violent than anyone had expected. In addition, for conservative militarists and right-wing nationalists, this talkie was the perfect opportunity to once again heighten the resentment between the United States and Germany so prevalent during the all too recent sound technology 'patent war'. Peace was as unstable as the economy.

Already in May 1930 another antiwar adaptation had premiered in Berlin and had caused some uproar: *Westfront 1918*. Its depiction of the 'monotonous', 'hellish' 'reality of war'[124] shook audiences, as Kracauer noted in his review for *Frankfurter Zeitung*. Based on Ernst Johannsen's novel *Vier von der Infanterie, ihre letzten Tage an der Westfront 1918* (Four Infantrymen on the Western Front, 1918) and on the script by Ladislaus Vajda and Peter Martin Lampel,[125] this early Nero produced, Tobis-Klangfilm talkie communicated the dehumanizing effect of war in a realism hitherto unachieved in German cinema. Pabst directed the 1929 adaptation and carefully composed images that dialectically depict war as ordinary and extraordinary, normal and abnormal, everyday and horrifyingly exceptional—for example, when two young soldiers sit at the edge of a crater chatting away while their legs dangle over the shell hole.[126] In *Berliner Tageblatt* Alfred Kerr praised Pabst's film as it unveils the 'truth' about war, and suggests that particularly the younger generation should be mandated to see this 'realistic' picture.[127] While again criticizing the quality of the sound (a consequence of the incompatibility of the above mentioned US recording system and German projection technology), particularly of spoken dialogue, Kracauer, too, acknowledged the impact of the film due to the audience's experience of the human suffering caused by war. But again, it is not language but the primal human sounds—sighs and moans, sobs and screams—that in Kracauer's mind had the most dramatic affective impact and caused numerous members of the audience to 'flee' the cinema while loudly objecting to this 'unbearable' representation of war.[128] The effects of this 'human sound' were arguably augmented by the almost complete absence of music from the film. In Hollywood, Herbert Brenon's pre-Code drama *The Case of Sergeant Grischa* (1930)—an adaptation of Arnold Zweig's antiwar novel *Der Streit um den Sergeanten Grischa* (The Case of Sergeant Grischa, 1927)—was well received and its use of sound widely praised. Sound director John Tribby and his RKO Radio Studio Sound Department were nominated by the Academy for Best Sound Recording, but lost to MGM's *The Big House*.[129]

Only a few weeks later in June 1930 the chairman of the MPPDA (Motion Picture Producers and Distributors of America), Will Hays, visited Berlin, and, according to an article published in *Film-Kurier*, gave a speech "embellished with the friendliest sort of flattery for Germany" in which he noted that "sound film could be the 'greatest peace instrument of mankind'."[130] Hays had been actively involved in achieving the aforementioned peace deal between the US American and European sound technology patent holders that allowed for Hollywood films to be screened again in German cinemas and vice versa, and possibly hinted at both—the affective impact and international relations' dimension of talking pictures. Universal's German-language version of *All Quiet on the Western Front* had been post-synchronized using Carl Robert Blum's 'rhythmographic apparatus'. When the Hollywood talkie was advertised in Germany, posters and the Hugenberg-controlled *Kinematograph* claimed at least partial ownership of the film not only with regard to the literary source by Remarque. They also announced that the soundtrack used both German and US American technology—"Licht- und Nadelton"—i.e., Tobis' recording method using light to record sound on film, and Western Electric's Vitaphone process.[131] Using in fact Blum's rhythmographic post-synchronization device, the film version screened in German-speaking countries did indeed involve both US American and German technology to great effect. Even some of the film's harshest critics acknowledged the convincing replacement of the original English voices with German ones and the overall quality of the sound.[132] The ambient sound of trench warfare was created by Universal's recording supervisor C. Roy Hunter in the studio and subsequently added to the film.[133]

The German public was most likely not aware of the technological intricacies of this adaptation of Remarque's famous text, which soon faded due to loud and sometimes violent protests following its premiere. Conservative and right-wing reviewers were aggravated not only by this American depiction of German suffering and defeat during the past war but used the differences between the original and the synchronized versions of the film to accuse Universal of deeply immoral and deceitful behavior. Alterations had indeed been made to the German-language rendering of the antiwar movie, which were meant to make the film more palpable for audiences in Germany. The nationalist press, of course, raged at what they considered "an alleged attempt to camouflage American malice," stating that "Germans will no longer tolerate it when propaganda is translated for the sake of political expediency or economic demands."¹³⁴ Diverting from their original objections to Remarque's *Im Westen nichts Neues*, which they considered 'a second stab in the back',¹³⁵ right-wing critics now directed their anger even more forcefully at the film. Considered a provocation and a deliberate effort by "Jewish" and left-wing Hollywood to soil Germany's reputation abroad,¹³⁶ *All Quiet on the Western Front* certainly did not serve as an 'instrument of peace' in the minds of nationalist critics and the wider conservative public.

Milestone's *All Quiet on the Western Front* premiered in Germany on December 4, 1930. During the screening in Berlin's Film-Theater at Nollendorfplatz, Joseph Goebbels is reported to have protested loudly and repeatedly. Hugenberg's Ufa cinemas boycotted the film.¹³⁷ As reported in *The Manchester Guardian* (December 10, 1930),

> [a]nti-pacifist demonstrations (for this is what they are) continued last night in the Nollendorfplatz, outside the picture theatre where 'All Quiet on the Western Front' is being shown. Further demonstrations are announced for this evening. The argument that the film is anti-German is a mere pretense. The film is nothing of the kind. [...] The film is a peace film so far as it reveals something of the nature of war, and that is the reason why the National Socialists [...] are making such attacks. There seems to be a chance that they will succeed in getting the film suppressed.

Goebbels organized demonstrations outside movie theaters, with Nazi youth regularly throwing stink bombs and releasing mice into the cinema—until screenings of the film were prohibited on 11 December. The ban was lifted again after cuts to particularly 'offensive' scenes had been made. Protests by Nazi supporters continued, however, and numerous cinema owners chose to avoid trouble and refrained from screening the adaptation in the first place.

While the vast majority of the liberal, left-wing press applauded the pacifist message of the film and praised the visualization of Remarque's bestselling novel as successful counsel for the youth, German nationalists continued to discredit the movie. On December 24, 1930, the "Kampfblatt der national-sozialistischen Bewegung" [lit. 'battle paper of the national-socialist movement'] *Völkischer Beobachter* published an old movie poster rather than a Christmas message on its front page. It was The Crystal cinema's advert for the melodramatic propaganda film *The Kaiser, the Beast of Berlin* (US, Rupert Julian, 1918).

One might question the relevance of this film twelve years after it was produced independently by Julian, who also starred in the silent picture as Kaiser Wilhelm II. But eventually the distribution rights were sold to Universal Pictures, and thus to German-American co-founding owner of the company Carl Laemmle (Karl Lämmle). Thus, the anonymous author of this front-page article in the Nazi paper (Adolf Hitler is named as editor) holds Jewish filmmaker Lämmle personally responsible for the spread of anti-German propaganda and draws on the English-language poster of a First World War silent film to discredit a modern talkie. The author refers to Laemmle as "the same Jew who in 1919 filmed [...] the malicious defamation film and disseminated this wickedness worldwide."[138] The writer of this short piece neither cared that it was Carl Laemmle Jr., the son of the above-named founder of Universal, who had overseen the adaptation of Remarque's novel as head of production, nor that Lämmle (Jr. or Sr.) did no filming of the project, especially in 1919.

But truth was never a concern for Nazis, who consistently discredited highly respected and widely read independent newspapers and journalists by calling them "Lügenpresse" ["lying press"] while vigorously spreading misinformation themselves. As Walter A. Berendsohn reminded readers in 1946, Hitler had clearly outlined his plans for propaganda, expansionism, and racial cleansing in his infamous manifesto *Mein Kampf*, and those bemoaning the suffering caused by another World War should have been well aware of the Nazis' methods and agenda. If Germany was to be 'great' again, necessary expansionism made war inevitable. In preparation, as Hitler explained, the opposition must be continually brought into disrepute, and information that can shape people's perception and generate support for the fascist cause should be repeated as often as possible no matter whether true or false.[139] In order to achieve this imagined rise to global supremacy, 'common threats' (such as communists and Jews) according to Hitler had to be identified, and especially the youth had to be prepared to fight for their nation on the battlefield. *All Quiet on the Western Front*'s depiction of young soldiers' unspectacular everyday, and their deaths, one after another, without a hint of heroic glamour, documented the dehumanizing effects and barbarism of war and thus negated Hitler's mythology. Both Remarque's source text and Milestone's film could only be understood as warnings about war as a senseless monstrosity. In addition, Universal's press releases on both sides of the Atlantic highlighted the fallacy of any warmonger's logic by depicting naïve boys 'heroically' choosing to fight as 'their fate was hunger, privation, pain, horror, death. No glory, no fame'.[140]

Hitler and his growing gang of followers tried to silence this cinematic promotion of pacifism and global peace. On January 15, 1931, the *Völkischer Beobachter* celebrated a ban of the adaptation in Austria and claimed it as 'a victory of the swastika over the Remarque-ignominy'.[141] Public screenings in Vienna had been discontinued after protests organized by local Nazi activists. While their numbers were in all probability exaggerated in the article, their success in suppressing Remarque's and Hollywood's messages of peace was celebrated as proof of the strength of the movement and the dedication of Austrians' willingness to keep in (goose)step with the Nazi movement of the Reich. In Germany, a number of states (Bavaria, Saxony, Württemberg, etc.) applied to the government in Berlin to issue a national ban of the film, arguing its detrimental effect on both public order locally and Germany's reputation abroad. In September 1931, the movie was released again with further cuts as directed by the German censorship board. Making the most of their power as the largest European market, Universal was pressured into agreeing to allow only this German-edited version to be screened internationally. In 1933, the Nazi government banned the film as well as the novel. Universal returned to distributing a nearly original version of approximately 130 minutes. Today, *All Quiet on the Western Front* is considered a "hard-hitting, timeless masterpiece," "one of the most influential antiwar films ever made," and "deserving [its] place in film history."[142] It is regularly listed as one of the 100 best Hollywood films ever made and has helped define the genre of antiwar talkies.[143]

In the aftermath of the political aggravation and commercial difficulties surrounding the release of *All Quiet on the Western Front* in Germany and Austria, Universal decided to move away from dubbed, post-synchronized talkies in favor of multi-language film versions, at a time when other Hollywood studios abandoned this costly practice in favor of dubbing.[144] For the German-language version of *The Boudoir Diplomat* (1930, directed by Malcolm St. Clair)—an adaptation of the German-language farce *Die Republik befiehlt* by Rudolf Lothar and Fritz Gottwald—Universal arranged for actors Olga Tschechowa, Johannes Riemann, Arnold Korff, and Hans Junkermann to travel to California to film *Liebe auf Befehl* (US, Ernst L. Frank, Johannes Riemann, 1931).[145] This seems to be the only Universal production, however, that was filmed in German in Hollywood. Normally, as Wedel confirms, Universal's European language versions were to be produced in Germany and in France ("under the umbrella of the Societé Internationale Cinématographique").[146] Its director outlined the company's objective "to produce films with themes appropriate to the countries in question, Germany, France, England, and America. [...] A well-organized production should make it possible that an interesting subject matter, elaborated in a proper way for each country, becomes a success"[147] as the *Film-Kurier* reported on June 22, 1931. But the company's crisis management also included an agreement with Tobis "to exclusively use Tobis-Klangfilm technology for production in their studios across Europe without having to pay license fees in cash. This deal allowed Universal to create a homogenous technological framework that avoided problems of adaptability and interchangeability."[148] When its ban was lifted in September 1931 and after additional cuts to the film were made in order to appease local audiences, *All Quiet on the Western Front* became the most successful foreign film in Germany well into the following year.[149]

With fascism and antisemitism unbearably on the rise in Germany and Austria, bestselling author Vicki Baum became the target of numerous vicious antisemitic attacks in the right-wing press. Eventually, Baum accepted MGM's invitation to come to Hollywood and write for the cinema screen.[150] Her Ullstein novel *Menschen im Hotel* (People at a Hotel, 1929) had become a runaway bestseller, was adapted for theater almost instantly under Max Reinhardt's direction, and translated into several languages. The English edition of the novel in Britain was followed by publication in the United States, now entitled *Grand Hotel* (1930). Greatly successful with American readers, Baum's novel was adapted for Broadway, co-produced by Harry Moses, who owned the adaptation rights, and by MGM. By helping to finance the stage production, MGM secured the film rights.[151] Vicki Baum's ironically subtitled 'colportage novel' takes place almost exclusively in one of Berlin's five-star hotels, most likely the Excelsior or the Bristol, where Baum spent several weeks working incognito as a chambermaid for research purposes. The lobby is the heart of both the hotel and Baum's narrative. It is here that individual protagonists are introduced and where their stories begin to collide—be it the gallant and amiable impostor Baron Gaigern, who wants to steal the jewels of the Russian prima ballerina with the help of his companion disguised as a chauffeur, or the terminally ill accountant Kringelein, who intends to spend his life's savings and some extra from his employer's cash box on a few days of self-indulgent luxury; his boss at the cotton factory in Fredersdorf, general manager Preysing, or typist Fräulein Flamm, called Flämmchen, who dreams of becoming a movie star and in the meantime engages in a bit of occasional prostitution for additional income. In the center of the lobby and at the core of the novel sits 'a long gentleman' with only half a face—one side a refined profile with a beautiful ear and a temple covered in grey hair, the other half absent, merely 'a lopsided, intertwined, chaotic tangle of seams and scars, from which a glass eye blindly gazed'. Dr. Otternschlag calls it 'a souvenir from Flanders'. This First World War veteran is lonely, traumatized, and addicted to morphine, asking daily for mail or telegrams that never arrive. He sits nearly motionless in the middle of this hectic and always fluid space, a monument to the destructiveness of war from which there is no escape or redemption.[152] Apart from Otternschlag, who forms the text's shattered yet stable spine within the novel's narrative continuum, the other protagonists as well as their fortunes are constantly in motion. The revolving door in the lobby resembles this cycle of money and people, an eternal recurrence of one and the same. Guests come and go, and hotel staff works shifts, one bad-tempered one-armed man operating the lift replaced in the evening by another grumpy, one-armed veteran. Despite moments of contact and connection, perhaps even love, the different narrative strands are marked by their fragmentary and transitory nature, thereby capturing the disjointed and fleeting soul of modern, urban life. In the end, Otternschlag sits again in the middle of the busy lobby, complaining about his isolation: 'The world has become a dead planet, there's no warmth anymore.'[153] The thief who

FIGURE 4.5 *The lobby in* Grand Hotel *(US, Edmund Goulding, 1932)*.

fell in love with the ballerina is dead, and Flämmchen left with Kringelein. But the revolving door spills new guests into the lobby, and with them the perpetual hope for human contact.

The star-studded cast of MGM's *Grand Hotel* (US, Edmund Goulding 1932) includes Greta Garbo as prima ballerina Grusinskaya, John Barrymore as the 'Baron', Joan Crawford as Flaemmchen the stenographer, Lionel Barrymore as Otto Kringelein, Wallace Beery as General Director Preysing, and Lewis Stone as Doktor Otternschlag. The adaptation, which opens as "Grand Hotel by Vicki Baum," follows the different narrative strands of the novel and was remarkably successful, winning a number of Academy Awards, including the Oscar for Best Picture, and exceeding even the most hopeful breaking box-office expectations. The focus of the movie camera is often on the Grand Hotel's lobby, an Art Deco inspired design like a roulette wheel by MGM Art Director Cedric Gibbons. It is a place where people meet, if only in passing. Here, too, modern society's anonymity poses risks, as one cannot distinguish between a thief and a baron, a CEO and a murderer. While for the most part only shot from his 'good', unscathed side, war memory here, too, is located in the center of the hotel's most public place. Dr. Otternschlag sits in the busy lobby, resigned to his solitude, engaging in conversations when the opportunity arises, a nearly immobile presence in the midst of the hustle and bustle of this microcosm's everyday. While the movie foregrounds connections and relationships between the different protagonists more than their fragmentation, here, too, proximity arises by chance or is bought, and everyone struggles with separation and loneliness in their own way.

Baum's depiction of modern society's fragmentation is emphasized in the film and repeatedly underscored by the use of sound. The novel, too, sets off with the hotel's worried doorman receiving a phone call—his pregnant wife had been brought to hospital—and from the beginning it is sound that frames Baum's introductions of her various characters. The lobby is the place of first fleeting encounters, where jazz music pours in from the tea rooms, merging with the romantic violin solo emanating from the conservatory, trickling sounds from the lobby's illuminated fountain enfold glasses clinging, wicker chairs crackling, silk dresses rustling, and amidst this subtle cacophony, voices emerge and overlap. Goulding's focuses especially on telephone conversations to convey Baum's literary depiction. The main characters are introduced by speaking in their respective telephone booths, providing insights into their current state of mind. But quickly sentences begin to overlap until all we hear are different voices and snippets of fragmented speech while looking through the camera's birdseye into the lobby.

This soundscape is repeated as a new day begins and again creates a symbolic aural representation of modernity's affliction and remedy in one. Like a lifesaving net for trapeze artists rolled out by the switchboard operators, invisible connections between modern city-dwellers are formed and conversations via telephones take place across far distances or even from one room to the next. In the film, the all-too-human story of the prima ballerina (Garbo) just past her prime who falls for the con artist Baron Gaigern (Barrymore) is foregrounded. But here, too, despite all the hustle and bustle, love and loss, life and death, war veteran Otternschlag complains: "Grand Hotel. Always the same. People come, people go, nothing ever happens."[154]

After the talkie's enthusiastic reception in the United States, it was successfully distributed internationally.[155] When the adaptation was screened in Germany in February 1933, there was only little mention of the source text by an Austrian Jew. The movie was marketed via its star-studded cast, but particularly as 'the new Greta Garbo-film', capitalizing on the popularity of the international celebrity in Germany. The film introduces her accordingly in a first close-up. She is the star of the picture, but it is no easy life for the aging dancer. "You know, Suzette," she says to her maid, "I've never been so tired in my life."

Across the Atlantic, reviews in Europe were generally as enthusiastic as in the United States. In Germany, critics were particularly delighted with the fact that the place of action was Berlin, the musical score—like the waltz that accompanies guests who come and go through the revolving doors—

was equally local and familiar, and the German names of the characters had been maintained. When the film premiered at Berlin's Capitol cinema with much glamor and several local luminaries in attendance, it was screened in the original with German subtitles. A post-synchronized version was in preparation—for the 'provinces', as one reviewer stated.[156] In February 1933, when Hitler had just been appointed the Reich's Chancellor, many in Germany's culture and, especially, film industry considered knowledge of English essential to their future and not merely their professional survival.

Literary Prestige Films and Universal-Appeal Pictures in Germany

In the early 1930s, German film producers still lamented the lack of suitable manuscripts. As Kracauer noted in the *Frankfurter Zeitung* in 1931, 'for some time now the film magazines have been crying out for good authors—but the authors are not forthcoming, and the manuscripts just do not emerge'. Kracauer blamed the 'slipshod nature' of the film industry, as he called it, which tended to focus too much on operettas or popular songs and produced films in which 'always the same actors' turned up 'in the same roles'.[157] In Hollywood at the same time, major film studios from MGM to Warner Brothers, Paramount and Twentieth Century Fox had the same "rapacious appetite for new material"[158] as Tom Leitch notes, and were constantly looking for suitable stories to adapt. Beyond these big film companies in the United States, only Germany's Ufa was equipped with adequate financial muscle and, with its integrated network of production, distribution and exhibition, able to compete successfully. Or so it seemed. For in order to maximize profits, which had to include income from their talkies' international distribution, the board of Germany's most powerful film company aimed for 'universal appeal'.

In an interview on "The Future of the Kinema" published in *The Observer* on September 4, 1932, Erich Pommer is reported to have "pointed to the new season's programme of Ufa productions as fully expressing his own views as producer."[159] According to the British paper's Berlin correspondent, Pommer wanted pictures that "interest and amuse" and did not believe that "problem films have any right to exist unless they are able to effect a direct change of social conditions. If they can only arouse controversy without bringing suggestions for improvement, they can only disturb and not soothe the imagination." The aim was thus not to produce films that merely propagated an idea, but rather to support film projects that promised "universal appeal to everybody in an audience, no matter what their different class, profession, opinion, or interests, than to indulge in the aggressiveness of one idea expressing the views of one particular section of the populace only." The story as such was of minor importance as, in Pommer's view, the "universal-appeal picture" or "amusement film" could "deal with a problem and present itself in a limited sense as a new artistic experiment: by applying new forms in the technical or artistic sense." Thus "any worn-out theme can be made singular or unusual, new and attractive." It all depended on the "producer as artist" and "the money placed at his disposal." The public, however, clearly preferred "the entertaining story interwoven with music." Escapist entertainment, in Pommers view, was the bedrock of cinema:

> The cinema has only obtained its present position—a matter of intense and impassioned interest for millions of people—because the desire for entertainment, recreation, and the need to forget the petty cares and worries of everyday life is inherent in every one of these millions. The demand for amusement is universal.

He fully accepted that "cinema is an industry and cannot afford to risk its valuable commercial power by deviating from the special purpose set for it in the world of art—which is distinct [...] because of this universal craving of the millions." Admitting to not having cared for talkies in the beginning, he now considered them "a joy in themselves." Of course, talking pictures have to avoid "the long speech and the monologue" (their place is on the theater stage) and must "visualize at a different angle" (as a painter would). Their success from a producer's point of view also depended on international collaborations, and Pommer highlighted Ufa's agreement with Gaumont-British "as the re-internationalization of the film. The language difficulty is being overcome by other countries liking our pictures and wanting them, when the German language is a definite drawback, in a medium they can understand."

The instability and arbitrariness of life are reflected in numerous German-language novels and plays of the late 1920s and early 1930s. Contemporary authors reflected on the consequences of the Wall Street crash for individuals, who struggle to make a decent life for themselves within the chaos of modern, urban spaces marked by economic crisis. Elisabeth Hauptmann/ Kurt Weill/Bertolt Brecht's *Dreigroschenoper* (Threepenny Opera, 1928), Alfred Döblin's *Berlin Alexanderplatz* (1929), Carl Zuckmayer's *Der Hauptmann von Köpenick* (The Captain from Köpenick, 1931), and Hans Fallada's *Kleiner Mann, was nun?* (Little Man, What Now?, 1932) may serve as the most prominent examples. All four texts were adapted to film and, as adaptations of very well received literary texts or plays, were among the most successful films of their time. These early talkies typically foregrounded social struggle and a milieu of an impoverished petit bourgeoisie, petty criminals, sometimes women having to make ends meet and resorting to occasional prostitution, and—as, famously, in *Berlin Alexanderplatz* and *Der Hauptmann von Köpenick*—former inmates who seek reintegration, but struggle with existential difficulties, anxieties, marginalization, and German bureaucracy.

The board of Ufa, as Pommer indicated above, had decided to put all bets on light, singing and dancing entertainment such as *Der Kongress tanzt*—which was criticized by Kracauer, who called for talkies that 'showed working people' and, instead of superficially escapist commodities, for films that are 'actually worth watching'.[160] An exception—which turned out to be one of Ufa's biggest international successes at the time—was *Emil und die Detektive* [Emil and the Detectives] (DE, Gerhard Lamprecht, 1931). In his bestselling children's book (1929), Erich Kästner had reimagined a genre formerly dominated by fairy-tales and moralizing prose. The story focuses on Emil from Neustadt and his diverse band of newly found friends in Berlin, who step up to help him get the crook who stole his single mom's hard-earned cash, which Emil was meant to bring to his grandmother in Berlin. Loved by children and adults alike, Kästner's first children's book was a huge success. Critics praised the mix of wit, great humor, authentic and yet elegant prose of this adventurous tale that never lacks awareness of the all-too-fragile aspects of life.[161] Prompted by international successes of films about children—such as Little Mary, i.e., Mary Pickford who became a much-loved child star from 1909, or Baby Peggy, i.e., Diana Serra Cary, who starred in over a 100 short films from 1921—but also encouraged by the Volksverband Filmkunst e.V., an association founded by G.W. Pabst that called for the production of children's films, Ufa decided on an adaptation of *Emil und die Detektive*.[162]

Kästner's novel was brought to the cinema screen by a team equipped with huge talent: Gerhard Lamprecht, who had directed *Buddenbrooks* in 1923 and was well known for his ability to capture a milieu shaped by social hardship and individual challenge, worked with an inspired script[163] by Billy Wilder (with Paul Frank), and Carl Mayer provided dramaturgical support in this Günther Stapenhorst production. The first of ten *Emil and the Detectives* adaptations[164] to date stayed true to Kästner's differentiated portrayal of children like Emil (Rolf Wenkhaus), and offered a (partly post-synchronized) highly entertaining and greatly praised talkie that featured a musical score by Allan Gray. Indeed a film of 'universal appeal', critics often praised the urban dynamism of the film's outdoor mass scenes of nearly a 100 children running, cycling, scooting through Berlin in pursuit of the despicable thief, and the horrifying and yet carnivalesque hallucinatory sequence on the train to Berlin, after Emil is drugged by evil Grundeis (Fritz Rasp, creepy as ever). According to film critic Philip French, *Emil and the Detectives* had an impact at least on two major British films: Hitchcock's *The Lady Vanishes* (1938) "copies the hallucinatory sequence on a train that follows the villain giving Emil a drugged sweet; and *Hue and Cry* (1947) borrows the notion of smart, organised schoolkids chasing a criminal in the big city."[165]

Apart from Ufa's *Emil und die Detektive*, it was smaller film companies that took full advantage of contemporary literary and theater successes and, despite difficult economic conditions affecting their overhead expenses, ensured that some of the most important literary texts of the time were brought to cinema screens. This is not to say that these adaptations were necessarily as important as their groundbreaking source texts. Case in point is Döblin's *Berlin Alexanderplatz* (1929), a *Bildungsroman* or novel of formation, which is considered a canonical literary representation of the modern metropolis. A changing world had brought forth new modernist literatures—such as, for example, Marcel Proust's *À la recherche du temps perdu* (In Search of Lost Time, 1913–27), the above-mentioned *Ulyssees* by Joyce, Thomas Mann's *Der Zauberberg* (The Magic Mountain, 1924), Woolf's *Mrs Dalloway* (1925), Kafka's *Das Schloss* (The Castle, 1922/1926), Musil's *Der Mann ohne Eigenschaften* (The Man without Qualities, part 1, 1930), and *Berlin Alexanderplatz*. Döblin uses free indirect discourse not only to capture his anti-hero Franz Biberkopf's experience of modern mass culture, but to reflect a multi-layered urban mass experience per se.[166] Applying the principle of montage to his novel, Döblin describes the journey of a violent and immoral man who forces his girlfriend into prostitution and, when she wants to leave, beats her so severely that she dies of her injuries. The novel begins as Biberkopf, full of good intentions, is released from prison after serving his sentence for manslaughter. Like so many of his generation affected by war, poverty, and class struggle, his experience of the modern city is intensified as he is suddenly faced with an acceleration of change brought about by his four-year separation from daily urban adjustments. Biberkopf's wish to lead an honest life collides not only with his personal demons, but with his fear and disorientation in modern, urban society. Only slowly and after repeated failings, he manages to adjust and, finally, learning and understanding begin to take root.

Sound plays an integral part in Döblin's prose, which is coined the last Expressionist novel and, at the same time, considered a prime literary example of New Objectivity, but also includes elements of the other two avant-garde movements of the time, Dadaism and Futurism. Beginning with the anti-hero's first tram ride as a free man, simply being in this fast-moving urban environment is depicted as a frightening and overwhelming experience due to a multitude of visual and aural sensations. Döblin's innovative novel had such an impact that two of the most outstanding actors at the time—Emil Jannings and Heinrich George—contacted the author and offered to play Biberkopf in an adaptation. The possibility of authenticity offered by sound film, which would allow his anti-hero to speak, excited Döblin as he wrote in *Film*-Kurier already in 1930,[167] and it looked as if an adaptation of the bestseller would follow without delay. Ufa had already agreed on an option with Döblin, but in the end decided against purchasing the rights to the novel.[168] Heinrich George noted at the time that 'to make a film, you need money. But investors are rare, and rarest when the project is a so-called literary film.'[169]

When George ran into Arnold Pressburger in London, he persuaded the founder of Allianz-Tonfilm GmbH, who had previously worked with directors such as Mihali Kertész (Michael Curtiz), G.W. Pabst, Carmine Gallone, and Hans Behrendt, to seize the opportunity and secure the film rights for *Berlin Alexanderplatz*. Phil (Piel) Jutzi, who had created such a convincing milieu of working-class Berlin in *Mutter Krausens Fahrt ins Glück* [Mother Krause's Journey to Happiness] (DE, 1929; based on stories and illustrations by Heinrich Zille), was chosen to direct the adaptation of the novel. Döblin himself worked on the screenplay together with Hans Wilhelm, and Karl-Heinz Martin was in charge of dialogues. Allan Gray composed the score, which often combined music with diegetic sounds such as songs and urban noise or "Geräuschmusik" [lit. noise music, i.e., ambient sound] that Germans were particularly fond of at the time.[170]

Berlin—Alexanderplatz (DE, Phil Jutzi, 1931) stars George as Biberkopf together with notable actors Maria Bard, Margarete Schlegel, Bernhard Minetti, Albert Florath, Hans Deppe, Käthe Haack, and others. The adaptation opens with an aerial shot of Alexanderplatz in Berlin, which is a visual reference to both the title of the film's source text and the beginning of cinema in Germany, i.e., to Max Skladanowsky's short documentary about *Leben und Treiben am Alexanderplatz in Berlin* [Life and Goings-on at Alexanderplatz in Berlin] (1896). More than three decades later, technology and the film medium had excelled, as the bird's-eye view from high above perhaps suggests in contrast to the well-known eye-level shots of the busy square by Skladanowsy all those years ago. In this opening sequence, the freedom of Alexanderplatz observed from one of the adjacent tall buildings almost jarringly cuts to a low angle shot of a high wall that leaves only a small sliver of sky in the upper left corner of the frame. Symbols of imprisonment— prison walls and a façade with symmetrically aligned, barred windows— lead to a door that opens to discharge our anti-hero. Franz Biberkopf is released with a handshake. His hesitation and sluggishness are placed in sharp contrast with the city's swiftly moving traffic. When Biberkopf takes a tram toward Berlin's urban center, he experiences the cacophony of urban space for the first time in four years. The montage of POV and traveling shots of rails, other trams, cars, horse-drawn carriages, buses, pedestrians, shops, buildings and people, movements and sounds is based on Nicolas Farkas and Erich Giese's camera work and Geza Pollatschik's editing. The montage's speed and rhythm suit the quickly moving tram and affectively communicate the threat of this hectic chaos that Biberkopf experiences. Soon unable to cope, he jumps off the tram, runs into a building, where he sits down in a sparsely furnished corridor next to a homeless man. 'I don't know my way around anymore, I lost my bearings', he stammers.

But as we follow Biberkopf's journey, the film's cinematography becomes increasingly conventional and its plot linear, focused almost entirely on our anti-hero. Those 'fleeting scenes, rapidly changing moods, kaleidoscopes of rolling, gliding events'[171] that Döblin had envisaged during his first conversation with George about an adaptation of his novel all too quickly subside after the film's beautiful opening sequence. Jutzi emphasized upon completion of the talkie that his intention had been to summarize Döblin's 'wealth of thought' into a film narrative that was as 'clear and convincing' as possible. For him, that meant the removal of anything 'superfluous and superficial'.[172]

When the film was released in October 1931 after a significant marketing effort by its first distributor Südfilm and a premiere that included representatives of Berlin's cultural avant-garde such as Käthe Kollwitz, Bertolt Brecht, Lion and Marta Feuchtwanger, and Heinrich Mann, to name but a few, the adaptation's undeniable success at the box office did not match the often negative reaction of reviewers in the press. While some critics praised the authenticity of some of the street scenes, particularly their 'natural noise' and dialects, most were disappointed, as Berlin's 'mood' had not been captured, being cast aside in favor of George as the star and focal point of the picture. This seemed particularly disappointing as the novel itself already offered a literary montage of images. Moreover, Ruttmann's *Berlin*-film (1927) could have been used as a model for urban cinematography, and Clair had already established a suitable film technique[173] in *Sous les toits de Paris* (1930), which convincingly recreated the enchanting mood of Paris almost entirely in a studio, and skillfully incorporated a city into a cinematic narrative. Thus, numerous reviewers regarded this first *Berlin Alexanderplatz* adaptation as a failed experiment that should have been entitled 'Heinrich George, as Franz Biberkopf' as critic Herbert Ihering[174] sardonically suggested at the time.

Considering the innovative style of the novel, which 'irresistibly captured today's Berlin with an innovative epic technique', as Kurt Pinthus[175] put it, an adaptation of *Berlin Alexanderplatz* would have offered an opportunity to be similarly inventive and groundbreakingly avant-garde. But compared to the expert novelist Döblin, scriptwriter Döblin was an 'amateur', as Ernst Jäger noted in *Film-Kurier* (October 9, 1931), calling the film a 'literary off-shoot', naïve, and lacking in complexity. A cutting-edge novel had been reduced to a straightforward 'crook and pimp story' and star-vehicle, that closes with the banal insight that it is better to sell suspenders than to be a crook and a pimp, as Hans Siemsen claimed.[176] Pinthus, the famous author and journalist, who had compiled the momentous anthology of Expressionist poetry *Menschheitsdämmerung* [The Twilight of Humanity] in 1919, nonetheless praised the project as courageous and important at a time of 'military and civilian distraction-films', but lamented its bowing to an assumed audience taste. The assumption that cinemagoers suffered history and politics fatigue led to a significant reduction of references to the First World War, for example, thus reducing the film's political dimension. In his review of *Berlin Alexanderplatz*, Kracauer criticized the adaptation's determined attenuation of Germany's current sociopolitical climate, willfully ignoring its real and present danger.[177]

Today, however, *Berlin Alexanderplatz* is considered one of the most important German films of the era—together with other adaptations such as *Die freudlose Gasse* (1925), *Varieté* (1925), *Faust* (1926), *Die Büchse der Pandora* (1929), *Tagebuch einer Verlorenen* (1929), *Der blaue Engel* (1930), *Die Drei von der Tankstelle* (1930), *Westfront 1918* (1930), *Die 3-Groschen-Oper* (1931), *Emil und die Detektive* (1931), *Mädchen in Uniform* (1931), *Liebelei* (1933), and *Das Testament des Dr. Mabuse* (1933).[178] A collaborative pilot project by filmportal.de and T-Online, inaugurated at the Berlinale in 2006, identifies the 'most important German films from the beginning of cinema to the present day.' Fifty-six percent of the films listed are adaptations and emphasize the importance of literature for German cinema in general and during this era of cinematic masterpieces from Murnau's *Nosferatu* to Lang's *Metropolis* (1927) and *M* (1931) in particular. *Der Hauptmann von Köpenick* [Captain of Cöpenick] (DE, Richard Oswald, 1931) is strangely missing from this list originally limited to 100 titles. Perhaps the sheer number of outstanding films of the decade and the universal appeal of this Carl Zuckmayer adaptation lessened its chance to be included.

At the time, however, as both a playwright and scriptwriter, particularly in comparison to Döblin, Zuckmayer was considered much more successful in his attempt to highlight an ex-offender's social hardship, even while poking fun at Germans' adoration of the military. The playwright had become a household name after the premiere of *Der fröhliche Weinberg* [lit. The Merry Vinyard] at Berlin's Theater am Schiffbauerdamm in December 1925 and receiving the prestigious Kleist-prize the same year. It was Fritz Kortner, famous film and theater actor and director, who suggested a collaborative project for both stage and screen that would tell the story of the infamous 'Captain of Cöpenick', a.k.a. unemployed ex-con shoemaker Wilhelm Voigt, who in 1906 had dressed up in a second-hand Captain's uniform and managed to order a group of soldiers to 'take' the cityhall in Köpenick (Berlin), to imprison the mayor, and, in the end, left with the city council's moneybox. Newspapers at the time were filled with satirical images and stories about this 'nobody' who had made such good use of his fellow Germans' blind deference to authority and all-too-willing submission to anyone wearing a uniform. Amused readers could not get enough of the story, which was soon represented in different media and performed in folk theaters.[179]

Kortner was starring in a Terra Film adaptation of Fyodor Dostoevsky's *The Brothers Karamazov* entitled *Der Mörder Dimitri Karamasoff* [The Murderer Dimitri Karamazov] (DE, Fedor Ozep, 1930) at the time and, as Helmut Asper[180] outlines, facilitated contact with the film company. Zuckmayer sold the film rights to his unfinished play and planned film script to Terra Film in July 1930, and then decided to focus on writing the play—without Kortner.[181] In December, however, financial difficulties and Goebbels' intense opposition to and successful campaign against *All Quiet on the Western Front* left its mark on the film company's readiness to proceed with a film that could be considered anti-militarist. Zuckmayer's play *Der Hauptmann von Köpenick: Ein deutsches Märchen* (Captain of Cöpenick: A German Fairy-Tale, 1931) meanwhile had taken shape and premiered at the Deutsches Theater in Berlin on March 5, 1931.[182] In the original stage production under Heinz Hilpert's direction, Werner Krauß starred as the 'Captain' to great audience amusement and critical acclaim. The play was to become one of the most outstanding theater successes of the early 1930s and, despite numerous antisemitic attacks on 'half-Jew Zuckmayer' in the right-wing press, was staged all over Germany in sold-out productions until the Nazis banned the writer's work in 1933.

Together with Albrecht Joseph, Zuckmayer adapted his play for the cinema screen, and presented Terra with the complete screenplay in July 1931. But the film company stalled, citing political concerns. Zuckmayer then contacted Ufa, but here, too, the topic was considered incompatible with the company's ideological outlook. Meanwhile Terra Film, also moving politically further and further to the right, was eager to wash its hands of the entire project and, in August 1931, sold its *Hauptmann von Köpenick*-contract with all rights and responsibilities to Richard Oswald.

Following the enormous success of the play, the adaptation project promised to be a financial success, but Terra Film was unwilling to take the imagined political risk involved, contractually securing only a 50 percent share of potential profits to be made in the United States, which at the time would most likely not be noticed by Goebbels and his Nazi thugs. Zuckmayer himself was shocked when he was informed of the deal made by Terra and, having envisaged Ewald André Dupont as director for 'his' adaptation, refused to supply Oswald with the script. Legally, however, Oswald had the upper hand and, encouraged by further, significant financial inducements (and the fact that his co-author Joseph was accepted as assistant director), Zuckmayer soon came on board. Oswald, his Roto-Film and G.P. Films production companies (co-producer Gabriel Pascal), and distributor Südfilm-Verleih were adamant that Zuckmayer's name and talents were to contribute to the success of the film. Clearly committed to keeping the author happy, Oswald and his production team agreed to use the script by Zuckmayer and Joseph and to work only with the two authors. But a film based on this first draft would have been at least five or six hours long, even at the fastest recording speed, as Zuckmayer wrote to Joseph after a reading of the script at the studio in Berlin-Tempelhof, stating that 'in this regard we were amateurs'. In an effort to create more than an adaptation of the play, Zuckmayer and Joseph had written several additional scenes, but now Oswald insisted on significant cuts. The director's changes unveil a vision of the planned adaptation that differed fundamentally from Zuckmayer's.[183]

New Objectivity was all the rage in avant-garde literary, theater, and film circles at the time, and Oswald envisaged Zuckmayer's play on screen as a historical reportage rather than a 'German fairy-tale'. His vast knowledge of filmmaking, particularly with regard to adaptations of literary texts, saved the project. Zuckmayer and Joseph aimed at differentiating the film script from Zuckmayer's play, but lacked the necessary experience, and eventually placed their trust in Oswald as the expert, who consistently respected and valued their input. The two authors produced a significantly shortened version and, while Oswald made further cuts, several new or expanded scenes were maintained in order to encourage the film's reception beyond an adaptation of Zuckmayer's play, which suited all involved. Oswald himself came up with the idea to omit Wilhelm II from the audience's vision toward the end of the film. Following a fabulous sequence of images of newspapers with superimposed headlines in different languages being drowned out by audible outbursts of gaiety as the world is laughing with the Germans about their 'uniform fetish', visibly concerned (uniformed) staff wait in the German Emperor's antechamber, where he is to be informed of the shoemaker's ruse. Again, sound plays a central role in this conclusion of the film narrative as, finally, the hearty, liberating laughter of the Kaiser allows even his subjects to enjoy the humor of the 'Captain's' mischievous act.[184]

The film about gentle ex-con shoemaker Voigt (sympathetically and skillfully played by Max Adalbert), who spent fifteen years in prison for document fraud and upon his release is caught in the 'carousel' or 'coffee grinder', as he calls it, of being considered unsuitable for a job for lack of papers, and unsuitable for papers for lack of a job, ends happily with a royal pardon and, finally, a passport. *Der Hauptmann von Köpenick* premiered at Berlin's Mozartsaal on December 22, 1931, only six weeks after Oswald's *Arm wie eine Kirchenmaus* [Poor as a Church Mouse], an adaptation of Hungarian Ladislas (Laszlo) Fodor's play (1927), which was among the most performed at German-language theaters during the late 1920s.[185] As Asper notes, Oswald was an astute entrepreneur and Zuckmayer admired his courage for taking on the project. Despite the fact that Oswald did not want to make a 'political film', the alarming growth of the Nazi movement must have shaped his outlook, as he exacerbated the play's critique of military supremacy.[186] In addition, he highlighted the individual's responsibility for society. Low camera angles emphasize the authority of the court, while an indifferent judge hands down a brutally harsh sentence. Other authoritarians are depicted as bullies that are, in close-up, little more than their silly, trembling whiskers or shiny baldness. Voigt's marginalization and humiliation due to his criminal record and shabby appearance are accentuated in the first part of the film. The disguise that follows contravenes the power dynamic and offers a highly entertaining critique of authority.

In an interview for *Reichsfilmblatt*[187] Oswald explained that he 'pulled apart the twenty-one pictures of Zuckmayer's play into eighty-six film scenes', but insisted that he stayed 'true to reality, nothing is added, nothing left out'. There was no need, in the director's mind, to film a parody. 'The thing itself is parody enough', Oswald said, and supported Zuckmayer's desire to focus on a human being, peeling away their outer layers until the audience not only understood this individual's core and foundation but recognized these inner workings in themselves. In his essay "Ich verfilme Bühnenwerke"[188] [I film stage plays], published in *Film-Kurier* on November 5, 1931, the day of the premiere of *Arm wie eine Kirchenmaus*, Oswald emphasized the importance of sustaining the source text while applying the laws of film. Rejecting any form of filmed or photographed theater, Oswald promoted a creative use of visual and acoustic means appropriate to film during the adaptation process—'an adaptation for cinema begins where the mobile camera, the continuous flow of images blows up spatial boundaries of the theater stage'. His 'poetic of theater adaptation'[189] reflects respect for the source text, which Oswald considered indispensable for any adaptive work, but also explains the changes Oswald and Zuckmayer made in order for the adaptation to come to life on screen. As Wedel summarizes, these 'condensations' go beyond the common emphasis on linear narrative structure and continuity or increased spatial mobility. Oswald's image compositions communicate the marginal hero's liminal existence and state of uncertainty, but also the genius of his masquerade and the public's amused respect for the implied criticism of their blind obedience to anyone in a uniform.[190] Furthermore, Oswald's seventh talkie was conventional in its narrative but innovative visually and aurally. To the dismay of Zuckmayer and Joseph, Oswald refused to include ambient sound or extra-diegetic music in favor of an 'objective' use of sound, that provided information rather than 'mood'.

As Wedel and other film scholars have emphasized, the most innovative aspects of this first adaptation of Zuckmayer's play include an animation, a montage of newspaper headlines and announcements, a rhythmical sequence of overlapping and competing sounds and images, and abrupt alterations of camera distances. Especially sudden cuts to extreme close-ups communicate the latent aggressiveness within society as "Wahrnehmungsschock" or 'perceptual shock', as Wedel convincingly argues.[191] Therefore, as Kanzog points out, despite the historically correct use of German Empire uniforms, Oswald's adaptation competently reflects the vein of the early 1930s and an unstable German society rife with racism and social deprivation that clings desperately to authoritarianism or anyone promising 'order'. By tracing this individual's impossible struggle for reintegration or, by way of a passport, the possibility of emigration, Oswald's Zuckmayer-adaptation is not just the depiction of a desperate prank but 'illuminates a system'.[192]

As the director/producer emphasized in an article published in *Lichtbild-Bühne* in November 1931, sound film is a creative force for a 'natural' or naturalistic depiction that depends greatly on the skill and instinctiveness of actors who manage to avoid affectation.[193] After the premiere of the film in December, critics praised not only Max Adalbert's and the cast's acting skills, but the film's attention to detail and time and again the authenticity of the performances. Hans Feld was clearly delighted that 'these great performances are made accessible to millions thanks to the mechanization of reproduction'. A critic in *Vorwärts* also praised the cast, but particularly Oswald's 'unflinching' and, compared to the play, more pronounced critique of a society and its 'insane belief in the uniform', whereas in *D.A.Z.* the film was called a 'caricature of an old Germany', missing entirely the timeliness of the film's critique. The review in *Berliner Börsen-Courier* praised the fruitful collaboration between Oswald and his scriptwriters Zuckmayer and Joseph. And, despite his apparent apprehensiveness regarding both adaptations and talkies, the critic believed this film would 'counter the current, seemingly unstoppable decline in quality cinema' not least due to the authenticity of spoken dialogues and natural sound.[194] While some reviewers from both margins of the political spectrum criticized the film as 'silly'[195] and a missed opportunity that lacked political vigor, or were offended by the humorous depiction of a wide-spread fixation and fetishization of uniforms, Oswald's focus on the human being—homeless and at the margins of society, who just wants a passport in order to start over elsewhere—skillfully foregrounds the frightening precariousness of existence and the normalization of social division and deprivation. Commercially, Oswald's talkie was a brief but significant success. Very popular abroad, the comedy won, for example, the New York Film Critics award when it was first released in North America. Theatrical aesthetics fueled the rise of the talkies in the United States, as Leitch[196] tells us. In Germany, too, quality theater and successful musicals or operettas lent themselves to adaptation due to the new sound technology. When a popular theater production offered both dialogue and songs, while having already established its commercial viability, studio heads and filmmakers were usually quick to act.

Brecht's *Dreigroschenoper* (1931) and the Threepenny Lawsuit

The Threepenny Opera (1928) was the most successful contemporary 'play with music', as Brecht called it, of the late 1920s. Based on John Gay's *The Beggar's Opera* (1728), Brecht adapted Elisabeth Hauptmann's translation of the eighteenth-century text, but also used ballads by (uncredited) François Villon. Kurt Weill composed the multi-facetted musical numbers, which are performed and adapted to this day. Marc Silberman, who made the most relevant "*Threepenny*-Material" available in English with introductory commentaries and contexualizing information, even calls it "the most popular play in Weimar Germany."[197] *The Threepenny Opera* suited Brecht's commitment to the theater stage as a place of thought or "Denkstätte". In 1929, he wrote about pedagogy as the 'new purpose' of a 'new art' that 'follows reality'. Brecht wanted to educate, and his epic theater envisaged critical thinking in 'the spectator as mass audience'.[198] But he also believed—long before Zuckmayer's *Hauptmann von Köpenick*— that Germans' 'somberness' was neither the opposite of triviality or frivolity, nor incompatible with light-hearted, playful gaiety.[199]

The plot of *The Threepenny Opera* focuses on the competition and struggle for survival of two 'businessmen'—Macheath, a successful criminal with excellent relations to London's Chief of Police Brown, and Peachum, the hardnosed leader of the begging mafia. Gay's beggar's opera, too, tells the story of villain Macheath (Mackie the Knife), who marries king of the beggars Peachum's daughter Polly, but Brecht's adaptation depicts Gay's delinquents as cold-blooded capitalists and his homeless beggars as ruined war veterans and representatives of the vast army of unemployed. Macheath is dressed impeccably, visually emulating an upstanding member of bourgeois society who did very well for himself during the years preceding the fatal burst of the economic bubble on the so-called Black Friday in 1929. He is key to the 'wellbeing' of those around him, from the members of his gang, his numerous prostitutes, to his wife Polly, and the play opens with the famous street ballad about Mackie the Knife. In its first stage production, which premiered on August 31, 1928, at the Theater am Schiffbauerdamm under the direction of Erich Engel and on a set designed by Caspar Neher, Erich Ponto and Rosa Valleti starred as Peachum and his wife, Harald Paulsen as Macheath, Kurt Weill's wife Lotte Lenya as Pirate Jenny, and Kurt Gerron as Chief of Police Brown. It was also Gerron who sang the introductory song about Mackie the Knife—"Oh, the shark has pretty teeth, dear / And it shows them pearly white."

By the autumn of 1928, the *Threepenny Opera* had become the hottest theater ticket in town, particularly due to songs such as "Seeräuberjenny"

[Pirate Jenny] and, of course, "Die Moritat von Mackie Messer" [The Ballad of Mack the Knife], which became immensely popular on the radio and was sung in German cabarets until 1933. To this day, the play and its songs are still performed and adapted. Lars von Trier, for example, "seduced by the great revenge motif in the song,"[200] mentioned repeatedly that "Pirate Jenny" inspired his film *Dogville* (DK/GB/SE/FR/DE/NL, 2003).

Following play's success, Brecht/Weill were offered a highly attractive sum for selling the film rights to their *Threepenny Opera* to Nero-Film. Founded in 1925 by Heinrich Nebenzahl (NE) and Richard Oswald (RO), Nero had been put on solid financial footing due to its production of highly popular Harry Piel-films, and by the late 1920s were investing heavily in aesthetically more ambitious productions, particularly in adaptations of German-language literature—such as *Die Büchse der Pandora* (1929) and *Westfront 1918* (1930)—and other innovative talkies such as Fritz Lang's *M* (1931), and stunning works of New Objectivity on screen such as *Menschen am Sonntag* [People on Sunday] (DE, Robert Siodmak, Edgar G. Ulmer, 1930).[201] Together with the left-wing, proletarian film company Prometheus, Nero-Film was quickly becoming the last bastion of arthouse cinema resisting the rise of National Socialism in Germany.[202] When Nebenzahl and Oswald acquired the rights to the *Threepenny Opera* in May 1930, G.W. Pabst was chosen to direct the adaptation. Pabst had an excellent track-record with films based on literary texts (from Hugo Bettauer and Frank Wedekind to Margarete Böhme) and most recently directed the highly popular *Skandal um Eva* [Scandalous Eva] (1930)—Henny Porten's first sound film—based on playwright and publicist Heinrich Ilgenstein's 1927 *Skandal um Olly*, for Nero-Film. While Ilgenstein's play did very well in theaters even beyond the German republic, its success paled in comparison with *The Threepenny Opera*.

As Silberman notes, in early August 1930, Nero-Film

> negotiated a further agreement [on Brecht's insistence] that allowed him to write a scenario with his theatre collaborators Caspar Neher and Slatan Dodow, as well as Léo Lania. Though the agreement accorded Brecht the right to demand changes if the final cut did not follow their scenario, it also obliged the filmmakers to follow the original play's text both in style and content.[203]

When Brecht presented the screenplay *Die Beule* [The Bruise] to the producers, conflict arose due to a number of significant alterations made to the narrative intended to strengthen the political message. Especially the new motif of the "Beule" or 'bruise', which structurally and visually linked the different competing factions of the *Threepenny*-film, was deemed a commercially problematic diversion from the original project and hence unacceptable. Brecht, however, insisted on this version, while Nero-Film was eager to proceed with the production, having already rented studio space, signed contracts with the German- and French-language cast, and "resold the rights to Tobis-Klangfilm and Warner Brothers in anticipation of an international release by the celebrated director Georg Wilhelm Pabst."[204] Finally, Brecht was removed from the development of the adaptation and Léo Lania, together with scriptwriters Ladislaus Vajda and Béla Balázs, rewrote the script. For producers—Nebenzahl and Oswald were no exception here—the literary work was not sacrosanct but essentially raw material. This was common across Europe and, especially, in Hollywood, of course, as the other volumes in this series elucidate.[205] In this case, however, the commercial success of the film was considered dependent on its proximity to its fantastically popular stage production.

Brecht sued the company even though he probably knew he had no chance of winning his case. What he did gain, however, was publicity—a public demonstration of the commodification of literature by the film industry or, as Brecht put it, "how far the process of transforming intellectual values into commodities has progressed."[206] By putting the movie company's adaptation practices on the pillory, Brecht intended to highlight the collaborative input of the cinemagoer—if "you buy a ticket for the sound film *Threepenny Opera*, [...] then you must know that this *Threepenny Opera* fell into a huge machine whose function it is to make commodities out of artistically formed works at enormous expense."[207] Brecht believed his contract with Nero-Film would prohibit the company's "meddling with the poetic substance" of his work, and that the screenplay would not only be "written in consultation with him," but that he would also be able to "control the adaptation of the sound film."[208] As his contract included no veto power, this proved naïve, and by the time the court delivered its verdict, the film under Pabst's direction had been completed without Brecht. Even though the court rejected Brecht's claim, Nero subsequently returned the film rights to Brecht and paid the cost of the court. The composer of the musical score, Kurt Weill, also sued the company. His contract had stated that his music would remain unchanged and, as a single sounding of a trumpet was added to the score of the film, Weill received a generous settlement out of court.[209]

As Timothy Corrigan points out, the case highlighted the fact that "both the legal and artistic rights of the filmic author superseded those of the literary author once a work had been sold to a filmmaker."[210] For Brecht, however, the court case was not only about defending his rights as an author but presented a perfect opportunity to bring the issue of cultural commodification to the attention of the wider public. He could have settled out of court for a very attractive sum of 30,000 Marks but refused. Never before had the topic of adaptation aroused such media attention. During the trial, the courtroom was filled with journalists who reported daily on the proceedings. Questions such as the impact of literature on film and the role of the author (as "supplier or equal partner") in the film industry were suddenly hotly debated in the public sphere.²¹¹

Brecht used the courtroom as a compelling and polemical stage from which the complex relationship between literature/art and film could be analyzed and displayed to expose the detrimental effect of a capitalist culture industry that had discovered 'public appeal' cinema as its most profitable investment. "Everyone agrees that film, even of the most artistic kind, is a commodity," Brecht put it, and literature, i.e., "art's function is precisely to liberate the cinema from this enslavement." If literary text is nothing more than a commodity to an industry only interested in making profit, authors or "intellectual workers" find themselves caught in a "horrible vicious circle of exploitation." They depend on "these means of production," but all that matters is whether or not "a thing is marketable."²¹² If their literary work is indeed considered commercially attractive, and the adaptation rights are purchased by a film company, "the buyers even purchased the right to destroy what they bought," as Brecht summarized the "economic and legal distinctions between literature and film" at the time.²¹³ It was an exercise in "interventionist thinking *(eingreifendes Denken)* [and] a sociological experiment not only about individual authorship under capitalism, but a materialist account of how the structure of the film industry itself determines the nature of the products."²¹⁴

While he lost in court, Brecht was certainly successful in highlighting the ambivalent role of 'art' within a modern culture industry and in encouraging authors to pay close attention to the contracts with film companies they might yet sign. Perhaps most importantly, he publicly challenged the core of all major adaptation projects: public appeal. As Pommer argued above, the taste of the audience must be a component in the shaping of an adaptation project, particularly for larger and more expensive productions that depended on international or, as he put it, "universal appeal."

Die 3-Groschen-Oper premiered in Berlin's Atrium cinema on February 19, 1931, and the star-studded cast of screen, theater, and cabaret artists included Rudolf Forster as Mackie, Carola Neher as Polly, Lotte Lenya as Jenny, Fritz Rasp and Valeska Gert as Mr. and Mrs. Peachum, and Reinhold Schünzel as Tiger-Brown. Pabst had simultaneously filmed a French-language version for export entitled *L'Opéra de quat'sous*, which starred Albert Préjean as Mackie, darling of cinema audiences since his role in Clair's *Sous les toits de Paris* the previous year. Silent film star Gaston Modot, who had also appeared in Clair's talkie, plays Peachum. The role of Peachum's daughter Polly brought Moulin Rouge singer and dancer Florelle fame and, in the 1930s, a second career in the movies. Margo Lion's (Jenny) successful career as cabaret singer began in Pabst's film and "Pirate Jenny" became a staple in her performances. Antonin Artaud, then film writer, avant-garde dramatist, and theater producer, who was to become one of the main innovators of twentieth-century theater, appears in the film as one of the beggars.

Despite Brecht's devastating criticism of Pabst's adaptation as an artistic sell-out, the MLV-film was a box-office success in German-language countries and in France, perhaps even due to the publicity created by the trial. In English-speaking countries, its impact at the time was minor.[215] As an adaptation, the musical film profited from cinema's effect on Weimar's avant-garde theater, and from Brecht's and Weill's efforts to illustrate this underbelly of society both in dialogues and in songs. Hence, as Winter emphasizes, the

> deficiencies of early sound-reproducing apparatus could not greatly militate against music whose idiom often had much of the stridency of beer-garden pianolas. With these elements Pabst directed a cynically brilliant operetta, counterpointing songs and images.[216]

For the next two years, the play and its adaptation, its songs and aesthetic, had a solid fan base from the socially most marginal to established intellectuals of the bourgeoisie, who embraced *The Threepenny Opera* for its song, its political message, its fashion, or simply its entertainment value. Even years later and long in exile from Nazi Germany, Lotte Laserstein, a Berlin painter and cinema-lover, depicted herself as Polly Peachum in a purple feather boa and hat, with Mack the Knife standing behind her. Perhaps a defiant gesture in light of the Nazi's criticism (and, in 1933, prohibition) of both the play and its adaptation while so many of the production's creative talent were forced into exile, Laserstein's self-portrait was exhibited for the first time in Sweden in 1939—the year Joseph Goebbels called Pabst's musical film 'a typical Jew product', nauseatingly priding himself for having 'removed that kind of rubbish' from Germany.[217]

Conclusion

With a focus on the impact of sound on adaptation practices and projects from first tentative experiments to international successes like *The Blue Angel*, filmed in Babelsberg's first custom-built sound studio, the so-called "Tonkreuz,"[218] this overview of adaptations in early sound film from remakes such as *Alraune* to films based on contemporary hit plays like *Der Hauptmann von Köpenick* and *Die 3-Groschen-Oper* sheds light on the challenges faced by innovators and the volatile successes of some of the most notable adaptations.

The appeal of sound film had been underestimated initially by executives in the German film industry due to the international renown of their silent cinema output. The introduction of sound and, especially, the enormous box-office success of *The Jazz Singer* subsequently led not only to a scramble for transnational collaborations but to intense competition between "fifteen different systems involving three thousand patents"[219] in Europe alone. Once European patent holders had joined forces in March 1929, the enormous success of *The Singing Fool* in Berlin in June that year triggered new anxieties regarding the possibility of an American patent monopoly in Europe. The ensuing patent war involved film companies and electronics industries on both sides of the Atlantic, until the 'Paris Sound Film Peace' treaty regulated the market and guaranteed distribution.[220]

Cinemagoers were eager to experience sound films in newly equipped cinema palaces like Berlin's Ufa-Palast am Zoo or Vienna's Zentral-Kino, later called Ufa Ton-Kino, from 1929 onwards. Major film companies, and especially Ufa with outstanding producers like Pommer, looked to maximize profits by investing into 'universal-appeal-pictures'. Enabled by new sound-film technology, musical comedies and operetta films became the most popular genre of the early 1930s as cinema owners were scrambling to equip their film theaters with sound.

In addition to the challenges outlined regarding the regulation of production and distribution of commodities based on new technologies and patented equipment, sound had also created language barriers that fundamentally changed the conditions for international distribution. MLV-films, an increase in transnational production agreements and international exchanges of talent from the late 1920s, had a direct impact on literary prestige films, musical comedies, and operetta films aimed at international audiences. The vast majority of early sound films based on German-language literature, however, emerged from within the language area. Only a decade after the First World War, Hollywood productions such as Milestone's Remarque adaptation *All Quiet on the Western Front* and Goulding's *Grand Hotel* based on Baum's *Menschen im Hotel* were the exception, warranted by the international bestseller status of both novels.

In Germany, as in other European countries and the United States, early sound filmmakers rarely adapted the literary canon but rather looked to contemporary playwrights, whose works had already proved popular with mass audiences. The adaptation co-op that enabled Winsloe's and Sagan's *Mädchen in Uniform* was highly successful; the Nero-production of *Die 3-Groschen-Oper* and the ensuing lawsuits and trial unveiled the challenging position of writers and other creatives within an industry, which systematically used literature as raw material and mere commodity, not as an author's intellectual property or even art. The stage production of *The Threepenny Opera* demonstrated the possibility of amalgamating the expectations of mass entertainment, the needs for social critique, and the desire to produce art. The majority of individual elements were well established by other avant-garde movements such as Expressionism, for example, that already had put prostitutes and beggars in the center of their canvases or prose. The Cabaret was a thriving place of musical entertainment in Berlin and other urban centers. But Brecht, Weigel, and other creatives such as Toller and Piscator sincerely believed in the power of theater and mass media as a potential force for change and a better society. Brecht's dismay at the adaptation by Nero-Film was an acknowledgment of the failure of the movie in this regard, and the trial successfully moved the debate into the public sphere. Never before in the history of adaptation had the meaning and position of literature on film been more widely considered in the national press and by the public than during the *3-Groschen*-trial in Berlin in 1930/1. Even in the twenty-first century, the protection of creatives in the industry is still an important question today and Joachim A. Lang's *Mackie Messer—Brechts Dreigroschenfilm* (DE, 2018) contributed to this debate and to the legal changes under consideration in Europe at the time, which the last chapter will briefly outline.

Films of this early period were often highly innovative in their use of sound, reflecting the challenges but also the joy of experimentation at the time. Whether it was a faint whimper or a desperate scream, sound enabled the communication of individual tragedy, while ambient sound created a hitherto unfamiliar realism in movies as accounts of cinemagoers' affective responses highlight. Both ambient sound and human noises fascinated audiences and provided the foundation for effective antiwar action and other forms of political agency on screens. New Objectivity dominated contemporary German literature at the time and an 'objective' use of sound that conveyed evidence rather than a 'mood' introduced an unfamiliar documentarity into feature films. Controversial topics woven into often melodramatic narratives triggered debates and were amplified by sound, unless silenced by censors, distribution companies, and even cinema owners.

Sound enabled a more effective use of cinema for political agency in the fight for the legalization of abortion, for example, but also allowed for a much more persuasive representation of complex and multifaceted urban realities that had become a major theme in contemporary literature. But as Oswald emphasized, sound film as a creative force for naturalistic depictions of human nature and everyday life hinged on the ability of actors to shed the mannerisms of silent cinema. Continuities of practices, visual aesthetics but also of *sujets* are all apparent in early sound films. But as before, escapism remained the most attractive commodity of the mass entertainment industry, which now flourished due to musical comedies and operetta films. The experience of war, postwar hyper-inflation, and from 1929, another and this time global economic collapse aggravated people's sense of uncertainty. Cinema responded to this anxiety not only by offering absorbing distractions in 'universal appeal' films, but by thematizing discrimination and inequality, the randomness of fate, and the uncertainties of modern life. But with the introduction of sound, Germany's "cinema of metaphor"[221] was, not surprisingly, losing out to more direct, unambivalently entertaining narratives.

This final chapter of Weimar cinema is rife with memorable women, but often refashions age-old stereotypes like the *femme fatale* to put a spotlight on the power of seduction and the duplicity of individuals in modern urban spaces. While many at the time still believed in the aesthetic superiority of silent cinema, the introduction of sound altered the conditions and potential for literature on film and triggered an energetic engagement with new texts and, especially, contemporary theater. More than half of the most prominent German-language films of this era cinema were adaptations. Films by Milestone and von Sternberg, Thiele, Oswald, Pabst, and Sagan, or Fritz Lang's superb first sound film *M*, shaped the rich tapestry of sound cinema in German-speaking countries, until the Nazis' rise to power fundamentally transformed not only German society, but the creative industries and the lives of millions of citizens involved in their output.

Notes

1 Erich Pommer, "The Future of the Kinema," *The Observer* (September 4, 1932), 17.
2 *1922—Das Wunderjahr der Worte* is the title of Norbert Hummelt's new book (Munich: Luchterhand, 2022).
3 Two earlier *Golem* films that Paul Wegener co-wrote and directed during the First World War (with H. Galeen and R. Gliese respectively) seem to be lost.
4 A notable exception to this would be Hermann Sudermann's works, which continued to prove popular in Hollywood (cf. Paramount's *Lily of the Dust*, 1924; MGM's *Flesh and the Devil*, 1927). The Faust-theme, however, readily applicable to the Germany's hubris and lust for power continues to be present internationally—cf., for example, Frederick Todd's *Faust* (US, 1921), Raoul Grimoin-Sanson's *Faust* (FR, 1922); Nestroy's *Lumpaci Vagabundus*, again a story of temptation and being led astray, found its way into the Swedish adaptation *Andersson, Pettersson och Lundström* (SE, Carl Barcklind, 1923), based on a play by the Swedish author Frans Hodell which had been inspired by Nestroy's text.
5 Walter Ruttmann patented a predecessor of the multiplane camera in 1920 and presented avant-garde, abstract animation sequences in 1921 (e.g., his *Opus*-films) that were presented with live music based on a score composed to emphasize the rythm of his animation. When working with Lotte Reiniger from 1923 on *Die Abenteuer des Prinzen Achmed* [*The Adventures of Prince Achmed*] (DE, Lotte Reiniger, 1926), she developed his patent into a *Tricktisch* or animation table and created three-dimensionality and introduced a novel experience of depth perception in animation. *The Adventures of Prince Achmed*, an adaptation of *Arabian Nights* and one of the very first feature-length animation films, meant to serve as an intercultural endeavor. Reiniger

and most of her team were members of Berlin's Institute for Cultural Research (Institut für Kulturforschung) that aimed at conducting cultural research and convey findings via written and visual media for the development of a 'global cultural community' based on 'mutual respect and appreciation'. Cf. Ulrich Döge, "Kulturfilm als Aufgabe. Hans Cürlis (1889–1982)," *Filmblatt-Schriften* 4 (Babelsberg: Cinegraph, 2005), 17–19; Dora Rappsilber-Kurth, *Lotte Reiniger als Scherenschnittkünstlerin, Schattenspielerin und Pionierin des Trickfilms mit ihrem Beitrag einer gelebten Humanität* (Tübingen: Stadtmuseum Tübingen, 2010), 12f.

6 Siegfried Kracauer was at the time film and literature editor at the *Frankfurter Zeitung*. In 1933 the Jewish writer and journalist fled to France and in 1941, as the German troops had invaded and were all over Paris, was enabled to emigrate to the United States with the help of the French ambassador and his wife and others.

7 Kracauer, "Tonbildfilm," *Frankfurter Zeitung* (October 12, 1928), in *Von Caligari zu Hitler* (appendix: Filmkritiken 1924 bis 1939; Frankfurt: Suhrkamp, 1984), 409–11, here p. 409. The screening in Frankfurt took place on October 11, 1928.

8 Corrigan, "Literature on Screen," 35.

9 Leitch, *The History of American Literature on Film*, 135.

10 Ibid., 147; Leitch quotes Ruth Vasey, *The World According to Hollywood*, 102.

11 The Tri-Ergon system was based on 42mm (non-standard) film that included the standard 35mm stock.

12 Bagier notes in his diary that all Ufa studios were filled with noise—shouting producers, knocking builders, whistling gaffers, droning spotlights, etc.; quoted in https://www.filmportal.de/thema/die-tri-ergon-abteilung-der-Ufa.

13 https://www.filmportal.de/film/das-maedchen-mit-den-schwefelhoelzern_71437801ff3540519c98a70e2faec607.

14 Bagier emphasized the suspicion of sabotage and noted how he stepped outside after the disastrous premiere, and overheard a man 'with a foreign accent' say to his buddy: "It worked—German sound film is over!" ("Die Sache hat geklappt—der deutsche Tonfilm ist erledigt!"). Cf. Guido Bagier, "'Ton mehr aufdrehen—verstärken!' Guido Bagier über die Tri-Ergon-Abteilung der Ufa," *Das Ufa-Buch*, ed. Hans-Michael Bock, Michael Töteberg, 247; in 1929 Bagier supervised sound for Ruttmann's *Melodie der Welt* (*Melody of the World*) film project.

15 Lang's *Nibelungen* (1922–4) and *Metropolis* (1924–7) also contributed to Ufa's financial crisis. The company's subsequent loan from and contract with Paramount and Metro-Goldwyn-Mayer—the Parufamet agreement (1925)—guaranteed access to American films in Ufa cinemas, but also the distribution of German films in the United States. Cf. Brockmann, *A Critical History of German Film*, 53. See also Thomas J. Saunders, *Hollywood in Berlin: American Cinema and Weimar Germany* (Berkeley: University of California Press, 1994). The Parufamet agreement led to the resignation of Erich Pommer—as Ursula Hardt outlines in *From Caligari to California: Erich Pommer's Life in the International Film Wars* (Oxford: Berghahn, 1996), 92f.)—and, as Pommer had foreseen, only temporarily alleviated the crisis Ufa found itself in.

16 Michael Wedel, *Der deutsche Musikfilm. Archäologie eines Genres 1914–1945* (Munich: text+kritik, 2007), 192–217; a summary in English can be found in Wedel, *Pictorial Affects*, 169–170.
17 Arthur Honegger composed a score for Abel Gance's *La Roue* (1922), and used Rierre Delacommune's Cinépupitre, an apparatus that "recorded the rhythm of successions of sounds. A later improvement was made by C. R. Blum, the Rhythmonome." Marian Hannah Winter, "The Function of Music in Sound Film," *The Musical Quarterly* 27.2 (1941): 146–64, here p. 147.
18 Ibid.
19 Douglas Gomery, "Tri-Ergon, Tobis-Klangfilm, and the Coming of Sound," *Cinema Journal* 16 (Autumn 1976): 51–61.
20 Cf. "Das Gründungsprogramm der Tobis," *Film-Kurier* 172 (July 20, 1928), which can be accessed via filmportal.de at https://www.filmportal.de/material/das-gruendungsprogramm-der-tobis.
21 "Kino—das große Traumgeschäft," *Der Spiegel* (December 20, 1950), cf. also "Das Gründungsprogramm der Tobis," *Film-Kurier* 172 (July 20, 1928).
22 Neubabelsberg outside Berlin was home to Deutsche Bioscop's studios. In 1911/12, the company had "transformed the site into one of Europe's largest studios through the addition of new buildings and massive exterior sets." After merging with Decla in 1920, Ufa started buying shares of its rival Decla-Bioscop until acquiring control of the company in 1923 and thus its vast studio space in Neubabelsberg.
23 Siegfried Kracauer, "Der erste deutsche Tonfilm," *Frankfurter Zeitung* (November 11, 1929), in *Von Caligari zu Hitler*, 415–17, here p. 416.
24 Stephen Brockmann, *A Critical History of German Film*, 55.
25 Hugo was author of *Berlin Alexanderplatz* Alfred Döblin's older brother.
26 Numbers of cinemas equipped with sound technology according to *Der Spiegel* (https://www.spiegel.de/spiegel/print/d-44451166.html) were 1,864 in December 1930, 2,320 in Dezember 1931, and 3,820 in Dezember 1932. Even then 1,251 cinemas in Germany were still only equipped for silent films.
27 Dayton Henderson provides insights into the patent war on the ground in his "11 December 1930 Ban of All Quiet on the Western Front Highlights Tensions over Sound Technology," in *A New History of German Cinema*, ed. Kapczinsky and Richardson, 219–25, especially 220–2.
28 Corinna Müller, *Vom Stummfilm zum Tonfilm* (Munich: Fink, 2003); Wolfgang Mühl-Benninghaus, *Das Ringen um den Tonfilm. Strategien der Elektro- und Filmindustrie in den 20er und 30er Jahren* (Düsseldorf: Droste, 1999); Peter Bächlin, *Der Film als Ware* (Frankfurt/M.: Fischer, 1975), 56–65.
29 René Clair's *Sous let toits de Paris* (1930) was produced by Tobis-Klangfilm and shot at its French studio.
30 pe., "Alraune," *Lichtbild-Bühne* 289 (December 3, 1930); can be accessed via filmportal.de at https://www.filmportal.de/node/27509/material/638405.
31 Illés' sequel to his original *Alraune, die Henkerstochter, genannt die rote Hanne* [Alraune, hangman's daughter, known as red Hanne] was released in 1919.
32 Semenza and Hasenfratz, *The History of British Literature on Film*, 166–71. As Semenza and Hasenfratz outline, it was Carl Laemmle, jr. at Universal, who "almost single-handedly reinvented the horror genre in the early 1930s under

the guidance of his father," beginning with Bram Stoker's *Dracula* (1931) and Mary Shelley's *Frankenstein* (1931). Semenza/Hasenfratz, *History of British Literature on Film*, 166.
33 Michael Wedel, *Filmgeschichte als Krisengeschichte* (Bielefeld: transcript, 2011), 150.
34 Wedel provides very valuable insights into Oswald's *Alraune* in his *Filmgeschichte als Krisengeschichte*, 174–6.
35 Richard Oswald, "Alraune," *Film-Kurier* 284 (December 2, 1930). Also quoted in Wedel, *Filmgeschichte als Krisengeschichte*, 174; Michael Geisler also makes the point in the context of Neue Sachlichkeit: "The randomization of life (and death) in the city, as expressed in such diverse works as Hermann Hesse's *Steppenwolf* (1927), Alfred Döblin's *Berlin Alexanderplatz* (1929), or Erich Kästner's *Fabian* (1931) closely resembles the experience of random injury and death in the trenches [...]." Geisler, "The Battleground of Modernity: *Westfront 1918*," in *The Films of G.W. Pabst*, ed. Rentschler, 91–102, here p. 99.
36 See, for example, pe., "Alraune" as above, and E. J., "Alraune," *Film-Kurier* 285 (December 3, 1930).
37 Richard B. Jewell, *The Golden Age of Cinema* (Oxford: Wiley, 2008), 95.
38 For further information on the film cf. Andre Sennwald's review in the *New York Times* (October 28, 1935), at https://www.nytimes.com/1935/10/28/archives/transatlantic-tunnel-the-drama-of-an-engineering-miracle-below-sea.html (accessed December 2018).
39 In Liechtenstein, movies were screened from 1908 onwards in pubs and restaurants. The first purpose-built cinema opened in Vaduz in 1944. See https://historisches-lexikon.li/Kino (accessed May 2020).
40 Bock/Töteberg, "A History of Ufa," 291.
41 Jan Christopher Horak, "German Film Comedy," *The German Cinema Book*, 43.
42 Bock/Töteberg, "A History of Ufa," 291.
43 Winter, "The Function of Music in Sound Film," 159.
44 Ibid., 160.
45 Ibid.
46 Siegfried Kracauer, "The Mass Ornament," in *The Mass Ornament, Weimar Essays*, trans./ed. Thomas Y. Levin (Cambridge, MA: Harvard University Press, 1995), 75.
47 Cf. *Gesellschaft* (=society) as defined by Ferdinand Tönnies and, especially, by Émile Durkheim in his *De la division du travail social* (1893).
48 Jewell, *The Golden Age of Cinema*, 95.
49 In 1927, a medical indication was included in §218 to allow doctors to end a pregnancy in a medical emergency.
50 Wolf's brochure was published by the German Arbeiter-Theater-Bund (the workers' theater association) in 1928. Cf. Emmi Wolf and Klaus Hammer, eds., *Cyankali von Friedrich Wolf. Eine Dokumentation* (Berlin: Aufbau, 1978).
51 See, for example, the contributions made by Erika Mann, Milena Jesenská, Gabriele Tergit, and Helen Wolff. Jesenská was murdered in Ravensbrück concentration camp, the other three fought to continue their careers in exile.

For decades, they were mostly remembered as 'the daughter of Thomas Mann' or the 'lover of Franz Kafka.' Thanks to Helen Wolff's niece, Marion Detjen, Wolff's *Hintergrund für Liebe* (1932) was published for the first time in 2020, and to scholars such as Irmela von der Lühe (*Erika Mann. Eine Biographie*, 2001) that we are reminded of their important work. My edited *Practicing Modernity: Creative Women in the Weimar Republic* (2006) might also be of interest in this context.

52 Lynda J. King, *Best-sellers by Design: Vicki Baum and the House of Ullstein* (Detroit: Wayne State University Press, 1988). King writes: "[Baum's] greatest fame came through her serialized novels in Ullstein's *Berliner Illustrierte Zeitung*, which was circulated nationally and in other German-speaking countries and had a readership of over 1.8 million in 1928. The magazine's circulation increased by 200,000 during the serialization of Baum's first great success, *stud. chem. Helene Willfüer* in 1928–29." King, *Best-sellers by Design*, 12.

53 Cf. Atina Grossmann's essay on the New Woman as social reality rather than a "media myth or a demographer's paranoid fantasy," 64; quoted in Ritta Jo Horsley, "'This Number Is Not in Service': Destabilizing Identities in Irmgard Keun's Novels from Weimar and Exile," in *Facing Fascism and Confronting the Past*, ed. Elke P. Frederiksen and Martha Kaarsberg Wallach (New York: SUNY, 2000), 37–60, here p. 37.

54 Keun, *Gigli*, 13f.; quoted in Gerd-Peter Rutz, *Darstellungen von Film in literarischen Fiktionen der zwanziger und dreißiger Jahre* (Münster: LIT, 2000), 142.

55 Gilgi's life as described by Keun is a "Zeitschicksal"—the typical fate of a woman of her time; cf. Horsley, "This Number Is Not in Service," 40. See also Rutz, *Darstellungen von Film in literarischen Fiktionen*, 142f.

56 Horsley, "This Number Is Not in Service," 40.

57 Rutz, *Darstellungen von Film in literarischen Fiktionen*, 143.

58 Ulrich L. Klaus, *Deutsche Tonfilme,* vol. 3, 45f.; quoted in Rutz, *Darstellungen von Film in literarischen Fiktionen,* 141.

59 The most detailed assessment of the film and its production history can be found in Michael Grisko, *Heinrich Mann und der Film* (Munich: Meidenbauer, 2008), esp. 220–81; cf. also: Richard A. Fierda, "Literary Origins: Sternberg's Film *The Blue Angel*," *Literature Film Quarterly* 7.2 (1979): 126–36; Gertrud Koch, "Between Two Worlds: Von Sternberg's *The Blue Angel*," in *Film and German Literature*, ed. Eric Rentschler (New York: Methuen, 1986), 60–72; Gilbert Carr, "'Mit einem kleinen Ruck, wie beim Kinematographen'. From the Unmaking of Professor Unrat to an Unmade *Der blaue Engel*," in *Processes of Transposition: German Literature and Film*, ed. C. Schönfeld (Amsterdam: Rodopi, 2007), 119–31.

60 Other actresses were considered for the role of Lola Lola—Trude Hesterberg, Brigitte Helm, Lucie Mannheim, Phyllis Haver, Blandine Ebinger, and Käthe Haack. Cf. Manfred Flügge, *Heinrich Mann. Eine Biographie* (Reinbek: Rowohlt, 2006), 237f.

61 Werner Sudendorf, *Marlene Dietrich* (Munich: dtv, 2001), 67; quoted in Grisko, *Heinrich Mann und der Film,* 223.

62 Not only actors such as Emil Jannings or Conrad Veidt followed Pommer to Hollywood, but a number of directors; cf. Hardt, *From Caligari to California: Erich Pommer's Life in the International Film Wars,* 94–6.

63 For his script's dialogues, Kräly also referred to Ashley Dukes' play *The Patriot*—which was based on Neumann's *Der Patriot* and had a very successful run at Broadway earlier that year—and Dmitry Merezhkovsky play *Paul I*. Naumann's *Der Patriot* was originally published in 1925 as "Erzählung" (short story), followed by revised versions as novel and "Drama."

64 In 2012, the French black-and-white and mostly silent *The Artist* was nominated and won the Oscar for Best Picture.

65 According to Bock and Töteberg, Ludwig Klitzsch, director general of Scherl Publishing and put in charge of Ufa by Hugenberg in 1927, invited Pommer back to Ufa, well aware of the producer's talents and networks. Cf. Bock/Töteberg, "A History of Ufa," 290f.

66 Heinrich Mann in his conversation with Raoul Plaquin, published in *Revue du Cinéma* 17 (1930), quoted in Grisko, *Heinrich Mann und der Film*, 223f. Flügge mentions that Mann had been in conversations, if unsuccessfully, with 'interested film producers' regarding his novels back in 1919 and again in 1926. Cf. Flügge, *Heinrich Mann*, 237.

67 As mentioned above, this was partly due to Ufa's major investments into grand cinema spectacles such as Murnau's *Faust,* Lang's *Nibelungen* and *Metropolis* brought Ufa to the brink of bankruptcy and to the Parufamet agreement with Paramount and Metro-Goldwyn-Mayer in 1925.

68 Heinz Umbehr outlines the innovative engineering of the "Tonkreuz" in an article published in the journal *Filmtechnik* in November 1929. See also Douglas Gomery, "Tri-Ergon, Tobis-Klangfilm, and the Coming of Sound," *Cinema Journal* 16 (Autumn 1976): 51–61.

69 The Berlin correspondent in "The Future of the Kinema," *The Observer* (September 4, 1932) 17. When Deutsche Bank refused to support Ufa's loans in 1927, "[b]oth Carl Laemmle and Paramount Pictures were interested in capturing the German film industry."

70 Grisko, *Heinrich Mann und der Film*, 227.

71 Flügge, *Heinrich Mann*, 238. Because of Emil Jannings' dreadful German accent, however, the German-language version became the more widely distributed at the time.

72 Grisko, *Heinrich Mann und der Film*, 229.

73 Born Jonas Sternberg, the director was not of noble heritage as the "von" in his name might indicate. Whether the nobiliary particle was added by himself or by those marketing *The Salvation Hunters* (1925), his directorial debut, could not be established. But since Sternberg filmed *Salvation Hunters* on a 'shoestring,' it is likely that the embellishment of his name was made by the director himself.

74 Cf. Sternberg's *Fun in a Chinese Laundry* (1965) in Grisko, *Heinrich Mann und der Film*, 233.

75 Heinrich Mann on March 15, 1930: "On The Blue Angel: Heinrich Mann to Karl Lemke," in *Authors on Film*, ed. Harry M. Geduld, 124.

76 The German adjective 'toll' can mean either fantastic or nuts, and the film title consciously infers both.

77 The year 1930 was a hugely successful year for Harvey due to *Liebeswalzer* [Waltz of Love] (DE, Wilhelm Thiele), and *Hokuspokus* (DE, Gustav Ucicky) the aforementioned adaptation of Curt Goetz's 1926 play, both with Willy Fritsch. An English version *Hokuspokus* entitled *The Temporary Widow* starred Lilian Harvey and Laurence Olivier.

78 Carr, "'Mit einem kleinen Ruck, wie beim Kinematographen': From the Unmaking of Professor Unrat to an Unmade *Der blaue Engel*," in *Processes of Transposition*, ed. Christiane Schönfeld (Amsterdam: Rodopi, 2007), 124 cf. note 59.
79 Doane, *Femme Fatales*, 101.
80 Cf. especially Petro, *Joyless Streets*.
81 Heinrich Mann, "*The Blue Angel* Is Shown to Me," in Geduld, ed., *Authors on Film*, 125–8, here p. 127.
82 Mann, "*The Blue Angel* Is Shown to Me," 126.
83 Heinrich Mann, "On *The Blue Angel*: Heinrich Mann to Karl Lemke," in *Authors on Film*, 123–5, here p. 124.
84 Ibid.
85 Ibid.
86 Victor Mann, *Wir waren fünf. Bildnis der Familie Mann* [1949] (Frankfurt/M.: Fischer, 1994), 437f.
87 Mann, "*The Blue Angel* Is Shown to Me," 127.
88 Ibid., 128.
89 Peter Baxter, "Fallen Angels," *Sight and Sound* 11 (2001): 65; also quoted by Carr, "Mit einem kleinen Ruck," 119.
90 Kracauer's *Die Neue Rundschau* (January 28, 1930) article is included in the Suhrkamp edition of *Von Caligari zu Hitler*, 418–21, here p. 418.
91 "The German Talkie Comes to London." *The Observer* (July 6, 1930): 15. The reviewer considers the other actors unable to translate "their emotions into a language that is not familiar enough to carry them. Only Marlene Dietrich comes out of the ordeal alive; the others lack inflection, colour and poetry."
92 Ibid.
93 Brockmann, *A Critical History of German Film*, 105; Mayne, "Marlene Dietrich, *The Blue Angel*, and Female Performance," in *Seduction and Theory: Readings of Gender, Representation and Rhetoric*, ed. Dianne Hunter (Urbana: University of Illinois Press, 1989), 28–46, here p. 35. Brockmann's chapter on *The Blue Angel* (*A Critical History of German Film*, 97–111) provides an excellent introduction and critical overview. Cf. also Carr, "'Mit einem kleinen Ruck," 124ff.
94 Flügge, *Heinrich Mann*, 239.
95 "The German Talkie Comes to London." *The Observer* (July 6, 1930): 15.
96 The film also promoted the new Bauhaus style. Otto Hunte designed the set and his interiors pay homage to "neues Bauen"; cf. Nils Warnecke, *Kino der Moderne*, 56. I am indebted to François Genton for the Remarque reference.
97 "The German Talkie Comes to London." *The Observer* (July 6, 1930): 15.
98 Cf. *The Observer* (September 4, 1932).
99 Peter Gay mentions "a dance on the edge of a volcano" in his *Weimar Culture: The Outsider as Insider* (New York: Norton, 2001, xiv). The German term "ein/der Tanz auf dem Vulkan" appears already in Goethe in his *Italienische Reise* (*Italian Journey*, 1786/7, published 1816/17), describing life in Herculaneum and Pompeii under the shadow of Vesuvius. It also recurs in *Wilhelm Meisters Wanderjahre* (*Wilhelm Meister's Journeyman Years, or the Renunciants*, 1821) and in his studies on volcanology.

100 Not even Louise Brooks, who had fascinated European audiences as seductive female lead in G. W. Pabst's German productions *Pandora's Box* and *Diary of a Lost Girl* (both 1929) and returned to Hollywood, could compete with Dietrich's depiction of the 'female archetype.' For a more detailed discussion, see my essay on "Women on Screen: A Short History of the Femme Fatale," *Women's Studies Review* 8 (2002): 29–46, on which this paragraph is based.
101 Winsloe also published a short novel on the topic entitled *Das Mädchen Manuela* (The Child Manuela) in 1933.
102 B. Ruby Rich, "Maedchen in Uniform: From Repressive Tolerance to Erotic Liberation," *Jump Cut* 24.25 (1981): 44–50; https://www.ejumpcut.org/archive/onlinessays/JC24-25folder/MaedchenUniform.html.
103 A leitmotif of Sagan's film and a recurring motif in Weimar cinema, as Lotte Eisner explains.
104 Winter, "The Function of Music in Sound Film," 155.
105 Eisner, *The Haunted Screen*, 326.
106 For example in Alfred Santell's *Bondage* (US, Alfred Santell, 1933) written by Austrian Arthur Kober and based on the book by Grace S. Leake.
107 See, for example, Nina Zimnik, "No Man, No Cry? The Film Girls in Uniform and Its Discourses of Political Regime," *Women in German Yearbook* 15 (2000): 161–83; Emily M. Danforth, "Mädchen in Uniform," *Quarterly Review of Film and Video* 27.5 (2010): 353–5; Veronika Mayer, "Lesbian Classics in Germany? A Film Historical Analysis of Mädchen in Uniform (1931 and 1958)," *Journal of Lesbian Studies* 16 (2012): 340–53.
108 Ilinca Iurascu, "Introduction: The Media Histories of *Girls in Uniform*," *Seminar* 55.2 (2019): 89–93.
109 Wedel, *Pictorial Affects*, 165; Wolfgang Mühl-Benninghaus, *Das Ringen um den Tonfilm. Strategien der Elektro- und der Filmindustrie in den 20er und 30er Jahren* (Düsseldorf: Droste, 1999).
110 Wedel, *Pictorial Affects*, 166; Mühl-Benninghaus, *Das Ringen um den Tonfilm*, 199–21.
111 Karl Wolffsohn, *Jahrbuch der Filmindustrie* 4 (1930): 109, quoted by Wedel, *Pictorial Affects*, 167; Mühl-Benninghaus, *Das Ringen um den Tonfilm*, 171.
112 Wedel, *Pictorial Affects*, 168; Thompson, *Exporting Entertainment*, 163.
113 Wedel, *Pictorial Affects*, 165.
114 Jewell, *The Golden Age of Cinema*, 265.
115 Claus Gigl, *Im Westen nichts Neues* (Stuttgart: Klett, 2014), 95. The novel's success was in part due to its focus on very young men enthusiastically joining the war effort in 1914, which resonated with many at the time. In addition, Remarque's publisher Propyläen ran a very effective marketing campaign.
116 "Deutsche Universal verfilmt *Im Westen nichts Neues*," *Film-Kurier* 158 (July 5, 1929); quoted in Wedel, *Pictorial Affects*, 174.
117 Maria Tatar, "The Poetics of the Combat Zone: Erich Maria Remarque's Im Westen nichts Neues," *German Quarterly* 92.1 (Winter 2019): 1–19, here p. 2.
118 Remarque, *Im Westen nichts Neues*, 249.
119 See apart from Lampel's aforementioned texts, for example, Georg von der Vring's *Soldat Suhren* (Private Suhren, written in 1924 but not published

until 1927), in 1928 Ernst Glaeser's bestselling *Jahrgang 1902* (Born in 1902) and Ludwig Renn's *Krieg* (War), as well as Alexander Moritz Frey's *Die Pflasterkästen* (The Plaster Boxes) in 1929. For more information, cf. Hans-Harald Müller, "Politics and the War Novel: The Political Conception and Reception of Novels about the First World War," in *German Writers and Politics, 1918–39*, ed. Richard Dove and Stephen Lamb (Houndmills: Macmillan, 1992), 103–20, here p. 110.
120 Toller, "Im Westen nichts Neues" (original published in *Die literarische Welt* on February 22, 1929), *Sämtliche Werke* 4: 603–4.
121 Jewell, *The Golden Age of Cinema*, 221.
122 Ibid., 221f.
123 A summary of the cuts is given in Gigl, *Im Westen nichts Neues*, 96. Censorship did not only affect the film in Germany, however. A scene in which the main character Paul Bäumer (played by Lew Ayros) stabs a French soldier had to be removed in France, and both novel and film were prohibited in fascist Italy. As the censorship report explains in a somewhat indignant tone, a Frenchman would not be killed by a German. Cf. Angela Gutzeit, "Verstümmelt und verboten," *Neue Osnabrücker Zeitung* (February 4, 1985).
124 Siegfried Kracauer, "Westfront 1918," *Frankfurter Zeitung* (May 27, 1930); cf. *Von Caligari zu Hitler* (appendix), 430–2, here p. 431.
125 Peter Martin Lampel was responsible for the dialogues; he was the author of a number of literary texts inspired by his own war experience, namely *Heereszeppeline im Angriff* (Zeppelins attack, 1917), *Bombenflieger* (Bombers, 1918), and *Wie Leutnant Jürgens Stellung suchte* (with a subtitle "Ein Filmroman aus den Spartakustagen," 'a filmnovel from the Spartacusdays'). His satirical and highly provocative play *Giftgas über Berlin* (Poison gas over Berlin) was adapted for cinema under the direction of Michail Dubson (1929). The silent film, which ends in catastrophe, was supported by the German League of Human Rights. Lampel and Natan Sarchi co-wrote the script, and Sergei Eisenstein helped design the closing sequence in which the dead of the First World War rise to condemn the use of poison gas. While popular at the box office despite significant cuts demanded by the censorship office that removed most of the political impetus, critics viewed the adaptation as clichéd, sensationalist, and embarrassing (cf. Kracauer, *Frankfurter Zeitung* (November 27, 1929); *Von Caligari zu Hitler*, 417f.) and, considering the power of the mass medium film, a missed opportunity (cf. *Die Weltbühne* (November 19, 1929); Karl Dahlke, ed. et al., *Deutsche Spielfilme von den Anfängen bis 1933* (Berlin: Henschel, 1993), 201f.).
126 See Geisler's discussion of the scene in "The Battleground of Modernity," 99–101.
127 Quoted in Christa Bandmann, Joe Hembus, "Westfront 1918," in *Klassiker des deutschen Tonfilms* (Munich: Goldmann, 1980), 19.
128 Kracauer, "Westfront 1918," 432.
129 The director of Metro-Goldwyn-Mayer Studio Sound Department Douglas Shearer received the Oscar, https://www.oscars.org/oscars/ceremonies/1931.
130 Quoted in and translated by Henderson, "11 December 1930," 222.

131 Dayton Henderson argues that "Tobis's technology was not used to make the film. Universal relied exclusively on Western Electric's apparatus while filming." Henderson, "11 December 1930," 223. This, however, ignores the use of German technology during the post-synchronization process, which the adverts referred to. With regard to *All Quiet on the Western Front* see chapter 8 of Wedel's *Pictorial Affects*, in which Wedel gives an excellent summary of the relevant facts and discourses relating to the adaptation of Remarque's novel as a sound film (160–79).

132 Deutsche Kinemathek, Schriftgut archive, folder of reviews; see also Wedel's summary in *Filmgeschichte als Krisengeschichte*, 204–9, or for the English translation *Pictorial Affects*, 169–76.

133 George J. Mitchell, "Making All Quiet on the Western Front," *American Cinematographer* 66.9 (1985): 34–6.; quoted in Wedel, *Pictorial Affects*, 174.

134 Henderson, "11 December 1930," 223. The second quote is Henderson's translation of a quote from "Zirkus-Nollendorfplatz," *Kinematograph* (11 December 1930): 2.

135 In Hans Zöberlein's 'answer by a front soldier to Remarque's book' evokes the stab-in-the-back myth (*Dolchstoßlegende*) in his highly critical "Im Westen nichts Neues," *Völkischer Beobachter* (August 14, 1929); quoted by Müller, "Politics and the War Novel," 114.

136 Henderson gives an excellent summary of selected criticism and skillfully places it in the context of sound film competition. I would, however, point out that the reviews examined in his article were published by the Scherl-group, which was owned by Hugenberg and thus belong to the conservative/nationalist camp. Numerous positive reviews celebrating the pacifist message of the film were published in a range of film journals and newspapers and can be accessed, for example, at the Deutsche Kinemathek in Berlin. For a selection see Bäbel Schrader, ed., *Der Fall Remarque: Im Westen nichts Neues, eine Dokumentation* (Leipzig: Reclam, 1997).

137 Bock/Töteberg, "A History of Ufa," 290.

138 Anon., "'Die Bestie von Berlin': Die Deutschhetze des Filmjuden Lämmle, des Produzenten des Remarquefilms," *Völkischer Beobachter* 305 (December 24, 1930): 1.

139 Cf. the critical edition of Hitler's *Mein Kampf* (especially the last three chapters), and Walter A. Berendsohn, *Die humanistische Front: Einführung in die deutsche Emigranten-Literatur*, vol. 1 (Zurich: Europa, 1946), 11.

140 Press briefing folder, Germany, 1950, DK archive.

141 Anon., "Der Sieg des Hakenkreuzes in Wien über die Remarque-Schande. Der Nationalsozialismus auch dort der Vorkämpfer für die deutsche Ehre," *Völkischer Beobachter* 327 (January 15, 1931): 2.

142 These quotes are taken from the description of the film on i tunes.

143 Produced by ITC Entertainment, *All Quiet on the Western Front* was adapted for television in 1979 under the direction of Delbert Mann. The film starred Richard Thomas, Donald Pleasence, Ian Holm, and Ernest Borgnine, among others, and was well received by critics. Awards included the Golden Globe Award for Best Motion Picture Made for Television.

144 Crafton, *The Talkies*, 436f.; Wedel, *Pictorial Affects*, 174f.

145 According to IMDb, the following adaptations of Lothar/Gottwald's *Die Republik befiehlt* were completed: the English *The Boudoir Diplomat* (US, Malcolm St. Clair, 1930), the Spanish *Don Juan diplomático* (US, George Melford, 1931), and the French *Boudoir diplomatique* (US, Marcel De Sano, 1931). For further information see Wedel, *Filmgeschichte als Krisengeschichte*, 210–12.
146 Wedel, *Pictorial Affects*, 175.
147 Wedel quotes from *Film-Kurier* 144 (June 22, 1931); Wedel, *Pictorial Affects*, 175.
148 Wedel, *Pictorial Affects*, 176.
149 Wedel, *Filmgeschichte als Krisengeschichte*, 209; Joseph Garnarz, "Hollywood in Germany. Die Rolle des amerikanischen Films in Deutschland 1925–1990," in *Der deutsche Film*, ed. Uli Jung (Trier: WVT, 1993), 200.
150 Initially, Baum was invited to provide a screenplay based on her novel, but having no experience with scriptwriting, the script was instead written by William A. Drake. Subsequently, Baum worked as a screenwriter in Hollywood and lived in Pacific Palisades close to fellow exiles Katja and Thomas Mann and Marta and Lion Feuchtwanger. She died in California in 1960.
151 Cf. for further information Leitch, *The History of American Literature on Film*, 145. See also p. 137 for a discussion of the move from a theatrical to a novelistic aesthetic in the film.
152 Vicki Baum, *Menschen im Hotel* (Klagenfurt: Kaiser, 1972), 7; cf. also 9, 13, 15, and 31 for previous references to the novel.
153 Baum, *Menschen im Hotel*, 309, 318f. "Wärme" (warmth) is used in the context of emotional comfort, "love," however, would be too strong.
154 Cf. Anne Massey, "This mixture of gender, social class and personal situation acts as a microcosm for the anxieties generated by life during the rise of modernity and, in this case, at the beginning of the Great Depression." Massey, "Learning from Los Angeles: Hollywood Hotel Lobbies," *Hotel Lobbies and Lounges: The Architecture of Professional Hospitality* (New York: Routledge, 2013), 49–58, here p. 54. See also Jörg Thunecke, "Kolportage ohne Hintergründe. Der Film *Grand Hotel* (1932). Exemplarische Darstellung der Entwicklungsgeschichte von Vicki Baums Roman *Menschen im Hotel*," in *Die Resonanz des Exils. Gelungene und mißlungene Rezeption deutschsprachiger Exilautoren*, ed. Dieter Sevin (Amsterdam: Rodopi, 1992), 134–53.
155 According to Tom Leitch, "only MGM turned a profit" during the 1932–3 season. Leitch, *The History of American Literature on Film*, 112.
156 "Menschen im Hotel. Capitol." Review by F. O.; Cf. also *Film-Journal* 8 (February 19, 1933) review and others in Deutsche Kinemathek archive, file F4756.
157 Kracauer, "Berliner Filmchronik," *Frankfurter Zeitung* (January 6, 1931), in *Von Caligari bis Hitler*, 473.
158 Leitch, *The History American Literature on Film*, 112.
159 "The Future of the Kinema," *The Observer* (September 4, 1932): 17. The following quotes are from the same Erich Pommer interview by "our Berlin Correspondent."

160 Kracauer, "Grenze 1919," in *Frankfurter Zeitung* (November 21, 1931), in *Von Caligari bis Hitler*, 515.
161 Cf. for example the review by Hans Sochaczewer published in *Berliner Tageblatt* (December 15, 1929).
162 See Pabst's November 1929 article in *Film und Volk*; also: Karin Herbst-Messlinger, "Kindheit," in *Kino der Moderne*, 34–9, here 35. Herbst-Messlinger rightly points out that among the few available films for children in Germany were Lotte Reiniger's silhouette films *Aschenputtel* (Cinderella, 1922) and *Die Abenteuer des Prinzen Achmed* (1926).
163 A first script was drafted by Emeric Pressburger, but Erich Kästner was opposed as it changed his characterization of Emil, who was close to his heart. Following further collaborations, Billy Wilder's reworking of the script captured the atmosphere of the novel and Kästner eventually approved. Cf. Helga Belach and Hans-Michael Bock, eds., *Emil und die Detektive. Drehbuch von Billy Wilder nach Erich Kästner zu Gerhard Lamprechts Film von 1931* (introductory essay by Helga Schütz and relevant documents by Gabriele Jatho; Munich: edition text+kritik, 1998); Ingo Tornow, *Erich Kästner und der Film* (Munich: dtv, 1998); Stefan Neuhaus, ed., *Erich Kästner* (Stuttgart: Metzler, 2023).
164 Further adaptations of Kästner's novel include *Emil and the Detectives* (GB, Milton Rosmer, 1935), *Toscanito y los detectives* (AR, Antonio Momplet, 1950), *Emil und die Detektive* (DE, Robert Adolf Stemmle, 1954), *Emil to tantei tachi* (JP, Mitsuo Wakasugi, 1956), *Pega Ladrão* (BR, Alberto Pieralisi, 1957), a first Disney adaptation (US, Peter Tewksbury, 1964), *Emiler Goenda Bahini* (Bangladesh, Badal Rahman, 1980), *Shakh-e gav* (Iran, Kianoush Ayari, 1995) and another adaptation in Germany (DE, Franziska Buch, 2001). Adaptations for television include the British, 1952, three episodes series adapted for TV by Godfrey Harrison.
165 Philip French, "Emil and the Detectives," *The Guardian* (September 8, 2013); https://www.theguardian.com/film/2013/sep/08/emil-detectives-classic-dvd-french.
166 Sabina Becker, *Experiment Weimar. Eine Kulturgeschichte Deutschlands 1918–1933* (Darmstadt: wbg academic, 2018), 168f. Especially Kafka, Joyce, and Schnitzler's use of first-person stream of consciousness narrative in *Leutnant Gustl* (None but the Brave, 1900) and *Fräulein Else* (1924) inspired Döblin. For more detail, see my article on the novel and its adaptations in *The Palgrave Encyclopedia of Urban Literary Studies*, ed. Jeremy Tambling (London: Palgrave, 2022), which is in part based on work done for this book; https://link.springer.com/referencework/10.1007/978-3-319-62592-8.
167 Cf. Döblin in *Film-Kurier* (August 16, 1930).
168 Gabriele Sander, *Erläuterungen und Dokumente zu Alfred Döblin: Berlin Alexanderplatz* (Stuttgart: Reclam, 1998), 229.
169 Quoted in Sander, *Alfred Döblin*, 230.
170 As Winter points out, Germans were particularly fond of "Geräuschmusik" [lit. noise music], composed by musicians such as Edmund Meisel, who had provided the musical score to Eisenstein's masterful Potemkin in 1925. "In his use of percussion instruments Meisel anticipated many effects of sound film; the use of noise—Geräuschmusik—was his special interest, and after sound film was an actuality he made a series of six records for Polydor which

incorporated various noises into 'effect music'—*Street Noises, The Start and Arrival of a Train, A Train Running till the Emergency Brake Is Pulled, Noises of a Railway Station, Machine Noises, a Bombardement and Music of the Heavenly Hosts*." Winter, "The Function of Music in Sound Film," 151.

171 Döblin wanted a radio play or a film "mit fliehenden Schaupätzen, schnell wechselnden Stimmungen, kaleidoskopartig abrollendem, dahingleitendem Geschehen." Quoted in Sander, *Alfred Döblin*, 230.

172 "Der Döblin Film im Werden," *Film-Bild-Bühne* 122 (May 22, 1931), quoted by Sander, *Alfred Döblin*, 233f.

173 This was pointed out by Georg F. Salmony especially. Quoted in Sander, *Alfred Döblin*, 236.

174 For a summary of contemporary reviews see Sander, *Alfred Döblin*, 234–42.

175 Kurt Pinthus in *8 Uhr Abendblatt der National-Zeitung* (October 9, 1931); quoted in Sander, *Alfred Döblin*, 235. Pinthus coins the term "Ablenkungsfilm" [lit. distraction movie].

176 Hans Siemsen in *Die Welt am Montag* (October 12, 1931); quoted in Sander, *Alfred Döblin*, 238.

177 Kracauer, "'Berlin-Alexanderplatz' als Film," *Frankfurter Zeitung* (October 13, 1931); included in appendix of Kracauer, *Von Caligari zu Hitler*, 508–10. For a contemporary assessment of the film's de-historicization (Bourdieu) see, for example, Claire Kaiser, "Berlin Alexanderplatz von Alfred Döblin zu Piel Jutzi," in *Die streitbare Klio: zur Repräsentation von Macht und Geschichte in der Literatur*, ed. Elizabeth Guilhamon (Bern: Lang, 2010), 140–50.

178 The films mentioned above are all listed on https://www.filmportal.de/thema/projekt-die-wichtigsten-deutschen-filme. Fifty-six percent of those chosen as 'historically most relevant German films' of the years 1925–32 are in fact adaptations of German literature.

179 See, for example, Max Brinkmann, "Der Räuber-Hauptmann von Cöpenick—oder: Der geschundene Bürgermeister," *Die Lustigen Blätter* (original flyer), October 1906, DK archive.

180 Asper's introduction to Zuckmayer's *Der Hauptmann von Köpenick* script can be accessed at https://www.helmut-g-asper.de/images/Einleitung_Hauptmann.pdf. The following account regarding Zuckmayer, Kortner, and Oswald is predominantly based on Asper's research.

181 Instead, Zuckmayer offered Kortner a temporary share of the royalties from all theater performances of the play. Their quarrel continued for years. Cf. Asper's research based on documents held in the Deutsche Literatur Archiv, Marbach am Neckar, and published correspondence: *Carl Zuckmayer Albrecht Joseph: Briefwechsel 1922–1972*, ed. Gunther Nickel (Göttingen: Wallstein, 2007), 489f.; cf. also Klaus Völker, *Fritz Kortner—Schauspieler und Regisseur* (Berlin: Hentrich, 1987), 155–9.

182 Max Reinhardt stepped back from directing in order to reduce the potential politization of the play, choosing non-Jewish Hilpert, who was a Berliner and not Austrian as Reinhardt. Asper quotes Gustl Mayer's letter to Zuckmayer. Asper, "Einleitung," 6.

183 The playwright initially considered Oswald's suggestions 'stupid' and 'primitive.' I'm here still referring to Asper's excellent introduction; cf. letter to Joseph, August 15, 1931. The previous 'quote' (my translation) refers to the same letter quoted by Asper.

184 Helmut G. Asper, "'Für Ihre files will ich Ihnen ein paar Facts geben.' Richard Oswald an Siegfried Kracauer über seine Filmarbeit in der Weimarer Republik und im amerikanischen Exil," *Filmblatt* 14 (2000): 22–7.
185 For Oswald, as Wedel emphasizes, the popularity of a play provided necessary assurance regarding potential adaptation projets' commercial viability. Cf. Wedel, *Filmgeschichte als Krisengeschichte*, 154.
186 Asper, "Einleitung," 18.
187 See Hans Taussig, "Köpenick!," *Reichsfilmblatt* (December 5, 1931).
188 "Ich verfilme Bühnenwerke," *Film-Kurier* 260 (November 5, 1931), quoted in Wedel, *Filmgeschichte als Krisengeschichte*, 156.
189 Wedel, *Filmgeschichte als Krisengeschichte*, 156.
190 Ibid., 157f., 160–1. For a detailed comparative analysis of Zuckmayer's play and Oswald's film, see Klaus Kanzog, "Aktualisiertung—Realisierung. Carl Zuckmayers *Der Hauptmann von Köpenick* in den Verfilmungen von Richard Oswald (1931) und Helmut Käutner (1956)," *Carl Zuckmayer und die Medien*, ed. Gunter Nickel (St. Ingbert: Röhrig, 2001), 249–308.
191 Wedel, *Filmgeschichte als Krisengeschichte*, 159.
192 Kanzog, "Aktualisiertung—Realisierung," 268–73.
193 Oswald, "Der Zwang zur Natürlichkeit," *Die Lichtbild-Bühne* 262 (November 2, 1931); quoted in Wedel, *Filmgeschichte als Krisengeschichte*, 158.
194 Most reviews were published the day after the premiere (December 23, 1931). Wedel provides a very useful account of the echo in the press in Wedel, *Filmgeschichte als Krisengeschichte*, 156–65.
195 For example Heinz Lisser, "Der Hauptmann von Köpenick und der Militarismus," *Der Vorstoß* 2.2 (January 10, 1932): 57. Michael Wedel provides further summaries of the criticism across the political spectrum in *Filmgeschichte als Krisengeschichte*, 162f.
196 Leitch, *The History of American Literature on Film*, 113.
197 Marc Silberman, trans./ed., *Bertolt Brecht on Film & Radio* (New York: Methuen, 2000). Despite the relevance of this film, I kept my summary brief due to Silberman's work already available in English.
198 Bertolt Brecht, *Werke in 5 Bänden*, vol. 5: *Schriften* (Berlin: Aufbau, ²1975), 59–60, 70, 72. Cf. Brecht's "Über Stoffe und Form" (1929), 58–60; "Notizen über die dialektische Dramatik" (1931), 61–75.
199 Brecht, *Schriften*, 8; cf. Brecht's "Über die deutsche Literatur" (1920). Ibid., 8–10.
200 Stig Bjorkman, "'It was like a nursery—but 20 times worse'. Lars von Trier on the highs and lows of making *Dogville*," *The Guardian* (January 12, 2004); https://www.theguardian.com/film/2004/jan/12/1.
201 This groundbreaking film is based on a story by Curt Siodmak, a screenplay by Billy Wilder, and exquisite matter-of-fact camera work by Fred Zinnemann and Eugen Schüfftan, who made film history when he invented the "Schüfftan-process" for Lang's *Metropolis* (1927).
202 Erika Wottrich, ed., *M wie Nebenzahl. Nero—Filmproduktion zwischen Europa und Hollywood* (Munich: text+kritik, 2002).
203 Silberman, *Bertolt Brecht on Film & Radio*, 131.
204 Ibid.

205 Leitch, *The History of American Literature on Film*, 112; cf. also Leitch's "Collaborating with the Dead: Adapters as Secret Agents," in *Adaptation Considered as a Collaborative Art*, ed. Bernadette Cronin, Rachel MagShamhráin, and Nikolai Preuschoff (Cham, CH: Palgrave, 2020), 19–38.
206 Brecht, "On the Discussion about Sound Film," in Silberman, *Bertolt Brecht on Film & Radio*, 144f., here p. 144.
207 Ibid., 145.
208 Brecht, "Meddling with the Poetic Substance," in Silberman, *Bertolt Brecht on Film & Radio*, 145f., here p. 145.
209 Cf. Thomas Elsaesser, "Transparent Duplicities: *The Threepenny Opera* (1931)," in *The Films of G. W. Pabst*, ed. E. Rentschler, 103–15, here p. 105.
210 Corrigan, "Literature on Screen," 37.
211 Cf. Brecht in Silberman, *Bertolt Brecht on Film & Radio*, 152; in his "The Threepenny Lawsuit" (147–99), Brecht quotes from newspapers such as *Magdeburgische Zeitung, Deutsche Allgemeine Zeitung* and *B.Z. am Mittag*.
212 Brecht in Silberman, *Bertolt Brecht on Film & Radio*, 168, 162, 169.
213 This opening of Brecht's polemic is often quoted, cf. "The Film, the Novel, and Epic Theatre," in *Brecht on Theatre* (New York: Hill & Wang, 1964), 47; quoted in Corrigan, "Literature on Screen," 43. In *Film and Literature* (p. 3), Corrigan also refers to Brecht/Nero's trial asking how it might have focused the "economic and legal distinctions between film and literature in the early 1930s".
214 Elsaesser, "Transparent Duplicities: *The Threepenny Opera* (1931)," 104.
215 "Pabst's *Dreigroschenoper* (1931), far in advance of anything achieved before or since, has had no perceptible influence in America. Given a limited showing here [GB], it gained tremendous enthusiasm from a small group of specialists." Winter, "The Function of Music in Sound Film," 159.
216 Ibid.
217 Goebbels, *Tagebücher (1924–1945)*, 1326; https://archive.org/details/JosephGoebbelsTagebucher.
218 UNESCO's "Creative City of Film"-award for Potsdam is largely due to the legacy of *The Blue Angel* and the Tonkreuz building at Babelsberg studios, where the movie was filmed.
219 Kreimeier, *The Ufa Story*, 179.
220 For more details see Kreimeier, *The Ufa Story*, 180f.
221 Elsaesser, "Transparent Duplicities," 110f. Elsaesser here refers to Michel Henry's *Le cinéma expressioniste allemand* (Fribourg: du Signe, 1971).

5

The Other German Cinema: Exile and the Second World War (1933–45)

> *We are exiles, displaced persons.*
> *And not a home, an exile shall be the country that took us in.*
> BERTOLT BRECHT[1]

Poverty, political extremism, and economic crises had destabilized Weimar society. And yet, stunning creativity emanated from this fundamentally unstable nation well into the early 1930s, despite the lasting fallout of the First World War, casino capitalism particularly in the United States and Western Europe, and the existential burden of the economic collapse in 1929. The latter was carried not by the military or political elite, but predominantly by the lower and middle classes, who saw their jobs, and life savings, disappear. Resentment and a profound craving for reassurance among the electorate prepared a most fertile ground for change and a subsequent empowerment of a confidently raging leader, who promised the German people vengeance for past humiliations and the strength to fight all enemies within and abroad. The sharp rise in support for Hitler and his National Socialist movement following the global economic crisis was a gamble for respect and security by an angry and disappointed electorate that had enough of political and economic instability and risk. As their movement grew, attacks on theater and film performances by Jewish and/or anti-fascist filmmakers, writers, actors, etc. increased dramatically. Inflammatory articles and smear-campaigns in antisemitic Nazi papers like *Der Stürmer*, the 'German weekly fighting for truth' as its subtitle proclaimed, further sidelined Jewish and anti-fascist talent. In 1932, German philosopher Ernst Bloch considered the surge in horror films screened in Berlin's cinemas—from early talkie *Alraune* (1930) discussed in the previous chapter, to *Frankenstein* (US, James Whale, 1931)—not 'romanticism, but prognosis' as their dystopic message exemplified a 'new fear, new insecurity'[2] among those now labeled a threatening Other by right-wing nationalists and antisemites. Vicki Baum left for Hollywood, and G.W. Pabst moved to Paris. On the eve of his departure, Pabst told the Berlin correspondent for the Observer "it will be easier to make films there with a definite ethical tendency than it is in Berlin."[3]

When Hitler was appointed Reich Chancellor on January 30, 1933, the empowerment of far-right extremists swiftly ended democracy in Germany and resulted in an immediate existential threat for many writers and filmmakers, whether they were Jewish or simply opposed to National Socialism. The Nazi leadership had been keeping lists of prominent members of the opposition, and arrests commenced that cold January night. Writers and filmmakers in Germany who had offended the Nazi leadership, contested its cause, or were friends with outspoken anti-fascist writers like Heinrich Mann, Ernst Toller, Bert Brecht, Kurt Tucholsky, Carl von Ossietzky, or Erich Mühsam to name but a few, were suddenly threatened with imprisonment or worse. The Nazis considered them 'cultural bolshevists' and a menace to their bizarre vision of pure Aryan culture. Brecht and Helene Weigel fled with their children to Czechoslovakia, finally ending up in California after an odyssey that brought them to Denmark, Finland, and the Soviet Union. Kurt Weill escaped to Paris, then to the United States. Those abroad when the Nazis came to power, like Toller and Feuchtwanger, could no longer return home. Ossietzky and Mühsam were among the many arrested and later died due to the injuries inflicted on them while imprisoned.

The first eliminations of 'undesired elements' in the German film industry happened instantly, but its focus was on those in political opposition. Soon antisemitic legislation followed. But even without legal grounds, the board of UFA decided already on March 29, 1933, that 'Jewish employees' would be terminated. Shortly after, 'a boycott of all German Jewish filmmakers was [...] instituted on April 1, 1933,' as Horak notes.[4] The aim was not only to remove Jews from the film industry, but to deprive them of their livelihood in Germany. For Germans who were lucky enough to find a new home in Hollywood, the industry provided a chance for survival. It also equipped this talent from abroad, at least theoretically, with hitherto unseen opportunities for transnational communication of an 'other Germany' now in exile, even though success would elude most of them.

Exodus

The exodus of creative individuals who had sustained Germany's film industry included directors such as Fritz Lang, Robert Siodmak, Max Ophüls, Paul Czinner, Friedrich Zelnik, Kurt (Curtis) Bernhardt, Karl Grune, Alfred Zeisler, producers Erich Pommer, Eugen Tuscherer, Alexander Korda, Max Schach, screenwriters Billy Wilder, Willy Haas, Carl Mayer, Irmgard von Cube, Robert Liebmann, Max Kolpe, Hans Wilhelm, Hans Kafka, Willy Haas, editors like Adolf Lantz, camera innovators such as Eugen Schüfftan, actors Kurt Gerron, Peter Lorre, Lilli Palmer, Fritz Kortner, Elisabeth Bergner, and many more.[5]

The ensemble of the *Threepenny Opera* film reflects the range of individual trajectories in 1933. Carola Neher, an avid anti-fascist, fled to Prague and later to the Soviet Union where she fell victim to one of Stalin's cleansing campaigns. Lotte Lenya emigrated with her ex-husband Kurt Weill to the United States in 1935. Reinhold Schünzel, being half-Jewish, was only able to work in Hitler's Reich with a special permit. He left for Hollywood in 1937, where he found work sporadically playing Nazis, such as in Fritz Lang's *Hangmen Also Die!* (1943). Valeska Gert fled to the United States via France and England, opening the 'Beggar Bar' in New York in 1941, where, for example, Tennessee Williams read his poetry. Ernst Busch and his wife Eva, a well-known singer, fled to the Netherlands at first, but settled in the Soviet Union, where he worked for Radio Moscow and in the Soviet film industry, before joining the fight against Franco in Spain with anti-fascist songs. Arrested by French police and handed over to the Gestapo in 1943, he survived imprisonment badly injured, and later worked with Brecht and Weigel at the Berliner Ensemble in East Berlin. Eva Busch, who was arrested in Paris after the German invasion of France in 1940, survived four years in Ravensbrück concentration camp, where Milena Jesenská, the Czech writer and resistance fighter remembered for her relationship with Kafka, died in 1944 and approximately 50,000 other women were murdered.

Among those who collaborated with Hitler's murderous regime was Pabst's 'Mack the Knife' Rudolf Forster, who returned to Austria after a stint on Broadway in the 1930s. Fritz Rasp and Hermann Thimig also continued their careers as actors in the German Reich. In 1944, Goebbels added Thimig to the Nazi's "Gottbegnadeten-Liste" or 'God-gifted list' of artists, recognized for their essential contributions to Nazi culture. Others on that list included Heinrich George, Gustaf Gründgens, and Werner Krauss. Harald Paulsen, the actor who had played Mack the Knife in the original stage production, in 1933 quickly reinvented himself as Nazi-supporter. His Jewish colleague Kurt Gerron, who could no longer work in Nazi-Germany, was arrested in

1943 during the German occupation of the Netherlands and, with his family, deported to Theresienstadt (Terezín) concentration camp, where he was forced by the SS to direct the pseudo-documentary entitled *Theresienstadt* (1945).

For 6 million Jews, the Nazi regime was a death sentence—among those murdered in Nazi death camps were actors Gerron, Alice Dorell, Fritz Grünbaum, Thea Sandten, Paul Morgan, and Dora Gerson, director and film architect Rudolf Bamberger, scriptwriter Curt Alexander, composer Willy Rosen, *Cyankali*'s Hans Tintner, director of Sternheim's *Underpants* adaptation, *Die Hose* (1927), Hans Behrendt, author of the *Jettchen Gebert* story Georg Hermann, and many more.[6] The 'lucky' ones, who found refuge elsewhere, still suffered the many challenges of exile, and some of them—such as authors Stefan Zweig, Ernst Toller, and Ludwig Fulda—chose to end their lives. Even very successful exiles, such as film composer Friedrich Hollaender, now Frederick Hollander, who worked with Ernst Lubitsch on *Angel* (1937) and *Bluebeard's Eighth Wife* (1938) in Hollywood, considered himself among *Those Torn from Earth*, as he entitled his autobiographical account of exile in 1941.[7]

As Günter Peter Straschek points out in his five-hour television series *Filmemigration aus Nazideutschland* [Film-emigration from Nazi Germany] (FRG television, WDR/SFB, 1975), about 2,000 filmmakers on Nazi blacklists had to flee. Many went to neighboring countries such as Austria (until 1938) and, especially, France (until 1939/40) at first. Eventually, up to 800 of them found (if often temporary) employment in Hollywood.[8] Exile was an arduous and unstable journey through countries such as Czecholslovakia, the Netherlands, Switzerland, France, Britain, Spain, until a more or less temporary home could be established in the United States, Cuba, Mexico, Brazil, Turkey, the Soviet Union, China (Jakob and Luise Fleck), Thailand (Arthur Gottlein), Palestine, or, in the case of Willy Haas, even India.[9] From 1933 onwards, adaptations of German-language literature produced outside Germany starring Jewish actors or anti-fascist intellectuals were banned in Hitler's Reich. Moreover, adaptations of literary texts by Jewish and/or blacklisted writers were no longer an option in Nazi Germany, and films that had been in production under the direction of German Jews and/or a predominantly Jewish cast usually no longer passed censorship.

After inciting students to purge libraries and burn books by Jewish or otherwise 'undesired' writers[10] such as Brecht, Kafka, the Mann brothers, Kästner, Döblin, Remarque, Schnitzler, Werfel, and Zuckmayer in May 1933, Nazi authorities began revoking German citizenships from their critics, thus depriving them of their human (including their property) rights and rendering them stateless. The names publicized in the *Deutscher Reichsanzeiger* from August 1933 included well-known writers like Lion Feuchtwanger, Heinrich Mann, Alfred Kerr, Kurt Tucholsky, Ernst Toller, Johannes R. Becher, Rudolf Leonhard, Theodor Plievier, Leonhard Frank, Klaus Mann, Arnold Zweig, and Oscar Maria Graf.[11] Interestingly, very few members of the film industry appeared on those expatriation lists—only Carola Neher, Erwin Piscator, and Gustav von Wangenheim—which might indicate that Goebbels and Hitler considered the film industry well under control and its remaining talent more pliable. Indeed, the majority of non-Jewish filmmakers opted to stay in Nazi Germany, either choosing to keep their heads down expecting an end of Nazi rule before long, or—like Veit Harlan, Wolfgang Liebeneiner, and Leni Riefenstahl—rather smelling their chance of success under the new leadership.

Nero's last film in Germany was the famous adaptation of Norbert Jacques' novel *Dr. Mabuses letztes Spiel* [lit. Dr. Mabuse's Last Play, adapted as *Das Testament des Dr. Mabuse*] directed by Lang and based on a script he had written with his wife Thea von Harbou. Produced by Seymour Nebenzahl, filming was completed in January 1933. On March 29, 1933, the day after Goebbels' speech calling for the removal of Jews from the film industry, the censorship board banned the film about evil madman manipulator Dr. Mabuse (Rudolf Klein-Rogge). The story of how he pulls the strings even from inside an insane asylum, and manages to control and destabilize at will, perhaps seemed too close to home. The film was given the green light for export, however, as the German government did not want to forego valuable foreign currency from international distribution, as was to be expected considering the success of previous *Dr. Mabuse*-films and the international fame of Fritz Lang.[12] But producer Nebenzahl was having none of that. He took the negative of the film and, helped by his car's Dutch license plate, managed to cross the border into the Netherlands. From there he drove on to Paris, where he reunited with his family, including his parents. Since Nero-Film had an office in the French capital, he was able to continue his business and produce nine more films between 1933 and 1939. *The Testament of Dr. Mabuse* premiered in a post-synchronized French version at the new Cinéma Marignan in Paris on April 21, 1933. According to Brigitte Berg and Margrit Frölich, Nebenzahl was sued subsequently by the Nazi government for his illegal removal of the film from German soil. Nero-Film in Germany went bankrupt.[13] "Apart from films financed abroad, [Horak notes] there were no films produced in the summer of 1933 involving Jewish filmmakers."[14]

In the meantime, Richard Oswald had completed his film *Ganovenehre* [Honor amongst Thieves], based on Charles Rudolph's popular play. The film had a short run from February 3, 1933, in two cinemas in Berlin, but was banned by the National Censorship Board after protests by some local Nazi authorities claiming the adaptation to be a danger to public order.[15] Oswald's subsequent *Ein Lied geht um die Welt* [A Song Goes around the World], starring the internationally famous (and Jewish) lyric tenor Joseph Schmidt, premiered at Ufa-Palast am Zoo in May 1933. Despite the musical film's popularity with cinemagoers, hateful attacks on the star of the picture, ridiculed due to his diminutive stature, were constant in the Nazi press. The film was banned in 1937, while Joseph Schmidt toured the United States. Unfortunately, Schmidt decided to return to Europe for family reasons, and died in 1942 at the age of thirty-eight in a Swiss refugee camp. Oswald left Germany for Vienna and Prague, where he directed *Abenteuer am Lido* [Adventure at the Lido] (1933), subsequently moving to the Netherlands for work, where he co-directed *Bleeke Bet* in 1934 with Aaf Bouber starring as Bleeke. After engagements in Britain and France, Oswald and his family were able to emigrate to the United States, hoping for a new life in Hollywood, in 1938. Fritz Lang directed the Molnár-adaptation *Liliom* (1934) in Paris, produced by Erich Pommer for Fox Europe, leaving for Hollywood soon after. Nebenzahl's cousin Robert Siodmak directed four Nebenzahl productions in Paris, but in order to cater to audiences in France turned to popular French literature, such as Edouard Bourdet's *Le sexe faible* [The Weaker Sex] (1933).

Other exiles like camera-innovator Eugen Schüfftan also found much-needed employment at Nebenzahl productions. Robert's brother Curt Siodmak co-wrote the script to *La crise est finie* [The Crisis Is Over], a 1934 musical comedy film starring Albert Préjean and Danielle Darrieux. Schüfftan was once again responsible for cinematography, the music was written by fellow exile Franz Wachsmann. The latter left for Hollywood in 1935 and made his name with the musical score for Hitchcock's *Rebecca* (1940). In 1951, Gene Kelly would present Waxman with the Academy Award for Best Scoring of a Dramatic or Comedy Picture for Billy Wilder's *Sunset Boulevard* (1950). Wilder had also fled to Paris in 1933, where he co-wrote and directed *Mauvaise Graine* [The Bad Seed], before moving to Hollywood in 1934. Here he began his career with a remake of his script for *Was Frauen träumen* [What Women Dream] (DE, Géza von Bolváry, 1933), which was produced by Universal Pictures as *One Exciting Adventure* (US, Ernst L. Frank, 1934). He became one of the most prominent scriptwriters and directors of Hollywood's Golden Age.

One of the last adaptations based on contemporary German literature prior to the exodus had been Kurt (Curt) Siodmak's novel *F.P.1 antwortet nicht* [Floating Platform 1 Does Not Answer] (1931). The novel was filmed in German, French, and English in 1932/3. Directed by Karl Hartl, the German-language version featured Hans Albers, Sybille Schmitz, Paul Hartmann, and Peter Lorre. It was both Lorre and Siodmak's last film project in Germany.[16] After working in England and France, Siodmak left for the United States in 1937. His screenplay for *The Wolf Man* (Universal, George Waggner, 1941; starring Lon Chaney Jr.) made his career in Hollywood. A number of horror movie scripts followed, such as *Frankenstein Meets the Wolf Man* (Roy William Neill, 1943; music by fellow exile Hans J. Salter) with Bela Lugosi as Frankenstein's monster, *House of Frankenstein* (Erle C. Kenton, 1944; written by Curt Siodmak, music by exiles Hans J. Salter and Paul Dessau), *House of Dracula* (Erle Kenton, 1945), and *Abbott and Costello Meet Frankenstein* (Charles Barton, 1948).[17]

Being invited to work in Hollywood was lifesaving, even before German troops invaded France in 1940. Quotas on foreign staff allowed only 10 percent of non-French employees per film and a maximum of 50 percent per department, which made finding continuous work in the French film industry a great challenge, not just for Hitler's exiles. But even in Hollywood, success eluded some of the most gifted filmmakers of the time. G.W. Pabst returned to France in 1936 after he had a disappointing run with *A Modern Hero* (1934) in the United States. In September 1939 while visiting family in Vienna, the German invasion of Poland and the beginning of another world war made it nearly impossible to leave the German Reich (which had annexed Austria in 1938). Pabst ended up working for Bavaria Film in Geiselgasteig near Munich, directing historical films or comedies with subtle ideological subtexts in line with Goebbels' propaganda system.

Adaptations in Austria and Switzerland

During the twelve years of Nazi dictatorship, the cinema screen was once again a contested space, especially when it came to adaptations. While Hitler, Goebbels, and their ideologically aligned film industry were busy associating their leadership with symbols of popular culture and the German-language literary canon alike as outlined in Chapter 6, only a few exiles were in a position to claim German-language literature for a cinema opposed to Hitler's Reich. Austria had remained a relatively safe place for Jewish writers until the 'Anschluss' of 1938, despite accelerating support for the Nazi movement and a sharp increase in antisemitic attacks. The Austrian film industry, however, depended on Germany as a market and hence largely abided by the rules of the Hitler regime. Fittingly, a fifth adaption of Johann Nestroy's *Der böse Geist Lumpazivagabundus* [The Evil Spirit L.] was produced by the Austrian Styria-Film in 1937, starring an elite of German/Austrian actors such as Heinz Rühmann, Paul Hörbiger, Hans Holt, and Hilde Krahl.[18] The film traces the three main characters' varying successes in withstanding the seductive and destructive power of evil spirit Lumpazivagabundus, but carefully avoids any clear reference to the rise of Nazism or the fate of exile. Nonetheless, censors required a number of cuts prior to screenings in Hitler's Reich. Both in Austria and in Germany, with its star-studded cast, the 'singing and talking' comedy had universal appeal and was praised for its entertainment value. Any mention of a possible political subtext was cautiously avoided.

Switzerland, the other at least partly German-speaking country, was only beginning to establish its film industry in the 1930s and was no option for filmmakers fleeing from Germany and Austria. Terra-Film in Berlin was under Swiss ownership, but the company's owner Eugen Scotoni and his son Ralph supported the fascist outlook of Germany's Nazi leadership and considered film an important medium in the 'spiritual defense' of Switzerland against left-wing, liberal intellectualism.[19] *Füsilier Wipf* [Fusilier Wipf] (1938) is an adaptation of Swiss writer Robert Faesi's novel (1917) that patriotically reflects on the definition of home and the need to protect one's geographical but also intellectual and ideological boundaries. The only other adaptation of German-language literature in Switzerland at the time was *Die missbrauchten Liebesbriefe* [The Misused Love Letters] (Leopold Lindtberg, 1940) by Gottfried Keller, one of Switzerland's most revered writers.[20]

The Literary Canon in French Exile

As outlined above, neither Austria nor Switzerland was a suitable country of exile for Jewish and anti-Nazi filmmakers. The vast majority of them moved to Paris first—such as producers Nebenzahl, Arnold Pressburger, Gregor Rabinowitsch, Eugen Tucherer, Max Glass—often building on existing relationships. Sound film had necessitated MLV-films and producers had either contacts in the industry due to French-language productions of their films or, in some cases, already a subsidiary company in Paris. They created vital employment and internationalization opportunities for exiles, and by December 1933, the *Pariser Tageblatt* noted ironically that 'thanks to Dr. Goebbels, the heavyweights of German filmmaking are now producing in Paris; [...] the truly representative German film will from now on be made in France.'[21] Unfortunately for all those exiles with expertise in filmmaking, the French film industry was struggling in the aftermath of the global economic crisis and, while guests were welcome, competition was not.[22]

Max Ophüls stands out in this context. He had directed an adaptation of Schnitzler's play *Liebelei* (Flirtation, 1895) in a high-profile production that starred Paul Hörbiger, Magda Schneider, Gustaf Gründgens, Olga Tschechowa, and Wolfgang Liebeneiner. The movie was released in Vienna on February 24, 1933. Ophüls left with his family for France shortly after, as his last German film *Lachende Erben* [Laughing Heirs], an Ufa-comedy based on a novella by forgotten writer Trude Herka, premiered in Berlin. In France, Ophüls, now Ophuls, released *Une histoire d'amour* [A Love Story], the French-language version of *Liebelei* shot at Joinville Studios in Paris, starring Abel Tarride and Simone Héliard, but also Magda Schneider, Gründgens, and Liebeneiner. Ophuls' Schnitzler-adaptation was immensely successful in France, a great gift to the director, who needed to establish himself in exile. But, due to the above-mentioned protests regarding the employment of German Jews in the French film industry, and an attractive invitation by newspaper mogul and film producer Emilio Rizzoli, Ophuls left France for Italy together with his scriptwriter Curt Alexander. Ophuls directed *La Signora di tutti* [Everybody's Woman] in 1934. Alexander[23] co-wrote the script based on a serialized novel by Salvator Gotta, but neither of the Jewish exiles was credited for the successful adaptation in fascist Italy.[24] In 1938, after directing in the Netherlands and back in France,[25] Ophuls returned to perhaps the ultimate representative of German literary culture, when he adapted *Die Leiden des jungen Werther* (The Sorrows of Young Werther, 1774) by Johann Wolfgang von Goethe.

Helmut Asper calls *Le Roman de Werther* [The Novel of Werther] (FR, 1938) a film *à clef* of exile as it showcases Germany's film culture in France. Produced by Nebenzahl and Nero-Film (Paris), *Le Roman de Werther* features Schüfftan at the camera, Paul Dessau as composer of the score with music by Bach, Mozart, Schubert, and Beethoven. As he did not have a work permit in France, Dessau, however, could not be mentioned in the credits.[26] But the film does more than reflect employment practices within the exile community. Ophuls and his collaborators on the one hand try to reclaim the culture of their pasts in Germany and Austria for that 'other' Germany and Austria in exile—an imagined community where humanist traditions and values are upheld. On the other hand, it is an acknowledgment of these values and traditions in France, which tie those grateful exiles to their host.[27] How important that link between the two countries and humanist outlooks were during the making of the film is exemplified by an added scene not contained in Goethe's epistolary novel, that focuses on the bond of Werther and Albert as an intellectual proximity, based on their shared belief of the fundamental value of freedom for any enlightened individual or community. A banned copy of the revolutionary *Du Contrat Social* by Jean-Jacques Rousseau, which they both secretly carry, symbolizes their connection, their idealism, and hope for a better future. Rousseau also had shared the fate of exile, prior to the French revolution (1789), which *The Social Contract* (1762) helped to inspire. In *Werther*, however, the two men's love for Lotte jeopardizes their friendship. As Frölich notes, the film received a positive echo in the press, but commercially the film was a disaster, associating its failure at the box office with French cinemagoers' lack of familiarity with Goethe's text, rather than Jules Massenet's opera. Five years into Hitler's reign, Ophuls' choice of canonical German literature for a non-German audience was a risk. While the project was deeply meaningful to the German exile community in Paris, the film completely lacked universal appeal, which Pommer had considered so essential. As a result, Nero-Film went bankrupt.[28]

From Historical Novel to Exile Literature on British Screens

In England, it was Lothar Mendes who turned to contemporary German literature in an effort to use cinema to combat the rising tide of Nazism and fascism in Europe[29] while also supporting an exiled writer by adapting his work.[30] In order to circumvent British censorship usually applied to pictures with a political subtext, Mendes chose Lion Feuchtwanger's novel *Jud Süß* [Jew Süss] as a source text and folded its political message into a costume drama. Feuchtwanger tells the story of historical figure Joseph Ben Issachar Süßkind Oppenheimer (1698–1738),[31] a successful businessman who became financial advisor and, eventually, Privy Councillor of Finance for Duke Karl Alexander of Württemberg in Stuttgart.[32] After the Duke's death in 1737, Joseph Süß Oppenheimer was arrested and accused of an array of crimes, chiefly of "Präpotenz" (i.e., the 'Court Jew's' supposedly preposterous assumption of being in charge of Württemberg). "Jud Süss," as he is derogatively called in most legal documents relating to the case, was hanged in Stuttgart on February 4, 1738, where his body remained gibbeted for six years.

Joseph Süß Oppenheimer became the main character in a number of German-language literary texts[33] including Wilhelm Hauff's 'naïvely antisemitic' novella of 1827.[34] Feuchtwanger used the historical figure in his 1925 novel (and previous play), but it was not his biography that really interested him.[35] It is a common story, Feuchtwanger said, about 'a man who is successful'[36] and, in this case, it focuses on the Jewish financial advisor who profits soundly from his collaboration with a noble lord and who is sent to the gallows as a scapegoat when problems arise. The author's imagination was captured by a small detail: Josef Süß Oppenheimer could have saved himself by converting to Christianity, but he did not. His fall is at the same time his achievement. In Feuchtwanger's mind it was the journey from the European will to power, to the Egyptian will to immortality to, finally, the Buddhist path to liberation[37] or, simply, the understanding of the emptiness of material possessions and power; consequently, the ability to accept one's destiny as a vital, inevitable step on the path of vision.[38] In Feuchtwanger's text, the focus is also on Süß as a father, who hopes to find meaning and a path that might reunite him with his dead child.[39]

Based on a screenplay written by Dorothy Farnum and Arthur Rawlinson, and produced by Michael Balcon, Mendes' historical drama *Jew Süss* (1934) highlights the workings of antisemitism as a cancerous growth in society in an effort to send an implicit political message in this otherwise close adaptation of Feuchtwanger's text. Germany's star actor Conrad Veidt agreed to play the lead. He was married to half-Jewish Ilona Prager [Lily Preger], had seen many of his friends and colleagues harassed and driven away by escalating antisemitism due to Nazi Germany's racist ideology, and embraced this opportunity to draw attention to atrocities committed against Jews.

Veidt's last role in Germany was the part of Hermann Gessler in Heinz Paul's biopic of the Swiss national hero *Wilhelm Tell* (1933), a role he had played a decade earlier in Willy Rath's adaptation of Schiller's play (DE, Rudolf Walther-Fein and Rudolf Dworsky, 1923).[40] The English-language version of the film had facilitated his move to England, where he and his wife set up home. Despite propaganda minister Goebbels' efforts to retain the celebrity for Nazi Germany's culture industry—ranging from an offer to provide his wife with fake Aryan credentials to house arrest when he returned to Berlin for the premiere of the *Wilhelm Tell* film—Veidt refused. This and his participation in Mendes' philosemitic Feuchtwanger-adaptation made him *persona non grata* in his homeland and provided an incentive to the Nazi leadership to pursue their own *Jud Süß* adaptation in 1940.[41]

Film critic C. A. Lejeune reported on Mendes' *Jew Süss* at the time, and emphasized in *The Observer* that Gaumont-British had acquired the production rights for an adaptation of Feuchtwanger's novel due to "the present political situation in Germany." Lejeune considered the film "impressive" and praised Veidt's "elegance" but was particularly moved by the final scene: "a five minutes' impression of an eighteenth century Inquisition that none of us is ever likely to forget." But herein laid the problem for the critic who questioned the significance of a historical film not meant "to make people happy, but to make them think." While being supportive of the movie's "plea for sympathy with an oppressed people," she wondered why spend "so generously on a film about a little German municipality of two hundred years ago."[42] In the end, this kind of "cultural" endeavor is nothing more than a "Costly Experiment in Horror" as she entitled her article, which must have reflected the attitude of the majority of viewers as, commercially, the film flopped both nationally and internationally.

Veidt, who played Germans in British thrillers such as *Dark Journey* (Victor Saville, 1937) and Michael Powell's *The Spy in Black* (1939) and *Contraband* (1940), became a British citizen in 1938. After starring as Jaffar in the greatly successful Technicolored Arabian fantasy film *The Thief of Baghdad* (1940), Veidt moved once again to Hollywood. He is today mostly remembered for his depiction of Cesare, the deadly somnambulist in *The Cabinet of Dr. Caligari* (1920) and of creepy Nazi-Major Strasser in Curtiz' *Casablanca* (1942). As Fritz Kortner notes in his memoirs, jobs for Veidt, himself, and other emigrants dried up mainly because Hitler's regime had threatened to boycott all films that starred exiled Germans, and many studio executives, just like publishers, were not inclined to lose out on potential profits to be made in Nazi Germany.[43]

Another adaptation of German-language literature produced by Michael Balcon in the UK was the previously mentioned Bernhard Kellermann science-fiction novel *Der Tunnel* (1913). Adapted by scriptwriters Kurt Siodmak, Clemence Dane, and Lawrence du Garde Peach, the film was directed by Maurice Elvey and premiered in New York and London in 1935. At a time of growing political division and instability, this British adaptation—which makes use of footage filmed for the previous German- and French-language adaptations directed by Curtis Bernhardt in 1933—emphasizes the need to collaborate in the interest of peace, and makes an effort to avoid Jewish stereotyping. Here, the transnational alliance between Britain and the United States is foregrounded, and the message is clear: projects of this magnitude are costly and require sacrifice, but are surely worth the effort. Günther Krampf was the Austrian cinematographer on the film, who had been working with Gaumont British since 1932. He is rarely remembered, despite his outstanding camera work on Murnau's *Nosferatu* (1922), Galeen's *The Student of Prague* (1926), Pabst's *Pandora's Box* (1929), Oswald's *Alraune* (1930), Tintner's *Cyanide* (1930), and Brecht's/Slatan Dudow's *Kuhle Wampe* (1932), to name but a few.

Collaborations among exiles led to plays such as *Gefängnis ohne Gitter* [Prison without Bars], written by Gina Kaus, Hans Wilhelm, Egon and Otto Eis in 1937, who hoped for an adaptation of their play by the film industry as a much-needed source of income.[44] *Gefängnis ohne Gitter* was adapted as *Prison sans barreaux* for French cinema in 1938 under the direction of Léonide Moguy. It was nominated for Best Foreign Film at the Biennale Film Festival in Venice but, not surprisingly, lost to Riefenstahl's *Olympia* at a competition under Fascist sponsorship. The film was remade into an English-language version entitled *Prison without Bars* (GB, Brian Desmond Hurst, 1938) the same year, enabling further income for struggling exiles. Produced by Alexander Korda, the film takes place in a reform school for girls reminiscent of Winsloe/Sagan's *Girls in Uniform*. It was released in Britain in September 1938 and in the United States in April 1939.

Kästner's *Emil and the Detectives* was brought to British cinema in 1935 in a Richard Wainwright production directed by Milton Rosmer. The adaptation follows an English translation of Billy Wilder's script that simply replaced references to Berlin with locations in London. The musical score by Allan Gray, who had left Berlin for London when the Nazi's came to power in Germany, was also reused. Many shots by fellow German émigré Mutz (Max) Greenbaum are reminiscent of Werner Brandes' innovative cinematography and Lamprecht's direction in the original adaptation.

Greenbaum was also the cinematographer on the first, and only, adaptation based on Ernst Toller's work. His final drama *Pastor Hall* incorporated commissioned scenes by fellow exile Hermann Borchart and puts an individual's courageous resistance against the inhuman Nazi-regime center-stage.⁴⁵ The adaptation by the Boulting brothers, who co-wrote the *Pastor Hall* script with Leslie Arliss, Anna Reiner, and Haworth Bromley, had its premiere in London in May 1940, about a year after the author's tragic death in New York, and eight months into the Second World War. The appeal for (Christian) humanity rings out beyond the protagonist's death in a Nazi concentration camp: "I cannot sacrifice the truth, even for you," Pastor Hall (Wilfried Lawson) says to his daughter Christine (Nova Pilbeam), who wished for her father to be more pragmatic and live.⁴⁶ Pastor Niemöller, who inspired Toller's and Hermann Borchardt's play, was arrested in 1938 and imprisoned in Sachsenhausen and Dachau, but survived the Nazi-regime. In 1940, the Boulting brothers' adaptation received mixed reviews, even though no one questioned the timeliness of its theme.

FIGURE 5.1 *Wilfried Lawson as* Pastor Hall *(GB, Roy Boulting, 1940)*.

German Exiles, Contemporary Literature, and Agitation in Soviet Cinema

The Soviet Union, an important place of exile for communists fleeing Nazi-Germany, provided refuge to Erwin Piscator, Gustav von Wangenheim, and Herbert Rappaport, and supported the production of three adaptations of contemporary German literature, beginning with Anna Seghers' first literary publication *Der Aufstand der Fischer von St. Barbara* [Revolt of the Fishermen of Santa Barbara], which had won the prestigious Kleist-prize in 1928. Piscator was a communist and left Berlin for the Soviet Union already in 1931. He had revolutionized German theater in the 1920s, particularly with Toller's *Hoppla, wir leben!* in 1927, which used film clips and groundbreakingly innovative stage design. In the Soviet Union, he worked on several theater projects, but also adapted Anna Seghers' novella for a new 'cinema of agitation'.

Piscator considered sound film the most 'lucrative' division of the entertainment industry, which in his opinion should be both art and agitation: "Machen wir es der Agitation dienstbar!"[47] His adaptation of Seghers' *Revolt of the Fishermen* or *Восстание рыбаков* was Piscator's first feature film, produced by the Russian-German Meschrabpom-Film company (1931–4). The German-language version, however, was never completed, to the great disappointment of its director. Piscator was clearly aware of and inspired by Russia's avant-garde cinema and its innovative principles of montage, but in his film creates an affective drift cultivated by a mobile camera and cinematographic techniques much more typical of Weimar cinema, which incensed Eisenstein who publicly rejected the adaptation.[48]

The film's affective rhetoric serves to highlight the plight of fishermen, their exploitation due to industrialized fishing practices, and the unspeakable hardship of their families, according to the focus of Seghers' literary narrative. *Revolt of the Fishermen* is reminiscent of Friedrich Zelnik's 1927 adaptation of Hauptmann's *Die Weber* [The Weavers] and reveals Piscator's familiarity with the cinematic language of social critique in German film of the 1920s, often embodied by marginalized and maltreated women. Here, too, a metaphor for violence and power, the police are integral to enforcing a system of abuse. Piscator depicts a deeply immoral arm of the state, as exemplified in a sequence following another fisherman's funeral: policemen start drinking in a pub and end up gang-raping a local woman. The camera pans along those witnessing the rape—some look on in disgust, others smile—until resting on the victim's face as she is pinned down on a table, her face now seen in close-up as initial horror turns to a blank stare during the ordeal. The rape scene is intercut with the faces of other desperate women, who had just attended another funeral of one of their men. The widow of this dead fisherman finds no comfort in the word of God and rips up the priest's bible. Piscator's montage-editing highlights the theme of exploitation and rape, and forges visual links between the dehumanizing disregard for women and male workers by the authorities. In the end, inevitably, violence escalates when the police use machine guns against protesters. The consequence of continuous exposure to humiliation and cruelty is foregrounded when the camera focuses on a despairing widow who repeatedly and violently hits a soldier with a rock. Although their battle seems as madly unequal as in Zelnik's Hauptmann-adaptation, in the end, the suppressed stand united, ready to rise up. In his adaptation, Piscator moves the film's focus from the fishermen and their families' misery, so central to Seghers' novella and its pessimistic conclusion, to a defiant gesture of overdue resistance as the film draws to a close.

Intended to appeal to the masses and create a popular front against Nazi Germany, Piscator's film of agitation, however, failed to meet his and his team's expectations. The picture premiered in the Soviet Union in October 1934. A subtitled version was shown in a few non-fascist countries in Europe such as Switzerland and France, but reception at the time was mixed. Some critics praised the documentary effect and the dynamics and rhythm of the film's mass scenes, highlighting the work of Pjotr Yermolov and Michail Kirillov that was reminiscent of Karl Freund's unchained camera, while evoking a Soviet film aesthetic. But exiled author Arthur Koestler considered the film deeply deceitful and unrealistic, as it suggested a linear trajectory from mass deprivation to glorious revolution seemingly without a hitch.[49] Leo Lania in Paris, however, deemed the adaptation a vital first step toward the development of significant political mass drama, which would be most effective on the cinema screen.[50] Disappointed with the reception of his film and due to increasing political difficulties, Piscator left the Soviet Union for France in 1936, migrating to the United States in 1939, where his *Revolt of the Fishermen* and the violence it portrayed would have been in breach of the Hays Code. Fortunately, Piscator was invited by Alvin Johnson to establish an acting school associated with The New School for Social Research in New York. Among the students of Piscator's Dramatic Workshop, which

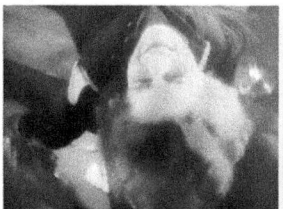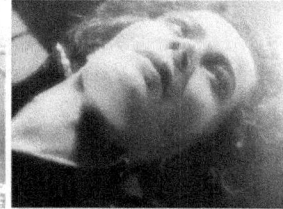

FIGURE 5.2 *The rape scene in* Revolt of the Fishermen/Восстание рыбаков *(USSR, Erwin Piscator, 1934)*.

opened the following year with a faculty that included Stella Adler and Lee Strasberg, would be Tennessee Williams, Marlon Brando, and Tony Curtis.[51]

Perhaps the most successful contribution to anti-fascist exile cinema was Herbert Rappaport and Adolf Minkin's adaptation of Friedrich Wolf's drama *Professor Mamlock* (written in French exile in 1933). Rappaport had seen the story of a respected Jewish surgeon, who is humiliated, exploited, and ultimately driven to suicide by the Nazis, in a Moscow theater and, together with scriptwriter Minkin, dramatized the narrative with agitation in mind. Профессор Мамлок (1938) depicts the brutal persecution of Professor Mamlock (played by Semyon Mezhinsky) and Jewish citizens in Nazi Germany, but also highlights the intimidation and torture endured by communists like Mamlock's son Rolf (Oleg Zhakov). Mamlock is shot dead by the SA after finally standing up and calling for resistance, but his son, who managed to escape his tormentors, evokes hope for a mass uprising and political change as the narrative concludes. The film was a box-office hit, not only in the Soviet Union, where 16 million people were reported to have seen the picture within the first eight months of its release. Initially banned in Britain, where in 1938/9 it was considered unwise to offend Hitler, US American censors in several cities also prohibited screenings of the film due to its communist leanings.[52] In New York, the picture opened two days before the November pogroms of 1938, and was praised by critics as an "engrossing, sincere" and "highly dramatic" movie. While applauding the actors and the values purported in the film, Frank Nugent criticized the "Soviet's customary insistence upon tossing a clove of propaganda into the brew," arguing that "none of its virtues completely counterbalances that propagandistic burden. Good as it is, it would have weighed more in our opinion if Comrade Stalin had removed his hand from the scales."[53]

Published in *The New York Times* on November 8, 1938, Nugent's claim that the film tells viewers "nothing new about Nazi persecution of the Jews in Germany" was to be disputed already the next day when pogroms in Germany commenced with "burnings and beatings, [...] assaults on defenseless and innocent people," as the London *Times* reported.[54] This orchestrated prelude to the intended genocide of Jews under Nazi leadership shocked the world. When images and reports of hundreds of burning synagogues all over Germany and tens of thousands of humiliated, beaten, and arrested Jews hit the press, Wolf's dramatic play seemed more than real and its adaptation a pertinent instrument to draw attention to the brutal and systematic persecution of Jews in Hitler's Reich.[55] The Nazi government did its best to curtail the impact of the film via the Reich's embassies, which issued immediate protests whenever the film was to be screened. In the interest of calming already tense diplomatic relations with Hitler's Germany in advance of another world war, the film was banned in France in 1939. Even the Soviet Union prohibited further screenings of the film together with all other anti-fascist propaganda after signing the Molotov-Ribbentrop

Pact in August 1939, a non-aggression agreement between Germany and the Soviet Union in place until June 1941, when Hitler's invasion of the Soviet Union rendered it obsolete. The Chinese government prohibited screenings at first due to Germany's diplomatic intervention, but then charged the German Embassy with "unreasonable interference in domestic affairs of China."[56] According to *The New York Times*, censors in Argentina simply rejected the protests coming from representatives of Hitler's Reich when *Professor Mamlock* was to be screened there, claiming that it was "not anti-German," thus notably if implicitly differentiating between "German" and 'Nazi-German'.[57]

By 1942, Germany and the Soviet Union were at war, and Bertolt Brecht's play *Furcht und Elend des Dritten Reiches* [Fear and Misery of the Third Reich], written and first performed in exile (Paris, 1938), was adapted for the screen by Manuel Bolshintsov and directed by Vsevolod Pudovkin and Yuri Tarich. Not so subtly entitled Убийцы выходят на дорогу [The Murderers Are Coming], the picture was banned by Soviet censors who feared its potentially unsettling effect on the public. Peter Rollberg calls the film "breathtakingly modern in its analysis of the inner workings of a totalitarian state," which in the Soviet Union at the time, however, was considered "subversive rather than patriotic."[58]

German-language Literature in Hollywood

In Hollywood, a few noteworthy adaptations of German-language literature were produced, but most had little impact. Beginning with a third adaptation[59] of Hermann Sudermann's 1908 novel *Das hohe Lied*, this *Song of Songs* (US, Rouben Mamoulian, 1933) stars Marlene Dietrich as Lily. For Paramount, however, and despite the popularity of Dietrich, this rather conventional pre-Code star vehicle was a commercial setback; perhaps Sudermann-fatigue was finally setting in among cinemagoers.

At Universal, Carl Laemmle Jr. was convinced that an adaptation of Hans Fallada's *Kleiner Mann—was nun?* [Little Man, What Now?] would surely appeal to a mass audience. The novel had been the author's breakthrough bestseller in 1932 with an English translation proving greatly successful among British and American readers. Fallada had had his share of difficulties (surviving a serious accident, typhoid, drug addition, a suicide attempt, and imprisonment) and his insightful study of mankind faced with the volatility of existence hit exactly the right notes for many readers during the depression era. The novel explores the effects of poverty and instability on a young couple, focusing particularly on Johannes Pinneberg and his precarious journey through difficult times. In 1933 and still in Germany, Fallada was asked to rewrite several passages of the novel and to remove all critical depictions of Nazi thugs. The production of a first adaptation of the novel in Nazi Germany, which Fallada did not approve, is discussed in the following chapter.

The US American adaptation of *Little Man, What Now?*, produced by Carl Laemmle Jr. and Frank Borzage, who also directed the 1934 drama film, maintains much of the German milieu and references Weimar[60] cinema, but clarifies the universal relevance of the question posed in a preface provided by Laemmle, in which he writes:

> On presenting 'LITTLE MAN, WHAT NOW?' to the screen, I strove to render a social service. The story of LITTLE MAN is the story of EVERY MAN—and the question of WHAT NOW? is the WORLD'S DAILY PROBLEM, a problem that men can only hope to overcome by a courage born of great faith in the hearts of women. Against the tide of time and chance, *all* men are little—but in the eyes of a woman in love, a man can become bigger than the whole world.

Margaret Sullavan and Douglass Montgomery star as Hans and Emma ("Lämmchen"/little lamb) Pinneberg. The screenplay was written by William Anthony McGuire, and Arthur Kay, who had migrated to the United States already in 1911, provided the music. The adaptation, which opens with an agitator protesting social inequality surrounded by avid listeners in the pouring rain, weaves moments of dissatisfaction among the less privileged into the film narrative from the outset, strangely juxtaposed with repeated scenes of Pinneberg gently drying or cleaning his pregnant lover's (and soon wife's) face with his white handkerchief.

Comic relief is provided by grumpy and demanding Kleinholz (played by DeWitt Jennings), a misogynistic patriarch, who terrorizes his family with his moods, demands, and his generally offensive behavior. The film offers an assemblage of different masculinities: mean, desperate, violent, angry, selfish, and corrupt on the one hand and—heralded as examples to us all— men like Heilbutt (played by G.P. Huntley, Jr.; confident, independent, kind, and professional with a social conscience) and Puttbreese (Christian Rub), who helps the decent young couple in dire straits whenever he can. But the focus is on Pinneberg, only twenty-three and trying to make a living in difficult times. He is confronted with the responsibility for a young wife and, soon, a child. The struggle of the kind-hearted and decent young husband is at the core of the narrative. At several instances he is close to giving up or turning to violence, but thanks to his solid moral foundation and a good, i.e., optimistic and loving woman by his side, he never loses his path and is rewarded for it in the end. The future is bright, the film seems to tell its audiences, as long as men choose the right kind of masculinity and do not lose sight of love as life's core. The young family's departure from Germany in the end is an addition that places the film in the context of the post-1933 exodus from Hitler's Reich. While the novel locates hope in the center of a loving relationship with the newborn child as its symbol of a better future, this somewhat saccharine adaptation highlights the importance of solidarity and attentiveness among friends, and migration as a potentially lifesaving opportunity.

The film was released on May 1, 1934, just before the Hays Code and PCA-approval requirement came into play. Nonetheless, the film disappointed at the box office; reviewers and audiences were not impressed. Caroline A. Lejeune, film critic for the British *Guardian* and *The Observer*, was less than enthusiastic about *Little Man, What Now?* for in her mind, the story did not migrate as well as so many Germans in the past year. This "film version of the Hans Fallada novel" depicts "post-war Germany and its troubles," she writes. This story is

> so obviously intelligent in conception, so anxious in asking its question, and earnest about supplying an answer, that one would like very much to be able to take it seriously. But I fear it is a national treatise which [...] does not travel. Even in the hands of that kindly German-American, Carl Laemmle, the film version is a trifle sickly, not a little incoherent, and occasionally absurd.[61]

The reason given by Lejeune pinpoints the viewers' expectations regarding Tinseltown talkies equated with enjoyable entertainment: This adaptation, however, "deals with an emotion and a psychology that is wholly alien to the Hollywood mood."[62]

Following this setback, three years passed until Universal produced another adaptation of German literature. This time, *Der Weg zurück* (The Road Back, 1931)—a sequel to Remarque's greatly successful *Im Westen nichts Neues*, i.e., Milestone's *All Quiet on the Western Front* (1930)—seemed to promise reliable success at the box office, particularly since war movies were still popular with audiences at the time. Nonetheless, when *The Road Back* hit cinemas in 1937, critics were lukewarm and, financially speaking, the project was a disaster. The film's focus on returning soldiers' PTSD and their difficulties of reintegration was supposed to communicate a strong pacifist and anti-fascist message. At least that was the original intention of scriptwriters Charles Kenyon and R.C. Sherriff and director James Whale. But when the production costs of Universal's Oscar Hammerstein musical film *Show Boat* (1936), also directed by James Whale, spiraled out of control, the company's creditors took over and ousted Carl Laemmle Jr. and Sr. It is rumored that the German consul in Los Angeles protested the adaptation of Remarque's novel—a blacklisted author whose works had been included in the public book burnings in Hitler's Reich in May 1933— and it is likely that new studio heads reacted. But whether they did indeed order scriptwriter Kenyon to remove all criticism of far-right extremism and instead add comedy scenes, and causing an appalled James Whale to leave Universal, could not be verified. Again, the film's reception was lukewarm. It was too German and another financial fiasco for the company.

MGM and Louis B. Meyer generously issued contract offers to exiles, but by and large avoided German themed pictures as they were rare to make a profit.[63] Among the refugees offered temporary employment, who could thus secure entry visa to the United States, were writers such as Ernst Toller, Heinrich Mann, and Alfred Döblin, and émigré filmmakers like Fritz Lang[64] and Wilhelm Thiele. While most screenplays written by German and Austrian refugees never made it to cinema screens,[65] a few adaptations based on the works by exiled authors were adapted by MGM.

Three Comrades (US, Frank Borzage, 1938) is an adaptation of *Drei Kameraden* (Three Comrades, 1936) by Remarque and partly based on a script by F. Scott Fitzgerald. The film about postwar struggles, bitterness, and friendship, as well as emigration and the search for happiness, stars Margaret Sullavan, Robert Taylor, and Franchot Tone. In contrast to the source text, the adaptation avoids political commentary or provocation of Nazi Germany. Remarque's popularity in the United States, however, paid off and the film turned a good profit for the company.

Two years passed until *The Ghost Comes Home* (1940), directed by exile William Thiele, was released in the United States. It is MGM's adaptation of an earlier, 1928 adaptation of Georg Kaiser's comedy play *Der mutige Seefahrer* (The Courageous Mariner, 1926). A Gregor Rabinowitsch adaptation, Thiele had directed the first adaptation entitled *Hurra! Ich lebe!* [Hurrah! I'm Alive!] for Ufa, and was hoping to repeat the success in Hollywood, but also wanted to claim his work and that of Georg Kaiser for the "other Germany" abroad. The Nazis considered Kaiser, once a celebrated Expressionist playwright, "degenerate", and blacklisted him. He was prohibited from publishing, his plays were banned, and his books burned. Thiele's adaptation of his play, however, was reshot in Nazi Germany in 1935, under the direction of Hans Deppe, who incorporated a stab at émigrés in its new conclusion. Without income, Kaiser struggled to leave Germany but eventually managed to flee to Switzerland in 1938. His visa application to the United States was denied because his son served in the German Wehrmacht.[66] But by buying the rights to make *The Ghost Comes Home*, MGM provided vital financial support to the exiled playwright.

In 1938, *New York Times* reporter Frank Nugent had criticized Hollywood's hesitation to tackle controversial subjects due to "its fear of jeopardizing foreign markets." When the United States joined the war against Nazi Germany and fascist Italy in 1941, topics such as Nazi brutality and their relentless persecution of Jews in Germany became part of the war effort. Fritz Lang directed four anti-Nazi films in the next few years—*Man Hunt* (Twentieth Century Fox, 1941), *Hangmen Also Die!* (United Artists, 1943), *Ministry of Fear* (Paramount, 1944), and *Cloak and Dagger* (Warner

Bros., 1946)—but none were as effective in communicating both the horror of Nazi persecution, and the human condition in a totalitarian state, as MGM's *The Seventh Cross* (Fred Zinnemann, 1944), based on Anna Seghers' novel *Das siebte Kreuz,* which she wrote in Mexican exile. As Birgit Maier-Katkin outlines, both Seghers and Zinnemann came from assimilated Jewish families, in respectively Germany and Austria, and were keen to use their art for social commentary, even though at the time, they could not have been aware on the extent and sheer monstrosity of the crimes committed under Hitler's leadership.[67]

Despite the fact that Seghers, as former member of Germany's communist party, had been prohibited from entering the United States and was under surveillance by the FBI, she had numerous American and exiled friends, like F.C. Weiskopf, who supported her work.[68] Her novel *The Seventh Cross* was published in an abridged English translation in 1942, with a staggering first print-run of 600,000. Within weeks it was selected by the Book-of-the Month Club and considered for an adaptation into a comic book.[69] American journalist and writer Helen Deutsch wrote a screenplay based on Seghers'

FIGURE 5.3 The Seventh Cross *(US, Fred Zinnemann, 1944) trailer: "The TRUE PICTURIZATION of the Vividly Exciting NOVEL ..."*

novel, which was bought by MGM. It is the story of seven concentration camp prisoners, who manage to flee. Six of them are recaptured and their broken bodies are hung on crosses prepared by their brutal guards. Only Georg Heisler's cross remains empty, and his story of survival offers the hopeful narrative trajectory of this devastating tale. Heisler makes it to the Netherlands thanks to the help of a few courageous individuals.

While Seghers weaves the escapees' stories into a multi-facetted portrayal of everyday German life under Nazi dictatorship, Deutsch's script and Zinnemann's film focus the adaptation on its lone survivor following a fairly linear and sequential trajectory of his escape. Played by Spencer Tracy, Heisler's fight for survival on the one hand and, integral to his perseverance, the 'good' Germans' selfless humanity on the other is foregrounded. As Zinnemann writes in his autobiography *A Life in the Movies* (1992), MGM's Louis B. Mayer had "collected the greatest stable of stars, superstars and starlets," and as Maier-Katkin notes, "film directors were instructed to superimpose a star's face even in a scene set at midnight in a tunnel."[70] Tracy was indeed central to the film's marketing strategy, adaptation, and financial success, generating a profit of over 1 million US dollars for the studio. A number of exiles from Nazi Germany and Austria such as Felix Bressart, Kaaren Verne, John Wengraf, and Brecht's wife Helene Weigel were employed on the set, mostly in small roles and partly uncredited, but paid a much-needed salary.[71] The film is a celebration of the human spirit, of the possibility of human kindness and selfless courage even under the most threatening circumstances. But in 1944, five years into the Second World War and a defeat of Hitler's Reich in sight, it also shed a differentiating and hopeful light on a Germany comprising more than evil Nazis.

The greatest success of German exile literature and adaptation, however, was Franz Werfel's *Das Lied von Bernadette* (1941).[72] Translated by Lewis Lewisohn, *The Song of Bernadette* was on the *New York Times* Best Seller list for over a year, and became the number one fiction title of 1942, according to *Publisher's Weekly*, remaining among the top ten fiction books in 1943. Twentieth Century Fox secured the film rights from the now California-based novelist and launched *The Song of Bernadette* (1943) under the direction of Henry King as their most expensive production of the year. The film, based on George Seaton's screenplay, follows Franz Werfel's novel, and stars Jennifer Jones as Saint Bernadette Soubirous of Lourdes or, rather, as poor and sickly peasant girl Bernadette, who is considered cognitively impaired by her teachers and—following her visions of the Virgin Mary—a fraud by authorities.

Werfel and his wife Alma Mahler-Werfel had found refuge in the French town of Lourdes during their arduous journey as refugees from Austria after the *Anschluss*. Inspired by the altruism and compassion they encountered in Lourdes, the Jewish writer vowed that, if he managed to escape Hitler's henchmen, he would tell the story of Bernadette. In the preface to his novel, Werfel writes:

> In the last days of June 1940, in flight after the collapse of France, the two of us, my wife and I, had hoped to elude our mortal enemies in time to cross the Spanish frontier to Portugal, but had to flee back to the interior of France on the very night German troops occupied the frontier town of Hendaye. The Pyrenean départements had turned into a phantasmagoria—a very camp of chaos. This strange migration of people wandered about on the roads in their thousands obstructing towns and villages: Frenchmen, Belgians, Dutchmen, Poles, Czechs, Austrians, exiled Germans; and, mingled with these, soldiers of the defeated armies. There was barely food enough to still the extreme pangs of hunger. There was no shelter to be had. Anyone who had obtained possession of an upholstered chair for his night's rest was an object of envy. In endless lines, stood the cars of the fugitives, piled high with household gear, with mattresses and beds. There was no petrol to be had. A family settled in Pau told us that Lourdes was the one place where, if luck were kind, one might find a roof. Since Lourdes was but thirty kilometres distant, we were advised to make the attempt and knock on its gates. We followed this advice and found refuge at last in the little town of Lourdes in the foothills of the Pyrenees.[73]

The adaptation follows the main narrative strands of Werfel's novel while accentuating the dichotomies presented in the literary text. As Fred Stanley observed in *The New York Times* in March 1943, it also exemplifies, together with MGM's *Quo Vadis*, "the Henryk Sienkiewicz story of early Christianity," "a new spiritual resurgence in Hollywood." This was indeed a programmatic decision by *The Song of Bernadette* producer William Perlberg and director Henry King. As "the country is going through a spiritual awakening, due to the war [...], they are certain that a picture dealing with miracles and religious faith will now be welcomed."[74]

The film's success proved them right. *The Song of Bernadette* was nominated for numerous awards, winning four Academy Awards (out of the twelve nominations)—for Best Actress in a Leading Role (Jennifer Jones), Best Art Direction (James Basevi, William S. Darling, and Thomas Little), Best Cinematography (Arthur C. Miller), and Best Music (Alfred Newman)—and winning the first three Golden Globes in 1944; Jennifer Jones and Henry King were honored as best motion picture actor and best director, and *The Song of Bernadette* won best motion picture in the drama category. The 155-minute-long movie glorifies Bernadette's simple faith, and puts her modesty, commitment, and integrity center stage. While it hints at the problem of commercialization of a miraculous occurrence and, by implication, religion, it clearly objects to those who obstruct 'true faith.' Numerous efforts by both church and state authorities to damage the trust of a swiftly growing number of believers in Bernadette fail—but at the same time reveal questionable ethics and the unprofessionalism of these institutions' representatives. Their bullying and even threats of Bernadette's removal to an asylum are juxtaposed with touching examples indicating the miraculous healing powers of the fount. Bernadette's critics are eventually swayed, and Catholicism as a religion, as well as inexplicable 'phenomena', are depicted in a positive light. While believing in something supernatural appears to address a human need, it is hope and faith that are foregrounded in this *Song of Bernadette* as human strength, be it divinely inspired or not. It is, as Werfel indicates in his preface, what helps individuals to overcome great challenges and fear. The couple's arduous journey into exile and the death[75] of their beloved daughter, to whom the novel is dedicated, provided the foundation to this text. Its context is fascism and an age filled with mockery, wrath, and indifference that had turned away from fundamental values such as 'divine mystery and human sanctity'. Twentieth Century Fox's Bernadette is a marginal, simple girl, who overcomes challenges due to her faith and never loses hope, and thus communicates values vital to the war effort.

As the Second World War was coming to an end, MGM produced *Weekend at the Waldorf* (US, Robert Z. Leonard, 1945) based on Guy Bolton's stage adaptation *Grand Hotel* derived from Baum's aforementioned novel. The screenplay was written by Samuel and Bella Spewack and situated the film in New York rather than Berlin. The lobby of the famous Waldorf-Astoria Hotel was rebuilt at MGM's studios in Hollywood, where the film was shot. This more light-hearted version of Baum's novel—starring Ginger Rogers, Lana Turner, and Walter Pidgeon—still incorporates the theme of war trauma into the film's narrative. But this time, it is injuries received during the Second World War, and Captain James Hollis (Van Johnson) is awaiting surgery to remove shrapnel precariously lodged near his heart. When the film was released in the United States on October 4, 1945, the tagline on posters (mostly showing the two couples and stating the names of the four lead actors) was: 'It's always exciting and romantic!—that weekend at the Waldorf' and reads like an ad campaign for the famous hotel. Baum's name was no longer mentioned on the marketing brochures or posters. Any reference to Germany would have potentially soiled the undertaking only a few months after the end of the war, which cost almost half a million American soldiers' lives. German literature, once a symbolic vernacular of culture and, for all those exiles working in Hollywood, of belonging and even pride, was now a heart-breaking reminder of war and genocide. German-language literature, which had been integral to successful film productions in Germany and Austria during the 1920s and 1930s, had become a liability.

Conclusion

Only a few adaptations of German-language literature were produced in exile countries between 1933 and 1945, when a large majority of notable authors and filmmakers were forced to leave their homes in Germany and soon Austria for an uncertain future abroad. Together with many thousands of Jewish and non-Jewish journalists, artists, anti-fascist political activists, as well as Germans and (following the 'Anschluss' in 1938) Austrians from all walks of life, they represented the 'other Germany' in exile. Many were saved by temporary contracts in the film industry in Paris, Amsterdam, and London, and, as the German troops invaded neighboring countries, Hollywood studios, especially Louis B. Mayer at MGM, but also Warner Bros. and Columbia. Some only made it to a safe haven after having been helped out of Vichy France by courageous individuals like Lisa Fittko and Varian Fry. But as authors like Döblin noted, there was no real interest in these German-speaking refugees' work, and temporary employment offers were charitable acts rather than investments into the creative potential of exiles.[76] A German Academy of the Arts and Letters in Exile was formed and aid organizations such as the American Guild for German Cultural Freedom provided vital support to many refugees. While some did find jobs in the film industry, many remained unemployed and dependent on the financial support provided by leading, anti-Nazi activists such Prinz Hubertus zu Löwenstein and the American Guild, and internationally successful authors like Thomas Mann, Lion Feuchtwanger, and Stefan Zweig. In 1938, the European Film Fund was set up by film agent Paul Kohner together with Lubitsch, Liesl Frank, and others, and financed by those on studios' payrolls, who donated part of their income every week.[77] German-born directors Henry Koster and Ernst Lubitsch as well as producers Eric Pommer, Wolfgang and Gottfried Reinhardt were among the most generous, but even struggling actors like Albert Bassermann or writer Gina Kaus made small donations whenever they could.

In desperate need of income, many exile authors actively sought adaptations of their works, but only rarely did they materialize, even for bestselling writers; Remarque, Seghers, and Werfel were among the lucky few. Exile director Ophuls' effort to preserve the German literary canon and ensure the survival of German culture abroad by filming Goethe's *Werther* remained an exception. Neither film studios nor audiences were interested in 'German culture' unless an exile writers' works provided useful and entertaining insights into the current challenges faced and had an established and wide-ranging readership. The impact of Fascism and National Socialism in Europe was devastating. In Nazi-Germany, the canon of German literature was celebrated in ideologically aligned adaptations as the following chapter outlines. For international cinema, German-language literature was now considered a liability.

Notes

1 From Brecht's poem "Über die Bezeichnung Exilanten," 1937.
2 Ernst Bloch, "Bezeichnender Wandel in Kinofabeln" [1932], in *Literarische Aufsätze* (Frankfurt: Suhrkamp, 1985), 75–8, here p. 77; quoted in Gerald Bär, *Das Motiv des Doppelgängers als Spaltungsphantasie in der Literatur und im Stummfilm* (Amsterdam: Rodopi, 2005), 522f.; cf. also Gerald Bär, "Perceptions of the Self as the Other: Double-Visions in Literature and Film," in Schönfeld, ed. *Processes of Transposition*, 89–117.
3 "The Future of the Kinema—Pabst on the Use of Symbolism, Strong Contrasts, Lessons from His New Film, Leaving for Paris," *The Observer* (September 18, 1932): 10.
4 Jan-Christopher Horak, "German Exile Cinema, 1933–1950," *Film History* 8 (1996): 373–89, here p. 375.
5 Until the German army invaded France in 1940, Tuscherer, Bernhardt, Kafka, Liebmann, Lantz, and many others worked in the Paris film industry. They collaborated, for example, on the French melodrama *Carrefour* (1938). See Horak, "German Exile Cinema, 1933–1950," 373–89.
6 Katinka Dittrich and Hans Würzner, eds., *Die Niederlande und das deutsche Exil 1933–1940* (Königstein: Athenäum, 1982); Jan-Christopher Horak, "German Exile Cinema, 1933–1950" and Horak, *Fluchtpunkt Hollywood. Eine Dokumentation zur Filmemigration nach 1933* (Münster: MAkS, 1986); Julia Friedrich, ed., *Günter Peter Straschek. Emigration—Film—Politics* (Cologne: Museum Ludwig, 2018).
7 Because of the Nazi's creation of a legal basis for the confiscation of property via their "Reichsfluchtsteuer" [Reich's escape tax] for those that fled, refugees were often broke upon arrival and in dire need of employment.
8 Cf. Asper's "filmexilhandbuch" at https://www.helmut-g-asper.de/index.php/2013-06-05-17-53-21/filme-und-themen/filmexilhandbuch. Horak counts only about 500 exiles among those working in Hollywood; Horak, *Fluchtpunkt Hollywood*; see also Julia Friedrich, *Günter Peter Straschek*.
9 For a useful list, see https://www.helmut-g-asper.de/index.php/2013-06-05-17-53-21/filme-und-themen/filmexilhandbuch.
10 Among them Albert Einstein, Sigmund Freud, Heinrich Heine, Karl Marx, August Bebel, Walther Rathenau, Kurt Tucholsky, Georg Kaiser, Max Brod, Franz Werfel, Theodor Plievier, Carl von Ossietzky, Else Lasker-Schüler, and Hermann Hesse, but also writers not from German-speaking countries, such as Jack London, Theodor Dreiser, Helen Keller, and Ernest Hemingway.
11 Graf had protested his lack of inclusion in the book burnings in a newspaper article entitled 'Burn Me!,' stating 'I do not want my books in the bloody hands and the rotten brains of the murderous brown mob.' Graf's article "Verbrennt mich!" was published on the cover of the Viennese Workers' newspaper the *Wiener Arbeiter-Zeitung* (May 12, 1933). A reprint can be found in Georg Bollenbeck, *Oskar Maria Graf* (Reinbek: Rowohlt, 1985), 98.
12 Margrit Frölich, "Die Nebenzahls, Nero-Film und Filmexil in Frankreich," in *Feuchtwanger und die Erinnerungskultur in Frankreich /Feuchtwanger et la culture mémorielle en France*, ed. Daniel Azuélos, Andrea Chartier-Bunzel,

and Frédéric Teinturier (London: Lang, 2020), 247–62, here p. 148. I refer to Frölich, Asper, and Berg in this paragraph.
13 Cf. Brigitte Berg, "Monsieur Nero: Seymour Nebenzahl in Paris," in *M wie Nebenzahl* (2002, 56), quoted by Frölich, "Die Nebenzahls," 251f.
14 Horak, "German Exile Cinema," 375–6.
15 Bock, "Biografie," in *Richard Oswald*, ed. H. Belach et al., 131.
16 Fred Gehler, "F.P.1 antwortet nicht," *Deutsche Spielfilme von den Anfängen bis 1933*, ed. Günther Dahlke/Günter Karl, 310.
17 Many more actors/filmmakers could have been mentioned here, such as Emeric Pressburger, who left Germany for Paris in 1933 and, in 1935, moved to Britain, where he created his renowned films in collaboration with Michael Powell including another adaptation of *The Tales of Hoffmann* (1952).
18 Nestroy's text had been adapted in 1911 (DK, Sören Nielsen; starring Oscar Stribolt as Lumpazi), in 1921 (AT, Carl Wilhelm), in 1923 (SE, Carl Barcklind).
19 Ralph Scotoni even became a member of the NSDAP. The statement on Wikipedia that "Scotoni automatically became a member of the Nazi Party (as was common for owners of large companies)" is nonsense. Pressure was applied on company owners to join the NSDAP due to their 'exemplary function' in society, and sometimes that pressure was severe, especially from the early 1940s, but membership was certainly not "automatic," and some business owners successfully kept their distance throughout.
20 The adaptation is based on Keller's novella, which is included in his canonical collection *Die Leute von Seldwyla* (The People of Seldwyla, 1865).
21 "Film-Berlin an der Seine. Streifzug durch das deutsche Filmschaffen in Frankreich," *Pariser Tageblatt* (December 15, 1933): 4; also quoted by Frölich, "Die Nebenzahls," 247. Horak counts at least forty-six exile films produced in France between 1933 and 1940; cf. Horak, "Exilfilm, 1933–1945. In der Fremde," *Geschichte des deutschen Films*, ed. Wolfgang Jacobsen, Anton Kaes, and Hans Helmut Prinzler (Stuttgart: Metzler, ²2004), 103.
22 Cf Helmut G. Asper, "Von der Milo zur B. U. P. Max Ophüls' französische Exilfilmproduktion 1937–1940," in *Hallo? Berlin? Ici Paris! Deutschfranzösische Filmbeziehungen 1918–1939*, ed. Sibylle M. Sturm and Arthur Wohlgemuth (Munich: text+kritik, 1996; accessed online).
23 Curt Alexander stayed in fascist Italy and was murdered in Auschwitz in 1944.
24 Mary Ann Doane, "The Abstraction of a Lady: La Signora di tutti," *Cinema Journal* 28.1 (1988): 65–84.
25 Ophuls' films of the time include *Divine* (FR, 1935, based on novel by Colette); *La Tendre ennemie* (FR, 1936, based on play by André-Paul Antoine); *Yoshiwara* (FR, 1937, based on novel by Maurice Dekobra).
26 Frölich, "Die Nebenzahls," 261; Helmut G. Asper, *Max Ophüls. Eine Biographie* (Berlin: Bertz+Fischer, 1998), here esp. 367–74; cf. also Asper's *Max Ophüls. Deutscher—Jude—Franzose* (Berlin: Hentrich & Hentrich, 2011). Pierre Richard-Willm stars as young Werther and Annie Vernay as his adored Charlotte.
27 Cf. Asper, *Max Ophüls*, 367–74; Frölich, "Die Nebenzahls," 260.
28 Frölich, "Die Nebenzahls," 261.

29 Cf. Anthony Clark at http://www.screenonline.org.uk/film/id/570808/index.html.
30 Feuchtwanger's income had been reduced to royalties received via his non-German publishers. He was among the few lucky ones among German-language exile writers—like Thomas Mann and Stefan Zweig—whose works were also being sold in translation.
31 See the biography by Hellmut G. Haasis, *Joseph Süss Oppenheimer, genannt Jud Süss: Finanzier, Freidenker, Justizopfer* (Rowohlt: Reinbek, 1998). Lion Feuchtwanger was familiar with Manfred Zimmermann's *Josef Süss Oppenheimer, ein Finanzmann des 18. Jahrhunderts. Ein Stück Absolutismus- und Jesuitengeschichte. Nach den Vertheidigungs-Akten und den Schriften der Zeitgenossen* (Stuttgart, 1874) when he wrote his play and novel *Jud Süß*.
32 For further information, see my article on the topic on which this part of the book is based: "Feuchtwanger, Jud Süß and the Nazis," in *Aesthetics and Politics in Modern German Culture*, ed. Brigid Haines, Steven Parker, and Colin Riordan (London: Lang, 2010), 39–52. Permission to reuse this research is gratefully acknowledged.
33 Regarding literary adaptations by Wilhelm Hauff, Paul Kornfeld, Klaus Pohl, see especially essays by Friedrich Knilli, Gabriele von Glasenapp, Itta Shedletzky, Britta Hermann, Mona Körte, and Anat Feinberg in: Alexandra Przyrembel and Jörg Schönert, eds., *'Jud Süß'—Hofjude, literarische Figur, antisemitisches Zerrbild* (Frankfurt/M.: Campus, 2006), 75–200.
34 Feuchtwanger in the afterword to his novel *Jud Süß*. Cf. Itta Shedletzky, 'Tragik verfrühter Emanzipation—Topography jüdischer Mentalität: Die Deutungen des 'Jud Süß' bei Selma Stern und Lion Feuchtwanger,' in *'Jud Süß'—Hofjude, literarische Figur, antisemitisches Zerrbild*, 137. In Hauff's novella, the dominant female figure is Lea, Josef Süss Oppenheimer's sister, who ends up drowning herself, when her love Gustav refuses to marry her, and her brother is hanged.
35 'Über *Jud Süß*,' *Freie Deutsche Bühne*, 11.1 (January 5, 1929), in: Lion Feuchtwanger, *Centum Opuscula* (Rudolstadt: Greifenverlag, 1956), 388f.
36 Feuchtwanger, 'Über die Ursachen meines Erfolgs,' typescript (2 pages), Feuchtwanger Memorial Library, Special Collections, University of Southern California, Box D8a, folder 4, p. 1.
37 Feuchtwanger calls it the "Lehre Asiens vom Nichtwollen und Nichttun"; Feuchtwanger, *Centum Opuscula*, 390. See also William Small, "In Buddha's Footsteps. Feuchtwanger's *Jud Süß*, Walther Rathenau, and the Path to the Soul," *German Studies Review* 12.3 (1989): 469–85.
38 Feuchtwanger was, however, not inspired directly by Tibetan Buddhism and the *Abhisamayalankara*, but by Alfred Döblin's Expressionist novel *Die drei Sprünge des Wang-lun* (1915).
39 Feuchtwanger, *Centum Opuscula*, 390. For further context see Frank Stern, "Aufklärende Dunkelheit: Filmische Metamorphosen vom Exil zur Diaspora," in *Feuchtwanger und Remigration*, ed. Ian Wallace (Oxford: Peter Lang, 2013), 465–74.
40 Hans Marr played the Swiss national hero Tell both in 1923 and in 1933. Veidt, Marr, Göring's future wife Emmy Sonnemann, Eugen Klöpfer, Maly Delschaft, Franziska Kinz, Carl de Vogt, and Käthe Haack appear both in

the English and in the German version of the 1933/4 Tell film. Because of insufficient language skills, Charles Cullum replaced Olaf Bach, and Dennis Aubrey Theodor Loos in the English-language version. The film was produced by Ralph Scotoni's Terra-Film AG (Berlin/Zurich).

41 See, for example, Kay Weniger's dictionary of film exiles: "Es wird im Leben dir mehr genommen als gegeben…," in *Lexikon der aus Deutschland und Österreich emigrierten Filmschaffenden 1933 bis 1945* (Hamburg: Acabus, 2011).

42 C. A. Lejeune, "*Jew Suss*. A Costly Experiment in Horror," *The Observer* (October 7, 1934): 18.

43 Kortner, *Aller Tage Abend*, 357. Famous playwright and poet Ernst Toller's *Eine Jugend in Deutschland* (A Youth in Germany, 1933), for example, was under contract with Orell Füssli in Zurich. But the Nazi government threatened to boycott all Orell Füssli books in Germany if Toller's text were to be printed, and the Swiss publisher backed down. This left Toller without publisher or income. 'As if Germany alone weren't reason enough to despair!' he wrote to his friend Luise Geissler. Cf. Ernst Toller, *Briefe 1915–1939* (Göttingen: Wallstein, 2018), 943.

44 Gina Kaus and Ladislas Fodor also collaborated on *Die Nacht vor der Scheidung* [The Night before the Divorce] which was published in Vienna by Georg Marton in 1937. Fellow exile Robert Siodmak directed *The Night before the Divorce* as a comedy film for 20th Century Fox in 1942.

45 *Pastor Hall* was produced by John Boulting and directed by Roy Boulting, who is also credited for editing the film. Toller's play was written in parts by fellow-exile Hermann Borchart. Cf. Irene Zanol, "'Da sitzt der Autor des neuen Toller-Stückes.' *Pastor Hall*—ein Plagiat?," in *"…doch nicht nur für die Zeit geschrieben": Zur Rezeption Ernst Tollers: Person und Werk im Kontext*, ed. Michael Pilz, Veronika Schuchter, and Irene Zanol (Würzburg: Königshausen & Neumann, 2018), 55–78.

46 Cf. my article on "Ernst Toller und das Kino," *text+kritik* 223 (2019): 47–57 (volume on *Ernst Toller*, ed. Hannah Arnold and Peter Langemeyer).

47 'Let's Use It for Agitation!'; Piscator, "Tonfilm Freund und Feind," *Schriften*, 70–2, here p. 72.

48 Klaus Gleber, *Theater und Öffentlichkeit. Produktions- und Rezeptionsbedingungen politischen Theaters am Beispiel Piscators 1920–1966* (Frankfurt/M.: Lang, 1979), 302f. For an enlightening theory of affective drift in the context of adaptation, see John Hodgkins, *The Drift: Affect, Adaptation, and New Perspectives on Fidelity* (New York: Bloomsbury, 2013).

49 Cf. Günther Agde, "Mit dem Blick nach Westen," in *Die rote Traumfabrik: Meschrabpom-Film und Prometheus (1921–1936)*, ed. Günter Agde and Alexander Schwarz (Berlin: Bertz+Fischer, 2012), 141–7; Jeanpaul Goergen, *Vosstanie rybakov (Aufstand der Fischer)* (Berlin: Selbstverlag, 1993).

50 Arthur Koestler, "Piscators Fischer von Sankt Barbara," *Das Neue Tage-Buch* (February 9, 1935); Leo Lania, "Piscator, Nicolai Ekk, Eisenstein, Pudowkin. Aus der sowjetischen Filmproduktion," *Pariser Tageszeitung* (June 14, 1936); Jasmin Arnold, *Die Revolution frisst ihre Kinder. Deutsches Filmexil in der UdSSR* (Marburg: Tectum, 2003); Peter Diezel, "Erwin Piscators Film *Aufstand der Fischer*," *Argonautenschiff. Jahrbuch der Anna-Seghers-Gesellschaft* 16 (2008): 68–79.

51. Peter M. Rutkoff, "Politics on Stage. Piscator and the Dramatic Workshop," in *New School: A History of the New School for Social Research*, ed. Peter M. Rutkoff and William B. Scott (New York: Macmillan, 1986).
52. Cf. Anette Insdorf, *Indelible Shadows. Film and the Holocaust* (Cambridge: Cambridge University Press, ³2010), 155.
53. Frank S. Nugent, "'Professor Mamlock,' a Russian Appraisal of Nazi Culture, Has Its Premiere at the Cameo," *The New York Times* (November 8, 1938): 26.
54. *Times* (November 11, 1938), n.p.
55. Jeremy Hicks, *First Films of the Holocaust: Soviet Cinema and the Genocide of the Jews, 1938–1946* (Pittsburgh: University of Pittsburgh Press, 2012), 18.
56. Cf. "German Role in China Hit," *The New York Times* (August 18, 1939): 5.
57. Cf. "Nazi Film Protest Is Rejected," *The New York Times* (November 10, 1941): 5: the article refers to three "not anti-German" pictures: *Professor Mamlock*, Fritz Lang's *Man Hunt* (1941), and James Whales' romantic war drama *They Dare Not Love* (1941)—as all three pictures are certainly anti-Nazi.
58. Peter Rollberg, *Historical Dictionary of Russian and Soviet Cinema* (Lanham, MA: Rowman & Littlefield, 2016), 595.
59. *The Song of Songs* (US, Joseph Kaufman, 1918) and *Lily of the Dust* (US, Dimitri Buchowetzki, 1924).
60. For example, when Pinneberg stares at the knife in his hand (which he then drops), which is reminiscent of the great psychological thrillers of the Weimar era; cf. portrayals by Emil Jannings in *Varieté* (DE, E. A. Dupont, 1925) or Peter Lorre in Fritz Lang's *M* (1931).
61. C. A. Lejeune, "The Pictures: 'One Night of Love.' Little Man Has Had a Busy Day," *The Observer* (September 30, 1934): 16.
62. Lejeune, "The Pictures," 16.
63. MGM's Sidney Franklin bought the film rights to Felix Salten's *Bambi* in 1933. On Salten see especially Beverly Driver Eddy, *Felix Salten. Man of Many Faces* (Riverside: Ariadne, 2010); for some additional facets, see Ernst Seibert and Susanne Blumesberger's edited volume *Felix Salten. Der unbekannte Bekannte* (Vienna: Praesens, 2006). Regarding *Bambi*, see Sabine Strümper-Krobb's excellent comparative study of the original novel, its translation into English, and its adaptation by Disney: Sabine Strümper-Krobb, "'I Particularly Recommend It to Sportsmen.' Bambi in America: The Rewriting of Felix Salten's *Bambi*," *Austrian Studies* 23 (2015): 123–42. Initially, *Bambi* failed at the box office and worsened the difficulties Disney corp was already experiencing. But its success after the end of the war lasted for decades. With regard to the copyright dispute between Salten's heirs/Twin Books and Disney, see Twin Books v Disney; U.S. 9th Circuit Court of Appeals, No. 95–15250v, documents can be accessed at https://web.archive.org/web/20090619060947/http://caselaw.lp.findlaw.com/scripts/getcase.pl?court=9th&navby=case&no=9515250.
64. For further information, see Palmier, *Weimar in Exile: The Antifascist Emigration in Europe and America*, especially 513–18.
65. For example, Ernst Toller; for further details on his work for MGM, see my article on "Ernst Toller's Film Projects," *German Life and Letters* 75.2 (2022): 250–65.

66 Renate Benson, *German Expressionist Drama: Ernst Toller and Georg Kaiser* (London: Macmillan, 1984), 103.
67 Birgit Maier-Katkin, "Literary and Cinematographic Reflections on the Human Condition by Anna Seghers and Fred Zinnemann," in *Processes of Transposition: German Literature and Film*, 141–56, here p. 142f. My short outline here follows Maier-Katkin's text, which offers an in-depth discussion of the source text and its adaptation. See also Birgit Maier-Katkin, "The Seventh Cross: Dignité humaine and Human Rights," *Anna Seghers. The Challenge of History*, ed. Helen Fehervary, Christiane Zehl Romero, and Amy Kepple Strawser, *German Monitor 80* (2019): 62–77.
68 Alexander Stephan, "Communazis," in *FBI Surveillance of German Emigré Writers*, trans. Jan van Heurck (New Haven: Yale University Press, 2000); Christiane Zehl Romero, "'Armer und lieber Sagetet', Anna Seghers and Franz Carl Weiskopf," in *Seghers in Perspective*, ed. Ian Wallace (Amsterdam: Rodopi, 1998).
69 See Ursula Emmerich and Erika Pick, "Beim Lesen eines Briefwechsels," in *Anna Seghers and Wieland Herzfelde*, ed. Ursula Emmerich and Erika Pick (Darmstadt: Luchterhand, 1985), 27; Alexander Stephan, "Ein Exilroman als Bestseller," *Exilforschung* 3 (1985): 239.
70 Fred Zinnemann, *An Autobiography. A Life in the Movies* (New York: Scribner, 1992), 45; quoted by Maier-Katkin, "Literary and Cinematographic Reflections," 148.
71 Bressart used to be one of the highest paid film actors of Weimar Germany; cf. Horak, *The German Cinema Book*, 43. Richard Oswald, one of the most productive filmmakers in Germany since the First World War, also felt the impact of exile. While he managed to find work in the film industries in neighboring countries, his output was small and of no real consequence. Invited to work in Hollywood in 1938, his remake of *Der Hauptmann von Köpenick* as *I Was a Criminal*—which highlights the desire for and the difficulty of exile if you don't have the right paperwork (as described in Anna Seghers' novel *Transit*)—could not find a distributor in 1941, and in 1945, disappeared from cinema screens before it was really noticed. US audiences had a hard time relating to themes of Prussian militarism, subservience, and lack of democracy [Cf. Kay Weniger, *Es wird im Leben dir mehr genommen als gegeben*, 381]. Albert Bassermann, who had worked with Oswald in films such as *Lucrezia Borgia* (1922), *Alraune* (1929/30), *1914. Die letzten Tage vor dem Weltbrand* (1930), and *Dreyfus* (1930), was one of the most famous German actors of his generation and now also a struggling exile, stars in the picture, speaking English with German accent. Thus "perhaps the most German of all exile films" as Horak puts it, but nonetheless "a considerable directorial accomplishment." For further discussion of the film, seen Horak, "German Exile Cinema," 387.
72 MGM's Irving Thalberg had secured the film rights for Werfel's *Die vierzig Tage des Musa Dagh* (The Forty Days of Musa Dagh, 1933)—a novel about 1915 and the Armenian genocide in Turkey during the First World War—soon after its publication in German. The adaptation was scrapped due to political pressure by the Turkish government. For further context and detail see Frank Stern, "Die jüdische und die armenische Erfahrung in Filmen nach Franz

Werfel," in *Franz Werfel und der Genozid an den Armeniern*, ed. Roy Knocke and Werner Treß (Berlin: de Gruyter, 2015), 140–7.
73 Franz Werfel, "A Personal Preface," in his *The Song of Bernadette* (New York: Viking, 1942).
74 Fred Stanley, "A New Spiritual Resurgence in Hollywood: Studios Now Look Favorably on Religious Themes," *The New York Times* (March 7, 1943): section X, 3.
75 The novel is dedicated to Manon Gropius, Alma's daughter from her second marriage to Walter Gropius. The girl contracted poliomyelitis in 1934 and passed away a year later. Her mother had cared for her together with Franz Werfel.
76 Alfred Döblin, *Schicksalsreise. Bericht und Bekenntnis* (Frankfurt/M.: Knecht, 1949).
77 See https://kuenste-im-exil.de/KIE/Content/EN/Topics/european-film-fund-en; for the 1941/2 donor list, see https://kuenste-im-exil.de/KIE/Content/EN/Topics/european-film-fund-en.html?catalog=1.

6

A History of Abuse: German-language Literature in Nazi Cinema (1933–45)

Film is one of the most effective ways to manipulate the public.
JOSEPH GOEBBELS (1934)[1]

Those who don't know, don't want to know.
Those that forget, want to forget.
ERNST TOLLER (1934)[2]

Adaptations of the German literary canon were integral to Nazi cinema, beginning with Hans Deppe/Curt Oertel's *Der Schimmelreiter* [Rider on a White Horse/The Dike Master] (1933/4) based on Theodor Storm's 1888 novella, and closing with the crime film *Der stumme Gast* [The Silent Guest], an adaptation of another novella of poetic realism, namely Theodor Fontane's *Unterm Birnbaum* (Under the Pear Tree, 1885), directed by Harald Braun in 1944/5. In this chapter on Nazi film, German literature on cinema screens is predominantly regarded in the context of its ideological function within and as mass culture. According to Adolf Hitler's minister for 'public enlightenment and propaganda' Joseph Goebbels, feature films were the ideal medium for a subtle, ideological education of the people. A focus on adaptation reveals the significance of both classic and popular literature as cultural heritage, integrated into a process of ideological alignment of not only the film industry, but of German society as a whole. A focus on adaptation as a genre yields new insights into the frequently explored shaping of national film culture under Hitler and Goebbels. Both were cinema enthusiasts and keenly aware of the power of film as a most effective, unique propaganda tool. Hitler was a 'film addict' according to his bodyguard Rochus Misch, watching everything from romantic comedies and historical dramas to Westerns and cartoons.[3] An avid Laurel and Hardy fan who also owned a number of Mickey Mouse animations, Hitler enjoyed film as entertainment, particularly in the privacy of his Berghof retreat in the Alps; but as Bill Niven argues convincingly, in "public, for the most part at least, he wanted to be associated only with films carrying a serious political message."[4] Together, Hitler and Goebbels controlled cinema as an ideological space, but also demanded effective entertainment for the masses and commodities suited for export.[5]

While Hitler, of course, had ultimate authority in the German Reich and in some respects was indeed "more important than Goebbels when it came to overseeing film production,"[6] as Niven states, when it came to adaptations of literary texts, he was normally not directly involved. While he occasionally ordered a feature to be banned, Hitler differentiated between fiction and documentary films or newsreels that would document his leadership for posterity—regularly vetting newsreel coverage, particularly during the Second World War.[7] Goebbels, as this chapter will outline, ultimately guided cinema as a national project, and the construction of a subtle propaganda message in feature films, particularly in adaptations. The film industry as a whole—from screenwriters and cameramen to actors and directors—either actively served their *Führer* and his propaganda minister, or self-censored and kept their heads down. Together, their films contributed to the most wide-ranging "fictionalization of politics and the politicization of fiction"[8] of motion picture history. Some adaptations of the literary canon included critical messages subtly woven into the dramatization of outwardly aligned motion pictures. Necessary as their inconspicuousness might have been, their ambiguity, however, defused any criticism implied, and rendered any opposition on cinema screens invisible compared to the onslaught of cinematic sustenance produced by and for the Hitler regime.[9]

Film became the most important propaganda instrument[10] of the national-socialist regime under Adolf Hitler, while politics became a driving force in every adaptation project undertaken by the German film industry between 1933 and 1945. Narratives were either shifted and shaped to fit a specific political purpose or focused on aspects of a specific literary text in order to promote aspects of Nazi ideology.[11] The German film industry produced films for all age groups, from children who enjoyed trustworthy and kind Nazi authorities in fairy tales to antisemitic propaganda films selling a much more deadly message to teenagers and adults alike. Of the forty Nazi films that are still banned in Germany today, the three usually mentioned in this context are *Hitlerjunge Quex* [Hitler Youth Quex] (1933), directed by Hans Steinhoff, and two Veit Harlan films: *Jud Süß* [Jew Süss] (1940) and *Kolberg* (1945). All three of these most prominent examples of Nazi propaganda on film are adaptations of German-language literature. The vast majority of the 1,086 feature films that premiered between 1933 and 1945 were not, of course, overtly political in their message, but rather lighthearted comedies or so-called "Revuefilme" (musicals with dance elements) meant to distract and entertain the German public.[12] Like adaptations of German-language literature, comedies and musicals provided a comforting sense of continuity with popular pre-Nazi film production. After 1933, significant investments were also made in high-quality adaptations of works by non-German authors such as Ibsen, Maupassant, Flaubert, Pushkin, or Tolstoy in order to promote German film internationally. This proved difficult, however, even prior to German invasions of neighboring countries, mass deportations of Jewish families, imprisonment or murder of political opponents, and other atrocities. But seemingly undeterred, filmmakers in Nazi Germany continued to exploit the literary canon for their purposes.

More than 100 feature films produced during this period were adaptations of German literary texts, and the vast majority of adaptation projects of the time incorporated the language of current debates and key terms clearly defined by ideological contexts. On the surface many adaptations produced by the Nazi film industry seem apolitical and tell a good yarn. It is only when examining in detail the film in comparison to its literary source that the differences between the original text and the Nazi product unveil shifts toward a normalization of Nazi thought and the communication of a specific set of values.

The German-language texts chosen by the political leadership and filmmakers in Nazi Germany fall into three categories: popular and *Heimat*-literature, nationalist and national-socialist literature, and, finally, the classics, i.e., the 'canon' of German literary culture. Numerically, the majority of adaptations belong to the category of entertainment film, often based on literary texts by Hermann Sudermann, Ludwig Thoma, Maximilian Böttcher, Ludwig Anzengruber, or on works by contemporary authors such as Heinrich Spoerl, Anton Hamik, and Austrian Alexander Lernet-Holenia. Remakes of Ganghofer[13] or Sudermann novels were common and communicated cultural continuity while maximizing the popular appeal of Nazi cinema. Contemporary author Hamik, for example, wrote traditional folkloric plays like *Weiberregiment* (Women's Rule, 1936) or the hugely popular *Der verkaufte Großvater* (Grandfather for Sale, 1942) under the pseudonym Franz Streicher. Adapting those plays ensured healthy profits for the film industry at German box offices, especially during the war, as they catered to an increasingly intense longing for escapism among the German public.[14] Much less interesting if perhaps informative are adaptations of nationalist and national-socialist literature, such as radio plays or prose by Hans Rothe, Hanns Heinz Ewers, the Austrian "Blood and Soil"-author Richard Billinger (who became a favorite during the war years 1942 to 1944), but also Walter von Molo, Gerhard Menzel, Walter Harlan, and Thea von Harbou. Their texts and all subsequent adaptations are usually linear and one-dimensional in their narrative as well as political focus. Because of the utter predictability of most of these movies in terms of their ideological outlook only little attention will be paid to them in this chapter. Much more thought-provoking are films based on the literary canon; the approximation of Nazi and traditional bourgeois culture in Germany in adaptations of texts by Gotthold E. Lessing, Friedrich Schiller, Johann Wolfgang von Goethe, Heinrich von Kleist, Theodor Storm, Theodor Fontane, Gottfried Keller, Friedrich Hebbel, Marie v. Ebner-Eschenbach, Gerhard Hauptmann, Arno Holz, Max Halbe, or even Ricarda Huch represents a significant aspect of Nazi propaganda and *Gleichschaltung* and arguably deserves a more considered analysis than this chapter can provide.

Repression, Censorship, and Ideological Alignment

Transposing literature to film in Nazi Germany was a practice integrated into the highly influential cultural industry overseen by Joseph Goebbels from 1933.[15] Appointed by Presidential Decree as 'Minister of Popular Enlightenment and Propaganda' on March 13, 1933, and selected by Hitler to head the *Reichsfilmkammer* or 'Reich Film Chamber'[16] soon after, he watched over film production and distribution processes from screenwriting to public performance. Within a couple of weeks after Hitler's appointment as Reich Chancellor, the new position of "Reichsfilmdramaturg" was created. Germany's film dramaturgue reported directly to Goebbels[17] and was to assess the 'suitability' of all film treatments suggested for production. On April 19 fanatically anti-Jewish Goebbels proudly noted in his diary that from now on he controlled the entire culture division of the interior ministry.[18]

Following German cinema's 'golden age' of the 1920s, film now constituted a valuable segment of the nation's cultural heritage. Moreover, as a vehicle for propaganda the film industry had an official function that was to be integral to the ideological stabilization of German society under Nazi rule. Hence, every person working in this industry had to submit proof of 'belonging' to the 'Reich' envisaged, as Hitler himself emphasized: "Whoever wishes to contribute to our German cultural resource film, must be of Aryan decent and a German citizen."[19] But that alone was not enough; loyalty to the Nazi cause was also considered of vital importance to the success of the film industry as an agent in the effective communication of far-right ideals to the widest possible audience. Goebbels' aim was to produce only movies in Germany that supported the Nazi agenda, and numerous scholars have convincingly argued that the apparatus of entertainment and manipulation controlled by Goebbels and, ultimately, Hitler significantly aided in the German public's support for the Nazi's exclusionary politics, another world war, and, if perhaps inadvertently, mass murder.[20]

When the leader of the NSDAP Adolf Hitler was appointed Chancellor of Germany by the increasingly frail President von Hindenburg on January 30, 1933, German literature and a high-quality film industry were already two significant parts of the Nazi leadership's vision for the construction of a national mass culture based on and aligned with Nazi ideology. In his first speech as Chancellor on February 1, 1933, Hitler evokes the 'highest goods of our past' that a deeply divided German people had forgotten at their own peril as this, according to the Nazi leader, resulted in 'external and internal deterioration'. In a typical rhetoric aimed at shaping nostalgic longing for a rose-tinted past amongst voters living in a not so perfect present, Hitler delivered his "Proclamation to the German people"[21] not in the Reichstag as expected for an inaugural speech, but via Berlin radio. Using progressive, state-of-the-art technology, the new Chancellor addressed the general public directly—in a domineering gesture that implicitly cast aside dated and redundant political (democratic) structures like the Reichstag—thereby laying the foundation for a personal relationship between the people and their soon-to-be *Führer*. In his undemanding address, Hitler blamed Marxism, anarchism, and bolshevism for the 'horrific suffering of our people', and held the division of the state's democratically elected representatives, i.e., an 'incompetent parliament', responsible for failing to protect the 'highest goods of human culture and civilization'. Pledging his commitment to foundational values such as 'honor and loyalty, [...] morality and faith' as well as—just to add a few more buzzwords to his populist speech—to 'family, [...] nation, culture and economy',[22] and proclaiming 'unity of spirit and will' as his first and highest aim, Hitler promised to protect Germany's foundation and bring the nation back to health and strength. The German *Volk* or 'people' here remain undefined and despite his obvious hatred of Marxists, other aspects of his pathological ideology such as antisemitism remain conveniently veiled. Only a month later, in an article published in the NSDAP newspaper *Völkischer Beobachter*, Hitler identifies film and literature as 'means to an end' in his 'systematic campaign to restore the nations' moral and material health.[23]

Despite the fact that the Reich Chamber of Culture was not established until September 22, 1933, which provided the legal basis for the exclusion of all non-Aryan artists, efforts to align the cultural industries with Nazi ideals or "Gleichschaltung" began as soon as the Reichstag Fire Decree (February 28, 1933) and the Enabling Act had legally equipped Hitler with plenary powers and established a Nazi dictatorship by March 1933. The 1920 "Lichtspielgesetz" or film law had provided for regulatory authorities and licensing processes, and enabled the prohibition of films deemed to endanger public order or to portray a negative image of Germany abroad.

While this existing legislation afforded the Nazi government with the basis for an elimination of their critics on screen, a new and much more empowering law was passed on February 16, 1934. Now only films could go into production, which had been confirmed as not offensive to 'national-socialist, religious, moral or artistic sentiments'.

The journal *Licht-Bühne* reported on March 16, 1934, that *The Song of Songs* (US, Rouben Mamoulian, 1933), a Paramount remake of Hermann Sudermann's novel *Das Hohe Lied* (The Hymn, 1908)—based on previous silent film adaptations *The Song of Songs* (US, Joseph Kaufman, 1918, based on Edward Sheldon's stage version of Sudermann's text) and *Lily of the Dust* (US, Dimitri Buchowetzki, 1924, starring Pola Negri)—would not be screened in Germany. Ernst Seeger, Head of the Film Department in the Propaganda Ministry, called the romantic drama an 'anti-German concoction [...] that would endanger Germany's reputation in the context of §7 of the new Cinema Act (February 16, 1934)'.[24] The real reason, however, was Marlene Dietrich, who starred in this new US American Sudermann adaptation alongside Hans Schumm, a German-Jewish actor who appeared here on cinema screen for the first time. Goebbels had been eager to get Dietrich back to Germany, but she steadfastly refused to return to Berlin and add glamor to Nazi culture despite great financial incentives. When Goebbels visited the Ufa film company in Neubabelsberg in April 1933, he left no doubt regarding his expectation of a complete 'Gleichschaltung' or political synchronization of the national film industry with his party's ideology. In his view, German film's most important duty was to be a "Vorkämpfer nationaler Kultur,"[25] a standard-bearer of Germany's new national culture.

As many scholars such as Ian Kershaw, Hilmar Hofmann, or David Welch have emphasized, propaganda was the Nazi Party's most important tool in creating and maintaining a mass base of support for Adolf Hitler as Germany's *Führer*.[26] The potential significance of film as a fantastically useful instrument of propaganda had been realized by the party leadership years before the NSDAP and Hitler came to power. In his *The Triumph of Propaganda*, Hofmann called film "the most influential among the mass media in the Third Reich [and] the means of artistic communication that Hitler used to greatest effect in bringing his political ideas to a mass audience."[27] As early as 1930, the Nazi Party created its own "Reichsfilmstelle" (film office), which produced numerous short 'documentaries' such as *Hitlers Kampf um Deutschland* [Hitler's Fight for Germany] (1931) or *Hitler über Deutschland* [Hitler on Germany] (1932) for propaganda purposes. In his infamous *Mein Kampf* Hitler emphasized that film could convey a message—or rather, as he put it, provide "Aufklärung" (enlightenment)—in an "instant", and was therefore the Nazi leadership's preferred propaganda medium.[28] Goebbels was instrumental in this effort to step up the party's impact on the German public via film and, from 1933, championed numerous adaptation projects while heading the newly established Reich Ministry of Public Enlightenment and Propaganda. Adolf Hitler himself had identified the Ministry's main responsibility as intellectual/spiritual manipulation of the nation as documented, for example, by Joseph Wulf.[29] In line with his *Führer*'s wishes, Goebbels and his Ministry also controlled film policy and production. In a speech delivered on March 28, 1933, Goebbels assured the representatives of the German film industry albeit with a little *caveat*: 'Art is free and will remain free. It must only get used to certain norms.'[30] As mentioned above, the creation of a preliminary Reich Film Chamber in July 1933 and a permanent *Reichsfilmkammer* in September 1933 was primarily to ensure the alignment of the industry and all its contributors with Nazi ideology and to allow for the exclusion of individuals based on racial or political grounds. In addition, Goebbels explicit aim was to communicate Adolf Hitler as the leader or *Führer* Germany and the German people needed. Both the required membership in the Reich Film Chamber and the political dependency of the Filmkredit-Bank GmbH, which supplied funding to virtually all film projects during the 'Third Reich', were meant to further encourage the ideological conformity of the film industry's creative talent.[31]

Politics of exclusion formed the core of this systematic campaign. Goebbels and his staff at the Propaganda Ministry took control of almost every aspect of film production and distribution in Germany as soon as they took office. Together with the Ministry of the Interior, Goebbels saw to the prohibition of cinematic masterpieces such as Fritz Lang's first sound film *M* (1930), and to the banning of the aforementioned adaptations *Die Büchse der Pandora* (1929), *Westfront 1918* (1930), *All Quiet on the Western Front* (1930), *Die Dreigroschenoper* (1931), or Sagan's *Mädchen in Uniform* (1931), to name but a few. The latter film was, however, at the same time available to Hitler himself for screenings at the Berghof and part of his personal film library.[32] On March 20, 1933 the Ministry of the Interior also banned Josef von Sternberg's *Der blaue Engel* (1930) from being distributed or screened anywhere in Germany. This elimination of another highly popular film from public culture was due to the novel's author Heinrich Mann who was openly opposed to Nazism and left Germany for France shortly after Hitler's appointment as Chancellor. After his departure the author was mocked on the title page of a Nazi magazine as having fallen 'head over heels for Judah', a reference to Marlene Dietrich's song in *The Blue Angel* "Falling in Love Again" or "Ich bin von Kopf bis Fuß auf Liebe eingestellt."[33] The magazine thus implies both the popular adaptation itself and the author's elective exile as evidence of transnational Jewish power and control.

As mentioned in the previous chapter, Heinrich Mann's books, including *Professor Unrat* (Small Town Tyrant, 1905) and *Der Untertan* (The Loyal Subject, 1914), were included in the Nazi's ceremonial book burning sessions in Mai 1933.[34] Together with Lion Feuchtwanger, Ernst Toller,

Kurt Tucholsky, and Alfred Kerr, his name appeared on the first of 359 *Ausbürgerungslisten* or 'expatriation lists'. The names of those listed and published in the official *Deutscher Reichsanzeiger* were no longer deemed worthy of German citizenship by the Nazi government that revoked all their rights and left them stateless.

How quickly even respectable newspapers and journals were bowing to the new leadership can be seen, for example, in a report about the ban of an adaptation of the novella "Amokläufer" (Running Amok, 1922) by the Austrian bestselling author Stefan Zweig. According to the journal *Film-Kurier* the *Amok*-film was prohibited by the Reich's minister for Public Enlightenment and Propaganda on April 28 due to 'significant internal and external political concerns [...]. The author Stefan Zweig was black-listed, and his books were burned publicly.'[35] By simply stating 'concerns' and implying public 'burning' as a consequence of wrongdoing, the author was criminalized and any oppression of his work appears, therefore, justified. By omitting to mention Zweig's Jewishness, the film journal became complicit in substantiating manufactured reasons that supposedly led to the ban.

As mentioned in the previous chapter, Fallada's break-through bestseller *Kleiner Mann—was nun?* (Little Man, What Now?, 1932) had almost immediately been marked for adaptation[36] due to its enormous popular success. The story of a young couple's struggles during the economic crisis following the stock market crash, their experiences of instability and potential ruin despite hard work, decency, and love for one another seemed to mirror the lives of so many, especially among the petit bourgeoisie—a class particularly open to the promises of national greatness made by Adolf Hitler. A first German adaptation of *Kleiner Mann* was 'in the pipeline' when the Nazis came to power. Initial director Erich Engel contacted Kurt Weill[37] inviting him to compose the film's score. But Fallada and Engel could not agree on the script, and the project was abandoned until R.N.-Filmproduktion GmbH under the headship of Robert Neppach took over and presented a new script by Herbert Selpin and Fritz Wendhausen. When Fallada rejected this script, too, the adaptation was pursued without the author's collaboration.[38]

Wendhausen had worked on adaptations of German-language literature before, having written the screenplay for *Heimkehr* [Homecoming] (1928) based on Leonhard Frank's novella *Karl und Anna* (1926) together with the film's director Joe May. His co-author Herbert Selpin would later co-write and direct the Nazi propaganda film *Carl Peters* (1940/1). *Kleiner Mann* stars Hertha Thiele as "Lämmchen," known for her performance as Manuela in the adaptation of Christa Winsloe's play *Mädchen in Uniform* [Girls in Uniform] (Leontine Sagan, 1931), as well as well-known and respected Austrian and German actors such as Hermann Thimig, Viktor de Kowa, Ida Wüst, Paul Henckels, and Theo Lingen. The adaptation of Fallada's novel should have had all the ingredients of a straight-forward box-office hit, especially due to the appearance of the most famous German vocal ensemble of the time: the Comedian Harmonists. The internationally renowned group had composed and recorded the title song "Kleiner Mann, was nun?" on May 8, 1933, and appeared in a few scenes. What should have enhanced the success and entertainment value of this early sound film, however, subsequently became a fundamental problem for the survival of the entire project.

When the movie was finally released by the "Filmprüfstelle" [board of film censors] on July 7, 1933, R.N.-Filmproduktion GmbH and the movie's producer Robert Neppach were ordered to cut all scenes depicting the Comedian Harmonists. The decision was solely based on antisemitic film politics as three of the members of the famous close harmony ensemble were Jewish. Their title song remained but the singers were edited from the film and thereby rendered invisible. Their absence was a chilling harbinger of the things to come under Germany's new fervently antisemitic, racist leadership. Probably every single adult German viewer of the movie at the time though would have recognized the title song as sung by Harry Frommermann, Erich A. Collin, Roman Cycowski, Ari Leschnikoff, Robert Biberti, and Erwin Bootz, and the vast majority—unaware of the visual eradication of the sextet and the butchery of the film—would have cared little about anything but the gifted singers' beautifully delivered music.

Literary texts framed Nazi cinema from beginning to end. Goebbels preferred films based on nationalist literature, but the choice here was limited. Gustav Ucicky's patriotic submarine-drama *Morgenrot* [Dawn] (1933) based on Edgar von Spiegel's First World War-diary *U 202* premiered on January 31, 1933, in the Schauburg-cinema in Essen—less than twenty-four hours after Adolf Hitler's appointment as the Reich's Chancellor. *Morgenrot* was filmed during the Weimar Republic, but as Thomas Kramer points out, already transmits a number of central motifs of national-socialist film-propaganda: an unconditional willingness to sacrifice oneself for one's nation, the celebration of the military collective as a most meaningful entity, and an almost mythical longing for death.[39] Goebbels excitedly quoted the film in his diary: 'We Germans might not know how to live, but we certainly know how to die.'[40] It was the perfect film to positively impact on the somewhat strained relationship between Ufa's media mogul and right-wing reactionary Alfred Hugenberg[41] and the new political leadership.

In this first phase of Nazi adaptations Gustav Ucicky, son of painter Gustav Klimt, and scriptwriter and Hitler-enthusiast Gerhard Menzel were a highly productive team. Their next film, based on Gerhard Menzel's novel, was an anti-Soviet propaganda film entitled *Flüchtlinge* [Refugees] (1933) that premiered on December 8, 1933, in Berlin's Ufa-Palast am Zoo. In this action adventure about the Volga-Germans' suffering under Soviet rule and the inefficiency of the League of Nations, Hans Albers plays the male lead and presents a picture of masculinity and heroism—unbending and tough as nails, yet humane in light of the plight of those deserving of his sympathy. Needless to say, he defeats his enemies decisively and helps the Volga-Germans find their way home to the Reich. Critic Oskar Kalbus praised the 'new spirit' of this film, which in his view epitomized both the moral ideal of self-help and the leadership principle.[42]

The leadership principle is also at the core of *Hitlerjunge Quex* [Hitler Youth Quex] (1933) and, as the movie's subtitle suggests, both Karl Aloys Schenzinger's 1932 novel and its adaptation focus on the spirit of sacrifice among the German youth. Dedicated to all young Germans devoted to Adolf Hitler and aiming to present a high-quality adaptation of national-socialist literature, critics hailed this film as the 'true birth of NS-cinema'. *Hitler Youth Quex* was aimed at the young generation, communicating values such as courage, will to sacrifice, camaraderie, and loyalty in the context of the Nazi movement to those children and young Germans, who had not yet been exposed to it in their homes, as Hilmar Hoffmann points out.[43] The power of adaptation projects produced during the Nazi era from *Der Schimmelreiter* [Rider on a White Horse/The Dike Master] (1933/4, based on Theodor Storm's novella) to Veit Harlan's *Der Herrscher* [The Ruler] (1936/7, based on Gerhard Hauptmann's *Vor Sonnenuntergang*/ Before Sunset) or *Jud Süß* (1940, based on Lion Feuchtwanger's play and novel of the same name) lies in what Theodor Adorno would later call their (pretense of) 'harmlessness'[44] and their integration by association into German high culture. By adapting well-known German literature, the Nazi film industry offered audiences an opportunity to root their unsettled present in a treasured and seemingly uncomplicated past. At the same time the literary canon provided a cultural foundation for the filmmakers' vision of a new Germany and an ideal vehicle for the communication of Nazi ideology. Film director Veit Harlan could be considered instrumental in this process, but only very few adaptations of German literature by the Nazi film industry fail to contain echoes of party-political messages and Nazi ideology and are always the product of a team of willing collaborators.

Moreover, the production of the commodity film had long become collaborative, of course, but in Hitler's Germany the team-work aspect of cinema was celebrated, not least because all members of the production team needed to function within a particular political, tightly controlled framework. The scriptwriter, director, producer, director of photography, art director, composer, editor, the actors, etc. all ensured that a literary text was adapted and communicated in a particular way, guiding the viewers' understanding by decisions made by the different members of the production team during the multi-facetted transposition and production process. In the case of the first adaptation of Theodor Storm's *Der Schimmelreiter*, this particular product was carefully planned as both cultural intervention and naissance of 'true' Nazi cinema.

Theodor Storm and Nazi Heritage Film

Theodor Storm's novella *Der Schimmelreiter* (Rider on a White Horse, 1888)[45] was well suited to Goebbels' idea of cultural propaganda, i.e., the distribution of Nazi ideology on the back of cultural heritage, as the majority of Germans at the time would have considered Theodor Storm one of the most important representatives of German literary culture.[46] Storm's *Zur Chronik von Grieshuus* (A Chapter in the History of Grieshuus, 1884), adapted by Thea von Harbou for the 1925 silent film[47] directed by Arthur von Gerlach (starring Lil Dagover, Rudolf Forster, and Paul Hartmann) with sets designed by Walter Röhrig and Robert Herlth,[48] had been very popular with cinemagoers. Storm's *Schimmelreiter* promised to be at least as successful on screen as it conveyed a rootedness, a comfortable sense of heritage, and was highly entertaining. An example of German literary realism, the novella tells the story of Hauke Haien, the son of a surveyor who grows up on a farm in Northern Frisia, but works hard to become proficient in surveying, mathematics, and geometry. The dikes that protect Germany's North Sea coast are of particular interest to him, and when he takes on the job of farmhand for the local 'Deichgraf' or dike reeve Tede Volkerts, his innovative ideas regarding more effective dike constructions lead to a close working relationship between the two men. This creates tension between Hauke and the senior hand Ole Peters, who views the young man as competition. This unpleasant situation intensifies further when Hauke and the Deichgraf's daughter Elke fall in love, and Hauke is chosen as her father's successor, i.e., new dike master after Volkert's death. Access to the job of "Deichgraf" requires not only expertise, but ownership of sufficient land, which Elke guarantees when announcing their wedding. The locals, however, remain ambivalent regarding their new dike reeve, not only due to all the changes and innovations he proposes, but because he rides a new white horse, which they believe might be bewitched. A horse skeleton that used to lie on a nearby island is no longer visible from the coast, and jealous Ole Peters uses the people's superstition to deepen their opposition to Hauke's work. Undeterred, Hauke implements the changes he had envisioned since his teens and a new dike is built. His deep fascination for this innovative project of his own, however, leads to a lack of attention to the existing dikes that are left to deteriorate. During a particularly violent storm, one of the old dikes breaks and Hauke witnesses his wife and their beloved mentally disabled daughter Wienke drowning in the ensuing, horrific flood. In desperation, he commits suicide by riding into the violent sea shouting 'Lord, take me, but spare the others!'. The schoolmaster, who functions as the narrator of this story in a framing narrative, concludes the novella by referring once again to the mysterious horse skeleton that strangely reappeared after Hauke's death. And, according to some, he tells

FIGURE 6.1 *Mathias Wieman as leader Hauke Haien in* Der Schimmelreiter *(DE, Hans Deppe/Curt Oertel, 1934).*

the reader, a ghostly rider on a white horse can be seen on stormy nights, riding along, and keeping watch on his dike that now had stood strong for 100 years and had surely saved hundreds of lives.

Theodor Storm (1817–88) spun a good yarn and was one of the most widely read authors in Germany throughout the twentieth century. Both his poetry and prose were staple texts in secondary school curricula during the Weimar Republic, and his last prose text *Der Schimmelreiter* is often viewed as the author's masterpiece. When the adaptation of Storm's famous novella premiered in the Ufa cinema at Berlin's Kurfürstendamm on January 29, 1934, the film was to mark the first anniversary of the Nazi regime's rise to power and was announced as "urdeutsche Filmkunst"[49] or 'original German film art'. Critics praised the filmmakers' ability to bring both the German coastal landscape and its inhabitants to life due to the very successful collaboration of the entire film team: 'The script, camera/photography, musical score, acting and directing all share the introversion and intensity of the artistic means used and contribute almost equally to the unusual impact of this film.' One of the journalists writing under the abbreviated "dr. loh." praised the film as 'a piece of Germany' that successfully conveys the roots and source of 'our power'.[50]

The team working on this first *Schimmelreiter* adaptation was officially led by Hans Deppe and Curt Oertel, who had written the script and were asked to co-direct the film. Alexander von Lagorio served as the director of photography, Winfried Zillig composed the musical score, Fritz Seeger was responsible for sound, and Gabriel Pellon designed the set. Mathias Wieman and Marianne Hoppe star in the adaptation as Hauke and Elke Haien, the so-called "Schimmelreiter" and his wife. Theodor Storm's implicit contribution to this film as author of the source text is made very much explicit, not only in the credits, but also in all promotional material published as well as in interviews conducted with members of the cast. When the film premiered in 1934, critics[51] praised its novelty and declared this *Schimmelreiter* adaptation proof that the German film industry had been imbued with 'new life'. The film's excellent artistic quality was seen as 'unusual', again marking the adaptation as the starting point for a new kind of excellent

(Nazi) cinema. Several critics remarked on the collaborative nature of this project that further heightened the film's 'relevance for today' and which would surely impact on both German and international audiences. The team was praised for producing a 'faithful adaptation', that appeared true to the 'spirit' of its source and, at the same time, a new prototype carved out of Storm's 'most perfect novella'. Only the North German locals, well familiar with Storm's famous tale, disapproved of added scenes not part of the original narrative as reported by Marianne Hoppe.[52]

According to Iris Kampf the original idea for an adaptation of Storm's text had come from film producer Dr. Carls, who had intended to collaborate with award-winning documentary filmmaker Curt Oertel on this project. As a Jew, however, Carls was unable to realize the film once the Nazis had come to power. He was forced out of the film industry and emigrated.[53] The project was taken over by producer Rudolf Fritsch, who supported Carls' choice of Oertel as scriptwriter, but asked—perhaps at the request of the Reich's film dramaturge or, indeed, Goebbels himself—that Hans Deppe, a 'loyal subject', joined the team as both co-author and director to ensure the political alignment of the film. Especially the addition of narrative elements such as two speeches that serve to promote Hitler as Germany's *Führer* was most likely Deppe's contribution to an otherwise quite intuitive transposition of Storm's work.

Storm's *Schimmelreiter* as a source text was a 'safe' choice by all involved in a number of respects. The story is set in typical Northern German landscape and rooted in local heritage, which suited the Propaganda Ministry's desire for the production of explicitly 'German' film. The juxtaposition of the potentially violent force of nature and the power of man in Storm's work could be used to popular effect as readily in a film about the North Sea coast as it had been very successfully employed in mountain films such as *Die weiße Hölle von Piz Palü* [The White Hell of Pitz Palu] (1929) and *Berge in Flammen* [Mountains on Fire] (1931), which were among the greatest box-office hits of the early 1930s. In addition, Storm's text was considered not only high and folk culture at the same time, which matched the Nazi's idea of German *Volkskultur*, but implied historical authenticity due to its implicit reference to a specific natural catastrophe such as the 'Great Flood' of 1756. The film omits the novella's narrator and framing narrative, but the audience's familiarity with the literary text ensured that the framing narrative's absence actually emphasized the documentary effect of the 1933 adaptation. Producer Rudolf Fritsch also saw the potential of Storm's story about a visionary, which could easily be molded into a plot that highlighted not only Germany's need for a strong ruler, but the importance of autonomous leadership.

Already in 1927 Eilhard Erich Pauls, a racist and fervent Nazi, had published on Storm's novella and its main character's courage and ability to lead and achieve greatness, which Pauls simply considered a 'natural' consequence of his racial make-up.[54] It was Pauls' interpretation that facilitated an easy integration of Storm's *Schimmelreiter* into the Nazi propaganda machine. Blindly ignoring the inherent ambivalence and multi-facetted nature of Storm's texts, Fritsch and many early supporters of the Nazi Party NSDAP considered Storm a writer of German 'Blood and Soil' who, in their minds, captured the ideals of perfect strength, visionary action, and true creativity in male protagonists such as Hauke Haien. In line with this interpretation and current ideology, Deppe and Oertel's adaptation indeed foregrounded leadership and aligned the concept with images of exceptional ability and noble sacrifice. Storm's *Schimmelreiter* is structured by juxtapositions such as man vs. nature, individual vs. community, reason vs. superstition—all themes also prevalent in Nazi ideology. However, in order to use the novella for an education in and appreciation of heroic leadership, the script needed to focus on Hauke Haien as leader. By reducing the novella's focus on superstition, myths and folklore, and juxtaposing reason with irrational emotions and human flaws, Deppe and Oertel created a more linear cinematic narrative that aimed at establishing a clear link between undeterred leadership and the survival of the community.

The film is frequently and for the most part analogous with the narrative structure and characterization of the main figures of Storm's literary text. However, in a clear diversion from the original text the scriptwriters Oertel and Deppe weave threads from Hitler's *Mein Kampf* throughout their adaptation of the nineteenth-century narrative. In their film, the main protagonist is portrayed not only an enlightened scientist and visionary who overcomes social division but is effectively distinguished as a selflessly persevering leader. The most significant additions[55] to the script are two speeches: Hauke Haien,[56] the former farmhand who wishes to become the visionary protector of his people asking for their support as the new dike project is going forward, and the confirmation of his 'genius' by Hauke's superior upon the dike's completion. Hauke promotes the "Volksgemeinschaft" or national (people's) community with modest but decidedly heroic pathos in his speech. He highlights the need to create "Lebensraum"/'living space' for his people and promises a rather uninspired crowd to 'tear' fertile ground from the sea. The use of the verb "entreißen" has, in this expansionist context, a violent and threatening ring to it, but at the time served to emphasize Hauke's determination and the significance of his work. This is stressed later on by the "Oberdeichgraf" [chief dike master], who emerges in the film to outline the impact and altruism of Hauke's work to the local community. In his speech, the chief dike master and highest authority in this film declares the young man a genius and visionary, and advises all to 'follow him' at the promise that only then will they 'harvest richly for many years to come'. During the chief dike master's speech, the camera comes to rest on Hauke Haien and his resolute face in a close-up, low angle shot, commanding the viewer's respect for their exceptional, hard-working, and trustworthy hero. Images of endless fertile fields and peacefully swaying reed underline their appeal. In contrast, in Storm's novella, the "Oberdeichgraf" is only in passing mentioned as having praised Hauke during his inspection of the new dike project.

While a number of narrative sequences are removed or severely shortened in comparison[57] to the literary text, the two speeches are not only added, but narrated time slows down or is expanded when Hauke's 'important work' is to become the focus of the viewers' attention. Oertel and Deppe's script clearly favors the work aspect and foregrounds it, too, in Hauke's speech that clarifies his intention and purpose for the well-being of all. At the same time, the opposition to his work is portrayed as the one and only element that could not only bring about the failure of the 'work' project, but the demise of the entire community. The choreography of this scene is striking: As the camera pans along the crowd of villagers that have come to the beach to listen to the new dike master's plans, we hear only Hauke's voice, promising that they will all profit from supporting the project and sharing his vision of those new and fertile fields. Again, it is Hauke's jealous competitor Ole Peters who rudely interrupts the speaker, accusing him of selfishness and greed. But Hauke retorts, now seen in an extreme long-shot dominated by the sea behind him and then standing slightly elevated in a long-shot when rejecting Peters' lies and slander. His voice is raised when he informs the crowd of 'the truth' ("die Wahrheit ist ...!") and the camera cuts to Peters who awkwardly casts his eye, before returning to Hauke now in a medium close-up, low angle shot. Hauke declares with a piercing gaze that the new dike will stand for a hundred and another hundred years—reminding us of the Reich that Hitler proclaimed would last a thousand. The camera moves closer and elevates Hauke further while keeping him in the centre of the frame as he shares his passion for the new project. When he is challenged once again by Peters and the first villagers begin to leave, he reminds the people of the imminent danger they are in, his face in a close-up and low angle shot spouting populist rhetoric. But despite his appeal to get to work as a community in order to address this looming threat, most of the villagers walk away. The lonely and misunderstood visionary remains on the beach and an extreme long-shot emphasizing the leader's loneliness and struggle concludes the scene. The affective impact of this and the final scene was repeatedly emphasized by reviewers at the time.

In the end, Hauke is swept away by the sea. Theodor Storm's protagonist is an ambivalent figure, who fails due to his own hubris, not primarily due to the community's lack of support. The film in contrast depicts Hauke's death as selfless sacrifice and in an epilogue raises the hero's status to savior whose dike 'will never break'. The adaptation closes only after once more declaring Hauke Haien divinely empowered, a visionary leader, a messiah-like figure, who triumphs in the end for the vital benefit of all. As Kurt

Sontheimer and many others after him pointed out, "'Heroic' leadership was a significant element in the ideas of the nationalist and *völkisch* Right long before Hitler's spectacular rise to prominence. It can justifiably be regarded as 'one of the central ideas of the anti-democratic movement in the Weimar Republic' and 'one of its indispensable articles of faith'."[58] As Sontheimer emphasizes, the parliamentary, pluralist system of the Weimar Republic created after the devastating World War and collapse of the German Empire had failed in overcoming the severe economic, social, and political crisis. Nationalist, right-wing groups fed the struggling people's desire for a new beginning or 'rebirth' that could only be achieved under the leadership of a strong and heroic individual.

Deppe and Oertel used Storm's protagonist in order to communicate the type of leadership envisaged by the German nationalists as early as 1920—a visionary hero who selflessly takes a stand in order to modernize the community's protective borders and ensure its safety effectively. As Sontheimer suggests, the true leader's mission must supersede all other desires. He is both radical and responsible, a straight-talker committed to the cause to a point of ruthlessness.[59] A year into Hitler's reign, many Germans remained critical of Nazi ideology and unconvinced of Nazi policies and institutions. But, as Ian Kershaw points out, "The adulation of Hitler by millions of Germans who might otherwise have been only marginally committed to Nazism meant that the person of the Führer, as the focal point of basic consensus, formed a crucial integratory force in the Nazi system of rule."[60] Like Leni Riefenstahl's *Triumph des Willens* [Triumph of the Will] (1935), the *Schimmelreiter*-film can be considered one of the first and a typical example of the Nazi-led film industry's effort to corroborate and increase Hitler's personal popularity and ensure that he was recognized as the "charismatic authority" and exceptional, heroic leader[61] matching exactly the Nazi's idea of 'true leadership'[62] that many Germans longed for when the economic and social crisis after 1929 led to the collapse of the Weimar Republic.[63] Moreover, the construction of the film's Hauke Haien underlines Germany's expansionist need for 'Lebensraum', and communicates clearly the obligation to elevate 'divinely' inspired visionaries (such as Hitler we are led to believe) to leadership status.

The woman by Hauke's side, Elke—stage actress Marianne Hoppe in her first major film role—is turned into an active partner and inevitable support for the modern leader in this film, while for the most part remaining firmly rooted in traditional gender stereotypes. She unquestioningly and fully supports Hauke from the very beginning, and is transformed from the brunette with dark eyes and a 'brownish' complexion[64] in Storm's text into a fair skinned, upright blonde with blue eyes in the film, squarely in line with the Nazi's ideal woman.[65] With her traditional dress and her blond hair braided, she seems to have stepped off a Nazi propaganda poster or even Karl Diebitsch's *Mutter* or *Germania* paintings for the Nazi cause. Elke in the film is no longer signified by motherhood, however, but her loving support of Hauke equally elevates her to an exemplary symbolic position. Elke and Hauke Haien's offspring is conspicuously absent from the film that makes no reference to the main protagonists' intellectually disabled child. Even though a child is born, it plays no part and is rendered invisible in this adaptation. The main protagonists' deep love and tender care for the child that are very explicit in Storm's novella[66] did not fit the Nazi's ideal of a healthy, Aryan German populace, and would have stained Hauke's reputation as an immaculate hero figure and contravened his representation as a visionary leader.[67] Six years later, the systematic murder of those already marginalized and often incarcerated and/or sterilized citizens commenced.

While it remains unclear whether Goebbels influenced the script directly, it must be assumed that at least Hans Deppe was a keen Hitler supporter, moving on to direct another thirty feature films before the final collapse of the genocidal regime. Curt Oertel, however, disappeared almost completely from the industry after one more Storm adaptation (*Pole Poppenspäler*, 1935) apart from some minor documentary work. The pressure on filmmakers to conform ideologically during the Nazi era was immense, even though in many cases not explicit. Self-censorship was rife and as the Storm-adaptation illustrates, the success of a film project depended almost entirely on its productive political alignment with Nazi rule. Oertel and Deppe drew attention to the life and the challenges of a 'proud, weather-hardened people' in Northern Frisia as a symbolic context in order to communicate the value principles or "völkisch-nationale Wertprinzipien"[68] of the far-right. The *Schimmelreiter*-film incorporated a number of key terms defined by ideological contexts into the cinematic narrative—from expansionism to a national (people's) community (*Volksgemeinschaft*)—and with the help of cameraman Alexander Lagorio successfully turned the main character into a heroic leader figure. It was hoped that Mathias Wieman's screen performance of the *Schimmelreiter* Hauke Haien—conveying strength of purpose and willingness to sacrifice himself for the greater good—could contribute successfully to a positive public reception of Hitler as *Führer*. Alexander von Lagorio's camera work not only promotes an affective relationship between landscape and audience but contributes significantly to the identification of Hauke Haien as both common man and exceptional individual, which is further emphasized by Winfried Zillig's melodramatic musical score.[69]

Critics applauded documentary filmmaker Oertel and director of photography Lagorio for creating landscape images full of narrative potential that seemed inspired by the poetry of Storm himself. An enthusiastic review published in *Berliner Börsenzeitung* on the first anniversary of the Nazi's election even claimed that it was in those shots that 'the best facets of the current ideology'[70] were conveyed. The Nazi leadership[71] was equally delighted with the finished product and actively promoted *Der Schimmelreiter* by presenting the film with an 'artistic and particularly valuable'-award via the politically synchronized 'Filmbewertungskammer' or film qualification board. A wave of ecstatic reviews further guided and shaped audiences' image-reception. Critics publishing in major newspapers and journals celebrated the film almost without exception, calling the film everything from 'wonderful' to 'biblical' and 'timely', its screenwriters/directors, the composer, and the director of photography experts verging on genius, Storm's dialogues as powerful as their use by the actors, and the whole collaborative effort resulting in an outstanding heroic epic and work of 'art'.

This Storm-adaptation not only provides a good example of the subtle manipulation of a literary text for purely political and ideological purposes but marks the beginning of a series of (ab)uses of German literary texts during the Nazi era, conveying not only the complexity of the relationships between those working in the film industry and the Nazi leadership, but their deliberate use of the medium film for its affective power. The contribution of adaptations such as Deppe/Oertel's *Schimmelreiter* to the rise of Hitler's popularity during the early years of the Führer's reign and to the increasingly chilling and finally lethal momentum of Nazi rule should not be underestimated.

The Literary Canon on Film: Friedrich Schiller

Friedrich Schiller (1759–1805), the young revolutionary who was to become the most celebrated German playwright of the nineteenth and early twentieth centuries, was being appropriated for the communication of Nazi ideology even before the Nazi party's rise to power. Already in August 1924, Goebbels wrote in his diary: 'We shall follow Schiller, because he is the titanic fighter against material matter, he represents the spirit of the resurrection from rubble and filth.'[72] And Hitler himself chose a demonstrative quote from Schiller's *Wilhelm Tell*—"Der Starke ist am mächtigsten allein," i.e., 'the strong one is most powerful alone'—as the title of one of the chapters in his autobiographical Nazi manual *Mein Kampf* (first published in 1925)[73]. Hitler thereby linked his personal antisemitic, racist, militarist, and nationalist motivation and ideology to a revered cultural icon.

In the Schiller year 1934, Alfred Rosenberg, the Nazi Party's principal ideologist, editor of the rampantly antisemitic Nazi paper *Völkischer Beobachter* and author of the infamous *Der Mythus des 20. Jahrhunderts* (The Myth of the Twentieth Century, 1930), was put in charge of the 'spiritual and philosophical education' of the Nazi party and its related organizations. Rosenberg had been one of the co-founders of the *Kampfbund für deutsche*

Kultur, which originated at the Nazi party rally in 1927 and was formally constituted as the first cultural political organization of the NSDAP two years later. Its aim was to address the perceived crisis of German culture and convey Nazi ideology to those who could not be reached at the mass rallies. This was to be achieved especially by way of cultural icons deeply rooted in what the majority of the population proudly believed to be intrinsically German. In Schiller, Rosenberg believed to have found the ideal representative and in 1934 the *Völkischer Beobachter* called the literary celebrity one of the 'Godfathers of the Third Reich.'[74] Consequently, quotations from Schiller's plays and poetry featured time and again in speeches by Hitler, Goebbels, and other Nazi officials. *Wilhelm Tell* became the most performed play on German stages and countless speeches during the time begin or end with Tell quotes evoking unity and patriotism.[75]

On November 10, 1934, to mark the 175th anniversary of Schiller's birth, mass spectacles and public celebrations as well as political events dedicated to the German poet took place all over Germany. According to Georg Ruppelt, these celebrations were intended to inspire a sense of kinship and community among German people with Friedrich Schiller as their irreproachable ally. During the live radio broadcast of the Schiller anniversary celebrations in Marbach, most speakers emphasized Schiller's relevance for the 'present times' and repeatedly pointed to the correlation between the poet's "Weltanschauung" and the ideology of National Socialism.[76] But the Schiller-year had to be marked by big budget movie productions, too. On September 9, 1934 Johannes Meyer's romantic adventure film *Schwarzer Jäger Johanna* [Black Hunter Johanna] premiered in Berlin's Capitol. Starring Marianne Hoppe, Paul Hartmann, and Gustav Gründgens, the adaptation of the popular novel by Georg von der Vring draws on both Schiller and anti-French propaganda. Hanns Johst—one of the co-founders of the Kampfbund für deutsche Kultur and known for his revanchist poetry and nationalist prose[77]—adapted Schiller's *Wilhelm Tell* (together with Hans Curjel, Wilhelm Stöppler, and Heinz Paul) and provided the screenplay for a first Schiller film that catered to the Nazis' desire to appropriate the German poet for their nationalist agenda: *Wilhelm Tell—Das Freiheitsdrama eines Volkes* [William Tell—A People's Drama of Freedom] (1934). Heinz Paul, who had written and directed an adaptation of Bruno Frank's popular novel *Trenck, der Roman eines Günstlings* (Trenck: Novel of a Favourite, 1932) together with Ernst Neubach in 1932, was appointed to direct this *Tell*-feature. While Schiller's play served as the main source text, Paul and the team of scriptwriters also referred to Aegidius Tschudi's chronicle of the historical events and Jeremias Gotthelf's narrative *Der Knabe des Tell* (The Son of Tell, 1846) for inspiration. But they also turned to the popular silent film adaptation of Schiller's play of 1923, directed by Rudolf Walther-Fein and Rudolf Dworsky, which is mentioned neither in the credits nor in any other marketing documentation. There are numerous similarities between the two films, not least due to the fact that the two main characters—Tell and his adversary, the imperial bailiff Gessler—are played by the same actors (Hans Marr and Conrad Veidt). Käte Haack also appears in both adaptations if in different roles. Emmy Sonnemann played the hero's wife; other collaborators were enacted by Eugen Klöpfer, Theodor Loos, and Carl de Vogt, to name but a few. Goebbels supported the high-profile project as he hoped to communicate the motivation of the NSDAP while rooting his party deeply in Germany's traditional cultural heritage. The marketing campaign for the film emphasizes Tell as the mature hero who will risk his life and livelihood for the next generation.

Numerous members of the crew of the film had either already joined the NSDAP or fully supported the reading of Schiller's *Wilhelm Tell* as a protofascist text: director Heinz Paul[78] was in the SA, Hans Marr who played Tell was an enthusiastic supporter of the Nazi party, Emmy Sonnemann (Frau Tell) was Minister Hermann Göring's lover and later became his wife. Conrad Veidt, in contrast, left Germany after filming was complete, together with his Jewish wife, Ilona Prager. He did, however, return to Berlin to attend the premiere of the film. Goebbels tried to persuade him

FIGURE 6.2 *Terra film poster for* Wilhelm Tell *(DE/CH, Heinz Paul, 1934)*.
Source: Deutsche Kinemathek Berlin.

to stay, informing his British employer that he was too sick to travel back to England.[79] Veidt, however, had no intention of selling his craft to the highest bidder nor of divorcing his wife, and subsequently starred in Lothar Mendes' adaptation of Lion Feuchtwanger's play and novel *Jud Süß* that rebukes antisemitism and autocratic leaders. Having outed himself as 'philo-Semitic' through both his personal and professional choices, the Nazi propaganda machine did its utmost to obliterate this outstanding actor's legacy in Germany.

In total, three of Schiller's plays were turned into Nazi films in big budget and high-profile productions: *Wilhelm Tell, Die Jungfrau von Orleans,* and, indirectly in Herbert Maisch's biopic, *Die Räuber* (The Robbers). *Das Mädchen Johanna* [The Girl Johanna] (1935) was adapted for the screen by Gerhard Menzel and directed by Gustav Ucicky, starring Gustav Gründgens, Heinrich George, Erich Ponto, Veit Harlan, Angela Salloker, and many more A-list actors of the time.[80] The film, which premiered in 1935, is a cynical, rather depressing take on the power-hungry few and the weakness of the masses. Johanna, i.e., the knowing 'Maid of Orléans' or Joan of Arc, is clearly depicted as a victim.

The "Rütlischwur" or Rütli Oath in Schiller's *Wilhelm Tell* became a staple of Nazi gatherings and was performed all over Germany on Schiller's anniversary in 1934. By reducing Tell to this grand gesture of resistance, the Nazis exploited Schiller's text to emphasize their own 'struggle' to re-establish Germany as a nation based on her 'eternal rights' or "ew'ge[n] Rechte."[81] The Rütli oath was not only instrumentalized to justify the Nazis' 'Blood and Soil' ideology, but to declare their claims on this soil as indisputable and based on the Germanic Aryan race's material ownership going back a thousand years: "Unser ist durch tausendjährigen Besitz der Boden" (*Wilhelm Tell*, line 1269). Casting their own position as an essentially defensive one, the Nazis maintained that their aim was merely to re-establish a time-honored natural state against its detractors and corruptors—just like Tell and his allies had done.[82]

As mentioned above, Schiller quotations featured time and again in speeches by Hitler, Goebbels, and other Nazi officials, and *Wilhelm Tell*-passages that evoked unity and patriotism were particularly popular. But in 1941, Hitler banned the play from both the stage and school curricula because its recent reception had indicated a growing focus on the play's depiction of separatist tendencies and, especially, tyrannicide.[83] Increasing numbers of individuals among cinema and theater audiences had been reported to start clapping the moment that Tell's arrow finally pierces Gessler's cruel heart, and Armgart, a poor mother of seven cheers: 'Dead, dead! He reels, he falls! ... Look children! This is how a tyrant dies!'

Literature as Mass Entertainment

Mass entertainment based on popular plays such as Arno Holz and Oskar Jerschke's *Traumulus* that turned the 1904 naturalistic tragicomedy into an educational narrative for a 'steeled' youth needed for the future (1935), or Heinrich Spoerl's and Hans Reimann's *Wenn wir alle Engel wären* [If We All Were Angels] (1936), both directed by Carl Froelich, proved to Reichsminister Goebbels that the most effective propaganda was subtle and entertaining. On March 5, 1937, Goebbels instructed German filmmakers at their first annual meeting that it was their responsibility to create art in the most 'modern' of all mass media. But at the same time their art had to serve the 'education of the people'. Interestingly, he clearly distinguished during his speech between feature films, documentaries, and newsreels. Only feature films were in fact responsible for the ideological education of the nation, he argued. One had to use subtle methods, however, because, as Goebbels told the filmmakers:

> The moment propaganda is noticeable as such, it loses effect. But if it remains in the background as propaganda, as a tendency, a character, as mind-set, and only becomes apparent through people, plot, sequence of events, basic statement, it will be effective in every respect. [84]

The film industry as the most popular mass medium has to provide 'inspiration and thrust'. Goebbels' objective was 'to win over the entire nation for the new state'. This was, he emphasized, the 'paramount responsibility of his ministry' and, therefore, of the German film industry.

Nazi ideology and support of autocratic leadership was clearly communicated via adaptations of texts by Nazi authors—such as, for example, Hans Heinz Ewers' *Horst Wessel* (Franz Wenzler, 1933) or Hans Rothe's radio play *Verwehte Spuren* (Veit Harlan, 1938)—as well as by 'Blood and Soil' adaptions of literary works by, for example, bestselling Austrian author Richard Billinger, such as the popular *Die goldene Stadt* [The Golden City] (1942, directed by the most prolific of Nazi filmmakers Veit Harlan and filmed as one of the first Agfa-colored features of the era). Walter von Molo's trilogy about Frederick the Great (*Fridericus Rex*, 1918–21) not only won praise by monarchists during the Weimar Republic but also was brought to cinema screens already in 1923 under the direction of Arzén von Cserépy as *Sanssouci* and, shortly after, the sequel *Schicksalswende* [Change of Fortune]. Here Otto Gebühr played the Prussian king for the first time, which was to become his recurring role on film. On February 8, 1937, *Fridericus* or *Der alte Fritz* [Old Fritz], directed by Johannes Meyer, premiered at Berlin's Ufa-Palast am Zoo.

One the Nazi film industry's most infamous directors, Veit Harlan, also emphasized the theme of autocratic leadership in his adaptation *Der Herrscher* [The Ruler] (1937), based on Gerhard Hauptmann's *Vor Sonnenuntergang* (Before Sunset, 1889). Here, Hauptmann's radically naturalistic play about generational conflict, alcoholism, milieu, and the difficulty of leading a good, principled life is turned into a persuasive presentation of the unflinching responsibility of a true, unselfish *Führer* for his national community.[85] The film's populist rhetoric combines values such as community and love with a vigorous resentment of lazy and apathetic capitalists and other 'fat cats', who must be removed, and leadership that is verbally associated with genius and visually with steel. Emil Jannings plays this 'inspired' industrial leader, who personifies unbending determination, and quotes almost verbatim from Hitler's 1934 decree directed at the "Deutsche Arbeitsfront" or 'German workers' front' commanding each individual to absolute loyalty toward their executive.[86] Those that remain are fully committed to submit to the will of the ruler and to serving the "Volksgemeinschaft" or national community, no matter the sacrifice. The film fulfills its purpose, as outlined by Goebbels above, with absolute efficiency.[87]

Emil Jannings who stars in Harlan's *Der Herrscher* also rooted for a screen adaptation of Heinrich von Kleist's canonical comedy *Der zerbrochene Krug* (The Broken Jug, 1808), having been celebrated in the role of Judge Adam many times on the theatre stage. In addition, Ufa had invested heavily in a previous adaptation based on Kleist (as well as on Plautus, Molière, and of course, Greek mythology): *Amphitryon—aus den Wolken kommt das Glück* [Amphitryon, happiness comes from the clouds]. Written and directed by Reinhold Schünzel, the project had not only been a very profitable project for Schünzel himself, but was filmed in multiple languages in 1935, aiming for international success, and making it Ufa's most expensive production of the year. And while many, like Thomas Mann, considered the adaptation quite 'juvenile'[88] and its success was no more than respectable, Jannings was determined to appear as Kleist's Judge Adam on cinema screens.

Goebbels, however, was unsure of the project from the start. On July 15, 1937, he wrote in his diary:

Jannings wants to make a film of the Broken Jug. In Kleist's language. A very risky project. But Jannings will be careful. I refuse to give it 200,000 Mark in advance. Kimmich has written the screenplay. It's not bad at all.

Gustav Ucicky was put in charge of the film, but after the premiere in October 1937 Goebbels commented in his diary: 'This is filmed theater, but no film art. Jannings didn't want to listen to my advice. He will have to face a great fiasco. He has to work hard and do well in order to make up for this.'[89] In light of this 'great fiasco' Jannings was obliged to deploy his enormous popularity more 'effectively' in national-socialist propaganda films such as *Ohm Krüger* (1941). Hitler himself, however, liked Ucicky's *Der zerbrochene Krug* and asked for it to be screened when, as Niven puts it, he was "in a bad mood."[90]

Fairy Tales as Mass Entertainment

By 1937 Hitler's government had seized full ownership of Ufa and the canon of German-language literature. Even the fairy tales collected by the brothers Grimm (*Kinder- und Hausmärchen*, 1812–58) were designated as vehicles for propaganda purposes. Perfectly suited in their doubled function as entertainment and education of children, fairy tales communicate danger and introduce forces of unknown evil, while representatives of the current regime are placed front and center as caring guardians not only of the younger members of society. *Rotkäppchen und der Wolf* (1937), Fritz Genschow's adaptation of the Grimm version of the well-known *Little Red Riding Hood*-fairy tale, for example, reveals the subtle means of manipulation directed at the youngest among German-speaking cinema audiences. The forty-minute Tobis-film features a black-and-white framing narrative in which little Liesel (Eva-Marianne Müller) dreams the fairy tale, which is then presented in color using Agfa-Biback-technology (a two-tone system), thereby embedding the color adaptation of the fairy-tale within a black and white NS-reality. This innovative visual mode of separating everyday life and fantasy by use of color anticipated the famous adaptation of L. Frank Baum's children's book *The Wizard of Oz* (US, Victor Fleming, 1939), but had been a trend in especially musical film production in the United States since *The Broadway Melody* in 1929.

In *The Wizard of Oz*, of course, it is a tornado rather than a dream that whirls Dorothy and her little dog Toto from her black-and-white quotidian life of the 1930s in Kansas into an Agfa-colored, sparkling dream world or land of Oz. But unlike Judy Garland, Eva-Marianne Müller is forgotten; Genschow's (ab)use of the *Little Red Riding Hood* story for propaganda purposes ensured that this fairy tale film was never screened after the end of Hitler's reign. At first glance, the dream narrative does not deviate from the narrative structure and content of the fairy tale in the Grimm-collection. The figure of the hunter, however, is worth a closer look.

Played by Fritz Genschow himself, the hunter not only saves the grandmother from being digested by the Big Bad Wolf, but also frees cute, innocent little Rotkäppchen from the beast's protruding belly. Without hesitation, the young girl calls their savior "Onkel Jäger" underscoring familiarity and trust. Having rescued them from certain death at the last minute and thereby ensuring the tale's happy end, the hunter's courage,

FIGURE 6.3 *Fritz Genschow as cheerful hunter in uniform in* Rotkäppchen *(DE, Fritz Genschow, 1937)*.

resoluteness, and dedication are undisputed. His uniform is adorned with the Reich's eagle and swastika, symbols clearly identifying this friendly and heroic 'Uncle' as representative of the Nazi state. Heartfelt expressions of gratitude by Little Red Riding Hood and her granny are mirrored in the framing narrative, when the same actor now appears as a policeman in a

1930s German town, who saves a little girl (also played by Eva-Marianne Müller) who had clearly underestimated the dangers of modern automobile traffic. Again, and this time in her contemporary Nazi Germany 'reality', Liesel is saved, because of the swift action of this very astute and effective policeman. No matter if fairy tale fiction or Reich reality, the film tells its young viewers that those adorned with the insignia of Hitler's Reich are reliably ensuring Liesel's and, by implication, the Aryan nation's protection.

This adaptation is only one of more than twenty fairy tale adaptations by the Nazi film industry, with an explicit brief of "Volkserziehung," i.e., education of the youngest of Hitler's subjects. The framing narrative of the *Little Red Riding Hood* film not only situates the Grimm brothers' fiction in 1930s Germany, but also addresses the naiveté of individuals who underestimate the risks that are supposedly threatening their livelihoods. The symbolic use of traffic and its youngest and most innocent of potential victims places the representative of Nazi authority in an utterly positive light and emphasizes his position of utmost importance. Without him, Liesel and all her Volksgenossen would be toast, the film tells its viewers, so calmly trust in the uniformed representatives of the state for your own benefit and safety. Hubert Schonger, an equally enthusiastic fairy tale filmmaker, who directed, among others, *Hänsel und Gretel* (1940, starring the young Gunnar Möller as Hänsel), *Das tapfere Schneiderlein* [The Valiant Little Tailor] (1941), and *Die Bremer Stadtmusikanten* [Town Musicians of Bremen] (1942/43), stated in a 1938 interview with *Film-Kurier*: 'Every fairy tale can be given a political spin without violating the original text.' The political mission of fairy tale films produced by the Nazi film industry was not only to induce trust in authority but to militarize German youth by presenting uniformed heroes as models of masculinity and ideal Germanness.

Sudermann, Rothe, and Rhon on Nazi Film

The majority of films based on German-language literature served the purpose of mass entertainment and were not overtly political, such as Otto Ernst Hesse and Hans Brennert's adaptation of Hermann Sudermann's hugely popular, melodramatic play *Heimat* [home/homeland] while nonetheless communicating a subtext of loyalty and rootedness. Harald Braun wrote the script and Carl Froelich directed the film that premiered in the Ufa-Palast in (today's Polish) port-city Danzig on June 25, 1938; a second Berlin premiere took place in the capital on September 1. Implicitly marking Gdańsk as *Heimat* or home, Zarah Leander plays single mother Magda von Schwartze who returns to her hometown after years of absence as a musical celebrity Maddalena dall'Orto. After a number of highly emotional encounters and difficult conversations the trauma of past wrongs is lifted and she reconciles with her father (played by Heinrich George), finally deciding to make her "Heimat" once again her and her daughter's home.

How the protection of the national community and their *Heimat* warrants even morally or legally dubious actions was the implicit message of *Verwehte Spuren* (Scattered Tracks, 1938), once again directed by Veit Harlan. Based on the radio play by Hans Rothe, the film tells the story of young Séraphine (Kristina Söderbaum) who searches for her mother in Paris after her disappearance without trace, turning a promising holiday into a traumatic ordeal. When the girl is finally informed of her mother's death due to the plague, she readily understands that suppression of the press, cover-up of facts, and elimination of the nameless dead were unavoidable and entirely in the nation's interest. Veit Harlan, ever the loyal and subservient director, followed his *Führer*'s lead, who wrote in *Mein Kampf*:

> Every propaganda must be down-to-earth, its intellectual level must be adjusted to the mental capacity of the most dull-witted among those it is to address. The larger the mass of people to which it directs itself, the lower its purely intellectual level must be gauged. It cannot be emphasized enough that in the event of creating propaganda to promote the perseverance of the people in times of war for instance, which is intended to bring an entire nation under its spell, it is absolutely essential to carefully avoid high intellectual expectations. [...] Propaganda must not only examine the truth, insofar as it is advantageous to the others, and be fed to the masses with doctrinaire sincerity, but it must also consistently serve one's own interests.[91]

When another adaptation of Hermann Sudermann's novella *Die Reise nach Tilsit* (The Journey to Tilsit, 1917) premiered in Tilsit (today part of the Kaliningrad Oblast in Russia) and Berlin in November 1939, Veit Harlan's film encouraged anti-Polish sentiments only weeks after the invasion of Poland by German troops. The male protagonist's mistress is here changed into an unscrupulous Polish woman, who is identified as a threat to the married couple and all Christian values. Already the opening sequence identifies the villain of this piece: 'Do you know that the Polish woman is back again?' asks a well-meaning friend. The pretty, blond, and seemingly immaculate wife (played by Harlan's now young wife Kristina Söderbaum) pales visibly as she names her competition: 'The Sabierska?'—'Yes, the Sabierska, the slut.' The designation could not be simpler, the juxtaposition of good and evil, family/familiar and alien, life and death not clearer. The Polish woman's selfishness and destructive energy dominate almost the entire narrative of the film. Sabierska openly and confidently tells the faithful and modest wife that she 'would never give up Hendrik', i.e., the other's husband. This Polish *femme fatale* is ruthless, without pity, self-centered, and strong-willed. Finally, the wife's father intervenes: 'We are not used to allowing

FIGURE 6.4 Der Fuchs von Glenarvon *(DE, Max W. Kimmich, 1940)*.
Source: Deutsche Kinemathek, Berlin.

someone to take away our honor', he says and hits her across the face with a whip. A female bystander exclaims enthusiastically: 'That's a real man at last!' thereby marking masculinity in the context of a constructed necessity of force against any threat to one's home and value system, in this case personified by 'vermin from Poland'. Anti-Polish propaganda rhetoric remains an undercurrent throughout the entire film, which rendering the melodramatic adaptation deeply political. Contrary to Sudermann's literary text, Harlan's film ends happily as the couple prevails in its fight to preserve their family and home.[92] This adaptation, distributed across the Reich, could not have been a more effective rallying cry as German troops were marching through Poland and another war began to engulf Europe.

Joseph Goebbels' brother-in-law Max W. Kimmich also supported the war effort by filming an adaptation of Nicola Rhon's novel *Der Fuchs von Glenarvon* (The Fox of Glenarvon, 1937), based on the screenplay Wolf Neumeister and Hans Bertram in 1939. Set in 1884 in the west of Ireland, the screenwriters turned "Nicola Rhon's affirmation of the Anglo-Irish order into a vehement critique of the British," as Eoin Bourke summarizes. Their adaptation of Rhon's popular crime novel foregrounds the threat of the British oppressors in the context of the Irish people's fight for independence. The audience is guided in focusing their sympathy on "Ireland, the Emerald Isle" as "one of the oldest victims of English tyranny."[93] The melodramatic vehicle is, once again, a love story starring 'State Actress of the Third Reich'[94] Olga Tschechowa, Karl Ludwig Diehl, and—as the evil oppressor—Ufa's "all-purpose alien"[95] Ferdinand Marian. The cover of *Illustrierter Filmkurier* announcing the film depicts Marian with a union jack superimposed on his face, hovering threateningly above the weary lovers.[96]

The Literary Canon on Film: Theodor Fontane

Theodor Fontane's novel *Effi Briest* (1894–5) is not only the most famous exploration of adultery and victimhood in German-language literature, but also one of the greatest German-language prose texts of the nineteenth century, and one of the most widely read German novels in the world. Of course, Fontane's *Zeitroman,* which critically foregrounds social and moral conventions of the time, had to be incorporated into the Nazi's entertainment industry. *Der Schritt vom Wege* [The False Step], directed by Gustaf Gründgens in 1938/9, is based on a screenplay by Georg C. Klaren and Eckart von Naso. The change of title from *Effi Briest* to *The False Step* (or, literally, the step away from the path) could be interpreted as a direct reference to the adaptive process, to a play-within-a-play,[97] but also as moral judgment. While the opening credits unmistakably identify the source of the film plot as 'based on the novel *Effi Briest* by Theodor Fontane', the opening of this first *Effi Briest*-adaptation differs significantly from Fontane's text. The film does not begin with a description of the Briest estate, nor does it depict the mother and daughter busy with their embroidery; it does not show seventeen-year-old Effi on her swing with childlike exuberance, but instead opens with a close-up of Effi's gravestone. As the camera moves away, the Briest's family dog Rollo becomes visible lying on the grave as well as Effi's parents (played by Paul Bildt and Käthe Haack), quietly sitting together on a bench. The novel's conclusion constitutes the narrative framework for the film, and the question of guilt, which thus dominates the beginning and end of the adaptation, is clearly emphasized. In this initial sequence, Briest, the father, declares as an irrefutable fact: 'We are not quite as much, as we believe.' And Mother Briest adds: 'Not a day goes by when I don't blame myself.'

This opening scene's declaration of moral bankruptcy and helplessness transforming 'questions'[98] into self-reproaches is followed by military music, which establishes an acoustic bond between the framing narrative defined by loss, guilt, and death and the actual film plot, which is told as flashback. Soldiers march past the Briest's estate while the girlish young Effi is on her swing, suggestive of her childlike playfulness. Swinging higher and higher, her exuberance emphasizes Effi's depiction by Fontane as a 'child of nature'.[99] The juxtaposition of elated play and the dull order of the military might be too implicit, but the association of blame and death with the military cannot be overlooked due to the various visual and auditory denotations. Effi is presented as a young teenager in the novel who marries the much older Baron Innstetten (Karl Ludwig Diehl) under pressure from her mother, because she wants to be seen as acting prudently within the confines of her class and according to social expectations and her own ambitions. The film follows the major narrative strands of the literary source and uses numerous dialogues verbatim. As in the novel, Effi suffers under the sinister atmosphere in her new home and the boredom in her marriage, but in contrast, her friend and local pharmacist Gieshübler (Max Gülstorff), 'aesthete and exceptional character' and 'kind human soul' here is not disabled by kyphosis. Also, Crampas (Paul Hartmann), her soon-to-be lover, is officially introduced to Effi without his military title of 'Major'. He appears in civilian attire of a bourgeois, since the portrayal of an officer behaving 'dishonorably' by seducing the wife of a state official would have been as unacceptable in Germany 1939 as the casting of a 'disabled person' in a positive role, and might have put the film project in jeopardy.

As in the literary source, repressive norms extend as far as the natural environment, and their apparent polarity captured, for example, by panorama shots of the sea juxtaposed with close-up of a sign bearing Innstetten's signature that prohibits access to the beach, reveals any hope for natural self-determination as illusion. The soundtrack emphasizes the significance of this moment with a pause or fermata, when extradiegetic, symphonic background music, underscoring the drama of the narration throughout the film, is almost reduced to silence. The confrontation of nature/emotion/ rebellion (individual identity) with society/convention/adjustment (social norm) as conceptual opposites structures the adaptation's cinematography, repeatedly emphasizing the incompatibility of freedom with subjugation, entrapment, and exclusion.[100] Effi's growing disappointment with married life, which she communicates occasionally by brief sulks, is juxtaposed with a close-up of the image of the 'Chinaman' sculpture in a cross-fade. It seems to nod and laugh at Effi maliciously while regarding her dissatisfaction as a well-deserved result of her social conformity. The extradiegetic music is increasingly charged with menace, and the occasionally clichéd images of natural scenes heighten the sense of imminent danger to the young woman.

Aesthetically the film reimagines nature in total or panoramic shots, for example during Effi's and Crampas' riding expeditions along the seashore, in reference to other Nazi-adaptations of German literature like the aforementioned *Schimmelreiter* or Max Halbe's *Jugend* (Veit Harlan, 1938). But Gründgens also uses nets symbolizing the danger of love entanglements as a visual reference to Josef von Sternberg's banned Heinrich Mann adaptation *The Blue Angel* (1930). Revolutionary playwright Heinrich von Kleist's *Käthchen von Heilbronn,* which was staged repeatedly in the 1930s at the State Theatre in Berlin under Gründgens' artistic direction, is here the play performed by Effi and Crampas, rather than Ernst Wichert's *Ein Schritt vom Wege* [A Step from the Path] in the novel. The film largely follows the plot of the novel when her digression from the 'path of virtue' is discovered by Innstetten years after their move to Berlin, but its more explicit polarization of Innstetten and Crampas marks death as a consequence of transgression. Effi's daughter Annie is kept from her mother following the divorce, and their reencounter highlighting their estrangement is followed by Effi's collapse. Her disgust with herself, but even more with 'your virtue!' is highly melodramatic. Effi is the victim almost throughout this adaptation. Action is reserved for men, and they fail spectacularly. The narrative concludes when Innstetten, who describes himself as a 'fool', receives news of his promotion and of Effi's death simultaneously. This juxtaposition of a successful career with a death notice highlights the tragedy of the fatal ambition-driven decisions by the two main protagonists.

Various changes provide evidence of the film's time and place of production. Especially striking, however, are two absences: the omission of the two most famous quotes from the novel referring to the "Angstapparat aus Kalkül" [the instrument/apparatus designed to instill fear], and the "tyrannisierenden Gesellschafts-Etwas" [social something which tyrannizes us].[101] Both references could have been understood as systemic criticism of the National Socialist dictatorship and were obligingly erased by Gründgens and his screenwriters.[102] Nonetheless, *Der Schritt vom Wege* avoids overt forms of affirmation of national-socialist ideology, especially when compared to other adaptations by the NS-film industry of canonical literature. Gründgens—who told Günter Gaus in a 1963 interview, he 'was not born to live against something', and that for him, the Nazi era was entirely void of 'reality'[103]—had allowed himself to be co-opted by the Hitler regime and integrated into the official culture industry for the sake of his career.

While Gründgens' potential disgruntlement with the political leadership could be interpreted as discernible, the film also complies with the expectations of Goebbels and his ministry. It presents high culture as both German and masculine while, for example, the performance of a French love song is depicted as vulgar.[104] Dualisms and polarities, which structure the film, are largely taking their cues from the novel. But Fontane's social criticism, which would have been quite apposite after six years of Nazi rule, especially with regard to a tyrannical apparatus instilling fear, is only present as an absence. Effi's misery and death tacitly become its substitute. Not surprisingly, none of the film critics dared to mention this blatant absence of Fontane's famous identification of the core of repressive structures, but rather praised the film's fidelity to the novel.[105] Especially Marianne Hoppe, who had married Gründgens in 1936 in order to protect both of them from persecution due to their respective bisexuality and homosexuality, and whose portrayal of Effi was understated and sensitive, was showered with praise. This adaptation of one of the most revered novels in the German language was a remarkable box-office success. The film cannot hide its compliance with the ideological and political framework set up by Goebbels and his ministry for the Nazi film industry, but also seems to struggle with its own conformity and support of the regime's official line.

Gründgens was one of the most well-known and respected theater and film actors during the Weimar Republic and the Hitler regime. He had starred as head of the underworld in Fritz Lang's *M* (1931), alongside Wolfgang Liebeneiner in Ophuls' *Liebelei* (1933), in the French- and German-language versions of Kurt Bernhardt's *Tunnel* (1933), but also in *Das Mädchen Johanna* (1935) and, to name just one more, as comedic performer Debureau, who takes on the French king over a woman and for a laugh in Hans Steinhoff's *Tanz auf dem Vulkan* [Dance on a Vulcano] in 1938.

The latter picture closes with Debureau's death sentence as the people rise up against tyranny. One of the songs here performed by a broadly smiling Gründgens mentions the 'men in their catacombs considering building bombs and whispering rebellion.'[106] Another comedic depiction of resistance against authority was the adaptation of Heinrich Spoerl's 1936 best-selling novel *Der Maulkorb* [The Muzzle] under the direction of Erich Engel. Both *Tanz auf dem Vulkan* and *Maulkorb* were greatly popular and could be read as implicit challenges to the Nazi leadership or calls to rebellion. But Hitler enjoyed great popularity among the Aryan masses at the time, and the Nazi regimes' confidence was at an all-time high—boosted by Hitler's enthusiastic welcome in Austria and the nation's "Anschluss" or incorporation into his 'German Reich' in 1938, the passivity of other nations despite the Nazi's disregard for basic human rights of its own citizens, its defiance of the Treaty of Versailles, and invasion of other countries. Clearly, a self-assured and seemingly all-powerful leadership felt it could join in the laughter of its subjects. This changed, of course, once German troops had attacked Poland in September 1939, thereby making another world war inevitable.

Friedrich Schiller at (World) War

But even a year later, a degree of ambivalence or even criticism could be carefully pushed past the censors by adapting the literary canon, with Schiller serving as the Trojan horse of choice. Goebbels had demanded more political films—'Less shallow entertainment. Enough of that!'—and the minutes of a Tobis Film executive board meeting[107] give evidence of a decidedly political intention behind a planned Schiller film now that Germany was at war. Herbert Maisch was absolutely delighted to be offered *Rebellen* [Rebels], the original title of the film, as he recounts in his autobiography.[108] He had established himself as successful and productive director not only of mostly light-hearted features and melodramas with works such as *Königswalzer* [King's Waltz] (1935), *Liebeserwachen* [Awakening of Love] (1936), *Boccaccio* (1936), *Starke Herzen* [Strong Hearts] (1937), and the Carmen-adaptation *Andalusische Nächte* [Andalusian Nights] (1938), but also directed films with a strong political subplot such as *Menschen ohne Vaterland* [People without Homeland] (1937)[109] or *D III 88* (1939), and was considered politically reliable. Nonetheless, Maisch's *Friedrich Schiller—Der Triumph eines Genies* [Friedrich Schiller. A Genius' Triumph] (1940), which is at the same time an adaptation of Schiller's famous play *Die Räuber* [The Robbers] as a paratext, raised some eyebrows in the Ministry for Propaganda.[110]

The film flaunts an all-star cast which includes the young and famous theater actor Horst Caspar as Friedrich, Hannelore Schroth as his love interest Laura, Heinrich George as Duke Karl Eugen von Württemberg, *Caligari*'s Lil Dagover as gentle and benevolent Franziska von Hohenheim, and Paul Dahlke as Feldwebel Rieß. Bernhard Minetti stars as Franz Moor in the premiere of Schiller's first play in Mannheim toward the end of the diegesis. The script was written by Walter Wassermann and C.H. Diller (the pen name of actress Lotte Neumann) based on an idea by Hans Josef Cremers, as well as on the novel *Leidenschaft* [Passion] and the exposé *Der Tyrann* [The Tyrant] by Norbert Jacques.[111] According to Maisch, the original title *Rebellen* was changed to *Friedrich Schiller—Der Triumph eines Genies* to ensure that the public realized that the film suggested Adolf Hitler as Schiller's successor and total genius, rather than a rebellion against Nazi rule. To guarantee that the audience would not rather identify Hitler with the unjust and brutal dictator Carl Eugen of the film, who was driving good people into exile, Maisch was ordered to cut the last word of the film: "Freiheit!" [Freedom] which the escapee whispers to his friend after having successfully fled to the neighboring country.[112]

Critics and scholars are divided when it comes to interpreting the film: is it merely an 'interesting episode from cultural history'; or is the depiction of Schiller's 'struggle with his time' to be read as a protest against tyranny and as an outcry against the lack of artistic freedom in Nazi Germany? Or does the representation of the Reich's 'Godfather' indeed amount to a politically effective propaganda vehicle? Erwin Leiser's documentary film *Deutschland, erwache!* [Germany, Awake!] (1968) considers Maisch's representation of Schiller clearly as that of a predecessor to Adolf Hitler. In his view, the director is at pains to foreground Schiller as a dazzling *Übermensch* who stands, by implication, above the law. Leiser's interpretation is partly based on Maisch's own description of Goebbels' minimal intervention during the making of the film and the director's opportunistic collaboration with the Nazis. In hindsight, it is difficult to believe that even a 1940s audience would identify Schiller with their self-proclaimed *Führer* Adolf Hitler.

In contrast to committed Nazi filmmakers such as Veit Harlan, Maisch's *Schiller*-film can be considered another example of a determined cinema of ambivalence or of *lavieren*, i.e., a safe maneuvering within a given restrictive framework filled with compromise, ensuring compliance and sufficient interpretative flexibility at the same time. Maisch's 1940 film opens with medium and long shots of soldiers on horseback wearing the uniforms of the eighteenth-century Duchy of Württemberg. They lead four shackled prisoners who struggle to remain on their feet, stumbling and running behind the easy gait of the riders who drag them along with ropes. The scene is rapidly cut, yet repetitive, and the four captives are dragged through the film frame several times. While these images clearly emphasize repression and violation, the camera remains at a distance and never rests on the faces of these maltreated figures. The soldiers and the prisoners are symbols of power and the absence thereof, respectively, indicating the hierarchy of terror in a totalitarian state. Maisch introduces these images of callousness and violence casually, spending little time on detail. No reason for the forced march is given, as if this were of minor importance in a country in which human rights violations are daily occurrences.

This opening sequence illustrating oppression and tyranny cuts to a long shot of five well-dressed gentlemen entering a tavern where the first words spoken in the film can be heard: 'Violence, destruction, pain and suffering, that's the glorious life which the Duke has in store for his country. [...] But things must change and they will change. I can feel it [...]: a storm is brewing!'[113] The voice belongs to Christian Friedrich Daniel Schubart (played by Eugen Klöpfer), who managed to flee Württemberg, but who would be lured back and arrested in Blaubeuren shortly after this defiant proclamation.[114] Enraged by Schubart's revolutionary articles and poems against autocratic rulers in general and the bully of Württemberg in particular, the Duke Karl Eugen had the poet incarcerated at Hohenasperg. By opening his film with Schubart rather than Schiller, Maisch sets the tone of the biopic and also hints at its purpose. In this opening sequence, Schubart drinks to the death of the tyrant and proclaims:

> Sound the horn to murder and death, you will be overcome, too! Build your injustices into a mountain of suffering, but at some point, you will die, too! Cover yourself in gloss and false gleam, but you cannot fool eternity! Only curses, tears, and hatred are yours, and terrible will be your judgment!

Schubart is introduced as Schiller's mentor, which is historically correct, his letters providing ample evidence of his love and admiration for the young poet.[115] He shared Schiller's understanding of the importance of freedom[116] as basic human need and the source of human dignity. Both poets were opposed to absolutism and, therefore, faced censorship, incarceration, and exile. Schubart, however, experienced the power of a totalitarian regime to a greater degree, spending ten years of his life imprisoned at Hohenasperg (1777–87)[117] while Schiller managed to escape the clutches of his "Landesvater." Indeed, Herbert Maisch's biopic of Friedrich Schiller (played by Horst Caspar) ends with the poet's escape from Württemberg together with his friend Andreas Streicher on the evening of September 22, 1782. The idea of freedom forms the core of the film, just as it permeated Schiller's understanding of nature, human reason, and dignity. At first glance, the concept of freedom, as it is represented in this film, remains vague and open to interpretation, and it seems that ambiguities are deliberately created and employed in order to ensure an apparent compliance of the film with the Nazi leaders' expectations.

The narrative focus on Maisch's biopic is on a young Schiller, whose passion for the art of writing, for poetry, and philosophy clashes with his forced education at the Hohe Karlsschule, the military academy in Stuttgart and the Duke of Württemberg's pet project. In the film, the Duke represents ultimate authority, but at the same time wishes to take on a paternal role for the promising boys and young men who are being trained to be the next generation of officers, doctors, and lawyers. The academy's structure is based on discipline and order, military drill, and categorical obedience. Predictably, there is no question of free speech or constructive criticism; open conversations are suppressed, books that do not pertain to the course of studies prescribed by the Duke himself are confiscated, and on the whole young minds are silenced and abused. In this atmosphere a desperate Schiller begins to resist and secretly writes his first drama *Die Räuber*. After its anonymous publication, Schiller attends a hugely successful premiere in Mannheim. Upon his return, he courageously faces the Duke and demands "Freiheit dem Geist, Freiheit dem Volk!," i.e., 'freedom of thought/speech/intellect, and freedom for the people!' It comes as no surprise that after this incident any reconciliation with the Duke fails and a prison sentence seems inevitable. Schiller chooses exile over prison and flees Württemberg. The film ends with his carriage crossing the border and traveling into the sunset—a conclusion that harks back to the opening sequence, Christian Friedrich Daniel Schubart, and the theme of freedom as a human right.

There are many similarities regarding the narrative and the cinematography of Maisch's 1940 film and the silent movie of 1923, *Schiller—Eine Dichterjugend* (Schiller, Youth of a Poet), directed by Curt Goetz. A number of scenes are almost identical in composition and mise-en-scène. Compared to *Friedrich Schiller—Der Triumph eines Genies*, however, Goetz's film lacks pathos; his depiction of Schiller (Theodor Loos) foregrounds the fragile physical constitution of the poet and portrays his illness as a result of the stress associated with the emotional encounter with his imprisoned hero Schubart on Hohenasperg. Maisch, in contrast, chooses to ignore biographical evidence and represents Schiller as the picture of health. In comparison to Götz's Schiller, Maisch's poet has undergone a transformation from the immature, weak genius to a truly visionary, if sensitive superhero. It is the poet rather than the Duke who possesses true authority. This is emphasized in most scenes that feature both Schiller and Duke Karl Eugen by the fact that it is Schiller who is regularly foregrounded and who dominates the film frame. Conflict only arises due to the Duke's efforts to contain and confine the poet's genius. Freedom from suppression becomes Schiller's main goal and drive. In hindsight, however, it may be tempting to interpret Schiller's strive for independence and liberation from a tyrannical ruler as the filmmaker's plea for an end to Hitler's dictatorial regime. Yet as the *Illustrierter Film-Kurier* clarified in 1940: 'Friedrich Schiller's vision, [...] was that there was something greater than the poor and rotting circumstances of his time. [...] And this ideal, which he believed in and for which he fought, was: Germany, one people, one country ("Vaterland").'[118]

Schiller is clearly the superior individual in Maisch's film. The Duke is called everything from a tyrant to a 'golden bull,' and when he visually enters the narrative for the first time, we see him in the center of the film frame, fat and sweaty, waddling along a magnificently decorated corridor. The camera only draws back once its focus is on Karl Eugen's big belly and his rather unattractive upper body fills the frame. Throughout the film, he is portrayed as an authoritarian, decadent pig. After Schiller's cursing of the Duke during his visit of the imprisoned and desperate Schubart, Maisch cuts from a profile shot of Schiller to a marble sculpture of a sitting male nude whose classical beauty resembles that of the poet. The sculpture is located in the Duke's dining room at his palace toward the left of the film frame, while on the right the shadow of a singing and drinking Duke dances on the wall. His physical attributes and behavior mirror the dictatorship portrayed. Karl Eugen is thus shown as merely a shadow of a ruler while Schiller is depicted as the true hero.

Maisch's Schiller film became one of the cornerstones of Goebbels' "Propaganda Aktion" in 1941 and 1942, when it was shown across the Reich and at the war front in mobile cinemas ("Tonbildwagen") together with antisemitic filth such as *Jud Süß*.[119] The ambivalent depiction of a just fight for freedom in Maisch's Schiller-film thus helped to sell a much more deadly message of racial purging. In 1941, 835 such mobile cinemas were in commission and sent into remote communities for propaganda purposes.[120] As the military crisis on the Eastern front deepened and the wider German public began to be directly affected by the war, entertainment for mass audiences was considered of utmost importance by the propaganda ministry, or, as Goebbels himself put it: 'Good humor is a military resource!'[121]

Although he claims in his autobiography not to have become part of Goebbels' "war-propaganda-machine,"[122] *Friedrich Schiller—Der Triumph eines Genies* was in fact in line with the political goals of Goebbels' propaganda apparatus. In Maisch's film, criticism remains implicit or goes underground: the 'rebels' listen to Schiller reading from Act V of his play *Die Räuber* (*The Robbers*) while hiding in a basement. The Duke and one of his officers, however, are aware of the rebellious ongoings and spy on them. They overhear Pastor Moser's words to Karl Moor[123]—

> 'Now do you really think that the Almighty will suffer a worm like you to play the tyrant in His world and to reverse all his ordinances? Do you think the nine hundred and ninety-nine were created only to be destroyed, only to serve as puppets in your diabolical game? Think it not! He will call you to account for every minute of which you have robbed them, every joy that you have poisoned, every perfection that you have intercepted.'[124]

This very part of *The Robbers* is evoked again toward the end of the film at the premiere of Schiller's play in Mannheim. But why did Maisch choose to present the same scene twice, a scene, furthermore, that was not actually performed in Mannheim in January of 1782 when only a shortened and somewhat less provocative version of Act V was staged? In his autobiography, Maisch voices his astonishment regarding the fact that both this 'forgery' and the cheers of the audiences in Berlin's cinemas that regularly accompanied this scene seemed to go unnoticed by Goebbels and his watchdogs.

The film is rife with ambiguities. During this time of repression, any participation in filmmaking meant working hand in hand with Hitler's henchmen, who were clear about their intentions. As Goebbels put it already in March 1933: 'We will not tolerate that those ideas that are currently being exterminated from this new Germany will return openly or somehow veiled.'[125] Peter Hoefer shed some light on the reception of the film after attending the YMCA screening in his POW camp, subsequently writing in the POW journal *Der Ruf*:

> 'We saw this movie in 1940 for the first time after its premiere and celebrated it as the Song of Songs to freedom. But how could one dare to stand up against tyranny, dictatorship, against the idea of the state, disguised, but nevertheless unequivocally? How does this make sense?' [If such a film could be screened], 'then surely much about the Nazi's terror is only gossip. They even recommended the film in the press. There could [therefore] be no doubt about the tolerance of the [Nazi] leadership.— That's what they wanted you and your opponents to believe. They let you call "freedom!" once with impunity in front of witnesses to camouflage all the "off-the-record" cases that ended up in concentration camps for the same reason.'[126]

Herbert Maisch continued his work for the Nazi regime until its collapse in 1945. Clearly an opportunist, he had evidently made a pact with the powers that were and directed two out of the three films on subjects identified by Goebbels as perfect for propaganda purposes: Bismarck, Schiller, and Ohm Krüger. The anti-British film *Ohm Krüger* (1941) can be read as a justification of genocide. The Night of Pogroms in November 1938 had been not only a turning point in regard to an increase of explicitly antisemitic attacks on Jewish citizens and synagogues in the German Reich, but also a move toward organized mass murder. The Nazi film industry produced a number of virulently antisemitic films in order to intensify the Germans' hatred and fear of the Jews—such as pseudo-documentary films like *Der ewige Jude* [The Eternal Jew] (1940) directed by Fritz Hippler, and the star-studded feature film *Jud Süß* [Jew Süss] (1940).

Adapting for Genocide and Final Victory: Veit Harlan

Following the aforementioned adaptations as well as *Maria, die Magd* [Maria, the maid] (1936) and *Das unsterbliche Herz* [The Undying Heart] (1939) based on trivial works by his father Walter, Veit Harlan turned to a particularly perfidious adaptation project, using Lion Feuchtwanger's phenomenally successful novel *Jud Süß* (1925) and his preceding *Jud Süß* play (1917). The source texts' Jewish exile author was shocked when reading about Harlan's latest endeavor in an article published in the NSDAP newspaper *Völkischer Beobachter* about the film's premiere at the Venice Film Festival, where the picture was enthusiastically received by the fascist press and awarded the Biennale's top prize, the Leone d'oro.[127] Realizing that the film must be an adaptation of his novel *Jud Süß* or *Power* (the title of Feuchtwanger's novel and Lothar Mendes' 1934 film in the United States), but one that blatantly perverted and reversed the intentions of his text, Feuchtwanger wrote an 'Open Letter to Seven Berlin Actors':

> I am reading in the *Völkischer Beobachter* that you starred in an award-winning *Jud Süß* film. The film unveils, the paper tells me, the true face of Judaism, its spine-chilling methods and devastating objectives. This is illustrated, for example, by showing how Jew Süss makes a young woman compliant by torturing her husband. In short, by adding a bit of Tosca. [...] You, gentlemen, have turned my novel *Power* (Jew Süss) into an obscenely antisemitic propaganda film in line with Streicher and his *Stürmer*.[128]

Even without having seen the film, Feuchtwanger had no doubt that Harlan and his collaborators had used his novel and adapted it to the purposes of Nazi propaganda. The synopsis of the film narrative provided in the review highlighted a perversion of the plot of Feuchtwanger's text that the author instantly recognized. He identifies the focal point of the distortion, when he refers to the desperate young woman and the sexual abuse she endures. She is, indeed, a prime example of the Nazis' ruthless misrepresentation, and her character, her rape, and tragic death prove the Nazis' deliberate abuse of the Jewish writer's work.[129] In the script of the 1940 film, written by Veit Harlan, Eberhard Wolfgang Möller, and Ludwig Metzger,[130] and slightly revised by Goebbels himself, not surprisingly, no mention of the Jewish author Lion Feuchtwanger is ever made. Nevertheless, the film features references to Feuchtwanger's play and novel that venture far beyond a mere link in history. Of course, Harlan and his team created an entirely negative and one-dimensional Josef Süß character that has nothing to do with Feuchtwanger but rather Nazi ideology formulated by anti-Semites such as Alfred Rosenberg, Hans Heinz Bader, or, indeed, Adolf Hitler.[131] The depiction of a power-hungry, ruthless, and determined Jew fit neatly into the Nazi's idea of a worldwide Jewish conspiracy that would cause the downfall of the Aryan race, which is the focus of films such as Fritz Hippler's aforementioned *The Eternal Jew* (1940) or Erich Waschneck's *Die Rothschilds* (The Rothschilds, 1940).

With Veit Harlan's film of the same year, the historical figure Süß Oppenheimer became the epitome of the threatening, ruthless Jew of antisemitic Nazi propaganda and perfect example of a carefully designed construction of deviance. Harlan's *Jew Süß* is probably the most infamous of all Nazi propaganda films and has been discussed by many scholars of this field.[132] The impetus for the film was given by both Lothar Mendes' 1934 adaptation of Feuchtwanger's *Jew Süß* novel discussed in the previous chapter, and the novel's phenomenal success. Lion Feuchtwanger's wife Marta refers to Mendes' film when asked about the Nazis' antisemitic version of *Jud Süß*:

> The Nazis had of course noticed this big success of the movie, and they thought that they would take advantage of it and also the success of the book. They made a movie and turned everything into the contrary. It was a very antisemitic movie, and the greatest actor, Werner Krauss, played I think four or five parts, each one more antisemitic than the other.[133]

As Marta Feuchtwanger infers, Goebbels, the crafty designer of the Nazis' politics of entertainment, was indeed aware of Lothar Mendes' 1934 adaptation of Lion Feuchtwanger's novel. He had arranged for a screening of Mendes' film during the pre-production phase of the Nazis' own version of *Jud Süß*. The audience included members of the production team, such as the director and scriptwriter Veit Harlan and the scriptwriter Ludwig Metzger.[134]

According to the film's designated director and eager supporter of the genocidal regime Veit Harlan, it was Goebbels who insisted that the Germans 'make their own version', since "Conrad Veidt, a German actor, has made an anti-German film in England on a German subject by the German classic writer Wilhelm Hauff."[135] While Feuchtwanger had read Hauff's 1827 novella, it is clear that Mendes' *Jew Süss* or *Power* is based on Feuchtwanger's novel, not Hauff's text. The spirit of Feuchtwanger's novel and Mendes' adaptation was diametrically opposed to the antisemitic core of Nazi ideology. While their representations of Joseph Süß Oppenheimer's marginalization, ambition, rise, and fall were critically motivated and contextualized by the early eighteenth-century historical figure's Jewishness, the focus of their representations was on a human being. Therefore, Goebbels was adamant that "a new film version had to be made."[136] His 'Ministry of Illusion'[137] oversaw the filming of *Jew Süss* in Berlin Babelsberg (Ufa studios) and in Prague (Barrandow atelier and Baroque castle Troja) from March to late June 1940 with a stellar cast that included Ferdinand Marian[138] (Jud Süß), Heinrich George (Herzog Karl Alexander), Werner Krauss (Rabbi Loew, Süß' assistant Levy, and other Jewish characters), Kristina Söderbaum (Dorothea Sturm), Eugen Klöpfer (her father, Landschaftskonsultent Sturm), Albert Florath (Obrist Röder), and Malte Jäger (Dorothea's fiancé Faber). Apart from Veit Harlan,[139] the actors Werner Krauss, Eugen Klöpfer, Heinrich George, and Albert Florath were well acquainted with Lion Feuchtwanger and had appeared in his *Jud Süß* play. Judging from his 'open letter' to these actors, Feuchtwanger was shocked when he learned that colleagues, men he had worked with in the past and who had all read, 'understood' and 'admired' his novel, would agree to participate in this antisemitic rendering of 'his' *Jud Süß*.[140] He had no doubt, however, that a hard-nosed entrepreneur such as Goebbels would not shy away from ignoring two-thirds of his book and 'nick' those elements suitable to augment antisemitic attitudes among the German people.[141]

Nazi propaganda films regularly emphasize the Jews' otherness and the Jewish race's threat to the German community.[142] In Harlan's film, Süß Oppenheimer changes his outward appearance, leaves the ghetto, and—masked as a Gentile—gains access to the community and the court. The journal *Der Film* (January 20, 1940) describes Ferdinand Marian's Süß Oppenheimer as 'the elegant financial advisor, the savvy politician, short: the disguised Jew.' In Harlan's adaptation Süß Oppenheimer's true skill is deceit, as he masquerades as a Christian gentleman, and all too quickly turns the Duke into a dependent puppet. Ruthlessly, Süß exploits and punishes the people, and, like a vampire, sucks the life spirit from the community. In the film, Marian's dark Jew Süss is placed early on in opposition to young, blond, healthy, and pure Dorothea Sturm (Kristina Söderbaum), who serves as a symbol of ideal womanhood[143] or as an Aryan version of Feuchtwanger's Tamar and Naemi in his play and novel. Süss accumulates fabulous riches and seemingly limitless power. It is not until he rapes the daughter of his political opponent Sturm that the exploited and suppressed community rises up against the 'ruthless parasite.' Only after this most violent transgression, the sullying and destruction of the symbol of purity, is he arrested, tried, and sentenced to death. Feuchtwanger's novel and Veit Harlan's film share a number of similarities—the characterization of Süß Oppenheimer as vain, ambitious businessman, the central female figure as ideal, the (attempted) rape and subsequent suicide as climax and turning point of the narrative—but also regarding the dialectics[144] of rejection and integration of the 'Other'. However, whereas Feuchtwanger depicts greed, vanity, and ambition as human weaknesses inevitably transpiring among both Jews and Gentiles, Harlan's film focuses entirely on the Jew as dangerous and recklessly underestimated threat. In a subversion of Feuchtwanger's novel and play, the ideal woman here is not Süss' adoring and adored daughter, but Süss's virgin victim, kind-hearted Dorothea Sturm, the symbol of Aryan purity and beauty.[145]

Following her death by suicide, her stone-faced husband carries her all the way to the castle, with an increasing number of citizens joining him—the wave of anger and rage against the Duke's Jewish advisor rising with

FIGURE 6.5 *Ferdinand Marian and Kristina Söderbaum in* Jud Süß *(DE, Veit Harlan, 1940).*

every step. The people of Stuttgart unite for the purpose of self-preservation and national renewal, Dorle's rape and death unambiguously signifying the imminent disintegration of their community. When an officer of the Duke's army appears, Faber apologizes for the commotion and clarifies: 'It's the Jew's doing' and gently lays his love's body down on the steps of the castle. The camera closes in on her face, resting on her 'ideal' form. For twelve long seconds the audience sees nothing but her lifeless, faultless features while Wolfgang Zeller's tragic score underlines the injustice of her untimely death. Twelve long seconds to clarify the Nazis' simple logic: it is time to act. When the officer proclaims: 'The Jew must be eliminated!', the masses enthusiastically shriek their approval.

Like all other propaganda films produced during the Hitler era, this film contributed to the maintenance of the *Volksgemeinschaft,* the community of German-speaking, Aryan people theoretically united under the colors of the Nazi flag, by "reverberation and of ethnic distinction"[146] as Werner Sollers put it. As others have stated, the Nazis' idea of this particular community emerged as a symbolic product after the 'humiliation of Versailles' and economic disaster, metaphorically evoking the bleeding, broken bodies that emerged from the Great War. The Nazis' idyllic suggestion of strength, beauty, youth, and health—personified by Dorothea Sturm in Harlan's film—contrasted the hardship and demise of the politically and economically weak and unstable Weimar era. Leni Riefenstahl manifests this celebration of the strong and healthy body in her propagandistic *Triumph des Willens* [Triumph of the Will] (1935) and her 1936 Olympic games films. In 1940, Veit Harlan suggests the Jew's deadly threat to this symbolic body, and was instrumental in evoking fear of the Jews' supposed detrimental, corrupting effects on the symbolic Aryan community.

In this vile and aggressively antisemitic propaganda film blood is, in the end, the measure of difference, and its purity declared imperative to the definition, containment, and protection of the *Volksgemeinschaft.* The film's message is entirely in line with Hans Heinz Bader's *Wir und die Anderen* [We and the Others] in which the Nazi ideologist outlines the threat of the 'racial elite.'[147] The German public at the time would have associated the title of the film predominantly with Feuchtwanger's bestseller, and even the font design of the 1940 *Filmkurier* announcing Veit Harlan's *Jud Süß* is virtually identical to the title design of the 1925/7 edition of Feuchtwanger's bestselling novel published by Drei Masken Verlag, implicitly marketing the film as adaptation of the bestseller so many Germans had enjoyed.

The mechanisms at work during the production of *Jud Süß* as cinematic entertainment and antisemitic propaganda illustrate the fanatical support for Hitler's ideology by some and the pragmatism of others working in the Nazi film industry. Individual (in)action, cowardly silences, and at the time perhaps seemingly minor compromises eventually lead to crimes before which, in the words of J.M. Coetzee, "our human understanding recoils in bewilderment."[148] Lion Feuchtwanger wished to "ameliorate the condition of mankind through literature."[149] Veit Harlan and his all too willing colleagues in the now fully aligned film industry[150] helped to prepare the ground for genocide.

While adaptations of the canon of German-language literature continued until the final collapse of Hitler's genocidal Reich in May 1945—such as *Das Fräulein von Barnhelm* (Hans Schweikart, 1940; based on Lessing's comedy *Minna von Barnhelm*, 1767) or *Kleider machen Leute* [Clothes Make People] (Helmut Käutner, 1940; based on 'motifs' of Gottfried Keller's 1874 novella and starring Heinz Rühmann and Hertha Feiler)—Harlan's 'kitschy adaptation' loosely based on Theodor Storm's novella *Immensee* as a star-studded 1943 color film sticks out. As Wiebke Strehl outlines, here *Heimat* or home becomes "Schutzraum," i.e., a sanctuary or otherwise protected space.[151] Once again, Harlan's wife Kristina Söderbaum is foregrounded as a model of a German woman; faithful and ready to sacrifice herself in order to safeguard the sanctity of her home. This is also the theme of Harlan's *Opfergang* (The Walk to the Sacrifice, 1944), a movie based on a short story by Rudof Binding. Kristina Söderbaum here stars as Aels, who—even as a seemingly independent amazon—is still willing to give up herself for a greater good. At the time, the Second World War made loss of life and loved ones an everyday occurrence, and Harlan once again contributed actively to the mass distribution of Nazi propaganda. In his film, death is marked as a restoration of order and sacrifice, and thus as a form of apotheosis. This narrative sustained the Nazi leadership while the devastating impact of the war was being felt both at the front and at home.[152]

The Nazis' early confidence regarding certain victory was beginning to show serious cracks, especially after the defeat at Stalingrad in January 1943, and Germans' support of the World War was dwindling, especially due to the frequent bombings and food shortages. Goebbels needed a film that would communicate the need for unity among all Germans, as he wrote in his diary,[153] no matter whether they fought at the front or tried to survive at home. In his mind, Germans had to persevere, and Paul Heyse's patriotic play *Colberg* (1865) about the small community now called Kołobrzeg in West Pomerania on the shore of the Baltic Sea seemed to provide the ideal plot. Kolberg's resistance in 1807 against Napoleon's troops became a widely revered David and Goliath tale in Prussian history and a founding myth that Goebbels intended to use for propaganda at this precarious and uncertain time, particularly in light of the Nazi's progressively ill-equipped army and Germany's often hungry and increasingly weary population. Goebbels personally ordered Heyse's play to be adapted for cinema and provided such generous funding via the state-owned Ufa that it exceeded all other previous productions of the past decade.[154] Goebbels instructed Harlan to make the film with an explicit aim to 'show that a people united at home and at the front can overcome all opposition.' Considering this film project 'spiritual warfare' in Agfacolor, Goebbels empowered Harlan to request support from the 'Wehrmacht, the State and the Party'.[155]

After films such as *Jud Süß*, Harlan was Hitler's and his propaganda minister's most trusted director. In 1941 he was given his own production team and in 1943 both himself and director and Ufa head of production Wolfgang Liebeneiner were awarded professorships. Both Heise's play and Harlan's film examine human nature in times of crisis, in this case during the city's siege by Napoleon's troops. Heyse's greatest literary success, this play features a strong female, Rose, and also investigates masculinity in its spectrum from weakness to strength. Rose's brother Heinrich is an ambivalent male hero, who is weak but rises to the challenge when the pressure is on and the home is threatened by a seemingly unassailable enemy. This depiction of human strength, both male and female, despite all odds and a clearly superior adversary provided the perfect narrative frame for a Nazi-*Volkssturm*- and perseverance film. The movie[156] premiered on January 30, 1945, the twelfth anniversary of the 'Machtergreifung'[157] both at the Western front in La Rochelle and in Berlin.[158]

In *Kolberg*'s opening credits, the audience is informed that the film 'was written in 1942'. This is either a mistake—or rather a deliberate lie that aims at distracting from Nazi Germany's defeat at Stalingrad and subsequent military calamities. In order to give a realistic picture of the impact of the siege on the city, a set depicting the center of Kolberg was recreated in Groß-Glienicke near Neu-Babelsberg. Kristina Söderbaum again played the female lead under her husband's direction. Other stars included Heinrich George, Paul Wegener, and Horst Caspar. The film's reception in Germany was, of course, supportive and placed the movie's narrative in the context of Germans' current war experience. The men's courage and determination are predictably hailed, and Maria's (Söderbaum) suffering in light of the loss of her beloved father (George) and brothers is indicative of her fidelity.[159] A reviewer in the Nazi paper *Völkischer Beobachter* delighted in the depiction of all this 'faithful bravery' and seems only too aware of the link between Heyse's play and this film made during a much more devastating war: 'On its own, the enemy all around, Germany fights then and now for her life and future.'[160] The historical fact of Kolberg's downfall once Napoleon's troops had defeated the Prussians was carefully omitted in both Heyse's patriotic play and its Nazi-adaptation.

Conclusion

Shortly after the collapse of Hitler's 'Reich', Theodor W. Adorno and Max Horkheimer published their *Dialectic of Enlightenment* (1947)[161] and in it offered a new interpretation of modern mass culture and the cultural industry. The aim of their groundbreaking work was not only to formulate a new critical theory in the aftermath of fascist totalitarianism, but to offer an analysis of the product 'culture' as such, as Adorno himself clarified in a radio speech which was aired in Germany in 1963. Their definition was in part based on the knowledge and experience of a culture industry shaped by Nazi ideology, and is especially relevant when analyzing adaptations produced in Germany between 1933 and 1945, that weave the familiar into a new fabric and produce a commodity of new and different quality.[162] Never in adaptation history in the context of German culture has this conscious leveling of aesthetic significance as formulated by Adorno been more evident than during the cinema of the Hitler era. As the political became the driving force in almost every collaborative adaptation process in the German film industry, its products provide ample prominent examples of narratives being shifted and shaped to fit a political purpose and promote a specific ideology. At the same time, most literary adaptations produced during the twelve years of National Socialist rule proved to be ambivalent enough so as not to appear as outright forms of propaganda. With the exception of Harlan's *Jud Süss*, most of the resulting films entertained first and foremost, while also nurturing the ground of a *völkisch*, masculine and martial ideology. Agfacolor—a significant investment at the time—underlines the consequence of German-language literature on film: nearly half of the thirteen color-features produced during the Hitler era were adaptations.[163] Adaptations of German-language literature by the Nazi's entertainment industry epitomize this flexibility of a cultural product, which is being consumed as apolitical, decades after the end of Germany's most devastating and heinous era—whether we consider the redefinition and repurposing of the *Heimat*-film-genre[164] or annual screenings of Hermann Weiss' 1944 adaptation of Heinrich Spoerl's *Die Feuerzangenbowle* [The Fire-Tongs Bowl] that has been providing 'timeless, cheerful escapism'[165] to millions of Germans every year around Christmas via public television—and continues to do so until the present day.

Notes

1 "Film [ist] eines der modernsten und weitreichendsten Mittel der Beeinflussung der Massen, die es überhaupt gibt." Goebbels to members of the 'Reichsfachschaft Film,' quoted in Hoffmann, "*Und die Fahne führt uns in die Ewigkeit.*" *Propaganda im NS-Film* (Frankfurt/M.: Fischer, 1988), 99.

2 "Jeder, der hören wollte, hat hören können. Jeder, der wissen will, muß wissen. Wer nicht hörte, wollte nicht hören, wer nicht weiß, will nicht wissen. Wer vergißt, will vergessen." Ernst Toller at the annual P.E.N. congress, Edinburgh, 1934. Toller, *Sämtliche Werke*, vol. 4.1, 348.

3 Quoted by Bill Niven in his *Hitler and Film: The Führer's Hidden Passion* (New Haven: Yale University Press, 2018), 9. Misch published his account *Der letzte Zeuge: Ich war Hitlers Telefonist, Kurier und Leibwächter* (Munich: Pendo, 2008).

4 Niven, *Hitler and Film*, 2.

5 For example, science fiction features such as *Gold*, filmed in both a French- and a German-language version in 1934 (under the direction of Austrian Karl Hartl) or another Kellermann adaptation *Der Tunnel* [The Tunnel] (DE/FR, Curtis Bernhardt, 1933). See also Nicholas Pronay, "Introduction," in *Propaganda, Politics and Film, 1918–45*, ed. N. Pronay and D. W. Spring (London: Macmillan, 1982), 14.

6 Niven, *Hitler and Film*, 2.

7 As Niven outlines, Hitler lost interest as defeat loomed from the battle at Stalingrad onwards. Cf. Niven, *Hitler and Film*, 7, and chapter 9 in his book. See also Eric Rentschler, *The Ministry of Illusion. Nazi Cinema and Its Afterlife* (Cambridge, MA: Harvard University Press, 1996); Lutz Koepnick, *The Dark Mirror. German Cinema between Hitler and Hollywood* (Berkeley: University of California Press, 2002).

8 Hake, "Lubitsch's Period Films," 82. Sabine Hake outlines this process beginning in the Weimar Republic that became a strategy during Hitler's reign. See also her article "The Münchhausen Complex: From Adaptation to Intermediality," *ILCEA* 23 (2015); https://doi.org/10.4000/ilcea.3310.

9 I consciously avoid the term "Third Reich" as it is tainted by fascist ideology. The announcement of "das dritte Reich" was an important element of Nazi propaganda as it declared their 'Reich' as legitimate heir and elevate Hitler's Germany to the level of the (1) the Holy Roman Empire (tenth century to 1806) and (2) the German Empire (1871–1918), thereby delegitimizing the (democratic) Weimar Republic as a viable state.

10 See Mary-Elisabeth O'Brien, *Nazi Cinema as Enchantment. The Politics of Entertainment in the Third Reich* (Rochester, NY: Camden House, 2004); Francis Courtade, *Geschichte des Films im Dritten Reich* (Munich: Hanser, 1975); Sabine Hake, *Popular Cinema of the Third Reich* (Austin: University of Texas Press, 2001); Hilmar Hoffmann, *Triumph of Propaganda: Film and National Socialism, 1933–1945*, trans. John Broadwin and Volker Berghahn (Oxford: Berghahn, 1996); Felix Moeller, *The Film Minister. Goebbels and the Cinema in the 'Third Reich'* (London: Menges, 2001); Robert C. Reimer, *Cultural History through a National Socialist Lens. Essays on the Cinema*

of Nazi Germany (Columbia, SC: Camden House, 2002); Rentschler, *The Ministry of Illusion*; Richard Taylor, *Film Propaganda. Soviet Russia and Nazi Germany* (New York: Tauris, 1998); Karl-Heinz Schoeps, *Literature and Film in the Third Reich* (Rochester, NY: Camden House, 2003); Linda Schulte-Sasse, *Entertaining the Third Reich: Illusions of Wholeness in Third Reich Cinema* (Durham: Duke University Press, 1996).

11 While scholars such as Sabine Hake (cf. *Popular Cinema of the Third Reich*, 2001) have in past criticized the close identification of Nazi film with fascist aesthetics and propaganda, adaptations of the literary canon produced during the Nazi era do in the vast majority of cases unveil ideological subtexts in careful comparative analyses. This is also true for a range of popular productions based on Hermann Sudermann, Ludwig Ganghofer, etc. Other notable appropriations of German-language literature include, to name but a few, Veit Harlan's *Jugend* (1938; based on Max Halbe's play), *Die Reise nach Tilsit* (1939; based on Hermann Sudermann's novel), Hans Schweikart's *Das Fräulein von Barnhelm* (1940; based on Lessing's *Minna von Barnhelm oder das Soldatenglück*), Harlan's *Jud Süß* (1940; based on Lion Feuchtwanger's play and novel) and *Kolberg* (1944), based on Paul Heyse's play. For further information see Karsten Witte, "How Nazi Cinema Mobilizes the Classics: Schweikart's *Das Fräulein von Barnhelm*," in *German Literature and Film*, ed. E. Rentschler, 103–16; Christiane Schönfeld, "Feuchtwanger and the Propaganda Ministry: The Transposition of Jud Süß from Novel to Nazi Film," in *Feuchtwanger and Film*, ed. Ian Wallace (London: Lang, 2009), 125–51.

12 See Hake, *Popular Cinema of the Third Reich*. Ernst Offermanns also calls for a more differentiated approach to Nazi cinema in his *Die deutschen Juden und der Spielfilm der NS-Zeit* (Frankfurt/M.: Lang, ²2008).

13 As Johannes von Moltke notes, "there is an astonishing continuity of basic texts to be adapted over and over again: Ostermayr acquired the rights to the bestselling novels of Ludwig Ganghofer in 1920 and managed to exploit most of these wildly popular alpine texts at least three times—producing his first 'Ganghofer series' in the early 1920s, then remaking the same films as an independent producer for Ufa between 1934 and 1940, and finally producing another set based on the same novels during the 1950s, now in wide screen in and color" and often involving "the same personnel." Cf. Moltke, "Evergreens: The *Heimat* Genre," *The German Cinema Book*, 17–28, here p. 20.

14 Much work still needs to be done in this area as Sabine Hake rightly points out. For more information about the Nazi entertainment industry, see O'Brien, *Nazi Cinema as Enchantment: The Politics of Entertainment in the Third Reich*.

15 See for example Felix Moeller's in-depth study *Der Filmminister: Goebbels und der Film im Dritten Reich* (Berlin: Henschel, 1998); trans. Michael Robinson as *The Film Minister. Goebbels and the Cinema in the 'Third Reich'* (Fellbach: Menges, 2001). Beginning in the 1990s, a number of experts in the field of film studies and literary and cultural studies, among them Eric Rentschler, Lutz Koepnik, Erica Carter, Sabine Hake, and others, have been publishing important research und evaluations on the subject of film during the national-socialist period. However, there has been no systematic analysis

to date of the recourse to literary texts in filmmaking during that time. This is surprising, since it is precisely while examining the transformational processes from basic text to screen that important conclusions can be drawn regarding strategic decisions and collaborative structures within the adaptation projects.

16 While this is the more common translation (used by Rentschler, Carter, Koepnick, etc.), Horak uses the term 'Reich's Film Guild.' Cf. Horak, "German Exile Cinema," 375.
17 Reichsfilmdramaturgues included Willi Krause (aka author Peter Hagen) from February 1934, Hans-Jürgen Nierentz (1936–7), Fritz Hippler, Carl-Dieter von Reichmeister (until 1943), Kurt Frowein, and finally Ewald von Demandowsky.
18 Goebbels, *Tagebuch*, 795: "die ganze Kulturabteilung des Reichsinnenministerium."
19 Cited in Zeller, *Klassiker in finsteren Zeiten*, 437, my translation (unless otherwise noted).
20 Hoffmann, *Triumph of Propaganda*, 1996; Rentschler, *The Ministry of Illusion*, 1996 and *The Use and Abuse of Cinema*, 2015; Laura Heins, *Nazi Film Melodrama* (Chicago: University of Illinois Press, 2013).
21 For a transcript of the speech, see: https://de.metapedia.org/wiki/Quelle_/_Rede_vom_1._Februar_1933_(Adolf_Hitler).
22 See Hitler's speech, as above.
23 Rentschler, *The Ministry of Illusion*, 227. See also Julian Petley, "Film Policy in the Third Reich," *The German Cinema Book*, 173–81, here p. 173.
24 Cf. document in Joseph Wulf, Theater und Film im Dritten Reich, *Eine Dokumentation* (Reinbek: Rowohlt, 1966), 306.
25 Goebbels' speech was published in *Film-Kurier* (27 April 1933), and is included in Wulf's anthology. See Wulf, *Theater und Film im Dritten Reich*, 292f.
26 Ian Kershaw, *The 'Hitler Myth.' Image and Reality in the Third Reich* (Oxford: Oxford University Press, 1989); Hoffmann, *Triumph of Propaganda*, 1996; Moeller, *The Film Minister*, 2001; Reimer, *Cultural History through a National Socialist Lens*, 2002; David Welch, *Propaganda and the German Cinema, 1933–1945* (London: Tauris, 2001); etc.
27 Hoffmann, *Triumph of Propaganda*, vi.
28 Hilmar Hoffmann, *"Und die Fahne führt uns in die Ewigkeit." Propaganda im NS-Film* (Frankfurt/M.: Fischer, 1988), 122.
29 Wulf, *Theater und Film im Dritten Reich*, 56.
30 "Dr. Goebbels' Rede im Kaiserhof am 28.3.1933," in Gerd Albrecht, *Film im 3. Reich*, 26–31; see also Joseph Goebbels, "Rede bei der ersten Jahrestagung der Reichsfilmkammer am 05.03.1937 in der Krolloper, Berlin," *Jahrbuch der Reichsfilmkammer* (1937): 74; Joseph Goebbels, "Rede in den Tennishallen in Berlin am 19.05.1933," in Curt Belling, *Der Film in Staat und Partei* (Berlin: Der Film, 1936), 31; Christian Schicha and Carsten Brosda, eds., *Politikvermittlung in Unterhaltungsformaten: Medieninszinierung zwischen Popularität und Populismus* (Münster: LIT, 2002), 79; Manuel Köppen and Erhard Schütz, eds., *Kunst der Propaganda. Der Film im Dritten Reich* (Bern: Lang, 2007), 23.

31 For further information see Wolfgang Mühl-Benninghaus, "The German Film Credit Bank, Inc.," *Film History* 3.4 (1989): 317–32. Regarding the Propaganda Ministry's impact on the German film industry after 1933, see especially Rentschler, *The Ministry of Illusion*, 1996 and *The Use and Abuse of Cinema. German Legacies from the Weimar Era to the Present*, 2015; David Bathrick, "State of the Art as Art of the Nazi State: The Limits of Cinematic Resistance," in *Flight of Fantasy: New Perspectives on Inner Emigration in German Literature*, ed. Neil H. Donahue and Doris Kirchner (Oxford: Berghahn, 2005), 292–304; and as listed in endnote 10.
32 Niven, *Hitler and Film*, 17.
33 Mentioned in Flügge, *Heinrich Mann*, 240.
34 The book burnings were often organized by students supportive of the NSDAP. Among the biggest events were the fires outside Humboldt University in Berlin and the Heidelberg University—on squares close to the Universities' libraries.
35 A copy of the *Film Kurier* article (published on August 10, 1933) can be found in Wulf, *Theater und Film im Dritten Reich*, 305.
36 William Anthony McGuire adapted this German movie and Fallada's bestselling 1932 novel for English-speaking audiences and Frank Borzage's *Little Man, What Now?* (1934) with Margaret Sullavan as Emma, i.e., "Lämmchen" and Douglass Montgomery as her clandestine husband Hans Pinneberg. Cf. chapter 4.
37 Panja Mücke, *Musikalische Filme—Musikalisches Theater* (Münster: Waxmann, 2011), 145.
38 Michael Grisko, *Hans Fallada: Kleiner Mann—was nun?* (Leipzig: Reclam, 2002), 95.
39 Thomas Kramer, *Lexikon des deutschen Films* (Stuttgart: Reclam, 1995), x. Starring in the film are Rudolf Forster, Adele Sandrock, Fritz Genschow, and Camilla Spira. Being half-Jewish Spira was deported to Westerbork together with her family only a few years later and was saved from Auschwitz and probable death by her mother's written confirmation that Camilla was the result of an affair with an Aryan actor and, therefore, not Jewish at all. Camilla Spira survived Hitler's reign in exile.
40 Goebbels, *Tagebuch*, February 1933.
41 Ufa under the leadership and influence of the right-wing nationalist Alfred Hugenberg had become increasingly "völkisch" or nationalist in outlook and invested more and more in so-called "vaterländische" (nationalistic/patriotic) productions. Hugenberg became the first finance minister of the Third Reich until June 1933.
42 Oskar Kalbus, *Vom Werden deutscher Filmkunst*, part II: *Der Tonfilm* (Berlin: Cig. Bilderdienst, 1935), 104. The movie poster features Albers as the ideal of indomitable masculinity ready to sacrifice for a threatened German national community, the latter represented here by the female body (Käthe von Nagy) in need of protection. Ufa producer Günther Stapenhorst—works include *Emil und die Detektive* (1931), romantic comedies such as *Das schöne Abenteuer* (Reinhold Schünzel, 1932), *Morgenrot* (Gustav Ucicky, 1933), and an adaptation of H.v. Kleist/Molière's *Amphytrion* (Reinhold Schünzel,

1935) —emigrated after Goebbels' rejection of the latter project. Stapenhorst then worked as producer for Alexander Korda and Gaumont British in London. In the autumn of 1939 after German troops had invaded Poland and the Second World War was unfolding, he moved to Switzerland, where he continued his work as producer, but nonetheless dreamt of a leadership position at Ufa—he applied in 1941, 1942, and 1943. However, he was considered unsuitable due to his previous collaboration with Jewish actors.

43 Hoffmann, 'Und die Fahne führt uns in die Ewigkeit,' 59f.
44 Cf. Theodor W. Adorno, "Résumé über die Kulturindustrie," in *Ohne Leitbild* (Frankfurt/M.: Suhrkamp, 1967), 60.
45 For a more in-depth analysis of the film see my essay "Collaborative Art with Political Intent: The 1933 Adaptation of Theodor Storm's *Der Schimmelreiter/The Rider on the White Horse* (1888)," in *Process and Practice: Adaptation Considered as a Collaborative Art*, ed. Bernadette Cronin, Rachel MagShamhráin, and Nikolai Preuschoff (London: Palgrave, 2020), 169–92. This part of the chapter is based on this previous publication and permission to reuse some of this material is gratefully acknowledged.
46 Cf. Corrigan on heritage films as "comfortable images of a literary past" during "a contemporary climate of political violence and social multiculturalism" in "Literature on Screen," 36; see also Ginette Vincendeau, *Film/Literature/Heritage: A Sight and Sound Reader* (London, London: BFI, 2001).
47 See Lotte Eisner's discussion of the film in *The Haunted Screen*, trans. Roger Greaves (New York: Thames & Hudson, [1969] 1973), 60–3.
48 Walter Röhrig is remembered for his Expressionist set design of *The Cabinet of Dr. Caligari;* he collaborated with Robert Herlth already on Murnau's *Last Laugh, Faust,* and *Tarüffe.* They went on to become successful art directors during the Nazi era working, for example, on literary adaptations for cinema such as Heinrich von Kleist adaptations *Amphitryon* (1935) and *Der zerbrochene Krug* (The Broken Jug, 1937), but also fairy tales or on Veit Harlan's *Der Herrscher* (The Ruler, 1937; script by Thea von Harbou) based on Gerhart Hauptmann's *Vor Sonnenuntergang.*
49 Deutsche Kinemathek, Schriftgut (text documents archive) file 1412; all translations from this file are my own. This file contains an array of different newspaper clippings; however, not all can be traced back to the author or even the newspaper in which they were originally published.
50 Cf. *Schimmelreiter* film reviews folder (file 1412) in the document archive (Schriftgutarchiv) at the Deutsche Kinemathek in Berlin.
51 Ibid.
52 See Günter Spurgat, *Die Bedeutung einer Kontextanalyse des Films für den medienkundlichen Unterricht. Eine Problemdarstellung an Hand von zwei Verfilmungen der Novelle* Der Schimmelreiter *von Theodor Storm* (Kiel: Diplomarbeit [typescript], 1978), 24; Rundell, "Literary Nazis?," 180. As Rundell points out, the filmmakers protected themselves by declaring the story 'freely' based on or "frei nach" Storm's text as they "wanted to avoid being condemned for infidelity." Rundell, "Literary Nazis," 178f.
53 Iris Kampf, *Literaturverfilmungen als Spiegel ihrer Zeit? Die drei filmischen Adaptionen nach Theodor Storms Novelle* Der Schimmelreiter *aus den*

Jahren 1933/34, 1977/78 und 1984 im Vergleich (Saarbrücken: VDM, 2008), 104.
54 Eilhard Erich Pauls, "Die Tragik des Schimmelreiters," *Volk und Rasse* 2 (1927): 126f., quoted in Kampf, *Literaturverfilmungen*, 102.
55 The Office for Film Classification praised the film's 'immediacy' which was made, as they said, 'without the aid of explicitly unartistic techniques like programmatic speeches by the performers.' This is debunked by the two added scenes discussed here.
56 Kampf and others (Denzer, *Untersuchungen zur* Filmdramaturgie, Spurgat, *Bedeutung einer Kontextanalyse*, etc.) rightly point to the significance of Hauke Haien's speech about the new dike project, which was added by Oertel and Deppe clearly as a vehicle for the communication of Nazi ideology. See Kampf, *Literaturverfilmungen*, 25.
57 For a discussion of the 20 percent of added narrative, see Kampf, *Literaturverfilmungen*, 20f. For further discussions regarding the propaganda message of the two speeches, see Rundell, "Literary Nazis," 181. Because of the absence of a narrator, the story seems more objective than subjective, and by removing Storm's specific references to dates (i.e., the flood in October 1756 and the time of the framing narrative) and adopting a documentary style of photography especially during the outdoor scenes, the film's narrative and 'objective' message gains general importance and impact, even though the film is still somewhat historical in appearance, mostly due to the actors' costumes. See especially Denzer, *Untersuchungen zur Filmdramaturgie des Dritten Reichs,* 281.
58 Kershaw, *The 'Hitler Myth,'* 13; quoting Kurt Sontheimer, *Antidemokratisches Denken in der Weimarer Republik: Die politischen Ideen des deutschen Nationalismus zwischen 1918 und 1933* (Munich: Nymphenburger, 1962), 268.
59 Sontheimer, *Antidemokratisches Denken*, 272, also cited by Kershaw, *The Hitler Myth*, 20.
60 Kershaw, *The Hitler Myth*, 1.
61 See also Jo Fox, *Film Propaganda in Britain and Nazi Germany* (Oxford: Berg, 2007), 196.
62 Ian Kershaw, "Hitler and the Uniqueness of Nazism," *Journal of Contemporary History* 39.2 (2004): 245; Fox, *Film Propaganda in Britain and Nazi Germany,* 196.
63 Max Weber, *Economy and Society*, ed. Guenther Roth and Claus Wittich (Berkeley: University of California Press, 1978), 214f.
64 Storm, *Schimmelreiter*, 270 ("das bräunliche Mädchen"), 303 ("ihre dunklen Augen"), etc.
65 Kampf, *Literaturverfilmungen*, 61.
66 Storm, *Schimmelreiter*, esp. 348f.
67 Spurgat, *Bedeutung einer Kontextanalyse*, 19; Kampf, *Literaturverfilmungen*, 28.
68 Kampf, *Literaturverfilmungen*, 88.
69 Zillig commented on his music in the *Hamburger Fremdenblatt* (October 15, 1933): "This film, which is constructed on atmosphere and mood, foregrounds images and music." In the composer's view, the latter plays a particularly

important role in communicating the essence of landscape and human nature and adds significantly to the dramatization of the plot as it reaches its climax. Zillig, "Meine Musik zum Schimmelreiter," DK, file 1412.
70 As reference to other contemporary *Schimmelreiter*-reviews, cf. DK, file 1412.
71 According to Bill Niven, Hitler was a fan of the film: "The gloomy supernaturalism [...] clearly appealed to him"; Niven, *Hitler and Film*, 13.
72 "Schiller mögen wir nachfolgen, den er ist der titanische Kämpfer gegen die Materie, der Geist der Auferstehung aus Schutt und Unflat"; see Goebbels, *Tagebücher*, vol. 1, 146. See https://archive.org/details/JosephGoebbelsTagebucher/page/n149.
73 *Mein Kampf*, vol. 2, chapter 8.
74 Georg Ruppelt, *Schiller im nationalsozialistischen Deutschland. Der Versuch einer Gleichschaltung* (Stuttgart: Metzler, 1979), 33f.
75 Especially popular were the *Wilhelm Tell* quotes "Ans Vaterland, ans teure, schließ dich an" and "Wir wollen sein ein einzig [often misquoted as 'einig'] Volk von Brüdern, in keiner Not uns trennen und Gefahr."
76 Ruppelt, *Schiller im nationalsozialistischen Deutschland. Der Versuch einer Gleichschaltung*, see esp. 33–45.
77 See, for example, Hanns Johst volume of revanchist poetry: *Rolandsruf* (München: Langen, 1919); or his drama: *Schlageter* (München: Langen-Müller, 1933), which tells the story of Nazi martyr Albert Leo Schlageter and is dedicated to Adolf Hitler 'in loving admiration and resolute loyalty.' In his powerful position as director of the Reichsschrifttumskammer, Johst was responsible for the persecution of all non-Aryan and anti-Nazi literatures.
78 Heinz Paul went on to direct a number of cheesy entertainment films for Terra film in Berlin, among them *Kameraden auf See* (1937/8)—a Nazi film that interweaves romantic a love story with an adventure plot focused on fighting communists and propagates not only the demise of the latter but the comradery among soldiers, which saves lives and loves.
79 While there are different versions of what actually occurred and whether a doctor was sent from London to establish Veidt's fitness to travel, it is clear that Goebbels did not want to lose another A-list movie actor and did his best to persuade Veidt to stay in Germany.
80 Bruno Duday was head of production for Ufa; he was the third of the "names to be noted" by Pommer in his previously mentioned 1932 interview. He produced a number of propaganda films for Ufa, but also *Zu neuen Ufern* with Zarah Leander, until enthusiastically volunteering for the war in 1939.
81 Schiller, *Wilhelm Tell*, II, 2, line 1278.
82 *Wilhelm Tell*, II, 2, lines 1281–7.
83 See the letter by Reichsleiter Martin Bormann to the head of the Reichskanzlei, Reichsminister Lammers; cited in: Bernhard Zeller, ed., *Klassiker in finsteren Zeiten*, 420.
84 Goebbels, "Rede bei der ersten Jahrestagung der Reichsfilmkammer am 5.3.1937 in der Krolloper, Berlin," 61–85. Quoted in Thymian Bussemer, "'Nach einem dreifachen Sieg-Heil auf den Führer ging man zum gemütlichen Teil über'. Propaganda und Unterhaltung im Nationalsozialismus. Zu den historischen Wurzeln eines nur vermeintlich neuen Phänomens," in *Politikvermittlung in Unterhaltungsformaten*, ed. Christian Schicha and Carsten Brosda (Münster: LIT, 2002), 73–87, here 78f.

85 For further information, see Heins' insightful analysis in *Nazi Film Melodrama*, 124–30; and Klaus Kreimeier, *Das Kino als Ideologiefabrik* (Berlin: Kinemathek, 1971), 41f.
86 Kreimeier, *Das Kino als Ideologiefabrik*, 42.
87 In Harlan's *Jugend* (Youth, 1938) based on the play by Max Halbe (screenplay: Thea von Harbou) the focus is also on the national community, but in particular on the responsibility of the youth, i.e., the importance of educating young people to become good and true Nazis, while communicating an anti-clerical message.
88 "albern" as Thomas Mann noted in his diary on September 27, 1935.
89 Cf. Ralph Georg Reuth, ed., *Joseph Goebbels Tagebücher*, vol. 3 (1935–9) (Munich: Piper, 1999), 1144f.
90 Niven, *Hitler and Film*, 12.
91 My translation.
92 Veit Harlan also adapted and directed *Das unsterbliche Herz* (The Immortal Heart, 1939) based on *Das Nürnbergische Ei* (The Egg from Nuremberg, 1913) by his father Walter Harlan. The story and film celebrate the German pocket watch inventor Peter Henlein's genius and devotion; another example of Harlan's efforts to strengthen nationalist pride and a sense of superiority among German audiences.
93 See Eoin Bourke's insightful essay about this film in "Two Foxes of Glenarvon," in *Processes of Transposition: German Literature and Film*, 157–68, here p. 160f.
94 A title endowed on Tschechowa (Chekhova) by Hitler 1936. Cf. Bourke, "Two Foxes of Glenarvon," 166.
95 Erica Carter, *Dietrich's Ghosts: The Sublime and the Beautiful in Third Reich Film* (London: BFI, 2004), 186. See Carter's illuminating study for further contexts and interpretations of Nazi icons and popular culture.
96 Cf. Bourke, "Two Foxes of Glenarvon," 162.
97 *Ein Schritt vom Wege* is the title of the play performed in the source text by Fontane.
98 Fontane, *Effi Briest* (Berlin: Aufbau, 1998), 349.
99 Ibid., 41.
100 See Anke-Marie Lohmeier, "Symbolische und allegorische Rede im Film. Die Effi Briest-Filme von Gustaf Gründgens und Rainer Werner Fassbinder," *Theodor Fontane*, ed. Heinz Ludwig Arnold (Munich: text+kritik, 1989), 229–41, here p. 230f.; cf. also Paul Coates, "National Socialism and Literary Adaptation: Gustav Gründgens's Der Schritt vom Wege and Helmut Käutner's Kleider machen Leute," *German Life and Letters* 53.2 (2000): 231–42; Eva Schmid, "War Effi Briest blond? Bildbeschreibungen und kritische Gedanken zu vier Effi Briest-Verfilmungen," in *Literaturverfilmungen*, ed. Franz-Josef Albersmeier and Volker Roloff (Frankfurt/M.: Suhrkamp, 1989), 122–54; Ulrike Schwab, *Erzähltext und Spielfilm* (Berlin: LIT, 2006).
101 Fontane, *Effi Briest*, 278 and 157.
102 For more information see my chapter on "Verfilmungen," in *Metzler Handbuch: Fontanes Effi Briest*, ed. Stefan Neuhaus (Stuttgart: Metzler, 2019), 131–49. This section is based on my contribution to the Handbook in German.

103 Gründgens to Gaus in the TV show *Zur Person* on July 10, 1963.
104 Cf. Coates, "National Socialism and Literary Adaptation," 236. The criticism voiced regarding Effi's separation from her child—expressed by Effi's father in the novel—is now spoken by the mother. Gründgens and his team thereby transformed Briest's literary easy-going and loving humanity into a masculinity that is driven by duty and strict social conformity.
105 For example, Werner Fiedler in *Deutsche Allgemeine Zeitung* (February 10, 1939).
106 "Die Nacht ist nicht nur zum Schlafen da," a clip is available on youtube: https://www.youtube.com/watch?v=XqzX-uZUtI4.
107 Quoted in Gerd Albrecht, *Nationalsozialistische Filmpolitik* (Munich: Hanser, 1969), 143.
108 Herbert Maisch, *Helm ab—Vorhang auf. Siebzig Jahre eines ungewöhnlichen Lebens* (Emsdetten: Lechte, 1968), 289.
109 *Menschen ohne Vaterland* is based on Gertrud von Brockdorff novella *Der Mann ohne Vaterland* (1936). Brockdorff was a popular and inexhaustible writer during the Hitler era. *Heiratsschwindler* [Marriage Swindler/Impostor] (1938) is based on her *Die rote Mütze* [The Red Hat] (1937).
110 This section is based on my article "Triumph des Genies (1940): Schiller in Third Reich Cinema," *Germanistik in Ireland* 1 (2006): 75–88.
111 Norbert Jacques (1880–1954) has a place in film history mainly due to his creation of Dr Mabuse. His novel *Dr Mabuse der Spieler* was published in 1921 and 1922 (and soon turned into a film script by Thea von Harbou). Fritz Lang directed *Dr Mabuse der Spieler* in 1922, followed by *Das Testament des Dr Mabuse* in 1933 and *Die Tausend Augen des Dr Mabuse* in 1960.
112 Maisch, *Helm ab*, 294.
113 For a full analysis of this film see my article "Triumph des Genies," 75–88.
114 Kurt Honolka, *Schubart* (Stuttgart: DVA, 1985), 177. Honolka describes the trap set for Schubart by the Duke (176f.) who ordered the Kloster-Oberamtmann Scholl to lure Schubart back to Württemberg under false pretenses. Scholl's compliance was, according to Honolka, based entirely on fear.
115 Schubart's letters are evidence to his love and admiration for Schiller, whom he calls 'the strong one' ("der Starke") and 'a great guy, I love him dearly' ("ein großer Kerl, ich lieb ihn heiß!"). See Christian Friedrich Daniel Schubart, *Briefe* (Munich: Beck, 1984), 275 and 168.
116 See R. D. Miller, *Schiller and the Ideal of Freedom* (Oxford: Clarendon, 1970).
117 Cf. Schubart's letters from this period; Schubart, *Briefe*, 168.
118 Quoted in Francis Courtade and Pierre Cadars, *Geschichte des Films im Dritten Reich* (Munich: Heyne, 1975), 99. See also Zeller, *Klassiker in finsteren Zeiten*, 446.
119 For details regarding the Nazi's 'propaganda action' 1941/42, see *Politischer Informationsdienst, Gauleitung der NSDAP* (Salzburg: Gaupropagandaamt 1, 1941), 9.
120 The Nazi Government invested more than 2.3 million Reichsmark in order to reach rural communities by screening films and newsreels with clear

propaganda purposes. See Curt Belling, *Der Film in Staat und Partei* (Berlin: Der Film, 1936), 90; Gerhard Stahr, *Volksgemeinschaft vor der Leinwand* (Berlin: Theissen, 2001), 75; Bernd Kleinhans, *Ein Volk, ein Reich, ein Kino. Lichtspiel in der braunen Provinz* (Cologne: PapyRossa, 2003), 165f.
121 "Die gute Laune ist ein Kriegsartikel!" Quoted in Felix Moeller, *Der Filmminister: Goebbels und der Film im Dritten Reich*, 264.
122 Maisch, *Helm ab*, 267.
123 Friedrich Schiller, *Sämtliche Werke*, vol. 1 (Munich: Hanser, 1965), 605. (Act 5, scene 1).
124 Schiller, *Die Räuber/The Robbers*, English translation available online via Project Gutenberg at https://www.gutenberg.org/files/6782/6782-h/6782-h.htm#link2H_4_0021.
125 Goebbels in a speech he delivered on March 28, 1933, in Hotel Kaiserhof in Berlin. Quoted in Kleinhans, *Ein Volk, ein Reich, ein Kino*, 31f.
126 Peter Hoefer, "Freiheit, die ich meine...! Ein Wort zum Schiller-Film," *Der Ruf* 18 (December 1, 1945), included in Zeller, *Klassiker in finsteren Zeiten*, 446–7.
127 For a detailed comparison between Feuchtwanger's texts and the Nazi film see my essay "Feuchtwanger and the Propaganda Ministry: The Transposition of Jud Süß from Novel to Nazi Film," in *Feuchtwanger and Film*, ed. Ian Wallace (London: Lang, 2009), 125–51. Permission to reuse parts of the article in this chapter is gratefully acknowledged.
128 Lion Feuchtwanger, 'Offener Brief an sieben Berliner Schauspieler,' Feuchtwanger Memorial Library, Special Collections, University of Southern California, Box D8a, typescript, 7 pages (here p. 1). Published in *Atlantic Monthly*, April 1941; German original in *Aufbau* (New York), July 4, 1941.
129 Film scholars in the 1980s and 1990s, however, considered the choice of rooting both literary and film text in a specific chapter of Württemberg history as the only factor that loosely ties the two narratives together. Consequently, the complexity of the relationship between the original and its perverted adaptation was largely ignored. See, for example, Dorothea Hollstein, *'Jud Suess' und die Deutschen: Antisemitische Vorurteile im nationalsozialistischen Spielfilm* (Frankfurt/M.: Ullstein, 1983), 78; Stefan Mannes, *Antisemitismus im nationalsozialistischen Propagandafilm*: Jud Süß und Der ewige Jude (Cologne: Teiresias, 1999), 27. See also Friedrich Knilli and Siegfried Zielinski, "Lion Feuchtwangers 'Jud Süß' und die gleichnamigen Filme von Lothar Mendes (1934) und Veit Harlan (1940)," in *Lion Feuchtwanger*, ed. Heinz Ludwig Arnold (Munich: text&kritik, 1983), 99–121, here p. 100.
130 The first script was written by Ludwig Metzger. Möller was brought on board when Metzger's script was considered lacking in antisemitic spirit. Harlan eventually reworked the screenplay. See Susan Tegel, "Veit Harlan and the Origins of 'Jud Süss', 1938–39: Opportunism in the Creation of Nazi anti-Semitic Film Propaganda," *Historical Journal of Film, Radio and Television* 16.4 (1996): 515–31. According to a number of collaborators on the film, Goebbels made changes to the script in green ink that were beyond discussion. Harlan, for example, refers in his autobiography to a several changes Goebbels demanded, among them to cut Süß's final curse of the

people of Württemberg. See Harlan, *Im Schatten meiner Filme* (Gütersloh: Mohn, 1966), 96. See also William Small, "*Jud Süß* between Art and Politics: Veit Harlan and Lion Feuchtwanger," in *Aliens—Uneingebürgerte: German and Austrian Writers in Exile*, ed. Ian Wallace (Rodopi: Amsterdam, 1994), 85–99, here p. 94.

131 For a comparison of Veit Harlan's *Jud Süß* and Hitler's *Mein Kampf*, see Daniel Knopp, *Wunschbild und Feindbild der nationalsozialistischen Filmpropaganda* (Tectum: Marburg, 1997), 50–70.

132 See, for example: David Stewart Hull, *Film in the Third Reich: A Study of the German Cinema 1933–45* (Berkeley: University of California Press, 1969); Dorothea Hollstein, *Antisemitische Filmpropaganda: Die Darstellung des Juden im nationalsozialistischen Spielfilm* (Munich: Saur, 1971); Schulte-Sasse, *Entertaining the Third Reich*, 1996; Daniel Knopp, *Wunschbild und Feindbild der nationalsozialistischen Filmpropaganda am Beispiel von Leni Riefenstahls "Triumph des Willens" und Veit Harlans "Jud Suess"* (Marburg: Tectum, 1997); Harro Segeberg, ed., *Mediale Mobilmachung: das Dritte Reich und der Film* (Munich: Fink, 2004). *Jud Süß* has become synonymous with Nazi propaganda, as in Rolf Giesen's book on Third Reich films: Rolf Giesen, *Hitlerjunge Quex, Jud Süss und Kolberg* (Berlin: Schwarzkopf, 2005); for Harlan's *Jud Süß*, see 254–9.

133 Marta Feuchtwanger, *An Émigré Life: Munich, Berlin, Sanary, Pacific Palisades*, interviewed by Lawrence M. Weschler, vol. 2, completed under the auspices of the Oral History Program (Los Angeles: University of Southern California, 1976), 552.

134 Work on the script commenced in February 1939, screen testing took place in October/November. The film premiered in Germany on September 24, 1940. After the end of the Second World War, Metzger declared not to have written the script, but only a treatment. For details regarding the production history see Tegel, "Veit Harlan and the Origins of 'Jud Süss', 1938–39," 520.

135 Tegel quotes Harlan's version of events. Ibid., 526.

136 Ibid.

137 Rentschler, *The Ministry of Illusion*.

138 Marian had famously played an elegant womanizer and rogue in Gerhard Lamprecht's *Madame Bovary* (with Pola Negri) and in Detlev Sierck's *La Habanera* (with Zarah Leander, both 1937). After the Second World War he was banned from working in the film industry and died in a car crash on August 7, 1946.

139 See Siegfried Zielinski, *Veit Harlan: Analysen und Materialien zur Auseinandersetzung mit einem Film-Regisseur des deutschen Faschismus* (Frankfurt/M.: Fischer, 1981).

140 Feuchtwanger, "Offener Brief an sieben Berliner Schauspieler," 1.

141 Ibid., 2 and 3.

142 See, for example, Dorothea Hollstein's *Antisemitische Filmpropaganda: Die Darstellung des Juden im nationalsozialistischen Spielfilm* for further information regarding the representation of Jews in propaganda films such as *Die Rothschilds*, *Der ewige Jude*, or *Ohm Krüger* but also in examples of mass entertainment such as *Robert und Bertram* (Hans Zerlett, 1939).

143 Regarding the Nazi's cinematic depiction of ideal womanhood, see a. o. Linda Schulte-Sasse, *Entertaining the Third Reich: Illusions of Wholeness in Third Reich Cinema*, 1996; Jo Fox, *Filming Women in the Third Reich* (Oxford: Berg, 2000); Antje Ascheid, *Hitler's Heroines: Stardom and Womanhood in Nazi Cinema* (Philadelphia: Temple University Press, 2003); Angela Vaupel, *Frauen im NS-Film. Unter besonderer Berücksichtigung des Spielfilms* (Hamburg: Kovac, 2005).
144 See Régine Mihal Friedmann, *L'image et son Juif. Le Juif dans le cinema Nazi* (Payot: Paris, 1983), 111f.
145 The Nazi film quotes from Feuchtwanger's play and novel on several occasions. For further details see my essay "Feuchtwanger and the Propaganda Ministry: The Transposition of *Jud Süß* from Novel to Nazi Film" mentioned above.
146 Werner Sollers, "Introduction," in *The Invention of Ethnicity* (Oxford: Oxford University Press, 1989), xx. Cf. also O'Brien, *The Politics of Entertainment in the Third Reich*, 263.
147 Hans Heinz Bader, *Wir und die Anderen. Eine völkerrechtliche Studie* (Berlin: Limpert, 1942). On the first page (p. 3) of his book, Bader quotes Goethe—"Sich im Unendlichen zu finden, Mußt unterscheiden und dann verbinden"—in order to justify the protection and maintenance of the Aryan community. Here, p. 91.
148 J. M. Coetzee, "Portrait of the Monster as a Young Artist," *NYRB* 54.2 (2007): 11.
149 Lion Feuchtwanger, "Speech upon arrival in England?" [no date, unclear orig.], typed, 1 page, corrections handwritten, not by Feuchtwanger himself. Feuchtwanger archive, USC Libraries.
150 In 1942 Ufa was merged with Tobis, Terra, Bavaria, and the Austrian Wien-Film to create one enormous production company called Ufa-Film GmbH or "Ufi"; no film was produced in Germany or Austria without the oversight of the Propaganda Ministry in Berlin.
151 Wiebke Strehl, *Theodor Storm's Immensee. A Critical Overview* (Rochester: Camden House: 2000), 101.
152 For further analysis of *Opfergang*, see Heins, *Nazi Film Melodrama*, 116–22.
153 Elke Fröhlich, ed., *Die Tagebücher von Joseph Goebbels*, vol. 15 (Munich: Saur, 1995), May 7, 1943.
154 The film budget was 7,655,300 Reichsmark, a significant investment at the time. Cf. a list of UFA costings regarding movies in production in 1944 at Bundesarchiv/Filmarchiv Berlin (BArch R/109/II).
155 Cf. a copy of the letter in Werner Maser, *Heinrich George. Mensch aus Erde gemacht. Die politische Biographie* (Berlin: edition q, 1998), 316. For more information regarding the use of color, cf. Russell A. Alt, "September 3, 1942," *A New History of German Cinema*, 294–9.
156 For an in-depth analysis cf. Ulrich Gehrke, *Veit Harlan und der "Kolberg"-Film* (Hamburg: self, 2011).
157 "Machtergreifung," i.e., grabbing or seizing of power is a term promoted by the Nazi leadership as it marked the supposed determination and strength of their *Führer*.
158 According to filmportal.de.

159 J. Sch., "*Kolberg*—ein Film? Ein Beispiel!" *Völkischer Beobachter* (January 31, 1945); DK Schriftgut archive.
160 Anon., in *Völkischer Beobachter* (January 31, 1945).
161 A first version of Adorno and Horkheimer's seminal work was published in 1944 as *Philosophische Fragmente* (New York: Social Studies Association). A revised version was published by Querido in Amsterdam entitled *Dialektik der Aufklärung*.
162 Adorno, "Résumé über die Kulturindustrie," 60.
163 *Die goldene Stadt* (1942), *Immensee* (1943), *Münchhausen* (1943), *Opfergang* (1944), Johann Strauss-operetta adaptation *Die Fledermaus* (1944), *Kolberg* (1945). For children, several fairy-tale films, puppet films, and animations were filmed in color. Cf. Gert Koshofer's list of Agfacolor-films accessible via filmportal.de at https://www.filmportal.de/sites/default/files/Agfacolor-Kinofilme_chronologisch.pdf.
164 Cf. Altmann, *German Cinema Book*, 21.
165 Georg Seeßlen, "Uraufgeführt vor 50 Jahren: Die Feuerzangenbowle," *epd Film* 3 (1994), http://www.filmzentrale.com/rezis/feuerzangenbowlegs.htm.

7

The Postwar Period: Reconstructions and Deconstructions (1946–61)

Oh Germany, pale mother! You sit defiled among nations.
BERTOLT BRECHT[1]

It's awful. It's ailing. It makes us look bad.
JOE HEMBUS ON GERMAN CINEMA IN 1961[2]

The Second World War ended in Europe on May 8, 1945, with Nazi Germany's total and unconditional surrender. By the time of Emperor Hirohito's public announcement of Japan's defeat on August 15, 1945, Nazi Germany's military aggression, rooted in Hitler's toxic desire for pure Aryan rule across a pugnaciously expanded Reich, had caused global conflict and a total of 45 million civilian and 15 million military fatalities. Among those directly and systematically murdered by Hitler's willing executioners were over 6 million Jews, hundreds of thousands of citizens with disabilities, Roma, and countless victims persecuted for their religious and political beliefs or sexual orientation. Finally, millions were left with life-changing injuries, both physical and mental. Culture, Germany's proudly celebrated bedrock of a young nation's imagined identity since 1871, had provided no protection from inconceivable moral deterioration and barbaric behavior. War criminals like Josef Mengele had reveled in the music of Ludwig van Beethoven and Robert Schumann, even while performing the most horrific experiments on Jewish children in Auschwitz concentration camp. The canon of German literature, the works of Goethe and Schiller, Kleist, Fontane, and Storm, to name but a few, were soiled by the Nazis conceited bellicosity and sadism not only by association, but also by their recent cinematic incorporation into the Nazi's propaganda and entertainment industry. By 1945, two world wars and the Holocaust had raised inevitable questions regarding the value of German literature, especially in the context of its potential incorporation into the entertainment industry and its significance for mass culture.

This chapter traces primarily the role played by German-language literature on cinema screens in the rehabilitation of 'culture' in Germany, first during the occupation, and in the wake of the creation of two German states in 1949. As the following pages will argue, the Cold War and the division of Germany into two countries separated by opposing ideologies affected German-language cinema in general, but adaptation projects based on German-language literature in particular. Thus, a focus on adaptation sheds new light on the significance of film and literature in the postwar reconstruction of both cultural heritage and the public sphere in the two newly formed political entities.

While a few outstanding contemporary filmmakers in postwar France began to turn away from literature and used their camera as 'pen' or "caméra-stylo"[3] to tell their stories, Germans struggled to salvage their soiled culture. The ways in which adaptation projects contributed to this cultural reconstruction of Germany on either side of the so-called 'Iron Curtain' will be of particular interest here. In both the German Democratic Republic (GDR) in the East and the Federal Republic of Germany (FRG) in the West, films based on the canon, but also on contemporary literature, were profoundly affected by political but also economic interests. Adaptations discussed in this chapter reflect diverging degrees of critical engagement with the past and present, indicating the emergence of a memory culture shaped by the specificities of time and place. Adaptations negotiated gender roles, reflected on civil society, contributed to the public sphere and in some cases even shaped political debates.

In the GDR, varying degrees of political pressure affected film projects throughout the country's forty-year history. Conflicts caused by some DEFA (Deutsche Film Aktiengesellschaft/Soviet zone) adaptations during this first decade of the country's existence reveal some of the challenges as the construction of a socialist culture and film industry in East Germany was to become an integral part of the political agenda. In the FRG, however, numerous film productions at the time served equally political purposes and implicitly served to stabilize capitalist West Germany as the country enjoyed significant economic growth during the *Wirtschaftswunder* years. The role of literature in German cinema of this era has long been underestimated and will be addressed in the pages to follow.

Numerous adaptations, of course, intentionally ignored present realities in favor of useful escapist visions of an idyllic past or an entertaining present. Remakes also emerged *en masse* in this initially quite confused battle to reimagine and reconstruct. Did such films attempt to reclaim cultural heritage and salvage literature used for propaganda during the Nazi era by way of adaptation? In West Germany under Chancellor Konrad Adenauer, the politics of integration (former SS, Wehrmacht soldiers, but also numerous former Nazi judges, teachers, etc.) aimed at consolidating the new state, but also accommodated the public's unwillingness to critically engage with their recent past. The West German film industry and its distributors, interested in maximizing profits while minimizing risk, catered to the public's desires by producing escapist movies for a mass audience. Hence, postwar remakes of adaptations popular during the Nazi era might have been more than well-meaning efforts to reincorporate German-language literature into a postwar cinematic canon.

It comes as no surprise that most international producers shunned German-language literature during the postwar period. Only a few adaptations based on the German canon were filmed abroad during this era and often transformed the literary text into a reflection on the political, economic, and intercultural consequences of the crimes against humanity committed in the name of Nazism and Aryan superiority. An exception in this context are adaptations of exile literature produced in Hollywood, South America, and in Europe. Highlighting the works by a few of the writers that had left Germany in 1933 or Austria after the 'Anschluss' in 1938, these adaptations helped to renegotiate both the writers' relationship to their former home and the German-language literary canon, while making important contributions to an emerging memory culture.

In the context of a history of German literature on film, it would be easy to dismiss this era of struggles and failures altogether. Only very few, usually international adaptations of German-language texts are today considered worth including in histories of cinema, even though a growing number of film scholars have in the recent past emphasized the significance of rubble films of the immediate postwar period, of East German DEFA productions and West Germany's efforts to reimagine an unscathed *Heimat* on film in the 1950s.[4] Here, the looking glass of adaptation sheds further light on this era and allows for new insights into postwar processes of reconstruction, political and cultural division, and integration. Especially in West Germany, adaptations played an integral part in this process.

The Significance of Film after the Second World War

When Germany finally surrendered, countless tasks—from denazification and re-education of the German people to challenges in delivering the basic requirements for life for the remaining populace—Holocaust survivors, refugees, and occupying troops had to be attended to.[5] Despite this array of duties and problems in the aftermath of the war, already in May 1945, members of the occupation forces examined conditions for film production and distribution as the Records of United States Occupation Headquarters reveal.[6] The German film industry, of course, was in tatters. Those previously working in the sector had to undergo denazification, and prominent filmmakers were initially blacklisted. Apart from some studios in Babelsberg (near Berlin in the Soviet sector) and in Geiselgasteig (near Munich in the US American sector), much of the country's film production and distribution infrastructure had been destroyed during bombing raids. The Office of U.S. Military Government in Germany (OMGUS) estimated that only around 900 cinemas in Germany were either still in working condition or could be repaired within less than six months.

There was no question among the Allies regarding the potential benefit of cinema during this period of grave instability and devastation. According to a memo from the British Office of War Information in London sent on March 27, 1945, the use of cinema in defeated Germany was recommended, as it would serve to "keep [...] the Germans off the streets." Perhaps surprisingly, the memo refers to Goebbels (who had understood film as "a first-rate medium of political guidance and education"), and thus advises the use of film in the Allies' reeducation program: "feature films will serve also as a form of entertainment which will have the people present when more serious information material is to be given to them."[7]

Within only a few weeks after the end of the war, allied military governments initiated a reorientation and re-education process with the explicit goals to (1) encourage Germans to recognize the crimes committed during the Hitler regime, and (2) to clarify to German audiences the connection between the destruction caused by Germans during the Second World War and the hardship they were facing now.[8] Film officers were appointed and production began with educational documentaries and re-education films.[9] In documentary films produced by OMGUS and the Soviet Military Administration in Germany (SMAD) during this early postwar period, emphasis was placed on the atrocities that had been committed in concentration camps. Films such as *Die Todesmühlen* (Death Mills, 1945) or the Soviet-licensed forty-minute DEFA documentary *Todeslager Sachsenhausen* (Death Camp Sachsenhausen, 1946), however, regularly encountered resistance. As OMGUS documents reveal, members of the audience closed their eyes or turned their heads away from the screen to avoid seeing what some Germans at the time considered mere propaganda.[10] The six-minute DEFA documentary about the Nuremberg trials *Vergeßt es nie—schuld sind sie!* (Don't ever forget, they're the guilty ones, 1946) 'stunned' cinema audiences according to OMGUS reaction reports.[11] But many Germans also took the film as a verdict that guilt had now been assigned, conveniently interpreting its message as separation between the perpetrators charged with heinous crimes committed in the name of Nazism and 'regular Germans' who had 'only' been following orders or keeping their heads down. In addition, their own suffering and loss was seen as, perhaps, just and entirely sufficient punishment. The 'defiled mother' of Brecht's poem above was ready to close the lid on the past and move on.

In an effort to address occupied Germans' deficient willingness to consider the monstrous violations committed and take responsibility, occupying military governments organized a host of events—from exhibitions and public debates to youth conferences. But it was cinema that became central to the Allies' attempt to teach civic values and counter that "process of selective remembering and forgetting"[12] by shaping Germans' awareness regarding their recent past. As OMGUS reports indicate, offering visual documents of the horror of war and Holocaust, and alternative visions of community and justice in American, British, French, and Soviet cinema, however, did very little initially to help Germans rethink their Nazi past. When filmmakers such as Billy Wilder and producers like Eric(h) Pommer returned to Germany as members of the US military to support the re-education effort and, in Pommer's case, to help rebuild the film industry, the contribution of German filmmakers was soon considered integral to a successful re-education process. According to Pommer, it was the US Military Government's "belief & policy that Germans of sincere intent can do more to reorient Germans than can foreigners."[13] In this process, several filmmakers would turn to the literary canon to nourish their audience's understanding of their recent past and, through familiar and cherished narratives, foster Germans' willingness to critically address their own culpability.

Consequently, during this immediate aftermath of the Second World War, cinema screens became a highly contested space once again. As soon as licenses for film productions[14] became available to Germans, Nazi filmmakers like Wolfgang Liebeneiner and Veit Harlan sought whitewashing in denazification trials, and, like several younger entrepreneurs, turned to German literature to reimagine, recreate, and thus reclaim German culture. This push for a relegitimization of German cinema initially hinged on permits provided by respective military offices that allowed for adaptive and performative endeavors on theater stages and cinema screens soon after the division of Germany into four sectors had been agreed upon at the Potsdam conference in the summer of 1945.

After a sluggish start mainly due to lack of resources, feature film production took off rapidly. After only nine productions in the western zones of occupation in 1947, West German annual feature film output increased to a stunning 150 by 1954. Nearly a quarter of films produced during this era were explicitly based on German-language literature. In the summer of 1954, *The Quarterly of Film, Radio and Television* published an article by the former head of European documentary film sections of US agencies Stuart Schulberg, who now worked as a producer for American Trans-Rhein Film located in Wiesbaden.[15] In his essay entitled

"The German Film: Comeback or Setback?," Schulberg considers the spectacular rise in German film production as a potential cause for concern for other countries. Overtaking all but Italy in terms of film productivity in Europe, the strength of West Germany's film landscape was due to the vast studio space available, he explains, "thanks to the unilateral policies of the occupation powers which encouraged regional studio expansion in each of the western zones." He also notes that Germany "is the exception to the rule that European audiences prefer American films. The Germans like German films best."[16]

After Weimar cinema's penchant for rational social critique and Nazi cinema's use of film for affective mass indoctrination, postwar cinema was initially divided between the use of film for dispassionate documentation and its need to communicate subjective trauma.[17] Several adaptation projects discussed in this chapter, however, offer another take on the notion that German film of this era is merely engrossed with its own wartime suffering, anxious to put the chaos of Germany's and Austria's immediate postwar years in order, by providing affirmation and validation to certain imaginary legacies and foundational myths.[18] Moreover, adaptations of the literary canon and films based on contemporary literature were essential components of cultural (and political) strategies integral to ideologically competing nation-building processes in East and West Germany.[19] In Austria and Switzerland adaptations were for the most part based on a 'national' canon. Although the war had exposed the ugly grimace of nationalism, both group loyalty and the desire to belong became once again explicit, especially when Austria and the two new Germanies returned to relative sovereignty. The literary canon offered soothing familiarity and catered to the need of attachment and reformulation of national identity and was used extensively by the respective film industries. Literary texts were adapted to political and educational cinema, but for the most part offered conventional entertainment and escapism.[20] This culturally inward-looking tendency of the adaptation industry mirrored practices elsewhere during the postwar era but affected particularly the German literary canon on film.

German Literature in Rubble Films (1946–9)

For all the scholarly attention bestowed on postwar Germany's so-called rubble film, the question of adaptation has been considered only marginally for obvious reasons.[21] Only two films produced during the immediate postwar era under military occupation were based on German literature. Two more were so-called Überläufer (lit. 'defector') films. *Münchnerinnen* [Women of Munich] is a 1944 adaptation of Ludwig Thoma's entertaining

1919 novel, filmed under the direction of Philipp Lothar Mayring, and was finally released in postwar Germany and Austria in 1949. A first adaptation of Swiss author John Knittel's 1934 novel *Via Mala* was also produced during the Hitler era, but not released in German-speaking countries until after the war. It is the story of a brutally abusive father and husband, who is killed by his long-suffering family. But the 'via mala' [the bad way] here is not a one-way street. The father's despicable and violent deeds are followed by his family's morally questionable decision to murder him, and their subsequent decision to keep his death a secret in turn jeopardizes their ability to form meaningful relationships and lead happy lives.

Ufa had bought the rights from Knittel already in 1941.[22] Thea von Harbou subsequently wrote the script for the adaptation, in which she foregrounds the process of alienation and the inevitability of guilt. Slowly but surely, the family's fear turns to hatred of the tyrannical despot, perhaps reflecting on the German people's changing relationship with their once-adored dictator. Harbou's melodramatic *Via Mala* adaptation, filmed under the direction of Josef von Báky, ends with an acknowledgment of past ills, truth, and thus, the possibility of a happy future. The killer here, however, is not a member of the family, but publican Lukas Bündner (Carl Kuhlmann). A witness to the abuse endured, he provides closure when he sacrifices himself for the good of the community.

The film was released for export but banned for cinemagoers in Hitler's expanding Reich by order of Joseph Goebbels, who considered this melodrama too dark and inappropriate for times of war, commanding substantial reworkings of the film.[23] It can only be assumed that Goebbels was also concerned about the adaptation's foregrounding of potentially lifesaving defiance against a tyrannical oppressor, which could have been read as an intimation of rebellion at of time of growing resistance against Hitler's regime. The film's official premiere took place in Switzerland in November 1946, and the picture was screened in Germany in January 1948, following its release by the sector's Soviet military government. A review in *Der Spiegel* notes enormous queues outside cinemas screening Baky's movie in rubbled Berlin, as if Knittel's catastrophic family dynamics were just the ticket among Germans either all too aware of having chosen the wrong path themselves, or simply eager to enjoy this remnant of a supposedly self-determined past and cherished film culture. Disagreements between von Baky and Goebbels, and the death of director of photography Carl Hoffmann, prior to the required reshooting of a number of scenes, were cited as reasons for the delayed release. The fact that members of the Soviet forces, who had found the negative of the film in Babelsberg, turned it over to their film department (DEFA) for completion without consulting the film's director Josef von Baky—who was by then working under a US license (Objektiv-Film)—hints at the fraught relationship between the US and Soviet forces in Germany.[24]

Baky had directed *Münchhausen* (1942/3), which was to be Nazi Germany's answer to Britain's enormously successful *The Thief of Bagdad* (1940, dir. Alex Korda). The adaptation of Rudolf Erich Raspe's Baron Munchausen narrative[25] as an Agfacolor film was produced with enormous expense to celebrate Ufa's 25th anniversary with pomp and circumstance, all during a time when casualties of the battle of Stalingrad were mounting to a staggering 2 million. *Münchhausen* could neither compete with the visual precision of Technicolor used by experts in the British film industry nor with the charm of their Arabian fantasy. But the employment of a 'Berthold Bürger' as screenwriter for the tall tales of Baron Munchausen's travels and conquests had been Baky's saving grace in the eyes of US authorities. 'Bürger' (German for 'citizen') was in fact author Erich Kästner, who had been opposed to the Nazi regime and thus officially prohibited to write or publish in Hitler's Reich. Seemingly in direct contravention of the ban, Baky was among those who helped ensure an income for Kästner, who had also continued his work for theater under a number of pseudonyms during the war.[26]

Once directors formerly working in the Nazi film industry were allowed to return to filmmaking, 'rubble films' such as Helmut Käutner's *In jenen Tagen* [In Those Days] (1947), Harald Braun's *Zwischen Gestern und Morgen* [Between Yesterday and Tomorrow] (1948), and Josef von Baky's *Und über uns der Himmel* [And above Us the Sky or City of Torment] (1947) clearly focused on the individual's choice with regard to moral behavior, which was essential if the film was to be granted a production permit by respective military government officers. Usually highlighting humanitarian deeds in times of crisis, and the obligation of the individual toward the other, while conveniently avoiding any clear reference to the real humanitarian disaster, namely the Holocaust, these films reveal complex shifts in the communication of national identity and cultural memory. Often harking back to Weimar cinema aesthetically while regularly featuring familiar actors from the Nazi era, the material destruction of Germany, especially of cities like Berlin and Munich, forms both a visual and a narrative presence in these films.

Baky's *Und über uns der Himmel*, for instance, opens with graphic symbols of bombing raids by depicting destroyed homes but also, if subtly, questions whether an entire culture would have to fall victim to a racist regime's preposterous sense of superiority. In the opening sequence of Baky's film, war veteran Hans Richter (played by celebrity of Nazi cinema Hans Albers) returns to his home in Berlin after years of absence. Exile Fritz Kortner, the former star actor on the stage and screen of the Weimar era, who had actually returned to Berlin at the time in order to support former UFA producer Pommer in the cultural reconstruction of Germany, called the city a 'hellhole' of hunger, destruction, and despair.[27] In contrast, Albers' fictional veteran in Baky's film takes the chaos in his stride, calls missing

FIGURE 7.1 *Hans Albers (l.) and Ralph Lothar in* Und über uns der Himmel *(DE, Josef von Baky, 1947).*

doors and gaping holes in the walls of his house a mere 'trifle', and informs his companion—while picking up a dust-covered, tattered book from the ground—that even his 'library' is still intact.

This cheerful return to a soiled and broken home exemplifies rubble films' ambiguous performance of optimism that collides with the reality of moral and material catastrophe. The bitter irony of Albers' character's casual emphasis on an uncomplicated reconstruction of reliable, canonical culture becomes all too apparent when considering adaptations of German-language literature after the Second World War.

The Return of Nazi Filmmakers and a Call for Contemporary Literature

Wolfgang Liebeneiner, with Veit Harlan the most prolific director in Nazi Germany's film industry, who helped to promote the Nazi's euthanasia program with his *Ich klage an* [I Accuse] (1941), was blacklisted by US American authorities after the Second World War. In 1948, Liebeneiner[28] was acquitted in a denazification trial in Hamburg, and afterwards was free to officially pursue work in the culture industry again.[29] He immediately sought permission to adapt Kleist's canonical novella *Die Marquise von O...* (The Marquise of O..., 1808), but his application was denied by the British authorities.[30] The story of a widow of impeccable reputation who puts an ad in the paper to identify the father of her unborn child after having been raped while unconscious (as it turns out, by the Russian officer who had 'saved' her) was all too clearly an effort to draw attention to mass rapes by Soviet soldiers of German women around the end of the Second World War. As Hester Baer notes, Liebeneiner had "hoped that a film based on a classic literary text predating the Nazi period would pass the film censors more easily" but chose "Kleist's famous story precisely because of its connections to contemporary reality [...] and the necessity of coming to terms with rape."[31]

While getting nowhere with Heinrich von Kleist, who had represented the rape in his early nineteenth-century text with what must be the most discordant "—" dash in German literary history, Liebeneiner did not give up on the idea of thematizing the trauma of rape via adaptation. He turned his attention to contemporary literature and the returning soldier—a favorite theme of rubble films beginning with *Die Mörder sind unter uns* [Murderers Among Us] (Soviet sector/DEFA, Wolfgang Staudte, 1946)—while incorporating a female perspective into his next project based on Wolfgang Borchert's play *Draußen vor der Tür* (The Man Outside, 1946/7).[32] A key representative of 'rubble literature,' Borchert wrote numerous prose pieces, poems, and his famous drama before he died at the age of only twenty-six in November 1947. When the text was first broadcast on the radio in February 1947 to great acclaim, and soon, equally successful on the theater stage, Borchert's unflinching depiction of a veteran's trauma of loss—of the familiar, of home, national identity, masculinity, even agency—turned the young author into the most important literary voice of this immediate postwar era. Borchert's play touched a nerve and became "*the* overwhelming success of the postwar German theater," as Gordon Burgess notes.[33] All too many shared the existential crisis of the play's anti-hero Beckmann, who calls himself a 'patsy' and 'ghost of yesterday—one that no one wants to see anymore'.[34]

Reflecting on the adaptation of the recently deceased author's work in 1949, the year of Johann Wolfgang von Goethe's 200th birthday, journalist Kurt Lothar Tank called to other contemporary authors to take up Borchert's baton and provide more of 'the right language' that could enable a resurrection of the German film industry. The language of the so-called 'prince among poets' Goethe was deemed useless after Karl-Heinz Stroux's adaptation of Goethe's epistolary novel *The Sorrows of Young Werther* had tanked earlier that year. Stroux's *Begegnung mit Werther* [Encounter with Werther] was the second most expensive film of the 'rubble era',[35] a significant investment by Georg Fiebiger's Nova-Film, who secured 'Schiller'-actor Horst Caspar and well-known stars like

Heidemarie Hatheyer[36] for the project. Stroux included a telling 1832 quote by Schelling as a preface to his script for the film, which reads: 'Germany was not orphaned, not impoverished, it was—despite all its weakness and inner turmoil—great, rich and spiritually powerful as long as Goethe lived'. But, while audiences seemed quite moved in test screenings, the film was criticized as much too theatrical upon its release and, as a determined and coordinated effort to resurrect Goethe for a postwar German culture via adaptation, the project failed to convince. As an investment, the film was a complete disaster and the end of the Nova-Film company.[37] For journalist Tank, this was ample evidence that any successful reconstruction of a respectable film industry in Germany required literature written by authors who had experienced war and loss, the trauma of twelve years of Nazi rule or exile:

> The right language for the right film is missing, and it is missing because it can't be had without literature. It is for this reason that the contemporary German novel is so important. But precisely in the area of the contemporary novel, we have not moved beyond the rudiments.[38]

Borchert's text had been an exception within the growing body of "Kahlschlagliteratur" (lit. clear-cutting literature) that consisted mainly of short prose texts and poems by a mostly younger generation of authors. Many of them former Wehrmacht soldiers like Borchert, they attempted to kick-start a new German literature that would not simply reconstruct the language of their Nazi past but start afresh, conscious of the devastation that surrounded them and the manipulative power of the written and spoken word.[39] Borchert's play also appealed to young producer Hans Abich, who was to become instrumental in bringing German literature back to local cinema screens. Founder of Filmaufbau GmbH in Göttingen together with his former college friend Rolf Thiele, producer Abich favored adaptations of German literature, which could serve as vehicle for a non-threatening gaze into the past while reclaiming German literature for mass entertainment.[40]

Abich and Thiele's efforts to construct [Aufbau = building, development] rather than 'reconstruct' film emphasize the fresh start, which they had outlined in their "Starnberger Denkschrift" [The Starnberg Exposé] soon after Nazi Germany's surrender. In their manifesto, they called for postwar film to function as an antidote to Nazi film and to "consciously turn away from the dishonesty of the dream factory." Realism, i.e., "the real human being as a document of this world" was the only possible subject if this new German cinema was to

> make palpable that the basic principles of our existence have been transformed. It must break through from appearance to reality. The self-purification of the German people can by all means be brought to

expression through the medium of the film camera. To unleash its magical powers is the task of the new German film. Our Aufbau Film Production Company must place its work in the service of truth. We are not calling for the filmic representation of the bleak tragedy of ruins, but rather it is imperative that we make clear that film, like any other art form, can and should follow intellectual, religious, and ethical imperatives. The contemporary film must seek answers to the pressing questions of our day: It must search for the reality of truth and the meaning of responsibility.[41]

Moving in with Abich's aunt in Göttingen, the pair—calling themselves "Aufbaugemeinschaft Film" or 'film construction community'—identified buildings at a former military airport, secured financial backing, and were granted a license for 'the production and synchronization/dubbing of all film genres' by the British military government in autumn 1946.[42] A second manifesto, compiled by Abich and Thiele in 1948, highlights that educational power of visual narratives, but also emphasizes the need to be didactically "subtle," and to go beyond "our own times, although we certainly must have knowledge of these times if we are to be qualified to make an artistic statement."[43] Their aim was to reclaim film as art that could at once help to shape a new democratic state and, at the same time, "relegitimate cinema after its 'distortion' by the Nazis."[44]

Aufbau Film's first project and first adaptation of contemporary German literature after the Second World War in Germany was *Liebe 47* [Love 47] (dir. Wolfgang Liebeneiner, 1949), based on Wolfgang Borchert's play *Draußen vor der Tür*. Inspired by Goethe's *Faust*, Georg Büchner's *Woyzeck*, the plays of Frank Wedekind, August Strindberg, and German expressionists like Georg Kaiser who "portray the frustrated and isolated individual on his way through a hostile world"[45] as Ernst Schürer put it, Borchert's play focuses on a traumatized, twenty-five year old German soldier, who cannot come to grips with his guilt and finds only loss upon his return—his child was killed in a bombing raid, his parents committed suicide, and his wife now lives with another man. Unable to make sense of it all, Beckmann is hurt, tired, and starved of answers. He tries to drown himself, but not even the river provides refuge; the Elbe spits him out again, forcing him to bear the life there is. Moreover, his attempt to speak the truth about war and its horrific consequence is thwarted by the director of a cabaret, who demands 'art' instead of truth. 'Who wants to hear the truth these days?' he asks rhetorically, and Beckmann finally concedes—in rubbled Germany, truth is indeed 'unpopular'.[46]

Wolfgang Liebeneiner wrote the script after the play had been aired on the radio in February 1947 and directed the film in 1948. His and Veit Harlan's exoneration by the British authorities that year caused significant outrage among parts of the German population[47] and is an indicator of the shifting attitude toward the crimes of war and Holocaust among Western (especially British) Allied governments. The film *Liebe 47*, which also caused considerable debate when it premiered in March 1949, opens with Death, appearing as a rotund figure and in great spirits, as people have been dying like flies, first on the battlefield, now by suicide. Collaborating with Liebeneiner on the script, Kurt Joachim Fischer expanded the narrative to include a female perspective, which subsumes and incorporates both the part of the girl or "Mädchen" and that of the Other or "des Anderen" in Borchert's play and emphasizes their status as victims. Suicidal Beckmann (Karl John) meets Anna Gehrke (Hilde Krahl) at the bank of the river. She is equally committed to ending her miserable existence, and the two begin to tell one another their life stories—his 'hell', which is fanned by memories of the war and feelings of guilt being compared to her "Hölle" of isolation, deprivation, and sexual victimization in the here and now.

While the film, as its source text, forcefully questions the humanity of the Nazi perpetrators, the female perspective in Liebeneiner's film foregrounds the suffering of German women, thus moving the focus away from Nazi crimes while highlighting the need of community and altruism: 'You help me and I help you', is the simple economy Anna proposes as the film closes. Her offer to pray with him is politely declined by Beckmann, who prefers to eat. For Liebeneiner, the film was an 'honest answer' to Borchert's sense of loss and separation displayed in the play.[48]

Commercially, the somewhat disjointed adaptation flopped, despite its accommodatingly conciliatory tone, its overt recognition of German

FIGURE 7.2 *Hilde Krahl in* Liebe 47 *(DE, Wolfgang Liebeneiner, 1949).*

suffering, and an optimistic ending. At the premiere in Göttingen's 'Capitol' cinema, however, audiences were in tears, among them Borchert's mother, a reviewer for *Der Spiegel* noted in March 1949.[49] Viewers seemed to appreciate the substitution of Borchert's desperate, lonely, and forever unanswered scream into darkness at the end of the play, with Liebeneiner's homely image of domesticity as Beckmann and his new companion Anna sit at a neatly set table as the film closes. But the currency reform of 1948, which led to improved living standards nearly overnight, further reduced audiences' readiness to engage with the deprivation of the immediate postwar era.[50] Abich stated in an interview that successful distribution for their first film project was crucial for the economic survival of their new company, and the narrative changes were thus inevitable. A 'pure Borchert' would not have made it to cinemas, he argued, 'only the figure of Anna made the distribution of the film possible'. Neither Liebeneiner nor Abich wanted a 'realization of literature' but felt that film had to be a form of "Umsetzung"[51]—'implementation' or 'transposition'—which 'necessitated change.' The introduction of a female counterpart, whose voice and gaze dominate much of the film, was important because it allowed for a critical reflection of the male experience of war. 'For my generation,' Abich said, 'Borchert was both duty and passion'.

At the premiere of *Liebe 47*, Liebeneiner announced his next project with Filmaufbau-Film—Austrian playwright Karl Schönherr's popular and rather misogynistic drama *Der Weibsteufel* (Devil Woman, 1914), adapted for the screen by Carl Zuckmayer, who had by then returned from exile in the United States.[52] Liebeneiner's plan to film another *Faust*—as a 'good' German's story of seduction and the perfect symbol for a revival of the German literary canon—had to be postponed for financial reasons. His hope that *Liebe 47* would provide the necessary commercial boost to Aufbau Film was shattered as the currency reform of June 1948 caused a temporary but nonetheless significant cultural crisis due to consumerist desires shifting toward now-available food and clothing.[53] In cinemas, "attendance decreased by 63 percent in the American sector, 44 percent in the British sector, 40 percent in the French sector, and 53 percent in West Berlin."[54] Liebeneiner's response to this nosedive was, again, literature—from canonical authors such as Ludwig Tieck's *Des Lebens Überfluss* (Life's Luxuries, 1839) in 1950 to Hermann Sudermann's story of return, love and redemption *Johannisfeuer* (Fire of St. John, 1900) as *Und ewig bleibt die Liebe* [Love Stays Forever] in 1954—as conventional mass entertainment. Liebeneiner directed several adaptations, but never managed to repeat his Nazi era successes, despite a pragmatic turn to popular literature and decent box-office returns with Maria Augusta Trapp's *Story of the Trapp Family Singers* as *Die Trapp Familie in Amerika* (1958) and Curt Goetz's entertaining play featuring a love triangle in *Ingeborg* (1960).[55]

Already in June 1947, fellow filmmaker Helmut Käutner insisted in an article on 'dismantling of the dream factory' that filmmakers should prioritize potential audiences' escapist desires: 'the German public wants relaxation, conflicts instead of problems, stories instead of experience', he wrote in *Film-Echo*.[56] His comedy *Der Apfel ist ab* [lit. The apple is off; The Original Sin] (Bizone, 1948) reflects his acknowledgment of the need for a critical assessment of the past, but clearly prefers light-hearted entertainment. An adaptation of a 1935 play written by the cabaret ensemble *Die Nachrichter*, which had been banned by the Nazi government, *Der Apfel ist ab* satirizes the past and aims to amuse at all cost. Produced by Käutner's and Helmut Beck-Herzog's Camera-Film company (Hamburg-München), Käutner's adaptation cheerfully reimagines the *Nibelungenlied* and shows Siegfried in hell, with a swastika on his lapel. Paradise is off-limits and surrounded by barbed wire. A sign reads: 'Closed due to fall into sin'. The cringe-worthy explanation given is conveniently perplexing: Lucifer (Arno Assmann) had caused havoc, because in 1933, God forgot to take off his rose-tinted glasses. But, alas, the narrative filled with amusing intertextual references from Goethe's *Faust* to Lang's *Metropolis* was all a dream, from which Adam (Bobby Todd) finally wakes. In a final sequence that evokes the collaborative masterpiece *Menschen am Sonntag* [People on Sunday] (Germany, Robert Siodmak, Rochus Gliese, Edgar G. Ulmer, 1930), his acute dilemma is solved when Adam's two women, ('good') Eva (his wife) and ('bad') Lilith (his secretary), are merged to create one ('normal') woman, which Herr Schmidt (Adam) promptly meets at a tram stop in the 'real world' as the film closes. The adaptation presents the fall of man as fact while reassuringly containing it within an outer-worldly realm. Once the artificial is replaced by an aesthetic reminiscent of Weimar cinema's New Objectivity, the 'real world' is void of any allusion to the Nazi era. The clear reference to *Menschen am Sonntag* (written by Billy Wilder and filmed by Eugen Schüfftan) was perhaps to serve as a reminder of all the talent that left for Hollywood or, rather, as a cheery promise of future love and the return of carefree Sundays.

Adaptation in the Soviet Zone: Georg Büchner

In the Soviet sector, film production commenced in Babelsberg outside Berlin soon after the Nazi government's surrender. In the spring of 1946, the *Augenzeuge* news program reported that German film had reason to celebrate: the new film company DEFA was announcing its first corpus of productions, while many actors, such as Hilde Körber and Paul Klinger, musicians, artists, journalists and representatives of the different military governments, including members of the OMGUS' film control division, were listening. In his introductory speech, Colonel Sergei Ivanovich Tiulpanov, SMAD's Head of the Propaganda and Information Department, declared: 'Film as popular, mass-produced art must become a sharp and powerful weapon in the struggle against reactionary forces', gregariously adding 'and for democracy, peace and friendship of all people in this world'. DEFA's first program included newsreels, ten feature films of either 'serious or light-hearted nature', one musical film, and a movie in color. Only one of the initial twelve DEFA productions openly promoted a link between a re-legitimized postwar cinema and the German literary canon: Georg Klaren's 1947 adaptation of Büchner's drama fragment *Woyzeck* (1836/7).

Klaren had planned an adaptation of Büchner's play already during the final years of the Weimar Republic. His *Wozzeck* not only reimagines much of Weimar cinema's avant-garde aesthetic, from chiaroscuro lighting to fast-paced montage editing, but also features some of the most creative practitioners of the era such as Paul Wegener as artistic advisor and set designer Hermann Warm, who had recently returned from exile. Klaren equips the tragic story of soldier Woyzeck with a framing narrative, in which the author Büchner himself (played by Max Eckard) advocates for a differentiation between legal and moral guilt, arguing that disadvantaged Woyzeck never stood a chance and was bound to be exploited, dehumanized, and eventually destroyed by the more educated, affluent, and powerful. His fate was already sealed the moment he was born. Klaren's conciliatory message suited an antifascist cinema as envisaged by its Soviet administrators,[57] but also criticized reactionary and imperialist forces on the one hand and the division of the working class on the other, which was entirely in line with the principles of the newly founded Socialist Unity Party (SED).[58] Moreover, *Wozzeck*'s allegorical reflection of a soldier and anti-hero addresses Germany's long-standing history of fetishization of heroic masculinity and victorious military aggression, beginning with its foundation as a united Empire under Prussian leadership in 1871. In his thoroughly melancholic adaptation, Klaren acknowledged the audience's multifarious traumas without delving into problematic specificities, while being supportive of a reconstruction of Germany under socialism that would welcome and unite those defeated and abused.[59] As Horak notes, Klaren's film hence offered "positive traditions for the creation of a non-fascist, German national identity"[60] and hoped to help communicate social justice in the context of a socialist utopia.

Like many DEFA films, Klaren's *Wozzeck* was not screened in the United States until the 1960s. Movies produced in the Bizone (American and British sectors) were usually exported to the United States and Britain with subtitles soon after their release to generate additional income, even though they received poor reviews overall.[61] But when the West German Film Control Board banned the Western *Colorado Territory* (USA, Raoul

Walsh, 1949) in 1950, because it supposedly glorified criminals or "antisocial elements,"[62] even West German imports to the United States were temporarily jeopardized.

German-Language Literature in International Cinema

As mentioned above, most international producers understandably shied away from using German literature in their films. Austrian literature was considered slightly more suitable, but nonetheless Argentinian filmmaker Carlos Hugo Christensen and his racy 1946 adaptation of Arthur Schnitzler's *Fräulein Else* provocatively entitled *El ángel desnudo* [The Naked Angel] ranges among the few exceptions. Even former Axis-ally Italy now showed little interest in the canon of German-language literature.[63] The picture changes slightly, however, when one considers Hitler's exiles. Director Max Ophüls, for example, turned to German-language literature repeatedly during this immediate postwar era, and the works of exile writers such as Stefan Zweig, Gina Kaus, B. Traven, Leonhard Frank, Curt Goetz and, of course, Erich Maria Remarque were brought to the cinema screens in Germany and abroad.

After completing the romantic adventure film *The Exile* (1947) with Douglas Fairbanks, Jr. in the lead, who also wrote and produced the picture based on Cosmo Hamilton's *His Majesty, the King* (1926), Max Ophüls adapted fellow Jewish exile and bestselling author, the late Stefan Zweig. In this wonderfully subtle and utterly devastating drama *Letter from an Unknown Woman* (1947), loss takes center stage—the loss of familiarity, love, memories, a child, and life—reminding viewers of the exiled author himself, and his *Die Welt von gestern* (*The World of Yesterday*, 1942), i.e., prewar, early-twentieth-century Austria, as well as Zweig's eponymous tragic tale. After two more Hollywood films (*Caught* and *The Reckless Moment*, both 1949), Ophüls returned to France and to Austrian literature in his next adaptation project. Having had his breakthrough as a director with his adaptation of Schnitzler's *Liebelei* in 1932 Ophüls filmed *La Ronde* (1950), based on Arthur Schnitzler's *Reigen* (1897), as a stunning critique of a sexually repressive society's moral hypocrisy. The film marked the 30th anniversary of the banned play and featured the *crème de la crème* of French actors that included Simone Signoret, Danielle Darrieux, and Gérard Philipe.

Ophüls celebrated both the survival of those ostracized and the adaptation as a French product. Taking ownership of a German-language text, exiles—from Ophüls, producer Ralph Baum, composer Oscar Straus(s), and Adolf Wohlbrück[64] (Anton Walbrook, who plays the 'conferencier' in the film)—and French nationals collaborated on the film in France to recreate Schnitzler's play as a transnational product for international postwar cinema.⁶⁵ The French-language title *La Ronde* was maintained even in English-speaking countries, serving a similar function as the rubber stamp in Michael Powell and Emeric Pressburger's *The Tales of Hoffmann* (1951). Powell and Pressburger brought Offenbach's opera⁶⁶ to film as a flamboyantly ironic and audacious visual and aural spectacle that still sets the standard for excellence in opera adaptations today. While the composer of the musical score was French, E.T.A. Hoffmann was German, and the adaptation thus a risky endeavor so soon after the end of the war in a country still bearing scars from the Blitz. But Powell and Pressburger's collaborative genius not only confidently presented their project as a multinational team's celebration of transnational culture but included a sassy gesture of ownership as the opera-film closes, when we see Thomas Beecham emphatically stamp "Made in England" on the cover of his Offenbach score.⁶⁷

Refugees from Hitler's Reich had sought to create and maintain that "other Germany"—a cultural space of ethics and humanism that, for example, Thomas Mann evoked in his "Deutsche Hörer!" [German Listeners!] broadcasts to Nazi Germany via BBC's long-wave radio in July 1942.⁶⁸ Literary works by German-language exiles were considered distinct from

FIGURE 7.3 *Moira Shearer as Olympia in* The Tales of Hoffmann *(GB, Michael Powell/Emeric Pressburger, 1951).*

Nazi culture and thus, at least potentially, suited for adaptation. By opting for their plays and novels, venturesome studio bosses and filmmakers chose either to support surviving exile writers financially or to remember those that had perished. They also, if implicitly, rebuffed those voices in Germany that, like celebrated conductor Furtwängler, called exiles 'shamefaced fugitives', who—in the words of so-called 'inner emigrant' Frank Thiess— 'had watched the German tragedy from the boxes and stalls', provocatively implying not only their safe distance but also voyeuristic pleasure as their home country was being devastated.[69]

Nonetheless, associating a motion picture with German-language literature was a risk so soon after the war, as illustrated, for example, by *Beware of Pity*, a first British adaptation directed and produced by Maurice Elvey in 1946 based on Stefan Zweig's novel *Ungeduld des Herzens* (Beware of Pity, 1939), which tanked on both sides of the Atlantic. Zweig's dramatic novella *Vierundzwanzig Stunden aus dem Leben einer Frau* (Twenty-Four Hours in the Life of a Woman, 1927), which had previously and successfully been adapted in Weimar Germany (Robert Land, 1931, starring Henny Porten) and Argentina (Carlos F. Borcosque, 1944, starring Amelia Bence), was brought to cinema under the direction of Victor Saville as *Affair in Monte Carlo* in 1952, thus marking the 10th anniversary of Zweig's death. The adaptation featured Richard Todd, Leo Glenn, Stephen Murray, and Alex Korda's partner Merle Oberon. Oberon had been celebrated for *Wuthering Heights* (USA, William Wyler, 1939), where she had played opposite Laurence Olivier. What seemed like a fairly safe bet financially was ripped to shreds by conservative critics in Britain and failed at the box office despite its racy title. In the United States, the adaptation was marketed as a romantic drama and star vehicle and fared slightly better at the box office. References to Zweig, who had taken his life in exile a decade earlier, were largely omitted.[70]

Other adaptation projects, however, such as John Huston's *The Treasure Of The Sierra Madre* based on B. Traven's very successful adventure novel *Der Schatz der Sierra Madre* (1927), were delayed by the war, but proved a tremendous hit upon its release with audiences and critics in the United States and abroad. In an unusual but profitable diversion from Warner Brothers' studio-approach to filmmaking, Huston's adventure movie was shot on location in Mexico. The adaptation won three Academy Awards in 1949, including Best Director and Best Adapted Screenplay for Huston.[71] Neither the literary source, however, nor its shadowy author[72] had been mentioned on posters advertising the adventure film. B. Traven, also known as Ret Marut, who was probably Otto Feige,[73] was considered a dubious alien with a shady past, who was suspected to be an anarchist with communist leanings. The omission of his name on much of the marketing material was at least as much due to the pressures of McCarthyism as with a problematic association with German culture. At the same time, the lack of clarity regarding his identity might have helped to de-emphasize the German origin of the source material.[74] The film itself names the author of the literary source in small letters while John Huston's directorial work is highlighted. In Mexico, Traven's home since the 1920s, his work was adapted to film several times, beginning with *La Rebelión de los colgados* [The Rebellion of the Hanged] (MX, Alfredo Crevenna, 1954).[75]

During the immediate postwar period, the majority of Hitler's exiles still remained in the United States. Among them was Austrian bestselling author Gina Kaus, who had been working as a Hollywood screenwriter since 1939. Her novel *Die Schwestern Kleh* (The Sisters Kleh, 1933) had been published in a well-received English translation entitled *Dark Angel* in 1934 and was considered for adaptation by some of the major players in Hollywood.[76] But Kaus gave the rights to the film to fellow Austrian emigré Edgar G. Ulmer, who had come to great acclaim when *The Black Cat* became Universal's highest grossing movie of 1934, but subsequently fell into disrepute due to his affair with and later marriage to Shirley Castle (née Kassler), the wife of Carl Laemmle's nephew.[77] Ulmer's Kaus adaptation *Her Sister's Secret* (1946) addresses the pain and hardship caused by fear of moral judgment and marginalization in the life of a young woman, when a one-night stand with a soldier (played by Phillip Reed) leads to pregnancy. The film focuses on the fate of the unwed mother (Nancy Coleman), who gives up her baby to be raised by her sister (Margaret Lindsay)—a topic that was considered rather provocative for the melodrama genre, even though the film articulated questions of morality that were integral to postwar discourses on gender and sexuality.[78]

Conservative critics rejected the 'Ulmer'-picture, and Catholic countries such as Ireland initially banned it altogether.[79] The director's controversial personal life, which almost destroyed his career in Hollywood, had a significant impact on the reception of the emotional drama in the United States. In sharp contrast, Paramount's competing weepie *To Each His Own* (USA, Mitchell Leisen, 1946) released six months prior was mostly well received by critics, even though almost identical conflicts were being highlighted on screen. Here, Olivia de Havilland stars as the pretty girl who falls for the fighter pilot and finds herself pregnant after their one night together. The story of the unwed mother who gives up her baby and subsequently is forced to suffer the separation from her child for most of her life is here told in flashback. The focus is on the consequences of her past actions, which are neatly encapsulated by the framing narrative. Charles Brackett's story was nominated for the Academy Award for Best Writing (Original Story), and Olivia de Havilland won the Best Actress award for her role.

Adaptations of German-language literature remained the exception in postwar Hollywood, and while romantic dramas and comedies proved popular with mass audiences, there was generally little interest in works by exiles. By the end of the war, MGM had accumulated scores of scenarios and screenplays by German and Austrian writers on one-year contracts, but only very rarely did their stories make it to production.[80] In 1947, only Leonhard Frank's dramatic love story *Karl und Anna* hit the cinema screens as MGM's *Desire Me* (USA, 1947) with Robert Mitchum and Greer Garson in leading roles. Following a difficult production history that saw four directors (Jack Conway, George Cukor, Mervyn Le Roy, and Victor Saville) come and go, the picture received a mixed reception when it was finally released.

Numerous exiles longed to return to Europe not only due to McCarthyism and growing resentment against foreigners amongst the American public. The Swiss German writer Curt Goetz and his wife, actor Valérie von Martens, left their chicken farm in California and work in Hollywood for Switzerland initially, and filmed[81] Goetz's play *Dr. med. Hiob Prätorius* (1934) in autumn 1949. Goetz wrote the film script together with Karl Peter Gillmann, and directed *Frauenarzt Dr. Prätorius* [(Gynecologist) Doctor Praetorius] (1950) with his wife in and around Göttingen (Hans Domnick Filmproduktion), in the newly founded West German republic. Strapped for cash, Goetz also played the good doctor alongside his wife in the female lead. Seasoned expert Fritz Arno Wagner was at the camera and Franz Grothe in charge of the music. An orchestral performance under Dr. Prätorius' conductorship of Johannes Brahms' "Academic Festival Overture" concludes the film. Goetz pays homage to Germany's proud history of classical music and not only knew of the enormous popularity of the rejoicing "Gaudeamus Igitur" as a famous carpe diem student hymn, but also had witnessed its very effective integration into film—from *The Wizard of Oz* (1939), *The Mortal Storm* (1940), and *Ball of Fire* (1941) to *A Song Is Born* (1948)—in Hollywood. *Frauenarzt Dr. Prätorius* became West Germany's first major box-office success of the postwar era.

The melancholic and witty story of love considered controversial issues such as the death penalty, pregnancy out of wedlock, and abortion, but at the same time offered a comfortable explanation for past challenges and the weakness of man—from Prätorius' search for a microbe that might explain the extent of human stupidity to a misconduct hearing that only serves to highlight the good doctor's competence, kindheartedness, and sense of humor. The small-minded, envious colleagues that put him on trial are told off by his young wife: 'Don't forget that you tried to make a man small, whom you will never reach, even if you stand on your toes!' In his confident rebuttal Prätorius emerges as exemplary of ideal manhood exactly because he trusts his own humanity and has little respect for repressive moral and authoritarian structures. Germans lapped it up. The film offered great entertainment, an unlikely solution for all problems, and an uplifting happy end. It thoroughly catered to the postwar audience's escapist needs. Following the resounding success of the adaptation, the appealing play and film were remade for 20th Century Fox under the direction of Joseph L. Mankiewicz as a romantic comedy entitled *People Will Talk* (1951). Heart-throb Cary Grant starred alongside Jeanne Crain as utterly charming Dr. Praetorius, who "defies convention and shatters taboos" as the trailer promised in this "picture that takes a new look at life!". The good doctor's name was changed from the challenged "Hiob" [Job] of the German original to a preserving "Noah" in this Darryl F. Zanuck production, but otherwise follows the main trajectory of its predecessor even though in rather different political circumstances. Mankiewicz's adaptation—filmed at a time of rampant McCarthyism and the Korean War—considers the iniquity of war and repressive moral standards, but also foregrounds the immorality of witch hunts as the film concludes.[82] The successful run of the adaptation in cinemas was followed by a radio version broadcast by Lux Radio Theater.[83]

The most enduring success by far in this context, however, was enjoyed by the aforementioned *Letter from an Unknown Woman*, the 1948 adaptation of Stefan Zweig's novella *Brief einer Unbekannten* (Letter from an Unknown Woman, 1922) under the direction of Max Ophüls (Opuls). The beautifully atmospheric, romantic film is regularly included in the list of the 100 greatest American movies of all time. While the motion picture is a superbly insightful adaptation of a text written years before Zweig's departure from Austria, it was at the same time a monument to the internationally renowned and celebrated author, whose suicide sent shockwaves through the exile community.[84]

Erich Maria Remarque on International Screens

But it was Erich Maria Remarque, whose name continued to capture the attention of readers and cinemagoers alike. *All Quiet on the Western Front* (1930) had made cinema history, and another Remarque-Milestone collaboration was intended to shed light on the privation of refugees and negotiate both memory and trauma of the past. *Arch of Triumph* (1948) was produced by Enterprise Studios, an independent company created by producers David L. Loew, Charles Einfeld, and actor John Garfield in 1946 with the explicit aim of empowering their colleagues in the field to use film as a tool for advocating humanitarian and civic values.[85] Adaptation played a prominent role in their early work and two of their first four productions involved Remarque, who had become a household name following his antiwar novel *Im Westen nichts Neues* and Milestone's famous adaptation *All Quiet on the Western Front*. Remarque's treatment 'Beyond' was produced by Enterprise Studios as *The Other Love* (Andre DeToth, 1947), followed by the adaptation of his novel *Arc de Triomphe* (Arch of Triumph,1945).[86]

Remarque had based his novel *Arc de Triomphe* on interviews he conducted with numerous exiles during the 1930s, speaking particularly to those much less fortunate than a bestselling author residing in Switzerland like himself. But even for him, losing his home had a dramatic impact as he told Heinz Liepmann in an interview:

'They took away my German citizenship. That was a great honor at that time, but of course professionally a great shock. A writer without a country? What was he supposed to write about? How would he earn a living? When Hitler drove me out of Germany, my third novel *Drei Kameraden* was almost finished. It was such a shock for me to have to leave Germany that it took me four years to complete the book. Without my own country I was like an animal deprived of food.'[87]

The rise of fascism and the Second World War had displaced over 11 million people. As poverty and cramped living conditions in many German and other European cities were aggravated by two particularly harsh winters following the end of the war, many considered refugees an undue burden, while nearly a million of them were still surviving in camps across Europe waiting to be offered a more permanent home. Across the Atlantic, with fascism defeated, the growing sentiment that exiles should now 'go back', took little notice of the extensive destruction caused by war and Holocaust, which left many refugees without a family or home to return to.

Milestone's *Arch of Triumph* highlights the fate of exiles in Paris and is based on the English-language pre-release of Remarque's novel in the New York magazine *Collier's Weekly* (6 issues, 1945); the screenplay was written by Milestone and Harry Browne. While the film follows the novel quite closely, it emphasizes the difficult romantic entanglement of Ravic and Joan Madou, while subtly communicating the manifold challenges faced by traumatized refugees, including their fears and memories of imprisonment and torture. Both novel and film take place mostly in Paris, but the adaptation's stylized set suggests this could be anywhere, and Paris' landmarks, rooted in the novel, now merely embellish the narrative on screen.

The film starts with clear references to the recent war, but without any criticism of hero worship as implied in the source text by Remarque, who called himself a 'militant pacifist'.[88] During the prologue of Milestone's film, Paris' triumphal arch forms the background to the memory of war as the camera comes to rest on the grave of the Unknown Soldier sheltered underneath. For Remarque, the eternal light on the tombstone, i.e., the memory of the dead, deserved protection, but the Arc de Triomphe de l'Étoile with its implication of battlefield heroism was, as he puts it, a 'gigantic portal of Hades', a sinister emblem of futile death and inhumane suffering.[89] In contrast, so soon after the end of the Second World War, Milestone pays respectful consideration to its many victims, before highlighting the actual message of his adaptation as the film opens.

As the first few bars of the Marseillaise provide a familiar musical reference and, with the words "allons enfants de la Patrie" calling to the 'children of the fatherland', a voiceover introduces the narrative: It is winter 1938, one year before the outbreak of the Second World War. Milestone shows teeming crowds on big city streets, "when Paris was still an island of light in the darkness of Europe. And everywhere, men saw the new European citizen: the refugee." Considering the significance of the *citoyen* during the French Revolution, the term "new European citizen" declares the fugitives, the state- and home-less refugees, to be an integral, active, and responsible part of the state and the community. Despite their conspicuousness, however, "no one cared if these men and women lived or died." This unambiguous and provocative statement poignantly placed at the beginning of the motion picture intends to engage the audience directly, because "history prepared the end of an era and the beginning of our times." For Milestone and his team, the film was not primarily concerned with a story from the past, it was meant to help set the course for "our times." The pertinence of the subsequent narrative is categorically stated—the following story concerns us all and demands the full interest of those potentially indifferent crowds filling the darkness of the cinema.

The experience of the refugee's suffering and trauma thus becomes part of a highly dramatized opening sequence: A newspaper vendor enters a restaurant and sells a copy to a middle-aged man. This customer (Ravic/Charles Boyer)—the invisible, illegal refugee or "ghost doctor"—is just opening the paper when he catches sight of a man (Haake/Charles Laughton) on the outside looking in. The perpetrator and his victim are still separated by a windowpane, but Ravic's expression freezes in recognition and a flashback ensues, explaining the reason for this violent reaction: a stylized montage of his and his beloved Sybill's cross-examinations and torture at the hands of the Gestapo agent. While presenting inmate Ravic with the dead body of his life companion, Haake's comment is aloof and dripping with irony: "Yes, she is dead. You're quite right, she didn't know anything ... it's a pity, my apologies." Ravic is about to throw himself on Sybill's murderer, but Haake whips him violently across the face. In a cross-fade Ravic's hand on the fresh wound next to the eye of the prisoner turns into the hand on the scarred temple of the refugee in Paris, who jumps up after a further moment of terror only to see a car drive away. The scar is a recurring theme in this film and the refugee's signifier.

Both novel and film focus on the themes of love and revenge, opposites that illuminate the significance of memory, the burden of trauma, and the impossibility of love for an exile during inhuman times. Remarque's illegal refugee is indeed a 'ghost', who must remain undetected by the authorities, and works as a badly paid surgeon by night in a local hospital, unable to rent a flat, not allowed to marry. Normality has no place in this life; he is 'a man without future', as Remarque writes.[90] In the 1948 adaptation, trauma and the complications of everyday life of refugees are illuminated by subtly staged affective images. Their legitimacy, also and especially in a life of illegality, is substantiated repeatedly by relating stories about the refugees' origin and their present circumstances.[91] While Ravic's experiences in the cellars of the Gestapo are not mentioned until after roughly 100 pages into the novel, Milestone's adaptation foregrounds the consequences of the war, of Nazi rule, and the brutality of the perpetrators. Memories of past suffering and questions of identity structure the film, in which romantic love is doomed to fail. Joan Madou (Ingrid Bergman) who is indeed 'beautiful like a meadow' as Ravic says in the novel shares the refugees' fate and knows what it means to lead a precarious life filled with fear born out of homelessness. While Remarque's novel implicitly champions the rights of refugees, the film explicitly highlights their suffering and incorporates, by means of reiteration, the trauma, and the rights of the dead into a cinematographically mediated memory culture.

The "distinguished motion picture" was announced as "the greatest screen event of our times." The trailer shown in cinemas did not offer selected scenes or even the briefest description of the narrative, but instead stated confidently: "so compelling is the emotional impact of 'Arch of Triumph', so great its performances, so sustained its suspense, that mere excerpts cannot do justice to its story and its stars." It refers instead to the well-known author of the source text: "Its impassioned love story, by Erich Maria Remarque, is the most widely-discussed, best-selling novel of our times." Finally, superimposed on the image of a copy of the novel, two years of adaptive work at Enterprise Studios are mentioned, and "distinguished director Lewis Milestone … who has twice won the Academy Award … brings it to the screen." The trailer promises a star-studded melodrama with such an affective impact that the adaptation will become "a part of the personal history of every person who sees it."

Bosley Crowther in his review in the *New York Times* (April 21, 1948), however, criticizes the reduction of Remarque's novel, for him "a story of the desperate disillusionment of not one but several battered refugees dragging out borrowed-time existences in Paris just before the recent World War." The comparison to the source text[92] motivates Crowther's critique of the "over-drawn picture" that in his mind communicated "no more than a mood," in which "a blighted romance is all that stands as the tragic symbol of a tottering world." The plight of millions of refugees, so emphasized in the picture's prologue, all too quickly turns to a "hermetically sealed love story" and thus sacrifices "the broader theme" to its "over-indulgence of personalized romance."

> And with Miss Bergman and Mr. Boyer playing it, it becomes a super-extroversion of high-powered love. It becomes a gold-plated, Chanel-perfumed version of down-at-heel boy-meets-girl, a full Hollywood

intensification of the poignancies of a doomed romance. From within Lewis Milestone's roving camera, we watch love as it is made by two of the movies' most able craftsmen, repetitiously and at exceeding length.[93]

Indeed, the film repeatedly tells of the scars, which visibly mark Ravic and which all refugees carry. When they speak of their nightmares or "dreams" about torn-out fingernails, narrow escapes and arrests, and their constant fear of the next catastrophe, the camera draws in and rests on their faces in close-up, constructing affective images aimed at the promotion of tolerance and understanding.

Before the "odious Nazi big-wig" Haake is eliminated and the victim–perpetrator dynamic is reversed, Ravic and his Russian friend Boris (Louis Calhern) consider the murder as a political and moral act. In their remarkable dialogue, Ravic insists "revenge is a personal thing. This is something bigger," and argues the necessity of the murder, even if it can never undo the damage or bring true "justice" to the perpetrator's victims. In the context of the Nuremberg trials, which were still taking place during the production of this film, Ravic's deed takes on an added significance: it justifies the death sentences for the Nazi leadership and throws a positive light on the decision to take the law into one's own hands.[94]

Remarque's novel about traumatized exiles ends with the outbreak of another war and a city engulfed in darkness. Milestone's adaptation in contrast concludes with the portrayal of unquestioning friendship, hope for a future and a reunion, and Paris' famous arch, which radiates within a triumphal gloriole denoting to the viewers in 1948: This war, too, was won. This deviation from the source text was to help make palpable to audiences the clear moral challenge they all faced. But while viewers appreciated the adaptation's stars and foregrounding of the love story between those two beautiful if broken individuals, there was little appetite among the

FIGURE 7.4 *Memories of torture in* Arch of Triumph *(USA, Lewis Milestone, 1948).*

general public for drawn-out depictions of the traumatized refugees. *Arch of Triumph* "which cost $5.2 million, was, according to the president of United Artists, the 'most outstanding disappointment in the year 1948'" and bankrupted Enterprise Studios.[95]

On other international screens, Remarque's presence continued throughout the 1950s. His novel *Liebe Deinen Nächsten* (Love Your Neighbor, 1939/41) became *Demir perde* [The Iron Curtain] in Turkey, written and directed by Semih Evin in 1951.[96] Together with Fritz Habeck, Remarque co-wrote *Der letzte Akt* [The Last Act] (Austria/Germany, G.W. Pabst, 1955), an adaptation of Michael A. Musmanno's book *Ten Days to Die* (1950) about Hitler's last days in his Berlin bunker in April 1945. As Michael Töteberg outlines, the movie was rebuffed outright in West Germany. Self-pitying complaints such as 'We are spared nothing: Hitler dies for the box office!' in the press were embellished with reports about financial gain—from director G.W. Pabst's 'selfish intention' to sell Germany's painful history abroad, to Remarque's enormous fees for a screenplay about a time and place the 'treacherous' exile and 'degradation writer' would have only known 'by hearsay'.[97] The film flopped in West Germany and in Austria, where it was deemed 'too early for Hitler films' as it was mildly put by *Süddeutsche Zeitung*. Remarque was appalled at being called that 'Hollywood-nightclub-type' who dared to touch Hitler, Germany's 'most holy cultural folk heritage' as he noted irately in his diary.[98] As Margarete and Alexander Mitscherlich outlined in 1967 in their seminal study of the Germans' collective *Unfähigkeit zu trauern* or incapability to mourn, repression of the past was the dominant defense mechanism against overwhelming guilt and shame. Abroad, the movie proved a hit and was sold to fifty-two countries.[99]

In Douglas Sirk's *A Time to Live and a Time to Die* (US, 1958) based on Remarque's Second World War drama *Zeit zu leben, Zeit zu sterben* (1954), Remarque even appeared himself on screen as a Professor critical of war and the Hitler regime. Orin Jannings wrote the screenplay of the Eastmancolor CinemaScope antiwar drama film, which starred John Gavin as Private Graeber and Liselotte 'Lilo' Pulver as his soon-to-be wife. The movie stands out as it addresses the killing of Russian civilians by the Wehrmacht, but also depicts 'good Germans' among the enemies—as Zinnemann's Anna Seghers' adaptation *The Seventh Cross* had done it a decade earlier—such as young Graeber and Professor Pohlmann, who reminds his former student that an order given by a superior does not abdicate the one acting out the order of moral responsibility. Together with *Me and the Colonel* (based on exile Franz Werfel's play *Jacobowsky und der Oberst*), *A Time to Love and a Time to Die* was nominated for "Best Film—Promoting International Understanding" at the 16th Golden Globes. The 1959 award, however, went to *The Inn of the Sixth Happiness* (USA, Mark Robson, 1958) with Ingrid Bergman and Curd Jürgens (i.e., Curt Jurgens in anglophone countries).

In the late 1950s, Remarque was also adapted to the new mass medium television, which was quickly becoming cinema's fiercest competitor, as other volumes in this series outline.[100] His play *Die letzte Station* (The Last Station, 1956) was directed by Helmut Dziuba, who had written the screenplay with Volodja Kitajskij, and premiered on Central Soviet television as *Из пепла* [*Iz pepla*; From the Ashes] in 1958. The adaptation helped to secure the play's lasting popularity in Russia's theater landscape and Remarque's continuing fame in the USSR. Brazilian television station Paulista (São Paulo) turned Remarque's *Im Westen nichts Neues* into *Sem novidades no front*, which aired in January 1959. Two years later and back on cinema screens, Al Pacino starred as racing driver Bobby Deerfield in Sydney Pollack's adaptation of Erich Maria Remarque's *Der Himmel kennt keine Günstlinge* (Heaven Knows no Minions, 1961). Pollack's *Bobby Deerfield* (USA, 1977) foregrounds the male lead and focuses on his transformation from a cold and ambitious egotist into a human being ready to embrace life.[101] Central to his incarnation is a woman, Lillian (Marthe Keller), and an amplified crisis that allows for introspection, change and, finally, true love. In the United States, Remarque continued to carry weight. Marketing material distributed in North America relating to *Bobby Deerfield* and other Remarque adaptations regularly utilized the author's name and the title of the film's source text, clearly aiming at a positive reception of the picture based on the author's fame. Apart from Remarque, however, adaptations based on exile writers' works were rare, even in Hollywood.

Franz Werfel in Germany and the United States

Nonetheless, nearly a decade after Milestone's *Arch of Triumph*, another US American adaptation project based on an exile writer's work highlighted the plight of refugees: Franz Werfel's aforementioned *Jakobowsky und der Oberst*, which had premiered in theaters in New York and Basel, Switzerland, in 1944, and was adapted for the screen by playwright Samuel Behrman and Austrian novelist George Froeschel. *Me and the Colonel* (1958) was directed by Peter Glenville and produced by William Goetz for Columbia. Three months after the movie's successful premiere in New York City, the 'comedy of a tragedy' was introduced to German audiences in Stuttgart on November 7, 1958. Perhaps surprisingly, the film's German premiere was a triumph, and the adaptation became a box-office hit throughout West Germany. The familiar and well-liked star Curd Jürgens[102] as Colonel Prokoszny certainly paved the way for this "modern fairy-tale," as did the comedic talent of Danny Kaye as Jacobowsky. Here, antisemitism and the plight of the refugee cannot dwarf life, love, and altruism. Kaye's sense of humor greatly appealed to German audiences who were all too eager to believe that as a people, they were no longer marked by war and Holocaust and could join an international community in laughter. In the United States, the film was equally successful, securing a Golden Globe for Danny Kaye and a Writers Guild of America Award for Berman and Froeschel.

The film's positive reception in Germany and Austria was helped by the German-language adaptation of Werfel's *Der veruntreute Himmel* [Embezzled Heaven] (FRG, 1958), directed by Austrian Ernst Marischka, who had come to fame on the back of his hugely popular *Sissi* trilogy about the Austrian Empress Elisabeth (1955–7), which he wrote and directed. As a reviewer in *Der Spiegel* remarked, Marischka had previously 'reduced historical tales of the last Austrian emperor couple to garden gnome level', and then busied himself turning Werfel's religious parable of an old cook hoping to use her savings for a place in heaven 'into a pathetic and colorfully outlined emotional showpiece, [...] an apotheosis of kitsch'. Audiences in Germany and Austria loved it. The film was a box-office hit not least due to the spiritual encouragement it received from Rome. Pius XII had allowed the color filming of one of his audiences in St. Peter's Church, which was considered a sensation. As the critic concluded, this adaptation of a novel by a Jewish writer who had converted to Catholicism 'will go down in cinema history as the only feature film with an apostolic blessing'.[103]

The National Canon on Screen in Switzerland and Austria

The devastation of the Second World War had triggered a period of reflection both in neutral countries such as Switzerland and those welcomed into the xenophobic and antisemitic folds of the Aryan Reich via annexation, such as Austria. It was a time of looking inward, which is clearly reflected in the choices made by local film companies. During this period of change, the cultural industry provided reassurance and emphasized the country's reliable foundations: its landscape, dialects, and literary heritage.

In Switzerland, adaptations for cinema and television of this era were almost entirely of Swiss authors, beginning with Friedrich Glauser's crime novel *Matto regiert* (Matto rules/In Matteo's Realm, 1936). It was brought to cinemas in Germany entitled *Paragraph 51—Seelenarzt Dr. Laduner* (CH, Leopold Lindtberg, 1946) and in English-language countries as *Madness Rules*. Lindtberg's adaptations of Swiss authors Gottfried Keller and Robert Faesi in the 1930s and 1940s helped to establish him as one of Switzerland's most prominent theater and film directors at the time. His successor was Swiss film director Franz Schnyder,[104] who brought Switzerland's most famous nineteenth-century authors Jeremias Gotthelf and Johanna Spyri to international cinema audiences. Gotthelf's *Uli der Knecht* (Uli the Farmhand, 1841) became the romantic comedy *Uli der Knecht* (1954) followed by a sequel based on Gotthelf's *Uli der Pächter* (Uli the Tenant, 1849) in 1955. Both adaptations were hits at the box office, in no small measure due to the films' female lead Lilo Pulver, who starred alongside Hannes Schmidhauser, an adored member of Switzerland's national soccer team. Relatively unknown at the time, Swiss-born Pulver subsequently became one of the most popular and sought-after female film stars in West Germany, where the adaptation was marketed as ... *und ewig ruft die Heimat* [... and Forever the Homeland Calls] evoking postwar Germans' favorite genre—the 'Heimatfilm'.[105]

Particularly popular during this period, however, was Schnyder's *Heidi und Peter* (1955), which followed Canadian-born US filmmaker Allan Dwan's 1937 Shirley Temple-film and Luigi Comencini's 1952 Swiss German (and German) adaptation of Johanna Spyri's bestselling novel *Heidi* (1881). After two world wars within a mere three decades, this outcast and yet kind and witty little Swiss girl won not only the heart of her sad and grumpy grandfather, but of an international mass audience. Her unwavering spirit, her sense of belonging and love for nature, family, and friends enabled her to make a home for herself and others, and thus provided welcome reassurance as well as beautiful Alpine imagery for the pleasure and edification of postwar viewers. In the 1950s alone, five more Spyri-adaptations exuding the unpredictable and yet eternal security of home in idyllic landscapes were produced in Austria, Germany, France, Britain, the United States, and India, including a BBC mini-series in 1959. Spyri's literary work—and first and foremost her *Heidi*—remains one of the most successful international cinematic exports to date.[106]

Austria, occupied but soon considered more a liberated than a defeated country by the Allies, turned mainly to its own national authors for inspiration and cultural consolidation in their postwar film production. Adaptations ranged from nineteenth- and early twentieth-century canonical writers Adalbert Stifter (*Der Wildschütz von Tirol*, 1949), Peter Rosegger (*Das Siegel Gottes*, 1948), and Ferdinand Raimund (*Der Verschwender*, 1952; *Der Bauer als Millionär*, 1961), to two particular favorites of the postwar era, contemporary author Alexander Lernet-Holenia (*Das andere Leben*; *Maresi*; *An klingenden Ufern*, all 1948), and nineteenth-century dramatist Johann Nepomuk Nestroy[107] (*Einmal keine Sorgen haben*, 1953; *Wenn Poldi ins Manöver zieht*, 1956; *Einen Jux will er sich machen*, 1958). The latter adaptation, a West German-Austrian co-production, was directed by Alfred Stöger, who had returned to Austria after filming numerous ideologically aligned short films and fairy tales for the Nazi film industry. Produced by his own Mundus Film Company in Vienna, Stöger's films of Schiller plays were valiant efforts to bring theater art into cinemas, but failed to generate much interest.[108] While Lernet-Holenia[109] had played an ambivalent role in the Nazi's culture industry, exiles—such as Roda Roda, Hans Adler (Paul Vulpius), Georg Kaiser, Fritz Hochwälder, Carl Zuckmayer, or Ödön von Horváth—fit the bill for a reimagined, integrative film industry during this immediate postwar period, and their works were regularly adapted for the cinema and, increasingly, also for television.[110]

The degree to which exile literature implicitly aided the negotiation of Austria's Nazi past, and eased the incorporation of former collaborators into the country's postwar film industry should be considered in more detail than this book can offer. Films like *Die Frau am Weg* [Woman by the Road] (1948), directed by Eduard von Borsody, produced by Willi Forst and starring Brigitte Horney, might serve as example and shed light on the complexities of this cultural and political conciliation within diverse memory discourses. Despite the fact that von Borsody, Forst, and Horney had worked in the Nazi's propaganda and entertainment industry, they were able to successfully continue their film careers in Austria after the war.[111] The movie is based on the work of Georg Kaiser and Fritz Hochwälder, who both fled to Switzerland in 1938, when Austria became part of Hitler's Reich. Kaiser had drafted the story, and encouraged the much younger Hochwälder, whose parents had been murdered in Theresienstadt concentration camp, to turn it into a play. *Der Flüchtling* [The Refugee] premiered in Munich's Volkstheater in July 1946 and its dramatic narrative of flight, fear, and sacrifice culminating in an act of true humanity was considered more than suitable for adaptation to film by an industry eager to reinvent itself.

Audiences, however, much preferred light-hearted entertainment to reminders of hardship. Austro-Hungarian-born playwright and novelist Ödön von Horváth had fled Austria after the 'Anschluss' or annexation by Hitler's Reich in 1938 and was killed the same year on the Champs Elysées during a storm. He had been on his way to meet Robert Siodmak to discuss the adaptation of his novel *Jugend ohne Gott* (Youth without God, 1937). A first adaptation of his work now set the tone for much of the box-office successes emerging from the Austrian film industry for the decade to come: *Hin und Her* [To and Fro] (1949, based on Horváth's 1933/4 play) was directed by Theo Lingen, who also starred in the comedy alongside his daughter Ursula and familiar celebrities O.W. Fischer and Curd Jürgens.

The same year, Gustav Ucicky, who had been blacklisted until 1947 due to his copious work for Goebbels' propaganda apparatus, turned to antifascist exile Carl Zuckmayer's work, and adapted his novella "Der Seelenbräu" [lit. The Soulbrew] into a comedy film, starring Paul Hörbiger and Heinrich Gretler as the two pig-headed adversaries. Zuckmayer's text, first published in 1945 by Bermann-Fischer, centers on the men's opposing professions and spiritual vs. corporal commitments; a theme brought to and beloved by a mass audience across Europe following the adaptations of Giovanni Guareschi's *Don Camillo and Peppone* novels of the 1950s and 60s, starring

Fernandel as the town's cheeky priest Don Camillo and Gino Cervi as its often-raging and yet good-hearted mayor Peppone. The popularity of Uckicy's adaptation *Der Seelenbräu* and Zuckmayer's controversial hit-play *Des Teufels General* (The Devil's General, 1946) made the former exile the most sought-after provider of source texts for both cinema and the emerging television industry in Austria and, especially, West Germany.

Divided 'Heimat': German-language Literature and the 'Iron Curtain'

When the French, British, and US American zones became West Germany in 1949, the new democratic republic's allegiance to Western capitalism and commitment to function as a bulwark against communism was paramount; it certainly superseded the Allies' desire to push Germany's negotiation of its Nazi past. Under Chancellor Konrad Adenauer, a steadfast antifascist before and during the Hitler era who subsequently prioritized recovery during this postwar era, the newly formed Federal Republic of Germany (FRG) became a 'superintegrationcountry'[112] in the interest of political and economic stability, incorporating millions of 'notjustnazis' as writer and journalist Christian Staas sarcastically calls them. In contrast, the German Democratic Republic (GDR), socialist East Germany, was not as welcoming, and promoted its antifascist stance also via film and adaptation projects within increasing political constraints.[113] The world's third largest film industry prior to the Second World War found itself in a deep crisis as the two Germanies were established. A West German parliamentary committee chaired by Rudolf Vogel advised that the federal government included a bank guarantee of 20 million marks in its 1950–1 budget in support of film productions and to encourage growth in the sector.[114] So-called "Bundesbürgschaften" would guarantee up to 35 percent of production costs initially.

Postwar East German film production was dominated by DEFA and under Soviet control. In western zones, film licenses had been granted to individuals by British, French and US American authorities, leading to dozens of 'dwarf companies'.[115] As the business newspaper *Wirtschaftszeitung* warned on July 16, 1949, the currency reform of the previous year had dramatically reduced profits at the box office in West Germany, and the absence of available credit meant threat of bankruptcy for these small firms after even just one dud. Pleasing a mass audience and making a profit at the box office became paramount and an irrefutable argument in productions of light entertainment or safely innocuous adaptations of respected literary works. Audiences in Germany—but increasingly also abroad—'rigorously rejected' the suffering depicted in rubble films, the 'milieu' of war and postwar, and demanded hope instead of hopelessness, the paper advised. As the new currency and its positive impact on consumer society in western zones fundamentally changed cinemagoers' outlook, it was believed that film companies should offer forward-looking narratives during this 'time of restoration for the soul'.[116] According to *Wirtschaftszeitung*, the most successful productions of the time were contemporary light-hearted Austrian productions filled with good humor and an amusing smattering of local dialect. Remakes, such as Willy Birgel's 1955 third adaptation of Otto Erich Hartleben's officer's drama *Rosenmontag* (Shrove Monday, 1900), were now often equipped with a soothing and profitable Happy End.[117] In conclusion, the production of thrillers, comedies, and circus-films were recommended, as they were often the most successful in bringing audiences back into cinemas and turning a profit for production companies.

Overall, West Germany's integrative spirit was mirrored by the country's film production and distribution. The conservative climate that preferred idyllic images of the past promoted light-hearted adaptations of 'Blood & Soil'-author Rudolf Binding (e.g., *Moselfahrt aus Liebeskummer* [Moselle Trip from Heartache], Kurt Hoffmann, 1953), of committed Nazi educator Hans Venatier's *Der Major und die Stiere* [The Major and the Bulls] (Eduard von Borsody, 1955), and Agnes Günther's *Die Heilige und ihr Narr* [The Saint and Her Fool] (Gustav Ucicky, 1957). The positive reception of this type of cinematic entertainment among conservative West German society and the press reveals not only the prevalence of Nazi sympathizers or unrepentant former Nazis, but the growing confidence of a country that had reinvented itself within a decade after the end of the war.[118] In addition to the majority of surviving former employees of the Nazi's culture industry returning to filmmaking, Ilse Kubaschewski's Gloria-Filmverleih company (founded in 1949) regularly distributed films produced in Nazi Germany that had been categorized as 'apolitical' by the Allies (particularly by OMGUS).[119]

Successful distributors such as Gloria and Herzog-Film bought the distribution rights to planned or ongoing film productions in bulk, provided much-needed capital, and thus greatly influenced the type of films to be produced. Kubaschewski was an astute entrepreneur who catered to the masses by supporting the most popular genres such as *Heimat*-films and musicals featuring pop songs (*Schlagerfilme*). When she founded her own production company, she continued to support projects with mass appeal beginning with *Ave Maria* (starring celebrity singer of the Nazi era Zarah Leander, 1953), and adaptations based on popular, bestselling novels—such as *08/15* (1954/5, based on Hans Hellmut Kirst's trilogy) and *Der Arzt von Stalingrad* [The Doctor of Stalingrad] (FRG, Géza von Radvanyi, 1958, based on a bestseller by Heinz G. Konsalik)—that typically humanized the 'good' German in uniform and clearly differentiated between him and 'bad' Nazis. But Kubaschewski also, together with the Interior Ministry in Bonn, co-financed an adaptation of the 1957 production of Goethe's

Faust at Hamburg's Deutsches Schauspielhaus (*Faust*; FRG, Peter Gorski, 1960) starring Gustaf Gründgens and Will Quadflieg. Irrespective of their collaboration with the Nazi regime, their outstanding theater performance was to be highlighted for both national and international audiences while being integrated into West Germany's cultural memory. Viewers abroad, however, were not impressed, and the film, which had been confidently submitted by West Germany for the Academy Awards competition in 1961, failed to be nominated for Best Foreign Language Film.[120] The Academy of Motion Picture Arts and Sciences clearly had little interest in allowing a former Nazi collaborator's Faustian narrative of seduction take center stage.

Proto-heritage Film

Despite the public's unwillingness to engage with their recent past, film production in both Germanies and in Austria[121] during the 1950s was often more than superficial entertainment and (re)constructions of national identity alongside ideological divisions, as Marc Silberman, Henning Wrage, Sabine Hake, and others have convincingly argued.[122] Particularly in West Germany and Austria, adaptations of German-language literature impacted all genres—from comedies to musical films, from war movies to crime films, children's pictures, fairy tales and, especially, *Heimat*-films. The *Heimat*-genre's foundation on mostly untainted, prewar literary heritage was integral to communicating stability, continuity, and traditional values. Following the runaway-success of *Schwarzwaldmädel* [Black Forest Girl] (FRG, Hans Deppe, 1950), works by authors such as the three Ludwigs (Ludwig Anzengruber, Ludwig Ganghofer, and Ludwig Thoma), whose popular stories evoke the arcadian spaces of the Bavarian and Austrian Alps, but also Hermann Löns—'the Poet of the Heath' and probably the most popular writer of 'homeland'-literature in Nazi Germany[123]—were adapted throughout the 1950s, and evoked a powerful sense of cultural belonging during this era of devastation and change.

The literary canon not only complemented the genre's core position but also provided the backbone to its stabilizing function. Not surprisingly, the vast majority of notable "Heimat"- or 'homeland'-films were based on nineteenth-century German and Austrian literature, texts written prior to the nations' false sense of superiority leading to the wars and genocides of the twentieth century. Psychological, moral, and physical challenges faced by 'average' Germans were acknowledged in these novels, and became proxies for the recent war on screen. First and foremost, however, *Heimat*-films were produced in West Germany and Austria to provide escapist entertainment in picturesque landscapes unscathed by war and deprivation. A ghost dance of a genre in which undying love is possible, and good women still fall for real men, *Heimat*-narratives inevitably end with order and a sense of 'home' restored, never mind those minor upheavals along the way. Profiting from a sizeable body of literatures by authors who celebrated local landscapes, people, and customs, the genre[124] proved hugely popular among German-speaking audiences.[125] Their works had been enjoyed by a mass readership in German-speaking countries throughout the first half of the twentieth century, and now lent complexity and weight to a genre that was quickly becoming formulaic.

Anzengruber's 'play with song' *Der Pfarrer von Kirchfeld* (The Priest of Kirchfeld, 1870) was adapted twice in 1955 alone—as *Der Kirchfeldpfarrer* in Austria under the direction of Alfred Lehner, and as *Der Pfarrer vom Kirchfeld* in West Germany, directed by Hans Deppe. Remakes were common at the time, promising commercial profit based on previous box-office successes during the Weimar Republic and the Hitler era as *Schwarzwaldmädel* had already indicated.[126] Based on the operetta by Leon Jessel and August Neidhart (1917), Deppe's 1950 musical film was already the fourth German *Schwarzwaldmädel* adaptation, following versions for cinema by Arthur Wellin (1920), Victor Janson (1929), and Georg Zoch (1933). Anzengruber's *Der Pfarrer von Kirchfeld* had been brought to the silent cinema screen already in 1914 by Luise Kolm(-Fleck) and Jakob Fleck. The famous Austrian filmmaking couple—who emigrated to Shanghai where they worked with Chinese director Fei Mu following Jakob Fleck's release from Buchenwald concentration camp—had also adapted Anzengruber's *Der Meineidbauer* [lit. the perjury farmer] in 1915, followed by *Der Schandfleck* [The Stain of Shame] and the farce *Der Doppelselbstmord* [Double Suicide] in 1917. Arthur Maria Rabenalt directed a remake of the latter comedy film in the Austrian-German co-production entitled *Hochzeit im Heu* [Wedding in the Hay] in 1951, before turning to another remake of the horror classic *Alraune* (1952). Following the success of Deppe's *Der Pfarrer von Kirchfeld* the previous year, in 1956, the remake of Anzengruber's *Der Schandfleck* drew mass audiences into cinemas in this Austrian-West German collaboration (Rex Film, Berlin, and Schönbrunn-Film, Vienna), produced by Robert Siepen and directed by Herbert Fredersdorf.

The same year, Rudolf Jugert directed *Der Meineidbauer* for Eichberg Film (Munich) in an Edgar G. Ulmer production, which proved the most interesting of all Anzengruber adaptations. Here, the cinematography of stunningly picturesque settings by the French camera team Roger Hubert and Max Dulac strangely competes with the unforgiving severity of the two main characters, well played by Heidemarie Hatheyer and Carl Wery, thus creating a layer of nonnarrative tension and lending dramatic complexity to this movie's rather straightforward plot of greed and betrayal. In this respect, Jugert's film is comparable only to the second adaptation of actress and bestselling author Wilhelmine von Hillern's *Geier-Wally* (The Vulture Wally, 1875), which was based on a script by Peter Ostermayr[127] and Wolf Neumeister and produced by Ostermayr-Film in West Germany under the direction of František Čáp (1956). The script of *Die Geierwally* follows the melodramatic narrative, which focuses on a hardened and marginalized young woman in the German Alps. Čáp's film evokes the drama of the popular 'Bergfilme' or mountain films of the 1920s and 1930s, while focusing on the girl called Geierwally and the consequences of her nongendered upbringing. Raised as a courageous tomboy by her father, Geierwally is left longing for love and the stability of a family of her own. The adaptation and its concluding outlook thus incorporated social debates around gender as a subtext, at a time when the last German POWs were returning from the Soviet Union, often to independent, hardworking women who had looked after their family or themselves for years on their own.[128]

Ludwig Ganghofer's late-nineteenth-century novels provided West Germany with much sought after drama and romance untouched by the knowledge of twentieth-century warfare and mass murder. Within the first decade following the Second World War, a total of ten adaptations[129] of Ganghofer's novels secured steady incomes for a several new film companies. Writer Helmut Weiss, who had authored *Das Geheimnis einer Ehe* [The Secret of a Marriage] for the theater stage and subsequently reshaped it into a screenplay, directed an adaptation of his own text in 1951, but soon specialized in Ganghofer adaptations: *Der Jäger von Fall* [The Hunter of Fall] (1954), *Schloß Hubertus* [Hubertus Castle] (1954), and *Das Schweigen im Walde* [Silence in the Woods] (1955). The latter, which had already been adapted in 1929 under the direction of Wilhelm (William) Dieterle and in 1937 by Paul May, was the first color film based on Ganghofer's literary work. This investment by Peter Ostermayr-Film indicates the producer's confidence in the commercial value of films based on "Heimat"- or 'homeland'-literature, setting a trend that continued well into the 1970s.[130]

Peter Rosegger's insightful narratives of life and human nature in the Austrian Alps had brought fame to the author beginning with his first book publication *Geschichten aus der Steiermark* (Tales from Styria, 1871). In Austria and Germany, his work, too, was adapted in an effort to safeguard traditional heritage on the one hand and help the transition to popular folklore irrespective either Austria's or Germany's Nazi past, beginning with Alfred Stöger's *Das Siegel Gottes* [God's Seal] (prod. by Stöger/Walter Tjaden's Mundus-Film company, 1949) based on Rosegger's novella.[131] Stöger's film was soon followed by Rosegger-adaptations in West Germany, namely Robert A. Stemmle's *Die Försterbuben* [The Boys of the Forrester] (1955) and Ferdinand Dörfler's *Die fröhliche Wallfahrt* [The Merry Pilgrimage] (1956).

Ganghofer's contemporary Ludwig Thoma, whose satires of everyday life in Bavaria and humorous tales of a young rascal in *Lausbubengeschichten* (Scoundrel Stories, 1904) and *Tante Frieda* (Aunt Frieda, 1906), delighted readers with dialogues in Bavarian dialect, their supposed authenticity and rootedness placed in satirical contrast to stuck-up High-German spoken by the city folk or other dubious and unsympathetic characters. Beginning with the atmospheric *Heimat, deine Sterne* [Homeland, your Stars] (FRG, Hermann Kugelstadt, 1951), adaptations of Ludwig Thoma's literary works were sure to yield positive returns at the box office and, in subsequent television productions, high audience ratings.[132] Kugelstadt's first Thoma adaptation was based on the author's *Der Jagerloisl* (Hunter-Loisl[133], 1921), but the movie's title was changed from the original to *Heimat, deine Sterne*. At the time, this must have been an easily recognizable intertextual reference to a very popular song, which had featured in the Nazi comedy hit *Quax, der Bruchpilot* [Quax the Crash Pilot] (1941).[134] In addition, the design of the poster advertising the film, promising 'An atmospheric homeland-film— based on a hunting novel by L. Thoma', is clearly reminiscent of the visual aesthetic often used in propaganda posters and thus incorporates the film culture shaped by Goebbels and Hitler into the genre.

Take 2: Veit Harlan and Theodor Storm

Not surprisingly, Veit Harlan also turned to the canon of German literature once he walked free after standing trial for helping to justify the Holocaust. The *New York Times* reported: "Veit Harlan, one of Germany's best-known film producers, was acquitted today for the second time by a Hamburg court on charges of crimes against humanity arising from his 'Jew Suess', an anti-Semitic version of a book by Lion Feuchtwanger."[135] His trials, both presided over by the same former Nazi-judge, caused significant controversy. After one of the witnesses was threatened and jeered as 'Jewish swine' outside the court, Chancellor Adenauer issued a public statement "expressing his 'deepest regret' about the 'shameful way' in which, his fellow-countrymen, 'even if they are few', were behaving towards Jews."[136]

Harlan's first postwar film *Unsterbliche Geliebte* [Immortal Beloved] (1951) was an adaptation of the tragic novella *Aquis submersus* by Theodor Storm, one of the most widely read nineteenth-century authors and a staple in every German school's curriculum. Upon its release, however, several politicians and the wider public boycotted Harlan's self-pitying film about true love, inevitable infidelity, and yet gruesome retribution, even though Harlan's sullied name was neither mentioned during marketing nor in the movie's credits.[137] As per usual starring his wife, Harlan's involvement in this 'Kristina-Söderbaum-picture' was all too transparent, and when the adaptation was finally shown in a few German cities, screenings were interrupted by hecklings and even stink bombs.

Erich Lüth, director of the National Press Office in Hamburg, had called for a boycott of Harlan's film and several journalists followed suit. August

Kerger, representative of the Social Democrats (SPD) in West Germany's capital Bonn, managed to prevent the Harlan/Söderbaum-picture to be shown on his turf, but as *Der Spiegel* reported at the time, it was only a short way to Bad Godesberg, where Chancellor Adenauer lived and *Unsterbliche Geliebte* screenings were taking place under police protection.[138] In his dismay about the pushback he and his picture faced, Harlan even wrote to West Germany's President Theodor Heuss, who assured him that the state would prevent any 'unjustified restriction' of his rights.[139] Harlan also sued for an injunction in order to prevent Erich Lüth from publicly insisting on a boycott of *Unsterbliche Geliebte*. The District Court in Hamburg granted the injunction in 1951. It was not until seven years later that the decision was overturned by the Federal Constitutional Court confirming the critic's freedom of expression.

Heinrich Mann on Film in the Two Germanies

In the GDR, turning the literary canon into a political instrument via adaptation proved more difficult than anticipated by the political leadership. Their vision of a unified socialist and antifascist community struggled with a (self-)critical assessment of the country's recent past. But while the GDR government never officially acknowledged East Germans' involvement in the Holocaust or the two Germanies' shared Nazi past, surviving exiles and returning members of the communist party and German-Jewish authors like Hedda Zinner, Anna Seghers, and others successfully contributed to a more sophisticated East German memory culture both via their literary texts and adaptations of their work for cinema and television.[140]

The production and reception of a first adaptation of exile Heinrich Mann's novel *Der Untertan* (The Loyal Subject, 1914/18) sheds light on the ideological division between the two Germanies, but also on the complexities and pressures of shaping a memory culture on either side of the new border. Already in October 1949, only weeks before the creation of the GDR, DEFA sought the rights to adapt Mann's novel and contacted the author in his Californian exile. Heinrich Mann—bestselling writer, stateless exile, a politically progressive bourgeois, and sufficiently left-wing humanist—had been designated to help shape the culture and institutions of the future East German state.[141] The GDR's leadership actively sought out exiles and encouraged them to help turn their utopian vision of an antifascist community into reality. Mann was appointed President of the East German Academy of Arts in 1949 but died in Californian exile in 1950 before he could return to East Berlin. His satisfyingly sardonic novel *Der Untertan* about the petty bourgeois climber and 'loyal subject' Dietrich Hessling in Wilhelmine Germany had been partly released in the satirical magazine *Simplicissimus* in 1914, but even those excerpts caused such an uproar, especially among the conservative (male) bourgeoisie, that the novel was not published in its entirety in Germany until after the end of war and Empire in 1918. Mann's depiction of ultra-nationalism, antisemitism, xenophobia, and bigotry as ills of a morally bankrupt society unfit to survive, struck a core with disillusioned readers in the postwar Weimar Republic, and again in postwar East Germany. The main character of his socio-critical novel is a monarchist, a nationalist, but more than anything, he is a self-important opportunist, who uses his connections to get rid of unwanted competition, knows when to buckle, and lashes out at those less powerful whenever he can. In his novel, Heinrich Mann created the epitome of a class-conscious bourgeois who is both coward and a bully and who frequently speaks of Christian values but lives in blatant contradiction to them. He is the type associated with the rise of fascism, and the opposite of the ideal socialist citizen envisaged by the GDR political leadership.

The adaptation project was part of the government's cultural strategy, which sought to legitimize the GDR as an antifascist German state by linking well-known writers such as Heinrich Mann and Arnold Zweig and their works to their political vision.[142] Johannes R. Becher had personally encouraged numerous exiles to return and, as head of publishing at Aufbau Verlag, promoted exile literature by authors such as Anna Seghers, Alfred Döblin, Lion Feuchtwanger or Bertolt Brecht. Becher, who had spent the twelve years of Nazi rule mostly in the Soviet Union, was also one of the founders of the humanist "Kulturbund zur demokratischen Erneuerung Deutschlands" [Cultural Association for the Democratic Renewal of Germany] in 1945. The "Kulturbund" became integral to creating and supporting antifascist, socialist culture in the GDR from 1949 onwards, and both literature and film were considered essential components in the communication of socialist ideals.[143]

After the GDR's first prestige picture *Familie Benthin* [Family Benthin] (GDR, Kurt Maetzig, Slatan Dudow, Richard Groschopp, 1950),[144] antifascist exiles Heinrich Mann and Arnold Zweig provided the source texts for the GDR's two most notable adaptations of the decade: *Der Untertan* (Wolfgang Staudte, 1951) and *Das Beil von Wandsbek* (Falk Harnack, 1951).

Staudte wrote the script based on Heinrich Mann's *Der Untertan* together with his father Fritz and directed the adaptation. His film (released in English as *The Kaiser's Lackey*)[145] dissects human nature and, more specifically, German masculinity, which built on his previous *Rotation* (1949) and his analysis of hierarchical power dynamics and the human desire to conform during the Hitler era. While the burden of guilt in *Rotation* is so fundamental that the call for forgiveness almost rings hollow, Diederich Hessling (Werner Peters) in Staudte's *Der Untertan* is as disagreeable and creepily successful in his endeavors for most of the film as in Mann's text. Not surprisingly,

FIGURE 7.5 *Werner Peters in* Der Untertan *(GDR, Wolfgang Staudte, 1951) as the heavens open during his nationalist 'blood and iron' speech at the inauguration of Wilhelm I's equestrian statue.*

Staudte's adaptation was praised as 'faithful' to its source text and 'respectful' of the memory of Heinrich Mann.[146] Herbert Ihering even celebrated the late Heinrich Mann as the 'innovator', who had provided a new German cinema with inspiration and momentum.[147]

Werner Peters stars in Staudte's film as the Kaiser's 'loyal subject' Diederich Hessling. He is a caricature of a citizen, and the film's epilogue unambiguously links his behavior to the rise of National Socialism and the destruction of Germany. The adaptation was praised as Staudte's 'masterpiece'.[148] When screened by some film societies in the West, reviews generally echoed the gist of reactions internationally. *The Manchester Guardian*'s London film critic wrote, for example, that while the film "expressed hatred of German nationalism, as it was interpreted under the Hohenzollerns and Hitler," he was pleased to report that Staudte's adaptation "bangs no specifically Soviet drum."[149] In the GDR, however, the leadership rebuked Staudte's lack of explicit political commitment, and questioned the adaptation's intellectual and affective contribution to the construction of a socialist community.[150] The film's aesthetic mastery and critical engagement with Germans' penchant for cynical authoritarianism did not satisfy those looking for a clear antifascist message that foregrounded communist and socialist victimhood.

On the other side of the border, the West German political leadership dismissed the film's deconstruction of a petty bourgeoisie and the epilogue's clear reference to the rise and consequence of National Socialism as East German propaganda. The reception of the film sheds light on the fraught relationship between the two Germanies during the Cold War era, and on control mechanisms pursued and implemented on both sides. Officially, feature films were to be exchanged between the two Germanies—for example, the beautifully elaborate Agfacolor feature *Das kalte Herz* [The Cold Heart] based on Wilhelm Hauff's fairy tale (GDR, Paul Verhoeven, 1950) was to be made available to West Germany in exchange for the adaptation of the popular children's film based on Erich Kästner's *Das doppelte Lottchen* [Two Times Lottie] (FRG, Josef von Baky, 1950).[151] But, concerned that a socialist infiltration could be taking place via cinema screens, the West German ministry for trade made it increasingly difficult to exchange feature films for mutual benefit, mirroring practices of the McCarthy-era in the United States, adamant in suppressing the spread of 'communism'. There was little doubt about the power of film, but after twelve years of fascist rule many considered censorship and other forms of cultural control mechanisms highly problematic.[152]

On September 25, 1952, the West German weekly *Die Zeit* reported that a censorship law had been accepted in the West German parliament (Bundestag) despite the Social Democrats' vehement opposition. The proposed regulation smacked of the 1920s censorship law, which formed the basis of the new Cinema Act passed by National Socialists in 1934. *Die Zeit*'s Richard Tüngel lamented: 'So we're back here'. The vast majority of delegates supported the proposed protection of minors from indecent and disturbing texts and films, but also considered the potential for censorship of politically undesired publications and releases via this "Schmutz- und Schundgesetz" [dirt and trash law]. As the debates were dragging on, the FRG's government under Konrad Adenauer created a "West-Ost-Filmaustausch"-committee in 1953 that was to oversee the exchange of movies between the two Germanies. Here, films could be eliminated without due process, and as Michael Grisko reveals, several DEFA films were unofficially banned by the committee in closed sessions.[153]

In West Germany, Staudte's *Der Untertan* was released in a truncated version that most notably omitted the final sequence (images of ruins and the 'Horst-Wessel'-song, a favorite of the Nazi movement), which clarified the connection between the toxic chauvinism of the German Kaiser's loyal subject and the catastrophic consequence of National Socialism. It was not until 1957 that West German cinemas (rather than film societies) distributed the film. Conservative critics and Cold Warriors generally considered the DEFA product 'tendentious propaganda', but even some of them admitted to the reality of the 'obedient sycophant' and 'small tyrant' and the 'truth' in Staudte's persuasive portrayal of this particular type.[154]

Arnold Zweig, Falk Harnack, and the GDR

The second noteworthy adaptation of 1951 supported by GDR's state film company also caused political controversy and became the first banned feature film in the history of DEFA.[155] Based on Arnold Zweig's *Das Beil von Wandsbek* (The Axe of Wandsbek, 1943) and a script by Wolfgang Staudte, this project was focused on Germany's Nazi past and should have addressed the cultural industry's antifascist brief. Zweig's antiwar novel *Der Streit um den Sergeanten Grischa* (The Case of Sergeant Grischa, 1927)[156] had achieved international acclaim during the late 1920s. The Jewish, pacifist writer left Nazi Germany in 1933 and spent his exile mostly in the British Mandate of Palestine, before returning to the Soviet sector in 1948. As a committed socialist, Zweig supported the young GDR as Member of Parliament, as a delegate to the World Peace Council in 1950, and he also replaced the late Heinrich Mann as President of the GDR's Academy of Arts the same year.

The exile's novel *Das Beil von Wandsbek* was inspired by a newspaper report about a butcher, who agreed to carry out executions of communists on the day of Hitler's visit to Hamburg. The actual executioner had fallen ill, and the local government was eager not to 'spoil' the Führer's visit by postponing the event. Arnold Zweig's story focuses on the butcher Albert Teetjen, who faces bankruptcy and accepts the job of temporary executioner primarily for monetary reasons, hoping for anonymity. But his act has dire consequences—it destroys his family, and isolates him from his peers. His wife ends her life in despair and, eventually, the butcher follows suit. As Zweig wrote to fellow writer and exile F.C. Weiskopf, his aim was to 'make transparent the German bourgeoisie during the peak of fascism in 1937/38', and to outline the fatality of Germans' collective enthusiasm for Adolf Hitler.

Wolfgang Staudte wrote the film script in 1950, but Falk Harnack[157] directed the adaptation, which starred Berliner Ensemble actor Erwin Geschonneck[158] as Albert Teetjen. Harnack—Wehrmacht soldier in a penal battalion, resistance fighter and, finally, active member of the Greek partisan organization ELAS during the Second World War—had lost several family members to the viciousness of the SS and the Nazi courts. A committed antifascist, he served as artistic director as DEFA from 1949. But, as Joshua Feinstein highlights:

[R]egardless of their artistic merit, films dealing with morbid themes and moral dilemmas were of little interest to the Party. Political functionaries called for "socialist realism" and insisted on films brimming with confidence, populated with exemplary "positive heroes", and able to convince viewers that socialism was triumphing.[159]

Moreover, DEFA's Russian adviser General Igor Tschekin opposed Harnack's *Das Beil von Wandsbek*, expecting the film to have "a detrimental effect on East Germany's population, as it does not create hatred against fascism, but pity for the murderers."[160]

Thus, *Das Beil von Wandsbek* (1951) contributed significantly to the first ideological rupture and political crisis at DEFA. Empathy for the adaptation's tragic anti-hero was deemed entirely unacceptable and the film was pulled after only four weeks.[161] DEFA productions were to support the permeation of East German society with socialist ideology while contributing to a transnational socialist culture. On July 27, 1952, the Politburo Central Committee of the Socialist Unity Party issued a resolution that announced the promotion of 'progressive German film art.' At the same time, Harnack's film was renounced as fatally flawed due to its depiction of Teetjen, who was not the heroic fighter for the working class as envisaged by the GDR's political leadership but rather its executioner.[162] Deeply disappointed, Harnack resigned as DEFA's artistic director, and left for West Germany.

Film/Adaptation and Political Control East/West

On January 1, 1953, DEFA became a "volkseigener Betrieb" or 'company owned by the people'. Film production in East Germany was now fully nationalized and politics "began to truly impact reality at the studio," as Heiduschke states.[163] For cinema and adaptations to be produced and distributed, depended not merely on their quality, but on how convincingly they serviced socialist ideals and society. "Many films were banned for falling out of lockstep with the current artistic guidelines set by the SED, and for some artists, opposition was costly, ending their careers in East German cinema for good. Being blacklisted with the monopoly studio DEFA often meant unemployment—or the hope to receive a one-way visa to West Germany."[164] As Hake, Silberman, and others have outlined, Stalinist cinema and debates regarding socialist realism shaped GDR film from the early 1950s[165] until mass demonstrations in June 1953 led to the announcement of a 'New Course'. This "granted movie professionals somewhat more autonomy and also revitalized contacts with the West in order to respond to strong audience demand for more and better entertainment"[166] at least for a short while until political concerns began once more to outweigh pragmatic integration.

The fact that West German government increased its bank guarantee for film productions to 100 percent in 1953 was no coincidence, as it enabled more political control. West German producers, who collaborated with DEFA, were usually denied support.[167] Planned East- and West-German co-productions based on Kurt Tucholsky's *Rheinsberg* or Thomas Mann's *Buddenbrooks* failed to materialize. Even a renowned Nobel-laureate like Mann, who favored a collaboration between Abich's Filmaufbau and the GDR's DEFA for a new *Buddenbrooks* adaptation, was denied, despite the German public's interest in this adaptation of 'their last great classic' on both sides of the border.[168] For three years Hans Abich tried to gain the West German government's approval for the transnational project, but Bonn refused. According to State Secretary in the Ministry for Pan-German Affairs Franz Thedieck, this kind of co-production would have buttressed DEFA's wish for 'social and political respectability and credit-worthiness in West Germany', which Adenauer's government was not inclined to support at the time.[169] Nonetheless, GDR cinema was not insulated but, as Silberman and Wrage emphasize, in fact "its media landscape [was] characterized by constant dialogue, if not competition, with both the capitalist West and socialist East."[170]

Competing Ideologies and Owning the Canon I—from Lessing to Hauff

Questions of literary heritage became indeed integral to the definitions of culture in both Germanies, and adaptation—from period films to fairy tales— became an instrument of laying claim. After 1949, the role of adaptations of both canonical and contemporary literature in divided Germany must be considered in the context of competing political systems that nonetheless aimed at mass impact. Both Germanies competed for 'their' authors via cinema and television screens and filmmakers usually altered the literary texts' trajectories according to the current political climate. While West Germany generally preferred apolitical interpretations, the GDR's interest remained clearly in the promotion of a socialist ethos and community. Filmmakers often struggled with either form of conformism.

The global success of the Soviet fairy-tale adaptation Каменный цветок or *The Stone Flower* (USSR, Aleksandr Ptushko, 1946) charmed the DEFA board into approving the production of *Das kalte Herz* [lit. The Cold Heart; released as *Heart of Stone*], a Wilhelm Hauff-adaptation by Paul Verhoeven, who also directed the feature.[171] DEFA made a significant investment into the high-value, intricate production, which tells the story of poor Peter Munk, who sells his heart for endless wealth to an evil spirit and only realizes after the utmost catastrophe has occurred that he must win back his heart and humanity. The team responsible for the East German film company's first color-film included experienced cameraman Bruno Mondi, and Ernst Kunstmann, a specialist in animation. Mondi had been at the camera for Veit Harlan's *Jud Süß* (1940), *Die goldene Stadt* (1942), *Immensee* (1943), *Opfergang* (1944), *Kolberg* (1945), but was able to reinvent himself when filming the aforementioned *Wozzeck* (1947) under the direction of Georg C. Klaren, followed by outstanding features such as *Rotation* (DEFA, Wolfgang Staudte, 1949) and *Biberpelz* (DEFA, Erich Engel, 1949, based on Robert A. Stemmle's adaptation of Gerhart Hauptmann's 1893 play). Particularly due to the superb, but costly and time-consuming trick sequences (credited to Ernst Kunstmann), the project went vastly over budget and ended Verhoeven's collaboration with DEFA. *Das kalte Herz*, however, was a commercial success, and not only provided the foundation for fairy-tale film productions in the GDR, but the film's humanistic substance set the tone for the communication of a particular value system for years to come. The film encapsulates Germans' anxieties and desires far beyond escapist entertainment. As Silberman rightly notes, "Traumatic experiences being transformed into happy memories through goodwill and dependable labor indicates an early, wishful pattern of 'coming to terms with the past' in German postwar popular culture."[172]

In the FRG, Hubert Schonger, who had specialized in fairy-tale adaptations during National-Socialism, returned to the genre after the war, producing a series of Grimm adaptations for West German audiences during the late 1940s and 1950s.[173] He adapted *Zwerg Nase* [Dwarf Nose] (Francesco Stefani, 1952), for example, but Schonger's Hauff-adaptation was nowhere near as popular as Wolfgang Staudte's East German *Der kleine Muck. Ein Abenteuer aus 1001 Nacht* [The Story of Little Muck] the following year. DEFA's 1953 production of Hauff's 1826 Arabian fantasy[174] became DEFA's most successful production during the forty years of GDR filmmaking.[175]

This transnational Wilhelm Hauff-competition continued a few years later, when Kurt Hoffmann's *Das Wirtshaus im Spessart* [The Spessart Inn] broke West German box-office records in 1957. The musical comedy starring Lilo Pulver, who helped to imbue the feature with self-reflective irony and a sufficient dose of eeriness, was based on the framing narrative in Hauff's fairy-tale almanac of 1828. The GDR followed suit with the amusing satire *Der junge Engländer* [The Young Englishman, based on Hauff's *Der Affe als Mensch*/The Monkey as Man] (GDR/DEFA, Gottfried Kolditz, 1958), but was trumped once again by Kurt Hoffmann and his West German "Grusical" [spooky musical] sequel *Das Spukschloß im Spessart* [The Haunted Castle in the Spessart Mountains; distributed internationally as *The Haunted Castle*] in 1960 with music composed by Friedrich Hollaender, who had returned to Munich from Hollywood.

West German fairy-tale films of the time were mostly based on the Grimm brothers' classic transnational collection of *Children's and Household Tales* (1812/15). While many of the folk tales were not originally German at all but from other European countries, they had become part of Germany's cultural heritage due to the Brothers Grimm and their publication. As Dieter Wiedemann argues, quoting Christa Wolf, fairy-tale films and their promise of good prevailing over evil were integral to societies, especially during difficult times of change. As indicated above, in both Germanies, fairy tales were adapted to film regularly during this era. Only in 1951, following the enormous success of Walt Disney's *Cinderella* (1950), no new fairy-tale film was released in West Germany.[176] While Walter Oehmichen's *Brüderchen und Schwesterchen* [Brother and Sister] and *Die goldene Gans* [The Golden Goose] were well received in 1953, as was Fritz Genschow's *Rotkäppchen* [Little Red Riding Hood] (1953)—a fictionally revisionist remake of his 1937 adaptation—it became clear that West German fairy-tale films could not compete with Disney on the one side and DEFA on the other. Nonetheless, demand continued, especially with the increasing availability of television as the economy surged. Genschow continued to dominate the fairy-tale adaptation scene in the 1950s, with *Frau Holle* [Mother Holle] and *Hänsel und Gretel* [Hansel and Gretel] (both 1954), *Aschenputtel* [Cinderella], *Dornröschen* [Sleeping Beauty] (both 1955), and *Die Gänsemagd* [The Goose Girl] (1957). But other filmmakers, too, turned to this financially relatively dependable genre, among them Herbert Fredersdorf (*König Drosselbart* [King Trushbeard], 1954; *Der gestiefelte Kater* [Puss in Boots], and *Rumpelstilzchen* [Rumpelstiltskin], 1955), Walter Janssen (*Rotkäppchen* [Little Red Riding Hood], 1954), Otto Meyer (*Der Froschkönig* [The Frog Prince], 1954), Erich Kobler (*Schneeweißchen und Rosenrot* [Snow White and Rose Red]; *Schneewittchen und die sieben Zwerge* [Snow White and Seven Dwarfs], 1955; *Die Heinzelmännchen* [The Shoemaker and the Elves], 1956), Hans Wilhelm (*Der Teufel mit den drei goldenen Haaren* [The Devil with Three Golden Hairs], 1955), Jürgen von Alten (*Tischlein deck' dich* [The Wishing Table], 1956), Peter Podehl (*Der Wolf und die sieben Geißlein* [The Wolf and the Seven Young Goats], 1957), and Rainer Geis (*Die Bremer Stadtmusikanten* [The Bremen Town Musicians], 1959).

Adaptations of children's books in West Germany also included Heinrich Hoffmann's nineteenth-century authoritarian picture book and horrendous educational bestseller *Der Struwwelpeter* [Shaggy Peter], reimagined for the screen by Fritz Genschow in 1954. The same year, even a racist nursery rhyme was adapted to film: Rolf von Sydow's *Zehn kleine Negerlein* [Ten Little Niggers]. Considered a 'harmless' children's musical, the live-action feature tells the story of little African kids who endure their chief's tyrannical (and magical) power until they manage to free themselves from his dictatorship. The parallels to a comforting reimagination of recent German history in this film are as obvious as its colonial and racist inclination is unsettling. Genschow's and Sydow's adaptations could be regarded as products of the 'superintegration'-society's right-wing conservatism, and as active investments into the continuation of repressive educational structures and racism in West Germany. Thankfully, much more public support was granted to adaptations of Erich Kästner's amiable and insightful children's books, which the majority of cinemagoers clearly preferred. *Das doppelte Lottchen* (FRG, Josef von Baky, 1950), *Pünktchen und Anton* (FRG/A, Thomas Engel, 1953), *Das fliegende Klassenzimmer* (FRG, Kurt Hoffmann, 1954), and, especially, another adaptation of *Emil und die Detektive* (FRG, Robert A. Stemmle, 1954) tell stories of friendships among children across social and other divides, exemplifying solidarity, loyalty, and a willingness to work hard for those we love and to support those pushed to the margins.[177] Adaptations of Kästner's works have remained popular since Gerhard Lamprecht/Billy Wilder's fabulous *Emil und die Detektive* [Emil and the Detectives] in 1931, and are still reimagined for cinema and television screens today.[178]

As the West German 'economic miracle' accelerated, an adaptation of Hans Sachs' fairy-tale *Aufruhr im Schlaraffenland* [Riot in the Land of Plenty] (FRG, Otto Meyer, 1957) offered an intriguing and comical critique of prosperity that conveyed a simple logic: overeating leads to stomach pains, riches to resentment, and excess to boredom. It is the children, of course, who realize the need for change and finally take charge, attaining the help of the teacher (education), the doctor (healthcare), and a clever princess (there is a trustworthy 'elite' among the powerful) in order to rectify and reform in Sachs' land of plenty.[179]

From the mid-1950s the canon of German literature became the focus of filmmakers in both Germanies. As televisions became more affordable and an increasingly attractive entertainment option within the private sphere, TV studios "were busy cultivating associations with the theatrical and literary past" as Semenza and Hasenfratz convincingly argued in the context of British literature on television screens.[180] In both Germanies, too, the literary canon served to establish television as a meaningful pastime. In 1959, for example, Schiller's *Kabale und Liebe* was adapted twice for television—in West Germany under the direction of Harald Braun, and for East German cinema under the direction of Martin Hellberg. Competition also ensued over Lessing's work, when West German television adapted *Minna von Barnhelm oder Das Soldatenglück* (Minna von Barnhelm or the Soldiers' Happiness, 1767) under the direction of Ulrich Erfurth, and DEFA's Martin Hellberg directed an adaptation of the bourgeois tragedy *Emilia Galotti* (1772) at the same time. West Germany followed up with their *Emilia Galotti*-adaption for television in 1960, and another *Minna von Barnhelm*-adaptation for cinema entitled *Heldinnen* [Heroines] (FRG, Dietrich Haugk, 1960) the same year. Again, it was Hellberg who was put in charge of a follow-up: under his direction, yet another *Minna von Barnhelm* was brought to East German cinemas in 1962. The two film industries' wrangling over poor Minna continued as Lessing's comedy became a staple on both East and West German television screens with regular adaptations until 1979 in the FRG and 1984 in the GDR.

Owning the Canon II—Literary Realism

Master of realism Conrad Ferdinand Meyer is another canonical author who was brought to postwar television in both Germanies. His moving ballad "Die Füße im Feuer" (Feet in the Fire, 1867) was adapted west of the border as *Der Gast* [The Guest] (FRG, Konrad Wagner, 1956) and in the east as *Du sollst nicht töten* [You Shalt Not Kill] (Erich-Alexander Winds, 1957). The ballad's 'guest', who is being sheltered during a stormy night, turns out to be the torturer and murderer of the host's wife, who some years ago tried to force the lady of the manor to give up a suspected Hugenotte-refugee. Clearly reminiscent of those that were brave enough to shelter Jews during the Nazi era, both adaptations evoke the pain and losses suffered, and weigh the moral of the law of hospitality. In Meyer, it is a rule fundamental to the survival of society, and it cannot be broken as the last stanza reads: "Mein ist die Rache, redet Gott"—'Revenge is mine, speaks God'. As so often during this era, adaptation allowed for an implicit and yet public discourse about traumatic events of the recent past.

Meyer's novella *Gustav Adolfs Page* (Gustav Adolf's Page, 1882) was turned into a feature film for cinema in 1960, by scriptwriters Juliane Kay, Tibor Yost, and Peter Goldbaum. Filmed in autumn 1960 in picturesque Rothenburg ob der Tauber, the Altmühl-valley and in Wien-Film studios in Vienna, the adventure film was directed by Rolf Hansen in a West-German-Austrian co-production (Peter Goldbaum Produktion, Munich, and Stöger's Viennese Mundus-Film). Here, popular Swiss starlet Liselotte Pulver plays Gustl Leubelfing, a tomboy and ardent fan of Gustav Adolf, king of Sweden. When Gustav Adolf (Curd Jürgens) comes to Nuremberg, where Gustl lives with her uncle, she dresses as a boy to serve her idol as his page. This interesting act of deception and entertaining gender-bending roleplay, however, offers Gustav Adolf's enemies an opportunity of conspiracy aimed at the king's downfall. While critics were not enthusiastic about the adaptation, they praised the co-production's effort in providing "gehobene Filmunterhaltung"[181]—upscale film entertainment. Once again, it was the canon of German-language literature that was to substantiate mass entertainment, assure cultural 'sophistication' on film, and—as it had done with cinema decades before—elevate German television on both sides of the border to the status of mediator of high culture.

Theodor Storm, another prominent representative of literary realism, was adapted already in 1950 by Veit Harlan as mentioned above. In 1954, the East German DEFA brought Storm's novella *Pole Poppenspäler* (1874) to cinemas. Arthur Pohl, who had helped adapt Thea von Harbou's *Das indische Grabmal* [The Indian Tomb] for Nazi Germany's cinema in 1938, wrote the script based on Storm's novella and directed the romantic drama for DEFA in Potsdam/Babelsberg. The film was successfully exported and screened in West Germany in 1956, this time entitled *Das Dorf in der Heimat* [The Village in the Homeland]—relating the Storm adaptation to other *Heimat*-films, West Germany's financially most successful genre. In East Germany, audiences were particularly taken with the use of puppets in the live-action film, and the following year, Herbert Schulz wrote and directed the puppet-animation *Der kleine Häwelmann* [Little Havelman] for DEFA, based on Storm's eponymous fairy tale, further expanding DEFA's expertise and standing in the area of animation and children's films. Subsequently, in West Germany, Veit Harlan once again tried his luck with an adaptation of a Storm novella. His 1958 film *Ich werde dich auf Händen tragen* is based on *Viola tricolor* (1874) and turns Storm's story about the difficulty of loss and remembrance into a tear-jerking melodrama once again featuring his wife Kristina Söderbaum.

Considering adaptations of the German-language canon during the 1950s, the movement of literary realism proved attractive to filmmakers, who anticipated audiences' longing for a past untouched by two world wars. Storm's, but also Theodor Fontane's depictions of individuals' and families' everyday lives across the social spectrum appealed to readers and cinemagoers alike both in East and West Germany. Arthur Pohl's adaptation of Fontane's *Frau Jenny Treibel* (Mrs Jenny Treibel, 1893) for DEFA foregrounds class in a politically conscious reworking of the source text and is typical in its effort to meet the expectations of the GDR's leadership. Pohl's film is named not after the upper-class Jenny Treibel (Trude Hesterberg), but is here entitled *Corinna Schmidt* (1951) after the daughter of the novel's secondary school teacher (Hans Hessling). Accordingly, the film emphasizes the need to choose human decency, strength of character, and education (represented by Corinna's father and her cousin Marcell), rather than waste one's life striving for social status and material riches. Pohl supplemented his adaptation with socialist ethics and views, and thus links the revered author to GDR society, culture, and a socialist value system. Cousin Marcell (Peter Podehl) is an example of a decent human being who is expelled from the country for his political activism, thus providing a canvas for the memory of socialist and communist victims of Nazism.

Fontane's *Effi Briest* was also adapted to film in West Germany. It was 1954, the year the FRG and the GDR were allowed back into the international community of sport, which sent a nearly forgotten wave of national enthusiasm through the divided country, especially when the West German soccer team brought home the World Cup after beating Hungary in the 'miracle of Bern' in Switzerland in the final. Following the tremendous financial success of Hans Hellmut Kirst's *08/15* trilogy and its adaptation starring Joachim Fuchsberger as the 'good, clean' Wehrmacht soldier—another most useful narrative to be discussed below—the Divina-Film company in Munich invested heavily into their adaption of Fontane's famous novel. Entitled *Rosen im Herbst* [Roses in Autumn] (1955) and directed by Rudolf Jugert, the movie featured star actor Ruth Leuwerik[182] as (a slightly too mature) Effi and Bernhard Wicki as Innstetten. Jugert had worked with and studied direction under Helmut Käutner, and his mentor's influence is clearly visible in the film. Jugert designed *Rosen im Herbst* as a lavish color film that stands firmly on the shoulders of Gründgens' previous adaptation of Fontane's novel (1939; Ch. 5) without, however, wishing to focus on the 'question of guilt' merely a decade after the war. To this end Horst Budjuhn re-scripted the dialogues and actualized the film plot by adding new passages. Political commentaries or shades of social criticism were to be strictly avoided on the producer's behest that 'all political issues had to disappear'. This even included references to Bismarck, which were all cut.[183] This new *Effi Briest* is a sentimental film about love in a regional setting, a melodrama and a typically escapist product of the West German film industry of the 1950s.[184] The choice of actors, too, was the usual mixture of postwar stars like Leuwerik and Wicki, supported by familiar greats of the silent film (Lil Dagover) and particularly of Nazi cinema (Carl Raddatz, Paul Hartmann, Dagover, etc.). Hartmann, who had played the lead in Karl Ritter's atrocious propaganda film *Pour le Mérite* (1938) and shortly after Major Crampas in Gründgens' *Der Schritt vom Weg* (1939), turns up here as Effi's likeable father. Franz Grothe, producer and conductor of numerous musical scores for Nazi-films (from *Zwei im Sonnenschein* [Two in the Sun], 1933, to *Rätsel der Nacht* [Riddles of the Night], 1945), composed the music that underscores the adaptation's melodrama.

The film imitates elements of Gründgens' dramaturgy but fails to reimagine its predecessor's ambivalent complexity. The emphasis of this adaptation is on Effi; vivacious and striving for independence, she brings suffering and destruction upon herself and her loved ones with her mixture of ambition and thirst for adventure. Critical memory culture, present in numerous West German feature films at least as an inoffensive subtext, is here displaced by the failing love story between Innstetten and Effi. Two additions by Budjuhn, however, are noteworthy: a conversation on the beach between Effi and her lover Crampas about Heinrich Heine—German-Jewish poet, politically persecuted and exiled—and his poem "Die Heimkehr" [The Return] from the *Buch der Lieder* [Book of Songs] and, as a focal point of this adaptation of Fontane's novel first published in 1894/5, a speech by the minister during a New Year's Eve party—celebrating the year 1900 and the dawn of a new era. In his speech, the minister expresses his gratitude for the innovations of the past century: the telephone invented by a Scot, the lightbulb by an American, and Otto Lilienthal's 'flight apparatus', which 'has carried us Germans up high, because no one has ever risen to such heights as Otto Lilienthal'. References to Britain and the United States, important partners of the young West German state, and the pioneering aviator Lilienthal, replace military or political figures of the nineteenth century such as Bismarck. In conclusion, the minister wishes everyone a new century of 'joy, progress [and after an evocative pause, with emphasis:] and peace'.

The fatal consequences of putting career and Fontane's 'social something' that exacts proper behavior, wealth and social standing before love and community, are highlighted dramaturgically in the final sequence, when the news of Effi's death, relayed to Innstetten via telephone call by Gieshübler, arrives almost simultaneously with a sealed letter informing her widower of his promotion. In the final sequence of the film, the camera zooms from Innstetten's palpable agitation to a shot of Effi's empty swing in the fog and, a clichéd cut if there ever was one, to heaving waves accompanied by a sentimental musical score. 'Love is the highest form of religion'—quoting the inscription of the Chinese grave at Kessin—is presented to the postwar audience like an intercultural motto to take home with them, for the tragedy here does not lie in the conformity of the individual to prevailing norms, but simply in the breakdown of a bourgeois marriage. Despite its overall positive reception, critics repeatedly implied the adaptation's 'mediocrity' or even 'triviality', which owed much to its producers' obedience to and anticipation of viewers' tastes and sensibilities in the emerging "cinema of consensus."[185]

Living Greats of a Bygone Era

Famous since the early twentieth century, Nobel prize-winning author Gerhart Hauptmann had been included in Hitler's 'God-gifted list' during the Second World War and considered integral to German culture under National Socialism. His works had been adapted to cinema screens since *Atlantis* (1913) and were popular source texts in the Nazi film industry.[186] Nonetheless, his literary works were thought of highly in the Soviet Union, and Wilhelm Pieck, Johannes R. Becher, and Sergei Ivanovich Tiulpanov attended and spoke at the funeral service for Hauptmann in Stralsund in 1946. But it was West German film companies that undertook adaptations of his works, beginning with the musical drama *Königin der Arena* [Queen of the Arena], a loose adaptation of his novel *Wanda* (FRG, Rolf Meyer, 1952). Six major productions based on Hauptmann's works followed during the 1950s. In contrast to *Königin der Arena,* the adaptation of his play *Die Ratten* [The Rats] (FRG, Robert Siodmak, 1955) was a high-profile project shaped by the courage of its producer Artur Brauner, scriptwriter Jochen Huth, and director Robert Siodmak. With Maria Schell and Curd Jürgens in the lead, the film tells the tragic story of Pauline Karka (Schell), who is pregnant, homeless, and utterly destitute. Jürgens manages not to succumb to the glamour of previous screen appearances and convincingly portrays a heartless and lazy brute. Producer Brauner was adamant that Huth's script should emphasize female agency rather than portray martyrs or victims. Following international criticism that German films all too often promoted compassion and even highlighted former perpetrators' victimhood, his film attempts to avoid a "Mitleidstour" ['pity tour'] and instead shows strong individuals who are hardened by the suffering they endure.[187]

1956 alone saw the premieres of three Hauptmann adaptations— *Fuhrmann Henschel* (Josef von Baky), *Vor Sonnenuntergang* (Gottfried Reinhardt), and Wolfgang Staudte's *Rose Bernd*. Staudte's first West German adaptation after his *Mutter Courage* [Mother Courage, based on Brecht's play] (GDR/Sweden) was aborted, starred Maria Schell. In the early 1950s, the actor was considered the ticket when it came to pulling West German film from the 'bog of mediocrity'[188] but neither the press nor cinemagoers in West Germany appreciated scriptwriter Walter Ulbrich's and Staudte's depiction of Rose as a vulnerable Silesian refugee, who is sexually harassed, raped, marginalized, and exploited. Only the Protestant film journal *Evangelischer Filmbeobachter* praised the adaptation's 'suggestion of overcoming guilt and suffering through forgiving love'.[189] The ability for unconditional love and forgiveness is represented by August Keil (Hannes Messemer), a "meek and modest printer, a skinny, bespectacled little guy," as the reviewer in the *New York Times* called him in 1959.[190] Internationally, the adaptation did surprisingly well and received some excellent reviews. While the positive connotation of "bespectacled little" August and his (nonheroic) masculinity and kindness did not meet the expectations of West German audiences, abroad this renegotiation of male gender norms in a German movie was clearly welcomed.

In the meantime, Hans Abich of Aufbau Film continued his efforts to renew and reform German cinema.[191] Central to this undertaking was another Nobel-laureate, Thomas Mann, who had always been interested in cinema and continued to be eager to sell the rights to his literary work for adaptation. Films such as *Königliche Hoheit* [Royal Highness] (Harald Braun, 1953), *Bekenntnisse des Hochstaplers Felix Krull* [Confessions of Felix Krull] (Kurt Hoffmann, 1957),[192] *Buddenbrooks* (Alfred Weidenmann, 1959), and *Tonio Kröger* (directed by Abich's long-time friend Thiele in 1964) successfully incorporated bourgeois literary and exile culture into West-Germany's cinema landscape. Mann had spent his exile with his family in France and the United States and refused Walter von Molo's invitation to return to Germany after the end of the war. The reintegration of the internationally acclaimed author into the West German cultural industry via adaptation was significant, especially as several high-profile exile writers such as Lion Feuchtwanger and Heinrich Mann were considered culturally and politically affiliated with the GDR, and other left-leaning authors, like Bertolt Brecht and Friedrich Wolf, had returned from exile to make a new home in East Berlin rather than in West Germany.[193]

While *Bekenntnisse des Hochstaplers Felix Krull* remains the most interesting of Thomas Mann-adaptations of the decade, the author's reaction to the adaptation project was rather ambivalent. Both in his diary and in letters, Mann considered an adaptation of his unfinished novel ludicrous and a whim. Erica Mann, however, who negotiated the rights on her father's behalf, repeatedly emphasized her father's enthusiasm for and enjoyment of the project.[194] Once production of this adaptation had commenced, Erica remained deeply involved, and even appears briefly as Eleanor Twentyman's English governess.[195] The reception of the film was very positive, despite the usual criticism of the screen version's lack of the subtleties of parody and linguistic brilliance so typical for Mann's literary work.[196] The film's successful amalgamation of cultural sophistication and witty entertainment enabled audiences to celebrate once again an imagined continuation of world-class German-language prewar literary and film culture. Horst Buchholz, who played the charming dreamer Krull with plenty of sex appeal, was celebrated in the German press. Abroad, the adaptation disappointed. Bosley Crowther considered the film all too "tame" and blamed "the late Thomas Mann, from whose pathetically weak last novel this not very sparkling film was made. And apparently neither he nor Robert Thoeren and Erika Mann, who wrote the script, could endow their plainly Teutonic playboy with real romantic spirit or even wit."[197]

Shortly before he passed away in 1955, Thomas Mann wrote about cinema and his 'eagerness to see my own narrative works transferred to the screen—provided that it is done with as much love and tact as the adaptation of *Royal Highness*.' He considered Harald Braun's 1953 film 'a truly tasteful showpiece that pleases the eye, amuses the crowd, and even transposes quite a bit of my intellectual intentions.' He had 'high hopes' for the future of cinema, but as Mann considered it a place of entertainment rather than of high culture, he remained ambivalent toward the medium, even if he 'did not believe, that a good novel would necessarily be ruined by its adaptation'.[198]

The success of *Die Bekenntnisse des Hochstaplers Felix Krull* enabled Filmaufbau to adapt Hugo Hartung's 1957 satirical novel *Wir Wunderkinder* [lit. We Miracle Children] for Constantin, Germany's distributor of Columbia and United Artists' movies at the time. The story of two quite dissimilar schoolmates serves to recount and explain German history of the first half of the twentieth century and was exactly the kind of contemporary voice Abich had been looking for. This comedic adaptation of the novel was a hit, both in West Germany and abroad. Marketed as *Aren't We Wonderful?* in the United States, old stager Kurt Hoffmann was awarded the Golden Globe for the best 'Foreign Film' in 1960. Postwar heartthrob Hansjörg Felmy plays the idealist journalist Hans, who loses his job when the Nazis come to power. His classmate Bruno (Robert Graf) is a selfish opportunist, who manages to navigate successfully through dictatorship and also occupation, emerging as a wealthy business man, who enjoys life and power during West Germany's economic miracle. Thanks to a Jewish friend, who returned to the 'old fatherland' from his 'new home' as part of the US military, Hans is offered work as a journalist to the delight of his young family. When he publishes an article about Bruno's Nazi past, his self-serving and inattentive former classmate confronts him and threatens to take legal action. But his angry threats ring hollow when he, still reeling from indignation, falls to his death into an elevator shaft. Hoffmann's film appears firmly in the tradition of Robert A. Stemmle's internationally successful rubble film and social satire *Berliner Ballade* (1948)[199] as it addresses the need to eliminate unrepentant former Nazis by way of comedy. But a decade later Hoffmann foregrounds much more directly if no less amusingly the fatal consequence of Germans' unwillingness to 'open their eyes' and think critically about their past. Among his handwritten notes on the draft of the screenplay is an anti-'all persons fictitious'-disclaimer, which was to follow the opening credits: "Die handelnden Personen haben mit lebenden Personen viel zu tun" [The acting individuals have a lot to do with living persons]. While the disclaimer subsequently included in the film still states that the identification with actual living persons is intended and should be inferred, parallels to present-day West Germany portrayed in the film are merely 'coincidental'[200] as the intertitle states. Hoffmann prioritized the creation of a role model (Hans) and a product suitable for mass entertainment, and had no interest in causing a scandal. But the film was criticized nonetheless—for its depiction of the Nazis' rise to power as an 'operational accident' that lacks any significant analysis of the reasons for the masses' enthusiastic support for Hitler and his venomous ideology.[201]

Rearmament and Redefinitions of Masculine Agency in (Anti-)War Film

When the Second World War ended, the three 'Ds'—demilitarization, denazification, and democratization—were identified as central to the Allies' function during the occupation of Germany. During the escalating Cold War with the Soviet Union and not least due to the Korean War, however, West Germany's geographical position at an ideological frontline quickly energized the debate around remilitarization in the early 1950s. After a couple of years of heated deliberations in the context of the

Bonn-Paris conventions, the way for rearmament of the FRG, including the establishment of a "Bundeswehr" (Federal Army), was paved by the ratification of the treaty at the Allied High Commission's last meeting in Bonn on May 5, 1955. Now a sovereign state, West Germany agreed to the continued military presence of French, British, and US American troops on its soil, and became a member of NATO, thus "marking the official return of Germany to the company of civilized nations"[202] as Lawrence S. Kaplan put it. The rearmament debate, however, continued in parliament for another year until the Bundeswehr was officially established. Both literature and film contributed to this debate and in some cases, as the final part of this chapter outlines, were instrumentalized to communicate a remodeled and positive image of a new generation of German soldiers.

Drama romance war films had become a successful genre on both sides of the Atlantic—from *Es kommt ein Tag* [A Day Will Come] (FRG, 1950, Rudolf Jugert)[203] based on Ernst Penzoldt's 1941 novella *Korporal Mombour*, to the second highest grossing film of 1953[204] *From Here to Eternity* (USA, F. Zinnemann, based on the 1951 novel by James Jones). Conveying the shock of war and the reality of death and destruction as a backdrop, these romance movies had mass appeal and critics repeatedly praised their 'make love not war' rhetoric. In the context of the rearmament of West Germany, contemporary German literature played a considerable role in the debate, most prominently Carl Zuckmayer's play *Des Teufels General* (The Devil's General, 1954) and Hans Hellmut Kirst's three *08/15* novels (1954/5)[205]—particularly once the texts' message had been amplified via adaptations to cinema screens. The two male leads—Joachim Fuchsberger in Paul May's adaptation of Kirst's hugely popular *08/15* trilogy (1954/5), and Curd Jürgens as Hitler's air force General in Helmut Käutner's adaptation of Carl Zuckmayer's *Des Teufels General* [The Devil's General] (1955)—both put critical, independent thought center stage and, together with depictions of human decency as integral values of any 'good' soldier, these films consider the possibility of keeping one's hands 'clean' even in the Wehrmacht. This was a significant shift from earlier German films about the Second World War and reflected debates about the crisis of conventional masculinity and traditional gender roles in postwar Germany's public sphere at the time.[206]

The struggle to reassert masculine agency is particularly interesting in the context of *08/15*. Kirst's war novels and, if to a lesser degree, May's adaptation foreground a different kind of masculinity, which is based on humanist ethics rather than ideology, thus enabling a smooth transfer of those values and male agency into civic engagement in post-Second World War West Germany. The novels and their adaptations offer a chronological review of Germany's military history with a focus on three periods: from the annexation of Austria in 1938 to the invasion of Poland in September 1939 (part 1); the war winter of 1941/2 (part 2); and, finally, the end of the war in April/May 1945 and the immediate postwar era (part 3). Both literary text and adaptation differentiate clearly between the "military" and the ideologues among them, while highlighting Nazi ideology as responsible for turning good Germans into bad humans no matter their rank. In the films, good, critically minded men who despised Hitler's "dishonest war" like Private Asch and Major Luschke (Wilfried Seyfert) are placed opposite bad, i.e., unthinking, selfish, and sadistic brutes like Hauptmann Witterer (Rolf Kutschera), SD-officer Greifer (Michael Janisch), or SS-officer Hauk (Hannes Schiel). Symbolic images serve to indicate a history and Nazi present of toxic masculinity imbued by military heroism and destructive ideologies.

Kirst's bestselling satirical novels focus on Private Asch, a young soldier in Hitler's military, and convey the dynamics of repression and subversion during his army training, during the war, and into the postwar period.[207] Asch is everything but the outstanding and heroic German soldier the Nazis had in mind. He is nothing special, a cog in the machine of a system that is distinguished by permanent, mindless drill, symbolized by the '08/15' machine gun, first used in the First World War, and once again cheaply mass-produced during the Second World War. Central to their pointless everyday as they shoot, clean, and reassemble the weapon, the machine gun exemplifies average. "Gefreiter Asch" reminded readers in the 1950s of the German figure of speech "Schütze Arsch im letzten Glied" ['Private Ass in the last row']. With this expression, soldiers referred to their position of disempowerment and dependency, while conveniently releasing themselves from responsibility in the context of the Second World War and the Holocaust. According to Walter Nutz, no other war novel sold more copies in Germany than Kirst's *08/15*, which had been published in serialized form in *Die neue Illustrierte* first, significantly increasing the magazine's print-run.[208]

The run-away bestseller, of course, recommended itself for adaptation. Fuchsberger, an unknown actor[209] who played Private Asch in the adaptations, became the face of the 'clean' Wehrmacht soldier, who did not lose his sense of humor or sight of his own humanity while becoming increasingly aware of the madness of war and National Socialism. The tremendous success of Kirst's novels and their adaptations hinged on both the texts' and the films' skilled and unthreatening portrayal of a familiar and yet difficult past. Highly entertaining and imbued with sardonic wit, May's films suggested a productive engagement with the recent war effected by a dictatorial and inhumane system. Both Kirst's novels and their adaptations implicitly encouraged participation in a political present that imagined a better future. An awareness of the past was integral to this future, even if only in the interpretative context of a systemic preparation of Germany's moral and material catastrophes by a 'misled' military. Fuchsberger as Private Asch was instrumental in providing a sympathetic canvas for this engagement of everyone who had been swept along, inadvertently or intentionally becoming a cog in Hitler's murderous machine.

The *08/15* trilogy was shaped by the team's interest in commercial success, which at the time still hinged on a palpable message for the wider public. The director and his scriptwriter Ernst von Salomon[210] prepared to show the consequences of 'the evil of power in the wrong hands' while emphasizing the separation between those mighty perpetrators and the majority of average Germans. The opening sequence sets the tone, when it foregrounds the wall of the military training facility, identifying the ideologically driven space as a closed entity by voiceover: 'Walls have always been symbols of insularity. Walls create a boundary and mark a world within a world.' The message was clear and made the depiction of Germans' crimes palpable: the evil purported in the years 1933–45 is not Germany, but the Nazi regime. Not the German people should feel guilty; it is the fanatics that are responsible. Nonetheless, their crimes are part of a shared past, which must be acknowledged. In an interview May said: 'A People that fails to respect its past does not have a future.'[211]

The trilogy's convenient narrative about the 'clean' Wehrmacht, filled with regular human beings and usually sound and humane leaders, is unrealistic, as scholarship and the Wehrmacht exhibition of 1995 have shown.[212] Four decades earlier, the narrative about loyal but harmless subjects sat very well indeed with a generation of Germans, with millions drafted into the Wehrmacht, who had to come to terms with their support of a murderous regime. Despite the novels' enormous commercial success, von Salomon toned down the source texts' criticism of war as an event only to be enjoyed by 'animals', as Kirst notes. Notably, the screenwriter also eliminated most references to crimes against humanity—including rapes, enslavement and, in particular, the 'shooting of Jews' by those blinded by 'megaphones, bellowing, [...] printer's ink'.[213] War here is neither the heroic adventure of the Nazi's 'Landser'-books, nor is it the nightmare and paralyzing trauma of *Die Mörder sind unter uns* (1946). It is simply a "Scheißkrieg," an inconvenient and 'shitty war'. Robert G. Moeller convincingly argues that the adaptation of *08/15* was a reaction to popular US imports such as *The Desert Fox* (Henry Hathaway, 1951) and the aforementioned *From Here to Eternity* (Fred Zinnemann, 1953), and may well serve as a measure of Germans' willingness to deal with their past and to integrate selected aspects or interpretations into their present.[214]

The enthusiastic reception of the trilogy both among cinemagoers and film critics unveils the problematic nature of this adaptation project. As the minutes of parliamentary debates of the time indicate, those who insisted on pacificism and reminded others of their nation's moral failure under Hitler were labeled unrealistic dreamers suffering from 'neurosis'. Instead, most conservative representatives believed that positive traditions in the military

FIGURE 7.6 *Joachim Fuchsberger as 'citizen in uniform' Asch, challenging authority in* 08/15 *(FRG, Paul May, 1954).*

upheld by 'mentally stable' Germans—as foregrounded in the novels and, especially, in the films—could very well form the basis of a Bundeswehr.[215]

With Fuchsberger as their poster boy, the *08/15*-adaptations succeeded in affirming male agency and reinventing the archetypal postwar heroic narrative at the same time. Gunner Asch is young, rebellious, and thinks for himself. His moral compass remains intact throughout, his humanity and decency are emphasized repeatedly, as is his good humor and his ability to move on. The message is clear: war is to be avoided at all cost; and reason and human ethics as guiding principles should enable integration rather than exclusion. Asch became postwar West Germany's moral anti-hero, an educator who climbs the walls that intend to contain him and looks beyond ideology and discipline to communicate a form of citizenship compatible with the new capitalist sovereign state. As Moeller outlines in his insightful essay, the *08/15* trilogy is for its time and of its time, and was of utmost relevance for West Germany's rearmament debate in the mid-1950s.[216]

The director of *08/15* was awarded West Germany's media prize—a "Bambi"—for 'his vision and creativity that affected and inspired the German public' in 1955. The son of Ufa-producer Peter Ostermayr, Paul worked in the Nazi film industry as an editor and (co-)director and changed his name to May after the war.[217] His *08/15* films and a remake of John Knittel's *Via Mala* (1960) made his career in the FRG and are considered his most notable achievements. Commercially, his *08/15*-films were the most successful war-movies of the decade.[218] Their suggestion, that the problem of the past was an ideologically driven military insulated from society, and that no atrocities could have been committed if Germany had had more Aschs, more 'citizens in uniform', proved a most useful narrative, which paved the way for the approval of rearmament and the creation of a 'Bundeswehr'.

By the time *Die Brücke* [The Bridge] (FRG, 1959)—perhaps the most compelling antiwar film ever made in Germany—was screened in cinemas, the FRG's new ministry of defense and armed forces had been established.[219] Bernhard Wicki's film is an adaptation of a third-person autobiographical novel by journalist Manfred Dorfmeister (Manfred Gregor), published by Kurt Desch in 1958. The adaptation unmistakably depicts war as moral and human tragedy—and gives a voice to the many committed pacifists in Germany who saw rearmament with great concern. Both book and film tell the story of seven German boys of fifteen or sixteen years of age, drafted into the Wehrmacht during the final days of the Second World War, and ordered to defend a strategically insignificant bridge against advancing American troops. Only the narrator survives the event, and his traumatic memories remain an eternal hell from which there is no escaping, as the author states in the afterword to his novel.[220]

Both the book and its adaptation engage with the liminal nature and tragedy of war, but Wicki's film focuses particularly on the unraveling of children, men, and humanity during battle. The last twenty-five minutes of the film are devoted entirely to the boys' fear and pain, their wounds, violence, and disintegration. By clarifying the structure of the novel into a sequentially unfolding film narrative, Wicki managed to represent the consequences of war, i.e., the radical shift from life to death, from animate to inanimate, from joy and laughter to sheer horror and unbearable screams of pain. Creating an aesthetic informed by the unobstructed view of the documentary and the affective rhetoric of the melodrama alike, Wicki radically reduced camera-distances, and forced audiences to witness close-up the distorted faces of these boys, as they weep and soil themselves, overwhelmed by the horror of battle. In this film, Wicki turned his back on the light and rosy future of a booming West Germany, entering the darkness of the past by telling a 'true story' that never made it into any of the military records as he states at the end of this film. This conclusion is another intertextual reference to Remarque's novel that pays homage to and integrates his own film into the tradition of antiwar cinema beginning with Milestone's *All Quiet on the Western Front* in 1930.

In an interview in *Der Spiegel* in 1959 Wicki said: 'In most westerns and war films, men die quietly and without pain. They are hit, fall over and are dead. [...] I wanted to show how one really died—not quickly and

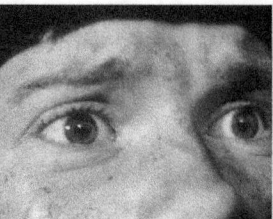

FIGURE 7.7 *Volker Lechtenbrink scared in* Die Brücke *(FRG, Bernhard Wicki, 1959)*.

heroically but suffering and screaming.'[221] Wicki's highly effective semiotic acknowledges the boys' fears and their deaths as painful, messy, and crude. His work can be seen as *Trauerarbeit*—work of mourning or grieving—a term introduced by Sigmund Freud in his text *Trauer und Melancholie* (1916) and taken up in 1967 by Margarete and Alexander Mitscherlich in their aforementioned bestselling study on the German people's inability to mourn the heinous crimes committed in the name of National Socialism: *Die Unfähigkeit zu trauern. Grundlagen kollektiven Verhaltens* (*The Inability to Mourn: Principles of Collective Behavior*). Wicki demands that his audience look. His images of war speak of the madness of voting antisemitic, racist brutes into office, of the horror of war, and of the need to speak about the crimes and trauma. As Elie Wiesel wrote in his memoirs *And the Sea Is Never Full*: "Human silence is at the core of inhumanity."

As indicated above, neither antiwar literature nor films all too critical of Germany's Nazi past were particularly welcome in West Germany, while the young country was busy enjoying its US Marshall-plan and currency reform induced 'economic miracle'. It took Dorfmeister/Gregor four years to find a publisher for his autobiographical text. When Vicki Baum's 1929 novel *Menschen im Hotel* was adapted once again in 1959 with a star-studded cast that included O.W. Fischer, Heinz Rühmann, and Gert Fröbe, the German-French co-production of CCC-Film GmbH (Berlin) and Les Films Modernes S.A. (Paris) eliminated war memory altogether. Director Gottfried Reinhardt[222]—the son of celebrity theater and film director and producer Max Reinhardt and actor Else Heims[223]—had learned his craft early on at MGM in Hollywood. He had been praised highly for his first German film, an adaptation of Gerhart Hauptmann's play *Vor Sonnenaufgang* [Before Sunrise] (1956). Also produced by Holocaust-survivor Artur Brauner's CCC-Film, with Hans Albers starring as elderly industrialist Mathias Clausen, Jochen Huth's script and Reinhardt's direction ensured that the remake unveiled the tragedy of human conflict, and, if implicitly, the shameless use of German-language literature for propaganda purposes by the Nazi's film industry.

Exile Writers and Films about War and Trauma

Brauner and Reinhardt's new adaptation of Baum's *Menschen im Hotel* reflects the challenges faced when addressing a traumatic past. Still a country with an unspoken undercurrent of antisemitism at the time, the adaptation of a Jewish writer's text, produced and directed by Jews, was considered perhaps commercially risky enough in West Germany, even without a focus on the devastation brought about by war. In both novel and its previous 1932 Hollywood adaptation *Grand Hotel*, personified by disfigured veteran Dr. Otternschlag as the immobile heart within the hotel's hustle and bustle, the memory of war is a manifest, conspicuous presence. Now, in the adaptation's 1959 remake, Dr. Otternschlag is absent, eliminated from the script, together with his traumatic past. It seems war memory has no place in economically flourishing West Germany, not even a marginal one. In the end, dead Baron Gaigern is carried out the back of the luxury abode and witnesses of the murder are asked to keep silent—'The reputation of the hotel, you understand ...' the director explains, which might also be read as an ironic, self-referential remark regarding contemporary film production and consumption practices. The façades are to be kept intact, and the survivors retreat into the private sphere. This denial of war memories and atrocities is consistent with the West German film industry's commitment to entertaining the masses which, from the mid-1950s onwards, localized the self in the private sphere. Aleida Assmann called this vacancy a "Brachland des Vergessens"[224] or 'wasteland of oblivion' as memory fell victim to a society and culture increasingly unwilling—and as the Mitscherlichs suggested—unable to remember and thus work through and cultivate an understanding of their recent past.[225]

As this *Menschen im Hotel* adaptation exemplifies, exile writers were integrated into the West German cultural landscape, too, but especially if they had returned and were willing to support the cultural reconstruction of their former home. Carl Zuckmayer was one of the most revered of these exiles, especially among the younger generation, largely because he sought to inspire the German youth with hope for the future. Celebrated by an enthusiastic audience of more than two thousand when appearing as the keynote speaker at the International Youth Congress in Munich in June 1948, the stateless exile[226] acknowledged the challenges to be faced but, at the same time, conveyed his confidence in his young listeners, who would in his opinion effect a spiritual and moral renewal due to the 'strength, honesty and good will' of the next generation. Significantly, he rejected the notion of collective German guilt for the crimes against humanity committed in their recent past. Zuckmayer's speech was remembered by many as marking a new beginning for those who had been raised during National Socialism.[227] His magnanimous and empathetic attitude toward postwar Germany and his enormous talent as a writer of comedies, crime dramas, and love stories with human depth made him one of the most adapted contemporary writer in postwar Germany.

Already in 1948, Zuckmayer's then-unpublished novella *Nach dem Sturm* [After the Storm] was turned into screen drama under the direction of Gustav Ucicky. The adaptation by Ucicky and Peter Wyrsch premiered first in Switzerland in November 1948 and in Austria and West Germany the following year.[228] Ucicky's aforementioned Zuckmayer adaptation *Der Seelenbräu* (1950) was followed by *Der fröhliche Weinberg* [The Merry Vineyard] (FRG, Erich Engel, 1952), *Eine Liebesgeschichte* [A Love Story] (FRG, Rudolf Jugert, 1953/4), and *Des Teufels General* [The Devil's General] (FRG, Helmut Käutner, 1954).[229] As Zuckmayer recounts in his autobiographical text *Als wär's ein Stück von mir*, he had given up his job as a Hollywood screenwriter and moved to a farm near Barnard, Vermont, when he read about the 'accidental' death of his friend Ernst Udet. The life of this First World War flying ace, who became Colonel-General in the German Luftwaffe, serving the Hitler regime in order to fly, inspired Zuckmayer to write the story of the 'Devil's General' called Harras.[230]

Des Teufels General became the most popular play[231] of the postwar era but was not without controversy. Particularly the depiction of Harras, a man in uniform, who refuses to take a stand and in the end dodges responsibility, was criticized in the conservative press.[232] The play not only served as an antidote to the collective amnesia regarding Germans' collaboration with the genocidal regime but, as Edward Plater points out:

> provided a sorely needed outlet for those who were struggling with their conscience and for the confused and questioning youth of Germany. Issues of particular concern involved the guilt of those in influential positions (like General Harras) who did not attempt to stop what they knew was wrong and of those who (like Oderbruch) engaged in sabotage in order to bring about their country's defeat and knowingly sent 'innocent' compatriots to their death in the process.[233]

And with a view on autonomous subjectivity, Mariatte C. Denman notes, Zuckmayer's classic play "does not just criticize the National Socialist cult of heroism in order to proffer a new definition of humanism […]. Rather, in the final scene Zuckmayer conjoins particular notions of masculinity with a narrative of self-sacrifice and atonement."[234]

Already in 1949, Zuckmayer planned to bring his successful play to cinemas, but it took another five years for the adaptation to take shape under Käutner's direction and be produced at Real-Film Studios in Hamburg. According to the director himself, "Allied military experts" advised Käutner "on how to make the film more 'realistic' by omitting controversial political issues mentioned in the play, such as philo-Semitic notions, references to communism, and the pogroms at the eastern front."[235] The adaptation of Zuckmayer's play catered to a mass audience, the majority of which "rejected the notion of German war crimes." As Plater reminds us, "55 percent felt that German soldiers in World War II had nothing to reproach themselves for in their behavior regarding the countries they had occupied."[236] When the film premiered at the 1000+seater Weltspiele cinema in Hanover on February 23, 1955, the final product reflected "the parameters of German Cold War cultural politics in the wake of Germany's rearmament,"[237] and presented Harras as a "less reckless, more sensible man, more in keeping with the ideal of the responsible citizen-soldier envisioned for the Bundeswehr."[238]

The much-discussed adaptation of Zuckmayer's play resonated both nationally and internationally.[239] Jürgens is at his best when a well-oiled Harras lectures Hartmann, a young Lieutenant worried about the lack of 'racial purity' in his family. Declaring the young man's despair complete nonsense, Harras enthusiastically describes the genetic benefits of the Rhineland, a melting pot of different cultures and races for thousands of years. As it was here, Harras tells young Hartmann that the diverse DNA of countless individuals—from a black Roman legionary to a Jewish spice merchant, a Swedish horseman to a French actor—created a multicultural breeding ground from which 'Germany's greats' such as Gutenberg, Beethoven, and Goethe eventually sprung.

In his review[240] of "The Devil's General" in the *New York Times*, A.H. Weiler conveys his surprise at this German production a decade after "Hitler's Holocaust" but seems pleased that the movie "strongly criticizes [the Nazi leaders'] rottenness, intrigues, jealousies and hatreds," even if it is invested more in "melodrama than drama." The "adaptation of Carl Zuckmayer's play [...] paints a murky and occasionally disjointed picture of a Luftwaffe technical genius," Weiler writes, but emphasizes that the film leaves no doubt regarding

> the drama's objectives. It strikes at the viciousness of the schemers in the High Command while showing that General Harras, a tall, handsome hero with a sense of humor who has won his medals honorably and openly hates the Gestapo and the industrialists, who are vying for Hitler's favor. As Hermann Goering's World War I comrade in arms, he is caught in the machinations of the corpulent Nazi No. 2 and Heinrich Himmler to gain control of the Luftwaffe in November, 1941. He is shown, too, as being compassionate toward the Jews, who are being slaughtered.

Critical of the "Russian campaign," he also "learns at first hand of the Gestapo's insidiously cruel methods. [...] And, he discovers in a climactic scene that his technical assistant has been sabotaging planes, which killed his fliers, as a desperate gesture to save Germany from further bloodshed."[241]

Interestingly, Weiler refers to 6.3 ft-tall Jürgens as "an actor of regal bearing and classic profile, [who] gives force and vitality to the role of the harassed air chief who is tortured by the signs of doom for his air force, ideals and country." His nemesis is SS-Gruppenführer Schmidt-Lausitz played by Victor de Kowa, whom Weiler describes as "arrogant and hard." It is in this opposition that not primarily political positions, but masculinities are being negotiated on the cinema screen. As producer Abich put it in 1996, when referring to films of the 1950s: 'The strength of men had come under high suspicion.'[242] Filmmaker Dominik Graf described Jürgens' General Harras as an obstinate powerhouse with a death-wish, a man of the past, a womanizer.[243] This supposedly admired military leader in his tailor-made uniform was a drunkard, a collaborator, whose saving grace is that he burps into de Kowa's face when the Gestapo bully tries to recruit him into the SS. Both men represent a difficult past, but de Kowa's Schmidt-Lausitz is an all too familiar Nazi-type, who advertises the SS as an organization of 'real men', where order means power, and 'power' is the guarantor of Germany's future. In the 1950s, viewers knew well how that turned out. While *Heimat*-films of the early 1950s all too often still featured knights in shining armor, Käutner's *Des Teufels General* managed to communicate the inevitable death of this 'hero' type to a mass audience.[244]

Star actor Jürgens' popularity made both the demise of prewar heroic masculinity and the depiction of this ambivalent and suicidal German officer palpable to German audiences.[245] In contrast, the two resistance dramas based on Claus von Stauffenberg's assassination attempt on Adolf Hitler, which both premiered in 1955, turned out what film producers called "Kassengift" [box office toxin]. A decade after the assassination attempt on Adolf Hitler, Stauffenberg and his group were still considered traitors by many Germans. While the widow of infamous and fanatical Nazi judge Freisler[246] received a full pension with benefits, the widow of Generalmajor Hellmuth Stieff, one of the July 20, 1944, conspirators hanged in August 1944, was denied her right to receive her husband's pension in three different trials until finally in 1960, sixteen years after her husband's death, she was granted a pension by the court of appeals. The two feature films about the assassination attempt—G.W. Pabst's and Falk Harnack's Stauffenberg resistance dramas *Es geschah am 20. Juli* [It Happened on July 20] and *Der 20. Juli* [The Plot to Assassinate Hitler]—competed for the attention of a mostly disinterested public.[247]

Significantly more popular with audiences were more adventurous reassessments of the function of the German soldier in three films under the direction of Frank Wisbar, who had also returned from Hollywood exile: *Haie und kleine Fische* [Sharks and Small Fish] (1958), his Stalingrad drama *Hunde, wollt ihr ewig leben?* [Dogs, Do You Want to Live Forever?] (1959)[248] based on the provocatively entitled eponymous autobiographical novel by Fritz Wöss, and *Fabrik der Offiziere* (1960), an adaptation of another novel by Hans Hellmut Kirst. The fate of a generation of young soldiers that had little choice but to become cannon fodder for the Nazi leadership was gaining currency at the time. Seeking a differentiated portrayal of masculinity and heroism, Wisbar's *Haie und kleine Fische* was based on Wolfgang Ott's autobiographical novel (1954) and tells the story of four friends on a minesweeper and submarine during the Second World War. Both novel and film highlight the mind-numbing, disempowering everyday of war. But unlike *Unruhige Nacht* [Restless Night], Harnack's story of a military pastor (also 1958, based on Albrecht Goes' war novella first published in 1950), which foregrounds the problematic and ambiguous nature of decency at times of war, Wisbar's young soldiers are simply 'small fish', we're told, who will be eaten by the sharks, who in turn receive their orders from 'the greatest shark of all, the one who lives merely to kill'. This simple rhetoric of atonement and liability paid off at the box office as it once again catered to the many West Germans who considered themselves not perpetrators but merely victims of a crazed dictator.

As in the *08/15* novels and films before, Wisbar's adaptations reaffirmed decency as a moral possibility even during the Second World War and thus maintained an element of nostalgia, while insisting on a value system untainted by National Socialism even during the twelve years of Hitler's dictatorship.[249] Nonetheless, charged with establishing the Bundeswehr, arch-conservative Bavarian politician and current Defense Secretary Franz-Josef Strauß and the Bundeswehr's Inspector General Heusinger informed Wisbar that his Stalingrad-film *Hunde, wollt ihr ewig leben?* and thus the depiction of 'this greatest tragedy of the German army' would open many wounds. This would 'not be in the interest of the general public', nor 'in the interest of the Bundeswehr', and would 'lead to considerable controversy among the population', Strauß himself warned the filmmaker. In his mind, West German society was not ready for this kind of film, a project he considered 'hazardous', 'particularly in political terms'.[250]

To conclude, the significance of the impact of the rearmament debate on filmmakers may be illustrated by an unusual Rilke adaptation by Walter Reisch. The prose poem *Die Weise von Liebe und Tod des Cornets Christoph Rilke* (The Love and Death of Cornet Christopher Rilke, 1899/1912) tells the story of an eighteen-year-old cavalry member in the seventeenth century who is elevated to cornet shortly before he dies at the hands of the Turks. Even before *Der Cornet* [The Cornet] premiered in December 1955, the production company published an open letter stating that the film is neither pro-war or military, nor does it intend to let 'Rilke ride for Germany'.[251] Reisch, who had worked predominantly as scriptwriter for directors such as Alexander Korda and Géza von Bolváry in Vienna and Berlin in the 1920s, returned to West Germany after spending his exile in London (writing and directing *Men Are Not Gods*, 1936) and, from 1937, in Hollywood. Working with other exiles such as Lubitsch and Wilder (*Ninotchka*, 1939), he received an Oscar-nomination for co-writing *Comrade X* (USA, King Vidor, 1940)—in which Clark Gable quips that "Germany just invaded Russia," an assault that did not happen until the Gottfried Reinhardt production had made a solid profit for MGM the following year. Reisch won the Academy Award for Best Original Screenplay in 1953 for *Titanic* (USA, Jean Negulesco, 1953) together with his co-authors Charles Brackett and Richard L. Breen. When he returned to West Germany for the premiere of *Comrade X* in 1954, Reisch set out to adapt (and expand) Rainer Maria Rilke's prose poem to prove that 'German film can be better than its reputation'.[252]

Reisch, who also directed the Eastman-colored film, 'modernized' Rilke's notes of an adolescent spirit, twenty-nine pages of almost shorthand, dreamlike reflections of naïve male heroism and sexual desire, all wrapped in events surrounding the Great Turkish War between the Ottoman Empire and the so-called 'Holy League' (the Habsburg Empire, Poland, Russia, and Venice) in the 1660s. However, already during the production of the costume drama, critics accused Reisch of instrumentalizing Rilke as minstrel for the military and his adaptation as an advert for rearmament. But in his interview with *Der Spiegel*, Reisch was adamant his film would be entirely apolitical, telling Rilke's story 'with other means'. The production company Fama clarified their intentions to the press as mentioned above. In Austria, the adaptation was even released as *Zärtliches Abenteuer* [Affectionate Adventure], referring to the night the Cornet supposedly spends with the lady of the castle instead of defending Christendom against the Turks. The 'collapse of time' evoked in Rilke's text becomes a clichéd close-up of the Cornet's first lover's face, raptly musing: 'it is beautiful to be happy, we have so little time for that ...'. After its nationwide release, Göran Strindberg's cinematography was praised (he received the German Film Prize in 1955), but Reisch's efforts were considered 'a suicidal attempt to expand Rilke's overrated prose of love and death into a 90-minute movie spectacle'.[253] The release of the film was a debacle for Fama. In the 1990s, however, the adaptation received belated recognition. Praising its 'candour and serenity', Fritz Göttler called Reisch's Rilke-film 'the most beautiful of all remigration-films of German cinema'.[254]

Conclusion

As this chapter has outlined, German-language literature on film contributed to cultural reconstruction processes in all German-speaking countries following the Second World War. Cinema in general and adaptations in particular served two main purposes during this immediate postwar period: stabilization and consolidation. Films that offered an innocuous and nostalgic review of the past or simply light-hearted escapism ranged among the most popular, but within the first decade after the war, under the conservative leadership of Chancellor Adenauer in West Germany and the socialist government in the GDR, state subsidies (and in East Germany: state ownership) provided a solid footing to postwar German film production that regularly included features based on German literature. While East German cinema usually catered to the ideal of an antifascist, socialist collective, the 'Adenauer-Kino' all too often indulged in dreams of an unsullied and undamaged homeland in *Heimat*-films, but neither side had much interest in a self-critical assessment of their shared and recent past. In either of the newly founded states, adaptations served to establish a sense of cultural heritage, mediated values, and provided entertainment. Adaptations were commodities ideally suited both for a national mass audience and for export, and thus avoided potential irritants at a time when the international community had little patience for German culture.

In West Germany, adaptations were the backbone of an anticipated restoration of cultural heritage and a multifaceted enactment of renewal. The literary canon, but also contemporary literature, was instrumentalized by numerous film producers, scriptwriters, and directors to reassure postwar audiences of both the continued existence and value of literary culture in German-speaking countries. In addition, adaptation served as a mostly nonthreatening mnemonic mode of production that helped to shape difficult memories in the public sphere. However, as the films discussed in this chapter convey, there is a clear interrelation between envisaged audiences and their potential willingness to engage with the horror of recent German history.

Nonetheless, adaptations of contemporary literature in the 1950s—*08/15*, *Des Teufels General*, *Die Brücke*—contributed to a more differentiated assessment of the past, highlighted the importance of critical thought and personal responsibility instead of blind obedience, and integrated pacifist principles and transnational awareness in the public sphere. The positive depiction of the 'mill of nations of Europe' in *Des Teufels General* helped to relegitimize German cinema internationally, while adaptations like *Die Brücke* were central to keeping the topic of antiwar in the public sphere. The real big sellers, however, were *Heimat*-films, musical films, romantic comedies, and remakes. "Kassengift" or 'box office poison' were films that addressed the division of Germany, social hardship, neglected children and broken families, but also critical assessments of Germans' antisemitism and unapologetic engagements with the country's Nazi past.[255]

During the fourteen years of Adenauer's chancellorship in West Germany, the public's willful amnesia regarding the crimes committed under Hitler's reign was supported by most of the major players in the West German and Austrian film industry. Examining this era through the looking glass of adaptation not only reveals the commercial draw of *Heimat*- and *Schlager* [pop song]-films. It also exposes the desire to lay claim to particularly popular literary texts via adaptation in both Germanies, to wrest cherished authors such as Fontane, Storm, and Hauptmann[256] from Nazi cinema, and to produce numerous and usually profitable remakes that implicitly linked postwar with anti-fascist, pluralistic Weimar culture and the 'golden age' of German cinema—from Kästner's *Emil und die Detektive* (FRG, Robert A. Stemmle, 1954), Zuckmayer's *Der Hauptmann von Köpenick* (FRG, Helmut Käutner, 1956), Hauptmann's *Rose Bernd* (FRG, Wolfgang Staudte, 1957), and Winsloe's *Mädchen in Uniform* [Girls in Uniform] (FRG, Géza von Radványi, 1958), to name but a few.

Moreover, a decade after the end of the Second World War and particularly in the context of the FRG's rearmament debate, adaptations provided canvases for subtle renegotiations of male heroism and, in some cases, offered noteworthy counter-representations of a differentiated (inquisitive, sensible, and mindful) masculinity on cinema screens.[257] While addressing the trauma of Germany's genocidal past remained difficult, especially in a medium that manages to summon the past more realistically and directly than any other, the contribution of Holocaust survivors, exile authors, and returning filmmakers was instrumental in bringing war guilt and trauma to cinema screens. Producers like Artur Brauner, and directors such as Gerd Oswald, Gottfried Reinhardt, Robert Siodmak, and Max Ophüls repeatedly turned to exile literature to address the consequences of Nazism and fascist convictions.

Having left Nazi Germany as a child in 1938 with his parents—actor Katharina Paar (Käte Oswald/Waldeck) and director Richard Oswald—exile Gerd Oswald remigrated to postwar West Germany and initially worked with producer Ludwig 'Luggi' Waltleitner, soon directing his own films. Waldleitner had specialized in adaptations of popular fiction by authors such as Joseph Kessel, William von Simpson, John Knittel and, most famously, the highly controversial and politically charged account of the events leading to the murder of high-class prostitute Rosemarie Nitribitt by Erich Kuby (*Das Mädchen Rosemarie*, Rolf Thiele, 1958).[258] But he also agreed to produce Gerd Oswald's *Schachnovelle* [Chess Novella] (*Brainwashed*/The Royal Game; FRG, Gerd Oswald, 1960). Oswald co-wrote the script and directed this first adaptation of Stefan Zweig's last work in exile. An exceptional reflection on the torture of solitary confinement and the lasting impact of Nazi rule in Austria, the adaptation stars once again Jürgens as Dr. B., who gradually loses control when a stolen book of chess matches becomes his only pastime, and his identity begins to split into black and white. The climax of both the novella and the film is a match with a chess champion aboard the ship that would bring the victim of Nazi terror to safety as he once again loses his grasp on reality. While the Nazis' violence succumbs to the power of B.'s mind on one level, as he successfully resists the Gestapo's methods and is finally released, the impact of torture and the destruction of the protagonist are powerfully communicated.[259]

Despite Jürgens starring in the picture, Waldleitner's and Oswald's prestige project initially failed to impress in West Germany, where critics labeled the film mostly a trite copy of Zweig's outstanding literary work. Considering the significantly more positive reception abroad, the reviews indicate once again Germans' reluctance to engage honestly and openly with the consequences of National Socialism. Two years earlier, in 1958, the Ulm Einsatzkommando trial addressed crimes committed by Gestapo and SS for the first time since the creation of the FRG. Following the trial, the Central Office of the State Justice Administrations for the Investigation of National Socialist Crimes was set up by Konrad Adenauer's government. The vast majority of the German public, however, had no interest in films about Nazi crimes and did not approve of 'stirring up' the past.

The difficulties of dealing with the past, the unwillingness to critically evaluate the Second World War, and the resistance to acknowledge the genocide of the European Jewry among Germans and Austrians during this era are reflected time and again in the choices of literary texts for adaptation and the films' reception. But slowly, shifting demands on viewers, a new generation of cinemagoers, and growing awareness and acceptance of the crimes committed through extensive media coverage of the Auschwitz trials (1963–5) in particular triggered a process that was to bring about fundamental change. Still, it was not until May 8, 1985, that Richard von Weizsäcker, West Germany's President at the time, addressed the fortieth anniversary of Nazi Germany's defeat and in his remarkable speech proclaimed that 'the secret of salvation is called memory'.

During the 1950s, most feature films emerging from the highly productive West German movie industry were run-of-the-mill pieces of entertainment that, according to Stuart Schulberg, failed to make "a significant contribution outside Germany," due to the Nazi's "legacy of artistic mediocrity, which is still hindering the development of originality and individuality." In addition, distributors, who commonly aimed "at the lowest common denominator—the small-town audience," were generally not interested in film art or pictures that critically addressed the country's Nazi past. Finally, Schulberg notes, West German government's national and local subsidy bodies, which were "badly burned in the past with heavy-handed 'serious' pictures—are now avoiding risk by supporting only 'sure-fire' commercial ventures."[260] As a consequence, by the end of the decade the industry was at serious risk. Creative input from returning exiles, adaptations of reliable canonical works such as Sudermann's *Jons und Erdme* (IT/FRG, Victor Vicas, 1959), of successful comedy plays such as *Die Ehe des Herrn Mississippi* (The Marriage of Mr. Mississippi, 1950) by the Swiss writer Friedrich Dürrenmatt (CH/FRG, Kurt Hoffmann, 1961), and of bestselling popular literature by Mario Simmel[261] and Heinz G. Konsalik[262] could not sustain the economic miracle-induced cinema boom[263] once televisions became affordable and the consumption of films became Germans' favorite entertainment option within the private sphere. By 1961, increasing numbers of cinemas had closed or were being divided up into several smaller screens in order to address shrinking ticket sales and profits.

Especially West Germany's postwar production of literary adaptations was impressive. As the economy thrived, Germans flocked to cinemas, but soon increasing numbers bought televisions for their new homes. The literary canon was an integral component of television productions during this era, and proved useful in communicating the sense of 'sophisticated' entertainment from Gottfried Keller's *Regine* (Harald Braun, 1956) to Bertolt Brecht's *Der kaukasische Kreidekreis* [The Caucasian Circle] (FRG, Franz Peter Wirth, 1958).[264]

In East Germany, the political leadership marked Stalin's birthday on December 21, 1952, with the first postwar television broadcast. West Germany's ARD (Arbeitsgemeinschaft der Rundfunkanstalten Deutschland/ working group of the broadcasting corporations, founded in 1950) followed suit four days later. Until well into the 1950s, home television units were luxury items. The vast majority viewed events of global or at least European interest—such as the coronation of Elisabeth II in 1953 or the world soccer championship in 1954—in pubs and restaurants, or followed them on the radio, as Sönke Wortmann's *Das Wunder von Bern* [The Miracle of Bern] (2003) nicely illustrates. Ownership of a house and a television became synonymous with a successful reinvention in capitalist society. In 1955, only around 100,000 households in West Germany owned a television set—considering TV-sales in the United States, Britain, and France a comparatively small number. Two years later, that number had increased tenfold. West German sales of television sets peaked in 1959 with 5,000 per day. By 1960, 3.5 million private households in West Germany spent their evenings watching tele.[265] In East Germany, most television owners were able to receive West German broadcasts.

Television productions based on German-language literature included a new adaptation of Wolfgang Borchert's *Draußen vor der Tür* [The Man Outside] (FRG, Rudolf Noelte, 1957), and filmed theater or studio productions of plays by Friedrich Schiller, Heinrich von Kleist, Johann Nepomuk Nestroy, Christian Dietrich Grabbe, Wilhelm Raabe, Arthur Schnitzler, Georg Kaiser, Carl Sternheim, and Klabund, but also of contemporary German-language literature by authors such as Brecht, Alfred Andersch, Zuckmayer, Marieluise Fleisser, Remarque, Thomas Mann, Tankred Dorst, Barbara Noack, Ernst Wiechert, Kästner, Max Frisch, Dürrenmatt, and Heinrich Böll.[266] Fritz Umgelter should be mentioned here as instrumental in bringing literature to television productions, thus making adaptations an integral component of evening entertainment enjoyed by families at home. From 1958 to 1962 the number of both films produced and cinema tickets sold decreased by nearly 50 percent—a reduction by half in merely four years. At the same time, TV licenses increased from 2 million to over 7 million—i.e., they almost quadrupled.[267]

International co-productions became increasingly common as producers were eager to maximize budgets and distribution, while reducing financial risks. Notable adaptations of this era include films with high production value such as *Angst/La Paura* (FRG/IT, Roberto Rossellini, 1954) based on Stefan Zweig, *Christine* (FR/IT, Pierre Gaspard-Huit, 1958), another adaptation of Schnitzler's *Liebelei*, *Le dialogue des Carmélites* based on Gertrud von Le Fort's novella *Die Letzte am Schafott* (Last on the scaffold, 1931) (FR/IT, Philippe Agostini/R.L. Bruckberger, 1960), and Irmgard Keun's bestseller *Das kunstseidene Mädchen* (The Artificial Silk Girl, 1932) as *The High Life* (FRG/Italy/France, Julien Duvivier, 1960).[268] But it was two Austrian-Spanish co-productions that set the tone for the decade to come—*Die Sklavenkarawane/Caravana de esclavos* [Caravan of Slaves] (Georg Marischka/Ramón Torrado, 1958) and *Der Löwe von Babylon/ En las ruínas de Babilonia* [The Lion of Babylon] (Johannes Kai/Ramón Torrado, 1959), both based on late-nineteenth-century adventure novels by Karl May, a bestselling author, adored by generations of predominantly teenagers and young men.[269]

So-called 'sophisticated' films that might help postwar Germany and Austria to negotiate their Nazi past as well as an imagined future of prosperity, freedom, and justice continued to be nearly impossible to turn into profitable endeavors throughout this era, and distributors pressured production companies to support only light-hearted fares. German audiences on both sides of the 'iron curtain' preferred German to international productions during this time of 'looking forward' rather than into the darkness and shame of the Nazi past.[270] German-language literature was instrumentalized within diverging processes of nation building and identity formation in opposing ideological camps, for educational and political purposes and, of course, for entertainment. The number of adaptations in postwar East and West Germany also indicates calculated efforts to reclaim the literary canon on either side of the border, while suggesting fundamental questions regarding the new nations' cultural foundation. But despite the country's division, many of the topics negotiated on cinema screens, from war and suppression to exile and return, resonated in both East and West Germany.[271]

While auteur filmmakers such as Jean Luc Godard in France, Margaret Tait in Britain, Stan Brakhage in the United States, to name but a few, presented cinema as a novel art form, in Germany (and Austria) seasoned directors such as Kurt Hoffmann and Helmut Käutner continued to produce entertainment for the masses in a gradually declining cinema culture. At the same time, however, filmmakers such as Rudolf Jugert, Robert Siodmak and, especially, Vienna-born Herbert Vesely offered glimpses of a truly innovative cinema, paving the way for the so-called New German Cinema to follow.

Vesely's first film *Und die Kinder spielen so gern Soldaten* [And the Children Love Playing Solders, 1951] seems to be lost, but descriptions hint at a highly innovative adaptation of Kafka's short story "In der

Strafkolonie" (In the Penal Colony, 1914/19), which directly comments on the recent war by endlessly looping the death of a soldier, thus proposing a countermeasure against popular amnesia regarding Germany's and Austria's Nazi past. His next project *An diesen Abenden* [On Those Evenings] (AT, Herbert Vesely, 1952) takes inspiration from "Die junge Magd" (The Young Sevant, 1913) by Austrian poet Georg Trakl, and communicates the foul, sexually repressive atmosphere in a small, conservative village, and the threatening mood exerted by cowardly local men. The poem suggests a 'fallen' maid's suicide after rape, and its adaptation successfully conveys hardship and victimhood of a marginalized young woman.[272] By 1961, Vesely and Leo Ti were working on an adaptation of Heinrich Böll's novella *Das Brot der frühen Jahre* (The Bread of Those Early Years, 1955), a film that also marks the beginning of a new era of German-language cinema, as the next chapter will outline.

The German and Austrian film and adaptation industries during this era contributed actively to the "conspiracy of silence"[273] after the Second World War. They did, however, help to (re)construct the literary canon and to highlight aspects of contemporary literary culture via cinema screens. In 1961, the year of the construction of the Berlin wall that was to remain a symbol of division and repression for the nearly three decades to come, the international reputation of German-language film had dwindled, and a group of young West German and Austrian filmmakers demanded not only a new German-language cinema, but an honest engagement with the catastrophic consequences of Nazi rule and fascism.

Notes

1 Bertolt Brecht wrote his poem "O Deutschland, bleiche Mutter" in exile in 1933. Klaus Mann quoted fellow exile Brecht in an open letter to writers in Nazi Germany in 1939; cf. Klaus Mann, "An die Schriftsteller im Dritten Reich" (1939), in *Heute und Morgen. Schriften zur Zeit* (Munich: Nymphenburger, 1969), 244–64, here p. 251.
2 Joe Hembus, *Der deutsche Film kann gar nicht besser sein* (Bremen: Schünemann, 1961), 11.
3 French critic and film director Alexandre Astruc published an article in *L'Ecran français* (March 30, 1948) famously coining the term for a new literariness in filmmaking by a new generation of directors in France. See also *The History of French Literature on Film* by Kate Griffiths and Andrew Watts.
4 See, for example, the relevant research published and/or edited since 2005 by Hester Baer, Tim Bergfelder, Stephen Brockmann, Erica Carter, John Davidson and Sabine Hake, Jaimey Fisher, Johannes von Moltke, Jennifer M. Kapczynski, Paul Cooke, and Marc Silberman.

5   For further information, see Heide Fehrenbach, *Cinema in Democratizing Germany* (Chapel Hill: University of North Carolina Press, 1995).
6   Records of United States Occupation Headquarters, World War II, Information Control Division, Motion Picture Branch. Subsequent references to archival material found at the National Archives in Maryland are cited as NARA and RG (record group): NARA, RG 260.
7   NARA, RG 260. See also C. T. de Jaeger, "Re-educate Germany by Film," *Sight and Sound* 11 (1942): 33.
8   This section is a summary of my research on postwar film and based in parts on the following publications: "Memories of World War II in German Film after 1945," in *The Long Aftermath: Cultural Legacies of Europe at War, 1936–2016*, ed. Manuel Braganca and Peter Tame (Oxford: Berghahn Books, 2015), 200–18; "Being Human: Good Germans in Postwar German Film," in *Representing the 'Good German,'* ed. Christiane Schönfeld and Pól Ó Dochartaigh (Rochester, NY: Camden House, 2013), 111–37; "Fritz Kortner's Return to Germany and the Figure of the Returning Exile in Kortner's 'The Mission' and Josef v. Báky's *Der Ruf*," *Feuchtwanger Studien* 3 (2013): 475–94; "Erfolg und Misserfolg von Verfilmungen: Manfred Gregors *Die Brücke* und die Nahaufnahmen des Krieges in Kino und Fernsehen," *Germanistik in Ireland* 7 (2012): 81–102; "Pariser Exilromane im Film: Transnationale Neucodierungen von Erinnerungskultur," in *Feuchtwanger et la culture mémorielle en France*, ed. Daniel Azuélos, Andrea Chartier-Bunzel and Frédéric Teinturier (London: Lang, 2020), 229–46; "Verfilmungen," in *Metzler Handbuch: Fontanes Effi Briest*, ed. Stefan Neuhaus (Stuttgart: Metzler, 2019), 131–49.
9   For more information on film officers such as Robert Joseph or, especially, Stuart Schulberg, see Cora Sol Goldstein, *Capturing the German Eye: American Visual Propaganda in Occupied Germany* (Chicago: University of Chicago Press, 2009); and Maria Fritsche, *The American Marshall Plan Film Campaign and the Europeans* (London: Bloomsbury, 2019). Films produced in Allied countries were also selected for screenings for the benefit of both the armed forces and the wider population. The latter had a clear preference for German films, often mentioned in OMGUS' so-called Reaction Reports. A selection of Nazi films, deemed a-political by film officers, was soon shown in cinemas across the American and British sectors.
10 NARA, RG260; OMGUS docs match reports within my own family. In Regensburg, for example, food ration cards were only validated after attendance of a *Todesmühlen*-screening. This was deemed against regulations by the American authorities, however, and the local re-education officer was ordered to cease the practice.
11 NARA, RG260.
12 Paul Cooke and Marc Silberman, eds., intro., *Screening War: Perspectives on German Suffering* (Rochester, NY: Camden House, 2010), 2.
13 Handwritten addition to an OMGUS film production control officer document (corrective comments relating to the *New York Times* article "German Film Growth decried by U.S. Aid" (February 6, 1947). NARA, RG 260, box 293.
14 Germans could apply to the occupying governments for licenses in each of the four sectors from 1946. The first license for a film production under German

direction was granted by SMAD for Staudte's *Die Mörder sind unter uns* (East Berlin, October 1946).
15 Stuart Schulberg, "The German Film: Comeback or Setback?," *The Quarterly of Film, Radio and Television* 8.4 (1954): 400–4.
16 Schulberg, "The German Film," 401.
17 See Sabine Hake and John Davidson, eds., *Take Two: Fifties Cinema in Divided Germany* (New York: Berghahn, 2007).
18 I take inspiration here from Sabine Hake's essay on "Political Affects: Antifascism and the Second World War in Frank Byer and Konrad Wolf," in *Screening War: Perspectives on German Suffering*, ed. Paul Cooke and Marc Silberman, 102–22.
19 See Sabine Hake's "The Politicization of Cinema in the East" (106–11) and "The Depoliticization of Cinema in the West" (112–26) in her *German National Cinema* (London: Routledge, 2008).
20 Hake clarifies the significance of German and Austrian cinema of the 1950s in her excellent introduction to Davidson and Hake, eds., *Framing the Fifties*, 1–9.
21 Robert Shandley, *Rubble Films: German Cinema in the Shadow of the Third Reich* (Philadelphia: Temple University Press, 2001); Brockmann, *A Critical History of German Film*, 183–234; Bergfelder, Carter, Göktürk, *German Cinema Book*, 2002; Hake, *German National Cinema*, 2002, etc.
22 Boguslaw Drewniak, *Der deutsche Film 1938–1945* (Düsseldorf: Droste, 1987), 556.
23 Drewniak, *Der deutsche Film 1938–1945*, 479; cf. also Kay Weniger, *Das große Personenlexikon des Films*, vol. 1, 222f.; according to filmportal.de, new scenes were filmed in June/July 1944; Operation Valkyrie had been underway and Stauffenberg's failed assassination attempt on Adolf Hitler took place on July 20, 1944.
24 Anon., "Andrang vor der Schlimmen Straße," *Der Spiegel* (January 24, 1948), https://www.spiegel.de/spiegel/print/d-44415463.html.
25 Rudolf Erich Raspe's account was published in German in serialized form, and subsequently as a book in English entitled *Baron Munchausen's Narrative of his Marvellous Travels and Campaigns in Russia* (Oxford, 1785).
26 Kästner's clandestine involvement in the Nazi film industry had been tolerated by Goebbels due to the antifascist's talent for comedy, which in his view was needed during times of war. It was only *after* Ufa's extravagant twenty-fifth anniversary film *Münchhausen* in 1943 that Kästner was put under "Totalverbot," i.e., a complete ban in Nazi Germany. Cf. Hanuschek's introduction to Erich Kästner's *Das Blaue Buch. Geheimes Kriegstagebuch 1941–1945* (Zurich: Atrium, 2018), 8; Ingo Tornow's *Erich Kästner und der Film* (Munich: dtv, 1998), 20; for further contexts, see Stefan Neuhaus, *Das verschwiegene Werk. Erich Kästners Mitarbeit an Theaterstücken unter Pseudonym* (Würzburg: Königshausen & Neumann, 2000)and "Erich Kästner und der Nationalsozialismus: 'Gestern, heute und morgen' und 'Drei Männer im Schnee,'" *Wirkendes Wort* 49 (1999): 372–87.
27 Fritz Kortner (1892–1970) was born in Vienna as Fritz Nathan Kohn. For further information, see the following autobiographical and biographical

works: Fritz Kortner, *Aller Tage Abend. Autobiographie* [1959] (Munich: dtv, 1976), 458 for "Überbleibsel von Berlin" and "Hungerhölle" quote; Klaus Völker, *Fritz Kortner. Schauspieler und Regisseur* (Berlin: Hentrich, 1987); Peter Schütze, *Fritz Kortner* (Reinbek: Rowohlt, 1994).

28 The title of Jan Müller's article in *Der Tagesspiegel* (March 21, 1948), in which he protests Veit Harlan's 'scandalous' acquittal by the British authorities in Hamburg. Witness for the defense was Liebeneiner, who had been confirmed as blacklisted by OMGUS on June 14, 1946, and 'had even dirtier hands' than Harlan, was also acquitted by the same court shortly before—to the 'astonishment of all and may work again without any restriction.' See also Irina Scheidgen, "Nachkriegskarrieren II: Der Fall Liebeneiner," in *Mediale Mobilmachung III. Das Kino der Bundesrepublik Deutschland als Kulturindustrie (1950–1962)*, ed. Harro Segeberg (Munich: Fink, 2009), 91–121; Nicola Weber, *Im Netz der Gefühle: Veit Harlans Melodramen* (Münster: LIT, 2011).

29 Liebeneiner file, NARA, RG 260. Classification BLACK, June 14, 1946.

30 Kleist's novella was subsequently adapted as *La Marquise d'O* (FR, Claude Barma, 1959), *Die Gräfin von Rathenow* (FRG, TV, Peter Beauvais, 1973), *La marquise d'O* (FR, Éric Rohmer, 1975), *Die Marquise von O.* (DE, Hans-Jürgen Syberberg, 1989), *Julietta—Es ist nicht wie du denkst* (FRG, Christoph Stark, 2001), and *Il seme della discordia* (IT, Pappi Corsicato, 2008).

31 Quoted in Sobotka, "Die Filmwunderkinder," 77; and Baer, *Dismantling the Dream Factory*, 80.

32 Hester Baer discusses *Liebe 47* in her *Dismantling the Dream Factory*, 73–100. See also Sobotka, "Die Filmwunderkinder," 76f.; Meier, *Filmstadt Göttingen*, 52f.

33 Anthony Burgess, *The Life and Works of Wolfgang Borchert* (Rochester: Camden House, 2003), 220; quoted Baer, *Dismantling the Dream Factory*, 79.

34 Borchert, *Draussen vor der Tür*, 20.

35 According to an article in *Der Spiegel* only Käutner's *Der Apfel ist ab* was more expensive: "Pappmond über Leid und Liebe," *Der Spiegel* (August 11, 1949), https://www.spiegel.de/spiegel/print/d-44437355.html.

36 Horst Caspar had starred as the other German prince of poets in the aformentioned *Friedrich Schiller*-film (1940) and Heidemarie Hatheyer was a celebrity from the Nazi era. She had famously played "Geierwally" in the Nazi's take on the Wilhelmine von Hillern's famous novel in 1939/40. *Begegnung mit Werther* was supposed to ease her comeback as a film actress.

37 Cf. review of the film "Pappmond über Leid und Liebe" mentioned above.

38 Kurt Lothar Tank, "Falsche Sprache zu den richtigen Bildern," *Hannoversche Allgemeine*, December 10, 1949, quoted and translated by Baer, *Dismantling the Dream Factory*, 80.

39 Many of these contemporary writers were invited to meetings of the so-called Gruppe 47 (Group 47), organized by Hans Werner Richter between 1947 and 1967, which indeed helped a new generation of writers come to the fore.

40 For further information on the company, Christian Bauer's documentary for Bayrischer Rundfunk (BR), *Phönix aus der Asche. Hans Abich und die Filmaufbau Göttingen* (FRG, 1988); and Irmgard Wilharm, "Filmwirtschaft,

Filmpolitik und der 'Publikumsgeschmack' im Westdeutschland der Nachkriegszeit," *Geschichte und Gesellschaft* 28.2 (2002): 267–90.

41 The quote used here is based on Hester Baer's translation of the (reconstructed) manifesto, quoted in Baer, *Dismantling the Dream Factory*, 76. Cf. also Sobotka, "Die Filmwunderkinder," 49f.

42 Petzel and Schreivogel, *Filmstadt Göttingen*, 1999, http://www.filmstadt-goettingen.de/?show=chapter_1.

43 Quoted from the translation of the manifesto in Baer, *Dismantling the Dream Factory*, 77–8. Abich/Thiele's insight here is disturbingly reminiscent of Goebbels' understanding of effective propaganda via cinema.

44 Baer, *Dismantling the Dream Factory*, 78.

45 Ernst Schürer, "Introduction," in *German Expressionist Plays*, ed. Ernst Schürer, x.

46 Borchert, *The Man Outside*, scene 4.

47 See, for example, Jan Müller, "Hitlerregisseur Nr. 2," *Der Tagesspiegel* (March 21, 1948): n.p.

48 See (Anon./A.E.K), "Liebeneiner gibt Antwort," *Film Echo* (June 20, 1949), quoted by Gordon Burgess in his essay "The Failure of the Film of the Play. *Draussen vor der Tür* and *Liebe 47*," *German Life & Letters* 38.4 (1985): 155–64. For an extensive analysis of gender constructions in the film, see Baer, *Dismantling the Dream Factory*, 73–100, particularly 81–93.

49 "Beckmann trifft Anna. Der Faust wird kommen," *Der Spiegel*, March 12, 1949.

50 But reviewers at the time also criticized the incompatibility of the two narratives—Borchert's play depicting the male experience of war and homecoming that included nightmarish visions reminiscent of Expressionist theater and cinema, and Fischer's screenplay that tried to convey a realistic picture of a German woman's suffering during and after the Second World War. See, for example, Gunter Groll, "Borchert, Liebeneiner und der Zeitfilm. Der verlorene Maßstab," *Süddeutsche Zeitung* (May 28, 1949), quoted in Hilmar Hoffmann and Walter Schobert, ed., *Zwischen Gestern und Morgen: Westdeutscher Nachkriegsfilm 1946–1962* (Frankfurt/M.: Deutsches Filmmuseum, 1989, 348; quoted by Baer, *Dismantling the Dream Factory*, 94, who rightly considers the film an example of "clashing codes, disparate styles, and generic inconsistencies that characterized so many postwar films" (p. 95).

51 Hans Abich, "Zeigen, wie es sein soll. Ein Gespräch mit Hans Abich," in *Lichtspielträume. Kino in Hannover 1896–1991*, ed. Rolf Aurich et al. (Hannover: Gesellschaft für Filmstudien, 1991), 57–68. The previous and following quotes from this text are my translations.

52 This was already the third adaptation of Schönherr's *play*. The Austrian film industry at the time preferred adaptations suitable for a mass market, such as Heimat-films based on Karl Heinrich Waggerl's *Das Jahr des Herrn / Der Wallnerbub* (AT, Alfred Stöger, 1950) or *Cordula* [AT, Gustav Ucicky, 1950], based on Anton Wildgans' hexameter epos *Kirbisch oder Der Gendarm, die Schande und das Glück* (Kirbisch or the policeman, the shame and happiness, 1927).

53 *Der Spiegel* 11 (1949), http://www.spiegel.de/spiegel/print/d-44435878.html

54 Baer, *Dismantling the Dream Factory*, 94; Baer quotes from Johannes Hauser, *Neuaufbau der westdeutschen Filmwirtschaft 1945–1955 und der Einfluß der US-amerikanischen Filmpolitik* (Pfaffenweiler: Centaurus, 1989), 374f.
55 *Und ewig bleibt die Liebe* is a remake of Arthur Rabenalt's Nazi adaptation *Johannisfeuer* (1939). Liebeneiner directed adaptations of *Waldwinter*, based on the forgotten Silesian writer Paul Keller (1956); *Königin Luise* (1957; for Divina-Film, director of production: Heinz Abel, distributor: Gloria-Filmverleih GmbH, Munich), Walter von Molo's 1919 novel about the Prussian Queen; and *Taiga* (1958), based on former SS-officer Herbert Reinecker's work.
56 Helmut Käutner, "Demontage der Traumfabrik," *Film-Echo* 5 (June 1947).
57 Cf. Gerhard Lamprecht in *Der Augenzeuge* 8 (1946).
58 The party's program can be accessed at: https://www.cvce.eu/en/obj/political_programme_of_the_socialist_unity_party_berlin_21_and_22_april_1946-en-d9c5faf7-5c39-43fa-aa3f-88d5431e3746.html (21 and April 22, 1946).
59 At the same time, as Anke Pinkert demonstrates, "the official antifascist rhetoric of socialist renewal competed with the pragmatic social need to negotiate the trauma of returning soldiers." Anke Pinkert, *Film and Memory in East Germany* (Bloomington: Indiana University Press, 2008), 3. Her chapter 3 on "Psychotic Breaks and Conjugal Rubble" refers to *Büchners Wozzeck. In einem Film von Georg Klaren. Begleitmaterial* (Berlin: Sovexportfilm, 1947); Michael Hanisch, *"Um 6 Uhr abends nach Kriegsende" bis 'High Noon': Kino und Film im Berlin der Nachkriegszeit 1945–1953* (Berlin: DEFA, 2004), 6–25; Jan-Christopher Horak, "Postwar Traumas in Klaren's 'Wozzeck' (1947)," in *German Film and Literature: Adaptations and Transformations*, ed. Eric Rentschler, 132–45. Pinkert also addresses DEFA films focused on the suffering of women: Slatan Dudow's *Frauenschicksale* [Destinies of Women] (1952) and Kurt Maetzig's *Roman einer jungen Ehe* [lit. Novel of a Young Marriage/Story of a Young Couple] (1952).
60 Horak, "Postwar Traumas in Klaren's *Wozzeck*," 133.
61 To name but a few: *Und über uns der Himmel / City of Torment* (1947), Bosley Crowther, "The Screen: Quartett of Newcomers Arrives," *New York Times* (June 10, 1950): 11; *Mädchen hinter Gittern / Girls behind Bars* (Germany/OMGUS, Alfred Braun, 1949), "The Screen in Review," *New York Times* (May 10, 1950): 41. *Film ohne Titel / Film without a Name* was at least recognized as a "decent attempt" by *New York Times* film critic Bosley Crowther (October 20, 1950): 32. Even the vastly popular *Das weiße Rössl am Wolfgangssee / White Horse Inn* was considered a "stale Wiener Schnitzler" (*NYT*, December 4, 1957) with regard to its libretto in 1957. When *Des Teufels General / The Devils General* was imported to the United States the same year, however, the reception was generally positive.
62 "West Germans Ban U.S. Film," *New York Times* (May 27, 1950): 24. According to the *New York Times*, the "West German Film Control Board said that the picture 'Colorado Territory' was 'an excellent example of the gangster film by which anti-social elements are glorified.'"
63 In defeated Italy at the time, the Empire had come to an end and a republican constitution had been adopted in January 1948. Schiller's play about William Tell and the Swiss people's fight for independence seemed an appropriate topic

to Giorgio Pastina, who adapted and directed the historical drama *Guglielmo Tell* in 1948/9. Carmine Gallone, well-respected screenwriter and director, who had fallen into disrepute internationally due to his productions of pro-fascist and revisionist propaganda films under Mussolini, now reflected on human weakness and the seductive draw of power by once again adapting Faust as *La leggenda di Faust* [The Legend of Faust], released in 1949. At the same time René Clair transposed Faust into an allegorical tragicomedy *Beauté du diable* [lit. The Beauty of the Devil] set in the nineteenth century, released in Britain and the United States as *Beauty and the Devil*. Here, "handsome, dashing young Faust is played as a romantic hero" (Durrani, "Filmed Fausts," *Processes of Transposition,* ed. C. Schönfeld, 27–37, here p. 31). Audiences generally welcomed the adaptation's hopeful message. In Germany, the French-Italian production was entitled *Der Pakt mit dem Teufel* [The Pact with the Devil] lest the subtext of destruction caused by choosing the wrong bedfellow were to slip past audiences there.

64   Adolf Anton Wohlbrück had starred a.o. in *Regine*, a Gottfried Keller adaptation directed by Erich Waschneck (1935) and in the third adaptation of Hanns Heinz Ewers' *Der Student von Prag* (The Student of Prague, 1935; directed by Arthur Robison) in the Nazi film industry. At risk even in pre-1938 Austria due to his Jewish mother and his own homosexuality, he changed his name to Anton Walbrook, and emigrated to Britain. He starred in the psychological thriller *Gaslight* (GB, Thorold Dickinson, 1940) a. o., and worked repeatedly with Michael Powell and Emeric Pressburger (*The Life and Death of Colonel Blimp*, 1943; *The Red Shoes*, 1948, etc.) He also starred in Ophüls' *Lola Montez* as King Ludwig I of Bavaria (1955), and in *On Trial* (*L'Affaire Maurizius; Il caso Mauritius*, 1954), a French-Italian adaptation of Jakob Wassermann's novel *Der Fall Maurizius* (The Maurizius Case, 1928).

65   *La Ronde* won the 1951 BAFTA for Best Film and was also nominated for best screenplay (Max Ophüls/Jacques Natanson) at the 1952 Academy Awards. In France, films of this decade largely circumvented German literature. The French-Italian co-production *L'affaire Maurizius / Caso Mauritius / On Trial* (1954), the aforementioned adaptation of Wassermann's 1928 novel, must be considered an exception. The 1952 film *Le jugement de Dieu* [Judgment of God] (dir. Raymond Bernard, scr. Pierre Montazel) was based on the Agnes Bernauer-legend rather than a specific literary source— of which there are numerous (by Hans Sachs, Christian Hoffmann von Hoffmannswaldau, etc.). Most successful was Friedrich Hebbel's play *Agnes Bernauer* (1852).

66   Emigré Paul Czinner's adaptation of Hofmannsthal/Richard Strauß's *Der Rosenkavalier* [The Knight of the Rose] (GB, 1960) could not repeat the success of the flamboyant Pressburger/Powell adaptation.

67   For further information, see especially Andrew Moor, who considers the question of national identity in his "No Place Like Home: Powell, Pressburger Utopia," in *The British Cinema Book*, ed. Robert Murphy (London: Bloomsbury, 2019); Ian Christie and Andre Moor, ed., *Michael Powell: International Perspectives on an English Filmmaker* (London: BFI, 2005).

68   Listening to the BBC was considered treason in Nazi Germany and severely punished. Nonetheless, many were eager to get news not controlled by the

Nazi's propaganda machine and built their own radio antenna from a wire coat hanger allowing them to receive BBC broadcasts.

69 Cf. Thomas Mann, Frank Thiess and Walter von Molo, *Ein Streitgespräch über die äußere und innere Emigration* (Dortmund: Druckschriften Vertriebsdienst, 1946).

70 Further adaptations of Zweig's *24 Stunden aus dem Leben einer Frau* were directed by Dominique Delouche (1968, starring Danielle Darrieux), and by Laurent Bouhnik (2002, starring Agnès Jaoui and Michel Serrault). In 1961, the novella was adapted to television in the United States (starring Ingrid Bergman).

71 Best Director, Best Adapted Screenplay, and one for his Dad Walter Huston for Best Supporting Actor.

72 Little is certain about B. Traven, who was probably Ret Marut, an anarchist who supported the Munich Soviet in 1918/19 and left for Mexico in 1924. See Karl S. Guthke, *B. Traven. Biografie eines Rätsels* (Frankfurt/M.: Gutenberg, 1987); John Engell, "The Treasure of Sierra Madre: B. Traven, John Huston and Ideology in Film Adaptation," *Literature/Film Quarterly* 17.4 (1989): 245–52; James Goldwasser, "Ret Marut: The Early B. Traven," *The Germanic Review* 68 (1993): 133–42.

73 Roy Pateman, *The Man Nobody Knows: The Life and Legacy of B. Traven* (Lanham: University Press of America, 2005).

74 Thanks to Bob Hasenfratz for this take on the matter.

75 Other adaptations of this era include *Canasta de cuentos mexicanos* (MX, Julio Bracho, 1955/6), *Le destin / Macario* (MX, Roberto Gavaldón, 1959/60), and *Rosa Blanca* (MX, Roberto Gavaldón 1961).

76 The text was first adapted during her French exile in an Arnold Pressburger production under the direction of Léonide Moguy, who co-wrote the script for the film with Charles Gombault and Hans Wilhelm in 1938 entitled *Conflit* [Conflict].

77 Noah Isenberg, "Perennial Detour: The Cinema of Edgar G. Ulmer and the Experience of Exile," *Cinema Journal* 43.2 (2004): 3–25, here p. 10f.

78 Horak in his article on "German Exile Cinema" emphasizes the innovative take on the genre of melodrama in this adaptation. While the unwed mother relinquishes her child for the second time to her sister and her husband, a happy end is nonetheless implied for the fallen woman, who reunites with the little boy's father. This, according to Horak "ran counter to the unwritten moral laws of Hollywood, which would have required the unwed mother to be punished for her sins, rather than awarded with a nuclear family. The film was produced for Monogram by Arnold Pressburger's brother-in-law, the former Berlin businessman, Heinz Brasch. It was directed by Edgar G. Ulmer, another Austrian, and based on a novel by Gina Kaus who had written Pressburger's pre-War hit, *Prison sans barreaux*." Horak also points to the other "emigrés" working on the film, namely, the cameraman Franz Planer, the composer Hans Sommer, and "actors Felix Bressart, Fritz Feld and Rudolf Anders." Horak, "German Exile Cinema," 386.

79 Cf. Kevin and Emer Rockett, *Irish Film Censorship* (Dublin: Four Courts, 2004); and Horak, "German Exile Cinema," 386. Gina Kaus' novel *Der Teufel*

nebenan (Amsterdam: Allert de Lange, 1940) was adapted under the direction of Rolf Hansen in West Germany in 1955.

80 See, for example, the case of Ernst Toller: C. Schönfeld, "Ernst Toller's Film Projects," *German Life and Letters* 75.2 (2022): 250–65.

81 Fritz Arno Wagner had worked with Murnau, Lang, Pabst, and other outstanding directors during the Weimar Republic, filmed for Ufa—from *Das Testament des Dr. Mabuse* and *Flüchtlinge* (both 1933) to Nazi propaganda such as *Der Fuchs von Glenarvon* and *Friedrich Schiller* (both 1940)—and after the war for Soviet controlled DEFA, until leaving for West Germany together with Paul Verhoeven in 1950/1.

82 See, for example, James Travers' review at http://www.frenchfilms.org/review/people-will-talk-1951.html.

83 According to imdb.

84 Cf. Tim Dirks, Filmsite, at https://www.filmsite.org/momentsindx.html; twenty-two critics give the film a 100 percent approval on Rotten Tomatoes.

85 Andre Spicer and Helen Hanson outline the studios difficulties with HUAC in their *Companion to Film Noir* (Hoboken, NJ: Wiley, 2013).

86 The American film noir romance *The Other Love* (1947) directed by Andre DeToth is not, as often repeated, based on a short story entitled "Beyond," but instead on a treatment Remarque wrote while in Hollywood. Cf. the website of the Remarque archive at https://www.remarque.uni-osnabrueck.de. For a discussion of the impact of the literary works of Karl May on De Toth's Westerns, see Helmut Asper's essay at https://www.helmut-g-asper.de/index.php/2013-06-05-17-53-21/filme-und-themen/nicht-nur-karl-may.

87 Remarque, *Erich Maria Remarque. Ein militanter Pazifist. Texte und Interviews 1929–1966*, 112f.

88 Remarque in an interview with M. Feldmann, "Gespräch mit C. [sic] M. Remarque," *Europäische Rundschau* 1.5 (1946): 228–30. Reprinted in Erich Maria Remarque, *Ein militanter Pazifist. Texte und Interviews 1929–1966*, 84–90, here p. 85.

89 Tim Westphalen's afterword to Remarque's novel: "Das Tor des Hades. Nachwort," *Arc de Triomphe*, 491–505, here p. 491. E. M. Remarque, *Arc de Triomphe* (Cologne: KiWi, 2011), 194.

90 Remarque, *Arc de Triomphe*, 195.

91 A typescript of Remarque's essay "The Eye Is a Strong Seducer" is held in NYU's Fales Library, Remarque Collection [RC 1.305/001]; a German translation of the text can be found in Thomas F. Schneider, ed., *The Eye Is a Strong Seducer—Erich Maria Remarque and Film* (Osnabrück: Universitätsverlag Rasch, 1998), 106f.

92 In film criticism, the issue of fidelity is one of the most recurring. While the differences between a source text and its adaptation can be highly revealing, it is often a narrow perspective used to judge rather than interpret the complexities of the transmedial interchange. In their introduction (1–12) to *The Cambridge Companion to Literature on Screen* (2007), for example, Deborah Cartmell and Imelda Whelehan highlight the relationship between literature and film as intertextual rather than comparative.

93 Bosley Crowther, "Ingrid Bergman and Charles Boyer Are Seen in 'Arch of Triumph' at Globe," *New York Times* (April 21, 1948): 33.

94 In contrast, the occupying Soviet government in Germany feared that a similar logic depicted in the original final sequence in Wolfgang Staudte's *Die Mörder sind unter uns* (*Murderers among Us*, 1946) would lead to vigilante justice, and required a revised ending that calls for the notification of appropriate military authorities whenever a Nazi criminal had been identified.
95 Spicer/Hanson, eds., *The Companion to Film Noir*, 2013.
96 Semih Evin also directed *Kardes gibiydiler* (1963) based on Remarque's *Three Comrades*.
97 For a summary of the film's reception see Michael Töteberg, "Kann man Hitler verfilmen?," *film-dienst* 19 (2004), accessed online via filmportal.de at https://www.filmportal.de/node/57165/material/679776.
98 Ibid.
99 Ibid.; Töteberg also notes that it was Pabst's film or rather Albin Skoda as Adolf Hitler that proved to Bruno Ganz before Bernd Eichinger/Oliver Hirschbiegel's *Der Untergang / Downfall* (2004) that Hitler could indeed be portrayed on screen.
100 Semenza/Hasenfratz, *The History of British Literature on Film,* 228ff; Leitch, *The History of American Literature on Film,* 239ff.
101 Cf. Saskia Fares, "Filmanalyse Bobby Deerfield," in *Erich Maria Remarque und der Film*, ed. Thomas F. Schneider (Osnabrück: V&R unipress, 2012), 51–80.
102 Curd Jürgens also starred alongside May Britt in an ill-advised remake of *The Blue Angel* (USA, Edward Dmytryk, 1959), based on Heinrich Mann's *Professor Unrat*.
103 Anon., "*Der veruntreute Himmel* (Deutschland)," *Der Spiegel* 44 (1958); accessed via the *Spiegel* archive at https://www.spiegel.de/politik/der-veruntreute-himmel-deutschland-a-8f627df8-0002-0001-0000-000041759491. The novel was adapted to radio in 1951 (SWF) and 1957 (BR) and would have been quite well known in Germany at the time. Adaptations for television followed in Austria in 1958 and in Germany in 1990.
104 Schnyder also directed several adaptations of Swiss literature for television, among them Gotthelf's *Die Käserei in der Vehfreude* [The Cheese-dairy in Vehfreude] (1958), which was distributed to Germany as *Annelie vom Berghof oder Oh diese Weiber* [Annelie or Oh, these Women]. Gotthelf's famous text *Die schwarze Spinne* was adapted for television by Werner Düggelin in 1960.
105 Schnyder's Gotthelf-adaptations *Anne Bäbi Jowänger* were also released in two parts in 1960 and 1962 but could not repeat his previous successes.
106 See https://en.wikipedia.org/wiki/Heidi#Film_and_television for further *Heidi* adaptations from Japanese anime to Argentinian tele-novelas.
107 *The Matchmaker* (USA, Joseph Anthony, 1958) is based on the play by Thornton Wilder, which in turn adapts Nestroy's 'farce with singing' *Einen Jux will er sich machen* (He'll Have Himself a Good Time, 1842). But Nestroy had based his text on John Oxenford's play *A Day Well Spent* (1835). It came to the attention of an international audience with the musical *Hello Dolly!* (1964).

108 Stöger's Schiller films include *Wilhelm Tell* (1955), *Maria Stuart* (1956), and *Don Carlos* (1957).
109 Lernet-Holenia's novel *Ich war Jack Mortimer* (I Was Jack Mortimer, 1933) was first adapted in 1935; an Austrian remake (dir. Emil Edwin Reinert) and an English-language version *Stolen Identity* (AT/US, Gunther von Fritsch, 1953) followed in 1952 and 1953, respectively. Cf. also the television adaptation of his *Der 20. Juli* as *Land, das meine Sprache spricht* (AT/FRG, Michael Kehlmann, 1959).
110 See, for example, the third adaptation of Austrian exiles Roda Roda's *Feldherrnhügel* (AT, Ernst Marischka, 1953), or *Drei, von denen man spricht* (AT, Axel von Ambesser, 1953), based on Paul Vulpius [=Ladislas Fodor and László Lakatos] *Jugend voran oder Hau-ruck* [Youth at the Helm].
111 Borsody had worked as editor for Ufa, beginning with Gustav Ucicky's Nazi films *Morgenrot* [Sunrise] and *Flüchtlinge* [Refugees] and later as cinematographer for *Wunschkonzert* [Request Concert], one of the most successful musical films of the Nazi period. Borsody directed the Gottfried Keller adaptation *Jugendliebe* [Young Love] (1944/7), which was banned by Nazi censors, a fact that helped to kickstart his career when the war ended. After the end of the war Borsody had no trouble continuing his film career despite his previous involvement in propaganda films. Willi Forst, actor and director (particularly for Wien-Film) [Vienna-Film] effectively worked for the Nazi's entertainment industry after the German annexation of Austria and the collaboration between Wien-Film and Ufa. Horney had starred in propaganda films such as *Feinde* [Enemies] (1940).
112 Christian Staas, "Superintegrationsland," *Die Zeit* 53 (2014); online version.
113 While no Nazi film directors were employed by DEFA, much more leeway was given to much-needed technical personnel, from cutters to cameramen (such as the abovementioned Arno Wagner).
114 Even the *New York Times* reported on "German Films Face Home Market's Loss," *New York Times* (May 29, 1950): 22.
115 "Überholte Filme," *Wirtschaftszeitung* (July 16, 1949), accessed online at http://www.geschichte-projekte-hannover.de/filmundgeschichte/deutschland_nach_1945/zeitgenossische-spielfilme/die-filme-3/liebe-47/der-film-in-der-zeitgenossischen-kritik/k5-k7.html.
116 *Wirtschaftszeitung* (July 16, 1949) as above.
117 Hartleben's *Rosenmontag* was previously adapted by Rudolf Meinert (1924) and Hans Steinhoff (1930).
118 Venatier's adaptation foregrounds amusing cultural difficulties between the rural population in Bavaria and their US American occupiers. A former Nazi-functionary is the smartest of the lot and makes sure he maintains the upper hand. Venatier's *Der Major und die Stiere* had been published by Klosterhaus in Lippoldsberg, owned by Nazi-author Hans Grimm. Cf. Denis Schimmelpfennig, "Hans Venatier—der völkische Erzieher," in *Dichter für das Dritte Reich*, ed. Rolf Düsterberg, vol. 2 (Bielefeld: Aisthesis, 2011). Venatier was able to return to teaching after the war, but took his life in 1959, because those 'good forces among the Nazis' as he put it in his suicide note, were in his mind not sufficiently allowed to integrate into the West German state. Ernst Klee, *Kulturlexikon zum Dritten Reich*, 567.

119 These labels were given by members of the occupying forces after 1945. Garncarz mentions films such as *La Habanera,* directed by Detlef Sierck (1937) prior to his departure for Hollywood, or *Hallo Janine* (1939) in this context. Cf. Joseph Garncarz, "Spotlight: Gloria Filmverleih GmbH," *German Cinema Book*, 29–31.

120 Other box-office hit productions of Kubaschewski's Diana (later renamed Divina)-Film company include *Die Trapp-Familie* (1956) and *Nachts, wenn der Teufel kam* (1957) until the company folded in 1962 despite Kubaschewski's rather desperate efforts to contain the decline of cinema by producing erotic *Angelique*-movies; see Joseph Garncarz, "Spotlight: Gloria Filmverleih GmbH," *German Cinema Book*, 29–31; Knut Hickethier, "The Restructuring of the West German Film Industry in the 1950s," in *Framing the Fifties: Cinema in a Divided Germany*, ed. John Davidson and Sabine Hake (New York: Berghahn, 2009), 194–209.

121 On Austrian film of the 1950s, see Mary Wauchope, "The Other 'German' Cinema," *Framing the Fifties*, 210–22.

122 Marc Silberman and Henning Wrage, "Introduction," in *DEFA at the Crossroads of East German and International Film Culture* (Berlin: de Gruyter, 2014), 2.

123 Cf. West German adaptations of Hermann Löns' (1866–1914) work such as *Grün ist die Heide* [Green Is the Heath] (Hans Deppe, 1951), *Rot ist die Liebe* [Red Is Love] (Karl Hartl, 1956), and *Wenn die Heide blüht* [When the Heath Blooms] (Hans Deppe, 1960). The simplicity and plainness of these titles are an indication of the narrative depth of these stories and their adaptations by former Nazi filmmakers.

124 For further contextualization and evaluation of the *Heimat*-film genre, see especially Johannes von Moltke, *No Place Like Home: Locations of Heimat in German Cinema* (Berkeley: University of California Press, 2005); and Moltke, "Evergreens: The Heimat genre," *German Cinema Book*, 17–28.

125 It was not until April 2002 that many of the films of this era were shown for the first time in the United States. Sponsored by the Goethe Institute/German Cultural Center, thirty-one films were screened as part of the "After the War, before the Wall: German Cinema, 1945–60" exhibition at the Walter Reade Theater, Lincoln Center.

126 Numerous Weimar successes were remade during this era, from *Die tolle Lola* (FRG, Hans Deppe, 1954) to *Die Drei von der Tankstelle* (FRG, Hans Wolff, 1955), often by filmmakers implicated by their Nazi past.

127 Jan-Christopher Horak published an essay on Ostermayr's early (silent) work, another very much underresearched area of German film history; Horak, "Munich's First Fiction Feature: Die Wahrheit," in *A Second Life: German Cinema's First Decades*, ed. Thomas Elsaesser with Michael Wedel (Amsterdam: Amsterdam University Press, 1996), 86–92.

128 W. v. Hillern's novel was adapted to opera—Alfredo Catalani's *La Wally* (1892)—and to film: in 1921, 1940, 1956, 1967, 1988, and 2005. With regard to the portrayals of women in German cinema between 1945 and 1960, see Erica Carter's illuminating *How German Is She? Post-War West German Reconstruction and the Consuming Woman* (Ann Arbor: University of Michigan Press, 1998). Carter focuses on the significance of

women as domestic consumers and the role of cinema in the context of the reconstruction of Germany after 1945.

129 Ludwig Ganghofer adaptations in West Germany include *Der Geigenmacher von Mittenwald* (Rudolf Schündler, 1950), *Die Martinsklause* (Richard Häussler, 1951), *Die Alm an der Grenze* (Walter Janssen, 1951), *Der Herrgottschnitzer vom Ammergau* (Harald Reinl, 1952), *Der Klosterjäger* (Harald Reinl, 1953), *Der Jäger von Fall* (Helmut Weiss, 1954), *Schloß Hubertus* (Helmut Weiss, 1954), *Das Schweigen im Walde* (Helmut Weiss, 1955), *Der Edelweißkönig* (Gustav Ucicky, 1957) *Der Schäfer vom Trutzberg* (Eduard von Borsody, 1958).

130 For example, Paul May directed an adaption of *Waldrausch* in Austria in 1962, and Harald Reinl directed remakes of *Hubertus Castle* and *The Hunter of Fall* in 1973 and 1974, respectively. A remake of *Waldrausch* [Forest Murmur] was directed by Horst Hächler in 1977. A recent publication on the genre of *Heimat*-film is Sarah Kordecki, *Und ewig ruft die Heimat ...: Zeitgenössische Diskurse und Selbstreflexivität in den Heimatfilmwellen der Nachkriegs- und Nachwendezeit* (Göttingen: V&R, 2020).

131 Alfred Stöger's films of stage-productions of the canon of German literature in Vienna—from Goethe's *Der Götz von Berlichingen* (1955) to Schiller's *Wilhelm Tell* (1956), *Maria Stuart* (1959), and *Don Karlos* (1960)—are also of interest in this context.

132 *Der weißblaue Löwe* [The White-Blue Lion/a reference to the Bavarian coat of arms] (FRG, Olf Fischer/Werner Jacobs, 1952), and *Mit Schnurrbart und Korsett* (*O, diese Bayern*) [With Mustache and Girdle/Oh Those Bavarians] (FRG, Arnulf Schröder, 1960); productions for television include *Magdalena* and *Die Medaille* (both 1955), *Gelähmte Schwingen* (1956), *Moral* (1958), *Die Lokalbahn* (1960), and *Die kleinen Verwandten* (1961).

133 Loisl is a Bavarian abbreviation of Alois; High German: Ludwig.

134 The Nazi film starred a young Heinz Rühmann, who was still most Germans' favorite neighbor after the war, with his much-admired good humor and capacity to keep his head above water.

135 "German Freed again over Anti-Semitism," *New York Times* (April 30, 1950): 5.

136 Cf. "Hamburg Mob Jeers 'Jew,'" *New York Times* (April 15, 1950): 5; "Anti-Semitism Deplored," *New York Times* (April 16, 1950): 34. After Harlan was declared 'untarnished' or "unbelastet" in a denazification trial in Hamburg in 1947, two groups representing Holocaust survivors/victims of Nazims had taken Harlan to court in 1948. Harlan, who claimed that Goebbels was responsible for the strong antisemitic message of his *Jud Süss*, was acquitted in 1949 and again in 1950 (appeal). The judge on both trials was Walter Tyrolf, who had served in the Nazi's justice system and handed out death sentences to several individuals accused of *Rassenschande* (lit. racial shame, Nazi Germany's anti-miscegenation concept prohibiting sexual relationships between Aryans and non-Aryans). After the war he was employed once again as a judge in Hamburg's judicial system. This was not unusual—apart from Judge Ernst Lautz, who was convicted to ten years in prison during the Nuremberg trials in 1947, none of Hitler's 570 judges and public persecutors were ever accused of their crimes. Many found employment in the German

judicial system after the war. Cf. Jörg Friedrich, *Freispruch für die Nazi-Justiz* (Berlin: Ullstein, 1998); Arnim Ramm, *Der 20. Juli vor dem Volksgerichtshof* (Berlin: Wissenschaftlicher Verlag, 2007); Zuckmayer, *Geheimreport* (Stuttgart: dtv, 2004); Can Bozyakali, *Das Sondergericht am Hanseatischen Oberlandesgericht* (Frankfurt/M.: Lang, 2005); Zielinski, *Veit Harlan*.

137 Nicola Weber, *Im Netz der Gefühle: Veit Harlans Melodramen*, 107. In 1948, when attending the premiere of Kurt Maetzig's *Ehe im Schatten* (1948) in the British zone—the film that tells the story of famous actor Joachim Gottschalk and his Jewish wife's bullying and persecution by Nazi authorities that resulted in the couple's suicide together with their young child—Veit Harlan and Kristina Söderbaum were expelled from the cinema by a furious audience.

138 *Der Spiegel* (March 12, 1951), https://www.spiegel.de/spiegel/print/d-29193530.html.

139 In *Der Spiegel* (article on "Hitlers liebste Schwedin," September 5, 2012): https://www.spiegel.de/fotostrecke/nazi-filmikone-kristina-soederbaum-fotostrecke-107560.html.

140 For Hedda Zinner adaptations, see, for example, *Der Teufelskreis* [Vicious Circle] (Carl Ballhaus, 1956), *Nur eine Frau* [Only a Woman] (Carl Ballhaus, 1958), and especially *Die Schauspielerin* [The Actress] (Siegfried Kühn, 1988). Anna Seghers' works were adapted from 1968 by DEFA regularly, especially for GDR television.

141 Grisko, *Heinrich Mann und der Film*, 326–7. At the same time, Heinrich Mann was awarded the "Nationalpreis 1. Klasse," and conversations regarding his leadership of the East German Academy of Arts were underway, as Grisko points out.

142 Grisko, *Heinrich Mann und der Film*, 420. See also Elizabeth Ward, *East German Film and the Holocaust* (Oxford: Berghahn, 2021).

143 Becher became the Kulturbund's first President, Gerhart Hauptmann was declared honorary president, author of *Der Tunnel* Bernhard Kellermann was one of the VPs. Cf. Gerd Dietrich, "Kulturbund," in *Die Parteien und Organisationen der DDR. Ein Handbuch*, ed. Gerd-Rüdiger Stephan et al. (Berlin: Dietz, 2002), 537f.

144 *Familie Benthin* is based on a script by Becher and Dudow but was criticized for lacking in narrative sophistication.

145 It was not until the 1970s that further adaptations of Mann's novel were produced—as a radio drama by Westdeutscher Rundfunk public broadcaster in 1971, and as a six-part mini-series for television (BBC) in Britain entitled *Man of Straw* (1972).

146 Review in *Thüringer Tageblatt,* etc. Cf. Grisko for several quotes from a number of different newspapers in Grisko, *Heinrich Mann und der Film*, 398f.

147 Ibid., 399.

148 Ibid., 409.

149 "East German Film: Adaptation of Novel by Heinrich Mann," *The Manchester Guardian* (December 15, 1952), 3.

150 Klaus Kreimeier, *Kino und Filmindustrie in der BRD. Ideologieproduktion und Klassenwirklichkeit nach 1945* (Kronberg: Scriptor, 1973), 38f.;

Wolfgang Mühl-Benninghaus, "Vergeßt es nie! Schuld sind sie! Zu Kriegsdeutungen in den audiovisuellen Medien beider deutscher Staaten in den vierziger und fünfziger Jahren," in *Schuld und Sühne 2: Kriegserlebnis und Kriegsdeutung in deutschen Medien der Nachkriegszeit (1945–1961)* (Amsterdam: Rodopi, 2001), 743–57.

151 Cf. Richard Oehmig, *Besorgt mal Filme!*, 64. Regarding DEFA's prolific production of ideologically educational fairy-tale films, see Marc Silberman, "The First DEFA Fairy Tales: Cold War Fantasies of the 1950s," *Framing the Fifties*, 106–19; the second, revised edition of this book edited by Sabine Hake and John Davidson is entitled *Take Two: Fifties Cinema in Divided Germany* (New York: Berghahn, 2008).

152 Cf. Buchloh, "Pervers, jugendgefährdend, staatsfeindlich," 185; quoted in Grisko, *Heinrich Mann und der Film*, 405.

153 According to letters and minutes held in the Bundesarchiv Koblenz approx. 5 percent of DEFA films were effectively banned by the 'East-West Film Exchange Committee'; cf. Grisko, *Heinrich Mann und der Film*, 404.

154 Cf. reviews quoted in Grisko, *Heinrich Mann und der Film*, 401–8f.

155 Brockmann, *A Critical History of German Film*, 221.

156 Adapted to sound film in 1930: Herbert Brenon's pre-Code drama *The Case of Sergeant Grischa*.

157 Seán Allan / John Sandford, eds., *DEFA. East German cinema, 1946–1992*, 68f.

158 See Sabine Hake, "Public Figures, Political Symbols, Famous Stars: Actors in DEFA Cinema and Beyond," *DEFA at the Crossroads of East German and International Film Culture*, eds. Marc Silberman/Henning Wrage, 197–220.

159 Joshua Feinstein, *The Triumph of the Ordinary* (Chapel Hill: University of North Carolina Press, 2003), chapter 1.

160 Minutes, meeting of the DEFA commission, October 3, 1950; quoted in Sebastian Heiduschke, *East German Cinema. DEFA and Film History* (New York: Palgrave, 2013), 12. See also Deborah Vietor-Engländer, "Arnold Zweig, Lion Feuchtwanger und der Film *Das Beil von Wandsbek*," *Feuchtwanger und Film*, 297–314.

161 Shortened by twenty minutes, a truncated version of the film was released by DEFA in 1962. The complete film was not restored until 1981.

162 https://www.bpb.de/apuz/26959/ddr-alltag-im-film-verbotene-und-zensierte-spielfilme-der-defa.

163 Heiduschke, *East German Cinema*, 11.

164 Ibid., 12.

165 Hake, *Film in Deutschland*, 182.

166 Silberman/Wrage, "Introduction," 4.

167 During the rearmament debates, political control was also exerted via these bank guarantees when a film was deemed critical of rearmament. Zander, *Thomas Mann im Film*, 168f. Zander quotes Kreimeier, "Der westdeutsche Film in den fünfziger Jahren," 290.

168 According to *Stuttgarter Zeitung* in *Der Spiegel* 32 (1959), https://www.spiegel.de/politik/bonner-bedenken-a-b5d2dca5-0002-0001-0000-000042622204.

169 Franz Thedieck mentioned this in a television interview according to Manfred Barthel, *So war es wirklich*, 335.

170 Silberman/Wrage, "Introduction," *DEFA at the Crossroads*, 2.
171 https://www.defa-stiftung.de/filme/filme-suchen/das-kalte-herz/.
172 Silberman, "The First DEFA Fairy Tales," in *Framing the Fifties*, ed. Hake/Davidson, 106–19, here p. 114.
173 Among them the Grimm brothers' *Frau Holle* (1944/8); he produced *Hans im Glück* [Hans in Luck] for Peter Hamel (1949); filmed *Brüderchen und Schwesterchen* [Brother and Sister] and *Die goldene Gans* [The Golden Goose] with Walter Oehmichen (1953); produced *Hänsel und Gretel* [Hansel and Gretel] and *Rotkäppchen* [Little Red Riding Hood] for Walter Janssen (1954), *Schneeweißchen und Rosenrot* [Snow White and Rose Red] (1955), *Schneewittchen und die sieben Zwerge* [Snow White] (1955), *Die Heinzelmännchen* [The Shoemaker and the Elves] (1956) and *Rübezahl* (1957) for Erich Kobler; 1956 *Tischlein deck dich* [The Wishing-Table] for Jürgen von Alten; and in 1959 *Die Bremer Stadtmusikanten* [The Bremen Town Musicians] for Rainer Geis; and for Peter Podehl *Der Wolf und die sieben Geißlein* [The Big Bad Wolf] (1957) and *Frau Holle—Das Märchen von Goldmarie und Pechmarie* [Mother Holle] (1961). These fairy-tale adaptations are still regularly shown on German television and, also, in the United States.
174 Three previous adaptations had been released in 1921 (DE, Wilhelm Prager); 1938 (USSR, Olga Khodataeva); 1944 (DE/NS-Film, Franz Fiedler).
175 DEFA in the meantime produced increasingly for GDR television, beginning with Helmut Spieß's *Das tapfere Schneiderlein* [The Valiant Little Tailor], 1956. Adaptations for East German cinemas included Francesco Stefani's *Das singende, klingende Bäumchen* [The Singing Tree] (1957), Christoph Engel's *Das Zaubermännchen* [Rumpelstiltskin] (1960), and the very popular *Schneewittchen und die sieben Zwerge* [Snow White] (GDR, Gottfried Kolditz, 1961).
176 Dieter Wiedemann, "Es war einmal … Märchenfilme in der Bundesrepublik Deutschland und der DDR," in *Märchen im Medienwechsel,* ed. Ute Dettmar et al., 179–228, here p. 180.
177 Also, based on Kästner's novels for his more grown-up readers, the film comedies *Die verschwundene Miniatur* [The Lost Miniature] (FRG, Carl-Heinz Schroth, 1954) and *Drei Männer im Schnee* [Three Men in the Snow] (AT, Kurt Hoffmann, 1955).
178 Twenty-first-century German adaptations of Kästner's works include *Emil und die Detektive* (Franziska Buch, 2001); *Das fliegende Klassenzimmer* (Tomy Wigand, 2003); the 3D computer-animated comedy *Konferenz der Tiere (Animals United*, 2010); *Das doppelte Lottchen* (Lancelot von Naso, 2017); and *Fabian oder Der Gang vor die Hunde* (Dominik Graf, 2021). See the final chapter in this book for further information and my chapter on "Film" in Neuhaus, ed., *Erich Kästner Handbuch*, 2023.
179 The importance of the next generation is also highlighted in one of the most interesting fairy-tale adaptations of this decade, in which it is a young boy, who saves the day: *Petya and Little Red Riding Hood* (USSR, Boris Stepantsev and Evgeny Raykovsky, 1958).

180 Greg M. Colón Semenza and Bob Hasenfratz, *The History of British Literature on Film, 1895–2015* (New York and London: Bloomsbury, 2015), 233.
181 According to www.filmdienst.de.
182 Cinematographers Werner Krien and Gerhard Krüger had successfully collaborated before on the Thomas Mann adaptation *Königliche Hoheit* [Your Royal Highness] (FRG, Harald Braun, 1953), which also starred Ruth Leuwerik.
183 Cf. my essay on the topic in Neuhaus ed., *Effi Briest Handbuch*, 133–5, which provided the foundation for this section; the quote is derived from Heinkel, *Epische Literatur im Film*, 55–6.
184 Rare exceptions include *Die Sünderin* [The Sinner] (1951). Here, a teenage Marina (H. Knef) prostitutes herself out of loneliness and boredom more than greed, describing the "geometry" of the arrangement as 'He gave and I took, I gave and he took—it was a smooth calculation—and that's how it stayed my entire life.' A scene in which she posed nude for her partner (a painter) caused outrage among Church representatives and conservative Germans.
185 This is a term first used by film critic Georg Seeßlen, "Der Neo-Adenauer-Stil," *taz. die tageszeitung* (June 12, 1997): 15. See also Eric Rentschler, "From New German Cinema to the Post-Wall Cinema of Consensus," in *Cinema and Nation*, ed. Mette Hjort and Scott MacKenzie (London and New York: Routledge, 2000), 260–77.
186 Jürgen von Alten's *Der Biberpelz* [The Beaver Coat] (1937).
187 Jochen Huth (September 27, 1954), Artur Brauner-Archiv im Deutschen Filminstitut—DIF, https://www.filmportal.de/sites/default/files/DA4257AEF03D41ED81FD1FD626185524_F012181_ABA_026_PS_001.pdf.
188 Quoted in Bartel, *So war es wirklich*, 234.
189 *Rose Bernd* is a sort of "Heimatfilmdrama" as epd film notes: https://www.epd-film.de/tipps/2016/filmreihe-geliebt-und-verdraengt-das-kino-der-jungen-brd.
190 See, for example, Bosley Crowther, "Screen: Maria Schell in German Role; 'Sins of Rose Bernd' at Little Carnegie Well-Made Drama of Sin and Sorrow," *New York Times* (January 24, 1959).
191 Eric Rentschler, *West German Filmmakers on Film: Visions and Voices* (New York: Holmes & Meier, 1988).
192 Cf. Wedel, *Filmgeschichte als Krisengeschichte*, 192f.; Zander, *Thomas Mann im Kino*, 166f.
193 Wolf wrote the scripts for Kurt Maetzig's *Der Rat der Götter* (1950) and Martin Hellberg's *Thomas Müntzer* (1956). His Professor Mamlock was readapted in 1961 under the direction of his son Konrad.
194 Cf. Mann, *Tagebücher 1953–1955*, 306 (January 9 and March 11, 1955), quoted in Michael Wedel, who convincingly argues that it was Erica's own interest in the project that drove the positive depiction. Cf. Wedel, *Filmgeschichte als Krisengeschichte*, 230f.
195 See Wedel, *Filmgeschichte als Krisengeschichte*, 192–247; Zander, *Thomas Mann im Kino*, 166–72. Eleanor Twentyman is played by a young Heidi Brühl.

196 See for example: "Hervorragend missglückt. Ufa-Theater: Felix Krull, sehr frei nach Thomas Mann," *Kölnische Rundschau* (May 18, 1957).
197 B. Crowther, "The Screen: 'Felix Krull'. German Import Based on Novel by Mann," *New York Times* (March 5, 1958): 38.
198 Thomas Mann, *Nachlese. Prosa 1951—1955* (Berlin and Frankfurt/M.: Fischer, 1956), 227f. For a detailed analysis of postwar adaptations of Mann's works, see Yahya Elsaghe, *Thomas Mann auf Leinwand und Bildschirm* (Berlin: de Gruyter, 2019).
199 See Claudia Breger, "'Kampf dem Kampf': Aesthetic Experimentation and Social Satire in *The Ballad of Berlin*," in *German Postwar Films*, ed. W. Wilms and W. Rasch, 157–74.
200 The intertitle reads: "Die Handlung ist frei erfunden. Zufällige Ähnlichkeiten mit lebenden Personen sind beabsichtigt." The script and Hoffmann's notes can be accessed digitally thanks to filmportal.de at https://www.filmportal.de/sites/default/files/7D347B1778284E38B19131B59012133B_f007469_slg_hoffmann_wirw_01_02.pdf.
201 http://www.kulturarchiv.de/wunder.php.
202 Lawrence S. Kaplan, "NATO and Adenauer's Germany: Uneasy Partnership," *International Organization* 15.4 (1961): 618.
203 Produced by Abich, *Es kommt ein Tag* [A Day Will Come] (1950) was directed by Jugert, who had worked as assistant director under Helmut Käutner from 1939 onwards. The author of the source text Penzoldt had served in the German army in both world wars and in many of his works conveyed the shock of war, the reality of death, and the beauty of life and friendship in a way that appealed to a largely male audience during the Second World War. His story of Corporal Mombour, which was even printed in a front edition, takes place during the Prussian-French war of 1870/1 and is subtitled "A Soldier's Romance." In the script co-written by Hans Abich, Rolf Thiele, Thea von Harbou and Fritz Graßhoff, war is an inevitable reality, while romance is foregrounded. The adaptation starred Dieter Borsche and Maria Schell in their first film together, quickly establishing the pair as the first and perhaps most revered dream couple in Germany of the time.
204 The highest grossing was the biblical epic *The Robe* (USA, Henry Koster, 1953), based on Lloyd C. Douglas' 1942 novel; the screenplay adapted by exile Gina Kaus, blacklisted Albert Maltz, and Philip Dunne. https://archive.org/details/variety193-1954-01/page/n301/mode/2up?view=theater.
205 The three novels are *08/15 Die abenteuerliche Revolte des Gefreiten Asch* [The Adventurous Revolt of Private Asch], later entitled *08/15 in der Kaserne* [in the barracks], *08/15 Die seltsamen Kriegserlebnisse des Soldaten Asch* [The Strange War Experiences of Soldier Asch], later also more simply entitled *08/15 im Krieg* [at war], and finally *08/15 Der gefährliche Endsieg des Soldaten Asch* [The Dangerous Final Victory of Soldier Asch], later entitled *08/15 bis zum Ende* [till the end]. Volume 1 and 2 were published in 1954, volume 3 in 1955.
206 For further information about masculinity in postwar film, see especially Jaimey Fisher, "Deleuze in a Ruinous Context: German Rubble-Film and Italian Neorealism," *Iris* 23 (1997): 53–74; Erica Carter, "Men in Cardigans: Canaris (1954) and the 1950s West German Good Soldier," in *War-Torn*

Tales: Representing Gender and World War II in Literature and Film, ed. D. Hipkins and G. Plain (Oxford: Lang, 2007), 195–222; Jennifer M. Kapczynski, "Armchair Warriors: Heroic Postures in the West German War Film," in *Screening War: Perspectives on German Suffering*, ed. P. Cooke and M. Silberman (Rochester, NY: Camden House, 2010), 17–35; and Hester Baer, "'Das Boot' and the German Cinema of Neoliberalism," *The German Quarterly* 85.1 (2012): 18–39.

207 English translations of Kirst's novels followed almost immediately and were published as *The Revolt of Gunner Asch* (1955), *Forward, Gunner Asch!* (1956), *The Return of Gunner Asch* (1957), and *What Became of Gunner Asch* (1964).

208 Walter Nutz, "Der Krieg als Abenteuer und Idylle: Landser-Hefte und triviale Kriegsromane," *Gegenwartsliteratur und Drittes Reich*, ed. Hans Wagener (Stuttgart: 1977), 265; quoted by Robert G. Moeller, "Kämpfen für den Frieden: 08/15 und westdeutsche Erinnerungen an den Zweiten Weltkrieg," *Militärgeschichtliche Zeitschrift* 64 (2005): 359–89, here p. 359.

209 Mario Adorf was the other relatively unknown actor in the film who became one of the stars of FRG's cinema and television screens.

210 Ernst von Salomon is remembered for his involvement in the assassination of Weimar Germany's Jewish Foreign Minister Walther Rathenau in 1922 and his nationalist publications, such as his Freikorps novel *Die Geächteten* (The Outlaws, 1930). Moeller calls him an elitist fighting "the Weimar system" (Moeller, "Kämpfen für den Frieden," 359f.) His autobiographical *Der Fragebogen* (1951) became a bestseller after its publication. A reference to his novel is included in *08/15* (part 3) when a naïve young American soldier looking at a box filled with questionnaires filled out by Germans mockingly exclaims: 'Now we can find out the truth!'. See also R. G. Moeller, "Kämpfen für den Frieden," 377.

211 May was interviewed by the Munich newspaper *Süddeutsche Zeitung* (April 7, 1992); quoted in the original in Moeller, "Kämpfen für den Frieden," 374.

212 The exhibition "Die Verbrechen der Wehrmacht" [The Crimes of the Wehrmacht] in 1995 caused an uproar in Germany, especially among a whole generation of former soldiers that had lived quite contently with the 'clean soldier' narrative.

213 Kirst, *08/15* (part 2), 579; see also 565, 578, 594.

214 Moeller, "Kämpfen für den Frieden," 363f.

215 Cf. minutes of the Bundestag-debates (June 28, 1955), quoted in Moeller, "Kämpfen für den Frieden," 376.

216 Moeller quotes from an array of contemporary reviews that illustrate his well-argued point. Cf. Moeller, "Kämpfen für den Frieden," 375.

217 May was born on May 8, 1909; May 8, 1945, marked the end of National Socialism. The director chose the English/American spelling of the month (German: Mai) as a nod to Hollywood culture and the United States and Britain as allies.

218 Within the first month of the first of the trilogy's films, 5 million West Germans flocked to the cinema—even more viewers than Deppe's epitome of postwar Heimat-film *Schwarzwaldmädel* (1950). According to R. G. Moeller, the film, which had cost merely 200,000 USD, made 4 million dollars at the

box office within four weeks (Moeller, "Kämpfen für den Frieden," 363). According to Wolfgang Wegmann, up to 20 million watched part 1. Cf. Wegmann, Der westdeutsche Kriegsfilm der fünfziger Jahre (*PhD thesis, Cologne University, 1980*), 119; quoted by Moeller, Ibid., 363.

219 The following passage is based on my previous publications on the topic. For further analysis of this film, see my articles "Erfolg und Misserfolg von Verfilmungen: Manfred Gregors *Die Brücke* und die Nahaufnahmen des Krieges in Kino und Fernsehen," *Germanistik in Ireland* 7 (2012): 81–102; and "Representing Pain in Literature and Film: Reflections on Die Brücke (The Bridge) by Manfred Gregor and Bernhard Wicki," *Comunicação & Cultura* 5 (2008): 45–62.

220 Manfred Gregor, *Die Brücke* (Munich: DVA, 2005), 211.

221 Quoted in Reimer, *Nazi Retro Film*, 65f.

222 As producer at MGM, Reinhardt's work included King Vidor's *Comrade X* (1940) and Robert Siodmak's Dostojevsky-adaptation *The Great Sinner* (1949), and John Huston's *The Red Badge of Courage* (1951). During his time in the US Army (Signal Corps), he co-wrote *Here Is Germany* (1945), an educational if somewhat propagandistic documentary for the US troops, directed by Frank Capra.

223 Else Heims worked repeatedly with Richard Oswald, appearing in films such as *Es werde Licht* (part 3; 1918) and *Die Rothausgasse* (1928).

224 Assmann, *Erinnerungsräume*, 359f.

225 Alexander Mitscherlich and Margarete Mitscherlich, *Die Unfähigkeit zu trauern. Grundlagen kollektiven Verhaltens* (Munich: Piper, [1967] 2007).

226 Having his citizenship revoked by the Nazis, Zuckmayer was appalled that he was expected to apply and undergo a bureaucratic process of approval for German citizenship upon his return to his former home. He accepted US American citizenship in 1946 and moved to Switzerland in 1957.

227 This is based on my father's account of the event, who attended it as a seventeen-year old. Roland Schönfeld, *Carl Zuckmayer*, unpublished typescript.

228 The film premiered on November 17, 1948, in Switzerland, then in Austria on January 21, 1949, and, finally, in West Germany on October 28, 1949.

229 The popularity of Zuckmayer-adaptations continued well into the 1970s. His *Teufels General* was followed by several adaptations of his works for cinema: *Herr über den Tod* [Death's Master] (FRG, Victor Vicas, 1955), *Frauensee* [based on the 1937 prose text "Ein Sommer in Österreich" or "A Summer in Austria"] (FRG, Rudolf Jugert, 1958), three exceedingly successful adaptations for cinema under the direction of Helmut Käutner—*Ein Mädchen aus Flandern* [The Girl from Flanders, based on Zuckmayer's Engele von Loewen] (FRG, 1955), a remake of *Der Hauptmann von Köpenick* starring Heinz Rühmann (FRG, 1956), and a first adaptation of Zuckmayer's 1927 play *Der Schinderhannes* [Schinderhannes or Duel in the Forest] (FRG, 1958) dominated by Curd Jürgens' morose masculinity—, and the dramatic crime drama taking place during the carnival season in Mainz *Die Fastnachtsbeichte* [Carnival confession] (FRG, William Dieterle, 1960). William Dieterle's last feature film for cinema and the returning exile's last film in Germany stars Hans Söhnker, Gitty Daruga and Götz George.

Zuckmayer-adaptations for West German television included *Das kalte Licht* [The Cold Light] (Leo Mittler, 1955), *Der kleine Friedländer* [Little Friedländer] (Peter Horn, 1956), *Schinderhannes* (Peter Beauvais, 1957), another *Hauptmann von Köpenick* adaptation, this time starring Rudolf Plate (Rainer Wolffhardt, 1960), and *Der fröhliche Weinberg* (Hermann Pfeiffer, 1961). Cf. Hans-Michael Bock and Tim Bergfelder, *The Concise Cinegraph: Encyclopaedia of German Cinema* (Oxford: Berghahn, 2009), 91f.; filmportal.de.

230 Udet had committed suicide by shooting himself in the head, but his death was reported as accidental, and he was given a state funeral. Carl Zuckmayer, *Als wär's ein Stück von mir* (Frankfurt/M.: Fischer, 2006), 623f.

231 Edward Plater, "Helmut Käutner's Film Adaptation of *Des Teufels General*," *Literature/Film Quarterly* 22.4 (1994): 253–64. "The play was tremendously popular in the early postwar years. Even though it was not performed in Germany until November 1947, it nevertheless led all plays in number of performances for the 1947–8 season and the following year outdistanced its nearest competitor, *The Captain of Köpenick*, also by Carl Zuckmayer, by a margin of better than four to one." Ibid., 253.

232 For a good summary of the reactions in the press see Mariatte C. Denman, "Nostalgia for a Better Germany: Carl Zuckmayer's 'Des Teufels General'," *The German Quarterly* 76.4 (2003): 369–80, here p. 371f.

233 Plater, "Helmut Käutner's Film Adaptation of *Des Teufels General*," 254.

234 Denman, "Nostalgia for a Better Germany," 369.

235 Denman makes reference to Käutner. Ibid., 411.

236 See Plater, "Helmut Käutner's Film Adaptation of *Des Teufels General*," 259 and 263, also quoted by Denman, "Nostalgia for a Better Germany," 370. Cf. also Wolfgang Becker and Norbert Schöll, *In jenen Tagen. Wie der deutsche Nachkriegsfilm die Vergangenheit bewältigte* (Opladen: Leske+Budrich, 1995), 79–94; Anthony Wayne, "Carl Zuckmayer's *Des Teufels General* as a Critique of the Culture of Masculinity," *Forum for Modern Language Studies* 14.3 (1996): 258–70.

237 Denman, "Nostalgia for a Better Germany," 370; she makes reference here to Becker and Schöll, *In jenen Tagen*, 79–94.

238 Plater, "Helmut Käutner's Film Adaptation of *Des Teufels General*," 258.

239 The success of this adaptation had a multiplicatory effect as the long list of further Zuckmayer adaptations reveals. *Herr über Leben und Tod* (1955), *Das kalte Licht* (1955), *Ein Mädchen aus Flandern* (1956), *Der kleine Friedländer* (1956), *Der Hauptmann von Köpenick* (1956), *Der Schinderhannes* (1956), *Frauensee* (1958), *Der Schinderhannes* (1958), *Herbert Engelmann* (1959), *Die Fastnachtsbeichte* (1960), *Der Hauptmann von Köpenick* (1960), and *Der fröhliche Weinberg* (1961).

240 A. H. Weiler, "Luftwaffe Drama: 'The Devil's General' Is German Import," *New York Times* (April 16, 1957), 38.

241 Weiler, "Luftwaffe Drama," 38.

242 Abich is quoted by Dominik Graf, "Hunde, wollt ihr ewig leben? Einige Männerbilder und ihre Darstellungsstile im westdeutschen Nachkriegsfilm," in *Geliebt und verdrängt: Das Kino der jungen Bundesrepublik Deutschland*

von 1949 bis 1963, ed. Claudia Dillmann and Olaf Möller (Frankfurt/M.: Deutsches Filminstitut DIF, 2016), 132–59, here p. 140.
243 Graf, "Hunde," 141.
244 Ibid.
245 Curd Jürgens' popularity was at an all-time high. He starred in numerous films and many adaptations, and from the mid-1950s worked increasingly in international productions; he played, for example, the lead in *Die Ratten* [The Rats], an adaptation of Gerhart Hauptmann's 1911 play, which was transposed to 1950s West Germany by scriptwriter Jochen Huth and director Robert Siodmak. He also starred in the aforementioned *Teufel in Seide* (FRG, Rolf Hansen, 1956) based on Gina Kaus as well as the same year alongside Brigitte Bardot in *Et Dieu … créa la femme* [And God Created Woman] (FR, Roger Vadim, 1956). He also took on the role of Professor Rath in the 1959 remake of Sternberg's famous Heinrich Mann adaptation *The Blue Angel* (USA, Edward Dmytryk, 1959).
246 Fanatical Nazi and President of Hitler's so-called Volksgerichtshof or people's court from 1942, Roland Freisler was infamous for humiliating the accused during trial, especially members of resistance group such as the Scholl-siblings and other members of "Weiße Rose" [White Rose], or Stauffenberg and those involved in the assassination attempt on Hitler on July 20, 1944. Under Freisler's command over 5,000 death sentences were handed down. Killed during a bombing raid in 1945, Freisler's widow received a full pension after the war which included additional benefits that her husband would have acquired if his career had not been cut short. Johann Chapoutot, "The Nazi People's Court (1944)", in *The Scene of the Mass Crime*, eds. Christian Delage and Peter Goodrich, 101–12, here p. 111.
247 David Clarke, "German Martyrs: Images of Christianity and Resistance to National Socialism in German Cinema," *Screening War: Perspectives on German Suffering*, ed. P. Cooke and M. Silberman, 36–55, here p. 38f.
248 The review published in *Der Spiegel* ("Frei nach Schiller," April 15, 1959) claimed the project to be 'loosely based on Schiller.' Despite the fact that he considered it badly written, the text became an essential "Hebel" or 'lever' for Wisbar's concept of the *Stalingrad* film project, which takes its narrative composition from Schiller's *Wallenstein*.
249 Carter, "Men in Cardigans," 195–222; Kapczynski, "Armchair Warriors," 17–35.
250 According to the quotes from Strauß's letter to Wisbar published in *Der Spiegel*. "Frei nach Schiller," *Der Spiegel* 16 (April 15, 1959), https://www.spiegel.de/spiegel/print/d-42625075.html.
251 "Reitet für Rilke" in *Der Spiegel* 44 (October 26, 1955); https://www.spiegel.de/spiegel/print/d-41960501.html.
252 Quoted in the Cornet-review "Reitet für Rilke," ibid.
253 In "Neu in Deutschland: Der Cornet (Deutschland) […]," *Der Spiegel* 1 (January 4, 1956); https://www.spiegel.de/spiegel/print/d-31587107.html.
254 Fritz Göttler, "Westdeutscher Nachkriegsfilm," in *Geschichte des deutschen Films*, ed. Wolfgang Jakobsen et al., 171–210, here p. 198.
255 Examples of box-office hits include *Schwarzwaldmädel* (1950), *Grün ist die Heide* (1951), and *Der Pfarrer vom Kirchfeld* (1955); 'cash box poison'

would have included films such as *Der Verlorene* (FRG, Peter Lorre, 1951); *Der 20. Juli* (FRG, Falk Harnack, 1955) and *Schwarzer Kies* (FRG, Helmut Käutner, 1961).

256 Heinrich Spoerl's *Der Maulkorb* [The Muzzle] (FRG, Wolfgang Staudte, 1958) might also be mentioned in this context, but the 1938 film was read as critical of the Nazi regime at the time.

257 Horst Buchholz, for example, managed to create a struggling hero with scruffily stunning looks in Georg Tressler's 1959 adaptation of B. Traven's anarchic adventure novel *Das Totenschiff. Die Geschichte eines amerikanischen Seemanns* (The Death Ship. The Story of an American Sailor, 1926), which set the tone for an attractive new type that was recreated in German cinema and television well into the 1970s.

258 For more information on this film, see my essay on "Die verdinglichte Frau als Heimat im deutschen Film: Rolf Thieles *Das Mädchen Rosemarie*," in *Post/Nationale Vorstellungen von ‚Heimat' in deutschen, europäischen und globalen Kontexten*, ed. F. Eigler, J. Golec and L. Żyliński (Frankfurt/M.: Lang, 2012), 133–8.

259 According to Wikipedia, Zweig's novel also inspired the Czechoslovakian films *Šach mat* (1963) and *Královská hra* (1980).

260 Schulberg, "The German Film," 402.

261 Having written twenty-one screenplays between 1950 and 1961, adaptations of Simmel's popular literary work commenced across in the two Germanies and Austria in 1960 with *Mein Schulfreund* (FRG, Robert Siodmak), *Gerichtet bei Nacht* (GDR, Hans-Joachim Kasprzik), and *Mit Himbeergeist geht alles besser* (AT, Georg Marischka). French/West-German co-productions *Affäre Nina B.* (Robert Siodmak), *Es muß nicht immer Kaviar sein* (Géza von Radványi) and *Diesmal muß es Kaviar sein* (Géza von Radványi) followed in 1961. Nearly twenty more adaptations based on Simmel's work were produced, including a television series (FRG, ZDF, 1977).

262 So far fifteen adaptations based on Heinz G. Konsalik's bestsellers have been produced, beginning with the popular war novels *Der Arzt von Stalingrad* (FRG, Géza von Radványi, 1958) and *Strafbataillon 999* (FRG, Harald Philipp, 1960).

263 Cinema boomed until the affordability of televisions restructured Germans' entertainment landscape. By 1950, West Germany had reached the prewar level of 4,000 cinemas; nine years later, that number had nearly doubled again.

264 Disagreements during the pre-production of adaptations of his works meant that Bertolt Brecht's *Herr Puntila und sein Knecht Matti* was first adapted to film in Austria under the direction of Alberto Calvalcanti in 1955. Wolfgang Staudte, who had left for West Germany, followed with *Mutter Courage und ihre Kinder* (FRG, 1956). It was not until 1960 that Brecht's *Die Gesichte der Simone Machard* (GDR, Lothar Bellag, 1960) was brought to East German television audiences, and the long-planned *Mutter Courage und ihre Kinder* (GDR, Peter Palitzsch/Manfred Wekwerth, 1960) to cinemas in the GDR.

265 Knut Hickethier, with Peter Hoff, *Geschichte des deutschen Fernsehens* (Stuttgart: Metzler, 1998).

266 Among the relevant research available in English on adaptations for German-language television, see especially Gisela Holfter's work on Heinrich Böll: "From Bestseller to Failure? Heinrich Böll's *Irisches Tagebuch* (Irish Journal) to *Irland und seine Kinder* (Children of Eire)," in *Processes of Transposition: German Literature and Film*, ed. C. Schönfeld, 207–21; and for more context, her *Heinrich Böll and Ireland* (Newcastle upon Tyne: Cambridge Scholars, 2011).

267 Norbert Grob, Hans-Helmut Prinzler and Eric Rentschler, *Neuer Deutscher Film* (Stuttgart: Reclam, 2012), 12.

268 See Leo Lensing, "Cinema, Society and Literature in Irmgard Keun's Das kunstseidene Mädchen," *The Germanic Review* 60 (1985): 129–34.

269 For more on this topic, see Tim Bergfelder, *International Adventures. German Popular Cinema and European Co-Productions in the 1960s* (Oxford: Berhahn, 2004). Walter Berendsohn claimed that Karl May was also Hitler's favorite author. See W. B., *Die humanistische Front* (Zurich: Europa, 1946), 45.

270 Gottfried Reinhardt's successful adaptations/remakes (*Vor* Sonnenaufgang, 1956; *Menschen im Hotel*, 1959) and films such as *Liebling der Götter* (1960) and *Stadt ohne Mitleid* (starring Kirk Douglas and Christine Kaufmann, 1961) are a case in point.

271 Consider the relevant contributions by Steinle, von Moltke, Wauchope and Fisher in John Davidson, Sabine Hake, ed., *Framing the Fifties*.

272 This paragraph is based on Otto Scheugl's article "Der Film der frühen Jahre—Herbert Vesely und der Neue deutsche Film," which can be accessed at https://scheugl.org/website-von-hans-scheugl-startseite/texte-von-hans-scheugl/der-film-der-fruhen-jahre-herbert-vesely-und-der-neue-deutsche-film/.

273 As W. G. Sebald, for example, put it repeatedly.

8

Split Screens: Continuities and a New German Cinema (1962–89)

I'll return to Germany to make movies because they don't have any there.
VOLKER SCHLÖNDORFF TO JOE HEMBUS (1962)

Until we find out, why men act the way they do, everything is in doubt.
MARLENE DIETRICH IN BLACK FOX (1962)

The period following the construction of the Berlin Wall was marked by decisive changes in attitudes and values while a new generation of filmmakers began to reflect critically on a society that still struggled to face its past. The public trial of Adolf Eichmann in Jerusalem, his sentencing as one of the main perpetrators of genocide, the appeals process and, finally, his execution in June 1962 received considerable media attention. The trial, which opened on April 11, 1961, was televised and witness statements by survivors of the Holocaust were broadcast internationally. The following month, nearly 1 million East Germans went to see Konrad Wolf's remake of his father's play *Professor Mamlock*, which takes an unflinching look at antisemitism in Nazi Germany and the mechanisms of adjustment, marginalization, and repression that prepared the ground for genocide.

In West Germany, convenient bouts of amnesia regarding the Nazi era were increasingly difficult to sustain during the Eichmann trial and in light of public debates about definitions of guilt and the premeditated mass murder of Jewish citizens, including over 1 million children. The Auschwitz trials in Frankfurt/Main (1963–5) gave further impetus to shifting memory

FIGURE 8.1 *Wolfgang Heinz as* Professor Mamlock *(GDR, Konrad Wolf, 1961)*.

discourses in perpetrator countries. Finally, questions were being asked by sons and daughters who needed to know why their parents and grandparents let this happen, and "why men act the way they do," as Marlene Dietrich's voice puts it in Stouman's Goethe-adaptation and Hitler-era-documentary *Black Fox*.

As West Germany's 'phase of dealing with the past'[1] began, the dynamics of this era are reflected in the role of German-language literature on screen, from continued attempts by a profit-orientated film and television industry to use the literary canon for escapist entertainment, to innovative adaptations of contemporary literature that impacted the public sphere in a politically charged climate marked by substantial division. As this chapter will outline, most adaptations of this era were based on genre fiction and continued the postwar trend of mainstream fare from fairy tales to light-hearted comedies. In literature, however, the writers of *Gruppe 47* [Group 47] had begun to establish new traditions in their pursuit of an innovative language and offered a realism that was to refute the linguistic corruption of Nazi propaganda. In their literary texts, writers like Heinrich Böll, Ingeborg Bachmann, Peter Weiss, and Uwe Johnson, to name but a few, addressed the catastrophes of antisemitism and Nazism, war, and the Holocaust, and shed light on the consequences of these events as well as of their willful erasure from cultural memory for individuals and postwar German and Austrian society. By the 1960s, as one of the most prolific German filmmakers of the era Volker Schlöndorff put it in 2020, it was time for cinema to do the same and 'face its past', using this 'literary model' and thus creating 'a symbiotic relationship between literature and film'.[2] The impact of these adaptations by young West German filmmakers of contemporary literature, but also of selected texts of the German-language literary canon will be of particular interest here.

In the early 1960s, West Germans were losing interest in cinema. Profits at the box office in the FRG were merely half of what they had been six years earlier. After reaching an all-time high in 1956 with 818 million tickets sold in the FRG to a growing population of 53 million that year, only 443 million visits to the cinema were recorded in 1962. By 1976 ticket sales had plunged to a historic low of 115 million.[3] Young German filmmakers such as Schlöndorff, Werner Herzog, Alexander Kluge, Margarethe von Trotta, Rainer Werner Fassbinder, Doris Dörrie, Wim Wenders, and other innovators of the era renewed the public's interest in cinema and pushed ticket sales to 144 million in 1980.

This new generation's anger is reflected in many of the gritty adaptations of the 1970s and 1980s, and this chapter examines some of the main trends that surface in German-language cinema at the time. The emergence of the auteurist New German Cinema is deeply entwined with the state of commercial cinema, television culture, as well as political unrest, and state interventions in West Germany as the following pages will argue. Filmmakers considered themselves spectators of, but also active participants in the public sphere and repeatedly turned to literature to critically examine their nation's past and to engage with their unstable present, while raising questions about identity and integrity. A generation was coming of age that believed in the possibility of change, affected by the United States and President John F. Kennedy, the civil rights and antiwar movements at the outset. At the same time, far-right, nationalist sentiments were on the rise again in West Germany, especially following the resignation of chancellor Adenauer in October 1963, and fueled by the economic recession of 1966/7. Appalled by this willingness to once again embrace values that had brought about two world wars and mass murder, many young West Germans disillusioned with the conservative government, and then worried about the leadership of a Grand Coalition (1966–9), were becoming increasingly politicized, and in parts radicalized, due to police violence and other acts of suppression.

When numerous left-wing protesters were beaten by police and Benno Ohnesorg, a 26-year-old student, was shot and killed in West Berlin during demonstrations against the state visit of the Shah of Iran in June 1967, the protest movement spread across the country. On April 2, 1968 four students around Andreas Baader set fire to two department stores in Frankfurt/Main as an act of opposition to the Vietnam War, but also against the West

German Government, which they considered not more than an extension of the fascist state Germany had become thirty-five years earlier. These actions had a palpable impact on politics in the FRG. Former chancellor Adenauer's guiding principle of continuity and 'no experiments!', turned into the 'daring more democracy'-slogan under the new chancellor, social-democrat Willy Brandt (1969–74), who also promoted a more conciliatory stance toward the Eastern Bloc and is still remembered for his wordless gesture of humility during a state visit to Poland, when he fell on his knees in front of the Warsaw ghetto memorial in 1970.

The protests of 1968 had aimed at changing society peacefully and for the better. The supporters of the movement across Western Europe and the United States shared the conviction that a functioning democracy requires participation and naturally challenges existing power structures and hierarchies. A counter-public and counter-institutions (such as the 'outer-parliamentarian opposition' APO) emerged from this engagement, while a minority called for much more forceful resistance. The formation of the Rote Armee Fraktion [Red Army Faction/RAF] culminated in the violence of the 'German Autumn' of 1977. Film once again became the site of counterculture, negotiated by young filmmakers in collaborative projects such as *Deutschland im Herbst* [Germany in Autumn] (1977). As the following pages will demonstrate, several adaptations by New German Cinema emerged as intertextual masterpieces that share an acute political awareness while engaging with both canonical and contemporary literature, until West Germany's increasingly neoliberal film culture under Interior Minister Friedrich Zimmermann jeopardized art cinema in the FRG and pushed several of these outstanding filmmakers abroad.

East Germany in the meantime was facing the failure of socialist economic reforms instigated under First Secretary Walter Ulbricht. Following the economic crisis, Ulbricht was replaced by Erich Honecker in 1971, who promised a rise in material and cultural quality of life, founded on socialist production, and social and political reforms, aimed at increasing the workforce after the mass exodus prior to 1961.[4] Honecker was an ideologue and hardliner, however, and his failure to embrace Mikhail Gorbachev's liberal politics of glasnost and perestroika in the 1980s eventually led to mass protests in the GDR, which were documented at the time by Andreas Voigt in his film *Leipzig im Herbst* [Leipzig in Autumn] (1989). Honecker was forced to resign shortly before the 'fall' of the Berlin Wall in November 1989. During this era, filmmakers at the state-sponsored Deutsche Film Anstalt (DEFA) and the GDR's state television broadcaster Deutscher Fernsehfunk (DFF) carefully negotiated creative spaces constrained by political pressures. Their films, including some outstanding adaptations of both Germany's literary heritage and contemporary literature, were for the most part disregarded in the capitalist West, but have in recent years received a significant amount of scholarly attention.[5] Despite the fact that films based on German literature were in the minority, adaptations produced by DEFA during this period have dominated screenings of East German films in German and international cinemas in recent years.[6]

Following an overview of German literature on international screens, and of the significance of adaptations for commercial cinema during this period, the focus of this chapter will be on New German Cinema and young West German filmmakers' use of a politically and historically aware literature produced by authors who critically engaged with society as responsible citizens. This form of *littérature engagée*, as Jean-Paul Sartre[7] defined it, now played a significant role in productions by this new generation of young filmmakers, who declared their "Papas Kino" an obsolete corpse and demanded change.

Addressing the recent past—finding a language for the Holocaust and the devastation caused by National Socialism, but even more so the German people's unfathomable moral failure—had become the primary goal of the Group 47 writers. Now, as budding filmmakers like Schlöndorff saw it, it was high time for film to embark on that journey and take on the task of analyzing and communicating Germany's Nazi past. Wolfgang Koeppen's *Trilogie des Scheiterns* (Trilogy of Failure, 1951–4),[8] works like Böll's *Billiard um halb zehn* (Billiards at Half-Past Nine, 1959), and Günter Grass' *Die Blechtrommel* (The Tin Drum, 1959) were some of the novels that critically explored German lives during the Hitler era, individual and collective guilt, while advocating an awareness of the past and responsibility for the present. The *Spiegel*-affair of 1962—a political scandal that resulted in the resignation of Minister of Defense Franz-Josef Strauß after the owner and two editors of the weekly political magazine *Der Spiegel* had been arrested for publishing a supposedly 'seditious' article—was a stark reminder "why press freedom is worth fighting for."[9] The Eichmann trial and the *Spiegel*-affair dominated newspaper front pages and television debates for months and highlighted the importance of the public sphere and discursive engagements between individuals and the state as stakeholders in the betterment of society.

It was also in 1962 that promising young academic Jürgen Habermas published his *Structural Transformation of the Public Sphere*.[10] Here, the philosopher and sociologist emphasizes the importance of the public sphere as an integral part of civil society, and he refers to discussions about literary texts, such as those happening in the Salons of the eighteenth and nineteenth centuries, which not only entertained bourgeois citizens in their living rooms, but "served society."[11] From those rational-critical debates, he argues, democratic structures based on reason emerged. Moreover, public discourses and opinion play a significant role in controlling the domination by a government and the abuse of power. The use of literary texts by young filmmakers of this period reflects, consciously or not, Habermas' understanding of the importance of critical engagement with but also via literature and artistic representation, as one of the most fertile grounds out of which the public sphere may develop. Emphasizing his commitment as a writer to the public, Böll insisted in his 'Aesthetics of Humanity' lecture in 1964: 'without literature a society is dead'.[12] It is no surprise, therefore, that no other author was adapted more often by New German Cinema.

As indicated in the previous chapter, television culture was on the rise and cinema in crisis, a trend that continued during this period, while generational and political conflicts gained momentum. The period spanning from 1962 to 1989 was a time of significant sociopolitical upheaval on both sides of the Berlin Wall. By the time this manifestation of political and cultural separation crumbled in November 1989, the public sphere had affected fundamental change.[13] Whether German-language literature on film played a role in this process is the underlying question of this chapter. While a number of international adaptations by outstanding *auteur* filmmakers from Éric Rohmer to Luchino Visconti have received plenty of scholarly attention, German-language literature's impact on German film and its contribution to the formation of a new aesthetic have been thoroughly underestimated.[14]

German-language Literature on International Screens

The Holocaust continued to haunt the culture industry and only few adaptations of German-language literature were produced outside Germany and Austria during this period. International co-productions, such as Orson Welles' Kafka adaptation *The Trial* (US/FR/FRG/IT, 1962), reflect on fascism and, if implicitly, the Holocaust with the literary text at its core.[15] Welles insisted that an adaptation should be an "original work":

> A film should never be an illustration of a book or a play, it should be itself. And it cannot be itself unless its 'creator', [...] the 'picture-maker', [...] is after all engaged in an artform that is entirely different from literature and the theater. And he has not only the perfect right, but the obligation to turn the work into something a little different than what the author intended, not to perfectly realize it. If he perfectly realizes it, we might just as well have lantern slides and somebody with a lovely voice reading the book.[16]

Welles here follows Truffaut's insistence on the auteur's independence from 'traditional storytelling', and the rejection of 'quality cinema's' adaptations that diligently add moving pictures to a pre-existing narrative to transpose a literary into a cinematic mode of narration.[17]

French New Wave directors were less concerned with narrative than with cinema as art that could communicate a story by means truly its own. When challenged in the same interview regarding the "alarmingly different" way K. is killed and how he acts when he dies compared to Kafka's *Der Prozess* (The Trial, 1925), Welles replied sternly:

> Because the book was written before the Holocaust!—and I couldn't bear the defeat of K in the book after the Holocaust. I am not Jewish, but we are all Jewish since the Holocaust. And I could not bear for him to submit to death as he does in Kafka. Masochistically submit to death. It stank of the old Prague ghetto. I had to let him shout out defiance until he was blown up.

The knowledge of the past and an awareness regarding the challenges of the present inform most of the truly outstanding adaptations that in Welles' *Trial* reflect evil as a "contagion" while also signaling man's "slavish relationship" with modern technology.[18]

As Welles' *The Trial*, most of the highly acclaimed and noteworthy adaptations of German-language literature of this period were international productions often with recurring themes. Time and again, stories of human weakness and seductions of power, of return and justice were brought to cinema screens, implying the lessons to be learnt from recent history—for example, in *The Visit* (US/FR/IT/FRG, Bernhard Wicki, 1964) based on Swiss writer Friedrich Dürrenmatt's *Der Besuch der alten Dame*, and

FIGURE 8.2 *Anthony Perkins shouting at his killers in Orson Welles'* The Trial *(US/FR/FRG/IT, 1962)*.

Hungarian director István Szabó's *Mephisto* (HU, 1981), an adaptation of Klaus Mann's eponymous exile novel. Mann's text was inspired by his former brother-in-law Gustav Gründgens, the actor's star performance in Goethe's *Faust*, and his profitable collaboration with the Hitler regime.[19] Szabó's adaptation won the Academy Award for Best Foreign Film.[20]

In the United States, the Beat generation's discovery of recent Nobel laureate Hermann Hesse and the enormous subsequent popularity[21] of his novels in the original and in translation led to adaptations during the 1970s of the two most widely read of his texts, which resonated perfectly with the growing antimaterialistic counterculture at the time: *Siddharta* (US, Conrad Rooks, 1972), starring Shashi Kapoor in the title role with Sven Nykvist at the camera, and *Steppenwolf* (US/FR/CH/GB, Fred Haines, 1974), with Max von Sydow as the tortured, uncanny half-man, half-wolf Harry Haller, and "an impressive battery" of cutting-edge special effects.[22] Hesse's 1920s novels explore the psychological condition of man and invite us to follow his protagonists' journeys of self-discovery. Both adaptations of Hesse's ethical fiction[23] emerged from an existentialism-infused popular and avant-garde culture in the United States and profited from the esteem in which both the author and his works were held. But admiration is often counter-productive, too, and especially *Steppenwolf* was panned by film critics for emerging all too "dimly from the printed page," as Lawrence van Gelder asserted in *The New York Times*:

> Fred Haines, who wrote the screenplay and directed the movie, has approached the Nobel Prize-winning German author's exploration of the spiritual and sensual elements of human personality with the all-too-familiar translational reverence that preserves literature while creating stillborn cinema.[24]

In sharp contrast, Luchino Visconti's stunningly atmospheric *Morte a Venezia* [Death in Venice] (IT, 1971) based on Thomas Mann's novella reigns among the most accomplished adaptations of all time. Framed by the hauntingly exquisite adagietto of Gustav Mahler's 5th symphony, Visconti's film foregrounds Mann's theme of impossible desire—for perfection in art, for authenticity and intransience, but also for the beauty of adolescent male bodies.[25] The film was very well received by critics and won numerous awards, among them four Baftas, and was nominated for the Palme d'Or at the Cannes Film Festival. Éric Rohmer's Heinrich von Kleist adaptation *La Marquise d'O ...* (FRG/FR, 1976) won the Grand Prix at Cannes and the film remains one of his greatest critical successes.

In his collection of short stories *Six contes moraux* (Six Moral Tales, 1974), inspired by Murnau's *Sunrise* and Sudermann's *Die Reise nach Tilsit*,[26] Rohmer reflects on the French New Wave's critical stance toward adaptation and the 'double question': 'why film a story when one can write it? Why write it when one will film it?' In the preface to his collection, Rohmer announces his intention to dedicate his craft to 'a foreign cause' and 'someone else's creation' and explains that he learned German in order to adapt or 'actualize' Kleist in the original language.[27] Considering the complex relationship between France and Germany—a culturally deeply admired neighbor that the Prussians/Germans managed to invade three times between 1870 and 1940—Rohmer evokes the literary tradition of moral tales, which was popular in both countries during the late eighteenth century, the time in which Kleist's novella is set. Rohmer's adaptation is a transcultural experiment that focuses on the moral dilemma of the novella and the crisis of rejection based on conventions of outdated mores of a conservative society, while preserving the ambiguity of Kleist's conventional conclusion of his narrative and thus the irony of morality itself.

Finally, Black musician Coalhouse Walker Jr.'s story in E.L. Doctorow's historical novel and its adaptation *Ragtime* (US, Miloš Forman, 1981) reimagines Kleist's novella *Michael Kohlhaas*, even if the narrative here features a fancy Model T Ford rather than two black stallions as the trigger for damages sought, and for the tragic narrative to spiral out of control. While recreating an exemplary if tragic human being driven to violence in his fixated pursuit of justice, both Doctorow and Forman shift Kleist's focus to expose society's racism and Coalhouse's quest for justice in early twentieth-century New York as entirely warranted if, perhaps, naive.[28] By evoking this devastating climate of racism in the United States through Kleist and thus German culture, Nazism and the bitter consequences of racist ideologies shine through in Doctorow's text and Forman's film.

How German-language literature became a vehicle for innovative and unconventional German and Austrian filmmakers eager to explore new aesthetic possibilities and critically engage with their parents' past as well as

FIGURE 8.3 *Howard Rollins as Coalhouse Jr. in* Ragtime *(US, Miloš Forman, 1981).*

their own present will be outlined in more detail below. The spotlight will be on the impact of writer Heinrich Böll on film history and of German-language literature on highly innovative filmmakers such as Schlöndorff and Fassbinder that helped a new aesthetic in film to emerge. But first, the context to this creative development needs to be outlined, beginning with an overview of the role of adaptation in West German commercial cinema and television, as well as in the context of East Germany's state-controlled film production.

German-language Literature in Commercial Cinema and Public Television

By 1962, the consumption of moving pictures in the comfort of the private sphere had become an affordable luxury for many in the Global North. Televisions changed entertainment cultures and, as a result, countless film palaces were either carved into smaller units or closed entirely. To combat the downward trend of cinema admissions, Hollywood but also the British film industry invested in spectacular productions such as *Ben Hur* (US, William Wyler, 1959) or *Lawrence of Arabia* (GB, David Lean, 1962), and promoted their global stars in a variety of film genres. In France, the *Nouvelle Vague* of experimental filmmaking advanced aesthetic standards, and not only shaped international cinema for decades to come, but also, as Semenza and Hasenfratz emphasize, "film's relationship to literature."[29] Filmmakers such as Jean-Luc Godard, François Truffaut, Agnes Varda, Éric Rohmer, and Claude Chabrol presented their own aesthetically innovative and "genuinely personal"[30] film language or so-called auteur cinema in masterpieces such as *Les Quatre Cents Coups* [The 400 Blows] (FR, François Truffaut, 1959) or Swiss-French director Godard's *À bout de souffle* [Breathless] (FR, 1960). While literary texts were at first glance of little relevance for that generation of avant-garde filmmakers, their aesthetic but even more so their innovative spirit and insistence on film as "a serious cultural art form"[31] significantly shaped some young filmmakers' relationship to cinema in Germany and Austria. They, in contrast, very much embraced adaptations for a number of reasons, as this chapter will clarify.

In 1962, *The Longest Day* (US, Ken Annakin/Andrew Marton/Bernhard Wicki/Darryl F. Zanuck/Gerd Oswald), based on Cornelius Ryan's non-fiction book about D-Day, and the most high-profile epic war film of its time, initiated not only a novel take on the war film genre, but triggered countless debates in civil society on both sides of the Atlantic. A multi-lingual and collaborative endeavor of an international group of creative artists that could be labeled *cinéma engagée*, the project aimed to address the events leading up to this most significant military operation of the Second World War from

US American, British, French, and German perspectives with a clear antiwar message. The film, which conveyed the horror of war for victors and losers alike, premiered at a time of heightened political tensions between the Soviet Union and the United States that culminated in the Cuban Missile Crisis as the film was being released in Europe. The project and its box-office success demonstrated to a new generation of filmmakers the possibility of political activism through commercial cinema.[32] For now, the reality of commercial cinema and television in German-language countries, however, proved merely a continuation of established practices.

German literature maintained its presence in films of virtually all genres but remained, for the most part, within the German-language area. In West Germany, producers of adaptations usually aimed at film as high culture by way of association with the literary canon, but cut corners financially due to economic pressures, regularly releasing remakes while desperately trying to cater to popular tastes.[33] Apart from a few exceptions that drew millions into West German and Austrian cinemas—such as, for example, adaptations of Karl May's adventure novels featuring the 'noblest of American Indians' *Winnetou* (FRG, Harald Reinl, 1962–8), or Artur Brauner/CCC-Film's remake of the Germanic myth *Nibelungen* (FRG, Harald Reinl, 1966) starring supposedly scrumptious Olympic hammer thrower Uwe Beyer as Siegfried[34]—the majority of films' low production values meant that movies made for the big screen were little different from what was readily available on television. This fundamentally jeopardized German cinema's ability to compete. By the early 1960s, West German film production had slowed by 50 percent and ticket sales in cinemas had fallen by nearly 400 million as mentioned above.[35] During the same period, TV licences almost quadrupled.[36] After years of financial struggles, the once giant Ufa declared bankruptcy in 1962.[37]

The impact of television and, in particular, TV serials reached a climax with Francis Durbridge's *Das Halstuch* [The Scarf], a six-part mini-series produced by West German television, which proved a mega-hit and the epitome of a so-called "Straßenfeger" [Street Sweeper]-show. On those six evenings between January 3 and 17, 1962, streets in West German cities were as if swept clear—theaters and cinemas were empty, factories had to cancel night shifts, and political events were called off—because 90 percent of televisions in West Germany were tuned in. The public sat at home, glued to their television screens from one cliffhanger to the next.[38]

But despite the success of crime serials and whodunnits, television producers were adamant to establish the medium as a provider of sophisticated entertainment. Many referred to television as "Mattscheibe" [lit. matt screen; goggle-box], a disparaging term used at the time that insinuated mental numbness ensuing from the medium's consumption. Screening adaptations became as integral to television broadcasts as soccer games—in order to maximize the popularity of the commodity and confirm its educational potential—and the source texts chosen for adaptation were often as hotly debated as the decisions of a referee.[39]

When Bertolt Brecht's former assistant Egon Monk's adaptation of his late mentor's *Das Leben des Galilei* [The Life of (Galileo) Galilei] was broadcast on January 11, 1962, for example, the West German tabloid *Bild* even initiated a survey, provocatively inquiring: 'Following the building of the Berlin Wall, should Brecht's plays be televised?' Respondents in the capitalist FRG voted nearly 2:1 in favor of the socialist and antifascist exile, who had returned to East Berlin in 1949. But conscious of their predominantly conservative viewers, decentralized West German television producers also 'greatly accentuated'[40] literary events such as Gerhart Hauptmann's centenary, while subtly communicating the medium's educational potential. In celebration of the 'forgotten'[41] Nobel prize-winning author Hauptmann, a number of new adaptations of his works were produced and broadcast during the jubilee year, beginning in January 1962 with *Der Biberpelz* [The Beaver Coat] (John Olden), and ending on his 100th birthday with a new adaptation of *Rose Bernd* (adapted by Kuno Epple and directed by Gustav Burmester), which premiered on November 15.

When a second channel was introduced in 1963, color television became available in 1964, and several regional public channels were established from the mid-1960s onwards in West Germany, even more cinemas shut down. Increasingly, adaptations of German-language literature became the domain of public television, and they were produced in ever greater numbers. In West Germany, noteworthy adaptations of the canon included Büchner's *Woyzeck* (Bohumil Herlischka, 1962), Lenz's *Die Soldaten* [The Soldiers] (Harry Buckwitz, 1962), Robert Walser's *Jakob von Gunten* (adapted by Ror Wolf and co-written/directed by Peter Lilienthal, 1971), and Kleist's *Erdbeben in Chile* (Helma Sanders-Brahms, 1975). Some authors—such as Nestroy, J.M. Lenz, Robert Walser, Georg Kaiser, Franz Werfel, even Hermann Sudermann—were now entirely relegated to the small screen. For contemporary authors like Alfred Andersch, Martin Walser, Günter Eich, Wolfgang Hildesheimer, Tankred Dorst, Heinar Kipphardt, and Egon Erwin Kisch, the medium represented an attractive outlet that increased the readership and popularity of these almost exclusively male writers.[42]

It was only the most successful at the time whose literary works served as source texts for regular presences on both (for the most part commercially driven) cinema and television screens—among them, especially, Erich Kästner[43] and Heinrich Böll, Swiss contemporaries Friedrich Dürrenmatt and Max Frisch, and, of course, popular authors such as Siegfried Lenz.[44] Having achieved national and international acclaim by inventively and critically examining Germany's Nazi past, contemporary literature by Group 47 authors came to the fore and began to appeal even to seasoned filmmakers like Helmut Käutner, who turned to Andersch's eponymous novel in his *Die Rote* [The Red One] (FRG/IT, 1962) and collaborated with the author on the script.⁴⁵ On the light entertainment spectrum, bestsellers by Johannes Mario Simmel and Heinz G. Konsalik were selected for numerous adaptations for both cinema and television throughout the following decades. Swiss exile Curt Goetz, who had spent most of the Hitler era in California, was particularly popular during the 1960s with several of his works adapted for cinema by prolific directors such as Käutner (1963), Kurt Hoffmann (1964, 1965), Michael Pfleghar (1964), and Rolf Thiele (1967).⁴⁶

Following a postwar period of mostly willful amnesia regarding the crimes committed in the name of Nazism as outlined in the previous chapter, the vast majority of film productions for commercial cinema in West Germany and Austria in the early 1960s still shied away from critical engagement with their countries' past. While some international filmmakers turned to the canon of German literature to analyze recent events by, for example, combining documentary footage of the Nazi era with a retelling of Goethe's "Reineke Fuchs" (1794) in the brilliant *Black Fox: The Rise and Fall of Adolf Hitler* (US, Louis Clyde Stoumen, 1962),⁴⁷ it took the Auschwitz trials and a new generation of filmmakers for German-language film to follow suit. As to *Reineke Fuchs*, the first German adaptation of Goethe's epic poem about the cunning fox only followed in 1989 with Manfred Durinok's co-produced children's animation (FRG/CN, Zhuang Minjin/He Yumen) that displayed moderate pedagogical intent while trying to remain resolutely apolitical.

In this context, children's film is a genre that should receive much more attention than this book is able to provide. As mentioned above, adaptations of Kästner's works from *Emil and the Detectives* (US, Peter Tewksbury, 1964) to *Das fliegende Klassenzimmer* (FRG, Werner Jacobs, 1973) continued to delight audiences in cinemas and, increasingly, via television. Michael Ende's career as a bestselling author of children's books became manifest in the early 1960s, when his *Jim Knopf* adventures were turned into a televised puppet show by the Augsburger Puppenkiste (1961/2).⁴⁸ Black orphan Jim Knopf [Button], who is being raised on the small island of 'Morrowland', and his best friend Luke the Engine Driver are at the heart of the narrative and not only reflect on friendship and community, but on racism, fascist authoritarianism, and even on representation and perspective.⁴⁹ The horrid, Nazi-inspired dragon educator Frau Mahlzahn or 'Mrs. Grindtooth', who speaks of eugenics and indoctrinates her kidnapped and chained pupils, is finally captured and, to the great relief of everyone around her, awakes as 'Golden Dragon of Wisdom'. There is indeed much wisdom in Ende's fantasy novels, beginning with this German fairy-tale. Whether it is open-minded and compassionate Jim Button, or lonely Mr. Tur Tur—the illusionary giant, who seems frighteningly enormous but turns out to be a kind and gentle vegetarian close-up—or, indeed, the courageous little girl in Ende's novel *Momo* (1973), who fights 'Men in Grey', the time thieves of modern society. They, Otfried Preußler's robber *Hotzenplotz*, James Krüss'

Timm Thaler, and many others in Kästner's works, are characters few children ever forget once they had the privilege to encounter them on the page or cinema and, to this day, in countless reruns on television screens.[50]

Adaptation in the GDR: Ideology and Literary Heritage

In East Germany, the state-owned DEFA film studios and DFF television continued to produce high-quality films for grown-ups and children alike, while fulfilling an ideological function that included addressing the crimes of Germany's Nazi past and promoting an antifascist social utopia.[51] Film production was under constant political scrutiny, even though the degrees of the leadership's control varied according to internal and international political climates.[52] These fluctuating political constraints made working in the GDR's culture industry a potentially volatile endeavor. The 11th plenum of the Central Committee of the Socialist Unity Party (SED) in 1965, when party hardliners like Erich Honecker lashed out at 'politically unreliable' writers and filmmakers, resulted in the SED's order to withdraw nearly an entire year's feature film production.[53] Several films that had already been released were also banned, such as Konrad Wolf's 1964 adaptation of Christa Wolf's *Der geteilte Himmel* [Divided Heaven], a fate experienced repeatedly by this particular adaptation over the years to come as political climates varied.

Because of film's ideological function, adaptations were usually pursued by DEFA only if the literary work could "be made compatible with GDR cultural policies,"[54] and its definitions and representations of youth, individuals, and community corresponded to and complemented current priorities of the socialist leadership.[55] In his book *The Buchenwald Child*, Bill Niven offers unique insights into literature and film production in the GDR, when he examines Bruno Apitz's *Nackt unter Wölfen* (Naked among Wolves, 1958), a literary account of little Stefan Jerzy Zweig's survival at Buchenwald concentration camp, and its adaptation for television in 1960 and, subsequently, cinema. The bestselling novel became the first German film that focused on life in and everyday horror of a Nazi concentration camp while telling the story of a child's survival enabled by other inmates' courageous and selfless actions. But even Frank Beyer's outstanding adaptation *Nackt unter Wölfen* [Naked among Wolves] (1963) may serve as an example of political control exerted on an adaptation process as Niven outlines. While crucially highlighting the crimes against humanity in a concentration camp just outside Weimar—the city of Goethe and Schiller, and once proud symbol for the country's 'enlightened' culture—both the novel's and the adaptations' politically driven aim was to contribute to the making of a specific East German antifascist memory culture that foregrounded communist concentration camp inmates (rather than Jews) as heroes.[56]

A couple of years later, Beyer directed the equally intriguing *Spur der Steine* [Trace of Stones] (GDR, 1966), an adaptation of Erik Neutsch's 1964 novel, which became one of the most widely read literary texts of the GDR at the time. Despite the fact that Neutsch was awarded the national prize for art and literature for the novel in 1964, its adaptations for cinema by Beyer and for theater by Heiner Müller[57] were both banned following the 11th plenum of the Central Committee of the Socialist Unity Party, due to 'anti-socialist tendencies.' Beyer's masterful adaptation stars Manfred Krug as charismatic and initially unruly carpenter Hannes Balla, and hints at problematic labor conditions and party politics, but nonetheless supports socialism as a utopian concept deserving of reality. The film caused a scandal upon its premiere and was pulled by the political leadership shortly after. As Frank Beyer notes in his autobiography *Wenn der Wind sich dreht* (As the Wind Turns, 2001), since numerous copies of the film had already been produced and initial screenings announced, the film was allowed to premiere. But "between 80 and 100 people who already knew the film were sent [by the party leadership] to play 'the voice of the people'."[58] This practice reminded Beyer of a previous intervention aimed at public sabotage:

> I knew that at the beginning of the 1930s the Nazis had gone into movie theaters to shout down the pacifist American film *All Quiet on the Western Front*. [...] But I simply could not wrap my mind around the fact that the SED, of which I was a member, had organized a similar top-down 'provocation'.[59]

Following this orchestrated public scandal Beyer was banned from feature-filmmaking for years. *Spur der Steine* was not released again until 1989, when streets in cities like Leipzig were filled with GDR citizens peacefully marching for democracy and openness. But Hannes Balla's trajectory from unruly citizen to good socialist failed to put a dent into the public's demand for change, which resulted in the 'fall' of the Berlin Wall on November 9, 1989, the opening of the inner-German borders, and the end of the GDR the following year.

Throughout the forty years of the GDR's existence, leading figures in its government considered film an important propaganda medium, which was to be accessible as widely as possible, suitable for both cinema and television and, in selected cases, for export. While notably fewer literary texts were adapted by the GDR's industry compared to West Germany, productions designated for export often adapted the literary canon to increase their transnational market value.

Fontane's *Effi Briest* may serve as an example. Written and directed by Wolfgang Luderer for the DFF, and starring Angelica Domröse as Effi, this elaborate Fontane-adaptation premiered on GDR television in March 1970. The film was subsequently bought by West Germany's public television for 'hard currency', and broadcast in the FRG the following year. This *Effi Briest* was motivated by, and in turn profited from, a Fontane-Renaissance, which arose after the building of the wall in 1961 in both parts of Germany. Adaptations of the works of a 'cultural treasure' like Fontane helped to underscore basic ideologies and convictions of the political systems in either of the two German states, while laying claim to the nation's cultural heritage as outlined in the previous chapter. Appropriations of the literary canon from Lessing to Schiller[60] continued across the Berlin Wall, but productions shifted from cinema to television as their primary outlet.

Luderer's *Effi Briest* unveils the mechanisms by which the genre became an attractive commodity in the eyes of the GDR's political leadership.[61] The novel's class-based system of values and norms forms the conceptual structure of this adaptation.[62] The film critically reflects Wilhelmine society's hypocritical and inhuman code of honor and patriarchal power relations in copious dialogues, which is accentuated by both camera angles and a meticulous mise-en-scène. The catastrophic result of acting under the pressure of outdated social conventions within a class-based hierarchy is clearly communicated by this otherwise relatively unadventurous TV-adaptation. The film condemns superficial posturing, exploitative practices, and careerist behavior. Following the student revolts of 1968, many west of the border agreed with the need of a critical overhaul of society. Both in the FRG and the GDR, the film was frequently broadcast and became a lasting success.

As indicated before, productions for television and cinema based on the literary canon and fairy tales produced in the GDR not only functioned as vehicles for the communication of socialist ethics, but as a medial absorption of cultural heritage and, due to their potential suitability for export, as profitable commodities. Fairy-tale adaptations such as *Drei Haselnüsse für Aschenbrödel* [Three Wishes for Cinderella] (GDR/ČSSR, Václav Vorlíček, 1973), for example, broadcasted a contemporary female role model in the context of uncontroversial social(ist) ethics. This 'updated' version of the Grimm brothers' tale received much praise at the time and remains a staple of German and Czech television Christmas entertainment to this day.[63] From the early 1970s, increased confidence and a willingness to turn over a new leaf under the leadership of Ulbricht's successor Erich Honecker seemingly encouraged constructive criticism and dialogue with writers and filmmakers in the GDR, while West German chancellor Willy Brandt's new Eastern policies or "Ostpolitik" also reduced tensions and began to normalize relationships between the FRG and GDR.[64] In 1971, First Secretary Honecker confirmed the confidence of the socialist state in his famous 'no taboos' speech, which was widely read as the GDR's political leadership relaxing its grip on cultural production. But as Sabine Hake points out, film narratives that reflected contemporary reality could be realized only within categories that clearly differentiated between private and public, making any literary or cinematic portrayal of GDR society personal rather than political.[65]

Honecker at the time also demanded more entertaining and thrilling television programmes, which initially also led to a several high-production value adaptations of the literary canon following the success of *Effi Briest*. As hopes for a liberalization of GDR film policy were growing, Konrad Wolf turned to Lion Feuchtwanger's novel about the painter Goya, and adapted the text's antifascist and radically humanist message to film.[66] Seán Allan clarifies Wolf's ambition, when he writes: "with his screen adaptation of Feuchtwanger's [...] *Goya—oder der arge Weg der Erkenntnis*, Wolf attempted to produce a *Künstlerfilm* of international standing that could take its place alongside the work of directors such as Igor Talankin and Andrei Tarkovsky." The film was conceived as a "prestige production that would appeal to an international audience and enhance DEFA's standing. In addition, it was hoped that a successful production would lead to other important works of twentieth-century German literature (in particular those of Thomas Mann) being filmed in the GDR rather than in the Federal Republic."[67]

Despite political constraints and often difficult production histories, DEFA's fairy-tale adaptations and children's animations, but especially films such as Wolf's exceptional *Goya* (1971),[68] Beyer's remarkable Holocaust film *Jakob der Lügner* [Jacob the Liar] (1975) based on Jurek Becker's novel[69]—the only East German movie ever to be nominated for an Oscar— or deeply poetic and innovative takes on supposedly 'unadaptable' literary texts such as Johannes Bobrowski's *Levins Mühle* [Levin's Mill] (GDR, Horst Seemann, 1980) have left their mark on film history. Others were more conventional, but nonetheless internationally popular, for example, DEFA's only Thomas Mann adaptation *Lotte in Weimar* (Egon Günther, 1975), its success greatly aided by international celebrity Lilli Palmer as Goethe's once so adored Lotte.[70]

For writers that had chosen the socialist part of Germany as their home after returning from exile (Anna Seghers, Stefan Heym, Bert Brecht, etc.), or from war and imprisonment (Hermann Kant, Franz Fühmann, etc.), constructive engagement with the new state via their literary texts was an integral component to their potential success. Political activism and support of the GDR were rewarded not least by adaptations. Anna Seghers, for instance, was awarded numerous prizes in the GDR and a dozen of her works were adapted for cinema and television between 1968 (*Die Toten bleiben jung* [The Dead Stay Young], DEFA, Joachim Kunert) and 1988 (*Der Aufstand der Fischer von St. Barbara* [The Fishers' Revolt], DFF, Thomas Langhoff). Even in the 1980s at a time of liberalization and reform in the Soviet Union under Gorbachev, cultural policy and individual success in Honecker's GDR depended on a perception of political reliability. When acclaimed director Beyer returned to the GDR, for example, to direct an adaptation of Hermann Kant's autobiographical *Der Aufenthalt* [released as *The Turning Point*] (DEFA, 1983) based on a script by Wolfgang Kohlhaase, both the director's difficult relationship with the party's leadership and the narrative itself jeopardized the project. Novel and film focus on the protagonist's experiences as a prisoner of war in Poland, who is accused of war crimes, and examines themes such as authority and justice, denunciation, and abuse. Not surprisingly, the film caused some irritation in Poland, and was subsequently barred from being screened at the International Berlinale Film Festival, and only ran briefly in a few selected arthouse cinemas in the GDR.[71]

While theoretically welcoming constructive criticism and accepting authors as important building blocks of an antifascist, socialist society, East Germany's political leadership regularly disapproved and censored writers and filmmakers, often keeping them under Stasi-surveillance. Adaptations of the literary canon and of contemporary literature were frequently marked by controversy, and some collaborative projects and innovative adaptations were criticized as obscene and subsequently banned, such as the co-production *Ursula* (GDR/CH, Egon Günther, 1978) based on Gottfried Keller's novella. Consequently, Egon Günther,[72] like numerous writers and filmmakers before and after him, left the GDR.

The expulsion of 'inconvenient poet'[73] Wolf Biermann in 1976 caused an uproar within the GDR's creative community, and a letter of protest was delivered to General Secretary of the Socialist Unity Party Honecker and to the daily newspaper *Neues Deutschland*, signed by writers Jurek Becker, Christa Wolf, Franz Fühmann, Volker Braun, Stefan Heym, Heiner Müller, Ulrich Plenzdorf and others, but also actors such as Angelika Domröse, Armin Müller-Stahl, Katharina Thalbach, Eva-Maria Hagen, and Manfred Krug. Some of the signatories, like Jürgen Fuchs, ended up in prison; others could no longer publish or perform in the GDR and were forced to apply for exit visas.

East-West Rivalries and Collaborative Endeavors

Internationally esteemed directors such as Wolfgang Staudte or Paul Verhoeven had left the GDR early on, and worked not only in the film industry but, from the 1960s onwards, also for television, regularly adapting German-language literature, beginning with Joseph Roth's *Die Rebellion* [Rebellion] (FRG, Wolfgang Staudte, 1962), and *Ihr schönster Tag* [Her

Best Day], based on the play *Das Fenster zum Flur* by Curth Flatow (FRG, Paul Verhoeven, 1962). But it was Fallada's *Wer einmal aus dem Blechnapf frisst* [Once a Jailbird] (FRG, Fritz Umgelter, 1962), which caused significant debate that year. The transposition of Fallada's novel to the present day and Umgelter's unflinching focus on the novel's middle-aged anti-hero's inability to deal with guilt, change, and the challenges of the everyday was all too obvious in its desire to accentuate shamefaced West Germany's unwillingness to address the recent past and further involves film in promoting and supporting a climate of change.[74] Hence, adaptations of the literary canon helped television on either side of the Berlin Wall to become a respectable pastime for the broadest possible audience. The younger generation, however, generally preferred dubbed US American television series, such as NBC's 431 episodes of *Bonanza*, which were broadcast on German television (ARD) from October 1962 and for decades to come.

In cinemas, too, Wild West adventures—based on Karl May novels that had been enthusiastically devoured by generations of German-speaking teenagers since the late nineteenth century—became the winning ticket for Rialto-film's producer Horst Wendlandt and director Harald Reinl.[75] Son of an impoverished Saxon weaver May had several stints in prison before beginning to write and remained a controversial upstart in the eyes of the literary establishment. Equipped with a stunningly fecund imagination evoking adventures in foreign lands, his novels became enduring bestsellers. By 1962, half a century after his death, May was the most translated German-language writer after the Grimm brothers and Karl Marx, and considered "the most popular author in modern German history."[76] Wendtlandt and Reinl were well aware of the potential of a Karl May adaptation, but their spectacular *Der Schatz im Silbersee* [Treasure of the Silver Lake] (1962) exceeded even their most confident expectations.

The Italian and French co-produced adaptation reimagined Hollywood's Western but invigorated the familiar genre by celebrating exotic landscapes and people, and ethical values that transcended nationality and race. Shot in Croatia (then Yugoslavia) with up to 2,500 horses and 3,000 extras, the movie made box-office history and drew millions of cinemagoers back into deserted film palaces. As Bergfelder notes, the adaptation was "like all subsequent May films shot in Eastmancolor and CinemaScope, [and] was, with a budget of 3.5 million DM, the most expensive West German production up to this point."[77] The team shot four further equally spectacular May adaptations—the *Winnetou*-series (I-III, 1963–5) and *Winnetou and Old Shatterhand im Tal der Toten* [The Valley of the Dead] (1968)—that focus on the friendship between the strikingly beautiful and deeply noble American Indian Winnetou (played by French actor Pierre Brice) and the equally reliable and decent Old Shatterhand (former 'Tarzan' Lex Barker[78]), while the pair battle a string of evildoers. Representations of male

FIGURE 8.4 *Riding off into the sunset in* Winnetou *(FRG, Harald Reinl, 1962).*

heroism and true humanity on the one hand, and bad guys who get their comeuppance usually involving some form of pyrotechnics on the other, provided the popular formula for commercial success that led to a string of further Karl May-adaptations. Directed by Harald Philipp and, especially, Alfred Vohrer, they all drew from Reinl's idiosyncratic form of the Western, as did Sergio Leone's Italian versions and the Western all'Italiana from 1964 onwards.[79]

East Germany began producing its own version of "Indianerfilme" [American Indian films]—the term 'Western' was considered politically inappropriate—beginning with an adaptation of Liselotte Welskopf-Henrich's 1951 novel *Die Söhne der Großen Bärin* [The Sons of the Great (Female) Bear] with Gojko Mitić playing Chief Tokei-ihto, a role that was to define Mitić's career. *Die Söhne der Großen Bärin* (GDR, Josef Mach, 1966) became the most successful film in the GDR of the year and soon matched the tremendous popularity of Reinl's *Winnetou*-films west of the border. While preserving the core conventions of the Western genre, DEFA's "Indianerfilme" shifted "the perspective away from the colonizer to the canonized," as Heiduschke[80] argues. Stunning widescreen panorama shot of unspoiled nature and close-ups of strapping Serbian actor Mitić served to highlight the dire fate of the American Indians as a metaphor of destructive capitalism, and thus remained squarely within the remits of ideological messaging.[81]

Writers both in East and West Germany often functioned as their nation's political and moral 'conscience' and contributed actively and dynamically to their cultural environments, even if in the case of numerous GDR writers, their work could only be published in West Germany and was thus, at least officially, unavailable in the GDR. When it came to adaptations, filmmakers' creative autonomy was restricted by an ideological framework in the East and, particularly in the capitalist West, commercial considerations.

In Switzerland, Michel Soutter, Alain Tanner, and Claude Goretta made often highly poetic French-language Swiss films from the 1960s, inspired by Godard and the French New Wave. But it was not until Markus Imhoof's adaptation of Swiss author and journalist Alfred A. Häsler's literary account of Swiss migration policies during the Hitler era *'Das Boot ist voll.' Die Schweiz und die Flüchtlinge 1933–1945* (The Boat is Full: Switzerland and the Refugees, 1967) that a Swiss adaptation of a German-language text came to international attention and acclaim. *Das Boot ist voll* (CH, Markus Imhoof, 1980) won numerous European awards and was nominated for an Academy Award for Best Foreign Language Film in 1982.[82]

In West Germany and Austria, a new generation pushed ahead with various cultural interventions that had been brewing since the late 1950s. Their creative actions began, most famously, with the so-called 'Oberhausen Manifesto,' which was signed by twenty-six filmmakers—among them Alexander Kluge, Hansjürgen Pohland, Edgar Reitz, Peter Schamoni, Haro Senf, and Herbert Vesely. The declaration, which was read out at the Short Film Festival in the West German town of Oberhausen on February 28, 1962, denounced German-language film production of the past decade as useless, superficial engagements with life that had ruined cinema with its mediocre and conventional productions. In the years to come, it was them and even younger compatriots such as Rainer Werner Fassbinder, Werner Herzog, Helma Sanders-Brahms, Volker Schlöndorff, Margarete von Trotta, and Wim Wenders, who not only dared to remember and analyze the Hitler era and its legacy, but to address controversial themes such as, for example, homosexuality and homophobia, xenophobia and racism, domestic abuse and abortion. Often perceiving themselves as outsiders and misfits, and considering directors such as the greats of Weimar film and Hollywood's exiles Fritz Lang and Billy Wilder, Max Ophüls, G.W. Pabst, and Douglas Sirk as their role models, once again picaresque figures and outcasts moved from the margins into the center of big (and small) screens, as an avant-garde of filmmakers looked to their predecessors for inspiration while reviving a culture of decidedly individual expression.

The Death of 'Papa's Cinema' and the Birth of New German Film

German cinema was so traumatized by its own past, it took a new generation of filmmakers to offer their own, critical perspective of their country's history, its visual and literary culture, as well as the film industry. The "sharp pattern that has dominated most film production and film criticism as the direct result of the economic, stylistic, and industrial prevalence of literary narratives (short stories, drama, and novels) as the heart of cinema and cinema studies,"[83] to quote Tim Corrigan, began to change from the 1950s onwards, as the French New Wave film 'authors' confidently offered their individual film styles, rejected adaptation, and critically engaged with both past and present in feature films, but also in documentaries such as the stunning *Nuit et brouillard* [Night and Fog] (FR, Alain Resnais, 1955) about Nazi concentration camps and the Holocaust. Resnais, however, also looked to literature and collaborated with authors Marguerite Duras and Alain Robbe-Grillet in *Hiroshima, mon amour* (FR/JP, 1959) and *L'Année dernière à Marienbad* [Last Year at Marienbad] (FR/IT, 1961) respectively, films that transpose the structure and deeply personal perspective of the *Nouveau Roman* to film.

Utterly frustrated with their countries' simultaneously declining film culture in Germany and Austria, twenty-six young filmmakers staged an intervention at the Oberhausen Film Festival on February 28, 1962. They presented a manifesto—in "an expression of Oedipal outrage,"[84] as Rentschler puts it—against the "spiritually arid and intellectually bankrupt cinema"[85] of the previous generation. "Papas Kino," as these young filmmakers called it, was 'dead,' signified by the closure of Ufa and the conspicuous collapse of conventional cinema production. By 1960 even undoubtedly gifted directors like Staudte, Hoffmann, or Käutner were receiving little to no attention by the international film market and, in 1961, not a single film of that year's output had been deemed worthy of the *Deutscher Filmpreis*, West Germany's national film award.[86] The manifesto's signatories not only pronounced the dire need for, but also their belief in the possibility of, a renewal of German cinema. Committed to a new beginning, their manifesto became the "founding myth"[87] for New German Cinema. Virtually all film histories use the manifesto to mark the birth of Young German Film as it was called in this early stage, and this *History* is no different, even though the development of a new film language was already underway as two Heinrich Böll adaptations indicate: *Das Brot der frühen Jahre* [The Bread of Those Early Years] (FRG, Herbert Vesely, 1962) and the short *Machorka-Muff* (FRG, Danièle Huillet/Jean-Marie Straub, 1962).

Following the release of *Das Brot der frühen Jahre* (written by Vesely and Leo Ti, produced by Hansjürgen Pohland), the young Austrian filmmaker

Vesely was recognized as best up-and-coming director of the year in West Germany, mostly due to his unique style and innovative use of montage that was markedly different from the *Nouvelle Vague*'s preference for long takes with deep focus, but nonetheless providing opportunities to witness actions as they unfold, while productively problematizing perception and the core components of human relationships. When his Böll adaptation was screened at the renowned Cannes Film Festival and in German cinemas, however, the film flopped. Vesely's adaptation was seen as the manifest's aesthetic representative—a tall order for any film—and in that context it was, according to Vesely, rejected if not 'condemned' by the press.[88]

Not surprisingly, the cultural landscape did not change overnight and film producers for the most part clung to familiar formulas. Throughout the 1960s and well into the 1970s, most adaptations for cinema repeated previous styles and formats and were often based on the same supremely *Heimat*-heavy works by popular authors such as Ludwig Thoma (1964, 1965, 1966, 1969) or Ludwig Ganghofer (1962, 1973, 1974, 1976, 1977, 1986). Even Austrian blood-and-soil author Richard Billinger could still guarantee a profit and was thus considered more than suitable for cinema screens by old hands like Helmut Weiss.[89] More innovative directors such as Rolf Thiele who adapted Wedekind's provocative *Lulu*-plays for cinema (1962)[90] and Thomas Mann's *Tonio Kröger* and *Wälsungenblut* (1964) were neither commercial nor experimental enough and thus caught in an 'aesthetic vacuum.'[91] West Germany's public television channel ZDF created *Das kleine Fernsehspiel* in 1963 to fill that void and to promote young new talent at the same time. The section provided an important framework for avant-garde productions, supporting filmmakers such as Kluge, Fassbinder, or feminist writer/director Helke Sander to name but a few.[92]

In 1964, Hans Rolf Strobel in the German weekly *Die Zeit* appealed to young filmmakers to produce that new critical cinema they had promised in the Oberhausen manifesto. There was still way too much 'old German film,' which continued to provide 'life aid by life lies,' referring to conventional entertainment that provided comfortingly mendacious escapism, and thus welcome consolations to the perpetrator nations after the Second World War and Holocaust. Now, Strobel insisted, it was high time for truth.

> 'Our truths will be uncomfortable, but they will prove to be more helpful. By its mere existence, new German film will be critical, or it won't come into existence at all. No doubt the latter would be preferred by many.'[93]

A young writer, who had spent most of the Hitler era in Swedish exile, attended the Auschwitz trial during March and April that year, and subsequently wrote *Die Ermittlung* [The Investigation] as a document of horror for the theater stage. Peter Weiss' play features nine 'numbered' witnesses (a reference to the number tattooed into their forearms replacing their names and personal identity), eighteen 'named' accused, and facts uttered in the courtroom during the Auschwitz trial. Eleven Dantean 'cantos' encapsulate countless witness statements and offer an oratory of the trial, which provides an inventory of suffering and, by simply revealing the facts, an analysis of the everyday practice of mass murder in a devastating journey 'from the ramp' to the gas chamber ('Cyclone B.').

Adorno had just proclaimed it 'barbaric to write poetry after Auschwitz',[94] which further encouraged Weiss to reflect on these horrific crimes in sparse language that documented rather than aestheticized. On October 20, 1965, the play was performed by the Royal Shakespeare Company in London and premiered simultaneously in fifteen cities in both East and West Germany. Finally, the divided country was beginning to stand united in its acknowledgment and remembrance of the Holocaust. Theater functioned once more as a moral institution by staging an 'engaged' writer's documentary play that unequivocally condemned the crimes against humanity committed in the name of Nazism.

On October 20, East German television broadcast excerpts of the play filmed the previous evening at the "Volkskammer," the GDR's unicameral parliament. The production included well-known actors such as Ernst Busch, Erwin Geschonneck, Hilmar Thate, and Helene Weigel, artist Fritz Cremer, and writers Bruno Apitz, Stephan Hermlin, and Wieland Herzfelde. The entire material filmed was subsequently edited by a 'collective' (directors Lothar Bellag, Karl von Appen, Manfred Wekwerth, Erich Engel, Konrad Wolf, Ingrid Fausak) and was broadcast in November 1966.

A filmed version of the play's production in Hamburg had premiered in March 1966 on West German public television and more than a third of registered televisions were tuned in. The production included Ida Ehre, Hellmut Lange, Ursula Langrock, Konrad Mayerhoff, Siegfried Wischnewski, and others. It was filmed by six cameramen, and produced by Egon Monk for NDR, the public North German Broadcasting Company. Peter Weiss' documentary play directly confronts the horror of the crimes committed, which the film further emphasizes by including documentary footage, negotiating guilt, both individual and collective. Under Peter Schulze-Rohr's direction, the actors were as integral to this process of documentation as the film clips used. The opening scene, for example, evokes trains arriving and leaving Auschwitz, followed by a judge's questions posed to the accused. Their answers are almost mechanical repetitions of the same—'I was not aware,' 'I only did my job,' 'orders had to be followed'—reminiscent of the excuses given at previous trials of Nazi crimes in Germany and Israel.[95] The documentary style of the film melds with that of Weiss' play, and without pathos or melodrama both on stage and screen, the Holocaust is recounted step by step. A critic in the *Hörzu* magazine wrote at the time about television's task of contemporaneity and addressing the Holocaust in *Die Ermittlung*: 'one thing is clear: it fulfilled a task it had to fulfil. And it fulfilled it well.'[96]

Despite much criticism[97] of both Weiss' uncomfortable play and its filmed version in West Germany, an evolving political landscape and public sphere recognized the importance of contemporary voices within the culture industries. In order to support young talent and encourage a new generation to contribute to a lackluster German film landscape, the "Kuratorium junger deutscher Film" [foundation for young German cinema] was created in 1965. One of the first applicants to the foundation was Schlöndorff, who submitted his script for an adaptation of Musil's debut novel *Die Verwirrungen des Zöglings Törleß* (The Confusions of Young Törless, 1906). Having worked as assistant director under well-respected filmmakers such as Louis Malle and Alain Resnais, and having chosen a canonical text of German-language literature that not only explores sadistic bullying in an Austrian military academy and boarding school, but power mechanisms that lead to willing subservience, the young aspiring director was hopeful that his application would be successful. Schlöndorff's script and later film focused the narrative on these cancerous growths of an authoritarian system that leads to violence and inhumanity by design. Törless (Mathieu Carrière) is the bystander, an interested voyeur of homoerotic sadism, who finally comprehends the despicable malice of his classmates and his own complicity, and in the end is glad to be leaving the school.

To his surprise, Schlöndorff was denied funding. As the director reveals in his autobiography, it was twenty years later that he was told about the intervention by his own father, who had no time for Musil's introspective masterpiece and considered the financial support of his son's 'nonsense' a waste of taxpayers' money.[98] The film was made nonetheless, thanks to the financial support of Franz Seitz[99] and Louis Malle. Schlöndorff's *Der junge Törless* [Young Törless] won the critics' award, the FIPRESCI Prize, at the 1966 Cannes Film Festival, and brought a new German film language, crafted with the inspirational succor of the French avant-garde and a deep admiration for the cinema of Fritz Lang, to the attention of an international audience.

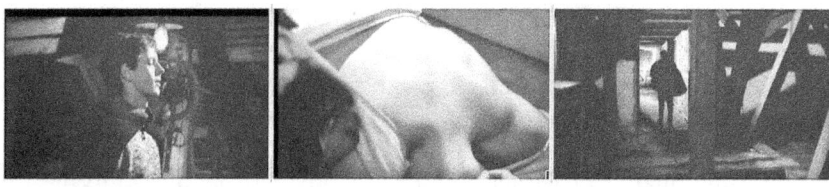

FIGURE 8.5 *Mathieu Carrière as bystander in* Der junge Törless *(FRG, Volker Schlöndorff, 1966)*.

The historical film's implicit parallels to pre-war Germany—from militarism and authoritarian educational systems, the significance of group dynamics and instruments such as fear and repression, to the role of the by-stander—made this adaptation one of the most relevant cultural contributions of the German film industry of the decade. *Törless* was well received, even in reluctant West Germany, and not only drew attention to the genre of adaptation as a means even for commercial cinema to shed light on the complexities of an uncomfortable past, but also to the canon of German-language literature as a useful dialectical supplement to a filmmaker's desire for contemporaneity. As the Group 47 authors of the previous two decades, these young filmmakers aimed at highlighting the disjuncture of present society regarding its past and the consequences of a nation's sense of dislocation in the context of the development of a reasonable collective identity.

Kluge's *Abschied von gestern* [Farewell to Yesterday/*Yesterday Girl*] (1966) in which the writer-director-producer adapted "Anita G.," a chapter from his own book *Lebensläufe* (1962), did receive funding from the Kuratorium. The film premiered at the Venice Film Festival, where it won the Silver Lion and the critic's award. The following year, Kluge's film was awarded the FRG's national film prize (Filmband in Gold) for best feature film, best direction, best lead actor, and best supporting actor. Kluge and Schlöndorff, together with Vesely and Straub/Huillet, created a diverse and very personal film language that was to define the style and aesthetics of the emerging New German Cinema. Literature, unlike in France, was integral to developing this new film language and a genre, which Semenza and Hasenfratz identify as "auteur adaptations."[100]

Public Funding and 'Amphibian' Films

When the West German government introduced a new film law or "Filmförderungsgesetz" in January 1968, it provided the legal foundation for national film funding. The "Filmförderungsanstalt" (FFA), a federal film board was created in March that year for the protection of film heritage and support of new film projects. In 1969, the West German government committed awards of up to 250,000 German marks to six feature films per year that would allow an 'artistically orientated' filmmaker to 'buy artistic freedom.'[101] Theoretically, the aim was to re-establish German film as art, more than a decade after the French New Wave filmmakers had shaped their nation's cinema history. While the initiative was designed to 'increase the quality of German film on a broad scale,' in reality it still linked funding awards to the production's likely box-office success. As Wolf Donner highlighted in his 'Money for the Obedient Ones' article in *Die Zeit*, at a time when box-office hits were rare, film companies interested in their economic well-being naturally prioritized those productions most likely to appeal to the masses. Consequently, young filmmakers eager to reinvent German film would once again be left without funding accessible to them, the critic feared.

Representatives of the 'industry', proudly if blindly defending their "Spitzenniveau" or sense of excellence, had publicly protested the choices for national German Film awards that year: Kluge's film collage *Die Artisten in der Zirkuskuppel—ratlos* [Artists in the Big Top: Perplexed] (1968), Peter Fleischmann's feature based on Martin Sperr's 1965 play *Jagdszenen aus Niederbayern* [Hunting Scenes from Bavaria] (1969), and Peter Zadek's adaptation of Thomas Valentin's 1963 novel *Die Unberatenen* [The Unadvised] as *Ich bin ein Elefant, Madame* [I'm an Elephant, Madame] (1969). As Donner recounted at the time, big studios considered these productions as either 'failing to educate or arrogantly abusing the audience' and noted that they would never amount to anything at the box office.[102] But the culture critic also expressed his concern regarding Interior Minister Ernst Benda's remarks that no film would be supported that reflected 'contempt for mankind,' a 'hostile attitude towards the object or the spectator,' or worked 'against society.' In his mind, this was a clear message for young filmmakers: avoid being 'too ambitious, too aggressive, too critical of society.' Donner feared that this would once again 'prune young German film to be positive and uplifting—and produce clichéd representations of which there are plenty already.'[103]

Not surprisingly, by 1970, the situation had still not changed dramatically, and critics were frequently bemoaning the national film debacle. Films like Schlöndorff's *Törless* had proven that this crisis was not due to a lack of creative talent, but that it had 'structural reasons,' as Donner argued in 1970 in his article 'For a Better Cinema.'[104] Taking a stab at powerful distributors such as Ilse Kubaschewski[105] (Gloria-Film), who rather invested in co-productions such as the popular *Angélique*-series (FR/IT/FRG, Bernard Borderie, 1964, 1965, 1966, 1967, 1968) based on French author Anne Golon's erotic novels, Donner outlines that state funding is little help if no distributor is willing to ensure that new German films are actually screened in cinemas.

Adaptations such as *Josefine Mutzenbacher* (FRG, Kurt Nachmann, 1970) based on the famous Austrian pornographic novel (1906) and the supposedly educational *Schulmädchen-Report* [The Schoolgirl Report] (FRG, Wolf C. Hartwig, 1970) caused what Donner describes as a "Sexschwemme," i.e., an excess of erotic and soft-core porn films that was bringing an already volatile cinema culture into disrepute in the public eye. In contrast, television seemed to the critic a 'constant film festival' with sophisticated and educational productions based on the literary canon, but also broadcasting rather quirky adaptations of, for example, Kleist's novella *Der Findling* [The Foundling] by American screenwriter/director George Moorse[106] (1967) in the ZDF's *Das kleine Fernsehspiel*. On the small screen, adaptations of popular and even controversial contemporary literature were becoming an increasingly common feature.[107]

Donner, who commends young filmmakers for being their own producers, despite the challenges this represents, also highlights the contribution of 'Young German Film' in this context. Their independence from distributors allowed for the development of film that was not primarily concerned with commercial profit, and thus promoted a generational shift with regard to film aesthetics and topics raised. But, as with Weiss' *Die Ermittlung*, television continued to play an important role in this context, and shaped film projects to a significant degree.

Public funding remained essential for young filmmakers' projects to come to fruition, and it became more readily available when the 'Film-Television-Agreement (FRG)' stipulated collaborations between the German film industry, the Federal Film Board and public television in 1974.[108] 200,000 German marks would normally be granted for a feature film at the time, which would usually amount to a significant contribution toward the production costs. Regional television stations would, however, not only contribute to the funding of a particular film project, but participate in the selection process and could, at least potentially, supervise the production. As the Bundeszentrale für politische Bildung [bpp; FRG's Federal Agency for Civic Education] suitably notes: 'As a result, West German television stations became midwives to a new era in West German cinema, which soon included internationally renowned filmmakers such as Wim Wenders, Werner Herzog, Volker Schlöndorff and Rainer Werner Fassbinder.'[109] Such co-funded films would be screened in cinemas for eighteen months, and subsequently returned to television for broadcast at the stations' discretion.

Co-funding practices enabled 'amphibian films,' as West German Broadcasting station WDR's Günter Rohrbach[110] called them, that suited both big and small screens. The Federal Agency for Civic Education gives two prominent examples for those more 'opulent cinema-television-coproductions'—*Die Blechtrommel* [Tin Drum] (Volker Schlöndorff, 1979) and *Das Boot* [The Boat] (Wolfgang Petersen, 1981)—that held their ground in both media.[111] The choice is telling. Television had been gradually and successfully established as a serious and respectable medium throughout the 1960s and 1970s. This was to no small degree due to feature films, many of which were based on literature, including several auteur adaptations. As Volker Schlöndorff confirmed, it was particularly West Germany's public television stations that supported adaptations of well-known literary texts as they were eager to ensure some sophistication to their programming. As producers of their own productions, young German filmmakers like Schlöndorff depended on state and television funding. Without this incentive, fewer adaptations would have seen the light of the projectors. Funding applications based on the nation's cultural heritage were simply more likely to be funded.[112]

'Young German Film' and Literary Heritage

Falsche Bewegung [Wrong Turn] (FRG, Wim Wenders, 1975) was a collaborative project based on Goethe's *Wilhelm Meisters Lehrjahre* (Wilhelm Meister's Apprenticeship, 1795/96) shaped by Austrian author Peter Handke, director of photography Robby Müller, and co-writer and director Wenders. The adaptation was labeled 'one of the most important German films since Lubitsch, Lang and Murnau' in the weekly magazine *Der Spiegel*. 'Something strangely contemporary and modern must be within Goethe's work' to inspire Wenders and Handke to make this film, a critic in *Der Spiegel* noted.[113] And, indeed, the figure of young Wilhelm, insecure and quiet, encounters an intriguing hodge-podge of characters on his journey of self-discovery, which now tellingly orients him toward Bonn, the FRG's capital city along the Rhine. The river and places along its bank like the Lorelei had in the past so frequently been used in German culture and politics to root common and unifying heritage but also, especially in the nation's recent past, to fuel a toxic sense of self-importance. In *Falsche Bewegung*, Wilhelm (Rüdiger Vogler) is a representative of the next generation, who struggles to communicate and mourns the past. His journey leads him to realize the need for critical self-reflection and political resistance, while the requirement of remembrance of the 'dead souls' of Germany (Goethe) now included 6 million Jews.

FIGURE 8.6 *Rüdiger Vogler and Hanna Schygulla in* Falsche Bewegung *(FRG, Wim Wenders, 1975) above the river Rhine.*

Together with Eberhard Itzenplitz's adaptation for television (ARD, 1976) of Ulrich Plenzdorf's *Die neuen Leiden des jungen W.* (The New Sorrows of Young W., 1972), in which his protagonist struggles with convention and, when reading Goethe's novel, identifies with young Werther, Wenders' contemporary take on Goethe in *Falsche Bewegung* stands out at the time. Most adaptations of the literary canon were still aiming at historical fidelity, causing one of West Germany's top film critics Hans C. Blumenberg to chastise filmmakers for turning to literature for inspiration in the first place. In his 'Fancy Dress Party and No End in Sight'-article, he wrote in 1978:

> German cinema loves German lessons. German directors adapt classic works of German literature, which is very noble, very culturally aware, and very boring. This tendency reached its low point last year with Heidi Genée's *Grete Minde* (based on Theodor Fontane) and Selma Sander's Kleist biopic *Heinrich*. Television recently screened *John Glückstadt* (1975) by Ulf Miehe (based on Theodor Storm), and even the veterans of the industry have recently begun to present themselves as educationally eager. Franz Seitz took on Thomas Mann's *Unordnung und Frühes Leid* [Disorder and Early Suffering], and soon Alfred Weidenmann will present a new *Schimmelreiter* [Rider on a White Horse]. Cinema hides from reality, fleeing straight into our ancestors' massive bookcases, where you cannot lose but win significantly (in terms of subsidies and federal film prizes).[114]

Blumenberg's criticism was not unfounded. It had become all too clear that an adaptation project was the most opportune for funding applications to be successful. Consequently, uninspired adaptations were 'gradually degrading the cinema to a middle-class provincial theater,' Blumenberg carped. In his view, only two films of the late 1970s at least attempted to break out of this 'vicious circle of Germanic consecrations' and an event culture, financially supported by the West German government and geared at reinventing its literary canon. They were Wolf Gremm's *Tod, oder Bernhard* (loosely based on Schiller's *Robbers*) and Bernhard Sinkel's *Taugenichts* [Good for Nothing] (an adaptation of Eichendorff's novella)—films that made literature 'fun' rather than a 'chore' or educational routine.[115]

Inspired by the student and sexual revolutions of 1968, Sinkel had intended to film Eichendorff's *Taugenichts* as a utopian narrative about a young, non-conformist hippie, 'who escapes the pressure of meritocracy by fleeing into a colorful nirvana, [stumbling] through flowering meadows towards every new and absolutely useless adventure.' When Sinkel finally managed to make the film nearly a decade later, Eichendorff's 'good-for-nothing' was still a 'dreamy flower child,' refracted however by the film's 1977 perspective. Reality had caught up with the young man, overtaxed and fidgeting, seeming 'more like a refugee than a seeker of happiness.' The film implies that Eichendorff's Taugenichts wouldn't stand a chance during this time of both terrorist and state violence.

Both Sinkel and Gremm reflect individual desires and art as a respected profession rather than ungainful occupation, 'But why *Taugenichts* [Good-for-Nothing], why *The Robbers*?,' Blumenberg asked.

> Why not a film about the angry freaks of the late seventies and their hopes, why not a film about the terrorists, in which one can no longer rely on a vague concept of *libertà*? Despite all the respectable attempts to sneak up on the present from behind [...], German cinema will have to end its endless costume party if it does not want to lose its last few viewers.[116]

Blumenberg was proved wrong in November 1979, when the US American *Holocaust* four-part series (1978) was broadcast by West German television. The series traces a regular German family's journey from moments of discrimination, racial legislation leading to unemployment, deportation and, finally, the last few steps into the gas chambers. The final part had viewers in tears due to the series' affective dramaturgy aimed at affinity and identification. The Weiss's, a family like any other, with the fundamental difference that they were made to endure unfathomable suffering and senseless death, finally opened the German public to empathy on a large scale, which had a tremendous impact on the country's memory culture, setting new standards for television serials in the FRG.[117] When the series was repeated in 2019, director of WDR-television Jörg Schönenborn remarked on the flood of engagement triggered by the series forty years prior. Most importantly, 'the generation of perpetrators [...] represented in all important positions in society, was now deprived of the authority to interpret their own history.'[118]

A critical reevaluation of the past and, especially, of the guilt of previous generations was integral to avant-garde filmmaking in the FRG during the 1970s and early 1980s especially. The role of public funding via the cinema-television agreement remained vital in supporting innovative and radical film projects, beginning with *Warum läuft Herr R. Amok* (FRG, Michael Fengler/R.W. Fassbinder, 1970), a seething critique of German society's hypocrisy that more than hints at a mendacious superficiality fueled by evenings in front of the goggle-box that culminate in Mr. R.'s bludgeoning a chatty neighbor as well as his family to death prior to his suicide. The triviality of *Heimat*-films and formulaic Karl-May-sequels eventually elicit this symbolic act of revenge, inflicted by the next generation.

Encouraged by the FRG's funding opportunities, young directors/writers repeatedly turned to German literature or the figure of the creative writer/artist as vital component of German culture. Television producers sitting on funding boards favored adaptations and hence the reinvention of German cinema and German-language literature are firmly intertwined. Adaptations of Georg Büchner's drama fragment *Woyzeck* by Werner Herzog (1979), Günter Grass's *Die Blechtrommel* [The Tin Drum] by Schlöndorff (1979), Alfred Döblin's *Berlin Alexanderplatz* by Fassbinder (1980) as well as writer-filmmaker collaborations (for example, Peter Handke and Wim Wenders)[119] not only led to a rebirth of German film as art, but to an invaluable social-political engagement of filmmakers with both their country's past and present. Even when not directly addressing the Hitler era—like Herzog's *Woyzeck*, Schlöndorff's *Törless* or Fassbinder's *Effi Briest*—filmmakers of New German Cinema confronted the German past by way of focusing on individuals that were struggling, abused and tortured, exposed to institutions that were anachronistic and their functionaries indifferent or cruel.[120]

Heinrich Böll on Screen

Heinrich Böll (1917–85) grew up in an impoverished Catholic family in Cologne that opposed the Hitler regime. Drafted into the Wehrmacht in 1939, much of his early work addressed the existential crisis experienced by many during the postwar era, following the trauma of war and death. He captured an illusive longing for home, safety, and for a language to put into words the destruction and the unfathomable abyss of inhumanity of Nazi ideology and practices—topics that were decidedly unpopular initially but won him the prize of the Group 47 writers in 1951.

In a lecture delivered at the University of Frankfurt/Main in 1964, Böll spoke about his desire to capture the 'poetics of the moment' ("Poetik des Augenblicks") and to create an 'aesthetics of the humane' ("Ästhetik des Humanen"). It is this aesthetic of the humane in his literary work that enables glimpses through the eyes of those rubbished by society.[121] Looking closely, noticing the margins, and those that have been discarded is a process at the center of his literary work.[122] Films based on his prose—by Vesely, Huillet/Straub and Schlöndorff/Trotta in particular—often adapt this perspective, but not necessarily via POV shots. It is the attention to detail, to small gestures or, sometimes, a power construct of looks and gazes that communicate the inhumanity of a system and/or the fragile humanity of a marginalized individual.

Gruppenbild mit Dame [Group Portrait with Lady] (FRG/FR, Aleksandar Petrović, 1977) may serve as one example of how Böll's literary aesthetic of the humane was adapted to film. In this adaptation of Böll's 1971 novel, the female protagonist Leni Gruyten (Romy Schneider) follows her own moral compass throughout the Hitler era, even though it leaves her with nothing but her memories in postwar Germany. The film's focus is on Leni's

FIGURE 8.7 *Following a cup of coffee in* Gruppenbild mit Dame *(FRG/FR, Aleksandar Petrović, 1977). Kremp: "He has his rations!"—Leni: "This is my coffee."—Kremp: "What? Your proper coffee for that one?"*

relationship with Russian POW Boris (Brad Dourif), and a short sequence in which war veteran and amputee Kremp (Wolfgang Condrus) refuses Boris a cup of coffee during their break. The scene beautifully translates this distinctly poetic moment of solidarity and humanity into film, as Leni quietly but firmly intervenes and the camera follows the filling of mugs, the angry spilling, and calm refilling of Boris' cup, this time with proper coffee, that Leni gently places in front of the POW.

As mentioned before, most Germans were all too eager to put the past behind them, but Böll's direct, uncomplicated language and insightful stories played a significant part in helping to address not only the past but also the problems of the present. Böll's works touch upon the everyday and reflect a deep love and understanding for humankind, inspired to some degree by his Catholic upbringing and social teaching regarding the common good, social justice, and human dignity. Deserving of our solidarity, those on the margins—traumatized or harassed individuals, struggling artists and single mothers, or those failing to make sense of it all—are the focus of his attention, and his literary works never fail to promote compassion and humanity. Daring to look behind those once again supposedly perfect bourgeois facades of a country enjoying its 'economic miracle,' Böll critically highlighted the destructive effects of collective amnesia, consumerism, and militarism in West Germany.

His focus on the isolation and anxieties experienced by alienated individuals caused him to be labeled a "Nestbeschmutzer," accused of running down his own country in novels such as *Haus ohne Hüter* (House without

Guardian, 1954), *Das Brot der frühen Jahre* (The Bread of Those Early Years, 1955), *Ansichten eines Clowns* (The Clown, 1963), or *Gruppenbild mit Dame* (Group Portrait with Lady, 1971). In 1972, Böll was awarded the Nobel Prize for Literature "for his writing which through its combination of a broad perspective on his time and a sensitive skill in characterization has contributed to a renewal of German literature."[123] In addition, however, Böll's work contributed to a rejuvenation of German film and thus deserves attention in this context.

Beginning with the aforementioned 1962 adaptations of Böll's *Das Brot der frühen Jahre* by Austrian filmmaker Vesely, and the story "Hauptstädtisches Journal" [Metropolitan Journal], which was turned into a short film by Danièle Huillet and Jean-Marie Straub the same year, Böll's works continued to be adapted for cinema or television with nearly annual regularity throughout the 1960s and 1970s, as Böll's popularity grew in West Germany and abroad. In total, there are fifteen adaptations of Böll's prose. They range from avant-garde, *Nouvelle Vague* inspired cinematic representations of his literary texts—such as Straub/Huillet's *es hilft nur gewalt, wo gewalt herrscht* [Where Violence rules, Only Violence Helps] (1965)—to quite conventional, but often very successful transpositions for West German television, such as, for example, the highly entertaining and equally hard-hitting *Nicht nur zur Weihnachtszeit* [Not Only at Christmas Time] (Vojtěch Jasný, 1970) or *Ende einer Dienstfahrt* (End of an Official Trip, Hans Dieter Schwarze, 1971). Böll is not only one of the most widely adapted German-language authors after the Second World War, but his political engagement and, especially, his work inspired young filmmakers, thus providing the literary foundation for what was to become known as New German Cinema, one of the most interesting creative movements of twentieth-century film history.[124]

Volker Schlöndorff and Margarethe von Trotta's famous adaptation of Böll's *Die verlorene Ehre der Katharina Blum oder: Wie Gewalt entstehen und wohin sie führen kann* [The Lost Honour of Katharina Blum, or: How violence develops and where it can lead] (FRG, 1975) remains one of the best-known film adaptations of a German-language text, especially outside of Germany. The story of Böll's prose on screen, however, began already in the late 1950s with *Die Stunde der Wahrheit* [The Hour of Truth], a television production based on Böll's radio play *Bilanz* [Taking Stock]. The 'Fernsehspiel' premiered on ARD television on April 22, 1958 under the direction of Gustav Burmester. The film is about the "Lebensbilanz," the balance sheet of life, of the main character Clara (played by Elisabeth Bergner), who takes stock on her deathbed. Her greatest regret is that she would have loved to really *know* someone. Böll's text and its adaptation focus particularly on the consequences of a life lived pretending, playing predesignated parts. As Clara's life is coming to an end, the construction and impact of human behavior come to the fore during an hour of truth that tests and, finally, realigns relationships.

A keen analyst of human nature, Böll is particularly interested in the aftereffects, the ripples, of decisions or actions taken at some stage in the past, that affect our sense of self and shape our relationships in the future, and this aspect is foregrounded in the adaptation. But the film also implicitly criticizes postwar West German society's obsession with bourgeois appearances and pretenses (as Böll's *Bilanz* had done). Not surprisingly, the reception of the film after its TV screening was lukewarm, even though actors Bergner and Heinz Klevenow were considered outstanding.[125] It was too early for that kind of critical self-reflection in West Germany, but the tide was beginning to change.

According to J.H. Reid's annotations in the Cologne edition of his works[126] Böll had written *Das Brot der frühen Jahre* in the summer of 1955 during his second prolonged visit to Ireland, while staying with his family in Keel on Achill Island. Ireland had provided an impetus for the narrative—or rather the socio-economic and cultural difference between his almost premodern, positive vision of Ireland on the one hand, and life determined by the capitalist market and mass consumption in booming West Germany on the other. Upon his return to Cologne after his previous visit to Ireland, he told follow writer Andersch in a letter how disgusted he felt when looking at his fellow Germans' eager consumerism.[127]

In contrast to Böll's distinct presence of the first-person narrator Walter Fendrich in *Das Brot der frühen Jahre*, Vesely creates a collage of visual and aural facets in his 1962 adaptation of Böll's text, that allow the viewer to gain insight into the complex nature of a 'false' existence. Walter's life is shaped by pragmatic opportunism, social norms, and expectations, chosen to ensure a deflection of previous misery. When he is asked by his father to collect Hedwig, a girl from his hometown, at the train station, the encounter has a deep impact on the young man, who decides to leave behind the security of permanent employment, and to break off the engagement to his boss' daughter. The film captures the fissures emerging from Walter's spontaneous decision to continue his life with Hedwig. The rupture is reflected in repeated queries over the telephone, fragmented and recurring searches, and in voice-overs mirroring the core and consequence of the decision to leave a pragmatic or opportunistic existence for something 'real.' Böll's story ends with Hedwig and Walter waiting to sneak up to her room to spend the night. We hear Böll's philosophical musings of the last page—'Never before did I realize that I was immortal and how mortal I was'—in a voice-over, but as viewers of Vesely's complex montage of narrative sequences we experience that "time is no longer an organic progression; events no longer look back on an unbroken past and forward to a radiant future"[128] as Reid writes about Böll's use of montage technique in his text. Moreover, it is the acknowledgment of rupture that allows for a glimpse of courage, chance, and renewal in the final sequence of this inspired adaptation.

Thus, Vesely's film not only touched on the core of Böll's literary work but caused heated public debates following its premiere. These were soon topped, however, by Huillet and Straub's adaptation of Böll's short-story *Hauptstädtisches Journal* which was turned into a short film entitled *Machorka Muff* in 1962, and premiered in 1963 in Oberhausen after a prolonged controversy with the Oberhausen film festival committee. Aesthetically reminiscent of French New Wave cinema—in black-and-white, no musical score, only diegetic sound, documentary camera style and an unruffled use of irony—the adaptation emphasizes the continuous presence of former Nazis in positions of political and economic power in West Germany. Rearmament has been decided and an only superficially reformed Nazi is to be made general; in addition, a war criminal is to be rehabilitated; 'diffamed' due to his 'losses,' he had been transferred to the seaside resort of Biarritz 'for disciplinary reasons,' where he died of 'lobster poisoning.' His Nazi buddies are fully integrated and doing well in capitalist West Germany, powerful families during the Hitler era are still powerful—now equipped with 'the confidence of this class of survivors'—and a complicit Catholic church does nothing to make them at least morally reflect on their evil deeds.

As Vesely's and Straub/Huillet's films indicate, Böll's literary work provided not only an impetus for young filmmakers to create adaptations that offered a new film language. It also inspired a critical engagement with complacent West German society that focused on economic success, traditional family values, closed private spheres, and perfected public pretenses, rather than the guilt, stink, and horror of its recent past.[129] The New German Cinema and, especially, films of this period by Vesely, Kluge, Huillet/Straub, Schlöndorff, von Trotta, and Fassbinder should be considered interventions in the interest of the public, and as efforts by the next generation of young Germans to recreate a 'literary public sphere' and critical debate via adaptation.

For Böll and the makers of New German Cinema, 'engagement' is the precondition and bedrock of creative production, as Böll told Horst Bienek in an interview in 1961.[130] Adaptations such as *Nicht versöhnt oder Es hilft nur Gewalt, wo Gewalt herrscht* based on Böll's *Billiard um halb zehn* [Billiards at half-past nine] (Huillet/Straub, 1965), *Nicht nur zur Weihnachtszeit* (1970), *Ende einer Dienstfahrt* (1971), *Haus ohne Hüter* [House without Guardians] (Rainer Wolffhardt, 1975), and *Ansichten eines Clowns* [The Clown] (Vojtěch Jasný, 1975) are all deeply personal and at the same time highly effective and aesthetically innovative, personal and at the same time critical engagements with Germany's past and present. They contributed to the public sphere by igniting and informing countless debates, encouraging a critical review of the construction of national identity and memory culture, gender roles, social and economic positioning, and marginalization, while highlighting normative structures and conventional behavior with a good dose of irony and resentment.[131]

Volker Schlöndorff, Margarethe von Trotta, and German-language Literature

Schlöndorff stands out in this history of German-language literature on film as its most prolific contributor, comparable to exceptional scriptwriters like Carl Mayer and directors who repeatedly turned to the genre like Richard Oswald, G.W. Pabst, F.W. Murnau, and Max Ophüls. His extensive filmography includes adaptations of Robert Musil (*Der junge Törless*, 1966), Heinrich von Kleist (*Michael Kohlhaas—Der Rebell*, 1969),[132] Bertolt Brecht (*Baal*, 1969, starring R.W. Fassbinder), Heinrich Böll (*Die verlorene Ehre der Katharina Blum*, with M.v. Trotta, 1975), Günter Grass (*Die Blechtrommel*, 1975), Nicolas Born (*Die Fälschung*, 1981), and Max Frisch (*Homo Faber*, 1991). His *Return to Montauk* (2017) was co-written with Irish author Colm Tóibín. It is an homage to Schlöndorff's friend, the Swiss author Max Frisch and springs from his novel *Montauk*, but is also a deeply personal encounter with a literary text and the reader's own reference points, wounds, and experiences.[133]

Throughout his filmmaking career, he also ventured into other language-cultures with adaption projects such as *Der Fangschuss* (FRG/FR, 1976, based on Marguerite Yourcenar's *Le Coup de grâce*) and *Eine Liebe von Swann* (FR/FRG, 1984, courageously based on the first volume of Marcel Proust's *A la recherche du temps perdu*), *The Ogre/Der Unhold* (FR/FRG/GB, 1996, based on Michel Tournier's novel *Le roi des aulnes*), and *Diplomacy/ Diplomatie* (FR/FRG, 2013, based on Cyril Gely's play), as well as *Death of a Salesman* (US, 1985, based on Arthur Miller), *A Gathering of Old Men* (US/GB/FRG, 1987, based on Ernest J. Gaines' novel), *The Handmaid's Tale* (US/FRG, 1990, based on Margaret Atwood), and *Palmetto* (US/FRG, 1998, based on James Hadley Chase's novel *Just Another Sucker*).

Schlöndorff is an auteur filmmaker who has managed to bring literary texts to the screen in an unmistakable aesthetic that is nonetheless distinct each time, infused as it is by a specific literary disposition. His multi-layered adaptations communicate the mood of their source texts and engage with the literary work in a deeply personal manner that nonetheless reflects the director's appreciation and respect for another's creative work. This is, perhaps, the reason why he is sometimes overlooked when Germany's auteurist New German Cinema is mentioned.[134] Or is it because he did not lose sight of the audience, especially when becoming his own producer beginning with his Brecht adaptation *Baal*? 'Due to the fact that we shouldered the entire financial risk, we had to keep an eye on the market and could not lose sight of the audience despite all our dreams,' he explains.[135] Nonetheless, for James M. Welsh and many other film historians, the

> movement known as the New German Cinema begins in 1966 with a film by Volker Schlöndorff, *Der junge Törless* (*Young Törless*), made by a German who had learned filmmaking in France and worked as assistant director with Alain Resnais on *Last Year at Marienbad* (1962) and Louis Malle on *Zazie dans le métro* (1960) and other talents of the French New Wave.[136]

When he returned to Germany, Schlöndorff contributed significantly to the reform of German cinema, not least due to the international success of his *Der junge Törless*.[137] Musil's story evokes the suppression and tangibly violent atmosphere in a boarding school at a military academy in Austria-Hungary around 1900. One of the pupils, Basini, is being bullied by his classmates and Törless, while disgusted by their actions, remains a passive observer. Musil's text is primarily a critique of an authoritarian system that breeds bullies and cowards, but at the same time explores the fate of those who do not belong and are crushed. Schlöndorff's adaptation depicts the *fin-de-siècle* boarding school as a system of violence and suppression that effects change in its inhabitants. The majority of the pupils participate in or at least tolerate the brutal actions against Basini (Marian Seidowsky), because their fear of exclusion and punishment outweighs their empathy with the victim. Even Törless (Mathieu Carrière), who is appalled by his classmates' viciousness and understands the difference between good and evil, has little confidence that those in authority would interfere and evoke change for the better. So, he remains passive and as detached as possible, having to live with the consequences of his inaction when he realizes that his curiosity, disgust, and voyeuristic pleasure made him complicit in his classmates' despicable actions. The film was widely praised as a critique of Germans' behavior between 1933 and 1945, when the Nazi's exclusionary politics and practices went from marginalization and incarceration of Jews to mass murder while significant fractions of the public submissively observed the crimes committed or actively ignored them, failing to muster the courage to oppose the brutally racist regime and thus abetting its crimes.

As Schlöndorff notes in his autobiography, he learned his craft from *Nouvelle Vague* filmmakers, especially Malle and Jean-Pierre Melville, who also provided insights into the process and collaborative practice of adaptation.[138] His enthusiasm for Weimar cinema—G.W. Pabst's *Freudlose Gasse* and *Die Büchse der Pandora* and, especially, Fritz Lang's *M*, films he had translated synchronously numerous times during screenings at the Cinemathèque française in Paris for the French-speaking audience—as well as the Russian cinema of Alexander Dovzhenko and Vsevolod Pudovkin, and the 1940s and '50s movies by Fritz Lang, Elia Kazan, and Akira Kurosawa affected his own film language.[139] But while these filmmakers and the French New Wave auteurs who use the camera as a pen or their individual 'caméra-stylo'[140] shaped his desire to find his own personal style, Schlöndorff also insists that 'every film should have its own language, its images their own syntax'.[141] This logic includes not only a specific montage of camera movement and distances, and a consistency and coherence to the composition of the narrative, but always already a personal engagement with a source text and the language of its author. In *Törless*, the use of inserts is Schlöndorff's link to Lang, but also to Eisenstein and Buñuel. The film's close-up of inanimate objects is reminiscent, too, of Dupont's aforementioned *Varieté* (1925), the camera work of Karl Freund, and Ophüls' French films of the 1950s.

Music is an essential component in most of Schlöndorff's adaptations. Speaking of specific images in Musil's literary work, he emphasizes the capacity of music to suggest, that which is 'suspended' between words, the 'uncertainty and deception behind the image.'[142] Producer Franz Seitz suggested composer Hans Werner Henze, who had recently supplied the film score for Resnais' *Muriel ou Le temps d'un retour* (1963). Deliberately avoiding sophistication, Henze's musical score for *Der junge Törless* makes use of old instruments like a hurdy-gurdy and a wooden flute, and superbly evokes the boys' crudity and awkwardness. Henze also composed the scores for *Die verlorene Ehre der Katharina Blum* (FRG, 1975) and *Un amour de Swann* (FR/FRG, 1983), contributing to the mood and narrative of each adaptation in a unique and idiosyncratic way.

Böll, Schlöndorff, and von Trotta

According to his autobiography, Schlöndorff and his partner von Trotta, who remains one of the most important representatives of new German women's cinema, had intended to adapt Böll's *Ansichten eines Clowns* but could not secure funding. When Böll asked them to consider his *Die verlorene Ehre der Katharina Blum* for adaptation, they did not hesitate.[143] It is a story that emanated from the author's deep anger about the sensationalist and manipulative tabloid press, which had fanned public hysteria regarding terrorism and labeled left-wing students—but also writers like Böll— RAF 'sympathizers.' After years of jaded reporting by *Bild*, Böll was fed up with the tabloid's unethical journalistic practices that in his view were incompatible with a constitutional state; they are 'fascist': 'this is pure fascism. Hate speech, defamation, filth, encouraging lynch law'.[144] In his 1972 article, he reminded the public of the State's but also the press's obligation to respect and protect human rights, as these rights and the freedom of the individual are the bedrock of any democratic society governed by the rule of law. Böll considered the hysteria created and fed by the tabloid press regarding those few far-left extremists around Andreas Baader and Ulrike Meinhof as preposterous and immoral. While he considered the RAF's 'war of 6 against 60 million'[145] as irrational and quite pointless, he also viewed the nation's hysteria and the government's willingness to declare a state of emergency as ludicrous. His suggestion—evoking Luther's recommendation for Michael Kohlhaas—to offer Ulrike Meinhof 'safe conduct'[146] in order to stop the escalation of violence and enable communication caused a scandal. "What followed was a storm of newspaper articles attacking my father, indeed our whole family," Böll's son René said. "There were tirades in German Parliament, where he was called insignificant and ignorant. And the right-wing press labelled him a Communist and an anarchist."[147]

Bild journalist Matthias Walden charged Böll with being 'the spiritual father of violence' which must have been extremely offensive to the author, who was a committed pacifist and whose literary texts often focused on those that had suffered injustice and violence and carried with them the scars. Böll decided to take Walden to court for slander, but Schlöndorff writes 'he lost in all the courts and lots of money, but in his eyes, he had lost especially his honor. He fought back by writing a 'pamphlet', which he sent to me. [...] The text pinpointed the disgust, which many of us felt in light of the public Baader-Meinhof-hysteria.'[148]

The 'pamphlet' consisted of the proofs of Böll's *Lost Honour of Katharina Blum* text with handwritten corrections in the margins. Here, Böll again turned to the marginalized and abused, as he had done so frequently in his previous literary texts.[149] After spending the night unknowingly with a 'terrorist,' his protagonist Katharina is exposed to a smear campaign by the tabloid press. Even her elderly mother is haunted by immoral journalists, and in the end, the young woman kills one of the most ruthless and offensive of them. The key question in Böll's text about a kind, single woman who ends up committing a violent crime is: 'How did this violence come about?' and to make sure that all his readers get this vital point, he highlights it in the subtitle of his story: 'How violence develops and where it can lead.' It explores the consequences of defamatory articles in press, the changes in perception of a human being that has been exposed to this kind of slander, the entanglement of the media and the police, and the desperate efforts of an innocent individual to protect her honor.

Böll, Schlöndorff, and von Trotta went through the script scene by scene. According to the directors, the original structure of the text—a matter-of-fact protocol that recounts the events of only four days—already provided the outline of the film. Böll was adamant to ensure the authenticity of the script (changing details such as, for example, the amount of money left in Katharina's mother's purse when she died) and intensified some of the dialogues. According to Schlöndorff, for Böll, the significance of this challenge to her reputation was fundamental: Katharina needed to defend her honor, because as a woman of her class and social background, her good reputation was her most important possession.[150]

Schlöndorff and von Trotta embraced Böll's desire for authenticity and truthful expression but aimed for maximum public impact of their adaptation. For this reason, the film's structure and style draw on the conventions of the thriller genre. But it is Angela Winkler's small gestures and physical expressions that reflect her humiliation and growing despair. Her humanity and the injustice of her destruction are communicated in those 'moments of truth,' as Schlöndorff puts it.[151]

Böll, Schlöndorff, and von Trotta were at this stage all considered 'sympathizers' with the terrorist RAF[152] but nonetheless the film project received nearly 50 percent of its 1.7 million German marks budget from public sources like the FRG's federal film board (FFA) and public television (WDR). *Die verlorene Ehre der Katharina Blum* premiered on October 10, 1975 and became by far the most successful of all Böll-adaptations, both nationally and internationally from the United States to the Soviet Union. To this day it is considered one of the prime examples of New German Cinema and one of the best-known film adaptations of a German-language text. Within the FRG, the film was considered rather conventional by the majority of 'new German' filmmakers and was not included in Reclam's *Neuer Deutscher Film* epoch volume.[153] Nonetheless, in his review published in the *Frankfurter Rundschau* Wolfram Schütte considered the adaptation the breakthrough film of New German Cinema, stating the movement had finally 'arrived in reality and with the audience.' The popularity of the film was like a referendum: the public voted for Böll, and against the hatred and demagoguery of *Bild* and the Axel Springer-press, against the hysteria and emergency laws; from bugging operations to high security prisons.[154]

Grass, Schlöndorff, and *The Tin Drum*

Schlöndorff said in an interview that literature is his 'life elixir.' The literary texts he adapted were often a challenge, but Günter Grass' *Die Blechtrommel* (The Tin Drum, 1959) proved particularly exigent. The novel told by a 'misshapen dwarf' about Gdansk/Eastern Pomerania during the Second World War and Germany after 1945 had landed like a bombshell in the country's public sphere and made Grass one of the most famous writers in the German language. When offered the project, Schlöndorff was hesitant to even attempt to adapt Grass' 'powerful language' and a novel of such complexity, but in the end the author managed to persuade the gifted director to put his vision into film. Schlöndorff's adaptation focuses the novel on Oskar Matzerath, the boy, who was born when Hitler began to rise, and who rejected the fascist world of the adults and refused to grow any further.

An odd little goblin, Oskar is a picaresque figure, who stands apart and yet center stage, sitting underneath the kitchen table, for example, observing, listening, and shattering windows with his scream when frustration gets the better of him or, sometimes, to display his power. For Schlöndorff, visualizing Grass' dream only became a 'reality' once he was introduced to David Bennent, actor Heinz Bennent's son, who was very small for his age. Suddenly, *Die Blechtrommel* on film seemed possible, but the adaptation had to end with the fall of Hitler's Reich, because Grass' Oskar decides to grow again once Nazi Germany is defeated. Since he develops into a hunchback after the so-called 'zero hour,' Schlöndorff believed this final part of the novel could not have been adapted convincingly without the availability of CGI.[155]

Die Blechtrommel (1979) became Schlöndorff's greatest international success to date. The adaptation was awarded the 'Oscar' for Best Foreign Film and the Palme d'Or in Cannes. As Schlöndorff told John Vinocur in an interview published in *The New York Times*:

> Grass said I made *The Tin Drum* because I asked the right questions and listenend to his answers. But I think there is something else. If you have a piece as original as *The Tin Drum* then you can't profane yourself by making something even more original out of it. [...] I had no need to put a personal label on this film. I think it was this approach that interested him: a professional filmmaker who did not try to make the film his own.[156]

FIGURE 8.8 *David Bennent in* Die Blechtrommel *(FRG, Volker Schlöndorff, 1979)*.

In the context of this adaptation project, Grass was more than the author of the source text. He edited the script (which Schlöndorff had written with Jean-Claude Carrière), worked on dialogues, and on the transposition of Oskar's grandmother's monologue in the closing sequence. He was also involved when the film had to be shortened by approximately sixty minutes. The adaptation had far exceeded the length stipulated in the contract and Grass helped with the editing in this final stage of the movie's production, while the director acknowledges especially the important contribution of Suzanne Baron in this process, who created the film's 'autonomous narrative flow' at the cutting table.[157] But Grass also insisted on certain details and shots, for example a close-up of Angela Winkler's "Geschleim," her vomit on the beach. Nonetheless, it was Schlöndorff's vision of Grass' text, his understanding of Oskar in the context of Chaplin's *The Kid* (1921), and his ability to transform a picaresque novel into a visual montage of historical events and deeply personal views and experiences. In his autobiography, he repeatedly highlights the contribution of his team, and in the same vein felt privileged to share authorship of his adaptation.[158]

As a filmmaker, Schlöndorff is interested in contemporaneity rather than historicity. At the same time, when adapting a literary text, he takes measure of his work by asking himself: 'Am I at the level of the literary text?' As a reviewer in *Die Zeit* admiringly notes: 'For Schlöndorff, cinema is a ladder. Step by step he climbs up to the great novels and plays, into the world of the sublime and meaningful—into the world of art.'[159] By writing with rather than about the source text, by considering the language of the literary text while making his film and allowing it to seep deeply into its mood and fabric rather than simply transposing the plot and retelling the narrative, Schlöndorff creates unique adaptations that differ fundamentally from one another in terms of their cinematic language. It is for that reason that he is sometimes overlooked in publications about the *auteurs* of New German Cinema. By sharing his unique creative voice with that of the source text, Schlöndorff places literature as a creative force at the very core of each of his adaptation projects. His ability to relinquish control over the adaptation project in this context, however, makes him one of the outstanding auteurs of the genre.

Fassbinder and the Canon of German-language Literature

Rainer Werner Fassbinder died in 1982, when he was just thirty-seven years old. He is considered one of the most important representatives of New German Cinema and stands out as a filmmaker, whose work remains "a touchstone of auteurist practice in twenty-first century (and international) arthouse film" as Bergfelder notes.[160] His more than forty feature films, three short films, and two television series, not to mention his plays for theater and radio, introduced an uncompromising and provocative passion for an all-consuming creative process that had little interest in making history but rather in mediating the public sphere, intervening in memory discourses, and shaking up his viewers' understanding of their here and now. His films were always political and, as German film director Christian Petzold explained in an interview, like "each great filmmaker—be it Truffaut, Godard, or Fassbinder—[Fassbinder] has made films about making films. That is, they placed themselves and their conditions of production center stage."[161]

During his time in the avant-garde Munich theater group Action-Theater, which reformed under Fassbinder's leadership as "antiteater" in 1968, this manically prolific filmmaker and *enfant terrible* of New German Cinema was already on the warpath 'against the state,' which according to him was synonymous with repressive, fascist, and militarist structures.[162] In this era of radical renewal of cinema culture following the Oberhausen Manifesto, Fassbinder played a central role in the realization of highly artistic, innovative films, from the seventies onwards until his untimely death. Fassbinder's contributions not only to New German Cinema, but also quality television with serialized adaptations[163] such as *Berlin Alexanderplatz* (1980), based on Döblin, and die *Welt am Draht* (World on a Wire) (1973), based on Daniel F. Galouye's science fiction novel *Simulacron-3*, are recognized in virtually all histories of German film published this century. His television mini-series *Acht Stunden sind kein Tag* [Eight Hours Don't Make a Day] (five episodes, 1972–3) raises themes such as rack renting and xenophobia, which seem as pertinent today as they were then. Fassbinder's work is both aesthetically innovative and deeply political when putting a spotlight on society's hypocrisy, homophobia, racism, and gender inequality, while his interest is also drawn to an individual's potential to muddle through and survive. As other young German filmmakers such as Schlöndorff, his work actively challenges established traditions of ideal worlds and happy ends in commercial cinema and television, and addresses the remnants of fascism in German society at every turn.

While also adapting Nabokov and Ibsen, German-language literature provided the foundation to several of his films, namely *Pioniere in Ingolstadt* (1971) based on Marieluise Fleißer's 1928 play, and *Wildwechsel* [Jailbait] (1972), based on Franz Xaver Kroetz's stageplay of the previous year, followed by *Fontane Effi Briest* (1974), a two-part adaptation of Oskar Maria Graf's 1931 novel *Bolwieser* (1977), and further commissions for public television.[164] Döblin's groundbreaking montage novel *Berlin Alexanderplatz* (1929) was a particularly prominent source of inspiration and identification for Fassbinder and a presence in his work nearly from the beginning of his career.[165] The literary text and its main protagonist ex-con Franz Biberkopf, who struggles desperately to be a better man, infused his first feature-length movie entitled *Liebe ist kälter als der Tod* [Love is Colder than Death] (1969) as much as the aesthetic of the French New Wave and Hollywood's *film noir*. The film is dedicated to innovative auteur filmmakers that inspired him: Claude Chabrol, Éric Rohmer, and Jean-Marie Straub. Fassbinder himself plays "Franz" (and uses the name "Bieberkopf" when checking into a hotel), a small-time pimp who wants to remain independent from a powerful syndicate, while getting entangled in a web of personal relations and criminal activity not unlike Döblin's Franz. As in *Warnung vor einer heiligen Nutte* [Beware of a Holy Whore] (FRG, R.W. Fassbinder, 1971), produced by antiteater-X-film, the film raises the question of independence and sets the tone for one of his oeuvre's main themes.[166]

The film *Händler der vier Jahreszeiten* [Merchant of Four Seasons] (FRG, Rainer Werner Fassbinder, 1971) made shortly before his outstanding adaptation of the German literary canon *Fontane Effi Briest* (1972–4), marks a turning point in Fassbinder's oeuvre toward a seemingly less complex way of storytelling about human action and agency.[167] The original title of the *Merchant of Four Seasons* had been 'Many things cause injuries— some things kill,' illustrating a theme Fassbinder continues to explore in *Effi Briest*, i.e., the consequences of trespassing against a patriarchal, authoritarian system of repression, marginalization, and exclusion. Fassbinder, who 'was more interested in literary themes,' described *Fontane Effi Briest* as an extremely important film for him personally.[168] Known as an indefatigable workaholic, Fassbinder often shot a film in less than two weeks. For his *Effi Briest* adaptation he allocated sixty days of shooting alone, which underlines the importance of the project for the director/ screenwriter.

To obtain funding for the project, however, proved difficult. There was no money available apart from the 'feature film award' of 250,000 German marks by the ministry of the interior. Public television station ARD (Channel 1) had recently bought Luderer's *Effi Briest* adaptation (GDR, 1969) and had no interest in another adaptation of the same Fontane novel. ZDF (Channel 2) insisted on color film and on Fassbinder collaborating with a production company of their choice to keep the unruly director in check.[169] Fassbinder decided to finance the film himself instead and was happy to pay for this 'luxury.'[170] In 1973 he commented:

> 'There are important films, especially those that have been fought for against certain obstacles. Among them *Fontane Effi Briest* is particularly important to me. I wanted to make this film in black and white at that time and no one wanted to give me a cent for it. Nobody wanted a black-and-white film. So I said I'll make it anyway and take my chances. It's something that has value for me personally.'[171]

On June 28, 1974, the film premiered at the International Film Festival in Berlin and was nominated for the *Goldener Bär*. The adaptation, which was screened across the country the following month, turned out to be an unexpected magnet for cineastes in West Germany and abroad. Its complex construct of narratives, which probes the multiple layers of Fontane's text, nevertheless circles around a thematic core. Fassbinder's screenplay indicates the film's intrinsic proximity to literature from the beginning and opens with black script on white background.[172] The title reads: '*Fontane Effi Briest* or Many who have an idea of their possibilities and needs, and yet accept the ruling system in their minds and through their actions consolidate and altogether confirm it.' The title alone illustrates the focus of this adaptation, which subtly radicalizes Fontane's skepticism toward the possibility of self-realization in the context of narrow social norms and ultimately rejects it as utopian.[173] Fassbinder investigates power structures of the disciplinary social order (Foucault)[174] as described by Fontane, from the aforementioned 'instrument designed to instill fear' to the 'tyrannical social something' in a differentiated and uncompromising cinematography that does not shy away from depicting a female protagonist who submits to this system and thus ultimately perpetuates it at great cost to herself.[175] "I made *Effi Briest*

FIGURE 8.9 *Hanna Schygulla in* Fontane Effi Briest *(FRG, Rainer Werner Fassbinder, 1974)*.

because Fontane's attitude to his society was a lot like my own, and I'm German, making films for German audiences," Fassbinder said in a *Sight & Sound* interview with Tony Rayns.[176]

The aesthetic starting point of this adaptation is the daguerreotype, represented in a portrait of Effi following the opening sequence.[177] With this type of mirror image, Fassbinder reflects on adaptation as a 'reversed copy' of the literary source, while his use of mirrors as idle surfaces exposes as a 'travesty' the 'utopian ideal of autonomous self-determination of a subject' within a repressive patriarchal system with a clearly contrastive binary morality.[178] Moreover, the film's lighting and color design, and especially the dubbing of most of the actors' voices, also echo the theme of reproduction and imitation. Fassbinder's interest in duplication is foregrounded in these facets, while his adaptation explores literature on screen as genre, practice, and experiment.

Fontane Effi Briest refers back to early photography and film history, and at the same time probes the essence of the narrative by the author he included in the title of his film. By means of a special lighting design, which reduces contrast and creates images with a high proportion of gray on a white background, the film aesthetically merges the chromatic medium film with the monochromatic printed text. This in turn reflects the colorlessness and rigidity of society, thus expressing this leitmotif not only in the direction of the different characters, but also in the very materiality of the film. The "artificiality of the theme" demanded a high degree of stylization, making the adaptation almost "hermetic," as Fassbinder explained.[179]

White faders 'mark chapters'[180] and intertitles ("Inserts") emphasize the proximity of film and text as well as the significance of literature for film history. As Fassbinder emphasized in an interview with Corinna Brocher, it was crucial

> for the viewer of the film to clearly notice that this is a novel and that the important thing about that novel is not that it tells a story but how it tells that story. It should always be clear that this story was told by someone. How and why this story was told, should be obvious from the film.[181]

Fade-outs to paper-white evoke leafing through a notebook and consciously accentuate the fragmentary character of an adaptation. Intertitles or text inserts between scenes quote from the literary source and are reminiscent of title plates in silent movies. At the same time, they draw the viewers' attention toward certain motifs of the novel and emphasize one of Fassbinder's main concerns once again by doubling: Fontane's 'an instrument designed to instil fear' appears twice on the film's intertitles.

Fassbinder takes on the role of the narrator and his relatively monotonous voiceover mostly complements the action, but at times also contradicts the adaptation's simulacrum. Fassbinder's screenplay begins with the following instruction:

From white screen fade-in panorama shot of the house. It must under no circumstances look like the house the narrator describes. There should be only some similarity. The house must be visible for a moment before the narrator begins.

The spoken text as well as the visual transposition of the novel contravenes each other here and in other scenes when the text read out does not correspond to what we see. Slow motion sequences or stills provide the opportunity to look closely and to grasp the image's discrepancy with the spoken (literary) text, producing moments of (critical) dissociation. Fassbinder and his team worked with a variety of alienation effects—the interruption of the narrative by inserts and white screens, unreliable narration, 'anti-realistic' direction and distanced demeanor of the cast, and the synchronization of individual actors—inspired by Brecht's epic theater.[182] Only Hanna Schygulla (Effi), Wolfgang Schenk (Innstetten), and Karlheinz Böhm (Wüllersdorf) speak their own parts, but Fassbinder insisted on monotone diction, which Schygulla found initially as problematic as Fassbinder's dictatorial directing style, until she realized that this controlled diction enabled her to portray the tensions in a young woman full of zest for life and sexual needs but fettered by social conventions.[183]

Reminiscent of the cinematography in Ophüls' *Le Plaisir* (FR, 1952) and *Madame de ...* (FR, 1953), the audience's view is obstructed repeatedly (by lace curtains, branches, window bars, etc.) and the composition of images thus dominated by barriers, dividing lines, and fragmentations.[184] Reflecting on film and literature alike, these techniques allow the literary source to be perceived in its historical remoteness and otherness, while providing the opportunity for a critical evaluation of the events observed, and of the audience's scopophilia, curiosity, and enjoyment of scandal.[185] In this highly personal work, Fassbinder communicates the tragedy of Effi's short life, reflects on adaptation and filmmaking, and settles the score with 1970s West Germany.[186]

Normative structures and a repressive morality which lead to the social exclusion of individuals appear as recurrent themes in Fassbinder's films (*Katzelmacher, Warnung vor einer heiligen Nutte, Angst essen Seele auf, Lola*, etc.), but his criticism is not only directed toward the "instruments of fear," but at those who do not contest the role of victim imposed on them and continue their existence in masochistic complicity and disenfranchisement.[187] Fassbinder's masterful adaptation about the tragedy of a doomed life and an individual's search for happiness, which is destined to fail within repressive (protofascist) social norms, was made at a time when the political opposition became increasingly radical and the first RAF generation around Baader and Meinhof was rounded up and jailed. After years of political dissatisfaction with affluent society and its immovable structures and fixed identities (Marcuse), West German society was shaken by RAF attacks and arrests of left-wing terrorists, economic crisis, protest actions, and violently suppressed strikes. In his adaptation, Fassbinder explores authoritarian personalities (Adorno) and directs his audience's attention toward the individual in view of a critical analysis of a reactionary system. *Fontane Effi Briest* rethinks the literary original in the context of Fassbinder's own experience of disillusion when the 1968 movement's creative utopias seemed to degenerate into violence or resignation. His unique depiction of repressive power structures and a ruling system's intransigence exposed the relevance of literature in the public sphere in general and of Fontane's novel in particular. 'Surprisingly popular' at the time, the film is still recognized as an 'ingenious adaptation.'[188]

Fassbinder's fifteen-and-a-half hour adaptation of Döblin's *Berlin Alexanderplatz* (1980), broadcast on public television in fourteen parts, wrote television history for being not only the most expensive public television series at the time, but "probably the single most controversial production ever to appear on German television" according to Anna Kuhn.[189] Because of its unusual level of sex and violence that thwarted expectations regarding the genre's "high-brow aspirations,"[190] the series was considered "unacceptably disturbing"[191] and appealed neither to critics in West Germany, nor to a mass audience. Today, if only occasionally, Fassbinder's auteur adaptation is still screened at film festivals in fifteen-hour marathons.[192]

Following his outstanding *Die Ehe der Maria Braun* (1979) and *Lili Marleen* (1981), the final movie in Fassbinder's FRG-trilogy *Lola* (1981) is an adaptation of an adaptation, namely of Josef von Sternberg's *The Blue Angel*, and thus loosely based on Heinrich Mann's novel *Professor Unrat*. The time of the narrative in Fassbinder's film, however, is the 1950s, and the adaptation functions as a political satire of West Germany, where free enterprise and consumerism, enabled by the so-called 'economic miracle,' are running amok. "The fat little bourgeois foxes are spoiling the vines in the fields, the buildings in the cities and everything else they can acquire through kickbacks, payoffs, fraud and, possibly, murder," as Vincent Canby summarized Fassbinder's caricature of capitalist West Germany in *The New York Times*.[193] At the same time, however, Fassbinder's anti-capitalist and anti-fascist take on Mann's novel necessitated its focus on Sternberg's *Der blaue Engel* and his subsequent *femme fatale* movies starring Marlene Dietrich in Hollywood. Barbara Sukowa is Lola, the Cabaret/brothel's star performer and potential ruin of the seemingly incorruptible head of the city's planning department von Bohm (Armin Mueller-Stahl), while her boss and building contractor Schuckert (Mario Adorf) ensures that Fassbinder's critique of class-based society reenters the fray. Leading ladies and deadly dolls, the depiction of ambition and social mobility, stars, movies like *The Blue Angel*, and literary texts such as *Professor Unrat* are all resources being developed for maximum profit, and Fassbinder's *Lola* is as much about commercial cinema and adaptation, as about working as an avant-garde director in capitalist West Germany.

When Fassbinder's first movies were screened, his understated images suggested a restrained film aesthetic that offered an attractive alternative to the superficial affectation and melodrama that had dominated much of West German postwar cinema. This does not mean that his films shy away from drama—quite the contrary. Violence is part of the everyday, cruelty part of human nature, and death part of life. Fassbinder wanted to change the world (or at least West German society) with his films, but at the same time he mistrusted revolutionaries as much as the state. Change benefits those in power, opportunism, and egotism rule. Themes such as power (derived from money, social status, and/or sex), love, and isolation reoccur in his works and clearly determined the choices of literary source texts for his adaptations. Fassbinder's goal, however, was to raise issues of contemporary relevance and bring them to life: 'Movies have to stop being movies at some point, have to stop being stories. They must come alive so that we ask ourselves, what does this actually mean for me and in my life?'[194]

Conclusion

German-language literature was an integral part of German film history during the era outlined in this chapter, no matter whether we consider the increasingly dire commercial West German movie industry, film in the GDR, television culture of the 1960s and 1970s, 'young German film' or New German Cinema. Adaptations of contemporary literature reign among the most successful internationally, from Beyer's *Jacob the Liar* to Schlöndorff's *The Lost Honour of Katharina Blum* and *Tin Drum*. In international cinema, some of the most superb adaptations of the German-language literary canon were written and directed by auteur filmmakers such as Welles, Visconti, and Rohmer.

While most productions for commercial cinema in Austria and West Germany had no appetite for a critical engagement with their countries' past, and East Germany's DEFA worked under the constraints of oscillating cultural policies and priorities of the political leadership, a new generation of young directors took stock of their present and set out to innovate German film.[195] Taking inspiration from Weimar cinema and Hollywood's *film noir*, the French New Wave and, especially, contemporary Group 47 literature, they created a new and personal, diagnostic, and rebellious film language that became internationally known as New German Cinema.

As this chapter hoped to show, both the literary canon—from Goethe, Büchner, Kleist, and Fontane to Musil and Döblin—and contemporary literature (Weiss, Born, Böll, Grass, etc.) inspired and guided filmmakers such as Vesely, Sanders-Brahms, Kluge, von Trotta, Schlöndorff, Fassbinder, Herzog, Wenders, and others. Thanks to public funding on the one hand,

and the creativity and dedication of this new generation of writers/directors on the other, several outstanding adaptations based on German-language literature came to fruition.

Raising controversial issues such as repressive social and moral structures, homosexuality, racism, antisemitism, and the German public's willful amnesia regarding their nation's Nazi past in the context of adaptation caused numerous heated debates in the public sphere. No matter if the adaptation was based on a text of the literary canon or on a contemporary novel or play, literature on film became a vehicle for these young filmmakers to examine contemporary society's deficits and the reasons for radicalization and violence in West Germany. The impact of adaptations, especially in the 1970s, was significant, as controversial issues raised in these films usually reached a sizable audience due to screenings of co-funded movies in cinemas and subsequently on television.

1982, the year of Fassbinder's untimely death, was a turning point. Thomas Mann's *Der Zauberberg* (The Magic Mountain, 1924), previously considered cinematically impregnable by directors such as Joseph Losey, Peter Zadek or Visconti, was adapted by Hans Werner Geißendörfer (FRG/AT/FR/IT, 1982), and his film not only tanked spectacularly, but became a platform for seething criticism of a cocky avant-garde's exploitation of complex literary works, funded by the taxpayer. Franz Seitz' adaptation of Mann's *Doktor Faustus* (FRG, 1982) faired only slightly better. But it was especially Herbert Achternbusch's *Das Gespenst* [The Ghost] (FRG, 1982) that scandalized bourgeois society in Bavaria and beyond. A media campaign in Axel Springer's tabloid *Bild* and the conservative weekly *Welt am Sonntag* in 1983 targeted film funding in the context of Achternbusch's Jesus-satire, and enabled the new federal Minister of the Interior, Friedrich Zimmermann of Bavaria's conservative CSU party, to present new government guidelines for film funding to the West German parliament.[196]

As *Der Spiegel* reported on January 2, 1984, social democrat Freimut Duve condemned those guidelines ("Richtlinien") as "Hinrichtungslinien," warning that Zimmermann's 'executionary course' would put an end to art cinema in the FRG. Under Zimmermann's guidance, the film political turn in the hands of a restructured funding commission ensured that 'intellectual shenanigans'[197] would no longer be financed by the taxpayer. Funding criteria now included 'public appeal' and 'economic promise.' Schlöndorff and Wenders left for the United States, but the future of aspiring auteurist filmmakers in the FRG suddenly looked a lot less promising.

Adaptations of German-language literature saw a sharp decline from the 1980s. The vast majority of remaining cinemagoers as well as television's mass audience were more interested in entertainment and glamour than in educational or intellectual art films. Overall, the era was still predominantly male; both literary canon and market were dominated by male authors and directors. Apart from Helma Sanders-Brahms and Margarethe von

Trotta, women filmmakers rarely turned to adaptation, avoiding the genre's potential obstruction of an authentic female voice.[198]

Nonetheless, New German Cinema offered a diverse film language inspired by writers that glanced unflinchingly at society's ills and its underlying systemic problems. During the 1960s and 1970s, young filmmakers looked to literature for experiences of coming-of-age and rebellion. From the early 1980s onwards, however, neoliberal economic practices in the industry quashed individualized impulses and instead prioritized bestsellers and encouraged transnational modes of production in order to reduce risk while maximizing available funds and potential profits. Lothar-Günther Buchheim's war novel *Das Boot* (The Boat, 1973) was promoted as 'a book like a tornado' and became a global bestseller within a few years despite its controversial focus on the Nazi's submarine war.[199] Günter Rohrbach saw the potential of the bestseller on screen and produced *Das Boot* (FRG, Wolfgang Petersen, 1981; TV mini-series 1985) with the financial support of public television SWR and WDR. The war film was a commercial hit due to the adaptation's high production value and Jost Vacano's superb cinematography that captures the claustrophobic space of the submarine and changing mood among its crew. Following its profitable first run in West Germany, the film was successfully distributed internationally by Columbia Pictures. In the context of *Das Boot*, Baer highlights the appropriation of "critical forces of art cinema" for neoliberal cinema and notes "the implications of the demise of art cinema, the so-called 'death of cinema,' along with the rise of television and digital culture, [...] must be understood in relation to global capitalism."[200]

This valid point will be explored further in the final chapter of this volume. While neoliberalism had a significant impact on adaptations of German-language literature as the following pages will outline, the genre continued to communicate sophistication and consequence. The relevance of literature and, by implication, adaptation for the public sphere may be illustrated in conclusion by *Die Geschwister Oppermann* (FRG/AT/CH, Egon Monk, 1983), a TV mini-series based on Lion Feuchtwanger's novel[201] about a bourgeois Jewish family during the rise of fascism in Germany and Hitler's empowerment in 1932/3. To mark the fiftieth anniversary of Hitler's appointment as Reich Chancellor, the first part of Monk's adaptation was screened at prime time. Nan Robertsen wrote in the *New York Times*:

> On Jan. 30, 1983, millions of Americans sat down before their television sets to immerse themselves in Superbowl Sunday. On the same day in Germany, millions of Germans sat down to watch *The Oppermanns*. The date marked the 50th anniversary of Adolf Hitler's accession to power. *The Oppermanns* is a film adaptation of the novel by Lion Feuchtwanger, one of the many Jewish artists who fled abroad from the Nazi threat. Set in Berlin during the winter of 1933, *The Oppermanns* tells of a sophisticated, successful, literate, assimilated Jewish family. Within

months, the Nazis had crushed the lives of them all and driven their brightest young hope to suicide.[202]

As times were changing in the FRG, the GDR's repressive cultural politics saw numerous writers, filmmakers, actors leave the country in the late 1970s. In addition to others mentioned above, writer Klaus Poche, and actors Armin Müller-Stahl and Jutta Hoffmann, for example, left the GDR after Frank Beyer's *Geschlossene Gesellschaft* (1978) was removed from public view after only one late-night screening. Numerous adaptation projects based on texts by contemporary GDR writers never saw the light of day. It was not until 1989, when the end of Honecker's socialist state was nigh, that Christa Wolf's *Selbstversuch* (Self-experiment, 1974) was considered for adaptation by East German television. By the time Peter Vogel's film about gender reassignment was broadcast on East and West Germany in January and May 1990 respectively, the process for German "reunification" was well underway. Konrad Wolf's aforementioned adaptation of Christa Wolf's novel *Der geteilte Himmel* [Divided Heaven] remains one of the most significant cinematic explorations of boundaries and division in the context of the construction of the Berlin Wall in 1961 and its consequences for individuals and the state.

During a time of neoliberal turns and political upheavals, literature continued to inspire cinema, if increasingly only in small independent productions. One of the most creative engagements with German-language poetry in the 1980s was Rosa von Praunheim's Anita Berber film project. In their 1988 film *Anita—Tänze des Lasters* [Anita: Dances of Vice] Praunheim—one of the German LGBTQ community's most prolific filmmakers since Fassbinder—not only created a montage of biographical events relating to Anita Berber and her then husband and creative collaborator Sebastian Droste but included poems and choreographies from Berber/Droste's book publication *Die Tänze des Lasters, des Grauens und der Ekstase* (The Dances of Vice/Depravity, Horror, and Ecstasy, 1923). Written and designed by Droste and Berber, the volume contains portrait drawings, photographs (from the d'Ora Studio in Vienna), Expressionist dance poems, manifestoes, and choreographies. In von Praunheim's film, Berber is an elderly woman who is institutionalized due to her unconventional behavior. The mad(wo)man, of course, plays a significant role in Expressionist literature (G. Heym *Der Irre* and numerous poems) and film (R. Wiene's *Das Cabinet des Dr Caligari*, 1920), and Praunheim takes his cue from one of Droste/Berber's dances called "Das Irrenhaus" [lunatic asylum], where elderly Berber is tied to a bed and has flashbacks of her glory days in 1920s Berlin. The choreography in the 1923 publication indicates that the dance started with lament and ended in destruction—a narrative structure Praunheim follows in his film. As in Expressionist literature, the marginalized individual here once again takes center stage.

The same year, Turkish director and Palme d'Or winner (1982 for *Yol*) Şerif Gören reimagined Zuckmayer's *Der Hauptmann von Köpenick* in West Berlin. His 1988 adaptation *Polizei* [Police] stars Turkish comedian Kemal Sunal as street sweeper Ali who joins a theater group and subsequently plays a policeman not only on- but off-stage, greatly cherishing the respect his new uniform affords. A "parody of ethnographic observation," as Göktürk[203] puts it, *Polizei* is a highly entertaining and insightful depiction of the (in)visibility of migrant workers in West Berlin, hybrid identities in former guest worker communities and, like its source text, mocks Germans' as well as Turkish-Germans' deference to authority. As these two last examples of adaptations indicate, by 1989, German cinema had become significantly more diverse and less somber, but not necessarily less rebellious.

Notes

1. "Phase der Vergangenheitsbewältigung"; Norbert Frei, *1945 und wir. Das Dritte Reich im Bewußtsein der Deutschen* (Munich: Beck, 2005), 26. This phase of acknowledging the crimes committed, of examining the structures and mechanisms that affected them, and of working through the guilt and shame is still ongoing. Cf. Susan Neiman, *Learning from the Germans. Race and the Memory of Evil* (New York: Macmillan, 2019), which is an excellent exploration of this ongoing phase of 'working through the past' in Germany in view of the United States' history of slavery and racism.
2. In my interview with Volker Schlöndorff via zoom on October 6, 2020, the director explained how literary texts provided the 'model' for German cinema's ability to address the past.
3. Nonetheless, a steady decline followed once again, reaching 102 million, the lowest number recorded in 1989. Statistics accessed at http://www.spio.de/?seitid=381&tid=3]: SPIO; Filmförderungsanstalt (FFA); Bundesverband Audiovisuelle Medien e.V.; Bundesamt für Wirtschaft: Filmexport und— import. A renewed interest in cinema in the late 1970s pushed ticket sales to 144 million in 1980, but this recovery could not be sustained for long. By 1989, ticket sales were back down to 102 million per year. At the same time, the population of the FRG had grown to 62 million.
4. According to the minutes of the 8th SED party congress in Berlin, June 1971.
5. Seán Allan's and John Sandford's work was essential in this context, beginning with their edited volume *DEFA, East German Cinema 1946–1992* (Oxford: Berghahn, 1999). See also Sabine Hake's excellent summary of "East German cinema 1961–1990" in her *German National Cinema*, 127–52; Claudia Sandberg's "DEFA—Desires, Possibilities, and Limitations," in *The German Cinema Book*, ed. T. Bergfelder, E. Carter, D. Göktürk and C. Sandberg (London: BFI, 2020), 297–300; David Clarke's "Constructing Victimhood in Divided Germany," *Memory Studies* 11.4 (2018): 422–36, and "Remembering National Socialism in the German Democratic Republic," in *A Companion to*

Nazi Germany, ed. S. Baranowski et al. (Hoboken, NJ; Chichester: Wiley-Blackwell, 2018), 599–613. Cf. also digitalized content made available by the DEFA foundation at https://www.defa-stiftung.de/en/.

6 For example, Herbert Ballmann's children's film *Tinko* (1957) based on Erwin Strittmatter's eponymous youth novel, Konrad Wolf's 1964 adaptation of Christa Wolf's novel *Der geteilte Himmel* (Divided Heaven, 1963) that highlights ideological divisions that impact directly on the lives of individuals even prior to the construction of the Berlin Wall, the Barlach-film *Der verlorene Engel* [The Lost Angel] (GDR, Ralf Kirsten, 1966), based on Franz Fühmann's novella *Ernst Barlach. Das schlimme Jahr* (E.B.: A Bad Year, 1963), to Horst Seemann's 1980 adaptation of Johannes Bobrowski's *Levins Mühle* (Levin's Mill, 1964), *Unser kurzes Leben* [Our Short Life], Lothar Warneke's 1981 adaptation of late Brigitte Reimann's novel *Franziska Linkerhand* (1974/98), Roland Gräf's 1982 tragicomedy *Märkische Forschungen*, based on Günter de Bruyn's bitter satire about the arrogance of the powerful (1978), etc.

7 Jean-Paul Sartre, *Qu'est que la littérature?* (Paris: Gallimard, 1948).

8 Koeppen's novels *Tauben im Grass* [Pigeons on the Grass], *Treibhaus* [The Hothouse], *Tod in Rom* [Death in Rome].

9 The affair was remembered by Amy Davidson Sorkin in her article "When Journalists Are Called Traitors" in the context of Edward Snowden and the NSA affair. See *The New Yorker* (October 11, 2013) at https://www.newyorker.com/news/amy-davidson/when-journalists-are-called-traitors.

10 Habermas' "Habilitationsschrift" (a second doctoral thesis required for a career as Professor in Germany) *Strukturwandel der Öffentlichkeit* examines the development and erosion of the 'public sphere.'

11 Jürgen Habermas, *The Structural Transformation of the Public Sphere*, trans. Thomas Burger et al. (Cambridge, MA: MIT, 1991), 45.

12 Cf. Böll's lectures given at Frankfurt/Main University during the summer semester of 1964; "Frankfurter Vorlesungen: Zur Ästhetik des Humanen in der Literatur," in Heinrich Böll, *Werke*, vol. 14 (Cologne: Kiepenheuer & Witsch, 2002). See also Manfred Lange, "Ästhetik des Humanen. Das literarische Programm Heinrich Bölls," in *Heinrich Böll* (Munich: text+kritik, 1982), 89–98.

13 For an insightful summary of the era, see Sabine Hake, "West German cinema 1962–1990," *German National Cinema*, 153–89.

14 Despite Eric Rentschler's efforts in the 1980s, it was not until recently that scholars such as Tim Bergfelder, Jaimey Fisher, and Hester Baer in particular began to explore the impact of adaptation as a genre in more detail. See Bergfelder, *International Adventures: German Popular Cinema and European Co-productions in the 1960s*, 85; highlights Constantin's "[s]equelisation of one-off box-office hits and the creation of generic cyles"; Hester Baer, "Producing Adaptations: Bernd Eichinger, *Christiane F.*, and German Film History," in *Generic Histories of German Cinema: Genre and Its Deviations*, ed. Jaimey Fisher (Rochester: Camden House, 2013), 173–96.

15 *The Trial* triggered a number of further Kafka-adaptations and deserves more attention than this chapter can provide. Productions for cinema include *Ein Brudermord* (FRG, Lothar Elsässer, 1967), *Das Schloß* (FRG, Rudolf Noelte,

1968), and *Klassenverhältnisse* (FRG, Danièle Huillet and Jean-Marie Straub, 1983). For television, productions included *Amerika oder Der Verschollene* (FRG, Zbynek Brynych, 1969), *Die Verwandlung* (FRG/AT, Jan Němec, 1975), and the outstanding Michael Haneke's *Das Schloss* (AT, 1997). See also TV series "Literarische Filmerzählung" [Literary Filmstory] produced by regional public television stations from 1965; Max Frisch's *Skizze eines Unglücks* (FRG, Hilde Bechert, 1984).

16 "Filming The Trial"; https://www.youtube.com/watch?v=n8BR034qDsk.
17 François Truffaut, "La politique des auteurs" (1954); see Marco Grosoli, "The Politics and Aesthetics of the 'politique des auteurs'," *Film Criticism* 39.1 (2014): 33–50.
18 As Welles outlines in the same interview, he cut an entire scene illustrating man's "slavish relationship" with the 'machine' on the afternoon of the opening night. For further information, see Anne-Marie Scholz, *From Fidelity to History: Film Adaptations as Cultural Events in the Twentieth Century* (New York: Berghahn, 2013), 93–116.
19 See Joachim Paech, ed., *Literatur und Film: Mephisto* (Frankfurt/M.: Diesterweg, 1984); Karina von Lindeiner-Strásky, *Die Mehrfarbigkeit der Vergangenheit: István Szabós Adaptation von Klaus Manns Roman 'Mephisto'* (Würzburg: Königshausen & Neumann, 2013).
20 Also nominated that year was the Swiss film *Das Bootist voll* [The boat is full] (CH, Markus Imhoof, 1980) based on the eponymous publication about refugees by Swiss author Alfred A. Häsler.
21 Theodore Ziolkowski's publications trace Hesse's rise in the United States; see "Saint Hesse among the Hippies," *American-German Review* 35.2 (1969): 19–23; "Hesse's Sudden Popularity with Today's Students," *University: A Princeton Quarterly* 45 (1970): 19–25; "Hesse and Film: The Seduction of a Generation," *Chronicle of Higher Education Review* (October 1, 1973): 9; "Cultivating Hesse," *Times Literary Supplement* (August 31, 1973): 989–91. For a critical reading of these texts and others, see Jefford Vahlbusch, "Toward the Legend of Hermann Hesse in the USA," *Hermann Hesse Today*, ed. Ingo Cornils and Osman Durrani (Amsterdam: Rodopi, 2005), 133–46.
22 Lawrence van Gelder, "'Steppenwolf' Emerges Dimly from Printed Page: The Cast," *The New York Times* (December 19, 1974): 60: "animation, Daliesque art, television superimpositions and color synthesizers."
23 Two further adaptations followed in the twenty-first century: Hesse's poem "Ich weiß von solchen …" in Ralf Schmerberg's film *Poem* (2003), and Stefan Ruzowitzky's *Narziss und Goldmund* (2020). Cf. the final chapter.
24 van Gelder, "'Steppenwolf' Emerges Dimly," 60.
25 According to Visconti, he wanted to depict 'the jarring conflict between art and life in an aging artist'; cf. Visconti, "Ich, Luchino Visconti," *Götterdämmerung. Luchino Viscontis deutsche Trilogie* (Berlin: Stiftung deutsche Kinemathek, 2003), 18. In his Morte a Venezia Visconti recounts the influence of German literature from Goethe and Schiller to Thomas Mann on his work and emphasizes that he considered Thomas Mann 'one of us'—one of the European 'Décadent' (Ibid., 20)—a label he proudly accepted for himself.

26 Richard Neupert, *A History of the French New Wave Cinema* (Madison: University of Wisconsin Press, 2002), 255.
27 Eric Rohmer *Six contes moraux* (Paris: Cahier du cinema, [1974] 1998), 6f. In his afterword to *The Marquise of O-: Film by Eric Rohmer, Story by Heinrich von Kleist* (New York: Ungar, 1985), Alan Spiegel writes that Rohmer "spent four years learning German in order to film the text in its original language with a cast of German actors." Spiegel, "The Marquise," 125–37, here p. 126.
28 In 1999, the novella was once again adapted, this time into an American Western by Dick Cusack, who wrote the script for *The Jack Bull* (US, John Badham, 1999). Featuring a *Black Beauty* and *Little House on the Prairie* aesthetic, the film stars his son John Cusack as decent and law-abiding horse trader Myrl Redding, who fights for his rights in a climate of corruption and injustice as Wyoming was being admitted into the Union in 1890.
29 Semenza and Hasenfratz, *The History of British Literature on Film*, 256. For a very useful summary of the impact of auteur theory and Truffaut's "A Certain Tendency" essay, see 255–7.
30 Edward Buscombe, "Ideas of Authorship," *Screen* 14.3 (1973): 76; quoted in Semenza and Hasenfratz, *The History of British Literature on Film*, 257.
31 Semenza and Hasenfratz, *The History of British Literature on Film*, 256.
32 In German-language countries, the focus shifted from antiwar films to the victims of Hitler's reign, which included Wehrmacht soldiers (cf. Theodor Plivier's novel *Stalingrad*, which was adapted for television by Claus Hubalek, dir. Gustav Burmester, 1963) until Wolfgang Petersen created an international box-office sensation with his adaptation of Lothar-Günther Buchheim's 1973 novel *Das Boot* (FRG, 1981).
33 Remakes based on post-World War I adaptations include the Jewish writer Georg Hermann, who was murdered in Auschwitz in 1943: *Kubinke* (FRG, R. A. Stemmle, 1966); *Jettchen Geberts Geschichte* (FRG, Reinhard Baumgart, 1978); *Grenadier Wordelmann* (GDR, Hans-Joachim Hildebrandt, 1980).
34 Most critics attacked this remake of the mythical tale for its evocation of male heroism and Germanic exceptionalism, but the masses flocked to cinemas once again (over 3 million cinema tickets were sold in the FRG in the first eighteen months alone). Not an actor by training, the Olympian had to be dubbed before the film could be released.
35 By 1966, that number had reduced by half once again to a little over 200 million. Production had fallen from 123 films in 1956 to 80 films in 1961 according to http://www.deutsches-filmhaus.de/chr_kino/ch_61.htm; these numbers match those mentioned in "Mattscheibe kontra Flimmerkiste: Die 'Krise' der deutschen Film Wirtschaft" in *Die Zeit* (May 27, 1960); Prinzler's estimates are slightly lower in *Chronik des deutschen Films*, 208 and 252; Zander, *Thomas Mann im Kino*, 79. DEFA produced twenty-five feature films in 1961.
36 During this period, television licenses in West Germany amounted to approx. 2 million in the mid-1950s to over 7 million five years later. Norbert Grob, Hans-Helmut Prinzler, and Eric Rentschler, *Neuer Deutscher Film* (Stuttgart: Reclam, 2012), 12. West German feature film productions for cinema fell from more than 120 in 1956 to sixty-four. In the years to come, West Germany produced between forty-nine (1980) and sixty-nine (1964); in East Germany,

DEFA's production of feature films fluctuated between twenty-five in 1962 and fourteen in 1989.

37 The financial situation of the company had become so dire, that "the UFA voted to cease theatrical film production and distribution altogether, reducing the once proud firm to a small chain of movie houses" [http://www.referenceforbusiness.com/history2/96/UFA-TV-Film-Produktion-GmbH.html]. Ufa was bought by the Bertelsmann group in 1964.

38 West German television could be received in most of East Germany. It was illegal for members of the police or military to tune into "Westfernsehen" or 'western telly.' For the large majority of the public, watching West German television was ideologically suspect, but not illegal.

39 Not unlike the use and effect of literature on film during the first decades of cinema.

40 *Gong* 15 (1962): 33.

41 Lupus, "Biberpelz und Roter Hahn an zwei Abenden," *Die Zeit* (April 6, 1962); https://www.zeit.de/1962/14/biberpelz-und-roter-hahn-an-zwei-abenden.

42 Cf. Andersch's *Sansibar oder der letzte Grund* (FRG, Bernhard Wicki, 1987); *Der Vater eines Mörders* (FRG, Carlheinz Caspari, 1987); Martin Walser's *Ein fliehendes Pferd* (FRG, Peter Beauvais, 1986); etc.

43 Following *The Parent Trap* (USA, David Swift, 1961), an adaptation of *Das doppelte Lottchen,* Kästner adaptations included *Liebe will gelernt sein* (FRG, Kurt Hoffmann, 1962), *Konferenz der Tiere* (FRG, Curt Linda, 1969), *Das fliegende Klassenzimmer* (FRG, Werner Jacobs, 1973), *Drei Männer im Schnee* (FRG, Alfred Vohrer, 1974), *Fabian* (FRG, Wolf Gremm, 1979), *Die verschwundene Miniatur* (GDR, Vera Loebner, 1989).

44 Pre-war popular literary texts were also (re)adapted for television. For example, a series of five of Hedwig Courths-Mahler's novels—*Die Bettelprinzeß* (Impoverished Princess, 1914), *Die Kriegsbraut* (War Bride, 1915), *Griseldis* (1917), *Eine ungeliebte Frau* (A Woman Unloved, 1918), *Der Scheingemahl* (Pretend Husband, 1919)—were adapted by Süddeutscher Rundfunk (SDR)/ARD. Their series of adaptations proved highly popular with viewers even though critics panned them as "Kitsch à la mode." See *Der Spiegel* 15 (1974): https://www.spiegel.de/kultur/oh-von-hedwig-a-2b123ebb-0002-0001-0000-000041751336.

45 The reception of adaptations of contemporary literature indicates the significance of the genre regarding critical assessments of the Second World War in the public sphere during this era: F. Dürrenmatt's *Die Physiker* (FRG, F. Umgelter 1962), Grass' *Katz und Maus* (FRG, Hansjürgen Pohland, 1967), F.-J. Degenhardt's novels *Zündschnüre* (FRG, R. Hauff, 1974) and *Brandstellen* (GDR, H. E. Brandt, 1978), A. Andersch's *Winterspelt* (FRG, E. Fechner, 1976), but also of *Das Boot* (1981). Dieter Noll's *Die Abenteuer des Werner Holt* (Adventures of W.H., 2 vols., 1960 and 1963) became one of the most popular antiwar films (DEFA, J. Kunert, 1964); also of interest in this context: Anna Seghers' *Die Toten bleiben jung* (The Dead Stay Young, 1949) (GDR TV, J. Kunert, 1968; Christa Wolf co-wrote the script); and Hermann Kant's *Der Aufenthalt* (F. Beyer, 1983).

46 In addition, several Curt Goetz adaptations were produced for television. Kurt Hoffmann's adaptations of Kurt Tucholsky's *Schloss Gripsholm* (FRG, 1963) and *Rheinsberg* (FRG, 1967) were produced for cinema, but soon made regular and much appreciated appearances on the small screen, just like many of the adaptations produced during the 1950s mentioned in the previous chapter. Similarly, adaptations of Vicki Baum's novels became popular on West German television; the only novel adapted to cinema was *Rendezvous in Paris* (FRG/FR, Gabi Kubach, 1982).

47 Narrated by Marlene Dietrich, Stouman's film uses documentary footage of the Second World War and Holocaust, Leni Riefenstahl's *Triumph of the Will*, as well as drawings and etchings that had from the nineteenth century illustrated Goethe's world of anthropomorphic animals. They suffer the sly fox's lies and crimes and still fall into his traps and become complicit. Creating a parallel structure, Stoumen uses Goethe's poem as a parable or scaffold by which to unveil Hitler's trajectory step by step. He won the Academy Award for Best Documentary Feature in 1962.

48 *Jim Knopf* adaptations by the Augsburger Puppenkiste began in 1961 with the black-and-white *Jim Knopf und der Lokomotivführer* [Jim Button and Luke the Engine Driver], a series repeated regularly due to popular demand throughout the next decade. The series was reshot in color in 1976–7. Adaptations of Ende's works also include cinema productions such the English-language adaptation of *Unendliche Geschichte* as *The Neverending Story* (FRG, Wolfgang Petersen, 1984; Michael Ende was unhappy about the melodramatic kitsch his book was being turned into and tried to halt the production or have at least the title changed, and eventually sued producers Neue Constantin and Bavaria, but lost); *Momo* (FRG/IT, Johannes Schaaf, 1985); and a life-action adaptation of *Jim Knopf und Lukas der Lokomotivführer* (FRG, Dennis Gansel, 2016/17).

49 In this context, see also Else Ury's *Nesthäkchen* [lit. nestling/baby of the family]. The first three volumes of this book series for teenage girls (orig. published 1913–25) were adapted by Gero Erhardt for ZDF in 1983. Despite her fame, the Jewish author was deported during the Nazi era, and murdered by Hitler's henchmen in Auschwitz in 1943.

50 Preußler's children's book *Räuber Hotzenplotz* was first adapted in 1967 by the aforementioned Augsburger Puppenkiste as a televised puppet show. A life-action adaptation with Gert Fröbe as the robber followed (FRG, Gustav Ehmck, 1974), with a sequel launched with a new cast in 1979. According to Wikipedia, an animated adaptation of Preußler's tale entitled 大盗贼 [The Big Robber] (China, Fang Run Nan, 1989) was produced in Shanghai. Krüss' novel *Timm Thaler oder Das verkaufte Lachen* (Timm Thaler or the Traded Laughter, 1962) became one of the most successful of West Germany's second public television channel ZDF's Christmas series (13 parts, Sigi Rothemund, 1979), turning Thomas Ohrner into a teen idol. The novel was adapted to film by Russian television in 1981. An adaptation for cinema was directed by Andreas Dresen (FRG, 2017).

51 Cf. Anke Pinkert's reading of Konrad Wolf's *Ich war neunzehn* [I Was Nineteen] (1968) and Jürgen Böttcher's *Jahrgang '45* [Born in '45] (1965),

or Manuel Köppen's essay on "Emplotting Antifascism," in *DEFA at the Crossroads of East German and International Film Culture*, ed. Marc Silberman and Henning Wrage (Boston: deGruyter, 2014), 107–32 and 45–66 respectively. The following adaptation for television of antifascist writers such as Johannes R. Becher [*Das Führerbild* as *Der Weg nach Füssen*, Fritz Bornemann, 1962; *Die Winterschlacht* (Fritz Bornemann, 1963); *Abschied* (Egon Günther, 1968)], or Otto Gotsche [*Das Lied vom Trompeter* (Konrad Petzold, 1964); *Tiefe Furchen* (Lutz Köhlert, 1965); *Die Fahne von Kriwoj Rog* (Kurt Maetzig, 1967)] would be of particular interest in this context.

52 Seán Allen and John Sandford, eds., *DEFA. East German Cinema 1946–1992* (Oxford: Berghahn, 1999); Silberman and Wrage, eds., *DEFA at the Crossroads of East German and International Film Culture*, 2014.

53 In his insightful discussion of Beyer's *Spur der Steine*, Stephen Brockmann embeds the 11th plenum's cultural intervention in the GDR's economic and political difficulties at the time as well as Honecker and his hard-line Politburo allies' implicit criticism of his rival Walter Ulbricht's New Economic System. See Brockmann, *Critical History of German Film*, 247–57.

54 Hermann Ernst Schauer, "Adaptationsprobleme des literarischen Erbes," in *Sozialistisches Menschenbild und Filmkunst* (Berlin: Henschel, 1970), 307; also quoted in William Walker, "GDR Film in Cultural Context," *Unterrichtspraxis* 15.2 (1982): 194–206, here p. 204.

55 For example, Walker writes, "the role of the women in each film is crucial to understanding the essential function of women in the creation of a socialist society and the definition of women within the contet of the socialist personality." Cf. Walker, "GDR Film in Cultural Context," 204.

56 Bill Niven, *The Buchenwald Child. Truth, Fiction, and Propaganda* (Rochester: Camden House, 2007); also useful in this context: Dagmar Schittly, "DDR-Alltag im Film. Verbotene und zensierte Spielfilme der DEFA," *Aus Politik und Zeitgeschichte* B17 (2002): 23–9; and Schittly's PhD thesis *Zwischen Regie und Regime. Die Filmpolitik der SED im Spiegel der DEFA-Produktionen* (Berlin: Links, 2002). Apitz's 1958 novel had already been adapted for television (GDR, Georg Leopold, 1960); another adaptation followed in 2015 under the direction of Philipp Kadelbach, produced by Nico Hofmann.

57 Heiner Müller wrote the adaptation entitled *Der Bau* for Deutsches Theater in Berlin in 1964/65. The play is a parable that traces Neutsch's text back to Kafka. The play begins with a question—'Why are you destroying the foundations?'—which clearly refers to the destruction of a socialist utopia by GDR politics.

58 I'm referring to Brockmann's translated passage from Beyer's autobiography here. Brockmann, *Critical History of German Film*, 256.

59 Ibid.

60 See, for example, Gotthold Ephraim Lessing (beginning with Martin Hellberg's DEFA feature *Minna von Barnhelm* in 1962), Friedrich Schiller [for television: *Wallenstein I & II* (FRG, Franz Peter Wirth, 1962); *Maria Stuart* (FRG, Hans Lietzau, 1963); *Don Carlos, Infant von Spanien* (FRG, Franz Peter Wirth, 1963); *Kabale und Liebe* (AT, Erich Neuberg, 1965); *Kabale und Liebe* (FRG, Gerhard Klingenberg, 1967); *Carlos* (FRG, Hans W. Geissendörfer, 1971); *Kabale und Liebe* (FRG, Heinz Schirk, 1980); *Die Räuber* (GDR, Celino

Bleiweiß, 1982); *Kabale und Liebe* (GDR, Piet Drescher, 1982); *Turandot* (GDR, Anne Eikke, 1984); *Maria Stuart* (FRG, Heinz Schirk, 1986); *Die Verschwörung des Fiesco zu Genua* (FRG, Franz Peter Wirth, 1986), and *Wallenstein* (FRG, Franz Peter Wirth, 1987)]; for cinema: Schiller's *Braut von Messina* as *Chamsin* (FRG, Veit Relin, 1970); Wolf Gremm's adaptation of *The Robbers* as *Tod oder Freiheit* (FRG, 1978); in the GDR: Rainer Bär's *Der Geisterseher* (GDR, 1987).

61 For example, Prussian representatives (Bismarck) and virtues (militarism, authoritarianism) are portrayed critically, but Roswitha is emphasized as particularly positive: as Effi's true friend and representative of exemplary (classless) humanity.

62 See for example Ulrike Schwab, *Erzähltext und Spielfilm. Zur Ästhetik und Analyse der Filmadaption* (Berlin: LIT, 2006), 276.

63 František Pavlíček wrote the script based on Božena Němcová's eponymous story. Cf. *Lexikon des internationalen Films*, available online via https://www.filmdienst.de. The most popular film that year, however, was *Die Legende von Paul und Paula* [The Legend of Paul and Paula] (GDR, Heiner Carow, 1973), a passionate, tragic love story that featured the East German rock band The Puhdys. Ulrich Plenzdorf's novel, which was based on his script for the film, subsequently became a bestseller.

64 Events like Willy Brandt's speechlessly falling on his knees in front of the Warsaw ghetto memorial during the FRG's first official visit to Poland in 1970, and the United Nation's membership of both GDR and FRG in 1973, contributed to the easing of tensions and, as Hake points out, an increased political confidence within East Germany. Hake, *Film in Deutschland*, 230.

65 Hake, *Film in Deutschland*, 230.

66 For further information see Frank Stern, "Visualizing Aufklärung," and Seán Allan, "'Der arge Weg der Erkenntnis': Konrad Wolf's *Goya* and its Relation to GDR Cultural Policy and the DEFA *Künstlerfilm*," in *Feuchtwanger and Film*, ed. Ian Wallace, 5–20 and 21–39.

67 Seán Allan, "Representations of Art and the Artist in East German Cinema," in *DEFA at the Crossroads of East German and International Film Culture*, 89–105, here 97 and 98. See also Larson Powell, "Breaking the Frame of Painting. Konrad Wolf's *Goya*," *Studies in European Cinema* 5.2 (2009): 131–41; Sebastian Heiduschke, *East German Cinema. DEFA and Film History* (New York: Palgrave, 2013).

68 See Ian Wallace, ed., *Feuchtwanger and Film* (Bern: Lang, 2009). Further Feuchtwanger adaptations followed: *Exil* (FRG/FR, Egon Günther, 1981), *Die Geschwister Oppermann* (FRG, Egon Monk, 1983), and *Narrenweisheit oder Tod und Verklärung des Jean Jacques Rousseau* (GDR, Jurij Kramer, 1989).

69 Heiduschke, *East German Cinema*, 107–13.

70 Günther's Thomas Mann adaptation was followed by *Die Leiden des jungen Werther* (GDR, Egon Günther, 1976), a costume drama starring Katharina Thalbach as Lotte, which conveys Goethe's epistolary novel in flashback induced by the couple's love letters.

71 Burkhard Olschowsky outlines the political complexities of the DEFA production in "Der DEFA-Film *Der Aufenthalt* und seine Rezeption in Polen,"

in *DEFA International*, ed. Michael Wedel et al. (Wiesbaden: Springer, 2013), 421–31.
72 Egon Günther was a writer in his own right. Most notably, his novel *Die schwarze Limousine* was adapted and directed by Konrad Petzold for DEFA as *Jetzt und in der Stunde meines Todes* (GDR, 1963). The narrative evolves with the Eichmann trial as backdrop. Cf. also Allan, in *DEFA at the Crossroads*, 177–96.
73 "Wolf Biermann ist ein unbequemer Dichter" is the first sentence of the letter of protest written by members of Berlin's creative community on November 17, 1976.
74 Umgelter worked for the federal state of Hesse's public broadcasting corporation Hessischer Rundfunk (Hesse Broadcasting; HR). His body of work of the time included a range of adaptations from children's books (Augsburger Puppenkiste) to Schiller's *Die Räuber*.
75 Constantin profited tremendously from the Karl May films and became Germany's top distributor until the company went bankrupt in 1977; it was revived by Bernd Eichinger as Neue Constantin in 1979.
76 Wilhelm Kosch, *Deutsches Literatur-Lexikon* (Bern: Francke, 1963), 268f.; quoted in Colleen Cook, "Germany's Wild West Author: A Researcher's Guide to Karl May," *German Studies Review* 5.1 (1982): 67–86, here p. 67.
77 Bergfelder, *International Adventures: German Popular Cinema and European Co-Productions*, 184.
78 Following the breakup of his marriage with Lana Turner, who had been told about his sexual abuse of her thirteen-year-old daughter Cheryl (cf. Cheryl Crane's *Detour: A Hollywood Story*), Barker moved to Europe, where he starred in *The Strange Awakening* (GB, Montgomery Tully, 1958), *Captain Fuoco* (IT/FR, Carlo Campogalliani, 1958) and, to name but one more, the aptly titled *La scimitarra del Saraceno* [The Pirate and the Slave Girl] (IT, Piero Pierotti, 1959), before moving to Germany to work with Reinl and appearing in his *Dr. Mabuse*-sequels before successfully reinventing himself as morally upstanding Old Shatterhand.
79 Bergfelder provides much intriguing and useful further information in his *International Adventures: German Popular Cinema and European Co-Productions*. He summarizes the films' narrative formula: "peace between Indians and white settlers is threatened by the evildoing of white racketters [...]. Old Shatterhald and Winnetou intervene and rescue the victims, often with the help of friendly Indians. The villains meet a horrible death (however, in order to preserve the heroes' saintly and pacifist credentials, villains usually perish in convenient accidents or kill themselves), and fire or explosions destroy their hide-outs. Old Shatterhand and Winnetou pontificate about their values of nature, peace, and friendship and then ride into the sunset." (185).
80 Heiduschke, *East German Cinema*, 93–105, here 95.
81 Jon Randaulen, "Spotlight: Indianerfilme," *The German Cinema Book*, 37–8. See also Gerd Gmünden, "Between Karl May and Karl Marx: The DEFA Indianerfilme (1965–1983)," *Film History* 10.3 (1998): 399–407; Friedrich von Borries and Jens-Uwe Fischer, *Sozialistische Cowboys. Der Wilde Westen Ostdeutschlands* (Frankfurt/M.: Suhrkamp, 2008); Thomas Kramer, *Heiner Müller am Marterpfahl* (Bielefeld: Aisthesis, 2006). The next "Indianerfilm"

Chingachgook, die große Schlange [Chingachgook, the Great Snake] (GDR, Richard Groschopp, 1967) was loosely based on James Fenimore Cooper's *Leatherstocking Tales*. Further "Indianerfilme" were based on orinial scripts, by Günter Karl and others, but also by the films' star Gojko Mitić himself.

82 In this context, film- and theater director Daniel Schmid is of interest. He had acted in films by Fassbinder (*Händler der vier Jahreszeiten, Lili Marleen*) and Wenders (*Der amerikanische Freund*), and directed Rossini's opera *Guglielmo Tell*, based on Friedrich Schiller's play for Swiss television in 1988.

83 Corrigan, "Literature on Screen," 36.

84 Eric Rentschler, "February 28, 1962: Oberhausen Manifesto Creates Founding Myth for New German Cinema," in *A New History of German Cinema*, ed. Kapczynski/ Richardson, 394–9, here p. 394.

85 Ibid.

86 Producer Kurt Ulrich, who had great hopes for a remake of Brecht/ Hauptmann/Weill's *Threepenny Opera,* considered first Käutner as director before deciding on Staudte. The original plan to change the time of the narrative to West Germany in the 1950s was thwarted by Helene Weigel's opposition, who had inherited the rights with Weill's widow Lotte Lenya, and demanded a 'faithful' adaptation. Despite stars like Curd Jürgens, Hildegard Knef, Gerd Fröbe, and (for the US release) Sammy Davis Jr., the German-French co-production was panned by critics when it was released in 1963. Another adaptation by Israeli (action) filmmaker Menahem Golan (*Mack the Knife*; US/H/NL, 1989) fared no better.

87 See the title of Rentschler's 2012 article quoted in note 84.

88 "verdonnert"; see Susanne Fuhrmann and Heinrich Lewinski, "Poesie ist das, was bleibt. Der Filmregisseur Herbert Vesely im Gespräch," *filmwärts* 27 (1993): 7.

89 Billinger's *Auf Wiedersehen am blauen Meer* [Farewell at the Blue Sea] (FRG, Helmut Weiß, 1962) was entitled *Manuela und der Förster* [M. and the forest ranger] in Austria; the romance was filmed in the Swiss Alps and in Italy and concludes with the reunited couples return to their homeland in the mountains, where decency is still possible and thus happiness will prevail.

90 Wedekind-adaptations for television followed in 1962, 1965, 1972, and 1979.

91 As Zander points out; Zander, *Thomas Mann im Kino*, 80.

92 *Das kleine Fernsehspiel* still provides support and a forum for young filmmakers, having supported outstanding talent in the more recent past such as Christian Petzold, Fatih Akin, Tom Tykwer, Sandra Nettelbeck, Valeska Grisebach, Burhan Qurbani, etc. In the 1970s, it was a vital in terms of financial support and media outlet for women directors Helke Sander, Jutta Brückner, Uschi Reich, Monika Funke-Stern, Elfi Mikesch, Chantal Akerman, Ulrike Ottinger, etc. Cf. Knut Hickethier, *Geschichte des deutschen Fernsehen* (Stuttgart: Metzler, 1998), 348f.; see also See Thomas Elsaesser, "Television and the Author's Cinema: ZDF's Das kleine Fernsehspiel," in his *European Cinema: Face to Face with Hollywood* (Amsterdam: Amsterdam University Press, 2005), 212–18.

93 Hans Rolf Strobel, "Deutschlands Film ist ohne Väter," *Die Zeit* 24 (1964), accessed online via *Die Zeit* archive at https://www.zeit.de/1964/24/deutschlands-film-ist-ohne-vaeter.

94 T. W. Adorno, "Kulturkritik und Gesellschaft," in *Prismen. Kulturkritik und Gesellschaft* (Munich: dtv, 1963), 7–26. As Klaus Hofmann and others have noted, Adorno's essay was originally published in 1951 in *Soziologische Forschung in unserer Zeit* and reprinted in *Prismen* in 1955. For further context, see Klaus Hofmann, "Poetry after Auschwitz—Adorno's Dictum," *German Life and Letters* 58.2 (2005): 182–94.

95 Eichmann trial (1961–2), Ulm Einsatzkommando trial (1958), Auschwitz trial (1963–5).

96 *Hörzu* 16 (1966): 61; quoted at http://krimiserien.heimat.eu/fernsehspiele/fernsehspiele/19660329ard-dieermittlung.htm. The theater-film was broadcast three more times in 1967, 1970, 1979. When the film was shown in 1979, the moderator introduced the film as 'a play one has to face up to.'

97 For example, Joachim Kaiser in *Süddeutsche Zeitung* (September 4, 1965). Cf. Robert Cohen, "The Political Aesthetics of Holocaust Literature: Peter Weiss's *The Investigation* and Its Critics," *History and Memory* 10.2 (1998): 43–67.

98 Volker Schlöndorff, *Licht, Schatten und Bewegung. Mein Leben und meine Filme* (Munich: Hanser, 2008), 133.

99 Franz Seitz was a successful producer of *Heimat*-Kitsch, Ludwig Anzengruber-adaptations, and Ludwig Thoma's *Lausbubengeschichten* (FRG, Helmut Käutner, 1964; sequel: Werner Jacobs, 1965), but also Erich Kästner's *Das fliegende Klassenzimmer* [The Flying Classroom] (FRG, Werner Jacobs, 1973) and Günter Grass' *Die Blechtrommel* [The Tin Drum] (FRG, Volker Schlöndorff, 1979). He was particular to Thomas Mann and produced adaptations of *Wälsungenblut* [The Blood of the Walsungs] (FRG, Rolf Thiele, 1964), *Unordnung und frühes Leid* [Disorder and Early Sorrow] (FRG, Franz Seitz, 1977), and *Der Zauberberg* [The Magic Mountain] (FRG, Hans W. Geißendörfer, 1982). Seitz also adapted Mann's *Doktor Faustus* (FRG, Franz Seitz, 1982) which tanked due to the complexity of the novel, and a montage technique, which included inserting documentary footage (clips from newsreels, Heimat-films, and soft-porn).

100 Semenza and Hasenfratz, *History of British Literature on Film*, 258ff.

101 Wolf Donner, "Geld für die Braven. Minister Benda und der deutsche Film," *Die Zeit* 28 (July 11, 1969); https://www.zeit.de/1969/28/geld-fuer-die-braven. This paragraph is based on his article.

102 Donner, "Geld für die Braven," 2.

103 Ibid.

104 Wolf Donner, "Für ein besseres Kino," *Die Zeit* 12 (1970): https://www.zeit.de/1970/12/fuer-ein-besseres-kino.

105 Kubaschewski was also responsible for a number of adaptations and remakes that were turned into superficial entertainment cinema for good profit, like Schnitzler's *Der Reigen* as a suggestive farce (AT/FRG, Otto Schenk, 1973), which she co-produced with Karl Spiehs.

106 George Moorse was a young American working in West-Berlin. He won a national film award for his short film IN-SIDE-OUT (1964, produced by Literarisches Colloquium Berlin), and wrote and directed adaptations of Heinrich von Kleist's novella *Der Findling* [The Foundling] (1967) and of Georg Büchner's *Lenz* (1971) for West German television. His innovative and

experimental film language was commended at the time, and he is regarded as an important contributor to 'young German film' or New German Cinema, as it was later called.

107 Kurt Nachmann wrote and directed two sequels: *Mutzenbacher II– Meine 365 Liebhaber* [My 365 Lovers] (1971) and *Auch Fummeln will gelernt sein* [Even Groping Must be Learned] (1972). A porn film *Josefine Mutzenbacher—Wie sie wirklich war* (FRG, Hans Billian, 1976) repeated previous successes and ensured further productions within the genre. Even more profitable proved the 'reports' based on Günther Hunold's publications about teenagers' first sexual experiences (inspired by reports of the 1960s by Kinsey and Masters/Johnson), which saw a total twelve sequels to the original *Schulmädchen*-Report within the decade. These adaptations became global hits and are arguably at least commercially the most successful German films to date. Cf. Rudolf Novotny, "40 Jahre Schulmädchenreport," *Frankfurter Rundschau*, January 24, 2019.
108 https://www.bpb.de/gesellschaft/medien-und-sport/deutsche-fernsehgeschichte-in-ost-und-west/245199/die-1970er-jahre.
109 Ibid.
110 Ibid.; quoted on website above.
111 The impact of television serial such as Fassbinder's *Berlin Alexanderplatz* and, especially internationally, Petersen's *Das Boot* should also be considered.
112 The conversation with Volker Schlöndorff took place on October 6, 2020.
113 Siegfried Schober, "Die Leiden des Wilhelm M.," *Der Spiegel* 11 (1975), https://www.spiegel.de/spiegel/print/d-41533771.html.
114 Hans C. Blumenberg, "Kostümfest ohne Ende: Literaturverfilmungen nach Eichendorff und Schiller," *Die Zeit* 5 (1978); accessed online via Die Zeit's digital archive: https://www.zeit.de/1978/05/kostuemfest-ohne-ende. Heidi Genée, daughter of Fritz Genschow, directed an adaptation of Fontane's *Grete Minde* with the suitably threatening subtitle *Der Wald ist voller Wölfe* [The forest is filled with wolves] in 1977. Eighteen-year-old Katerina Jacob played her first title role, later became a staple on West German television. Despite negative reviews, the film was awarded the German Filmpreis in Silber. Genée had worked as an editor on the T. Mann adaptation *Tonio Kröger* (1964) and on Ulf Miehe's *John Glückstadt* (1974) but also on the collaborative and highly political *Deutschland im Herbst* (1977).
115 Text in single quotation marks is, as before, my translation and here derived from Blumenberg's article.
116 Blumenberg, "Kostümfest ohne Ende."
117 Hickethier, *Geschichte des Fernsehens*, 341.
118 https://www1.wdr.de/unternehmen/der-wdr/unternehmen/schoenenborn-interview-tv-serie-holocaust-100.html.
119 This collaboration was examined in depth by Martin Brady and Joanne Leal in their *Wim Wenders and Peter Handke: Collaboration, Adaptation, Recomposition*. Particularly fascinating is "Parallel Texts" (chapter 2, 113– 62) on the transposition of Handke's *Die Angst des Tormanns vorm Elfmeter* (The Goalkeeper's Fear of the Penalty, 1970) in the context of collaboration and adaptation.

120 This is a translated summary of points made in Norbert Grob, Hans Helmut Prinzler, and Eric Rentschler, *Neuer Deutscher Film*, 53. Note also other Georg Büchner-adaptations such as *Woyzeck* (FRG, Bohumil Herlischka, 1962), *Lenz* (FRG, George Moorse, 1971), and *Wodzeck* (FRG, Oliver Herbrich, 1984). Numerous other adaptations could be mentioned here, for example Peter Schneider's *Der Mauerspringer* [Walljumper] which was adapted by Reinhard Hauff as *Der Mann auf der Mauer* [The Man on the Wall] (FRG, 1982).

121 Lit. those 'declared rubbish' or 'considered unfavorable' / "die für abfällig Erklärten" [Abfall = rubbish; abfällig = derogatory, unfavorable].

122 Interview with Dieter Wellershoff; cited in Manfred Lange, "Ästhetik des Humanen. Das literarische Programm Heinrich Bölls," in *Heinrich Böll* (Munich: text+kritik, 1982), 89–98, here 94: "Perspektive der von der Gesellschaft für abfällig Erklärten."

123 According to the Nobel website https://www.nobelprize.org/prizes/literature/1972/summary/.

124 Among the numerous publications on NGC, see especially Thomas Elsaesser, *New German Cinema: A History* (New Brunswick, NJ: Rutgers University Press, 1989); John Sandford, *The New German Cinema* (Oxford: Berg, 1980); James Franklin, *New German Cinema: From Oberhausen to Hamburg* (Boston: Twayne, 1983).

125 In *Gong* 19/1958; http://krimiserien.heimat.eu/fernsehspiele/fernsehspiele/19580422ard-stundederwahrheit.htm.

126 According to Hamish Reid's annotations in Heinrich Böll, *Werke*, vol. 9 (Cologne: Kiepenheuer & Witsch, 2006), 505.

127 Letter to Andersch (November 15, 1954); cf. J.H. Reid's commentary "Das Brot der frühen Jahre (1955)," Heinrich Böll, *Werke*; vol. 9, 503f.

128 Ibid., 480.

129 See Barton Byg's enlightening book on D. Huillet and J.-M. Straub for further information on these fascinating filmmakers: *Landscapes of Resistance* (Berkeley: University of California Press, 1995); especially chapters on *Not Reconciled*, Brecht's *The Business Affairs of Mr. Julius Caesar*, Kafka's *Amerika,* and Hölderlin's *The Death of Empedocles.*

130 Bienek cited in James H. Reid, "Time in the Works of Heinrich Böll," *The Modern Language Review* 62.3 (July 1967): 476–85, here p. 476.

131 Among the extensive literature on Böll and his impact, see especially Elsaesser, *New German Cinema*; Annette Kuhn, *Women's Pictures: Feminism and Cinema* (London: Routledge, 1982); E. Ann Kaplan, *Women and Film* (New York: Methuen, 1983); Julia Knight, *Women and the New German Cinema* (New York: Verso, 1992), here esp. 73–101.

132 'Too much, too soon' is Schlöndorff's verdict when he talks about his adaptation of the Kleist novella. He had intended to film a European Western, adapting the classic tale to a popular cinematic genre, but considers the result a failed attempt. Schlöndorff, *Licht, Schatten und Bewegung*, 172–5.

133 Schlöndorff's oeuvre also includes films for television such as an adaptation of Friedrich Ani's crime novel *Der namenlose Tag* [Nameless Day] (2017).

134 Malte Hagener, "German Stars since Reunification," *The German Cinema Book*, 157.

135 Schlöndorff, *Licht, Schatten und Bewegung*, 180.

136 James M. Welsh, "Volker Schlöndorff," in *The Encyclopedia of Filmmakers*, ed. John C. Tibbets and James M. Welsh, vol. 2 (New York: Facts on File, 2002), 567–70, here p. 567.

137 Ibid., 567. I would disagree with James M. Welsh, however, that Schlöndorff—no doubt a key agent—single-handedly reformed "moribund German cinema."

138 He worked under Louis Malle on *Zazie dans le Métro*, an adaptation of Raymond Queneau's recent novel (script: L. Malle and Jean-Paul Rappeneau, 92f.), which his friend Tavernier considered unfilmable. Jean-Pierre Melville, the 'spiritual father' of the French New Wave had inspired Godard and others with his documentary style and editing techniques such as jump cuts but had also worked on a number of adaptation projects since *Quand tu liras cette lettre* [When You Read This Letter] (FR, Jean-Pierre Melville, 1953).

139 Schlöndorff, *Licht, Schatten und Bewegung*, 88. He also notes Agnes Varda's *La Pointe Courte* (92) and working with his three 'masters' Louis Malle (92ff.), Alain Resnais, and Jean-Pierre Melville (104).

140 Cf. Alexandre Astruc's article "Naissance d'une nouvelle avant-garde: la caméra-stylo," *L'Ecran français* (March 30, 1948); this idea was fundamental to the concept of the "auteur" in essays by members of the *Nouvelle Vague*, published in *Cahiers du cinéma* from 1951; see also the previous chapter.

141 Schlöndorff, *Licht, Schatten und Bewegung*, 161.

142 Ibid., 164.

143 Heinrich Böll published *The Lost Honour of Katharina Blum* first in the weekly *Der Spiegel* (from July 29, 1974). But at that time, he had already sent a first draft of the story to Schlöndorff. Böll explicitly wished his story to be considered for adaptation. Schöndorff, *Licht, Schatten, Bewegung*, 212f.

144 The situation escalated after the publication of Heinrich Böll, "Will Ulrike Gnade oder freies Geleit?," *Der Spiegel* 3 (1972): 53–7, here p. 55.

145 Böll, "Will Ulrike Gnade oder freies Geleit?," 55.

146 Ibid., 57. The editor gave prominence to Böll's suggestion by making it the title of the article. The use of Ulrike Meinhof's first name only implied a familiarity that furthered the claim the Böll sympathized with terrorists.

147 René Böll talked about the backlash from his father's 'clemency' article in an interview with dw/Deutsche Welle: https://www.dw.com/en/on-heinrich-bölls-birthday-his-son-reflects-on-the-nobel-laureate/a-41878022.

148 Schöndorff, *Licht, Schatten, Bewegung*, 212.

149 Whether he focused on returning traumatized soldiers figuring out where or who they were as in *Wanderer, kommst du nach Spa ...* (*Stranger, Bear Word to the Spartans We ...*, 1950), on women bearing poverty and hardship after the war in silence in *Und sagte kein einziges Wort* (*And Never said a Word*, 1953), artists, intellectuals and, generally, outsiders as in *Ansichten eines Clowns* (*The Clown*, 1963) or *Gruppenbild mit Dame* (*Group Portrait with Lady*, 1971), his main characters are mostly individuals who do not quite belong or are pushed to the fringes of society due to their inability to fit the mould of what was considered the norm in postwar West German society.

150 Schöndorff, *Licht, Schatten, Bewegung*, 214.

151 Ibid., 217.

152 Public television station WDR and Paramount Orion paid 500,000 marks each; producer Willi Benninger contributed 400,000 marks; 300,000 marks provided by the Filmförderungsanstalt were returned to the public purse after the film's successful release. Cf. Schöndorff, *Licht, Schatten, Bewegung*, 218f.
153 Grob, Prinzler and Rentschler, *Neuer Deutscher Film*.
154 According to Schöndorff, *Licht, Schatten, Bewegung*, 219f.
155 Grass was critical of the use of CGI. As one of his assistants indicated in a conversation (on July 7, 2017 in the Grass Museum in Lübeck), the author least approved of Martin Buchhorn's adaptation of his novel *Die Rättin* (The Rat, 1986) for television (ARD, premiere October 14, 1997), chiefly due to the unsatisfactory use of digital technology.
156 John Vinocur, "After 20 Years, 'The Tin Drum' Marches to the Screen," *The New York Times* (April 6, 1980), II, 1, 17. Also quoted in Welsh, "Volker Schlöndorff," *The Encyclopedia of Filmmakers*, 570.
157 Schöndorff, *Licht, Schatten, Bewegung*, 299.
158 Ibid., 249. Cf. his 'Tin Drum' diary in *Licht, Schatten, Bewegung*, 249–305.
159 "Die Fälschung: *Homo Faber* oder Die Liebe zur Literatur," *Die Zeit* 13 (March 22, 1991); https://www.zeit.de/1991/13/die-faelschung.
160 Tim Bergfelder, "Introduction," *The Cinema Book*, 3.
161 Marco Abel, "The Cinema of Identification Gets on My Nerves: An Interview with Christian Petzold" *Cineaste* 33.3 (2008); https://www.cineaste.com/summer2008/the-cinema-of-identification-gets-on-my-nerves?rq=Petzold.
162 Robert Fischer, ed., *Fassbinder über Fassbinder: die ungekürzten Interviews* (Frankfurt/M.: Verlag der Autoren, 2004).
163 In both East and West German television, adapations were regularly produced as mini-series—such as Fallada's *Kleiner Mann, was nun?* (GDR, Hans-Joachim Kasprzik, 1967) in East Germany or Fontane's *Der Stechlin* (FRG, Rolf Hädrich, 1975) and Walter Kempowski's *Tadellöser & Wolff* (FRG, Eberhard Fechner, 1975) in the West. Other mini-series were based on: Siegfried Lenz's *Deutschstunde* (1971), Walter Kempowski's *Ein Kapitel für sich* (FRG, Eberhard Fechner, 1979), and Uwe Timm's *Morenga* (FRG, Egon Günther, 1985). *Enfant terrible* of New German Cinema R.W. Fassbinder used the format for his adaptation of Döblin's *Berlin Alexanderplatz* in 1980. His approximately 900 minutes of adaptation in fourteen parts, however, brought television audiences to their knees or, rather, to switch the channel, while the feature-length cinema version of his adaptation was celebrated by cineasts.
164 The author of the play Kroetz considered Fassbinder's adaptation to be obscene and tried to prevent its release. A theater production of his play by Theater der Courage in Vienna was filmed under the direction of Dieter Berner for Austrian television ORF in 1972. Péter Szász directed an adaptation of the play for Hungarian television entitled *Luxus-eljárás* in 1981.
165 *Nora Helmer* (1974) is based on Henrik Ibsen's Nora; *Despair—Eine Reise ins Licht* (1978, script mostly by Tom Stoppard) on Vladimir Nabokov's *Despair*; *Querelle* (1982) is based on the novel by Jean Genet. Fassbinder also adapted his own plays in *Katzelmacher* (1969), *Die bitteren Tränen der Petra von Kant* (1972), and *Bremer Freiheit* (1972).
166 In this film, the group of actors wait on location in Spain for their director and, equally important, the cheque from the federal funding agency, FFA.

167 Michael Töteberg, "Nachwort," in Töteberg's *Fassbinders Filme*, vol. 3 (Frankfurt/M.: Verlag der Autoren, 1990), 177–87, here p. 177.
168 Fassbinder, cited in Herbert Spaich, *Rainer Werner Fassbinder* (Weinheim: Beltz, 1992), 342.
169 Töteberg, "Nachwort," 186. The ZDF's *Kleine Fernsehspiel* became an important outlet for young auteur filmmakers and adaptation in the 1970s. See Elsaesser, "Television and the Author's Cinema," 212–18.
170 Töteberg, "Nachwort," 186.
171 Interview with Corinna Brocher, "Fassbinders Fontane," *Der Tagesspiegel* (February 11, 1973).
172 See Rainer Werner Fassbinder, "Fontane Effi Briest," in *Fassbinders Filme 3*, ed. M. Töteberg, 99–174.
173 See Anke-Marie Lohmeier, "Symbolische und allegorische Rede im Film. Die Effi Briest-Filme von Gustaf Gründgens und Rainer Werner Fassbinder," in *Theodor Fontane*, ed. Heinz Ludwig Arnold (Munich: text+kritik, 1989), 229–41, here p. 233f.
174 See especially Foucault's *Discipline and Punish*, which was published as *Surveiller et punir* (Paris: Gallimard, 1975).
175 Schwab, *Erzähltext und Spielfilm*, 301; on Effi's collusion, see also Christina Thürmer-Rohr, *Vagabundinnen* (Berlin: Orlanda, 1987), 38f.
176 Tony Rayns, "The Primary Need Is to Satisfy the Audience" [1974], *Sight and Sound* (May 2017): 30–1, here p. 31.
177 Daguerrotypes are early photographic images that appeared on highly polished silver-coated copper plates after a lengthy exposure time. See the image of Effi in *Fontane Effi Briest* [00:05:53-00:06:24].
178 Lohmeier, "Symbolische und allegorische Rede im Film," 236.
179 Rayns, "The Primary Need Is to Satisfy the Audience," 31; Elsaesser, *Rainer Werner Fassbinder*, 448; Andrew Webber, "The Stylist," *Sight and Sound* (May 2017): 29.
180 Spaich, *Rainer Werner Fassbinder*, 345.
181 Brocher, "Fassbinders Fontane," 1973.
182 See for example Anna Kuhn, "Modes of Alienation in Fassbinder's *Effi Briest*," *Seminar* 21.4 (1985): 272–85.
183 See also Carter, "The Ladies' Man," 25.
184 Fassbinder worked with two different cinematographers (Dietrich Lohmann replaced by Jürgen Jürges due to illness), but the style of the camera work remains even and indicates the director's control.
185 For instance, when Effi is partially obscured in *Fontane Effi Briest* [00:58:10 and 01:02:50].
186 For more detail, see Schönfeld, "Verfilmungen," 131–49.
187 Cf. Fassbinder in Rayns, "The Primary Need Is to Satisfy the Audience," 22; Carter, "The Ladies' Man," 25. Effi enters a marriage of convenience willingly and is therefore complicit in Fassbinder's eyes.
188 Cf. Helmut Schmitz in his review for *Frankfurter Rundschau* (October 4, 1974); Ulrich Greiner, "Effis erster Orgasmus," *Die Zeit* 8 (February 12, 2009).
189 Anna Kuhn, "Rainer Werner Fassbinder. The Alienated Vision," in *New German Filmmakers: From Oberhausen through the* 1970s, ed. K. Phillips

(New York: Ungar, 1984), 76–123, here p. 119. The film shot on 16 mm cost 13 million marks and is a dark (and low lit), grim vision of both Döblin's novel and society.
190 Elsaesser, "Television and the Author's Cinema," 213.
191 Thomas Elsaesser, *Fassbinder's Germany* (Amsterdam: Amsterdam University Press, 1996), 234; see also Elsaesser, *New German Cinema*, 1989.
192 For example, in a fifteen-hour-screening at the 2007 Berlinale. For further information, see Schönfeld, "Berlin Alexanderplatz," in *The Palgrave Encyclopedia of Literary Urban Studies*, ed. Jeremy Tambling, 210–26.
193 Vincent Canby, "Fassbinder Looks at the 50s," *The New York Times* (August 4, 1982), section C, 24.
194 Rainer Werner Fassbinder, "Kino oder Leben"; https://www.basisfilm.de/Fassbinder/PMFassb.pdf.
195 Joshua Feinstein in his *The Triumph of the Ordinary: Depictions of Daily Life in the East German Cinema, 1949–1989* (University of North Carolina Press, 2003) discusses "traditional activities as *Heimatpflege*, or the preservation of local identity and history" (p. 6) in the context of film, which could be productively examined with regard to adaptations of the literary canon.
196 Stefan Volk, *Skandalfilme: Cineastische Aufreger gestern und heute* (Marburg: Schüren, 2012), 125. Volk considers Achternbusch's film the most scandalous film of the decade.
197 Cf. "Mehr Glimmer: Am Beispiel der Filmförderung exekutiert Innenminister Zimmermann die kulturpolitische Wende—nach der Devise: Kommerz statt Kunst," *Der Spiegel* 1/1984 (January 1, 1984); https://www.spiegel.de/spiegel/print/d-13507725.html.
198 Helma Sanders-Brahms (1975 TV drama *Erdbeben in Chile/Earthquake in Chile*, based on Heinrich von Kleist's novella and her 1977 Kleist-film *Heinrich;* her *Deutschland bleiche Mutter/Germany, Pale Mother* takes its title from Brecht's aforementioned poem) and Margarethe von Trotta (apart from co-directing *Katharina Blum* film, she co-wrote and directed films such as *Rosa Luxemburg* [1986] and *Hanna Arendt* [2012]; in 2000 she adapted Uwe Johnson's *Jahrestage* for television) are exceptions here; for more information on the first International Women's Film Seminar in West-Berlin (1973), organized by filmmakers Helke Sander and Claudia von Alemann, and the support available to creative women during this era, see Hester Baer and Angelica Fenner, "Introduction: Revisiting Feminism and German Cinema," *Camera Obscura* 33.3 (2018): 1–19.
199 Gerrit Reichert, "Bestseller wider Erwarten," *NWZ* (October 27, 2016).
200 Baer, "Das Boot," 22.
201 The first adaptation of Feuchtwanger's text was *Semya Oppengeym* (USSR, Grigori Roshal, 1939).
202 Nan Robertson, "German TV Bids for U.S. Viewers," *The New York Times* (March 13, 1983): II, 1.
203 Deniz Göktürk, "Paternalism Revisited: Turkish German Traffic in Cinema," in the revised new edition of *The German Cinema Book*, ed. Tim Bergfelder, Erica Carter, Deniz Göktürk and Claudia Sandberg (London: BFI, 2020), 494–512, here p. 499.

9

The Walls Come Down: Entrepreneurs, Auteurs, and Arthouse Cinema (1990–2021)

> *What defines industrial art is not mechanical reproduction but the internalized relation with money.*
> GILLES DELEUZE (1985)[1]

> *Döblin by accident.*
> BURHAN QURBANI (2020)[2]

This chapter outlines recent trends and changes that have affected adaptations of German-language literature in neoliberal economies. Producer Bernd Eichinger plays a prominent role in this context, considering that his adaptations and remakes epitomize especially a thorough 'conciliation between capital and culture' as if Fassbinder and New German Cinema had never existed.[3] At the same time, however, auteur filmmakers brought some of the most outstanding adaptations of German-language literature to cinema screens. The final part of this book is devoted to their creative spirit and will close with an overview of a few mainstream and several niche films that stand out due to their innovative engagement with literature. Stanley Kubrick once said: "If it can be written, or thought, it can be filmed."[4] Because of advances in film technology, this has never been more true and is reflected in several adaptations based on novels widely considered 'unfilmable'. But as the twentieth century, the century of film, ended and CGI and digital filmmaking began to dominate the industry, the interest in the literary canon on film also continued to fade. Superhero franchises became Hollywood's global money-spinners, and glossy heritage films have been fanning a British sense of singularity in the UK while successfully functioning as attractive entertainment commodities abroad. At the same time, modes of production have become increasingly transnational to make films more lucrative and sustainable, echoing the global dimension of today's entertainment industries. During the past three decades, the vast majority of adaptations based on the canon of German-language literature have been produced for television—from another *Nibelungen* to Lessing's *Emilia Galotti*, Goethe's *Werther*, and Schiller's *Kabale und Liebe*, from Thomas Mann's *Mario und der Zauberer* and *Buddenbrooks*, Uwe Johnson's *Jahrestage* (Anniversaries, 1970–83) to award-winning contemporary literature such as Uwe Tellkamp's *Der Turm* (The Tower, 2008).[5] In the last few years, a renewed interest in the literary canon and, especially, contemporary literature by both commercial cinema and auteur filmmakers can be witnessed in German-speaking countries.[6] This most recent trend will be outlined further below.

Following the economic and political unification of Germany in 1990, national policies, globalization processes, and media conglomeration endeavors all shaped film projects based on German-language literature. The fall of the Berlin Wall caused great enthusiasm, relief, and joy in both Germanies and abroad, but unification also affected Germans' sense of national identity, and triggered well-founded sensitivities around the GDR and its culture as East Germans faced the insecurity of a capitalist, neoliberal economic environment. While numerous DEFA and DFF adaptation projects[7] based on works by GDR authors such as Brigitte Reimann, Christoph Hein, and Volker Braun were still being completed as unification was celebrated, the number of collaborative productions for cinema based on the canon of German-language literature continued its steady decline.[8] As Lutz Koepnick, Eric Rentschler, Hester Baer, and others have argued, cinema screens functioned as important sites of identification during the 1990s, when commercial cinema regularly offered reconstructions of a shared German past, in order to "reclaim sites of multicultural consensus from a history of intolerance and persecution, reconstructing an affirmative vision of German history that flies in the face of the Nazi past and elicits consensus for the Berlin Republic," as Koepnick maintains.[9] Most of the German-language literary canon was considered to be of little use in this context.

Because of the changes in national funding policies and subvention schemes outlined in the previous chapter, a profit-driven film industry looked for markets beyond the German-language area and was adamant to identify themes that would appeal to both national and international audiences. In terms of films inspired by German history, only the Nazi era was known to 'travel' well globally, but soon films about the GDR government's surveillance apparatus as depicted in *Das Leben der Anderen* [The Lives of Others] (DE, Florian Henckel von Donnersmarck, 2006) were celebrated internationally and, in this case, were even awarded a best foreign film Oscar. Critical explorations of German history and national identity through adaptation of the literary canon, however, that had given impetus to several international successes during the previous decades—from Schlöndorff's *Törless* (1966) to Fassbinder's *Lola* (1981)—were now resolutely ignored by popular cinema, which favored mostly 'feel-good' movies that could be sold globally.

As film experts such as Seeßlen and, subsequently, scholars such as Rentschler, Jaimey Fisher, and Baer[10] insisted, it was Bernd Eichinger, 'the prophet of neo-liberalism' who 'created successful German cinema for Europe, a cinema of consensus' for the masses[11] that reconciled audiences with 'Papas Kino' after the mere interlude afforded by New German Cinema. Seeßlen's 1997 article published in the left-wing Berlin newspaper *taz* highlighted the trajectory and effect of the internationally ambitious producer on German cinema. Indeed, Eichinger unleashed his Hollywood-inspired "Zutatenkino," a 'cinema of ingredients', with films such as the comic adaptation *Werner—Beinhart!* [Werner—Supertough!] (1990), which became the most successful German film that year, surpassed at the box office in Germany and Austria only by Hollywood blockbusters *Look Who's Talking* (USA, Amy Heckerling, 1989) and *Pretty Woman* (USA, Garry Marshall, 1990).[12] *Werner*-sequels and other comic-adaptations such as *Der bewegte Mann* [The Most Desired Man/Maybe ... Maybe Not] (DE, Sönke Wortmann, 1994) as well as films by and with comedians Bully Herbig and Otto Waalkes remain among the highest grossing German productions of the past three decades.[13] Producer Eichinger's choices were guided principally by the established marketability of a film project's individual components. Hence the preponderance of adaptations among his production list—bestsellers guaranteed name recognition and an established audience of fans. In this popularity contest, the genre itself was of little relevance. In addition to bestsellers from novels to comic books as source texts, as Seeßlen pointed out in 1997, Eichinger insisted on high production values, a well-known director, and a sprinkle of stars to maximize profits while minimizing commercial risk. With this profit-orientated 'cinema of ingredients', Eichinger contributed significantly to a proliferating and rather mundane culture of consensus that was aesthetically flexible and as conventional as a lucrative mass audience might require. More recently, a new generation of producers like Oliver Berben or Sarah Kirkegaard considered bestselling literature's potential for serialization and successfully brought novels such as Patrick Süskind's *Das Parfum* (Perfume, 1985) and Ferdinand von Schirach's *Schuld* (Guilt, 2010) to television and streaming services while creatively addressing the demands of the popular format.[14]

"Auteur Producer" Bernd Eichinger and Constantin Film

In 2001 Bernd Eichinger said: 'The only thing that counts in cinema is whether I have the right film that everyone wants to see.'[15] Frequently criticized for his all too enthusiastic embrace of neoliberalism, Eichinger remained an ambitious pragmatist who thrived on competition, fought for recognition and public subsidies, and considered 'uneconomical' films a waste of resources. Time was money, too, and in an interview given after the completion of *Das Mädchen Rosemarie* (1996) for the SAT1 German Classics series, he prided himself in writing the script for the television remake in ten days and filming the entire movie in less than a month.[16] As producer, he defined his job as identifying the 'perfect' material, focusing the script, and selecting the cast in collaboration with the director before, finally, overseeing the editing of the film.[17] When arthouse film had largely disappeared from German cinema screens as the new millennium dawned, Eichinger felt vindicated as a defender of narrative filmmaking who let 'the market' take the lead. Once co-producer of award-winning adaptations such as Wim Wender's Goethe-inspired road movie *Falsche Bewegung* (1975), Bernhard Sinkel's Eichendorff-adaptation *Taugenichts* (1977), Hans-Jürgen Syberberg's aesthetically innovative cultural-political critique *Hitler-Ein Film aus Deutschland* [Hitler: A Film from Germany] (1977), and Maximilian Schell's *Geschichten aus dem Wiender Wald* [Stories from the Vienna Forest] (FRG/AT, Maximilian Schell, 1979) based on Ödön von Horváth's tragic play, Eichinger turned from New German Cinema to popular literature in order to stabilize Constantin-Film, the company he took over in 1979. That year, the once-powerful production/distribution company famous for its Karl May and Edgar Wallace adaptations and genre series was on the brink of bankruptcy.[18] When Eichinger passed away in 2011, he had built Neue Constantin "into the biggest studio player in German cinema," as Fisher put it. And Eichinger, to quote Baer, "was considered the most significant German film producer, but also a singular figure in German filmmaking, a man who more than anyone else shaped the course of German cinema over the last forty years."[19]

As Bergfelder, Baer, and others have noted, Eichinger is considered instrumental in making German film internationally successful once again. In his world, the consumer was king, and every ticket sold at the box office was a vote that delivered the information required to develop more products that would entice and satisfy a mass audience. The market defined film projects' utility. When Eichinger took over Constantin, he was already eyeing the biggest seller and most discussed book of 1979: *Christiane F.— Wir Kinder vom Bahnhof Zoo* [Christiane F.—We Children from Zoo Station] for adaptation. Based on interviews with a teenage heroin addict and occasional prostitute, the book scandalized bourgeois parents as much as it fascinated teenagers at the time. Kai Hermann's and Horst Rieck's account of Christiane's descent into addiction, sexual exploitation, but also experiences of love and friendship was raw and authentic. Many feared that the book glamorized drug use and sex, and *Christiane F.* dominated debates in the public sphere for weeks.[20] For Eichinger it was the perfect commodity. He produced the adaptation of the book (FRG, Uli Edel, 1981), with his previous company Solaris and distributed it via Neue Constantin. The film quickly attained cult status, not least due to David Bowie's performance of "Station to Station" in a concert scene.[21]

Baer outlines Eichinger's previous productions of adaptation mostly of the literary canon, and highlights his "popular breakthrough" both nationally and internationally with *Christiane F.* and *Das Boot* (1981) that was to shape his career for decades to come, "laying the groundwork for a new producers' cinema that aimed to make a virtue of the tyranny of the market."[22] Adaptations of bestsellers, i.e., the transformation of popular culture, tested and approved by the market in terms of its transnational potential and commercial appeal, became core to his success:

> Eichinger reinvented the failing Constantin largely by combining two patented strategies of adaptation. Bringing to the screen internationally renowned literary texts, he created prestige pictures for Neue Constantin that reached a built-in global audience familiar with the original literary properties, thereby guaranteeing profitability. At the same time, by updating the original Constantin corporation's strategy, Eichinger also maintained a dedicated German audience with nonexportable genre films, relying strongly on sequelization and the production of series to maximize returns.[23]

Apart from internationally acclaimed historical dramas such as *Der Untergang* [Downfall] (DE/IT/AT/RU, Oliver Hirschbiegel, 2004) and *Baader Meinhof Komplex* (DE, Uli Edel, 2008), Eichinger's blockbuster successes range from comedy films like *Der bewegte Mann* [internationally marketed as *The Most Desired Man*, released in the United States as *Maybe ... maybe not*] (Sönke Wortmann, 1994) based on Ralf König's comic books *Der bewegte Mann* and *Pretty Baby*, to global prestige films based on internationally bestselling literature under auteur direction, from Umberto Eco's *Il nome della rosa* (FRG/FR/IT, Jean-Jacques Annaud, 1986), Peter Høeg's *Frøken Smillas fornemmelse for sne* [Miss Smilla's Feeling for Snow] (DK/DE, Bille August, 1997), and Patrick Süskind's *Das Parfum—die Geschichte eines Mörders* [Perfume—the Story of a Murderer] (DE/ES/FR/US, Tom Tykwer, 2006) to Donna Woolfolk Cross' bestselling novel *Pope Joan* [*Die Päpstin*] (DE/ES/US, Sönke Wortmann, 2009).[24] He also produced adaptations of the *Resident Evil* video games,[25] a digitally animated adaptation of Erich Kästner's *Konferenz der Tiere* (DE, Holger Tappe/Reinhard Klooss, 2010), and *The Three Musketeers* (DE/US/FR/GB, Paul Anderson, 2011), a 3D-adenture film based on the canonical French novel by Alexandre Dumas.²⁶

The mood of the market and box office successes were regularly and systematically monitored. Following Bavaria Film's managing director Günter Rohrbach's interest in the work of Helmut Krausser and the adaptation of his novel *Fette Welt* [Fat World] (Jan Schütte, 1998), Eichinger adapted and directed Krausser's *Der große Bagarozy* the following year.²⁷ His sense of 'the right film' was confirmed many times, but perhaps especially, when *Nirgendwo in Afrika* [Nowhere in Africa] (DE, Caroline Link, 2001) based Stefanie Zweig's autobiographical novel about her Jewish family's story of exile in Kenia won the Academy Award for Best Foreign Language Film and several German and Bavarian Film Awards. Eichinger co-produced the film with Peter Hermann and distributed it via Constantin Film. It was the first Academy Award for a German production since Schlöndorff's *Die Blechtrommel* in 1979.

After Eichinger's death in 2011²⁸, the company continued in the same vein, ensuring a steady income with serialized feature films for cinema based on popular children's and youth literature, such as British classic by Enid Blyton *Famous Five*, as *Fünf Freunde* (2012, 2013, 2014, 2015, 2018), and *Ostwind* [*Windstorm*], the horse-based series by Lea Schmidbauer and Kristina Magdalena Henn (DE, Katja von Garnier, 2013, 2015, 2017, etc.), but also films such as renowned director Andreas Dresen's *Timm Thaler oder Das verkaufte Lachen* (2017) based on James Krüss' 1962 eponymous children's novel and the hugely popular 1979 television series.²⁹

Constantin landed a surprise hit with *Fack ju Göhte* (2013, 2015, 2017) and the comedy's implication of a new generation's unruly opposition to

FIGURE 9.1 *Justus von Dohnányi as affluent Baron Lefuet coercing Timm (Arved Friese) to sell his infectious laugh in Andreas Dresen's* Timm Thaler oder Das verkaufte Lachen *(2017).*

(parental) convention and (literary) tradition. Despite the fact that the place of the narrative is a school named after Goethe, the film was released as *Suck Me Shakespeer* in English-speaking countries, which reflects the distributor's penchant for alliteration and an undeniable expectation of the target audience's ignorance regarding even the classical highlights of German literature. In the meantime, Constantin continued to be the main 'adapter' of German-language literature with films based on German-Icelandic author Kristof Magnusson's popular play *Männerhort* [Shelter for Men] (Franziska Meyer Price, 2014), and of Timur Vermes' bestselling novel *Er ist wieder da* [He is Back] (David Wnendt, 2015). The latter comedy about Adolf Hitler, who suddenly awakes on slightly scorched ground in twenty-first-century Berlin, drew over 1.4 million viewers into German cinemas during the first three weeks alone, after an advertising campaign built on the novel's economic status: 'global bestseller—millions of enthusiastic readers—no. 1 on *Der Spiegel*'s bestseller list for months!'[30] In Germany, *Er ist wieder da* became the second most successful film of 2015, surpassed only by *Fack ju Göthe 2*.[31]

One of the company's main interests is on adapting bestselling contemporary literature and updating canonical literary texts to contemporary settings both for cinema and television. Criminal defense lawyer Ferdinand von Schirach's literary work has been among the most adapted of contemporary German-language crime literature. Unusual for an author of that genre, von Schirach was awarded the Kleist-Preis, one of Germany's most prestigious literary prizes in 2010 for his work inspired by 'true crime', namely his volume of short-stories *Verbrechen* (Crime, 2009). The book topped bestseller's lists in Germany for nearly a year and was sold into more than thirty countries. Constantin secured the film rights to *Verbrechen* as well as to Schirach's second volume of short stories *Schuld* (Guilt, 2010) and, together with its subsidiary Moovie[32] (Oliver Berben), produced both highly popular mini-series for television[33] and feature films for cinema based on his work.

Adaptations for cinema include von Schirach's short story "Glück" [Happiness/Luck], which was the first to be adapted by acclaimed writer and filmmaker Doris Dörrie in 2012. Her take on the story of traumatized refugee and sex worker Irina (Italian arthouse 'shooting star' Alba Rohrwacher) and her homeless punk buddy Kalle (Vinzenz Kiefer) in Berlin, who makes the dead john in her flat disappear, foregrounds the precariousness of life among the marginalized in a Ken Loach aesthetic that grinds against the utopia of an imagined past. Having first worked with Eichinger on *Ich und Er* [Me and Him, based on Italian author Alberto Moravia's novel] in 1988 as an up-and-coming writer and director with plenty of public appeal, Dörrie agreed with her producer that a literary source text can potentially and significantly improve the quality of a film project while also maximizing financial returns.

Dörrie regularly adapted literary texts, from the popular Turkish-German culture-clash crime-comedy *Happy Birthday, Türke!* (1992) based on Jakob Arjouni's (Jakob Michelsen) novel, to her Brothers Grimm inspired *Der Fischer und seine Frau* [The Fisherman and His Wife] (2005), but also, perhaps following the example of Eric Rohmer, adapted her own, deeply insightful and satirical short stories and novels in films such as *Bin ich schön?* [Am I Beautiful?] (1998), *Nackt* [Naked] (2002), and *Alles inklusive* [All Inclusive] (2014).[34] She has frequently credited Eichinger for saving her financially, when she cancelled filming of *Bin ich schön?* to be with her dying husband, cinematographer Helge Weigel, while her insurance refused to cover the ensuing costs. Eichinger paid Dörrie's production company's debt by buying the script and all rights to the project. For Dörrie, this provided the lifeline to save the production company and its employees.

Detlev Buck, also a long-term Eichinger-collaborator, had appeared as an actor in Eichinger/Constantin-Film-adaptations from *Der große Bagarozy* (1999) and *Herr Lehmann* (2003) to *Ostwind* (2013) and *Mängelexemplar* [Damaged Goods] (written and directed by Laura Lackmann, based on the novel by Sarah Kuttner, 2016). He also worked as a producer with theater director Leander Haußmann (Haussmann) and writer Thomas Brussig on *Sonnenallee* [Sun Alley] (1999), with Haußmann on an updated *Kabale und Liebe* (2005)[35] for television, and with bestselling author Daniel Kehlmann, co-writing the script for adaptations of Kehlmann's novel *Die Vermessung der Welt* [Measuring the World] (DE/AT, Detlev Buck, 2012), and of Thomas Mann's *Die Bekenntnisse des Hochstaplers Felix Krull* (DE, Detlev Buck, 2021).[36] As a director, he has a clear knack for entertainment, but he rarely takes aesthetic or commercial risks. His well-crafted but all too sleek Krull adaptation failed to generate much interest. In contrast, Buck's cool neo-noir thriller *Asphaltgorillas* (2018) based on von Schirach's short-story from the volume *Schuld* was much more distinctive and was well received overall, but nonetheless criticized for its 'wild genre-mix', and for being 'not funny enough for a comedy, too predictable for a crime-flic, and too cynical for a drama.'[37]

In 2019, Constantin Film's *Der Fall Collini* [The Collini Case] (DE, Marco Kreuzpaintner) brought von Schirach's eponymous 2011 novel to cinema screens. The project was co-funded by the German national film funding institution Filmförderungsanstalt (FFA), the Bavarian film fund FilmFernsehFonds Bayern and Medienboard Berlin-Brandenburg, and became the most successful German film of the year.[38] With a cast that included *Fack ju Göthe*'s Elyas M'Barek alongside Heiner Lauterbach and Alexandra Maria Lara, the political thriller successfully merged the crime genre with a critical assessment of Germany's postwar failings in bringing Nazi perpetrators to justice. The tension-filled narrative navigates its viewers' attention to the reluctance of Germany's dealing with the crimes committed during the Hitler era, and communicates the need to remember, especially to a younger audience, as highlighted by the former president of the Jewish committee in Germany Charlotte Knobloch.[39] Martin Moszkowicz, Eichinger's former side-kick and Chairman of the Executive Board at Constantin Film, emphasized the significance of the adaptation, not only in the context of the Holocaust—his father survived Auschwitz, but several of his family members were murdered by the Nazis—and the need to remind younger generations of the Shoa, but also to inform them of legislation that had been proposed by justice ministry division head Eduard Dreher in 1968. The former Nazi persecutor designed a deliberately convoluted new law for misdemeanors, which in fact retroactively statute-barred nearly all Nazi murders and thus protected thousands of war criminals from punishment.[40] It was not until 1979 that murder became once again exempt from any statute of limitations in the FRG. For Constantin-Film CEO Moszkowicz, von Schirach's novel and Constantin Film's 2019 adaptation were important contributions to the public sphere that foreground the question of indelible guilt and crimes against humanity—especially at a time when atrocious antisemitic acts and hate crimes were once again on the rise.

Adaptations by Constantin Film are often co-productions and usually profit from collaborations with public television and subsidies by local and national film boards. When Swiss director Alain Gsponer decided to adapt Ödön von Horvath's novel *Jugend ohne Gott* (Youth without God, 1937) about the suppression of humanist values by a fascist society of obedient followers, he collaborated with Constantin Film, and received an unusually high subsidy of 1.8 million euro from the Bavarian film and television funding agency (FFF Bayern) and the national Deutsche Filmförderfonds, with further funding provided by HessenInvest Film and the FFA. Rather than focusing on the theme of racism so prevalent in Horvath's exile novel, however, Alain Gsponer's adaptation is set in the near future, when a young elite is being prepared for an oppressive meritocracy. As Gsponer emphasized repeatedly in interviews, it was his love for this novel since he was a teenager that led him to this project, but he wanted to make it 'relevant' for today's audience all too familiar with performance pressure, bullying, and rivalry. Replacing fascism with a society that knows only winners and losers, Gsponer reflects on a world that 'is divided into rich and poor' and in which social media 'put us in a permanent state of competition'.[41] The 'God' of Horvath's text is a value system based on truth, ethics, and love. In Gsponer's view, however, 'today's youth is no longer familiar with humanist ethics or principles' and the film is meant to critically and cynically highlight this presumed lack.[42] In his adaptation, young Zach (Jannis Niewöhner) dreams of 'a world without sectors: there is no malice and no envy, no one has to fight, not for their lives or their property, nor for justice', while the real world is ruled by ferocious competition and only the best and most ruthless get ahead.

Asked about his two previous films based on literary texts (*Lila Lila*, 2009, *Der letzte Weynfeldt*, 2010; both by Swiss author Martin Suter) in the same interview, Alain Gsponer highlights the 'appeal' of adaptation in Germany's neoliberal film industry:

> In order to be successful in Germany, you need a brand to market your product. Except for comedies. It is a reality I must deal with. Moreover, in adaptation you have a foundation for which there is feedback available, that of the readers. You can build on that. The story has already been warranted.

Baer also points to the prestige and "prepackaged legitimacy" that an adaptation could derive from its bestselling source text. This was, as previously mentioned, the motivation for many of the pioneers of filmmaking when turning to a well-known literary text and continued to be inseparable from many of the adaptation projects discussed in this volume. It was also common practice during the classical Hollywood era, as Baer notes, when "adapted works enabled studios to more easily develop the cultural capital and brand recognition to attract both talent and audiences, and thus to increase profitability."[43] In turn, the success of an adaptation greatly increased sales of the source text. This was the case with countless novels that provided the basis for a film, most notably in recent years with Stefanie Zweig's *Nirgendwo in Afrika* (1995) and Dietrich Schwanitz's *Der Campus* (1995). When Sönke Wortmann's 1998 adaptation of Schwanitz's novel about a university professor accused of raping a student was reviewed in *Der Spiegel*, Fritz Rumler praised the film in reference to its literary source: 'it is an intelligent film first and foremost because of its intelligent source text; it takes a very close look at the paws of the powerful and those addicted to imperiousness.'[44]

Eichinger's power and financial clout stemmed predominantly from investing in a range of adaptations of varying genres from comic books to literary texts that had proved popular with a large readership. For three decades from 1981 onwards, Eichinger was involved in most of the commercially successful films emerging from Germany and was not only instrumental in the successful renewal of German film as a commercially viable industry, but in shifting both nationally and internationally recognized adaptations away from arthouse to a high-production-value commercial cinema, establishing the genre as a highly lucrative endeavor. Baer rightfully concludes, "[h]is vision left an indelible imprint on the dominant narrative and stylistic trends in contemporary German and international film."[45] Constantin-Film continues to abide largely by Eichinger's approach to film production. Remakes have been one of the core activities in order to safeguard economy, but now streaming services are becoming important partners. Constantin capitalized on Eichinger's original investment in

Christiane F. Wir Kinder vom Bahnhof Zoo once again, for example, when a remake was produced in a now popular serialized format. The first season (eight episodes) of the new adaptation of *We Children from Bahnhof Zoo* was first screened on Amazon Prime from February 2021.

Trends and Figures

Eichinger's and Constantin Film's strategy is mirrored elsewhere, as producers seek collaborations with television and choose adaptations mostly once the market has indicated sufficient interest. Former director of WDR's Deutsches Fernsehspiel (1968–79) and managing director of Bavaria Film (1980–94) Günter Rohrbach[46] stands out in his support of adaptation projects, which also dominated his choices as an independent producer since 1994. His productions, however, have also followed the trends among potential readerships and across the commercial film industry. Beginning with an adaptation of commercially very successful children's book *Rennschwein Rudi Rüssel* [Racing Pig Rudi Snout] (Peter Timm, 1994), Rohrbach produced adaptations of popular, bestselling literature such as Ingrid Noll's *Die Apothekerin* [The (female) Pharmacist] (Rainer Kaufmann, 1996), Erica Fischer's tragic queer love story in Nazi Germany *Aimée und Jaguar* (Max Färberböck, 1997), "Wende"-novel Jens Sparschuh's *Der Zimmerspringbrunnen* (Peter Timm, 2001), Corinne Hofmann's autobiographical *Die weiße Massai* [The White Massai] (Hermine Huntgeburth, 2005), and journalist Hannes Wenger's amusing account of his daughter Carla in puberty *Das Pubertier—Der Film* (Leander Haußmann, 2017). The only film based on the literary canon was Huntgeburth's latest adaptation of Fontane's *Effi Briest* (2009), which will be discussed further below.

Overall, a downsized German cinema landscape recovered financially during the 1990s with a steady rise in ticket sales to 178 million in 2001. While the number of feature films increased significantly in the new millennium, an average of seventy-nine German productions and sixty-eight co-productions [with France, Austria, Switzerland, Belgium, and the United States] premiered per year during the past decade. Since 2010, productions plateaued at around 140 to 150 feature film productions per year.[47] But what kind of films are being produced and is German-language literature still considered in this process?[48]

Between 1997 and 2006, an average of 16.2 percent of all feature films produced or co-produced in Germany that grossed over 1 million euro were based on a 'book' or novel. This included international adaptations of bestselling literary texts such as Süskind's *Das Parfum* by Tom Tykwer, but also films based on bestselling autobiographical accounts such as Huntgeburth's

Die weiße Massai. Adaptations of contemporary literature, such as *Nichts als Gespenster* [Nothing but Ghosts] (DE, Martin Gypkens, 2006) based on Judith Hermann's short stories, the star-studded international production of *Night Train to Lisbon* (DE/CH/PT, Bille August, 2013) based on Pascal Mercier's bestselling work, or Eugen Ruge's beautifully melancholic portrayal of the GDR in his *In Zeiten des abnehmenden Lichts* [In Times of Fading Light] (DE, Matti Geschonnek, 2017), however, indicated potential pitfalls even of commercially successful literary texts at the box office.

Nonetheless, as Wilfried Berauer's statistical analysis of SPIO data (1997–2006) reveals, adaptations accounted for 22.5 percent of profits made by German film production companies, or, if comic book adaptations such as *Werner* or *Kleines Arschloch* [Little Asshole] are included, adaptions enabled an even greater slice of 27.5 percent or annual profits of 17.5 million euro. While films based on important historical events that are integral to German culture and identity proved financially the most successful—*Luther* (2003), *Das Wunder von Bern* [The Miracle of Bern] (2003), *Der Untergang* [Downfall] (2004), *Sophie Scholl, die letzten Tage* [Sophie Scholl: The Final Days] (2005)—adaptations accounted for a significant portion of film productions and gross income. Only a closer look reveals the near absence of what would commonly be considered the canon of German-language literature. During the decade considered in Berauer's report, 75 percent of adaptations are based on children's and youth literature, a segment of the genre that proved to be most lucrative at the box office, too. Approximately half of those adaptations are either based on bestselling contemporary children's literature by authors such as Joachim Masannek and, especially, Cornelia Funke,[49] or enduring 'classics' by Erich Kästner,[50] Otfried Preußler,[51] or Michael Ende.[52]

Cinema in Germany and Austria was comparatively slow to discover children's and youth literature, and the dominance of the genre in the twenty-first century is, perhaps, surprising. But children and young adults provide a significant portion of box office income, and in addition, adaptations of popular children's literature and young adult fiction are unproblematic in terms of subsequent distribution. Film companies producing for cinema (with a planned secondary release via television and online streaming platforms) clearly prefer economically safer adaptation projects based on popular fiction for children and young adults[53] or bestselling autobiographical accounts.[54] Meanwhile the canon of German-language literature has been increasingly relegated to the small screen.[55]

Changes to the guidelines for public funding were adapted in 2016 and a slight increase in adaptations of the literary canon has become evident, and films such as *Mackie Messer—Brechts Dreigroschenfilm* (DE/BE, Joachim A. Lang, 2018) and new adaptations of Siegfried Lenz's *Deutschstunde* [German Lesson] (DE, Christian Schwochow, 2019), Alfred Döblin's *Berlin Alexanderplatz* (DE, Burhan Qurbani, 2020), Stefan Zweig's *Die*

Schachnovelle [Chess Novella] (DE/AT, Philipp Stölzl, 2021), and Erich Kästner's *Fabian oder Der Gang vor die Hunde* [Fabian—Going to the Dogs] (DE, Dominik Graf, 2021) once again foreground the significance of the genre for the public sphere. Most explicitly, the former film about the *Threepenny Opera* project by Elisabeth Hauptmann, Brecht and Weill, as well as the 1930/1 Nero production based on the hit play, and Brecht's own adaptation *Die Beule* (The Bump, 1930), puts intellectual property, film as art, and the role of literature within the creative industry centerstage, while critically assessing adaptation as collage, interpretation, and commodity. Clearly aware of epic theater, the 2018 film especially offers a palimpsest and montage of the different stories and source texts, that incorporate and illustrate the historical past, while colliding with present processes and trends in the entertainment industry. Underlying the final product is Brecht's life, work, and theory, and the question of art as a political weapon. If it is the responsibility of the artist to produce works of art that can function as weapons of immeasurable value in the struggle against fascism, as Ernst Toller put it, how can the film industry resolutely support artists, this adaptation seems to ask, instead of commodifying their work and rendering it mute.[56] The film raises the question of 'intellectual property' and the creator's rights, which was most timely considering the changes to European copyright laws at the time.

FIGURE 9.2 *Jella Haase and Welket Bungué as Mieze and Franz/Francis in* Berlin Alexanderplatz *(DE, Burhan Qurbani, 2020).*

In 2020, the only notable adaptation based on the canon of German-language literature apart from Qurbani's outstanding *Berlin Alexanderplatz* was *Narziss und Goldmund*, directed by Oscar winner Stefan Ruzowitzky.⁵⁷ Based on Hermann Hesse's C.G. Jung and Nietzsche-inspired novel about close friends raised in a monastery who set out on very different trajectories, Ruzowitzky's opulent if conventional adaptation dramatizes the friendship between two very different psychological types, the extravert and the introvert, and turns their journey into an adventure narrative rather than an exploration of the fabric of the one's spirituality and the other's shadow and that which intertwines and connects the two. Considering the number of adaptations of the literary canon and contemporary literature produced in German-speaking countries and in Europe overall, a downward trend in the twenty-first century is undeniable, even though recent high value productions by auteur filmmakers—especially since the new film subsidy law of 2016—indicate that the tide may be changing once again.

Conglomerates and Consensus Cinema

As indicated above, the German-language adaptation landscape in the twenty-first century is dominated by children's literature, the occasional contemporary bestseller, and fairy-tale parodies, such as Sven Unterwaldt's *7-Zwerge*-comedies based on the Jacob and Wilhelm Grimm's *Snow White and the Seven Dwarfs*.⁵⁸ Berauer summarizes the 'core-recipe' for Unterwaldt's comedies as a well-known story, adapted with an air of persiflage, and involving a well-known comedian.⁵⁹ In general, cinema profited soundly from this kind of 'recycling' of popular stories of the public domain, particularly if the source text was known internationally and the high production value of the adaptation included medialized elements of the cultural canon and plenty of comedy.

The aforementioned post-wall 'cinema of consensus', which Rentschler⁶⁰ associates with filmmakers such as Rainer Kaufmann, Doris Dörrie, Dominik Graf, Sonke Wortmann, Katja von Garnier, Joseph Vilsmaier, Helmut Dietl, and Detlev Buck, is thriving exactly because it avoids problematic aspects regarding national identity or difficult questions about Germany's past. In contrast to the provocative auteurs of New German Cinema, their films aim at entertainment and enchantment. The literary canon is rarely considered in this context unless an anniversary promises additional interest and support by public film subsidy boards. Actor/director Sebastian Schipper turned to the classics in his 2009 film *Mitte Ende August* [Sometime in August], a modern-day romantic drama based on Goethe's novel *Wahlverwandschaften* (Elective Affinities, 1809), highlighting the 200-year anniversary of this outstanding text for cinemagoers and television audiences and its relevance for readers today. As Anna Arco emphasized in *The Guardian* at the time:

> Goethe's classic work uses the chemical metaphor to explore the conflict between bonds created by society and the bonds that are formed through chemical attractions. Controversial in its day, as it lent itself to the interpretation that love could be reduced to a chemical attraction, the novella continues to be relevant. Despite a shift in mores, contemporary readers will recognise the emotional pressures and the problems that Goethe explores through his characters and the Romantic landscape.[61]

Dominik Graf, widely known for his work for public television, particularly in police crime dramas, is one of Germany's most outstanding genre filmmakers. He ventured into adaptation with *Das Gelübde* (2007; based on Kai Meyer's contemporary novel), and raised eyebrows with his plush historical costume drama about Friedrich Schiller and his relationship with Charlotte and Caroline von Lengefeld; *Die geliebten Schwestern* [Beloved Sisters] (DE/AT, 2014)[62] celebrates enlightenment, the creative genius of Schiller, his love for revolution and for beautiful women. The film is deeply nostalgic and committed to bringing idyllic cultural heritage to a large audience, focusing on Schiller as a relatively unproblematic, admirable creator of some of the best dramas and poems in the German language rather than, perhaps, interrogating the idea of literary heritage and its contribution to an imagined national identity.

As Rentschler, Mette Hjort, and Scott MacKenzie highlighted in 2000, "subsidy policies favouring commercial films [...] enhanced co-operation between film and television, a radical transformation of the public sphere by new media, changing self-conceptions and significant investments in German film by five major American distributors."[63] In the twenty-first century, this trend continues. In 2019, for example, the New York-based investment firm KKR bought up the German production and distribution companies Tele München and Universum in order to create a "new German entertainment platform" overseen by former Constantin Film CEO and former head of entertainment at Germany's public television station ZDF Fred Kogel.[64] The trend toward the creation of ever bigger multinational media conglomerates no doubt benefits transnational collaboration, but also the distribution of US American productions in the German-language area, thus facilitating the widest possible distribution of English-language films and a limited distribution of German-language movies, which are swiftly "pushed into the arthouse sector, regardless of budget or style."[65]

As Ed Meza sees it, "U.S. distribution deals for German films are of great strategic value for international rollouts, but lucrative prospects largely depend on the type of film on offer.[66] The spectrum of German film continues to broaden, encompassing everything from arthouse, historical drama and family entertainment to animation, action and horror—not to mention English-language German productions." But these deals depend on the film's performance at international film festivals, and even then, especially more experimental German-language productions face an uphill battle. Moritz Hemminger, deputy head of sales and acquisitions at ARRI Media, points out: "With German-language dramas that do well at festivals and gain some prestige, you do have high chances of finding a passionate U.S. indie distributor who will release your film in limited cinemas in New York, L.A., Chicago and other major U.S. cities."[67] According to Julia Weber, head of theatrical sales and acquisitions at Global Screen, 'three kinds of films sell well in North America, namely, 'blue chip animated features, such as *Luis and the Aliens*, sophisticated and still entertaining films like *The Collini Case* or *Crescendo*, and well produced intriguing thrillers such as *Cut Off*.' And while the production value and script quality of German films are usually appreciated, Weber emphasizes that "English-language films enjoy much greater opportunities."[68] Hemminger agrees that German-language films are struggling in the context of international distribution. US distributors are finding it increasingly difficult "to convince exhibitors to program foreign-language movies in the US"[69] and this trend is evident elsewhere.

Multinational media conglomerates responded to this development by producing increasing numbers of adaptations in English rather than German, with much of the funding to be derived from public sources in German-language countries. Swiss author Pascal Mercier's *Nachtzug nach Lissabon* (Night Train to Lisbon, 2004) may serve as an example. The philosophical novel sold over 2 million copies in German-speaking Europe and became an international bestseller following its publication in Barbara Harshav's English translation. The novel's initial success led to over thirty further translations and its adaptation was produced by Studio Hamburg Filmproduktion, C-Films, Cinemate, TMG Tele München, SRF, Teleclub, ZDF, and the K5 Media Group Munich, with Concorde Filmverleih and Frenetic Films releasing the film in Germany and Switzerland, respectively. An international cast of established icons was chosen that included English actors Jeremy Irons, Christopher Lee, Charlotte Rampling and Jack Huston, Swedish actor Lena Olin, German actors Martina Gedeck and August Diehl, Swiss actor Bruno Ganz and others. Danish film veteran Bille August directed the adaptation. The narrative folds the Portuguese past under right-wing dictator Salazar into present day Bern and Lisbon and develops into a political mystery that is as much about the historical past and decisions already made as it is about their consequence and the opportunity to change their course, or perhaps, about one last chance of becoming another.

The reception of the film was lukewarm. In German-speaking countries reviewers called the adaptation a 'misunderstanding'[70] and mostly criticized it as too high-brow and 'upper-class kitsch'[71] personified by stiff-upper-lipped Irons in the lead. In the United States, the adaptation was considered "hopelessly page-bound" and overall "an antiquated throwback to the lumpy English-language Europuddings that mostly died out in the 1990s."[72] The 1989 Oscar winner for *Pelle the Conqueror* Bille August was criticized for his "outmoded storytelling approach, not to mention [the fact that he is] drawn to material of questionable screen viability."[73] Even though not quite considered "a train wreck," other reviews echoed much of the same criticism that repeatedly focused on the Swiss novel as being too intellectual and thus incompatible with the demands on current film entertainment.[74]

In the twenty-first century's cinema of neoliberalism, however, even bestselling 'good and easy reads' like Uwe Timm's *Die Entdeckung der Currywurst* (Invention of the Curried Sausage, 1993) were shaped into simplistic and superficial screen stories to indulge an imagined mass audience who wants to lean back and be amused. For the acclaimed author, writing is a process of remembering, which presupposes and at the same time requires 'the look back'. Writing is the art of memory, and *ars memoriae* requires recourse to 'sensually haptic experiences.'[75] The 'look back' for Timm is always already a fragmented one, and sensual memories that trigger affects (such as fear, hunger, or desire) have become signposts in the author's mediation of reality and/or historical truth. This hermeneutic thread is part of the fabric of his novella on the Zero Hour, because Timm recognized the need to remember and to confront the reader once more with the amnesia of Germany's postwar society. Ulla Wagner's 2008 adaptation, however, is an effort to retell only those aspects of a narrative that fit the increasingly narrow parameters of the entertainment industry and thus is far less productive.

Having sacrificed the story's enlightening framing narrative and flashbacks to facilitate the construction of a linear narrative, Wagner's film loses the complexity and self-irony of the novella and remains, despite its 3D-technology, one-dimensional. And yet the movie sometimes conveys the self-referentiality of memory, even if we must do without the elderly, always-knitting Mrs. Brücker. On screen, no stitches fall, the work of remembering hardly leaves a trace. It is the story of Lena Brücker (Barbara Sukowa) as a lonely, middle-aged woman in 1945 who hides a young deserter (Alexander Khuon) for seventeen days and nights, even after the war has ended, because his presence is all too satisfying in a number of respects. When he finally realizes that the war is over, he leaves the same day, but at least the mystery of the origin of Germany's famous *Currywurst* is revealed. The film provides insights into the time around the end of the Second World War; however, the greater significance of the silence and concealment in the context of West German postwar reality is no longer considered a relevant narrative feature in Wagner's cinema of consensus. The narrative interweaving of the approaching Allied troops and the union of two strangers does allow room for an examination of the past but remains a moment in time—one that neither truly reflects on nor questions itself. Timm's method of narration aims at an affective mediation of material reality and seeks 'moments of truth'[76] like Böll before him, helped along by the memory of the reader's own experience that has become 'palpable' in language. Martin Heidegger's thoughts also underlie the novella as a nearly invisible 'knitting pattern', and Timm's text can also be read as a clever and partly also very humorous examination of Heidegger's *Der Ursprung des Kunstwerks* (The Origin of the Work of Art, 1935).[77] Wagner's adaptation is only interested in the broad strokes and a good yarn. Like that of many other filmmakers, her approach reflects the desire of neoliberal, commercial cinema to cater to the market and provide uncomplicated, affirmative entertainment that most cinemagoers will opt for when out for a good time.[78]

Film Subsidies

By 2008, as *Der Spiegel* reports based on Germany's public film subsidy board numbers (Filmförderungsanstalt/FFA), cinema had once again become a popular pastime and, similar to the time of the Adenauer-era, i.e., the cinema of the 1950s and 1960s, some German productions proved more popular than even Hollywood blockbusters and contributed significantly to the positive trend. The highest grossing film of the year was the surprise box office hit *Keinohrhasen* [Rabbit without Ears], directed, co-written, and co-produced by Til Schweiger, who also starred in the romantic comedy, which was seen by nearly 5 million cinemagoers in Germany during the first year, even more than the new James Bond film *Quantum of Solace* and DreamWorks' *Madagascar 2*.[79] Nearly as successful, however, was *Der Baader Meinhof Komplex* (DE, Uli Edel, 2008), Eichinger's adaptation of *Der Spiegel*'s editor-in-chief Stefan Aust's book, which documents the Red Army Faction's first decade focusing on the group's radicalization and initial wave of terrorist activity (*Der Baader-Meinhof-Komplex*, 1985/97). For this adaptation project, Eichinger managed to secure 10 million euro from public television companies (in exchange for a longer two-part TV version of his feature), 6.5 million from local, and 2.7 million from national film subvention funds[80] in recognition and support of those 'true stories' that have proved increasingly popular with mass audiences.

Adaptations co-funded by German and Austrian film subsidy boards and public television, however, have also brought the literary canon of the second half of the twentieth century in particular to big and subsequently small screens—from the acclaimed Ingeborg Bachmann adaptation *Malina* (DE/AT, Werner Schroeter, 1991) to another adaptation of Martin Walser's *Ein fliehendes Pferd* [Runaway Horse] (DE, Rainer Kaufmann, 2007)[81] and Siegfried Lenz's *Deutschstunde* [German Lesson] (DE, Christian Schwochow,

2019)[82]—but a significant downward trend is undeniable. Commercial cinema has increasingly mobilized popular rather than literary culture in an effort to maximize profits in domestic and international markets. At the 2008 Berlinale Film Festival, Medienboard managing director Petra Mueller recognized the dynamic within shifting interests: 'studios are going on shopping sprees in the games industry, the internet is the new leading medium: Web 2.0 and computer games are the driving forces behind the radical change we're witnessing in the industry.'[83] Changes to the availability of public funding as outlined in the previous chapter had already dramatically reduced filmmakers' and producers' interests in adaptations based on German-language literature. Transnational modes of production "heighten[ed] sensitivity to cultural specificity,"[84] as Randall Halle explained, which provided additional momentum that moved film projects away from the literary heritage of Germany, Austria, and Switzerland,[85] unless the source text had a clear marketability due to its promise of satisfaction of desired fantasies or nostalgic longing for idyllic landscapes and alternative trajectories as in Johanna Spyri's *Heidi*.[86] Furthermore, adaptations of Germany's literary heritage seemed to nearly guarantee bad reviews in the national press, as filmmakers from Hans W. Geissendörfer to Dominik Graf and Detlev Buck would tell us. Even stunning and timely adaptations such as Christian Petzold's *Transit* (2018) and *Undine* (2020) or Burhan Qurbani's *Berlin Alexanderplatz* (2020) were not immune to repeated bashings in respected newspapers' culture sections for attempting to bring literary masterpieces (here, by Anna Seghers, Friedrich de la Motte Fouqué, and Alfred Döblin respectively) to cinema screens. All three projects were enabled by public film subsidies and tell complex stories in an aesthetically innovative film language, while providing entertainment that includes an invitation to think critically about contemporary society, good communities, and the challenges those on the margins face.

On November 10, 2016, the German Bundestag passed a new federal "Filmförderungsgesetz" [Film Subsidies Act]. The law ringfenced 44 million euro in order to 'secure the structure of the German film industry and to strengthen German film as an economic and cultural asset. It also aims to maintain and further develop the quality and diversity of German filmmaking.'[87] While the German language and German production elements are integral to fulfilling the necessary 'cultural criteria' in order to be eligible for public funding, co-productions with other, especially EU, countries are actively encouraged, as they 'contribute to intercultural understanding [...], promote the exchange of films between the countries involved, and to make German filmmaking more competitive internationally by increasing production budgets.' Overall, the federal government's law aims at 'increasing the artistic quality of German films and supporting the distribution of German films of artistic quality, while promoting the cinema as a cultural venue.' Monika Grütters, the German government's

Commissioner for Culture and the Media (2013–21), oversaw the changes that foregrounded gender equality and artistic excellence. Essential criteria for funding now include the following: the film's language either must be German or, alternatively, the director is German or lives in Germany; at least one of the producers must reside in Germany or be an EU or Swiss national; the contribution of the 'German'/EU producer must be at least as high as foreign investments; and, finally, the film has to premiere in Germany and be distributed in Germany first.[88]

Excluded from funding are film projects that 'contain unconstitutional or unlawful content, have a pornographic focus, promote violence, or are obviously deeply and inappropriately offensive to religious feelings of others'.[89] Compared to previous guidelines passed during the film political turn under Minister of the Interior Friedrich Zimmermann discussed in the previous chapter, there is no longer any allusion to commercial viability, even though the expected range of distribution, particularly in cinemas, is still being considered. The definition of German 'society and culture' is deliberately free from guidance or potential framing, and cultural or 'literary heritage' is no longer mentioned.[90] Nonetheless, in 2017, the FFA's commission for subsidizing film productions allocated nearly a quarter of its budget of 1.6 million euro to support the adaptation of Siegfried Lenz's novel *Deutschstunde* by Christian and (his mother) Heide Schwochow.[91]

When the 'Moviepilot' community recently rated the seven best adaptations of German-language literature since 2000, all seven had received public funding via Germany's state and federal film subsidy boards.[92] Top of the list is *Herr Lehmann* (Leander Haußmann 2003), an adaptation of Sven Regener's bestselling and very amusing debut novel about a young man working in a pub in the socially diverse area of Berlin-Kreuzberg in 1989. Regener won the German film award for best screenplay in 2004. Sven Taddicken's award-winning adaptation of Claudia Schreiber's novel *Emmas Glück* [Emma's Happiness/Luck] (2006) follows in second place, surpassing even big budget, international productions such as *The Reader/Der Vorleser* (US/DE, Stephen Daldry, 2008)[93] and Tykwer's multinational, English-language *Perfume: The Story of a Murderer* (2006), starring Ben Whishaw as olfactory prodigy and fixated mastermind next to Alan Rickman, Rachel Hurd-Wood, Dustin Hoffman, and others.[94]

Süskind's bestselling psychological thriller, and Tykwer's star-studded period drama, also inspired the television series *Parfum* (Philipp Kadelbach, 2017/18 and, for a second season, 2020/1).[95] But Eva Kranenburg's script locates the story in a contemporary rather than historical setting. Commissioned by public German television station ZDF, the series is an international collaboration between Constantin Film, Moovie, and Beta in Germany and Netflix, and received financial support from several public subsidy boards. Public television channels like ZDF, and regional German broadcasting companies in collaboration with ARD and the Austrian ORF, as well as Swiss radio and television SRF,[96] have continued to invest in adaptations of German-language literature as well as non-German texts, particularly British or Swedish romance and crime literatures, and have profited from the aforementioned subsidy schemes. In terms of German-language literature, public television—often collaborations between German, Austrian,[97] and Swiss companies or with the German-French channel ARTE—has been instrumental in bringing adaptations of contemporary literature, such as Juli Zeh's 2016's bestselling novel *Unterleuten,* to the small screen.[98] They have also continued to invest in adaptations of the literary canon, producing heritage films and costume dramas, which include another take on Zuckmayer's *Der Hauptmann von Köpenick* (Frank Beyer, 1997, script Wolfgang Kohlhaase), Schiller's *Kabale und Liebe* (DE/AT, Leander Haußmann, 2005), and Heinrich Breloer's lengthy new adaptation of Thomas Mann's *Buddenbrooks* (2008) with much attention to descriptive detail. *Emilia,* Henrik Pfeifer's adaptation of Lessing's 1772 play—a transposition project inspired by Michael Almereyda's *Hamlet* (US, 2000)—is an experimental Swiss-German co-production for ARTE, which generated much interest due to the creative integration of a past literary language into a present setting and an updated narrative.[99] Other innovative adaptations of important twentieth-century texts by the Austrian ORF include Kafka's *Das Schloss* (Michael Haneke, 1997), Ingeborg Bachmann's *Ihr glücklichen Augen* (Margaretha Heinrich, 1992), or Vicki Baum's *Hotel Shanghai* (as *Shanghai 1937,* Peter Patzak, 1996).[100] In the context of the Austrian cinema/television agreement (Film/Fernseh-Abkommen), ORF continues to support adaptation projects—in 2021 nearly 2 million euro were allocated to bring Austrian literature to film, from Robert Seethaler's *Ein ganzes Leben* (A whole life, 2014) and Doris Knecht's *Wald* (Forest, 2015) to children's series such as Christine Nöstlinger's *Geschichten vom Franz* (Stories of Franz, 1984–2011).[101]

In Germany, together with ZDF's "Das kleine Fernsehspiel," the series "Literarische Filmerzählung" [Literary Filmstory] founded by the ARD's regional partner Bavarian Broadcasting subsidiary BR in 1965 stood out for many years among public television companies in their promotion of auteur film and literature, but only few adaptations of the German-language literary canon followed after an adaptation of Austrian and exile author Stefan Zweig's *Leporella* (BR, Dagmar Damek) in 1991.[102] In the context of often transnational cinema-television agreements, it has been bestselling contemporary literature—such as Katharina Hagena's *Der Geschmack von Apfelkernen* (The Taste of Apple Seeds, 2008) adapted to cinema in 2013 under the direction of Vivian Naefe, Daniel Kehlmann's *Ruhm* (Fame, 2009; DE/AT/CH, Isabel Kleefeld, 2011), or Claudia Schreiber's aforementioned award-winning *Emmas Glück* (Emma's Bliss, 2003)— that proved more attractive, and was regularly and generously subsidized, especially if coupled with up-and-coming filmmakers. *Emmas Glück,* for example, was adapted under the direction of Sven Taddicken in 2005, with Jördis Triebel and Jürgen Vogel in the lead, and co-produced by the public broadcasting company SWR for its 'new talent' series.[103] Very popular in Germany, the well-acted and rather quirky take on a *Heimat*-film deals with illness and death in the strangely charming idyll of a small pig farm. While the film grossed over $3 million in Germany, it was far less successful abroad, even in neighboring Austria and Switzerland.[104] When Annette Pehnt's novel *Mobbing* (Bullying, 2008) was selected for adaptation by ARTE, the topic seemed to complement a desire to shed light on the devastating effects of bullying in the workplace. Pehnt's source text, however, was only mentioned in passing when the film was announced in 2012, which mirrored the subsequent reception of it in newspapers.

The trend points clearly toward popular literature on film. Crime films in particular have become a staple, not only in German-language television, and especially in serialized form. Filmmakers have been adapting crime novels to film for over a century, but the *Heimat*-crime-film is a recent subgenre that has gained traction with adaptations of popular novels by Rita Falk. Produced by Kerstin Schmidbauer/Constantin TV (Munich) for public television (ARD, BR) and Degeto Film, the first adaptation of Falk's *Dampfnudelblues* [Steamed Dumpling Blues] in 2013 proved so successful with national television audiences that her entire 'provincial' Franz-Eberhofer-series (2010ff.) is successively being adapted. The feature films (seven to date[105]) are all set in rural Bavaria, where dialect is spoken, local dishes are enjoyed, and crimes are regularly committed and inevitably solved—all in all a profitable scenario that is as unrealistic as it is comforting.

A much more urban take on the historical notion of 'Heimat' during the Weimar Republic in the crime genre are Volker Kutscher's Gereon Rath novels beginning with *Der nasse Fisch* (The Wet Fish, 2008), which have been adapted and successfully sold internationally: *Babylon Berlin* (DE, co-written/co-directed by Henk Handloegten, Tom Tykwer, Achim von Börries, 2017–20 for season 1–3) by X-Filme Creative Pool. Known for its internationally successful productions *Run Lola Run* and *Goodbye Lenin*, directors Tom Tykwer, Dani Levy, and Wolfgang Becker as well as producer Stefan Arndt founded the company in 1994. Because of its public-private financing model and successful collaboration between X-Filme, Warner Bros. Pictures Germany, and a few public and private television channels, the series has been widely distributed. While the production of a fourth season was delayed due to the Covid-19 pandemic, It was shown on German television and available via streaming networks in 2022. The most expensive German television series to date, the adaptation project has been supported financially by Medienboard Berlin-Brandenburg (MBB) in Potsdam, the Film- und Medien Stiftung NRW in Düsseldorf, the German Motion Picture Fund in Berlin, and the EU's Creative Europe MEDIA programmein Bruxelles.[106] Currently one of Germany's most successful film exports, the adaptation project would not have been viable initially without public funding sources.

Filmmaker/writer/author and lecturer Julia von Heinz emphasizes the important role of public television and highlights the broadcasting companies' role in supporting unpopular, critical, uniquely creative projects, as they did, for example, with Rosa von Praunheim's films about homosexuality, feminist films by Helke Sander, and German-Turkish films by Fatih Akin.[107] In her 2017 article in *Die Zeit*, she pleads:

> Public television must continue to leverage its unique position. Since it is not subject to the demand of 'the market', it is here that commercially risky films can be made that reflect our highly complex and vulnerable present without lulling the viewer into a false sense of security.[108]

But Heinz, who directed an adaptation of Hape Kerkeling's bestselling *Ich bin dann mal weg* (I'm Off Then, 2006) in 2015, also emphasizes the role of cinema, when controversial social issues need to be artistically explored in a format that is free from genre limitations. In order to enable these 'experiments with an uncertain outcome,' i.e., 'an experimental laboratory far removed from the market', television as a financial partner and public subsidies are crucial. Without them, exciting and important films such as *Victoria* (DE, Sebastian Schipper, 2015) or *Toni Erdmann* (DE/AT, Maren Ade, 2016), or adaptations such as *In den Gängen* [In the Aisles] (DE, Thomas Stuber, 2018), based on Clemens Meyer's short story, or Kästner's timely *Fabian oder Der Gang vor die Hunde* [Fabian—Going to the Dogs] (DE, Dominik Graf, 2021) would most likely not have been made. Their relative independence from the market is public television's greatest asset and by supporting fringe productions and experimental films, their contribution to the public sphere remains significant even if viewing practices have moved largely from cinemas to streaming services as welcome alternatives during lockdowns and limitations during the Covid-19 pandemic.

Nonetheless, the commercial pressure on filmmakers is increasingly enormous. Production and distribution companies are looking predominantly for 'projects with regional roots, that can be easily related to a sense of home, preferable in dialect', Heinz writes. According to the writer/filmmaker and comparable to tendencies in the film production landscape elsewhere in the Global North, in Germany, comedies are clearly favored, but 'dramedies' might also be considered. Serious topics are produced only if 'tackled light-heartedly, ideally with a wink, as long as the conclusion offers resolution and healing of all conflicts', as she puts it pointedly. Scripts that focus on historical topics or times that might unsettle have little chance of being produced, she insists. In her experience, complex and difficult film proposals face an uphill battle while the producers' imagined viewer simply 'wants answers, not more questions and problems!'[109]

The Berlin School

Filmmakers of the so-called "Berliner Schule" never shied away from asking questions and with their work established the most significant German film movement since the 1990s. Beginning with films such as Thomas Arslan's *Mach die Musik leiser* [Turn Down the Music] (1994), Christian Petzold's *Pilotinnen* [Female Pilots] (1995), and Angela Schanelec's *Das Glück meiner Schwester* [My Sister's Good Fortune] (1995), this "nouvelle vague allemande"[110] reflected on its creative output in a bi-annual publication, *Revolver*, a magazine founded by Benjamin Heisenberg, Christoph Hochhäusler, and Sebastian Kutzli, who studied together at the Munich Film Academy (Hochschule für Film und Fernsehen).[111] Marco Abel summarizes the movement astutely as "a counter-cinema that refuses to make films 'for' an already existing German people and instead seeks to address a people in their collective becoming."[112] Directors such as Arslan, Schanelec, Petzold, Heisenberg, and Hochhäusler, but also, more recently, Maren Ade and Valeska Grisebach do not focus on the consensus or that which we might all share, but instead address the fissures and margins in our society while expressing their own creative imagination and skill. Their films make room for overlooked individuals and stories missing from the nation's repetitive medial re-enactment of a unified culture, particularly in the context of a globally successful cinema of identification.[113] The Berlin School has been recognized internationally "for its revitalization of art cinema via techniques of filmic realism attentive to the forms of subjectivity and relationality produced among Germans and Europeans in the era of late capitalism and globalization"[114] as Baer and Fenner note.

The Berlin School's director-producers bring their truth and contemporaneity to cinema screens, and it cannot surprise that they have had little interest in turning to a male-dominated literary canon for inspiration. Especially Christian Petzold used to be rather outspoken in his rejection of 'literary films' and collaborative cinema-television productions[115] so popular among the auteurs of New German Cinema. In 2018, however, his adaptation of Anna Seghers's *Transit* (1944) became one of the most widely discussed films in German feuilletons of the year. As Petzold mentioned in interviews, *Transit* was both his and his former teacher at the Deutsche Film- und Fernsehakademie in Berlin, Harun Farocki's favorite novel. They had discussed adapting the text before filming *Phoenix* (2014) but agreed that a novel this good had already found its "perfection of form, its definite form," as Hitchcock put it in a conversation with Truffaut about adaptation.[116] 'We were both of the opinion [...] that *Transit* is a great novel and hence always kept a bit of distance', he explains, but nonetheless they collaborated on a treatment for an adaptation, reading Georg Karl Glaser's account of persecution and exile *Geheimnis und Gewalt* (Secret and Violence, 2 vols., 1951/3) alongside, an autobiographical novel they also both cherished.[117] After Farocki passed away in 2014, Petzold 'had the idea of bringing this story into the present time, as kind of a ghost story', as he remarks in an interview. 'Ghosts' of the past in the present and the theme of exile run through his work like a thread—calling his films *Die innere Sicherheit* [lit. 'Inner' but also 'Homeland' Security/The State I Am In] (2000), *Gespenster* [Ghosts] (2005), both co-written with Farocki, and *Yella* (2007), his 'ghost-trilogy'. In *Transit* (2018), which finally emerged from Petzold's collaboration with his late friend and mentor, and inspired by Glaser's term "Geschichtsstille" [historical silence], the filmmaker's interest and focus is on individuals who 'have no present' and 'hang around in liminal spheres, who can go no further and cannot go back.'[118] As a metaphor for the state of being in exile, the term evoked for Petzold the state of being 'out at sea. There is no longer a breeze that could carry one forward. History has taken the wind out of your sails, you are no longer needed.'[119]

Transit, the most remarkable Anna Seghers-adaptation since Piscator's *Revolt of the Fishermen* (1934), will be discussed further below.

Petzold's opposition to the "entire neoliberal nonsense"[120] is well documented. In an interview with Abel published in *Cineaste*, Petzold outlines neoliberalism's impetus as "to destroy all well-established social institutions, even though the reunification in 1990 momentarily disguised that trend. The polis, the public space, the common, all sexy terms such as the 'lean state'—all of these were merely synonyms for the essential desire of neoliberals to destroy the political society." For the film industry, a cinema of affect and identification has proven commercially most attractive, but for Petzold, they are outdated and misleading representations reminiscent of narratives of the "eighteenth century, or the worst of the nineteenth!" that contribute little to the public sphere.

FIGURE 9.3 *Paula Beer and Franz Rogowski in* Transit *(DE, Christian Petzold, 2018)*.

In his article "Schluss mit der Anpasserei!"[121] (Stop the Alignment, 2003) published in *Die Zeit*, Volker Schlöndorff also addressed the crisis of German cinema since the 1990s. Focused too much on "globale Leitkultur" or leading global culture and constantly trying to secure public subsidies and television co-financing agreements, German cinema 'imitates what has been successful' and shies away from 'any theoretical engagement', the veteran director argues. Instead, most filmmakers follow standardized formats and styles, particularly regarding television. Hence, in Schlöndorff's view, German cinema is, for the most part, devoid of personal style, characterless, uninspiring, and thus largely ignored internationally. In contrast, he argues in view of Wolfgang Becker and Tom Tykwer, those who do not care about the material safety promised by following the norms have gained international recognition, and Schlöndorff clearly hopes that more young filmmakers will follow suit.

Not surprisingly, Petzold took issue with Schlöndorff's assessment, and especially disagreed with the value of theory in this context. In fact, he blamed Germany's auteurs such as Schlöndorff for contributing to the crisis:

> They participated in this pigeonholing—art house over here, mainstream over there, nonstars vs. stars, etc. Those who participated in divvying up cinema this way were the death of cinema. And the cinema for which Schlöndorff stands was involved in this process because it began to focus on adapting great German literature. Hitchcock said that you couldn't film a great novel, only a bad one. I find myself agreeing with this, for cinema is not literature. But towards the end of the 1970s, all of a sudden everyone made films based on novels by Uwe Johnson or Thomas Mann, and this was the most boring and impoverished cinema imaginable. Thus, by the end of the 1980s we had two kinds of cinema: the miserable cinema of literature and an escapist, lowbrow cinema, which wanted to be the opposite of this literary cinema. And before you knew it someone like Dominik Graf, for whose attempt at making intelligent genre films I have the utmost respect, found himself in an incredibly lonesome position.[122]

While the international success of masterful adaptations by auteur filmmakers beginning with Schlöndorff's *Törless* indeed triggered numerous less inspired films based on the literary canon as discussed in the previous chapter, Petzold's point regarding the division of "escapist, lowbrow cinema" and "literary cinema" is an important one. During the past three decades, a neoliberal film industry favored the commercially more profitable cinema with universal appeal, from comedies to the cinema of identification, as outlined above. The Berlin School emerged from a new generation of auteur filmmakers who chose to tell their own stories, rather than using their voice for re-creating a literary cinema now considered a different if no less problematic version of "Papas Kino." But at the same time, a new transnational German cinema emerged with international adaptation projects such as Schlöndorff's *Homo Faber* (1990) and *Return to Montauk* (2017) respectively based on and inspired by Max Frisch or Tom Tykwer's aforementioned Süskind adaptation *The Perfume* (2006), that could serve as examples of films produced by a globalizing media industry, merging the demands of a consumer-driven market, i.e., a high-production-value commercial cinema aimed at mass entertainment, with the nuanced aesthetics of art cinema and a director's auteurist expression.[123]

Most notably, by turning to the literary canon, Petzold has redefined adaptations in the context of their contemporaneity by critically examining canonical literary texts and thus a historical presence in contemporary cinema culture. In his wonderful *Undine* (2020) inspired by Friedrich de la Motte Fouquée's story[124] Petzold reflects on myths and adaptations during the era of Romanticism as well as on society, entertainment culture, and the spaces we create and inhabit. His story takes place in a twenty-first-century Berlin, a capitol struggling with urban cultural transformations that problematically reimagine or even celebrate an imperial past, while exhibiting film as a medium that is critical and magical, personal and yet

FIGURE 9.4 *Paula Beer as urban historian in* Undine *(DE, Christian Petzold, 2020).*

exemplary. His film functions as an adaptation and is a unique cinematic work of art. Petzold's *Transit* and *Undine* comment on adaptation practices of Germany's postcapitalist cinema of neoliberalism and counter the notion that 'only what can be (re)narrated in cinema is really literature. Everything else is merely mannerism, eccentricity, masquerade, and experiment' as culture and film critic Andreas Kilb put it:

> Ever since cinema has learned to talk, it has been eating books. Big books, small books, thick and thin books, classics and trash, and above all novels. Because novels tell stories. Stories that the film camera can continue to tell. The form and style, the narrative technique and its rhythm, cinema is not interested in that. It reads a classic like a dime novel and a dime novel like a classic.[125]

In contrast to Kilb's assessment, Petzold's adaptations *Transit* and *Undine* are negotiations of literature on film that reflect awareness of both the stories' 'narrative technique and [...] rhythm' and the function of cinema within the public sphere. His films reimagine the literary text as art and could not be further from commercial cinema's use of a suitable and ideally bestselling narrative.

Pandemic Adaptations and Copyright Regulations

It is undeniable that our cinema of neoliberalism has only little interest in anything but bestselling German-language literature when considering the production of an adaptation. Yet some of the most outstanding films of the past thirty years have been literary films, as the list of 'solitaires' at the end of this chapter hopes to illustrate. From March 2020, the Covid-19 pandemic and necessary lockdowns have had a serious impact on film productions and cinemas. Productions were delayed, hygiene requirements made filming more difficult and time-consuming, and financially the business became even more precarious, especially for the independent creatives involved in filmmaking.

In Germany alone, about 40 percent fewer feature films were released during 2020 compared to previous years. Because of closures of cinemas and an array of 'safer' streaming options during the pandemic even when lockdowns had ended, ticket sales fell by a staggering 70 percent the same year.[126] This taxing development was mirrored globally to varying degrees. While the pandemic has been affecting film and cinema in general from 2020 onwards, the 'Act to adapt copyright law to the requirements of the

Digital Single Market' might have a more direct impact on adaptations of German literature specifically.[127]

Already in 2016, while the reform of the copyright law was being considered by the German government, author/producer Alfred Holighaus—who co-produced an adaptation of Brussig's highly entertaining 'Wende'-novel *Helden wie wir* [Heroes like us] (DE, Sebastian Peterson, 1999)—gave a keynote at the Institut für Europäisches Medienrecht [European Media Law Institute] in Berlin in 2016. Here, he outlined the potentially dire consequences of the new law for the film industry, which would see a 'bow wave' of financial and administrative pressures that, in his estimation, would significantly hinder growth within the industry.[128] In their press release, Constantin Film warned that aspects of the reform were simply unrealistic. The rights to review, revocation, and ongoing renumeration of authors and publishers in accordance with the success of a particular film project would be untenable. In the context of practical applicability, Holighaus emphasized that even the legal uncertainty was already jeopardizing potential film projects. The reform under consideration caused significant debate within the film production industry, but whether the expectation of a changing legal framework already impacted films based on contemporary literature—that might now come with a high and ongoing price-tag—could not be established.

After years of consultations, the revised Copyright Law was passed in the German parliament (Bundestag) and has been legally binding since June 2021. Most importantly in the context of adaptations, the rights of the 'creators' especially, but also those of the publishers are strengthened, and authors must be 'appropriately' compensated for the use of their creative work. In case of a disparity between the payment received and the success of the 'utilization' ("Verwertungserfolg") of an author's work, subsequent claims to remuneration must be considered. Now not only authors, but publishers, and other creators such as screenwriters, must be 'fairly' compensated, and 'exploiters' must inform 'creators' in much more detail about the ways in which they intend to make use of their texts.[129] The clarity of the law passed in 2021, the removal of certain aspects most detrimental to adaptation projects in the eyes of producers, and the industry's unquenchable hunger for stories will most likely circumvent an end of adaptations in general and of films based on German-language literature in particular. Overall, the significant reduction of productions and premieres during the Covid-19 pandemic meant that fewer adaptations of German-language literature made it to commercial cinema. But television's interest in popular stories and arthouse cinema's newfound attention to the canon of German literature means that overall, adaptation still reigns among the most common practice of filmmaking.

Adaptations of German-language Literature Abroad

Viewed from across the Atlantic, German cinema seemed "on a roll" since the turn of the millennium, Abel wrote in 2008, with numerous appearances at international film festivals, four Academy Award nominations and Oscars for Best Foreign Language Film for *Nirgendwo in Afrika* [Nowhere in Afrika] (DE, Caroline Link, 2001) and *Das Leben der Anderen* [The Lives of Others] (DE, Florian Henckel von Donnersmarck, 2006).[130] Apart from Caroline Link's *Jenseits der Stille* [Beyond Silence] (1997), the Academy clearly preferred German and Austrian films that addressed the dark sides of the German past with stories dealing with the repression experienced by individuals during the Hitler era, or by the East German secret police Stasi. As Abel puts it: "American audiences especially seem to love such German films, as if to perpetuate the stereotype that German culture can essentially be reduced forever to its totalitarian legacies of the twentieth century."[131] Academy Award nominations for Best Foreign Film between 1990 and 2005 went to German and Austrian films—Michael Verhoeven's *Das schreckliche Mädchen* [The Nasty Girl] (1990), Helmut Dietl's *Schtonk!* (1992), Oliver Hirschbiegel's *Der Untergang* [Downfall] (2004), Marc Rothemund's *Sophie Scholl—The Final Days* (2005)—that all deal directly or indirectly with the Hitler era and German Nazism. The first Austrian win went to Stefan Ruzowitzky's Holocaust-film *Die Fälscher* [The Counterfeiters] in 2007.[132]

Anglophone adaptations of German-language texts during the past three decades have been rare and were mostly inspired by commercial successes of either a previous adaptation abroad or a translation of the literary text, while usually dealing with events in Nazi Germany and/or during the Holocaust. Frank Beyer's adaptation of Jurek Becker's *Jakob der Lügner* [Jacob the Liar] in 1976 became the first East German film nominated for a Best Foreign Film Oscar since the creation of the GDR. In 1999, the tragicomedy about Jakob's comforting fake radio broadcasts in a Jewish ghetto during the Holocaust was remade in Hollywood under the direction of Peter Kassovitz and starring Robin Williams. But the remake struggled to match Beyer's outstanding first adaptation despite Williams' empathetic and convincing portrayal of main protagonist Jakob Heym.[133] Overall strikingly well-fed if dusty looking ghetto inmates failed to convince internationally.

Bestselling English-language versions of a German-language novel have also and repeatedly led to adaptations by Hollywood studios and in Europe as the previous chapters have shown. When Fallada's anti-Nazi novel *Jeder stirbt für sich allein* (1947), for example, was published by Penguin in English as *Alone in Berlin* (EU)/*Every Man Dies Alone* (USA) in an outstanding translation by Michael Hofmann in 2009, it received rave reviews. Vincent Pérez and Stefan Arndt acquired the film rights and, with the help of

Master Films and X Filme Creative Pool as well as funding provided by Medienboard Berlin-Brandenburg, DFF, FFA, and others, *Alone in Berlin* (DE/GB/FR, Vincent Perez) premiered at the Berlin Film Festival in 2016, starring international celebrities Emma Thompson and Brendan Gleeson as the Quangels, whose small acts of resistance lead to imprisonment and death in Nazi Germany. Despite excellent performances by the leading aforementioned actors and by Daniel Brühl as Gestapo inspector Escherich charged with finding the authors of antifascist and pacifist sentiments scribbled on postcards that were being inconspicuously left in public spaces around Berlin, the adaptation received mixed reviews.

Among all the Holocaust-literature in German, Bernhard Schlink's *Der Vorleser* (The Reader, 1995) has been the most successful commercially. A global bestseller translated into more than fifty languages, Schlink's story of former concentration camp guard Hanna focuses on her affair with a fifteen-year-old schoolboy, who reads to her, and ends with an intriguing twist when years later, Michael attends the Auschwitz-trials as a young law student and recognizes Hanna as one of the accused. Schlink's morally complex parable about guilt, agency, and coming to terms with the past was translated into English by Carol Brown Janeway and sold over 2 million copies after being presented in Oprah's Book Club in 1999. Despite labels such as "Holocaust-Kitsch" and much criticism focused on Schlink's narrative choice to reveal Hanna as illiterate—which implicitly calls Hanna's culpability as a former concentration camp guard into question—millions of copies sold in Anglophone countries alone made the book a candidate for adaptation. David Hare wrote the screenplay based on the novel, and Stephen Daldry directed the Weinstein Company and Babelsberg film co-production (producers Anthony Minghella, Sydney Pollack, Donna Gigliotti, and Redmond Morris), which benefitted from film subsidies from several German film boards. In 2009, the adaptation was nominated for five Academy Awards (including Adapted Screenplay) and won the Actress in a Leading Role Oscar for Kate Winslet as Hanna Schmitz.

When considering films based on German-language literature of the past three decades, certain trends from commercial interests (bestsellers) to historical concerns (memory culture) can easily be identified. But there are adaptations that defy categorization and stand out. Exceptional filmmakers from Brazil, China, the United States, Russia, France, Greece, Italy, Senegal, and Japan—namely Wes Anderson, Constantin Costa-Gavras, Xu Jinglei, Stanley Kubrick, Arnaud des Pallières, Sean Penn, Djibril Diop Mambéty, Fernando Meirelles, Aleksandr Sokurov, the Taviani brothers, and, to name just one more outstanding talent, the Japanese animator Kōji Yamamura—have all turned to German and Austrian literature and reimagined not only the stories of Kleist and Goethe, Kafka, Schnitzler, and Stefan Zweig, but also more recent literary texts by Hochhut and Dürrenmatt. Their films are what I would consider 'solitaires'—unique engagements of creative

FIGURE 9.5 *David Kross as young Michael Berg reading Lessing's* Emilia Galotti *to Kate Winslet as Hanna Schmitz in* The Reader *(US/DE, Stephen Daldry, 2008).*

individuals with a text (or texts) that inspired them. But even they reflect and inadvertently calcify the male domination of the literary canon and its reception abroad. Implicitly, publishing houses and adaptations thus perpetuate male-dominated literary traditions, and reinforce exclusionary practices that saw writers like Emmy Hennings, Vicki Baum, Gina Kaus, Gabriele Tergit, and many others labeled as 'trivial'—an adjective that most effectively separated an author's work from the literary canon.[134] Only a few directors such as Werner Schroeter, Michael Haneke, and Julian R. Pölsler have in the last few decades brought the work of highly acclaimed writers like Ingeborg Bachmann, Elfriede Jelinek, and Marlen Haushofer to film.[135] More adaptations of marginalized and nearly forgotten authors will hopefully follow and in turn revitalize the literary canon.

Solitaires

Before concluding this book, I would like to draw attention to some of the outstanding 'solitaires' of the last three decades, gems among the vast number of films produced that happen to be based on German-language literature. This is a personal curation of films, of course, fundamentally shaped by genre-related contexts and interests. The films to follow are ordered chronologically and indicate the adaptation genre's vast range—from close re-imaginings, playful meta-adaptations to hybrid, bi- or transcultural experimentations. The films to follow once more reflect the impact of German-language literature on film and indicate its possibilities: begetting new forms and breaking new ground aesthetically, leaving traces for others to follow, or using a 'foreign' piece of literature to navigate one's way through the complexity of a familiar 'home.' They hopefully mark a transition to a future for adaptations based on German-language literature that not only celebrates but also sustains creative autonomy.

Malina (Germany/Austria, Werner Schroeter, 1991)

Two decades after the publication of Austrian writer Ingeborg Bachmann's 'imaginary autobiography' *Malina,* Werner Schroeter directed an adaptation of the novel based on a script by Elfriede Jelinek. The novel situates the female narrator in relation to men—her often absent lover Ivan, her flatmate Malina, and her father as a representative of masculinity during Nazism—exposing the nexus between fascism and patriarchy. The horror of the Second World War and Holocaust, rapes, and other moments of utter destruction haunt her dreams. Her struggle to be and to write 'after Auschwitz' culminates in her disappearance—and both novel and its adaptation end with the same unambiguous three words: 'it was murder'. Jelinek and Schroeter offer an adaptation that follows Bachmann in allowing for internal and external disassemblage, laying bare the fissures, and inferring archetypes of the human psyche as well as patriarchy as a social system entangled in the moral abyss of recent Nazi history. The adaptation stars Isabelle Huppert as the nameless writer, Mathieu Carrière (Malina), Can Togay (Ivan), and Fritz Schediwy (as her father); it won numerous awards, among them Best Film, Best Director, Best Screenplay, Best Editing (Juliane Lorenz), and Best Actor (Huppert) at the German Film Awards in 1991, and the Deutscher Kamerapreis (Elfi Mikesch) in 1992.

Hyènes [Hyenas] (Senegal, Djibril Diop Mambéty, 1992)

Considered one of Africa's greatest auteurs, Djibril Diop Mambéty or 'DDM' (1945-98) turned to Friedrich Dürrenmatt's satirical play *Der Besuch der alten Dame* (The Visit, 1956) to create a sequel to his masterful first feature-length film *Touki Bouki* [The Hyena's Journey] (1973), the second part of a planned "trilogy about ordinary people."[136] In the "human drama" *Hyène* DDM recreates Dürrenmatt's story of revenge and human weakness as a deeply personal narrative that never loses sight of the marginalized. Africa's history and neocolonialism are at the core of this adaptation. "For me, filming is remembering," DDM said in an interview, a return to the "place you come from." Screened at the 1992 Cannes Film Festival, the movie pays "homage to the beauty of Africa" and clearly focuses on local concerns, while accentuating them as transnational and global. DDM wanted to make a "continental film, one that crosses boundaries." He adapts Dürrenmatt's story to highlight the universal theme of "the vanity of vengeance," but also "borrowed elephants from the Masai of Kenya, hyenas from Uganda, and people from Senegal" to make *Hyènes* even more continental.

> And to make it global, we borrowed somebody from Japan, and carnival scenes from the annual Carnival of Humanity of the French Communist Party in Paris. All of these are intended to open the horizons, to make the film universal. The film depicts a human drama. My task was to identify the enemy of humankind: money, the International Monetary Fund, and the World Bank. I think my target is clear.[137]

Nearly half a century after it was first staged in Zurich, Dürrenmatt's drama ties all these facets relevant to a Senegalese filmmaker together—the false promises of Western materialism, the tragedy of corruption and African consumerism, the cowardice of human greed, and the inhumanity of marginalization, exploitation, and vengeance.

FIGURE 9.6 *Ami Diakhate as the 'old lady' Linguère Ramatou in* Hyènes *(Senegal, Djibril Diop Mambéty, 1992)*.

Schlafes Bruder [The Brother of Sleep] (Germany/Austria, Joseph Vilsmaier, 1995)

In Greek mythology, sleep's brother is Thanatos, the god of death. The film, based on Robert Schneider's bestselling eponymous 1992 novel, tells the story of Elias, an abject genius in an early nineteenth-century Austrian village. Schneider wrote the script for the adaptation in collaboration with the director. Elias (André Eisermann) can hear all the sounds of the universe and his ability to play the organ in the local church displays an uncanny power. The adaptation focuses the story about difference and marginalization, on love and friendship, and the destructive effects of ignorance and jealousy—motifs prevalent in Vilsmaier's equally atmospheric if much more affirmative adaptation of Adalbert Stifter's 1845 story *Bergkristall* (DE, 2004). Also starring Dana Vávrová and Ben Becker, *Schlafes Bruder* was widely criticized primarily due to the narrative reduction and conventional streamlining of Schneider's source text. Even so, Vilsmaier creates captivating images to communicate the oppressive atmosphere of closed communities, the grotesque power of human prejudice and cruelty, but also the beauty of nature and the possibility of growth in the face of failure and destruction. The film was nominated for a Golden Globe and received Austrian, German, and Bavarian film awards.

Le affinità elettive [Elective Affinities] (Italy/France, Paolo and Vittorio Taviani, 1996)

The Taviani brothers' elegant adaptation of Goethe's 1809 novel *Die Wahlverwandtschaften* is an unusually restrained if, for the most part, conventional period drama, here set in Tuscany, during the Napoleonic era. The precision and control of the film's aesthetic and acting make this adaptation stand out as an exploration of human order and discipline, but also of love as nothing more than a chemical reaction. The Tavianis' adaptation employs film as Goethe utilized fiction to create a scientific parable that examines the forces of attraction between individuals. The existing bond of marriage between Carlotta (Isabelle Huppert) and Edoardo (Jean-Hugues Anglade) is jeopardized when his friend (Fabrizio Bentivoglio) and her goddaughter (Marie Gillain) come to stay. As the composition of the four elements changes and, finally, tragedy strikes, the human dimension of these elected affinities is masterfully displayed.

Eyes Wide Shut (USA, Stanley Kubrick, 1999)

Following outstanding adaptations such as *2001: A Space Odyssey* (1968), *Barry Lyndon* (1975), and *The Shining* (1980), in his final movie Kubrick offers a luminous psychosexual meditation on Schnitzler's avant-garde *Traumnovelle* (lit. Dream Novella, 1926). The film, which took a staggering 400 days of shooting, stars Tom Cruise and Nicole Kidman as the main protagonists. The great American filmmaker passed away before the adaptation was released but his brother-in-law Jan Harlan said he "regarded *Eyes Wide Shut* as his greatest contribution to cinema." [138] By unraveling the subconscious of a good-looking, wealthy doctor with a beautiful wife during a nocturnal odyssey through present-day New York, Kubrick's adaptation muses not only about bourgeois (and celebrity) posturing and sexual (dys) function, but about the film industry as dream factory.[139] Schnitzler was inspired by Sigmund Freud's *Traumdeutung* (The Interpretation of Dreams, 1899), which integrated the subconscious into the conscious and thus enabled ordering access to an individual's mental state. But Schnitzler's literary display of Freud's book of dreams was at the same time a parody of the married bourgeois' ambivalent desire for sex and power, which is foregrounded when the male protagonist's eyes devour veiled and masked but otherwise naked women at a party, tortured by the obscurity of their otherwise exposed bodies. Their masks' over-dimensional eyes appear like a riddle of spectatorship. Kubrick's actualized adaptation is more than an exploration of looking and longing, it is about US American class-based society, where traditional values clash with sexual and monetary aspirations, celebrity culture, and neoliberal excess. The pleasure of the voyeur is here always-already the torture of unquenched desire, and Kubrick's adaptation of Schnitzler's text is not only a cinematic masterpiece but a deeply political critique of his country and its impossible dream. While critics were less enthused about the film in the United States than in Europe, the film grossed over $162 million worldwide.[140]

The Pledge (USA, Sean Penn, 2001)

In the late 1950s, Swiss novelist and playwright Dürrenmatt wrote a treatment for a haunting story about a serial killer, and a detective, who promises a disconsolate mother to bring her young daughter's murderer to justice. *Es geschah am hellichten Tag* [It Happened in Broad Daylight] (CH/ES/FRG, Ladislao Vajda, 1958) is one of the most powerful and highly acclaimed thrillers in German-language film history. The detective's successful delivery, which concludes the movie narrative, however, deviated fundamentally from Dürrenmatt's original idea, leading the Swiss author to write a novel that reflected on detective fiction and concessions of the entertainment industry in *Das Versprechen: Requiem auf den Kriminalroman* (The Pledge: Requiem for the Detective Novel, 1958) based on his film script. While numerous remakes[141] of the commercially very successful *Es geschah am hellichten Tag* were made internationally, it was Sean Penn who turned to *Das Versprechen* and adapted Dürrenmatt's work without losing sight of the audience's genre-related expectations. In one of the final scenes of his stunning neo-noir thriller, the viewer witnesses the car accident that kills the murderer. While the audience is relieved to know he will no longer harm young girls, the detective (Jack Nicholson) remains oblivious and thus haunted by an unfulfilled promise that leaves him a broken alcoholic. Chris Menges' cinematography constructs landscapes that seem as forbidding as that longing for resolution that will never be satisfied. Filmed mostly in British Columbia, Penn caters to the audience, while faithfully reimagining Dürrenmatt's detective, who succumbs to the desire to make a promise to comfort another, but for the rest of his life suffers the misery caused by his inability to keep it.

Le Pianiste [The Piano Teacher] (France/Austria/Germany/Poland, Michael Haneke, 2001)

This adaptation of Elfriede Jelinek's breakthrough novel *Die Klavierspielerin* (lit. The Female Piano Player, 1983) under Haneke's direction is as unsettling and powerful as its source text. The psychosexual drama focuses on a middle-aged piano teacher (Isabelle Huppert), whose life of discontent and frustration swings rhythmically, like a metronome, between the home she shares with her mother in bizarre symbiosis and the conservatory in Vienna, where she teaches. Longing for satisfaction, creatively and professionally as much as sexually, the repressed and disciplined protagonist has a sadomasochistic relationship with one of her male students that summons violence and ends in disaster. Like so many of his other films, Haneke's adaptation is an unflinching and in parts brutal exploration of human nature. As in Jelinek's self-harming protagonist, the piano teacher on screen struggles with obsessive disorders, auto-aggression, and her fixation with pornography. Haneke unveils the depths of misery and frustration in the life of a woman raised in emotional dependency and taught that only repression and sacrifice can yield recognition and success. Brilliantly conveyed by Huppert, the piano teacher's desires are askew and collide with the reality of an average life that is devoid of great achievement, of profound love or children. She is filled with self-loathing and Haneke highlights the destructive effects of a repressed and an unfulfilled existence, which causes the piano teacher to harm not only herself but others. *Le Pianiste* won the Grand Prix at the 2001 Cannes Film Festival and numerous other film awards. It was the Austrian submission to the Academy Awards that year, but the deliberately provocative and scathingly critical film would not be nominated.

Amen (France, Constantin Costa-Gavras, 2002)

Rolf Hochhuth's play *Der Stellvertreter* (The Deputy, 1963) about Pope Pius XII's role in the Second World War and the Vatican's collaborative silence about the Nazis' mass murder of Jewish citizens was first staged and directed by Erwin Piscator in Berlin in 1963. In his preface to the publication of the play, Piscator calls Hochhuth's work 'one of the few essential contributions to coming to terms with the past. It relentlessly calls a spade a spade, [...] it assigns their measure of responsibility to the guilty; it reminds all concerned that they did indeed decide, even if they did not.'[142] Piscator, one of the most important innovators of theater, insists that documentary and art have become inseparable in this play.[143] The year that Roman Polanski's Holocaust film *The Pianist* was awarded the Palme d'Or at Cannes, Costa-Gavras brought his adaptation of Hochhuth's play to cinemas and thus contributed significantly to ongoing memory discourses and important debates about the Holocaust and questions of accountability. Hochhuth's and Costa-Gavras' provocative spotlight on the Vatican's ultimate moral failure received plenty of criticism, but even though the adaptation had nowhere near the explosive effect of its source text, Costa Gavras' portrayal of individuals like SS-officer Gerstein (Ulrich Tukur) and the young Jesuit priest Fontana (Mathieu Kassovitz) invites contemplation. The film's critical energy is directed at the Catholic Church's leadership and the Vatican as a powerful institution that chose to protect its own standing in Germany and Austria, to ignore the organized murder of millions of innocent citizens, and finally, to help senior Nazis flee persecution via the so-called 'rat line'.[144]

Poem—Ich setzte den Fuß in die Luft und sie trug [Poem: I Set My Foot Upon the Air and It Carried Me] (Germany/USA, Ralf Schmerberg, 2003)

The title of this film refers to the motto preceding Hilde Domin's first volume of poetry *Nur eine Rose als Stütze* (Nothing but a rose for support, 1959) and highlights the core of the project, which consists of adaptations of nineteen different poems written over two centuries. *Poem* begins with Schmerberg's collaborator Antonia Keinz's "Alles" and ends with Schiller's *Ode to Joy* (1785)—with Beethoven's musical adaptation of the poem in 1824 evoking Europe and standing in as the European anthem since the 1970s. Joy is indeed a recurring theme in this project, even though a kaleidoscope of emotions as well as visual styles, rhythms, methods, places, and subjects are displayed in the different shorts. Schmerberg said in an interview[145] that poems should be a joy and pleasure, not a chore, and with their film hoped to foreground the pleasure and timelessness of the genre. The award-winning director, known for his music videos in particular, does not merely illustrate the poems but rather brings a tapestry of images and sounds to film. With the help of experts at the camera such as Robby Müller and Darius Khondji and major actors Jürgen Vogel, Meret Becker, Klaus Maria Brandauer, Anna Thalbach, and others, the poems chime and oscillate between their past and our imaginative here and now. These diverse and brief visual glimpses into narratives also illustrate how poetry as art is not bound to time and place, reflecting life and human experience in all its facets, no matter whether the poem is recited off-screen (while we watch someone carry a fellow traveler in the Himalaya mountains) or directly into the camera from a theater stage somewhere in Germany. Schmerberg and his team bring these poems to life on screen, no matter whether the individual short adapts a poem by Goethe, Heine, Rilke or Hesse, Claire Goll, Ernst Jandl, or exiles and victims of Nazi terror such as Selma Meerbaum-Eisinger, Mascha Kaléko, Else Lasker-Schüler, Kurt Tucholsky, Erich Kästner, Paul Celan, or Ingeborg Bachmann. Some of their short adaptations are filled with color, others come in shades of gray, some are loud, others gentle, either bursting with something to tell or hermetic and very personal, but all display inspiring creativity.

一个陌生女人的来信, Letter from an Unknown Woman (China, Xu Jinglei, 2004)

Xu Jinglei offers a delicate reimagining of the story, now set in China, in this fifth film[146] based on Stefan Zweig's *Brief einer Unbekannten* (Letter from an Unknown Woman, 1922) and clearly inspired by Max Ophüls' adaptation. Here, a celebrated author (Jiang Wen) receives a letter from a woman in 1948, the year Ophüls' film premiered. The letter outlines their relationship in a conventional voice-over and the story of unrequited love and memory is accentuated as world literature in a stunning visualization of Zweig's literary style. The story here begins in Sichuan in the 1930s and introduces a teenager (Lin Yuan) infatuated with the famous writer who lives nearby. Years later, they meet in Beijing. He is flattered by the young woman's admiration and has a brief affair with the college student (now played by Xu). While the womanizer forgets their encounter all too quickly, she finds herself pregnant and moves back to Sichuan to give birth to a boy during the time of the Second Sino-Japanese War. Finally, she is back in Beijing, working as a high-class prostitute to support her son. During their final encounter, the author fails to recognize her. In her letter, to be delivered after her death, she recounts their failed relationship and highlights the importance of communication and memory. Xu chooses to transpose the narrative to the 1930s and 1940s rather than the 1960s and 1970s or even the present-day, thus avoiding any indications of suicide, deprivation, single motherhood, and survival sex in the context of the Cultural Revolution or twenty-first-century China. Perceived by some as 'anticipated obedience' in light of potential censorship and other political pressures, the adaptation was criticized, while doing very well at the box office. As a transcultural adaptation that pays homage to Zweig and Ophüls, however, this film offers a unique and aesthetically stunning reading of the Austrian writer's novella. Taiwanese cinematographer Mark Lee Ping-bing's exceptional cinematography galvanizes as a reimagination of the reserve and crispness of Zweig's style of writing in exquisitely composed shots and graceful camera movements. Xu Jinglei was presented with the Best Director award at the 2004 San Sebastián International Film Festival.

Willenbrock (Germany, Andreas Dresen, 2005)

This adaptation of Christoph Hein's novel *Willenbrock* (2000) by scriptwriter Laila Stieler and director Andreas Dresen tells the story of successful car salesman Bernd Willenbrock (Axel Prahl) in Germany's east, a few years after the so-called 'Wende'. In 1990, then Chancellor Helmut Kohl had promised economic success and used the image of "blühende Landschaften" [flowering/flourishing landscapes] to evoke idyllic and happy lives for former East German citizens following the integration of the socialist GDR into capitalist West Germany. Hein, one of the GDR's most significant chroniclers, and Dresen, a filmmaker who had worked in East German theatres and for DEFA in the 1980s before graduating from Konrad Wolf College of Film and Television in Potsdam-Babelsberg in 1991, subtly draw out the fissures within the main protagonist's seemingly settled and 'flourishing' life in capitalist society some years after the fall of the Berlin wall and the disintegration of the Eastern Bloc. Dresen relocates the narrative from Berlin to Magdeburg, where societal changes in view of global capitalism are more pronounced than in the nation's rapidly transforming capital. Brilliantly transposing Hein's documentary style on film, Dresen and his team compose images and sequences that communicate the bleakness of everyday life, but also increasing anxiety and despair. A break-in becomes a seemingly existential threat that brings to the fore Willenbrook's distress and self-doubt as well as the volatility and instability of façades promising success and happiness in capitalist society. "Hein explores the societal cause and effect of Willenbrook's deep-rooted insecurities and lack of agency and their psychological impact on his life"[147] as Jean Conacher summarizes. Dresen and his ensemble explore this dynamic with the tools for filmmaking, from contrasting images of material culture to sound.[148] At the same time, the adaptation comments on community and collaborative practices that shaped much of the GDR's cultural production. Dramatic techniques inspired by Brecht and Stanislavsky are here linked and allied—two very different approaches that nonetheless invite and encourage a critical reading of the story shown and the themes addressed—providing insights and fostering awareness.[149] *Willenbrock* was awarded the Internationaler Literaturfilmpreis at the 2005 Frankfurt Book Fair.

Perfume: The Story of a Murderer (Germany/France/Spain, Tom Tykwer, 2006)

Patrick Süskind's 1985 novel was translated into forty-eight languages, sold more than 20 million copies, and was deemed unsuitable for cinema. In 2006, Tom Tykwer presented his vision of the literary text in a film that works very well as costume drama and psychological thriller but might also be considered an exploration of the post-human condition in reference to its past atrocities. Here, the female body becomes the ultimate commodity. Olfactory prodigy Jean-Baptiste Grenouille (Ben Whishaw) murders beautiful young women and distills their bodies to bottle their alluring scent, thus creating a product that entices and excites more than any perfume ever could. If used in larger quantities, however, people exposed to this ultimate, enthralling scent are not only driven to ecstasy, but cannibalism. The film's final climax depicts the consumption of the self and the other in an orgiastic dystopian image that might serve as an incisive metaphor for self-destructive practices of hyper-consumption. Eichinger had bought the film rights to the novel in 2000 and began to write a screenplay of Süskind's text together with Andrew Birkin. Tykwer joined them in 2003 as director and revised the script. Despite fairly dire reviews, 5.5 million went to see Tykwer's *Perfume* in Germany alone, a fact celebrated in the German press as proof that filmmakers could win back a mass audience they had assumed lost to Hollywood.[150] The fact that *Perfume* was based on an 'upscale' literary text was outweighed by more than 20 million copies of the novel sold worldwide and its considerable readership in German-speaking countries. In addition, "German cinema's bright new hope" (Rotten Tomatoes) Tykwer, internationally celebrated auteurist filmmaker since *Lola rennt* [Run Lola Run] had co-written the script, composed the score, and directed this transnational, big-budget production.[151] The marketing campaign foregrounded not only the novel, but Tykwer's unique vision, as well as Hollywood royalty such as Dustin Hoffmann. With the backing of Eichinger and Constantin Film in addition to financial support from several German and European film boards, the adaptation proved a well-calculated risk, grossing $135 million worldwide.[152]

カフカ 田舎医者, Franz Kafka's A Country Doctor (Japan, Kōji Yamamura, 2007)

Kafka's writings have inspired several amazing animations beginning with Caroline Leaf's *The Metarmorphosis of Mr. Samsa* (Canada, 1977) as well as highly original live-action short films like Kirsten Peter's SAMSAS (DE, 1999), and feature films such as Jochen Alexander Freydank's uncompromising cinematic vision of paranoia in *Der Bau* [The Burrow] (DE, 2014).[153] This Japanese anime short film visualizes and interprets Franz Kafka's surreal tale *Ein Landarzt* (A Country Doctor, 1917/19), drawing out conflicts between the rational and irrational in a dramatic and magical evocation of the desire to help in adverse circumstances. Sequences that illustrate an individual's battle against nature—from the journey through a blizzard to a patient's mysterious illness—are as evocative as they are sparse, and imaginatively illustrate the impossibility of circumventing disappointment and failure in this profession. This stunning anime short film received numerous awards, including the 2007 Grand Prize at International Animation Festival in Ottawa and the 2008 Ōfuji Noburō Award.

Synecdoche, New York (USA, Charlie Kaufman, 2008)

This postmodern film, emanating from one of Rilke's most famous poems, might not be an adaptation at all so much as an utterly original film—and that is exactly the point. In Charlie Kaufman's masterful debut film as director (he had previously written the screenplay for *Adaptation,* 2002, among others), soon-to-be McArthur Fellowship recipient Caden Cotard (Philip Seymour Hoffman) is a theater director who spends most of the film working on his first original play, a massive production focused on the representation of 'reality'. This Cotard hopes to achieve by producing the conditions for an imitation of the large ensemble's mundane lives within an enormous factory building. The film opens with the protagonist lying in bed and listening to a radio show about "fall" in literature, a melancholic avowal of the "beginning of the end" that concludes with a reading of Rilke's "Herbsttag" (Autumn Day, 1902): "Whoever has no house now, will never have one./Whoever is alone, will stay alone./Will sit, read, write long letters to the evening,/and wonder the boulevards up and down,/ restlessly, while the dry leaves are blowing."[154] "Goodness, that's harsh," the radio host remarks. Caden still has a 'house', but his family is about to disintegrate, like his exhausted body. Introspection drives the narrative, while mirrors regularly structure its individual elements, reflecting the person standing before it, but also their body as a mirror of age, illness, abuse, and basic functions. The body becomes a canvas—literally in the case of Caden/Adele's daughter—and the canvas becomes a body. Caden's partner Adele (Catherine Keener), a painter of simulacra or trompe-l'œil of mostly naked bodies in tiny formats that can only be seen through magnifying glasses, creates art that is praised as "more real" than the person we see impersonating the character in the film. She leaves the playwright for a show in Berlin never to return. He later sees his daughter's picture in a magazine, with much of her body tattooed. Everything is a canvas and a simulacrum, a reflection of life in the face of death, of the everyday, of actors playing themselves while reality and fiction constantly collide—questioning original representation always-already as adaptation. Written texts—performed (like Miller's *Death of a Salesman*), appearing in typeface in newspapers and magazines, read and spoken—impact the narrative as they affect the individual reading, working, hearing, and speaking of them. Rilke's poem describes a sense of an ending as nature gives into the hesitant cold of the season and the individual retreats into solitude. Incorporated into the opening sequence as spoken words emanating from the radio in translation, the literary text—canonical, hybrid, and flexible at once—provides the film's imaginative core and evokes Rilke's state of mind at the time like a daguerreotype in reverse.

Effi Briest (Germany, Hermine Huntgeburth, 2009)

Following four previous feature films (1939, 1955, 1970, 1974) and even Lego animations on YouTube (*Effi Briest to go*, 2015) as well as satirical short films for television such as *Letzte Stunde vor den Ferien: Effi Briest* [Final lesson before the holidays] (2017, Neo Magazin Royale), this formally quite conventional adaptation of Fontane's *Effi Briest* confronts the revisionism of the costume drama with a radical reformulation of Effi's traditional female trajectory and thus stands out. Together with screenwriters Nina Kötter and Volker Einrauch, Huntgeburth tells Fontane's novel first and foremost as a 'coming-of-age' story about Effi (Julia Jensch) who grows from a naïve and obliging teenager into an independent individual, who finally refuses to be destroyed by the patriarchal authorities' heart-breaking marginalization and isolation following the revelation of her long past affair. This modification of the original narrative has political valence but also evokes Fontane's utopian spirit. A pioneering author for the twentieth century, Fontane hoped for a society and a justice system that protected the rights of all citizens. The recourse in this film to the ideal of freedom as formulated in the eighteenth century, and the dismissal of the rigid social roles of the nineteenth and twentieth centuries, transforms this Effi—who strives for self-determination—into a tangible utopia for the twenty-first century. By virtue of this actualization, the film does not only answer Fontane's question whether it is possible for the individual to lead a self-determined life within a restrictive society, but it also recalls Fontane's theory of realism, which states that a positive or affective involvement among an audience or readers can only be guaranteed by adjusting the text to the reality of the recipients. Elisabeth von Ardenne, Fontane's inspiration for his literary figure Effi, did not die from a broken heart but at the advanced age of ninety-nine years, despite her divorce, her forced separation from her child, and her exclusion from 'good society'. Fontane's Effi and the life of von Ardenne, fiction and reality, and past and present all form the palimpsest of Huntgeburth's adaptation.

360 (Brazil/Austria/France/UK, Fernando Meirelles, 2011)

Schnitzler's scandalous play *Reigen* (La Ronde, 1897) was first banned and then adapted numerous times to theatre, opera, cinema, and television, and even served to highlight the spread of AIDS in *Chain of Desire* (US, Temístocles López, 1992). *360* adds to the more than two dozen previous cinema productions based on Schnitzler's play, but in this latest depiction of *Der Reigen*, screenwriter Peter Morgan and director Meirelles break some new ground formally and aesthetically. Schnitzler's narrative ends where it begins—with a focus on the sex worker—but as a comment on a hypocritical, class-based society and its repressive morality, it nonetheless has a linear trajectory. Morgan and Meirelles transform Schnitzler's clearly structured linearity into a circular—though sometimes messy—narrative, like a twenty-first-century Viennese roundabout. Making excellent use of the visual medium with a star-studded cast that includes Rachel Weisz, Anthony Hopkins, Jude Law and others, this film plays with the "Reigen" as a circular dance, both in terms of the adaptation's fundamental structure and its aesthetic means.

Faust (Russia, Aleksandr Sokurov, 2011)

This new take on *Faust* by one of the most innovative directors of the twenty-first century offers a disturbing and enlightening journey into Goethe's canonical narrative. Faust (Johannes Zeiler), bored and exhausted, searches in vain for knowledge and the meaning of it all. He is here placed in a community eroded by greed, hunger, self-interest, and violence. This is not a portrait of the Biedermeier era so often conjured in heritage films where the bourgeoisie live happily in their well-ordered private sphere. Sokurov summons a time of deprivation and exploitation that emphasizes the rigidity and narrowness of mental, spiritual, and physical space. This place stinks, and rats surround Mephistopheles (Anton Adassinski), who is the usurer who profits soundly from the misery of the masses. Following Sokurov's 'power' trilogy *Молох/Moloch* (1999), *Телец/Taurus* (2001), and *Сóлнце/Solntse/The Sun* (2005) about Hitler, Lenin, and Japanese emperor Hirohito respectively, this fourth installment looks at the mechanisms that make the masses pliable and easy to manipulate, while radically rethinking Faust as a driven, lonely, and preoccupied *flâneur*, who observes history as it unfolds, rather than taking action and responsibility.[155] This adaptation is rife with layered meanings and, sometimes simultaneously references both parts of *Faust*, thus cinematographically transposing the semantic ambiguities of Goethe's play brilliantly onto film. Sokurov uses narrative elements and motifs mostly from *Faust I* (1808), but also *Faust II* (1832)—such as the homunculus in a glass container—and in addition weaves a myriad of visual references, mostly to the cinema of Expressionism, into his adaptation. This resonant narrative is about literature and film, culture and society, but also offers a critical space of reception by challenging the body-mind dualism and foregrounding human responses to physical deprivation. Hunger is a much more effective driver of change than Faust's search for answers and knowledge, Sokurov's film seems to imply. People that are exhausted and insecure are easily manipulated, and thus the body takes center stage. Here, it is the physical apparatus that Faust would like to shed, because he understands its power. Physical desires, the need for food, sleep, warmth, but also the representation of sensual perceptions of smelly bodies at close proximity equip the film with a physicality that effectively communicates the utterly destructive effect of poverty for society. Sokurov's film was awarded the Golden Lion in Venice in 2011.

Die Wand [The Wall] (Austria/Germany, Julian Pölsler, 2012)

A woman finds herself closed in by a transparent and impenetrable wall which separates her from a world that seems suddenly frozen in place. She describes her life in a small cabin in the Alps, her struggles to survive, her weaknesses and moments of joy. Marlen Haushofer's 1968 novel is a unique contemplation, a narrative and formal reduction, that nonetheless describes this sudden metamorphosis with great precision and attention to detail. Julian Pölsler's adaptation is a haunting transposition that conveys the main protagonist's new reality with a sense of urgency and looming threat, while creating a world that is as appealing as it is solitary. As in the novel, the remoteness and isolation but also nature itself shape the unfolding narrative. The 'Woman' (Martina Gedeck) identifies dignity as core to the experience depicted—in relation to herself, the animals, nature, life itself—and Pölsler's

FIGURE 9.7 *Martina Gedeck as the protagonist writing her story in* Die Wand *(AT/DE, Roman Pölsler, 2012).*

adaptation builds on the protagonist's desire to bear witness, creating a visual and narrative connection between the need to account and the willingness to do so accurately while knowing that this might not be enough, implicitly raising questions about artistic representation and authenticity. In this collaboration with Austrian public television ORF, Pölsler seeks to create 'a platform for this fantastic text'—which has been translated into nineteen languages and sold over a million copies—and for Haushofer's language. He decided to use voice-over, knowing full well that this all-too-common technique in literary adaptations would entice major criticism. But, as he put it in an interview, he also 'wanted to make space for this great language, because our language is getting poorer all the time'.[156] This film is indeed enriched by Gedeck not only acting and writing but speaking Haushofer's words. Pölsler felt the novel deserved many more readers, 'especially today'.[157] His excellent adaptation deserves many more viewers.

Michael Kohlhaas (France/Germany, Arnaud des Pallières, 2013)

Marketed as *Age of Uprising* in English-speaking countries (sometimes with the subtitle The Legend of Michael Kohlhaas), Arnaud des Pallières' new adaptation of Heinrich von Kleist's famous novella is an auteurist costume drama filled with stunning and visually affective panorama shots that cut an ocular path into the protagonist's soul. A good and responsible husband, father, neighbor, and subject, Kohlhaas (Mads Mikkelsen) is driven to violent action in his inevitable fight for justice that will never repair or bring back what is lost. The film's cinematography is both sensual and direct, carefully outlining Kleist's conundrum that questions how a human being can be the most exemplary and horrifying ["entsetzlich"] creature at the same time. Pallières foregrounds human desire for justice, but also control, and offers an astute analysis that highlights the contemporaneity of Kleist's tale. Denis Lavant is a superb choice as the theologist in the film, who knows about a decent individual's need for agency, fairness, and reason, but is equally aware of the rulers' and their institutions' persistence when it comes to safeguarding power. Failure is human and systemic, making the destruction of a principled individual seem inevitable. The film was nominated for the Palme d'Or at Cannes and won two César awards among others.

The Grand Budapest Hotel (USA, Wes Anderson, 2014)

An "homage to Stefan Zweig," as Nikolai Preuschoff notes, "Anderson's *Grand Budapest Hotel* is a film *about* adapting and adaptation."[158] Featuring a fireworks of acting talent that includes Saoirse Ronan, Jason Schwartzman, Léa Seydoux, Bill Murray, Tilda Swinton, Edward Norton, Ralph Fiennes, F. Murray Abraham, Adrien Brody, Willem Dafoe, Jeff Goldblum, Harvey Keitel, Jude Law, and Owen Wilson, this beautifully lit and (like all of Anderson's movies) uniquely colored work (re)creates a wonderfully ambivalent album of remembrance, of a lost world, an exiled Jewish author, and a community threatened by fascism. Anne Washburn compares *The Grand Budapest Hotel* to Viennese pastry, "a confection of curious depth and substance," which allows viewers to experience "the lightest, airiest movie about cataclysm."[159] This narrative and visual assemblage inspired by works of the internationally renowned author and, following Austria's 'Anschluss', despairing exile—from Zweig's novel *Ungeduld des Herzens* (Beware of Pity, 1939), novellas *Rausch der Verwandlung* (The Post Office Girl), *24 Stunden aus dem Leben einer Frau* (Twenty-four Hours in the Life of a Woman), and his memoir *Die Welt von Gestern* (The World of Yesterday, 1942)—reveals both the author's and the filmmaker's "love of the tale" as much as "the love of telling it."[160] In the film, which he co-wrote with Hugo Guinness, Anderson celebrates literature and the visual arts, especially film, from Lubitsch's aforementioned *Die Puppe* (The Doll, 1919) to Hollywood films of the 1930s. His uniquely creative way of telling Zweig's stories conveys an understanding of the author as humanist and pacifist, but also reflects on the joy of collaboratively building a story. At the same time the film's undercurrent of melancholy and growing threat imagines the possibility of an end of our dreams of humanism, pacifism and a good society, an end of those illusions consumed joyfully and gratefully by cinemagoers for over a century. According to IMDb, *The Grand Budapest Hotel* was produced on a budget of 25 million USD and grossed over 172 million USD world-wide. It won four Academy Awards.[161]

Tschick (Germany, Fatih Akin, 2016)

Being able to create an adaptation of Wolfgang Herrndorf's wonderful and highly acclaimed youth novel *Tschick* (*Why We Took the Car*, 2010) was a dream project for outstanding Turkish-German director Fatih Akin, who shook up German-language cinema with courageous and provocative films such as *Gegen die Wand* (*Head-On*, 2004), *Auf der anderen Seite* [On the Other Side] (*The Edge of Heaven*, 2007), and *Aus dem Nichts* (*In the Fade*, 2017). Akin's film (script co-written with Hark Bohm based on Lars Hubrich's screenplay) remains close to the source text's narrative overall, while a few added scenes only emphasize the nuances and mood of the novel. Standing on the shoulders of the genre's most treasured figures such as Tom Sawyer and Huckleberry Finn, the two protagonists here are fourteen-year-old Maik Klingenberg (Tristan Göbel) and his new classmate, Russian-German Andrej 'Tschick' Tschichatschow (Anand Batbileg). Maik is a loner, who is considered strange and unapproachable by his peers, while he just thinks of himself as embarrassingly dull. While Tschick is a recent migrant and on the bottom of the social ladder, Maik represents white, well-to-do-Germany—but his life is far from perfect. His mother is an alcoholic who checks into rehab when school closes for the summer and his father prefers trips with his 'assistant' to looking after Maik at home. When Tschick shows up with a 'borrowed' car—an old Lada—the two boys counter neglect with agency and decide to drive across Germany's East toward Walachia. Like some of the most outstanding youth novels by Mark Twain, adventures begin with travels while guardians are left behind. Writer and artist Herrndorf (1965–2013) did not live to see his *Tschick* on screen. Akin's road movie stands out not only as an adaptation of a best-selling youth novel, but as a highly entertaining thematization of friendship, puberty and the masculine body, intergenerational conflict and migration for younger audiences and the public sphere.[162]

Les beaux jours d'Aranjuez (Germany/France, Wim Wenders, 2017)

At some point, the writer (Jens Harzer) gets up and runs from the terrace into the garden, shouting: 'Hey, didn't we agree no action? Only dialogue?' Indeed, it is words that make this film, beginning with a clear reference to the end of carefree times from Schiller's *Don Carlos* in the title of this latest collaboration between Wim Wenders and Peter Handke, a project that recounts dialogues straight from the latter's eponymous 2012 two-person-play. It is summer, a man (Reda Kateb) and a woman (Sophie Semin) sit in a garden and talk. The film records their conversation about past experiences, relationships, and perspectives on life—while Nick Cave plays the piano inside and Handke is briefly seen trimming the bushes in the back. The writer types what they speak. One hundred and twenty years after the first adaptation of a German-language text for the cinema screen, when action was all there was and words only existed in the readers/viewers' minds to complete the narrative on screen, Wenders' now takes us full circle and highlights the specificities of the medium and its paradoxical twinning of image and words, while Handke alludes to the illusionary practice of separation between reality and fiction in literature. The fact that Handke's wife plays the 'woman' or man's partner in the film emphasizes this inevitable overlap. Much of the conversation between the man and the woman seems banal and all too everyday, and 'boring' was probably the adjective most frequently used by critics in their reviews of the film. Wenders' cinematography, however, creates scenes that seem staged and yet utterly familiar. Is there no need for action in Handke's play or Wenders' film, because we all write our own stories whether we are reading a literary text, watching a play on stage or a film in the cinema or even on our computer or TV screens? The author and filmmaker are unmistakably present in this film that exposes transcultural practices in both literature and film, and suggests adaptations are palimpsests of texts and images, stories and memories, fiction and non-fiction. Handke wrote the play for his wife in French and the film could be seen to address the transnational nature of so many adaptations, while questioning the definition of a nation-based literary canon. In German-language literature, as this book will hopefully have shown, the separation of German and Austrian literature, for example, is historically and culturally problematic as borders shift, writers move, and cultures overlap. Many texts written in German are considered world literature, and although this adaptation project was not originally written in German, it is inherently European.

Return to Montauk (Germany/France/Ireland, Volker Schlöndorff, 2017)

Constructed from Swiss author Max Frisch's autofictional narrative *Montauk* (1975) as its underlying fabric, Schlöndorff revisits his late friend's most personal work in this film, which he co-wrote and directed. *Return to Montauk* tells Frisch's story in retrospect as it evolved and left its protagonists stranded in their respective lives on both sides of the Atlantic. On screen, the protagonist is not 'Max Frisch', but Max Zorn, a writer now in his early sixties and once again in New York City to promote his latest work. The film indeed returns to the literary text as well as to the lost lover within it and explores the devastating consequences of decisions made in the past. The adaptation thus reconsiders Frisch's text while updating and perpetuating it. The male protagonist (Stellan Skarsgård) is back in the city, where he fell in love nearly two decades ago. He insists on meeting his former partner (Nina Hoss), and dreams of a potential future together as they spend one more weekend at Montauk. The film reflects on authorship, in the context of both auteurist cinema and life itself. Typically for an individual, life is imbued with meaning and purpose by way of reconstructions of past events and memories that provide the foundation for a coherent imagination of a desired future. But while comforting, that kind of narrative identity is a chimera, the film implies, as it unforgivingly confronts the male protagonist with the impact of his choices on the life of another. It also calls into question auteurist filmmaking by highlighting its collective process and collaborative aspects of art cinema. Here, literature on film is underscored by the explicit multiplication of developmental processes; Irish author Colm Tóibín wrote the screenplay together with Schlöndorff, whose point of departure is the novel *Montauk* by the Swiss writer. Fiction becomes (auto)biographical both with regard to the male protagonist called Max Zorn, whose equally monosyllabic last name not only parallels the novel's author, but Zorn (meaning outrage) looks back in anger at the mistakes made in the past. Adding personal history as an integral element of the fabric of the adaptation to the debate, Schlöndorff's *Return to Montauk* is perhaps the most intimate of all of the veteran adapter's works. The meticulously multi-layered narrative and its impressive cinematography constitute an exquisite addition to Schlöndorff's adaptation oeuvre and life-long engagement with literature on film.

In den Gängen [In the Aisles] (Germany, Thomas Stuber, 2018)

Following Andreas Dresen's 2015 film based on Clemens Meyer's debut novel *Als wir träumten* (*As We Were Dreaming*, 2006), this adaptation of Meyer's short story "In den Gängen" (In the Aisles, 2008) left several critics puzzled. One of them called it a "peculiar not-quite comedy from Germany" and a "shaggy-dog tale that treats crisscrossing forklift traffic as a sight worthy of the Blue Danube waltz,"[163] while missing the point entirely. This film is not supposed to be a love story or even one of individuals longing for fulfillment, even though the desire for happiness, self-realization, and belonging provides the background melody to both Meyer's narrative and Stuber's direction (who co-wrote the script with the author) as we catch glimpses of the meaning of the precarity of life in post-Wende East Germany (Saxony). The focus is on economically disenfranchised citizens, who work in a huge wholesale store and barely make ends meet. At the core of the film is former neo-Nazi Christian (Franz Rogowski), recently released from prison and still on parole, who is offered support and reintegration by a team of individuals that form an unlikely but still vital form of community. There is little conversation and hardly any laughter, but at the end of the day, the foreman shakes the hand of every employee, just like in one of the VEBs [state-owned companies] during GDR times. Adversity—illness, the death of a partner, alcoholism, domestic violence—is personal and endured. Stuber[164] and his team underscore a form of comradery that is respectful of the guardedness of each individual worker. Christian's supervisor and forklift instructor at the megastore Bruno (Peter Kurth) sarcastically calls himself a "Wendegewinner" [Wende profiteur] as he is still in employment after reunification. We begin to understand the struggles and sense of loss in Meyer's and Stuber's carefully constructed script that treats this often invisible class of German citizens with respect and fondness, without any drama or maudlin romanticism. It is a story of the possibility of integration, life, and perhaps even love, that moves marginalized human beings into the center of the screen, forcing the audience to recognize their humanity and their lifelong contribution to society. Only the neo-Nazi thugs, who come to the store trying to bully Christian out of employment and back into their far-right, violently xenophobic group, are shown for what they are: selfish and destructive types who contribute absolutely nothing.

Transit (Germany, Christian Petzold, 2018)

According to Petzold, Anna Seghers' exile novel *Transit* is an outstanding piece of literature. As previously mentioned, he and Harun Farocki always wanted to keep 'a bit of distance' from their favorite book. The adaptation only came to fruition after Farocki's death in 2014 and therefore could be considered an homage to Petzold's late friend and collaborator.[165] In his film, Petzold creates the exiles' temporary refuge as a liminal or transitional space,[166] an 'intermediate realm', that offers neither a way forward nor back, as he explains, leaving the individuals stranded and 'without a present'.[167] But at the same time, the refugee narrative's mise-en-scène is marked by temporal collapse and folds the story of Seghers' main protagonists—exiles Georg (Franz Rogowski) and Marie (Paula Beer)—into the present day, while the place of most of the narrative, modern-day Marseilles, stays the same. "This is both stranger and less strange than it sounds," writes film critic Donald Clarke and calls *Transit* "a five-star, art-house modern-day Casablanca," an "existential riddle" that "keeps the audience on edge throughout."[168] For the auteur filmmaker, the theme of flight, refuge, the loss of home, etc. is deeply personal, due to his parents' refugee experiences toward the end of, and just after, the Second World War.[169] As a refugee, you need to pack lightly, he says, also referring to memories, which cause sadness and melancholia, and thus a dangerous state to be in as an exile. Petzold's Cinemascope film 'shows' what the novel's dialogues 'tell'—the protagonists' 'dance with words, gestures and looks' becoming the 'actual language' of the adaptation.[170] The outcome is not only a beautifully shot and aesthetically inspiring film, but an important contribution to the public sphere. By folding today's refugee discourses into Europe's history of migration, war and suffering, and reminding us of "the kindness of strangers"[171] as Salka Viertel put it, without which one would be lost, this adaptation makes us aware of the importance of memory and reflection. As Abel points out: "Petzold confronts his viewers with the need to reflect on our own perspective on both the past represented in the film and the past as it is effective in our own present" and adds "in *Transit,* Petzold renders this need more explicit than in any of his previous films."[172] Interested in critical reflection while exploring the practices of genre cinema,[173] Petzold's *Transit* repeatedly supplants spectorial identification by distanciation techniques. Abrupt cuts from a shot depicting a potentially emotional encounter between the two main protagonists to a view of the same individuals through a surveillance camera, for example, not only incorporate Germany's own past experiences, but subtly introduce the concept of 'biopower' (Foucault) to discourses on migration and exile. The surveillance camera provides a documentary-like view of those that are rarely considered from a neutral position, inviting us as spectators to take into account our own subjective perception. Within this highly heterogeneous visualization of contemporaneity, Petzold rediscovers Seghers' work, our history and culture, memory and agency, as fundamental to the development of sustainable modes of life-saving mobility and coexistence by way of a transnational cinema that functions within and beyond history and time, looking back and forward at the same time.[174]

Berlin Alexanderplatz (Germany/Netherlands/ Canada, Burhan Qurbani, 2020)

Transnational/bicultural filmmaker Burhan Qurbani's *Berlin Alexanderplatz* is the latest adaptation of Döblin's masterful novel. The son of political refugees from Afghanistan, who co-wrote the script with Martin Behnke, here reimagines Döblin's Franz Biberkopf as a refugee from Guinea-Bissau in modern day Germany. Francis/Franz (Welket Bungué) arrives in Berlin after a harrowing trip across the Mediterranean, suffering from PTSD and having lost everything. All he wants now is to make a decent life for himself and the most of this opportunity. But this place of refuge is filled with challenges and temptations. Francis/Franz carries the trauma of flight and loss and the guilt of survival into Germany's capitol, a place struggling with its own culpability and shameful history. Qurbani and his team skillfully interlink the city itself with the marginal individual and call into question Berlin's ethical urbanism while refugees are eliminated from the public sphere, and all too often step into illegality in their struggle to survive. Like the source text's disadvantaged protagonists, their lives are dominated by marginalization, instability, and violence. Franz here emerges just as 'battered' from his ordeal as Biberkopf in Döblin's eponymous novel, but there is hope in community and integration, driven mainly by the humanity of other marginalized citizens and 'survivors'. Wanting to highlight the plight of asylum seekers in Germany and being aware that a documentary about them can easily be ignored, Qurbani turned to *Berlin Alexanderplatz* as 'an important part of our educated bourgeois canon'. By adapting one of the most significant German-language novels of the twentieth century, 'you have to pay attention to these men, you have to look these people in the face'.[175] As Qurbani outlines in the same interview, editor Philip Thomas cut the first five-hour version of the film down to 183 minutes. This reductive process brought the project 'suddenly back to Döblin and the way he shifted images, scenes, and time into one another'[176] highlighting the avant-garde author's innovative use of montage to film almost 'by accident'.[177] Sadly, due to the Covid-19 pandemic, this adaptation has received far less attention than it deserves. The film's important theme, its excellent cast that includes Albrecht Schuch as tormented psycho Reinhold, Jella Haase as Mieze, and Joachim Król as duplicitous gang leader Pums, as well as an innovative aesthetic and high production values that all help to shed light on the challenges refugees face and to question the meaning of integrity when one is forced to survive in illegality. This outstanding adaptation reflects the potential and ongoing significance of the genre for the public sphere.

Conclusion

As Siobhan O'Flynn notes in reviewing Linda Hutcheon's scholarly work, adaptation as a "transcoding process that encompasses recreations, remakes, remediations, revisions, parodies, reinventions, reinterpretations, expansions, and extensions"[178] has been, in the twenty-first century, "further complicated by the emergence of transmedia as a media conglomerate production strategy."[179] So far, it is especially children's, young adult, and fantasy literatures written in German that expands into or overlaps with other narrative platforms with both fan-generated content in the digital sphere and commercial endeavors. The latter might even include quite traditional boardgames, such as one based on Otfried Preußler's internationally famous and much adapted *Das kleine Gespenst* (The Little Ghost, 1966), which won the Best Kid's Game of the Year award in

2005.[180] The canon of German-language literature also has seen a number of "remediations"—from mashups such as Susanne Picard's *Die Leichen des jungen Werther* (The corpses of young Werther, 2011), a Zombie adventure novel based on Goethe's *The Sorrows of Young Werther*, to "Sommers Weltliteratur to go" on YouTube. The channel features more than 300 short films with Lego figurines that enact summaries of canonical German-language texts such as Lessing's *Nathan der Weise*, Schiller's *Wilhelm Tell*, Goethe's *Faust*, Büchner's *Woyzeck*, Brecht's *Der gute Mensch von Sezuan*, Hesse's *Steppenwolf*, as well as more recent outstanding literary texts such as Jenny Erpenbeck's *Gehen, ging, gegangen* (To go, went, gone, 2015). Each of Michael Sommer's shorts condenses the literary text to around ten minutes, and as the comment sections indicate, his amusing digests generate delight among millions of secondary school pupils preparing for classes and exams.[181] But even in the more traditional practices in the context of literature on film, and although the production and reception landscape has been changing considerably here, too, literary adaptation remains a deeply embedded process that no film history should ignore.

In the last three decades, an increasingly multicultural and transnational cinema has offered narratives of division and (re)unification in adaptations of works by, for example, Sven Regener, Thomas Brussig, Torsten Schulz, Eugen Ruge, Clemens Meyer, and Juli Zeh.[182] We have also seen a multiplication of a range of transnational literatures on film—such as fantasy thrillers like *Die Tür* [The Door] starring Mads Mikkelsen and Heike Makatsch (DE, Anno Saul, 2009), based on Turkish-German author Akif Pirinçci's novel *Die Damalstür* (2001), Bettina Blümner's 2012 adaptation of Russian-German Alina Bronsky's debut novel *Scherbenpark* (Broken Glass Park, 2008), or *Feuchtgebiete* [Wetlands] (DE/ES, David F. Wnendt, 2013), an adaptation of the British-German author Charlotte Roche's provocative debut novel. The world's biggest-selling fiction book of 2008 and the "scandal of the season,"[183] *Feuchtgebiete* spent thirty weeks topping the literature charts in Germany and was marked for immediate adaptation due to its phenomenal success on the literary scene. "Clearly sex sells, even if it is in German?"[184] *The Economist* asked in 2008. Public funding body Medienboard Berlin-Brandenburg supported Roche, Claus Falkenberg, and David F. Wnendt in the development of the script. Five years later at the box office, however, the adaptation failed to repeat the success of its source text, which addresses female desire and sexual fantasy, as well as documenting bodily functions, experiences, odors, and flavors. Books are enjoyed mostly in the privacy of one's home, and while both the original text and its translations generated notable profits, it did not work as well in cinemas, where consumption is public, if low-lit. Nonetheless, in Germany, where the film was released for sixteen-plus audiences, nearly a million went to see it in cinemas, even though visualizations of the eighteen-year-old protagonist Helen's (Carla Juri) sensual explorations of her own body had to be kept brief to avoid a pornography label. More recently, however, profits once again surged due to the adaptation's availability for private streaming via several major online services.

Apart from selected international adaptations of German-language literature, and innovative contributions to the genre by directors of the Berlin School and other auteur filmmakers, among the most exciting developments in this context are cinematic takes on the literary canon by transnational filmmakers—especially when second-generation migrants such as Burhan Qurbani share their experience and their reading of German-language culture on cinema (or pandemic television and computer) screens. Working with literature is as much about belonging and creating as it is about recreating, reclaiming, and restructuring. But what differentiates filmmakers of conventional adaptations for a mass audience and the directors of the 'solitaires' listed above? Apart from their particular vision and unique creativity, it is the desire of the latter artists to present a creative engagement with literature that is hospitable and fertile, but in its actualization also autonomous, critical, and anti-nostalgic. Perhaps due to the (right-wing) political dimension of (national) nostalgia, many progressive auteurs have no interest in and successfully circumvent any fetishization of the literary canon and, by implication, a particular nation's history and supposed identity. Neither literature nor culture is ever homogenous. The fantasy of homogeneity not only differentiates reality and fiction, but in many ways also literature and film as art on the one hand and a functional, profit-driven mass culture on the other.[185]

In her *Berlin and Beyond* film festival talk in 2020, film scholar and expert in German-Turkish cinema Deniz Göktürk addressed the transformation of filmmaking and film consumption in the context of on-demand streaming, stating that streaming had "radically transformed our sense of time and place" and wondering if the concept of a "national cinema" is actually "obsolete in the age of global internet television?"[186] While this is a valid point and the idea of a 'national' cinema is indeed questionable in many ways, looking closely at adaptation practices in this context reveals, however, how deeply engrained the 'national' still is when it comes to Germany in particular, which to some degree is a consequence of the country's violent history and ongoing processes of "working through the past" (Adorno).[187] While viewing practices are indeed changing, and production practices are becoming ever more transnational and multi-facetted, German-language literature is still adapted regularly, and predominantly by filmmakers in Germany, Austria, and Switzerland. It is the language they share, even though German, too, of course, comes in many forms, dialects, and registers.

As this book has worked to outline, German-language literature provided the narrative core to thousands of films since the late nineteenth century, and many of German cinema's most influential masterpieces are adaptations of the literary canon. In addition to countless literary films produced by the entertainment industry, filmmakers have turned to German-language literature to address difficult pasts, negotiate identities, challenge clichés, and provoke public discourses. Production companies time and again made use of the comforting stability of a literary canon during times of uncertainty. And not surprisingly, especially since the 1980s, commercial cinema's adaptation practices have foregrounded economic interests and reacted to the preferences and volatility of the "market." In united Germany since the 1990s, adaptations fall mostly in three categories: bestselling novels, from youth literature to contemporary fiction with a wide readership; literary texts that contribute to the memory culture of that new and now united Germany; and, finally, the literary canon as narratives reimagined as costume dramas and/or actualized into contemporary settings.

Sometimes the choice of a canonical text might be a pragmatic one, aiming at maximizing the audience for a story that matters. Throughout its history, the cinema has been a forum that provoked, encouraged, and sometimes amplified debates. Qurbani's retelling of *Berlin Alexanderplatz*, for example, puts a migrant center stage and links his fate to all those marginalized individuals that populate the literary canon from Büchner's Woyzeck to Erpenbeck's Osarobo, Awad, Rufu and all the others in limbo and stranded on their way to a better life. Qurbani bridges the gap between past and present, center and margin, inside and outside in his work, and considers the significance of literature *and* film for society. This transnational filmmaker, but also many others named in this book, turns to literature to remember, challenge, and retell these stories on cinema screens, not only because they entertain and warrant an audience, but as a creative contribution to our vibrant literary and visual cultures on the one hand, and to the public sphere on the other, marking adaptation practice, at least potentially, as a form of active citizenship.[188]

As scholars, readers, and viewers, we should continue to interrogate adaptations as reflections on national literary culture, to better understand the layered notions of the transnational. Furthermore, by revealing the many overlaps and cross-border inspirations, we might counter objectives of an "insular cultural nationalism" as Erica Carter puts it, on both sides of the Atlantic.[189] In the last three decades, adaptations of German-language literature look back on a stunningly diverse and rich history, despite the impact of neoliberal production strategies. The story of adaptation provides an opportunity to rethink the idea of a national literary and film culture, while the sheer number of distinct examples easily dissipates any notion of national homogeneity. What has become apparent in this language-based cultural endeavor, however, is the enormous impact of the catastrophes of two world wars, fascism, and the Holocaust not only on German society, but on German-language literary and film culture. Adaptation has played an important role in this ongoing process of reflection and working through a past darkened by racism, antisemitism, xenophobia, unspeakable violence, and psychological entitlement. The contemporaneity of many recent adaptations is undeniable, no matter whether we look at novels about Austria's 'Anschluss' or courtroom dramas by contemporary authors—like *Der Trafikant* (Tobacconist, 2012) by the Austrian writer Robert Seethaler (DE/AT, Nikolaus Leytner, 2018) and von Schirach's *Der Fall Collini* (The Collini Case, 2011), brought to cinemas in 2019 under the direction of Marco Kreuzpaintner[190]—or recent adaptations of classics such as Seghers' *Transit* (2018), Zweig's *Schachnovelle* (2021), or Kästner's *Fabian* (2021).[191]

In the opening shot of Dominik Graf's adaptation of Kästner's *Fabian*, for example, we watch today's (underground) Berlin turn into the capitol of the Weimar Republic in a POV shot that takes us from the subway tunnel up into the past. While we watch the protagonist (Tom Schilling) drift through Berlin in 1931, at one point the camera rests on the so-called "Stolpersteine"[192] or 'stumbling blocks' on the sidewalk and unmistakably directs our attention to the former homes of those soon-to-be victims of Nazi terror.

The victim's names, dates of deportation or, if known, the year of their murder mark these small brass plates and Graf's visual inclusion of artist Gunter Demnig's memorial project (which commenced in 1992 and is

FIGURE 9.8 *Stumbling stones in* Fabian oder Der Gang vor die Hunde *(DE, Dominik Graf, 2021)*.

still ongoing) conveys his commitment to adaptation as art and practice in contemporaneity. As mentioned above, the majority of adaptations of German-language literature today are based on bestselling novels and popular children's books. But among the most interesting projects are those that include intertextual disruptions, and creatively engage with the literary text to remember and recuperate the past and navigate the present.[193]

In 1994, another Thomas Mann adaptation, *Mario und der Zauberer* [Mario and the Magician] (DE/FR/AT, Klaus-Maria Brandauer), warns of fascism and quotes Brecht's *Arturo Ui* play: 'The womb from which this crawled is fertile still'. When neoliberalism took hold of societies and funding policies, morally instructive visualizations of the literary past became increasingly unpopular in commercial cinema and television.[194] Nonetheless, both within German-language countries and on international screens, the memory of Germany's and Austria's Nazi past and the Holocaust lingers, especially as civil society faces ongoing challenges to democracy and equality. In this context the humanism of Bia Lessa and Dany Roland's Brazilian adaptation of Mann's *Der Erwählte* (The Holy Sinner, 1951) as *Crede-mi* (1997) might be considered. Aforementioned adaptations like *The Reader* (2008), *The Grand Budapest Hotel* (2014), and *Alone in Berlin* (2016) could also serve as examples of critical engagements with and the international relevance of toxic nationalism and other sources of evil that threaten what contemporary social theories define as 'good society'.[195] Adaptations emerge from a rich tapestry of past reimaginings, and films as diverse as *Hyènes, Eyes Wide Shut, The Pledge,* and *Berlin Alexanderplatz* reflect not only an awareness of their own history but also their visual and literary ancestry.

As I wrote parts of this volume, the Covid-19 pandemic had closed cinemas at the same time that more viewers than ever partook in visual entertainment. Do "remediations" of the film screen, as Thomas Elsaesser called the offerings on YouTube and via easily consumable on-demand streaming services, impact on adaptation cultures? Surely. Co-chief executive and chief content officer for Netflix Ted Sarandos said in a 2016 keynote that Netflix "brings the world's stories to the world's people," outlining their work with storytellers around the globe and in different languages. In his view, Netflix provided proof that even non-English-language productions could be successful. But whether streaming giants like Netflix or Amazon Prime turn to the canon of German-language literature depends largely on the recognition factor of a specific literary text. Netflix's film production portfolio for 2021 included adaptations of novels by John Preston, Robert Harris, AJ Finn, and Thomas Savage, a bestselling lineup that strikes me as very male and—were it not for the Indian writer and Man Booker Prize winner Aravind Adiga—very white.[196] Crime and science fiction continue to dominate, but in 2022 a third take on Remarque's globally famous antiwar novel *Im Westen nichts Neues* under the direction of *Deutschland 83*'s

Edward Berger premiered in select cinemas and was made available on Netflix.¹⁹⁷ The fame of both novel and Milestone's *All Quiet on the Western Front* might even help viewers navigate seemingly endless streaming options.

Commercial cinema and streaming networks continue to perfect the measure and type of 'ingredients' (Seeßlen) and content discussed in this final chapter—from employing the 'right' actors to delivering the appropriate measure of cliché—in order to satisfy narrative expectations, minimize commercial risk, and maximize profits. An imagined global mass audience drives much of the design of content and aesthetic of film products. Authenticity, however, remains a challenge for commodities aiming at the greatest common denominator within specific genres, and especially Hollywood has addressed this issue by producing an increasing number of films lately that are "based on a true story." This proclamation of real and authentic human experience clearly sells. It seems 'based on the play by Friedrich Schiller' does not have the same effect, even though literary texts are abundant with heroic journeys, challenging encounters, life-changing experiences, and truths. In Germany, some of the most acclaimed television serials were adaptations of autobiographical novels, such as Erwin Strittmatter's trilogy *Der Laden* (The Shop, 1983–92) which follows the Matt family from the Weimar Republic to the early years of the GDR and was brought to film as a transnational mini-series by Ulrich Plenzdorf and Jo Baier in 1998.¹⁹⁸

Authenticity has also been an increasingly popular component in recent productions subsidized by public funding bodies. In April 2019, for example, the FFA allocated 75 percent of script development subsidies to two adaptation projects based on autobiographical bestsellers: Robert Gold and Frieder Wittich's adaptation of Benjamin von Stuckrad-Barre's *Panikherz* (Panik heart, 2016) and Sonja Heiss's screenplay based on Joachim Meyerhoff's *Wann wird es endlich wieder so, wie es nie war* (When will things finally get back to the way they never were, 2013).¹⁹⁹ Subsequently, the FFA supported further adaptations of 'true stories' such as Gesa Neitzel's autobiographical *Frühstück mit Elefanten* (Breakfast with elephants, 2016), the young Berliner's account of her time as a ranger in Africa.²⁰⁰ Perhaps the appeal of supposedly fact-based narratives provides welcome relief to audiences suffering declarations of 'fake news' and deceitful soundbites by populism's frightful rulers in this so-called 'post-truth' era.²⁰¹

The origins and consequences of mass support for far-right populists are also the narrative undercurrent to the internationally successful *Babylon Berlin* television series, and indicative of the directors/producers' creativity. The neo-noir detective drama deftly satisfies current viewers' interests in the extravagance of nocturnal entertainment as a stylized artifice that merges contemporary and 1920s music, dance, film, and fashion, while supplementing it with the grit of social hardship. Thus, bridging a century of artistic production, capitalist dynamics, political volatilities, issues of class, social mobility, and changing definitions of gender, the series effortlessly highlights the past in view of our present, while following a who-dunnit from one cliff-hanger to the next.

The past decade has seen a rejuvenation of German cinema, and—at least in a minor key—of adaptation, thanks to directors such as Christian Petzold, Maren Ade, Fatih Akin, Burhan Qurbani, Maria Schrader, Dominik Graf, Philipp Stölzl, and others.[202] In 2008, Petzold remarked that

> cinema as such does not exist anymore. There are films, but there is no public for them. [...] You cannot invent a film infrastructure with films, since the infrastructure is determined by television, which rules everything, certainly in Germany. The large trusts and monopolies homogenized everything; as a result, one makes films in niches. But if you dwell too long on this fact you go crazy.[203]

Since 2016, public funding helped to enable adaptations like *Transit, Undine, Berlin Alexanderplatz,* or *Fabian* to emerge from that "niche." Their visualizations of literary narratives offer a critical view of our society and reflect on the meaning of citizenship, thus making important contributions to the public sphere, while proving Arnold Hauser wrong, who stated in the 1950s that the film business and the 'anarchy inherent in art' were simply 'incompatible'.[204] Like authors Brecht or Seghers, Döblin and Kästner, many of the auteur filmmakers mentioned in this book do not shy away from pointing their cameras at invisible individuals and perhaps forgotten narratives to unveil underlying dynamics and exclusionary mechanisms, while sharing their critical gaze into the dark corners of the past as well at the present of our society, which we inhabit and shape as individuals and as a community.[205]

Transnationality is integral to today's film production practices, but also to many of the literary texts that are adapted to film. The history of German-language literature on film, and this book, commenced with Goethe's *Faust* in 1897 and the French pioneers of filmmaking who probably chose the narrative due to the popularity of French composer Gounod's opera based on Goethe's play. *Undine,* one of the most widely read and translated German stories of the nineteenth century, also managed to cross language- and cultural boundaries more easily due to its numerous adaptations. In his 2020 *Undine,* Petzold refers to German Romanticism's literary representations of the water spirit especially in Friedrich de la Motte-Fouqué's novella *Undine* (1811), while also reminding us of traditions and practices of renarration and, by implication, our so-called national cultural heritage, as innately transnational. Fouqué also supplied the libretto for E.T.A. Hoffmann's magical opera *Undine* (1816), and the story continued to reverberate in European culture throughout the nineteenth, but also in both the twentieth and twenty-first centuries, while having also inspired cinema from 1916 onwards.[206] Petzold's film about the water spirit ponders the illusion of certainties and the reality of myths. It reflects on heteronormative structures of a patriarchal system but also on the reconstruction of Berlin's castle—perhaps as a symbol of society's tendency to hold on to the supposed certainties of the past rather than embrace the challenges of the here and now.

Petzold delves into the literary canon beginning with German Romanticism and Fouqué, but Ingeborg Bachmann's short story *Undine geht* (Undine walks/leaves, 1961) has also left its mark, particularly on the strong female protagonist. Undine (Paula Beer) is an urban historian and tour guide, who tells us about the development of Berlin from the Middle Ages on land wrested from the swamp or what the Slavs called 'brlo'. She explains the city's reconstruction after the Second World War and after the fall of the Berlin wall, and informs groups of visitors about the rebuilding of the sizeable Hohenzollern castle in the center of the city. Acknowledging the messiness but also the wonder of life and love, the plot structure weaves the water being's story of passion, truth, sacrifice, and death into a critique of the inability or unwillingness of some to live with the bitter complexities of the past and rather push for the recreation of a seemingly perfect present (the reconstruction of the old Berlin castle being a case in point).

Petzold's superb adaptation once again accentuates the significance of literary culture for cinema, and at the same time reminds us of the magic of films that reinvent and rethink these narratives and, sometimes, turn them into new and autonomous works of art.[207] While neoliberal motivations of a market-driven film industry surely dominate decisions made about productions to be pursued, a merely economic focus is surely insufficient to explain what informs and motivates artistic practice in the context of adaptation.[208] From the spring of 2020, changes to the public sphere in our social media infused world were amplified by the Covid-19 pandemic as cinemas and theaters closed, and streaming sites shaped viewing practices more than ever before. The desire to adapt literature and avail of the mass medium film to contribute to debates and the public sphere did not end, of course, but shifted toward available outlets. The adaptation for public television of von Schirach's play *GOTT* (God, 2020) about the right to die may serve as an example.[209] Thematizing a controversial topic such as assisted suicide, this high-value production with its star-studded cast communicated legal as well as emotional dimensions of the debate and invited further discussions. As in theaters before, the adaptation of the play concluded with an opportunity to voice one's preference and the result of the public vote was subsequently published on the ARD website.[210] As several newspapers reported the next day, nearly 71 percent of viewers voted in favor of the main character's right to die.[211]

Debates triggered by films that previously took place on the street, outside cinemas, in cafés and pubs, have now modified and moved predominantly to virtual spaces, but have perhaps even increased the accessibility of a wider public. The presence of adaptations of literary texts in cinema, on television screens and streaming sites in the meantime continues, while the heterogeneity of adaptors and adaptive practices in the context of German-language literature as well as the genre's impact on cinema has been significant. While this book hopefully succeeded in drawing attention to the key position of German-language literature on film and in outlining the most relevant contexts that shaped its place in cinema history, the impact of two World Wars and the horror of the Holocaust on the transmedial reception of German-language culture should be looked at in far greater depth as this book can offer. These pages hope to be useful as a foundation for further research. Apart from the socio-political, relevant socio-economic environments must also be considered when telling the story of film. The late Thomas Elsaesser, who contributed enormously to our understanding of cinema history in general and German-language film in particular, pointed repeatedly to the "materialist conditions" that both facilitate and limit the production of films.[212]

The industry's hunger for stories will never be quenched, but for films to continue to exist as art, public subsidies are absolutely essential. Perhaps some filmmakers embark on adaptation projects to facilitate funding awards, but this matters little as long as 'fidelity' to the source text is neither aim nor requirement. Several of the adaptations discussed in this volume, for example by greats of the profession like Murnau, Fassbinder, Wes Anderson, Sokurov, or Petzold, are works of art and deserve their place in cinema history. They and other auteur filmmakers like them turned to literature as inspiration, rather than restriction to their creative imagination. "Authority and freedom," as art critic Jed Perl tells us, are the essence and "lifeblood" of the arts.[213] Experts in the craft of filmmaking, their "authority" is evident. But is a literary source sometimes a hindrance to creating art on film? What is in fact the difference between Petzold's *Undine* and other adaptations of the narrative? And if autonomy is art's condition, how can film, always a costly endeavor, ever be sovereign, and—as an adaptation—entirely independent?

Adaptations of the literary canon during the Nazi era make the destructive effect of the promotion of an ideology on the back of a well-known novel evident; the annihilation of the possibility of creating art, of course, being only the beginning of the cataclysm. But Pearl also considers works that set out to "perform some clearly defined civic or community service"[214] problematic in view of art's freedom and authenticity. When Paula Beer as Undine talks about Berlin and the contested reconstruction of the Hohenzollern castle in the capitol's busy center, the thematization of both memory culture and the critical recalibration of our urban spaces may be considered pragmatic if desirable contributions to the public sphere. But when Undine guides us, Petzold places the poets of German Romanticism by her side. Writers like de la Motte-Fouqué and E.T.A. Hoffmann, Novalis,

Karoline von Günderrode, and Wilhelm Hauff—just like Mary Shelley, Hugo, Poe or Gogol and many others of the epoch—embraced the idea of the creative self and the endless possibilities (and chasms) unfolding when boundaries are questioned and transgressed, between disciplines as much as between our perception of myths or the darkness of dreams and the paradoxes inherent in everyday reality. Their groundbreaking aesthetics was as much personal and subjective as it was steeped in a specific cultural past and sociopolitical present. The freedom inherent in their works of art reverberates. And so does art cinema that remediates and "reshape[s] experience"[215] in view of literature, film, and ourselves.

Cinema's history provides plenty of evidence that taking a literary text as source does not need to burden the freedom of creation. Literature can inspire art in terms of form and content, but creative impression remains limited if fidelity to the source text, box-office success, or the promotion of a particular message is too much of a concern. Auteurs but also some more commercial filmmakers who turned to German-language literature have greatly enriched cinema history, culture and, time and again, the public sphere with their imagination and skills. While literature will without doubt continue to provide inspiration, both "industrial art['s] [...] internalized relation with money" (Deleuze) and the trend toward serialization on television and streaming platforms will increasingly shape adaptation projects. Hopefully society will continue to support and enable conditions for the creation of art cinema, while preserving the stunning diversity of our cultural heritage in literature and film, not only in the privileged Global North, for the growth, education, and wonder of future generations.

Notes

1   Gilles Deleuze, *Cinema 2: The Time-Image* [1985], trans. Hugh Tomlinson and Robert Galeta (London: Athlone Press, 1989), 77.
2   Qurbani in "Vollbild—das Filmmagazin—Deutschlandfunk Kultur" (July 11, 2020); iTunes podcast.
3   This paragraph is based on film expert Georg Seeßlen, "Der Neo-Adenauer-Stil," *taz. die tageszeitung* (June 12, 1997): 15; https://taz.de/Der-Neo-Adenauer-Stil/!1396796/. Remakes became increasingly popular in television during this era. They range from Uwe Janson's Brecht-adaptation *Baal* (2004) and *Die Brücke*—a remake of B. Wicki's pacifist M. Gregor-adaptation *The Bridge*—(Wolfgang Panzer, 2008) to *Nackt unter Wölfen* (Philipp Kadelbach, 2015). *Die Brücke* was produced by Jürgen Hebstreit and Wolfgang Herold (Lionheart Entertainment, Munich/Pixomondo Studios, Frankfurt) for the private Pro7 Television company. The remake ignored most of what made Wicki's adaptation so compelling, ensured that military action commenced early on, included some sex, and completely lost sight of Wicki's

critique of heroic masculinity. The remake does little to convince as an antiwar film and reinforced clichés regarding superficial entertainment provided by private television. *Nackt unter Wölfen*, produced by Nico Hofmann, on the other hand tries to set the record straight and offer a historically more accurate narrative based on Apitz's 'original' story. Hofmann produced several adaptations, including Christoph Stark's *Julietta* (DE, 2001), which transposes the historical setting of Kleist's *Marquise von O …* 'from a war context in a small unidentified Italian town around 1800 to the 'Love Parade' in a peaceful, post-unification Berlin; from a patriarchal, sexually repressed society to a liberal, hedonistic one,' as Ricarda Schmidt notes in "The Swan and the Moped. Shifts in the Presentation of Violence from Kleist's 'Die Marquise von O …' to Christoph Stark's Julietta," *Processes of Transposition*, ed. C. Schönfeld, 39–58, here 39.

4   The quote was central to the concept of the Deutsches Filminstitut's (Frankfurt/M.) and Centre de Cultura Contemorània de Barcelona's Kubrick exhibitions in 2018/2019. https://www.cccb.org/en/exhibitions/file/stanley-kubrick/228237.

5   *Nibelungen* (DE, Uli Edel, 2004); *Emilia* (CH/DE, Henrik Pfeifer, 2005); *Werther* (DE, Uwe Janson, 2008), *Kabale und Liebe* (DE, Leander Haußmann, 2005), *Mario und der Zauberer* [Mario and the Wizard] (DE/FR/AT, Klaus Maria Brandauer, 1994); *Buddenbrooks* (DE/AT, Heinrich Breloer, 2008); *Jahrestage* [Anniversaries] (DE/AT, Margarethe von Trotta, 2000); *Der Turm* [The Tower] (DE, Christian Schwochow, 2012).

6   Filmmaker Leander Haußmann might serve as an example. He adapted canonical works such as Schiller's *Fiesco* (1991) and *Kabale und Liebe* (2005) as well as contemporary literature: *Herr Lehmann* (2003) based on Sven Regener's bestseller; *Robert Zimmermann wundert sich über die Liebe* (Robert Zimmermann wonders about love, 2008) based on a novel by Gernot Gricksch, who also wrote the script; and Jan Weiler's *Das Pubertier* (2014) as *Das Pubertier—Der Film* (2017).

7   DEFA and DFF adaptations include *Der Fall Ö* (Franz Fühmann's *König Ödipus*; DE/ČSSR/GR/FR, Rainer Simon, 1991), Brigitte Reimann's *Die Frau am Pranger* as *Erster Verlust* (DE, Maxim Dessau, 1990); Christoph Hein's *Der Tangospieler* (DE, Roland Gräf, 1990); Frank Beyer's adaptation of Volker Braun's *Unvollendete Geschichte* as *Der Verdacht* (1990); Hermann Kant's *Bronzezeit: Geschichten aus dem Leben des Buchhalters Farssmann* as *Farssmann oder Zu Fuß in die Sackgasse* (DE, Roland Oehme, 1991); Jurij Koch's *Die Augenoperation* as *Tanz auf der Kippe* (DE, Jürgen Brauer, 1991); at the same time, Walter Kempowsky's *Herzlich willkommen* was adapted in the 'west' (DE, Hark Bohm, 1990).

8   Among the productions for cinema were Friedrich de la Motte-Fouqué's *Undine* (DE/IT, Eckhart Schmidt, 1991), E.T.A. Hoffmann's *Der Sandmann* (DE, Eckhart Schmidt, 1993), and, a more recent addition to the literary canon, Friedrich Dürrenmatt's *Der Richter und sein Henker* as *Justiz* (DE/CH, Hans W. Geissendörfer, 1993). Public funding made available by the Berlin senate (Berliner Filmförderung) enabled a number of arthouse films until the fund closed in 1995: Danièle Huillet and Jean-Marie Straub adapted Brecht/Hölderlin/Sophokles *Antigone* (1991); Gottfried Keller's *Der grüne Heinrich*

(CH/DE/FR, Thomas Koerfer, 1993), Thomas *Mann's Mario und der Zauberer* (DE/FR/AT, Klaus Maria Brandauer, 1994), and Lienhard Wawrzyn's GDR legacy drama *Der Blaue* [The Blue One] (DE, Lienhard Wawrzyn, 1994).

9   Lutz Koepnick, "Reframing the Past: Heritage Cinema and the Holocaust in the 1990s," *New German Critique* 87 (2002): 47–82, here p. 57. Also quoted in Baer, "Das Boot," 27. See also Bergfelder, *International Adventures,* 2005.

10 Hester Baer has published fundamental and important research in this area. As I am writing this book, Hester Baer's *German Cinema in the Age of Neoliberalism* (Amsterdam University Press) has not as yet become available, but her aforementioned previous publications on the neoliberal German film industry and Eichinger as a producer of adaptations have been essential sources for me and provided much useful information for this chapter.

11 Seeßlen, "Der Neo-Adenauer-Stil," 15. Hester Baer, who also quotes from Seeßlen's article, published an excellent piece on *Das Boot*, which is discussed in this context. Cf. Baer, "Das Boot," 22. Eric Rentschler, "From New German Cinema to the Post-Wall Cinema of Consensus," in *Cinema and Nation,* ed. Mette Hjort and Scott MacKenzie (London and New York: Routledge, 2000), 260–77.

12 Films based on Rötger Feldmann's popular *Werner*-comics (1990, 1996, 2003) were immensely successful; http://www.insidekino.com/DJahr/DAlltimeDeutsch50.htm. A *Werner*-sequel (*Werner—Das muss kesseln*, 1996) remains the sixth highest grossing opening week in German cinema history.

13 Cf. statistics "Die erfolgreichsten deutschen Filme seit 1962"; https://www.insidekino.com/DJahr/DAlltimeDeutsch50.htm.

14 *Parfum* (DE, Philip Kadelbach, since 2018) premiered on ZDF neo and is being distributed internationally by Netflix. *Schuld* was also produced for ZDF (DE, Maris Pfeiffer/Hannu Salonen, 2015).

15 "Im Kino zählt nur, ob ich den einen richtigen Film habe, den alle sehen wollen." Interview with Bernd Eichinger: "Ich bin mein erster Zuschauer," *Der Tagesspiegel* (February 11, 2001); https://www.tagesspiegel.de/wirtschaft/interview-mit-bernd-eichinger-ich-bin-mein-erster-zuschauer/202056.html. The term *auteur producer* is Hester Baer's in "Producing Adaptations: Bernd Eichinger, Christiane F., and German Film History," in *Generic Histories of German Cinema: Genre and Its Deviations*, ed. Jaimey Fisher (Rochester: Camden House, 2013), 173–96, here p. 173.

16 Cf. Interview with Eichinger in *Cinema* at https://www.cinema.de/stars/news/bernd-eichinger-im-cinema-interview-11291_ar.html. Eichinger's TV-remakes of 1950s box office hits included *Die Halbstarken* (Urs Egger, 1996), starring Til Schweiger as reincarnation of former heartthrob Horst Buchholz in the 1956 classic; *Das Mädchen Rosemarie* (Bernd Eichinger, 1996), with Nina Hoss starring as Rosemarie Nitribitt in the Rolf Thiele-remake; and *Es geschah am hellichten Tag* (Nico Hofmann, 1996), a remake of the 1958 film based on Dürrenmatt's script which the author then turned into the novel *Das Versprechen* [The Pledge].

17 https://www.cinema.de/stars/news/bernd-eichinger-im-cinema-interview-11291_ar.html.

18 Tim Bergfelder, *International Adventures*, 85f.; Baer, "Producing Adaptations," 183.

19 See Jaimey Fisher's "Introduction" to his *Generic Histories of German Cinema: Genre and Its Deviations*, 1–26, here p. 2; and Baer, "Producing Adaptations," 173.
20 The book was fought hard about in families, too. Like many other parents at the time, my mother took it away from me, (unsuccessfully) forbidding me to continue reading it, but read it herself and insisted that this account would lead to more teenagers falling prey to drugs and engaging in prostitution to feed their habit.
21 Constantin Film still successfully produces modern interpretations of world-renowned bestsellers and is bringing a serialized remake of *Wir Kinder vom Bahnhof Zoo* [Us Children of Zoo Station] to Prime Video (DE, Philipp Kadelbach, 2021).
22 Baer, "Das Boot," 19. The adaptation deserves more than this chapter can offer, please see Baer's excellent article instead.
23 Baer, "Producing Adaptations," 184, 183f.
24 His adaptation of Isabel Allende's *The House of Spirits* (DE/DK/PT, Bille August, 1993) disappointed, and Eichinger, ever the entrepreneurial producer, swiftly turned to the former box-office hits of the Adenauer era, remaking films such as *Das Mädchen Rosemarie* [The Girl Rosemarie], *Es geschah am hellichten Tag* [It Happened in Broad Daylight/The Pledge], and *Die Halbstarken* [Teenage Wolfpack], for a German television audience united in nostalgic longing for their youth and the illusion of an uncomplicated past. His remake of *Die drei von der Tankstelle* [The Three from the Filling Station] was 'updated' to *Die drei Mädels von der Tankstelle* [The Three Girls from the Petrol Station] (DE, Peter F. Bringmann, 1997), sporting a 'hip soundtrack' and international star Franka Potente.
25 Cf. also their adaptation of the fantasy role-playing video game *Monster Hunter* (CA/CN/DE/GB/JP/US, Paul W.S. Anderson, 2020).
26 *Der Baader Meinhof Komplex* is based on Stefan Aust's non-fiction book; other adaptations include Michel Houellebecq's highly controversial *Les Particules élémentaires* as *Elementarteilchen* (Oskar Roehler, 2006); Eichinger also co-wrote the script with Ruth Toma for the Constantin-produced *3096 Tage* [3096 Days] based on Natascha Kampusch's autobiographical account of her ordeal after being kidnapped as a ten-year-old (DE, Sherry Hormann, 2013).
27 *Einsamkeit und Sex und Mitleid* [Loneliness, Sex and Empathy] (2017) is an adaptation of Helmut Krausser's novel. Lars Montag wrote the screenplay in collaboration with the author and directed the film. Inspired by the German national anthem, which proclaims "Einigkeit und Recht und Freiheit für das deutsche Vaterland," i.e., unity, justice, and freedom, it reflects on the state of contemporary Germany by following fifteen citizens in a German metropolis.
28 Eichinger had been bought out in 2006 but continued to work with Constantin as one of the company's directors, as screenwriter and producer until his death in 2011. For more information, see Hester Baer's article on Eichinger and "Producing Adaptations."
29 See Julian Preece and Nick Hodgin, eds., *Andreas Dresen* (Oxford: Peter Lang, 2017).
30 Cf. the film's trailer at https://www.youtube.com/watch?v=fm81Ml8STZg.

31 http://www.filmstarts.de/nachrichten/18498832.html.
32 The company was founded by Berben in 1996 and became a subsidiary of Constantin Film in 1999. On its website, the Berlin film company defines its core production principle according to Eichinger's leadership—high-profile fictional formats, quality television that can guarantee strong ratings. https://www.constantin-film.de/unternehmen/moovie/.
33 Cf. the ZDF series *Schuld* [Guilt] (three seasons, 2014–19; DE, Nils Willbrandt; with Moritz Bleibtreu in the lead), and the mini-series *Verbrechen* [Crime] for ZDF. Directed by one of crime film genre's experts Hannu Salonen and starring audience favorite Josef Bierbichler as criminal defense lawyer Friedrich Leonhardt, the series did extremely well not only in German-language countries, but also abroad, especially in Asia, where von Schirach's novels are also bestsellers [https://www.prisma.de/filme/Verbrechen-nach-Ferdinand-von-Schirach-Faehner,184011]. "Der Äthiopier" [The Ethiopian], included in his volume of short stories *Verbrechen*, was adapted for public television ARD under the direction of Tim Trageser, and broadcast in 2016 with highly acclaimed German actor Jürgen Vogel in the lead. The adaptation not only won the audience award at the Festivals des Deutschen Films but also the Gold World Medal at the New York Film Festival.
34 For further information, see Paul M. Malone's "Transposition or Translation? Fiction to Film in Doris Dörrie's *Nobody Loves Me* and *Am I Beautiful?*" and Peter M. McIsaac's "Taking Doris Dörrie Seriously: Literature, Film, Gender," in *Processes of Transposition*, 333–46; 347–61.
35 A Schiller-adaptation just trivial enough for desired mass appeal, *Cabal and Love* tanked due to changes to the plot (especially the ending), which indicated a lack of understanding of the important source text. According to critics, the film failed in its attempt to perform a balancing act between classical theater and Hollywood.
36 The film was overall badly received. See for example https://www.spiegel.de/kultur/kino/felix-krull-von-detlev-buck-klassiker-mit-zuckerguss-filmkritik-a-a2be7dce-0002-0001-0000-000178959766.
37 https://www.kino-zeit.de/film-kritiken-trailer-streaming/asphaltgorillas-2018.
38 As announced in a press release by FilmFernsehfonds on July 19, 2018; cf. https://www.fff-bayern.de/no_cache/fff-bayern/presse/pressemitteilungen/pressemitteilungen/news/glaube-liebe-und-die-rettung-der-welt-fff-foerdert-49-filmprojekte-mit-63-mio-euro.html?tx_news_pi1%5Baction%5D=detail&tx_news_pi1%5Bcontroller%5D=News&cHash=18ff5d8fd3e26bb4e39f18f1592e40b9&sword_list%5B0%5D=collini.
39 Her support for the film was quoted in most reviews at the time; for example: https://www.mathaeser.de/mm/hollywood/starnews/das-ist-der-erfolgreichste-deutsche-film-des-jahres/404453.
40 Martin Moszkowicz in an interview by Louis Lewitan, "Fehler sind Teil unseres Geschäftes und unseres Lebens," *Zeitmagazin* 27 (2019), https://www.zeit.de/zeit-magazin/2019/27/martin-moszkowicz-constantin-film-rettung. For a more in-depth assessment see Jörg Friedrich, *Die kalte Amnestie: NS-Täter in der Bundesrepublik* (Frankfurt/M.: Fischer, 1984). For a summary of the debate in the West German parliament, see https://www.bundestag.de/dokumente/textarchiv/ns-verbrechen-199958.

41 https://www.tagblatt.ch/kultur/film/regisseur-alain-gsponer-die-jugend-kennt-keine-werte-mehr-ld.1447319.
42 Alain Gsponer in an interview with Corina Gall: "*Jugend ohne Gott*: Regisseur Alain Gsponer: Die Jugend kennt keine Werte mehr," *Aargauer Zeitung* (August 27, 2017); https://www.aargauerzeitung.ch/kultur/film/regisseur-alain-gsponer-die-jugend-kennt-keine-werte-mehr-131643976.
43 Baer, "Producing Adaptations," 183.
44 Fritz Rumler, "Die Hölle der Frauen," *Der Spiegel* 6 (1998); https://www.spiegel.de/spiegel/print/d-7811137.html; for the impact of the adaptation on the novel's sales, cf. https://www.abendblatt.de/kultur-live/buecher/article107623601/Der-Campus.html.
45 Baer, "Producing Adaptations," 173.
46 For WDR's Deutsches Fernsehspiel [more info in Chapter 7] Rohrbach produced, for example, Wenders' Handke adaptation *Die Angst des Tormanns vorm Elfmeter* (1972) and his Goethe-inspired *Falsche Bewegung* (1975). As managing director of Bavaria film, adaptations of German literature included Fassbinder's *Berlin Alexanderplatz* (1980), Petersen's *Das Boot* (1981–5), and *Die unendliche Geschichte* (1984).
47 Cf. SPIO data at http://www.spio.de, and numbers published by the German Federal Film Board (FFA); https://www.ffa.de/kinoergebnisse-uebersicht.html.
48 The following numbers are based on Wilfried Berauer's statistical analysis for SPIO. Cf. Wilfried Berauer's SPIO report (November 2, 2007): "Quellenanalyse deutscher Film. Woher kommt der Stoff der deutschen Traumfabrik," which can be downloaded at: http://www.spio.de/media_content/777.pdf.
49 Adaptations of Cornelia Funke's bestselling children's and youth literature include: *Inkheart*, based on Funke's *Tintenherz* (US/DE, Iain Softley, 2008; starring Brendan Fraser, Paul Bettany, Helen Mirren, Jim Broadbent, etc., the film had a budget of $60 million and a somewhat disappointing return at the American box office, but by now has grossed $62 million worldwide according to IMDb), *Herr der Diebe* [The Thief Lord] (DE/LU/GB, Richard Claus, 2005), *Hände weg von Mississippi* (DE, Detlev Buck, 2007), Funke's teeny series *Die wilden Hühner* [Wild Chickens] (DE, Vivian Naefe, 2006), *Die wilden Hühner und die Liebe* [Wild Chickens and Love] (DE, Vivian Naefe, 2007), *Die wilden Hühner und das Leben* [Wild Chickens and Life] (DE, Vivian Naefe, 2009), *Als der Weihnachtsmann vom Himmel fiel* (DE, Oliver Dieckmann, 2011, and as a puppet film, 2017), *Gespensterjäger* or *Ghost Hunters—On Icy Trails* (DE/AT/IE [Lucky Bird Pictures (Munich), Lotus-Film GmbH (Vienna), and Ripple World Pictures Ltd [Dublin], with comedian Anke Engelke, Milo Parker, etc., dir. Tobias Baumann, 2015), and the animated feature film *Drachenreiter* [Dragonrider] (DE/BE, Tomer Eshed, 2020). For Masannek's *Die wilden Kerle* [The Wild Soccer Bunch] see the six live-action films directed by the author of the series (DE, Joachim Masannek, 2003ff.). Public German television ZDF also produced a 26-episode animated series in 2012, which was also sold abroad, for example to the United States (Primo TV, 2017).
50 Among the many adaptations based on children's books by Erich Kästner are: *Charlie & Louise* (DE, Joseph Vilsmaier, 1994), *It Takes Two* (US, Andy Tennant, 1995), *The Parent Trap* (US, Nancy Meyers, 1998), *Mania czy*

Ania (PL, Jerzy Bielunas, 1999), *Pünktchen und Anton* (DE, Caroline Link, 1999), *Emil und die Detektive* (DE, Franziska Buch, 2001), *Das fliegende Klassenzimmer* (DE, Tomy Wigand, 2003), *Tur & Retur* (SE, Ella Lemhagen, 2003), *Ein Zwilling ist nicht genug* (DE, Brigitte Müller, 2004), the animated *Das doppelte Lottchen* (2007) and *Konferenz der Tiere* (2010), and the public (SWR) television production *Das doppelte Lottchen* (Lancelot von Naso, 2017).

51 The past three decades have seen films based on Otfried Preußler's beloved children's books such as *Das kleine Gespenst* (DE, Curt Linda, 1992), live-action adaptations *Der Räuber Hotzenplotz* (DE, Gernot Roll, 2006), *Krabat* (DE, Marco Kreuzpaintner, 2008), Das kleine Gespenst/S'Chline Gspängst [The Little Ghost] (DE/CH, Alain Gsponer, 2013), and *Die kleine Hexe* [The Little Witch] (DE/CH, Michael Schaerer, 2018).

52 Michael Ende's *Unendliche Geschichte* sold 16 million copies and was adapted under the auspices of Bernd Eichinger (DE/US, Wolfgang Petersen, 1984). Ende was so unhappy with the adaptation that he took legal action and did not want to be mentioned in the credits. Two recent Ende adaptations are *Jim Knopf und Lukas der Lokomotivführer* (DE, Dennis Gansel, 2018) and *Jim Knopf und die Wilde 13* (DE, Dennis Gansel, 2020).

53 Children's and youth literature on film: Walter Moers' *Käpt'n Blaubärs Seemannsgarn* (animation; DE, 1990); followed by *Käpt'n Blaubär—der Film* (DE, Hayo Freitag, 1990); Christine Nöstlinger's *Der Zwerg im Kopf* (DE, Claudia Schröder, 1991); Peter Härtling's *Krücke* (DE, Jörg Grünler, 1992); Erich Kästner's *Das doppelte Lottchen* (DE, Joseph Vilsmaier, 1993) and *Pünktchen und Anton* (DE, Caroline Link, 1999); more recently Andreas Steinhöfel's award winning youth novels about Rico and Oskar were brought to the cinema screens as *Rico, Oskar und die Tieferschatten* (DE, Neele Vollmar, 2014), *Rico, Oskar und das Herzgebreche* (DE, Wolfgang Groos, 2015), and *Rico, Oskar und der Diebstahlstein* (DE, Neele Vollmar, 2016).

54 The most recent adaptation in this context is *Gott, du kannst ein Arsch sein!* [God, you can be such an ass!] (DE, André Erkau, 2020), based on Frank Pape's bestselling autobiographical account using his fifteen-year-old daughter's diary subsequent to her terminal cancer diagnosis. The bestseller was adapted with acting heavyweights Heike Makatsch and Jürgen Vogel. The title is derived from a tattoo that Steffi (Sinje Irslinger) gets during the last few months of her life, placed right above her heart. Like many films nowadays, it makes the most of its authenticity—'based on a true story'—and emotional appeal.

55 Television adaptations since 1990 include works by Heinrich von Kleist, Friedrich de la Motte-Fouqué, E.T.A. Hoffmann, Adalbert Stifter, Thomas Mann, Arthur Schnitzler, Kurt Tucholsky, Stefan Zweig, Lion Feuchtwanger, Bruno Frank, Hans Fallada, Georg Hermann, Hermann Broch, Bert Brecht, Max Frisch, Friedrich Dürrenmatt, Wolfgang Koeppen, Christoph Hein, Ingeborg Bachmann, Siegfried Lenz, Peter Härtling, Felix Mitterer, Milo Dor, and Tankred Dorst.

56 Ernst Toller, "Film und Staat," *Berliner Volkszeitung* 60 (February 5, 1924), n.p.

57 Stefan Ruzowitzky received the Oscar for his 2007 *Die Fälscher / The Counterfeiters*. As the FFA announced on September 12, 2017, his new project—an adaptation of Hermann Hesse's *Narziss und Goldmund* (Mythos Film Produktions)—was awarded 568,400 euro in German public film funding. At the same meeting, half a million euro was allocated to the adaptation of Cornelia Funke's bestselling children's book *Drachenreiter* (dir. Tomer Eshed; script: Johnny Smith).

58 Based on the novels by German veteran comedian Otto Waalkes, *7 Zwerge—Männer allein im Wald* [7 Dwarves—Men Alone in the Woods] (DE, Sven Unterwaldt Jr., 2004) and *7 Zwerge—Der Wald ist nicht genug* [7 Dwarves—The Forest Is Not Enough] (DE, Sven Unterwaldt Jr., 2006), the adaptations written by Unterwaldt and Bernd Eilert range among the most successful at the box office since 1968, when ticket sales were first recorded. In 2004, *7 Zwerge* was the second most successful movie in Germany, ranging at eleventh place overall since 1968. The film was co-funded by the Filmstiftung NRW (NRW Film Fund). Cf. http://www.insidekino.com/DJahr/DAlltimeDeutsch50.htm.

59 Berauer, "Quellenanalyse," 4. The same 'recipe' applies to other comedians such as Bully Herbig.

60 Rentschler, "From New German Cinema to the Post-Wall Cinema of Consensus," 260–77.

61 https://www.theguardian.com/books/2009/aug/23/elective-affinities-books.

62 Cf. Marco Abel, "The Cinema of Identification Gets on My Nerves: An Interview with Christian Petzold," *Cineaste* 33.3 (2008); https://www.cineaste.com/summer2008/the-cinema-of-identification-gets-on-my-nerves?rq=Petzold.; and Klaus H. Kiefer, "Weltliteratur zu Pferde—Philipp Stölzls Film, Goethe!," in *Goethezeitportal* (May 11, 2013; newsletter no. 5); http://www.goethezeitportal.de/fileadmin/PDF/db/wiss/goethe/kiefer_weltliteratur_zu_pferde.pdf.

63 Hjort/MacKenzie, "Introduction," *Cinema and Nation*, 12.

64 Andreas Wiseman, "KKR Continues German Spree with Acquisition of Key Film Distributor Universum," *Deadline* (February 25, 2019); https://deadline.com/2019/02/universum-germany-kkr-film-distributor-vice-hateful-eight-1202564689/.

65 Ed Meza, "Tough to Crack," *Variety* (November 7, 2019); https://variety.com/2019/film/global/u-s-market-german-cinema-1203398023/.

66 Meza, "Tough to Crack."

67 Quoted by Meza, "Tough to Crack."

68 Julia Weber, in Meza, ibid.

69 Moritz Hemminger, deputy head of sales and acquisitions at ARRI Media, as quoted by Meza.

70 Lars-Olav Beier, "Die Hand am Hebel," *Der Spiegel* 10 (March 3, 2013); https://www.spiegel.de/kultur/die-hand-am-hebel-a-bfccd81c-0002-0001-0000-000091346616.

71 "Edel-Kitsch." Cf. Simon Broll, "Stars auf Kaffeefahrt," *Der Spiegel* (March 7, 2013); https://www.spiegel.de/kultur/kino/bille-augusts-literaturverfilmung-nachtzug-nach-lissabon-a-886176.html.

72 David Rooney, "Night Train to Lisbon: Berlin Review," *The Hollywood Reporter* (February 13, 2013); https://www.hollywoodreporter.com/movies/movie-reviews/berlin-review-night-train-lisbon-421224/.
73 Ibid.
74 For example, Boyd van Hoeij, "Night Train to Lisbon," *Variety* (February 13, 2013); https://variety.com/2013/film/markets-festivals/night-train-to-lisbon-1117949248/.
75 Uwe Timm, *Von Anfang und Ende. Über die Lesbarkeit der Welt* (Cologne: Kiepenheuer & Witsch, 2009), 83.
76 Cf. Timm's lectures on poetics (Frankfurt/Main University, 2009) *Von Anfang und Ende* as above.
77 Heidegger's lecture on the "Origin of the Work of Art" (1935) was published in *Holzwege* (1960); cf. Martin Heidegger, *Der Ursprung des Kunstwerkes* (Ditzingen: Reclam, 1986), 93–114.
78 Matti Geschonneck's 2010 adaptation of Torsten Schulz's novel *Boxhagener Platz* (Boxhagen Square, 2004) may serve as another example of an adaptation of a successful contemporary novel that skillfully recreates a particular period in time (here, East Berlin in the 1960s), but foregrounds the comedic elements to maximize box office returns. Schulz's sometimes nostalgic and often very amusing coming-of-age tale centers around twelve-year-old Holger, who is played by Samuel Schneider, and his grandmother Oma Otti (Gudrun Ritter). Berlin's specific dialect greatly supports the milieu's authenticity as the protagonists' lives under socialism unfold during a time of political and social change.
79 According to *Der Spiegel;* the article can be accessed at https://www.spiegel.de/kultur/kino/kinobilanz-2008-der-deutsche-film-ein-kassenschlager-a-605477.html. Anika Decker supplied the script.
80 Cf. Volker Gunske, "Das RAF-Business: Abgerechnet wird zum Schluss," *tip* 20 (2008): 28–31; Katharina Dockhorn: "Subventionierte Lobbyarbeit," *epd Film* 7 (2008): 6.
81 Following the TV-adaptation of Walser's 1978 novel in 1984/85, the author of the source text complained that Plenzdorf's script for the film (FRG, Peter Beauvais, 1985) was too faithful to the literary text. Walser argued—implicitly building on Fontane's literary theory—'If a film sticks too closely to the source text, it is bound to fail. You have to use the novel as a quarry, which you break, destroy, take apart and remove piece by piece. Otherwise, it won't be a film, only a documentation.' See Walser's interview with Jan Freitag, "'Gottschalk ist ein göttlicher Bub': Martin Walser über TV-Realitäten, Literaturverfilmungen, Hape Kerkeling und Bilderstürmer," *Die Zeit* (March 16, 2007), https://www.zeit.de/online/2007/12/interview-martin-walser. Walser was much happier with the 2007 adaptation and its A-list cast (Ulrich Noethen, Katja Riemann, Ulrich Tukur), and complemented director Rainer Kaufmann on successfully transposing his novel about a marriage to the present day.
82 Siegfried Lenz's literary work has led to numerous successful adaptations, especially for television; most notably *Die Flut ist pünktlich* [High Tide's on Time] (ZDF, 2013) and *Schweigeminute* [Minute of Silence] (ZDF,

2016); In 2020, *Der Überläufer*—a novel about a deserter that West Germany's publishers suppressed during the Cold War—was produced by ARD. Director and co-author of the script Florian Gallenberger notes in an interview available on the ARD Mediathek, that adaptation, too, is a defector or renegade ("Adaptation as Überläufer") both historically and in terms of the original narrative. Christian Granderath (Redaktionsleiter Film, NDR) explained the reason for the extension of the narrative and the inclusion of a love story as not wanting to 'only tell a men's story' ("eine Männergeschichte").

83 *BFV-Newsletter* 1 (2008); https://filmunion.verdi.de/++file++551538ceaa698e3 ffc000655/download/BFV-Newsletter%202008.pdf.

84 Randall Halle, *German Film after Germany: Towards a Transnational Aesthetic* (Urbana: University of Illinois Press, 2008), 86; also quoted in Baer, "Affectless Economies," 74.

85 Liechtenstein, as the fourth German-speaking country in Europe, should be mentioned here, too; but Liechtenstein's filmmakers such as Arno Oehri [*Der Eidechsenkönig*], or Isolde Marxer have not turned to local literature in their work. Austrian Georg Tressler's 1958 *Heimat*-film *Ein wunderbarer Sommer* [A Wonderful Summer] based on Paul Gallico's short novel *Ludmila. A Legend of Liechtenstein* (1955) seems to be the most recent adaptation related to the small Alpine country.

86 Johanna Spyri's *Heidi* (1880) is estimated to have sold more than 50 million copies worldwide. Alain Gsponer directed a beautiful if conventional new adaptation starring Bruno Ganz (DE/CH, 2015), which is interesting especially due to the secularization of the text on screen, in which nature is that which heals and inspires goodness.

87 https://www.bafa.de/DE/Wirtschafts_Mittelstandsfoerderung/Film_Technik/ Filmfoerderung/filmfoerderung_node.html.

88 A film's planned premiere at the Berlinale is insufficient to qualify for funding.

89 Cf. "Filmförderung" (film funding) guidelines listed by Bundesamt für Wirtschaft und Ausfuhrkontrolle; links to the relevant laws can also be found here: https://www.bafa.de/DE/Wirtschafts_Mittelstandsfoerderung/Film_ Technik/Filmfoerderung/filmfoerderung_node.html.

90 Subsidies awarded by the federal government for culture and media (BKM) are considered an award, not a loan, and do not have to be paid back. Up to 1 million euro may be awarded for a feature length film for either adults or children, while both genres are to be treated equally. Numerous films and adaptations of the last few years have received funding via the Medienboard Berlin-Brandenburg (MBB), which requires not only 50 percent of the film project's funding to be sourced elsewhere but also regional relevance in terms of the film's content, in contrast to the BKM's funding the MBB's subsidy is only a loan: https://www.medienboard.de/fileadmin/user_upload/ Medienboard_Fo__rderrichtlinie.pdf.

91 The film received 500,000 euro by the Filmförderungsanstalt (FFA); https:// www.ffa.de/aid=1365.html?newsdetail=20171205-488_neun-neue-kinoprojekt e&highlight=Literaturverfilmung.

92 https://www.moviepilot.de/news/top-7-der-besten-deutschen-literaturverfilmungen-nach-2000-157547.

93 A Weinstein Company film in collaboration with Babelsberg Film GmbH (Potsdam-Babelsberg) and Mirage Enterprises (Los Angeles), *The Reader* was produced by Anthony Minghella, Sydney Pollack, Donna Gigliotto, Redmond Morris. Kate Winslet won an Academy Award for her depiction of Hannah Schmitz, the former concentration camp guard, who has an affair with much younger Michael Berg (David Kross), who reads to her. When he sees her again, he is not only confronted with her past, but also begins to understand her own emerging sense of guilt. Numerous critics lamented the focus on the love story between the two main characters as a highly problematic trivialization of mass murder.

94 The ranking continues with *Lila, Lila*, an adaptation of Swiss author Martin Suter's 2004 novel about an author's success based on someone else's work, starring Daniel Brühl (DE/CH, Alain Gsponer, 2009) in fifth place, followed by the mystery-thriller *Die Tür* (DE, Anno Saul, 2009) based on Akif Pirinçci's aforementioned novel, and *Die Wolke* (DE, Gregor Schnitzler, 2006) based on Gudrun Pausewang's 1987 youth novel about fear of a nuclear catastrophe.

95 Specialized in romance and crime serials, Constantin TV also produces combinations of the two genres, most successfully in a feature-length adaptation of a *Heimat*-crime novel by Rita Falk, *Winterkartoffelkönig* [Winterpotatoking] (Ed Herzog, 2014). The original 2017/18 series of *Parfum* was written by Eva Kranenburg, who moved the setting from the Middle Ages to modern day and directed by Philipp Kadelbach. Kadelbach made a name for himself by adapting popular novels (like Iny Lorentz *Die Wanderhure* [The Wandering Whore] as *Die Pilgerin* [The Pilgrim] (DE/CZ, 2013), mini-series such as *Unsere Mütter, unsere Väter* [distributed internationally as *Generation War*] (2012), and remakes such as *Nackt unter Wölfen* [Naked among Wolves] (DE/CZ, 2015) and the serialized *Wir Kinder vom Bahnhof Zoo* [Us Kids from Zoo Station] (DE/IT/CZ, 2020). *Parfum* received mixed reviews that ranged from 'aesthetically impressive' to 'complete catastropy' (*Stern*, November 12, 2018; *Spiegel online*, November 13, 2018).

96 In Switzerland, it is heritage cinema that is being supported predominantly, for example, together with Cinémateque Suisse, SRF invested in the restoration and digitalization of one of the classics of Swiss cinema, the 1941 adaptation of Paul Ilg's autobiographical novel *Das Menschlein Matthias* (The little human Matthias, 1914). In 2020/1 SRF celebrated 100 years of Swiss author Dürrenmatt by screening several films based on his works, from *The Visit* (IT/US/FRG/FR, Bernhard Wicki, 1964) to the SRF's own adaptation of *Der Besuch der alten Dame* (CH, Max Peter Ammann, 1982), this time with Maria Schell rather than Ingrid Bergman as Claire Zachanassian.

97 German-Austrian co-productions include Erich Hackl's *Abschied von Sidonie: Sidonie* (Karin Brandauer, 1990) and Julian Roman Pölsler's Anzengruber adaptation *Der Schandfleck* (1999); Pölser's *Heimat*-film is the fourth adaptation of Anzengruber's text. More recently, Hesse's *Die Heimkehr* [Homecoming] (AT/DE, Jo Baier, 2012) praised as a sensitive period adaptation for television. See also Helga Schreckenberger, "Mit der Kamera erzählen: Xaver Schwarzenbergers Verfilmung von Gerhard Roths Roman *Der Stille Ozean*," *Modern Austrian Literature* 34 (2001): 79–87.

98   The novel was marked for adaptation due to its mass appeal and financial success by ZDF. *Unterleuten—das zerrissene Dorf* [U.- the torn village] was produced as a three-part mini-series (DE, Matti Geschonneck, 2020).

99   Rolf Teigler's *Penthesilea Moabit* (DE, 2008) is a free adaptation that also integrates the original literary language of the early nineteenth century into an urban, twenty-first-century setting. In this case, Ensemble 21, a group of amateur actors from different nationalities and cultural backgrounds perform Kleist's play about Penthesilea, the mythological queen of the Amazons, in the Moabit district of Berlin, where they all lived at the time.

100   This *Buddenbrooks* adaptation is available in a 150-minute version for cinema, and a three-part, 180-minute mini-series for television; Breloer's adaptation was praised for its attention to detail, that recreates features down to the wallpaper just like Thomas Mann depicted it in his novel, but was also sharply criticized, not least for its elimination of an entire generation, but also for its lack of independence from its admired source text. For the majority of critics, the film had to fall flat in comparison to Thomas Mann's important novel, and no one, not even Armin Müller-Stahl, would ever be able to do justice to Mann's Johann 'Jean' Buddenbrook. The film was co-produced by German public television broadcasting companies BR, WDR, NDR, SWR, Austrian public television ORF, ARTE, Bavaria Film, etc., and distributed internationally by Warner Bros., Bavaria Int., among others.

101   According to the announcement on the ORF website; https://der.orf.at/unternehmen/aktuell/oefi136.html.

102   Subsequent to the publication of his novel *Gantenbein* (published in English as *A Wilderness of Mirrors* and *Gantenbein*, 1964), Max Frisch developed the script *Zürich—Transit* (1966) in the context of a planned collaboration with journalist and director Erwin Leiser, but insisted that the project should not be considered an adaptation of his novel. When the collaboration with Leiser ended, Bernhard Wicki was supposed to take over, but the film was never made until Hilde Bechert took it on. Bechert's *Zürich—Transit. Skizze eines Films* (1992) was broadcast in the "Literarische Filmerzählung" series. Cf. H. W. Ohly's interview with Max Frisch in *Evangelischen Filmbeobachter* (1965), reprinted in: Luis Bolliger, ed., *jetzt: max frisch* (Frankfurt/M.: Suhrkamp, 2001), 182f.

103   "Debüt im Dritten" [debut in channel 3; the third channel was reserved for regional television, which was introduced after the two main German public TV channels ARD and ZDR. *Emmas Glück* premiered on July 16, 2006, at the Munich Filmfest and subsequently, in 2008, on SWR.

104   According to IMDb, *Emma's Bliss* received a 7.5 out of 10 rating, and grossed only $62,000 in Austria and $70,000 in Switzerland. Further afield, the film made $26,523 in Argentina, $22,000 in Brazil, $54,000 in Mexico, $62,000 South Korea, $14,000 in Taiwan, and not even $1,000 in Uruguay. The adapation proved comparatively popular in Spain, where it grossed $289,000.

105   *Dampfnudelblues* was followed by *Winterkartoffelknödel* (2014), *Schweinskopf al dente* (2016), *Grießnockerlaffäre* (2017), *Sauerkrautkoma* (2018), *Leberkäsjunkie* (2019), and *Kaiserschmarrndrama* (2021).

106 According to filmportal.de, public funding for the third season of *Babylon Berlin* was provided by Medienboard Berlin-Brandenburg (MBB) (Potsdam) and Film- und Medien Stiftung NRW (Düsseldorf) only.
107 For example, *Nicht der Homosexuelle ist pervers, sondern die Situation in der er sich befindet* [It Is Not the Homosexual Who Is Perverse, but the Society in Which He Lives] (FRG, Rosa von Praunheim, 1971); *Krieg und sexuelle Gewalt* [War and Sexual Violence] (DE, Helke Sander, 1993); *Solino* (DE, Fatih Akin, 2002). Julia von Heinz highlighted the impact of public television on German film in her PhD thesis *Die freundliche Übernahme—Der Einfluss des öffentlich-rechtlichen Fernsehens auf den deutschen Kinofilm von 1950 bis 2012* (Baden-Baden: Nomos, 2012).
108 Julia von Heinz, "Neue deutsche Gemütlichkeit," *Die Zeit* (January 10, 2017); https://www.zeit.de/kultur/film/2017-01/filmfoerderung-kinofilme-oeffentlich-rechtlicher-rundfunk.
109 Heinz, "Neue deutsche Gemütlichkeit," online.
110 Quoted in Abel, "The Cinema of Identification Gets on My Nerves."
111 For an excellent overview of the Berlin School, see Marco Abel, "The Berlin School," *German Cinema Book* (²2020), 252–61.
112 Abel, "The Berlin School," 255.
113 Abel uses Deleuze/Guattari's 'minor culture' concept to define the Berlin School's "'collective assemblage of enunciation'of a people that is still missing." Ibid., 256.
114 Baer/Fenner, "Introduction: Revisiting Feminism and German Cinema," 1–19, here 6f.; see their *Camera Obscura* 99 (2018) volume, which focuses on the women director-producers prevalent in the Berlin School: *Women's Film Authorship in Neoliberal Times: Revisiting Feminism and German Cinema*.
115 Baer points out that films are shot on 35 mm and are not meant for television in terms of their form or content; Baer, "Affectless Economies," 74f.
116 Petzold refers to Hitchcock's view that one can't film a good novel, only a bad one. The conversation between Hitchcock and Truffaut has been quoted often, especially in adaptation research, but also by, for example, Jonathan Coe, "Good Book, Great Film," *The Guardian* (April 1, 2011); https://www.theguardian.com/books/2011/apr/01/book-adaptations-film-jonathan-coe.
117 Liane von Billerbeck in *Deutschlandfunk Kultur*: "Wie man lernt, wieder Mensch zu sein"; https://www.deutschlandfunkkultur.de/christian-petzold-ueber-seinen-film-transit-wie-man-lernt.1008.de.html?dram:article_id=414659.
118 For example, in the above-mentioned interview in *Deutschlandfunk Kultur*.
119 Ibid.
120 Abel, "The Cinema of Identification Gets on My Nerves," online.
121 Volker Schlöndorff: "Schluss mit der Anpasserei!" *Die Zeit* (May 22, 2003); https://www.zeit.de/2003/22/CannesSchl_9andorff.
122 Abel, "The Cinema of Identification Gets on My Nerves," online. Several Thomas Mann-adaptations are discussed in the previous chapter; Uwe Johnson's a tetralogy of novels *Jahrestage* [Anniversaries: From a Year in the Life of Gesine Cresspahl] (1971–83) was only adapted for television as a four-part mini-series by Margarethe v. Trotta in 1999/2000.

123 See Bergfelder, *International Adventures*, 2005; Hester Baer examines these strategies in her article on *Das Boot*, referring to Bergfelder, 21. The strategies and practices of transnational productions aimed at appealing to an international audience are worth a closer look in this context, especially where they produce transnational modes of identification offering what Lutz Koepnick defined as "heritage identity"; this places "the nation's subjects outside of their own culture, asking them to look at their own lives like tourists who typify different cultures sites of radical—and, hence, pleasurable—alterity." See Lutz Koepnick, "'Amerika gibt's überhaupt nicht': Notes on German Heritage Film," in *German Pop Culture: How American Is It?*, ed. Agnes C. Mueller (Ann Arbor: University of Michigan Press, 2004), 191–208, here p. 199. Hester Baer calls it "an objectified, eminently consumable of self-representation that appeals to global tourists and local inhabitants alike." Baer, "Das Boot," 28.

124 The book can be downloaded via Project Gutenberg: https://www.gutenberg.org/ebooks/18752.

125 Andreas Kilb: "Eine neue Runde im ewigen Kampf des Kinos mit dem Buch," *Die Zeit* 7 (1997); https://www.zeit.de/1997/07/kinobuch.txt.19970207.xml.

126 According to SPIO statistics; cf. https://www.spio.de/?seitid=24&tid=3 and https://www.spio.de/?seitid=26&tid=3. See also Wilfried Berauer, *Filmstatistisches Jahrbuch 2021* (Wiesbaden: SPIO, 2021).

127 Gesetz zur Anpassung des Urheberrechts an die Erfordernisse des digitalen Binnenmarkts; https://www.bundesregierung.de/breg-de/suche/urheberrechtsreform-1845042.

128 See http://www.spio.de/?seitid=2841&tid=2782 for a transcript of Holighaus' keynote (January 28, 2016) on the "Reform des Urhebervertragsrechts—Zu den praxistauglichen Regelungen für die Beteiligten."

129 Cf. the German Parliament's Committee for Legal Affairs and Consumer Protection of the German Parliament resolution (May 19, 2021) at https://dip21.bundestag.de/dip21/btd/19/298/1929894.pdf and the Q&A doc relating to the new law [Umsetzung der Urheberrechtsrichtlinien (EU) 2019/790 ("DSM-Richtlinie") and (EU) 2019/789 ("Online-SatCab-Richtlinie"), June 7, 2021]. Thanks to Georg von Wallis (Berlin) for his take on the matter.

130 Abel, "Cinema of Identification."

131 Ibid.

132 The only other nomination to an Austrian film also dealt with the Nazi past: *38—Auch das war Wien* (AT, Wolfgang Glück, 1986). This tendency shifted with the nominations of Uli Edel's *Der Baader Meinhof Komplex* and Götz Spielmann's *Revanche* in 2008 and Haneke's *Das weiße Band* [The White Ribbon] in 2009; and (after a seven year lull) Maren Ade's *Toni Erdmann* in 2016, but returned in 2018 with the nomination of von Donnersmarck's *Werk ohne Autor* [Never Look Away].

133 Cf. Robert and Carol J. Reimer, *Historical Dictionary of Holocaust Cinema* (Toronto: Scarecrow Press, 2012), 99: "The film is less stylized than Beyer's, the humor a bit broader, and the Nazi guards more caricatured, all changes that fit Robin William's comedic style. The film closes with a variation of Becker's ficticious ending. Jakob is executed, not for trying to escape, but

rather for refusing to deny his friends hope and admit that the Russians are not coming. The Jews board the trains but are rescued by Russian tanks. The film closes with women resembling the 1940s U.S. trio the Andrew Sisters singing the 'Beer Barrel Polka'."

134 Fortunately, some publishers promote marginalized and forgotten women writers. For example, Wallstein has been publishing the works of Emmy Hennings since 2017 and an English-language translation of her novel *Das Brandmal* (1920) is being published by Broadview as *Branded*, edited and translated by Katharina Rout (2022).

135 Herta Müller's first novel *Der Fuchs war damals schon der Jäger* (The Fox Was the Hunter, 1992) about Ceaușescu's dictatorship in Rumania is based on her script for *Vulpe—vânător* (RU, Stere Gulea, 1993).

136 N. Frank Ukadike, "The Hyena's Last Laugh: A Conversation with Djibril Diop Mambety," *Transition* 78 (1999): 136–53, here p. 53.

137 DDM's interview with N. Frank Ukadike can be accessed here: http://newsreel.org/articles/mambety.htm.

138 According to Katherine Jane Alexander, "Debunking the Myths around *Eyes Wide Shut*, Stanley Kubrick's Final Film" (July 30, 2019); https://www.anothermag.com/design-living/11844/debunking-the-myths-of-eyes-wide-shut-stanley-kubricks-final-film.

139 As Kristina Jaspers points out, already a never realized early 1930s adaptation by G. W. Pabst imagined a "modernized" version of Schnitzler's *Rhapsody: A Dream Novel* (aka *Dream Story*) with cars rather than carriages and electricity rather than gas lighting. See Jaspers, *Kino der Moderne*, 108.

140 According to IMDb. Numerous scholars have written about this adaptation. See Jack Vitek, "Another Squint at *Eyes Wide Shut*. A Postmodern Reading," *Modern Austrian Literature* 34.1/2 (2001): 113–24; Pamela Saur, "*Eyes Wide Shut* and Its Literary Forebear: Tom Cruise Got Off Easy," *Lamar: Journal of the Humanities* 26.2 (2001): 53–61; Siobhan Donovan, "'Inspired by Schnitzler's *Traumnovelle*': The Intersemiotic Represeentaiton of Figural Consciousness in *Eyes Wide Shut*," *Processes of Transposition: German Literature and Film*, 59–79.

141 *La promessa* (IT, Alberto Negrin, 1979); *Szürkület* (HU, György Fehér, 1990); *The Cold Light of Day* (NL, Rudolf van den Berg, 1995); Nico Hofmann directed a German remake for television in 1997.

142 Erwin Piscator, "Vorwort zum 'Stellvertreter'," *Schriften* (Berlin: Henschel, 1968): 301–5, here p. 301.

143 Piscator, "Vorwort," 305.

144 Other Hochhuth adaptations include: *Berliner Antigone* (FRG, Rainer Wolffhardt, 1968); *Élő Antigoné* (HU, László Nemere, 1968); *Die Hebamme* (FRG, Wolfgang Spier, 1976); *Eine Liebe in Deutschland* (FRG/FR, Andrzej Wajda, 1983); *Ärztinnen* (GDR, Horst Seemann, 1984); *Effis Nacht* (DE, August Everding, 1998).

145 *Die Welt* (February 1, 2003).

146 Max Ophüls' outstanding 1948 adaptation was followed by further films based on Zweig's novella in 1957 (*Feliz Año, Amor Mío*; MX), 1962 (*Risala min Imra'atin Maghula*; EG), and in 2001 (TV, *Lettre d'une inconnue*;

FR). According to Wikipedia, an adaptation by Mongolian film director Naranbaatar premiered in 2011.
147 Jean E. Conacher in her enlightening article on 'Adapting Hein's *Willenbrock*: Andreas Dresen and the Legacy of the GDR 'Ensemble' Tradition,' in *Adaptation as Collaborative Art*, 193–213, here p. 196.
148 Dresen talks about the adaptation and the need to represent the protagonist's transformation with "visual material"; see Dresen, "Verdrängung ist lebenserhaltend," interview with Katharina Dockhorn, *filmecho-filmwoche* (March 10, 2005); translated and quoted by Conacher, "Adapting Hein's *Willenbrock*," 197.
149 Ibid.; Conacher discusses this point in detail; see her article (especially 198–204) for an in-depth discussion of this aspect of Dresen's adaptation.
150 Günter Rohrbach, "Das Schmollen der Autisten. Hat die deutsche Filmkritik ausgedient?," *Der Spiegel* 4 (2007); Tykwer's adaptation is one of the examples Rohrbach uses to question the validity of film reviews.
151 Under the leadership of Bernd Eichinger, the film was a co-production of Constantin Film Produktion GmbH (München), Castelao Producciones S.A. (Madrid), Nouvelles Éditions de Films S.A. (Paris), in collaboration with VIP Medienfonds GmbH & Co. KG (München-Geiselgasteig), Rising Star Entertainment (New York), Ikiru Films S.L. (Barcelona), and according to filmportal.de received public subsidies from the following film boards: FilmFernsehFonds Bayern, Bayerischer Bankenfonds, Filmförderungsanstalt (FFA, Berlin), Film- und Medien Stiftung NRW (Düsseldorf), and the EU's Eurimages.
152 According to IMDb the film only made $2 million of its 60 million budget in the United States and Canada.
153 http://kafkas-der-bau.de/#.
154 "Wer jetzt kein Haus hat, baut sich keines mehr. / Wer jetzt allein ist, wird es lange bleiben, / wird wachen, lesen, lange Briefe schreiben / und wird in den Alleen hin und her / unruhig wandern, wenn die Blätter treiben."
155 Mara Rusch, *Die Filme von Aleksandr Sokurov. Ein Rückblick auf die russisch-europäische Geschichte* (Munich: text+kritik), 2018.
156 Lida Bach, "Die Wand—Interviews mit Julian Pölsler und Martina Gedeck," *Negativ* (October 1, 2012); http://www.negativ-film.de/die-wand-interviews-mit-julian-polsler-und-martina-gedeck/. In 2017, Pölsler's adaptation of Haushofer's novella *Wir töten Stella* (Killing Stella, 1958) premiered, again starring Martina Gedeck.
157 Ibid.
158 Nikolai Preuschoff, "'His world had vanished long before he entered it': Wes Anderson's Homage to Stefan Zweig," in *Adaptation as a Collaborative Art*, 147–66, here p. 148.
159 Anne Washburn, "A 1,418 Word Introduction," in *The Wes Anderson Collection: The Grand Budapest Hotel*, ed. Matt Zoller Seitz (New York: Abrams, 2015), 9–11, here p. 9.
160 Washburn, "Introduction," 9. In an interview with Matt Zoller Seitz, Anderson states that he had "never heard of [Stefan Zweig] until six or seven years ago" but became interested after coming across a copy of *Beware of Pity*: "I really love his stories, and also his memoir *The World of Yesterday*."

See "The 7.269-Word First Interview," in *The Wes Anderson Collection: The Grand Budapest Hotel*, 31–62, here p. 31.

161 Zweig's works are regularly adapted for television (especially in Germany and Austria), for example: *Rausch der Verwandlung* (1988), *Leporella* and *Der verwandelte Komödiant* (both 1992), *Clarissa—Tränen der Zärtlichkeit* (1997). International adaptations of his works include *A Coleção Invisível* [The Invisible Collection] (BR, Bernard Attal, 2012), *Mary Queen of Scots* (CH, Thomas Imbach, 2013), *A Promise* (FR, Patrice Leconte, 2013), and the short film *Crepúsculo* (US, Clemy Clarke, 2017).

162 According to dpa-infocom, dpa:200916-99-580864/3, *Tschick* has been adapted more often in theatre productions than Kafka and Fallada and nearly reached the popularity of Goethe's *Faust* and Schiller's *Robbers* during 2018/19; accessed via https://www.azonline.de/welt/kultur/zehn-jahre-tschick-schon-heute-ein-klassiker-814525.

163 Ben Kenigsberg, 'In the Aisles' Review: A Store with Everything, Except Fulfillment, *The New York Times* (June 13, 2019).

164 In 2018, Stuber directed a high-quality adaptation of Lutz Seiler's novel *Kruso* (2014), which beautifully captures the mood of the literary text and the GDR's last moments on the island of Hiddensee. Thomas Kirchner, having successfully adapted Uwe Tellkamp's *Der Turm* (2008) for its television production, wrote the script.

165 See Petzold on Deutschlandfunk Kultur: "Wie man lernt, wieder Mensch zu sein: Christian Petzold im Gespräch mit Liane von Billerbeck" at https://www.deutschlandfunkkultur.de/christian-petzold-ueber-seinen-film-transit-wie-man-lernt.1008.de.html?dram:article_id=414659.

166 For an excellent analysis of this type of space in Petzold's so-called 'ghost trilogy' (*Die innere Sicherheit*, 2000; *Gespenster*, 2004; *Yella*, 2007) that takes inspiration from theoretical approaches by David Henry and Henri Lefebvre, see Jaimey Fisher, "Globalization as Uneven Geographical Development: The 'Creative' Destruction of Place and Fantasy in Christian Petzold's Ghost Trilogy," *Seminar* 47.4 (2011): 447–64.

167 Petzold in the same Deutschlandfunk interview with von Billerbeck as noted above.

168 Donald Clarke, "Transit: A Five-Star, Art-House Modern-Day Casablanca," *The Irish Times* (August 15, 2019); https://www.irishtimes.com/culture/film/transit-a-five-star-art-house-modern-day-casablanca-1.3985004.

169 His mother had to flee from the Sudentenland and never 'fully arrived,' he said on Deutschlandfunk Kultur: "Wie man lernt, wieder Mensch zu sein: Christian Petzold im Gespräch mit Liane von Billerbeck" at https://www.deutschlandfunkkultur.de/christian-petzold-ueber-seinen-film-transit-wie-man-lernt.1008.de.html?dram:article_id=414659.

170 Ibid.

171 Salka Viertel, *The Kindness of Strangers* (Montreal: Holt, Rinehart & Winston, 1969).

172 Abel, "The Berlin School," in *The German Cinema Book* (^{2}2020), 259.

173 Jaimey Fisher compellingly outlines how Petzold's films reflect on and "explicitly work with the tradition of genre cinema"; Abel, "The Berlin

School," 254; see Jaimey Fisher, *Christian Petzold* (Urbana: University of Illinois Press, 2013).

174 Petzold addressed his interest in migration and transit zones: "It is these people who are being pushed out of societies or are put in motion, but they do not even know where to go, where all of this is supposed to lead. They consequently end up in transitional spaces, transit zones where nothingness looms on one side and the impossibility of returning to what existed in the past on the other. These are the spaces that interest me. [...] I am interested in the mobile immobilities, the so-called transit zones, these non-places: that's where something modern is happening. And they expand in a metastatic way." Abel, "The Cinema of Identification." For an in-depth analysis and further contextualization of the adaptation, see Margarete J. Landwehr, "Empathy and Community in the Age of Refugees: Petzold's Radical Translation of Seghers' *Transit*," Arts 9.118 (2020): 1–22; https://www.mdpi.com. In an interview with Robert Fischer and Jaimey Fisher, Petzold is asked about Klee's 'Angelus Novus' in his film *Phoenix* (2014), reference to Walter Benjamin's essay about Klee's painting. Petzold notes "it's the angel that is being pushed forward but that looks back at us. I think that's the historical drama, that we are driven forward but that we do look back. That's how the historical drama should be." Christian Petzold, Robert Fischer, and Jaimey Fisher, "The Cinema Is a Warehouse of Memory: A Conversation," *Senses of Cinema* 84 (2017); http://www.sensesofcinema.com/2017/christian-petzold-a-dossier/christian-petzold/. In the previously mentioned interview in *Cineaste*, Petzold refers to the importance of Benjamin's "Theses on the Philosophy of History." See Walter Benjamin, "Theses on the Philosophy of History," in *Illuminations: Essays and Reflections*, ed. Hannah Arendt, trans. Harry Zohn (New York: Schocken, 1969), 253–64.

175 Burhan Qurbani in conversation with Knut Elstermann, "Berlin Alexanderplatz," in *Lola Talk: Der Filmpreis Podcast. Deutsche Filmakademie*, podcast (accessed via i tunes).

176 For a more detailed summary, see my "Berlin Alexanderplatz," in the living edition of Jeremy Tambling's *Encyclopedia of Urban Literary Studies*. This paragraph is a shorter version of the encyclopedia entry. Thanks are due also to Beta Cinema Gmbh and Dirk Schürhoff for sharing a screener-link and thus enabling me to view this new adaptation despite the pandemic lockdown on the emerald isle in 2020.

177 Qurbani in "Vollbild—das Filmmagazin—Deutschlandfunk Kultur" (July 11, 2020); iTunes podcast.

178 Linda Hutcheon, *A Theory of Adaptation*, 171; quoted in the revised edition of *A Theory of Adaptation*, in Hutcheon and Flynn, 2013, 181.

179 Ibid.

180 In addition to audiobooks, puppet shows, games, and reading aids, the children's book was translated into forty-four languages and adapted to television both in Germany and in the Soviet Union. Curt Linda, who adapted and directed an animation film based on Kästner's *Die Konferenz der Tiere* (Animal Conference, 1949) in 1969, produced an animated adaptation of *The Little Ghost* in 1992, followed by the 2013 release of the Swiss and German

production in both languages *S'Chline Gspängst/Das kleine Gespenst* (CH/DE, Universum Film, Alain Gsponer). A first computer animated version of *Die Konferenz der Tiere* was released in Germany in 2010. Internet-stars Heiko and Roman Lochmann appeared in *Takeover—voll vertauscht* (Florian Ross, 2020) as the twins that were raised by their parents in separate households, the 25th adaptation/remake of Kästner's Das doppelte Lottchen (Two times Lotte/The Parent Trap, 1949). When they meet, they decide to switch places—a gender-bent take on Kästner's classic. Produced by Pantaleon Films and Warner Bros. Pictures Germany (Hamburg), the action-packed adaptation was supported by public funding body Deutscher Filmförderfonds (DFFF).

181 See hits and comments on YouTube, for example: Lessing's *Nathan der Weise* at https://www.youtube.com/watch?v=60kNNVHeYTU.

182 Thomas Brussig co-wrote the script with Leander Haußmann and Detlev Buck, and released his novel *Am kürzeren Ende der Sonnenallee* [At the Shorter End of Sonnenallee] in 1999. His work and others—such as Uwe Johnson's *Jahrestage* (1970–83; Margarethe v. Trotta's adaptation for television followed in 1999/2000), Peter Schneider's *Der Mauerspringer* (adapted by Reinhard Hauff, *Der Mann auf der Mauer/The Man on the Wall*, 1982), etc.—contributed to public discourses and critical reflections of national identity in both divided and unified Germany. While German cinema has moved away to some degree from issues related to the country's division and/or reunification in 1990, the view and memory of the GDR in particular are still an integral and important part of German film history as adaptation projects of twenty-first-century novels such as Torsten Schulz's *Boxhagener Platz* (Matti Geschonneck, 2010) and Eugen Ruge's *In Zeiten des abnehmenden Lichts* (Matti Geschonneck, 2017) but also, to name just one more, the ZDF mini-series *Unterleuten* based on Juli Zeh's novel exemplify. For further context, see Paul Cooke, *Representing East Germany since Unification* (New York: Berg, 2005), especially 74–81 on Brussig's *Helden wie wir* and 111–19 on Haußmann's *Sonnenallee*. See also Nick Hodgin, *Screening the East: Heimat, Memory and Nostalgia in German Film Since 1989* (Oxford: Berghahn, 2011), and Muriel Cormican, "Thomas Brussig's Ostalgie in Print and on Celluloid," in *Processes of Transposition*, 251–67.

183 Carsten Heidböhmer, "*Feuchtgebiete* als Film. Es wird ekelig und explizit," *Stern* (June 19, 2013); https://www.stern.de/kultur/film/charlotte-roche---feuchtgebiete-als-film--es-wird-explizit-3049888.html.

184 "Laid Bare," *The Economist* (April 3, 2008); https://www.economist.com/books-and-arts/2008/04/03/laid-bare.

185 See Italian philologist/anthropologist Maurizio Bettini's *Wurzeln—die trügerischen Mythen der Identität* (trans. Rita Seuß; Bonn: bpb, 2018); and Nils Markwardt's essay "Sehnsucht nach Retropia," *DIE ZEIT* (August 30, 2018); https://www.zeit.de/kultur/2018-08/nostalgie-vergangenheit-politisierung-trend/komplettansicht.

186 https://www.youtube.com/watch?v=yKj6KEgDTyI&feature=youtu.be.

187 Adorno's essay "Was bedeutet: Aufarbeitung der Vergangenheit?" was published in an English translation by Henry W. Pickford, "The Meaning of

Working through the Past," in *Critical Models: Interventions and Catchwords* (New York: Columbia University Press, 2005), 89–104. See also Susan Neiman, *Learning from the Germans: Race and the Memory of Evil* (New York: Farrar, Straus and Giroux, 2019), for the ongoing significance of these processes of critically engaging with the past.

188 The new edition of *The German Cinema Book* skilfully reveals these cinematic practices.

189 November 20, 2020, Berlin and Beyond film festival, panel on "National Cinema in the Age of Netflix," see https://www.youtube.com/watch?v=yKj6K EgDTyI&feature=youtu.be.

190 Leytner is known for his adaptation of Dürrenmatt's *The Visit* (*Der Besuch der alten Dame*, DE/AT, 2008); Kreuzpaintner previously adapted Gudrun Pausewang's apocalyptic *Die Wolke* (script, 2006) and Preußler's children's book *Krabat* (script/dir., 2008).

191 See, for example a review of Dominik Graf's adaptation of Kästner's *Fabian* (2021), which followed Wolf Gremm's 1980 adaptation of the same text: "Dieser *Fabian* geht uns etwas an," *Leipziger Volkszeitung* (August 5, 2021), 24. The experience of Nazism in Germany and the horror of dictatorship and two World Wars continues to affect the German-language film production landscape. More recently, not only adaptations for cinema and television such as *Deutschstunde* (German Lesson, 1968) by Lenz, but also Remarque's antiwar novel *Im Westen nichts Neues* (All Quiet on the Western Front, 1929) for Netflix indicate the continuing interest in the wisdom communicated through literature and in stories that show us what happens when we forget our humanity.

192 https://en.wikipedia.org/wiki/Stolperstein. Gunter Demnig started this decentralized memorial project in 1992 and it is still ongoing.

193 Cf. Walter Benjamin's angel of history; "Theses on the Philosophy of History," *Illuminations*, 253–64.

194 How problematic efforts in rewriting history can be was exemplified by private television channel Pro7's remake of *Die Brücke/The Bridge*, which reimagines Wicki's antiwar film as an action soap that turns up the drama to reinstate boys as heros, marking their death as martyrdom rather than the consequence of Nazi rule and misguided criminal negligence by Hitler's willing henchmen as I tried to tease out in "Erfolg und Misserfolg von Verfilmungen: Manfred Gregors *Die Brücke* und die Nahaufnahmen des Krieges in Kino und Fernsehen," *Germanistik in Ireland* 7 (2012): 81–102.

195 For an excellent summary of the relevant theories and their challenges see Maeve Cooke, *Re-Presenting the Good Society* (Cambridge, MA: MIT Press, 2006).

196 According to Donald Clarke's list in the Irish Times: https://www.irishtimes.com/culture/film/netflix-25-films-to-watch-out-for-in-2021-1.4457144.

197 Following Milestone's antiwar classic *All Quiet on the Western Front* (US, 1930) and the adaptation for television (US, 1979).

198 Jo Baier adapted other literary texts for television, among them Oskar Maria Graf's *Heimat*story "Die Geschichte von der buckligen Hölleisengretl" as *Hölleisengretl* (1994) and Hermann Hesse's *Die Heimkehr* [Homecoming] (2012).

199 Already Stuckrad-Barre's debut pop novel *Soloalbum* (1998) was brought successfully to cinema by Gregor Schnitzler in 2003. In April 2019, the FFA awarded half a million to a fifth installment of the film series *Ostwind*, Simon Verhoeven's Berlin-film *Nightlife*, and to an adaptation of the French comedy *Le Brio*. Gold/Wittich and Heiss received 25,000 euro each for the development of the two scripts. The fantasy genre for children and young adults is increasingly serialized and subsequently adapted to film. For example, *Wolf-Gäng* is a vampire film for children based on Wolfgang Hohlbein's successful book series (DE, Tim Trageser, 2020). Alex Rühle's book series for younger audiences featuring the friendly ghost Zippel is also being adapted to film.

200 Svenja Rasocha was supported by the FFA in 2019; also, well-known actor Josef Bierbichler's *Mittelreich* (2013), a novel inspired by his own family in Bavaria and a century of German history was generously supported by the FFA and was directed by Bierbichler himself in a cinema/television co-production as *Zwei Herren im Anzug* [Two men in suits] and released in 2018. https://www.ffa.de/aid=1365.html?newsdetail=20190913-701_musik-mehr-ffa-vergibt-17-mio-euro-fuer-fuenf-filmprojekte-fuenf-drehbuecher-und-zwei-treatments.

201 Fittingly, three adaptations of Carlo Collodi's 1881 children's book *Pinocchio* have already premiere or are currently underway (IT, Roberto Benigni, 2021; Disney working on another live-action adaptation with Tom Hanks as Geppetto; and Guillermo del Toro is working on an adaptation for Netflix. No wonder that this moral tale is picked up again in our worryingly 'post-truth' era. Who would not like to escape into Collodi's illusionary world and see liars' noses lengthen by several inches?

202 Maria Schrader directed *Vor der Morgenröte* (DE/AT/FR, 2016), a film about Austrian writer Stefan Zweig's last years in exile in the United States and in South America, and his death in Brazil. She adapted Zeruya Shalev's novel *Love Life* (translated into German from the original Hebrew by Mirjam Pressler) together with Laila Stieler and directed the German-Israeli film (2007). Two of the most successful women directors of recent entertainment cinema are Julia von Heinz (see her afore mentioned adaptation of Hape Kerkeling's autobiography *Ich bin dann mal weg*) and Karoline Herfurth (*SMS für dich* [Text for You], 2016; an adaptation of Sofie Cramer's 2009 bestselling novel).

203 Petzold interviewed by Abel in *Cineaste* 33.3 (2008).

204 Arnold Hauser, *Sozialgeschichte der Kunst und Literatur* (Munich: Beck, 1983), 1016.

205 Agamben explains the meaning of contemporaneity as dipping your pen into the darkness in *Nacktheiten* (Fischer: Frankfurt/M., 2010), 21.

206 One of the most recent film adaptations of the myth in Ireland, the 'selkie,' is Neil Jordan's romantic drama *Ondine* (IE, 2009), starring Alicja Bachleda and Colin Farrell. Literary adaptions include retellings by Christian August Vulpius (1805), Achim von Arnim (1806), Hans Christian Andersen (1836), Oscar Wilde (1891), Kurd Laßwitz (1905), Jean Giraudoux (1939), Ingeborg Bachmann (1961), and Peter Huchel (1972). In recent decades, the figure appears most prominently in fantasy literature.

207 The public film funding body FFA awarded 2.5 million euro in April 2019 and Petzold's *Undine* received the fourth largest amount with 346,080.22 euro (most of the allocated amount went to the already popular children's and youth entertainment sector and comedies for a mass audience).
208 Of course, economic factors play a dominant role. On March 26, 2018, the FFA allocated 600,000 euro to an international remake of Til Schweiger's adaptation of well-known former comedian Dieter Hallervorden's *Honig im Kopf* as *Honey in the Head* (script British bestseller author Jojo Moyes) with Nick Nolte in the lead. The original adaptation was a box office hit with 7.2 million cinemagoers enjoying the film in 2014 in Germany alone; https://www.ffa.de/aid=1365.html?newsdetail=20180326-522_ffa-foerdert-neue-filme-von-caroline-link-und-anne-zohra-berrached.
209 Produced by MOOVIE (Heike Voßler, Oliver Berben) in collaboration with German television ARD Degeto Film and Rundfunk Berlin-Brandenburg, the Austrian ORF, and the Swiss SRF, as well as Constantin Film. The film starred, among others, Lars Eidinger, Christiane Paul, Matthias Habich, and Ulrich Matthes.
210 https://www.daserste.de/unterhaltung/film/gott-von-ferdinand-von-schirach/voting/index.html.
211 The film generated articles in well-respected weekly papers like *Die Zeit* (Thomas E. Schmidt: "Ethik ist keine Abstimmungssache," November 23, 2020) as well as in local dailies like *Gießener Allgemeine* (Florian Dörr: "'Gott' [ARD]: Ergebnis zu Schirach-Film ist da—so lief die Abstimmung," November 24, 2020).
212 Elsaesser, *Weimar Cinema and After*, 438.
213 Jed Pearl, *Authority and Freedom. A Defense of the Arts* (New York: Knopf, 2021). This section is inspired by his arguments and John Banville's review of Pearl's book in *The New York Review of Books* 69.7 (April 21, 2022), 22–4.
214 Pearl, *Authority and Freedom*, 16.
215 Ibid., 6. Also quoted in Banville's review, 24.

BIBLIOGRAPHY

NB: This selected bibliography lists the main scholarly sources that informed this book. For other texts, newspaper articles, and archival materials used, please see endnotes.

Abel, Marco. "The Cinema of Identification Gets on My Nerves: An Interview with Christian Petzold." *Cineaste* 33.3 (2008), https://www.cineaste.com/summer2008/the-cinema-of-identification-gets-on-my-nerves.
Adorno, Theodor W. and Max Horkheimer. *Dialektik der Aufklärung*. Frankfurt/M.: Suhrkamp, [1947] 1981.
Agde, Günter and Alexander Schwarz, eds. *Die rote Traumfabrik: Meschrabpom-Film und Prometheus (1921–1936)*. Berlin: Bertz+Fischer, 2012.
Albersmeier, Franz-Josef and Volker Roloff, eds. *Literaturverfilmungen*. Frankfurt/M.: Suhrkamp, 1989.
Albrecht, Gerd. *Nationalsozialistische Filmpolitik*. Munich: Hanser, 1969.
Allan, Seán. 'Auf einen Lasterhaften war ich gefaßt, aber auf keinen — Teufel'. Heinrich von Kleist's, *Die Marquise von O …*'. *German Life and Letters* 50 (1997): 307–22.
Allan, Seán and John Sandford, eds. *DEFA. East German Cinema, 1946–1992*. Oxford: Berghahn, 1999.
Allan, Seán and Sebastian Heiduschke, eds. *Re-imagining DEFA: East German Cinema in Its National and Transnational Contexts*. New York: Berghahn, 2016.
Arnold, Jasmin. *Die Revolution frisst ihre Kinder. Deutsches Filmexil in der UdSSR*. Marburg: Tectum, 2003.
Ascheid, Antje. *Hitler's Heroines: Stardom and Womanhood in Nazi Cinema*. Philadelphia: Temple University Press, 2003.
Asper, Helmut G. "Von der Milo zur B. U. P. Max Ophüls' französische Exilfilmproduktion 1937–1940." In *Hallo? Berlin? Ici Paris! Deutsch-französische Filmbeziehungen 1918–1939*, edited by Sibylle M. Sturm and Arthur Wohlgemuth, 111–26. Munich: text+kritik, 1996.
Asper, Helmut G. *Max Ophüls. Eine Biographie*. Berlin: Bertz+Fischer, 1998.
Asper, Helmut G. "'Für Ihre files will ich Ihnen ein paar Facts geben.' Richard Oswald an Siegfried Kracauer über seine Filmarbeit in der Weimarer Republik und im amerikanischen Exil." *Filmblatt* 14 (2000): 22–7.
Asper, Helmut G. *Max Ophüls. Deutscher—Jude—Franzose*. Berlin: Hentrich & Hentrich, 2011.
Assmann, Aleida. *Erinnerungsräume*. Munich: Beck, 1999.
Assmann, Aleida. *Der lange Schatten der Vergangenheit. Erinnerungskultur und Geschichtspolitik*. Munich: Beck, 2006.

Aurich, Rolf and Susanne Fuhrmann, eds. *Lichtspielträume. Kino in Hannover 1896–1991*. Hannover: Gesellschaft für Filmstudien, 1991.
Aurnhammer, Achim, Barbara Beßlich, and Rudolf Denk, eds. *Arthur Schnitzler und der Film*. Würzburg: Ergon, 2010.
Bächlin, Peter. *Der Film als Ware*. Frankfurt/M.: Fischer, 1975.
Baer, Hester. "Das Boot and the German Cinema of Neoliberalism." *The German Quarterly* 85.1 (2012): 18–39.
Baer, Hester. *Dismantling the Dream Factory: Gender, German Cinema, and the Postwar Quest for a New Film Language*. Oxford: Berghahn, 2012.
Baer, Hester. "Producing Adaptations: Bernd Eichinger, *Christiane F.*, and German Film History." In *Generic Histories of German Cinema: Genre and Its Deviations*, edited by Jaimey Fisher, 173–96. Rochester: Camden House, 2013.
Baer, Hester. *German Cinema in the Age of Neoliberalism*. Amsterdam: Amsterdam University Press, 2021.
Baer, Hester and Angelica Fenner. "Introduction: Revisiting Feminism and German Cinema." *Camera Obscura* 33.3 (2018): 1–19.
Bär, Gerald. *Das Motiv des Doppelgängers als Spaltungsphantasie in der Literatur und im Stummfilm*. Amsterdam: Rodopi, 2005.
Barnouw, Erik. *The Magician and the Cinema*. Oxford: Oxford University Press, 1981.
Bauer, Matthias and Stefan Keppler-Tasaki. *Handbuch Literatur & Film*. Berlin, Boston: De Gruyter, 2015.
Becker, Sabina. *Experiment Weimar. Eine Kulturgeschichte Deutschlands 1918–1933*. Darmstadt: wbg academic, 2018.
Becker, Wolfgang and Norbert Schöll. *In jenen Tagen. Wie der deutsche Nachkriegsfilm die Vergangenheit bewältigte*. Opladen: Leske+Budrich, 1995.
Belach, Helga and Hans-Michael Bock, eds. *Emil und die Detektive. Drehbuch von Billy Wilder nach Erich Kästner zu Gerhard Lamprechts Film von 1931*. Munich: text+kritik, 1998.
Belach, Helga and Wolfgang Jacobsen, eds. *Richard Oswald. Regisseur und Produzent*. Munich: text+kritik, 1990.
Benjamin, Walter. *Illuminations. Essays and Reflections*. Ed. Hannah Arendt. Trans. Harry Zohn. New York: Schocken, 1969.
Benjamin, Walter. *Illuminationen. Ausgewählte Schriften*. Frankfurt/M.: Suhrkamp, 1977.
Berger, Jürgen et al., eds. *Zwischen Gestern und Morgen—Westdeutscher Nachkriegsfilm 1946–1962*. Frankfurt/M.: Deutsches Filmmuseum, 1989.
Bergfelder, Tim. *International Adventures: German Popular Cinema and European Co-productions in the 1960s*. New York: Berghahn, 2005.
Bergfelder, Tim, Erica Carter, and Deniz Göktürk, eds. *The German Cinema Book*. London: BFI, 2002 (^{2}2020; in collaboration with Claudia Sandberg).
Bieberstein, Rada, ed. *Beyond Prince Achmed: New Perspectives on Animation Pioneer Lotte Reiniger*. Marburg: Schüren, 2021.
Bock, Hans-Michael and Michael Töteberg, eds. *Das Ufa-Buch*. Frankfurt/M.: Zweitausendeins, 1992.
Bock, Hans-Michael and Tim Bergfelder, eds. *The Concise Cinegraph: Encyclopaedia of German Cinema*. Oxford: Berghahn, 2009.

Bohnenkamp, Anne and Tilman Lang. *Literaturverfilmungen*. Stuttgart: Reclam, ²2012.
Borries, Friedrich von and Jens-Uwe Fischer. *Sozialistische Cowboys. Der Wilde Westen Ostdeutschlands*. Frankfurt/M.: Suhrkamp, 2008.
Bourke, Eoin. "Two Foxes of Glenarvon." In *Processes of Transposition: German Literature and Film*, edited by C. Schönfeld, 157–68. Amsterdam: Rodopi, 2007.
Brady, Martin and Joanne Leal. *Wim Wenders and Peter Handke: Collaboration, Adaptation, Recomposition*. Amsterdam: Rodopi, 2011.
Braganca, Manuel and Peter Tame, eds. *The Long Aftermath: Cultural Legacies of Europe at War, 1936–2016*. Oxford: Berghahn Books, 2015.
Braun, Michael. *Wem gehört die Geschichte?: Erinnerungskultur in Literatur und Film*. Münster: Aschendorf, 2012.
Braun, Michael. *Prometheus unchained: Beiträge zum Film*. Würzburg: Königshausen & Neumann, 2016.
Braun, Michael and Werner Kamp, eds. *Kontext Film: Beiträge zu Film und Literatur*. Berlin: Erich Schmidt, 2006.
Brockmann, Stephen. *A Critical History of German Film*. Rochester, NY: Camden House, 2010.
Bronfen, Elisabeth. *Over Her Dead Body: Death, Feminity and the Aesthetic*. London: Routledge, 1992.
Bronfen, Elisabeth. *Spectres of War: Hollywood's Engagement with Military Conflict*. New Brunswick: Rutgers, 2012.
Byg, Barton. *Landscapes of Resistance. The German Films of Danièle Huillet and Jean-Marie Straub*. Berkeley: University of California Press, 1995.
Carter, Erica. "Sweeping Up the Past: Gender and History in the Postwar German Rubble Film." In *Heroines without Heroes: Reconstructing Female and National Identities in European Cinema*, edited by U. Sieglohr, 91–110. London: Cassell, 2000.
Carter, Erica. *Dietrich's Ghosts: The Sublime and the Beautiful in Third Reich Film*. London: BFI, 2004.
Carter, Erica. "Men in Cardigans: *Canaris* (1954) and the 1950s West German Good Soldier." In *War-Torn Tales: Representing Gender and World War II in Literature and Film*, edited by D. Hipkins and G. Plain, 195–222. Oxford: Lang, 2008.
Cartmell, Deborah and Imelda Whelehan, eds. *The Cambridge Companion to Literature on Screen*. Cambridge University Press, 2007.
Cherchi-Usai, Paolo and Lorenzo Codelli, eds. *Before Caligari. German Cinema 1895–1920*. Pordenone: Edizioni Biblioteca dell'Immagine, 1990.
Clarke, David. "German Martyrs: Images of Christianity and Resistance to National Socialism in German Cinema." In *Screening War: Perspectives on German Suffering*, edited by P. Cooke and M. Silverman, 36–55. Rochester, NY: Camden, 2010.
Clarke, David. "Constructing Victimhood in Divided Germany." *Memory Studies* 11.4 (2018): 422–36.
Clarke, David. "Remembering National Socialism in the German Democratic Republic." In *A Companion to Nazi Germany*, edited by S. Baranowski et al., 599–613. Hoboken/Chichester: Wiley-Blackwell, 2018.

Conacher, Jean E. "Adapting Hein's Willenbrock: Andreas Dresen and the Legacy of the GDR 'Ensemble' Tradition." In *Adaptation as Collaborative Art*, edited by B. Cronin, R. MagShamhráin and N. Preuschoff, 193–213. Cham: Palgrave, 2020.

Cook, Colleen. "Germany's Wild West Author: A Researcher's Guide to Karl May." *German Studies Review* 5.1 (1982): 67–86.

Cook, David A. *A History of Narrative Film*. New York and London: Norton, ³1996.

Cooke, Paul. *Representing East Germany since Unification*. New York: Berg, 2005.

Cooke, Paul and Marc Silberman, eds. *Screening War: Perspectives on German Suffering*, Rochester, NY: Camden House, 2010.

Cornils, Ingo and Osman Durrani, eds. *Hermann Hesse Today*. Amsterdam: Rodopi, 2005.

Corrigan, Timothy. "Literature on Screen, a History. In the Gap." In *The Cambridge Companion to Literature on Screen*, edited by Deborah Cartmell and Imelda Whelehan, 29–43. Cambridge University Press, 2007.

Corrigan, Timothy, ed. *Film and Literature*. London: Routledge, ²2012.

Courtade, Francis. *Geschichte des Films im Dritten Reich*. Munich: Hanser, 1975.

Craciun, Iona. *Die Dekonstruktion des Bürgerlichen im Stummfilm der Weimarer Republik*. Heidelberg: Winter, 2015.

Crafton, Donald. *The Talkies: American Cinema's Transition to Sound 1926–1931*. Berkeley: University of California Press, 1999.

Creed, Barbara. *The Monstrous-Feminine. Film, Feminism, Psychoanalysis*. London: Routledge, 1993.

Cronin, Bernadette, Rachel MagShamhráin, and Nikolai Preuschoff, eds. *Adaptation Considered as a Collaborative Art*. Cham, CH: Palgrave, 2020.

Dahlke, Günther and Günter Karl, eds. *Deutsche Spielfilme von den Anfängen bis 1933. Ein Filmführer*. Berlin: Henschel, ²1993.

Davidson, John and Sabine Hake, eds. *Framing the Fifties: Cinema in a Divided Germany*. New York: Berghahn, 2007.

Davidson, John and Sabine Hake, eds. *Take Two: Fifties Cinema in Divided Germany*. New York: Berghahn, 2008.

Decker, Christof. *Hollywoods kritischer Blick: Das soziale Melodrama in der amerikanischen Kultur 1840–1950*. Frankfurt/M.: Campus, 2003.

Deleuze, Gilles. *Cinema 1: The Movement-Image* [1983]. Trans. Hugh Tomlinson and Barbara Habberjam. London: Athlone Press, 1989.

Deleuze, Gilles. *Cinema 2: The Time-Image* [1985]. Trans. Hugh Tomlinson and Robert Galeta. London: Athlone Press, 1992.

Denman, Mariatte. "Nostalgia for a Better Germany: Carl Zuckmayer's 'Des Teufels General'." *The German Quarterly* 76.4 (2003): 369–80.

Dettmar, Ute, Claudia Maria Pecher, and Ron Schlesinger, eds. *Märchen im Medienwechsel: Zur Geschichte und Gegenwart des Märchenfilms*. Stuttgart: Springer, 2018.

Diezel, Peter. "Erwin Piscators Film Aufstand der Fischer." *Argonautenschiff. Jahrbuch der Anna-Seghers-Gesellschaft* 16 (2008): 68–79.

Dillmann, Claudia and Olaf Möller, eds. *Geliebt und verdrängt: Das Kino der jungen Bundesrepublik Deutschland von 1949 bis 1963*. Frankfurt/M.: Deutsches Filminstitut DFF, 2016.

Dittrich, Katinka and Hans Würzner, eds. *Die Niederlande und das deutsche Exil 1933–1940*. Königstein: Athenäum, 1982.
Drewniak, Boguslaw. *Der deutsche Film 1938–1945*. Düsseldorf: Droste, 1987.
Durrani, Osman. *Faust. Icon of Modern Culture*. Mountfield: Helm, 2004.
Eigler, Friedericke, Janusz Golec, Maria Kłańska, and Irmela von der Lühe, eds. *Post/Nationale Vorstellungen von 'Heimat' in deutschen, europäischen und globalen Kontexten*. Frankfurt/M.: Lang, 2012.
Eisner, Lotte H. *The Haunted Screen: Expressionism in the German Cinema and the Influence of Max Reinhardt*. Trans. Roger Greaves. Berkeley: University of California Press, 1969.
Elliott, Kamilla. *Rethinking the Novel/Film Debate*. Cambridge: Cambridge University Press, 2003.
Elsaesser, Thomas. *New German Cinema: A History*. New Brunswick, NJ: Rutgers University Press, 1989.
Elsaesser, Thomas, ed. *A Second Life: German Cinema's First Decades*. Amsterdam: Amsterdam University Press, 1996.
Elsaesser, Thomas. *Fassbinder's Germany*. Amsterdam: Amsterdam University Press, 1996.
Elsaesser, Thomas. *Weimar Cinema and After: Germany's Historical Imaginary*. New York: Routledge, 2000.
Elsaesser, Thomas. *Rainer Werner Fassbinder*. Amsterdam: Amsterdam University Press, 2001.
Elsaesser, Thomas. *European Cinema: Face to Face with Hollywood*. Amsterdam: Amsterdam University Press, 2005.
Elsaesser, Thomas and Adam Barker, eds. *Early Cinema. Space, Frame, Narrative*. London: BFI, 1990.
Elsaesser, Thomas, Adam Barker, and Michael Wedel, eds. *Kino der Kaiserzeit. Zwischen Tradition und Moderne*. Munich: text+kritik, 2002.
Elsaghe, Yahya. *Thomas Mann auf Leinwand und Bildschirm: Zur deutschen Aneignung seines Erzählwerks in der langen Nachkriegszeit*. Göttingen: de Gruyter, 2019.
Engell, John. "*The Treasure of Sierra Madre*: B. Traven, John Huston and Ideology in Film Adaptation." *Literature/Film Quarterly* 17.4 (1989): 245–52.
Estermann, Alfred. *Die Verfilmung literarischer Werke*. Bonn: Bouvier, 1965.
Faber, Marion. "Hofmannsthal and the Film." *German Life and Letters* 32 (1979): 187–95.
Fay, Jennifer. *Theatres of Occupation: Hollywood and the Reeducation of Postwar Germany*. Minneapolis: University of Minnesota Press, 2008.
Fehrenbach, Heide. *Cinema in Democratizing Germany: Reconstructing National Identity after Hitler*. Chapel Hill: University of North Carolina Press, 1995.
Feinstein, Joshua. *The Triumph of the Ordinary: Depictions of Daily Life in the East German Cinema, 1949–1989*. Chapel Hill: University of North Carolina Press, 2003.
Fischer, Robert, ed. *Fassbinder über Fassbinder: die ungekürzten Interviews*. Frankfurt/M.: Verlag der Autoren, 2004.
Fisher, Jaimey. "Deleuze in a Ruinous Context: German Rubble-Film and Italian Neorealism." *Iris* 23 (1997): 53–74.

Fisher, Jaimey. "Globalization as Uneven Geographical Development: The 'Creative' Destruction of Place and Fantasy in Christian Petzold's Ghost Trilogy." *Seminar* 47.4 (2011): 447–64.
Fisher, Jaimey, ed. *Generic Histories of German Cinema: Genre and Its Deviations*. Rochester: Camden House, 2013.
Flügge, Manfred. *Heinrich Mann. Eine Biographie*. Reinbek: Rowohlt, 2006.
Foucault, Michel. *History of Sexuality*. Trans. Robert Hurley, vol. 1. New York: Vintage, 1990.
Fox, Jo. *Film Propaganda in Britain and Nazi Germany*. Oxford: Berg, 2007.
Franklin, James. *New German Cinema: From Oberhausen to Hamburg*. Boston: Twayne, 1983.
Frederiksen, Elke and Martha Kaarsberg, eds. *Facing Fascism and Confronting the Past*. Wallach, NY: SUNY, 2000.
Frei, Norbert. *1945 und wir. Das Dritte Reich im Bewusstsein der Deutschen*. Munich: Beck, 2005.
Friedmann, Régine Mihal. *L'image et son Juif. Le Juif dans le cinema Nazi*. Payot: Paris, 1983.
Friedrich, Julia, ed. *Günter Peter Straschek. Emigration—Film—Politics*. Cologne: Museum Ludwig, 2018.
Frölich, Margrit. "Die Nebenzahls, Nero-Film und Filmexil in Frankreich." In *Feuchtwanger et la culture mémorielle en France*, edited by Daniel Azuélos, Andrea Chartier-Bunzel and Frédéric Teinturier, 247–62. London: Lang, 2020.
Fuchs, Anne. *Phantoms of War in Contemporary German Literature, Films and Discourse*. New York: Palgrave, 2008.
Gaudreault, André. "Showing and Telling. Image and Word in Early Cinema." In *Early Cinema. Space, Frame, Narrative*, edited by Thomas Elsaesser and Adam Barker, 274–81. London: BFI, 1990.
Gay, Peter. *Weimar Culture: The Outsider as Insider*. New York: Norton, 2001.
Geduld, Harry, ed. *Authors on Film*. Bloomington: Indiana University Press, 1972.
Gersch, Wolfgang. *Film bei Brecht. Bertolt Brechts praktische und theoretische Auseinandersetzung mit dem Film*. München: Hanser, 1975.
Giddings, Robert, Keith Selby, and Chris Wensley. *Screening the Novel: The Theory and Practice of Literary Dramatization*. Houndmills: Macmillan, 1990.
Giesen, Rolf. *Hitlerjunge Quex, Jud Süss und Kolberg*. Berlin: Schwarzkopf, 2005.
Gleber, Klaus. *Theater und Öffentlichkeit. Produktions- und Rezeptionsbedingungen politischen Theaters am Beispiel Piscators 1920–1966*. Frankfurt/M.: Lang, 1979.
Gmünden, Gerd. "Between Karl May and Karl Marx: The DEFA Indianerfilme (1965–1983)." *Film History* 10.3 (1998): 399–407.
Göktürk, Deniz. "18 December 1913: *Atlantis* Triggers Controversy about Sinking of Culture." In *A New History of German Cinema*, edited by Jennifer Kapczynski and Michael Richardson, 51–6. Rochester, NY: Camden House, 2012.
Goldstein, Cora Sol. *Capturing the German Eye: American Visual Propaganda in Occupied Germany*. Chicago: University of Chicago Press, 2009.
Gomery, Douglas. "Tri-Ergon, Tobis-Klangfilm, and the Coming of Sound." *Cinema Journal* 16 (Autumn 1976): 51–61.

Gomery, Douglas and Clara Pafort-Overduin. *Movie History: A Survey*. New York: Routledge, 2011.
Greffrath, Bettina. *Gesellschaftsbilder der Nachkriegszeit. Deutsche Spielfilme 1945–49*. Pfaffenweiler: Centaurus, 1995.
Greve, Ludwig, Margot Pehle, and Heidi Westhoff, eds. *Hätte ich das Kino!— Die Schriftsteller und der Stummfilm. Eine Ausstellung des Deutschen Literaturarchivs im Schiller-Nationalmuseum Marbach a.N.* München: Kösel, 1976.
Grieveston, Lee and Peter Krämer, eds. *The Silent Cinema Reader*. London: Routledge, 2004.
Griffiths, Kate and Andrew Watts. *The History of French Literature on Film*. New York and London: Bloomsbury, 2021.
Grisko, Michael. *Hans Fallada: Kleiner Mann—was nun?* Leipzig: Reclam, 2002.
Grisko, Michael. *Heinrich Mann und der Film*. Munich: Meidenbauer, 2008.
Grob, Norbert. *Vom Gesicht der Welt. Essays zur Filmgeschichte*. Baden-Baden: Nomos, 2013.
Grob, Norbert, Hans-Helmut Prinzler and Eric Rentschler. *Neuer Deutscher Film*. Stuttgart: Reclam, 2012.
Gunning, Tom. "The Cinema of Attraction: Early Film, Its Spectator and the Avant-Garde." *Wide Angle* 8.3 (1986): 63–70.
Gunning, Tom. *The Films of Fritz Lang*. London: BFI, 2000.
Guttinger, Fritz, ed. *Kein Tag ohne Kino. Schriftsteller über den Stummfilm*. Frankfurt/M: VERLAG, 1984.
Habermas, Jürgen. *The Structural Transformation of the Public Sphere* [1962]. Trans. Thomas Burger and Frederick Lawrence. Cambridge: Polity, 1989.
Haines, Brigid, Steven Parker, and Colin Riordan, eds. *Aesthetics and Politics in Modern German Culture*. London: Lang, 2010.
Hake, Sabine. "Chaplin Reception in Weimar Germany." *New German Critique* 51 (1990): 87–111.
Hake, Sabine. *The Cinema's Third Machine: German Writings on Film 1907–1933*. Lincoln: University of Nebraska Press, 1993.
Hake, Sabine. *Popular Cinema of the Third Reich*. Austin: University of Texas Press, 2001.
Hake, Sabine. *Film in Deutschland. Geschichte und Geschichten seit 1895*. Reinbek: Rowohlt, 2004.
Hake, Sabine. *German National Cinema*. London: Routledge, 2008.
Halle, Randall. *German Film after Germany: Towards a Transnational Aesthetic*. Urbana: University of Illinois Press, 2008.
Hanisch, Michael. *"Um 6 Uhr abends nach Kriegsende" bis "High Noon": Kino und Film im Berlin der Nachkriegszeit 1945–1953*. Berlin: DEFA, 2004.
Hansen, Miriam. "Early Silent Cinema: Whose Public Sphere?." *New German Critique* 29 (1983): 147–84.
Harding, Colin and Simon Popple, eds. *In the Kingdom of Shadows. A Companion to Early Cinema*. London: Madison, 1996.
Hardt, Ursula. *From Caligari to California: Erich Pommer's Life in the International Film Wars*. Oxford: Berghahn, 1996.
Hauser, Arnold. *Sozialgeschichte der Kunst und Literatur*. Munich: Beck, 1983.

Heiduschke, Sebastian. *East German Cinema. DEFA and Film History*. New York: Palgrave, 2013.
Heins, Laura. *Nazi Film Melodrama*. Chicago: University of Illinois Press, 2013.
Heller, Heinz-B. "Literatur und Film." In *Neues Handbuch der Literaturwissenschaft. Zwischen den Weltkriegen*, edited by Thomas Koebner et al., 161–94. Wiesbaden: Athenaion, 1983.
Heller, Heinz-B. *Literarische Intelligenz und Film*. Tübingen: Niemeyer, 1985.
Hembus, Joe. *Der deutsche Film kann gar nicht besser sein*. Bremen: Schünemann, 1961.
Hickethier, Knut and Peter Hoff. *Geschichte des deutschen Fernsehens*. Stuttgart: Metzler, 1998.
Hicks, Jeremy. *First Films of the Holocaust: Soviet Cinema and the Genocide of the Jews, 1938–1946*. Pittsburgh: University of Pittsburgh Press, 2012.
Hipkins, Danielle and Gill Plain, eds. *War-Torn Tales: Representing Gender and World War II in Literature and Film*. Oxford: Lang, 2007.
Hjort, Mette and Scott MacKenzie, eds. *Cinema and Nation*. London and New York: Routledge, 2000.
Hodgkins, John. *The Drift: Affect, Adaptation, and New Perspectives on Fidelity*. New York: Bloomsbury, 2013.
Hoefert, Sigfrid. *Gerhart Hauptmann und der Film*. Berlin: Erich Schmidt, 1996.
Hoffmann, Hilmar. *"Und die Fahne führt uns in die Ewigkeit": Propaganda im NS-Film*. Frankfurt/M.: Fischer, 1988.
Hoffmann, Hilmar. *Triumph of Propaganda: Film and National Socialism, 1933–1945*. Trans. John Broadwin and Volker Berghahn. Oxford: Berghahn, 1996.
Hoffmann, Hilmar and Walter Schobert, eds. *Zwischen Gestern und Morgen: Westdeutscher Nachkriegsfilm 1946–1962*. Frankfurt/M.: Deutsches Filmmuseum, 1989.
Hollstein, Dorothea. *Antisemitische Filmpropaganda: Die Darstellung des Juden im nationalsozialistischen Spielfilm*. Munich: Saur, 1971.
Horak, Jan-Christopher. *Fluchtpunkt Hollywood. Eine Dokumentation zur Filmemigration nach 1933*. Münster: MAkS, 1986.
Hutcheon, Linda. *A Theory of Adaptation*. London: Routledge, 2013.
Insdorf, Anette. *Indelible Shadows. Film and the Holocaust*. Cambridge: Cambridge University Press, ³2010.
Isenberg, Noah. "Perennial Detour: The Cinema of Edgar G. Ulmer and the Experience of Exile." *Cinema Journal* 43.2 (2004): 3–25.
Isenberg, Noah, ed. *Weimar Cinema: An Essential Guide to Classic Films of the Era*. New York: Columbia University Press, 2008.
Iuraşcu, Ilinca. "Introduction: The Media Histories of *Girls in Uniform*." *Seminar* 55.2 (2019): 89–93.
Jacobsen, Wolfgang, Anton Kaes, and Hans Helmut Prinzler. *Geschichte des deutschen Films*. Stuttgart: Metzler, 1993.
Jaspers, Karl. *Die Schuldfrage: ein Beitrag zur deutschen Frage*. Munich: Artemis, 1947.
Jewell, Richard B. *The Golden Age of Cinema*. Oxford: Wiley, 2008.
Kaes, Anton, ed. *Kino-Debatte. Texte zum Verhältnis von Literatur und Film, 1909–1929*. Munich: dtv, 1978.

Kaes, Anton. "Literary Intellectuals and the Cinema. Charting a Controversy (1909–1929)." *New German Critique* 40 (1987): 7–33.
Kaes, Anton. "Silent Cinema." *Monatshefte* 82.3 (1990): 246–56.
Kaes, Anton, Nicholas Baer, and Michael Cowan, eds. *The Promise of Cinema: German Film Theory, 1907–1933*. Berkeley: University of California Press, 2016.
Kammer, Manfred. *Das Verhältnis Arthur Schnitzlers zum Film*. Aachen: Cobra, 1983.
Kampf, Iris. *Literaturverfilmungen als Spiegel ihrer Zeit? Die drei filmischen Adaptationen nach Theodor Storms Novelle Der Schimmelreiter aus den Jahren 1933/34, 1977/78 und 1984 im Vergleich*. Saarbrücken: VDM, 2008.
Kanzog, Klaus, ed. *Erzählstrukturen—Filmstrukturen. Erzählungen Heinrich von Kleists und ihre filmische Realisation*. Berlin: Erich Schmidt Verlag 1981.
Kanzog, Klaus. "An der Literatur zeigen, was der Film kann: *Phantom* (1922)." In *Von den Anfängen bis zum etablierten Medium 1895–1924*, edited by Werner Faulstich and Helmut Korte, 377–93. Frankfurt/M.: Fischer, 1994.
Kanzog, Klaus. "Missbrauchter Heinrich Mann? Bemerkungen zu Heinrich Manns *Professor Unrat* und Josef von Sternbergs *Der blaue Engel*." *Heinrich Mann-Jahrbuch* 14 (1996): 113–38.
Kanzog, Klaus. "Aktualisierung—Realisierung. Carl Zuckmayers *Der Hauptmann von Köpenick* in den Verfilmungen von Richard Oswald (1931) und Helmut Käutner (1956)." In *Carl Zuckmayer und die Medien*, edited by Gunter Nickel, 249–308. St. Ingbert: Röhrig, 2001.
Kapczynski, Jennifer. "Armchair Warriors: Heroic Postures in the West German War Film." In *Screening War: Perspectives on German Suffering*, edited by P. Cooke and M. Silberman, 17–35. Rochester, NY: Camden House, 2010.
Kapczynski, Jennifer and Michael D. Richardson, eds. *A New History of German Cinema*. Rochester: Camden House, 2012.
Kaplan, E. Ann. *Women and Film*. New York: Methuen, 1983.
Kappelhoff, Hermann, Bernhard Groß and Daniel Illger. *Demokratisierung der Wahrnehmung: Das westeuropäische Nachkriegskino*. Berlin: Vorwerk 8, 2010.
Keiner, Reinhold. *Hanns Heinz Ewers und der phantastische Film*. Hildesheim: Olms, 1987.
Keppler-Tasaki, Stefan and Fabienne Liptay, eds. *Grauzonen. Positionen zwischen Literatur und Film 1910–1960*. Munich: text+kritik, 2010.
Kershaw, Ian. *The "Hitler Myth." Image and Reality in the Third Reich*. Oxford: Oxford University Press, [1989] 2001.
Kittler, Friedrich. *Grammophon, Film, Typewriter*. Munich: Brinkmann, ²1987.
Kittler, Friedrich. *Die Wahrheit der technischen Welt. Essays zur Genealogie der Gegenwart*. Frankfurt/M.: Suhrkamp, 2013.
Kittler, Friedrich and Horst Turk, eds. *Urszenen*. Frankfurt/M.: Suhrkamp, 1977.
Kluge, Alexander. *Geschichten vom Kino*. Frankfurt/M.: Suhrkamp, 2007.
Knight, Julia. *Women and the New German Cinema*. New York: Verso, 1992.
Knopf, Jan. *Brecht-Handbuch. Bd. 3: Prosa, Filme, Drehbücher*. Stuttgart: Metzler, 2002.
Knopp, Daniel. *Wunschbild und Feindbild der nationalsozialistischen Filmpropaganda am Beispiel von Leni Riefenstahls "Triumph des Willens" und Veit Harlans "Jud Suess."* Marburg: Tectum, 1997.

Koebner, Thomas. "Der Film als neue Kunst. Reaktionen der literarischen Intelligenz." In *Literaturwissenschaft—Medienwissenschaft*, edited by Helmut Kreuzer, 1–28. Heidelberg: Quelle & Meyer, 1977.
Koebner, Thomas. "Liebe, Leidenschaft, Identitätszerfall. Thomas Mann und der Film." *Filmdienst* 6 (1994): 4–8.
Koepnick, Lutz. *The Dark Mirror. German Cinema between Hitler and Hollywood*. Berkeley: University of California Press, 2002.
Koepnick, Lutz. "Reframing the Past: Heritage Cinema and the Holocaust in the 1990s." *New German Critique* 87 (2002): 47–82.
Köppen, Manuel and Erhard Schütz, eds. *Kunst der Propaganda: Der Film im Dritten Reich*. Frankfurt/M.: Lang, 2008.
Kordecki, Sarah. *Und ewig ruft die Heimat …: Zeitgenössische Diskurse und Selbstreflexivität in den Heimatfilmwellen der Nachkriegs- und Nachwendezeit*. Göttingen: V&R, 2020.
Kortner, Fritz. *Aller Tage Abend. Autobiographie*. Munich: dtv, 1976.
Kracauer, Siegfried. *Von Caligari zu Hitler. Filmkritiken von 1924–39*. Frankfurt/M.: Suhrkamp, 1984.
Kracauer, Siegfried. *The Mass Ornament, Weimar Essays*. Translated and edited by Thomas Y. Levin. Cambridge, MA: Harvard University Press, 1995.
Kracauer, Siegfried. *From Caligari to Hitler: A Psychological History of the German Film*. Princeton: Princeton University Press, [1947] 2004.
Kramer, Thomas. *Lexikon des deutschen Films*. Stuttgart: Reclam, 1995.
Kreimeier, Klaus. *Kino und Filmindustrie in der BRD. Ideologieproduktion und Klassenwirklichkeit nach 1945*. Kronberg: Scriptor, 1973.
Kreimeier, Klaus. *The Ufa Story: A History of Germany's Greatest Film Company, 1918–1945*. Berkeley: University of California Press, 1999.
Kuhn, Anna. "Modes of Alienation in Fassbinder's *Effi Briest*." *Seminar* 21.4 (1985): 272–85.
Kuhn, Annette. *Women's Pictures: Feminism and Cinema*. London: Routledge, 1982.
Kuhn, Markus. *Filmnarratologie*. Berlin: de Gruyter, 2013.
Lange, Jasmin. *Der deutsche Buchhandel und der Siegeszug der Kinematographie 1895–1933: Reaktionen und strategische Konsequenzen*. Wiesbaden: Harrassowitz, 2010.
Lange, Manfred. "Ästhetik des Humanen. Das literarische Programm Heinrich Bölls." In *Heinrich Böll*, edited by Heinz Ludwig Arnold, 89–98. Munich: text+kritik, 1982.
Ledig, Elfriede. *Paul Wegeners Golem-Filme im Kontext fantastischer Literatur*. Munich: Verlegergemeinschaft SBL, 1990.
Leitch, Thomas. *Film Adaptation and Its Discontents*. Baltimore: John Hopkins University Press, 2007.
Leitch, Thomas. *The History of American Literature on Film*. New York: Bloomsbury, 2019.
Lensing, Leo A. "Cinema, Society and Literature in Irmgard Keun's *Das kunstseidene Mädchen*." *The Germanic Review* 60 (1985): 129–34.
Leppmann, Wolfgang. *Gerhart Hauptmann*. Berlin: Ullstein, 2007.
Lindeiner-Strásky, Karina von. *Die Mehrfarbigkeit der Vergangenheit: István Szabós Adaptation von Klaus Manns Roman Mephisto*. Würzburg: Königshausen & Neumann, 2013.

Lohmeier, Anke-Marie. "Symbolische und allegorische Rede im Film. Die *Effi Briest*-Filme von Gustaf Gründgens und Rainer Werner Fassbinder." In *Theodor Fontane*, edited by Heinz Ludwig Arnold, 229–41. Munich: text+kritik, 1989.
Lowenthal, David. *The Past Is a Foreign Country*. Cambridge: Cambridge University Press, 1985.
Lowenthal, David. "Preface." In *The Art of Forgetting*, edited by A. Forty and S. Küchler, xi–xiv. Oxford: Berg, 1999.
Luserke-Jaqui, Matthias, ed. *Schiller-Handbuch*. Stuttgart: Metzler, 2001.
Mahne, Nicole. *Transmediale Erzähltheorie*. Göttingen: V&R, 2007.
Maier-Katkin, Birgit. "Literary and Cinematographic Reflections on the Human Condition by Anna Seghers and Fred Zinnemann." In *Processes of Transposition: German Literature and Film*, edited by C. Schönfeld, 141–56. New York: Rodopi, 2007.
Maier-Katkin, Birgit. "*The Seventh Cross*: Dignité humaine and Human Rights." In *Anna Seghers. The Challenge of History*, edited by Helen Fehervary, Christiane Zehl Romero and Amy Kepple Strawser. *German Monitor* 80 (2019): 62–77.
Malthête, Jacques and Laurent Mannoni. *L'oeuvre de Georges Méliès*. Paris: Éditions de la Martinière, 2008.
Mitchell, George. "Making *All Quiet on the Western Front*." *American Cinematographer* 66.9 (1985): 34–6.
McMahan, Alison. *Alice Guy-Blaché: Lost Visionary of the Cinema*. New York: Bloomsbury, 2002.
Mitscherlich, Alexander and Margarete Mitscherlich. *Die Unfähigkeit zu trauern. Grundlagen kollektiven Verhaltens*. Munich: Piper, [1967] 2007.
Moeller, Felix. *The Film Minister. Goebbels and the Cinema in the "Third Reich."* London: Menges, 2001.
Moeller, Robert G. *War Stories: The Search for a Usable Past in the Federal Republic of Germany*. Berkely: University of California Press, 2001.
Moeller, Robert G. "Kämpfen für den Frieden: *08/15* und westdeutsche Erinnerungen an den Zweiten Weltkrieg." *Militärgeschichtliche Zeitschrift* 64 (2005): 359–89.
Moltke, Johannes von. *No Place Like Home: Locations of Heimat in German Cinema*. Berkeley: University of California Press, 2005.
Mühl-Benninghaus, Wolfgang. "German Film Censorship during World War I." *Film History* 9.1 (1997): 71–94.
Mühl-Benninghaus, Wolfgang. *Das Ringen um den Tonfilm. Strategien der Elektro- und Filmindustrie in den 20er und 30er Jahren*. Düsseldorf: Droste, 1999.
Mueller, Agnes C., ed. *German Pop Culture: How American Is It?* Ann Arbor: University of Michigan Press, 2004.
Müller, Corinna. *Vom Stummfilm zum Tonfilm*. Munich: Fink, 2003.
Murray Bruce, A. and Christopher J. Wickham, eds. *Framing the Past: The Historiography of German Cinema and Television*. Carbondale: Southern Illinois University Press, 1992.
Naremore, James, ed. *Film Adaptation*. New Brunswick, NJ: Rutgers University Press, 2000.
Neiman, Susan. *Learning from the Germans. Race and the Memory of Evil*. New York: Macmillan, 2019.
Neuhaus, Stefan. *Das verschwiegene Werk. Erich Kästners Mitarbeit an Theaterstücken unter Pseudonym*. Würzburg: Königshausen & Neumann, 2000.

Neuhaus, Stefan, ed. *Literatur im Film. Beispiele einer Medienbeziehung.* Würzburg: Königshausen & Neumann, 2000.
Neuhaus, Stefan. *Märchen.* Tübingen/Basel: Francke, 2005.
Neuhaus, Stefan. *Grundriss der Neueren deutschsprachigen Literaturgeschichte.* Tübingen/Basel: Francke, 2017.
Neuhaus, Stefan, ed. *Effi Briest Handbuch.* Stuttgart: Metzler, 2019.
Neuhaus, Stefan. *Der Krimi in Literatur, Film und Serie. Eine Einführung.* Tübingen/Basel: Francke, 2021.
Neuhaus, Stefan and Nicole Mattern, eds. *Metzler Handbuch: Thomas Manns "Buddenbrooks".* Stuttgart: Metzler, 2018.
Neupert, Richard. *A History of the French New Wave Cinema.* Madison: University of Wisconsin Press, 2002.
Nickel, Gunter, ed. *Carl Zuckmayer und die Medien.* St. Ingbert: Röhrig, 2001.
Niven, Bill. *The Buchenwald Child. Truth, Fiction, and Propaganda.* Rochester: Camden House, 2007.
Niven, Bill. *Hitler and Film: The Führer's Hidden Passion.* New Haven: Yale University Press, 2018.
O'Brien, Mary-Elisabeth. *Nazi Cinema as Enchantment. The Politics of Entertainment in the Third Reich*, Rochester. NY: Camden House, 2004.
Ó Dochartaigh, Pól. *Germany since 1945.* Basingstoke: Palgrave, 2003.
Ó Dochartaigh, Pól and Christiane Schönfeld, eds. *Representing the "Good German" in Literature and Culture after 1945: Altruism and Moral Ambiguity.* Rochester, NY: Camden House, 2013.
Olick, Jeffrey. *In the House of the Hangman.* Chicago: University of Chicago Press, 2005.
Paech, Joachim, ed. *Literatur und Film: Mephisto.* Frankfurt/M.: Diesterweg, 1984.
Paech, Joachim. *Literatur und Film.* Stuttgart: Metzler, 1988.
Palmier, Jean-Michel. *Weimar in Exile: The Antifascist Emigration in Europe and America.* New York: Verso, 2017.
Pearl, Jed. *Authority and Freedom.* New York: Knopf, 2021.
Petro, Patrice. *Joyless Street. Women and Melodramatic Representation in Weimar Germany.* Princeton: Princeton University Press, 1989.
Petzold, Christian, Robert Fischer, and Jaimey Fisher. "The Cinema Is a Warehouse of Memory: A Conversation." *Senses of Cinema* 84 (2017), http://www.sensesofcinema.com/2017/christian-petzold-a-dossier/christian-petzold/.
Phillips, Klaus, ed. *New German Filmmakers: From Oberhausen through the 1970s.* New York: Ungar, 1984.
Pick, Erika, ed. *Schriftsteller und Film. Dokumentation und Bibliographie. Aus den Sammlungen der Sektion Literatur und Sprachpflege.* Berlin: Akademie der Künste der DDR, 1979.
Pinkert, Anke. *Film and Memory in East Germany.* Bloomington: Indiana University Press, 2008.
Pinthus, Kurt, ed. *Das Kinobuch.* Zürich: Arche, [1913] 1963.
Piscator, Erwin. *Schriften*, 2 vols. Berlin: Henschel, 1968.
Plater, Edward. "Helmut Käutner's Film Adaptation of *Des Teufels General*." *Literature/Film Quarterly* 22.4 (1994): 253–64.
Popple, Simon and Joe Kember, eds. *Early Cinema: From Factory Gate to Dream Factory.* London: Wallflower, 2004.

Prawer, Siegbert. *Between Two Worlds: The Jewish Presence in German and Austrian Film, 1910–1933.* London: Berghahn Books, 2007.
Preece, Julian and Nick Hodgin, eds. *Andreas Dresen.* Oxford: Peter Lang, 2017.
Preuschoff, Nikolai. "'His World had Vanished Long before he Entered it': Wes Anderson's Homage to Stefan Zweig." In *Adaptation as a Collaborative Art,* edited by B. Cronin et al., 147–66. Cham, CH: Palgrave, 2020.
Prodolliet, Ernest. *Faust im Kino. Die Geschichte des Faustfilms von den Anfängen bis in die Gegenwart.* Freiburg: Universitätsverlag Freiburg/CH, 1978.
Pronay, Nicholas and D. W. Spring, eds. *Propaganda, Politics and Film, 1918–45.* London: Macmillan, 1982.
Raw, Laurence. *Translation, Adaptation and Transformation.* New York: Bloomsbury, 2012.
Reimer, Carol and Robert Reimer. *Nazi Retro Film.* New York: Twayne, 1992.
Reimer, Carol and Robert Reimer. *Historical Dictionary of Holocaust Cinema.* Toronto: Scarecrow Press, 2012.
Reimer, Robert. *Cultural History through a National Socialist Lens. Essays on the Cinema of Nazi Germany.* Columbia, SC: Camden House, 2002.
Rentschler, Eric, ed. *German Film and Literature.* New York: Methuen, 1986.
Rentschler, Eric. *West German Filmmakers on Film: Visions and Voices.* New York: Holmes & Meier, 1988.
Rentschler, Eric, ed. *The Films of G.W. Pabst.* New Brunswick: Rutgers University Press, 1990.
Rentschler, Eric. *The Ministry of Illusion: Nazi Cinema and Its Afterlife.* Cambridge: Harvard University Press, 1996.
Rohmer, Eric. *Six contes moraux (1974).* Paris: Cahier du cinema, 1998.
Rollberg, Peter. *Historical Dictionary of Russian and Soviet Cinema.* Lanham, MA: Rowman & Littlefield, 2016.
Rother, Rainer. *Zeitbilder: Filme des Nationalsozialismus.* Berlin: Bertz+Fischer, 2019.
Rusch, Mara. *Die Filme von Aleksandr Sokurov. Ein Rückblick auf die russisch-europäische Geschichte.* Munich: text+kritik, 2018.
Rutz, Gerd-Peter. *Darstellungen von Film in literarischen Fiktionen der zwanziger und dreißiger Jahre.* Münster: LIT, 2000.
Sander, Gabriele. *Erläuterungen und Dokumente zu Alfred Döblin: Berlin Alexanderplatz.* Stuttgart: Reclam, 1998.
Sandford, John. *The New German Cinema.* Oxford: Berg, 1980.
Sauer-Kretschmer, Simone, ed. *Körper kaufen? Prostitution in Literatur und Medien.* Berlin: Bachmann, 2016.
Saunders, Thomas J. *Hollywood in Berlin: American Cinema and Weimar Germany.* Berkeley: University of California Press, 1994.
Scheunemann, Dietrich, ed. *Expressionist Film. New Perspectives.* Rochester, NY: Camden House, 2003.
Schicha, Christian and Carsten Brosda, eds. *Politikvermittlung in Unterhaltungsformaten: Medieninszinierung zwischen Popularität und Populismus.* Münster: LIT, 2002.
Schittly, Dagmar. *Zwischen Regie und Regime. Die Filmpolitik der SED im Spiegel der DEFA-Produktionen.* Berlin: Links, 2002.

Schlöndorff, Volker. *Licht, Schatten und Bewegung. Mein Leben und meine Filme.* Munich: Hanser, 2008.

Schlüpmann, Heide. "Asta Nielsen and Female Narration: The Early Films." In *A Second Life: German Cinema's First Decades*, edited by Thomas Elsaesser and Michael Wedel, 118–22. Amsterdam: Amsterdam University Press, 1996.

Schlüpmann, Heide. "The Brothel as an Arcadian Space? Diary of a Lost Girl (1929)." In *The Films of G.W. Pabst*, edited by Eric Rentschler, 80–90, here p. 85.

Schmidt, Klaus M. and Ingrid Schmidt. *Lexikon Literaturverfilmungen.* Stuttgart: Metzler, ²2001.

Schmitz, Helmut, ed. *A Nation of Victims? Representations of German Wartime Suffering from 1945 to the Present.* Amsterdam: Rodopi, 2007.

Schoeps, Karl-Heinz. *Literature and Film in the Third Reich.* Rochester, NY: Camden House, 2003.

Scholz, Anne-Marie. *From Fidelity to History: Film Adaptations as Cultural Events in the Twentieth Century.* New York: Berghahn, 2013.

Schönfeld, Christiane. "Women on Screen: A Short History of the *femme fatale*." *Women's Studies Review* 8 (2002): 29–46.

Schönfeld, Christiane and Carmel Finnan, eds. *Practicing Modernity: Female Creativity in the Weimar Republic.* Würzburg: Königshausen & Neumann, 2006.

Schönfeld, Christiane. "*Triumph des Genies* (1940): Schiller in Third Reich Cinema." *Germanistik in Ireland* 1 (2006): 75–88.

Schönfeld, Christiane, and Hermann Rasche, eds. *Processes of Transposition: German Literature and Film.* Amsterdam and New York: Rodopi, 2007.

Schönfeld, Christiane. "Representing Pain in Literature and Film: Reflections on *Die Brücke* (*The Bridge*) by Manfred Gregor and Bernhard Wicki." *Comunicação & Cultura* 5 (2008): 45–62.

Schönfeld, Christiane. "Erfolg und Misserfolg von Verfilmungen: Manfred Gregors *Die Brücke* und die Nahaufnahmen des Krieges in Kino und Fernsehen." *Germanistik in Ireland* 7 (2012): 81–102.

Schönfeld, Christiane. "'Alle Qual vom Herzen Schreiben.' Performative Ästhetik von Lust und Schmerz in Margarete Böhmes *Tagebuch einer Verlorenen* (1905) und *Dida Ibsens Geschichte* (1907) in Text und Film." In *Schmerz, Lust, Weiblichkeit und Avantgarde in Deutschland*, edited by Lorella Bosco and Anke Gilleir, 51–78. Bielefeld: Aisthesis, 2015.

Schönfeld, Christiane. "Memories of World War II in German Film after 1945." In *The Long Aftermath: Cultural Legacies of Europe at War, 1936–2016*, edited by Manuel Braganca and Peter Tame, 200–18. Oxford: Berghahn Books, 2015.

Schönfeld, Christiane. "Von einer Ästhetik des Hässlichen zu einer Ethik des Ähnlichen: Prostituierte in Kunst, Literatur und Film." In *Komparative Ästhetiken*, edited by Meher Bhoot, Vibha Surana, Ernest Hess-Lüttich, 275–90. Mumbai: University of Mumbai Press, 2018.

Schönfeld, Christiane. "*Buddenbrooks* im Stummfilm." In *Metzler Handbuch: Thomas Manns Buddenbrooks*, edited by Stefan Neuhaus and Nicole Mattern, 58–63. Stuttgart: Metzler, 2018.

Schönfeld, Christiane. "Verfilmungen." In *Metzler Handbuch: Fontanes Effi Briest*, edited by Stefan Neuhaus, 131–49. Stuttgart: Metzler, 2019.

Schönfeld, Christiane. "Collaborative Art with Political Intent: The 1933 Adaptation of Theodor Storm's *Der Schimmelreiter/The Rider on the White Horse* (1888)." In *Process and Practice: Adaptation Considered as a Collaborative Art*, edited by Bernadette Cronin, Rachel MagShamhráin and Nikolai Preuschoff, 169–92. Cham/CH: Palgrave, 2020.

Schönfeld, Christiane. "Pariser Exilromane im Film: Transnationale Neucodierungen von Erinnerungskultur." In *Feuchtwanger et la culture mémorielle en France*, edited by Daniel Azuélos, Andrea Chartier-Bunzel, Frédéric Teinturier et al., 229–46. London: Lang, 2020.

Schulte-Sasse, Linda. *Entertaining the Third Reich: Illusions of Wholeness in Third Reich Cinema*. Durham: Duke University Press, 1996.

Schwab, Ulrike. *Erzähltext und Spielfilm. Zur Ästhetik und Analyse der Filmadaption*. Berlin: LIT, 2006.

Schweinitz, Jörg, ed. *Prolog vor dem Film. Nachdenken über ein neues Medium*, Leipzig: Reclam, 1992.

Segeberg, Harro, ed. *Die Mobilisierung des Sehens. Zur Vor- und Frühgeschichte des Films in Literatur und Kunst*. Munich: Fink, 1996.

Segeberg, Harro, ed. *Mediale Mobilmachung: das Dritte Reich und der Film*. Munich: Fink, 2004.

Semenza, Greg M. Colón and Bob Hasenfratz. *The History of British Literature on Film, 1895–2015*. New York and London: Bloomsbury, 2015.

Seeßlen, Georg. *Faust—Materialien zu einem Film von Peter Gorski*. Duisburg: Atlas Film, 1992.

Shandley, Robert. *Rubble Films: German Cinema in the Shadow of the Third Reich*. Philadelphia: Temple University Press, 2001.

Silberman, Mark. *German Cinema. Texts in Contexts*. Detroit: Wayne State University Press, 1995.

Silberman, Mark, trans./ed. *Bertolt Brecht on Film & Radio*. New York: Methuen, 2000.

Silberman, Mark and Henning Wrage, eds. *DEFA at the Crossroads of East German and International Film Culture*. Berlin: de Gruyter, 2014.

Simmel, Georg. *Brücke und Tor. Essays des Philosophen zur Geschichte, Religion, Kunst und Gesellschaft*. Stuttgart: Koehler, 1957.

Simmel, Georg. *Philosophie des Geldes*. Frankfurt/M.: Suhrkamp, [1900] 1989.

Sollers, Werner. *The Invention of Ethnicity*. Oxford: Oxford University Press, 1989.

Spaich, Herbert. *Rainer Werner Fassbinder*. Weinheim: Beltz, 1992.

Stephan, Gerd-Rüdiger, ed. et al. *Die Parteien und Organisationen der DDR. Ein Handbuch*. Berlin: Dietz, 2002.

Storch, Wolfgang, ed. *Die Nibelungen: Bilder von Liebe, Verrat und Untergang*. Munich: Prestel, 1987.

Strehl, Wiebke. *Theodor Storm's Immensee. A Critical Overview*. Rochester: Camden House: 2000.

Tambling, Jeremy, ed. *Encyclopaedia of Urban Literary Studies*. London: Palgrave, 2021.

Tatar, Maria. "The Poetics of the Combat Zone: Erich Maria Remarque's *Im Westen nichts Neues*." *German Quarterly* 92.1 (Winter 2019): 1–19.

Taylor, Richard. *Film Propaganda. Soviet Russia and Nazi Germany*. New York: Tauris, 1998.

Thunecke, Jörg. "Kolportage ohne Hintergründe. Der Film *Grand Hotel* (1932). Exemplarische Darstellung der Entwicklungsgeschichte von Vicki Baums Roman *Menschen im Hotel*." In *Die Resonanz des Exils. Gelungene und mißlungene Rezeption deutschsprachiger Exilautoren*, edited by Dieter Sevin, 134–53. Amsterdam: Rodopi, 1992.

Tibbets, John C. and James M. Welsh, eds. *The Encyclopedia of Filmmakers*, 2 vols. New York: Facts on File, 2002.

Tornow, Ingo. *Erich Kästner und der Film*. Munich: dtv, 1998.

Töteberg, Michael. *Fassbinders Filme*. Frankfurt/M.: Verlag der Autoren, 1990.

Turner, Graeme. *Film as Social Practice*. London: Routledge, ²1993.

Ukadike, N. Frank. "The Hyena's Last Laugh: A Conversation with Djibril Diop Mambety." *Transition* 78 (1999): 136–53.

Vaupel, Angela. *Frauen im NS-Film. Unter besonderer Berücksichtigung des Spielfilms*. Hamburg: Kovac, 2005.

Volk, Stefan. *Skandalfilme: Cineastische Aufreger gestern und heute*. Marburg: Schüren, 2012.

Völker, Klaus. *Fritz Kortner. Schauspieler und Regisseur*. Berlin: Hentrich, 1987.

Wallace, Ian, ed. *Seghers in Perspective*. Amsterdam: Rodopi, 1998.

Wallace, Ian, ed. *Feuchtwanger and Film*. Bern: Lang, 2009.

Webber, Andrew J. *Doppelgänger: Double Visions in German Literature*. Oxford: Oxford University Press, 1996.

Weber, Dana. "From Glorious Nibelungs to Inglorious Basterds: Quentin Tarantino's Refractive Retelling of Fritz Lang's Epic." *German Studies Review* 42.3 (2019): 537–60.

Weber, Nicola. *Im Netz der Gefühle: Veit Harlans Melodramen*. Münster: LIT, 2011.

Wedel, Michael. "Messter's Silent Heirs: Sync Systems of the German Music Film 1914–1929." *Film History* 11.4 (1999): 464–76.

Wedel, Michael. *Filmgeschichte als Krisengeschichte*. Bielefeld: transcript, 2011.

Wedel, Michael, ed. et al. *DEFA International*. Wiesbaden: Springer, 2013.

Wedel, Michael. *Pictorial Affects, Senses of Rupture: On the Poetics and Culture of Popular German Cinema, 1910–1930*. Berlin/Boston: de Gruyter, 2019.

Welch, David. *Propaganda and the German Cinema, 1933–1945*. London: Tauris, 2001.

Weniger, Kai. *"Es wird im Leben dir mehr genommen als gegeben …" Lexikon der aus Deutschland und Österreich emigrierten Filmschaffenden 1933 bis 1945*. Hamburg: Acabus, 2011.

Wilharm, Irmgard. "Filmwirtschaft, Filmpolitik und der 'Publikumsgeschmack' im Westdeutschland der Nachkriegszeit." *Geschichte und Gesellschaft* 28.2 (2002): 267–90.

Wilms, Wilfried and William Rasch, eds. *German Postwar Films. Life and Love in the Ruins*. New York: Palgrave Macmillan, 2008.

Witte, Karsten, ed. *Theorie des Kinos. Ideologie der Traumfabrik*. Frankfurt/M: Suhrkamp, 1972.

Wolf, Claudia. *Arthur Schnitzler und der Film*. Karlsruhe: KTI, 2017.

Wottrich, Erika, ed. *M wie Nebenzahl. Nero—Filmproduktion zwischen Europa und Hollywood*. Munich: text+kritik, 2002.

Wulf, Joseph. *Theater und Film im Dritten Reich. Eine Dokumentation.* Reinbek: Rowohlt, 1966.
Zander, Peter. *Thomas Mann im Kino.* Berlin: Bertz+Fischer, 2005.
Zeller, Bernhard, ed. *Klassiker in finsteren Zeiten, 1933–1945. Eine Ausstellung des Deutschen Literaturarchivs im Schiller-Nationalmuseum, Marbach am Neckar.* Marbach: Deutsche Schillergesellschaft, 1983.
Zielinski, Siegfried. *Veit Harlan: Analysen und Materialien zur Auseinandersetzung mit einem Film-Regisseur des deutschen Faschismus.* Frankfurt/M.: Fischer, 1981.
Zinnemann, Fred. *An Autobiography: A Life in the Movies.* New York: Scribner, 1992.
Zipes, Jack. *The Irresistible Fairy Tale: The Cultural and Social History of a Genre.* Princeton: Princeton University Press, 2012.
Zipes, Jack, ed. *The Oxford Companion to Fairy Tales.* Oxford: Oxford University Press, 2015.
Zischler, Hanns. *Kafka geht ins Kino.* Reinbek: Rowohlt, 1996.
Zoller Seitz, Matt, ed. *The Wes Anderson Collection: The Grand Budapest Hotel.* New York: Abrams, 2015.

INDEX

Abbott and Costello Meet Frankenstein (1948) 249
Abel, Alfred 109
Abel, Heinz 409 n.55
Abel, Marco 496 n.161, 522–3, 528, 550, 568 n.62, 573 nn.110–13, 573 n.120, 573 n.122, 574 n.130, 577 nn.172–3, 578 n.174, 581 n.203
Abel, Richard 30 n.14
Abenteuer am Lido/Adventure at the Lido (1933) 248
Abich, Hans 343–4, 346, 376, 384–5, 396, 408 n.43, 408 n.51, 421 n.203, 424 n.242
Abraham, F. Murray 545
Abschied von gestern/Farewell to Yesterday/Yesterday Girl (1966) 454
Abschied von Sidonie: Sidonie (Hackl) 571 n.97
abstract public 3
Abwege/The Devious Path (1928) 146
Achternbusch, Herbert 479, 498 n.196
Acht Stunden sind kein Tag/Eight Hours Don't Make a Day (1972–3) 472
Action-Theater 472
The Actor's Children (1910) 128
Adalbert, Max 156 n.13, 218, 220
Adaptation (2002) 540
Adaptation Considered as a Collaborative Art (Cronin, MagShamhráin & Preuschoff) 242 n.205, 576 n.147, 576 n.158
Ade, Maren 521–2, 558, 574 n.132
Adenauer, Konrad 335, 364, 369–70, 373, 376, 399, 401, 431–2, 516, 564 n.24

Adler, Hans 363
Adler, Stella 258
Adolf, Gustav 380
Adorf, Mario 422 n.209, 477
Adorno, Theodor W. 166 n.170, 284, 319, 324 n.44, 332 nn.161–2, 452, 492 n.94, 579 n.187
AEG 84 n.115, 175
Aesthetics and Politics in Modern German Culture (Haines, Parker & Riordan) 270 n.32
Affair in Monte Carlo (1952) 351
Afgrunden/The Abyss (1910) 46
Agamben, Giorgio 8 n.8, 581 n.205
Agde, Günther 271 n.49
Age of Uprising (2013) 544
Agfa-Biback-technology 298
Agnes Bernauer (Hebbel) 410 n.65
Agostini, Philippe 403
Aimée und Jaguar (1997) 509
Akerman, Chantal 491 n.92
Akin, Fatih 491 n.92, 521, 546, 558, 573 n.107
Albers, Hans 106–7, 191, 248, 283, 323 n.42, 340–1, 392
Albersmeier, Franz-Josef 327 n.100
Albrecht, Gerd 322 n.30, 328 n.107
Alexander, Curt 246, 251, 269 n.23
Alexander, Katherine Jane 575 n.138
Alexander, Tzar 183
Alice Guy-Blaché (1873–1968): la première femme cinéaste du monde (Bachy) 31 n.31
Alice Guy-Blaché: Lost Visionary of the Cinema (McMahan) 31 n.31, 31 n.33
Allan, Max 55
Allan, Seán 418 n.157, 445, 482 n.5, 488 n.52, 489 nn.66–7, 490 n.72

Allende, Isabel 564 n.24
Aller Tage Abend. Autobiographie (Kortner) 271 n.43, 407 n.27
Alles inclusive/All Inclusive (2014) 506
Allgeier, Sepp 147, 169 n.216
Allianz-Tonfilm GmbH 214
All Quiet on the Western Front (1930) 174, 200–6, 217, 226, 237 n.131, 261, 281, 354, 391, 443, 557, 580 n.197
All Quiet on the Western Front (1979) 237 n.143
All Quiet on the Western Front (Remarque) 198, 226, 354, 360, 580 n.191
Almereyda, Michael 519
Alone in Berlin (2016) 528–9, 556
Alraune (1928) 154, 177, 187
Alraune (1930) 177–80, 187, 231 n.34, 244, 254, 273 n.71
Alraune (1952) 367
Alraune (Ewers) 154, 177, 179–80
Alraune, die Henkerstochter, genannt die rote Hanne/Alraune, Hangman's daughter, known as red Hanne (1919) 230 n.31
Alraune und der Golem (1919) 142
Als der Weihnachtsmann vom Himmel fiel/When Santa Fell from Heaven (2017) 566 n.49
Also sprach Zarathustra/Thus Spoke Zarathustra (Nietzsche) 161 n.96
Als wär's ein Stück von mir/A Part of Myself (Zuckmayer) 394, 424 n.230
Als wir träumten/As We Were Dreaming (Meyer) 548
Alten, Jürgen von 378, 419 n.173, 420 n.186
Altenloh, Emilie 36, 77 n.19
alterity 72, 574 n.123
Alt-Heidelberg (1901) 170 n.233
Alt, Russell A. 331 n.155
Ambesser, Axel von 414 n.110
Ambrosio-Torino, Arturo 77 n.22
Amen (2002) 536
American Film Institution 166 n.174

American Guild for German Cultural Freedom 267
The American Marshall Plan Film Campaign and the Europeans (Fritsche) 405 n.9
Amerika (Kafka) 494 n.129
Am kürzeren Ende der Sonnenallee/At the Shorter End of Sonnenallee (Brussig) 506, 579 n.182
Ammann, Max Peter 571 n.96
Amok (1927) 141
Amok (Zweig) 141, 171, 282
Amphitryon (1668) 297, 323 n.42
Amphitryon (1807) 297, 323 n.42, 324 n.48
Amphitryon-aus den Wolken kommt das Glück/Amphitryon, happiness comes from the clouds (1935) 297, 323 n.42, 324 n.48
amusement film 57, 211
Andalusische Nächte/Andalusian Nights (1938) 307
Andam, F. D. (Friedrich Dammann) 196
Andere Frauen/Other Women (1928) 164 n.135
Anders als die Anderen/Different from the Others (1919) 67, 95
Andersch, Alfred 402, 440, 463, 486 n.42, 486 n.45, 494 n.127
Andersen, Hans Christian 174, 581 n.206
Anderson, Carolyn 8 n.3
Anderson, Lisa Marie 163 n.128
Anderson, Paul 504, 564 n.25
Anderson, Wes 529, 545, 560, 576 n.158, 576 n.160
Andersson, Pettersson och Lundström (1923) 228 n.4
Andréani, Henri 37
Andreas-Salomé, Lou 141
Andrew, Dudley 9 n.12
Angel (1937) 246
Angélique-series (1964–68) 415 n.120, 455
Angst essen Seele auf/Ali: Fear Eats the Soul (1974) 476
Angst/*La Paura*/Fear (1954) 403

Ani, Friedrich 494 n.133
animation films 76 n.16, 165 n.157, 228 n.5, 332 n.163, 514, 578 n.180
Animatograph 15
Anita Berber: Ein getanztes Leben (Fischer) 87 n.146
Anita-Tänze des Lasters/Anita: Dances of Vice (1988) 481
Ankerstjerne, Johan 47, 129
An klingenden Ufern/On Resonant Shores (1948) 362
Anna Boleyn (1920) 98, 158 n.43
Annakin, Ken 438
Annaud, Jean-Jacques 503
Anne Bäbi Jowänger (1978) 413 n.105
Anne Bäbi Jowänger (Gotthelf) 413 n.105
Annelie vom Berghof oder Oh diese Weiber/Annelie or Oh, these Women (1958) 413 n.104
À nous la liberté/Freedom for Us (1931) 182
Anschluss (1938) 249, 264, 267, 307, 335, 363, 545, 555
Ansichten eines Clowns/The Clown (1975) 464
Ansichten eines Clowns/The Clown (Böll) 462, 467, 495 n.149
Antalffy, Alexander von 58–9
Anthony, Joseph 413 n.107
anti-capitalist effect 119, 477
Antigone (1991) 562 n.8
antisemitism 180, 198, 252–3, 279, 295, 360, 371, 393, 399, 429–30, 479, 554
    fascism and 206
    and marginalization 120–2
    nationalism and 173
anti-war film 199, 206, 391, 485 n.32, 486 n.45, 562 n.3, 580 n.194
    rearmament/redefinitions of masculine agency 386–92
Antoine, André-Paul 269 n.25
anxieties 212, 226, 238 n.154, 377, 461, 538
    cultural 6, 50
    women and sexual identity 144–52

Anzengruber, Ludwig 1, 60–1, 277, 366–7, 492 n.99, 571 n.97
Anz, Thomas 167 n.191
Apitz, Bruno 442, 452, 488 n.56, 562 n.3
Appandurai, Arjun 7, 9 n.13
Apparition de Méphistophélès/Appartition of Mephisto (1897) 17
Appen, Karl von 452
Aquis submersus (Storm) 369
Arabian Nights (1974) 228 n.5
Arbeitsgemeinschaft der Rundfunkanstalten Deutschland (ARD) 402
Arc de Triomphe/Arch of Triumph (Remarque) 354–60, 412 nn.89–90
Arch of Triumph (1948) 354–60
Arco, Anna 513
ARD Degeto Film 402, 447, 458, 462, 473, 486 n.44, 496 n.155, 518–20, 559, 565 n.33, 570 n.82, 572 n.103, 582 n.209
Arendt, Hannah 578 n.174
Arliss, Leslie 255
Arm wie eine Kirchenmaus/Poor as a Church Mouse (1931) 218–19
Arndt, Stefan 520, 528
Arnim, Achim von 581 n.206
Arnold, Hannah 271 n.46
Arnold, Heinz Ludwig 327 n.100, 329 n.129, 497 n.173
Arnold, Jasmin 271 n.50
ARRI Media 514, 568 n.69
Arslan, Thomas 522
Artaud, Antonin 224
ARTE 169 n.222, 519–20, 572 n.100
Arthur Schnitzler und der Film (Aurnhammer, Beßlich & Denk) 81 n.65
Arthur Schnitzler und der Film (Wolf) 81 nn.59–60, 81 nn.62–4, 81 n.67, 81 n.69
The Artist (2012) 233 n.64
Arturo Ui (Brecht) 556
Ärztinnen (1984) 575 n.144
Ascheid, Antje 331 n.143

Aschenputtel/Cinderella (1922) 157 n.22, 239 n.162, 378
Asper, Helmut G. 217–18, 240 nn.180–3, 241 n.184, 241 n.186, 251, 268 n.8, 269 n.12, 269 n.22, 269 nn.26–7, 412 n.86
Asphalt (1929) 138
Asphaltgorillas (2018) 506
asphalt literature 3
Assmann, Aleida 393, 423 n.224
Astaire-Rogers films 183
Astruc, Alexandre 404 n.3, 495 n.140
Atlantik (1929) 175
Atlantis (1913) 40, 46–51, 81 n.71, 82 n.74, 129, 383
Atlantis (Hauptmann) 42–50, 82 n.80, 84 n.117, 129, 165 n.162, 383
Atrium cinema 224
Attal, Bernard 577 n.161
Atwood, Margaret 465
Auch Fummeln will gelernt sein/ Even Groping Must be Learned (1972) 493 n.107
Audran, Edmond 66, 93
Aufbau Film Production Company 344, 346, 384
Aufbaugemeinschaft Film 344
Auf der anderen Seite/On the Other Side (2007) 546
Aufklärungsfilme 66
Aufruhr im Schlaraffenland/Riot in the Land of Plenty (1957) 379
Auf Wiedersehen am blauen Meer/ Farewell at the Blue Sea (1962) 491 n.89
Augsburger Puppenkiste 441, 487 n.48, 487 n.50, 490 n.74
August, Bille 503, 510, 514–15, 564 n.24
Aurich, Rolf 163 n.120, 408 n.51
Aurnhammer, Achim 81 n.65
Auschwitz trials 401, 429, 441, 451–2, 492 n.95, 529
Aus dem Nichts/In the Fade (2017) 546
Austen, Jane 141
Austria 1, 4, 37, 42, 55–6, 61–2, 73, 87 n.158, 95, 101, 120, 153, 173, 205–6, 263, 266, 338–9, 349, 359, 366, 403, 426 n.261, 426 n.264, 434, 441, 449–50, 510, 531, 533, 535, 542–4, 572 n.104, 577 n.161
adaptations 249–50, 398, 400, 413 n.103
national canon on screen in 361–4
Aust, Stefan 516, 564 n.26
auteur adaptations 454, 456
auteur producer 502–9, 563 n.15
auteurs 467, 471, 512, 522, 524, 531, 553, 561
Authority and Freedom. A Defense of the Arts (Pearl) 9 n.11, 560, 582 nn.213–14
Authors on Film (Geduld) 161 n.56, 161 n.92, 166 n.168, 233 n.75
An Autobiography. A Life in the Movies (Zinnemann) 264, 273 n.70
automaton 26–7, 65–6, 94, 154
Autorenfilme 40
avant-garde 4, 35, 43, 50, 86 n.146, 90, 108, 114, 131, 150, 152–4, 173, 196, 213, 215, 218, 224, 226, 228 n.5, 256, 348, 436, 449, 451, 453, 459, 462, 472, 477, 479, 534, 551
avant la lettre 17
Ayros, Lew 236 n.123
Azuélos, Daniel 268 n.12, 405 n.8

Baal (1969) 465
Baal (2004) 561 n.3
Baal (Brecht) 465
Babelsberg Film GmbH 529, 571 n.93
Babylon Berlin (2017) 520, 557, 573 n.106
Bachleda, Alicja 581 n.206
Bach, Lida 576 n.156
Bächlin, Peter 230 n.28
Bachmann, Ingeborg 430, 516, 519, 530–1, 537, 559, 567 n.55, 581 n.206
Bach, Olaf 271 n.40
Bachy, Victor 31 n.31
Bacon, Lloyd 172

Bader, Hans Heinz 313, 316, 331 n.147
Badham, John 8 n.6, 485 n.28
Baer, Hester 8 n.3, 342, 404 n.4, 407 nn.31–3, 407 n.38, 408 n.41, 408 nn.43–4, 408 n.48, 408 n.50, 409 n.54, 422 n.206, 483 n.14, 498 n.198, 498 n.200, 500–2, 508, 522, 563 n.15, 563 nn.10–11, 564 nn.22–3, 564 n.28, 566 n.43, 566 n.45, 573 nn.114–15, 574 n.123
Bagier, Guido 174–5, 229 n.12, 229 n.14
Baier, Jo 557, 571 n.97, 580 n.198
Báky, Josef von 339–41, 373, 379, 384, 405 n.8
Balázs, Béla 125, 223
Balcon, Michael 252–3
Ballhaus, Carl 417 n.140
Ballmann, Herbert 483 n.6
Ball of Fire (1941) 353
Baluschek, Hans 99
Bamberger, Rudolf 246
Bambi (Salten) 40, 272 n.63
Bammé, Arno 169 n.221
Bandmann, Christa 236 n.127
Banville, John 582 n.213, 582 n.215
Baranowski, S. 483 n.5
Barcelona 20, 576
Barcklind, Carl 228 n.4, 269 n.18
Bard, Maria 214
Bär, Gerald 268 n.2
Barma, Claude 407 n.30
Baron Munchausen's Narrative of his Marvellous Travels and Campaigns in Russia (Raspe) 406 n.25
Bär, Rainer 489 n.60
Barry Lyndon (1975) 533
Barrymore, John 208
Barrymore, Lionel 208–9
Barthel, Manfred 419 n.169
Barthes, Roland 68
Barton, Charles 249
Basch, Felix 78 n.30
Bassermann, Albert 151, 178, 180, 267, 273 n.71

Batten, John 182
Baudelaire, Charles 141
Bauer, Christian 407 n.40
Baumann, Tobias 566 n.49
Baumgart, Reinhard 485 n.33
Baum, L. Frank 298
Baum, Ralph 349
Baum, Vicki 3–4, 160 n.72, 185–6, 198, 206–9, 226, 232 n.52, 238 n.150, 238 nn.152–3, 244, 266, 392–3, 487 n.46, 519, 530
Bavaria Film (Geiselgasteig) 106, 249, 487 n.48, 504, 509, 566 n.46, 572 n.100
Baxter, Peter 234 n.89
Bayrischer Rundfunk (BR) 407 n.40
Bazar de la Charité (Paris) 12
Beaumont, Harry 182
Beauté du diable/Beauty and the Devil (1950) 410 n.63
Beauvais, Peter 407 n.30, 424 n.229, 486 n.42, 569 n.81
Bebel, August 268 n.10
Becce, Guiseppe 99
Becher, Johannes R. 246, 371, 383, 417 nn.143–4, 488 n.51
Bechert, Hilde 484 n.15, 572 n.102
Becker, Ben 533
Becker, Jurek 445–6, 528
Becker, Meret 537
Becker, Sabina 54, 239 n.166
Becker, Theodor 61
Becker, Wolfgang 424 nn.236–7, 520, 524
Beck-Herzog, Helmut 347
Bed and Sofa/Третья Мещанская (1927) 119
Beecham, Thomas 350
Beer, Paula 523, 525, 549, 559, 560
Beery, Wallace 208
Beethoven, Ludwig van 251, 333
Before Caligari. German Cinema 1895–1920 (Cherchi Usai & Codelli) 80 n.54
Begegnung mit Werther/Encounter with Werther (1949) 342, 407 n.36
The Beggar's Opera (1728) 221

Behnke, Martin 550
Behn, Manfred 83 n.104
Behrendt, Hans 155, 170 n.233, 214, 246
Behrman, Samuel 360
Beicken, Peter 83 n.92
Beier, Lars-Olav 568 n.70
Bekenntnisse des Hochstaplers Felix Krull/Confessions of Felix Krull (1957) 384
Belach, Helga 85 n.126, 157 n.25, 239 n.163, 269 n.15
Bellag, Lothar 426 n.264, 452
Belling, Curt 322 n.30, 329 n.120
Bence, Amelia 351
Benda, Ernst 455
Ben Hur (1907) 34
Ben Hur (1959) 34, 438
Benigni, Roberto 581 n.201
Benjamin, Walter 5, 76 n.6, 131, 163 n.125, 166 n.169, 578 n.174, 580 n.193
Bennent, David 470
Bennent, Heinz 470
Benninger, Willi 496 n.152
Benson, Renate 273 n.66
Berauer, Wilfried 510, 512, 566 n.48, 568 n.59, 574 n.126
Berben, Oliver 501, 505, 565 n.32, 582 n.209
Berber, Anita 45, 70, 86–7 n.146, 95, 122–3, 143, 154, 165 nn.146–7, 168 n.200, 168 nn.202–3, 180, 190, 481
Berendsohn, Walter A. 205, 237 n.139, 427 n.269
The Berg (1929) 175
Berg, Brigitte 247, 269 n.13
Berge in Flammen/Mountains on Fire (1931) 287
Berger, Edward 557
Berger, Grete 53, 176
Berger, Ludwig 130, 166 n.167
Bergfelder, Tim 84 n.113, 404 n.4, 406 n.21, 424 n.229, 427 n.269, 447, 472, 482 n.5, 483 n.14, 490 n.77, 490 n.79, 496 n.160, 498 n.203, 502, 563 n.9, 563 n.18, 574 n.123

Bergfilme 368
Berghahn, Volker 320 n.10
Bergkristall (2004) 533
Bergman, Ingrid 357, 359, 411 n.70, 571 n.96
Bergner, Elisabeth 149, 151, 169 nn.223–4, 245, 462–3
Berlin 11–12, 20, 24, 39–40, 42, 44, 50, 52, 54–6, 62, 66, 69, 72, 92–3, 101, 105, 122–3, 149–50, 172–3, 183, 202, 205, 209–12, 215, 227, 244, 247, 254, 311, 340, 480, 525, 541, 555, 560, 569 n.78
Berlinale Film Festival 517
Berlin-Alexanderplatz (1931) 214–16
Berlin-Alexanderplatz (1980) 460, 472, 477, 493 n.111, 496 n.163, 566 n.46
Berlin Alexanderplatz (2020) 510–12, 517, 550–1, 554, 556, 558, 566 n.46
Berlin Alexanderplatz (Döblin) 211–13, 230 n.25, 231 n.35, 460, 472, 477, 496 n.163, 510
Berlin and Beyond film festival 553, 580 n.189
Berliner Ballade/The Ballad of Berlin (1948) 386
Berliner Börsen-Courier newspaper 100, 117, 220
Berliner Illustrierte Zeitung magazine 186, 232 n.52
Berliner Tageblatt newspaper 49, 62, 92, 157 n.18, 202
Berlin School 521–6, 553, 573 n.111, 573 n.113
Berlin. Sinfonie einer Großstadt/Berlin. Symphony of a Metropolis (1927) 109, 172, 175
Berlin Wall 432, 443–4, 447
construction 404, 429, 440, 481, 483 n.6
fall of 432, 443, 500, 538, 559
Berlioz, Hector 17–18, 21, 24
Bernard, Raymond 410 n.65
Bernhardt, Fritz 69

Bernhardt, Kurt (Curtis) 245, 254, 306, 320 n.5
Bertolt Brecht on Film & Radio (Silberman) 241 n.197, 241 n.203, 242 n.206, 242 n.208, 242 nn.211–12
Bertram, Ernst 161 n.90
Bertram, Hans 303
Besorgt mal Filme! (Oehmig) 418 n.151
Beßlich, Barbara 81 n.65
Best-sellers by Design: Vicki Baum and the House of Ullstein (King) 232 n.52
Beta Cinema Gmbh 518, 578 n.176
Bettany, Paul 566 n.49
Bettauer, Hugo 103, 119–20, 122, 153–4, 164 nn.134–5, 222
Bettini, Maurizio 579 n.185
Between Two Worlds: The Jewish Presence in German and Austrian Film, 1910–1933 (Prawer) 160 n.73
Betz, Louis 30 n.20
Beware of Pity (1946) 351
Beware of Pity (Zweig) 351, 545, 576 n.160
Beyer, Frank 442–3, 445–6, 478, 481, 486 n.45, 488 n.53, 519, 528, 562 n.7, 574 n.133
Beyer, Uwe 439
Beyond Prince Achmed: New Perspectives on Animation Pioneer Lotte Reiniger (Bieberstein) 83 n.94, 156 n.4
Bhatti, Anil 87 n.155
Biberpelz/Beaver Coat (1949) 377
Biberti, Robert 283
Bible 2
Bieberstein, Rada 83 n.94
Biebrach, Rudolf 85 n.125, 105
Bielunas, Jerzy 567 n.50
Bienek, Horst 464, 494 n.130
Biennale Film Festival (Venice) 254
Bierbaum, Otto Julius 100, 158 n.48
Bierbichler, Josef 565 n.33, 581 n.200
Biermann, Wolf 446
The Big House (1930) 203

The Big Parade (1925) 198
Bilanz/Taking Stock (1958) 462–3
Bild 440, 467–9, 479
Bildt, Paul 78 n.30, 99, 304
Bild-und Filmamt (BUFA) 57
Bildungsbürgertum 34
Bildungsphilister 23, 155
Billian, Hans 493 n.107
Billiard um halb zehn/Billiards at Half-Past Nine (Böll) 433, 464
Billinger, Richard 277, 296, 451, 491 n.89
Binding, Rudolf 317, 365
Bin ich schön?/Am I Beautiful? (1988) 506
biopower 550
Bioscop studios 52
Bioskop 11
Birgel, Willy 365
Birkin, Andrew 539
Bíró, Lajos 188
Birth of a Nation (1915) 55, 76 n.18
Bizone 347–8
Bjorkman, Stig 241 n.200
Blaché, Herbert 31 n.32
Black Beauty 485 n.28
The Black Cat (1934) 352
Black Fox: The Rise and Fall of Adolf Hitler (1962) 430, 441
Black Friday 221
Blackton, James Stuart 35
Black Widow (1954) 195
Bleeke Bet (1934) 248
Bleibtreu, Moritz 565 n.33
Bleiweiß, Celino 488–9 n.60
Bloch, Ernst 244, 268 n.2
Bloch, Iwan 67, 86 n.141
Blom, August 40–1, 43–4. See also *Atlantis* (1913)
Blonde Venus (1932) 195
The Blue Angel (1930). See *Der blaue Engel*/The Blue Angel (1930)
Bluebeard's Eighth Wife (1938) 246
Blum, Carl Robert 175, 203, 230 n.17
Blumenberg, Hans C. 458–9, 493 nn.114–16
"Fancy Dress Party and No End in Sight" 458

Blumesberger, Susanne 272 n.63
Blümner, Bettina 552
Blyton, Enid 504
Bobby Deerfield (1977) 360
Bobrowski, Johannes 445, 483 n.6
Boccaccio (1936) 307
Bock, Hans-Michael 85 nn.126–7, 114, 156 nn.5–6, 162 n.100, 170 n.232, 181–2, 229 n.14, 231 n.40, 231 n.42, 233 n.65, 237 n.137, 239 n.163, 269 n.15, 424 n.229
Böhme, Margarete 37, 67–72, 86 n.142, 86 n.145, 94–5, 98, 119, 145–6, 148–9, 153–4, 159 n.57, 169 nn.220–1, 222
Bohm, Hark 546, 562 n.7
Boito, Arrigo 17
Bollenbeck, Georg 268 n.11
Böll, Heinrich 402, 404, 430, 433–4, 440, 450–1, 467–9, 483 n.12, 494 nn.126–7, 494 n.131, 495 nn.143–6, 516
  Aesthetics of Humanity 434
  on screen 460–5
Bolliger, Luis 572 n.102
Böll, René 495 n.147
Bolshintsov, Manuel 259
Bolten-Baeckers, Heinrich 97
Bolt, Peter 176
Bolváry, Géza von 248, 397
Bolwieser (1977) 472
Bolwieser (Graf) 472
Bombenflieger/Bombers (1918) 236 n.125
Bonanza 447
Bondage (1933) 235 n.106
Bond, James 516
Bonsels, Waldemar 157 n.22
Bootz, Erwin 283
Borchart, Hermann 254, 271 n.45
Borchert, Wolfgang 342–6, 402, 407 n.34, 408 n.46, 408 n.50
Borcosque, Carlos F. 351
Borderie, Bernard 455
Borgnine, Ernest 237 n.143
Bormann, Martin 326 n.83
Bornemann, Fritz 488 n.51

Born, Nicolas 465
Börries, Achim von 520
Borries, Friedrich von 490 n.81
Borsche, Dieter 421 n.203
Borsody, Eduard von 363, 365, 414 n.111, 416 n.129
Borzage, Frank 198, 260, 262, 323 n.36
Böttcher, Jürgen 487 n.51
Böttcher, Maximilian 277
The Boudoir Diplomat (1930) 206, 238 n.145
Bouhnik, Laurent 411 n.70
Boulting, John 255, 271 n.45
Boulting, Roy 255, 271 n.45
Bourdet, Edouard 248
Bourdieu, Pierre 32 n.41, 32 n.44
bourgeois/bourgeoisie 12–13, 23, 27, 33, 35, 37, 45, 47, 50, 67, 70–2, 78 n.29, 90, 94–6, 105–6, 108, 112, 123, 125, 144, 148–50, 153, 155, 169 n.219, 187, 189–93, 221, 225, 278, 282, 304, 370–1, 373–4, 379, 384, 433, 461, 463, 477, 479–80, 534, 542, 551
Bourke, Eoin 303, 327 nn.93–4, 327 n.96
Bourke, Eva 160 n.74
À bout de souffle/Breathless (1960) 438
Bovenschen, Silvia 85 n.118
Bowie, David 503
Boxhagener Platz/Boxhagen Square (2010) 569 n.78, 579 n.182
Boxhagener Platz/Boxhagen Square (Schulz) 569 n.78, 579 n.182
Bozyakali, Can 417 n.136
Bracho, Julio 411 n.75
Brachvogel, Carry 163 n.126
Brachvogel, Heinz Udo 118, 163 n.126
Brackett, Charles 352, 398
Brady, Martin 493 n.119
Braganca, Manuel 405 n.8
Brakhage, Stan 403
Brandauer, Karin 571 n.97
Brandauer, Klaus Maria 537, 556, 562 n.5, 563 n.8

Branded (Hennings) 575 n.134
Brandlmeier, Thomas 164 n.143, 165 n.151
Brando, Marlon 258
Brandstellen/Scenes of Fire (1978) 486 n.45
Brandstetter, Gabriele 76 n.13
Brandt, H. E. 486 n.45
Brandt, Nils 565 n.33
Brandt, Willy 432, 444, 489 n.64
Brasch, Heinz 411 n.78
Brauer, Jürgen 562 n.7
Braun, Alfred 409 n.61
Braun, Curt J. 186
Brauner, Artur 383–4, 392, 400, 439
Brauner, Ludwig 56–7, 84 n.106
Braun, Harald 275, 300, 340, 379, 384–5, 402, 420 n.182
Braun, Michael 8 n.2
Braun, Volker 446, 500, 562 n.7
Braunwarth, Peter Michael 81 n.66
Brecht, Bertolt 6–7, 153, 173, 184, 211, 215, 221–5, 227, 241 nn.198–9, 242 n.206, 242 n.208, 242 nn.211–13, 243, 244–6, 254, 260, 268 n.1, 333, 337, 371, 402, 404 n.1, 426 n.264, 440, 445, 465, 476, 491 n.86, 494 n.129, 498 n.198, 511, 539, 552, 556, 558, 561 n.3, 562 n.8, 567 n.55
Breen, Richard L. 398
Breger, Claudia 421 n.199
Breloer, Heinrich 519, 562 n.5
Bremer Freiheit/Bremer Freedom (1972) 496 n.165
Brennert, Hans 300
Brenon, Herbert 203, 418 n.156
Brentano, Bernhard von 133–4, 166 n.178
Breslauer, Hans Karl 121, 164 n.131, 164 n.135
Bressart, Felix 264, 273 n.71
Brice, Pierre 447
Briefe 1915–1939 (Toller) 271 n.43
Briefe II (Schnitzler) 81 n.63
Brief einer Unbekannten/Letter from an Unknown Woman (1948) 349, 354, 537

Brief einer Unbekannten/Letter from an Unknown Woman (Zweig) 349, 354, 537
Bringmann, Peter F. 564 n.24
Brink, Elga 176
Brinkmann, Max 240 n.179
The British Cinema Book (Murphy) 410 n.66
British Office of War Information (London) 336
Britt, May 413 n.102
Broadbent, Jim 566 n.49
The Broadway Melody (1929) 182, 298
Broadwin, John 320 n.10
Brocher, Corinna 475, 497 n.171, 497 n.181
Broch, Hermann 567 n.55
Brockdorff, Gertrud von 328 n.109
Brockmann, Stephen 166 n.182, 194, 229 n.15, 230 n.24, 234 n.93, 404 n.4, 406 n.21, 418 n.155, 488 n.53, 488 n.58
Brod, Max 268 n.10
Brody, Adrien 545
Broll, Simon 568 n.71
Bromley, Haworth 255
Bronfen, Elisabeth 85 n.118
Bronsky, Alina 552
Bronzezeit: Geschichten aus dem Leben des Buchhalters Farssmann (Kant) 562 n.7
Brooks, Louise 145–6, 148–9, 169 n.218, 195, 235 n.100
Brooks, Peter 87 n.151, 164 n.139
Brosda, Carsten 322 n.30, 326 n.84
The Brothers Karamazov (Dostoevsky) 217
Browne, Harry 355
Brown, Eric C. 166 n.166
Browning, Elizabeth Barrett 126, 165 n.158
Browning, Tod 178
Bruckberger, R.L. 403
Brücke und Tor. Essays des Philosophen zur Geschichte, Religion, Kunst und Gesellschaft (Simmel) 79 n.35

Brückner, Jutta 491 n.92
Bruck, Reinhard 58, 61, 164 n.142
Brüderchen und Schwesterchen/Brother and Sister (1953) 378, 419 n.173
Brühl, Daniel 529, 571 n.94
Brühl, Heidi 420 n.195
Brüning, Heinrich 198
Brussig, Thomas 506, 527, 552, 579 n.182
Bruun, Cajus Zeuthen 43
Brynych, Zbynek 484 n.15
Buch der Lieder/Book of Songs (Heine) 382
The Buchenwald Child. Truth, Fiction, and Propaganda (Niven) 442, 488 n.56
Buch, Franziska 239 n.164, 419 n.178, 567 n.50
Buchheim, Lothar-Günther 480, 485 n.32
Buchholz, Horst 385, 426 n.257, 563 n.16
Buchhorn, Martin 496 n.155
Büchner, Georg 5, 8 n.6, 106, 152, 344, 347–9, 440, 460, 478, 492 n.106, 552, 554
Buchowetzki, Dimitri 106, 163 n.117, 272 n.59, 280
Buck, Detlev 506, 512, 517, 566 n.49, 579 n.182
Buckwitz, Harry 440
Buddenbrooks (1923) 109–12, 152, 160 n.82, 212
Buddenbrooks (1959) 384
Buddenbrooks (2008) 519, 562 n.5, 572 n.100
Buddenbrooks (Mann) 108, 110, 112–13, 160 nn.80–1, 376, 500, 519
Budjuhn, Horst 382
Bulwer-Lytton, Edward 79 n.44
Bummerstedt, Christian 155
Bundesbürgschaften 364
Bürger, Gottfried August 53, 79–80 n.45
Bürger Schippel/Citizen Schippel (1913) 104
Burger, Thomas 8 n.4, 483 n.11
Burgess, Anthony 407 n.33
Burgess, Gordon 342, 408 n.48
Burgtheater (Vienna) 80 n.59
Burmester, Gustav 440, 462, 485 n.32
Busch, Ernst 245, 452
Busch, Wilhelm 90
Buscombe, Edward 485 n.30
The Business Affairs of Mr. Julius Caesar (Brecht) 494 n.129
Bussemer, Thymian 326 n.84
Byg, Barton 494 n.129

Cabal and Love 565 n.35
Cabale et Amour/Intrigue and Love (1911) 37
The Cabaret (Berlin) 227
Cadars, Pierre 328 n.118
Cahiers du cinéma magazine 495 n.140
Calmettes, André 37, 83 n.91
Calnek, Roy 119
Calvalcanti, Alberto 426 n.264
The Cambridge Companion to Literature on Screen (Cartmell & Whelehan) 29 n.4, 412 n.92
camera 14, 18, 20, 27, 43, 47, 49, 66, 70, 77, 93, 109, 122, 124, 151, 195, 228 n.5, 289, 461, 467, 558
  distance 16, 22, 42, 71, 73, 129, 147, 151, 219, 391
  kinematographic 15
  mobile 129, 147, 219, 256
  for twentieth-century cinema 52–3
  "unchained camera" technique 164 n.143, 257
Camera Obscura (2018) 498 n.198, 573 n.114
Campogalliani, Carlo 490 n.78
Canasta de cuentos mexicanos (1956) 411 n.75
Canby, Vincent 477, 498 n.193
Capellani, Albert 36
Čáp, František 368
capitalism 13, 105, 111, 126, 224, 243, 364, 448, 480, 522, 538
Capitol cinema (Berlin) 197, 210
Capra, Frank 423 n.222
Captain Fuoco/Captain Falcon (1958) 490 n.78

Capturing the German Eye: American Visual Propaganda in Occupied Germany (Goldstein) 405 n.9
Carlos und Elisabeth (1924) 114
Carl Peters (1940/1) 282
Carlsen, Fanny 125
Carl Zuckmayer (Schönfeld) 423 n.227
Carl Zuckmayer Albrecht Joseph: Briefwechsel 1922–1972 (Nickel) 240 n.181
Carrefour/Crossroads (1938) 268 n.5
Carr, Gilbert 191, 232 n.59, 234 n.78, 234 n.89, 234 n.93
Carrière, Jean-Claude 471
Carrière, Mathieu 453, 466, 531
Carter, Erica 84 n.113, 321 n.15, 322 n.16, 327 n.95, 404 n.4, 406 n.21, 415 n.128, 421 n.206, 425 n.249, 482 n.5, 497 n.183, 498 n.203, 554
Cartmell, Deborah 9 n.12, 29 n.4, 412 n.92
Cary, Diana Serra 212
Casablanca (1942) 253
Casa paterna/Paternal Home (1910) 78 n.30
The Case of Sergeant Grischa (1930) 203, 418 n.156
Caserini, Mario 36, 39, 77 n.28, 79 n.44
casino capitalism 243
Caspar, Horst 307, 309, 318, 342, 407 n.36
Caspari, Carlheinz 486 n.42
Castelao Producciones S.A. (Madrid) 576 n.151
Catalani, Alfredo 415 n.128
Caught (1949) 349
CCC-Film GmbH (Berlin) 392, 439
Celan, Paul 537
celebrities of theater 65–6
Cellier, Léon 30 n.20
Centum Opuscula (Feuchtwanger) 270 n.35, 270 n.37, 270 n.39
Cervantes, Miguel de 30 n.18
C-Films 514
Chabrol, Claude 438, 473
Chain of Desire (1992) 542
Chamisso, Adelbert von 51–3, 59, 64, 106

Chamsin (1970) 489 n.60
Chaney, Lon, Jr. 248
Chaplin, Charlie 113, 471
Charell, Erik 183
Charlie & Louise (1994) 566 n.50
Chartier-Bunzel, Andrea 268 n.12, 405 n.8
Chase, James Hadley 465
Chautard, Émile 78 n.30, 87 n.157
Cherchi Usai, Paolo 80 n.54
Children in Uniform (1932) 196
Children's and Household Tales (Grimm brothers) 378
children's film 157 n.22, 212, 373, 381, 441, 483 n.6
Chrisander, Nils 142
Christensen, Benjamin 131
Christensen, Carlos Hugo 349
Christiane F. (1981) 503
Christiane F.-Wir Kinder vom Bahnhof Zoo/Christiane F.-We Children from Zoo Station (Hermann & Rieck) 502–3
Christian Petzold (Fisher) 578 n.173
Christians, Mady 109
Christie, Ian 410 n.66
Christine (1958) 402
chronic dualism 143
Cinderella (1950) 378
Cineaste magazine 523, 578 n.174, 581 n.203
cinema 27, 33, 36, 38–9, 74, 101, 152, 171, 176, 337, 384, 447, 516, 542, 558–9
  art 4–6, 14, 36, 50, 53–5, 60, 89, 98, 172, 224, 344, 401, 432, 435, 454, 460, 480, 511, 522, 525, 548, 553, 561
  attraction 13–14, 20
  birth of 11, 17, 29, 450–4
  of consensus 383, 512–16
  corruption 25, 117
  as cultural rupture 24
  education 37, 60, 62, 144, 338
  entertainment 3, 11–12, 23–4, 27, 38, 58, 73, 94, 99, 152, 211, 338, 492 n.105, 512, 515, 525, 581 n.202

escapism 58, 211, 227, 277, 319, 338, 399, 451
high culture 23–5, 74, 96, 102, 106, 114, 130–1, 439
immoral 146, 203, 256, 354, 468
provocation 12, 95, 204, 262, 443
reform movement 33, 37
sensation 14, 20, 30 n.15, 50
as space of agitation ("Agitationsraum") 67, 256
spectacle 14, 114, 153, 233 n.67
technology and marketing 14, 17–18, 50, 63, 66, 131, 133
vaudeville 12
Cinema and Nation (Hjort & MacKenzie) 420 n.185, 563 n.11, 568 n.63
Cinema in Democratizing Germany (Fehrenbach) 405 n.5
Cinema 1: L'Image-Mouvement (Deleuze) 87 n.148
Cinema's Third Machine: German Writings on Film 1907–1933 (Hake) 79 n.40
Cinemate 514
Cinematographe 12, 15, 22
Cinépupitre 230 n.17
Cines-Film 101
Cineteca del Comune di Bologna 169 n.222
Clair, René 182–3, 215, 224, 230 n.29, 410 n.63
Clara Kimball Young Film Corporation 74
Clarissa (Zweig) 577 n.161
Clark, Anthony 270 n.29
Clarke, Clemy 577 n.161
Clarke, David 425 n.247, 482 n.5
Clarke, Donald 549, 577 n.168, 580 n.196
Clausen, Mathias 392
Cloak and Dagger (1946) 262
Coates, Paul 327 n.100, 328 n.104
Codelli, Lorenzo 80 n.54
Coe, Jonathan 573 n.116
Coetzee, J. M. 317, 331 n.148
Cohen, Robert 492 n.97
Cohl, Émile 35, 38
Colberg (Heyse) 317

The Cold Light of Day (1995) 575 n.141
Cold War 334, 373, 386, 395, 570 n.82
A Coleção Invisível/The Invisible Collection (2012) 577 n.161
Coleman, Nancy 352
Colette, Sidonie-Gabrielle 269 n.25
collaboration 63, 92, 108, 113, 153, 175–7, 211, 226, 254, 269 n.17, 286, 354, 367, 414 n.111, 456, 460, 493 n.119, 507, 509, 518–20, 544, 564 n.27, 571 n.93, 572 n.102, 582 n.209
Collier's Weekly magazine 355
Collin, Erich A. 283
Collodi, Carlo 581 n.201
Colorado Territory (1949) 348, 409 n.62
Columbia Pictures 480
Comedian Harmonists 283
comedies 33, 61, 66, 73, 85 n.125, 92, 117–18, 121, 134, 140, 153, 155, 181–3, 226–7, 248–9, 262, 271 n.44, 276–7, 297, 317, 323 n.42, 347, 352, 354, 362–3, 365–7, 369, 377, 380, 386, 394, 399, 401, 406 n.26, 419 nn.177–8, 430, 503–6, 512, 516, 521, 524, 581 n.199, 582 n.207
Comencini, Luigi 362
commercial cinema and public television 438–42, 472, 517, 525–6, 554, 556–7
commodification 13, 49–50, 154, 223
Commodities of Desire: The Prostitute in Modern German Literature (Schönfeld) 157 n.30
The Companion to Film Noir (Spicer & Hanson) 412 n.85, 413 n.95
A Companion to Nazi Germany (Baranowski) 482–3 n.5
competition 175–7, 226, 254, 285, 301, 338, 366, 376–80, 502, 507
Comrade X (1940) 398, 423 n.222
Conacher, Jean E. 538, 576 nn.147–9
The Concise Cinegraph: Encyclopaedia of German Cinema (Bock & Bergfelder) 424 n.229

Concorde Filmverleih 514
The Condemnation of Faust (1903) 21
Conflit/Conflict (1938) 411 n.76
conglomerates and consensus cinema 512–16
Congress of Vienna 1
Constantin Film Produktion GmbH (Munich) 487, 490 n.75, 502–9, 518, 520, 527, 539, 564 n.21, 565 n.32, 576 n.151, 582 n.209
consumerism 477, 532
   eager 463
contemporaneity 6, 453–4, 471, 522, 525, 545, 550, 555–6, 581 n.205
contemporary plays and prose 39–41, 92–3, 173, 225, 479
continuity 20, 73, 219, 277, 321 n.13, 366, 432
Contraband (1940) 253
Conway, Jack 353
Cook, David A. 15, 24, 30 n.11, 30 n.13, 30 nn.15–17, 31 n.22, 31 n.25, 32 n.36
Cooke, Maeve 580 n.195
Cooke, Paul 404 n.4, 405 n.12, 406 n.18, 422 n.206, 425 n.247, 579 n.182
Cooper, Gary 199
Cooper, James Fenimore 491 n.81
Coppélia ou La Fille aux yeux d'émail (1870) 26
Coppélia ou la Poupée animée/ Coppélia or the Animated Puppet (Méliès) 26–7
copyright law 21, 34, 511, 526–7
Cordula (1950) 408 n.52
Corinna Schmidt (1951) 381
Cormican, Muriel 579 n.182
Cornils, Ingo 484 n.21
Correll, Ernst Hugo 189
Corrigan, Timothy 29 n.4, 32 n.42, 34, 76 n.10, 76 n.18, 170 n.230, 173, 223, 242 n.210, 242 n.213, 324 n.46, 450, 491 n.83
Costa-Gavras, Constantin 529, 536
A Country Doctor/カフカ 田舎医者 (2007) 540

Courtade, Francis 320 n.10, 328 n.118
Courths-Mahler, Hedwig 156 n.7, 486 n.44
Covid-19 pandemic 520–1, 526–7, 551, 556, 559
Craciun, Iona 83 n.92
Crafton, Donald 76 n.15, 166 nn.182–3, 237 n.144
Crain, Jeanne 354
Crainquebille (1922) 141
Cramer, Sofie 581 n.202
Crane, Cheryl 490 n.78
Crawford, Joan 195, 208
Creative Europe MEDIA programmein Bruxelles 520
Crede-mi (1997) 556
Creed, Barbara 168 n.201
Cremer, Fritz 452
Cremers, Hans Josef 307
Crepúsculo (2017) 577 n.161
Crescendo 514
Crevenna, Alfredo 352
A Critical History of German Film (Brockmann) 166 n.182, 229 n.15, 230 n.24, 234 n.93, 406 n.21, 418 n.155, 488 n.53, 488 n.58
Critical Models: Interventions and Catchwords (Adorno) 580 n.187
Cronin, Bernadette 242 n.205, 324 n.45
Crosland, Alan 171
Cross, Donna Woolfolk 503
Crowther, Bosley 357, 385, 409 n.61, 412 n.93, 420 n.190, 421 n.197
Cruise, Tom 534
The Cry of the Children (1912) 126, 128
Cserépy, Arzén von 296
Cuban Missile Crisis 439
Cube, Irma (Irmgard) von 187, 245
Cukor, George 353
Cullum, Charles 271 n.40
cultural capital 28, 32 n.44, 114, 508
cultural consumption 36

Cultural History through a National Socialist Lens. Essays on the Cinema of Nazi Germany (Reimer) 320–1 n.10, 322 n.26
cultural intervention 4, 284, 449, 488 n.53
cultural palimpsest 12, 34
Cultural Revolution 538
culture 1–2, 4, 6, 12, 57, 75, 106, 210, 249, 251, 266–7, 277, 293, 319, 333, 334, 343, 351, 370, 376, 381, 432, 438, 457, 459, 472, 526, 528, 553, 559–60, 574 n.123. *See also* high culture
  and capitalism 13
  commodification of 13
  memory 3, 334–5, 357, 370, 382, 443, 459, 464, 529, 554, 560
  national heritage 59–61
  rehabilitation 334
Curjel, Hans 293
Curtis, Tony 258
Curtiz, Michael 43, 177, 214
Cusack, Dick 485 n.28
Cusack, John 485 n.28
Cut Off (2018) 514
Cyankali/Cyanide (1930) 254
Cyankali/Cyanide (Wolf) 184–5, 246
Cyankali von Friedrich Wolf. Eine Dokumentation (Wolf & Hammer) 231 n.50
Cycowski, Roman 283
Czinner, Paul 149–51, 245, 410 n.66

Dadaism 213
Dafco (Danish-American Films-Corporation) 113
Dafoe, Willem 545
Dagover, Lil 285, 307, 382
daguerreotype 497 n.177
Dahlke, Günther 159 n.67, 269 n.16
Dahlke, Karl 236 n.125
Dahlke, Paul 307
Daldry, Stephen 518, 529
Dall'Asta, Monica 31 n.31
Dalliance (Stoppard) 81 n.59
Damek, Dagmar 519

Dammann, Friedrich 196
Dampfnudelblues/Steamed Dumpling Blues (2013) 520, 572 n.105
Dane, Clemence 254
Danforth, Emily M. 235 n.107
Dangel-Pelloquin, Elsbeth 76 n.13
Danish Film Institute 81 n.68, 169 n.222
Dantons Tod/Danton's Death (1920) 106
Dantons Tod/Danton's Death (Büchner) 106
d'Arc, Jeanne 77 n.28
"daring more democracy" slogan 432
Dark Angel (1934) 352
Dark Journey (1937) 253
The Dark Mirror. German Cinema between Hitler and Hollywood (Koepnick) 320 n.7
Dark Romanticism 51, 141–2
Darrieux, Danielle 248, 349, 411 n.70
Darstellungen von Film in literarischen Fiktionen der zwanziger und dreißiger Jahre (Rutz) 232 nn.54–5, 232 nn.57–8
Daruga, Gitty 423 n.229
Das Abenteuer der Sybille Brant/The Adventure of Sybille Brant (1925) 164 n.135
Das Abenteuer der Sylvester-Nacht/The New Year's Eve Adventure (Hoffmann) 52, 64
Das andere Leben/The Other Life (1948) 362
Das Beil von Wandsbek/The Axe of Wandsbek (1951) 371, 374–5
Das Beil von Wandsbek/The Axe of Wandsbek (Zweig) 374–5
Das Blaue Buch. Geheimes Kriegstagebuch 1941–1945/The Blue Book. Secret War Diary (Kästner) 406 n.26
Das Boot ist voll/The Boat is Full (1980) 449
Das Boot/The Boat (1981) 456, 480, 484 n.20, 485 n.32, 486 n.45, 493 n.111, 503, 563 n.11, 566 n.46, 574 n.123

Das Boot/The Boat (Buchheim) 480, 485 n.32
Das Brandmal/Branded (Hennings) 575 n.134
Das Brot der frühen Jahre/The Bread of Those Early Years (1962) 450, 463
Das Brot der frühen Jahre/The Bread of Those Early Years (Böll) 404, 450, 462, 494 n.127
Das Cabinet des Dr. Caligari/The Cabinet of Dr. Caligari (1920) 35, 55, 61, 78 n.28, 104, 131, 135, 142, 150, 172, 253, 324 n.48, 481
Das doppelte Lottchen/Two Times Lottie (1950) 373, 379
Das doppelte Lottchen/Two Times Lottie (1993) 567 n.53
Das doppelte Lottchen/Two Times Lottie (2007) 419 n.178, 567 n.50
Das doppelte Lottchen/Two Times Lottie (Kästner) 373, 486 n.43, 579 n.180
Das Dorf in der Heimat/The Village in the Homeland (1956) 381
Das eiserne Kreuz/The Iron Cross (1914) 61
Das Fenster zum Flur/Her Most Beautiful Day (Flatow) 447
Das fliegende Klassenzimmer/The Flying Classroom (1954) 379
Das fliegende Klassenzimmer/The Flying Classroom (1973) 441, 486 n.43, 492 n.99
Das fliegende Klassenzimmer/The Flying Classroom (2003) 419 n.178, 567 n.50
Das fliegende Klassenzimmer/The Flying Classroom (Kästner) 492 n.99
Das Fräulein von Barnhelm (1940) 317, 321 n.11
Das Fräulein von Scuderi (Hoffmann) 79 n.44
Das fremde Mädchen/The Foreign Girl (Hofmannsthal) 40

Das Geheimnis einer Ehe/The Secret of a Marriage (1951) 368
Das gelbe Haus/The Yellow House (1919) 95, 165 n.147, 190
Das Gelübde/The Vow (2007) 513
Das Gespenst/The Ghost (1982) 479
Das Glück meiner Schwester/My Sister's Good Fortune (1995) 522
Das Halstuch/The Scarf (1962) 439
Das Haus ohne Lachen/The House without Laughter (1923) 108
Das Haus zur roten Laterne/Red Lantern House (1928) 120
Das hohe Lied/The Song of Songs (1914) 74, 163 n.117
Das hohe Lied/The Song of Songs (1933) 163 n.117, 259, 280
Das hohe Lied/The Song of Songs (Sudermann) 74, 163 n.117, 259, 272 n.59, 280
Das indische Grabmal/The Indian Tomb (1959) 82 n.73
Das indische Grabmal/The Indian Tomb (Harbou) 43, 82 n.73, 381
Das Jahr des Herrn/Der Wallnerbub (Waggerl) 408 n.52
Das kalte Herz/The Cold Heart (1950) 373, 376–7
Das kalte Licht (1955) 424 n.229, 424 n.239
Das kalte Licht/The Cold Light (Zuckmayer) 424 n.229, 424 n.239
Das Kino als Ideologiefabrik (Kreimeier) 327 nn.85–6
Das kleine Fernsehspiel (1963) 451, 455, 491 n.92, 497 n.169, 519
Das kleine Gespenst (1992) 561 n.51, 567 n.51, 579 n.180
Das kleine Gespenst/The Little Ghost (Preußler) 551, 561 n.51
Das kunstseidene Mädchen/The Artificial Silk Girl (Keun) 403
Das Leben der Anderen/The Lives of Others (2006) 501, 528
Das Leben des Galilei/The Life of Galilei (1938) 6–7, 440

Das Liebesglück der Blinden/Blind Lover's Happiness (1910) 97
Das Lied von Bernadette/The Song of Bernadette (Werfel) 264
Das Mädchen aus der Ackerstraße/The Girl from Ackerstreet (1920) 92, 105–6
Das Mädchen Johanna/The Girl Johanna (1935) 295, 306
Das Mädchen Manuela/The Girl Manuela (Winsloe) 197, 235 n.101
Das Mädchen mit dem Goldhelm/The Girl with the Golden Helmet (1919) 157 n.23
Das Mädchen mit dem Goldhelm/The Girl with the Golden Helmet (Land) 157 n.23
Das Mädchen Rosemarie/A Girl Called Rosemary (1996) 502, 563 n.16, 564 n.24
Das Mädchen Rosemarie/Rosemary (1958) 400, 563 n.16
Das Menschlein Matthias/The Little Human Matthias (1941) 571 n.96
Das Menschlein Matthias/The Little Human Matthias (Ilg) 571 n.96
Das Motiv des Doppelgängers als Spaltungsphantasie in der Literatur und im Stummfilm (Bär) 268 n.2
Das Nibelungenbuch (Harbou) 161 n.98
Das Nürnbergische Ei/The Egg from Nuremberg (1913) 327 n.92
Das Parfum. Die Geschichte eines Mörders/Perfume: The Story of a Murderer (2006) 503, 509, 518, 525, 539
Das Parfum. Die Geschichte eines Mörders/Perfume: The Story of a Murderer (Süskind) 501, 503, 509
Das politische Theater (Piscator) 165 n.159
Das Pubertier (Weiler) 562 n.6
Das Pubertier-Der Film (2017) 509, 562 n.6
Das Ringen um den Tonfilm. Strategien der Elektro- und der Filmindustrie in den 20er und 30er Jahren (Mühl-Benninghaus) 230 n.28, 235 nn.109–11
Das Schauspiel meines Lebens (Krauß) 66
Das Schloß/The Castle (1968) 483 n.15
Das Schloss/The Castle (1997) 484 n.15, 519
Das Schloss/The Castle (Kafka) 213, 483 n.15, 519
Das schöne Abenteuer (1932) 323 n.42
Das schreckliche Mädchen/The Nasty Girl (1990) 528
Das Schweigen im Walde/Silence in the Woods (1955) 368, 416 n.129
Das Schweigen im Walde/Silence in the Woods (Ganghofer) 368, 416 n.129
Das Sexualleben unserer Zeit/Sexual Life in our Time (Bloch) 86 n.141
Das siebte Kreuz. See The Seventh Cross (1944)
Das siebte Kreuz/The Seventh Cross (Seghers) 263, 359
Das Siegel Gottes/God's Seal (1949) 368
Das Siegel Gottes (Rosegger) 362
Das singende, klingende Bäumchen/The Singing Tree (1957) 419 n.175
Das Spukschloß im Spessart/The Haunted Castle (1960) 377–8
Das tapfere Schneiderlein/The Valiant Little Tailor (1941) 300
Das tapfere Schneiderlein/The Valiant Little Tailor (1956) 419 n.175
Das Testament des Dr. Mabuse (1933) 216, 247, 328 n.111
Das Totenschiff. Die Geschichte eines amerikanischen Seemanns/ The Death Ship. The Story of an American Sailor (Traven) 426 n.257

Das Ufa-Buch (Bock & Töteberg) 83 n.104, 84 n.110, 84 nn.112–13, 229 n.14
Das unsterbliche Herz/The Immortal Heart (1939) 312, 327 n.92
"*Das verlorene Paradies*"/Paradise Lost (Berger) 130
Das Versprechen: Requiem auf den Kriminalroman/The Pledge: Requiem for the Detective Novel (Dürrenmatt) 534–5, 563 n.16
Das wandernde Licht/The Wandering Light (1916) 61
Das Weib als Verbrecherin und Prostituirte [sic] (Lombroso & Ferrero) 71, 168 n.214
Das Widmann'sche Faustbuch/ Widmann's Faustbook (1599) 26
Das Wirtshaus im Spessart/The Spessart Inn (1957) 377
Das Wunder von Bern/The Miracle of Bern (2003) 402, 510
Das Zaubermännchen/Rumpelstiltskin (1960) 419 n.175
The Daughter of Evil (1930) 177
Davidson, John 404 n.4, 406 n.17, 406 n.20, 415 n.120, 418 n.151, 427 n.271
Davidson, Paul 40, 57, 82 n.78
Davis, Sammy, Jr. 491 n.86
A Day Well Spent (1835) 413 n.107
D.A.Z. 220
D-Day 438
DDM (Djibril Diop Mambéty) 531–2, 575 n.137
Dea-Film 108
Death of a Salesman (1985) 465
Death of a Salesman (Miller) 465, 541
death of cinema 480, 524
The Death of Empedocles (Hölderlin) 494 n.129
The Death of Julius Cesar (1907) 30 n.18
de Bruyn, Günter 483 n.6
Decarli, Bruno 61
Decker, Christof 72, 87 nn.151–2
Decla-Bioscop 130, 161 n.99, 166 n.167, 230 n.22

Decla-Ufa 114
DEFA at the Crossroads of East German and International Film Culture (Silberman & Wrage) 415 n.122, 418 n.158, 419 n.170, 488 nn.51–2
DEFA. East German cinema, 1946–1992 (Allan & Sandford) 418 n.157, 482 n.5, 488 n.52
Defoe, Daniel 30 n.18
Degenhardt, Franz Josef 486 n.45
Degeto Film 520
Deines Bruders Weib/Your Brother's Wife (1921) 156 n.7
Deines Bruders Weib/Your Brother's Wife (Courths-Mahler) 156 n.7
de Jaeger, C. T. 405 n.7
Dekobra, Maurice 269 n.25
Delacommune, Charles 230 n.17
De la division du travail social (Durkheim) 231 n.47
Deleuze, Gilles 71, 87 n.148, 499, 561 n.1
Delouche, Dominique 411 n.70
Delschaft, Maly 124, 270 n.40
del Toro, Guillermo 581 n.201
Demandowsky, Ewald von 322 n.17
demilitarization 155 n.2, 386
de Mille, Cecil B. 78 n.28
Demir perde/The Iron Curtain (1951) 359
Demnig, Gunter 555, 580 n.192
de Musset, Alfred 51
Denk, Rudolf 81 n.65
Denman, Mariatte C. 394, 424 n.232, 424 nn.234–7
Denmark 34, 36, 38, 56, 73, 78 n.30, 95, 244
  Nordisk 41
  practice and process 47
  solitaires 5, 529
Den okända/The Unknown (1913) 40
Denzer, Kurt 325 n.57
de Palma, Brian 195
Deppe, Hans 214, 262, 275, 286–8, 290–2, 325 n.56, 366–7, 415 n.123, 415 n.126, 422 n.218
de Putti, Lya 124–5, 187

Der absolute Film (1924/25) 76 n.16
Der Affe als Mensch/The Monkey as Man (Hauff) 377
Der alte Fritz/Old Fritz (1937) 296
Der Andere/The Other (1913) 40, 51, 142
Der Andere/The Other (Lindau) 40
Der Apfel ist ab/The Original Sin (1948) 347, 407 n.35
Der Arzt von Stalingrad/The Doctor of Stalingrad (1958) 365, 426 n.262
Der Arzt von Stalingrad/The Doctor of Stalingrad (Konsalik) 365, 426 n.262
Der Aufenthalt (Kant) 446, 486 n.45
Der Aufenthalt/The Turning Point (1983) 446, 486 n.45
Der Aufstand der Fischer von St. Barbara/Revolt of the Fishermen of Santa Barbara (1988) 256–7, 445
Der Aufstand der Fischer von St. Barbara/Revolt of the Fishermen of Santa Barbara (Seghers) 256–7, 445
Der Augenzeuge 347, 409 n.57
Der Baader Meinhof Komplex (2008) 503, 516, 564 n.26, 574 n.132
Der Bankkrach unter den Linden/The Bank Crash of Unter den Linden (1926) 164 n.135
Der Bauer als Millionär/The Peasant as a Millionaire (1961) 362
Der Bau/The Burrow (Kafka) 488 n.57, 540
Der belagerte Tempel/The Besieged Temple (Harbou) 161 n.98
Der Besuch der alten Dame/The Visit (1982) 571 n.96
Der Besuch der alten Dame/The Visit (2008) 580 n.190
Der Besuch der alten Dame/The Visit (Dürrenmatt) 435, 531, 580 n.190
Der bewegte Mann (König) 503
Der bewegte Mann/The Most Desired Man (1994) 501, 503

Der Biberpelz/The Beaver Coat (1937) 420 n.186
Der Biberpelz/The Beaver Coat (1962) 440
Der Blaue/The Blue One (1994) 563 n.8
Der blaue Engel/The Blue Angel (1930) 3, 125, 187–97, 216, 225, 242 n.218, 281, 305, 413 n.102, 425 n.245, 477
Der böse Geist Lumpaci Vagabundus (1922) 106–7
Der böse Geist Lumpazivagabundus (Nestroy) 38, 106, 228 n.4, 249
Der brennende Acker/Burning Soil (1922) 135, 171
Der Campus (Schwanitz) 508
Der Cornet/The Cornet (1955) 397
Der deutsche Buchhandel und der Siegeszug der Kinematographie 1895–1933 (Lange) 156 nn.8–9
Der deutsche Hinkemann (Toller) 56
Der Doppelselbstmord/Double Suicide (1918) 367
Der Dummkopf/The Blockhead (1921) 92
Der Edelweißkönig/Edelweissking (1957) 416 n.129
Der Eid des Stephan Huller/The Oath of Stephan Huller (Hollaender) 92, 122, 165 n.145
Der Erlkönig/The Erlking (Goethe) 60
Der Erwählte/The Holy Sinner (Mann) 556
Der ewige Jude/The Eternal Jew (1940) 312–13, 330 n.142
Der Fall Collini/The Collini Case (2019) 506, 514, 555
Der Fall Collini/The Collini Case (von Schirach) 506, 555
Der Fall Maurizius (Wassermann) 410 n.64
Der Fall Ö (1991) 562 n.7
Der Fall Remarque: Im Westen nichts Neues, eine Dokumentation (Schrader) 237 n.136
Der Fangschuss/Coup de Grâce (1976) 465

Der Film als Ware (Bächlin) 230 n.28
Der Film journal 67, 84 n.110, 315
Der Filmminister: Goebbels und der Film im Dritten Reich (Moeller) 321 n.15, 329 n.121
Der Findling/The Foundling (Kleist) 455, 492 n.106
Der Fischer und seine Frau/The Fisherman and His Wife (Brothers Grimm) 506
Der Flüchtling/The Refugee 363
Der Fragebogen (Salomon) 422 n.210
Der Friedhof der Lebenden/Cemetery of the Living (1921) 108
Der fröhliche Weinberg/The Merry Vineyard (1952) 216, 394
Der fröhliche Weinberg/The Merry Vineyard (1961) 424 n.229, 424 n.239
Der fröhliche Weinberg/The Merry Vineyard (Zuckmayer) 216, 394, 424 n.229, 424 n.239
Der Froschkönig/The Frog Prince (1954) 378
Der Fuchs von Glenarvon/The Fox of Glenarvon (1940) 302–3, 412 n.81
Der Fuchs von Glenarvon/The Fox of Glenarvon (Rhon) 303
Der Fuchs war damals schon der Jäger (Müller) 575 n.135
"Der Gang nach dem Eisenhammer" (Schiller) 77 n.22
Der Gast/The Guest (1956) 380
Der Geigenmacher von Mittenwald/The Violinmaker of Mittenwald (1950) 416 n.129
Der Geisterseher/The Ghost-Seer (1987) 489 n.60
Der Geisterseher/The Ghost-Seer (Schiller) 63, 489 n.60
Der Geschmack von Apfelkernen/The Taste of Apple Seeds (Hagena) 519
Der gestiefelte Kater/Puss in Boots (1955) 378
Der geteilte Himmel/Divided Heaven (1964) 442, 481, 483 n.6

Der geteilte Himmel/Divided Heaven (Wolf) 442, 481, 483 n.6
Der Golem (1915, 1917 & 1920) 51, 85 n.120, 87 n.147, 135, 142, 172
Der Golem (Meyrink) 60
Der Götz von Berlichingen (1955) 416 n.131
Der Götz von Berlichingen (Goethe) 77 n.27, 416 n.131
Der große Bagarozy (1999) 504, 506
Der große Bagarozy (Krausser) 504
Der grüne Heinrich (Keller) 562 n.8
Der grüne Heinrich/Green Henry (1993) 562 n.8
Der Günstling von Schönbrunn/The Favorite of Schönbrunn (1929) 176
Der gute Mensch von Sezuan/The Good Person of Szechwan (Brecht) 552
"Der Handschuh"/The Glove (Schiller) 77 n.22
Der Hauptmann von Köpenick/The Captain from Köpenick (1931) 211, 216–18, 225, 240 n.180, 423 n.229
Der Hauptmann von Köpenick/The Captain from Köpenick (1956) 400, 423 n.229, 424 n.239
Der Hauptmann von Köpenick/The Captain from Köpenick (1997) 519
Der Hauptmann von Köpenick/The Captain from Köpenick (Zuckmayer) 211–12, 217, 240 n.180, 241 n.190, 400, 424 n.239, 482, 519
Der heilige Skarabäus/The Sacred Scarab (Jerusalem) 120, 144
Der Herrgottschnitzer vom Ammergau/The Carver of Ammergau (1952) 416 n.129
Der Herrscher/The Ruler (1937) 284, 297, 324
Der Himmel kennt keine Günstlinge/Heaven Has No Favorites (Remarque) 360

Der Irre/Insane (Heym) 481
Der Jagerloisl/Hunter-Loisl (1921) 369
Der Jäger von Fall/The Hunter of Fall (1954) 368, 416 n.129
Der Jäger von Fall/The Hunter of Fall (1974) 416 n.130
Der Jäger von Fall/The Hunter of Fall (Ganghofer) 368, 416 n.129
Der 20. Juli/The Plot to Assassinate Hitler (1955) 396, 426 n.255
Der junge Engländer/The Young Englishman (1958) 377
Der junge Törless/Young Törless (1966) 6, 453–4, 465–7
Der junge Törless/Young Törless (Musil) 6, 465–6
Der Katzensteg/The Cat's Bridge (1913) 78 n.30
Der Katzensteg/The Cat's Bridge (1915) 78 n.30
Der kaukasische Kreidekreis/The Caucasian Circle (1958) 402
Der kaukasische Kreidekreis/The Caucasian Circle (Brecht) 402
Der Kinematograph journal 40, 57, 62, 63, 80 nn.53–4, 85 n.129, 87 n.150, 101, 157 n.24, 189, 203
Der Kirchfeldpfarrer 367
Der kleine Friedländer/Little Friedländer (1956) 424 n.229, 424 n.239
Der kleine Häwelmann/Little Havelman (Storm) 381
Der kleine Muck. Ein Abenteuer aus 1001 Nacht/The Story of Little Muck (1953) 377
Der Klosterjäger/The Monastery's Hunter (1953) 416 n.129
Der Knabe des Tell/The Son of Tell (Gotthelf) 293
Der Kongreß tanzt/Congress Dances (1931) 183, 212
Der Laden/The Shop (1983–92) 557
Der letzte Akt/The Last Act (1955) 359
Der letzte Mann/The Last Laugh (1924) 135, 151, 156 n.15, 164 n.143, 187, 324 n.48

Der letzte Weynfeldt/The Last Weynfeldt (2010) 508
Der letzte Zeuge: Ich war Hitlers Telefonist, Kurier und Leibwächter (Misch) 320 n.3
Der Löwe von Babylon/En las ruínas de Babilonia/The Lion of Babylon (1959) 403
Der Major und die Stiere/The Major and the Bulls (1955) 365
Der Major und die Stiere/The Major and the Bulls (Venatier) 365, 414 n.118
Der Mann auf der Mauer/The Man on the Wall (1982) 494 n.120, 579 n.182
Der Mann mit den sieben Masken/The Man with Seven Masks (1918) 85 n.125
Der Mann ohne Eigenschaften/The Man without Qualities (Musil) 213
Der Mann ohne Vaterland/The Man without a Country (Brockdorff) 328 n.109
Der Mauerspringer/The Wall Jumper (Schneider) 494 n.120, 579 n.182
Der Maulkorb/The Muzzle (Spoerl) 306, 426 n.256
Der Meineidbauer/The Perjuring Farmer (1915) 61, 367
Der Mörder Dimitri Karamasoff/The Murderer Dimitri Karamazov (1930) 217
Der mutige Seefahrer/The Courageous Mariner (1926) 262
Der Mythus des 20. Jahrhunderts/The Myth of the twentieth Century (Rosenberg) 292
Der namenlose Tag/Nameless Day (Ani) 494 n.133
Der nasse Fisch/The Wet Fish (Kutscher) 520
Der Pakt mit dem Teufel/The Pact with the Devil (1949) 410 n.63
Der Patriot (Neumann) 233 n.63
Der Pfarrer vom Kirchfeld/The Priest of Kirchfeld (1955) 367, 425 n.255

Der Pfarrer von Kirchfeld/The Priest of Kirchfeld (Anzengruber) 61, 367
Der Präsident (Franzos) 95
Der Prozess/The Trial (Kafka) 434–5, 483 n.15
Der Rat der Götter/The Council of the Gods (1950) 420 n.193
Der Rattenfänger von Hameln/The Pied Piper of Hamelin (1918) 84 n.113
Der Räuber Hotzenplotz/The Robber Hotzenplotz (1974) 487 n.50
Der Räuber Hotzenplotz/The Robber Hotzenplotz (2006) 567 n.51
Der Räuber Hotzenplotz/The Robber Hotzenplotz (Preußler) 441, 487 n.50, 567 n.51
Der Richter und sein Henker/The Judge and His Hangman (Dürrenmatt) 562 n.8
Der Ring des Nibelungen/The Ring of the Nibelung (1848–74) 115
Der Rosenkavalier/The Knight of the Rose (1960) 410 n.66
Der Rubin-Salamander/The Red Salamander (1918) 85 n.125
Der Sandmann/The Sandman (Hoffmann) 26, 32 n.39, 94, 143, 562 n.8
Der Schäfer vom Trutzberg/The Shepherd of Trutzberg (1958) 416 n.129
Der Schandfleck/The Stain of Shame (1999) 571 n.97
Der Schandfleck/The Stain of Shame (Anzengruber) 367, 571 n.97
Der Schatz der Sierra Madre/The Treasure of the Sierra Madre (1948) 351
Der Schatz der Sierra Madre/The Treasure of the Sierra Madre (Traven) 351
Der Schatz im Silbersee/Treasure of the Silver Lake (1962) 447
Der Scheingemahl/Pretend Husband (Courths-Mahler) 486 n.44
Der Schimmelreiter/Rider on a White Horse/The Dike Master (1934) 275, 284–8, 292

Der Schimmelreiter/The Rider on the White Horse (1978) 458
Der Schimmelreiter/The Rider on the White Horse (Storm) 275, 284–6, 324, 458
Der Schinderhannes (1958) 424 n.239
Der Schinderhannes (Zuckmayer) 424 n.239
Der Schritt vom Wege/The False Step (1938/9) 303, 305, 382
Der Seelenbräu (1950) 394
Der Seelenbräu (Zuckmayer) 363–4, 394
Der Spiegel 230 n.26, 339, 346, 361, 370, 391, 398, 407 n.35, 408 n.49, 408 n.53, 417 nn.138–9, 425 n.248, 425 nn.250–1, 433, 457, 479, 493 n.113, 495 n.143, 505, 508, 516, 569 n.79
Der Stechlin (Fontane) 496 n.163
Der Stellvertreter/The Deputy (1963) 536
Der Streit um den Sergeanten Grischa/The Case of Sergeant Grischa (Zweig) 203, 374
Der Struwwelpeter/Shaggy Peter (Hoffmann) 378
Der Student von Prag/The Student of Prague (1913) 40, 51–3, 129, 142–3
Der Student von Prag/The Student of Prague (1926) 254
Der Student von Prag/The Student of Prague (1935) 410 n.64
Der Student von Prag/The Student of Prague (Ewers) 40, 142, 410 n.64
Der stumme Gast/The Silent Guest (1945) 275
Der Sturz der Menschheit. Die Memoiren des Satans/The Fall of Man. Satan's Memoirs (1918) 58
Der Tangospieler/The Tango Player (1990) 562 n.7
Der Tangospieler/The Tango Player (Hein) 562 n.7
Der Tanz ins Dunkel/Dancing into Dark (Berber) 165 n.146

Der Teufel mit den drei goldenen Haaren/The Devil with Three Golden Hairs (1955) 378
Der Teufel nebenan/The Devil Next Door (Kaus) 411–12 n.79
Der Teufelskreis/Vicious Circle (1956) 417 n.140
Der Trafikant/The Tobacconist (2018) 555
Der Trafikant/The Tobacconist (Seethaler) 555
Der Tunnel/The Tunnel (1933) 306, 320 n.5
Der Tunnel The Tunnel (Kellermann) 53–5, 83 n.97, 181, 253, 320 n.5, 417 n.143
Der Turm/The Tower (2012) 562 n.5
Der Turm/The Tower (Tellkamp) 500, 577 n.164
Der Tyrann/The Tyrant (Jacques) 307
Der Überläufer/The Defector (2020) 570 n.82
Der Unhold/The Ogre (1996) 465
Der Untergang/Downfall (2004) 503, 510, 528
Der Untertan/The Loyal Subject (1951) 371–3
Der Untertan/The Loyal Subject (Mann) 120, 189, 281, 370–1
Der Ursprung der Syphilis/The Cause of Syphilis (Bloch) 86 n.141
Der Ursprung des Kunstwerks/The Origin of the Work of Art (Heidegger) 516
Der Vater eines Mörders/The Father of a Murderer (1987) 486 n.42
Der Vater eines Mörders/The Father of a Murderer (Andersch) 486 n.42
Der Verdacht/Suspicion (1990) 562 n.7
Der verkaufte Großvater/Grandfather for Sale (1942) 277
Der Verlorene/The Lost One (1951) 426 n.255
Der verlorene Engel/The Lost Angel (1966) 483 n.6
Der verlorene Schatten/The Lost Shadow (1921) 106
Der verlorene Schuh/The Lost Shoe (1923) 130

Der Verschwender/The Spendthrift (Raimund) 362
Der veruntreute Himmel/Embezzled Heaven (1958) 361
Der veruntreute Himmel/Embezzled Heaven (Werfel) 361
Der verwandelte Komödiant/The Transformed Comedian (1992) 577 n.161
Der Vorleser/The Reader (2008) 518, 530, 556, 571 n.93
Der Vorleser/The Reader (Schlink) 529
Der Wald ist voller Wölfe/The Forest is Full of Wolves (1977) 493 n.114
Der wandernde Blumentopf/The Wandering Flower Pot (1916) 61
Der Weg zur Hölle/The Road to Hell (1906) 190
Der Weg zurück/The Road Back (Remarque) 261
Der Weibsteufel/Devil Woman (1914) 346
Der weißblaue Löwe/The White-Blue Lion (1952) 416 n.132
Der Wildschütz von Tirol/Bergkristall/Mountain Crystal (1949) 362
Der Wolf und die sieben Geißlein/The Wolf and the Seven Young Goats (1957) 378, 419 n.173
Der Zauberberg/The Magic Mountain (1982) 492 n.99
Der Zauberberg/The Magic Mountain (Mann) 213, 479, 492 n.99
Der zerbrochene Krug/The Broken Jug (1808) 297
Der zerbrochene Krug/The Broken Jug (1937) 298, 324 n.48
Der Zimmerspringbrunnen (2001) 509
Der Zimmerspringbrunnen (Sparschuh) 509
Der Zwerg im Kopf (1991) 567 n.53
Der Zwerg im Kopf (Nöstlinger) 567 n.53
De Sano, Marcel 238 n.145
The Desert Fox (1951) 389
Desire Me (1947) 353
Des Lebens Überfluss/Life's Luxuries (Tieck) 346
Despair (Nabokov) 496 n.165

Despair-Eine Reise ins Licht (1978) 496 n.165
des Pallières, Arnaud 8 n.6, 529, 544–5
Dessau, Maxim 562 n.7
Dessau, Paul 249, 251
destabilization 6, 13, 38, 67, 243, 247
Des Teufels General/The Devil's General (1954) 394, 396, 399
Des Teufels General/The Devil's General (Zuckmayer) 364, 387, 394–6, 399, 409 n.61
DeToth, Andre 354, 412 n.86
Detour: A Hollywood Story (Crane) 490 n.78
Dettmar, Ute 166 n.167, 419 n.176
Deutsche Bioskop AG 57, 161 n.99, 230 n.22
Deutsche Film Aktiengesellschaft/ Soviet zone (DEFA) 334, 364, 373–5, 377, 379, 381, 414 n.113, 417 n.140, 418 n.153, 418 n.161, 419 n.175, 485 n.35, 486 n.36, 500, 562 n.7
  adaptations 347–9
Deutsche Film Anstalt (DEFA) 432–3, 442, 445, 448, 478
Deutsche Film-Gemeinschaft GmbH (Berlin) 197
Deutsche Kinemathek (Berlin) 161 n.89, 237 n.132, 237 n.136, 324 nn.49–50
The Deutsche Lichtbild Gesellschaft (Deulig) 84 n.115
Deutscher Reichsanzeiger 282
Deutscher Fernsehfunk (DFF) 432, 442, 500, 529, 562 n.7
Deutscher Filmförderfonds (DFFF) 579 n.180
Deutsches Fernsehspiel (1968–79) 509, 566 n.46
Deutsches Filminstitut 83 n.94, 83 n.99, 562 n.4
Deutsche Spielfilme von den Anfängen bis 1933. Ein Filmführer (Dahlke & Karl) 159 n.67, 236 n.125, 269 n.16
Deutsches Schauspielhaus 366
Deutsches Theater (Berlin) 65–6, 122, 217, 488 n.57
Deutsche Tonfilm A.G. 175
Deutsche Tonfilme (Klaus) 232 n.58
Deutsche Universal 199
Deutsch, Helen 263
Deutschkunde und Kinodrama/ German Studies and Drama at the Cinema (1921) 106
Deutschland 83/Germany 83 556
Deutschland bleiche Mutter/Germany, Pale Mother (1980) 498 n.198
Deutschland, erwache!/Germany, Awake! (1968) 308
Deutschland im Herbst/Germany in Autumn (1977) 432, 493 n.114
Deutschnationale Volkspartei (DNVP) 168 n.204, 189
Deutschstunde/German Lesson (2019) 510, 516–18
Deutschstunde/German Lesson (Lenz) 496 n.163, 510, 516–18, 580 n.191
The Devil Is a Woman (1935) 195
de Vogt, Carl 270 n.40, 294
De Waber/*Die Weber*/The Weavers (Hauptmann) 35, 125–9
d'Hulst, Lieven 30 n.20
Dialektik der Aufklärung/Dialectic of Enlightenment (Adorno & Horkheimer) 166 n.170, 319
Dialogues of the Courtesans/Ἑταιρικοὶ Διάλογοι (Lucian of Samosata) 35
Diary of a Lost Girl (1918) 68–9, 165 n.147
Diary of a Lost Girl (1929) 169 n.219, 197, 235 n.100
Dickinson, Thorold 410 n.64
Dickson, William Kennedy 15, 172
Dida Ibsens Geschichte. Ein Finale zum Tagebuch einer Verlorenen (Böhme) 35, 67–9, 72, 86 n.140, 86 n.143
Dida Ibsens Geschichte/The Story of Dida Ibsen (1918) 70, 72, 103
Die Abenteuer des Prinzen Achmed/ The Adventures of Prince Ahmed

(1926) 157 n.22, 173, 228 n.5, 239 n.162
Die Abenteuer des Werner Holt/The Adventures of Werner Holt (Noll) 486 n.45
Die Alm an der Grenze/The Alpine Pasture on the Border (1951) 416 n.129
Die Angst des Tormanns vorm Elfmeter/The Goalie's Anxiety at the Penalty Kick (1972) 566 n.46
Die Angst des Tormanns vorm Elfmeter/The Goalie's Anxiety at the Penalty Kick (Handke) 493 n.119, 566 n.46
Die Apothekerin/The (female) Pharmacist (Noll) 509
Die Artisten in der Zirkuskuppel:Ratlos/ Artists in the Big Top: Perplexed (Kluge) 455
Die Augenoperation/Eye Surgery (Koch) 562 n.7
Die Befreiung der Schweiz 78 n.28
Die Bekenntnisse des Hochstaplers Felix Krull (2021) 385, 506
Die Bekenntnisse des Hochstaplers Felix Krull/Confessions of Felix Krull (Mann) 385, 506
Die Bettelprinzeß/Impoverished Princess (Courths-Mahler) 486 n.44
Die Beule/The Bump/The Bruise (1930) 222, 511
Die Biene Maja und ihre Abenteuer/ Bee Maja and her Adventures (Bonsels) 157 n.22
Diebitsch, Karl 290
Die bitteren Tränen der Petra von Kant (1972) 496 n.165
Die Blechtrommel/The Tin Drum (1979) 6, 456, 460, 470, 478, 492 n.99, 504
Die Blechtrommel/The Tin Drum (Grass) 433, 460, 465, 469–71, 492 n.99
Die Braut Nr. 68/Bride No. 68 (Bolt) 176

Die Braut von Messina (Schiller) 489 n.60
Die Bremer Stadtmusikanten/The Bremen Town Musicians (1959) 378, 419 n.173
Die Bremer Stadtmusikanten/The Bremen Town Musicians (Grimm brothers) 300, 419 n.173
Die Brücke/The Bridge (1959) 391–2, 399, 561 n.3, 580 n.194
Die Brüder Schellenberg/The Brothers Schellenberg (1926) 129
Die Brüder/The Brothers (Lindau) 85 n.125
Die Büchse der Pandora/Pandora's Box (1929) 145, 176, 195, 216, 222, 235 n.100, 254, 281, 466
Die Büchse der Pandora/Pandora's Box (Wedekind) 45, 58, 119, 125, 145–6
Die Bürgschaft/The Pledge (Schiller) 77 n.22, 77 n.28
Die Damalstür/The Back Door (Pirinçci) 552
Die Dekonstruktion des Bürgerlichen im Stummfilm der Weimarer Republik (Craciun) 83 n.92
Diederich, Helmut 80 n.54
Die deutschen Juden und der Spielfilm der NS-Zeit (Offermanns) 321 n.12
Die Dreigroschenoper/The Threepenny Opera (1931) 281
Die drei Mädels von der Tankstelle/ The Three Girls from the Petrol Station (1997) 564 n.24
Die drei Sprünge des Wang-lun/ The Three Leaps of Wang Lun (Döblin) 270 n.38
Die Drei von der Tankstelle/The Three from the Filling Station (1930) 181–2, 194, 216
Die Drei von der Tankstelle/The Three from the Filling Station (1955) 415 n.126
Die Drei von der Tankstelle/The Three from the Filling Station (1997) 564 n.24

Die Ehe der Maria Braun/The
   Marriage of Maria Braun (1979)
   477
Die Ehe des Herrn Mississippi/The
   Marriage of Mr. Mississippi
   (1950) 401
Die Ehre/Honor (Sudermann) 78 n.30
Die Entdeckung der Currywurst/
   Invention of the Curried Sausage
   (Timm) 515
Die Entstehung der Eidgenossenschaft/
   The Emergence of the
   Confederation (1924) 160 n.71
Die Ermittlung/The Investigation
   (Weiss) 451, 453, 456
Die Fälscher/The Counterfeiters (2007)
   528, 568 n.57
Die Fälschung/Circle of Deceit (1981)
   465
Die Fälschung/The Deception (Born) 465
Die Fastnachtsbeichte/Carnival
   Confession (1960) 423 n.229,
   424 n.239
Die Fastnachtsbeichte (Zuckmayer)
   423 n.229, 424 n.239
Die Feuerzangenbowle/The Fire-Tongs
   Bowl (Spoerl) 319
Die Fledermaus/The Bat (1944) 332
   n.163
Die Flut ist pünktlich/High Tide Is
   Dead on Time (2013) 569 n.82
Die Försterbuben/The Boys of the
   Forrester (1955) 368
Die Frau am Pranger/The Woman in
   the Pillory (1990) 562 n.7
Die Frau am Weg/Woman by the Road
   (1948) 363
Die Frau im Mond/Woman in the
   Moon (1929) 161 n.98
Die freudlose Gasse/Joyless Street
   (1925) 87 n.147, 103, 119,
   145–6, 159 n.63, 164 nn.135–7,
   168 n.206, 164 n.139, 164
   n.141, 216, 234 n.80, 466
Die freudlose Gasse/Joyless Street
   (Bettauer) 103, 119
Die fröhliche Wallfahrt/The Merry
   Pilgrimage (1956) 368

Die Gänsemagd/The Goose Girl
   (1957) 378
Die Geächteten/The Outlaws
   (Salomon) 422 n.210
Die Geierwally (1956) 368
Die Geier-Wally (von Hillern) 98, 367
Die Geier-Wally/The Vulture Wally
   (1921) 98
Die geliebten Schwestern/Beloved
   Sisters (2014) 513
Die Geschwister Oppermann/The
   Oppermanns (1983) 480, 489
   n.68
Die Gesichte der Simone Machard/
   The Visions of Simone Machard
   (Brecht) 426 n.264
Die Gezeichneten/The Stigmatized
   (1922) 119
Die Glocke/The Bell (Schiller) 77 n.21,
   106, 139
Die goldene Gans/The Golden Goose
   (1953) 378, 419 n.173
Die goldene Stadt/The Golden City
   (1942) 296, 332 n.163, 377
Die Gräfin von Rathenow/The
   Countess of Rathenow (1973)
   407 n.30
Die 3-Groschen-Oper (1931) 216,
   224, 225–6
*Die grüne Manuela-Ein Film aus dem
   Süden* (1923) 160 n.85
Die grüne Manuela/Green Manuela
   (Ratzka) 160 n.85
Die Halbstarken/Teenage Wolfpack
   (1996) 563 n.16, 564 n.24
Die Heilige und ihr Narr (Günther)
   365
Die Heilige und ihr Narr/The Saint and
   Her Fool (1957) 365
Die Heimkehr/Homecoming (1928)
   571 n.97, 580 n.198
Die Heimkehr/Homecoming (2012)
   571 n.97, 580 n.198
Die Heimkehr/Homecoming (Hesse)
   571 n.97, 580 n.198
Die Heinzelmännchen/The Shoemaker
   and the Elves (1956) 378,
   419 n.173

Diehl, August 514
Diehl, Karl Ludwig 303
Die Hose/The Pants (1927) 246
Die Hose/The Pants (Sternheim) 155, 246
Die humanistische Front: Einführung in die deutsche Emigranten-Literatur, vol. 1 (Berendsohn) 237 n.139
Die innere Sicherheit/The State I Am In (2000) 523
Die Insel magazine 100
Die Jungfrau von Orleans/The Maid of Orleans (Schiller) 295
Die Käserei in der Vehfreude/The Cheese-dairy in Vehfreude (1958) 413 n.104
Die Käserei in der Vehfreude/The Cheese-dairy in Vehfreude (Gotthelf) 413 n.104
Die Kinotechnik journal 143
Die Klavierspielerin/The Piano Teacher (Jelinek) 535
Die kleine Hexe/The Little Witch (2018) 567 n.51
Die kleinen Verwandten/Small Relatives (1961) 416 n.132
Die Konferenz der Tiere/Animal Conference (1969) 579 n.180
Die Konferenz der Tiere/Animals United (2010) 579 n.180
Die Konferenz der Tiere (Kästner) 579 n.180
Die Kriegsbraut/War Bride (Courths-Mahler) 486 n.44
Die Kunst zu heiraten/The Art of Marrying 85 n.125
Die Legende von Paul und Paula/The Legend of Paul and Paula (1973) 489 n.63
Die Leiden des jungen Werther/The Sorrows of Young Werther (1976) 489 n.70
Die Leiden des jungen Werther/The Sorrows of Young Werther (Goethe) 29 n.3, 77 n.27, 251, 267, 342, 489 n.70, 500, 552, 562 n.5

Die Letzte am Schafott/Last on the Scaffold (1960) 403
Die Letzte am Schafott/Last on the Scaffold (Le Fort) 403
Die letzte Station/The Last Station (1956) 360
Die Leute von Seldwyla/The People of Seldwyla (Keller) 269 n.20
Die Lichtbild-Bühne journal 38, 55–6, 62, 83 n.98, 83 n.101, 92, 101, 118, 156 n.17, 159 n.52, 220, 230 n.30
Die Lokalbahn (1960) 416 n.132
Die Marquise von O./The Marquise of O. (1920) 106
Die Marquise von O./The Marquise of O. (1989) 407 n.30
Die Marquise von O./The Marquise of O. (Kleist) 106, 342, 407 n.30, 562 n.3
Die Martinsklause/The Cloister of St. Martin's (1951) 416 n.129
Die Martinsklause (Ganghofer) 416 n.129
Die Medaille/The Medal (1955) 416 n.132
Die Mehrfarbigkeit der Vergangenheit: István Szabós Adaptation von Klaus Manns Roman Mephisto (Lindeiner-Strásky) 484 n.19
Die Memoiren des Satans I: Dr. Mors (1917) 58
Die Memoiren des Satans II: Fanatiker des Lebens (1917) 58
Die Memoiren des Satans III: Der Fluchbeladene (1917/18) 58
Die Memoiren des Satans/Memoirs of Beelzebub (Hauff) 85 n.119, 87 n.156
Die missbrauchten Liebesbriefe/The Misused Love Letters (1940) 250
Die Mörder sind unter uns/Murderers among Us (1946) 342, 389, 413 n.94
Die Nachrichter (1935) 347

Die Nacht vor der Scheidung/The Night before the Divorce (1937) 271 n.44
Die neue Illustrierte magazine 388
Die neuen Leiden des jungen W./The New Sorrows of Young W. (Plenzdorf) 458
Die Nibelungen (1861) 114
Die Nibelungen (1924) 1, 80 n.45, 114–17, 153–4, 229 n.15, 233 n.67
Die Nibelungen (1966) 439
Die Nibelungen (2004) 562 n.5
Die Nibelungen. Ein deutscher Stummfilm (Hoppe) 8 n.1
Die Niederlande und das deutsche Exil 1933–1940 (Dittrich & Würzner) 268 n.6
Die Päpstin/Pope Joan (2009) 503
Die Päpstin/Pope Joan (Cross) 503
Die Pflasterkästen/The Plaster Boxes (Frey) 236 n.119
Die Physiker/The Physicists (1962) 486 n.45
Die Pilgerin/The Pilgrim (2013) 571 n.95
Die Privatsekretärin/The Private Secretary (1931) 182
Die Prostitution (Bloch) 86 n.141
Die Puppe/The Doll (1919) 66, 93–4, 545
Die Ratten/The Rats (1955) 383, 425 n.245
Die Rättin/The Rat (Grass) 496 n.155
Die Räuber/The Robbers (1982) 488 n.60
Die Räuber/The Robbers (Schiller) 36–7, 77 n.21, 78 n.28, 295, 307, 310–11, 329 n.124, 458–9, 488 n.60, 490 n.74, 577 n.162
Die Rebellion/Rebellion (1962) 446
Die Rebellion/Rebellion (Roth) 446
Die Reglementierung von Prostitution in Deutschland (Gleß) 158 n.31
Die Reise nach Tilsit/The Journey to Tilsit (1939) 321 n.11

Die Reise nach Tilsit/The Journey to Tilsit (Sudermann) 135–6, 301, 321 n.11, 436
Die Republik befiehlt (Lothar & Gottwald) 206, 238 n.145
Die Resonanz des Exils. Gelungene und mißlungene Rezeption deutschsprachiger Exilautoren (Sevin) 238 n.154
Die Rote/The Red One (Andersch) 440
Die rote Mütze/The Red Hat (1962) 440
Die rote Mütze/The Red Hat (Brockdorff) 328 n.109
Die Rothausgasse/The Green Alley (1928) 120, 144–5, 423 n.223
Die Rothschilds/The Rothschilds (1940) 313, 330 n.142
Die Sage von Wilhelm Tell/The Legend of William Tell 78 n.28
Die Schachnovelle/Chess Novella (1960) 400, 510–11
Die Schachnovelle/Chess Novella (2021) 510–11, 555
Die Schachnovelle/Chess Novella (Zweig) 400, 510–11, 555
Die Schauspielerin/The Actress (1988) 417 n.140
Die schöne Miss Lilian/Beautiful Ms Lilian (1920) 156 n.7
Die schönste Frau der Welt/The Most Beautiful Woman in the World (1924) 164 n.135
Die schwarze Limousine/The Black Sedan (Günther) 490 n.72
Die schwarze Spinne/The Black Spider (Gotthelf) 413 n.104
Die Schweiz und die Flüchtlinge 1933–1945/Switzerland and the Refugees (1967) 449
Die Schwestern Kleh/The Sisters Kleh (Kaus) 352
An diesen Abenden/On Those Evenings (1952) 404
Die Sieger/The Victors 85 n.125
Die Sklavenkarawane/Caravana de esclavos/Caravan of Slaves (1958) 403

Diesmal muß es Kaviar sein/This Time It Must Be Caviar (1961) 426 n.261
Die Söhne der Großen Bärin/The Sons of the Great (Female) Bear (1966) 448
Die Söhne der Großen Bärin/The Sons of the Great (Female) Bear (Welskopf-Henrich) 448
Die Soldaten/The Soldiers (1962) 440
Die Soldaten/The Soldiers (Lenz) 440
Diessl, Gustav 187
Die Stadt ohne Juden (Bettauer) 120, 164 n.135
Die Stadt ohne Juden/City without Jews (1924) 164 n.135
Die Strasse/The Street (1923) 145
Die Stunde der Wahrheit/The Hour of Truth 462
Die Sünderin/The Sinner (1951) 420 n.184
Die Tagebücher von Josef Goebbels (Fröhlich) 331 n.153
Die Tänze des Lasters, des Grauens und der Ekstase/Dances of Vice, Horror, and Ecstasy (Berber & Droste) 143, 168 n.202, 481
Die 1000 Augen des Dr Mabuse/The Thousand Eyes of Dr. Mabuse (1960) 328 n.111
Dieterle, Wilhelm/William 78 n.28, 83 n.100, 125, 368, 423 n.229
Dietl, Helmut 512, 528
Die Todesmühlen/Death Mills (1945) 336
Die tolle Lola/Fabulous/Crazy Lola (1954) 415 n.126
Die tolle Lola/Fabulous/Crazy Lola (1927) 190
Die Toten bleiben jung/The Dead Stay Young (1968) 445, 486 n.45
Die Toten bleiben jung/The Dead Stay Young (Seghers) 445, 486 n.45
Die Trapp Familie in Amerika (1958) 346
Die Trapp-Familie/The Trapp Family (1956) 415 n.120
Dietrich, Gerd 417 n.143

Dietrich, Marlene 3–4, 168 n.200, 187–8, 191, 193–5, 234 n.91, 234 n.93, 259, 280–1, 429–30, 487 n.47
Dietrich's Ghosts: The Sublime and the Beautiful in Third Reich Film (Carter) 327 n.95
Die Tür/The Door (2009) 552, 571 n.94
Die Unberatenen/The Unadvised (Valentin) 455
"Die Verbrechen der Wehrmacht"/The Crimes of the Wehrmacht 422 n.212
Die Verfilmung literarischer Werke (Estermann) 77 nn.22–3, 78 n.28, 78 n.30, 79 nn.33–4, 81 n.71, 159 n.56, 159 n.61
Die verlorene Ehre der Katharina Blum oder: Wie Gewalt entstehen und wohin sie führen kann (Böll) 462, 465, 467–9, 495 n.143
Die verlorene Ehre der Katharina Blum/The Lost Honor of Katharina Blum (1975) 462, 465, 469
Die Vermessung der Welt/Measuring the World (2012) 506
Die Vermessung der Welt/Measuring the World (Kehlmann) 506
Die Verschwörung des Fiesco zu Genua (1986) 106, 489 n.60
Die Verschwörung zu Genua/The Conspiracy in Genoa (1921) 106
Die verschwundene Miniatur/The Lost Miniature (1954) 419 n.177
Die verschwundene Miniatur/The Lost Miniature (1989) 486 n.43
Die Verwandlung/Metamorphosis (1975) 484 n.15
Die Verwirrungen des Zöglings Törleß/The Confusions of Young Törless (Musil) 453
Die vierzig Tage des Musa Dagh/The Forty Days of Musa Dagh (Werfel) 273 n.72
Die Waffen nieder!/Down with the Weapons! (Suttner) 55

628   INDEX

Die Wahlverwandtschaften/Elective Affinities (Goethe) 533
Die Wahrheit der technischen Welt (Kittler) 32 n.40, 82 n.84
Die Wand/The Wall (2012) 543–4
Die Wandlung/Transformation (Toller) 104
Die Weber/The Weavers (1927) 125–8, 256
Die Weise von Liebe und Tod des Cornets Christoph Rilke/The Love and Death of Cornet Christopher Rilke (Rilke) 397
Die weiße Hölle von Piz Palü/The White Hell of Pitz Palu (1929) 287
Die weiße Massai/The White Massai (2005) 509–10
Die weiße Massai/The White Massai (Hofmann) 509–10
Die weißen Blätter magazine 60
Die Welt von gestern/The World of Yesterday (1942) 349, 545, 576 n.160
Die wilden Hühner/Wild Chickens (2006) 566 n.49
Die wilden Hühner und das Leben/Wild Chickens and Life (2007) 566 n.49
Die wilden Hühner und die Liebe/Wild Chickens and Love (2009) 566 n.49
Die wilden Kerle/The Wild Soccer Bunch (2003) 566 n.49
Die Wilde Ursula/Wild Ursula (1917) 156 n.7
Die Wolke/The Cloud (2006) 571 n.94, 580 n.190
Die Zeit newspaper 373, 451, 454, 471, 493 n.114, 521, 524, 582 n.211
Diezel, Peter 271 n.50
digital technology 496 n.155
D III 88 (1939) 307
Diller, D. H. 307
Dillmann, Claudia 425 n.242
Dinesen, Marie 43
Dinesen, Robert 43

Diplomatie/Diplomacy (2013) 465
Dirks, Tim 412 n.84
Dirnentragödie/Tragedy of the Street/of the Prostitute (1927) 145
Discipline and Punish (Foucault) 497 n.174
Dishonoured (1931) 195
Dismantling the Dream Factory (Baer) 407 n.38, 407 nn.31–3, 408 n.41, 408 nn.43–4, 408 n.48, 408 n.50, 409 n.54
"distinguished motion picture" 357
Dittrich, Katinka 268 n.6
Divina-Film company (Munich) 382
Divine (1935) 269 n.25
Django Unchained (2012) 1
Dmytryk, Edward 413 n.102, 425 n.245
Doane 168 n.213, 234 n.79
Doane, Mary Anne 146, 168 nn.210–11, 269 n.24
Döblin, Alfred 75, 87 n.159, 211, 213–15, 230 n.25, 231 n.35, 239 n.167, 240 n.171, 246, 262, 270 n.38, 274 n.76, 371, 460, 472, 477–8, 496 n.163, 498 n.189, 510, 517, 550–1, 558
Döblin, Hugo 176
Dockhorn, Katharina 569 n.80, 576 n.148
Doctorow, E. L. 437
Dodow, Slatan 222
Döge, Ulrich 229 n.5
Dogville (2003) 222
Doktor Faustus (1982) 479, 492 n.99
Doktor Faustus (Mann) 479, 492 n.99
Domin, Hilde 536
Domröse, Angelica 444, 446
Donahue, Neil H. 323 n.31
Don Camillo and Peppone (Guareschi) 363
Don Carlos (1910) 37
Don Carlos (1957) 414 n.108
Don Carlos (Schiller) 36–7, 197, 414 n.108, 488 n.60, 546
Don Carlos, Infant von Spanien (1963) 488 n.60
Donisthorpe, Wordsworth 15

Don Juan diplomático (1931) 238 n.145
Don Karlos (1960) 416 n.131
Donner, Wolf 454–6, 492 nn.101–2, 492 n.104
Donovan, Siobhan 575 n.140
Don Quichotte (Cervantes) 30 n.18
Doppelgänger 27, 51–3, 82 n.86, 129, 142–3, 154, 167 n.196, 169 n.226
The Doppelgänger: Double Visions in German Literature (Webber) 167 n.196
Dorell, Alice 246
Dörfler, Ferdinand 368
Dorfmeister, Manfred 391
Dorian Gray (Wilde) 51
Dor, Milo 567 n.55
Dornröschen/Sleeping Beauty (1955) 378
Dörrie, Doris 431, 505–6, 512, 565 n.34
Dorst, Tankred 402, 440, 567 n.55
Dostoevsky, Fyodor 82 n.86, 141, 217
doubles. *See Doppelgänger*
The Double/Двойник (Dostoevsky) 82 n.86
Douglas, Kirk 427 n.270
Douglas, Lloyd C. 421 n.204
Dove, Richard 236 n.119
Dovzhenko, Alexander 466
Doyle, Arthur Conan 61–2
Drachenreiter/Dragon Rider (2020) 566 n.49
Drachenreiter (Funke) 568 n.57
Dracula (1931) 178, 231 n.32
Drake, William A. 238 n.150
Draußen vor der Tür/The Man Outside (1957) 402
Draußen vor der Tür/The Man Outside (Borchert) 342, 344, 402, 408 n.46
DreamWorks 516
Dreher, Eduard 507
Dreigroschenoper/Threepenny Opera (1928) 211, 221–6, 245, 491 n.86, 511
Dreigroschenoper/Threepenny Opera (1931) 221–5, 242 n.215, 281

Drei Haselnüsse für Aschenbrödel/Three Wishes for Cinderella (1973) 444
Drei Kameraden/Three Comrades (Remarque) 262, 355
Drei Männer im Schnee/Three Men in the Snow (1955) 419 n.177
Drei Männer im Schnee/Three Men in the Snow (1974) 486 n.43
Drei Masken Verlag 317
Dreiser, Theodor 268 n.10
Drei, von denen man spricht/Three, Being Talked About (1953) 414 n.110
Dresen, Andreas 487 n.50, 504, 538–9, 548, 576 nn.148–9
Drewniak, Boguslaw 406 nn.22–3
Dreyer, Carl Theodor 55, 94–5, 101, 119
Dreyfus (1930) 178, 273 n.71
Dr. Fausts großer und gewaltiger Höllenzwang (Faust) 26
The Drift: Affect, Adaptation, and New Perspectives on Fidelity (Hodgkins) 271 n.48
Dr. Mabuse, der Spieler/Dr. Mabuse, the Gambler (1922) 115–16, 152, 171–2, 328 n.111, 490 n.78
Dr. Mabuses letztes Spiel/Dr. Mabuse's Last Game (Jacques) 247
Dr. med. Hiob Prätorius (1934) 353
Drössler, Stefan 160 n.73
Droste, Sebastian 143, 168 n.202, 168 n.203, 481
Dubson, Michail 236 n.125
Du Contrat Social/The Social Contract (Rousseau) 251
Duday, Bruno 326 n.80
Dudow, Slatan 254, 371, 417 n.144
Düggelin, Werner 413 n.104
Dukes, Ashley 233 n.63
Dulac, Max 367
Dumas, Alexandre 504
Duncan, Isadora 44
Dünnebeil (Hauptmann) 167 n.193
Dunne, Philip 421 n.204

Dupont, Ewald André 67, 98, 122–5, 143, 160 n.85, 164 n.143, 165 n.153, 175, 217, 272 n.60, 467
Durand, Jean 37
Duras, Marguerite 450
Durbridge, Francis 439
Durch Liebe erlöst/Redeemed by Love (Courths-Mahler) 156 n.7
Durinok, Manfred 441
Durkheim, Émile 231 n.47
Durrani, Osman 484 n.21
Dürrenmatt, Friedrich 401–2, 435, 440, 486 n.45, 529, 531–2, 534–5, 562 n.8, 567 n.55, 571 n.96, 580 n.190
Du sollst nicht töten/You Shalt Not Kill (1957) 380
Düsterberg, Rolf 414 n.118
Duve, Freimut 479
Duvivier, Julien 403
Dwan, Allan 362
Dworsky, Rudolf 253, 293
Dziuba, Helmut 360

Early Cinema: From Factory Gate to Dream Factory (Popple & Kember) 30 n.14
early cinema, reception 11, 16, 24, 29, 75 n.4, 141
East and the Federal Republic of Germany (FRG) 334
East German Cinema (Heiduschke) 418 n.157, 418 n.160, 418 n.163, 490 n.80
East German Film and the Holocaust (Ward) 417 n.142
East-West rivalries and collaborative endeavors 446–9
Ebermayer, Erich 194
Ebinger, Blandine 232 n.60
Ebner-Eschenbach, Marie von 96–8, 158 nn.32–3, 278
Eckard, Max 348
Eckermann, Johann Peter 30 n.19
Eckstein, Franz 156 n.7
Eco, Umberto 503
Eddy, Beverly Driver 272 n.63
Edel, Uli 503, 516, 562 n.5, 574 n.132

The Edge of Heaven (2007) 546
Edgerton, Gary R 8 n.3
Edison Manufacturing Company 31 n.26
Edison motion pictures 1890–1900 (Musser) 31 n.26
Edison, Thomas A. 13, 15–16, 20, 31 n.26, 40
Edwards, Kyle 8 n.3
Effi Briest (1971) 444–5, 473, 509, 541–2
Effi Briest (1974) 382, 445, 460, 472–4, 477
Effi Briest (2009) 509, 541–2
Effi Briest (Fontane) 303–6, 327 n.98, 327 n.101, 381–3, 444, 475, 477, 509, 541
Effi Briest Handbuch (Neuhaus) 420 n.183
Effis Nacht/Effi's Night (1998) 575 n.144
Egénieff, Franz 109
Eggeling, Viking 76 n.16
Egger, Urs 563 n.16
Ehe im Schatten/Marriage in the Shadows (1948) 417 n.137
Ehmann, Karl 164 n.135
Ehmck, Gustav 487 n.50
Ehre, Ida 452
Eichberg, Richard 82 n.73, 160 n.71, 164 n.135, 190
Eichendorff, Joseph von 458–9
Eich, Günter 440
Eichinger, Bernd 490 n.75, 499, 501–9, 516, 563 n.16, 564 n.24, 564 n.26, 564 n.28, 565 n.32, 567 n.52, 576 n.151
Eichmann trial (1961–2) 429, 433, 490 n.72, 492 n.95
Eidinger, Lars 582 n.209
Eigler, Friedericke 426 n.258
Eikke, Anne 489 n.60
Eiko-Film 57
Eilert, Bernd 568 n.58
Ein Brudermord/Fratricide (1967) 483 n.15
Eine Jugend in Deutschland/A Youth in Germany (Toller) 271 n.43

Eine Liebe in Deutschland/A Love in Germany (1983) 575 n.144
Eine Liebesgeschichte/A Love Story (1953/54) 394
Eine Liebe von Swann/Swann in Love (1984) 465
Eine lustige Geschichte aus einer Spielzeugschachtel/A Funny Story from a Toy Box (Willner) 93
Einen Jux will er sich machen/He'll Have Himself a Good Time (1958) 362
Einen Jux will er sich machen/He'll Have Himself a Good Time (Nestroy) 413 n.107
Eine ungeliebte Frau/A Woman Unloved (Courths-Mahler) 486 n.44
Eine von uns/One of Us (1931) 187
Einfeld, Charles 354
Ein fliehendes Pferd (Walser) 486 n.42, 516
Ein fliehendes Pferd/Runnaway Horse (1986) 486 n.42
Ein fliehendes Pferd/Runnaway Horse (2007) 516
Ein ganzes Leben/A Whole Life (2014) 519
Ein Kapitel für sich/A Chapter in Itself (1979) 496 n.163
Ein Landarzt/A Country Doctor (1917/19) 540
Ein Mädchen aus Flandern/The Girl from Flanders (1956) 423 n.229, 424 n.239
Ein Mädchen aus Flandern/The Girl from Flanders (Zuckmayer) 423 n.229, 424 n.239
Einmal keine Sorgen haben/No Worries for Once (1953) 362
Einrauch, Volker 541
Einsamkeit und Sex und Mitleid/Loneliness, Sex and Empathy (2017) 564 n.27
Ein Schritt vom Wege/One Step from the Path (Wichert) 305, 327 n.97
Einstein, Albert 268 n.10

Ein wunderbarer Sommer/A Wonderful Summer (1958) 570 n.85
Ein Zwilling ist nicht genug/One Twin is not Enough (2004) 567 n.50
Eis, Egon 254
Eisenstein, Sergei 6, 108, 111, 119, 125–6, 128, 160 n.83, 196, 236 n.125
Eisner, Lotte H. 51, 83 nn.89–90, 83 n.93, 121, 124, 131, 145, 149, 162 n.106, 163 n.120, 166 n.171, 167 n.196, 168 n.207, 168 n.215, 169 n.218, 169 n.227, 197, 235 n.103, 235 n.105, 324 n.47
Eis, Otto 254
Ekman, Gösta 131–2
El ángel desnudo/The Naked Angel (1946) 349
Elementarteilchen/Atomised (2006) 564 n.26
El ingenioso hidalgo don Quijote de la Mancha (Cervantes) 30 n.18
Elisabeth (1955–7), Austrian Empress 361
Elliott, Kamilla 9 n.12
Elliot, T.S. 171
Élo Antigoné (1968) 575 n.144
Elsaesser, Thomas 8 n.2, 9 n.10, 14, 29 n.8, 30 n.10, 30 n.14, 75 n.3, 80 n.52, 82 n.78, 85 n.123, 131, 134, 165 n.149, 166 n.173, 166 n.181, 168 n.213, 242 n.209, 242 n.214, 242 n.221, 415 n.127, 491 n.92, 494 n.124, 494 n.131, 497 n.169, 497 n.179, 498 nn.190–1, 556, 560, 582 n.212
Elsaghe, Yahya 421 n.198
Elsässer, Lothar 483 n.15
Elsker hverandre/Love each other (1922) 119
Elsker hverandre/Love each other (Madelung) 119
Elskovsleg/Dalliance (Schnitzler) 41–2
Elvey, Maurice 181, 254, 351
Emile Cohl, Caricature, and Film (Crafton) 76 n.15

Emilia 519, 562 n.5
Emilia Galotti (1913) 78 n.29
Emilia Galotti (Lessing) 58, 379, 500, 530
Emil to tantei tachi/Emil and the Detectives (1956) 239 n.164
Emil und die Detektive. Drehbuch von Billy Wilder nach Erich Kästner zu Gerhard Lamprechts Film von 1931 (Belach) 239 n.163
Emil und die Detektive/Emil and the Detectives (1931) 212–13, 216, 323 n.42, 379
Emil und die Detektive/Emil and the Detectives (1935) 254
Emil und die Detektive/Emil and the Detectives (1954) 239 n.164, 379, 400
Emil und die Detektive/Emil and the Detectives (1964) 441
Emil und die Detektive/Emil and the Detectives (2001) 419 n.178, 567 n.50
Emil und die Detektive/Emil and the Detectives (Kästner) 212–13, 254, 419 n.178, 441
Emmas Glück/Emma's Bliss (2006) 518–20, 572 nn.103–4
Emmas Glück/Emma's Bliss (Schreiber) 518–20
Emmerich, Ursula 273 n.69
Encyclopedia of Urban Literary Studies (Tambling) 156 n.4, 498 n.192, 578 n.176
Ende einer Dienstfahrt/End of an Official Trip (1971) 462, 464
Ende, Michael 441, 487 n.48, 487 n.50, 510, 567 n.52
enemy culture 73
Engel, Christoph 419 n.175
Engel, Erich 282, 306, 377, 394, 452
Engel, Fritz 62
Engelke, Anke 566 n.49
Engell, John 411 n.72
Engel, Thomas 379
The English Faust Book (1592) 16
Engl, Joseph (Jo) 172, 174
enlightenment films 66, 94

Enterprise Studios 354, 357, 359
Entertaining the Third Reich: Illusions of Wholeness in Third Reich Cinema (Schulte-Sasse) 321 n.10, 330 n.132, 331 n.143
Epple, Kuno 440
Epstein, Jean 141
Erdbeben in Chile/Earthquake in Chile (1975) 440, 498 n.198
Erdbeben in Chile/Earthquake in Chile (Kleist) 58, 440, 498 n.198
Erdgeist/Earth Spirit (1895) 58, 119, 145
Erdgeist/Earth Spirit (1923) 145
Erfolg verblüffend/Astonishing Success 108
Erfurth, Ulrich 379
Erhardt, Gero 487 n.49
Erich Kästner und der Film (Tornow) 239 n.163, 406 n.26
Erika Mann. Eine Biographie (Lühe) 232 n.51
Eriksen, Erik 156 n.7
Erinnerungsräume (Assmann) 423 n.224
Er ist wieder da/He is Back (2015) 505
Er ist wieder da/He is Back (Vermes) 505
Erkau, André 567 n.54
Erläuterungen und Dokumente zu Alfred Döblin: Berlin Alexanderplatz (Sander) 239 nn.168–9, 240 nn.171–6
Erlkönigs Töchter/The Erlking's Daughters (1914) 60
Ernst Barlach. Das schlimme Jahr/Ernst Barlach. The Bad Year (Fühmann) 483 n.6
Ernst, Max, *graffage* process 7
Erpenbeck, Jenny 552
Ersatz/Substitution 101
Erster Verlust/First Loss (1990) 562 n.7
Er und Sie (He and She) journal 121
Erzähltext und Spielfilm (Schwab) 327 n.100, 489 n.62, 497 n.175
Es geschah am hellichten Tag/It Happened in Broad Daylight (1958) 534

Es geschah am hellichten Tag/It Happened in Broad Daylight/ The Pledge (1996) 563 n.16, 564 n.24
Es geschah am 20. Juli/It Happened on July 20 396
Eshed, Tomer 566 n.49, 568 n.57
es hilft nur gewalt, wo gewalt herrscht/ Where Violence rules, Only Violence Helps (Straub & Huillet) 462, 464
Es kommt ein Tag/A Day Will Come (1950) 387, 421 n.203
Es muß nicht immer Kaviar sein/It Can't Always Be Caviar (1961) 426 n.261
Esser, Peter 109
Estermann, Alfred 77 nn.22–3, 78 n.28, 78 n.30, 79 nn.33–4, 81 n.71, 159 n.56, 159 n.61
Es werde Licht!/There will be Light! (1917) 67–8, 71, 95, 423 n.223
ethics of similarity 73, 87 n.155
Eugen, Carl 308
eurhythmics 86 n.146
Europe 1, 3, 13–15, 21, 36, 41, 43, 49–50, 75, 77 n.18, 91, 153, 155, 176, 182–3, 188, 192–4, 223, 226–7, 243, 248, 303, 335, 338, 355–6, 439, 501, 534
  fascism 198–210, 252, 267
  history of migration 550
  National Socialism 267
European Cinema: Face to Face with Hollywood (Elsaesser) 8 n.2, 491 n.92
European Film Alliance (EFA) 113
European Film Fund 267
Everding, August 575 n.144
Every Man Dies Alone (USA) 528
"The Evil Darkroom"/*Eine bösartige Dunkelkammer* (Proskauer) 94
Evin, Semih 359, 413 n.96
Ewers, Hanns Heinz 33, 40, 51–3, 75 n.2, 81 n.70, 142, 154, 177, 179–80, 277, 296, 410 n.64
The Exile (1947) 349

exiles 2, 225, 238 n.150, 244, 246, 248–9, 343, 349, 351–2, 363, 370–1, 451, 537, 549, 581 n.202
  contemporary literature, and agitation 256–9
  historical novel to literature 252–5
  literary canon in French 250–2
  writers and films 393–8
exodus 245–9, 261, 432
Experiment Weimar. Eine Kulturgeschichte Deutschlands 1918–1933 (Becker) 54, 239 n.166
Exporting Entertainment (Thompson) 235 n.112
Expressionism 24, 35, 51, 55, 76 n.14, 131, 135–6, 151, 226, 543
Expressionist Film (Scheunemann) 82 n.86, 156 n.16, 167 n.195, 167 n.198
The Eye Is a Strong Seducer-Erich Maria Remarque and Film (Schneider) 412 n.91
Eyes Wide Shut (1999) 533–4, 556, 575 n.138
Eyes Wide Shut (Schnitzler) 534

Faber, Marion 158 n.50
Fabian oder Der Gang vor die Hunde/ Fabian-Going to the Dogs (1979) 486 n.43, 580 n.191
Fabian oder Der Gang vor die Hunde/ Fabian-Going to the Dogs (2021) 419 n.178, 511, 521, 555, 580 n.191
Fabian oder Der Gang vor die Hunde/ Fabian-Going to the Dogs (Kästner) 231 n.35, 419 n.178, 486 n.43, 511, 521, 555, 580 n.191
Fabrik der Offiziere (1960) 396
Fabrik der Offiziere (Kirst) 396–7
Facing Fascism and Confronting the Past (Frederiksen) 232 n.53
Fack ju Göhte (2013, 2015, 2017) 504–6
Faesi, Robert 250, 361
Fairbanks, Douglas, Jr. 349

Falkenberg, Claus 552
Falk, Rita 520, 571 n.95
Fallada, Hans 211, 259–61, 282, 323 n.36, 447, 496 n.163, 528, 567 n.55, 577 n.162
"fallen women" films 35, 58, 71, 95–7, 119, 131–2, 144, 147, 154, 191
Falsche Bewegung/Wrong Turn (1975) 457–8, 502, 566 n.46
Familie Benthin/Family Benthin (1950) 417 n.144
Famous Five/*Fünf Freunde* series (Blyton) 504
Famous Players-Lasky 74, 113
Fanck, Arnold 169 n.216
Fantasie- und Nachtstücke (Hoffmann) 29 n.3
Fantasmagorie (1907) 35
Färberböck, Max 509
Fares, Saskia 413 n.101
Farkas, Nicolas 214
Farnum, Dorothy 252
Farocki, Harun 522–3, 549
Farrell, Colin 581 n.206
Farssmann oder Zu Fuß in die Sackgasse/Farssmann or Walking to a Dead End (1991) 562 n.7
fascism 134, 155 n.2, 197–210, 252, 266–7, 355, 371, 374–5, 400, 404, 433–4, 467, 472, 480, 507, 511, 531, 545, 554, 556
Faßbender, Max 67
Fassbinder, Rainer Werner 2, 431, 438, 449, 451, 456, 459–60, 464–5, 471–9, 491 n.82, 493 n.111, 496 nn.164–5, 497 n.168, 497 n.172, 497 n.184, 497 n.187, 498 n.194, 499, 501, 560, 566 n.46
Fassbinder's Germany (Elsaesser) 498 n.191
Fatal Attraction (1987) 195
Fatal Woman (Quentin) 195
Faulstich, Werner 167 n.193
Fausak, Ingrid 452
Faust (1898) 20
Faust (1906) 24
Faust (1910) 37
Faust (1921) 228 n.4
Faust (1922) 228 n.4
Faust (1926) 129–34, 153, 174, 187, 216, 233 n.67, 324 n.48
Faust (1960) 366
Faust (2011) 542–3
Faust (folk tale) 13, 133
Faust (Gounod) 17, 28
Faust (music) 17
Faust and Marguerite (1900) 20–1
Faust aux enfers/Faust in hell (1903) 18–19, 21–2, 24
Fausten, D. Johann 26
Faust et Marguerite (1911) 37–8
Faust et Marguerite/Faust and Gretchen (1897) 18
Faust et Méphistophélès/Faust and Mephisto (1903) 21–4
Faust I (Goethe, 1808) 12–13, 16–17, 20–1, 24–5, 83 n.88, 85 n.119, 87 n.156, 129–34, 152, 165 n.164, 344, 366, 436, 542–3, 552, 577 n.162
Faust II (Goethe, 1832) 12–13, 16–17, 20–1, 24–5, 87 n.156, 129–34, 152, 166 n.177, 344, 366, 436, 542–3, 552, 577 n.162
Faust im Kino (Prodolliet) 31 n.35
Faust, Johann Georg 16
Faustrecht/Law of the Fist (1922) 164 n.135
Faustrecht/Law of the Fist (Bettauer) 164 n.135
Faust Symphony (1857) 17
Fechner, Eberhard 486 n.45, 496 n.163
Federal Agency for Civic Education 456
Federal Film Board (FFA) 456, 469, 566 n.47
Federal Republic of Germany (FRG) 334, 364, 381, 387, 391, 400–1, 422 n.209, 431–2, 440, 444, 454, 457, 459, 479, 482 n.3, 485 n.34, 489 n.64, 507
Fehér, Friedrich 77 n.21, 78 n.28, 78 n.29
Fehér, György 575 n.141
Fehervary, Helen 273 n.67
Fehrenbach, Heide 405 n.5

Feichtinger, Johannes 87 n.155
Feiler, Hertha 317
Fei Mu 367
Feinberg, Anat 270 n.33
Feinde/Enemies (1940) 414 n.111
Feinstein, Joshua 374, 418 n.159, 498 n.195
Fekete, Alfred 108, 160 n.82
Feld, Hans 220
Feldherrnhügel/Grandstand for General Staff (1953) 414 n.110
Feldmann, M. 412 n.88
Feldmann, Rötger 563 n.12
Felix Salten (Seibert & Blumesberger) 40, 272 n.63
Felmy, Hansjörg 386
Feme (1927) 160 n.72
femme fatale films 45, 58, 103, 136, 145, 154, 178, 195, 228, 301, 477
Femme Fatales (2002) 195
Femme Fatales (Doane) 234 n.79
Fendrich, Walter 463
Fengler, Michael 459
Fenner, Angelica 498 n.198, 522, 573 n.114
Ferdinand, Archduke Franz 55
Ferguson, Elsie 74
Ferrero, Gugliemo 71–2, 168 n.214
Fette Welt/Fat World (1998) 504
Fette Welt/Fat World (Krausser) 504
Feuchtgebiete/Wetlands (2013) 552
Feuchtwanger and Film 489 n.68
Feuchtwanger, Lion 4, 215, 238 n.150, 246, 252–3, 267, 270 n.30, 270 n.31, 270 nn.34–9, 281, 284, 295, 313–15, 317, 321 n.11, 329 nn.127–8, 330 n.140, 331 n.145, 331 n.149, 369, 371, 385, 445, 480, 498 n.201, 567 n.55
Feuchtwanger, Marta 215, 238 n.150, 314, 330 n.133
Feyder, Jacques 141
fidelity 7, 28, 140, 152, 306, 318, 412 n.92, 458, 560–1
Fiebiger, Georg 342
Fiedler, Corinna 81 n.71
Fiedler, Werner 328 n.105

Fiennes, Ralph 545
Fierda, Richard A. 232 n.59
Fiesco (Schiller) 562 n.6
Fiesko (1913) 78 n.28
film(s) 14, 81 n.70, 119, 240 n.178, 405 n.9. See also specific films
 actualité/actuality 16, 43, 239 n.170
 censorship 38–9, 49, 55, 57, 62, 90, 92, 94–5, 140, 145, 153, 185, 206, 252, 278–84, 373, 538
 commodity 3, 23, 43, 53–5, 172, 284
 cultural expression 14
 documentary 12, 43, 119, 123, 151, 172, 196, 214, 246, 257, 276, 287, 291, 308, 312, 336–7, 430, 452, 487 n.47, 538, 551
 early narrative film 12–13, 33
 effects/special effects 16, 20, 52, 66, 134, 135, 239 n.170, 436
 illusion 12, 20, 26–7, 127, 152
 and impact of censorship legislation 102–6
 and impact of war 55–9
 mainstream 13, 94, 499
 mass entertainment (*see* mass entertainment)
 moving *tableaux* 20
 narrative 7, 13–14, 108, 110, 129, 131, 133, 154, 215, 218, 260, 313, 391, 445, 490 n.79
 new medium 12–13, 16, 20–1, 23–5, 28, 34, 37–40, 60, 65, 73–4, 95, 108, 113, 127, 130
 reflective practice 24
 sensation 12, 14, 18, 20, 30 n.15, 50, 115, 213, 485 n.32
 short films 11–13, 17, 22, 30 n.18, 61, 212, 362, 462, 464, 472, 492 n.106, 540–1, 552, 577 n.161
 silent film 4, 11–12, 14, 21, 27–8, 30 nn.14–15, 41, 51, 56, 61, 73–4, 80, 90, 92–3, 102, 108, 131, 134, 139, 141–2, 152–3, 155, 160 n.72, 162 n.117, 171, 177, 188, 190, 201, 205, 224, 227–8, 230 n.26, 280, 285, 293, 367, 382

subsidies 516–21
technological innovation 46, 50, 52–3, 90, 101, 188
transcultural 2, 13, 531, 538, 547
world 18, 60, 115
Film and Memory in East Germany (Pinkert) 409 n.59
Film and the Arts in Symbiosis (Edgerton) 8 n.3
Filmaufbau GmbH (Göttingen) 343
Filmbewertungskammer 292
Filmemigration aus Nazideutschland/ Film-emigration from Nazi Germany (1975) 246
FilmFernsehFonds Bayern 506, 576 n.151
Filmförderungsanstalt (FFA) 454, 482 n.3, 496 n.152, 506, 516, 518, 529, 557, 568 n.57, 570 n.91, 581 nn.199–200, 582 nn.207–8
Filmförderungsgesetz/Film Subsidies Act 454, 517
Film in Deutschland (Hake) 160 n.75, 418 n.165, 489 nn.64–5
Filming Women in the Third Reich (Fox) 331 n.143
Filmkredit-Bank GmbH 281
Film Kurier 199, 203, 206, 215, 219, 230 nn.20–1, 231 n.36, 282, 300, 317, 322 n.25, 323 n.35
Film/Literature/Heritage: A Sight and Sound Reader (Vincendeau) 324 n.46
filmmakers/filmmaking 5, 27, 34, 37, 60, 73, 74, 78 n.29, 92, 97, 101, 105, 119, 152, 153, 172, 376, 431, 520, 527
  choice of cinematic realism 46–7
  as cinema of sensation 30 n.15
  Jewish 4, 204–5, 243–7, 250–1, 349
  modern 173
  pioneers of 11–16, 22, 24–5, 27–38, 30 n.15, 34, 36, 79 n.33, 86 n.146, 123, 508, 558
The Film Minister. Goebbels and the Cinema in the "Third Reich" (Moeller) 320 n.10, 321 n.15, 322 n.26

film noir 195, 412 n.86, 473, 478
Filmpaläste 36
Film Propaganda in Britain and Nazi Germany (Fox) 325 nn.61–2
Film Propaganda. Soviet Russia and Nazi Germany (Taylor) 321 n.10
Filmprüfstelle 283
The Films of Fritz Lang (Gunning) 163 n.121
Filmstiftung NRW (NRW Film Fund) 568 n.58
Filmtechnik journal 233 n.68
Film-Television-Agreement (FRG) 456
Film-Theater (Nollendorfplatz) 204
Film- und Medien Stiftung NRW (Düsseldorf) 520, 573 n.106
Filmwelt journal 189
Finger, Willy 106
Finler, Joel Waldo 135, 166 n.185
Finn, AJ 556
Finnan, Carmel 76 n.14
Finn, Huckleberry 546
First Austrian Republic 1
First Films of the Holocaust: Soviet Cinema and the Genocide of the Jews, 1938–1946 (Hicks) 272 n.55
First World War 1, 3, 34, 51, 54–6, 58–9, 69, 73–5, 77 n.28, 81 n.71, 84 n.108, 84 n.113, 85 n.119, 87 n.156, 87 n.158, 89–92, 94, 101, 113, 118, 120, 141, 142, 152, 172, 198, 200, 205, 216, 226, 228 n.3, 236 n.125, 243, 273 nn.71–2, 388, 394
Fischer, Erica 509
Fischer, Jens-Uwe 490 n.81
Fischer, Kurt Joachim 345
Fischer, Lothar 87 n.146
Fischer, Olf 416 n.132
Fischer, O. W. 363, 392
Fischer, Robert 496 n.162, 578 n.174
Fischinger, Oskar 76 n.16
Fisher, Jaimey 8 n.3, 404 n.4, 421 n.206, 427 n.271, 483 n.14, 501, 563 n.15, 564 n.19, 577–8 n.173, 577 n.166, 578 n.174
Fittko, Lisa 267

Fitzgerald, F. Scott 262
The Flames of Johannis (1916) 74, 78 n.30
Flamm, Fräulein 207
Flatow, Curth 447
Flaubert, Gustave 141, 277
Fleck, Jakob 102, 367
Fleck, Luise 102
Fleischack, Hermann 105
Fleischmann, Peter 455
Fleisser, Marieluise 402
Fleißer, Marieluise 472
Fleming, Victor 187, 298
Flesh and the Devil (1927) 228 n.4
Flohr, Lilly 106
Florath, Albert 214, 314–15
Flöten und Dolche/Flutes and Daggers (Mann) 79 n.38
Flüchtlinge/Refugees (1933) 283, 414 n.111
Flüchtlinge/Refugees (Menzel) 283
Fluchtpunkt Hollywood (Horak) 268 n.6, 268 n.8
Flügge, Manfred 232 n.60, 233 n.66, 233 n.71, 234 n.94, 323 n.33
Fock, Gorch (Johann Wilhelm Kinau) 105
Fodor, Ladislas 271 n.44
Fontane Effi Briest (1974) 472–7, 497 n.177, 497 n.185
Fontane, Theodor 4, 275, 278, 303–7, 327 n.101, 327 nn.97–8, 333, 381–3, 400, 444, 458, 478, 493 n.114, 496 n.163, 509, 541–2, 569 n.81
Forest-Film 175
Forman, Miloš 437
Forster, Rudolf 170 n.234, 224, 245, 285, 323 n.39
Forst, Willi 176, 363, 414 n.111
Forward, Gunner Asch! (Kirst) 422 n.207
Foucault, Michel 68, 86 n.144, 157 n.27, 497 n.174
Fouqué, Friedrich de la Motte 517, 525, 558–60, 562 n.8, 567 n.55
Fox Europe 248
Fox, Jo 325 n.61, 331 n.143

Fox, William 134–5
F.P.1 antwortet nicht/Floating Platform 1 Does Not Answer (1932) 248
F.P.1 antwortet nicht/Floating Platform 1 Does Not Answer (Siodmak) 248
Framing the Fifties: Cinema in a Divided Germany (Davidson & Hake) 406 n.20, 415 nn.120–1, 418 n.151, 419 n.172, 427 n.271
Framing the Past: The Historiography of German Cinema and Television (Murray Bruce & Wickham) 159 n.60
France 13, 24, 28, 34, 36–7, 56, 73, 77 n.27, 117, 173, 177, 206, 225, 236 n.123, 245–6, 248–51, 257–8, 334, 362, 384, 402, 404 n.3, 410 n.65, 437, 454, 529, 533, 535–6, 539, 542, 544–8
filmmakers in postwar 334
literary canon in French exile 250–1
Franchini, M. 8 n.6
Frank, Bruno 83 n.100, 293, 567 n.55
Frankenstein (1931) 177, 231 n.32, 244
Frankenstein (Shelley) 177, 178, 231 n.32, 244
Frankenstein Meets the Wolf Man (1943) 248
Frank, Ernst L. 206, 248
Frankfurter Illustrierte Zeitung 189
Frankfurter Rundschau newspaper 469
Frankfurter Zeitung newspaper 118, 133, 140, 176, 202, 210, 229 nn.6–7, 236 n.125
Frank, Leonhard 246, 282, 349, 353
Frank, Liesl 267
Franklin, James 494 n.124
Franklin, Sidney 272 n.63
Franz-Eberhofer-series 520
Franziska Linkerhand (Reimann) 483 n.6
Franzos, Karl Emil 94
Fraser, Brendan 566 n.49
Frauenarzt Dr. Prätorius (1950) 353–4

Frauensee (1958) 423 n.229, 424 n.239
Frauen unter Kontrolle: Prostitution und ihre staatliche Bekämpfung in Hamburg vom Ende des Kaiserreiches bis zu den Anfängen der Bundesrepublik (Freund-Widder) 158 n.31
Frau Holle-Das Märchen von Goldmarie und Pechmarie/ Mother Holle (1961) 419 n.173
*Frau Holle/*Mother Holle (Grimm brothers) 378, 419 n.173
*Frau Jenny Treibel/*Mrs Jenny Treibel (Fontane) 381
Fräulein Else (Schnitzler) 149–50, 153, 239 n.166, 349
Fredall, H. 81 n.71
Frederiksen, Elke P. 232 n.53
Frederiksen, Lily 43
Fredersdorf, Herbert 367, 378
freedom of expression 89, 370
  and adaptations 92–4
  freedom of speech 90
Freisler, Roland 425 n.246
Freitag, Hayo 567 n.53
French New Wave/*Nouvelle Vague* 435–6, 438, 449–51, 454, 462, 464, 466–7, 473, 478, 495 n.138, 495 n.140
French, Philip 167 n.186, 212, 239 n.165
French Revolution 63, 251, 356
Frenetic Films 514
Freud, Sigmund 18, 44, 141, 143–4, 167 n.191, 167 n.197, 169 n.226, 268 n.10, 392, 534
Freund, Karl 61, 77 n.21, 78 n.30, 92, 122–5, 129, 151, 155, 161 n.99, 164 n.143, 165 n.153, 467
Freund-Widder, Michaela 158 n.31
Frey, Alexander Moritz 236 n.119
Freydank, Jochen Alexander 540
Freytag, Gustav 124
Fridericus Rex (1918) 296
Friedell, Egon 38, 79 n.40
Friedmann-Frederich, Fritz 63
Friedmann, Régine Mihal 331 n.144
Friedrich, Caspar David 47
Friedrich, Ernst 92
Friedrich, Jörg 417 n.136, 565 n.40
Friedrich, Julia 268 n.6, 268 n.8
Friedrich Schiller-Der Triumph eines Genies/Friedrich Schiller. A Genius' Triumph (1940) 307–11, 407 n.36, 412 n.81
Frischknecht, Arthur 175
Frisch, Max 402, 440, 465, 484 n.15, 525, 547–8, 567 n.55, 572 n.102
Fritsche, Maria 405 n.9
Fritsch, Gunther von 414 n.109
Fritsch, Rudolf 287–8
Fritsch, Willy 181–2, 233 n.77
Fritz Kortner-Schauspieler und Regisseur (Völker) 240 n.181, 407 n.27
Fröbe, Gerd/Gert 392, 487 n.50, 491 n.86
Froelich, Carl 60, 164 n.135, 197, 296, 300
Froeschel, George 360
Fröhlich, Elke 331 n.153
Fröhlich, Gustav 144
Fröhlich, Rosa 190
Frøken Smillas fornemmelse for sne/ Miss Smilla's Feeling for Snow (1997) 503
Frøken Smillas fornemmelse for sne/ Miss Smilla's Feeling for Snow (Høeg) 503
Frölich, Margrit 247, 251, 268 n.12, 269 n.12, 269 n.21, 269 n.26, 269 n.28
From Caligari to California: Erich Pommer's Life in the International Film Wars (Hardt) 229 n.15, 232 n.62
From Caligari to Hitler: A Psychological History of the German Film (Kracauer) 134, 162 n.114, 164 n.144, 197
From Fidelity to History: Film Adaptations as Cultural Events in the Twentieth Century (Scholz) 484 n.18
From Here to Eternity (1953) 387, 389

From Here to Eternity (Jones) 387
Frommermann, Harry 283
Frowein, Kurt 322 n.17
Frühlings Erwachen/Spring Awakening (1929) 102, 120
Frühlings Erwachen/Spring Awakening (Wedekind) 102, 120
Frühstück mit Elefanten/Breakfast with Elephants (Neitzel) 557
Fry, Varian 267
Fuchsberger, Joachim 382, 387–8, 390
Fuchs, Jürgen 446
Fuglsang, Frederik 126
Fühmann, Franz 445, 446, 483 n.6, 562 n.7
Fuhrmann Henschel (Hauptmann) 384
Fuhrmann Henschel/Drayman Henschel (1956) 384
Fuhrmann, Susanne 491 n.88
Fulda, Ludwig 92, 156 n.13, 246
Fuld, Werner 83 n.97
Funck, Werner 160 n.70
Fun in a Chinese Laundry (Sternberg) 190, 233 n.74
Funke, Cornelia 510, 566 n.49, 568 n.57
Funke-Stern, Monika 491 n.92
Furcht. Das Gespräch der Tänzerinnen/ Fear. The Conversation of the Dancers (Hofmannsthal) 35
Furcht und Elend des Dritten Reiches/ Fear and Misery of the Third Reich (Brecht) 260
Füsilier Wipf/Fusilier Wipf (1938) 250
Füsilier Wipf/Fusilier Wipf (Faesi) 250
Füssli, Orell 271 n.43
Futurism 213

Gad, Urban 46, 78 n.30, 131
Gaines, Ernest J. 465
Gaines, Jane 31 n.31
Galeen, Henrik 51, 59–60, 142, 154, 177–9, 228 n.3, 254
Galen, Philip 69
Galeta, Robert 561 n.1
Galilei, Galileo 6
Gall, Corina 566 n.42
Gallico, Paul 570 n.85

Gallone, Carmine 176, 214, 410 n.63
Galouye, Daniel F. 472
Gance, Abel 230 n.17
Ganghofer, Ludwig 321 n.11, 321 n.13, 366, 368, 416 n.129, 451
Ganovenehre/A Scoundrel's Honor (1933) 247
Gansel, Dennis 487 n.48, 567 n.52
Gantenbein (Frisch) 572 n.102
Ganz, Bruno 514, 570 n.86
Garat, Henri 183
Garbo, Greta 87 n.147, 121, 208, 209
Garde, Axel 43
Garfield, John 354
Garland, Judy 298
Garncarz, Joseph 30 n.14, 238 n.149, 415 n.119, 415 n.120
Garnier, Katja von 504, 512
Garson, Greer 353
Gärtner, Adolf 78 n.30
Gary, Cohen 87 n.155
Gaslight (1940) 410 n.64
Gaspard-Huit, Pierre 403
A Gathering of Old Men (1987) 465
A Gathering of Old Men (Gaines) 465
Gaudreault, André 14, 29 n.9
Gaumont, Léon 22, 24–5
Gaus, Günter 306, 328 n.103
Gauß, Karl-Markus 121, 164 n.133
Gavaldón, Roberto 411 n.75
Gavin, John 359
Gay, John 221
Gaynor, Janet 137
Gay, Peter 234 n.99
Gebühr, Otto 106, 190, 296
Gedeck, Martina 514, 544, 576 n.156
Geduld, Harry M. 40, 80 nn.56–7, 161 n.92, 233 n.75
Gefängnis ohne Gitter/Prison without Bars (Kaus) 254
Gegen die Wand/Head-On (2004) 546
Geheimnis und Gewalt/Secret and Violence (Glaser) 522–3
Gehen, ging, gegangen/To go, went, gone (Erpenbeck) 552
Gehler, Fred 269 n.16
Gehrke, Ulrich 331 n.156
Geisler, Michael 231 n.35, 236 n.126

Geis, Rainer 378, 419 n.173
Geißendörfer, Hans Werner 479, 488 n.60, 492 n.99, 517, 562 n.8
Geissler, Luise 271 n.43
Gelähmte Schwingen (1956) 416 n.132
Gely, Cyril 465
Genée, Heidi 458, 493 n.114
Generation War (2012) 571 n.95
Generic Histories of German Cinema: Genre and Its Deviations (Fisher) 8 n.3, 483 n.14, 563 n.15, 564 n.19
Genet, Jean 496 n.165
Génin, Eugénie 15, 25
genocide 6, 258, 266, 273 n.72, 312–19, 366, 401, 429
Genschow, Fritz 298–9, 323 n.39, 378–9, 493 n.114
George, Götz 423 n.229
George, Heinrich 213, 214, 245, 295, 301, 307, 314–15, 318
Gérard de Nerval: L'homme et l'oeuvre (Cellier) 30 n.20
Geräuschmusik 214, 239 n.170
Gerhart Hauptmann (Leppmann) 158 n.45
Gerhart Hauptmann und der Film (Hoefert) 80 n.58
Gerichtet bei Nacht/Judged at Night (1960) 426 n.261
Gerlach, Arthur von 156 n.14, 285
German Arbeiter-Theater-Bund 231 n.50
The German Cinema Book (Bergfelder, Carter & Göktürk) 84 n.113, 231 n.41, 273 n.71, 321 n.13, 322 n.23, 332 n.164, 406 n.21, 415 n.119, 482 n.5, 490 n.81, 498 n.203, 573 n.111, 577 n.172, 580 n.188
German Cinema in the Age of Neoliberalism (Baer) 563 n.10
German Democratic Republic (GDR) 334, 364, 370–1, 374–5, 381, 399, 432, 449, 452, 478, 489 n.64, 500
  ideology and literary heritage 442–6

German Empire 38–9, 55, 61–2, 89–90, 196, 290, 320 n.9
German Expressionist Drama: Ernst Toller and Georg Kaiser (Benson) 273 n.66
German Film after Germany: Towards a Transnational Aesthetic (Halle) 570 n.84
German Film & Literature: Adaptations and Transformations (Rentschler) 8 n.3, 409 n.59
German League of Human Rights 236 n.125
German Legacies from the Weimar Era to the Present (Rentschler) 323 n.31
German Motion Picture Fund (Berlin) 520
German National Cinema (Hake) 30 n.11, 406 n.19, 406 n.21, 482 n.5, 483 n.13
German Pop Culture: How American Is It? (Mueller) 574 n.123
German Reich 1–2, 4, 13, 245, 261, 276, 307, 312
German Romanticism 47, 51, 59, 63, 66, 129, 143, 181, 525, 558–9, 560
German-Soviet trade agreement (1922) 165 n.156
Germany 1, 4–6, 13, 34–7, 39, 45, 54–7, 60–2, 73–4, 75 n.4, 77 n.28, 90, 95–7, 119–20, 134, 140, 153, 155, 173, 206, 226, 307, 333, 360–1, 432, 514, 520, 531, 533, 535–7, 538–9, 541–51
  literary prestige films 210–20
  other Germany/das andere Deutschland 243–67
  rubble films 338–41
  sound film experiments 174–5
  universal-appeal pictures 210–20
Gerron, Kurt 191, 221, 245–6
Gerson, Dora 246
Gerstenberger, Katharina 68, 86 n.143
Gerstenbräun, Martin 163 n.128
Gert, Valeska 121, 224, 245

Gesamtkunstwerk 73, 104
Geschichte des Films im Dritten Reich (Courtade) 320 n.10, 328 n.118
Geschichten aus der Steiermark/Tales from Styria (Rosegger) 368
Geschichten vom Franz/Stories of Franz (Nöstlinger) 519
Geschichten vom Kino (Kluge) 8 nn.4–5
Geschichte und Systematik der Psychologie (Schönpflug) 167 n.190
Geschichtsstille 523
Geschlossene Gesellschaft/Closed Society (1978) 481
Geschonneck, Erwin 374, 452
Geschonneck, Matti 510, 569 n.78, 572 n.98, 579 n.182
Geser, Guntram 164 n.131
Gespenster/Ghosts (2005) 523, 566 n.49
Gespensterjäger/Ghost Hunters-On Icy Trails (2015) 566 n.49
Gespensterjäger/Ghost Hunters-On Icy Trails (Funke) 566 n.49
Gestern und heute/Yesterday and Today (1931) 196
The Ghost Comes Home (1940) 262
Gibbons, Cedric 208
Giese, Erich 214
Giftgas über Berlin/Poison Gas over Berlin (1929) 236 n.125
Gigl, Claus 235 n.115, 236 n.123
Gigliotti, Donna 529, 571 n.93
Gilgamesh 2
Gilgi. Eine von uns/Gilgi, One of Us (Keun) 186–7, 232 n.54
Gillmann, Karl Peter 353
Giovanna d´Arco (1909) 77 n.28
Giraudoux, Jean 581 n.206
Gish, Lillian 132, 166 n.174
Gladysz, Thomas 86 n.143
Glaeser, Ernst 236 n.119
Glasenapp, Gabriele von 270 n.33
Glaser, Georg Karl 522
Glass, Max 250
Gleber, Klaus 271 n.48
Gleeson, Brendan 529
Gleichschaltung 278–80
Glenn, Leo 351
Glenville, Peter 360
Gleß, Sabine 158 n.31
Gliese, Rochus 85 n.120, 106, 135, 228 n.3, 347
global cultural community 229 n.5
Gloria-Filmverleih company 365, 409 n.55
"Glück"/Happiness/Luck (2012) 505
"Glück"/Happiness/Luck (von Schirach) 505
Glück, Wolfgang 574 n.132
Gmünden, Gerd 490 n.81
Godard, Jean-Luc 403, 438, 449, 472, 495 n.138
Goebbels, Joseph 116, 118, 162 n.113, 204, 217, 225, 242 n.217, 245, 247, 253, 275–6, 278–81, 283, 285, 291–3, 295–7, 303, 306–8, 314–15, 317–18, 322 n.18, 322 n.25, 322 n.30, 323 n.40, 324 n.42, 326 n.84, 329 n.125, 329 n.130, 336, 339, 363, 369, 406 n.26, 408 n.43
"Propaganda Aktion" 311
propaganda system 116, 249, 253, 275–6, 280–1, 283, 296, 311–12, 318, 363, 369
Goergen, Jeanpaul 271 n.49
Goering, Hermann 395
Goes, Albrecht 397
Goethe Institute/German Cultural Center 415 n.125
Goethe, Johann Wolfgang von 1, 6, 12, 16, 24, 28, 30 n.19, 37, 39, 60, 73, 74, 77 n.27, 102, 130, 152, 165 n.164, 166 n.177, 234 n.99, 251, 267, 278, 331 n.147, 333, 342–4, 347, 365, 416 n.131, 436, 441, 457–8, 478, 487 n.47, 500, 512–13, 529, 533, 537, 543, 552, 558, 577 n.162
Faust I 16–17, 21, 24, 83 n.88, 131, 133, 543
Faust II 133, 166 n.177, 543
on film 129–34
Wilhelm Meisters Lehrjahre 457

Goetz, Curt 182, 233 n.77, 310, 346, 349, 353, 441, 487 n.46
Goetz, William 360
Göktürk, Deniz 30 n.10, 45, 50, 81 n.71, 82 nn.76–7, 82 n.81, 406 n.21, 482, 482 n.5, 498 n.203, 553
Golan, Menahem 491 n.86
Gold (1934) 320 n.5
Goldbaum, Peter 380
Goldblum, Jeff 545
Golden Age 4, 90, 114, 153, 248, 278, 400
The Golden Age of Cinema (Jewell) 231 n.37, 231 n.48, 235 n.114, 236 n.121
Gold, Robert 557
Goldschmidt, Siegbert 63
Goldstein, Cora Sol 405 n.9
Goldwasser, James 411 n.72
Golec, Janusz 426 n.258
Goll, Claire 537
Goll, Yvan 89, 155 n.1
Golon, Anne 455
Gombault, Charles 411 n.76
Gomery, Douglas 30 n.11, 230 n.19, 233 n.68
Goodbye Lenin (2003) 520
Goodrich, John F. 188
Gorbachev, Mikhail 432
Gordon, Mel 168 n.203
Gören, Şerif 482
Goretta, Claude 449
Gorski, Peter 366
Göske, Daniel 81 n.61
Gotsche, Otto 488 n.51
GOTT/God (2020) 559
Gotta, Salvator 251
Gott, du kannst ein Arsch sein!/God, you can be such an Ass! (2020) 567 n.54
Gotthelf, Jeremias 293, 362, 413 n.104
Göttler, Fritz 398, 425 n.254
Gottschalk, Joachim 417 n.137
Gottwald, Fritz 206, 238 n.145
Goulding, Edmund 208–9, 226
Gounod, Charles 17, 24, 28, 73

Goya-oder der arge Weg der Erkenntnis/Goya or the Hard Way to Enlightenment (1971) 445, 489 nn.66–7
Goyert, Georg 169 n.225
G.P. Films production 217
Grabbe, Christian Dietrich 402
Graf, Andreas 156 n.7
Graf, Dominik 396, 419 n.178, 424 n.242, 425 n.243, 511–13, 517, 521, 524, 555, 558, 580 n.191
Graf Michael (1918) 81 n.71
Graf, Oscar Maria 246, 268 n.11, 472
Gräf, Roland 483 n.6, 562 n.7
The Grand Budapest Hotel (2014) 545, 556
Grand Coalition (1966–9) 431
Granderath, Christian 570 n.82
Grand Hotel (1932) 207–8, 226, 393
Grand Hotel (Baum) 198, 207–8, 226, 266
Grant, Cary 354
Grass, Günter 6, 433, 460, 465, 469–71, 486 n.45, 492 n.99, 496 n.155
Graßhoff, Fritz 421 n.203
Gray, Allan 212, 254
"Great Flood" of 1756 287
The Great Sinner (1949) 423 n.222
Great Turkish War 398
Greaves, Roger 83 n.89, 324 n.47
Greenbaum, Mutz (Max) 254
Gregor, Manfred 423 n.219, 423 n.220
Greiner, Ulrich 497 n.188
Gremm, Wolf 458–9, 486 n.43, 489 n.60, 580 n.191
Grenadier Wordelmann (1980) 485 n.33
Grete Minde (1977) 458, 493 n.114
Grete Minde (Fontane) 458, 493 n.114
Gretler, Heinrich 363
Greve, Ludwig 75 n.1, 157 n.17, 166 n.178, 167 n.188, 167 n.194, 168 n.209
Gricksch, Gernot 562 n.6
Grießnockerlaffäre (2017) 572 n.105
Grieveston, Lee 30 n.14
Griffith, D. W. 55, 76 n.18

Griffiths, Kate 20, 31 n.21, 32 n.41, 167 n.192, 404 n.3
Grillparzer, Franz 53
Grimm, Jacob 300, 419 n.173
Grimm, Wilhelm 300, 419 n.173, 512
Grimoin-Sanson, Raoul 228 n.4
Grisebach, Valeska 491 n.92, 522
Griseldis (Courths-Mahler) 486 n.44
Grisko, Michael 165 n.161, 189, 232 n.59, 232 n.61, 233 n.66, 233 n.70, 233 n.72, 233 n.74, 323 n.38, 373, 417 n.146, 417 nn.141–2, 418 nn.152–4
Grob, Norbert 427 n.267, 485 n.36, 494 n.120, 496 n.153
Groos, Wolfgang 567 n.53
Gropius, Manon 274 n.75
Gropius, Walter 274 n.75
Groschopp, Richard 371
Grossmann, Atina 232 n.53
Grossmann, Stefan 160 n.84
Grosz, Georges 125
Grothe, Franz 187, 353, 382
Grünbaum, Fritz 246
Gründgens, Gustaf 245, 250, 293, 295, 303, 305–6, 328 nn.103–4, 366, 382, 436
Grune, Karl 129, 145, 245
Grün ist die Heide/Green is the Heath (1951) 415 n.123, 425 n.255
Grünler, Jörg 567 n.53
Gruppe 47/Group 47 407 n.39, 430, 433, 440, 454, 478
Gruppenbild mit Dame/Group Portrait with Lady (1977) 460–2
Gruppenbild mit Dame/Group Portrait with Lady (Böll) 460–2, 495 n.149
Grütters, Monika 517
Gsponer, Alain 507–8, 566 n.42, 567 n.51, 570 n.86, 571 n.94, 579 n.180
Guareschi, Giovanni 363
Guderian, Paul Gerd 117
Guglielmo Tell 37, 410 n.63, 491 n.82
Guilhamon, Elizabeth 240 n.177
Guillaume Tell et le clown/William Tell and the clown (1898) 25–6, 28

Guillaume Tell/Wilhelm Tell (1903) 28, 36, 77 n.28
guilt 4, 111, 136, 148, 304, 336, 339, 344–5, 348, 359, 371, 382, 384, 393–4, 400, 429, 433, 447, 452, 459, 464, 482 n.1, 501, 505, 507, 529, 550, 565 n.33, 571
Guinness, Hugo 545
Gulea, Stere 575 n.135
Gullivers Travels (Swift) 30 n.18
Günderrode, Karoline von 561
Gunning, Tom 14, 29 n.9, 163 n.121
Gunske, Volker 569 n.80
Günter Peter Straschek. Emigration-Film-Politics (Friedrich) 268 n.8
Günther, Agnes 365
Günther, Egon 8 n.6, 445, 446, 488 n.51, 489 n.68, 489 n.70, 490 n.72
Gürster, Eugen 140, 167 n.189
Gustav Adolfs Page/Gustav Adolf's Page (1960) 380
Gustav Adolfs Page/Gustav Adolf's Page (Meyer) 380
Guthke, Karl S. 411 n.72
Gutzeit, Angela 236 n.123
Guy, Alice 13, 22–5, 28, 31 n.30, 36–7, 50
Gypkens, Martin 510

Haack, Käthe 214, 232 n.60, 270 n.40, 294, 304
Haandvaerkersvendens Eventyr/ The Journeymen's Adventure (1911/12) 38
Haase, Jella 551
Haasis, Hellmut G. 270 n.31
Haas, Willy 125, 134, 142, 166 n.179, 167 n.194, 245
Habeck, Fritz 359
Habermas, Jürgen 3, 8 n.4, 433, 483 n.10, 483 n.11
Habich, Matthias 582 n.209
Hächler, Horst 416 n.130
Hackl, Erich 571 n.97
Hädrich, Rolf 496 n.163
Hagena, Katharina 519
Hagener, Malte 494 n.133

Hagen, Eva-Maria 446
Haie und kleine Fische/Sharks and Small Fish (1958) 396–7
Haie und kleine Fische/Sharks and Small Fish (Ott) 396–7
Haines, Brigid 270 n.32
Haines, Fred 436
Hake, Sabine 30 nn.10–11, 75 n.3, 159 n.60, 160 n.75, 161 n.95, 168 n.208, 320 n.8, 320 n.10, 321 nn.11–12, 321 n.14, 321 n.15, 366, 375, 404 n.4, 406 nn.17–21, 415 n.120, 418 n.151, 418 n.158, 418 n.165, 427 n.271, 445, 482 n.5, 483 n.13, 489 nn.64–5
Halbe, Max 41, 278, 305, 327 n.87
Halbwelt/Demimonde (1911) 61
Halle, Randall 517, 570 n.84
Hallervorden, Dieter 582 n.208
Hall, Mordaunt 167 n.187
Hallo Janine (1939) 415 n.119
Hall, Sara 159 n.63
Halm, Alfred 78 n.30, 96, 97, 98–9, 101
Halm, Harry 190
Hamburger Abendblatt newspaper 169 n.221
Hamel, Peter 419 n.173
Hamik, Anton 277
Hamilton, Cosmo 349
Hamlet (2000) 519
Hamlet (Shakespeare) 30 n.18
Hammer, Klaus 231 n.50
Hammerstein, Oscar 261
Hammonia-Film-Verleih 101
Hände weg von Mississippi (2007) 566 n.49
Handke, Peter 457, 460, 493 n.119, 546–7, 566 n.46
Händler der vier Jahreszeiten/Merchant of Four Seasons (1971) 473
Handloegten, Henk 520
The Handmaid's Tale (1990) 465
The Handmaid's Tale (Atwood) 465
Haneke, Michael 484 n.15, 519, 530, 535, 574 n.132
Hangmen Also Die! (1943) 245, 262

Hanisch, Michael 62–3, 65–6, 86 n.137, 86 nn.132–4, 409 n.59
Hanks, Tom 581 n.201
Hannah Arendt (2015) 498 n.198
Hanns Heinz Ewers und der phantastische Film (Keiner) 80 n.52
Hansch, Gabriele 158 n.37
Hans Domnick Filmproduktion 353
Hänsel und Gretel/Hansel and Gretel (1940) 300
Hänsel und Gretel/Hansel and Gretel (1954) 378, 419 n.173
Hänsel und Gretel/Hansel and Gretel (Grimm brothers) 300, 378, 419 n.173
Hansen, Miriam 37, 75 nn.4–5, 76 n.6, 77 n.26, 80 n.51, 82 n.82, 83 n.103, 87 n.159
Hansen, Rolf 380, 425 n.245
Hans im Glück/Hans in Luck (1949) 419 n.173
Hanson, Helen 412 n.85, 413 n.95
Hanstein, Adalbert von 63
Hanus, Heinz 164 n.135
Happy Birthday, Türke! (1992) 506
Happy Birthday, Türke! (Arjouni) 506
Harbou, Thea von 43, 82 n.73, 85 n.121, 114, 116, 118, 142–3, 161 nn.97–9, 162 n.102, 168 n.199, 172, 247, 278, 285, 324 n.48, 327 n.87, 328 n.111, 339, 381, 421 n.203
Harder, Emil 160 n.71
Hardt, Ursula 229 n.15, 232 n.62
Hare, David 529
Harlan, Jan 534
Harlan, Veit 86 n.133, 170 n.234, 247, 276, 284, 295, 296–7, 301–2, 305, 308, 312–19, 321 n.11, 324 n.48, 327 n.87, 327 n.92, 329–30 n.130, 330 n.131, 330 n.135, 337, 341, 344, 369–70, 377, 381, 407 n.28, 416 n.136, 417 n.137
Harlan, Walter 277, 312, 327 n.92
Harnack, Falk 371, 374–5, 396, 426 n.255

Harrison, Godfrey 239 n.164
Harris, Robert 556
Harris, Victoria 158 n.31
Harry Piel-films 222
Harshav, Barbara 514
Hartleben, Otto Erich 365, 414 n.117
Härtling, Peter 567 n.53, 567 n.55
Hartl, Karl 248, 320 n.5, 415 n.123
Hartmann, Paul 248, 285, 293, 304, 382
Hartung, Hugo 385
Hartwig, Wolf C. 455
Harvey, Lilian 182, 183, 190, 233 n.77
Harwig, Martin 160 n.70
Harzer, Jens 546
Hasenfratz, Bob 5, 8 n.7, 32 nn.41–4, 76 n.18, 162 n.101, 165 n.158, 169 n.229, 173, 178, 230 n.32, 231 n.32, 379, 411 n.74, 413 n.100, 420 n.180, 454, 485 nn.29–31, 492 n.100
Häsler, Alfred A. 449, 484 n.20
Hathaway, Henry 389
Hatheyer, Heidemarie 343, 367, 407 n.36
Hatot, Georges 17, 73
Hätte ich das Kino! Die Schriftsteller und der Stummfilm 75 n.1, 157 n.26, 157 n.29, 157 nn.17–19, 158 n.47, 158 n.49, 158 n.51, 159 n.58, 166 n.175, 166 n.178, 167 n.194, 167 nn.188–9, 168 n.209, 169 nn.223–4
Hätte ich das Kino!/If (Only) I Had the Cinema (Mierendorff) 95, 157 n.29
Hauff, Reinhard 486 n.45, 494 n.120, 579 n.182
Hauff, Wilhelm 58, 85 n.119, 87 n.156, 252, 270 nn.33–4, 314, 373, 376–80, 561
Haugk, Dietrich 379
The Haunted Hotel (1907) 35
The Haunted Screen: Expressionism in the German Cinema and the Influence of Max Reinhardt (Eisner) 51, 83 nn.89–90, 83 n.93, 162 n.106, 162 n.108, 164 n.137, 165 n.150, 166 n.171, 168 n.207, 168 n.215, 169 n.218, 169 n.227, 235 n.105, 324 n.47
Hauptmann, Elisabeth 211, 221, 511
Hauptmann, Gerhart 35, 37, 40, 42–50, 81 nn.71–2, 82 n.72, 82 n.75, 82 n.80, 84 n.117, 93, 98–9, 102, 125, 127–9, 133, 142, 153, 157 n.19, 165 n.162, 166 n.175, 167 n.193, 256, 278, 284, 297, 324 n.48, 377, 383–4, 392, 400, 417 n.143, 425 n.245, 440, 491 n.86
Hauptstädtisches Journal 462, 464
Hauser, Arnold 558, 581 n.204
Hauser, Heinrich 140
Hauser, Johannes 409 n.54
Haushofer, Marlen 530, 543–4, 576 n.156
Haus ohne Hüter/House without Guardians (1975) 464
Haus ohne Hüter/House without Guardians (Böll) 461–2, 464
Häussler, Richard 416 n.129
Haußmann, Leander 506, 509, 518–19, 562 nn.5–6, 579 n.182
Haver, Phyllis 232 n.60
Havilland, Olivia de 352
Hays Code 257, 261
Hays, Will 203
Hayworth, Rita 195
Head Full of Honey (2018) 582 n.208
Hebbel, Friedrich 53, 60, 114, 278, 410 n.65
Hebstreit, Jürgen 561 n.3
Heckerling, Amy 501
Hedwig Courths-Mahler (Graf) 156 n.7
Hereszeppeline im Angriff/Zeppelins Attack (Lampel) 236 n.125
Heidböhmer, Carsten 579 n.183
Heidegger, Martin 516, 569 n.77
Heidi (2015) 570 n.86
Heidi (Spyri) 3, 362, 517, 570 n.86
Heidi und Peter (1955) 362
Heiduschke, Sebastian 418 n.160, 418 n.163, 489 n.67, 489 n.69, 490 n.80

Heilborn-Körbitz, Luise 108, 112, 160 n.79, 160 n.82
Heimat, deine Sterne/Homeland, your Stars (1951) 369
Heimat films 7, 319, 364–6, 381, 396, 399, 408 n.52, 459, 520, 570 n.85, 571 n.95
Heimat/Home/Homeland (1912) 78 n.30
Heimat/Home/Homeland (Sudermann) 74, 78 n.30, 101, 105, 300–1, 317, 319, 335
Heims, Else 392, 423 n.223
Hein, Christoph 500, 538, 562 n.7, 567 n.55, 576 n.148
Heine, Heinrich 268 n.10, 382, 537
Heiner Müller am Marterpfahl (Kramer) 490 n.81
Heinrich Böll and Ireland (Holfter) 427 n.266
Heinrich Mann. Eine Biographie (Flügge) 232 n.60, 233 n.71, 234 n.94, 323 n.33
Heinrich Mann und der Film (Grisko) 165 n.161, 232 n.59, 232 n.61, 233 n.66, 233 n.70, 233 n.72, 233 n.74, 417 n.146, 417 nn.141–2, 418 nn.152–4
Heinrich, Margaretha 519
Heins, Laura 322 n.20, 327 n.85, 331 n.152
Heinz, Julia von 521, 573 nn.107–9, 581 n.202
Heisenberg, Benjamin 522
Heisler, Georg 264
Heiss, Sonja 557
Helden wie wir/Heroes Like Us (1999) 527
Helden wie wir/Heroes Like Us (Brussig) 527, 579 n.182
Heldinnen/Heroines (1960) 379
Héliard, Simone 250
Hellberg, Martin 379, 420 n.193, 488 n.60
Heller, Heinz B. 80 n.54
Hello Dolly! (1964) 413 n.107
Helm, Brigitte 143, 178–80, 187, 232 n.60

Hembus, Joe 236 n.127, 333, 404 n.2, 429
Hemingway, Ernest 268 n.10
Hemminger, Moritz 514, 568 n.69
Henckels, Paul 282
Henderson, Dayton 230 n.27, 236 n.130, 237 n.131, 237 n.134, 237 n.136
Henlein, Peter 327 n.92
Hennings, Emmy 530, 575 n.134
Henn, Kristina Magdalena 504
Henry, David 577 n.166
Henry, Michel 242 n.221
Henze, Hans Werner 467
Herbert Engelmann (1959) 424 n.239
Herbert Engelmann (Zuckmayer) 424 n.239
Herbig, Bully 501, 568 n.59
Herbrich, Oliver 494 n.120
Herbst-Messlinger, Karin 157 n.22, 239 n.162
Here Is Germany (1945) 423 n.222
Herfurth, Karoline 581 n.202
heritage identity 574 n.123
Herka, Trude 250
Herlischka, Bohumil 440, 494 n.120
Herlth, Robert 285, 324 n.48
Hermann, Britta 270 n.33
Hermann, Georg 72, 246, 485 n.33, 567 n.55
Hermann, Judith 510
Hermann, Kai 503
Hermann, Peter 504
Hermlin, Stephan 452
Herold, Wolfgang 561 n.3
Herr der Diebe/The Thief Lord (2005) 566 n.49
Herr Lehmann (2003) 506, 518, 562 n.6
Herr Lehmann (Regener) 562 n.6
Herrndorf, Wolfgang 546
Herr Puntila und sein Knecht Matti (Brecht) 426 n.264
Herr Puntila und sein Knecht Matti/Mr. Puntila and his Man Matti (1955) 426 n.264
Herr über den Tod/Death's Master (1955) 423 n.229

Herr über den Tod/Death's Master
(Zuckmayer) 423 n.229
Herr über Leben und Tod (1955) 424
n.239
Her Sister's Secret (1946) 352
Herzfelde, Wieland 452
Herzlich willkommen (Kempowsky)
562 n.7
Herzlich willkommen/Crossing Borders
or Welcome Indeed! (1990) 562
n.7
Herzog, Ed 571 n.95
Herzog, Werner 5, 431, 449, 456, 460,
478
Hesse, Ernst 300
Hesse, Hermann 141, 171, 231 n.35,
268 n.10, 436, 484 n.23, 490
n.74, 512, 537, 552, 568 n.57,
571 n.97, 580 n.198
Hessischer Rundfunk 490 n.74
Hesterberg, Trude 232 n.60
Heurck, Jan van 273 n.68
Heuss, Theodor 370
Heymann, Robert 58, 85 n.119, 87
n.156
Heymann, Werner 182
Heymel, Alfred Walter 100
Heym, G. 481
Heym, Jakob 528
Heym, Stefan 445–6
Heyse, Paul 317, 318–19, 321 n.11
Hickethier, Knut 415 n.120, 426
n.265, 491 n.92, 493 n.117
Hickman, Alfred 74
Hicks, Jeremy 272 n.55
Hiepko, Andreas 8 n.8
high culture 12, 14, 28, 34, 37, 74, 76
n.18, 96, 102, 106, 114, 154,
284, 306, 380, 385, 439
  adaptation as 62–4, 106–13
  cinema *vs.* 23–5
  consumption of 13, 59
  and mass entertainment (*see* mass
    entertainment)
  traditional forms of 27, 130
The High Life (1960) 403
Hildebrandt, Hans-Joachim 485 n.33
Hildesheimer, Wolfgang 440

Hilpert, Heinz 217
Hintergrund für Liebe (Wollf) 232
n.51
Hin und Her/To and Fro (1949) 363
Hin und Her/To and Fro (Horváth)
363
Hipkins, D. 422 n.206
Hippler, Fritz 312, 313, 322 n.17
Hiroshima, mon amour (1959) 450
Hiroshima, mon amour (Duras &
Robbe-Grillet) 450
Hirschbiegel, Oliver 503, 528
Hirschfeld, Magnus 95
Hirsch, Hugo 190
Hirsch, Rudolf 161 n.90
His Majesty, the King (Hamilton) 349
*Histoire de la sexualité. La volonté de
savoir* (Foucault) 86 n.144, 157
n.27
Historia von D. Johann Fausten (Spies)
16, 26
*Historical Dictionary of Holocaust
Cinema* (Reimer & Reimer) 574
n.133
*Historical Dictionary of Russian and
Soviet Cinema* (Rollberg) 272
n.58
*The History of American Literature
on Film* (Leitch) 167 n.192, 229
n.9, 238 n.151, 238 n.155, 238
n.158, 241 n.196, 242 n.205,
413 n.100
*The History of British Literature on
Film, 1895–2015* (Semenza &
Hasenfratz) 8 n.7, 32 nn.41–4,
76 n.18, 162 n.101, 165 n.157,
169 n.229, 230 n.32, 231 n.32,
413 n.100, 420 n.180, 485
nn.29–31, 492 n.100
*The History of French Literature on
Film* (Griffiths & Watts) 20, 31
n.21, 32 n.41, 167 n.192, 404
n.3
A History of Narrative Film (Cook) 30
n.11, 30 n.13, 30 nn.15–17, 31
n.22, 31 n.25, 32 n.36
*A History of the French New Wave
Cinema* (Neupert) 485 n.26

Hitchcock, Alfred 212, 248, 524, 573 n.116
Hitler, Adolf 2, 4, 6, 79 n.41, 118, 161 n.98, 164 n.131, 169 n.216, 170 n.234, 173, 198, 205, 210, 237 n.139, 243, 244, 245, 247, 249, 258–9, 261, 263, 275–6, 278–83, 287–8, 290, 292–3, 295, 298, 313, 320 n.8, 320 n.9, 322 n.22, 326 n.71, 326 n.77, 327 n.93, 330 n.131, 339, 369, 374, 396, 406 n.23, 505
  external and internal deterioration 279
  megalomania 116
  'Proclamation to the German people' 279
Hitler and Film: The Führer's Hidden Passion (Niven) 320 nn.3–4, 320 nn.6–7, 323 n.32, 327 n.90
Hitler-Ein Film aus Deutschland/ Hitler: A Film from Germany (1977) 502
Hitlerjunge Quex/Hitler Youth Quex (1933) 276, 284
Hitler's Heroines: Stardom and Womanhood in Nazi Cinema (Ascheid) 331 n.143
Hitlers Kampf um Deutschland/Hitler's Fight for Germany (1931) 280
Hitler über Deutschland/Hitler on Germany (1932) 280
Hjort, Mette 420 n.185, 513, 563 n.11, 568 n.63
Hochhäusler, Christoph 522
Hochhuth, Rolf 529, 536, 575 n.144
Hochwälder, Fritz 363
Hochzeit im Heu/Wedding in the Hay (1951) 367
Hockenhull, O. 8 n.6
Hodell, Frans 228 n.4
Hodgin, Nick 564 n.29, 579 n.182
Hodgkins, John 271 n.48
Hoefer, Peter 312, 329 n.126
Hoefert, Sigfrid 80 n.58
Høeg, Peter 503
Hoeij, Boyd van 569 n.74
Hofer, Franz 106

Hoffman, Dustin 518
Hoffmann, Carl 100, 117, 161 n.99, 339
Hoffmann, E.T.A. (Ernst Theodor Amadeus) 12, 13, 26–7, 29 n.3, 51–3, 59, 64, 79 n.44, 93–4, 141, 143, 350, 452, 558, 560, 562 n.8, 567 n.55
  adaptation as high culture 62–4
  Der Sandmann 26–7, 32 n.39, 94, 143, 562 n.8
  magical doublings and 65
Hoffmann, Hilmar 284, 320 n.10, 322 n.20, 322 nn.26–8, 324 n.43, 408 n.50
Hoffmann, Jutta 481
Hoffmann, Kurt 365, 377, 379, 384–6, 401, 403, 419 n.177, 441, 486 n.43, 487 n.46
Hoffmanns Erzählungen. See *Tales of Hoffmann* (1881)
Hoffmannswaldau, Christian Hoffmann von 410 n.65
Hoff, Peter 426 n.265
Hofmann, Corinne 509
Hofmann, Henri Chatin 123
Hofmann, Hilmar 280
Hofmann, Klaus 492 n.94
Hofmann, Michael 528
Hofmann, Nico 488 n.56, 562 n.3, 563 n.16, 575 n.141
Hofmannsthal, Hugo von 35, 37, 40, 77 n.26, 101
Hohlbein, Wolfgang 581 n.199
Hokuspokus (1930) 182, 233 n.77
Holch, Christel 41
Hölderlin, Friedrich 494 n.129, 562 n.8
Holfter, Gisela 427 n.266
Holighaus, Alfred 527, 574 n.128
Hollaender, Felix 92, 122, 165 n.145
Hollaender, Friedrich/Frederick 100, 194, 246, 378
Hölleisengretl (1994) 580 n.198
Holl, Gussy 95
Hollstein, Dorothea 329 n.129, 330 n.132, 330 n.142

Hollywood/Hollywood films 4, 8 n.3, 43, 92, 102, 113, 134, 155, 173, 176, 188, 223, 246, 249, 267, 335, 349, 360, 411 n.78, 438, 473, 478, 508, 545, 557
  German-language literature in 134–41, 155, 259–66
  "Golden Twenties" 172
Hollywood in Berlin: American Cinema and Weimar Germany (Saunders) 229 n.15
Hollywoods kritischer Blick: Das soziale Melodrama in der amerikanischen Kultur 1840–1950 (Decker) 87 nn.151–2
The Hollywood Story (Finler) 166 n.185
Holm, Ian 237 n.143
Holocaust 4, 334, 340, 433–5, 451, 453, 487 n.47, 507
Holocaust series (1978) 459
Holt, Hans 249
Holy League 398
Holy Roman Empire 320 n.9
Holz, Arno 278, 296
Homer 2
Homo Faber (1991) 465, 525
Homo Faber (Frisch) 465, 525
homo oeconomicus 108, 111
homosexuality and abortion 120, 184–6, 306, 449, 521
Homunculus (1916–17) 142
Honecker, Erich 432, 442, 444–5, 446, 481
Honegger, Arthur 230 n.17
Honig im Kopf/Honey in the Head (2014) 582 n.208
Honolka, Kurt 328 n.114
Hopkins, Anthony 542
Hoppe, Felicitas 8 n.1
Hoppe, Marianne 286–7, 290, 293, 306
Hoppla, wir leben! (1927) 165 n.159, 256
Horak, Jan-Christopher 231 n.41, 244, 268 n.8, 268 nn.4–6, 269 n.14, 269 n.21, 273 n.71, 322 n.16, 348, 409 nn.59–60, 411 nn.78–9, 415 n.127

Hörbiger, Paul 249, 250, 363
Horkheimer, Max 166 n.170, 319, 332 n.161
Hormann, Sherry 564 n.26
Horn, Camilla 132
Horney, Brigitte 363
Horn, Peter 424 n.229
Horsley, Ritta Jo 186–7, 232 n.53, 232 nn.55–6
Horst Wessel (1933) 296
Horst Wessel (Ewers) 296
Horváth, Ödön von 363, 502, 507
Hörzu magazine 452, 492 n.96
Hoss, Nina 563 n.16
Hotel Imperial (1927) 198
Hotel Shanghai (Baum) 519
Houellebecq, Michel 564 n.26
The Hound of the Baskervilles (Doyle) 61
House of Dracula (1945) 249
House of Frankenstein (1944) 248
The House of Spirits (1993) 564 n.24
The House of Spirits (Allende) 564 n.24
Hubert, Roger 367
Hubmann, Gerhard 81 n.66
Hubrich, Lars 546
Huchel, Peter 581 n.206
Huch, Ricarda 278
Hue and Cry (1947) 212
Hugenberg, Alfred 80 n.53, 168 n.204, 189, 193–4, 204, 233 n.65, 237 n.136, 283, 323 n.41
Hugon, André 164 n.135
Hugo, Victor 83 n.100, 230 n.25, 561
Huillet, Danièle 450, 462, 464, 484 n.15, 494 n.129, 562 n.8
Hull, David Stewart 330 n.132
Hummelt, Norbert 228 n.2
Hunchback of Notre Dame (1939) 83 n.100
Hunchback of Notre Dame (Hugo) 83 n.100
Hunde, wollt ihr ewig leben?/Dogs, Do You Want to Live Forever? (1959) 396–7
Hunold, Günther 493 n.107
Hunte, Otto 117, 234 n.96

Hunter, C. Roy 202
Hunter, Dianne 234 n.93
Huntgeburth, Hermine 509, 541–2
Huntley, G. P. Jr. 260
Huppert, Isabelle 531
Huppertz, Gottfried 117
Hurd-Wood, Rachel 518
Hurra! Ich lebe!/Hurrah! I'm Alive! (1928) 262
Hurst, Brian Desmond 254
Huston, Jack 514
Huston, John 351–2, 423 n.222
Huston, Walter 411 n.71
Hutcheon, Linda 9 n.12, 551, 578 n.178
Huth, Jochen 383–4, 392, 420 n.187, 425 n.245
Hyènes/Hyenas (1992) 531–2, 556

Ibsen, Henrik 277, 472, 496 n.165
Ich bin dann mal weg/I'm Off Then (Kerkeling) 521, 581 n.202
Ich bin ein Elefant, Madame/I'm an Elephant, Madame (1969) 455
Ich klage an/I Accuse (1941) 341
Ich küsse Ihre Hand, Madame/I Kiss Your Hand, Madame (1929) 194
Ich lasse dich nicht/I Won't Let You Go (1919) 156 n.7
Ich und Er/Me and Him (1988) 505
Ich war Jack Mortimer/I Was Jack Mortimer (1935) 414 n.109
Ich war Jack Mortimer/I Was Jack Mortimer (Lernet-Holenia) 414 n.109
Ich war neunzehn/I Was Nineteen (1968) 487 n.51
Ich werde dich auf Händen tragen/I'll Carry You in My Arms (1958) 381
Ihering, Herbert 99, 112, 117, 161 n.88, 215, 372
Ihr glücklichen Augen (Bachmann) 519
Ihr glücklichen Augen/You Happy Eyes (1992) 519
Ihr schönster Tag/Her Best Day (1962) 446–7
Ikiru Films S.L. (Barcelona) 576 n.151

Ilgenstein, Heinrich 222
Ilgner, Julia 81 n.65
Ilg, Paul 571 n.96
Il guanto/The Glove (1910) 77 n.22
Illés, Eugen 73, 177, 230 n.31
Illiad (Homer) 2
Illustrierter Filmkurier 303, 310
Il nome della rosa (Eco) 503
Il nome della rosa/The Name of the Rose (1986) 503
Imbach, Thomas 8 n.6, 577 n.161
Imedashvili, Aleksandre 142
Imhoff, Hildegard 109
Imhoof, Markus 449, 484 n.20
Immensee (1943) 317, 332 n.163, 377
Immensee (Storm) 317
Im Netz der Gefühle: Veit Harlans Melodramen (Weber) 407 n.28, 417 n.137
Im Westen nichts Neues/All Quiet on the Western Front (Remarque) 174, 198–9, 204, 235 nn.115–16, 235 n.118, 236 n.123, 261, 354, 360, 556, 580 n.191. *See also All Quiet on the Western Front* (Remarque)
In den Gängen/In the Aisles (2018) 521, 548–9
"In der Strafkolonie"/In the Penal Colony (Kafka) 403–4
industrialization 13, 55, 108–9, 125–6, 128
inflation 109, 112–13
Ingeborg (1960) 346
Inglorious Basterds (2018) 117
In jenen Tagen/In Those Days (1947) 340
Inkheart (2008) 566 n.49
The Inn of the Sixth Happiness (1958) 359
innovations 50, 52–3, 84 n.113, 90, 101, 114, 125, 149, 152, 181, 188, 285, 382
Insdorf, Anette 272 n.52
Institute for Cultural Research/Institut für Kulturforschung 173, 229 n.5

Institut für Europäisches Medienrecht/ European Media Law Institute (Berlin) 527
insular cultural nationalism 554
International Adventures. German Popular Cinema and European Co-productions in the 1960s (Bergfelder) 427 n.269, 483 n.14, 490 n.77, 490 n.79, 563 n.9, 563 n.18, 574 n.123
international cinema/internationalization 3–4, 141, 250, 267, 433, 438, 478
  German-language literature in 349–54, 434–8
  Remarque on 354–60
Internationale Cinematographen-und Licht-Effect-Gesellschaft 37, 77 n.21
Internationale Maatschappij voor Sprekende Films Amsterdam 175
international language (silent cinema) 57, 74
international marketability 103, 504
Internet Movie Database (IMDb) 238 n.145, 545, 566 n.49, 572 n.104, 575 n.140, 576 n.152
intertitles 36, 41–2, 44–6, 66, 82 n.74, 93, 110, 124, 126, 133, 169 n.222, 386, 475
The Invention of Hugo (Selznick) 29 n.1
In Zeiten des abnehmenden Lichts/In Times of Fading Light (2017) 510, 579 n.182
Irish Film Censorship (Rockett) 411 n.79
iron curtain 334, 364–6, 403
Irons, Jeremy 514
Isenberg, Noah 159 n.63, 411 n.77
ITC Entertainment 237 n.143
It Takes Two (1995) 566 n.50
Itzenplitz, Eberhard 458
Iurascu, Ilinca 235 n.108
I Was a Criminal (1945) 273 n.71

The Jack Bull (1999) 485 n.28
Jacobi, Jos. Max 84 n.109
Jacobowsky und der Oberst (Werfel) 359
Jacobsen, Frederik 41
Jacobsen, Wolfgang 30 nn.10–11, 85 n.126, 160 n.86, 269 n.21
Jacob's Room (Woolf) 171
Jacobs, Werner 416 n.132, 441, 486 n.43, 492 n.99
Jacques, Juliet 159 n.65
Jacques, Norbert 115, 172, 247, 307, 328 n.111
Jagdszenen aus Niederbayern/Hunting Scenes from Bavaria (1969) 455
Jäger, Ernst 215
Jäger, Georg 76 n.12
Jäger, Malte 315
Jäger, Moritz 125, 127
Jahrestage/Anniversaries (2000) 498 n.198, 500, 562 n.5, 573 n.122, 579 n.182
Jahrgang '45/Born in '45 (1965) 487 n.51
Jahrgang 1902/Born in 1902 (Glaeser) 236 n.119
Jakob der Lügner/Jacob the Liar (1975) 445, 478, 528
Jakob der Lügner/Jacob the Liar (Becker) 528
Jakobowsky und der Oberst (Werfel) 360
Jakob ten Brinken 177–8, 180
Jakob von Gunten (Walser) 440
Jandl, Ernst 537
Janeway, Carol Brown 529
Janisch, Michael 388
Jannings, Emil 3, 58, 61, 78 n.30, 99, 122, 131–2, 187–90, 193–4, 213, 232 n.62, 233 n.71, 272 n.60, 297
Jannings, Orin 359
Janson, Uwe 561 n.3, 562 n.5
Janson, Victor 157 n.23, 367
Janssen, Walter 378, 416 n.129, 419 n.173
Jaoui, Agnès 411 n.70
Jaques-Dalcroze, Émile 45, 86 n.146
Jasný, Vojtěch 462, 464
Jaspers, Kristina 575 n.139

Jatho, Gabriele 239 n.163
The Jazz Singer (1927) 171–2, 194, 226
Jeder stirbt für sich allein (Fallada) 528
Jelinek, Elfriede 530, 531, 535
Jenbach, Ida 120
Jennings, DeWitt 260
Jenseits der Stille/Beyond Silence (1997) 528
Jentsch, Ernst 27, 32 n.40
Jerschke, Oskar 296
Jerusalem, Else 119, 144, 153
Jesenská, Milena 231 n.51, 245
Jessel, Leon 367
Jessner, Leopold 101, 145
Jettchen Geberts Geschichte/Jettchen Gebert's Story (1918) 72
Jettchen Geberts Geschichte/Jettchen Gebert's Story (1978) 485 n.33
Jettchen Geberts Geschichte/Jettchen Gebert's Story (Hermann) 72, 246
Jetzt und in der Stunde meines Todes (1963) 490 n.72
Jewell, Richard B. 180, 201, 231 n.37, 231 n.48, 235 n.114, 236 n.121
Jim Knopf und der Lokomotivführer (2016/17) 441, 487 n.48
Jim Knopf und die Wilde 13 (2020) 567 n.52
Jim Knopf und Lukas der Lokomotivführer/Jim Button and Luke the Engine Driver (2018) 567 n.52
Joan of Arc/Joan the Woman (1916) 78 n.28
Johannes Brahms' "Academic Festival Overture" 353
Johannisfeuer/Fire of St. John (1916) 74
Johannisfeuer/Fire of St. John (1939) 409 n.55
Johannisfeuer/Fire of St. John (Sudermann) 74, 78 n.30, 346
Johannsen, Ernst 202
John Glückstadt (1975) 458, 493 n.114
John, Karl 345

Johnson, Alvin 257
Johnson, Nunnally 195
Johnson, Uwe 430, 498 n.198, 500, 524, 561 n.3, 562 n.5, 573 n.122, 579 n.182
Johst, Hanns 293, 326 n.77
Joinville Studios (Paris) 250
Jolson, Al 172
Jones, James 387
Jones, Jennifer 264, 265
Jons und Erdme (1959) 401
Jons und Erdme (Sudermann) 401
Jordan, Neil 581 n.206
Josefine Mutzenbacher (1970) 455
Josefine Mutzenbacher-Wie sie wirklich war (1976) 493 n.107
Joseph, Albrecht 217–19
Joseph Goebbels Tagebücher (Reuth) 327 n.89
Joseph, Robert 405 n.9
Joyce, James 150, 169 n.225, 171, 213, 239 n.166
Jud Süß/Jew Süss (1940) 86 n.133, 252–3, 276, 284, 312–18, 321, 330 n.132, 377
Jud Süß/Jew Süss (Feuchtwanger) 252–3, 270 n.31, 270 n.34, 270 n.37, 284, 295, 311–13, 315
Jugendliebe/Young Love (1944/7) 414 n.111
Jugend ohne Gott/Youth without God (Horváth) 363, 507
Jugend/Youth (1938) 305, 321 n.11, 327 n.87
Jugert, Rudolf 367, 382, 387, 394, 403, 421 n.203, 423 n.229
Jugo, Jenny 155
Julian, Rupert 204
Julietta (2001) 562 n.3
Jung, C. G. 512
Jünger, Ernst 75
Junghans, Wolfram 157 n.22
Jung, Uli 238 n.149
Junkermann, Hans 206
Jürgen, Habermas 8 n.4
Jürgens, Curd 359–60, 363, 383, 387, 396, 400–1, 413 n.102, 423 n.229, 425 n.245, 491 n.86

Jürgensen, Christoph 81 n.61
Just Another Sucker (Chase) 465
Justiz (1993) 562 n.8
Jutzi, Phil (Piel) 78 n.28, 214–15

Kabale und Liebe/Intrigue and Love (1913) 77 n.21, 78 n.28
Kabale und Liebe/Intrigue and Love (1959) 379
Kabale und Liebe/Intrigue and Love (1965) 488 n.60
Kabale und Liebe/Intrigue and Love (1967) 488 n.60
Kabale und Liebe/Intrigue and Love (1980) 488 n.60
Kabale und Liebe/Intrigue and Love (1982) 489 n.60
Kabale und Liebe/Intrigue and Love (2005) 506, 519, 562 nn.5–6
Kabale und Liebe/Intrigue/Love or Luise Miller (Schiller) 77 n.21, 78 n.28, 500, 519, 562 n.6
Kadelbach, Philipp 488 n.56, 518, 561 n.3, 563 n.14, 564 n.21, 571 n.95
Kadelburg, Gustav 190
Kaes, Anton 30 nn.10–11, 34, 73, 76 nn.8–9, 77 n.24, 79 nn.35–6, 79 nn.38–40, 80 n.58, 87 n.153, 158 n.39, 160 n.86, 167 n.196, 269 n.21
Kafka, Franz 213, 239 n.166, 246, 403, 434–5, 494 n.129, 519, 529, 540, 577 n.162
Kafka, Hans 245
Kai, Johannes 403
Kaiser, Claire 240 n.177
Kaiser, Georg 92, 100, 104–5, 136, 153, 159 nn.68–9, 218, 262, 268 n.10, 344, 363, 402, 440
Kaiser, Joachim 492 n.97
Kaiserschmarrndrama (2021) 572 n.105
The Kaiser's Lackey (1951) 371
The Kaiser, the Beast of Berlin (1918) 204
Kaiser-Titz, Erich 60, 66
Kalbus, Oskar 165 n.163, 284, 323 n.42

Kaléko, Mascha 537
Kameraden auf See (1937/8) 326 n.78
"Kampfblatt der nationalsozialistischen Bewegung" (1930) 204
Kampfbund für deutsche Kultur 292–3
Kampf, Iris 287, 324 n.53, 325 nn.56–7, 325 n.65, 325 nn.67–8
Kampusch, Natascha 564 n.26
Kant, Hermann 445, 486 n.45, 562 n.7
Kanzog, Klaus 167 n.193, 220, 241 n.190, 241 n.192
Kapczynski, Jennifer M. 8 n.2, 81 n.71, 162 n.102, 230 n.27, 404 n.4, 422 n.206
Kaper, Bronisław 178
Kaplan, E. Ann 494 n.131
Kaplan, Lawrence S. 387, 421 n.202
Kapoor, Shashi 436
Käpt'n Blaubär-der Film (1990) 567 n.53
Käpt'n Blaubärs Seemannsgarn (1990) 567 n.53
Kardes gibiydiler (1963) 413 n.96
Karl Alexander of Württemberg 252
Karl, Günter 159 n.67, 491 n.81
Karl Henning (1912) 167 n.193
Karl und Anna (Frank) 282, 353
Kasprzik, Hans-Joachim 426 n.261, 496 n.163
Kassovitz, Peter 528
Kasten, Jürgen 167 n.196
Kästner, Erich 1, 212, 231 n.35, 239 nn.163–4, 246, 254, 340, 373, 379, 400, 402, 406 n.26, 419 nn.177–8, 440–2, 486 n.43, 492 n.99, 504, 510–11, 521, 537, 555, 558, 566 n.50, 567 n.53, 578 n.180, 579 n.180, 580 n.191
Käthchen von Heilbronn (Kleist) 305
Katzelmacher (1969) 476, 496 n.165
Katz und Maus (Grass) 486 n.45
Katz und Maus/Cat and Mouse (1967) 486 n.45
Kaufman, Charlie 540
Kaufman, Joseph 74
Kaufmann, Christine 427 n.270

Kaufmann, Rainer 509, 512, 516, 569 n.81
Kaus, Gina 3, 254, 267, 271 n.44, 349, 352, 411 nn.78–9, 421 n.204, 530
Käutner, Helmut 317, 340, 347, 382, 387, 394, 396, 403, 407 n.35, 409 n.56, 421 n.203, 423 n.229, 426 n.255, 440–1, 450, 491 n.86, 492 n.99
Kay, Arthur 260
Kaye, Danny 360–1
Kay, Juliane 380
Kayßler, Friedrich 55
Kazan, Elia 467
Kehlmann, Daniel 506, 519
Kehlmann, Michael 414 n.109
Keiner, Reinhold 80 n.52
Keinohrhasen/Rabbit without Ears (2007) 516
Keinz, Antonia 536
Keitel, Harvey 545
Keller, Gottfried 160 n.71, 250, 269 n.20, 278, 317, 361, 402, 410 n.64, 414 n.111, 446, 562 n.8
Keller, Helen 268 n.10
Kellermann, Bernhard 53–5, 83 n.97, 129, 181, 253, 320 n.5, 417 n.143
Keller, Paul 409 n.55
Kelly, Gene 248
Kember, Joe 30 n.14
Kempowski, Walter 496 n.163, 562 n.7
Kenigsberg, Ben 577 n.163
Kennedy, John K. 431
Kent, Crauford 74
Kenton, Erle C. 248–9
Kenyon, Charles 261
Keppler-Tasaki, Stefan 80 n.54
Kerger, August 369–70
Kerkeling, Hape 521, 581 n.202
Kerr, Alfred 202, 246, 282
Kershaw, Ian 280, 290, 322 n.26, 325 nn.58–60, 325 n.62
Kertész, Mihály 43, 177, 214
Kessel, Joseph 400
Kessler, Frank 29 n.8
Kettelhut, Erich 117

Keun, Irmgard 185, 186, 187, 232 nn.53–5, 403
Khondji, Darius 537
The Kid (1921) 471
Kidman, Nicole 534
Kiening, Christian 76 n.7
Kienlechner, Karl 78 n.28
Kienzl, Hermann 38
Kießlich, Curt Wolfram 90
Kilb, Andreas 526, 574 n.125
Kimmich, Max W. 303
Kinder- und Hausmärchen (Grimm Brothers) 298
The Kindness of Strangers (Viertel) 577 n.171
Kinematographische Rundschau journal 60
Kinetophon 40
King, Henry 264–5
King, Lynda J. 232 n.52
Kintopp/Kintöppe 33, 36–9, 155
Kinz, Franziska 147, 270 n.40
Kipling, Rudyard 36
Kipphardt, Heinar 440
Kirchner, Doris 323 n.31
Kirchner, Thomas 577 n.164
Kirillov, Michail 257
Kirkegaard, Sarah 501
Kirsch, Egon Erwin 440
Kirsten, Ralf 483 n.6
Kirst, Hans Hellmut 365, 382, 387–9, 397, 422 n.207, 422 n.213
Kitajskij, Volodja 360
Kitsch 114
Kittler, Friedrich A. 29 n.3, 29 n.7, 32 n.40, 51, 82 n.84
KKR 513
Klabund 402
Klangfilm GmbH (Sound Film Co.) 175–6
Klaren, Georg C. 303, 348, 377
Klassenverhältnisse (1983) 484 n.15
Klassiker des deutschen Tonfilms (Bandmann & Hembus) 236 n.127
Klassiker in finsteren Zeiten, 1933–1945 (Zeller) 166 n.167, 322 n.19, 326 n.83, 328 n.118

Klaus, Ulrich L. 232 n.58
Klee, Ernst 414 n.118, 578 n.174
Kleefeld, Isabel 519
Kleider machen Leute/Clothes Make the Man (1921) 160 n.71
Kleider machen Leute/Clothes Make the Man (1940) 317
Kleider machen Leute/Clothes Make the Man (Keller) 160 n.71, 317
Kleiner Mann-was nun?/Little Man, What Now? (1933) 283
Kleiner Mann-was nun?/Little Man, What Now? (1934) 323 n.36
Kleiner Mann-was nun?/Little Man, What Now? (1967) 496 n.163
Kleiner Mann-was nun?/Little Man, What Now? (Fallada) 211, 259–61, 282, 496 n.163
Kleines Arschloch/Little Asshole (1997) 510
Kleines Theater 66
Kleinhans, Bernd 329 n.120, 329 n.125
Klein-Rogge, Rudolf 115, 117
Kleist, Heinrich von 5, 8 n.6, 35, 58, 102, 106, 152, 278, 297, 305, 323 n.42, 324 n.48, 333, 342, 402, 407 n.30, 436, 437, 440, 455, 458, 465, 478, 492 n.106, 494 n.132, 498 n.198, 529, 544–5, 562 n.3, 567 n.55, 572 n.99
Klevenow, Heinz 463
Klimt, Gustav 283
Klingenberg, Gerhard 488 n.60
Klinger, Paul 347
Klitzsch, Ludwig 233 n.65
Klooss, Reinhard 504
Klöpfer, Eugen 270 n.40, 294, 309, 314–15
Klosterhaus 414 n.118
Kluge, Alexander 3, 8 nn.4–5, 431, 449, 451, 454–5, 464, 478
K5 Media Group Munich 514
Knecht, Doris 519
Knef, Hildegard 491 n.86
Knight, Julia 494 n.131
Knilli, Friedrich 270 n.33, 329 n.129

Knittel, John 339, 391, 400
Knobloch, Charlotte 507
Knocke, Roy 274 n.72
Knopf, Jim 441
Knopp, Daniel 330 nn.131–2
Knoth, Nikola 83 n.102
Kober, Arthur 235 n.106
Kober, Erich 142
Köberer, Julian 566 n.49
Kobler, Erich 378, 419 n.173
Koch, Gertrud 232 n.59
Koch, Jurij 562 n.7
Koch, Robert 44
Koebner, Thomas 30 n.10
Koepnick, Lutz 320 n.7, 321 n.15, 322 n.16, 500, 563 n.9, 574 n.123
Koeppen, Wolfgang 433, 483 n.8, 567 n.55
Koerber, Martin 85 n.123
Koerfer, Thomas 563 n.8
Koestler, Arthur 257, 271 n.50
Kogel, Fred 513
Köhlert, Lutz 488 n.51
Kohlhaase, Wolfgang 446, 519
Kohner, Paul 267
Kokoschka, Oskar 34, 76 n.12
Kolberg (1945) 276, 318–19, 321 n.11, 332 n.163, 377
Kolditz, Gottfried 377, 419 n.175
Kollwitz, Käthe 215
Kolm(-Fleck), Luise 367
Kolpe, Max 245
König Drosselbart/King Trushbeard (1954) 378
Königin der Arena/Queen of the Arena (1952) 383
Königin Luise/Queen Luise (1957) 409 n.55
Königliche Hoheit/Your Royal Highness (1953) 384, 420 n.182
König Nicolo oder So ist das Leben/King Nicolo or That's Life (1919) 93
König Nicolo oder So ist das Leben/King Nicolo or That's Life (Wedekind) 93

König Ödipus (Fühmann) 562 n.7
König Ödipus/King Oedipus (1991) 562 n.7
Königswalzer/King's Waltz (1935) 307
Konsalik, Heinz G. 365, 401, 426 n.262, 441
Köppen, Manuel 322 n.30, 488 n.51
Körber, Hilde 347
Korda, Alexander 245, 254, 324 n.42, 340, 351, 397
Korean War 354, 386
Korff, Arnold 206
Kornfeld, Paul 270 n.33
Korporal Mombour (Penzoldt) 387
Korsten, Lucien 30 n.16
Korte, Helmut 167 n.193
Körte, Mona 270 n.33
Kortner, Fritz 61, 146, 176, 216–17, 240 n.181, 245, 253, 271 n.43, 340, 406–7 n.27
Kosch, Wilhelm 490 n.76
Koshofer, Gert 332 n.163
Koster, Henry 267, 421 n.204
Kötter, Nina 541
Kowa, Victor de 282, 396
Krabat (2008) 567 n.51, 580 n.190
Kracauer, Siegfried 76 n.6, 117–18, 122, 128, 134, 162 n.114, 163 nn.124–5, 164 n.144, 165 n.163, 166 n.180, 172, 176, 183, 193, 197, 202, 210, 212, 216, 229 nn.6–7, 230 n.23, 231 n.46, 234 n.90, 236 n.124, 236 n.125, 236 n.128, 238 n.157, 239 n.160, 240 n.177
Krahl, Hilde 249, 345
Královská hra/The Royal Game (1980) 426 n.259
Kräly, Hanns 187–8, 233 n.63
Kramer, Jurij 489 n.68
Krämer, Peter 30 n.14
Kramer, Thomas 283, 323 n.39, 490 n.81
Krampf, Günther 254
Kranenburg, Eva 518, 571 n.95
Krause, Frank 76 n.14
Krause, Willi 322 n.17
Kraus, Karl 77 n.26

Krausser, Helmut 504, 564 n.27
Krauss (Krauß), Werner 63, 65–6, 68, 70, 86 n.133, 99, 106, 155, 217, 245, 314–15
Kreimeier, Klaus 67, 86 n.139, 156 n.12, 242 nn.219–20, 327 nn.85–6, 417 n.150
Kretzer, Max 85 n.125
Kreuzpaintner, Marco 506, 555, 567 n.51, 580 n.190
Krieg und sexuelle Gewalt/War and Sexual Violence (1993) 573 n.107
Krieg/War (Renn) 236 n.119
Krien, Werner 420 n.182
Kristina-Söderbaum-picture 369
Kroetz, Franz Xaver 472, 496 n.164
Kröger, Consul 110
Król, Joachim 551
Krücke (1992) 567 n.53
Krücke (Härtling) 567 n.53
Krüger, Gerhard 420 n.182
Krug, Manfred 443, 446
Kruso (2018) 577 n.164
Kruso (Seiler) 577 n.164
Krüss, James 441, 504
Kubaschewski, Ilse 365, 415 n.120, 455, 492 n.105
Kubrick, Stanley 2, 134, 499, 529, 533–4
Kuby, Erich 400
Küchenmeister, Heinrich J. 175
Küchenmeister-Tobis group 175
Küchenmeister-Tobis-Klangfilm-group 177
Kugelstadt, Hermann 369
Kugel, Wilfried 80 n.52
Kuhle Wampe (1932) 254
Kuhlmann, Carl 339
Kuhn, Anna 477, 497 n.182, 497 n.189
Kuhn, Annette 494 n.131
Kühne, Friedrich 65–6
Kühn, Siegfried 417 n.140
Külpe, Oswald 141
Kulturbund zur demokratischen Erneuerung Deutschlands (Cultural Association for the Democratic Renewal of Germany) 371

Kulturlexikon zum Dritten Reich (Klee) 414 n.118, 415 n.119
Kunert, Joachim 445, 486 n.45
Kunst der Propaganda. Der Film im Dritten Reich (Köppen & Schütz) 322 n.30
Kunst ist Waffe (Wolf) 184
Künstlerfilm 445
Kunstmann, Ernst 377
Kunstmärchen 59
Kunstwart journal 140
Kuntze, Reimar 197
Kurosawa, Akira 467
Kurt Desch 391
Kurtz, Rudolf 162 n.106
Kutschera, Rolf 388
Kutscher, Volker 520
Kuttner, Sarah 506
Kutzli, Sebastian 522
Kyser, Hans 106, 130, 133–4, 157 n.19, 166 n.175, 174

Laban, Rudolf von 44
La Chanson de Roland/Song of Roland 82 n.79
Lachende Erben/Laughing Heirs (1933) 250
Lackmann, Laura 506
La crise est finie/The Crisis is Over (1934) 248
La Damnation de Faust/The Damnation of Faust (1898) 17–18, 21, 24
La Damnation du docteur Faust/The Damnation of Dr. Faust (1904) 19, 21
The Lady Vanishes (1938) 212
Laemmle, Carl, Jr. 178, 205, 230 n.32, 259–61
Laemmle, Carl, Sr. 261
L'affaire Maurizius/Caso Mauritius (1953) 410 n.65
Lagorio, Alexander von 286, 291
La Habanera (1937) 330 n.138, 415 n.119
Lähn, Peter 82 n.78
La laterne magique/The Magic Lantern (1903) 11–12, 27

La leggenda di Faust/The Legend of Faust (1949) 410 n.63
La Marquise d'O (1959) 407 n.30
La Marquise d'O (1976) 436
La Marquise d'O (Kleist) 407 n.30, 436
Lamb, Stephen 236 n.119
Lammers, Reichsminister 326 n.83
Lampel, Peter Martin 202, 235 n.119, 236 n.125
Lamprecht, Gerhard 108–12, 152, 160 nn.76–7, 160 n.79, 161 n.89, 212, 254, 330 n.138, 379, 409 n.57
L'andata alla fucina/Going to the Forge (1910) 77 n.22
Land, Hans 32 n.37, 37, 40, 157 n.23
Land ohne Frauen/Land without Women (1929) 176
Land, Robert 194, 351
Landsberger, Hugo 37
Landwehr, Margarete J. 578 n.174
Lange, Allert de 412 n.79
Lange-Fuchs, Hauke 31 n.35
Lange, Hellmut 452
Lange, Jasmin 91, 156 nn.8–9
Lange, Manfred 483 n.12
Langemeyer, Peter 271 n.46
Lang, Fritz 1, 2, 45, 80 n.45, 86 n.136, 108, 114–18, 142–3, 153–4, 161 n.98, 162 n.103, 162 nn.105–7, 163 n.120, 171–2, 178, 191, 216, 222, 228, 229 n.15, 233 n.67, 241 n.201, 245, 247–8, 262, 272 n.57, 272 n.60, 281, 306, 328 n.111, 347, 412 n.81, 449, 453, 457, 466–7
Langhoff, Thomas 445
Lang, Joachim A. 227
Lang, Peter 270 n.39
Langrock, Ursula 452
Lania, Léo 165 n.146, 222–3, 257, 271 n.50
L'Année dernière à Marienbad/Last Year at Marienbad (1961) 450, 466
Lantz, Adolf 102, 245
"La Nuit de Décembre"/Night in December (de Musset) 51

La Pointe Courte (1956) 495 n.139
La Poupee/The Puppet (1896) 66, 93
La promessa/The Promise (1979) 575 n.141
Lara, Alexandra Maria 506
La Rebelión de los colgados/The Rebellion of the Hanged (1954) 352
À la recherche du temps perdu/In Search of Lost Time (Proust) 213, 465
La Ronde (1950) 349–50, 410 n.65
La Roue/The Wheel (1922) 230 n.17
L'Arrivé d'un train en gare/Arrival of a train in the station (1895) 15
L'Arroseur arrosé/The Sprinkler Sprinkled (1895) 15
Larsen, Viggo 36, 77 n.28, 85 n.125, 164 n.142
La rue sans joie (1938) 164 n.135
La scimitarra del Saraceno/The Pirate and the Slave Girl (1959) 490 n.78
Laserstein, Lotte 225
La Signora di tutti/Everybody's Woman (1934) 251
Lasker-Schüler, Else 268 n.10, 537
La Sortie des ouvriers de l'usine Lumière/Workers Leaving the Lumière Factory (1895) 15
L'assassinat du duc de Guise/The Assassination of the Duke de Guise (1908) 83 n.91
Laßwitz, Kurd 581 n.206
The Last Command (1928) 188
Last Days of Pompeii (1913) 79 n.44
La Tendre ennemie/The Tender Enemy (1936) 269 n.25
laterna magica (magic lantern) 11–14
L'Auberge rouge (1923) 141
Lauret, René 170 n.231
Lausbubengeschichten/Scoundrel Stories (1964) 492 n.99
Lausbubengeschichten/Scoundrel Stories (Thoma) 368
Lauste, Eugène 172
Lautensack, Heinrich 60
Lauterbach, Heiner 506

Lautz, Ernst 416 n.136
La Wally (1892) 415 n.128
Law, Jude 542, 545
Lawrence, Francis 195
Lawrence, Frederick 8 n.4
Lawrence of Arabia (1962) 438
Leaf, Caroline 540
Le affinità elettive/Elective Affinities (1996) 533
Leake, Grace S. 235 n.106
Leal, Joanne 493 n.119
Lean, David 438
Leander, Zarah 300, 326 n.80, 330 n.138, 365
Learning from the Germans. Race and the Memory of Evil (Neiman) 482 n.1, 580 n.187
Leatherstocking Tales (Cooper) 491 n.81
Le Bargy, Charles 83 n.91
Lebensläufe (Kluge) 454
Lebensraum 288, 290
Leben und Treiben am Alexanderplatz in Berlin/Life and Goings-on at Alexanderplatz in Berlin (1896) 214
Leberkäsjunkie (2019) 572 n.105
Le Brio (2017) 581 n.199
Le Cabinet de Méphistophélès/Mephisto's Laboratory (1897) 18
Lechner, Maria 121
Le cinéma expressioniste allemand (Henry) 242 n.221
Leconte, Patrice 577 n.161
Le Coup de grâce (Yourcenar) 465
Lederer, Franz/Francis 146
Le destin/Macurio (1959/60) 411 n.75
Ledige Mütter/Single Mothers (1928) 186
Lee, Christopher 514
Lee Ping-bing, Mark 538
Lee, Robert G. 162 n.114
Le "Faust" de Goethe (Goethe) 30 n.20
Lefebvre, Henri 577 n.166
Lefevere, Andre 157 n.28
Le Fort, Gertrud von 403

Legband, Paul 93, 106
Lehmann, A. 8 n.6
Leidenschaft/Passion 190, 307
Leipzig im Herbst/Leipzig in Autumn (1989) 432
Leisen, Mitchell 352
Leiser, Erwin 308, 572 n.102
Leitch, Thomas 9 n.12, 167 n.192, 229 nn.9–10, 238 n.151, 238 n.157, 241 n.196, 242 n.205
Leitch, Tom 210, 238 n.155
Lejeune, Caroline A. 253, 261, 271 n.42, 272 nn.61–2
Le jugement de Dieu/Judgment of God (1952) 410 n.65
Lemhagen, Ella 567 n.50
Lemke, Karl 190, 193
Leni, Paul 100–1, 106
Lenk, Sabine 29 n.8
Lensing, Leo 427 n.268
Lenya, Lotte 224, 245
Lenz (1971) 492 n.106, 494 n.120
Lenz (Büchner) 5, 8 n.6, 492 n.106, 494 n.120
Lenz, J. M. 440
Lenz, Siegfried 440, 496 n.163, 510, 516, 518, 567 n.55, 569 n.82, 580 n.191
Leonard, Robert Z. 266
Leone, Sergio 448
Leonhardt, Friedrich 565 n.33
Leonhardt, Rudolf 149, 168 n.215, 169 n.221, 246
Leopold, Georg 488 n.56
Lepage, Marquise 31 n.33
Le Pianiste/The Piano Teacher (2001) 535
Le Plaisir (1952) 476
Leporella (1991) 519, 577 n.161
Leporella (Zweig) 519, 577 n.161
Leppmann, Wolfgang 158 n.45
Le Prince, Louis 15
Lernet-Holenia, Alexander 277, 362–3, 414 n.109
Le roi des aulnes/The Erl-King (Tournier) 465
Le Roman de Werther (1938) 251
Le Roy, Mervyn 353

Les aventueres de Robinson Crusoé (Defoe) 30 n.18
Les beaux jours d'Aranjuez (2017) 546–7
Leschnikoff, Ari 283
Les contes d'Hoffmann (Offenbach). See Tales of Hoffmann (1881)
Le sexe faible/The Weaker Sex (1933) 248
Le sexe faible/The Weaker Sex (Bourdet) 248
Les Films Modernes S.A. (Paris) 392
Les Hallucinations du baron de Münchhausen (1911) 79 n.45
Les Particules élémentaires (Houellebecq) 564 n.26
Les Quatre Cents Coups/The 400 Blows (1959) 438
Lessa, Bia 556
Lessing, Gotthold E. 37, 58, 78 n.29, 106, 278, 317, 321 n.11, 376–80, 488 n.60, 500, 519, 552, 579 n.181
Le tout petit Faust/The Very Small Faust (1910) 38
Letter from an Unknown Woman/一个陌生女人的来信 (2004) 537–8
Letzte Stunde vor den Ferien: Effi Briest (2017) 541
Leutnant Gustl (Schnitzler) 239 n.166
Leuwerik, Ruth 382, 420 n.182
Levins Mühle/Levin's Mill (1980) 445, 483 n.6
Levins Mühle/Levin's Mill (Bobrowski) 445, 483 n.6
Levin, Thomas Y. 231 n.46
Le Voyage dans la Lune/A Trip to the Moon (1902) 26
Le voyage de Gulliver à Lilliput et chez les géants/Gulliver's Journey to Lilliput (1902) 30 n.18
Levy, Dani 520
Lewinski, Heinrich 491 n.88
Lewis, Edgar 74, 78 n.30
Lewisohn, Lewis 264
Lewitan, Louis 565 n.40
Lexikon des deutschen Films (Kramer) 323 n.39

Leytner, Nikolaus 555, 580 n.190
Library of the World's Best Literature 82 n.72
Lichtenstein, Manfred 159 n.67
Licht, Schatten und Bewegung (Schlöndorff) 494 n.132, 494 n.135, 495 n.139, 495 n.141, 495 n.143, 495 n.148, 495 n.150, 496 n.154, 496 n.157
Lichtspiele 36
Lichtspielgesetz (cinema law) 103, 279
Licht- und Nadelton technology 202
Liebe 47/Love 47 (1949) 344–6
Liebe auf Befehl/Love on Command (1931) 206
Liebe Deinen Nächsten/Love Your Neighbor (Remarque) 359
Liebe ist kälter als der Tod/Love is Colder than Death (1969) 473
Liebelei (1933) 216, 250, 306
Liebelei/Flirtation (Schnitzler) 41–2, 80 n.59, 81 n.66, 250, 349, 403
Liebeneiner, Wolfgang 247, 250, 318, 337, 341–2, 344–6, 407 n.28, 409 n.55
Liebeserwachen/Awakening of Love (1936) 307
Liebeswalzer/Waltz of Love (1930) 181–2, 233 n.77
Liebe und Trompetenblasen/Love and Trumpets (1925) 190
Liebe will gelernt sein (Kästner) 486 n.43
Liebe will gelernt sein/Love Has to Be Learned (1962) 486 n.43
Liebknecht, Karl 89
Liebling der Götter (1960) 427 n.270
Liebmann, Robert 189, 190, 245
Liechtenstein (LI) 1, 181, 231 n.39, 570 n.85
Liedtke, Harry 190
Liepmann, Heinz 355
Lietzau, Hans 488 n.60
Lieutenant Gustl (Schnitzler) 150
The Life and Death of Colonel Blimp (1943) 410 n.64
The Life and Works of Wolfgang Borchert (Burgess) 407 n.33

Lignose-Hörfilm 175
Lila Lila (2009) 508, 571 n.94
Lila Lila (Suter) 508, 571 n.94
Lilienthal, Otto 382–3
Lilienthal, Peter 440
Lili Marleen (1981) 477, 491 n.82
Liliom (1934) 248
Liliom (Molnár) 248
Lilith und Ly (1919) 142
Lily of the Dust (1924) 162–3 n.117, 228 n.4, 272 n.59, 280
Linda, Curt 486 n.43, 567 n.51, 578 n.180
Lindau, Paul 40, 85 n.125
Lindeiner-Strásky, Karina von 484 n.19
Lindsay, Margaret 352
Lindtberg, Leopold 250, 361
Lingen, Theo 282, 363
Link, Caroline 504, 528, 567 n.50, 567 n.53
Lintz, Eduard 80 n.53
Lippmann, Hanns 100
Liptay, Fabienne 80 n.54
Lisser, Heinz 241 n.195
Liszt, Franz 17
literacy 25, 37
"*Literarische Filmerzählung*"/Literary Filmstory (1965) 484 n.15, 519, 572 n.102
literary canon 3, 12, 24–5, 27–8, 33, 36, 58–9, 90, 96, 100, 114, 130, 141, 152, 226, 249, 275–8, 284, 321 n.11, 335, 338, 346, 370, 379, 399, 402–4, 430–1, 439, 443–6, 458, 478, 500, 503, 509–10, 512, 516, 524, 547, 553–4, 560
   Fassbinder and 471–8
   Fontane 303–7
   in French exile 250–2
   male domination 522, 530
   Schiller 292–5, 444
   Ufa 74
literary heritage 3–4, 6, 33, 366, 376, 432, 442–6, 457–60, 513, 517–18
literary public sphere 464
literary realism 285, 380–3

literary scandals 100–2
literature
  bestselling/bestseller 6–7, 17, 22–3, 54, 73, 97, 105, 119–20, 149, 153, 156 n.13, 157 n.22, 173, 185, 187, 191, 204, 207, 212–13, 226, 236 n.119, 296, 317, 321 n.13, 323 n.36, 362, 365, 388, 392, 401, 441–2, 480, 501, 503, 505, 508–10, 519, 521, 526, 554, 556, 564 n.21, 565 n.33, 566 n.49, 568 n.57
  bridge/bridging effect of 23, 63, 73
  canon of (*see* literary canon)
  classical 4, 102, 130, 154, 505
  cultural capital of 28, 32 n.41, 32 n.44, 114, 508
  familiarity of 17, 20, 178, 251, 256, 287, 338, 349
  as high culture (*see* high culture)
  popular 3, 7, 16, 22, 36–8, 59, 61, 69, 78 n.30, 92, 102, 119, 129, 133, 153–4, 156 n.7, 173, 176, 187, 275, 277, 293, 303, 346, 365, 383, 400–1, 426 nn.261–2, 486 n.44, 502, 504, 509–10, 520, 556, 571 n.95
  tradition(s) of 18, 74, 472, 530
  as transcultural 2, 437, 531, 538, 547
Literature and Film in the Third Reich (Schoeps) 321 n.10
Literatur im Film. Beispiele einer Medienbeziehung (Neuhaus) 8 n.2
Literatur und Film: Mephisto (Paech) 76 n.7, 484 n.19
Little House on the Prairie 485 n.28
The Little Match Girl (Andersen) 174–5
Little Red Riding Hood 298–300
live-action revolution 128
Livingston, Margaret 137
Lloyd-Film (Berlin) 60
Loach, Ken 505
Loacker, Armin 164 n.131
Lochmann, Roman 579 n.180
Lodemann, Jürgen 8 n.6

Loebner, Vera 486 n.43
L'oeuvre de Georges Méliès (Malthête & Mannoni) 29 n.2, 31 n.23
Loew, David L. 354
Lohmann, Dietrich 497 n.184
Lohmeier, Anke-Marie 327 n.100, 497 n.173, 497 n.178
Lola (1981) 477, 501
Lola Montez (1955) 410 n.64
Lola rennt/Run Lola Run 539
Lombroso, Cesare 71, 168 n.214
London 12, 17, 20, 24, 28, 182–3, 194, 196, 214, 254–5, 258, 267, 324 n.42, 336, 397, 452
London, Jack 268 n.10
The Long Aftermath: Cultural Legacies of Europe at War, 1936–2016 (Braganca & Tame) 405 n.8
The Longest Day (1962) 438
Löns, Hermann 366, 415 n.123
Look Who's Talking (1989) 501
Loos, Theodor 117, 125, 271 n.40, 294, 310
L'Opéra de quat'sous (1931) 224
López, Temístocles 542
Lorre, Peter 245, 248, 272 n.60, 426 n.255
Losee, Frank 74
Losey, Joseph 479
The Lost Garden: The Life and Cinema of Alice Guy-Blaché (1995) 31 n.33
Lothar, Rudolf 206, 238 n.145
Lotte in Weimar (1975) 445
Lotte in Weimar (Mann) 445
Lotus-Film GmbH (Vienna) 566 n.49
Love Life (Shalev) 581 n.202
The Love Waltz (1930) 182
Lowe-Porter, H. T. 161 n.93
Lübeck 108–9, 161 n.89
Lubin, Arthur 195
Lubin Manufacturing Company (Philadelphia) 74
Lubin, Siegmund 74, 78 n.30
Lubitsch, Ernst 4, 57, 61, 66, 91, 98, 117, 158 n.43, 159 n.60, 172, 187, 246, 267, 397, 457, 545
Lucian of Samosata 35

Lucky Bird Pictures (Munich) 566 n.49
Lucrezia Borgia (1922) 171, 273 n.71
Ludendorff, Erich 57, 84 n.111, 84 n.113
Luderer, Wolfgang 444, 473
Ludmila. A Legend of Liechtenstein (Gallico) 570 n.85
Lugosi, Bela 248
Lühe, Irmela von der 232 n.51
Luis and the Aliens 514
Lukas, Wolfgang 81 n.61
Lulu (1917) 58–9
Lulu (1962) 451
Lulu. Tragödie in 5 Aufzügen/Lulu, a Tragedy in five Acts (Wedekind) 58, 451
Lumière brothers 13, 15–17, 22, 24–5, 28, 46, 50, 73
Lumière, Louis 13, 15–17, 50
Lumpensammler 163 n.125
Luna-Film 58, 102
Luserke-Jaqui, Matthias 85 n.130
Luther (2003) 510
Lüth, Erich 369–70
Luxemburg, Rosa 89
Lux Radio Theater 354
Luxus-eljárás (1981) 496 n.164
Lyne, Adrian 195

M (1931) 216, 222, 228, 272 n.60, 281, 306, 466
Mach die Musik leiser/Turn Down the Music (1994) 522
Mach, Josef 448
Machorka-Muff (1962) 450, 464
MacKenzie, Scott 420 n.185, 513, 563 n.11, 568 n.63
Mackie Messer-Brechts Dreigroschenfilm (2018) 227, 510
Mack, Max 40, 51, 58, 78 n.30, 142
Mack the Knife (1989) 491 n.86
Madagascar 2 (2008) 516
Madame Bovary (1937) 330 n.138
Madame Dubarry/Passion (1919) 172
Mädchen in Uniform/Girls in Uniform (1931) 196–7, 216, 226, 254, 281–2

Mädchen in Uniform/Girls in Uniform (1958) 400
Madelung, Aage 119
Madness Rules 361
Maetzig, Kurt 371, 409 n.59, 417 n.137, 420 n.193, 488 n.51
Magda (1917) 78 n.30
Magda (Sudermann & Winslow) 74, 78 n.30
Magdalena (1955) 416 n.132
magic lantern 11–14, 20
Magnusson, Kristof 505
MagShamhráin, Rachel 242 n.205, 324 n.45
Mahler, Gustav 436
Mahler-Werfel, Alma 264
Maierhofer, Ferdinand 121
Maier-Katkin, Birgit 263–4, 273 n.67, 273 n.70
Maigne, Charles 74
Maisch, Herbert 295, 307–12, 328 n.108, 328 n.112, 329 n.122
Makatsch, Heike 552, 567 n.54
Malina (1991) 516, 531
Malina (Bachmann) 516, 531
Malle, Louis 453, 466, 495 n.138, 495 n.139
Malone, Paul M. 565 n.34
Malthête, Jacques 29 n.2, 31 n.23
Maltz, Albert 421 n.204
Mambéty, Djibril Diop 529, 531–2
Mamoulian, Rouben 259, 280
The Manchester Guardian newspaper 204, 372
Manet, Édouard 35
Mängelexemplar/Damaged Goods (2016) 506
Man Hunt (1941) 262, 272 n.57
Mania czy Ania (1999) 566–7 n.50
Mania czy Ania (Kästner) 566–7 n.50
Mankiewicz, Herman J. 188
Mankiewicz, Joseph L. 354
Mann, Delbert 237 n.143
Männerhort/Shelter for Men (2014) 505
Männerhort/Shelter for Men (Magnusson) 505
Mann, Erika 231 n.51

Mannes, Stefan 329 n.129
Mannheim, Lucie 176, 232 n.60
Mann, Heinrich 2, 79 n.38, 120, 154, 163 n.130, 165 n.161, 187–94, 196, 215, 233 n.66, 233 n.75, 234 nn.81–3, 234 n.87, 244, 246, 262, 281, 305, 385, 413 n.102, 417 n.141, 417 n.145, 425 n.245, 477
   film in two Germanies 370–4
Mann, Klaus 165 n.146, 246, 404 n.1, 436
The Man Nobody Knows: The Life and Legacy of B. Traven (Pateman) 411 n.73
Mannoni, Laurent 29 n.2, 31 n.23
Mann, Thomas 79 n.41, 108, 130–1, 141, 153, 160 n.71, 160 n.78, 160 nn.80–1, 161 n.91, 161 n.93, 166 n.168, 213, 238 n.150, 246, 267, 270 n.30, 297, 327 n.88, 350, 376, 384–5, 402, 411 n.69, 420 n.182, 420 n.194, 421 n.198, 436, 445, 451, 458, 479, 484 n.25, 489 n.70, 492 n.99, 500, 506, 519, 524, 556, 563 n.8, 567 n.55, 572 n.100, 573 n.122
Mann, Victor 193, 234 n.86, 246
Man of Straw (1972) 417 n.145
Manuela und der Förster/Manuela and the Forest Ranger 491 n.89
Manz, Peter 165 nn.154–5
Marchais, D. 8 n.6
Maresi (1948) 362
Marey, Étienne-Jules 15
Margarete-die Geschichte einer Gefallenen/Margarete: A Fallen Woman's Tale (1919) 96–7
Maria, die Magd/Maria, the Maid (1936) 312
Marian, Ferdinand 303, 314–15, 330 n.138
Maria Stuart (1957) 414 n.108, 416 n.131
Maria Stuart (1963) 488 n.60
Maria Stuart (1986) 489 n.60
Maria Stuart (Schiller) 414 n.108, 416 n.131

Mario und der Zauberer/Mario and the Magician (1994) 556, 562 n.5, 563 n.8
Mario und der Zauberer/Mario and the Magician (Mann) 500, 556, 563 n.8
Marischka, Ernst 361, 414 n.110
Marischka, Georg 403, 426 n.261
Marjanishvili, Kote 141
marketability 103, 125, 501, 517
Märkische Forschungen (1982) 483 n.6
Marlene Dietrich (Sudendorf) 232 n.61
Marlowe, Christopher 16, 130
Marmorhaus-Lichtspiele 62
Marr, Hans 270 n.40, 294
Marshall, Garry 501
Martens, Valérie von 353
Martin, Karl Heinz 35, 92, 104, 214
Marton, Andrew 438
Marton, Georg 271 n.44
Marut, Ret 411 n.72
Marxer, Isolde 570 n.85
Marx, Karl 268 n.10, 447
Mary, Little 212
Mary Queen of Scots (2013) 577 n.161
Mary Queen of Scots (Zweig) 577 n.161
Masannek, Joachim 510, 566 n.49
Maser, Werner 331 n.155
Massary, Fritzi 55, 83 n.100
Massenet, Jules 251
mass entertainment 3, 12, 23, 36, 62, 73, 90–1, 130, 152, 171, 226–7, 330 n.142, 346, 386, 525
   fairy tales as 298–300
   literature as 296–8, 343
   and voyeurism 122–5
Massey, Anne 238 n.154
mass media 3, 95, 227, 280, 296
Massolle, Joseph 174
The Mass Ornament, Weimar Essays (Kracauer) 231 n.46
Master Films 529
Masters, Past 161 n.93
The Matchmaker (1958) 413 n.107

Mattern, Nicole 160 n.74
Matthes, Ulrich 582 n.209
Matto regiert/Matto rules/In Matteo's Realm (Glauser) 361
Mattscheibe 439
Maupassant, Guy de 277
Mauvaise Graine/The Bad Seed (1934) 248
Max Ophüls. Deutscher-Jude-Franzose (Asper) 269 nn.26–7
Max und Moritz (1923) 90
Max und Moritz (Busch) 90
Mayer, Carl 92, 135–7, 149–50, 156 nn.14–15, 161 n.99, 166 n.184, 212, 245, 465
Mayer, Gustl 240 n.182
Mayerhoff, Konrad 452
Mayer, Louis B. 264, 267
Mayer, Veronika 235 n.107
May, Joe 43, 61, 82 n.73, 138, 282
May, Karl 403, 412 n.86, 427 n.269, 439, 447–8, 490 n.75, 502
Mayne, Ethel Colburn 86 n.143
Mayne, Judith 194
May, Paul 368, 416 n.130, 422 n.217
Mayring, Philipp Lothar 339
M'Barek, Elyas 506
McCarthyism 351, 353–4
McGuire, William Anthony 260, 323 n.36
McIsaac, Peter M. 565 n.34
McMahan, Alison 31 n.31, 31 n.33
Me and the Colonel (1958) 359–60
Medical Society for Sexual Research 67
Medienboard Berlin-Brandenburg (MBB) 506, 520, 529, 552, 570 n.90, 573 n.106
Meerbaum-Eisinger, Selma 537
Mefistofele (Boito) 17
Meier, Aneka 83 n.94, 156 n.4
Meinert, Rudolf 55, 147, 414 n.117
Meinhof, Ulrike 468, 495 n.146
Mein Kampf/My Struggle (Hitler) 198, 205, 237 n.139, 280, 288, 292, 301, 330 n.131
Mein Schulfreund (1960) 426 n.261
Meirelles, Fernando 529, 542

Meisel, Edmund 175, 239 n.170
Melanchthon 141
Melford, George 238 n.145
Méliès, Georges 2, 15–28, 29 n.1, 30 nn.15–16, 31 nn.21–2, 31 n.27, 36–8, 50, 65, 73, 77 n.28, 79 n.45, 80 n.45, 117
and magic of E.T.A. Hoffmann 26–7
reality and illusion 27
"Star Film" 20
Melodie der Welt/Melody of the World (1929) 173, 229 n.14
Melodie des Herzens/Melody of the Heart (1929) 181–2
The Melodramatic Imagination. Balzac, Henry James, Melodrama, and the Mode of Excess (Brooks) 87 n.151, 164 n.139
Melville, Jean-Pierre 466, 495 n.138, 495 n.139
memory culture 3, 334–5, 357, 370, 382, 443, 459, 464, 529, 554, 560
Men Are Not Gods (1936) 397
Mendel, Georg Victor 156 n.7
Mendes, Lothar 252–3, 295, 313–14
Mengele, Josef 333
Menges, Chris 535
Menschen am Sonntag/People on Sunday (1930) 222, 347
Menschen im Hotel/People at a Hotel (1959) 392, 427 n.270
Menschen im Hotel/People at a Hotel (Baum) 198, 207, 226, 238 nn.152–3, 392–3
Menschen ohne Vaterland/People without Homeland (1937) 307, 328 n.109
Menschheitsdämmerung/The Twilight of Humanity (1919) 215
Menzel, Gerhard 277, 283, 295
Mephisto (1981) 436
Mephistophela (1920) 66
Mercier, Pascal 510, 514
Merezhkovsky, Dmitry 233 n.63
Merzbach, Paul 164 n.135

Meschrabpom-Film company 256
Mes Memoires (Méliès) 31 n.22
Messter-Film/Messter production 57, 60–1
Messter, Oskar 15, 56, 78 n.30, 85 n.123, 85 n.125, 98
Messters Projektion GmbH 61
Métamorphose de Faust et apparition de Marguerite/Transformation of Faust and appearance of Gretchen (1897) 17
The Metarmorphosis of Mr. Samsa (1977) 540
Metro-Goldwyn-Mayer (MGM) Studio 174, 182, 188, 203, 207–8, 210, 228 n.4, 229 n.15, 233 n.67, 262–7, 272 n.63, 272 n.65, 273 n.72, 353, 392, 398, 423 n.222
Metropolis (1927) 45, 86 n.136, 108, 143, 152, 161 n.98, 178, 187, 191, 216, 229 n.15, 233 n.67, 241 n.201, 347
Metropolis (Harbou) 143, 161 n.98, 168 n.199
Metzger, Ludwig 312, 314, 329 n.130, 330 n.134
Metzler Handbuch: Thomas Manns Buddenbrooks (Neuhaus & Mattern) 160 n.74
Meyer, Clemens 521, 548–9, 552
Meyer, Ferdinand 380
Meyer-Förster, Wilhelm 170 n.233
Meyerhoff, Joachim 557
Meyer, Johannes 187, 293, 296
Meyer, Kai 513
Meyer, Louis B. 262
Meyer, Otto 378–9
Meyer, Rolf 383
Meyers, Nancy 566 n.50
Meyrink, Gustav 60, 85 n.120, 172
Meza, Ed 513, 568 nn.65–8
Mezhinsky, Semyon 258
Michael Kohlhaas (2013) 544–5
Michael Kohlhaas (Kleist) 5, 8 n.6, 437, 465, 544–5
Michael Kohlhaas-Der Rebell (1969) 8 n.6, 465

Michael Powell: International Perspectives on an English Filmmaker (Christie & Moor) 410 n.66
Miehe, Ulf 458, 493 n.114
Mierendorff, Carlo 95, 157 n.29
Mignon (1906) 24
Mikesch, Elfi 491 n.92
Mikkelsen, Mads 552
Milestone, Lewis 2, 174, 199–200, 204–5, 226, 228, 261, 354–8, 360, 391, 557, 580 n.197
Miletty, Anny 121
Miller, Arthur C. 265, 465, 541
Miller, R. D. 328 n.116
Millet, Jean-François 35
Milton on Film (Brown) 166 n.166
Minder, Robert 163 n.127
Minetti, Bernhard 214, 307
Minghella, Anthony 529, 571 n.93
"Minister of Popular Enlightenment and Propaganda" 278
Ministry of Fear (1944) 262
The Ministry of Illusion: Nazi Cinema and Its Afterlife (Rentschler) 162 n.114, 320 n.7, 321 n.10, 322 n.20, 323 n.31, 330 n.137
Minkin, Adolf 258
Minna von Barnhelm (1962) 488 n.60
Minna von Barnhelm oder Das Soldatenglück/Minna von Barnhelm or the Soldiers' Happiness (1767) 317, 321 n.11, 379–80
miracle year of words 171
Mirage Enterprises (Los Angeles) 571 n.93
Mirren, Helen 566 n.49
Misch, Rochus 276, 320 n.3
Mitchell, George J. 237 n.133
Mitchum, Robert 353
Mit Himbeergeist geht alles besser/Everything Goes Better with Raspberry Brandy (1961) 426 n.261
Mitić, Gojko 448, 491 n.81
Mitscherlich, Alexander 359, 392–3, 423 n.225

Mitscherlich, Margarete 359, 392–3, 423 n.225
Mit Schnurrbart und Korsett/O, diese Bayern/Oh, Those Bavarians (1960) 416 n.132
Mitte Ende August/Sometime in August (2009) 512
Mitteilungen aus den Memoiren des Satans (Hauff) 58
Mittelreich (2013) 581 n.200
Mitterer, Felix 567 n.55
Mittler, Leo 424 n.229
Mobbing/Bullying (Pehnt) 520
mobility 2, 4, 20–1, 42, 136, 164 n.143, 195, 219, 477, 550, 558
Möbius, Paul 103, 159 n.64
A Modern Hero (1934) 249
modernity/modernist age 35, 51, 54, 90, 100, 105, 131, 136, 139, 141–2, 167 n.196, 186, 209, 238 n.154
modern life 38–9, 86 n.146, 227
Modot, Gaston 224
Moeller, Felix 320 n.10, 321 n.15, 322 n.26, 329 n.121
Moeller, Robert G. 389–90, 422–3 n.218, 422 n.208, 422 nn.210–11, 422 nn.214–16
Moers, Walter 567 n.53
Moest, Hubert 58
Moguy, Léonide 254, 411 n.76
Moisson, Charles 15
Molière 134, 156, 297, 323 n.42
Möller, Eberhard Wolfgang 312, 329 n.130
Möller, Gunnar 300
Möller, Olaf 425 n.242
Moloch/Молох (1999) 543
Molotov-Ribbentrop Pact (1939) 258–9
Molo, Walter von 38–9, 79 nn.41–2, 277, 296, 384, 409 n.55, 411 n.69
Moltke, Johannes von 321 n.13, 404 n.4, 415 n.124, 427 n.271
Momo (1985) 487 n.48, 487 n.50
Momo (Ende) 441, 487 n.48, 487 n.50
Momplet, Antonio 239 n.164

Mondi, Bruno 377
Monk, Egon 440, 452, 480, 489 n.68
Monster Hunter 564 n.25
The Monstrous-Feminine. Film, Feminism, Psychoanalysis (Creed) 168 n.201
Montag, Lars 564 n.27
Montauk (Frisch) 465, 547–8
Montazel, Pierre 410 n.65
Montez, Lola 190
Montgomery, Douglass 260
Monumentalfilm 99
Moor, Andre 410 n.66
Moor, Andrew 410 n.66
Moor, Karl 311
Moorse, George 8 n.6, 455, 492 n.106
MOOVIE 518, 582 n.209
Moral (1958) 416 n.132
morality 12, 67, 71, 103, 105, 112, 119–21, 138, 148–9, 154, 279, 352, 437, 475–6, 542
Mörder, Hoffnung der Frauen/Murderer, Women's Hope (Kokoschka) 34, 76 n.12
Morell, A. 8 n.6
Morena, Erna 58, 69
Morenga (1985) 496 n.163
Morenga (Timm) 496 n.163
Morgan, Paul 246
Morgan, Peter 542
Morgenrot/Dawn (1933) 283, 323 n.42, 414 n.111
Morocco (1930) 168 n.200, 195
Morris, Redmond 529, 571 n.93
The Mortal Storm (1940) 353
Morte a Venezia/Death in Venice (1971) 436
Moselfahrt aus Liebeskummer/Moselle Trip from Heartache (1953) 365
Moser, Hans 121
Moses, Harry 207
Mosheim, Grete 144, 184–5
Mosse, George L. 156 n.11
The Most Desired Man (1994) 503
Moszkowicz, Martin 507, 565 n.40
Mother (1926) 128
motherhood 69, 71–2, 186, 197, 291, 538

Motion Picture Producers and
  Distributors of America
  (MPPDA) 203
Movie History: A Survey (Gomery &
  Pafort-Overduin) 30 n.11
Moviepilot 518
Movietone sound film system 134,
  139–40
moving images 12, 14, 40, 57, 61, 63,
  101, 109, 173–4
Moyes, Jojo 582 n.208
Mozart, Wolfgang Amadeus 251
Mrs Dalloway (Woolf) 213
Mücke, Panja 323 n.37
Mueller, Adeline 117, 162 n.102, 162
  n.111, 163 n.118, 163 nn.120–2
Mueller, Agnes C. 574 n.123
Mueller, Petra 517
Mühl-Benninghaus, Wolfgang 39, 50,
  80 nn.46–8, 80 n.52, 199, 230
  n.28, 235 nn.109–11, 323 n.31,
  418 n.150
Mühsam, Erich 244
Müller, Brigitte 567 n.50
Müller, Corinna 98, 158 n.38, 158
  nn.42–4, 230 n.28, 237 n.135
Müller, Eva-Marianne 298, 300
Müller, Hans-Harald 236 n.119
Müller, Heiner 443, 446, 488 n.57
Müller, Herta 575 n.135
Müller, Jan 407 n.28, 408 n.47
Müller, Robby 457, 537
Müller-Stahl, Armin 446, 481, 572
  n.100
multiple-language versions (MLV)-
  films 183, 225–6, 250
multi-shot narrative films 18, 20, 28
Münchhausen (1911) 117
Münchhausen (1943) 332 n.163, 340,
  406 n.26
Münchnerinnen/Women of Munich
  (1944) 338, 340
Mundus Film Company (Vienna) 362,
  368, 380
The Murderers Are Coming/Убийцы
  выходят на дорогу (1942) 259
Muriel ou Le temps d'un retour (1963)
  467

Murnau, Friedrich Wilhelm 87 n.147,
  92, 105, 129–35, 139–40, 142,
  153, 164 n.143, 171, 174,
  187, 216, 233 n.67, 254, 324
  n.48, 412 n.81, 436, 457, 465,
  560
  cinematographic work 130
  Sunrise project 136
Murphy, Robert 410 n.66
Murray, Bill 545
Murray, Bruce A. 159 n.60
Murray, Stephen 351
musical chronometer 175
music(ians) and operetta(s) 93, 111,
  172, 180–3, 190, 194, 210, 220,
  225–7, 367, 437
Musil, Robert 6, 141, 213, 453, 465–6,
  478
Musmanno, Michael A. 359
Musser, Charles 31 n.26
Mutter Courage/Mother Courage
  (Brecht) 384, 426 n.264
Mutter Courage und ihre Kinder
  (1960) 426 n.264
Mutter Krausens Fahrt ins Glück/
  Mother Krause's Journey to
  Happiness (1929) 214
*Mutzenbacher II-Meine 365
  Liebhaber*/My 365 Lovers
  (1971) 493 n.107
Muybridge, Eadweard/Edward 14–15,
  111

Nabokov, Vladimir 472, 496 n.165
Nach dem Sturm/After the Storm
  (Zuckmayer) 394
Nachmann, Kurt 455, 493 n.107
Nachts, wenn der Teufel kam/The
  Devil Strikes at Night (1957)
  415 n.120
Nachtzug nach Lissabon/Night Train
  to Lisbon (Mercier) 514
Nackt/Naked (2002) 506
Nackt unter Wölfen/Naked among
  Wolves (2015) 561–2 n.3,
  571 n.95
Nackt unter Wölfen/Naked among
  Wolves (1963) 442, 571 n.95

Nackt unter Wölfen/Naked among Wolves (Apitz) 442
Naefe, Vivian 519, 566 n.49
Napoleonic wars 59
Naranbaatar 576 n.146
Narrenweisheit oder Tod und Verklärung des Jean Jacques Rousseau (1989) 489 n.68
Narziss und Goldmund (2020) 484 n.23, 512, 568 n.57
Narziss und Goldmund (Hesse) 484 n.23, 512, 568 n.57
Naso, Eckart von 303
Naso, Lancelot von 419 n.178, 567 n.50
Natanson, Jacques 410 n.65
Nathan der Weise/Nathan the Wise (2009) 171
Nathan der Weise/Nathan the Wise (Lessing) 106, 552, 579
National Censorship Board 247
national cinema 553
national cultural heritage 558
national culture 54, 60, 74, 130, 280
National Film Center (Tokyo, Japan) 104
national funding policies/subvention schemes 5, 500
national heritage 7, 59–61, 74
national identity 26, 113–18, 338, 340, 342, 348, 366, 410 n.67, 464, 500–1, 512–13, 579 n.182
nationalism 26, 55, 114, 118, 173, 189, 198, 200, 338, 372, 554, 556
National Socialism 4, 243, 267, 293, 372–3, 383, 388, 392, 393, 397, 401, 433
Nazi cinema (1933–45) 116, 275–319
  (ab)use of German literature 4, 275–319
  "Blood and Soil" ideology 288, 295–6
  filmmakers, return of 341–7
  ideological alignment 275, 278–84
  political leadership and filmmakers 277
  repression and censorship 278–84
  Storm and heritage film 285–92
  Sudermann, Rothe, and Rhon on 300–3
Nazi Cinema as Enchantment: The Politics of Entertainment in the Third Reich (O'Brien) 320 n.10, 321 n.14, 331 n.146
Nazi Film Melodrama (Heins) 322 n.20, 327 n.85, 331 n.152
Nazi Germany 106, 225, 245–7, 253, 256–8, 260, 262, 267, 277–8, 300, 308, 318, 333, 340–1, 343, 350, 365–6, 381, 400–1, 410 n.68, 416 n.136, 429, 470, 528
Nazi movement 155 n.2, 198, 205, 218, 249, 284, 373
Nazi propaganda 4, 86 n.133, 278, 282, 288, 290, 295, 313–15, 317, 320 n.9, 330 n.132, 412 n.81, 430
Nebenzahl, Heinrich 186, 222–3
Nebenzahl, Seymour 247–8, 250–1
Ned med våbnene (1914) 56
Ned med våbnene (Suttner) 56
Negrin, Alberto 575 n.141
Negri, Pola 117, 162 n.117, 280
Negulesco, Jean 398
Neher, Carola 224, 245, 247
Neher, Caspar 221, 222
Neidhart, August 367
Neill, Roy William 195, 248
Neiman, Susan 482 n.1, 580 n.187
Neitzel, Gesa 557
Nemere, László 575 n.144
neoliberal film industry 5–6, 432, 508, 515, 524, 526, 563 n.10
Neppach, Robert 105, 282, 283
Nero-Film (Paris) 202, 222–3, 226–7, 247, 251, 511
Nerval, Gérard de 17, 30 n.20
Nest, Anni 87 n.147
Nesthäkchen (1983) 487 n.49
Nesthäkchen (Ury) 487 n.49
Nest, Loni 70, 87 n.147
Nestroy, Johann Nepomuk 1, 38, 106, 228 n.4, 249, 269 n.18, 362, 402, 413 n.107, 440

Netflix 518, 556–7, 563 n.14, 580 n.191, 581 n.201
Nettelbeck, Sandra 491 n.92
Neubach, Ernst 293
Neuberg, Erich 488 n.60
Neuer Deutscher Film 427 n.267, 469, 485 n.36, 494 n.120, 496 n.153
Neue Sachlichkeit/New Objectivity/New Sobriety 43, 111, 151, 180, 186, 213, 218, 222, 227, 231 n.35, 347
Neues Deutschland newspaper 446
Neuhaus, Stefan 8 n.2, 160 n.74, 327 n.102, 405 n.8, 406 n.26
Neumann, Alfred 188, 233 n.63
Neumeister, Wolf 303, 368
Neupert, Richard 485 n.26
Neutsch, Erik 443
The Neverending Story (1984) 487 n.48
New Economic System 488 n.53
"new European citizen" 356
New German Cinema 5, 343, 372, 403, 431–4, 462, 464–6, 469, 477–8, 480, 493 n.106, 499, 501–2
    auteurs 471, 512, 522
    death of "Papa's Cinema" and birth of 450–4
    public funding and "amphibian" films 454–6
The New German Cinema (Sandford) 494 n.124
New German Cinema: A History (Elsaesser) 494 n.124, 494 n.131, 498 n.191
New German Cinema: From Oberhausen to Hamburg (Franklin) 494 n.124
A New History of German Cinema (Kapczynski & Richardson) 8 n.2, 81 n.71, 162 n.102, 230 n.27, 331 n.155, 491 n.84
Newman, Alfred 265
The New School for Social Research (New York) 257
"New Woman" 74, 137, 186–7, 194, 232 n.53

New York 2, 12, 17, 20, 24, 42–3, 46–7, 49–50, 56, 139, 245, 254, 258, 266, 360, 437, 514, 547
The New York Times newspaper 139, 231 n.38, 258–9, 262, 264–5, 357, 369, 384, 405 n.13, 409 n.62, 414 n.114, 416 n.136, 436, 470, 477, 480
Nibelungenlied 1, 39, 347
Nichols, George O. 126
Nicht der Homosexuelle ist pervers, sondern die Situation in der er sich befindet/It Is Not the Homosexual Who Is Perverse, But the Society in Which He Lives (1971) 573 n.107
Nicht nur zur Weihnachtszeit/Not Only at Christmas time (1970) 462, 464
Nichts als Gespenster/Nothing but Ghosts (2006) 510
Nicht versöhnt oder Es hilft nur Gewalt, wo Gewalt herrscht (1965) 464
Nickel, Gunter 240 n.181, 241 n.190
Nielsen, Asta 46, 78 n.30, 87 n.147, 121, 145, 151
Nielsen, Sören 38, 269 n.18
Nierentz, Hans-Jürgen 322 n.17
Nietzsche, Friedrich 23, 105, 155, 161 n.96, 512
The Night before the Divorce (1942) 271 n.44
Nightlife (2020) 581 n.199
Night Train to Lisbon (2013) 510
1922-Das Wunderjahr der Worte (Hummelt) 228 n.2
1914. Die letzten Tage vor dem Weltbrand (1930) 273 n.71
Ninotchka (1939) 397
Nipperdey, Thomas 80 n.47
Nirgendwo in Afrika/Nowhere in Africa (2001) 504, 528
Nirgendwo in Afrika/Nowhere in Africa (Zweig) 504, 508
Niven, Bill 276, 298, 320 nn.3–4, 320 nn.6–7, 323 n.32, 326 n.71, 327 n.90, 442, 488 n.56

Noack, Barbara 402
Noack, Victor 77 n.26
Noa, Manfred 106, 171
Noelte, Rudolf 402, 483 n.15
Noethen, Ulrich 569 n.81
Noll, Dieter 486 n.45
Noll, Ingrid 509
Nolte, Nick 582 n.208
Nonguet, Lucien 28, 36
No Place Like Home: Locations of Heimat in German Cinema (Moltke) 415 n.124
Nora Helmer (1974) 496 n.165
Nordisk production 41–2, 44–5, 49–50, 56, 95
Norrensen, Eric 70
Norton, Edward 545
Nosferatu (1922) 87 n.147, 171, 216, 254
Nöstlinger, Christine 519, 567 n.53
Nouveau Roman 450
Nouvelles Éditions de Films S.A. (Paris) 576 n.151
Nova-Film 342–3
Novalis 560
November revolution 89
Novotny, Rudolf 493 n.107
NSDAP/National Socialistist German Workers' Party 152, 160, 198, 269 n.19, 279–80, 288, 294, 313, 323 n.34
Nugent, Frank S. 258, 262, 272 n.53
Nuit et brouillard/Night and Fog (1955) 450
Nur eine Frau/Only a Woman (1958) 417 n.140
Nur eine Rose als Stütze/Nothing but a Rose for Support (Domin) 536
Nutz, Walter 388, 422 n.208
Nykvist, Sven 436

Oberdeichgraf 288–9
Oberhausen Film Festival 449–50, 464
Oberhausen Manifesto 449, 451, 472
Oberländer, Hans 60
Oberon, Merle 351
Objektiv-Film 339
O'Brien, George 137
O'Brien, Mary-Elisabeth 320 n.10, 321 n.14, 331 n.146
The Observer newspaper 194, 210, 228 n.1, 253
Ode to Joy (Schiller) 536
Ó Dochartaigh, Pól 405 n.8
Odyssee (Homer) 2
Oehme, Roland 562 n.7
Oehmichen, Walter 378, 419 n.173
Oehmig, Richard 418 n.151
Oehri, Arno 570 n.85
Oertel, Curt 275, 286–8, 290–2, 325 n.56
Offenbach, Jacques 26, 63–4, 350
Offermanns, Ernst 321 n.12
The Office of U.S. Military Government in Germany (OMGUS) 336–7, 348, 365, 405 nn.9–10, 405 n.13, 407 n.28
O'Flynn, Siobhan 551
Ohm Krüger (1941) 298, 312, 330 n.142
Olcott, Sidney 34
Olin, Lena 514
Olivier, Laurence 233 n.77, 351
Olschowsky, Burkhard 489 n.71
Oltermann, Philip 164 n.132
Olympia (1938) 254
Ondine (2009) 581 n.206
One Exciting Adventure (1934) 248
O'Neil, Nance 74
The Only Living Boy in New York (2018) 165 n.157
Operation Valkyrie 406 n.23
Opfer der Liebe/Victims of Love (Courths-Mahler) 156 n.7
Opfergang (1944) 317, 332 n.163, 377
Ophüls, Max 2, 81 n.59, 245, 250–1, 267, 269 n.25, 306, 349, 354, 400, 410 nn.64–5, 449, 465, 467, 476, 537–8, 575 n.146
Oppenheimer, Joseph Ben Issachar Süßkind 252, 270 n.34, 314–15
The Oppermanns (1933) 480
The Oppermanns (Feuchtwanger) 480
optical sound technology 174
Opus-films 228 n.5

ORF, Austrian 496 n.164, 518–19, 544, 572 n.100, 582 n.209
"Organisation Consul" 106
Orloff, Ida 45, 82 n.75
Ossietzky, Carl von 244, 268 n.10
Ostermayr-Film 368
Ostermayr, Peter 321 n.13, 367, 390, 415 n.127
Ostwind film series 504, 506, 581 n.199
Oswalda, Ossi 57, 66, 91, 94
Oswald, Gerd 400, 438
Oswald, Richard 61–2, 65–71, 72, 86 n.133, 86 n.145, 94–6, 98, 101, 103, 112, 114, 118–20, 123, 144–5, 153, 159 n.57, 160 n.72, 165 n.147, 171, 177–80, 190, 216–20, 223, 227–8, 231 nn.34–5, 240 n.183, 241 nn.184–5, 241 n.190, 241 n.193, 247–8, 254, 273 n.71, 400–1, 423 n.223, 465
  adaptation as high culture 62–4
  and literature on film 61–2
  "sensible public education" 67
Othello (Shakespeare) 58
The Other Love (1947) 354, 412 n.86
Ottinger, Ulrike 491 n.92
Ott, Wolfgang 397
Over Her Dead Body: Death, Feminity and the Aesthetic (Bronfen) 85 n.118
Oxenford, John 413 n.107
Ozep, Fedor 217

Paar, Katharina 400
Pabst, G. W. 87 n.147, 103, 119, 121–2, 125, 145–9, 159 n.63, 169 n.221, 183, 195, 197, 202, 212, 214, 222–5, 228, 235 n.100, 239 n.162, 242 n.215, 244–5, 249, 254, 359, 396, 412 n.81, 413 n.99, 449, 465–6, 575 n.139
Pacino, Al 360
Paech, Joachim 34, 76 n.7, 484 n.19
Pafort-Overduin, Clara 30 n.11

The Palgrave Encyclopedia of Urban Literary Studies (Tambling) 239 n.166
Palitzsch, Peter 426 n.264
Palmer, Lilli 245, 445
Palmetto (1998) 465
Palmier, Jean-Michel 272 n.64
Panikherz/Panik heart (Stuckrad-Barre) 557
Pantaleon Films 579 n.180
Panzer, Wolfgang 561 n.3
"Papas Kino" 433, 450, 501, 524
Pape, Frank 567 n.54
Paragraph 51-Seelenarzt Dr. Laduner (1946) 361
Paramount 174, 177, 187–8, 195, 210, 228 n.4, 229 n.15, 233 n.67, 233 n.69, 259, 262, 280, 352
The Parent Trap (1961) 486 n.43
The Parent Trap (1998) 566 n.50
Parfum/Perfume (2018) 518, 563 n.14, 571 n.95
Paris 2, 4, 12, 15, 17, 24, 26, 35, 42–3, 46, 121, 149, 177, 183, 229 n.6, 248, 250–1, 257, 267, 355–8, 466, 532
Pariser Tonfilmfrieden 177, 226
Paris Sound Film Peace 177, 226
Parker, Milo 566 n.49
Parker, Steven 270 n.32
Parlo, Dita 181
Partie d'ecarte/Card Party (1895) 46
Parufamet agreement 174, 229 n.15, 233 n.67
parvenu 13
Pascal, Gabriel 217
Pastina, Giorgio 410 n.63
Pastor Hall (1940) 254–5, 271 n.45
Pateman, Roy 411 n.73
patent war 202, 226, 230 n.27
Pathé/Pathé Frères 24, 36, 56, 77 n.28
The Patriot (1928) 187, 233 n.63
patriotism 25, 74, 293, 295
Patzak, Peter 519
Paul, Christiane 582 n.209
Paul, Heinz 253, 293–4, 326 n.78
Paul I (Merezhkovsky) 233 n.63
Paul I of Russia 188

Paul, Robert William 13, 15, 28, 36
Pauls, Eilhard Erich 287–8, 325 n.54
Paulsen, Harald 221, 245
Pausewang, Gudrun 571 n.94, 580 n.190
Pavlíček, František 489 n.63
Pawlowa, Vera 146
Peach, Lawrence du Garde 254
Pearl, Jed 9 n.11, 582 nn.213–14
Pearson, Roberta 76 n.18
Pecher, Claudia Maria 166 n.167
Pega Ladrão (1957) 239 n.164
Pehle, Margot 75 n.1, 157 n.17
Pehnt, Annette 520
Pelle the Conqueror (1987) 515
Pellon, Gabriel 286
Penn, Sean 529, 534–5
Penthesilea Moabit (2008) 572 n.99
Penzoldt, Ernst 387
People will Talk (1951) 354
Peregini, Frank 119
Pérez, Vincent 528–9
Perlberg, William 265
Perl, Jed 560
Peter, Kirsten 540
Peter Schlemihls wundersame Geschichte/Peter Schlemihl's Miraculous Story (Chamisso) 59, 64, 106
Petersen, Wolfgang 456, 480, 485 n.32, 487 n.48, 493 n.111, 566 n.46, 567 n.52
Peter, Shaggy 378
Peters, Ole 289
Peterson, Sebastian 527
Peters, Werner 372
Petro, Patrice 122, 145, 164 n.136, 164 n.139, 164 n.141, 168 n.206, 234 n.80
Petrović, Aleksandar 460
Pettenkofer, Max Joseph 44
Petya and Little Red Riding Hood (1958) 419 n.179
Petzel, Michael 408 n.42
Petzold, Christian 472, 491 n.92, 517, 522–6, 549–50, 558–60, 573 n.116, 577 nn.165–7, 577 n.169, 577 n.173, 578 n.174, 581 n.203, 582 n.207

Petzold, Konrad 488 n.51, 490 n.72
Pfeifer, Henrik 519, 562 n.5
Pfeiffer, Hermann 424 n.229
Pfeiffer, Maris 563 n.14
Pfemfert, Franz 31 n.34, 33, 75 n.1
Pfitzner, Felix 187
Pfleghar, Michael 441
Pflughaupt, Friedrich 197
Phantom. Aufzeichnungen eines ehemaligen Sträflings/Phantom. Notes by a Former Prisoner (Hauptmann) 142, 167 n.193
Philipe, Gérard 349
Philipp, Harald 426 n.262, 448
Philippi, Felix 85 n.125
Phillips, Klaus 497 n.189
Philosophie des Geldes/Philosophy of Money (Simmel) 70, 160 n.87
Philosophische Fragmente (Adorno & Horkheimer) 332 n.161
Phoenix (2014) 522, 578 n.174
The Pianist (2002) 536
Picard, Susanne 552
Picasso, Pablo 34
Pick, Erika 273 n.69
Pickford, Henry W. 579 n.187
Pickford, Mary 212
Pick, Lupu 65–6, 92, 156 n.13
Pictorial Affects, Senses of Rupture: On the Poetics and Culture of Popular German Cinema (Wedel) 230 n.16, 235 nn.109–13, 235 n.116, 237 n.131, 237 n.132, 237 n.133, 237 n.144, 238 nn.146–8
Picture of Dorian Gray (Wilde) 61
Pidgeon, Walter 266
Pieck, Wilhelm 383
Pieralisi, Alberto 239 n.164
Pierotti, Piero 490 n.78
Pilotinnen/Female Pilots (1995) 522
Pilz, Michael 163 n.128, 163 n.130, 271 n.45
Pinkert, Anke 409 n.59, 487 n.51
Pinneberg, Johannes 259–60, 272 n.60
Pinocchio (Collodi) 581 n.201
Pinthus, Kurt 98, 158 nn.39–40, 215, 240 n.175

pioneers 11–16, 22, 24–5, 27–38, 30
n.15, 34, 36, 79 n.33, 86 n.146,
123, 508, 558
Pioniere in Ingolstadt (1971) 472
Pirinçci, Akif 552, 571 n.94
Piscator, Erwin 67, 104, 127, 159
n.66, 165 n.159, 184, 227, 247,
256–7, 523, 536, 575 nn.142–3
Dramatic Workshop 257
Plain, G. 422 n.206
Planer, Franz 411 n.78
Plaquin, Raoul 233 n.66
Platen, Karl 109
Plater, Edward 394–5, 424 n.231, 424
n.233, 424 n.236, 424 n.238
Plate, Rudolf 424 n.229
Pleasence, Donald 237 n.143
The Pledge (2001) 534–5, 556
Plenzdorf, Ulrich 446, 458, 489 n.63,
557, 569 n.81
Plievier, Theodor 246, 268 n.10, 485
n.32
Poche, Klaus 481
Podehl, Peter 378, 381, 419 n.173
Poe, Edgar Allen 51, 141, 561
*Poem-Ich setzte den Fuß in die Luft
und sie trug*/Poem: I Set My Foot
Upon the Air and It Carried Me
(2003) 484 n.23, 536–7
Pohland, Hansjürgen 449, 450, 486
n.45
Pohl, Arthur 381
Pohl, Klaus 270 n.33
Pole Poppenspäler (1935) 291
Pole Poppenspäler (1954) 381
Pole Poppenspäler (Storm) 291, 381
Polizei/Police (1988) 482
Pollack, Sydney 360, 529, 571 n.93
Pollatschik, Geza 214
Pölsler, Julian Roman 530, 543–4,
571 n.97
Pommer, Albert 108
Pommer, Eric(h) 114–15, 117, 130,
162 n.116, 171, 181–3, 187–9,
190, 210, 211–12, 224, 228 n.1,
229 n.15, 232 n.62, 233 n.65,
238 n.159, 245, 248, 251, 267,
326 n.80, 337
Ponto, Erich 221, 295

Popple, Simon 30 n.14
Popular Cinema of the Third Reich
(Hake) 320 n.10, 321 n.11, 321
n.12
popularity 3, 7, 16, 22, 36–8, 59, 61,
69, 78 n.30, 92, 102, 119, 129,
133, 153–4, 156 n.7, 173, 176,
187, 275, 277, 293, 303, 346,
365, 383, 400–1, 426 nn.261–2,
486 n.44, 502, 504, 509–10,
520, 556, 571 n.95
Porten, Henny 61, 91, 97–100, 153,
156 n.7, 158 n.38, 158 n.43,
222, 351
Porten, Rosa 97, 156 n.7, 158 n.37
Porter, Edwin S. 13, 20, 31 n.26
postwar cinema/era 75, 91, 96, 109,
112, 151–2, 195, 335, 338, 342,
349, 352–3, 362–4, 388, 394,
398, 424 n.231, 441, 460
adaptation and political control
East/West 375–6
hyper-inflation 227
ideologies and owning canon
376–83
mass indoctrination 338
rearmament and redefinitions of
masculine agency in 386–92
reconstruction 334
society 100–2, 515
stabilization and consolidation 398
volatility and hyperinflation 153
Potemkin (1925) 111, 128, 239 n.170
Potente, Franka 564 n.24
Potjomkin, Bronenosez 111
Pour le Mérite (1938) 382
Powell, Larson 489 n.67
Powell, Michael 253, 269 n.17, 350,
410 n.64
*Practicing Modernity: Creative Women
in the Weimar Republic* (2006)
232 n.51
Praesidenten/The President (1919) 94,
101
Prager, Wilhelm 419 n.174
Praunheim, Rosa von 481, 521, 573
n.107
Prawer, Siegbert S. 160 n.73,
167 n.196

Preece, Julian 564 n.29
Preger, Lily 252
Préjean, Albert 224, 248
Pressburger, Arnold 250, 411 n.76, 411 n.78
Pressburger, Emeric 187, 239 n.163, 269 n.17, 350, 410 n.64
Press Law (1874) 39
Pressler, Mirjam 581 n.202
prestige films 210–20, 226, 503
Preston, John 556
Pretty Baby (König) 503
Pretty Woman (1990) 501
Preuschoff, Nikolai 242 n.205, 324 n.45, 545, 576 n.158
Preußler, Otfried 441, 510, 551, 567 n.51, 580 n.190
Price, Franziska Meyer 505
Prien, Niels 100
Prince Achmed (1926) 157 n.22
principle of secrecy 68, 95
Prinz Hubertus zu Löwenstein 267
Prinz Kuckuck!/Prince Cuckoo (1919) 100–1
Prinz Kuckuck. Leben, Taten, Meinungen und Höllenfahrt eines Wollüstlings/Life, Deeds, Opinions and Descent into Hell of a Voluptuary (Bierbaum) 100
Prinzler, Hans Helmut 30 n.11, 76 n.16, 160 n.86, 269 n.21, 427 n.267, 485 n.36, 494 n.120, 496 n.153
Prison sans barreaux (1938) 254, 411 n.78
Problematische Naturen/Problematic Natures (Spielhagen) 60
Processes of Transposition: German Literature and Film (Schönfeld, Finnan & Rasche) 232 n.59, 234 n.78, 268 n.2, 273 n.67, 327 n.93, 410 n.63, 427 n.266, 565 n.34, 575 n.140, 579 n.182
Prodolliet, Ernest 31 n.35
production, distribution and reception 2, 4, 15–16, 21, 23, 25, 34, 36–7, 56–7, 73–5, 79 n.41, 90–2, 98, 101, 103, 113–14, 119, 129, 172, 174, 195, 210, 229 n.15, 266, 276, 278, 281, 298, 334, 336–8, 364–5, 376–7, 399, 403, 439, 441–2, 486 n.37, 502, 510, 513–14, 517, 521, 526, 556
Professor Mamlock (1961) 420 n.193, 429–30
Professor Mamlock/Профессор Мамлок (1938) 258–9
Professor Unrat/Small Town Tyrant (Mann) 2, 120, 165 n.161, 187–9, 193–4, 281, 413 n.102, 477
Projektions A.G.-Union (PAGU) 40, 57, 84 n.113, 157 n.23
Prometheus 222
Prometheus unchained: Beiträge zum Film (Braun) 8 n.2
A Promise (2013) 577 n.161
The Promise of Cinema: German Film Theory, 1907–1933 (Kaes) 158 n.39
Promo-Film A.G. 102
Pronay, Nicholas 320 n.5
Propaganda and the German Cinema, 1933–1945 (Welch) 322 n.26
Proskauer, Martin 94, 157 n.21
Pro7 Television company 561 n.3, 580 n.194
proto-heritage film 366–9
Proust, Marcel 213, 465
Przyrembel, Alexandra 270 n.33
Psilander, Valdemar 41
psyche/psychoanalysis 18, 129, 141, 144, 151, 167 n.191, 193, 531
psychology, doubles, and adaptations 141–4
Ptushko, Aleksandr 376
"public appeal" cinema 224, 479, 505
public funding 5, 454–6, 459, 479, 510, 517–18, 552, 557–8, 562 n.8, 573 n.106, 579 n.180
public sphere 3, 23, 67, 90, 152, 154–5, 185, 224, 227, 334, 387, 399, 430–1, 433–4, 453, 464, 469, 472, 477, 479–80, 483 n.10, 486 n.45, 503, 507, 511,

513, 521, 523, 526, 546, 550–1, 554, 558–61
publishers and German film industry 91–2, 153, 253
Publisher's Weekly magazine 264
Pudovkin, Vsevolod 125–6, 128, 196, 259, 466
Pulver, Lilo 377
Pünktchen und Anton (1953) 379
Pünktchen und Anton (1999) 567 n.50, 567 n.53
puppet theater 25–6, 38, 65–6, 332 n.163, 381, 441, 487 n.50, 578 n.180
Pushkin, Alexander 277

Quadflieg, Will 366
Quantum of Solace (2008) 516
The Quarterly of Film, Radio and Television 337, 406 n.15
Quax, der Bruchpilot/Quax the Crash Pilot (1941) 369
Queneau, Raymond 495 n.138
Quentin, Patrick 195
Querelle (1982) 496 n.165
Querelle (Genet) 496 n.165
Quo Vadis (1951) 265
Qurbani, Burhan 491 n.92, 499, 510, 512, 517, 550–1, 553–4, 558, 561 n.2, 578 n.175, 578 n.177

Raabe, Wilhelm 402
Rabenalt, Arthur Maria 367, 409 n.55
Rabinowitsch, Gregor 250, 262
Raddatz, Carl 382
Radványi, Géza von 365, 400, 426 nn.261–2
Ragtime (1981) 437
Ragtime (Doctorow) 437
Rahn, Bruno 145
Raimund, Ferdinand 362
Rainer Werner Fassbinder (Spaich) 497 n.168, 497 n.180
Ralph, Hanna 117
Ramm, Arnim 417 n.136
Rampling, Charlotte 514
Randaulen, Jon 490 n.81

Rank, Otto 51, 82 n.85, 143, 167 n.197
Rappaport, Herbert 256, 258
Rappsilber-Kurth, Dora 229 n.5
Rasch, William 421 n.199
Rasocha, Svenja 581 n.200
Raspe, Rudolf Erich 340, 406 n.25
Rasp, Fritz 147, 224, 245
Rassenschande 416 n.136
Rathenau, Walther 106, 160 n.72, 268 n.10, 270 n.37, 422 n.210
Rath, Gereon 520
Rath, Willy 253
Rätsel der Nacht/Riddles of the Night (1945) 382
Ratzka, Clara 160 n.85
Rausch der Verwandlung/The Post Office Girl (1988) 577 n.161
Rausch der Verwandlung/The Post Office Girl (Zweig) 545, 577 n.161
Rauscher, Ulrich 39
Raw, Laurence 9 n.12, 157 n.28
Rawlinson, Arthur 252
Raykovsky, Evgeny 419 n.179
Raymond, Ernest 175
Rayns, Tony 475, 497 n.176, 497 n.179
RCA Photophone group 199
Reaction Reports 405 n.9
Real-Film Studios (Hamburg) 394
Rebecca (1940) 248
Rebellen (Rebels). *See Friedrich Schiller-Der Triumph eines Genies*/Friedrich Schiller. A Genius' Triumph (1940)
The Reckless Moment (1949) 349
The Reckoning (1986) 81 n.59
The Red Badge of Courage (1951) 423 n.222
Redding, Myrl 485 n.28
The Red Shoes (1948) 410 n.64
Red Sparrow (2018) 195
"Red Vienna" 120
Reed, Phillip 352
Reenberg, Holger 41
reframing 16
Reframing Culture: The Case of the Vitagraph Quality Films (Pearson & Uricchio) 76 n.18

Regener, Sven 518, 552, 562 n.6
Regine (1935) 410 n.64
Regine (1956) 402
Regine (Keller) 402, 410 n.64
Reichert, Gerrit 498 n.199
Reichmann, Max 176
Reichmeister, Carl-Dieter von 322 n.17
"Reich Ministry of Public Enlightenment and Propaganda" 281
Reich-Ranicki, Marcel 83 n.97
Reichsfilmkammer 278, 281
Reichsfilmstelle 280
"Reichsfluchtsteuer" 268 n.7
Reichstag Fire Decree 279
Reich, Uschi 491 n.92
Reid, Hamish 494 n.126
Reid, James H. 463, 494 n.130
Reigen (1920) 159 n.57
Reigen (Schnitzler) 349, 492 n.105, 542
Reimann, Brigitte 483 n.6, 500, 562 n.7
Reimann, Hans 296
Reimer, Carol J. 574 n.133
Reimer, Robert C. 320 n.10, 322 n.26, 423 n.221, 574 n.133
Reinecker, Herbert 409 n.55
Reineke Fuchs (1989) 441
Reineke Fuchs (Goethe) 441
Reiner, Anna 255
Reinert, Emil Edwin 414 n.109
Reinhardt, Gottfried 267, 384, 392, 398, 400, 423 n.222, 427 n.270
Reinhardt, Max 65, 122, 207, 240 n.182, 392
Reiniger, Lotte 83 n.94, 157 n.22, 173, 228 n.5, 239 n.162
Reinl, Harald 416 nn.129–30, 439, 447–8
re-internationalization 211
Reisch, Walter 397–8
Reitz, Edgar 449
Relin, Veit 489 n.60
remakes 1, 7, 21, 177–80, 225, 277, 334–5, 365, 367, 399–400, 416 n.130, 427 n.270, 439, 485 n.33, 492 n.105, 499, 508, 534, 551, 561 n.3, 571 n.95
of Ganghofer/Sudermann novels 277
postwar 335
Remarque, Erich Maria 174, 198–202, 204–5, 226, 235 n.115, 235 n.118, 237 n.131, 237 n.135, 246, 261–2, 267, 349, 354–60, 391, 402, 412 nn.87–91, 413 n.96, 556, 580 n.191
Rendezvous in Paris (1982) 487 n.46
Renn, Ludwig 236 n.119
Rennschwein Rudi Rüssel/Racing Pig Rudi Snout (1994) 509
Rentschler, Eric 8 n.3, 121, 162 n.114, 164 nn.137–8, 169 n.219, 231 n.35, 232 n.59, 242 n.209, 320 n.7, 321 nn.10–11, 321 n.15, 322 n.16, 322 n.20, 322 n.23, 323 n.31, 330 n.137, 409 n.59, 420 n.185, 420 n.191, 427 n.267, 483 n.14, 485 n.36, 491 n.84, 494 n.120, 496 n.153, 500–1, 512–13, 563 n.11, 568 n.60
Representing East Germany since Unification (Cooke) 579 n.182
Re-Presenting the Good Society (Cooke) 580 n.195
Resident Evil 503
resistance 22, 25, 73, 96, 118, 128, 189, 197, 245, 254, 257–8, 295, 306, 318, 336, 339, 374, 396, 401, 425 n.246, 432, 457, 529
Resnais, Alain 450, 453, 466, 467, 495 n.139
The Return of Gunner Asch (Kirst) 422 n.207
Return to Montauk (2017) 465, 525, 547–8
Reuth, Ralph Georg 327 n.89
Revanche (2008) 574 n.132
The Revolt of Gunner Asch (Kirst) 422 n.207
Revolt of the Fishermen (1934) 256–7, 523
revolution (1918/19) 89

Revolver magazine 522
Revuefilme 277
Rex, Eugen 156 n.13
Rex Film Company 92, 156 n.13, 367
Rhapsody: A Dream Novel (Schnitzler) 575 n.139
Rheinsberg (1967) 487 n.46
Rheinsberg (Tucholsky) 376, 487 n.46
Rhon, Nicola 300–3
Richard Oswald Production LLC (G.m.b.H.) 67, 145
Richard Oswald. Regisseur und Produzent (Belach & Jacobsen) 85 n.126, 269 n.15
Richardson, Michael D. 8 n.2, 81 n.71, 162 n.102, 230 n.27
Richard-Willm, Pierre 269 n.26
Rich, B. Ruby 196, 235 n.102
Richter, Hans Werner 76 n.16, 340, 407 n.39
Richter, Paul 117
Richter, Simon 83 n.87
Rickman, Alan 518
Rico, Oskar und das Herzgebreche (2015) 567 n.53
Rico, Oskar und der Diebstahlstein (2016) 567 n.53
Rico, Oskar und die Tieferschatten (2014) 567 n.53
Rieck, Horst 503
Riefenstahl, Leni 169 n.216, 247, 254, 290, 316, 487 n.47
Riemann, Johannes 206
Riemann, Katja 569 n.81
Rilke, Rainer Maria 398, 537, 540–1
Ring (Wagner) 1
Ringende Seelen/Struggling Souls (1918) 73
Ringende Seelen/Struggling Souls (Schmidt) 73
Riordan, Colin 270 n.32
Rippert, Otto 51, 142
Ripple World Pictures Ltd (Dublin) 566 n.49
Rising Star Entertainment (New York) 576 n.151
Ritscher, Wolfgang 42, 81 n.69
Rittau, Günther 117, 143

Ritter, Karl 382
Ritter Nérestan/Knight Nérestan (1930) 196
Rizzoli, Emilio 251
R.N.-Filmproduktion GmbH 282–3
Robbe-Grillet, Alain 450
The Robe (1953) 421 n.204
Robertson, Nan 480, 498 n.202
Robert und Bertram (1939) 330 n.142
Robert Zimmermann wundert sich über die Liebe/Robert Zimmermann wonders about Love (2008) 562 n.6
Robinson Crusoe (Defoe) 30 n.18
Robinson, Michael 321 n.15
Robison, Arthur 410 n.64
Robson, Mark 359
Roche, Charlotte 552
Rockett, Emer 411 n.79
Rockett, Kevin 411 n.79
Rockwell, Alexandre 8 n.6
Roda Roda 363, 414 n.110
Rodewald, Dierk 81 n.71
Roehler, Oskar 564 n.26
Roellinghoff, Charlie K. 179
Rogers, Ginger 195, 266
Rohmer, Éric 130, 165 n.165, 407 n.30, 434, 436–7, 438, 473, 478, 485 n.27, 506
Rohrbach, Günter 456, 480, 504, 509, 566 n.46, 576 n.150
Röhrig, Walter 285, 324 n.48
Rohrwacher, Alba 505
Roland, Dany 556
Rollberg, Peter 259, 272 n.58
Roll, Gernot 567 n.51
Roloff, Volker 327 n.100
Roman einer jungen Ehe/Story of a Young Couple (1952) 409 n.59
Romero, Christiane Zehl 273 nn.67–8
Ronan, Saoirse 545
Rooks, Conrad 436
Rooney, David 569 n.72
Roos, Julia 158 n.31
Rosa Blanca (1961) 411 n.75
Rosa Luxemburg (1986) 498 n.198
Rose Bernd (1919) 98–100
Rose Bernd (1957) 384, 400

Rose Bernd (Hauptmann) 98, 384, 400, 420 n.189, 440
Rosegger, Peter 362, 368
Rosenberg, Alfred 292–3, 313
Rosenfeld, Herbert 186
Rosen im Herbst/Roses in Autumn (1955) 382
Rosenmontag (1924) 365, 414 n.117
Rosen, Willy 246
Roshal, Grigori 498 n.201
Rosher, Charles G. 139–40
Rosmer, Milton 239 n.164, 254
Rossellini, Roberto 403
Ross, Florian 579 n.180
Rossini, Gioachino 37, 491 n.82
Rotation (1949) 371, 377
Rote Armee Fraktion/Red Army Faction (RAF) 432
Rote Fahne 125
Rothe, Hans 277, 296, 300–3
Rothemund, Marc 528
Rothemund, Sigi 487 n.50
Rother, Rainer 30 n.10
Roth, Guenther 325 n.63
Roth, Joseph 446
Rothstock, Otto 164 n.134
Rot ist die Liebe/Red is Love (1956) 415 n.123
Rotkäppchen/Little Red Riding Hood (1954) 378, 419 n.173
Rotkäppchen und der Wolf (1937) 298–9
Roto-Film 217
Rotter, Fritz 187
Rouge, Moulin 19
Rousseau, Jean Jacques 251
Rout, Katharina 575 n.134
Rovenský, Josef 146
Rowland, Herbert 43
Royal Shakespeare Company (London) 452
rubble films (1946–9) 335, 338–42, 365, 386
Rubble Films: German Cinema in the Shadow of the Third Reich (Shandley) 406 n.21
Rübezahl (1957) 419 n.173
Rubiner, Ludwig 38

Rudolph, Charles 247
Ruge, Eugen 510, 552, 579 n.182
Rühle, Alex 581 n.199
Rühmann, Heinz 182, 249, 317, 392, 416 n.134, 423 n.229
Ruhm/Fame (Kehlmann) 519
Rumfort, Grete 121
Rumler, Fritz 508, 566 n.44
Rumpelstilzchen/Rumpelstiltskin (1955) 378
Rundell, Richard 324 n.52, 325 n.57
Rundfunk Berlin-Brandenburg 582 n.209
Run Lola Run (1998) 520
Ruppelt, Georg 293, 326 n.74, 326 n.76
Rusch, Mara 576 n.155
Rutkoff, Peter M. 272 n.51
Ruttmann, Walter 76 n.16, 108, 109, 172–3, 175, 215, 228 n.5, 229 n.14
Rutz, Gerd-Peter 186, 232 nn.54–5, 232 nn.57–8
Ruzowitzky, Stefan 484 n.23, 512, 528, 568 n.57
Rye, Stellan 40, 52, 59–60, 82 n.83, 142

Šach mat/Checkmate (1963) 426 n.259
Sachs, Hans 379, 410 n.65
Sagan, Leontine 196–7, 226, 228, 235 n.103, 254, 281, 282
Saint-Saëns, Camille 83 n.91
Salloker, Angela 295
Salmony, Georg F. 240 n.173
Salomon, Ernst von 389, 422 n.210
Salonen, Hannu 563 n.14, 565 n.33
Salten, Felix 40, 80 n.55, 272 n.63
Salter, Hans J. 248
The Salvation Hunters (1925) 233 n.73
SAMSAS (1999) 540
Sandberg, Claudia 482 n.5, 498 n.203
Sander, Gabriele 239 nn.168–9, 240 nn.171–6
Sander, Helke 451, 491 n.92, 498 n.198, 521, 573 n.107
Sanders-Brahms, Helma 440, 449, 478, 479, 498 n.198

Sander, Selma 458
Sanders, Julie 9 n.12
Sandford, John 418 n.157, 482 n.5, 488 n.52, 494 n.124
Sandrock, Adele 323 n.39
Sandten, Thea 246
Sansibar oder der letzte Grund (1987) 486 n.42
Sansibar oder der letzte Grund (Andersch) 486 n.42
Santell, Alfred 235 n.106
Sarandos, Ted 556
Sarchi, Natan 236 n.125
Sartre, Jean-Paul 433, 483 n.7
Sascha-Film Sascha Kolowrat-Krakowsky 84 n.108
Saudners, Thomas P. 161 n.95
Sauerkrautkoma (2018) 572 n.105
Sauer-Kretschmer, Simone 76 n.14
Saul, Anno 552, 571 n.94
Saunders, Thomas J. 229 n.15
Saur, Pamela 575 n.140
Savage, Thomas 556
Saville, Victor 253, 351, 353
Sawyer, Tom 546
The Scarlet Empress (1934) 195
The Scar of Shame (1929) 119
Scattered Tracks 301
Schaaf, Johannes 487 n.48, 487 n.50
Schach, Max 245
Schaerer, Michael 567 n.51
Schäfer, Horst 166 n.167
Schamoni, Peter 449
Schanelec, Angela 522
Schanze, Helmut 130, 165 n.165, 166 n.172
Schauer, Hermann Ernst 488 n.54
Schediwy, Fritz 531
Scheffel, Michael 81 n.61
Scheidgen, Irina 407 n.28
Schell, Maria 383–4, 421 n.203, 571 n.96
Schell, Maximilian 502
Schenzinger, Karl Aloys 284
Scherbenpark/Broken Glass Park (2012) 552
Scherbenpark/Broken Glass Park (Bronsky) 552

Scherl (Berlin) 168 n.199, 168 n.204, 189, 237 n.136
Scheugl, Otto 427 n.272
Scheunemann, Dietrich 82 n.86, 156 n.16, 165 n.165, 167 n.195, 167 n.198
Schicha, Christian 322 n.30, 326 n.84
Schiel, Hannes 388
Schiller and the Ideal of Freedom (Miller) 328 n.116
Schiller-Eine Dichterjugend/Schiller, Youth of a Poet (1923) 310
Schiller, Friedrich 1, 4, 13, 25, 28, 37, 39, 63, 74, 77 n.21, 77 n.22, 77 n.28, 102, 106, 114, 139, 152, 158 n.46, 160 n.71, 197, 253, 278, 326 n.81, 329 nn.123–4, 333, 379, 402, 409 n.63, 416 n.131, 425 n.248, 458, 489 n.60, 490 n.74, 500, 513, 519, 536, 546, 552, 557, 562 n.6, 577 n.162
 on film 25–6
 literary canon on film 292–5
 at (World) War 307–12
 Wilhelm Tell (see *Wilhelm Tell* (Schiller))
Schiller-Handbuch (Luserke-Jaqui) 85 n.130
Schilling, Tom 555
Schimmelpfennig, Denis 414 n.118
Schipper, Sebastian 521
Schirk, Heinz 488–9 n.60
Schittly, Dagmar 488 n.56
Schlafes Bruder/The Brother of Sleep (1995) 533
Schlafes Bruder/The Brother of Sleep (Schneider) 533
Schlageter, Albert Leo 326 n.77
Schlegel, Margarete 214
Schlemihl, Peter 51, 59, 64
Schlesinger, Ron 166 n.167
Schlettow, Hans Adalbert 117
Schlink, Bernhard 529
Schlöndorff, Volker 5–6, 8 n.6, 429, 431, 433, 438, 449, 453–5, 456, 460, 462, 464–72, 478–9, 482 n.2, 492 nn.98–9, 493 n.112,

494 nn.132–3, 494 n.135, 495
  n.139, 495 n.141, 495 n.143,
  495 n.148, 495 n.150, 496
  n.154, 496 n.157, 501, 504,
  524–5, 547–8, 573 n.121
Schloss Gripsholm (1963) 487 n.46
Schloss Gripsholm (Tucholsky) 487
  n.46
Schloß Hubertus/Hubertus Castle
  (1954) 368, 416 n.129
Schloß Hubertus/Hubertus Castle
  (1973) 416 n.130
Schloß Hubertus/Hubertus Castle
  (Ganghofer) 368
Schloss Vogelöd (1921) 92, 105
Schlüpmann, Heide 30 n.10, 82 n.78,
  169 n.219
Schmerberg, Ralf 536–7
Schmidbauer, Kerstin 520
Schmidbauer, Lea 504
Schmid, Daniel 491 n.82
Schmid, Eva 327 n.100
Schmidt, Eckhart 562 n.8
Schmidt, Erich 80 n.58
Schmidt, Joseph 247–8
Schmidt, Lothar 73
Schmidt, Ricarda 562 n.3
Schmidt, Thomas E. 582 n.211
Schmitz, Hannah 571 n.93
Schmitz, Helmut 497 n.188
Schmitz, Sybille 248
Schneewittchen und die sieben Zwerge/
  Snow White (1961) 419 n.175
Schneewittchen und die sieben Zwerge/
  Snow White and Seven Dwarfs
  (1955) 378, 419 n.173
Schneider, Magda 250
Schneider, Peter 494 n.120, 579 n.182
Schneider, Robert 533
Schneider, Samuel 569 n.78
Schneider, Thomas F. 412 n.91, 413
  n.101
Schneider, Tilly 190
Schnitzler, Arthur 1, 41–2, 81 n.59,
  81 nn.61–3, 81 n.66, 102, 141,
  149–51, 153, 159 n.57, 169
  nn.223–4, 169 n.226, 239 n.166,
  246, 250, 349, 402–3, 492

n.105, 529, 534, 542, 567 n.55,
  575 n.140
Schnitzler, Gregor 571 n.94, 581 n.199
Schnyder, Franz 361–2, 413 nn.104–5
Schober, Siegfried 493 n.113
Schobert, Walter 408 n.50
Schoeps, Karl-Heinz 321 n.10
Schöll, Norbert 424 n.236
Scholz, Anne-Marie 484 n.18
Scholz, Gerhard 163 n.128
Schönbrunn-Film 367
Schönenborn, Jörg 459
Schönert, Jörg 270 n.33
Schönfeld, Christiane 83 n.94, 232 n.59,
  234 n.78, 321 n.11, 405 n.8, 410
  n.63, 427 n.267, 562 n.3
Schönfeld, Roland 423 n.227
Schonger, Hubert 300, 377
Schönherr, Karl 346, 408 n.52
Schönhuber, Franz 96
Schön, Margarete 117
Schönpflug, Wolfgang 167 n.190
Schrader, Bäbel 237 n.136
Schrader, Maria 558, 581 n.202
Schreckenberger, Helga 571 n.97
Schreiber, Claudia 518, 519
Schreivogel, Sven 408 n.42
Schröder, Arnulf 416 n.132
Schröder, Claudia 567 n.53
Schröder, Karl Ludwig 41–3, 81 n.63,
  81 n.67
Schroeter, Werner 516, 530, 531
Schroth, Carl-Heinz 419 n.177
Schroth, Hannelore 307
Schtonk! (1992) 528
Schubart (Honolka) 328 n.114
Schubart, Christian Friedrich Daniel
  309, 328 n.115, 328 n.117
Schubert, Franz 17, 251
Schuch, Albrecht 551
Schuchter, Veronika 271 n.45
Schüfftan, Eugen 86 n.136, 241 n.201,
  245, 248, 347
Schüfftan process 86 n.136, 241 n.201
Schuhpalast Pinkus/Shoepalace Pinkus
  (1916) 66
Schulberg, Stuart 337–8, 401, 405 n.9,
  406 nn.15–16, 426 n.260

Schuld/Guilt (2015) 563 n.14, 565 n.33
Schuld/Guilt (von Schirach) 501, 505–6
Schulmädchen-Report/The Schoolgirl Report (1970) 455, 493 n.107
Schulte-Sasse, Linda 321 n.10, 330 n.132, 331 n.143
Schulze-Rohr, Peter 452
Schulz, Franz 155
Schulz, Herbert 381
Schulz, Torsten 552, 569 n.78, 579 n.182
Schumann, Robert 333
Schumm, Hans 280
Schundfilm/Schundfilme 58–9
Schündler, Rudolf 416 n.129
Schünzel, Reinhold 61, 92, 106, 224, 245, 297, 323 n.42
Schürer, Ernst 344, 408 n.45
Schürhoff, Dirk 578 n.176
Schütte, Jan 504
Schütte, Wolfram 469
Schütze, Peter 407 n.27
Schütz, Erhard 322 n.30
Schütz, Helga 239 n.163
Schwab, Gustav 186
Schwab, Ulrike 327 n.100, 489 n.62, 497 n.175
Schwanitz, Dietrich 508
Schwartzman, Jason 545
Schwarz, Alexander 271 n.49
Schwarze, Hans Dieter 462
Schwarz, Hanns 181
Schwarzer Jäger Johanna/Black Hunter Johanna 293
Schwarzwaldmädel/Black Forest Girl (1917) 367
Schwarzwaldmädel/Black Forest Girl (1920) 367
Schwarzwaldmädel/Black Forest Girl (1929) 367
Schwarzwaldmädel/Black Forest Girl (1933) 367
Schwarzwaldmädel/Black Forest Girl (1950) 366–7, 422 n.218, 425 n.255
Schweigeminute/Minute of silence (2016) 569 n.82

Schweigeminute/Minute of silence (Lenz) 569 n.82
Schweiger, Til 516, 582 n.208
Schweikart, Hans 317, 321 n.11
Schweinitz, Jörg 13, 29 n.5, 32 nn.37–8, 76 n.17, 77 n.24, 78 n.32, 79 n.36, 79 n.42, 79 n.45, 80 n.55
Schweinskopf al dente (2016) 572 n.105
Schwentner, Isabella 81 n.66
Schwochow, Christian 510, 516, 562 n.5
Schwochow, Heide 518
Scotoni, Eugen 250
Scotoni, Ralph 269 n.19, 271 n.40
Scott, William B. 272 n.51
Screening War: Perspectives on German Suffering (Cooke & Silberman) 405 n.12, 406 n.18, 425 n.247
Seaton, George 264
Sebald, W. G. 427 n.273
A Second Life: German Cinema's First Decades (Elsaesser) 29 n.8, 30 n.10, 30 n.14, 75 n.3, 82 n.78, 85 n.123, 415 n.127
Second Sino-Japanese War 537
Second World War 1, 4, 54, 255, 264, 266, 276, 317, 324 n.42, 330 n.134, 330 n.138, 333, 335–8, 341–2, 344, 355–6, 359, 364, 368, 383, 387–8, 398, 400–1, 404, 408 n.50, 421 n.203, 438, 451, 462, 486 n.45, 487 n.47, 515, 549, 559
  ELAS during 374
  reorientation and re-education 336–7
  significance of film after 335–8
secularization 13, 570 n.86
Seduction and Theory: Readings of Gender, Representation and Rhetoric (Hunter) 234 n.93
Seeba, Hinrich C. 162 n.114
Seeber, Guido 52, 129, 143, 167 n.198
Seefahrt ist not!/Seafaring Is Necessity (Fock) 105

Seeger, Ernst 159 n.62, 280
Seeger, Fritz 286
Seemann, Horst 445, 483 n.6
Seeßlen, Georg 332 n.165, 420 n.185, 501, 561 n.3, 563 n.11
Seethaler, Robert 519, 555
Segeberg, Harro 30 n.10, 330 n.132, 407 n.28
Seghers, Anna 256–7, 263–4, 267, 273 nn.67–8, 273 n.71, 359, 370–1, 417 n.140, 445, 486 n.45, 517, 522–3, 549–50, 555, 558, 578 n.174
Seghers in Perspective (Wallace) 273 n.68
Seibert, Ernst 272 n.63
Seidlin, Oskar 30 n.20
Seiler, Lutz 577 n.164
Seitz, Franz 453, 458, 467, 479, 492 n.99
Selbstversuch/Self-experiment (1974) 481
self-referentiality 75 n.3, 515
Selling Sex in the Reich. Prostitutes in German Society, 1914–1945 (Harris) 158 n.31
Selpin, Herbert 282
Seltzer, Adele 82 n.72
Seltzer, Thomas 82 n.72
Selznick, Brian 29 n.1
Selznick, Lewis J. 74
Semenza, Greg M. Colón 5, 8 n.7, 32 nn.41–4, 76 n.18, 162 n.101, 165 n.158, 169 n.229, 173, 178, 230–1 n.32, 379, 413 n.100, 420 n.180, 454, 485 nn.29–31, 492 n.100
Semya Oppengeym (Feuchtwanger) 498 n.201
Semya Oppengeym/The Oppermanns (1939) 498 n.201
Senf, Haro 449
Sennwald, Andre 231 n.38
Sensationsfilm 115
The Serapion Brethren/Serapionsbrüder (Hoffmann) 51–2, 64
Serrault, Michel 411 n.70

The Seven Addictions and Five Professions of Anita Berber (Gordon) 168 n.203
The Seventh Cross (1944) 263, 359
Seventh Heaven (1927) 198
7 Zwerge-Der Wald ist nicht genug/7 Dwarves-The Forest Is Not Enough (2006) 568 n.58
7 Zwerge-Männer allein im Wald/7 Dwarves-Men Alone in the Woods (2004) 568 n.58
Sevin, Dieter 238 n.154
sexual exploitation 45, 68, 95–6, 102–3, 149, 154, 503
Seydoux, Léa 545
S. Fischer Berlin 167 n.193
Shakespeare, William 30 n.18, 58, 79 n.44
Shalev, Zeruya 581 n.202
Shandley, Robert 406 n.21
Shanghai 1937 (1996) 519
Shanghai Express (1932) 195
Shearer, Douglas 236 n.129
Shedletzky, Itta 270 n.33, 270 n.34
Sheldon, Edward 74, 163 n.117, 280
Shelley, Mary 141, 177, 231 n.32, 561
Sherriff, Robert Cedric 261
The Shining (1980) 533
Show Boat (1936) 261
Siddharta (1972) 436
Siddharta (Hesse) 171, 436
Siemsen, Hans 175, 215, 240 n.176
Sienkiewicz, Henryk 265
Siepen, Robert 367
Sierck, Detlev 330 n.138
Sigfrido (1912) 39
Sight and Sound magazine 234 n.89, 405 n.7, 475, 497 n.176, 497 n.179
Signoret, Simone 349
Silberman, Marc 221, 222, 241 n.197, 241 n.203, 366, 375–7, 404 n.4, 405 n.12, 406 n.18, 415 n.122, 418 n.151, 418 n.158, 418 n.166, 419 n.170, 419 n.172, 422 n.206, 425 n.247, 488 nn.51–2

silent cinema 4, 11–12, 14, 21, 27–8, 30 nn.14–15, 41, 51, 56, 61, 73–4, 80, 90, 92–3, 102, 108, 131, 134, 139, 141–2, 152–3, 155, 160 n.72, 162 n.117, 171, 177, 188, 190, 201, 205, 224, 227–8, 230 n.26, 280, 285, 293, 367, 382. *See also specific silent films*
The Silent Cinema Reader (Grieveston & Krämer) 30 n.14
Simmel, Georg 38, 70, 79 n.35, 112, 160 n.87
Simmel, Johannes Mario 401, 426 n.261, 441
Simon, Rainer 562 n.7
Simplicissimus magazine 371
Simpson, William von 400
Simulacron- 3 (Galouye) 472
The Singing Fool (1928) 172, 181, 226
Singing Pictures 79 n.33
Sinkel, Bernhard 458–9, 502
Siodmak, Kurt (Curt) 241 n.201, 248, 254
Siodmak, Robert 222, 245, 248, 271 n.44, 347, 363, 383, 400, 403, 423 n.222, 425 n.245, 426 n.261
Sirk, Douglas 359, 449
Sissi trilogy (1955–7) 361
Six contes moraux/Six Moral Tales (Rohmer) 436, 485 n.27
Sjöström, Victor 108, 131
Skandal um Eva/Scandalous Eva (1930) 222
Skandal um Olly (1927) 222
Skarsgård, Stellan 548
Skizze eines Unglücks (1984) 484 n.15
Skizze eines Unglücks (Frisch) 484 n.15
Skladanowsky, Emil 11, 16, 22, 123
Skladanowsky, Max 11, 16, 22, 50, 123, 214
Skoda, Albin 413 n.99
slapstick 25
Small, William 270 n.37, 330 n.130
Smith, George Albert 13, 20

Smith, Johnny 568 n.57
SMS für dich/Text for You (2016) 581 n.202
SMS für dich/Text for You (Cramer) 581 n.202
Snow White and the Seven Dwarfs (Grimm brothers) 512
Sochaczewer, Hans 239 n.161
The Social Contract (Rousseau) 251
social hygiene films 66–8
socialist society 446, 488 n.55
Socialist Unity Party (SED) 348, 375
social practices of marginalization/ exclusion 72
social problem films 90, 118–20, 128, 154
social-reform movements 86 n.146
Societa Italiana Pineschi Roma 77 n.21
Societé Internationale Cinématographique 206
Societé Lumière 17
society and culture 35, 393, 518
socio-political conditions 5, 25, 54
Söderbaum, Kristina 314, 317–18, 381, 417 n.137
Softley, Iain 566 n.49
Söhnker, Hans 423 n.229
Sokurov, Aleksandr 529, 542–3, 560
Soldat Suhren (von der Vring) 235 n.119
Solino (2002) 573 n.107
solitaires 5, 526, 530–1, 553
Sollers, Werner 316, 331 n.146
Solntse/The Sun (2005) 543
Soloalbum (2003) 581 n.199
Soloalbum (Schnitzler) 581 n.199
Solomon, Matthew 31 n.27
Sommer, Hans 411 n.78
Sommer, Michael 552
Sonderbare Heilige/Strange Saints (Harbou) 161 n.98
A Song is Born (1948) 353
The Song of Bernadette (1943) 264–6
The Song of Bernadette (Werfel) 264–6, 274 n.73
The Song of Songs (1918) 272 n.59, 280

Sonnemann, Emmy 270 n.40, 294
Sontheimer, Kurt 289–90, 325 nn.58–9
Sophie Scholl, die letzten Tage/Sophie Scholl: The Final Days (2005) 510, 528
Sophokles 562 n.8
Sorkin, Amy Davidson 483 n.9
sound and internationalization (1922–32) 171, 173, 200
    film experiments (1920s) 174–5
    and political agency 183–8
sound film technology 166 n.182, 174, 188, 226
Sous les Toits de Paris/Under the Roofs of Paris (1930) 182, 215, 224, 230 n.29
Soutter, Michel 449
Soviet Military Administration in Germany (SMAD) 336, 348, 406 n.14
Soviet revolutionary films 128
Sozialistische Cowboys. Der Wilde Westen Ostdeutschlands (Borries & Fischer) 490 n.81
Spaich, Herbert 497 n.168, 497 n.180
Sparschuh, Jens 509
Sperr, Martin 455
Spewack, Bella 266
Spewack, Samuel 266
Spicer, Andre 412 n.85, 413 n.95
Spider Woman (1944) 195
The Spider Woman Strikes Back (1946) 195
Spiegel, Alan 485 n.27
Spiegel, Edgar von 283
Spiehs, Karl 492 n.105
Spielhagen, Friedrich 60, 85 n.122
Spielmann, Götz 574 n.132
Spier, Wolfgang 575 n.144
Spies, Johann 16, 26
Spieß, Helmut 419 n.175
Spikher, Erasmus 64
SPIO data 510, 566 nn.47–8, 574 n.126
Spira, Camilla 323 n.39
Spoerl, Heinrich 277, 296, 306, 319, 426 n.256
Spring, D. W. 320 n.5

Springer, Axel 479
Spur der Steine/Trace of Stones (1966) 443, 488 n.53
Spurgat, Günter 324 n.52, 325 n.66
The Spy in Black (1939) 253
Spyri, Johanna 1, 3, 362, 517, 570 n.86
SRF 514, 519, 571 n.96, 582 n.209
Staas, Christian 364, 414 n.112
Stadt ohne Mitleid/Town without Pity (1961) 427 n.270
Stahl-Nachbaur, Ernst 93, 186
Stahr, Gerhard 329 n.120
Stalingrad (1959) 425 n.248
Stalingrad (Plivier) 485 n.32
Stam, Robert 9 n.12
The Standard Edition of the Complete Psychological Works of Sigmund Freud (Freud) 167 n.197
Stanley, Fred 265, 274 n.74
Stanwyck, Barbara 195
Stapenhorst, Günther 212, 323 n.42
Stark, Christoph 407 n.30, 562 n.3
Stark, Curt A. 97
Starke Herzen/Strong Hearts (1937) 307
State Theatre (Berlin) 305
Stationendrama 104
Staudte, Wolfgang 342, 371–4, 377, 384, 400, 406 n.14, 413 n.94, 426 n.256, 426 n.264, 446, 450
Stauffenberg, Claus von 396, 406 n.23
St. Clair, Malcolm 206, 238 n.145
Stefani, Francesco 377, 419 n.175
Steinhöfel, Andreas 567 n.53
Steinhoff, Hans 160 n.71, 276, 306, 414 n.117
Steinle, Matthias 427 n.271
Steinrück, Albert 151
Stein unter Steinen/Stone among Stones (1916) 78 n.30
Stemmle, Robert Adolf 239 n.164, 368, 377, 379, 386, 400, 485 n.33
Stepantsev, Boris 419 n.179
Stephan, Alexander 273 n.68, 273 n.69
Steppenwolf (1974) 436
Steppenwolf (Hesse) 231 n.35, 436, 552

Sternberg, Jonas 125, 190, 192, 195–7, 233 n.73, 233 n.74, 425 n.245
Stern, Frank 270 n.39, 273 n.72, 489 n.66
Sternheim, Carl 104, 153, 155, 246, 402
Stevenson, Robert Louis 62
Stieler, Laila 538, 581 n.202
Stifter, Adalbert 362, 533, 567 n.55
Stiller, Mauritz 40, 108, 131, 198
Stock, Valeska 125
Stöger, Alfred 362, 368, 408 n.52, 414 n.108, 416 n.131
Stoker, Bram 231 n.32
Stolen Identity (1953) 414 n.109
Stölzl, Philipp 511, 558
The Stone Flower/Каменный цветок (1946) 376
Stone, Lewis 208
stop-motion animation 18, 22, 35, 125
Stoppard, Tom 81 n.59, 496 n.165
Stöppler, Wilhelm 293
Storch, Wolfgang 161 n.97
Storm, Theodor 1, 4, 86 n.142, 275, 278, 284, 317, 325 n.57, 325 n.64, 325 n.66, 333, 369–70, 381, 400
  and Nazi heritage film 285–92
Story of the Trapp Family Singers (Trapp) 346
Stoumen, Louis Clyde 441, 487 n.47
Stöwer, Willy 49
Stow, Percy 84 n.113
Strachey, James 167 n.197
Strack, Heinrich 44
Strafbataillon 999 (1960) 426 n.262
Strafbataillon 999 (Konsalik) 426 n.262
Stramm, August 75
The Strange Awakening (1958) 490 n.78
Strasberg, Lee 258
Straschek, Günter Peter 246
Stratz, Rudolf 105
Straub, Jean-Marie 450, 462, 464, 473, 484 n.15, 494 n.129, 562 n.8
Straus(s), Oscar 349

Strauß, Franz-Josef 397, 425 n.250, 433
Strawser, Amy Kepple 273 n.67
Strehl, Wiebke 317, 331 n.151
Streicher, Andreas 309
Stresemann, Gustav 57, 84 n.110, 117, 163 n.119
Stribolt, Oscar 38, 269 n.18
Strindberg, August 344
Strindberg, Göran 398
Strittmatter, Erwin 483 n.6, 557
Strobel, Hans Rolf 451, 491 n.93
Stroheim, Erich von 141
Stroux, Karl-Heinz 342–3
Strukturwandel der Öffentlichkeit/Structural Transformation of the Public Sphere (Habermas) 8 n.4, 433, 483 n.10, 483 n.11
Strümper-Krobb, Sabine 272 n.63
Struss, Karl 139–40
Stuber, Thomas 521, 549, 577 n.164
Stuckrad-Barre, Benjamin von 557, 581 n.199
Stud. chem. Helene Willfüer (Baum) 186, 232 n.52
Studio Hamburg Filmproduktion 514
Stümke, Bruno 157 n.18
Sturm, Dorothea 316
Stürme/Storms (Landsberger) 37
Sturmflut, ihr Söhne (1917) 81 n.71
Sturm, Sibylle M. 269 n.22
Suck Me Shakespeer 505
Süddeutscher Rundfunk (SDR) 486 n.44
Süddeutsche Zeitung newspaper 102, 121, 159 n.58, 359, 422 n.211, 492 n.97
Sudendorf, Werner 232 n.61
Sudermann, Hermann 37, 53, 74, 78 n.30, 101, 102, 135–6, 140, 163 n.117, 228 n.3, 259, 277, 280, 300–3, 321 n.11, 346, 401, 436, 440
Südfilm 215
Südfilm-Verleih 217
Südwest Rundfunk (SWR) 480, 520, 567 n.50, 572 n.100, 572 n.103

Sukowa, Barbara 477
Sullavan, Margaret 260, 262, 323 n.36
Sunal, Kemal 482
Sunrise. A Song of Two Humans (1927) 134–6, 140, 436
Sunset Boulevard (1950) 248
Supper, Walter 197
Supreme Board of Film Censors 145
Süskind, Patrick 501, 503, 509, 518, 539
Suter, Martin 508, 571 n.94
Suttner, Bertha von 41, 55–6
Swift, Jonathan 30 n.18
Swinton, Tilda 545
Switzerland 1, 26, 87 n.158, 151, 175, 257, 262, 382, 449, 514, 517, 520, 571 n.96, 572 n.104
    adaptations 249–50, 338
    national canon on screen in 361–4
Syberberg, Hans-Jürgen 407 n.30, 502
Sydow, Max von 436
Sydow, Rolf von 378–9
Syndikat, Tobis-Tonbild 182
Synecdoche, New York (2008) 540–1
Szabó, István 436
Szasz, Peter 496 n.164
Szirtes, A. 8 n.6
Szürkület (1990) 575 n.141

Taddicken, Sven 518, 520
Tadellöser & Wolff (1975) 496 n.163
Tadellöser & Wolff (Kempowski) 496 n.163
Tagebuch einer Verlorenen/Diary of a Lost Girl (Böhme) 69, 86 n.145, 119, 145–6, 149, 169 n.220
Tagebücher (1924–1945) (Goebbels) 242 n.217, 326 n.72
Taiga (1958) 409 n.55
Tait, Margaret 403
Takeover-voll vertauscht (2020) 579 n.180
Take Two: Fifties Cinema in Divided Germany (Davidson & Hake) 406 n.17, 418 n.151
Talankin, Igor 445
Tales of Hoffmann (1881) 62–3, 65, 86 nn.133–4

Tales of Hoffmann (1916) 62–6
Tales of Hoffmann (1951) 269 n.17, 350
The Talkies: American Cinema's Transition to Sound 1926–1931 (Crafton) 166 nn.182–3, 237 n.144
talking picture 172, 175, 184, 203, 211
Tambling, Jeremy 156 n.4, 239 n.166, 578 n.176
Tame, Peter 405 n.8
Tank, Kurt Lothar 342–3, 407 n.38
Tanner, Alain 449
Tante Frieda/Aunt Frieda (1906) 368
Tanz auf dem Vulkan/Dance on a Vulcano (1938) 306
Tanz auf der Kippe (1991) 562 n.7
Tappe, Holger 504
Tarantino, Quentin 1, 117
Tarich, Yuri 259
Tarkovsky, Andrei 445
Tarride, Abel 250
Tartüffe (1664) 134, 156 n.15
Tartüffe (1925) 134–5, 156 n.15, 324 n.48
Tatar, Maria 200, 235 n.117
Tauben im Grass/Pigeons on the Grass (Koeppen) 483 n.8
Taugenichts/Good for Nothing (1977) 458–9, 502
Taugenichts/Good for Nothing (Eichendorff) 458–9, 502
Taurus/Телец (2001) 543
Taussig, Hans 241 n.187
Taviani, Paolo 529, 533
Taviani, Vittorio 529, 533
Taylor, Richard 321 n.10
Taylor, Robert 262
technological-functional societies 183
Tegel, Susan 329 n.130, 330 n.135
Teigler, Rolf 572 n.99
Teinturier, Frédéric 269 n.12, 405 n.8
Teleclub 514
Tele München 513–14
Tellkamp, Uwe 500, 577 n.164
Tell, Wilhelm/William 25–6, 409 n.63
Tempelhof studios (Berlin) 109, 162 n.116, 184, 218

The Temporary Widow (1930) 182, 233 n.77
Ten Days to Die (Musmanno) 359
"Tendenzdrama" 67, 183
Tennant, Andy 566 n.50
Ten Nights in a Barroom (1926) 119
Tergit, Gabriele 3, 231 n.51, 530
Terra-Film AG 217, 250, 271 n.40
The Testament of Dr. Mabuse (1933) 247
Teufel in Seide (1956) 425 n.245
Teufel in Seide (Kaus) 425 n.245
Tewksbury, Peter 239 n.164, 441
Thalbach, Anna 537
Thalbach, Katharina 446, 489 n.70
Thalberg, Irving 273 n.72
Thalia journal 63
Thanhouser 126, 128
Thate, Hilmar 452
theater and popular literature 36–8
Theater Censorship of 1850 39
Theater der Courage (Vienna) 496 n.164
Thedieck, Franz 376, 419 n.169
Theodor Fontane (Arnold) 327 n.100, 497 n.173
A Theory of Adaptation (Hutcheon) 578 n.178
Theresienstadt (1945) 246
They Dare Not Love (1941) 272 n.57
The Thief of Bagdad (1940) 253, 340
Thiele, Hertha 196, 282
Thiele, Rolf 343–4, 400, 408 n.43, 421 n.203, 441, 451, 492 n.99
Thiele, Wilhelm/William 181–3, 228, 233 n.77, 262
Thiess, Frank 351, 411 n.69
Thimig, Hermann 94, 245, 282
Third Reich 280–1, 320 n.9
Thoma, Ludwig 277, 338, 366, 368–9, 451, 492 n.99
Thomas Mann auf Leinwand und Bildschirm (Elsaghe) 421 n.198
Thomas Mann im Kino (Zander) 160 n.83, 160 n.86, 418 n.167, 420 n.192, 420 n.195, 485 n.35, 491 n.91
Thomas Müntzer (1956) 420 n.193

Thomas, Philip 551
Thomas, Richard 237 n.143
Thompson, Emma 529
Those Torn from Earth (Hollander) 246
360 (2011) 542
Three Comrades (1938) 262
Three Comrades (Remarque) 262, 413 n.96
The Three Musketeers (2011) 504
Threepenny Lawsuit (Brecht) 221–5
3096 Tage/*3096 Days* (2013) 564 n.26
Throta, Renée 109
Thunecke, Jörg 238 n.154
Thürmer-Rohr, Christina 497 n.175
Tibbets, John C. 495 n.136
Tibetan Buddhism 270 n.38
Tieck, Ludwig 141, 346
Ti, Leo 404, 450
Tiller Girls 183
A Time to Love and a Time to Die (1958) 359
Timm, Peter 509, 569 n.75
Timm Thaler oder Das verkaufte Lachen (2017) 487 n.50, 504
Timm Thaler oder Das verkaufte Lachen (Krüss) 442, 487 n.50, 504
Timm, Uwe 496 n.163, 515–16, 569 nn.75–6
The Tin Drum. See Die Blechtrommel/ The Tin Drum (1979)
Tinko (1957) 483 n.6
Tintenherz (2008) 566 n.49
Tintenherz (Funke) 566 n.49
Tintner, Hans 184, 246, 254
Tischlein deck dich/The Wishing Table (1956) 378, 419 n.173
Titanic (1953) 398
Tiulpanov, Sergei Ivanovich 348, 383
Tjaden, Walter 368
T. K. Tonfilm 187
Tobis-Klangfilm group 177–8, 187, 197, 199, 202, 206, 223, 230 n.29
Todd, Frederick 228 n.4
Todd, Richard 351

Todeslager Sachsenhausen/Death Camp Sachsenhausen (1946) 336
Tod in Rom/Death in Rome (Koeppen) 483 n.8
Tod in Venedig/Death in Venice (1921) 160 n.71
Tod in Venedig/Death in Venice (Mann) 160 n.71
Tod, oder Bernhard (Gremm) 458
Tod oder Freiheit/Death or Freedom (1978) 489 n.60
To Each His Own (1946) 352
Togay, Can 531
Tóibín, Colm 465, 548
Toller, Ernst 7, 9 n.13, 56, 75, 84 n.107, 104, 118–19, 122, 127–9, 136, 144, 153–4, 163 nn.128–9, 165 n.159, 184, 187, 200, 227, 236 n.120, 244, 246, 254, 256, 262, 271 n.43, 271 n.45, 272 n.65, 275, 281, 320 n.2, 412 n.80, 567 n.56
Tolstoy, Leo 277
Toma, Ruth 564 n.26
Tomlinson, Hugh 561 n.1
Tonbilder 79 n.33
Tonbildfilm 229 n.7
Ton-Bild-Syndikat AG (Sound Pictures Sydicate/Tobis) 175–6
Tone, Franchot 262
Tönende Welle/Sound Wave (1928) 172
"Tonfilm-Bühne Babylon" (Bülowplatz) 184
Toni Erdmann (2016) 521
Tonio Kröger (1964) 384, 451, 493 n.114
Tonio Kröger (Mann) 384, 451, 493 n.114
Tonkreuz 188, 225, 233 n.68
Tönnies, Ferdinand 231 n.47
Tornow, Ingo 239 n.163, 406 n.26
Torquato Tasso (Goethe) 77 n.27
Torrado, Ramón 403
Toscanito y los detectives (1950) 239 n.164
Toscanito y los detectives (Kästner) 239 n.164

Töteberg, Michael 82 n.83, 83 n.104, 84 n.110, 84 nn.112–13, 114, 156 nn.5–6, 156 n.15, 162 n.100, 170 n.232, 181–2, 229 n.14, 231 n.40, 231 n.42, 233 n.65, 237 n.137, 359, 413 n.97, 413 n.99, 497 n.167, 497 nn.169–70, 497 n.172
Touki Bouki/The Hyena's Journey (1973) 531
Tournier, Michel 465
Tracy, Spencer 264
Trageser, Tim 565 n.33, 581 n.199
Tragical History of the Life and Death of Doctor Faustus (Marlowe) 16
Trakl, Georg 404
Trans-Atlantic Tunnel (1935) 181
Transit (2018) 517, 522–3, 526, 549–50, 555
Transit (Seghers) 273 n.71, 522–3, 555, 558, 578 n.174
Translation, Adaptation and Transformation (Raw) 157 n.28
transnational and intercultural contexts 2, 34, 41, 558
Trapp, Maria Augusta 346
Trauer und Melancholie (Freud) 392
Traumdeutung/The Interpretation of Dreams (Freud) 534
Traumnovelle (Schnitzler) 534, 575 n.140
Traumulus (Holz & Jerschke) 296
Traven, B. 349, 351–2, 411 n.72, 426 n.257
Travers, James 412 n.82
The Treasure of the Sierra Madre (1948) 351
Treaty of Versailles 89, 202, 307
Treibhaus/the Hothouse (Koeppen) 483 n.8
Trenck, der Roman eines Günstlings/Trenck: Novel of a Favourite (Frank) 293
trends and figures 6–7, 298, 368, 430–1, 434, 438, 499–500, 508–14, 516–17, 520, 523, 529, 561
Treptow, Otto 156 n.13
Tressler, Georg 426 n.257, 570 n.85

Treß, Werner 274 n.72
The Trial (1962) 434–5
Tribby, John 203
Tribüne (1919) 104
Tricktisch 228 n.5
Triebdrama 122
Triebel, Jördis 520
Tri-Ergon-Musik-AG 175
Tri-Ergon system 134, 174–5, 229 n.11
Trier, Lars von 222, 241 n.200
Trilogie des Scheiterns/Trilogy of Failure (Koeppen) 433
A Trip to the Moon. See Le Voyage dans la Lune/A Trip to the Moon (1902)
Triumph des Willens/Triumph of the Will (1935) 290, 316, 487 n.47
The Triumph of Propaganda (Hofmann) 280, 320 n.10, 322 n.20, 322 nn.26–7
The Triumph of the Ordinary: Depictions of Daily Life in the East German Cinema, 1949–1989 (Feinstein) 418 n.159, 498 n.195
Truffaut, François 434, 438, 472, 484 n.17, 485 n.29, 522, 573 n.116
Truth to Tell: German Women's Autobiographies and Turn-of-the-Century Culture (Gerstenberger) 86 n.143
Tschechowa, Olga 186, 206, 250, 303
Tschekin, Igor 375
Tschick (2016) 546, 577 n.162
Tschick/Why We Took the Car (Herrndorf) 546
Tucherer, Eugen 250
Tucholsky, Kurt 50, 95, 100, 157 n.26, 158 n.47, 244, 246, 268 n.10, 282, 376, 487 n.46, 537, 567 n.55
Tucker, Harry 167 n.197
Tukur, Ulrich 569 n.81
Tüngel, Richard 373
Turk, Horst 29 n.3
Turnbull, Margaret 87 n.157
Turner, Lana 266, 490 n.78
Tur & Retur (2003) 567 n.50

Tuscherer, Eugen 245
Twentieth Century Fox/20th Century Fox 210, 262, 264, 266, 271 n.44, 353
20000 lieues sous les mers (Verne) 30 n.18
Twentyman, Eleanor 385
2001: A Space Odyssey (1968) 134, 533
Tybjerg, Casper 82 n.83
Tykwer, Tom 2, 491 n.92, 503, 509, 518, 520, 524–5, 539, 576 n.150
Tyrolf, Walter 416 n.136

U 202 (Spiegel) 283
Über das Marionettentheater (Kleist) 35
Über den physiologischen Schwachsinn des Weibes (Möbius) 159 n.64
Ucicky, Gustav 182, 233 n.77, 283, 295, 297–8, 323 n.42, 363–5, 394, 408 n.52, 414 n.111, 416 n.129
Uco-Productions 92
Udet, Ernst 394, 424 n.230
Ufa (Universum Film AG) 57, 74, 91–2, 98, 106, 109, 113, 117, 130, 133–4, 153, 161 n.99, 162 n.116, 168 n.204, 172, 174, 181–4, 187, 193, 204, 210–13, 229 n.12, 230 n.22, 233 n.65, 233 n.67, 233 n.69, 239 n.164, 262, 283, 286, 297, 318, 321 n.13, 323–4 n.42, 323 n.41, 326 n.80, 331 n.150, 339–40, 406 n.26, 412 n.81, 414 n.111, 439, 513, 579
  cultural mission 91
  financial crisis 174, 229 n.15
  right-wing leadership 189–95, 290
  Tauentzienpalast 108
  Ton-Kino 226
  Tri-Ergon system 174–5
Ufa-Palast am Zoo (Berlin) 115, 226, 247, 283, 296
The Ufa Story: A History of Germany's Greatest Film Company (Kreimeier) 156 n.12, 242 nn.219–20

Ukadike, N. Frank 575 nn.136–7
Ulbricht, Walter 432, 444, 488 n.53
Uli der Knecht/Uli the Farmhand (1954) 362
Uli der Knecht/Uli the Farmhand (Gotthelf) 362
Uli der Pächter/Uli the Tenant (1955) 362
Uli der Pächter/Uli the Tenant (Gotthelf) 362
Ullstein 91–2, 176, 186, 207, 232 n.52
Ulm Einsatzkommando trial (1958) 401, 492 n.95
Ulmer, Edgar G. 222, 347, 352, 367, 411 n.78
Ulrich, Kurt 491 n.86
Ulysses (Joyce) 150, 169 n.225, 171, 213
Umbehr, Heinz 233 n.68
Umgelter, Fritz 402, 447, 486 n.45, 490 n.74
Un amour de Swann (1983) 467
"unchained camera" technique 122, 124, 151, 164 n.143, 257
Unda, Emilie 196
Und die Kinder spielen so gern Soldaten/And the Children Love Playing Solders (1951) 403
Understanding Multiculturalism and the Habsburg Central European Experience (Gary & Feichtinger) 87 n.155
Und ewig bleibt die Liebe/Love Stays Forever (1954) 346, 409 n.55
Undine (1991) 562 n.8
Undine (2020) 517, 525–6, 558, 560, 582 n.207
Undine (Motte-Fouqué) 558, 562 n.8
Undine geht/Undine walks/leaves (Bachmann) 559
Und sagte kein einziges Wort/And Never said a Word (1953) 495 n.149
Und über uns der Himmel/And above Us the Sky or City of Torment (1947) 340–1, 409 n.61
Une histoire d'amour/A Love Story (1933) 250
Unendliche Geschichte (Ende) 567 n.52
Unendliche Geschichte/The Neverending Story (1984) 487 n.48, 566 n.46, 567 n.52
UNESCO 242 n.218
Ungeduld des Herzens/Beware of Pity (1946) 351, 545
Ungeduld des Herzens/Beware of Pity (Zweig) 351, 545
Unholy Love (1930) 177
United Artists 262, 359, 385
universal-appeal pictures 210–20, 224, 226–7, 249, 524
Universal Pictures 204, 248
Unordnung und frühes Leid/Disorder and Early Sorrow (1977) 458, 492 n.99
Unordnung und frühes Leid/Disorder and Early Sorrow (Mann) 458, 492 n.99
Unruhige Nacht/Restless Night (1958) 397
Unsere Mütter, unsere Väter (2012) 571 n.95
Unser kurzes Leben/Our Short Life (1981) 483 n.6
Unsterbliche Geliebte/Immortal Beloved (1951) 369–70
Unterleuten (2020) 572 n.98, 579 n.182
Unterleuten (Zeh) 519, 572 n.98, 579 n.182
Unterm Birnbaum/Under the Pear Tree (1944/5) 275
Unterm Birnbaum/Under the Pear Tree (Fontane) 275
Unterwaldt, Sven, Jr. 512, 568 n.58
Unvollendete Geschichte (Braun) 562 n.7
urban cinematography 215
urbanization 13
Uricchio, William 76 n.18
Ursula (1978) 446
Ury, Else 487 n.49
USA 280, 348, 351–3, 358–60, 387, 398, 413 n.102, 413 n.107, 421 n.204, 425 n.245, 484 n.21, 486 n.43, 501, 518, 528, 533–7, 540–1, 545

The Use and Abuse of Cinema
  (Rentschler) 322 n.20, 322 n.23,
  323 n.31
The U.S. National Archives and
  Records Administration (NARA)
  405 nn.6–7, 405 nn.10–11,
  405 n.13

Vachnadze, Nato 141
Vadim, Roger 425 n.245
Vahlbusch, Jefford 484 n.21
Vajda, Ladislao 534
Vajda, Ladislaus 176, 202, 223
Valentin, Thomas 455
Valetti, Rosa 106, 221
Vallentin, Hermann 55
van den Berg, Rudolf 575 n.141
van Gelder, Lawrence 436, 484 n.22,
  484 n.24
van Gogh, Vincent 124
Vanina (1922) 156 n.14
Vanina Vanini (Stendhal) 156 n.14
Vanity Fair magazine 166 n.174
Varda, Agnes 438, 495 n.139
Varieté (1925) 92, 122–3, 143, 151–2,
  164 n.143, 216, 272 n.60, 467
Vatsal, Radha 31 n.31
vaudeville 12
Vaupel, Angela 331 n.143
Vávrová, Dana 533
Veidt, Conrad 70–1, 100, 129, 176,
  232 n.62, 252–3, 270 n.40,
  294–5, 314, 326 n.79
Venatier, Hans 365, 414 n.118
Venice Film Festival 313, 454
Verbrechen/Crime (2009) 505,
  563 n.33
Vergeßt es nie-schuld sind sie!/Don't
  ever forget, they're the guilty
  ones (1946) 336
Verhoeven, Michael 528
Verhoeven, Paul 373, 376–7, 412 n.81,
  446–7
Verhoeven, Simon 581 n.199
Vermes, Timur 505
Verne, Jules 26, 30 n.18, 54
Verne, Kaaren 264
Vertov, Dziga 108

Verwehte Spuren (1938) 296, 301
Vesely, Herbert 403–4, 449–51, 454,
  462–4, 478
Vespermann, Kurt 109
Via Mala (1945) 339
Via Mala (1960) 391
Via Mala (Knittel) 339, 391
Vicas, Victor 401, 423 n.229
Victoria (2015) 521
Victorian system of regulation 96
Vidor, King 198, 398, 423 n.222
Viebig, Clara 40–1
Vienna 45, 56, 60, 98, 120–1, 149, 160
  n.71, 205, 226, 249–50, 380,
  416 n.131, 496 n.164, 535
Viennese workers 268 n.11
Viertel, Salka 550, 577 n.171
*Vierundzwanzig Stunden aus dem
  Leben einer Frau*/Twenty-Four
  Hours in the Life of a Woman
  (1931) 351
*Vierundzwanzig Stunden aus dem
  Leben einer Frau*/Twenty-Four
  Hours in the Life of a Woman
  (1968) 411 n.70
*Vierundzwanzig Stunden aus dem
  Leben einer Frau*/Twenty-Four
  Hours in the Life of a Woman
  (Zweig) 351, 411 n.70, 545
*Vier von der Infanterie, ihre letzten
  Tage an der Westfront 1918/
  Four Infantrymen on the
  Western Front* (Johannsen)
  202
Vietnam War 431
Villon, François 221
Vilsmaier, Joseph 512, 533, 566 n.50,
  567 n.53
Vincendeau, Ginette 324 n.46
Vinocur, John 470, 496 n.156
Viola tricolor (Storm) 381
VIP Medienfonds GmbH & Co. KG
  (München-Geiselgasteig) 576
  n.151
Visconti, Luchino 434, 436, 478–9,
  484 n.25
The Visit (1964) 435, 571 n.96
visual culture 2, 117, 125, 554

Vitaphone sound-on-disk system 172, 203
Vitascope production 55
Vitek, Jack 575 n.140
Vogel, Jürgen 520, 537, 565 n.33, 567 n.54
Vogelöd Castle. See *Schloss Vogelöd* (1921)
Vogel, Peter 481
Vogel, Rudolf 364
Vogt, Hans 174
Vohrer, Alfred 448, 486 n.43
Voigt, Wilhelm 216, 218–19
Völker, Klaus 240 n.181, 407 n.27
Völkischer Beobachter newspaper 204–5, 237 n.135, 279, 292–3, 313, 318
völkisch nationalism 198, 290, 319, 323 n.41
Volkserziehung 300
Volksfilm 117
Volksgemeinschaft 288, 291, 297, 316
Volksstück 38
Volk, Stefan 498 n.196
Vollbrecht, Karl 117
Vollmar, Neele 567 n.53
Vollmar, W. 8 n.6
Vollmöller, Karl 189–90
Voltaire 197
Vom Stummfilm zum Tonfilm (Müller) 230 n.28
von Alemann, Claudia 498 n.198
von Ardenne, Elisabeth 542
von Billerbeck, Liane 573 n.117, 577 n.167
Von Caligari zu Hitler (Kracauer) 166 n.180, 229 nn.7–8, 234 n.90, 236 nn.124–5, 240 n.177
von der Hellen, Eduard 29 n.3
von der Vring, Georg 235 n.119, 293
von Donnersmarck, Florian Henckel 501, 528, 574 n.132
von Hillern, Wilhelmine 98, 102, 367, 407 n.36
Von morgens bis mitternachts/From Morning to Midnight (1920) 35, 92, 104
Von morgens bis mitternachts/From Morning to Midnight (Kaiser) 92, 104, 159 nn.68–9
von Schirach, Ferdinand 501, 505–7, 555, 559, 565 n.33
von Sternberg, Josef 3, 168 n.200, 188, 205, 228, 281, 477
von Trotta, Margarethe 431, 449, 462, 464–9, 478–80, 498 n.198, 562 n.5, 573 n.122, 579 n.182
Vorderhaus und Hinterhaus 78 n.30
Vor der Morgenröte (2016) 581 n.202
Vorlíček, Václav 444
Vor Sonnenaufgang/Before Sunrise (1956) 392, 427 n.270
Vor Sonnenaufgang/Before Sunrise (Hauptmann) 392
Vor Sonnenuntergang/Before Sunset (1956) 384
Vor Sonnenuntergang/Before Sunset (Hauptmann) 284, 297, 324 n.48, 384
Vorwärts newspaper 220
Vossische Zeitung newspaper 62
Voßler, Heike 582 n.209
Vosstanie rybakov/*Aufstand der Fischer* (Goergen) 271 n.49
Vulpe-vânător (1993) 575 n.135
Vulpius, Christian August 581 n.206
Vulpius, Paul 414 n.110

Waalkes, Otto 501, 568 n.58
Wachsmann, Franz 248
Wagener, Hans 422 n.208
Waggerl, Karl Heinrich 408 n.52
Waggner, George 248
Wagner, Arno 414 n.113
Wagner, Elsa 176
Wagner, Fritz Arno 353, 412 n.81
Wagner, Konrad 380
Wagner, Richard 1, 114
Wagner, Ulla 515–16
Wahlverwandschaften/Elective Affinities (Goethe) 512
Wainwright, Richard 254
Wajda, Andrzej 575 n.144
Wakasugi, Mitsuo 239 n.164
Walbrook, Anton 349

Wald/Forest (2015) 519
Walden, Matthias 468
Waldleitner, Ludwig (Luggi) 400–1
Waldrausch (1962) 416 n.130
Waldrausch (1977) 416 n.130
Waldwinter (1956) 409 n.55
Walker, William 488 nn.54–5
Wallace, Edgar 502
Wallace, Ian 273 n.68, 321 n.11, 329 n.127, 330 n.130, 489 n.66, 489 n.68
Wallach, Martha Kaarsberg 232 n.53
Wallenstein (1962/1987) 488–9 n.60
Wallenstein (Schiller) 37, 425 n.248
Wallis, Georg von 574 n.129
Wallstein 575 n.134
Wall Street crash of 1929 152, 183, 195, 198, 211
Walser, Martin 440, 486 n.42, 516, 569 n.81
Walser, Robert 37, 78 n.31, 440
Walsh, Raoul 348–9
Wälsungenblut/The Blood of the Walsungs (1964) 451, 492 n.99
Walt Disney 378
Walter Reade Theater 415 n.125
Walther-Fein, Rudolf 253, 293
Waltz, Christoph 1
Wanda (1952) 383
Wangenheim, Gustav von 247, 256
Wann wird es endlich wieder so, wie es nie war/When will things finally get back to the way they never were (Meyerhoff) 557
war
  film, and impact of war 55–9
  First World War 1, 3, 34, 51, 54–6, 58–9, 69, 73–5, 77 n.28, 81 n.71, 84 n.108, 84 n.113, 85 n.119, 87 n.156, 87 n.158, 89–92, 94, 101, 113, 118, 120, 141, 142, 152, 172, 198, 200, 205, 216, 226, 228 n.3, 236 n.125, 243, 273 nn.71–2, 388, 394
  Second World War (*see* Second World War)
  and trauma 393–8
Ward, Elizabeth 417 n.142

Ward, Warwick 124
Warm, Hermann 55, 348
Warnecke, Nils 234 n.96
Warneke, Lothar 483 n.6
Warner Bros. 172, 176, 181, 210, 223, 262–3, 267, 351, 520, 572 n.100, 579 n.180
Warnung vor einer heiligen Nutte/Beware of a Holy Whore (1971) 473, 476
war-time adaptations 59–61, 85 n.125
  and definitions of alterity 72
Warum läuft Herr R. Amok (1970) 459
Waschneck, Erich 176, 313, 410 n.64
Was Frauen träumen/What Women Dream (1933) 248
Washburn, Anne 545, 576 nn.159–60
Wassermann, Jakob 410 n.64, 410 n.65
Wassermann, Walter 307
Wasteland (Elliot) 171
Watts, Andrew 20, 31 n.21, 31 n.24, 32 n.41, 167 n.192, 404 n.3
Wauchope, Mary 415 n.121, 427 n.271
Wauer, William 55, 85 n.119, 87 n.156
Wawrzyn, Lienhard 563 n.8
Wayne, Anthony 424 n.236
The Way of All Flesh (1927) 187
Waz, Gerlinde 158 n.37
The Weavers. See *De Waber/Die Weber* (Hauptmann)
Webber, Andrew J. 167 nn.196–7, 497 n.179
Weber, A. Dana 162 n.115
Weber, Julia 514, 568 n.68
Weber, Max 325 n.63
Weber, Nicola 407 n.28, 417 n.137
We Children from Bahnhof Zoo (2021) 509
Wedekind, Frank 45, 58, 93, 119–20, 125, 145–6, 153, 159 n.57, 195, 222, 344, 451, 491 n.90
Wedekind, Tilly 102
Wedel, Michael 8 n.2, 79 n.33, 80 n.52, 82 n.78, 85 n.123, 175, 199, 206, 219, 230 n.16, 231

nn.33–4, 235 n.116, 235
nn.109–13, 237 nn.131–3, 237
n.144, 238 nn.145–9, 241 n.185,
241 n.188–9, 241 n.191, 241
nn.193–5, 415 n.127, 420 n.192,
420 nn.194–5, 490 n.71
Weekend at the Waldorf (1945) 266
Wegener, Paul 51–3, 59–60, 83 n.94,
84 n.113, 85 n.120, 87 n.147,
106, 125, 135, 142, 172, 177,
228 n.3, 318, 348
Wegmann, Wolfgang 423 n.218
Wehrmacht exhibition of 1995 389
Weiberregiment/Women's Rule (1936)
277
Weidenmann, Alfred 384, 458
Weigel, Helene 184, 227, 244, 245,
264, 266, 452, 491 n.86
Weihmayr, Franz 197
Weiler, A. H. 395–6, 424 nn.240–1
Weiler, Jan 562 n.6
Weill, Kurt 211, 221–3, 225, 244–5,
282, 491 n.86, 511
*Weimar Cinema and After: Germany's
Historical Imaginary* (Elsaesser)
9 n.10, 165 n.149, 166 n.173,
166 n.181, 582 n.212
*Weimar Cinema: An Essential Guide
to Classic Films of the Era*
(Isenberg) 159 n.63
*Weimar Culture: The Outsider as
Insider* (Gay) 234 n.99
*Weimar in Exile: The Antifascist
Emigration in Europe and
America* (Palmier) 272 n.64
Weimar Republic 54, 57, 91–2, 95,
102–3, 112, 154, 155 n.3, 187,
192, 286, 296, 320 nn.8–9, 348,
367, 371, 412 n.81, 520, 555
anti-democratic movement 290
cinema 99, 123, 134, 181, 228, 235
n.103, 256, 338, 340, 347–8,
466, 478
Criminal Code 183
pervasive sexual cynicism 146
system 422 n.210
*Weimar through the Lens of Gender.
Prostitution Reform, Woman's
Emancipation, and German
Democracy, 1919–33* (Roos)
158 n.31
Weinmann, Friedrich 126
Weinstein Company film 529, 571 n.93
Weisbach, Robert 179
Weiskopf, Franz Carl 263, 273 n.68,
374
Weiß, Helmut 368, 416 n.129, 451,
491 n.89
Weiss, Hermann 319
Weiss, Josef 52
Weiss, Peter 430, 451–3, 456, 459,
478
Weisz, Rachel 542
Weizsäcker, Richard von 401
Wekwerth, Manfred 426 n.264, 452
Welch, David 280, 322 n.26
Wellershoff, Dieter 494 n.122
Welles, Orson 2, 434–5, 478, 484
n.18
Wellin, Arthur 367
Wellman, William 198
Wells, H. G. 54
Welsh, James M. 466, 495 nn.136–7
Welskopf-Henrich, Liselotte 448
Weltanschauung 293
Wenders, Wim 431, 449, 456–8, 460,
478–9, 491 n.82, 502, 546–7,
566 n.46
Wendhausen, Fritz 282
Wendlandt, Horst 447
Wenger, Hannes 509
Wengraf, John 264
Weniger, Kay 271 n.41, 273 n.71, 406
n.23
Wenn der Wind sich dreht/As the Wind
Turns (2001) 443
Wenn die Heide blüht/When the Heath
Blooms (1960) 415 n.123
Wenn Poldi ins Manöver zieht/When
Polidi Goes to Manoeuvre
(1956) 362
Wenn wir alle Engel wären/If We All
Were Angels (1936) 296
Wenzler, Franz 296
Wer einmal aus dem Blechnapf frisst
(Fallada) 447

Wer einmal aus dem Blechnapf frisst/ Who Once Eats Out of the Tin Bowl (1962) 447
Werfel, Franz 246, 264–5, 267, 268 n.10, 273 n.72, 274 n.73, 274 n.75, 359, 360–1, 440
Werk ohne Autor/Never Look Away (2018) 574 n.132
Werner-comics (1990, 1996, 2003) 501, 510, 563 n.12
Wertheimer, Max 141
Wery, Carl 367
The Wes Anderson Collection: The Grand Budapest Hotel (Zoller Seitz) 576 n.159, 577 n.160
Weschler, Lawrence M. 330 n.133
Westdeutscher Rundfunk (WDR) 417 n.145, 456, 459, 469, 480, 509, 566 n.46
Western Electric 177, 187, 199, 237 n.131
   sound technology 176
   Vitaphone process 203
Westfront 1918 (1930) 202, 216, 222, 281
West German Film Control Board 348
West German Filmmakers on Film: Visions and Voices (Rentschler) 420 n.191
Westhoff, Heidi 75 n.1, 157 n.17
West-Ost-Filmaustausch 373
Westphalen, Tim 412 n.89
Whale, James 178, 244, 261–2, 272 n.57
What Became of Gunner Asch (Kirst) 422 n.207
Whelehan, Imelda 9 n.12, 29 n.4, 412 n.92
Whishaw, Ben 518
Wichert, Ernst 305
Wickham, Christopher J. 159 n.60
Wicki, Bernhard 382, 391–2, 423 n.219, 435, 438, 486 n.42, 561 n.3, 571 n.96, 572 n.102, 580 n.194
Widmann, Faustbook 26
Wiechert, Ernst 402
Wieck, Dorothea 196

Wiedemann, Dieter 378, 419 n.176
Wiegmann, Marie 87 n.146
Wie interpretiert man einen Film? (Beicken) 83 n.92
Wieman, Mathias 286, 291
Wien, du Stadt der Lieder/Vienna, City of Songs (1930) 178
Wiene, Konrad/Conrad 61
Wiener Arbeiter-Zeitung newspaper 268 n.11
Wiener Kunstfilm 41, 80 n.59
Wiene, Robert 35, 61, 78 n.28, 135, 161 n.99, 481
Wien-Film studios 380, 414 n.111
Wiesel, Elie 392
Wiesenthal, Grete 86–7 n.146
Wigand, Tomy 419 n.178, 567 n.50
Wigman, Mary 45
Wildenbruch, Ernst von 61
Wilde, Oscar 51, 61, 581 n.206
Wilder, Billy 212, 239 n.163, 241 n.201, 245, 248, 254, 337, 347, 379, 397, 449
Wilder, Thornton 413 n.107
Wildgans, Anton 408 n.52
Wildwechsel/Jailbait (1972) 472
Wilharm, Irmgard 407 n.40
Wilhelm, Carl 106, 269 n.18
Wilhelm, Hans 214, 245, 254, 378, 411 n.76
Wilhelm II 49, 61, 89, 202, 218
Wilhelmine era (cinema reform movement) 33
Wilhelm Meisters Lehrjahre/Wilhelm Meister's Apprenticeship (Goethe) 457
Wilhelm Meisters Wanderjahre/ Wilhelm Meister's Journeyman Years, or the Renunciants (Goethe) 234 n.99
Wilhelm Tell (1923) 158 n.46, 253
Wilhelm Tell (1934) 253, 294
Wilhelm Tell (1956) 414 n.108, 416 n.131
Wilhelm Tell (Schiller) 25, 28, 36, 77 n.28, 158 n.46, 160 n.71, 253, 292–5, 326 n.75, 326 nn.81–2, 414 n.108, 416 n.131, 552

Wilhelm Tell-Das Freiheitsdrama eines Volkes/William Tell-A People's Drama of Freedom (1934) 293
Wilke, Sabine 162 n.114
Willbrandt, Nils 565 n.33
Willenbrock (2005) 538–9
Willenbrock (Hein) 538–9
Williams, Robin 528, 574 n.133
Williams, Tennessee 245, 258
Willkomm, Änne 117
Willner, Alfred Maria 93
Wilms, Wilfried 421 n.199
Wilson, Owen 545
Wim Wenders and Peter Handke: Collaboration, Adaptation, Recomposition (Brady & Leal) 493 n.119
Winds, Erich-Alexander 380
Wings (1927) 198–9
Winkler, Angela 469
Winnetou and Old Shatterhand im Tal der Toten/The Valley of the Dead (1968) 447
Winnetou-series (I-III, 1963–5) 439, 447–8
Winslet, Kate 529, 571 n.93
Winsloe, Christa 196–7, 226, 235 n.101, 254, 282, 400
Winslow, C. E. A. 74
Wintergarten theater 12, 122–4, 172
Winterkartoffelknödel (2014) 572 n.105
Winterkartoffelkönig/Winterpotatoking (2014) 571 n.95
Winter, Marian 182–3, 230 n.17, 231 n.43, 235 n.104, 239 n.170
Winter Olympics (1928) 151
Winterspelt (1976) 486 n.45
Winterspelt (Andersch) 486 n.45
Wir Kinder vom Bahnhof Zoo/Us Kids from Zoo Station (2020) 564 n.21, 571 n.95
Wirth, Franz Peter 402, 488–9 n.60
Wirtschaftswunder 334
Wirtschaftszeitung newspaper 364–5
Wir und die Anderen/We and the Others (Bader) 316, 331 n.147
Wir Wunderkinder (Hartung) 385
Wisbar, Frank 396–7, 425 n.248, 425 n.250
Wischnewski, Siegfried 452
Wiseman, Andreas 568 n.64
Witte, Karsten 30 n.10, 321 n.11
Wittich, Claus 325 n.63
Wittich, Frieder 557
The Wizard of Oz (1939) 298, 353
Wnendt, David F. 505, 552
Wodzeck (1984) 494 n.120
Wohlbrück, Adolf 349, 410 n.64
Wohlgemuth, Arthur 269 n.22
Wolf, Christa 378, 442, 446, 481, 483 n.6, 486 n.45
Wolf, Claudia 41, 81 nn.59–60, 81 nn.62–4, 81 n.67, 81 n.69
Wolf, Emmi 231 n.50
Wolff, Hans 415 n.126
Wolffhardt, Rainer 424 n.229, 464, 575 n.144
Wolff, Helen 231–2 n.51
Wolff, Kurt 60
Wolf, Friedrich 183, 184, 258
Wolffsohn, Karl 235 n.111
Wolf-Gäng (2020) 581 n.199
Wolf, Konrad 429, 442, 445, 452, 481, 483 n.6, 487 n.51, 489 n.67
The Wolf Man (1941) 248
Wolf, Ror 440
Wollenberg, Hans 165 n.163
Wolowski, Kurt 63
"Woman of the City" 137–9
women 35, 69, 111, 121, 184, 368, 415 n.128, 467, 488 n.55
 isolation and objectification 124, 155
 on screen (1919–20) 94–7, 103
 and sexuality 144–52
 unnatural aspirations 159 n.64
 in urban society 90
Women and Film (Kaplan) 494 n.131
Women and the New German Cinema (Knight) 494 n.131
Women Film Pioneers Project 31 n.31
Women's Pictures: Feminism and Cinema (Kuhn) 494 n.131
women's rights movement 90

Woolf, Virginia 171, 213
Worbs, Michael 167 n.191
Worker's Welfare Association 90
World Peace Conference (Vienna) 56
World Peace Council (1950) 374
Wortmann, Sönke 402, 501, 503, 508, 512
Wöss, Fritz 396
Wottrich, Erika 241 n.202
Woyzeck (1962) 440
Woyzeck (1979) 460
Woyzeck (Büchner) 344, 348, 460, 494 n.120, 552, 554
Wozzeck (1947) 377
Wrage, Henning 366, 376, 415 n.122, 418 n.158, 418 n.166, 419 n.170, 488 n.51, 488 n.52
Wrobel, Ignaz 100
Wulffen, Erich 85 n.125
Wulf, Joseph 281, 322 n.24, 322 n.29, 323 n.35
Wunderbare Reisen zu Wasser und zu Lande-Feldzüge und lustige Abenteuer des Freiherrn von Münchhausen (Bürger) 79–80 n.45
Wundt, Wilhelm 141
Würzner, Hans 268 n.6
Wüst, Ida 282
Wuthering Heights (1939) 351
Wyler, William 351, 438
Wyrsch, Peter 394
Wysbar, Frank 197
Wysling, Hans 161 n.90

X-Filme Creative Pool 520, 529
Xu Jinglei 529, 537–8

Yamamura, Kōji 529, 540
Yella (2007) 523
Yermolov, Pjotr 257
Yoshiwara (1937) 269 n.25
Yost, Tibor 380
Young, Clara Kimball 74
Young German Film 450, 455–6, 478, 493 n.106
  and literary heritage 457–60
Yourcenar, Marguerite 465

Zadek, Peter 455, 479
Zaïre (Voltaire) 197
Zander, Peter 111–12, 160 n.83, 160 n.86, 418 n.167, 420 n.192, 420 n.195, 485 n.35, 491 n.91
Zanetti, Sandro 8 nn.8–9
Zanol, Irene 163 n.128, 271 n.45
Zanuck, Darryl F. 354, 438
Zarathustra 155
Zärtliches Abenteuer/Affectionate Adventure 398
Zazie dans le métro (1960) 466
Zazie dans le Métro (Queneau) 495 n.138
Zeh, Juli 519, 552, 579 n.182
Zehn kleine Negerlein/Ten Little Niggers (1954) 378
Zeisler, Alfred 245
Zeiß 175
Zeitroman (Fontane) 303
Zeit zu leben, Zeit zu sterben (1954) 359
Zeller, Bernhard 166 n.167, 322 n.19, 326 n.83, 328 n.118, 329 n.126
Zeller, Wolfgang 173, 176, 316
Zelnik, Friedrich (Frederic) 96–8, 101, 119, 125–9, 154, 245, 256–7
Zentral-Kino (Vienna) 226
Zerlett, Hans 330 n.142
08/15 trilogy (1954) 365, 382, 387–91, 397, 399, 421 n.205, 422 n.210, 422 n.213
Zerstreuung (distraction) 34, 76 n.6
Zeyn, Willy 81 n.71
Zhakov, Oleg 258
Zielinski, Siegfried 329 n.129, 330 n.139, 417 n.136
Zille, Heinrich 214
Zillig, Winfried 286, 291, 325–6 n.69
Zimmermann, Friedrich 432, 479, 518
Zimmermann, Manfred 270 n.31
Zimmermann, Robert 562 n.6
Zimnik, Nina 235 n.107
Zinnemann, Fred 241 n.201, 263–4, 273 n.67, 273 n.70, 387, 389
Zinner, Hedda 370, 417 n.140
Ziolkowski, Theodore 484 n.21
Zöberlein, Hans 237 n.135

Zoch, Georg 367
Zohn, Harry 578 n.174
Zoller Seitz, Matt 576 nn.159–60
Zoopraxiscope 14–15
Zopp, Rudolf del 110
Zuckmayer, Carl 189–90, 211, 216–21, 240 nn.180–2, 241 n.190, 246, 346, 363–4, 387, 393–5, 402, 417 n.136, 423 n.226, 423 n.229, 424 nn.230–1, 424 n.239, 482, 519
Zündschnüre (Degenhardt) 486 n.45
Zündschnüre/Fuses (1974) 486 n.45
Zur Chronik von Grieshuus/A Chapter in the History of Grieshuus (1925) 285
Zur Chronik von Grieshuus/A Chapter in the History of Grieshuus (Storm) 285
Zürich-Transit (Frisch) 572 n.102
Zürich-Transit. Skizze eines Films (1992) 572 n.102
Zweig, Arnold 203, 246, 371, 374–5
Zweig, Stefan 141, 153, 171, 246, 267, 270 n.30, 282, 349, 351, 354, 400–3, 411 n.70, 426 n.259, 442, 510, 519, 529, 537–8, 545, 555, 567 n.55, 575 n.146, 576 n.160, 577 n.161, 581 n.202
Zweig, Stefanie 504, 508
Zwei Herren im Anzug/Two Men in Suits (2018) 581 n.200
Zwei im Sonnenschein/Two in the Sun (1933) 382
Zweites Deutsches Fernsehen (ZDF) 169 n.222, 455, 497 n.169, 514, 518–19, 565 n.33, 566 n.49, 569 n.82, 572 n.98
Zwerg Nase/Dwarf Nose (1952) 377
Zwischen Gestern und Morgen/ Between Yesterday and Tomorrow (1948) 340
Zwischen Gestern und Morgen: Westdeutscher Nachkriegsfilm 1946–1962 (Hoffmann & Schobert) 408 n.50
Żyliński, Leszek 426 n.258

www.ingramcontent.com/pod-product-compliance
Lightning Source LLC
Chambersburg PA
CBHW050320020526
44117CB00031B/1283